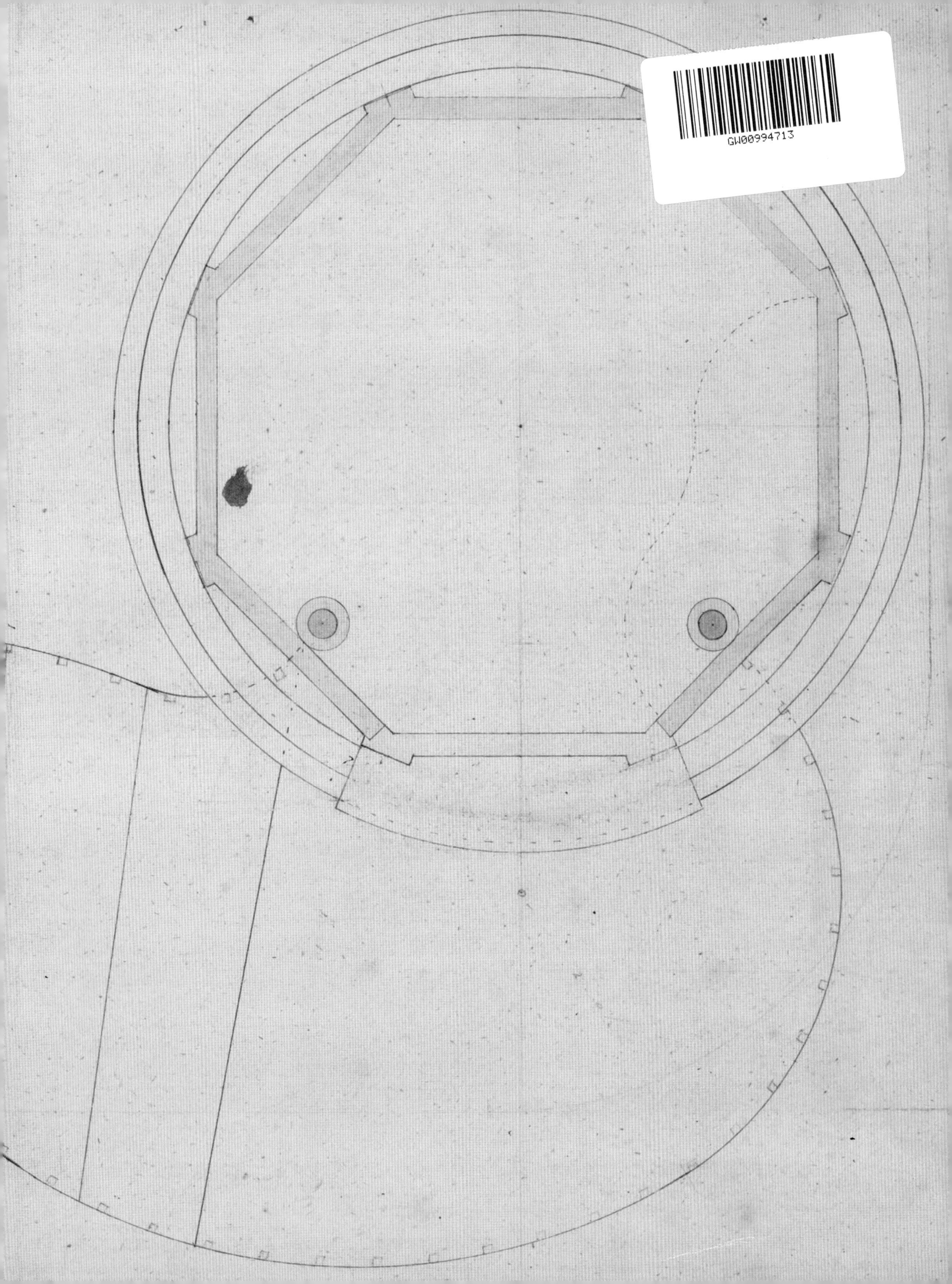

THE EIGHTEENTH-CENTURY CHURCH IN BRITAIN

amongst the several kinds of Buildings by which Great Citys are Adorn'd;
Churches, have in all Ages, and with all Religions been placed in the first Rank.

'Mr. Van-Brugg's Proposals about Building ye New Churches', 1712

THE EIGHTEENTH-CENTURY CHURCH IN BRITAIN

Terry Friedman

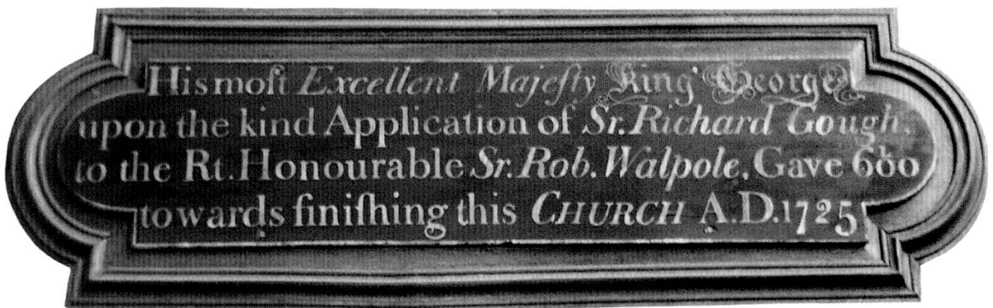
His moſt Excellent Majeſty King George
upon the kind Application of Sr. Richard Gough,
to the Rt. Honourable Sr. Rob. Walpole, Gave 600
towards finiſhing this CHURCH A.D. 1725

Published for
The Paul Mellon Centre for Studies in British Art
by
Yale University Press
New Haven and London

Designed by Gillian Malpass

Printed in China

Library of Congress Cataloging-in-Publication Data

Friedman, Terry.
The eighteenth-century church in Britain / Terry Friedman.
p. cm.
Includes bibliographical references (p.) and index.
ISBN 978-0-300-15908-0 (cl : alk. paper)
1. Church architecture–Great Britain–History–18th century.
2. Christianity and culture–Great Britain–History–18th century.
3. Great Britain–Church history–18th century. I. Title.
NA5466.F75 2010
726.50941'09033--dc22
2010027877

A catalogue record for this book is available from
The British Library

Endpapers St John, Hackney, London. Plan design for the pulpit, detail, 1796, pen and ink. Sir John Soane's museum, London, Drawer 47, set 8. James Spiller architect.

Page i A commemorative tablet at St Alkmund, Whitchurch, Shropshire, 1713

Page ii Edward Edwards. *Interior view of Westminster Abbey taken at the Commemoration of Handel from the Manager's Box*, detail, 1793. Oil on canvas. Yale Center for British Art, New Haven, Paul Mellon Collection. James Wyatt, architect, 1784.

Page iii A commemorative tablet at St Philip, Birmingham, Warwickshire, 1725

Facing page A commemorative tablet at St Helen, Wheldrake, Yorkshire, 1779

To the creators of eighteenth-century churches
– the heroes and heroines of this story

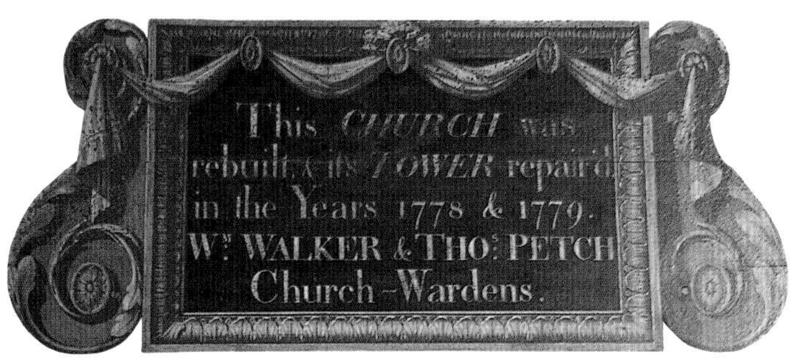

Artist unknown. View of an unidentified church interior towards the chancel, late eighteenth or early nineteenth centuries. Pencil and watercolour. Author's collection.

Contents

Part Four The Classical Traditions

Acknowledgements

No study of such wide scope could have been researched and written over two decades without the support and encouragement of many people. Above all, I am greatly indebted to the staff of record offices, archives and libraries throughout Britain and beyond, too numerous to name here individually. They are the dedicated guardians of remarkable holdings of manuscript and printed material dealing with church matters – not least of all parish records – without whose unfailing assistance and expertise this book would have proven immeasurably more difficult to produce. Special gratitude must be extended to Birmingham City Archives; the British Library; English Heritage (National Monuments Record); Lambeth Palace Library, London (His Grace the Archbishop of Canterbury and the Library Trustees); Bodleian Library, Oxford University; British Architectural Library Drawings Collection; Department of Prints and Drawings, Victoria and Albert Museum; Muniment Room, Westminster Abbey (by kind permission of the Dean and Chapter); York Minster Archives; Borthwick Institute of Historical Research, York University; Bristol Record Office; Centre for Kentish Studies; Lancashire Record Office; Lincolnshire Archives; London Metropolitan Archives; Guildhall Library, London; Shropshire Records and Research Centre; Somerset Archives and Record Service; Southampton Archive Service; Staffordshire Record Office; Warwickshire Record Office; Worcestershire Record Office; West Yorkshire Archive Service; The Trustees of Sir John Soane's Museum, London; World Monuments Fund, Britain; The National Trust; and the Yale Center for British Art, New Haven, Connecticut.

Individually, much good will and advice has been received from Dr Simon Bradley, Anthony M. Carr, Marcus Cooper, Katherine Eustace, Tom and Penny Friedman, Penelope Fussell, Delia Gaze, Erik Goldstein, Melanie Hall, Alastair Harper, Vaughan Hart, Richard Hewlings, Charles Hind, Peter Howell, Julia Ionides, Dr John Lord, Richard Mortimer, Dr Timothy Mowl, Susan Palmer, Thea Randall, Marshall and Ingrid Roscoe, David Sheard, Evelyn Silber and Christopher Webster. I wish to pay special tribute to the late Sir Howard Colvin, Professor Andor Gomme and Professor Derek Linstrum who over many years had been unstinting in their encouragement. My family has been a constant pillar of support. Dr Brian Allen, Director of the Paul Mellon Centre for Studies in British Art, and Gillian Malpass of Yale University Press, London, and their colleagues, expertly and sympathetically guided this endeavour to its final destination. I thank them all from the bottom of my heart.

Terry Friedman
Leeds, 2010

Architect unknown. Underbank Presbyterian Chapel, Stannington, Yorkshire, 1742.

Preface

While researching the career of the great early Georgian architect James Gibbs (the book was published by Yale University Press in 1984), I became suspicious of criticism of St Martin-in-the-Fields (1720–27; pl. 416) on the grounds of the 'undeniable incongruity of the temple-like church and the steeple which rushes up through the roof' – a view perhaps prompted by a biased neoclassicist's censure of the steeple as appearing 'to stand upon the roof [with] no other support' – which, however, is contradicted by a careful reading of unusually fulsome and explicit documentary evidence.[1] I also questioned attempts to isolate this masterpiece from the mainstream of British avant-garde church design (Sir John Summerson's magisterial *Architecture in Britain, 1750–1830*, first published in 1953, segregated it in a chapter devoted to the architect's 'Individual Contribution'), finding this approach unhelpful because it failed to recognise St Martin's brilliantly daring summation of the widely held, uniquely British notion of a Christian place of worship, complete with its ubiquitous but mandatory steeple, taking the form of an antique pseudoperipteral temple. This innovation had also occupied the imaginations of Gibbs and several of his contemporaries at least since the early 1710s and out of which St Martin emerged as a magnificent *idée fixe*, as revealed in chapter 21.

Approaching such iconic buildings in this way exposes the limitations of conventional architectural surveys and highlights one of the frustrations of a paucity of detailed studies of the eighteenth-century church as a major building type in its own right.[2] Categorising classical church design under the single umbrella of Anglo-Palladianism proves too simplistic. While it is true that the patterns of Andrea Palladio and Inigo Jones played vital roles in providing models, particularly for the work of the leading metropolitan architects, such as Henry Flitcroft, George Dance Sr, James Paine, James Wyatt and Thomas Hardwick, and their provincial followers – most notably John Wood Sr of Bath and John Carr of York – Nicholas Hawksmoor, the most talented baroque architect of the period, also pioneered classical alternatives inspired by late antique and early Christian temple forms, historical eras never plundered for the domestic market, as we shall see in chapter 20. A broader, more detailed treatment of the subject safeguards against ignoring works not conveniently fitting preconceived stylistic or theoretical categories, or those falling outside the official chronology, or slipping through historical cracks. This is particularly true of the plain idiom favoured not only by Sir Christopher Wren in many of his London churches, which, though largely completed by 1700 continued to undergo various improvements and remained almost universally revered throughout the century, but also by James Gibbs's smaller churches and chapels, which enjoyed an equally fruitful progeny. A fascinating manuscript diary (now in the British Library, Add. MS 22926) entitled 'Some Observations made in A Journey, begun June the 7th, and finish'd July the 9th. 1742' between Norfolk and London and back to home base (see Appendix A), perhaps compiled by an aspiring builder or architect, describing many recently completed churches in considerable detail with simple schematic plans, may help to explain how these buildings maintained and spread the conservative Wren-Gibbs formulas, as we shall see in chapter 23.

In chapters 12 to 17 we discover that Georgian gothic was not an insular and, by Puginian reckoning, largely disastrous anomaly divorced from true medieval traditions but rather part of an unbroken flow stretching from the major restoration and improvement programmes initiated at Westminster Abbey and St Mary, Warwick, in the early decades of the eighteenth century to the proto-Ecclesiological harangues of John Carter's 212 articles published in the *Gentleman's Magazine* between 1797 and 1817 under the title 'On the Pursuits of Architectural Innovation'. A crucial aspect of this activity concerned the great cathedrals and abbeys, the scholarly study of which is still principally the preserve of modern antiquarians and learned journals with little attempt to understand its broader impact on church design lower down the ecclesiastical hierarchy. In fact, few medieval fabrics of whatever size or function escaped improvements entirely during our period. I suggest that this gothic had little to do with the processes of either survival or revival promoted in conventional architectural history, and I am even reluctant to apply these murky distinctions, which in any case seem hardly to have interested the eighteenth century. Moreover, this part of the story involves the oft-discredited, yet compelling, phenomena of churches inhabiting a hybrid world of mixed gothic and classical styles, neither black nor white but a promiscuous mingling of architectural vocabulary in symbiotic relationship, which has barely undergone serious historical scrutiny. It is discussed in chapter 17.

A compulsive desire to redress these imbalances and to recover lost architectural continuities, as well as to provide the same comprehensiveness enjoyed by other building types, prompted me to write the present book. Its scope is as broad and detailed as time and space permit. Covering the entire eighteenth century, it deals principally with Anglican parish churches, the *sine qua non* of the English religious experience, but also with cathedrals, chapels of ease and those associated with colleges, hospitals, asylums, prisons and private houses, in both town and country. These latter, 'hidden rooms' have normally been included if at all as minor adjuncts of residential buildings by historians more enthralled with chronicling the appearance of domestic quarters, not to mention gossip in the drawing room, gluttony in the dining room, sexual peccadilloes in the bedroom and the daily toils of kitchen, laundry, stables, kennels and latrines. It also nominally explores Nonconformist meeting houses (an often handsome but architecturally humble output), as well as Catholic chapels and Jewish synagogues. Occasionally, these categories received a poor press. Ned Ward remarked in 1709, for example, of 'the Salamanca Doctor's meeting-house' in Penitent Street: 'we espied a sumptuous tabernacle, which being built so distinguishably from the House of the Lord, and contrary to the form of Solomon's Temple . . . Who does this . . . belong to? . . . A wicked congregation . . . Who is their teacher? The Devil.'[3] The book considers both new-builds on virgin sites and replacements of medieval and later fabrics reduced to obsolescence through structural collapse, fire or storm damage and sheer neglect, as well as repairs and refurbishments to existing buildings as part of ongoing restoration programmes. Here the architectural life of the great cathedrals is particularly enlightening. Unsuccessful attempts to advance beyond the drawing stage, for which an impressive body of evidence survives, also find a prominent place here. Geographically, I have occasionally strayed across the borders into Scotland (for we should not necessarily be put off by Thomas Pennant's Sassenach assertion regarding 'the slovenly and indecent manner in which Presbytery keeps the house of GOD'),[4] as well as Ireland,[5] Wales and beyond the British Isles.

Since governance of society in the eighteenth century was controlled through parish councils, houses of worship tended to be the most important and conspicuous structures in both town and countryside. The book therefore opens with a detailed account of the relationships between church architecture and worship, churches in their settings, and crucial aspects of church-going and church building. It will become clear to readers, however, that some of these topics would benefit immeasurably from more detailed exploration.

Detailed discussions of 272 ecclesiastical buildings of every denominational and stylistic variety, gleaned from a considerably larger number that form the basis of the present book, feature in the DOCUMENTS section presented in CD-ROM format attached to the back inside cover, and listed on pages 785–7 of the printed text. This offers a remarkable range of surviving evidence, since all architectural and decorative work, however incidental, required diocesan approval, which obliged the Vestry (members of an Anglican parish governing body that met to discuss parochial business) to submit applications and, if successful, to conduct regular meetings and record deliberations in minute books and churchwardens' accounts; in turn, architects, builders and craftspeople undertook work by written estimates and contracts, presenting finished products in the form of itemised bills. This practice was memorialised in a directive of 1785 that 'the Register Bookes in all Churches must be preserved and sauffly kept, whereby the memorie of such things as are recorded therein may successively descend in all ages into the knowledge of the posteritie to come'.[6] Also included are relevant entries from the published *Journals of the House of Commons*, contemporary descriptions extracted from local histories, guidebooks and diaries, which, while often repeating earlier accolades and censures (for this was well before the advent of copyright legislation), are useful barometers of changing fashion, and evidence printed in the popular press and the invaluable anthological *Gentleman's Magazine*, published monthly from 1731. In all this the original spellings have been retained, allowing the voices of the past to come through unadulterated. Architectural drawings and engraved views, post-1800 work and modern bibliographies, too, are listed. Other churches lacking such breadth and minutia are recorded more briefly within the main text.

Much of this material, representing the bedrock of research, is now deposited conveniently in county record offices and other public repositories, or in the case of cathedrals in their respective libraries.[7] The principal holdings for Greater London are the Guildhall Library and London Metropolitan Archives. The Papers of the Commission for Building Fifty New Churches in London, Westminster and suburbs (the so-called Queen Anne Churches), of 1711–59, a vast collection unrivalled in the history of British ecclesiastical architecture dealing with probably the most spectacular episode during the entire century (discussed in chapters 19 to 21), are held at Lambeth Palace Library, London.[8] They represent an extraordinary cornucopia of technological information, evocative in their frequently idiosyncratic spelling and now obscure vocabulary (see Glossary, pp. 739–45), and, of particular pertinence to the niceties of the economics of church work: costs of materials, construction, transportation, architects' and builders' fees. (Readers should also consult Appendix B.) Such source material also helps to bring to the fore the important contributions of the builders' trades in the creation of churches, so long ignored by architectural historians.[9] An inevitable consequence of this more in-depth exploration of documentary material reveals subtle, unexpected differences of emphasis in meaning and style, particularly, for example, in the interpretation of diverse phases of classicism. As the saying may go: God is in the detail.

One of the surprising results of this study is that it dispels a long-standing misperception of eighteenth-century England as a period of only modest church building activity.[10] Demographics reveal a very different conclusion. As noted above, few medieval churches escaped the 'improver's' hand, ranging from the completion of fabrics and major structural repairs to the introduction of galleries, organs, new altarpieces, pulpits, fonts, pews and painted glass. Victorian and later restorations, however, make it difficult to quantify this work. Similar operations characterise post-medieval fabrics up to 1700, including the majority of Wren's London churches, begun after the Restoration but finally receiving their steeples between 1700 and 1720 and continuing to undergo a variety of improvements through the rest of the century, as did St Paul's Cathedral. Their wholesale demolition began only under the Victorians and climaxed with the Blitz.[11] Most of the great cathedrals underwent alterations during our period, though work on only seven can still be seen, ranging from localised remodelling, such as the collapsed romanesque north-west door of Ely, replaced by a Wrenian classical insertion, to James Essex's impressively authentic choirscreen in Lincoln, to the spectacular completion of Westminster Abbey's west front under the direction of Nicholas Hawksmoor. While the huge number of new buildings erected by Nonconformists has been fully documented elsewhere, this study nevertheless offers a rare opportunity to see how the achievements of these often anonymous, inaccessible buildings fit into the wider scope of ecclesiastical architecture.[12]

Of new-builds, including replacements of earlier fabrics and maiden efforts on virgin sites, however, statistics are more easily calculated. In London, of ninety such buildings, comprising Anglican, Catholic and Jewish places of worship, all but fifty-six have survived intact. In the provinces there are 130 losses out of 441. While Bath, Bristol, Gloucester, Shrewsbury and Worcester have miraculously lost little, tragically nearly the entire stocks have vanished from the industrial conurbations of Birmingham, Liverpool, Manchester, Sheffield and Leeds, with the last preserving only one of twenty-four. In Wales, where new building activity was dominated by Nonconformist sects that showed little interest in architectural niceties, of only five major works three have been demolished, most notably John Wood Sr's remarkable early Christian interpolation at gothic Llandaff. Scotland and Ireland, which I have researched less comprehensively (and so remain ripe for further exploration), saw at least forty-three and fifty new ventures, with eight and six losses, respectively. Altogether, this comprises 629 new creations, of which 462 survive, from which, with the addition of the uncalculated category and an impressive amount of work on existing fabrics, much can be learnt.

The reputation of the eighteenth-century British church has not fared well. The Ecclesiologists attacked gothic Cottesbrooke, Northamptonshire, for being 'encumbered with . . . well-barricaded pens' (Georgian box pews).[13] Hawksmoor's inherently pagan classicism of St Mary Woolnoth (pl. 373) was considered 'far from . . . good taste', and St George, Bloomsbury (pl. 354), the subject of a recent dazzling restoration by the World Monuments Fund, 'the most pretentious and ugliest edifice in the metropolis'.[14]

Dickens famously ridiculed Archer's St John, Westminster (pl. 365), as 'a very hideous church with four towers at the four corners . . . resembling some petrified monster, frightful and gigantic, on its back with its legs in the air'.[15] *Murray's Guide* (1879) described the neoclassical masterpiece of St Chad,

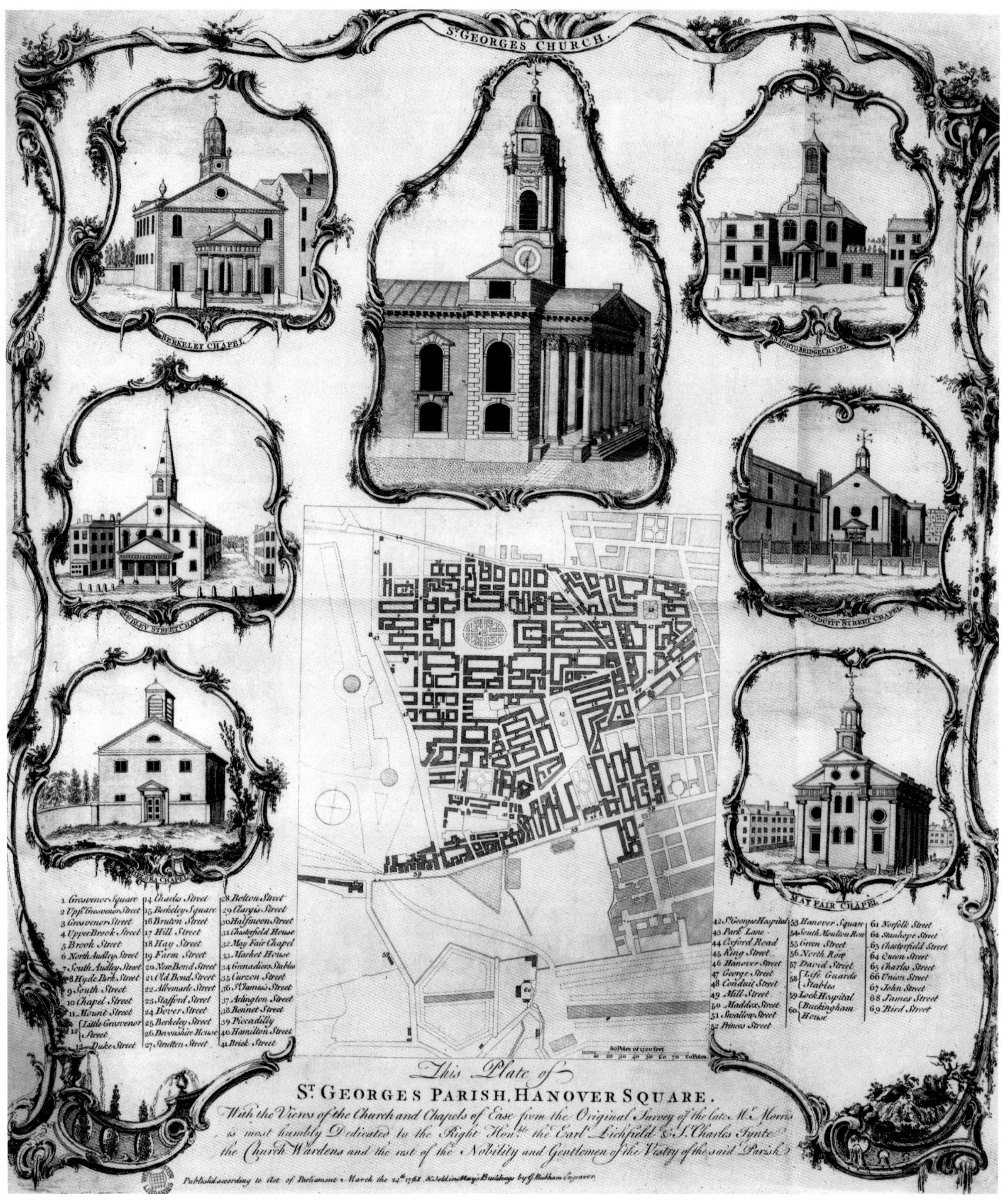

1 George Bickham after Morris. 'St George Parish, Hanover Square. With the Views of the Church and Chapels of Ease', published 24 March 1768. Engraving. City of Westminster Archives Centre, T. Pennant, London, III, extra-illustrated, f. 338. Top centre: St George (John James, architect, 1721–5); from top left: Berkeley Chapel (William Jones, architect, *c.*1750, demolished), Audley or Grosvenor Chapel (Benjamin Timbrell, architect, attributed, 1730), Chelsea Chapel (demolished); from top right: Knightsbridge Chapel (1699, demolished), Conduit Street Chapel (1716, demolished), May Fair Chapel (John James, architect, attributed, demolished).

Shrewsbury (pl. 679), as of an 'execrable taste'. Perhaps most telling is C. R. Cockerell's panoramic watercolour, *The Professor's Dream* (1848; Royal Academy of Arts, London), displaying elevations of 100 buildings dating from ancient Egyptian to modern times, where British eighteenth-century ecclesiastical achievements are represented perversely by John James's mimetic and dull St George, Hanover Square (pls I, II).[16]

Yet, such jaundiced perceptions were not exclusive to the Victorians. That inveterate wag Ned Ward remarked in *The London Spy* (1709) that St Paul's Cathedral, Sir Christopher Wren's consummate achievement, the labour of thirty-five years, was 'more by half like a goose pie I have seen at my landlord's, and this embroidered hole in the middle of the top is like the place in the upper crust where they put in the butter', while 'a Negro woman' seen at a fair sported 'thighs, as fleshy as a baron of beef . . . so much too big for her body that they looked as gouty as the pillars of St Paul's'. Furthermore,

> wretched *Wren* . . . taught by bungling *Jones*,
> To murder mortar, and disfigure stones . . .
> hate vile Cathedral, *Paul*!
> The choirs too big, the cupola's too small

reproached James Bramston's *The Man of Taste* (1733).[17] Yet, few doubted its primacy as an iconic expression of British church architecture. Soon after completion in 1710, it was proclaimed 'the most ample and celebrated Piece of Architecture in the whole World . . . built . . . upon the highest Ground of all the City and the greatest Prospect of any in Europe'.

> Nor can the Seven Hills of *Rome*
> Boast such a Church, with such a Dome
> Where Strength and Beauty nobly join,
> And in promiscuous Order shine
> Such light, great Paul! shall pour upon thy dome,
> That countries round with stupid eyes shall stare.
> To see thy tow'ring temple shine so fair
> Through the night-flaming, elemental air[18]

It distilled the essence of Anglicanism and might well have been the very building that prompted Robert Morris to muse in 1728 that

> no Science but Architecture is, or has been permitted to contain the sacred Deity, for which we are furnish'd with the noblest Buildings that have Adorn'd the several Countries of the World: It is this which has set Men at work on Temples and publick Places of Worship . . . that they might, by the Magnificence of the Building, invite the Deity to reside within it . . . Besides, it likewise opens the Mind to vast Conceptions, and fits it to converse with the Divinity of the Place; for every thing that is majestick, imprints Awfulness and Reverence on the Mind of the Beholder, and strikes it with the natural Greatness of the Soul.[19]

S.H.Grimm
fecit 1788

Part One

CHURCHGOING

facing page
Samuel Hieronymus Grimm. *View of the interior towards the west of Bath Abbey, Somerset,* detail of pl. 42.

2 Antonio Canaletto. *View of St Paul's Cathedral, London, from the north-west*, 1754. Oil on canvas. Yale Center for British Art, New Haven, Paul Mellon Collection. Sir Christopher Wren, architect, 1675–1710.

One

CHURCHSCAPES

towns and villages each of them nailed down to the earth by a tall,
tapering church spire[1]

this church is . . . a chief ornament in the modern improvements of Newcastle,
and will be, for ages, a proof of the good taste and munificence of the parishioners.
There is a beautiful area, sown with grass, and planted with poplar,
and other ornamental trees, with a border of flowering shrubs,
which give a lightness and elegance to the whole building[2]

In the eighteenth century the unrivalled physical presence of St Paul's Cathedral in the heart of the City of London (pl. 2) was not its only distinction. It was also likened to a Christian beacon:

Lo! in the midst *Wren's* wond'rous pile appears,
Which, like a mountain, its huge bulk uprears;
Such sure to sailors on a distant stream,
The lofty pike of *Tenerif* must seem.[3]

Domes and towers, of course, made churches the focus as well as the most conspicuous buildings in both town and country scapes: 'What is a Church?' asked the vicar-poet George Crabbe, ''Tis a tall building, with a tower and bells.'[4]

. . . now the Chappel's silver Bell you hear.
That summon you to all the Pride of Prayer's[5]

Alexander Pope's eulogy on 'glitt'ring spires' in *Windsor-Forest* (1713) written twenty-six years later became in turn

A hundred temples for devotion rise,
A hundred steeples glitter in the skies[6]

William Hogarth recognised one of their paramount functions when 'raised higher than ordinary, that they may be seen at a distance above the other buildings; and the great number of them dispersed about the whole city, adorn the prospect of it and give it an air of opulence and magnificence: on which account their shapes will be found to be particularly beautiful.'[7]

Wren's London steeples particularly took on a poetic air:

O'er all conspicuous with its beauteous spires,
London, th' Emporium of the busy world.[8]

Proud town! the noblest scene beneath the skies.
O'er *Thames* her thousand spires their lustre shed[9]

Or viewed from the impossibly long distance of the Isle of Wight off the south coast:

From where *Augusta* crown'd with towers appears,
And to the skies the Dome [of St Paul's] majestick
rears![10]

While from its crowning sphere, at least in Georgian times, 'you may agreeably observe the immense largeness of the Town, [and] the vast number of Churches':[11]

Whence *Pigmy-like*, he now may freely gaze,
The noblest *Scene*, beneath the Sky that meets,
Of cluster'd *Buildings*, *Lanes* and crouded *Streets*;
A world of *Squares* and *Courts* the Prospect tires,
Palaces, Churchs and their glist'ring *Spires*.[12]

Even the Abbé Pierre-Jacques Fougeroux, visiting from France in 1728, who found so little to admire in London's churches – 'When you have seen one, you have seen a hundred' – conceded the steeples were 'in an agreeable variety of design'.[13] One of the peculiarities of the topographical view at this time is the steeples' exaggerated height soaring unnaturally above

3a and b Mathias Read. Bird's-eye view of Whitehaven, Cumberland, 1738, details of pl. 3c, showing the churches of Holy Trinity, 1713 (left) and St Nicholas, 1687–93 (right), architects unknown, both demolished.

all other public and domestic buildings. Even when this was not the case, churches still dominated townscapes (pl. 3).[14]

Little wonder that steeples were essential elements of church design:

> That avenue will most delight the Sight
> That on some beauteous object shapes its way,
> Such is a Temple whose high towring Spire
> Divides the hovering cloud

bringing to mind

> the God, whose awfull Shrine
> These sacred walls enclose and where
> With thankfull Heart you often should resort[15]

At St Martin-in-the-Fields (pl. 416), the logic and beauty of James Gibbs's memorable dovetailing of monumental prostyle portico, temple body and 170-foot-high steeple are revealed on examining the conditions of the site as it then existed. Prior to the creation of Trafalgar Square in the nineteenth century, the church, hemmed within its irregular churchyard, could be approached only from acute north and south angles along St Martin's Lane, then closely packed with houses and shops, so that only the portico, with its steps projecting to the edge of the pavement, the westernmost part of the body and the steeple were ever fully in view. As we will see in chapter 21, it was precisely at this conjunction that Gibbs concentrated his ingenious repetition of free-standing columns *in antis*, which were considered 'very well conceiv'd, and a very fine effect in the profile of the building'.[16] The 165-foot-high, St Martin's-inspired steeple of nearby St Giles-in-the-Fields (pl. 562) also made the best of an awkward approach along Broad St Giles westward from Bloomsbury, fulfilling the expectation that 'a good church . . . at the farthest end of that part of the town [fronting] the great thoroughfare for all the persons who travelled the Oxford or Hampstead Roads [present-day Oxford Street and Tottenham Court Road], would be as great an ornament and as much exposed to view as any church which could be built in town'.[17] It was for these reasons that Sir John Vanbrugh recommended to his fellow New Churches Commissioners in 1711 that

> for the Ornament of the Towne, and to shew at a distance what regard there is in it to Religious Worship; every Church . . . may have a Tower . . . all of Stone or Brick; High and Bold Structures; and so form'd as not to be subject to Ruin by fire, but of such Solidity and Strength, that nothing but Time, and scarce that, shou'd destroy them.[18]

Timber construction was sometimes seen as a handicap. '*On the Design of pulling down the Wooden Tower of St Michael's Church in* St[am]ford, *and building a Steeple of Stone*':

> Do you call this a church? Why the tow'r's made
> of wood,
> I'm sure such a church can produce nothing good;
> Then away with this wood for a steeple of stone,
> Our fathers were wooden contrivers we own;
> But we are grown wiser, – have money to spare,
> Be the charge what it will we do not much care
> It will shew the whole town what we'd have
> understood,
> That we are, or at least would be thought, to be
> good,
> But soon the poor parson we'll leave in the lurch,
> Tho' we build up the steeple, we'll ne'er go to
> church.[19]

The working drawing for the steeple to St Swithin, Bath, demonstrates the building technology (pl. 4). Stunted steeples were also a handicap: that of St Mary, Truro, was a 'pitiful little thing . . . looking rather like a pidgeon-hut'.[20] Even worse: 'A beggarly people! A church and no steeple!'[21]

Finally, steeples were vehicles of (sometimes unsavoury) civic celebrations, as when the master masons at St Mary-le-Strand in London (pl. 378) were reprimanded by the building committee because 'the work-

3c Mathias Read. Bird's-eye view of Whitehaven, Cumberland, 1738, detail. Oil on canvas. Yale Center for British Art, New Haven, Paul Mellon Collection.

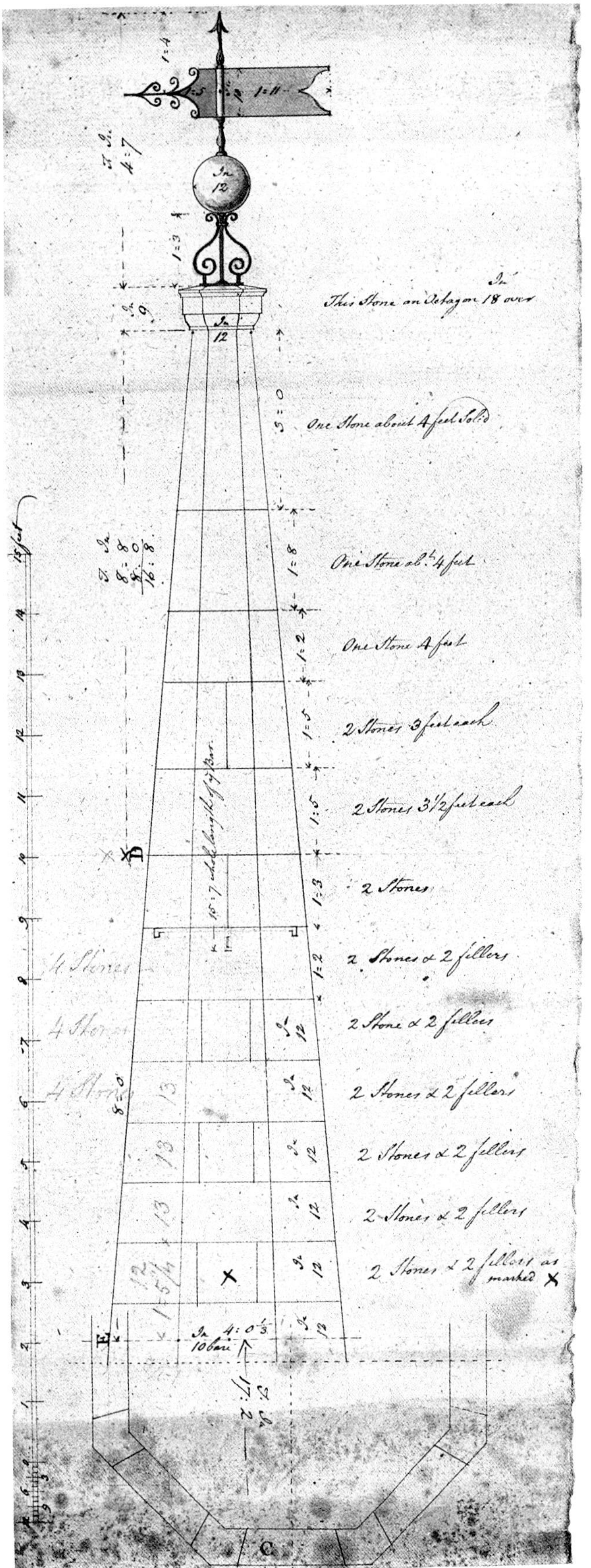

men were guilty of great disorder . . . upon finishing the Tower' (presumably they got intoxicated),[22] while at Salisbury Cathedral (pl. 143) a Whitsun fair custom involved the populous, 'heated with liquor', climbing the soaring spire to practise 'certain sports' where 'those who were the highest had the pleasure of discharging their urine on those below' and 'rambling all over the roofs . . . cut their names . . . date . . . and other foolish devices . . . through the lead', both hastening the fabric's decay; the authorities stopped these 'fool-hardy practices, by which many lives were hazarded'.[23] Or the tragic fate of Robert Cadman, who in the winter of 1740, having repaired the weathercock atop medieval St Mary, Shrewsbury, undertook 'several diverting Tricks and Trades upon the Rope' stretched from its pinnacle to Corbets Gay Field across the River Severn. While sliding down belly-first firing a pair of pistols, unfortunately the rope snapped, dashing his body to the icy pavement, which 'rebounded upwards several feet . . . amid thousands of spectators', including his horrified wife, who was collecting money.

> Twas not for want of skill
> Or courage to perform the task he fell;
> No, no, a faulty Cord being drawn too tight
> Hurried his Soul on high to take her flight
> Which bid the Body here beneath good Night[24]

Robert Cadman was one of several daredevils including the 'Italian Flyer' Thomas Cadman, who in 1727 successfully performed the feat from the top of the tall steeple of St Martin-in-the-Fields, grasping burning torches (pl. 5), as well as Mr Gillinoe from the 178-foot-high tower of All Saints, Derby, in 1732, and three years later a 'high flying Stranger' at Bromham, Wiltshire.[25]

Church touring proved a favourite Georgian pastime. Few were as industrious as the Irish clerics Jeremiah Milles, who made six excursions between 1735 and 1743, and Richard Pococke, who travelled through England, Ireland and Scotland during the 1740s, 1750s and 1760s; both are quoted throughout this book.[26] John Byng, 5th Viscount Torrington, a renowned diarist, confessed to a 'Greediness to visit Churches [which] hourly increases, as they all can furnish somewhat of Antiquity or of curiosity'.[27] The two most popular London venues were St Paul's Cathedral and Westminster Abbey (pl. 6):

4 (*left*) John Palmer. Working drawing for the construction of the steeple, St Swithin, Bath, Somerset, 1789. Pen and ink and wash. Original held at Somerset Record Office, D/P/wal.sw 8/4/1.

5 Anonymous. 'June 1727. The Italian Flyer, Flew from ye top of ye Steeple of St. Martins Church into the Meuse, ye Torches used when he Flew from ye upper Gallery to ye end of ye Stage' (St. Martin-in-the-Fields, London). Engraving. City of Westminster Archives Centre, Box 2, no. 18d.

> Next, to the Abbey let's repair,
> And view the sacred Relicks there;
> Th' Antiquities of *England* see,
> Well worth our Curiosity.[28]

One of the earliest guidebooks, Jodicus Crull's *The Antiquities of St Peter's; or, The Abbey-Church of Westminster . . . Adorned with Draughts of the Tombs, curiously Engraved*, published in two handy pocket-size volumes in six editions between 1711 and 1742, price 15s., which contains 'the Eulogies of the greatest Princes, Patriots, Heroes, Divines, Philosophers, and Poets' and engravings of their tombs, was issued for the benefit of the 'daily Concourse of People, of all Ranks [and] the great Number of Natives and Foreigners, that flock thither to be satisfied in the Sight of these Ancient, as well as Modern Repositories of the Bodies of so many great and illustrious Personages'. Joseph Addison's 'Remarks upon the Monuments' (reprinted in *The Spectator*, 30 March 1711) opens:

> When I am in a serious Humour, I very often walk by myself in *Westminster*-Abbey; where the Gloominess of the Place, and the Use to which it is applied, with the Solemnity of the Building, and the Condition of the People who lie in it, are apt to fill the Mind with a kind of Melancholy, or rather Thoughtfulness, that is not disagreeable . . . After having . . . surveyed this great Magazine of Morality . . . I examined it more particularly by the Accounts . . . on . . . Monuments . . . raised in every Quarter of that ancient Fabrick . . . Entertainments of this Nature are apt to raise dark and dismal Thoughts in timorous Minds, and gloomy Imaginations . . .

and so on.[29] The Revd George Reeves's *A New History of London . . . By Question and Answer* (1764) asked: 'How are we affected, at first entering the aisle?' – 'With admiration, at the strong and grand perspective; with the vast range of antique and modern monuments, which in a forcible, yet a pleasing manner, fills us with the most serious reflections.'[30] The German Karl Philipp Moritz visited 'on a dark and melancholy day, in keeping with the character of the place'.[31] The Birmingham historian William Hutton found that the 'distinguished collection of the dead stimulates the living';[32] the Lancastrian Richard Hodgkinson that they 'furnish an endless fund of entertainment to the Artist, the Poet, Historian, Biographer & the Scholar'.[33]

Soon after St Paul's completion in 1710 (pl. 2), the Leeds antiquary Ralph Thoresby climbed to the lantern, 'whence we had a surprising view of the vast extent of the City'. César de Saussure found it

> the most truly magnificent of all [churches in] London and England . . . At the base of the lantern there is a little gallery . . . From [where] on a fine

6 (*right*) Charles Taylor. 'Inside of Westminster Abbey' towards the chancel, 2 May 1796. Engraving. Author's collection.

day, when the atmosphere is clear, you can see the whole of London . . . and the pastures around . . . one of the finest views in the world.

A New Guide to London (1726) drew attention to the 'exquisite Workmanship and Taste' of the west portico, the 'extraordinary Fine . . . Ornaments and Sculpture' of the choir, Thornhill's painted dome, which cost 6d. to visit, and 'the immense largeness of the Town [and] vast number of Churches' seen from the lantern; an Irish cleric in 1761 was 'Lost in thought . . . wth. Regard to the Sublime taste & Grandeur . . . observd in this Glorious structure'; Richard Hodgkinson visiting in 1794 thought it 'a most amazing Structure . . . The Dome . . . surpasses anything of the sort I ever saw', though noting that worship was restricted to 'one corner of the Church only; & the rest is filled with gazing spectators who ramble about & pay no attention to the service'.[34] On the other hand, Moritz found the experience boring:

I must confess that on first entering . . . its emptiness damped rather than stimulated the feeling of majesty I desired . . . Everything I saw . . . cost me no more than a little over a shilling, paid out bit by bit in pennies and half-pennies as determined by the set fees payable for the privilege of seeing the various things of interest . . . I was shown over the church by a guide, whose rigmarole about how long it took to build, and all the rest of it, he delivered so mechanically that I wished he had kept it to himself.

The architect Thomas Harrison remarked that the fabric 'will sustain great injury from the *doors* being so constantly kept shut, which is done to oblige people to pay for admittance . . . for want of a due circulation of Air, that which is enclosed is generally so damp that it must corrode the walls'.[35] In the Revd William Hanbury's megalomaniac and unrealisable cathedral-like parish church planned for Church Langton, Leicestershire, in the 1770s, boys attending the adjacent, equally untenable school would be given the tasks of providing 'matts and scrapers . . . properly placed by the doors' and seeing that 'nobody chews Tobacco in . . . the Church', as well as serving as guides at fixed rates: ascending the crossing tower 2d., seeing the choir and Lady Chapel 3d. Tourism in full flower![36]

In *The Spectator* of 1711 Joseph Addison published a Ciceronian satire on the state visit to London of four Iroquois chiefs (an historical event in which the English sought to gain an Indian alliance in the war against France in Canada), describing how they were 'wonderfully struck with the sight of every thing that is new or uncommon', particularly St Paul's Cathedral, 'designed by God & carved from a mountain' – and perhaps to be read as an allegory of the savage's inability to comprehend man-made structures of Christian worship. 'On the most rising part of the town [Ludgate Hill] their stands a huge house, big enough to contain the whole nation of which I am king', observed E Tow O Koam, who was 'of opinion it was made by the hands of that great God to whom it is consecrated'. Granajah believed that 'it was created with the earth, and produced on the same day with the sun and moon', while Sa Ga Yean Qua Rash Tow thought that

this prodigious pile was fashioned into the shape it now bears by several tools and instruments . . . It was probably at first an huge misshapen rock that grew upon the top of the hill, which the natives . . . after having cut it into a kind of regular figure, bored and hollowed with incredible pains and industry, 'til they had wrought in it all those beautiful vaults and caverns . . . As soon as this rock was thus curiously scooped to their liking, a prodigious number of hands must have been employed in chipping the outside . . . as smooth as the surface of a pebble; and is in several places hewn out into pillars that stand like the trunks of so many trees bound about the top with garlands of leaves.[37]

Though indisputably the central architectural masterwork of a sprawling metropolis, what equally enchanted eighteenth-century visitors was the cathedral's setting within the wider natural landscape – indeed, for our bewildered Indian diplomats it was veritably a natural object and even for the English could become some sort of supernatural phenomenon. Dr Edmond Halley's 'Account of Light seen in the Air', published in the *Philosophical Transactions of the Royal Society* in 1716, recounted how, as it grew dark,

the Beginning of this wonderful Sight was seen; out of what seem'd a dusky Cloud . . . the Edges . . . tinged with a reddish Yellow, like as if the Moon had been hid behind it, there arose very long luminous Rays . . . perpendicular to the Horizon . . . Many . . . seeming to concur near the *Zenith*, formed there a *Corona* . . . which drew the Attention of all Spectators. Some liken'd it to that Representation of *Glory* wherein our Painters in Churches surround the Holy *Name of God* . . . Many compar'd it to the *Concave* of the great *Cupola* of St Paul's . . . having in the middle a Space less bright . . . resembling the Lantern.[38]

The cathedral itself was the subject of several unsuccessful planning proposals. Fougeroux in 1728 not only found it 'too much hemmed in by the surrounding houses' but the western approach also 'too narrow to afford a view of it, as is not only curved itself, but leads up to the façade at an angle, so that it cannot be seen until you are quite close'. An Italian visitor writing to a friend in Naples in 1762 condemned the 'aukward' site, neither square, round nor oval, as the 'worst design of the most barbarous people'. In 1711–12 Nicholas Hawksmoor suggested a bell-shaped enclosure of a continuous four-storey terrace in the manner of Inigo Jones's Covent Garden Piazza, with a free-standing, domed rotunda baptistery closing off the western opening. The Jacobite 6th Earl of Mar, exiled in Paris in 1726, offered as a solution creating a series of 'great' formal avenues linking his proposed new royal palace in Hyde Park (for the ill-fated James III) culminating at St Paul's dome. In 1734 the architectural writer James Ralph reminded readers that Wren in his post-Fire design for resurrecting the devastated City had envisaged a 'large street' stretching from Temple Bar in the west eastward to Aldgate, bisecting a 'large square' containing the cathedral 'with a proper distance for the view all round it; whereby that huge building would not have been cooped up . . . in such a manner as no where to be seen to advantage at all; but would have a long and ample vista at each end . . . and give it one great benefit which . . . it must now want for ever', while Ralph's erstwhile nemesis Batty Langley agreed that 'Nothing certainly can contribute more to such august structures than spacious avenues'.[39] Furthermore, the soaring domes and spires of churches were both integral to the urban setting and inseparable from the Anglican vision of a prosperous Christian community:

> There shall broad streets their stately walls extend,
> The circus widen, and the crescent bend;
> There, rayed from cities o'er the cultured land,
> Shall bright canal and solid roads expend
>
> Embellished villas crown the landscape scene,
> Farms wave with gold, and orchards blush
> between:-
> There shall tall spires and domed-capped towers
> ascend

rhapsodised Erasmus Darwin in *Visit of Hope to Sydney Cove, near Botany-Bay* (1789).[40]

This wider urban context was forcibly expressed in the New Churches manifestos of 1711 by Wren in a 'Letter to a Friend on the Commission' and by John Vanbrugh in 'Proposals about Building'.[41] Wren recommended purchasing ground not in 'the Extremities of the Suburbs . . . where vacant Ground may be cheapest [but] among the thicker Inhabitants, for Convenience of the better sort, although the Site . . . should cost more', since these parishioners would contribute to the cost of future repairs and other parish charges. He was perhaps echoing Palladio's observation in Book Four of *I quattro libri d'architettura*, Chapter 1, 'On the Site to be Selected for Building Temples', regarding choosing 'the most dignified and prestigious part of the city, far away from unsavory areas'. Palladio favoured sites 'on beautiful and ornate squares where many streets end, so that every part of the temple can be seen in all its majesty and arouse devotion and awe in whoever sees and admires it'.[42] Thomas Archer's unrealised rotunda church placed in the centre of the stately seventeenth-century square of Lincoln's Inn Fields (pl. 7), with six *in antis* porticoes aligned with walks fanning out to the perimeter, epitomised this aspiration. It was believed that the 650 by 450 foot square 'wants only a Church for its convenience & Ornament, to make it Equal any Piazza in Christendome'.[43] Its form carried not only a Palladian authority – Palladio's reconstruction of the Temple of Vesta at Rome is described as 'a round shape so as to resemble the mass of the earth which nurtures humanity'[44] – but also an Albertian one: 'It is obvious from all that is fashionable . . . under her influence, that Nature delights primarily in the circle.' Alberti had also written about situating the temple in 'a busy, well-known, and . . .

7 Thomas Leverton Donaldson. Plan no. 13, 1843, of Thomas Archer's lost wooden model for a church in Lincoln's Inn Fields, London, 4 January 1713. Pen and ink and wash. RIBA Library Drawings Collection, os5/9 (13).

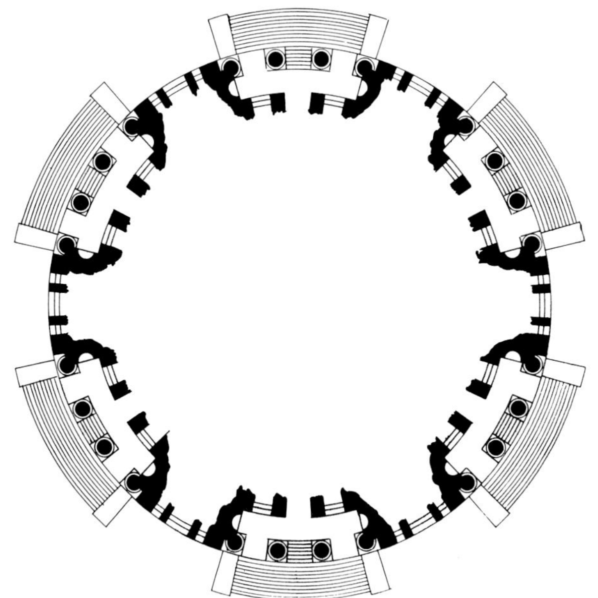

proud place, free of any profane contamination', as in 'a large, noble square . . . surrounded by spacious streets, or, better still, dignified squares, so that it is perfectly visible from every direction', and suggested raising it 'above the level of the city [which gives it] a greater air of dignity'.[45] This was the common currency of renaissance town planning theory based on Vitruvius' observation that 'the widest possible view of the city may be had from the sanctuaries of the gods'.[46]

The New Churches Commissioners, who included Wren and Vanbrugh, expressed interest in insularity where the sites were appropriate,[47] in response to Wren's idea – first explored without success in his post-Fire plan of redistributing the haphazard, devastated City churches on 'conspicuous and insular' sites along main thoroughfares[48] – of bringing this second bout of buildings 'as forward as possible into the larger and more open Streets, not in obscure Lanes, nor where Coaches will be much obstructed in the Passage'.[49] Vanbrugh recommended that 'their Situation may be ever Insulate', which not only gives them 'that Respectfull Distinction & Dignity which Churches Always ought to have; but makes the Access to them easy, and is a great Security from Fire' (an ever present concern since the 1666 catastrophe), and 'so plac'd, to be fairly View'd at such proper distance, as is necessary to shew their Exterior Form, to the best Advantage, as at the ends of Large and Strait Streets, or on the Sides of Squares and Other open Places'.[50] This idea was still powerful enough in 1771 for the author of *Critical Observations on the Buildings and Improvements of London* to hope that Sir William Chambers's parish church proposed (but never built) for up-market St Marylebone (pl. 620) would 'not be huddled into a bye corner; but appear as it ought, with a magnificence proper for the religious worship of an opulent people'.[51]

As in 1666, such ambitions largely failed to materialise, and one of its unfortunate victims was the imaginative programme initiated in 1713 of placing fifty statues of Queen Anne, the reigning monarch, 'made by the best hands' (Francis Bird and Grinling Gibbons), 'in the most conspicuous & convenient part of each of the . . . Churches' (pl. 404); but in the following year the scheme was condensed to a single, 10-foot-high bronze figure commissioned from G. B. Foggini in Florence to crown a 200-foot-high Corinthian column to be located in the middle of the Strand before Gibbs's church of St Mary (pl. 377). This was abandoned on the queen's sudden death in 1714, with the completed statue, stranded in Florence, then proposed for the domical west porch of the island church itself (pl. 378), before finally being shelved altogether in the following year.[52] Gibbs, who only a few years earlier (1703–8) had trained in Rome, was familiar first-hand with the prototypes, describing in his unpublished 'A few Short Cursory Remarks on some of the finest Antient and modern Buildings in Rome' Trajan's Column standing before Santa Maria di Loreto as 'one of the finest peeces of Architectur . . . now extant in the World . . . the beauty and grandeur of it appears to the spectator like a wonder', and the entry into the Piazza del Popolo, with the 'high Obelisque . . . in the Middle . . . And at the same time seeing [the twin churches of Santa Maria dei Miracoli and Santa Maria di Montesanto] and the three long streets all at one view', which 'certainly is one of ye finest Scenes can be seen, and strikes one with admiration at first coming in to that famous City'.[53]

The immediate concern of the Commissioners, who first met formally on 3 October 1711, was to identify the new churches across twenty-three parishes and to acquire appropriate sites.[54] Many of these were rejected as unsuitable. Mr White's ground in St Giles Cripplegate, though 'capatious enough for a Church & Ministers House', was untenable because of the 'black Mudd & water'.[55] The fashionable parish of St James's, Westminster, proved particularly frustrating. Various private properties were viewed, including Madam Panton's on Windmill Street fronting Haymarket, nearby Lady Clarges's and Lady Dover's, and the Duchess of Monmouth's on Soho Square, who demanded an excessively high £3,000.[56] On 15 May 1713 Thomas Archer, another Commissioner-cum-architect, reported to the Earl of Oxford on ground in Piccadilly adjacent to Green Park 'over against Devonshire House that would be beautified by such a structure to terminate the house, and . . . put a stop to any further building on that site', and that the 'impossibility of finding another . . . in this part of town . . . has forced the commissioners to apply to you to intercede with the Queen for her approval', which she refused.[57] A number of church plans, without elevations, were prepared by an early Commission surveyor, William Dickinson, none of which went beyond the drafting stage, though some are linked with subsequently successful building programmes, as we shall see later in chapter 19.[58] Some are pertinent in the present context. The most influential is Hawksmoor's scheme of 1711 for a basilica church 'after the Primitive Christians' for a site in Bethnal Green (pl. 383), which features a rectangular body with an apsidal chancel, prominently projecting side entrances and a semi-detached west block containing a baptistery surmounted by a tower. The walled burial ground with its

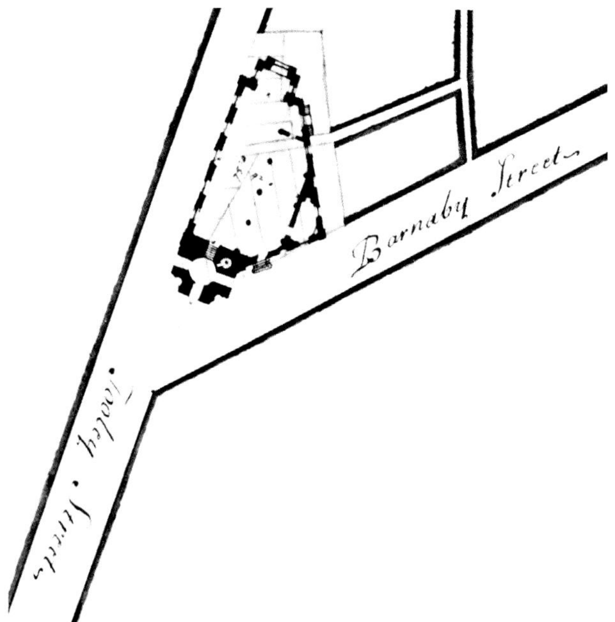

8 William Dickinson. Plan for an unrealised church at the intersection of Tooley Street and Barnaby Street, St Olave, Southwark, London, 1711–13, detail. Pen and ink. Lambeth Palace Library, MS 2750/76.

enclosed 'Sleeping place' and 'Cloyster for inscriptions' is isolated from the church, according with the Commissioners' recommendation, but linked to it by a short avenue, and beyond is the cemetery.[59] Though unrealised, many features of this remarkable scheme soon reappeared in more concrete form in Hawksmoor's preliminary and executed designs for St Alfege, Greenwich. His spectacular provision for the Via Regia, a straight, broad, east–west avenue linking the church's monumental portico (situated at the building's east end due to the unique orientation of the site) to Greenwich Hospital (pl. 357), also came to naught, presumably because of a reluctance to disturb the town's ancient, irregular street pattern.[60] For an awkward site in Southwark (pl. 8), Dickinson proposed a clever solution with a monumental tower (judging from the wall thickness) at the tip of the triangle, entrances on three sides and a side aisle and vestry room inserted along one side, but this filled up nearly all the available ground and would have proved irksome in terms of public access.[61] The site approved in 1711 for St George-in-the-East, Wapping, was bound by 'free Land Northward', Radcliffe Highway to the south and Cannon Street to the west. Hawksmoor reported that

> there is but one approach to it, vizt . . . out of . . . Cannon Street (which Street is but narrow, and the way from it to the Church not wide enough to turn a Coach or Horse) . . . But these impediments will be taken away if [the Commissioners] purchase 4 houses and Gardens by Mr Poulten, and that will open an approach from . . . Ratcliffe-highway of 54 foot wide and about 100 foot Long, by which the South front of the Church will be Layd open to the great Street . . . and the beauty and Conveniency of the Situation much increased.[62]

Hawksmoor's St Mary Woolnoth particularly suffered from the confinement of unreformed pre-Fire street patterns:

> It would be impossible . . . to find a place in the whole city where the principal ornaments of a building could be more completely concealed. The tower can no where be seen to advantage, and can scarce any where be seen at all . . . a great deal of expence has therefore been here thrown away in ornament, to very little purpose.[63]

There were, however, two notable successes. In 1713 Dickinson and Hawksmoor reported favourably that Henry Smith's ground in Westminster would 'admit of a good foundation for a Church' (the future St John, Smith Square), and Vanbrugh was invited to devise 'the Avenue to be made', eventually with Archer's memorable quadrupedal towered structure approached on the east from Church Street linked to Mill Bank along the Thames, and another from North Street aligned with (but not directly leading to) Westminster Abbey (pl. 365).[64] An early proposal for St George's parish, Hanover Square (pl. 9), placed a rectangular, apsidal-ended church in the centre of a *rond-point*, with one avenue leading axially into the square, a unique layout within the New Churches programme. John James's executed church (pl. 11) placed it less effectively to one side of the avenue, within restricted ground measuring 70 by 100 feet with 'publick Streets on three Sides and an Ally on the fourth'.[65] Nevertheless, the vista was considered 'one of the most entertaining in the whole city . . . the breaks in the building [and] the beautiful projection of the portico . . . are . . . circumstances that unite in beauty, and make the scene perfect'.[66]

Hawksmoor immediately applied the New Churches recommendations to radical re-planning at both universities in 1712–13, among the earliest important provincial schemes involving churches. Oxford was to be reconstructed on antique lines following Palladio's recommendation that houses of worship built outside the capital should have the main façade 'made to look out over public streets . . . so that passersby can see

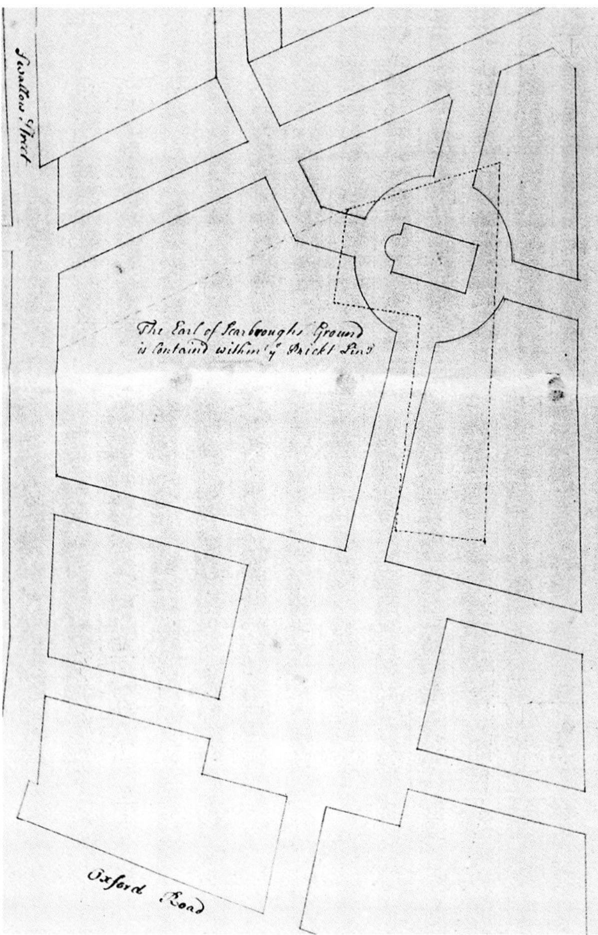

9 Anonymous. Plan for an unrealised church on 'The Earl of Scarbroughs Ground', St George Hanover Square parish, London, 1714–20, detail. Pen and ink. Lambeth Palace Library, MS 2750/23.

them and demonstrate their respect and reverence in front of them'.[67] The 'Capella Universitatis' was conceived as a huge rectangular, temple-like structure of twelve by fourteen columns sited to the east of and aligned to the Schools (pl. 10).[68] At Cambridge he proposed creating a central forum in the area fronting King's College approached by cross-axial avenues, one extending west–east from the east end of the College chapel passing through a colonnaded screen and along a straightened Petty Cury to Christ's College, the other north–south from the forum across a *piazza* with monumental obelisks linking the university church, Great St Mary, to All Saints (later demolished) and culminating at the romanesque round church of Holy Sepulchre. In his sketch for 'The town . . . as it now ought to be reformed', Hawksmoor begged 'pardon for Making such a plan, and hope I may be excused because Cavalier Fontana and others have done the same in Case of Like Nature', alluding to Domenico Fontana's remodelling of Rome under Sixtus V.[69]

Birmingham received a grand new parish church (designed by Thomas Archer, 1709–25) situated in a 'well chosen spot [on] the summit of the highest eminence' surrounded by wealthy residential terraces, a rectory and a charity school for eighty boys and girls, forming 'one of the finest church yards in Europe' (pl. 12), though there were complaints that 'admidst all the excellencies' the church was on axis neither with the yard nor the adjacent buildings along the seven streets leading in to it.[70] In 1777, however, it was aligned northward along the 36-foot-wide Church Street to the Newhall Estate's 300 by 235 foot churchyard with its centrally placed St Paul's Chapel, surrounded by handsome terrace houses, a sequence that survives to this day.[71] The catalyst for this layout in a town that until then retained much of its haphazard medieval street patterns may have been the display there in 1772 of an 18-foot-square wooden model of 'all the Squares, Streets, Churches' and so forth of the city and suburbs of Paris.[72]

Creating such strong formal links became a much-admired solution. The neatly gridded coal town of Whitehaven, Cumberland, laid out by the earls of Lowther at the close of the seventeenth century, recorded in a panorama painted at the zenith of the early Industrial Revolution (pl. 3), reveals how its two

10 Nicholas Hawksmoor. 'Regio Prima Aecademia Oxoniesis amplificata et oxornata', plan for reorganizing Oxford University, *c.*1713–14, detail. Pen and ink. Bodleian Library, University of Oxford.

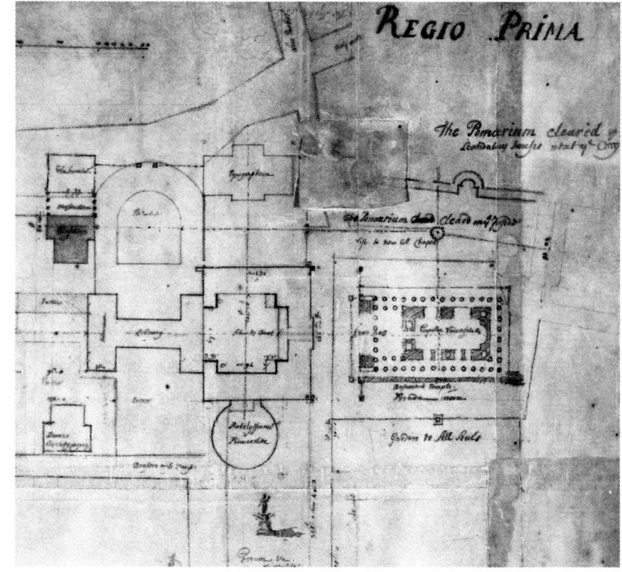

11 Thomas Malton Jr. *View of St George, Hanover Square, Mayfair, London*, from south-west, 1785–95. Watercolour. Museum of London, 002643. John James, architect, 1721–25.

classical churches, St Nicholas (1687–93) and Holy Trinity (1713–15), were given prominence within enclosed, manicured churchyards situated along major thoroughfares, a pattern that still survives.[73] Jacob Leroux's Polygon, Southampton, designs for which he exhibited at the Royal Academy in 1771–2, comprised a twelve-sided speculative development of houses, one in each segment, their fronts facing outward and gardens converging on a central water basin, with a chapel and an additional building outside the ring consisting of an 'elegant tavern, with assembly, and card rooms' linked by colonnades to two outer hotel blocks 'to accommodate the Nobility and gentry', the elevated ensemble commanding 'a most delightful prospect' of the town, and which, if completed, it was claimed, 'would be one of the first places in the kingdom, perhaps in the world, regarded in the view of modern architecture'. Nothing of this now remains.[74] At Great Yarmouth, Norfolk, John Price father and son built a new chapel integrated within the urban landscape by employing the same Doric order and round-headed windows in their contemporary Town Hall and Assembly Rooms (pl. 13), promoted by the same Corporation-led committee dipping into the same building fund. This is an outstanding example of reciprocity between Church and State and the influence of secular, particularly mercantile forces within a liberated, post-Puritan society, in a town rich from herring fishing and renowned as the 'finest and best furnished of any . . . market in England'.[75] A similar symbiotic relationship existed in Leeds, Yorkshire, the northern centre of cloth manufacture, between Holy Trinity Chapel (pl. 419) and the nearby Moot Hall (1710, demolished 1825), both designed by William Etty and employing giant order pilasters, and at Pontefract (pl. 14), between St Giles (1704–8, *circa* 1770), with its robust

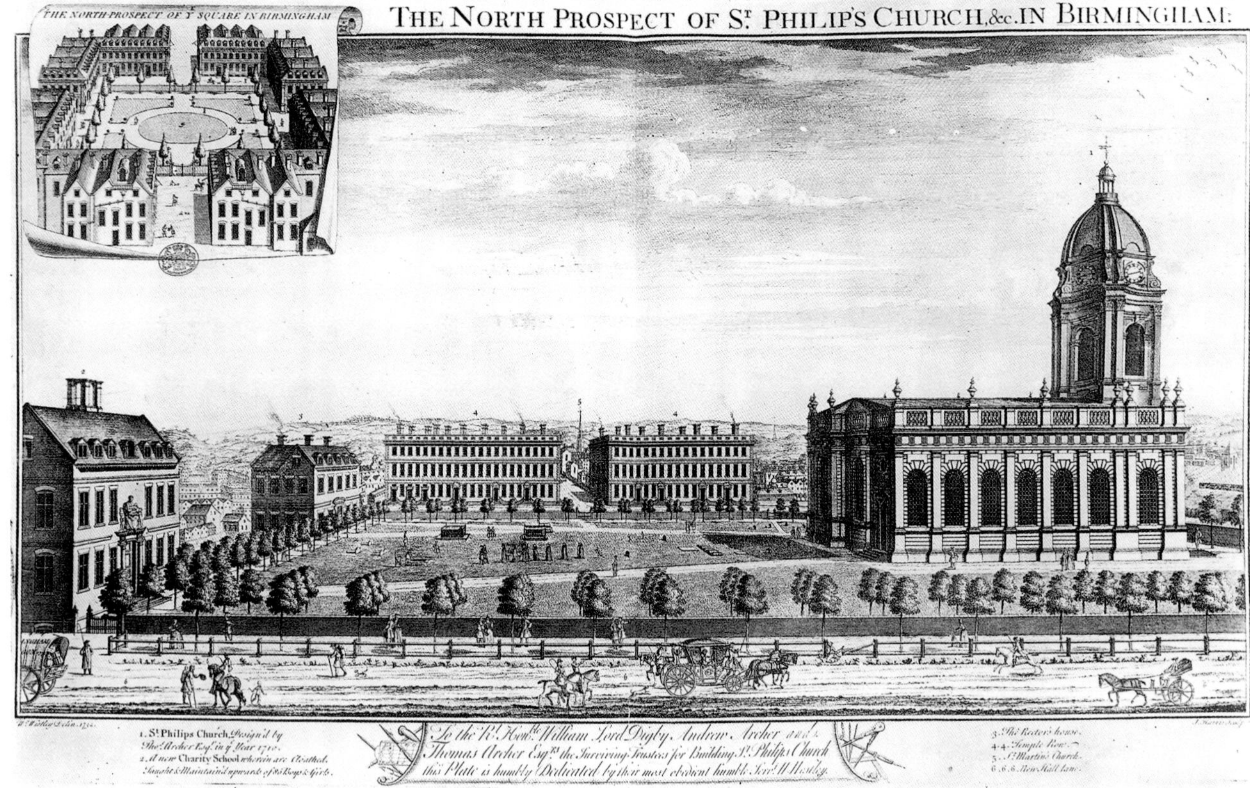

12 John Harris after William Westley. 'The North Prospect of St. Philip's Church, &c. In Birmingham', Warwickshire, 1732. Engraving. Author's collection. Thomas Archer architect, 1709–25.

Gibbs-surround windows, and the boldly rusticated Vanbrughian Market Cross (1734).[76]

Churches sited in the centre of newly created squares, like St Andrew, Glasgow (pl. 427), and St Paul, Liverpool (pl. 477), the latter an imposing, centrally planned, neoclassical reworking of the western section of Wren's Great Model (pl. 476), seen 'to much better advantage than its namesake' and 'a noble addition to the view of the town, from whatever point it is taken', became increasingly fashionable during the second half of the century.[77] The *Critical Observations on the Buildings and Improvements of London* (1771) advocated the idea that

> a perfect square [should] appear to open naturally out of the street, for which reason all the avenues should form *radii* to the centre of the place. The . . . circumference should be built in a stile above the common; and churches and other public edifices ought to be properly introduced. In the middle there ought to be some fountain . . . or statue.

It cited St James's Square and Wren's church (pl. 478), which 'strikes the mind . . . with something of more ease and propriety than any square in London'. John Dyer was already in 1757 poeticising 'Of busy Leeds':

> The stroke of axe and hammer; scaffolds rise,
> And growing edifices; heaps of stone,
> Beneath the chisel, beauteous shapes assume
> Of frieze and column. Some, with even line,
> New streets are making in the neighb'ring fields,
> And sacred domes of worship[78]

These urban formations reached a climax at the end of the century. In the 1790s the Bishop of Bristol donated land on what was then the western boundary of fast-expanding Leeds, which was developed as Park Square, with 'a fine large row of elegant houses . . . extremely neat and well built [in] by far the best part' of the town, adjacent to the 'large and fine . . . new church' of St Paul (pl. 668).[79] An agreement of 1791 with Revd Miles Atkinson, who financed its construction, specified 'not to suffer any . . . Buildings to be erected within Twenty seven Feet of the Pallisadoes along the west End', leaving this as 'a Foot and Carriage Road', and within 42 feet on the north, nor was the area immediately surrounding the church to be 'broke

13a and b John Harris after J. Corbridge. 'The South [and] West Prospect of St. George's Chappel' and 'New Hall' vignettes in 'West Prospect of the Town of Great Yarmouth in Norfolk', 1724, details. Engraving. Images courtesy of Norfolk Library and Information Service, Local Studies, Drawer 397. John Price Sr. and Jr. architects, 1715–16, latter demolished.

14 Thomas Malton. 'Market Place, Pontefract', Yorkshire, 1776, detail. Pen and ink and wash, preparatory drawing for S. T. Sparrow's engraving issued 1 November 1777. Pontefract Museum. St Giles, body attributed to Theophilus Shelton, 1704–8, south aisle *c.*1770 architect unknown, steeple remodelled by Bernard Hartley I, 1790–91, with Market Cross, 1734 architect unknown.

into for the purpose of Burying Ground'.[80] With its monumental engaged temple portico, the church dominated this verdant square overlooking open fields; by tradition, the choice of the Ionic order, with its frieze 'enriched with leaves, and the volutes of its capitals with festoons of fruits and flowers, alluding to its rural situation', was regarded as the 'most proper [for] a church in the country'.[81]

Meanwhile, other, mostly impractical urban improvements were contemplated. In 1713 Wren had found 'little Encouragement to begin to make' the principal, north transept front of Westminster Abbey 'magnificent . . . whilst it is so much incumbered with private Tenements, which obscure and smoke the Fabrick, not without danger of fireing it' (pl. 285).[82] James Ralph proposed in 1734 creating a grand open space for the abbey, 'surrounded with stone buildings all in a taste, raised on a piazza or colonnade, with suitable decorations: and the middle . . . adorned with a group of statues, answerable to the extent of the circuit round it, [which would] be to the honour and credit of the nation'. More radically, he would demolish St Margaret's church in order to bring Henry VII's Chapel 'into play, and be attended as it deserves', then detach it from the east end of the abbey, give it a new entrance front aligned to the old House of Lords, complemented by a new Parliament House, with a 'vista laid open to [St John, Smith Square]', creating a 'group of beauties in building and decoration, which few cities in *Europe* could parallel'.[83] In 1734, too, the *Grub-street Journal* suggested erecting a pair of 'quadrangular colonades [linked by] an open pallisade of iron' at the entrance to St Bartholomew-the-Less, Smithfield, as a way of creating 'a very magnificent aspect'.[84] As well, it recommended a Tuscan triumphal arch raised on the Southwark bank of London Bridge 'to denote the strength of the city', and opposite, adjacent to Wren's St Magnus the Martyr, a Corinthian arch 'enriched with festoons, hieroglyphics, & to represent its trade, riches, and elegance'.[85] Nothing was done, however, until after the church was severely damaged by fire in 1760, when George Dance Sr, the City of London clerk of the works, as part of a widening programme initiated by the London Bridge Committee, reduced the western end of the north and south aisles by one bay to expose the sides of the tower base, through which tall arches were cut to make a footpath leading on to the widened bridge, creating a sort of triumphal Ionic-engaged temple porticoed pavilion, with the steeple rising above.[86]

Wren's St Clement Danes was to have undergone a spectacular improvement to rectify its 'unlucky twist' resulting from the meandering medieval axis of the Strand as it merged into Fleet Street at Temple Bar. Ralph had observed in 1734 that this 'grand channel of communication [which] could not be too large and spacious [but was] incumber'd . . . in a most scandalous degree' by projecting buildings, and particularly the church, even whose 'beauty and magnificence' could not make 'amends for [the] inconvenience' of having its 'backside . . . crowded . . . into the face of the people . . . even tho' they had room enough to . . . prevent so capital a nuisance'. In 1793 a London Corporation committee chaired by Alderman William Pickett promoted George Dance Jr's scheme to 'bring about a commodious west entrance into the city' by setting back the houses on the south side of the thoroughfare to make it 50 feet wide in a straight line, except at St Clement, where 'it will be necessary to make a circular bend to the southward, in order to preserve the width in that part'; or, alternatively (pl. 15), 'in a more extensive and complete manner' by taking down the church and the nearby houses on the north side of the Strand, and building 'a row of handsome houses to form . . . a triangle', in the base of which the church would be rebuilt, enclosed by iron railings, 'so as to become a beautiful object to passengers', with a new street cut to the north 'in a direct line' to Lincoln's Inn Fields. The church work was estimated at £10,000. Preference was for the latter scheme as an expression of 'a more noble, extensive, and permanent improvement, and more congenial with the dignity and consequence of this country'. In 1796 the committee adopted Dance's pared-down version, with the north range of houses erected, though not without serious financial difficulties and the church left untouched. Nevertheless, the project was considered 'both useful and elegant', forming 'one great and extensive avenue from Charing cross to the Cathedral'.[87]

The unlikelihood of achieving such visionary designs is epitomised in the Revd Hanbury's failure between 1769 and 1777 to realise in his modest Leicestershire parish of Church Langton a scheme breathtaking in its colossal extravagance, comprising a gothic cathedral-size church and college complex, which would have taken more than sixteen years to build and cost

15 W. Thomas. 'View of the North and South Side from the West of St. Clement Church', London. *Gentleman's Magazine*, January 1794, p. 1093. Engraving. Author's collection. Sir Christopher Wren and James Gibbs architects, 1680–1720, with George Dance Jr's proposed straightening of the Strand and addition of new terraces.

£400,273. No drawings have been traced, though he cited as a reasonable comparison £373,291 spent on the Escorial near Madrid, a vital clue to his intention at Langton, where the church alone would measure some 750 feet long, nearly a third larger than York Minster, possessing in his vivid words 'the greatest Air of Majesty . . . that it may afford a most surprising prospect, saluting this Country, in the most astonishing and pleasing manner'. To the south would be a 780-feet-square 'Grand Quadrangle' leading to Broad Street, as wide as the church's length and bisected by an 'Eliptic Street' 900 feet wide and 1,200 feet long, a churchyard free of gravestones and 'always kept neat and level by constant mowing', 'Public Schools', offering the curricula of antiquity, botany, grammar, mathematics, music, poetry and writing taught by professors sustained by salaries, 'to the End of the World', with facilities for a 'Statuary' and a 'Drawing Master to Exercise his Art', a library 'forming an Equilateral square of 200 yards . . . each side', an observatory, a museum of curiosities, a printing house, a county hospital, a convent for '60 poor Women, and such others as may choose the like kind of Devout Life', a 'Temple of Religion and Virtue' decorated with paintings maintained by a keeper, a 'Grand Mausoleum', 'Two Pompous Inns', and a 'Square composed of Houses, appropriated for the taking in [of] Boarders'. These were ranged around four quadrangles featuring 'Grand Domes . . . over the four Grand Entrances', with smaller passages graced by cupolas, turrets, pinnacles, pyramids, skylights, globes, crosses and 'Elevated Towers . . . at the Corners of each Square' enclosed by 'Piazzas' and 'Ornamental Statues [of] the great Luminarys of the Literary World . . . properly arranged along the several Buildings', in effect a modern secular equivalent to the cathedral cloister. Hanbury began staking out the vast site on 3 October 1777, but the project had to be abandoned at his death the following spring.[88] However fascinating, one should not imply too much significance to this crackpot project.

The realities of situating new churches in townscapes are exemplified so strikingly by the frustrations the architect Thomas Telford experienced in 1791 during the preliminary stages of rebuilding the decayed medieval fabric of St Mary Magdalene, Bridgnorth, Shropshire, as recorded in his long letter to the building committee, that it is worth recounting here in some detail. Telford reported on nine potential sites, objected to six for unspecified reasons and explored the remainder. The otherwise advantageously situated Bowling Green was rejected for its approach across the old churchyard, while another site thrust the church 'entirely out of the Town'. A third, at the end of Castle Street, fronting the High Street,

> has the advantage of being much more intimately connected with the Town, [and] the Church would form an Object of considerable importance to the High Street especially when the projected improvement is made on the west side of the narrow passage, and it would occupy a desireable Station at the separation of two Streets which would diverge from behind it.

Though this removed the church from the old burial ground, proving inconvenient for funerals, it was not regarded 'as sufficient to weigh against its superior advantages', and Telford recommended it 'as an embellishment to the Town'. The committee objected to removing the church 'to a greater distance from the Inhabitants in the lower Town & the View of it would be entirely hid from the best Streets'. Telford was asked if it was 'altogether impractible to build upon the old ground . . . not . . . exactly where the present Church stands, it may be brought close up to the Castle Street with a flight of steps up to it'; 'sensible of a great many disagreeable things that must happen in removing the Old and making a new foundation besides a great additional expence but if necessity drives us to it what can be done [yet] shudder at the thought!'. Telford expressed disappointment, since 'I had conceived that a Structure adapted to that peculiar situation might have been so contrived as to have a very grand effect, and I can not resist still entertaining some hopes.' Then suddenly he recognised the true potential of the old churchyard and of reusing part of the medieval foundations as 'the most eligible and certainly by far the least expensive', though it entailed rotating the new rectangular building 180 degrees, reorientating it on an unorthodox north–south axis, with the entrance portico and tower, among the most stunning neoclassical ensembles of its day, located at the south end and closer to Castle Street (pl. 662). He later described the church as standing 'very romantic on the Banks of the Severn . . . the Entrance End . . . is to front & nearly fill the end of one of the principal Streets and one side is to shew itself to the lower Town & adjacent Country – the Tower & Cupola will be seen in all directions'.[89]

Finally, two visionary philanthropic experiments, which, though modest in scope, succeeded in going beyond the drawing stage. In *A Tour Through the Whole Island of Great Britain* (1724) Defoe advertised his scheme proposed to Sidney Godolphin, Lord Treasurer,

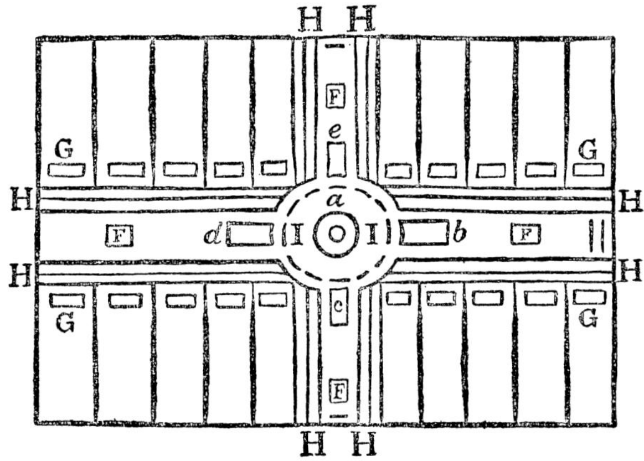

16 Daniel Defoe. 'Scheme for a new town at Lyndhurst, Hampshire' in D. Defoe, *A Tour Through the Whole Island of Great Britain*, 1724.

for a new 4,000-acre town to accommodate poor German refugees at Lyndhurst, Hampshire (pl. 16), which situated the church (marked a) at the crossroads between the shambles (b), market house (c) and town hall (d), surrounded by houses and lands (G, H).[90] In 1795 the London architect John Plaw published a 'Plan for a Village . . . made for a gentleman in Yorkshire' (pl. 17), intended for an unnamed and unidentified location in the 'vicinity of lead mines', which united 'symmetry and utility', with houses for labouring families and those of 'more independent circumstances' ranged along 'one continued street' and facing open gardens, thereby preserving their views and allowing a freer circulation of air, and 'the centre of the parallelogram' forming an enclosed oval, in the middle of which was a chapel or church, 'both convenient and picturesque'. Its plan and elevation owe much to Plaw's earlier Paddington parish church (pls 696–7). Both these schemes foreshadow the late Victorian garden suburb.

17 John Plaw. 'Plan for a Village . . . made for a gentleman in Yorkshire', dated 1 January 1795 in J. Plaw, *Ferme Ornee; or Rural Improvements*, 1803, pl. 33, detail. Engraving.

18 W. Ellis and I. Roffe after Frederic Nash. 'Choir of St. George's Chapel', Windsor Castle, Berkshire. Aquatint engraving. Author's collection. B. West's *Resurrection* window, painted glass, 1790, removed *c.*1846.

Two

THE ARCHITECTURE OF RELIGION

Nothing inspired me with more reverence than St George's Chapel [Windsor, pl. 18] . . . it raised within me by its very appearance memories of the centuries that had flowed past while it had stood Outside and inside, the chapel has an aspect of the deepest . . . melancholy . . . The disgusting boar who showed me round . . . for a shilling ruined the impression of the place itself by his claptrap.[1]

After Prayers all the Company appear on the Walks in the greatest Splendor, Musick playing all the Time; and the Ladies and Gentlemen divert themselves with Raffling, Hazard, drinking of Tea, and walking till Two, when they go to Dinner.[2]

'No!' roars the Huntingdonian Priest – 'No, no!
Lovers are liars – Love's a damned trade;
Kissing is damnable – to hell they go –
The Devil's claws await the rogue and jade.

'My chapel is the purifying place:
There let them go to wash their sins away

. . . toil six days beneath the galling load,
Poor souls! And then, the seventh be forced to go
And box the Devil, in Blackfriars Road![3]

Many of the fundamental features of eighteenth-century Anglicanism, the official state system of Protestant worship (the Church of England) secured by the Act of Uniformity in 1549 and refined in 1552 in the Book of Common Prayer, as much a political as a religious upheaval, were characterised by repudiation of the doctrines of the Church of Rome, particularly those concerning papal authority, many of the sacraments – notably transubstantiation and the Mass – and devotion to the Virgin and saints. These were replaced by personal responsibility solely to God (the Catholic Church also teaches this, although understands it in a different way, because of its teaching on the authority and ministry of the Church), acceptance of the Bible as the only source of revealed truth and congregational involvement in the communion service (exposed by the removal of pre-Reformation chancel screens). The emphasis now lay on preaching and receiving the Word rather than reception of the sacraments, expressed by bringing the pulpit and reading desks forward into the nave.

These activities were governed by a clerical hierarchy descending from archbishops based at Canterbury and York, who were responsible for provinces, down to bishops controlling jurisdiction over individual dioceses, archdeacons looking after parishes, rectors maintaining rectory, chancel, service books and vestments, to vicars, curates and churchwardens safeguarding the daily religious life of parishioners, with deans and chapters enjoying separate administrative control of cathedrals, all methodically chronicled in various writings, which, as we shall discover in this study, form rich sources about the architectural life of church buildings.[4]

As Protestantism evolved in an atmosphere of toleration during the next hundred or so years, a variety of breakaway sects emerged. As early as 1550 groups of

Independents met together as Separatists, the 'gathered Church' or Congregationalists, who opposed state intervention in religious matters. Ten years later the Presbyterian Church of Scotland was founded, advocating the principle of government by committees of elected overseers (presbyters) modelled on the New Testament, becoming the official national church in 1647. In 1612 the Baptists, stressing the individual's responsibility to work for the salvation of his or her own soul, established a church in London, splintering into groups believing in predestination and individual redemption. In 1668 the Society of Friends ('Quakers'), formed by George Fox, rejected the sacraments, formal services and paid ministers, and maintained a strong commitment to pacificism. They were all subsequently persecuted under the Conventicle Act of 1664, the Test Acts of 1673 and 1678, and the Act of Toleration of 1689.[5]

Architecturally, these developments formed an unbroken continuity into the eighteenth century.[6] Among the crucial monuments are the renaissance screen (1533–5) inserted into the gothic glory of King's College chapel, Cambridge, and Inigo Jones's classical re-casing of medieval St Paul's Cathedral (1633–2), foretastes of things to come: the classicism of Jones's Queen's Chapel, St James's (1623–7), Stoke Park chapel, Northamptonshire (1629–35), and St Paul's, Covent Garden, London (1631–3); Wren's Pembroke College chapel, Cambridge (1663), St Paul's Cathedral (1675–1710) and a succession of London churches, most notably St James, Westminster (1676–84), and St Andrew, Holborn (1684–90), as well as Ingestre, Staffordshire (1673–7), the King's Chapel, Windsor Castle (1680–84), Chatsworth House chapel, Derbyshire (1687–93), Trinity College chapel, Oxford (1692), and the Danish Church, London (1694–6). Representing the still living gothic traditions are Groombridge, Kent (1623), Lincoln College chapel, Oxford (1629–31), Charles Church, Plymouth (1643–57), Bishop Auckland, County Durham (1660), and Wren's St Alban, Wood Street, London (1683–98). As well, there is the idiosyncratic gothic-classical mixture of Peterhouse College chapel, Cambridge (1625–32), Laudian St Katherine Cree, London (1628–31), St John, Leeds, Yorkshire (1632–3), and St Mary, Warwick (1694–1704).

By the eighteenth century the success of Anglicanism could not disguise a growing pessimism. The more vulgar aspects of divine worship were conjured up by Ned Ward in *The London Spy*:

> we overtook abundance of religious lady-birds, armed against the assaults of Satan with Bible and Common Prayer Book, marching with all good speed to Covent Garden Church. Certainly . . . the people of this parish are better Christians than ordinary, for I never observed, upon a weekday . . . such a sanctified troop of females flocking to their devotions . . . walk the other way, you might meet as many young gentlemen from the Temple and Gray's Inn [the haunts of lawyers], going to join with them . . . They stood ogling one another with as much zeal and sincerity as if they worshipped the Creator in the creature, and whispering to their next neighbours, as if, according to the Liturgy, they were confessing their sins to one another. This . . . was only to make assignations, and their chief prayers is that Providence will favour their intrigues.

He added: 'A Beau . . . is as constant a visitor of a coffee-house as a Drury Lane whore is of Covent Garden Church'.[7] Nor does the opinionated John Byng, 5th Lord Torrington, an inveterate churchgoer, paint a pretty picture: at Lincoln Minster '6 o'clock morning prayers . . . have been disused about 5 years; (sad proof of idleness, and irreligion;) for nobody came but those who were obliged'; one Sunday morning at Higham Ferrers, Northamptonshire, he was

> shewn into a good pew amidst some farmers. A large church; but a small congregation. – Mr Dundas . . . or somebody very like him, drawled the prayers; and deliver'd a sermon. – Our service is most fatiguing, and ill put together, too tedious for age, or for youth . . . Some poor weakling singing. The Catholic service is much better then ours. I would be of the religion of the country I dwelt in, a R. Catholic, or a Mahometan; but let it be well kept up, and the pastors well maintain'd. Most people slept at the sermon; I was often on the brink.

The morning prayer at Christ Church, Oxford, was also 'miserably perform'd! Our Church is terribly upon the decline, which as a gentleman, and a Churchman I grieve for . . . Every minister of a sectory comforts himself with a deanery; whilst the slumb'ring Dean or the sporting curate equally disgrace our Church!!'[8] Valentine Green reported in 1796 that the creation of a passage around the west end of Worcester Cathedral 'effectively removed . . . the indecent annoyance of passengers conveying every sort of burden through the principal north entrance across the nave . . . to the cloisters, even during divine service'.[9] Churches even occasionally became crime scenes. The *Gentleman's Magazine* reported how vandals broke into St Paul's Cathedral vestry, stole £12, destroyed the sacred vestments and became intoxicated drinking sacramental wine, while at St Martin-in-the-Fields a 'well-dressed man, during divine service . . . was detected in attempting a rape upon two girls, the eldest not more than nine years old, on the stair-case leading to the belfry. He was taken into custody, and committed to prison.'[10] Yet, for the vast majority, attending worship was one of the central focuses of daily life, as Karl Philipp Moritz, a German traveller in 1782, makes amply clear:

> the parson arrived . . . The boys took off their hats and bowed low to him . . . The furnishing of the church was quite simple. Right above the altar were displayed the Ten Commandments in large letters on two tablets . . . there can be no better way of impressing the essential qualities of the faith on a waiting congregation than this . . . I gave my heart unrestrainedly to devotion and was often touched to tears . . . A few soldiers . . . seemed thoroughly ashamed – saying it was a most contemptible church . . . I took the liberty to tell them that no church was contemptible if it held well-behaved and sensible people.[11]

The extent of the Church's involvement in parish morale is revealed in Episcopal Visitations and Returns. The York diocese, for example, enquired how often divine service and the sacrament were performed, the 'Care . . . taken to instruct . . . Children . . . in the Principals of the Christian Religion, according to the Doctrine of the Church of England', if there was 'Suspicion of Adultery Fornification or Incest . . . common Swearers . . . Drunkards or any open, and notorious evil Livers . . . who suffer Persons to tipple in their Houses, or who keep open Shops, who follow their Callings, or Ordinary Labour on Sundays . . . who refuse to pay their Dues'.[12] Bishop Thomas Secker was informed by his Oxfordshire ministry that 'Many . . . Farmers and Labourers stay idle at Home, others go to the Ale House' instead of church, but the 'Constable does not care to complain . . . to the justices, for he knows some are unwilling and some dare not punnish them for fear of lessening the revenue of the excise'; 'too many . . . absent themselves from publick Worship . . . chiefly Servants, employing themselves in Fishing, Fowling and such like Exercises'; 'this Neglect does not proceed from any Contempt or disregard of the manner of Worship used in the Church of England but is rather the Effect of Sloth and Idleness'.[13] The vital proselytising function of churches is made explicit in a petition of 1711 from the inhabitants of Limehouse in east London for building a substantial fabric 'by reason . . . a Great Number . . . who are Dissenters . . . have declared they would constantly frequent the . . . New Church', while the parishioners of Blackburn, Lancashire, 'zealous to promote the established Religion', petitioned in 1726 to build a new, larger church 'speedily', since the 'great increase of Dissenters is an immediate growing Evil'.[14] The *Weekly Journal or the British Gazette* in 1727 praised the proposed erection of new churches in Old Street and Horselydown, London, as showing 'such a Regard to Religion, that it is hoped, from such virtuous Beginnings, his [George II's] Auspicious Reign will be attended with the Encouragement of Religion, to the Extirpation of Vice and Immorality'.[15] Indeed, church building prompted a general sense of well-being among the parishioners. When the first stone was laid for Holy Trinity, Leeds, in 1722, despite the 'loud huzza [which] seemed carnal to some', there was 'much spiritual rejoicing'.[16]

The Frenchman Françoise de la Rochefoucauld, son of the duc de Liancourt, observed in 1784 that 'All religions are practised' in London, which then comprised '315 different churches . . . 103 parish churches . . . 69 chapels of the established church, 21 for the French protestants, 11 for the Dutch, Germans, Danes, etc; 33 for the Baptists, 26 for the Independents, 28 for the Presbyterians, 19 chapels of the papists religions (counting those of the foreign ambassadors) and three Jewish synagogues'.[17]

The chapel of ease, a 'sort of little Church where an Incumbent, under the Denomination of a Chaplain, officiates', provided for 'an immense number of respectable families in a middling station of life . . . precluded from attending divine service, either on account of their distance from the parish church, or from their want of interest to procure seats in . . . proprietary chapels built by private landowners'.[18] Such buildings came into their own in the eighteenth century, for we learn from *The Case of The Erectors of a Chapel, or Oratory; In the Parish of St Andrew's, Holborn. And A Defence of their Proceedings therein. With a farther Consideration of the Case of Chapels in General, As Annexed, or Unannexed to Parochial Churches* (1722) that due to population increase parish churches failed to accommodate one eighth of their parishioners and the cure lay in erecting these secondary structures: 'Few . . . of the Kind [having] been made since the Reformation', and thus with scant precedents.[19] A visual expression of this is Morris's engraving of 1768 of Mayfair showing these satellites surrounding the mother church (pl. 1). Their subordinate function, however, did not necessarily condemn them to an aesthetic wilderness, as can be seen here and at Holy Trinity, Leeds (pl. 419), or at St Bartholomew, Birming-ham, a handsome Palladian box, which accommodated 800 and was the setting for a celebration of the signing of the Peace Treaty of Paris in 1763, ending the Seven Years War, marked by a performance of 'the late famous Mr Henry Purcell's Te Deum, Jubilate, and Anthem; also the late Mr Handel's celebrated Coronation Anthem: The Vocal Parts by a Society belong to the Chapel, accompanied with Instruments by Gentlemen whose Abilities render'd the Performance compleat'.[20]

Further insight into the close ties between religious observance and architecture comes from private country house chapels. 'Now,' said Mrs Rushworth, 'we are coming to the chapel', reported Fanny Price, visiting the Great House at Sotherton, in chapter 9 of Jane Austen's *Mansfield Park* (1814).

> They entered. Fanny's imagination had prepared her for something grander than a mere, spacious, oblong room, fitted up for the purpose of devotion – with nothing more striking or more solemn than the profusion of mahogany, and . . . crimson velvet cushions . . . I am disappointed, said she, in a low voice . . . This is not my idea of a chapel. There is nothing awful here, nothing melancholy, nothing grand.

She was informed that it had been

> formerly in constant use both morning and evening. Prayers were always read in it by the domestic chaplain . . . But the late Mr Rushworth left it off. Every generalization has its improvements, said Miss Crawford. It is a pity, cried Fanny, that the custom should have been discontinued. It was a valuable part of former times. There is something in a chapel and chaplain so much in character with a great house, with one's ideas of what such a household should be! A whole family assembling regularly for the purpose of prayer, is fine!

Perhaps she was meant to recall the frisson of Horace Walpole's *The Castle of Otranto* (1764): 'We must go down here, said Isabella: follow me; dark and dismall as it is, we cannot miss our way; it leads directly to the church'; Manfred 'hastened secretly to the great church. Gliding softly between the aisles, and grided by an imperfect gleam of moonshine that shone faintly through the illuminated windows, he stole towards the tomb of Alfonso.'[21] Or Torrington day-dreaming:

> I have seen many grand chapels in several of the great houses . . . which have all been lumb'ring marble monuments; and not to my idea of taste. Were I to build a chapel in my house . . . for no house of size can be otherwise complete, I wou'd send for drawings of several cathedral quires, and of several college chapels of Oxford and Cambridge; from them, I shou'd select one, and then build mine of a size equal to my house . . . with Gothic pillars, roof, and windows, *richly dight*; I cou'd first have a small exact model made; perhaps one of Kings College Chapel of Cambridge.[22]

Horrific social stigma was attached to the neglect of such facilities, as we learn from Torrington on a visit to Raby Castle, County Durham: 'I was met by a fat house-keeper; and shewn into the Gt Hall . . . "Have you any picture gallery?" "No." "No chapel?" "No. That was taken with the hall." "No library?" "Yes, one up stairs, kept lock'd" ', which though 'a stranger' drove him to ask the owner, Lord Darlington's permission 'to lay out £20,000, for "I, then, think that I could make your house a wonder of beauty . . . the hall should be in eternal warmth; I should build a chapel; and a Gothic stair-case" '.[23] The necessity of a chapel 'in a household of any size', Nicholas Le Camus de Mezières explained in *The Genius of Architecture; or, The Analogy of That Art with our Sensations* (1780), lay

> in order that the duties of religion may be performed in all circumstances and that the Masters may set a good example. Where it is impossible . . . to have one, it will be replaced by an oratory . . . the place must be conducive to meditation and inspire the profoundest respect. Severe forms, segmental arches, ceilings a little low, profiles with few moldings, a half-light, an altar in the shape of a tomb, a good picture hung in a recess and lit from unseen windows, all would contribute to this precious illusion . . . Such a room, open at particular times, is a stimulus and incitement to piety. What could be more conducive to the maintenance of good order? Where architecture produces such effects, in alliance with painting and sculpture, it engenders a magic that acts upon the soul, imparting to it sentiments, impressions, and especially those tender sensations that we savor with such delight.[24]

The intimacy between living quarters and chapel was palpable in the eighteenth century. In his petition to the Bishop of Gloucester for a faculty to replace dilapidated medieval St Mary, Dodington, Christopher Bethel Codrington pointed out that he was 'now making many principal Additions Improvements and Alterations in and about his Mansion . . . which partly adjoins to the Church Yard', and claimed that the new church attached to the main residence by a quadrant-shaped greenhouse would be 'of very great Benefit

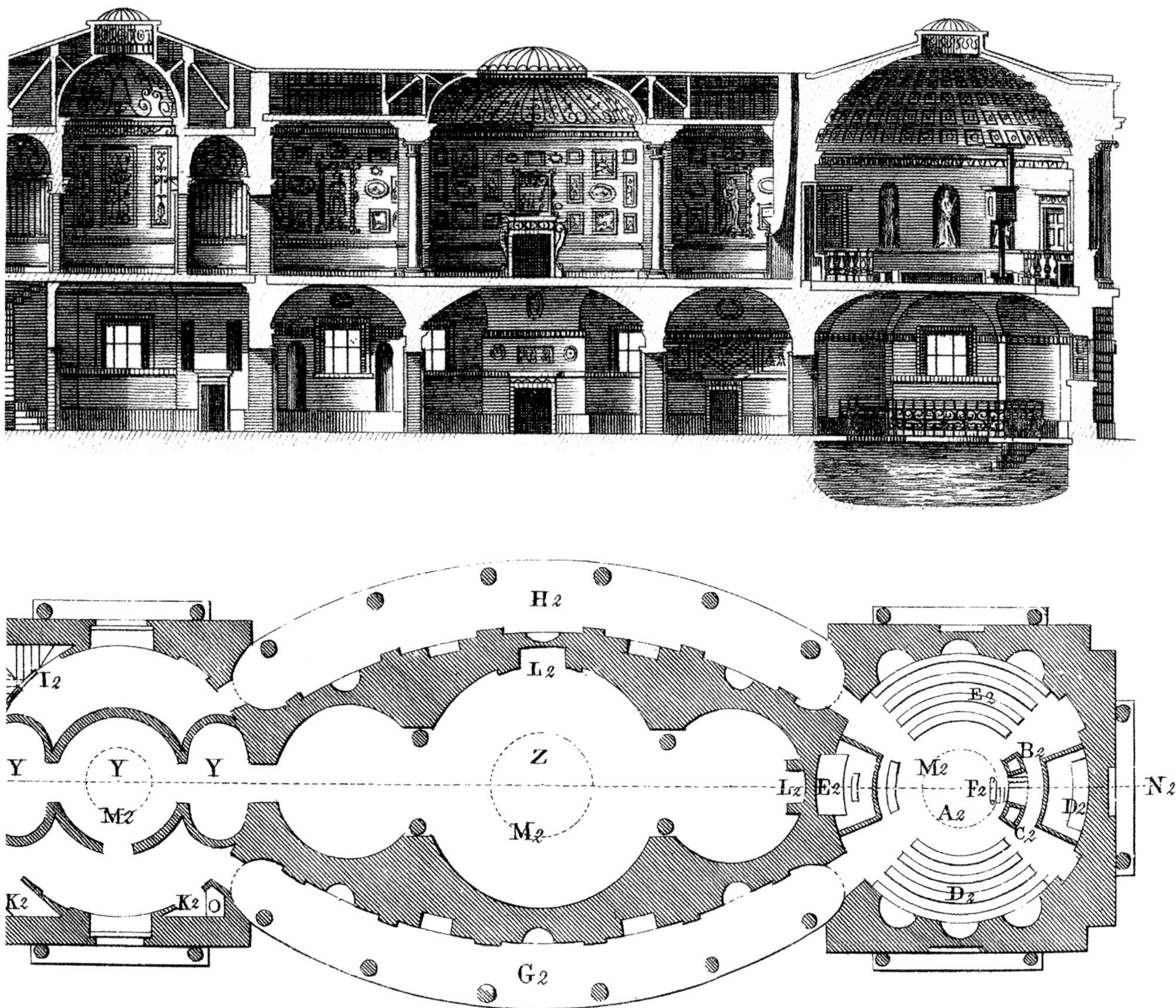

19 John Carter. Design for a 'Villa', Bywell, Northumberland, in 'A Society of Architects', *The Builder's Magazine*, 1776, XXXIII, detail. Engraving. Author's collection.

and Advantage to the present and future Minister Inhabitants and parishioners . . . and be the Means of accommodating [himself] without Injury to any person whomsoever'.[25] Its architectural and social dynamics are demonstrated in John Carter's unrealised 'Villa, designed at the Request of John Fennick, Esq; of Bywell', Northumberland (pl. 19), which features in one of a pair of wings projecting from the sides of the central block an enfilade of eccentrically shaped, first-floor rooms culminating in a Pantheon-like domed rotunda chapel, approached by segmental colonnades open to the landscape, marked G2, 'leading to the gentleman's side', and H2, to the servants' side, with a 'Private Stair-case for servants to go to the chapel', each caste occupying separate banks of pews (D2 and E2) facing one another across a central area containing the pulpit, reading desk, communion table and organ (B2, C2, D2). Beneath is the bath house.[26] Following Alberti's socio-religious recommendation that in 'Country houses . . . inhabited by gentlemen . . . There should be a consecrated chapel, immediately visible, with an altar; here any guest on entry may make a pledge of friendship, and here the head of the family on his return home may pray to the gods above for peace and calm for his family',[27] Giacomo Leoni's 1755 English translation of *De Re Aedificatoria* (1485) gave greater prominence to the space's function by locating it as 'the first Room' beyond the vestibule, where 'Strangers and

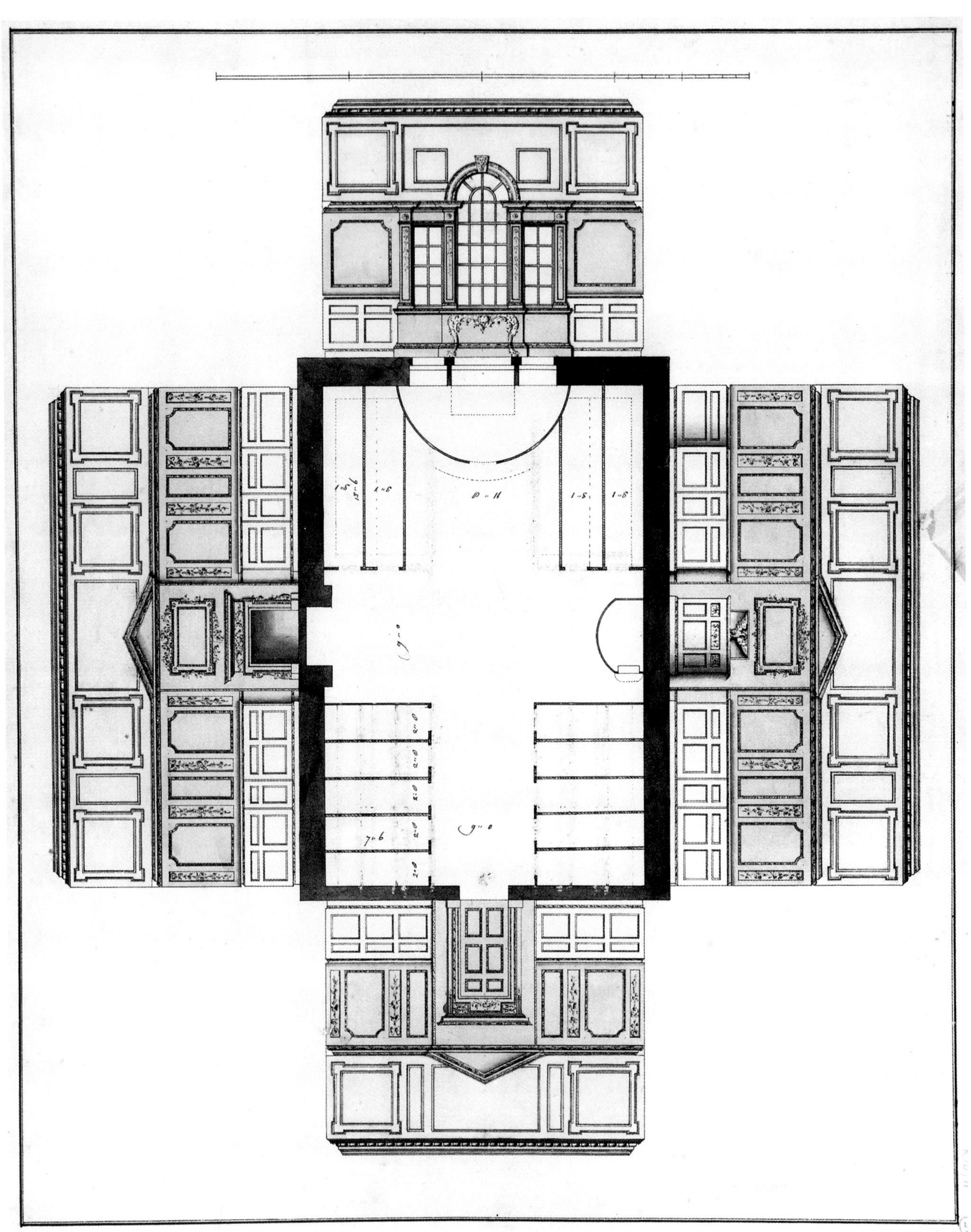

20 David and William Hiorne. Design for Gopsall Hall chapel, Leicestershire, *c.*1760. Pen and ink and wash. RIBA Library Drawings Collection, K10/11(21).

21 David and William Hiorne. Design for 'Front of reading desk over Pulpit' for Gopsall Hall chapel, Leicestershire, detail, *c.*1760. Pen and ink and wash. RIBA Library Drawings Collection, K10/11(22)

Guests may offer their Devotions, beginning their Friendship by Religion [and] the Father of the Family may put up his Prayers for the Peace of his House and the Welfare of his Relations'. Where Alberti's owner 'may embrace anyone who has come to greet him [in] the vestibule', Leoni even more poignantly relocated the welcome in the chapel itself, this only a few years after the Jacobite defeat at Culloden (1746) and the Treaty of Aix-la-Chapelle (1748).[28] Internally, these rooms could vie with state apartments in their elaborateness, as in the case of the rumbustious rococo decoration seething around the walls and across the ceiling at Gopsall Hall (pl. 20), the seat of Charles Jennens, 'Solyman the Magnificent' and Handel's librettist for *Messiah*, which included furniture like the pulpit-cum-reading desk with its 'eagle of burnished gold' (pl. 21) inspired by Thomas Chippendale's 1754 edition of *The Gentleman and Cabinet-Maker's Director*.[29]

Independent buildings within the estate grounds were usually simple, red brick, stone-trimmed boxes, like Biddlesden Park, Buckinghamshire (pl. 22), and Moreton, Shropshire, the latter erected by an annual endowment from Mrs Charlotte Bridgman of Coleshill and other aristocratic benefactions, which attracted £200 from Queen Anne's Bounty (a fund set up in 1704 to augment the livings of impoverished clergymen). Perhaps it was designed by the 'Undertaker', John Jones, who received £255 for 'Rebuilding' the old fabric and was 'at no Expence of Lime, Coal Burr Stone, for the Foundation, Clearing of Rubbish, Sand and Carriage of Materials', an account set out in a beautifully penned and bound folio.[30] The architecture may have been sober, but not necessarily the humour:

> By *Ovid*, 'mongst many more wonders, we're told
> What chanc'd to *Philemon* and *Baucis* of old;
> How their cot to a temple was changed by *Jove*:
> So a Chapel was chang'd to a Kitchen at *Grove*.
>
> The lord of the mansion most rightly conceiting,
> That his guests lov'd good prayers much less than
> good eating;
>
> A dresser sprung out of the communion table;
> Which, instead of the usual repast, bread & wine,
> Is stor'd with rich soup, and good *English* sirloin.[31]

Daniel Defoe published the epitome of a more public expression of the domestic chapel in 1724 in a 'Scheme for a Royal Palace in the Place of White-Hall' (burnt in 1698), perhaps his own but never realised, which incorporated two 'private chapels' for the king and queen and their respective households, as well as 'a large church or chapel royal, for the service of the household, and for preaching before the Houses of Parliament on publick days'. It featured a large gilded copper-covered stone dome, galleries supported on marble pillars 'of the finest and most beautiful workmanship', and a pair of 18-foot-high marble columns with gilt capitals crowned by life-size statues of *St Peter* and *St Paul* standing on each side of the steps leading up to the communion table. All the walls, entablatures, mouldings, choir-stalls and organ case were carved and

22 Francis Smith, attributed. Biddlesden Park chapel, Buckinghamshire, south elevation, 1735.

23 Architect unknown. George's Meeting House (Presbyterian), Exeter, Devon, west front, 1759–60.

gilt wood, the ceiling 'one great oval . . . carved as St Paul's' with the 'middle painted by the best masters, with either a figure of the ascention or the resurrection, the device to be new'.[32]

The eighteenth century also witnessed the appearance of new religious building types that deserve closer examination. Chief among these is an assortment of Nonconformist chapels struggling to escape intolerance. A Visitation reply from Newnham Courtney, Oxfordshire, in 1771, while reporting despondently that 'Too many greatly neglect the public Service . . . some by way of excuse the want of better Cloaths, but I rather Fear, from the want of better Hearts' and 'My Parishioners don't send their Servants & Children . . . to be instructed in their Catechism, I wish they would, for I should instruct them with great Pleasure', nevertheless affirmed, as if in compensation, 'There's not one Papist in the Parish nor hath any one here in my Memory been perverted to Popery'; 'I know not of any One' Presbyterian, Independent or Anabaptist 'for certain. Nor is there any Quakers'.[33] The Church of England greatly feared the repercussions from a variety of sects that were rife during the eighteenth century and from an alarming increase in their building activity. In particular, their less class-ridden seating arrangements were part of their social appeal, in contrast to Established Church practices, as will be seen in the next chapter.

Architectural modesty, together with an absence of steeples legislated under the Toleration Act of 1689, served the practical expediency of maintaining anonymity in the face of a hostile world by discouraging elaborate decoration and fittings, made clear by an 'Inscription for a Dissenters' Meeting-House in the Country' published in the *Gentleman's Magazine* in 1799:

> ALTHOUGH within this holy hall
> The beauteous Arts have never stood,
> To image on the storied wall
> Our Pilgrim-prophet doing good;
> We need no painting's gaudy show
> To print the kindness on our heart,
> Who, while he wept at human woe,
> Pour'd balsam on the sufferer's smart.
> Though here no sculptor's pious hands
> Engrav'd the mighty Victim's death,
> We can obey the lov'd commands
> Taught by his last, his dying breadth.
> We claim no organ's solemn tone
> To wing our praises to the sky;
> The incense of the heart alone
> Climbs with a welcome wing on high.
> Not on the marble altar's brink
> Only descends Devotion's tear;
> Simplicity high thoughts may think,
> To God the simple mind is dear.[34]

These structures rarely strayed far from conventional domestic repertory – at the Underbank Presbyterian Chapel, Stannington, Yorkshire (1742–3), only the pair of doors with their crowning oculi and tall, round-headed windows flanking the centrally placed pulpit on the internal south wall hints at its religious function (p. x).[35] Sometimes they were distinguished by sophisticated, delightfully quirky touches, like the serpentined attic of George's Meeting House (Presbyterian), Exeter (pl. 23).[36] Architectural restraint also expressed fundamental religious doctrine. James Boswell believed that 'the great success that the Methodists have . . . owing to their preaching in a plain, vulgar manner, which was the only way to do good to common people, and which men of learning and genius ought to do, as their duty; and for which they would be praised by men of sense'.[37]

The chapels of Selina, Countess of Huntingdon, an evangelical Calvinist who had been drawn to Methodism through her spinster sister-in-law, Lady Elizabeth ('Betty') Hastings, and who attracted fashionable society to her Connexion, following a cooling of friendship with John Wesley by 1764, took advantage of the Conventicle Act of 1664, which permitted a peeress to

24 William Hamilton after Thomas Thornton. 'View of Mr. Whitefield's Tabernacle near Moorfield', London, 1 August 1783. Engraving. ©The British Library Board, K.Top. XXVII-30-1. Matthew Pearce architect, 1753–4, demolished.

maintain her own private chapel provided the door was closed to the public.[38] She preferred plain classical forms, though the Bath chapel is distinguished by its choice of gothic (pl. 182). Ownership could be precarious, even in the case of a relatively sophisticated premise like the Connexion's octagonal Zion Chapel, Leeds, which opened in 1794, but within two years its ministers went bankrupt. The building was then purchased by two other clergymen, fearful that 'some Dissenters of different Denominations are striving to outbid . . . in order to prevent The Building becoming a Place under the Established Church', but this enterprise too failed and in 1801 it was finally taken under the Anglican wing (only to vanish in 1952 to make way for a car park, an all-too-familiar fate).[39]

The charismatic Revd George Whitefield, who converted to Methodism in 1735, dazzled Londoners, as his diary entries of 1739 reveal: 29 April: 'Preached . . . at Kennington Common . . . where no less than thirty thousand people were . . . present. The wind being for me, carried the voice to the extremest part of the audience. All stood attentive . . . The Word came with power'; 2 May: 'to about ten thousand'; 5 May, to 'twenty thousand hearers', and the next day for an hour and a half: 'Such a sight I never saw before. I believe there were no less than fifty thousand people . . . There was an awful silence'; 8 May, despite rain on the Common: 'To my great surprise . . . I saw about twenty thousand', and so on day after day; then on 13 May at Moorfields: 'near sixty thousand . . . Many went away because they could not hear'; 30 May at Mayfair: 'near eighty thousand . . . by far, the largest I ever preached to yet'; on 29 July, again despite rain: 'Nearly thirty thousand stood their ground, and God, I believe, watered them with the dew of His heavenly blessing'.[40] Between 1753 and 1756 he erected two nearly identical permanent 'Tabernacles' – a term employed 'because, perhaps, we may be called to move our tents'.[41] The first was at Moorfields, measuring 80 feet square (pl. 24), the second in the then still rural region of Tottenham Court Road (1756–60, razed 1857); both had lantern-crowned pyramidal roofs supported inside by four clusters of three full-height piers, while giant order pilasters on the external corners and three-bay entrance centrepieces did little to mitigate the starkness of the block with its uniform, unframed doors and windows. The architect for both was almost certainly an obscure bricklayer-builder named Matthew Pearce, a member of the latter congregation. His model was the Protestant Temple at Charenton near Paris (1623–4, demolished by an anti-Huguenot mob in 1685 but recorded in engravings), designed by the great French architect Salomon De Brosse as a three-storey, 100 by 50 foot rectangle with two superimposed galleries sup-

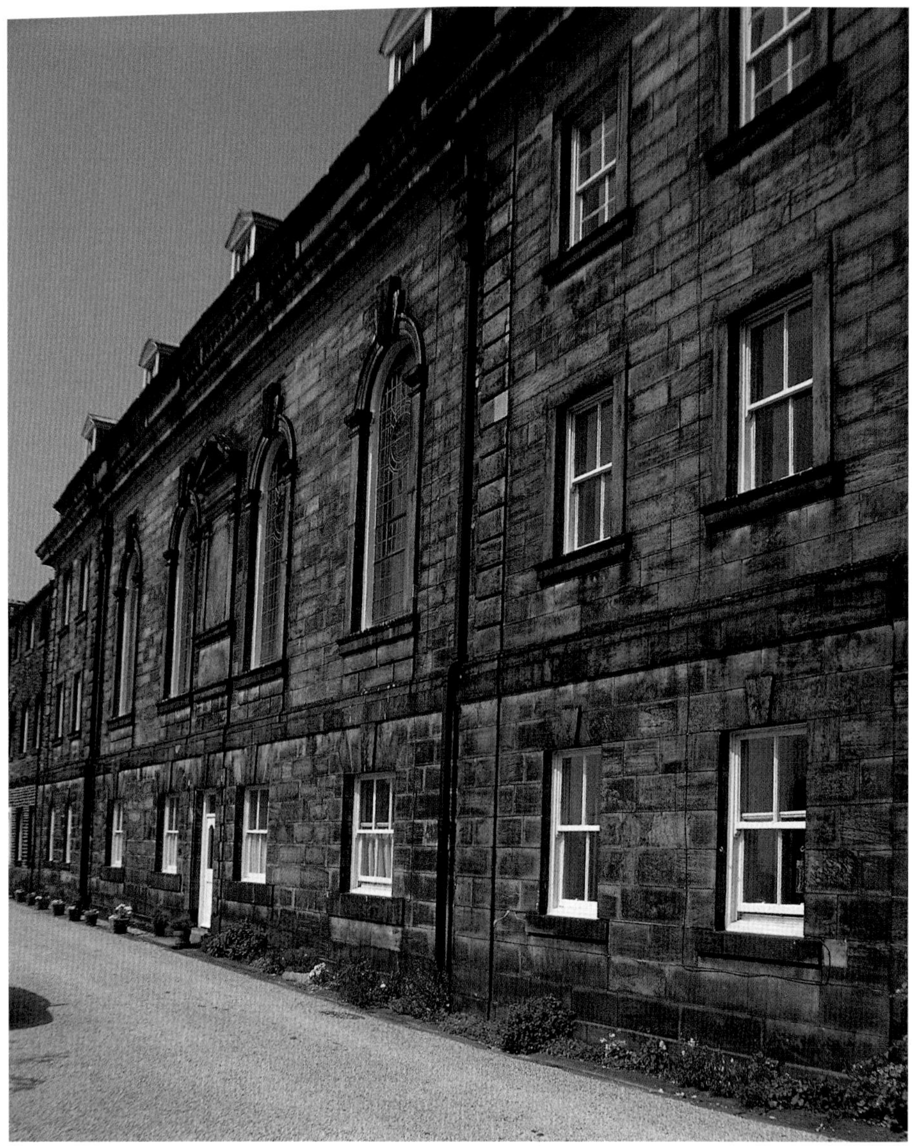

25 Architect unknown. Grace Hall, Fulneck, Yorkshire, 1746–8, south terrace elevation.

ported on giant order columns and then piers on all four sides, perhaps inspired by paper reconstructions of Vitruvius' famed Basilica at Fano.[42]

Methodism, established in 1740, which originated in the evangelistic movement inspired by John and Charles Wesley and propounded individual communion with God without intervention of a priest, of particular interest to the present study for its adoption of octangularity as a signature form, described later, remained part of the Church of England until its formal separation in 1791.[43] Nor was it a unique case. The Unity of the Brethren (Moravians) is a pre-Lutheran Protestant separatist sect founded in 1457 in Bohemia by followers of the martyred Jan Hus, which successfully reconstituted itself in 1722 on the Herrnhut estate near Dresden of Nikolaus Ludwig, Graf Zinzendorf, who founded a settlement at Fulneck, Yorkshire, in 1744, which five years later was officially recognised by Parliament as a true episcopal church. Stone-built Grace Hall (pl. 25) forms the centrepiece of the most complete and best-preserved expression of the Moravian building experiences in Britain. The double-storeyed and galleried chapel lit by prominent arched windows occupies the nucleus, flanked by congregational living spaces (an amalgamation with no parallel in the English Protestant tradition), the equivalent of the *Kaisersaal* in

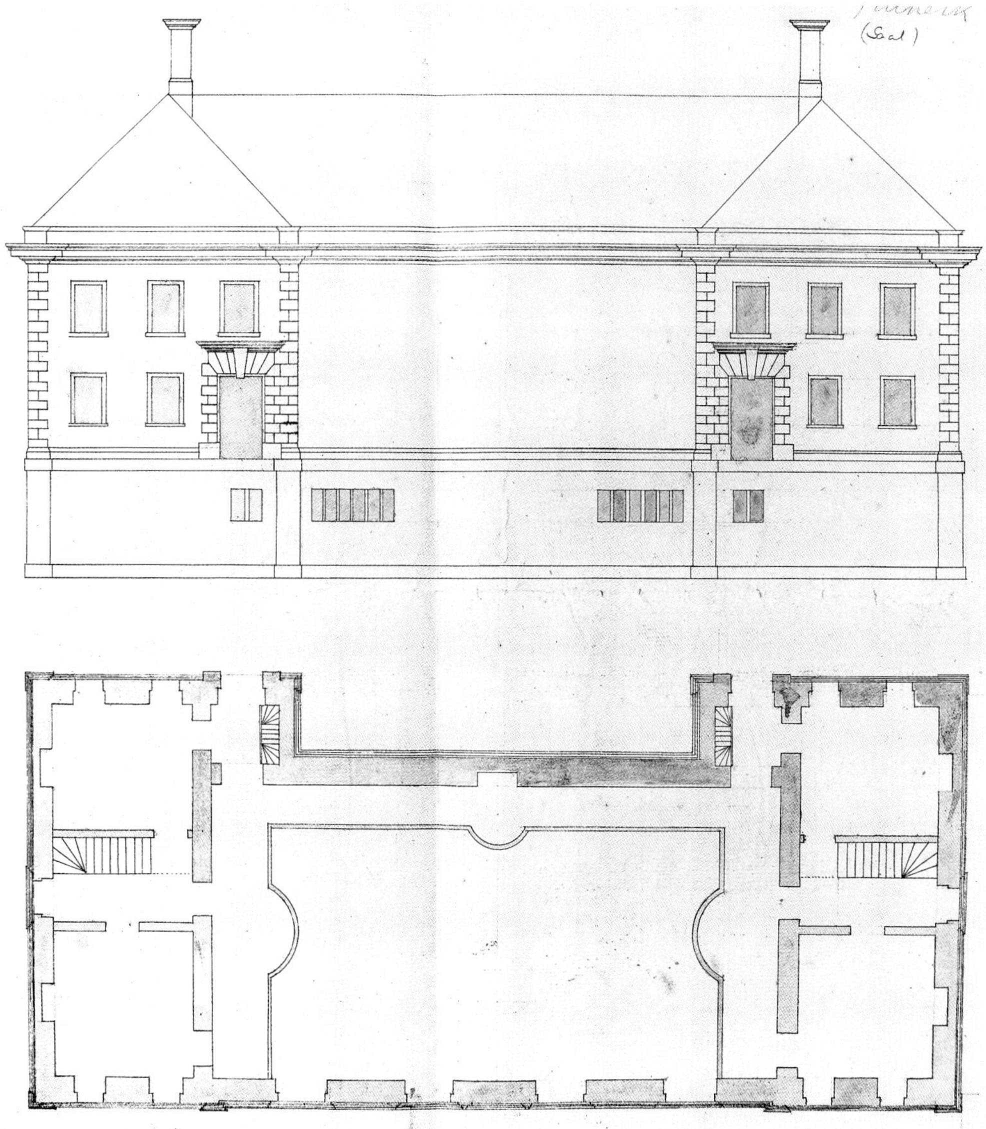

26 Architect unknown. Design for the north front elevation and first floor of Grace Hall, Fulneck, Yorkshire, *c.*1745. Pen and ink and wash. Moravian archive, Herrnhut, Germany, BA 1816b.

a German *Schloss*, though of course having none of its secular splendour. Benjamin Ingham, founder of the Yorkshire Ingamites, remarked in 1746 that the 'Unitas Fratrum' 'are building a finer House here than my Lord Huntingdon has' at Ledstone Hall, near Leeds.[44] The entirely domestic character of the block, divided by rusticated piers into a stately two–five–two bay system, recalls Cusworth Hall near Doncaster (1740–49), some 30 miles to the south-east, by the Rotherham architects George and John Platt Jr, suggesting that one or both may have had a hand in designing Grace Hall.[45] Several contemporary presentation drawings sent to Herrnhut for Zinzendorf's approbation survive. One (pl. 26) is remarkable in showing the central section of the north front above the sunken basement level left entirely blank; it was not finally filled in until 1779, when Brethren Clifford Swertner provided a design for the present cupola-crowned Corpse Chamber.[46]

Many Nonconformist chapels were prone to destruction during riots, such as the 'great Disorders' in Staffordshire in 1715, on spurious claims that Dissenters had 'ruined Trade, on Purpose to make the Nation out of Love with the late Peace' (the Treaty of Utrecht of 1713), for which Parliament proposed: 'the Sufferers may have full Compensation . . . for . . . Damages'.[47] In May 1745, provoked by the French declaration of war on

Britain and Marshal Saxe's victory over the Duke of Cumberland at Fontenoy, an incensed Exeter mob invaded the Waterbury Lane Chapel, previously used as a theatre,

> beat upon the Seats and Wainscot with their Hands and Sticks . . . kick'd the Bretheren, pull'd them by the Hair, spit on them . . . some crying out, *No Methodists! No Methodists!* . . . While up in the Galleries . . . others pelted [them] with hard Pieces of Mortar and Potatoes [and] piss'd down upon the People . . . Mrs *P. Hill* was met . . . by one who called her *Whitefieldite Bitch*.[48]

On 14 July 1791 a group of dissenters privately celebrating the second anniversary of the storming of the Bastille, 'the auspicious day which witnessed the Emancipation of Twenty-six Million People from the Yoke of Despotism', sparked off the infamous five days of 'Church and King' riots in Birmingham, during which four chapels, as well as twenty-seven private houses, including Dr Joseph Priestley's, were burnt down.[49]

Lest readers receive a false impression of universal discontent there is the press evidence of the foundation-stone laying at the parish church of St John, Wakefield, on 3 November 1791, when 'amidst thousands of . . . exulting spectators . . . joined with great devotion . . . singing . . . psalms . . . accompanied by a band of music' followed by a 'superb entertainment . . . at the Assembly-Rooms . . . Many loyal and other suitable toasts were drank. – All invidious distinctions were laid aside; many . . . dissenters, much to their credit . . . affording . . . convincing proof of the liberality of their sentiments', with the day 'spent with the most perfect harmony and conviviality'.[50] In *A Sentimental Tour through Newcastle; By a Young Lady* (1794), Jane Harvey and 'Edmond', though preferring

> the service of the church of England . . . yet . . . were by no means so bigoted as to refuse joining in the public worship of any other christian sect: for . . . we well know, that error in judgment, is not sin . . . I greatly admired the hymns and manner of singing at the Hanover Square Chapel . . . This . . . said I to Edmund, is really a neat place. A very neat place indeed, replied he.[51]

Moreover, Nonconformity inadvertently made a positive contribution by encouraging further Establishment building programmes. A petition in 1724 from the parishioners of Bethnal Green, London, hoping to take advantage of the New Churches Act, pointed out that 'there hath been Erected . . . a Meeting = house now near finished and which to [their] great Grief and fear will not be the only one that will be erected there'. Nothing less than a new Anglican church 'would effectually putt a stop to so growing an Evil'.[52]

Exceptions to the rule of Nonconformist architectural austerity were, of course, Catholic chapels and Jewish synagogues, both wholly new building types in post-Reformation Britain. The former are especially interesting as a reminder of how the Church of England may have defined itself in response, as will become clear in chapter 8.

The incredulous episode described in *Screw-Plot Discover'd; or, St Paul's Preserved* (1710), a spurious assassination attempt on Queen Anne while attending worship at St Paul's Cathedral by removing the iron bolts securing the roof timbers, which would then crash down on her head, was attributed to the machination of the devil or the pope. (For further details, see pp. 167–8.) Little wonder that Catholic chapels, for most of the century proscribed by the government, represented the architectural embodiment of Protestant phobia of a feared papist resurgence.[53] *A Letter to the Patriot, Relating to the Pretender, and the Growth of Popery in the City of York, and other Parts of Great Britain* (1714) claimed that Catholics resorted to a Mass House in Blake Street just by the Minster 'with Impunity in great Numbers several times a Day' and 'are very Assiduous in making *New Converts*, to the great Grief of Protestant Parents, who have their Children inveigled from them, and taught to embrace a Religion which obliges them to be *Parricides*'.[54] Anglican clergymen were regularly ordered by their bishops to identify the often elusive presence of private chapels within their parishes. Thus, the minister of Oulston, Yorkshire, reported in 1743 that 'There is said to be a Popish Chapel . . . but what Number assemble in it, I know not; One Mr Smith is said to be the Priest'; in Newtown, Hampshire, in 1765 a gardener, his wife and a maid 'go to mass at Lord Fingal's family, as I am informed', and in Havant in 1788 'There are supposed to be upwards of a hundred Papists with a chapel.'[55] Even in the case of grand, openly recusant country houses the presence of a private chapel might be discreetly camouflaged. John Adams, the future United States president, visiting Lord Petre's Thorndon Hall, Essex, in 1786, designed in a handsome neoclassical style by James Paine (1764–6), remarked that the family were Catholic since the 'Chapel furnishes full proof', while the 'very elegant . . . semicircular' library leading to it was 'contrived more as an ornamental Passage . . . than for Study'.[56]

London, where the Romanist population had reached 12,320 by 1767,[57] could be rabidly and sometimes even ridiculously anti-Catholic in architectural matters, as exposed in a muddled, apocryphal story first published in *Critical Observations on the Building and Improvements of London* (1771), subsequently appropriated by the popular press as a 'Genuine Anecdote' and repeated in the 1783 edition of James Ralph's *A Critical Review of the Publick Buildings, Statues and Ornaments in, and about London and Westminster.* The tale regarded the City's Common Council's rejection of an 'original design of Palladio' submitted by Lord Burlington in 1735 for the new Mansion House on the grounds that the famous Italian renaissance architect was a papist and not a freeman![58] This was exacerbated by the reality of the Gordon Riots, flamed by fears of the government's proposed repeal of the Catholic penal laws and a nationwide break-out of destruction in 1779, which climaxed in June 1780 when a hysterical mob plundered and burned the Sardinian Embassy Chapel in Lincoln's Inn Fields, the Bavarian Embassy Chapel near Golden Square and Moorfield's Chapel, while the new Roman Catholic Chapel in Bath was looted, leaving standing 'nothing but the bare walls'.[59] Many were killed and Horace Walpole regarded the whole episode as a 'savage outrage . . . Nothing ever surpassed the abominable behaviour of the ruffian apostle [Lord George Gordon, subsequently executed] that preached up this storm [which] will be a black spot in our annals as long as time will last.'[60] Nor were craftsmen immune to the dangers of such unrest. Take the notorious case of the London iron-founder Richard Jones, who in 1700 was accused with five others of murdering Robert Newey 'by striking him on the head during an anti-pope riot'. He escaped justice, and in 1709 received £11,000 for fashioning the magnificent cast-iron fence surrounding St Paul's Cathedral.[61]

The range of Mass Houses was wide and varied. In 'Countrey-places' they were sometimes 'just large enough to contain an Altar and Priest, the Congregation attending whilst in the field'.[62] The Catholic firm of Gillow, based in Lancaster, supplied thriving north of England recusant families with high-quality chapel furniture, including an ingenious tabernacle disguised as a domestic bookcase with the interior painted white and gilt and hung with green silk curtains, exposed when the front panel was lowered to form an altar top, a microcosm of the prayer rooms themselves.[63] James Paine's chapel in Robert Edward, 9th Lord Petre's London mansion in Park Lane (1766–70, demolished 1877) was discreetly positioned along one side at the rear of the principal floor; it was approached from the drawing room through a small waiting room into the screened apsidal end of the chapel proper, with the chaplain's apartment adjacent.[64]

Long vanished, what these rooms may have looked like can be gauged from a description of the Petre chapel at Thorndon, Essex, an earlier mansion remodelled by the Italian architect Giacomo Leoni (1733–9, dismantled 1763), which featured an altar table of 'several sorts of curious marbles' with a painting of the *Holy Family* flanked by bas-reliefs of *St Joachim* and *St Anne*, statues of the *Four Evangelists* 'by an Italian hand' placed in niches, and white marble chancel rails.[65] From a unique manuscript entitled 'Rules to be observ'd in the Chapple' dated 1741 we learn for a Mass performed on 17–18 November 1739 that this altar was furnished with 'a rich canopy wth. Lights and many other Ornaments, Suitable to the decency of the place, & expressive of the greatest Zeal & Religion in the Noble Owner'. On Epiphany it

> must be dressd wth. Flowers: The Canopy . . . set on the Tabernacle . . . A stand wth. a veil . . . before the Venerable in time of reading & instructing. Six carvd stands wth. Candles . . . Set within the rails . . . Two branches in the gallery. Four plain stands without the rails, over against the four first Pilasters. The best Vestment &c &c must be used at all the Mases on days of Exposition.

The document continues: on Candlemas, the '2d. best white Vestment & linnen. The best Chalice & Crewets. The Candles that are to be blessd . . . laid in a basket, & Set upon a little table coverd wth. a clean white cloth'; in Lent, the 'best purple Vestment'; on the Saturday before Passion Sunday, 'The Picture must be coverd, the Crucifix, the Tabernacle & Steps wth. purple'; on Palm Sunday, the 'Palms . . . put in a basket & set on a little table . . . The Six Silverd Candlesticks wth. Yellow Candles . . . Set upon the Altar instead of the gilt ones . . . On Wednesday in H[oly]. Week, the triangular Candlestick . . . prepard for Tenebrae, at wch. a Surplice & purple Stole must be used'; on Maunday Thursday, the 'best white Vestment, & lac'd linnen . . . The best Chalice . . . Set in the Canopy . . . After Mass the marble Steps . . . coverd wth. Black, & the Curtains let down . . . Six Small Silver Candlesticks . . . placed on the marble Steps'; on Good Friday,

> The Altar remains dressd wth. the . . . Sacraments in the Canopy till after the kissing the Cross is over, only the drapery before the Picture in the Sepulcher is let down, & 2 white ribbons pinnd on it like a cross . . . The best black Vestments must be used & plane Linnen. Cushions coverd wth black . . . laid upon the marble Steps, for the Priest to prostrate on.

On Easter Sunday, the 'best white Vestments, lac'd linnen: the best Chalice & Crewetts, all other things the best of their kind . . . If day-light only the Candles upon the Altar, & instead of Candlesticks Set two flower pots in the great Urns'; on Whit Sunday, the 'best red Vestment, all other ornaments the best in their kind'; at midnight on Christmas Day 'ten stands wth. Candles on them . . . The Altar dressd, & best ornaments must be us'd'.[66]

Mother Magdalen Davis, who became procuratress of the Bar Convent in York in 1735, recorded that the former chapel (replaced in 1766) was fitted out over the years with a variety of dazzling ornaments, none of which has survived: in 1742 'a new set of paper &c: flowers . . . for Easter' and a pair of 'silver cruibs for ye Altar'; in 1745 'A sett of Lyllys for ye Altar', 'The Old sett of. Silver flowers new vamped up with ye old silk Roses &c:', 'A new Garland for ye Holy Cross' and '6 tall flower glasses'; in 1750 '4 large silk spriggs'; in 1751 'a sett of crimson riband roses & strings to tye ye muslin to ye Arches. A Red frill at the bottom of Sepulchre steps' and a 'new tabernacle & Steps white & gold' costing £46; in 1752 the 'Candle steps of Sepulchre covered [in] Silver paper. & painted under neath'; in 1753 'Crimson silk to cover ye tops of ye Sepulchre steps', a 'new pedistall for ye Holy Cross covered with silver paper & some of ye old flowers yt came off ye old Vendarium', and the 'steps belonging to ye Veridarium new vamp'd up with crimson silk ground & spangles'; in 1756 'New ornaments of flowers & bugles to put upon ye 3 figures at ye tope of ye Sepulchre. two spriggs to stand in pots of worsted flowers [and] 3. New ribband french popies, for ye middles of ye 3. top figures' and '4. large Spriggs of Worsted flowers for ye great Altar' and '4. for ye little Altar'; in 1757 'a new crown of worsted flowers for ye Paschal Candle', '6. white glass flower pots for ye great Altar'; in 1758 '6. polished steel candlesticks' costing £16, 'a new silver Cyborium gilt in ye inside' and 'ye old frame at our Ladys Altar new painted blue & gold, & a new chect cover'; in 1759 a 'silver pissina' costing £2; in 1760 '2 Silver candlesticks one fixt under St Ignatiu's [*sic*] picture, the other under St Xaverius's'; and in 1763 a 'new gold frame for ye noble Altar piece, & five gold roses placed about it'.[67] Thomas Atkinson, the Catholic architect of the succeeding chapel (1765–9), discussed later, was paid £1 11s. 6d. for supplying 'the Glory at the Large Alter' and £2 18s. 0d. for 'Altering the Glory to small Swags of Leaves and ribands Ionic Capitals and flowers' in 'Burnished Gold'.[68] Nevertheless, the nuns remained cautious: Ann Aspinal, the mother superior, thanking the generaless for 'your cardinal wishes to send us some ornaments for our new chapel', warned her that there were 'innumerable dangers'.[69] The York and Thorndon documents transform one's perception of the appearance of Catholic chapels in the eighteenth century radically.

There is also the indisputable evidence of Wardour Castle chapel, Wiltshire, erected for Henry Bellings, 8th Earl of Arundell, an immensely rich Catholic, who had toured Italy in 1758–60 under the tutelage of the Yorkshireman Fr John Thorpe, English penitentiary at St Peter's, agent for the English Province of the Jesuits and the guiding light in the chapel's glamorous creation between 1769 and 1792. Some items, such as the altar crucifix, had to be smuggled through English customs, though Thorpe confessed 'the impossibility of making a secret' of the fixture, since on the occasion of its temporary erection for public viewing in 1776 the altar had been 'mentioned in the printed diary of Rome'.[70] Arundell's suggestion to place an inscription on the inside of the tabernacle door was regarded as 'very just considering the present state of religion'.[71] Thorpe recommended the Scottish Jacobite Catholic architect James Byres, a leading antiquary and cicerone resident in Rome employed by British milords on the Grand Tour, as 'a person more qualified to satisfy your Lordships elegant taste for whatever belongs to the fine arts . . . also as good a Christian as he is an ingenious Virtuoso'.[72] By 1767 he was sending designs for the high altar, the most flamboyant with a crucifix-crowned tabernacle canopied by a festooned, semicircular-headed *baldacchino* illuminated by the Holy Spirit and *putti* floating in clouds (pl. 27).[73] Four years later Thorpe reported seeing 'a grand piece . . . that might serve . . . for the Corp: Sant: if placed under the altar' consisting of 'Rock work of cast brass richly gilt . . . upon a slab of Giallo Antico' measuring 3 by 2 feet high with 'broken branches of shrubs & leaves . . . finely done . . . especially two or three lizards cast from the life', with an open 'Grotto' surmounted by a 'large Urn of silver of a good design & well wrought', together with a silver Crucifix, 'a Serpent . . . winding round the foot', all resting on a *verde antico* table embellished with an 'elegant border of silver'. But on reflection, Thorpe concluded, Byres's 'manner . . . will perhaps . . . appear . . . to rich for such a country as ours' and opted instead for what was 'elegant but with few costly ornaments as possible'.

> An elegant plainness will . . . be preferable to much ornament, & gilt brass to silver . . . Angels holding Candlesticks or Crucifix may look pretty in a Drawing, yet if executed on an Altar will have too

27 James Byres. Design for high altar, Wardour Castle chapel (Catholic), Wiltshire, 1767, unexecuted. Pen and ink. Wiltshire & Swindon Archives, Arundell family collection (photograph: Courtauld Institute of Art, 706/3/17).

> much of the Puppet show in England. Many say, nothing ought to be on or about an Altar, but what is majestick & elegant, or . . . as nobly simple as Art can make it.

Later Thorpe advised Arundell that his reputation 'will certainly make many noblemen and others desire to peep into your chapel; upon this account as well as for observing a noble decorum . . . I wish it to have as little a gaudiness and trumpery as possible'.[74] I know of no more subtle appreciation of the differences between Italian and English Catholic artistic tastes. Subsequently, the commission was successfully carried out by the renowned Italian architect Giacomo Quarenghi (pl. 632) as a simplified, uncanopied version of Byres's, with a silver crucifix enshrined in a subtly coloured variegated marble and ormolu domed tempietto, costing 600 guineas. It was finally dispatched in 1787, together with candlesticks and a pair of sumptuous silver and gilt sanctuary lamps made by the 'celebrated' Luigi Valadier, 'the first workman of these things in Europe', which 'have a magnificent effect', and Giuseppe Cades' *Deposition* altar painting (1776–80), which had been 'exposed in the Pantheon for the public'.[75] Thorpe hoped 'it soon will be placed over the Altar for which it was made', referring to an iconographic association between the subject and the sarcophagus-encased altar table.[76] Cades also proposed filling the elaborate geometric vaulting designed by James Paine (pl. 632) with panels depicting *Christ's Charge to Peter, The Resurrection, Four Evangelists, The Virgin and Mary Magdalene*, cherubs bearing instruments of the Passion and the *Holy Lamb* with Jehovah's name in Glory above the altar, the full panoply of Italian Roman baroque imagery, which, however, was not carried out. A sensible tactic in pre-Catholic Emancipation England.

Liberated from architectural mundanity after the Catholic Relief Act of 1791 (31 Georgii, c.32), buildings became both more conspicuous and ambitious. John Robert's Waterford Cathedral in Ireland (1792–6), which cost £20,000 and was sanctioned by the Corporation in 'the earnest wish and desire . . . to accommodate every description of their fellow citizens with every advantage which can tend (by facilitating the publick Worship of the Deity) to promote Religion and Virtue', adapted Gibbs's ranges of elaborately carved Corinthian dosseret columns from St Martin-in-the-Fields.[77] St Wilfrid, Preston (pl. 670), replaced a woefully inadequate fabric that had become

> quite too small [and] often so crowded that many cannot get within the doors. Several miss hearing Mass because they cannot bear the heat. Others complain that their clothes are soiled, almost torn off their backs and that they are nearly pressed to death. Some hundred wish for seats, who cannot have them [and] kneel in the crowd.[78]

Despite restrictions and other difficulties, sophisticated Catholic building during the eighteenth century was by no means fallow. Take four notable examples.

Brough Hall chapel, Yorkshire, erected by 1734 as part of Sir John Lawton, 3rd Baronet's remodelling from 1725 of the Elizabethan mansion (the room was destroyed by fire in 1979), is an early manifestation of the second phase of Burlingtonian Palladianism in which French-inspired rococo decoration, perhaps dating as late as the 1750s, was not regarded as incompatible (pl. 28).[79] It is uncertain who the architect was. The flamboyant treatment of the ceiling plasterwork sketched in pencil on the rectangular grid points to Isaac Ware, a senior official of HM Board of Works in

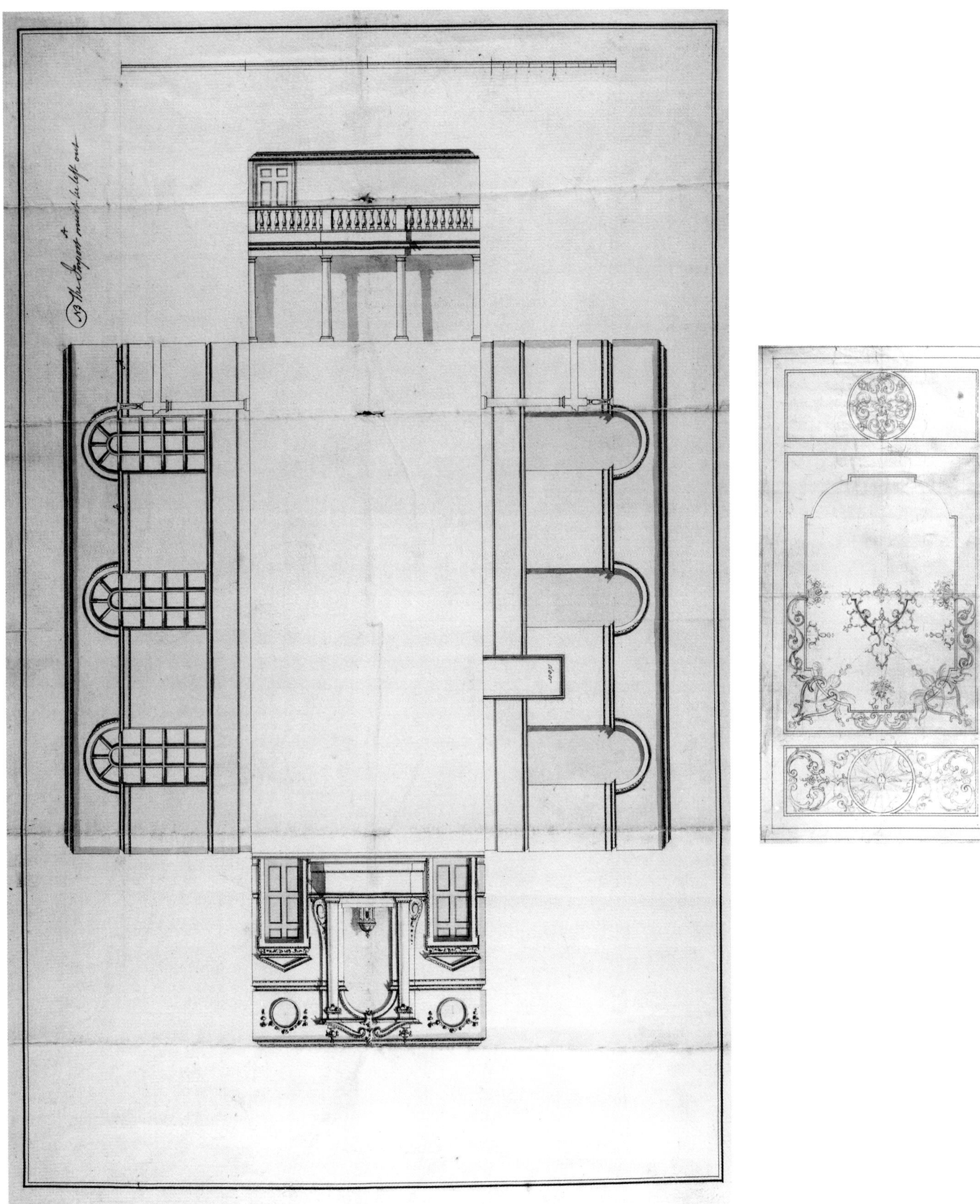

28a, b and c (*above and facing page*) Isaac Ware. Exploded plan and ceiling design for Brough Hall chapel (Catholic), Yorkshire, 1734. Pencil, pen and ink and wash. North Yorkshire County Record Office, ZRL 13/114-115.

29 'The Roman Catholick Chapple Tyburn Road as Design'd by Willm Jones Architect', arms dated 1753, subsequently demolished. Engraving. Author's collection.

London, with close ties to Burlington, who was Lord Lieutenant of the East and West Ridings of Yorkshire. Ware collaborated with the amateur architect Sir Thomas Robinson in the creation of the latter's mansion at Rokeby Park (1725–31), 15 miles to the north of Brough, and both buildings share an ardour for a Palladian vocabulary borrowed from William Kent's *The Designs of Inigo Jones* (1727), to which Robinson and Ware were subscribers.[80] Brough's altarpiece and flanking doors surmounted by festooned roundels are based on plates 46–7 in the First Volume, while its inverted scroll pediment relates to patterns published in Ware's *Designs of Inigo Jones and Others* (1731). These motifs were shared with James Paine, who also enjoyed Yorkshire Catholic patronage, though not until the following decade, and interestingly both he and Ware were members of the rococo-orientated St Martin's Lane Academy in London from its founding in 1735.[81]

Foreign embassy chapels in London alone were immune from official censure; nor were their services secretive, but, as a Swiss traveller reported in 1729, 'always crowded' and 'freely attended' by English Catholics.[82] The *Gentleman's Magazine* reported in 1751 that 'Many persons of distinction were at the *Portuguese* ambassador's chapel in *South-street* [Mayfair] . . . to hear the music and the dirge for the late lord *Aston*', and in 1789 'Was sung at the Portuguese chapel . . . a solemn High Mass and Te Deum, in thanksgiving to Divine Provinence for the happy recovery of his Royal Highness . . . Heir Apparent to the Crown of Portugal'. In 1799 'a grand Requiem and solemn Dirge' was performed in the Sardinian Embassy chapel on the occasion of Pope Pius VI's death, where a 'splendid mausoleum was erected . . . and the whole ceremony was truly graceful and magnificence'.[83]

The earliest of the grand embassy initiatives was the new building erected by the Spanish in Tyburn Road, Marylebone (near the traditional site used for Jacobite hangings), which was in hand in 1749 when the ambassador, Ricardo (or Richard) Wall, an Irishman, commissioned Gianbattista Tiepolo to paint the *St James of Compostela* altarpiece, which arrived the following year but was not hung due to a preference for another subject, *Christ Crucified*. Predictably, the chapel's exterior is unrecorded, though the interior is known from a unique engraving (pl. 29), which features the royal arms of King Ferdinando VI on the ceiling bearing the date 1753, presumably marking its completion, and identifying the architect as William Jones, of Ranelagh Gardens Rotunda fame.[84] He was a conservative classicist – his Berkeley Chapel, Mayfair, *circa* 1750 (pl. 1), is a close copy of Gibbs's Marylebone Chapel (pl. 506). Tyburn's architecture derived from Wren's St Clement Eastcheap (1683–7), but with the obligatory tabernacle and candlesticks framed in a Serliana, perhaps inspired by the Queen's Chapel, St James (pl. 66), by Jones's Stuart namesake.[85] With the two nations entering a period of peace following the Treaty of Aix-la-Chapelle of 1748 and the Anglo-Spanish Commercial Treaty of 1750, this choice of vocabulary suggests an attempt to create an architecturally safe building sympathetic to popular English taste.

The rectangular Sardinian Embassy chapel, Duke Street, Lincoln's Inn Fields, though also of unknown external appearance, was apparently about the same length as the north–south axis of St George, Bloomsbury, and internally as spatially complex. Its building history is uncertain. The 'finest Chapel for *Roman* Catholicks Worship in *England*', erected during the reign of Catholic James II (1685–8), was accidentally burnt down in 1759, rebuilt around 1762 by the ambassadorial secretary and obscure 'amateur' architect Jean Baptiste Jaques (his sole recorded work), then again, or at the very least internally restored, following

30 A. Pugin and T. Rowlandson. View of Sardinian Embassy Chapel, Lincoln's Inn Fields, interior towards chancel, in R. Ackermann, *The Microcosm of London*, 1808–9, p. 15. Coloured engraving. Jean-Baptiste Jaques architect, 1759–62, demolished 1907.

the infamous Gordon Riots of July 1780, when it was reported 'totally consumed' by fire. Quickly repaired and reopened the following February, we catch a glimpse of the chancel hung with J. F. Rigaud's *Deposition* altarpiece (1781), candelabrum, lamps and altar rail in an engraving of 1784, and more comprehensively from the western nave in Pugin's view (pl. 30).[86] Unclear if this reflects Jaques' pre-Riot appearance, it is an amalgam of double tiers of galleries accommodating both local and peripatetic worshippers, recalling seventeenth-century Amsterdam examples,[87] and a grand central space defined by four giant order Ionic columns or piers and covered by a huge octagonal, top-lit dome, which may owe something to Brunelleschi's celebrated dome of Florence Cathedral.[88] Monumental Serliana openings on the west, east and south sides had pendentives articulated by circular panels, the western ones punctured as oculi, to throw much-needed light into the topmost galleries of the four-bay nave, a motif that held special fascination in Piedmontese architecture.[89]

Sir Thomas Gascoigne, born at Cambrai in northern France, the scion of an old, well-established recusant family with Jacobite sympathies, taking up his inheritance at Parlington, Yorkshire, in 1772, commissioned John Carr to design a gothic chapel and chaplain's house linked by a walled enclosure complete with crenellation, turrets and arrow-loops (pl. 31). Not inappropriately, it is based on a published scheme for 'Facades to place before disagreeable Objects' (pl. 32).

31 John Carr. Design for 'The North Front' of Parlington Park Chapel (Catholic), Yorkshire, 1772. Pen and ink and coloured wash. West Yorkshire Archives Service (Leeds), WYL, 115/MA56.

32 Timothy Lightoler. 'Facades to place before disagreeable Objects' in *The Gentleman and Farmer's Architect*, 1762, pl. 25, detail. Engraving.

This may be the first occasion in post-Reformation Britain of a free-standing Catholic domestic chapel, though the project was abandoned in 1780 when Gascoigne became Protestant in order to run for Parliament in support of the prosecution of the end of war with the American colonies by a fellow Yorkshireman, the Earl of Rockingham.[90]

Three further English Catholic enterprises, the early Christian-inspired Bar Convent, York, the neoclassical Wardour Castle and the gothic St Peter, Winchester (of which only the carcass survives), are discussed in later chapters. It is, however, worth remarking here that in the last the windows were raised well above the ground to avoid its furnishings 'being seen through them', and a separate entrance at the east end gave access by a staircase to a 'private gallery', which was screened by arches with gilt mouldings hung with silk curtains for 'the benefit of those persons who attend the divine service' requiring concealment from 'the sight of the congregation', and no doubt from spying eyes.[91]

The secrecy surrounding pre-Emancipation popish places of worship was diametrically opposite to Diaspora synagogue design. One of its compelling aspects across eighteenth-century Europe was its ability to assimilate Christian architectural ideas of the adopted countries while preserving uniquely essential features of its ancient Near Eastern origins.[92] These are the Aron Kodesh (Ark) housing the Scrolls of the Law (Torah), which was not required to follow the traditional Christian custom of a liturgical eastern position;[93] the Bimah or reading desk, a centrally placed railed enclosure where portions of the Torah are read aloud during services; and the women's lattice-screened upper gallery. (César de Saussure, a Swiss Protestant visitor in London in 1729, 'curious enough' to attend Duke's Place Synagogue, was particularly struck by the custom where 'women do not mix with the men, but stood . . . in a sort of shut-off gallery'.[94])

It is hardly surprising that among Anglican architects there was a good deal of flexibility of interpretation. Robert Morris, for example, perhaps with tongue in cheek, described his scheme for a centrally planned cold bath published in *Rural Architecture* (1750) ambiguously:

> The Oddity of this Design has a little puzzled me to determine its Name and Uses. – I have consulted a very grave Jewish Rabbin, who informs me very little is wanting to make it a compleat Synagogue. – An honest plain-meaning *Dervise* commends it, and wishes me to send a Copy of it, (by him,) to *Constantinople*, as a Model for a Mosque. One zealous for the Propogation of his own Tenets, informs me, it is extremely well suited for a Chapel, and its Confessionals. – A Puritan of modern Growths entreats me not to make any Alterations in it, for it is the best he could ever wish to see, executed to perform their Devotions in.[95]

It was widely but incorrectly believed that the romanesque round churches in Cambridge and Northampton, built in imitation of the Holy Sepulchre at Jerusalem, were 'most probably, & rather demonstrable . . . erected by the Jews, who swarmed in[to] England soon after the Norman Conquest, [as] their Synagogues', and following their expulsion in the thirteenth century 'converted into Christian Temples'.[96] Furthermore, on 11 August 1753 the *Gray's-Inn Journal*, responding to the public outcry that followed the passing of an Act of Parliament – then quickly repealed – enabling individual Jews to apply for naturalisation, but distorted by its opponents as an attempt to undermine the very fabric of English culture and the Protestant religion, reported under 'TRUE INTELLIGENCE': 'We hear that a Scheme is on foot among the *Jews* to purchase St *Paul*'s Church [the cathedral] in order to hold a Synagogue there.'[97] This absurd episode of anti-Semitic scaremongering highlights the confusion over the different architectural needs of the two faiths during the eighteenth century.

In fact, Georgian synagogues bear little relationship architecturally to Anglican churches, much less to the National Cathedral. If anything, they resemble the discreet, tower-less exteriors of Nonconformity. Their internal furnishings, however, is another matter. Take the case of Bevis Marks, Aldgate (pl. 33), erected for the Spanish and Portuguese (Sephardic) community and little changed to the present day. The architect, Joseph Avis, was a Quaker who had worked at Wren's St Bride, Fleet Street (1675–92), where the original altarpiece, consisting of '6 carved Columns (painted Flake-stone colour) with Entablature and circular Pediment . . . embellish'd with Lamps, Cherubims, etc. all gilt with gold', provided a suitable model.[98] The Aldgate building contract reads much like its Christian counterpart: 'one large building with a gallery round . . . as . . . discribed in the modell' (untraced), 80 by 50 by 32 feet high, constructed of 'well burnt bricks', covered with 'good plain tyles', glazed with 'good English glass', 'stone door case'; the interior with Tuscan 'cullums . . . of firr with stone baces' and 'a true freece and cornish' etc. built 'in a good and workmanlike manner . . . with good sound materiells' for £2,650; and it was agreed not to work on 'Jewish Festival days or Saturdays'.[99] Bevis Marks is an authentic and poignant record of Jewish late Stuart religious architecture.

Anglo-Jewish prosperity during the eighteenth century is demonstrated by the growth of the German (Ashkenazi) émigré's Great Synagogue in nearby Duke's Place. The building started out in 1722 as a simple 60 by 63 foot box. It was doubled in size in the years 1762–6 under the direction of George Dance Sr, employing a Catholic contractor, by removing one entire outside wall, extending the interior from four to eight bays, inserting latticed women's galleries supported on columns along the sides, and repositioning the Bimah at the intersection of old and new, flanked by a pair of free-standing, full-height Corinthian columns, perhaps intended as reminders of the biblical twin columns in Solomon's Temple in Jerusalem. Gerhard Schott's spectacular 13-foot-high wooden model (1694, now in the Museum für Hamburgische Geschichte), based on reconstructions in J. B. Villalpando's and J. Prado's *In Ezechielem Explanationes* (1596–1605), had been exhibited in the Royal Exchange in London in 1730. The *Daily Courant* directed attention to the 2,000 chambers, the 7,000 pillars, the 'great Altar . . . Sanctum Sanctorum . . . Ark of the Covenant [and] the two famous Pillars, called Joachim and Boas', also advertising a 'printed Description . . . with 12 fine Cuts'

33 D. Havell after Isaac Mendes Belisario. 'Interior of The Spanish and Portugese Synagogue, London' (Bevis Marks), 1 January 1817. Coloured engraving. Jewish Museum, London. Joseph Avis architect, 1700–01.

priced 5s., while another model appeared in 1759–60.[100] Moreover, the Corinthian order was closely associated with the biblical Temple.[101]

In James Spiller's complete rebuilding of Duke's Place (pl. 34), ranges of monumental Ionic columns with attached grilled galleries forming side aisles recall its Amsterdam brethren, the Esnoga (1670–75).[102] Yet it also reflected contemporary British architectural fashions, particularly in abandoning the traditional pedimented Ark in favour of a coffered apsidal enclosure screened by paired columns supporting a straight entablature embellished with neoclassical ornament in the Adam manner.

Interestingly, ancient synagogue architecture played a reversed role in the Anglican repertory. The underlying geometry of the Congregationalists' Square Chapel, Halifax, Yorkshire (1771–3; pl. 558), is a 240-foot cube, precisely eight times the volume of the Holy of Holies containing the Ark of the Covenant in Solomon's Temple at Jerusalem as described in 1 Kings 6:19–20. It also features twin columns (of cast iron) flanking the entrance, which the client, Revd Titus Knight, explicitly associated with its biblical forebears:

> What is this Building, so magnificent
> With spacious Area, and this grand Ascent;
> With Pillars on each Hand? One might suppose
> The one was *Jachin*, and the other *Boaz*.

Criticised by his detractors for lavishing 'vast Expence . . . in Ornaments . . . to no End', the poem offered a vindication:

> But since you deem this House too large and fine,
> I'll lead your envious Thoughts to Palestine.

View foolish *Solomon*, at vast Expence,
Erect a House, which for Magnificence,
For Elegance, and Ornament, as far
Excell'd this House, as doth the Sun, a Star.[103]

Nonetheless, the chapel's overall appearance is suitably prosaic, and only the detailing of its internal pilasters, with their capitals copied from Robert Adam's *Ruins of the Palace of the Emperor Diocletian at Spalatro* (1764), hint at awareness of fashionable neoclassical taste.

A chancel screen introduced by Thomas Hardwick Jr at Wanstead, Essex (1787–90), in the form of 'a light Network of Iron or Eldorado Work', supplied by Francis Underwood and Co. of London, called '*cancelli* or lattic-work' had its origin in what Eusebius, the third-century commentator, described as early Christian furnishings composed of 'certain rails of wood, curiously and artificially wrought in the form of net-work, to make [the chancel] inaccessible to the multitude'. Perhaps this grew out of the Jewish tradition of the women's enclosure noted at both Bevis Marks and the Duke's Place synagogues.[104]

Another spectacular new building type to appear in the eighteenth century, evolving out of the medieval hospice-almshouse tradition, was the public hospital, offering the philanthropic benefits of care and cure of

34 A. Pugin and T. Rowlandson. View towards the Bimah and Holy Ark of the Great Synagogue, Duke's Place, Aldgate, London, in Rudolph Ackermann, *The Microcosm of London*, vol. 3, 1809, pl. 168. Coloured engraving. London Metropolitan Archives (Guildhall Library, 2064). James Spiller architect, 1788–90, destroyed in the Blitz, 1941.

35 John Saunders. 'View of the Inside of the Chapel of the Foundling Hospital', Holborn, London, 7 January 1774. Engraving. The British Library Board, K. Top. XXV-23-f. Theodore Jacobson architect, 1738–53, demolished 1925.

the sick complemented by 'a Consciousness of having been the Instruments, under GOD, of the Restoration of such Objects from Misery to Ease, from Impotence to Strength, and from Beggary and Want, to a Capacity of getting an honest Livelihood, and comfortable Subsistence'.[105] This encouraged scope for more sophisticated architectural forms, including integral spaces for Christian worship. As an expression of social reform this was embodied in the substantial, semi-detached chapel block at the centre of the Hospital for the Maintenance and Education of Exposed and Deserted Young Children, commonly known as the Foundling Hospital, in Lambs Conduit Fields, Holborn, on the northern fringe of the City of London, launched in 1739 and opened in 1753 (pl. 35). It was 'earnestly desirous that the children . . . should be early instructed in the principles of Religion and Morality',[106] but the complex additionally served as a venue for musical performances – 1,200 tickets were sold at 10s. 6d. each for a benefit performance of Handel's *Messiah* on 9 April 1752 – as well as for displaying paintings and sculpture presented gratis by leading artists such as William Hogarth, Thomas Gainsborough, Joshua Reynolds, Louis François Roubiliac and Michael Rysbrack. The hospital's designer was Theodore Jacobsen, a successful City merchant and 'amateur' architect, who subscribed to William Kent's *The Designs of Inigo Jones* (1727) and dipped into its utilitarian patterns for the details of doors, columns, windows and ranges of Serliana. Orphans occupied the galleries, which featured a recess to one side of the organ 'for solitary confinement of misbehaving children' and offered direct access to the wards to avoid 'mixing with the Congregation'.[107] In the case of the Magdalen House for Penitent Prostitutes proposed for London, for which an extraordinary scheme was initially proposed (pl. 493), its moralistic foundation is enshrined in the mottoes chosen by the architects invited to submit competition designs under noms de plume: 'There is more Joy in Heaven over one Sinner that repenteth, than over Ninety and nine just Persons that need no Repentance', 'No complaining no begging in the Streets', 'Evils may be more easily prevented than cured' and so on.[108] Nor should one forget the myriad of traditional almshouse chapels, of which Berkeley Hospital, Worcester, is a particularly charming example (pl. 36).[109]

The spectacular success of the Foundling Hospital chapel failed to percolate into the penitentiary system, which otherwise made innovatory strides in penal reforms: 'it cannot but be even more incumbent on us, to endeavour in all Ways, to reclaim those Offenders, who are to return again into the World, than those who are to be removed out of it: and the only effectual Means of Reclaiming them, is to instil into them a Principle of Religion'.[110] Earlier prisons had made little if any attempt to ameliorate the grimness of incarceration, but as early as 1702 Dr Thomas Bray, a member of the Society for the Promotion of Christian Knowledge (SPCK), in *An Essay Towards ye Reformation of Newgate and Other Prisons in and about London*, noting this neglect of worship, recommended the appointment of a 'sober pious' minister, daily prayer and Sunday sermons.[111] The new, reformed prisons were based on the principle of redemption through hard work and controlled religious observance, hence the alternative term penitentiary. The first purpose-built in the country, Debtors' Prison, York (1701–5, now a museum), was a 'most magnificent structure . . . so noble and compleat as exceeds all others, of its kind, in *Britain*; perhaps in *Europe*', but though incorporating 'a handsome chapel, neatly and beautifully adorned with suitable furniture', double-storeyed and galleried (no longer intact), it was architecturally undistinguished and, like the majority of British prison chapel interiors, mainly interesting in respect of planning as a reflection of a more sympathetic interaction between architecture and worship.[112]

In 1777 John Howard set out his programme for promoting improvements in his highly influential book *The State of Prisons in England and Wales*, exposing the 'great error in the management of some institutions: want of food, lack of water and air, absence of sewers, confining men, women, felons and debtors together, and, therefore, recommending separate wards with each prisoner having his or her own sleeping cells'. In particular, 'A CHAPEL is necessary in a Gaol', and in his ideal

36 Architect unknown. Berkeley Hospital chapel, Worcester, Worcestershire, 1703.

'Plan for a County Gaol . . . chose . . . a proper situation at the end of the central axis beyond the Gaoler's House and Garden', surrounded by segregated wards and an infirmary. 'It should have a gallery for debtors or women; and the rest may be separated below. Bibles and prayer-books should be chained at convenient distances: those who tear or otherwise damage them should be punished'; the chaplain should 'converse with the prisoners; admonish the profligate; exhort the thoughtless; comfort the sick; and make known to the condemned that *Mercy* which is revealed in the *Gospel*'. 'I have proposed nothing to give them an air of *elegance*, or *pleasantness*. On the contrary, I have censured the plan of some modern *Gaols* as too shewy and splendid', preferring 'perfect *plainness* and *simplicity*'.[113] Architecturally adventurous schemes atrophied. There was Henry Fielding's *Proposal for Making an Effectual Provision for the Poor, For Amending their Morals, and for Rendering them useful Members of the Society* (1753), drawn by Thomas Gibson and consisting of a vast Palladian multi-court complex housing 6,000 inmates with a 85 by 180 foot, double-apsed and galleried chapel (the equivalent size of St Martin-in-the-Fields), in which 'Prayers shall begin . . . precisely at five; at the Conclusion of which, on every *Wednesday* and *Friday*, some short Lecture, or Exhortation of Morality shall be read to the People', thereby 'instilling into them Notions of Religion . . . (a Matter as it appears to me of the highest Consequence)'.[114] In 1782 John Soane proposed a hexagonal chapel with alternating straight

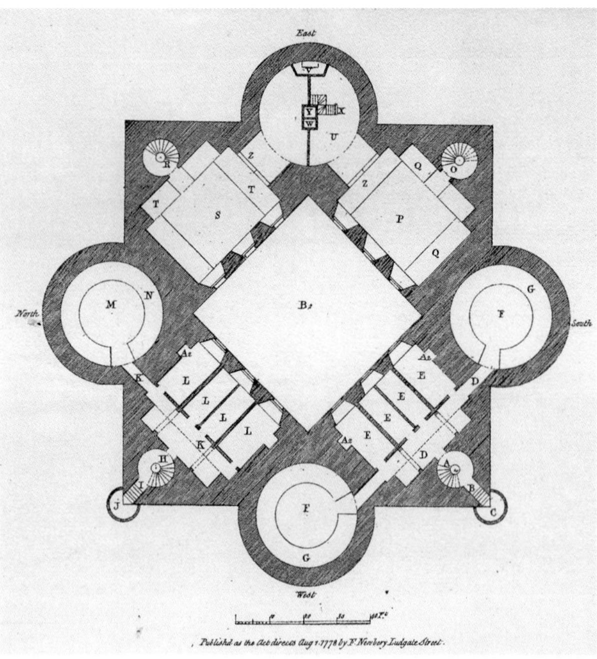

37 John Carter. 'Design for a County Goal', plan, in 'A Society of Architects', *The Builder's Magazine*, 1 August 1778, pl. CLXXX. Engraving. Author's collection.

and concave sides for a male prison for 600 inmates located in Wandsworth Fields, London, while in Battersea a clover-leaf plan expressive of 'feminine roundness' for 3,000 females, a competition stipulating 'plain, strong and substantial . . . Houses' providing 'solitary Imprisonment, accompanied by well-regulated Labour, and religious Instruction [as] the means, under Providence, not only of detering others from the Commission of the like Crimes, but also of reforming the Individuals, and inuring them to Habits of Industry'; in the chapel the chaplain 'shall read Morning and Evening Prayers . . . preach a Sermon both Morning and Afternoon, on every *Sunday* . . . *Christmas*-day and *Good-Friday*'.[115] Jeremy Bentham's visionary D-shaped Panopticon Penitentiary House (1787–91), as interpreted by Willey Reveley, contained a three-storey circular chapel with 'very little decoration' apart from quatrefoil gallery fronts and a moveable pulpit, its 'Great Annular Skylight' supported on tall, slender columns. In a reversal of earlier planning where inmates were transported to segregated positions within the chapel, here they remained in cells positioned along the outer perimeter, each with iron grating enclosing the inner circumference 'in a state of continued safe custody' while enjoying 'an uninterrupted view of the minister'. The circular galleries between grating and chapel accommodated visitors, a 'picturesque . . . scene' that encouraged 'prospect of contributions that might be collected . . . to keep the establishment in a state of exemplary neatness and cleanliness'.[116]

Adoption of progressive yet modest, practical solutions, if at all, is typified by John Carter's 'Design for a Country Goal' (pl. 37), in which the circular, subdivided chapel (marked U) is accessed from flanking male and female felons' 'Sleeping rooms' (P, S) via folding doors (Z) opened during divine service, with a shared altar, reading desk and pulpit (V–Y). Inmates were allocated in the following manner: 'felons . . . sent up to the second story, where, from a gallery . . . lighted from the sky-light . . . they may hear the service'; debtors from cells in E, F, L, M 'go into the chapel after the service is over'.[117]

Finally, because the parish vestry in the eighteenth century was the basic unit of local government, it was unsurprising to find conjugality of civic and mercantile aspirations present in a single structure erected largely for religious purposes. Thus it was reported in 1720 in connection with rebuilding St Michael Cornhill's tower in London that the adjacent porch was 'much abused & injured by the Vile Building raised upon it . . . for a Tenem[en]t. And . . . Shops for Trade in the Very Porch', despite Wren's estimate of £6,000 having included costs of 'removing these Nusances & making good' to the benefit of its 'great Beauty & Security'.[118] At St George, Derby Square, Liverpool (pl. 38), designed by Thomas Steers, builder of wet and dry docks that laid the foundation of the town's greatness as a seaport,[119] its semicircular chancel, rather than its tower, faced towards the main thoroughfare of Castle Street (from 1754 terminated by John Wood Sr's Exchange, now the Town Hall), with its south side supported on a rusticated arched terrace, the undercroft of which was occupied by market traders, flanked by a pair of semi-detached domed octagons used as the market clerks' office and temporary lock-up for delinquents.[120] The idea was probably inspired by Palladio's description of his Basilica at Vicenza, which stands 'on vaults in which are arranged shops for the various trades and businesses of the city; the prison and other places essential for public life'.[121] Steere's ensemble, marked by obelisk-shaped street lights, appears to have been unique in Britain.

This interaction reached a climax towards the end of the century when worship and trade collided. At All Saints, Pavement, York, following the curtailment of the medieval chancel in a road-widening scheme in 1778, Thomas Atkinson suggested but failed to realise replacing the free-standing baroque Market Cross with a

38 Thomas Malton after G. Perry. 'View of Castle Street Liverpool from the upper end of Pool Lane', Lancashire, with south elevation of St George, 20 March 1792. Engraving. © The British Library Board, K. Top. XXVIII-76-o. Thomas Steers architect, 1725–34, demolished.

39 Thomas Atkinson. Plan and elevation of a design for a new Market Cross attached to All Saints Pavement, York, Yorkshire, 1778. Pen and ink and wash. Borthwick Institute, York University, PR Y/ASP. F.17/9.

charming gothic arcade attached to the church's east end (pl. 39).[122] In Glasgow – where Smollett's Humphrey Clinker found 'marks of opulence . . . in every quarter of this commercial city'[123] – James Adam proposed one of the most adventurous schemes in social architecture of the age for the Tron or Laigh Church, a 59-foot-square congregational space with segmental flanks screened by a front block containing four two-room shops and a narrow central lobby. The façade closely resembles the Trades Hall in Glasgow (1791–4) by his late brother, Robert. This was preferred to a more palatial scheme (pls 40–41) in which an 80-foot-diameter galleried octagon lit on five sides by large Serliana is fronted by a pair of identically planned (but reversed) residences integrated into a terrace block and approached through a grand Roman triumphal arch framing a coffer-vaulted, column-screen *in antis* porch. Externally, only the elaborate domed cupola hints at an ecclesiastical presence.[124] At Inveraray, Argyllshire, Robert Mylne planned the parish church (1792–1802), which required accommodating separate Highland Gaelic-speaking and Lowland English-speaking congregations under one roof but with their separate entrances, as back-to-back rectangles sharing a common wall (a sort of equivalent to the Roman temple of Venus and Rome). On the austere external long walls at the conjunction of the two spaces he proposed introducing, but failed to realise, the novelty of a semicircular, double-entrance Tuscan portico echoed opposite by a blind equivalent incorporating tiered seats for the trone, or marketplace, complete with 'Market Seats' and 'exposure of Wares'.[125]

40 (*facing page top*) James Adam. Entrance elevation of a design for the Tron or Laigh Church, Glasgow, Strathclyde, Scotland, 1794. Pencil. Sir John Soane's Museum, London, AD 48/19.

41 (*facing page bottom*) James Adam. Ground plan of a design for the Tron or Laigh Church, Glasgow, Strathclyde, Scotland, 1794. Pencil. Sir John Soane's Museum, London, AD48/ 21.

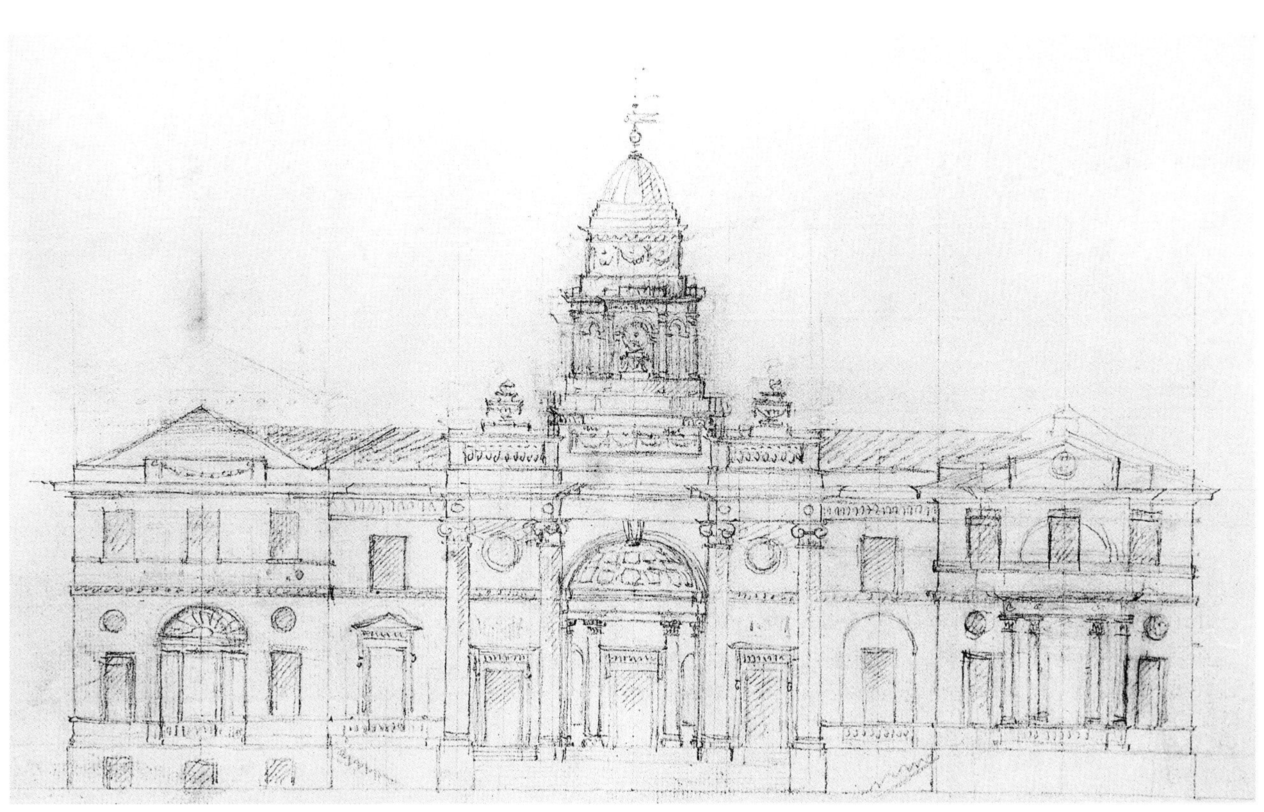

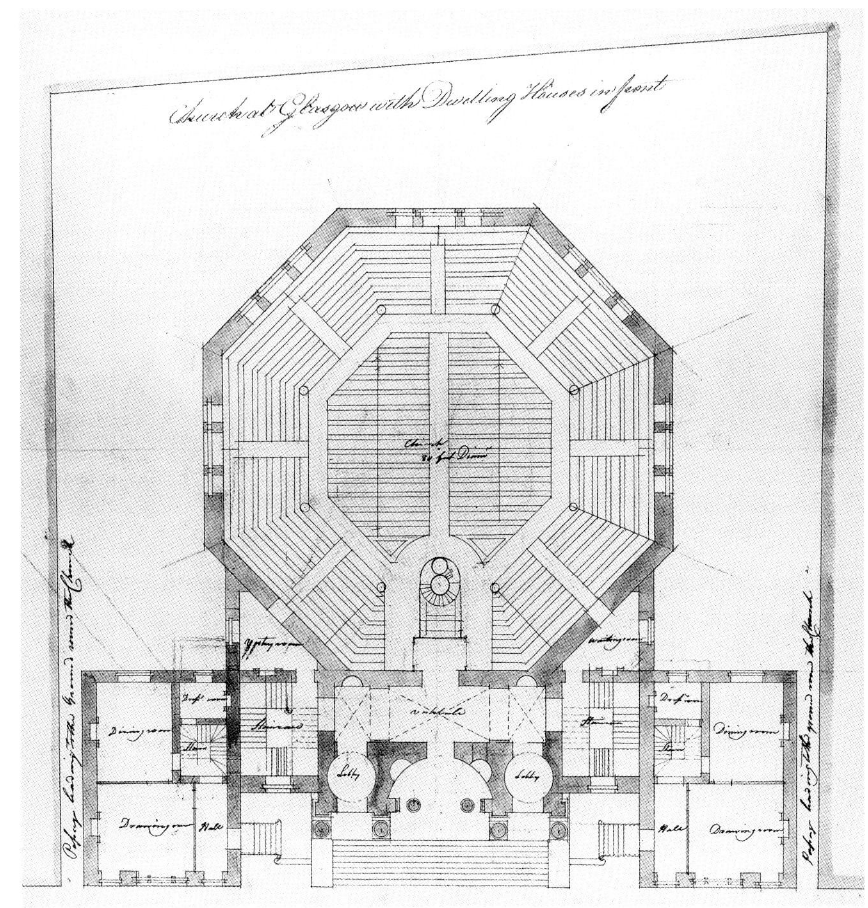
Church at Glasgow with Dwelling Houses in front

42 Samuel Hieronymus Grimm. *View of the interior towards the west of Bath Abbey, Somerset,* 1788. Pen and ink and wash. © The British Library Board, Kaye Collection, x, Add. MS 15546, f. 101.

Three

ACCOMMODATING THE CONGREGATION

Frequent the Church, in decent Dress,
There offer up religious Vows;
Yourself to none but GOD address;
Avoiding foppish Forms and Bows.
When you've your due Devotion paid,
Walk on the North or South Parade[1]

The flourishing, elegant spa society of Georgian Bath (pl. 42) – such a contrast to its metropolitan rival. Addison's Iroquois, whom we first met in chapter 1, on leaving St Paul's Cathedral in 1712, ventured into another 'holy house' but

> could not observe any circumstances of devotion . . . there was indeed a man in black who was mounted above the rest, and seemed to utter something with a great deal of vehemence; but as for those underneath him, instead of paying their worship to the deity of the place, they were most of them bowing and curtsying to one another, and a considerable number of them fast asleep

– a scenario later brilliantly satirised by Hogarth (pl. 43).[2] Foreigners were not always welcome in English churches. John Macky, author of *A Journey Through England*, first published in 1714, complained that 'one great Fault . . . which we no where meet with abroad . . . that is . . . a Stranger cannot have a convenient Seat without paying . . . and particularly at . . . St *James'* [Piccadilly], where it costs one almost as dear as to see a Play'.[3] Readers of the *Grub-street Journal* were informed irreverently and tongue-in-cheek by a 'Physician' that 'there is no more Danger of getting the Piles at Church than at a Play-House, especially if soft primitive Velvet Cushions can be had' and proposed between services on Sunday and holidays an entertainment

> sometimes with a New Minuet, sometimes a Rigadoon, but above all a reviving Jig after the Sermon. And . . . not . . . refrain'd from the Violin, Hautboy, Trumpet, French Horn, Flute &c. any more than the Organ, which is modern Music, when com-

43 William Hogarth. *Credulity, Superstition and Fanaticism*, detail, 1762. Etching and engraving.

par'd with some others [but] no vocal Music . . . unless *Italian* Eunuchs might be imported . . . and one or more plac'd in every Parish, to sing a favourite Song from one of our best Operas.

Furthermore, 'Dancing, that such People may be brought to hear divine Service, upon the prospect of seeing it, as at present don't know what the Inside of a Church is like; and that Bashfulness may be no Obstruction . . . allowing People of Quality to come in Masquerade'. Also during prayers:

> Gentlemen are displaying their Snuff-Boxes, Rings, &c. and . . . Ladies are employ'd in adjusting their Dresses; and both Sexes in twenty other Amusements. He knows Attempts have been made to deprive them of this Freedom, as well as that of coming into and going out of Church at their Pleasure, on Pretence of its hindering other People's Devotion. Poor silly Creatures! . . . if they were to have their Ways . . . we must not be allowed to go to above one Church in a Morning; whereas, with good Management, we may now pay Visits to four or five before Dinner, besides short Compliments to the Chapels and Tabernacles in our way; and, if Occasion be, to two or three Meeting Houses.

In this way, 'Churches would be fill'd with the most polite People, and their Assemblies be accounted as entertaining and genteel as any other, not excepting even Masquerades and Operas.'[4]

Not only that. Churches also attracted disreputable elements, so that, for example, at Wragby, Lincolnshire, 'a small private Isle . . . altogether fallen to decay, which was of no use but a receptacle of idle people and Boys to loyter in during the time of divine service' was demolished in 1756,[5] while at St George, Bloomsbury, 'if any Boys or other Persons . . . make . . . Disturbance in the porch or other places in time of Divine Service Beadles [are ordered to] carry them before some Justice of the peace to their being prosecuted and punished'.[6] At St Peter, Leeds, 'a Door [was] struck out at the Bottom of the Belfry Stair Case into the Church Yard to prevent some disorders Committed in the Church by disorderly people'.[7] Woodnewton, Northamptonshire, had 'two Hatch Doors . . . put up at the Entrance . . . Porch . . . to prevent . . . Boys . . . playing and doing . . . other Indecencies there'.[8] On the other hand, a meeting held at St Paul's Cathedral on 23 April 1789 attracted 2,000 spectators to view 6,398 boys and girls, all educated, clothed and supported by the voluntary contributions of the public, assembled under the dome, 'So glorious a picture . . . no country but England can boost'.[9]

This social structure is encapsulated in Grimm's interior view of Bath Abbey of 1788 (pl. 44a), depicting the minister and parish clerk in their respective pulpit and reading desk surrounded by blocks of kneeling charity children and scattered adults at prayer, with fashionable visitors attending the spa congregating at the west end. This could virtually be the scene recorded

44a and b Samuel Hieronymus Grimm. *View of the interior towards the west of Bath Abbey, Somerset*, details of pl. 42.

by Katherine Plymley, a visitor from Shropshire, who one Sunday afternoon in company with her friends, Rose Istead and a Miss Adams, made the rounds of voguish churches, including the abbey, 'to hear service perform'd for the different charity schools. The children . . . amounted to about seven hundred [who] sang to the Organ the 100th psalm & are taught to repeat amen, audibly at the end of each prayer.'[10]

Foreign travellers tended to generalise about congregational participation in the Anglican service of worship. François de La Rochefoucauld, visiting in 1784, observed that the English

> don't go to confession, they very rarely approach the Holy Table, and when they do . . . they do not believe they are eating the body of Jesus Christ . . . but . . . go . . . as a commemorative enactment. They are not bound to go to church every Sunday: rain, fog, heat – the least thing keeps them away. But they are obliged to read the Bible as often as possible . . . [The service] lasts an hour and a half and consists of a prayer with all the people making responses to the minister, then a reading from the Bible, then a sermon. There are always two ministers, one in a pulpit and the other below him . . . Evening service is shorter. Everything that is read, or spoken, or preached, is in English, to be within reach of everyone . . . The whole religion is based on the principle of political equality . . . All religions are tolerated in England – in fact, though not in law.[11]

This liberalism was manifest in concerns about seating accommodation, which more than anything apart from dress defined wealth and social status. Macky, visiting Maidstone in Kent, 'never was better pleas'd in any Place than this, which made me stay here some Days; for the Company is good, and the Families for ten Miles round are worth amongst them fifty thousand pounds a Year. Every body gives good Equipages; and at Church it's hardly to be express'd the Fineness of the Assembly.'[12] Box pews, which often filled both the body and the galleries (the latter a Protestant innovation) in order to provide increased seating as a remedy to non-attendance,[13] were identified by numbered labels and their allocation determined by set rates issued by public subscription and sometimes recorded in plans and views (pls 45, 63). Typical is this advertisement appearing in the *Leeds Intelligencer* on 3 March 1794:

> CHURCH PEWS and VAULTS, To be SOLD. On Monday, March 10th, at Ten o'Clock in the Forenoon, the PROPRIETOR of St PAUL'S CHURCH, in this Town, proposes to open the SALE of the PEWS and VAULTS. The Act of Parliament and Conditions of Sale, may be seen in the Vestry of the said Church, any Day of the Week (except Sunday) till the Sale opens.[14]

Pew sales were a vital source of income for supplementing ministers' salaries, as well as financing repair and rebuilding programmes. Though Wren would have preferred churches 'should not be so fill'd with Pews [so] that the Poor may have room enough to stand and sit in the Alleys, for to them equally is the Gospel preach'd', he recognised that there was 'no stemming the Tide of Profit, and the Advantage of Pew-Keepers'.[15] Rates varied. At Banbury, Oxfordshire, in 1797 ten double pews 'first class' fetched £100, thirty-three '2nd class' £50, forty-three '3rd class' £30, and fifty-five '4th class' £10, a total of £190.[16] In 1774 the total rents at St Mary, Birmingham, were fixed at £130 4s. 0d. on the ground floor and £193 17s. 0d. in the galleries.[17] On the occasion of the consecration of St Philip, Birmingham, the Vestry ordered that to 'avoid all disturbance . . . every person shall take their places in their seats as they come not to strive for any particular place [but] Should there be any disagreement between the parties . . . the person which subscribed most to the church shall be preferred'.[18]

At St Nicholas, Worcester, townspeople were permitted to occupy 'figured seats'; itinerant lodgers and others agreed to pay a weekly sum for sitting or kneeling, while widows and unmarried women 'may make use of the Seat marked with the second figure'.[19] Richard Barlow, pew-holder no. 31 in St James, Manchester, in 1788, agreed

> at all times . . . in a regular uniform and decent Order and Manner [to] well and sufficiently repair the . . . Pew . . . and shall not . . . at any time make any Additions to or Alterations . . . so as to destroy prejudice or affect the Uniformity of the Church . . . or prejudice hinder or obstruct any other person or Persons in his or their Property.[20]

At St Paul, Birmingham, Joseph Green was allowed to 'take down the partition between his two Seats . . . to make it more convenient' at a charge of £10, and should 'not be molested in the enjoyment of the seat in the manner . . . now alter'd',[21] but at Holy Trinity, Clapham, London, the Vestry ordered that 'no curtains be put on the tops of pews [as shown on p. vi], nor no hatpins be fix'd in the pillars, nor no holes made in the tops of the pews to stick Christmas in'.[22] In a revealing letter of 23 March 1713 from James Lowther in London to his agent at Whitehaven, Cumberland, regarding proposals for rebuilding Holy Trinity church in that prosperous mercantile town (pl. 3), he suggested:

> You may . . . consider . . . the numbers of the different sorts of Pews, according to wch we must agree upon a draught, I see none can hold more than our old Church wth Pews under the side Walls, but if it be necessary to have a great number of Pews of the highest rate the Modell of a chappel in Devonshire Street wil answer . . . there are 4 tire of Seats between the East side & the West side not cover'd by the Gallerys & consequently little difference in the goodness . . . this with the front Seats of the Galerys wil make abundance more of the 1st Rate Seats, but the other sort wil hold more People.[23]

The Revd John Penrose, visiting Bath in 1766, observed that 'People frequent the Churches, as well as the Assembly Rooms' on Sundays, citing some who 'offered Money for a Seat [at St James] but could not be admitted for Want of Room', and he learnt from the minister that there 'Prayers begin half an hour later than at the other Churches . . . that Servants might go thither, setting out after and getting Home before their Masters and Mistresses, who went to the Abbey'.[24]

Some parish records and seating plans particularised this social distribution. The parishioners of St Peter, Nottingham, petitioned 'that there is a great want of good suitable and convenient Seats where in to place severall Substantial Inhabitants . . . as now want room, or such others as shall be thought fitt to be placed there', which should be 'Built Uniform and commodious'.[25] At St Cuthbert, Carlisle, appointment was according to 'respective Degrees Estates and Condition' with an obligation to maintain the seats 'in good and Sufficient repair', with those 'in the Windows . . . left open for such Inhabitants . . . as have no particular Seats allotted to them, such Accomodation being thought necessary to Encourage them to attend Divine Worship'.[26] There was an underlying philanthropic liberalism behind pew allocation. John Stanhope, lord of the manor of Horsforth, Yorkshire, dictated that

> Our Chapel is now so far finished, that we can make Use of it & the Seats are distributed amongst the Landowners. In the old Chapel there were some few Seats wch had been always enjoyed by the Inhabitants of particular Houses: but for the most part the Seats were common to all. Indeed I could never find that any . . . were so appropriated that any Man could make a good Title to them. In the present Chapel we have endeavoured to distribute all the Seats (Except a few wch we purposely left unappropriated for the benefit of Cottagers who pay no assessment) amongst the Landowners in proportion to their respective share of the Church rate . . . in such a manner that I can with pleasure tell you, every body seems perfectly well satisfied with it . . .

having signified 'an entire pew of Nine Seats for the Use of the Tenants & Servants belonging [to] the Estate [together with owners] in the very best part of the Chappel'.[27] Just down the road at St Matthew in the Leeds suburb of Chapel Allerton, 'the Montpelier of Yorkshire', however, Thomas Webster, a Quaker leasing a local estate, claimed he 'always had a right to an entire Pew . . . without paying any consideration for the same either to the curate or upon any other occation'; nevertheless, the present incumbent 'discharged . . . Websters servant from siting . . . & has let the Pew to a person who resides in Potter Newton' (the adjacent village), charging one guinea a year. Webster's solicitor enquired if he was 'compelable to contribute towards the Assesmt. for the repairs . . . & how he must proceed to obtain a quiet enjoyment of the Pew?' The answer was that if the church had been founded 'within time of legal memory (viz. since the time of Richard the first)' he was not compelled to pay repair charges but 'may cite the person that disturbs him into the Spiritual Court, or . . . maintain an Action at Law against him'. The outcome of the dispute is unrecorded.[28]

An amusing incident took place in 1791 during preparations to pull down and rebuild dilapidated medieval All Saints, Milwich, Staffordshire. Benjamin Robinson, 'the Owner of a very good Estate . . . and . . . the best House in the parish . . . for many years . . . past destitute of a Seat . . . in the Church or Chancel', insisted on a case being heard for not 'rebuilding the Body . . . Tower . . . Pulpit reading Desk font and Seats'.[29] This was countered by a vociferous parishioner, who claimed that

> If Vice and a Life of Malpractices constitute a Gentlemen I readily admit . . . Robinson . . . to be one; he never goes to any Church or place of Worship . . . he has for years, and now does live in an open and notorious state of Adultery or fornication; he was recently out-lawed in an Action of Debt; is now so involved by a train of folly and profligacy that he is rarely visible but on a Sunday; he never would or did attend any of the Vestry Meetings respecting the Church, tho' . . . they were held and conducted in the most candid manner; and has repetedly declared that he did not care a farthing for the church, but would oppose, only to plague the petitioners; should then such a Man as this be permit-

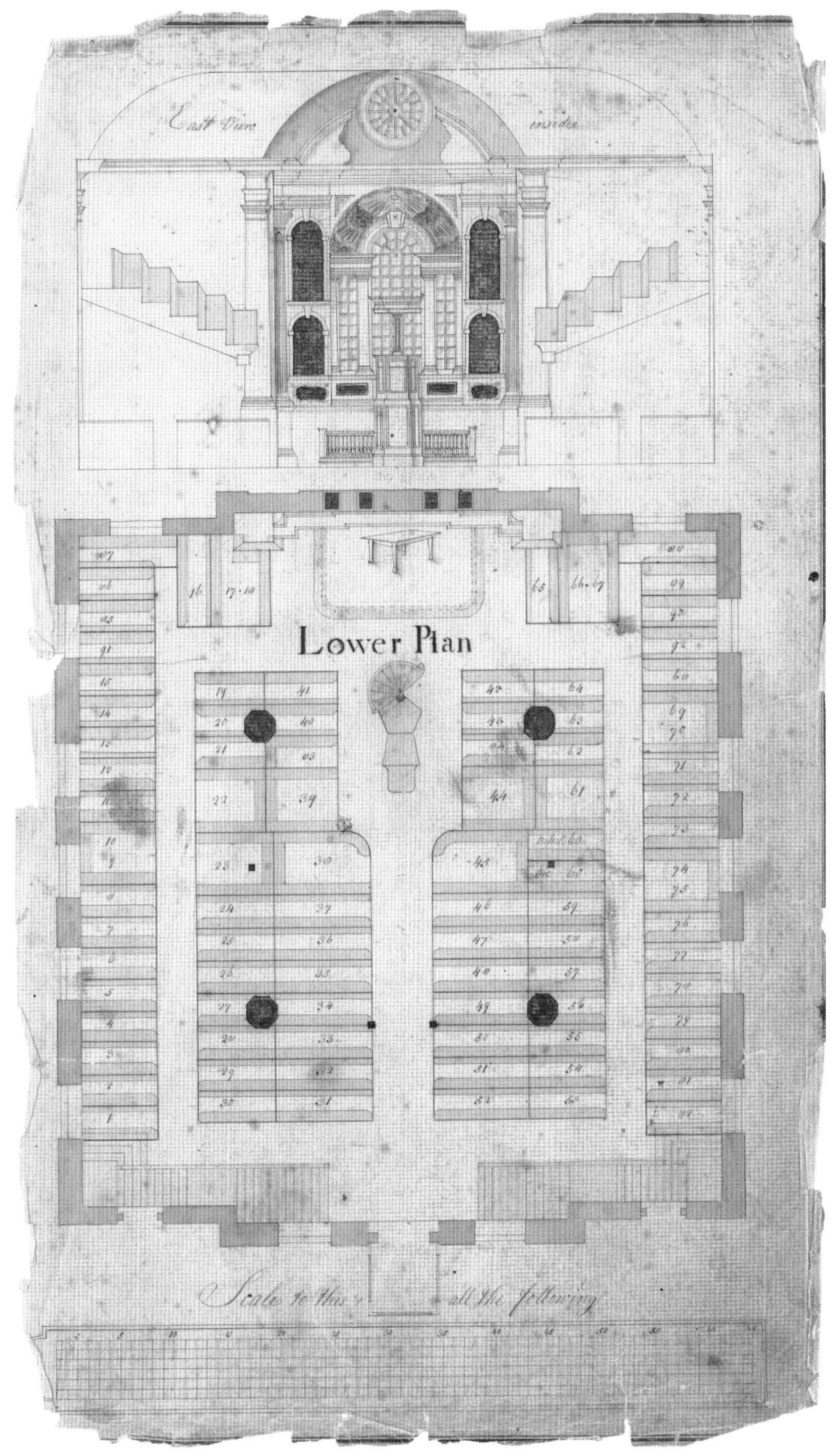

45 Nicholas Vass. 'East View inside' and 'Lower Plan' with seating allocations, St George, Portsea, Hampshire, 1753. Pen and ink and wash. Portsmouth City Record Office, CHU 4/2/1.

ted to trifle with the Court, and prevent the obtaining of a faculty for the most pious and laudable of purposes?

Moreover, he 'is such a Man . . . to control a whole parish and by such artful and frivolous means deprive them of paying their Devotion to God . . . In a Word it is clearly evident . . . that this Manoeuvring . . . is merely calculated for Vexation and delay.'[30] Robinson withdrew his 'Objections'.

The implications of a confusing or random seating arrangement are demonstrated in William Nicholson, Bishop of Carlisle's 'Perambulation' report of 1704 on three new pews installed in the chancel of medieval St Andrew, Penrith, Cumberland, which

brings a present Inconvenience; Especially, when great Numbers (as at Visitations, Confirmations, &c.) are to be admitted at once [the body] is basely Seated: For . . . as Familyes have decay'd or risen in this Tradeing Town, the pews have been neglected or improv'd. So that there's now no Uniformity in the whole . . . the Merchant's Pew, on the left hand comeing out of the Quire, has a Canopy which is a very great Nusance; and ought to be removed: Since it not onely drowns the Minister's Voice . . . but . . . hinders the Congregation's seeing the Consecration of the Elements . . .

though shortly all the seats were to be 'Regulated, and every man provided for according to his Quality'.[31]

As the Yorkshire incidents reveal, household servants were looked after. On the West Woodhay estate in Berkshire, males and females, including children, 'who pay no Seat or Lot in the . . . parish', were benched separately on either side of the west tower;[32] at St George, Bloomsbury, three 'Livery Servants belonging to the Gentlemen or Ladies renting Seats in the West Gallery' were allowed 'to sit in the Back Seats in the North Gallery Gratis';[33] at St John, Hackney, London, the Vestry resolved that 'pew openers in the Gallery be directed not to permit any Servants to come into the pews . . . which are appropriated to the Inhabitants';[34] whereas 'It would be to no Purpose to send servants to keep our pews clear for us', observed a pamphlet of 1759 issued by St Dunstan-in-the-West in Fleet Street, 'To disencumber the Passage and free it from the Crowd . . . would require half a regiment of soldiers with their Bayonets fixed'.[35]

A seating plan of 1735 for Apethorpe, Northamptonshire, places ladies and gentlemen attending communion at the entrance to the chancel, segregated according to sex, with churchwardens, overseers of the poor, constables and farmers concentrated in a large pew at the east end of the north aisle directly behind the pulpit, the 'Lords Uppermen Servants & Strangers' in an equivalent enclosure at the south-east, 'servants within doors', 'Liverry Servants of Stable [and] Servants of Husbandry' along the south wall, 'Coppy holders & Cottagers' opposite along the north wall, 'Children and farmers maidservants' on benches flanking the central aisle and 'former servants [and] singers' flanking the west door.[36] At Wendlebury, Oxfordshire, 'Land-owners or occupiers and their grown sons or kinsmen' were seated in the chancel and south transept, together with their 'Men-servants' in the latter, their 'Wifes &c.' and 'Maid-servants' in the north transept, and 'Children under the age of 12 or 14' in the fronts of both, on either side of the pulpit and desks placed at the crossing, while in the nave were 'Tradesmen . . . Labourers' and their wives; with 'a Gallery designed at present for the Singers . . . Hereafter for a parochial Library' and the west tower 'to serve for town meetings on Parish business'.[37]

Those categorised as 'the poorer Sort of People' were catered for as part of the parish philanthropic policies towards the disenfranchised.[38] At Rochdale, Lancashire, seats were ordered 'built form-size for the ease and benefit of the Poor only';[39] at St Nicholas, Warwick, pews nos. 45–8 were 'set apart for the Use of the Singers, if wanted; if not they may be us'd for the Conveniency of the Poor'.[40] 'A Bench fixed up' in Congleton, Cheshire, was 'for the Use of poor Inhabitants and such as stand in need of Seats . . . as the Mayor and Justice and Minister shall think most proper'.[41] At St Peter, Sheffield, the burgesses appropriated 'what ever pews and vacant spaces for benches remain at the extreme parts of the church . . . to the use of the poor . . . for their sole benefit without paying any rent',[42] or stored them under stationary pews; the new church at Aynho, Northamptonshire (1723–5), held approximately 370 persons 'besides what may be gain'd by draw-seats in the Isles';[43] in the Quaker Meeting House, The Friars, Bristol, each end of the pews had 'a Sliding Seat to Draw out 14 Inches'.[44] But issues concerning the impoverished also had unpleasant reverberations. At St Botolph, Bishopsgate, London, complaints about the 'Poor Standing to Begg' outside the entrance so that the congregation 'cannot with Ease Gett Out of the . . . Doores, after Divine Service' led to the appointment of six 'Beareres . . . To keep Off The Poor from making A Stopp'.[45] Early bouncers!

The relative merits of stationary pews and movable benches were debated. Joseph Farington recounted dining with the Bishop of Durham during which the latter observed that he 'thought pews in Churches a bad custom; and prefers benches. In a Church under his direction, He has adopted benches, from designs by [James] Wyatt'.[46] The priest of Claughton Roman Catholic Chapel, Lancashire, insisted on placing benches not bespoken at 'Convenient good places to kneel & sit in for those who are old & poor', and though drawing the line at providing 'loose Cushions', permitted 'the board they kneel on . . . covered with Cloath & stuff'd'.[47]

While the importance of succouring impoverished communities was acknowledged, this was not always achieved. Well-intentioned John Hunter published *Adius Templum; or, The pathway to Church, being a preparation for a more solemn devotion of the public worship of God in the Church; a New Year's gift to the parishioners of Hampton-Poyle and South-Weston, Oxon* (1737), somehow failing to realise that they were 'generally illiterate People and of the meaner sort, tho', I hope, good Christians [who] neither can purchase, nor spare time to peruse large Treatises', as he was obliged to confess to his bishop.[48]

In some parish documents the poor are specifically identified. 'Cottagers, Labourers, work-people in the Linnen and Cotton manufactories and Tenants at Rack Rents' at the ominously named Blackrod, Lancashire.[49] At Woolwich on the Thames 6,500 'very poor' parishioners belonging to approximately 1,200 families employed as 'Artificers and Laboureres' at the Navy Dockyard, Ropeyard and Ordnance service attended the ancient, 'rotten and mouldering' parish church of St Mary, which was capable of holding no more than 600, and 'apprehensive that [it was] in great Danger of falling' and they would be 'destitute of a Place to attend Divine Service', proposed in 1718 to erect a plain, five-bay, two-storey, galleried church of stock brick 'with the utmost frugality' for £5,069.[50] Lady Elizabeth Hastings, sister-in-law of the Evangelical Countess of Huntingdon, 'commiserating the State of the Inhabitants [of Beeston, Leeds] deprived of both Prayer and Preaching . . . it being to be justly dreaded, that the Zeal of the subterraneous Colliers (who are numerous there) would scarce surmount the easy Task of walking to any other neighbouring Church or Chapel', and in full knowledge that 'the poorer Sort, for want of such Conveniencies, were discouraged from attending . . . publick Worship . . . and thereby are in great Danger of sinking into gross Ignorance or grievous Errors, and into all manner of Impiety and Prophaneness, to the high Displeasure of Almighty God, and the great Scandal of Christianity, and of all good Men', subscribed £50 towards improving the chapel 'that they might enjoy the publick Worship of God both before and after Noon'.[51] W. Matthews's *The New History, Survey and Description of the City and Suburbs of Bristol* (1794) recollected that

> 40 or 50 years ago . . . the colliers of the forest, were . . . so barbarous and savage, that they were a terror to . . . Bristol . . . but by the labours of . . . *Whitefield* and *Wesley* [and] the erection of a parish Church and some meeting houses . . . are much civilized and improved in principals, morals and pronunciation.[52]

Aware of the growing population around Kingswood 'by reason of larger Collieries, and several extensive Manufactures' and the need to provide 'a plain, strong Fabrick' capable of accommodating 800 persons, a subscription was launched that attracted such luminaries as the Duke of Beaufort of Badminton, Ralph Allen of Bath and the Bristol Society of Merchants, raising £2,324 11s. 9d. of a required £5,400 and encouraging the city's clergy to 'speedily . . . preach a Sermon in . . . their . . . Parish to Exhort their Congregations to a Liberal Contribution', as well as aldermen 'to appear personally . . . in their . . . Wards and to go from House to House at the time of the Collection taking to their assistance such Gentlemen . . . as they in their discretions shall think proper'. The result, designed by a local carpenter named Samuel Glascodine and described as 'a handsome building of stone, in a modern stile', was a Wrenian, triple-aisled basilica with lofty west tower and Gibbs-surround doors and windows. Unsurprisingly, the Bishop of Bristol instructed that for the consecration service 'there ought to be a . . . Flaggon and two Chalices, with two plates . . . of Block Tin, 'till some future Benefactor shall bestow better . . . and some Tolerable floor shou'd be laid [though] Decorations may be postponed'.[53] A dispute broke out at Darrington, Yorkshire, in 1767–9 when John Holroyd opposed the parishioners for 'Enlarging their parish Gallery for the use of . . . poor people . . . Servants and others That has no . . . Sittings', fancying it for 'his Family Seat' and offering to erect another 'which might serve the poor'. The churchwardens rejected this, recommending instead that 'he had much better Build a Gallery for Himself. As there was room enough in the North Aisle' (presumably a less advantageous position). Holroyd offered the wardens 6s. to 'Drink with the parishioners if that he could prevail with them . . . to Exchange', but 'the people in general is quite against any Exchange, As it is thought an Unreasonable Request', suggesting he negotiate with another pew-holder as being 'much better. Then turning the poor . . . out off the Gallery'. The 'Freeholders Farmers and

Others' were petitioned on the matter 'Before . . . Holroyd took Violent possesion of it [and] there was not one Voice' in support of him. 'As many falshoods have been propagated', he called a meeting at the local alehouse but only nineteen of the fifty families attended and voted for retaining the gallery on grounds that 'There are . . . Betwixt 18. and 24 Cottages . . . which have no Seats . . . in the Body . . . Besides The Servants of most of the Farmers Which Can Claim No Other Seats . . . But a part in the Gallery.'[54]

The Salopian Miss Plymley, visiting Bath in 1796, reported the exceptional case of Christ Church, which was erected as

> a free church, where the poor & strangers may worship the Almighty. The idea is said to have originated with [William] Wilberforce, who shocked to find the poor entirely excluded from the Octagon [Chapel], too little room for them anywhere, & that strangers knew not where to go to church (indeed, two seats in St James's excepted, they cannot go anywhere without paying) advertised an offer of 300£ . . . numbers have subscribed & a handsome building, in the gothic stile, is now in great forwardness. It is . . . to cost perhaps somewhat more than 3000£. The whole body . . . is for the poor & strangers. Some seats in the gallery are to be set for a low rent, to pay a clerk, sexton & . . . a small stipend to a clergyman . . . The body . . . consists of benches, free to all poor & strangers, it will hold twelve hundred persons.

On a later visit, in 1807, however, having paid a shilling for a gallery pew, she noticed the body 'principally filled with Livery Servants & Ladies maids which . . . was not the original intention; it was meant for the real poor'.[55] Evidently Christ Church had gone upmarket. Box pews on the floor and in the galleries were important architectural elements, the subject of both detailed contractual specifications and aesthetic scrutiny, and, like much else in Georgian churches, the brunt of satire: 'Bombastry and Buffoonry, by Nature lofty and light, soar highest of all, and would be lost in the Roof, if the prudent Architect had not with much Foresight contrived for them a fourth Place, called the *Twenty-Penny-Gallery*, and there planted a suitable Colony, who greedily intercept them in their Passage.'[56]

The lack of suitable seating became a source of bitter internecine disputes. Here are two particularly heated examples. By 1751 the great increase in the population of Leeds meant that 'many . . . for want of room' in Holy Trinity (1723–7) were 'obliged to go to Divine Worship at inconvenient distances', while 'others go to Separate Congregations [or] no place . . . at all to the great encouragement of Prophaness and Immorality'. These fears were exacerbated by reports of the presence of five Dissenters' meeting houses and 'a large Building . . . Erecting . . . for the use of a Sect who call themselves Methodists'.[57] To remedy 'in some Degree this great Evil', it was proposed to erect galleries in the side aisles. A lone 'Gentleman', Henry Pawson, vehemently contested the scheme in the York Consistory Court on grounds that it was not 'Intended that Lofts should be built' and they would be of advantage only to the 'arrogant and haughty' curate, who would let seats to persons who were 'his Friends or he could Influence'; moreover, while providing 'more Room', the galleries 'will Occasion a Material Inconvenience to the proprietors of the Seats . . . within the Body . . . as they will Darken [them] by depriving them of the light from the . . . attick Windows'. The Revd Scott countered by observing that although

> there will be before and after service upon the people's coming into and going out of the . . . Galleries . . . an unavoidable noise so far from being a prejudice to the Body . . . will be of real Service by interrupting a proper portion of light it being notoriously true that the [church] is at present so glaring that it has been found convenient for many years occasionally to darken two of the . . . Attick windows by Curtains . . .

and that light as well as 'wholsome Air' will be supplied by 'the great West Door and Casements in the lower Class of Windows'. In a vote, forty-one out of fifty-five 'Proprietors' agreed to the proposal, and galleries were erected in 1755–6.[58]

In the second example the heritors (proprietors of a heritable parochial property) of Kirriemuir, Angus, Scotland, became embroiled with their architect, James Playfair, in a bureaucratic battle that raged between 1786 and 1790, proving explosive enough for the disputants to publish a thirty-two-page, illustrated explanation. The brief for the new church (pl. 46), an austere version of Wren's St James, Westminster, well suited to the ascetic needs of Scottish Presbyterianism, specified accommodating 1,600. Difficulties arose when the architect offered alternative solutions with and without a western tower, the former decreasing the internal seating space. Blame fell on the hapless minister, despite Playfair's apology that it had been 'entirely *my fault*', though it transpired that the heritors had 'never been at the trouble of examining' either the plan or the building itself, since they avowed 'One of the advantages contracting with . . . Playfair . . . a person, upon

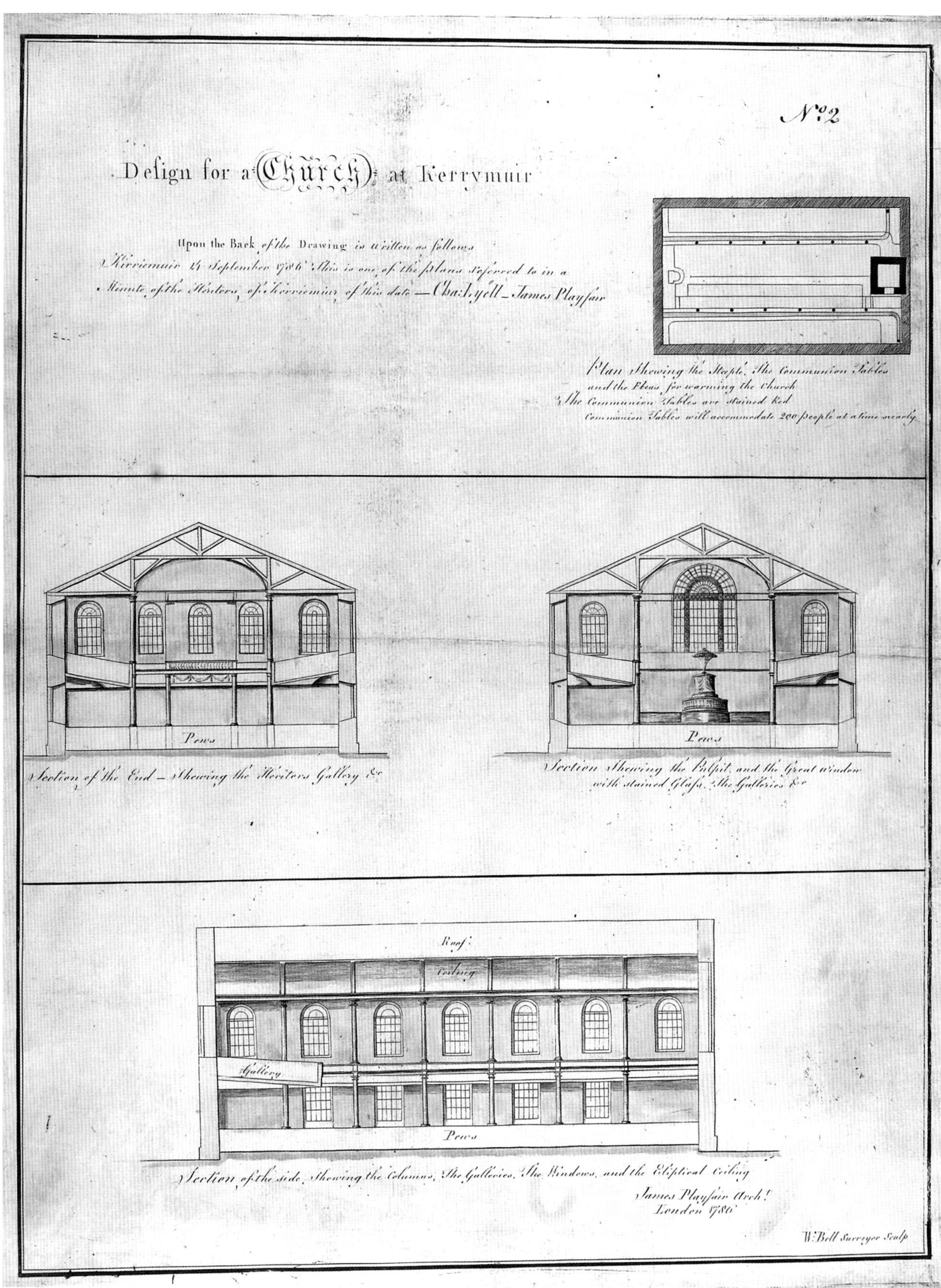

46 William Bell. Plan and section of a 'Design for a Church at Kerrymuir No.2' (Kerriemuir), Angus, Scotland, 1786. Engraving. National Archives of Scotland, RHP 176/3. James Playfair architect.

whose professional abilities and integrity, [they] might thoroughly rely . . . was that of being saved such trouble [and] very naturally led them to think . . . his plan . . . a good and sufficient one'. Nor would they have interfered but for a potentially 'very fatal' catastrophe when on the first Sunday service the gallery 'filled with people . . . threatened to give way; and . . . the congregation . . . immediately rushed out'. An independent survey exposed 'gross negligence' by the architect's overseer, who in making 'some trifling alteration' moved the supporting pillars 4 inches from the outside wall, leaving the beams short to bind with the structure. A Dundee wright named Samuel Bell recommended inserting 'a false girder . . . to join into the pillars' in preference to additional iron pillars, which, he feared, would 'make the kirk *like a fir park*'. It was then discovered that the pillars, 'thrown some inches off the perpendicular', endangered the roof they supported. A further survey undertaken by Playfair's friends concluded that the work had been 'executed agreeably to the contract, and in a sufficient manner'. This the by now incensed heritors rejected as 'very absurd and untenable' and in turn revealed the crux of their objections, that 'many . . . seats are incommodious . . . too narrow from back to breast' and that there was only room to accommodate 1,462. The surveyors were asked a series of predetermined questions concerning 'ease and convenience' and methods of rectification such as introducing seating 'flaps in the passages', expanding to considerations of the low pitch of the roof, durability of window frames and so on. Citing St Andrew, Edinburgh, as an example where seat depths measured 30–32 inches, compared to Kirriemuir's 27 inches, was regarded as evidence of Playfair's breach of contract, his insistence that the heritors were not entitled to object after approving the design as 'ungracious'. Moreover, the architect's revised solution of inserting an additional gallery and other similar alterations 'could not have been admissible at any time, far less at this advanced stage [and] utterly impossible without entirely disfiguring the church [rendering it] not only extremely unelegant, but exceedingly disagreeable' and producing an 'irregular, dark, and incommodious [building] very little better . . . than the old church'. The issue was never resolved.[59]

There were other concerns. 'NO SEATS . . . should be granted for a longer time than the Lives of the Parishioners; and they ought not to be annexed to Houses, because the Lands may be sold away from these Houses, and so in time the meanest People may sit uppermost, which will occasion much Confusion'; nor should pews be 'built so high as to hid Persons from being seen by the whole Congregation', unambiguous testimony to the social prerequisites of churchgoing and the fundamental importance attached to class.[60] The east gallery in St Peter, Nottingham, was 'very Incomodiously placed and Inconvenient in many respects both for the Minister and Congregation and . . . an hindrance to the Beauty and Ornament of the . . . Church',[61] whereas Watlington Vestry in Oxfordshire petitioned for a faculty to erect a new gallery in a 'void space' contingent with an existing one, 'without incommoding any Person, or injuring the regularity and Beauty of the . . . Church, but rather improving' it.[62] Galleries were the *bête noire* of the antiquary when imposed on pre-Reformation fabrics, the most flagrant surviving example being St Mary, Whitby, Yorkshire, where these interlopers, picturesquely cluttering the interior, were erected during several campaigns between 1700 and 1763. On one occasion a faculty specified the 'Underside . . . well ceiled with plaister to improve the Light of those who sit below and to prevent their being incommoded with Dust', while on two others breaking through the roof to create skylights.[63] An old gallery at Aston, Yorkshire, was 'so low that People who sit under it can't stand upright in their Pews', while it obscured daylight falling from windows on the pulpit.[64]

At Cherry Hinton, Cambridgeshire, windows containing armorial glass were 'destroyed to make way for more light',[65] while Torrington, visiting medieval St George, Doncaster, noted 'now that stain'd glass is removed, (which was intended for obstruction of the sun, and for meditation) must be like a greenhouse'.[66] Light, which carried compelling theological connotations – 'The Almighty Architect having in his Eternal Wisdom survey'd the *Chaos* in its rude and shapeless Condition, shew'd the first Instance of his Power in creating Light' and 'No sooner had the Light display'd its cheerful Beams, but it gave Birth to the first Day'[67] – was transformed into architectural concepts. '*Light (God's Eldest Daughter) is a principal Beauty in Building.* Yet it shines not alike from all parts of the Heavens. An *East window* gives the infant Beams of the *Sun* before they are of Strength to do any harm, and is offensive to none but a Sluggard.'[68] Yet, the glare of day needed to be curtailed. The Friends Meeting House, Carlisle (pl. 47), was provided with wooden shutters, though they may also have served as a security measure during times that still witnessed public unrest in response to Dissenting places of worship, as described in chapter 2.[69] Occasionally, curtains were used, as at St George, Bloomsbury, where the churchwardens were ordered to provide them for two western windows 'to prevent the

47 Architect unknown. 'A Plan of Carlisle Meeting House 1776', Cumberland. Pen and ink and wash. Cumbria Record Office, DFCF 2/49.

very Great Light coming through' into the chancel.[70] Robert Adam's design for 'a Church for the North part of Edinburgh' (1788, unrealised) shows the attic Diocletian windows hung with swagged curtains, a feature rarely indicated in presentation drawings and especially pertinent here because of worries about his brother James's nearby octagonal gothic St George's Episcopal Chapel, York Place (built 1792–4, later altered), concerning the 'want of light' emanating from the upper windows, which were blocked by the gallery fronts, casting part of the interior into 'darkness'.[71] Blinds were sometimes favoured. For example, Gillow and Co. supplied a 'Large brown Holland blind with strong green line brass pulleys [and] large Roller with Ironwork' at £4 for Amersham, Buckinghamshire.[72] At St Margaret, Westminster, the Vestry took the unusual measure to 'grind off the Polish of the Glass to the South Windows . . . to render the use of Sun-Curtains unnecessary'.[73]

Chandeliers of cast brass were the chief source of artificial illumination and many such fixtures still survive *in situ*. James Gibbs prepared meticulously rendered working drawings for St Martin-in-the-Fields (pl. 48), and he probably also designed the magnificent carved and gilt wood example for Cannons House chapel, formerly at Kirkleatham (pl. 503).[74] Two chandeliers were given by the Duke of Portland to Penrith parish church, Cumberland, as a reward to its parishioners for their 'loyalty and proper conduct' during the Jacobite rebellion of 1745.[75] The pair of 'magnificent' thirty-six-light chandeliers noted in *London and Its Environs Described* in 1761 still hang in St Giles-in-the-Fields.[76] The churchwardens of St Margaret, Westminster, ordered the sale of the 'Two oldest Sconces' to buy a '36 Branch Light' for £45.[77] Simpson & Co. supplied 'Pulpit Candlesticks' at £4 4s. 0d. for St Mary, Battersea.[78] As part of the refurbishment of Wren's St Michael Cornhill in 1789, George Wyatt recommended

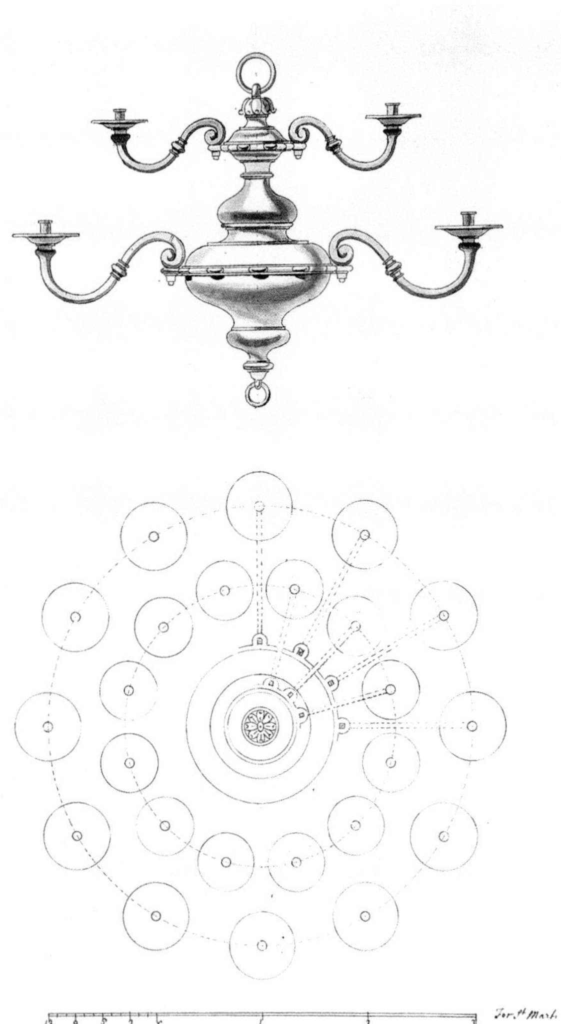

48 James Gibbs. Design for a 24-branch chandelier for St Martin-in-the-Fields, London, 1724. Pen and ink and wash. Ashmolean Museum, Oxford, Gibbs Collection, vol. IV, f. 28.

that 'six new Branches . . . of eighteen Lights in each Branch will add much to the Appearance & Elegance of the Church and give a much better Light than the old Method of lighting . . . by Means of brass Socketts placed at the Top of the several Pews'.[79]

Complaints about draughts – at Horsforth, Yorkshire, 'common people give . . . the Extreme Coldness . . . as a reason for frequenting the *Methodist Meeting house* "because it is much warmer" '[80] – were variously redressed. Many windows at Ashbourne, Derbyshire, were merely bricked up;[81] the entrances to St Paul, Covent Garden, were shut 'as soon as the Minister enters the Reading Desk, and not opened again until [he] has finished in the Pulpit';[82] while at St Chad, Shrewsbury, Shropshire, it was resolved that 'if light inner Doors Were put up in the different Entrances . . . covered with Green Baize . . . the evil complained of wod. be remedied'.[83] The dean and chapter of Chester Cathedral ordered 'Almsmen [to] stand at each of the small doors in the Side Isles to prevent them being kept open in the winter'.[84]

Technological advancement became increasingly prominent. A correspondent to the *Gentleman's Magazine* in 1755 recounted how 'during the late severe weather' he attended divine service at

> a chapel near *Piccadilly* . . . and . . . was most agreeably surprised to find a comfortable warmth surround me [emanating] from a couple of stoves . . . I could not but reflect upon the disadvantages that attend our churches in very cold or wet weather, especially those that are large, and not well filled. We are too apt in this lukewarm age to find any excuse to absent ourselves from the house of God . . . Yet . . . many persons who are weakly and infirm, or whose natural constitution is tender, are gradually brought into an habitual neglect of public worship, by the dampness or coldness of our churches in winter . . . the valitudinarian might attend without danger, the robust . . . without punishment, and the minds of all would be freed from the intrusion of uneasy sensations, which cannot but interrupt the exercise of devotion.[85]

Popularly known as American Stoves for their inventor, Benjamin Franklin, subsequently improved by a Mr Sharp of Leadenhall Street, London, these comforting cast-iron contraptions with frames ornamented in fashionable Adamesque flourishes were the subject of an

49 'American Stoves on the Improved Construction' in a 'Description of the Pensylvania Fire-Place' (no. 5), *Gentleman's Magazine*, October 1781, pp. 453–4, detail. Engraving.

50 Designer unknown. 'Sundry curious Plans for attaching New Vestries to Old Churches, with ornamental Designs for Chimneys' in A. and J. Hare 1825, pl. 6. Hand-coloured engraving. Author's collection.

illustrated article (pl. 49). This cited two large-size specimens in St John, Southwark, 'placed opposite to each other, about the middle of the church [with] the funnels . . . carried strait up through the galleries and roof', with interesting observations that previously 'it had been usual to employ women every Sunday morning with cloths to wipe and dry the pillars and walls before the congregation assembled', and that Sharp believed this the 'first stone building of its kind and size, that has ever been made comfortably warm by fires'.[86] A Mr Moser proposed in 1792–3 'Warming' the recently built St Peter-Le-Poer, London, by installing a stove for £45, instructing 'the Fire be made & kept up with 3 parts Cinders & 1 part Coal . . . lightened in the day Time only on Friday Saturday & Sunday' and guaranteeing that if this was 'disapproved by the Trustees in two Months after being finished [he] agrees to take away his Apparatus without requiring any payment or Satisfaction'; indeed, there were 'complaints' of insufficient heat, and 'with the approbation' of the architect he caused 'the Outward Air to be conducted to the Stove and . . . afterwards Experiments . . . made by Thermomiters . . . to determine whether it answers the purpose'.[87] Abraham Buzaglo, who had a shop in the Strand in London and advertised 'warming machines' suitable for 'Churches', as well as domestic and public premises, which heated the body without burning the face and legs, and were odourless as well as aesthetically pleasing, supplied Margaret Chapel, Bath, and St Mary, Lewisham.[88] In the final years of the century stoves 'fixed up to air' St Margaret, Westminster, were deemed 'mean, liable to great Defects . . . very disagreeable to those . . . seated near . . . Funnells that convey away the smoke [and] very improper', so it was recommended that the interior 'might be . . . more effectually warmed by fflues under the Pavement in the Aisles with fire Places to them . . . near the four Stair-cases to the Galleries . . . in a wholesome . . . comfortable manner' at an estimated £206.[89] At St Paul, Birmingham, Samuel Wyatt (renowned innovator in the use of cast iron and steam power) installed 'a flew under the middle Isle . . . so that by putting a fire into a kind of furnace Grate the day before it will keep the Church Warm'.[90] The exquisitely sophisticated neoclassical interior of St Botolph, Aldersgate, London (pl. 666), featured 'perforated brasses' set into the Portland stone paving to 'admit air from fires beneath, during the inclement season; a method far more decent in appearance than the exhibition of enormous chimney-places, generally introduced throughout London in churches and chapels'.[91] This improvement is illustrated in a view on page vi. In *Hints to Some Churchwardens, With a Few Illustrations, Relative to the Repair and Improvements of Parish Churches. With Twelve Plates* (1825), a thirty-one-page pocket-size book costing 10s. 6d. (with a wonderfully deadpan manner disguising obvious satire and, while dating outside the parameters of the present study, still reflecting eighteenth-century temperament), plate 6 (pl. 50) recommended 'carrying the chimney to the top of the spire' (marked A). The preface refers sar-

51 Designer and maker unknown. West gallery clock case, *c.*1740. Carved and gilt wood, metal. St Leonard, Shoreditch, London.

castically to 'very many splendid . . . zealous undertakings . . . which have emanated from those [unnamed] churchwardens who have attained perfection as planners and architects'.[92]

Worshippers were occasionally provided with the convenience of gallery clocks, some elaborately designed like the gorgeous rococo fixture at St Leonard, Shoreditch (pl. 51), perhaps part of the furnishing programme of 1740.[93]

Interiors were also rendered comfortable by extensive use of furnishing fabrics, though few examples survive *in situ*; and these are rarely considered by church historians.[94] The Duke of Chandos's palatial chapel at Cannons House, Middlesex, referred to with equal enthusiasm in 1728 as the 'rich Profusion of a Royal Mind' and 'in the worst taste in the world',[95] dispersed by public auction in 1747, just prior to demolition, featured chairs and cushions covered in crimson velvet, hangings of the same material with gilt-lace trim and so forth, all vanished except for a pair of chairs that subsequently found their way to Kirkleatham Hospital chapel, Yorkshire (pl. 503).[96] Ralph Thoresby described Leeds parish church in 1715 as possessing a 'most noble Pulpit-Cloth and Cushion of very rich Purple Velvet, with a deep and weighty Gold Fringe, &c. and a Character for the blessed Jesus surrounded with Glory . . . two others for the Curate and Clerk, of the same Materials, but proportionably less', as well as a 'new Altar-piece with Intercolumn [of] Scarlet Cloth Adorn'd with Gold Fringe' (pl. 52).[97] Such furnishings were still in vogue during the Regency period (p. vi). Here, as elsewhere, the fashion established at St Paul's Cathedral was paramount. At the turn of the century Celia Fiennes noted the velvet and gold altar with the dean's 'large crimson velvet elbow chair',[98] the mercers Richard Turner supplying 16¼ yards of 'Crimson Damask for the Organ-Loft' at 13s. 6d. per yard, totalling £10 19s. 4½d. in 1701.[99] These were often among the most expensive items in fitting out churches: at Hodnet, Shropshire, 'Super fine Crimson in grain broad Cloth . . . Crimson & Gold . . . fringe . . . Large Tosseles . . . Gold orrice binding . . . linen bound wth Lace' etc. costing £39 12s. 0d. was sent down from London in 1732; £34 15s. 0d. was spent on 'Crimson Silk Damask Cover. & Cushion' for the communion table, window curtains and so forth for St George, Portsea, Hampshire; for King's College chapel, Cambridge, Philip Palmer & Co., Ludgate Hill, London, supplied 33¼ yards of 'Crimson Rich damask' at £23 5s. 0d., and 26½ yards of 'Crimson Rich Genoa Velvet' at £35 15s. 0d., and B. Barrett, Laceman, Craven Street, London, 4½ yards of 'rich gold Crape turne Fringe' at £7 10s. 9d., 11½ yards of 'rich gold scallop'd Heading for . . . fringes' at £5 3s. 6d., and £1 5s. 0d. for '4 Rich Gold & Crimson Tossels', both craftsmen charging their 'very lowest price'; Frederick, Prince of

52 Joseph or John Rhodes. 'View of the Nave Looking East', St Peter, Leeds, Yorkshire, *c.*1838. Watercolour. Leeds Library and Information Service, F5 759.2 R346, no. 1.

Wales gave to St James, Westminster, 'Crimson Velvet Furniture for the Communion Table & the Pulpit', described as 'Magnificent draperies . . . embroidered with gold, and trimmed with gold fringe', valued at £700.[100] Sometimes existing materials were recycled. At St Nicholas, Warwick, the 'old Velvet Pulpit-Cloth [was] us'd for the Pulpit Reading [and] Clerks Desk & Altar Table as far as . . . can be made serviceable'; at St Michael Cornhill, London, the 'present Scarlet Pew Lineing to be new dyed & replaced'; the velvet and cloth of gold altar-cloth at Gainsborough, Lincolnshire, was a spoil of the Battle of Dettingen given by one of the officers.[101] Not all parishes could afford to indulge in such luxuries. A Visitation of 1765 to St Mary, Rowner, Hampshire, reported that the communion table 'has no covering and looks indecent'.[102]

The most fashionable colours were crimson and purple, with their royal associations. The sovereign's stall in St George's Chapel, Windsor, was upholstered in purple velvet and cloth of gold; the pulpit in St Clement, Hastings, Sussex, a survival of George I's Westminster Abbey coronation in 1714, featured 'flowered silver tissue, with a gold fringe at the bottom, and silver . . . at the top of the canopy'; George II presented 'a very rich crimson velvet, adorned with gold tassels, lace and fringe' for the altar table and pulpit of Inigo Jones's Banqueting House in Whitehall, long in use as the Chapel Royal.[103] Sometimes these colours combined with others. David Easton & Co. of Glasgow supplied St Andrew with £3 18s. 11d. worth of crimson and blue velvet.[104] Though the Vestry of St Michael Paternoster, London, decided that 'crimson worsted damask Curtains be fixed to the Pews at the Eastend . . . instead of green worsted damask and . . . Crimson Silk and Stuff damask Curtains . . . to the Churchwardens Pews instead of green Silk and Stuff damask',[105] green was not unpopular: at Gloucester Cathedral 'Just by the high altar . . . a small pew hung with green damask, with curtains of the same'; at St Margaret, Westminster, a west gallery 'Lined in a Uniform manner . . . of a Green Colour [and] Green Squab for the Step before the Alter'; at Holy Trinity, Guildford, Surrey, 'if any one shall be minded to Line their pews they may soo doo as the lining be . . . Green and . . . no . . . other . . . except those belonging to the Bishop and . . . Corporation'; at All Hallows, London Wall, Nathaniel Dance's *Ananias Restoring the Sight of St Paul upon His Conversion* in an 'elegantly carved and gilt frame' was 'preserved from injury by a curtain of green silk' (only the painting now remains *in situ*); at St Peter-Le-Poer, London, 'Merine [marino] Cushions of Pea Green Colour for the pews', with a Bible 'new bound in Royal Purple Coloured Leather'.[106]

The use of textiles as internal embellishment was particularly promoted by women, who were enthusiastic churchgoers: the Revd Penrose wrote from fashionable Bath that the abbey attracted 'a Congregation of fine Ladies. Your Sister saw . . . at one view more Ladies, than she had ever seen before in her Life-time put all together'.[107] Two fine examples of many will suffice here. Mrs Prowse, daughter of the Bishop of Wells, devoted seven years (1713–20) to embroidering the communion table frontal for Axbridge, Somerset, depicting images of a table laid out with plate beneath a draped and tasselled canopy supported on four Solomonic columns.[108] Catherine Owen of Condover, Shropshire, left funds in 1744 to provide for a gold-fringed, crimson velvet communion table cover and pulpit cloth and cushion for her parish church.[109] Efforts were particularly concentrated in the chancel. Mrs Owen's bequest of £550 also provided for an altarpiece with the Lord's Prayer, Ten Commandments and Creed, new railings, 'a large Brass Branch . . . the . . . Model . . . taken from those . . . in St Peter's Church in Cheshire' and 'a handsome Monument . . . made by some eminent hand in or near London, in memory of my . . . Husband and . . . Daughter . . . to be put up in the . . . Chancel'.[110] Stately altarpieces were gifted to Abbotsbury, Dorset, by Susan Strangways Horner,[111] while Bridget Price, 'a good Benefactor', gave St John, Gloucester, the 'handsome Altar-Piece with . . . Wainscotting for the side Walls . . . the Communion table & Rails', designed en suite with the church (still intact), for which she, her family and tenants were allocated pew no. 25, where they 'may sit, stand, kneel, hear & attend Divine Service & sermons Peaceably & without the interruption or molestation of Any Person or Persons Whomsoever'.[112] Women contributed in other ways. The late Miss Bower bequeathed her harpsichord to Chapel-en-le-Frith, Derbyshire, together with an annual salary of £20 for an organist; her mother had already lengthened the chancel and built 'a very handsome stone front, with a *Venetian* window'.[113] Mary Frewen replaced communion plate stolen from Sapcote, Leicestershire.[114] Moreover,

> She has enough to make her clean,
> At publick workship to be seen;
> Can give a little to the poor;
> Both privately, and at Church-door[115]

Occasionally, aristocrats as well as wealthy commoners financed the construction of entire churches. The most celebrated were Selina, Countess of Huntingdon (pl. 182)[116] and her sister-in-law, Elizabeth Hastings, 'the incomparably pious and ingenious Lady . . . whose greatest Delight is in doing Good . . . so very generous . . . In building and restoring holy shrines', whose timely intercession with a gift of £1,000 in 1721 salvaged the scheme to build Holy Trinity, Leeds (pl. 419).[117] Dowager Lady Middleton commissioned Richard Cassels to design Knockbreda church, County Down (1747); Marchioness Carnaervon financed Avington church, Hampshire, but died in 1768 shortly before work began, when, according to her epitaph, 'it pleased God to remove her to a better World';[118] Viscountess Glenorchy erected a chapel in Edinburgh named after herself (1774); she and Lady Hope founded Hope Chapel, Bristol (1788), which was opened by Lady Maxwell (pl. 339); Elizabeth Parkin of Ravenfield, Yorkshire, was an early client of John Carr (pl. 185).

Dorothy and Mary Weaman financed St Mary, Birmingham (pl. 623), while its trustees publicly paid

> their sincere and hearty Thanks to that kind and generous Benefactress, Mrs Elizabeth Walker, a Widow of moderate Fortune, for her Benefaction of Five Hundred Pounds towards building . . . an Instance of Generosity . . . scarce to be paralleled . . . without any View of Self-Interest, Ostentation, Popularity, or Applause, and paid . . . with so much Chearfulness, Affability, and Good Nature, as gave infinite Pleasure to the Receiver . . . may her Example excite an Emulation in all others of affluent Fortune to contribute as cheerfully towards erecting another Chapel.[119]

Mrs Elizabeth Wingfield, a 'woman of much taste', was responsible for the extraordinary creation of romanesque revival Tickencote (pl. 347).[120] The occasonal roles of women in the building trades are discussed in chapter 10.

At the opposite end of the social scale were the crews of female maintenance workers, who included, as already mentioned, those employed every Sunday to 'wipe and dry the pillars and walls' of St John, Southwark (p. 63); the 'Six Women for Cleaning and Washing' twice at Holy Trinity, Guildford, in preparation for its opening in 1763;[121] Mrs Mitten, who was responsible for cleaning the church at Walthamstow, Essex, and its sconces, and conveying plate to and from the premises;[122] Mrs Weaver, who was paid £9 18s. 7d. for cleaning St Michael Paternoster, London;[123] Joan Philpot and Ann Tanner 1s. 4d. per day each for the same at St George, Portsea, Hampshire.[124] Mary Jones of St George, Hanover Square, received an annual salary of £5 as 'Organ Blower', £2 2s. 0d. for 'Sweeping round the Church', £1 for 'keeping the Portico clean' and 8s. for 'Shovels & Brooms';[125] Ann Brown and Ann Howel mopped and cleaned St John, Wolverhampton, Staffordshire, for nine days at 9s. each;[126] while Elizabeth Hughes was paid £2 12s. 6d. annually for cleaning St Alkmund, Shrewsbury, for which she was 'allowed Brooms and Brushes'.[127]

In short, within the bustling Georgian social structure women's participation was very much more poignant than might be suggested by an episode reported in the *Morning Post* on 5 April 1775 concerning how in

> a church near Piccadilly . . . a lady of a military officer, and the wife of a brandy merchant . . . sit in a pew adjoining to each other; the latter, it seems, has lately worn a bunch of feathers in her hair of such an amazing height, as well as breadth, as to obscure the other's sight of the parson . . . the captain's lady in vain remonstrated; till last Sunday, after sermon, they coming to high words, the former, who is a little spirited woman, got upon a hassock, and in pulling the other's finery off, brought down her hair and a large quantity of wool, and other combustibles. The congregation not being half out, it occasioned a loud laugh, and the poor female . . . was obliged to wait in the sexton's room till after dark, before she could go home.[128]

Women, of course, were fair game for such ridicule. Joseph Addison 'very much admire[d] . . . those female architects, who raised such wonderful structures out of ribands, lace, and wire . . . sometimes they rise in the shape of a pyramid . . . and sometimes like a steeple [and] might . . . have carried this Gothic building much higher' but for evangelical preaching.[129] Indeed, it was reported in 1775 that a 'women-preacher, who accompanied . . . John Wesley to Plymouth, held forth upon the Parade, and brought together the greatest concourse of people that had ever been seen there; the novelty of a woman methodist-preacher having drawn half Plymouth to hear her'.[130]

53 Longmate. 'Two Views of the Rectory', Bruntingthorpe and Sadlington, 1795, in Nichols 1807, vol. iv, pt. i, pl. xvii. Engraving.

Four

THE VICAR'S LIFE

The temporal concerns of our family were chiefly to my wife's management, as to the spiritual I took them entirely under my direction. The profits of my living which amounted to but thirty-five pounds a year, I made over to the orphans and widows of the clergy of our diocese; for having a sufficient fortune of my own, I am careless of temporalities, and felt a secret pleasure in doing my duty without reward.

The description of a 'village preacher's modest mansion' in an anonymous 'Country Clergyman. In Imitation of Dr Goldsmith' (*The Vicar of Wakefield*, 1766, chapter 2) might have been the dwelling of the contented Dr Primrose and his family:

> The walls on the inside were nicely whitewashed, and my daughters undertook to adorn them with pictures of their own designing. Though the same room served us for parlour and kitchen that only made it the warmer. Besides, as it was kept with the utmost neatness . . . the eye was agreeably relieved, and did not want richer furniture . . . My farm consisted of about twenty acres of excellent land . . . Nothing could exceed the neatness of my little enclosures, the elms and the hedgerows appearing with inexpressible beauty.[1]

Perhaps it resembled the rectory of Bruntingthorpe and Saddington (pl. 53), or John Carr's residence for William Mason, canon of York Minster and poet, at Aston-cum-Aughton (1770–71), which he described to Horace Walpole: 'my curate and I are neither of us the dupes of fashion, but speak what we think in all simplicity. Treat us therefore with something more to *our* gout, and the world, even the great world, will not disdain to follow our plain Yorkshire taste'.[2] To be sure, less paradisiacal than Church Langton (pl. 54),[3] yet superior to that occupied by a destitute clergyman named Slender responsible for a 'poor village' together with his wife and a

> quiverful of brats to nurse
> To feed for weeks on herbs and broth
> Or, if his better stars incline,
> On the sweet scrags itself to dine
>
> No passions rack his carcase frail
>
> His brains, all sober and sedate,
> Ne'er teem with plans for church or state.
> His fancy, in its worst confusion,
> Ne'er rais'd the goblin, revolution
> He leaves the foundling stately sects
> To grave Utopian architects[4]

Even worse:

> Deep in the mire with tawny rush beset,
> Where bleak sea-breezes echo from the shore

54 Architect unknown. Front elevation of the Rectory, Church Langton, Leicestershire, *c.*1785.

And foggy damps infect the noontide heat,
There lies a country curate's dismal seat:
View well those barren heaths with sober eye,
And wonder how a man can live so wretchedly.[5]

Or:

Climb to the Curate's cottage, and look in;
And if you enter, stoop, and save you head,
And on th' uneven floor with caution tread.
Survey the motly furniture

But, gentle reader, think not here to find
Luxurious pomp, and rooms of various kind;
His Study, Kitchen, Parlour, and Saloon,
Contain'd in twelve feet square, so make but one

A little chink admits a little light,
Barely enough to eat, and read, and write.

His mouldy walls and roof imbibe the rain.[6]

55 Timothy Lightoler. 'Plan and Elevation of Parsonage or Farm House' in Lightoler 1762, pl. 2. Engraving

The Plan and Elevation of Parsonage or Farm House.

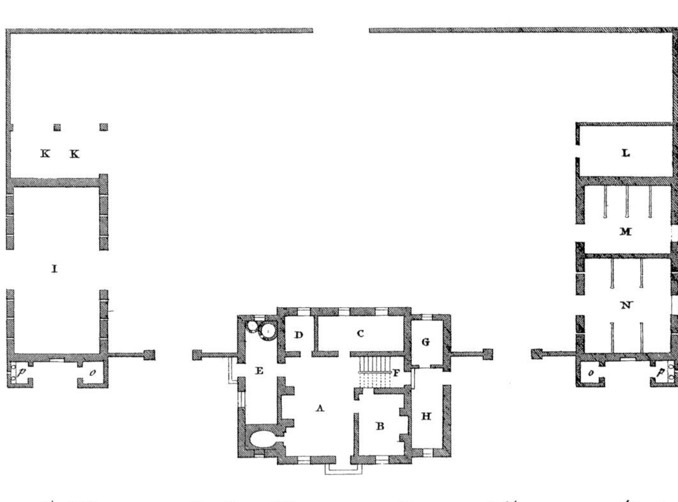

These melancholy poems reflect realities recorded in the Returns of Archbishop Herring's archdiocese of York Visitations (periodic inspections by episcopal authorities) of 1743: Kilburn, 'so very bad it is scarce habitable by the poorest Tenant'; Kirkby Sigston, 'being low & damp . . . we have frequent floods upon any great rain'; Veroom, 'only a low Thatch'd Cottage not proper for my Family'; Elkesley, 'a very mean one', Kayingham: 'only a Poor mud Cottage . . . built upon ye Lords' wast'; Bramham, 'not in Repair & the Income . . . so small, that . . . it wd. be an Advantage . . . if the House was to drop'.[7] To expiate such injustices, Queen Anne's Bounty, a fund established in 1704 to augment the livings of impoverished clergymen, was made more effectual by an Act of Parliament, paralleled in Ireland in 1707–8 by the so-called Board of First Fruits, which appropriated forfeited impropriations for building churches and augmenting poor vicarages 'to make good such Deficiencies', which had a rough ride through Parliament.[8] During the years 1774–82 it passed the Gilbert's Act 'to promote the Residence of the Parochial Clergy by making Provision for the most speedy and effectual building, rebuilding, repairing, or purchasing Houses, and other necessary Buildings and Tenements, for the Use of the Benefices'.[9]

While the Georgian vicarage has received due attention as a sociological phenomena, it has largely escaped the notice of architectural historians.[10] In the eighteenth century, however, it enjoyed special prestige as a distinct building type, so much so that architectural pattern books increasingly devoted space to its design. Here are three examples. In *A Complete Body of Architecture* (1756), Isaac Ware, who designed the vicarage at Rokeby, Yorkshire, advised that if built on 'dry wholesome soil' the ground floor may contain parlours on each side of the entrance door, and a study (a sure indication of the building type), together with a kitchen and wash house at the rear, 'which need be no more than a shed well covered', as well as a stable, with a front staircase leading to lodging rooms.[11] Timothy Lightoler developed this standard arrangement into an expanded, formal Palladian complex (pl. 55).[12]

We learn even more from a group of ten vicarages designed between 1714 and 1745 for the New (or so-called Queen Anne) Churches in London, the most important ecclesiastical building project of the period. In 1711 parishes were surveyed in an 'endeavour to find out proper Scites for . . . Ministers houses [and] fix upon Such as lye amongst or near the better Sort of the Inhabitants'.[13] Of these, five were remodelled fabrics, including St Mary Woolnoth, which was 'endanger'd' during the removal of the medieval church steeple and had £3 0s. 8d. spent on 'five Iron Dogs with Nuts and Screws for securing the . . . House',[14] and St Anne Limehouse, purchased for £550 and provided with a new timber roof, kitchen and 'Necessary House', which involved 'fetching Clay from the Street Tempering & treading it in the Cellar to Pave upon to prevent the Tide getting in', the operation, however, taking so long that in 1738 the builders were ordered that it be 'performed in as frugal a manner as possibly could be'.[15] The then existing fabric at St George, Wapping, was 'very small [with] no Garrets, and only four Chambers in which Beds can be set up'. Improvements included inserting 'Partition Dressers & Shelves in the kitchin' and 'a New Necessary house and Wash-house'.[16]

Thomas Archer, who served in the dual role as a Churches Commissioner and designer, described the earliest and architecturally most singular of these parsonages, at Deptford (pl. 362), as a 'triangular figure'. Each frontage measured 66 feet. Built of grey stock brick with rubbed, gauged brick detailing and containing forty-six windows in all, the rectory comprised two main floors, each with six rooms surrounding a central triangular staircase lit by a windowed lantern; three of the rooms were semicircular in shape (including the vestibule), while the three linking them were coved octagons. The polygonal bays were among the first appearance of the motif in English domestic architecture, and while one cannot avoid the Trinitarian symbolism of the plan, apparently the novel form arose from the restricted site within its own walled enclosure in the south-west corner of the churchyard rather than, as Archer stressed, 'from any fancy of mine'.[17] The total cost was £2,500.

The most fully documented of the new dwellings is Nicholas Hawksmoor's restrained, noble, grey stock brick block at Southwark, built for the minister of St John Horselydown, which, unlike the church, escaped the Blitz. A site plan (pl. 56) shows how the church was walled within side courts approached from Fair Street, with the Vestry House placed in a corner of the cemetery and the Minister's House with its garden in a separate, 142 by 57 foot enclosure to the east. An Act of Parliament passed in 1733 allocated £3,500 for the minister's 'Maintenance' and £1,100 for constructing 'a convenient Dwelling . . . paving the Church Yard . . . and setting up Gates and Rails'. On 23 July 1733 the architect was instructed to prepare an estimate and 'Model for the . . . House'; the 'Plans Upright and explanation' delivered on 13 August survive.[18] The contract with John Arnot, bricklayer, and William Coates, carpenter, both members of the Vestry, specified a great

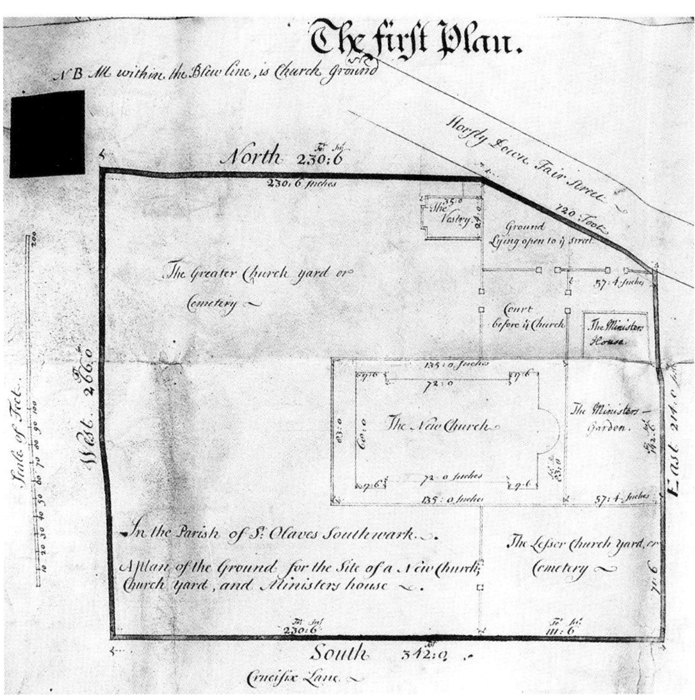

56 Nicholas Hawksmoor. 'The first Plan' for St John Horselydown, Southwark, London, 8 February 1732. Pen and ink. London Metropolitan Archives, P71/JH/42.

parlour 'wainscotted with good yellow Deal' and a 'Marble Chimney piece', a study and a little parlour 'with wainscotting of Deal and 4 portland chimny pieces', a 'Best Bedchamber [with] a handsome Alcove to receive a Bed with door on each side Leading to two Closetts', a 'little Attic', staircases of 'Sound best Deal Boards with a handsome . . . Rail, and Ballusters . . . neatly painted', 'Window Seats . . . in all the Rooms where required by the Surveyors', 'Sills of all the Sash frames . . . of good English Oak', glazing with 'best Crown Glass', the cellars with 'Newcastle Glass (in Squares)', together with wash and necessary houses.[19]

Outside London parsonages took various forms. Charles Sloane, a builder and carpenter of Gravesend, Kent (designer of St George parish church in 1731–3), reported in 1738 that 'the old Rectorial House' at Ash-next-Rudley was 'in so ruinous a State, that . . . there would be great danger in repairing a Building that seems to stand in need of so many shores as are now made use of', and offered a scheme for a new structure that 'will not be any Detriment, Inconvenience, or Disadvantage to the Rector' (pl. 57).[20] Accommodating two parlours, the ubiquitous study and a kitchen, with seven bedrooms on three floors, a brew house, dairy and pantry in a lean-to, the front elevation is old fashioned for its date, still clinging to late Stuart forms.[21]

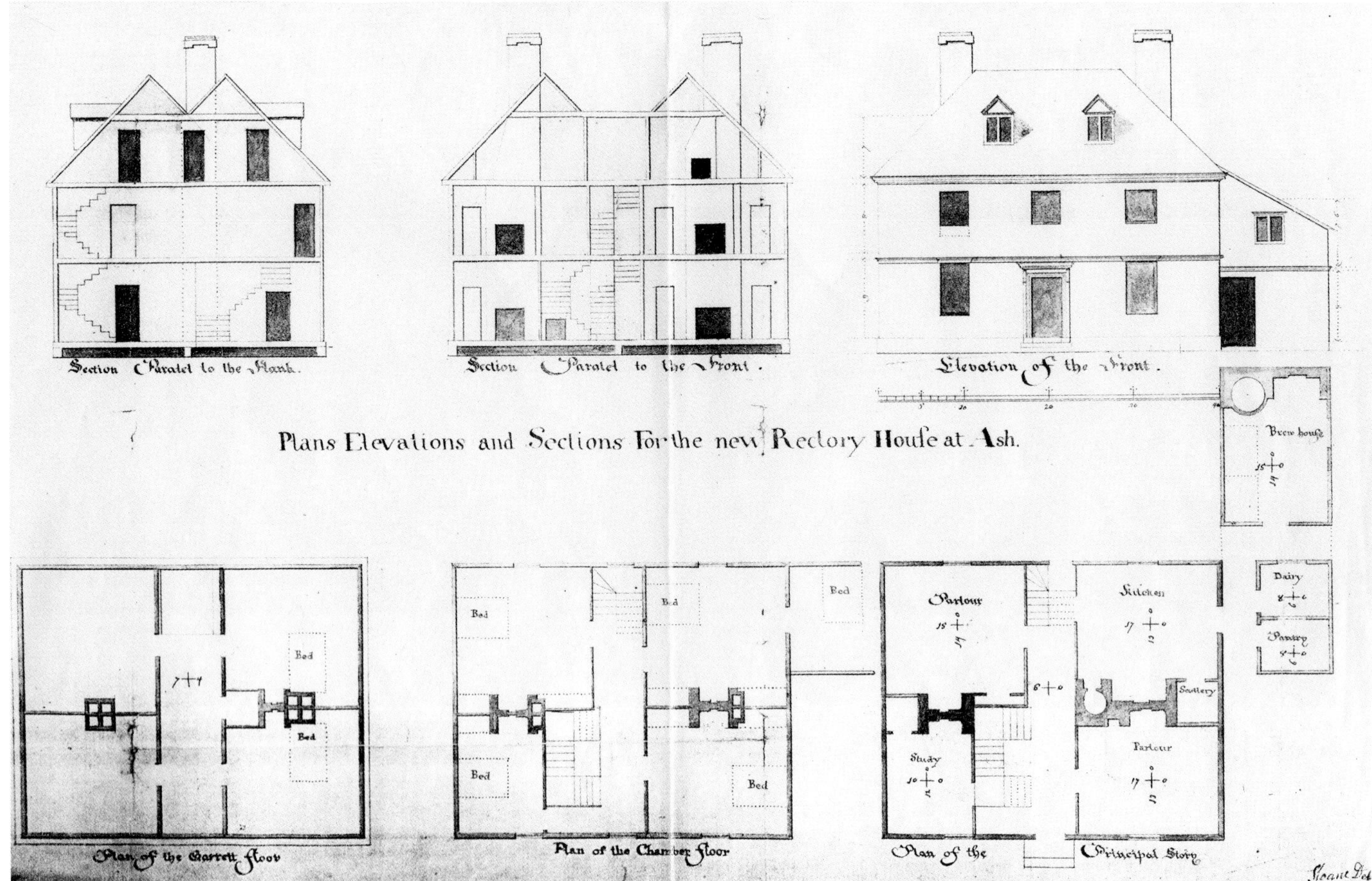

57 Charles Sloane. 'Plans Elevations and Sections For the new Rectory House at Ash', Kent, 1738. Pen and ink and wash. Centre for Kentish Studies, Drb /Acl.

It is surprising that before the nineteenth century gothic-style parsonages were deeply unfashionable, even where medieval churches remained. In S. B.'s poem '*To the Rev. Mr* LIONEL SEAMAN, *M.A., on his building a new Vicarage House at Froom, on the Ruins of the Old one*',

> Here *sense* and *symmetry* in every part,
> Commands the eye, and captivate the heart.
> Now in a cornice, or a light we trace
> *Romano*'s style, and here *Vitruvius'* grace[22]

The antiquary William Cole, who settled at Blecheley Parsonage, Buckinghamshire, in 1753, however, later erected in the garden

> an elegant, light & airy Chinese & Gothic Temple or Seat of an Hexagon Form . . . with Gothic pointed Arches, & a Frize of open Lace Work above the Pillars, which support 3 large Gothic Ornaments, like Mitres with Cabbage Work & Fleurs de Leis at Top . . . The Roof is arched in Rib Work, with a Rose of Plaister of Paris in the Centre & Escallop Shels at the Termination of the Ribs, & the Back of Stoko, done by one Page an ingenious Mason of Woburn . . . the Wood Work . . . by . . . John Bent, a very ingenious common Carpenter & Joyner of Whaddon, under my Direction.

Alas, it has since vanished (pl. 58). The architect is unrecorded but may have been Cole's friend James Essex, and it obviously belonged to Horace Walpole's brand of gothic.[23]

The unaffected kindness and generosity of Goldsmith's Dr Primrose may not have been typical of the species if we are to take seriously the satirist Dean Swift, who on a visit to Bristol in 1735 described its clergy as

> grave, proud and insolent: they constantly wear long Gowns, monstrous Hats, and grove-like Periwigs, for a Bob Wigg, even in a riding habit is an abomination unto them: they also pretend to good manners,

> but like Virtue it has fled from them . . . with all the force I was able I maintained the Dignity of Man against the encroachments of an insatiable Priesthood.[24]

Or the Swiss César de Saussure, who remarked that a

> foreigner is surprised to find the clergy in public places, in taverns, and eating-houses, where they smoke and drink just like laymen; but as they scandalise no one, you quickly get accustomed to this sight. The greater number . . . are stout and ruddy, and their comfortable appearance convinces you that they lead pleasant and not fatiguing lives. They pass for being rather lazy . . . their sermons do not seem to give them much trouble . . . in the pulpit they are modest and sincere and have none of the transports and gesticulations that make preaching seem so exaggerated in France.[25]

'The English clergy, especially in London', reported Karl Philipp Moritz, 'are notorious for their free and easy way of life . . . the . . . habit of getting up late in the morning accounts for divine service not commencing until half-past ten . . . many . . . wear wigs.'[26] While Lord Torrington was 'not averse from the clergy enjoying rational pleasures . . . I like not to see their names stand foremost in encouraging idle debaucherie, which come not to comfort their parishioners, but only to pick their pockets, and to lead their minds astray.'[27]

From two vicious poems published in the *Gentleman's Magazine*:

> In southern climes there lies a village,
> Where of the vicar, fond to pillage . . .
> And whilst o'er all his neighbours' ground,
> Striding, he throws his eyes around;
> Surveying, with a look most blithe,
> The growing riches of his tythe
>
> From pulpit high, MODERNUS doth advise
> That we be honest, virtuous, and wise;
> But in this conduct (which he should revere),
> He's neither just, nor honest, nor sincere:
> In manners wicked, and in vice compleat,
> His life's the very index of a cheat.[28]

The first, of course, was the result of a combination of inadequate salaries among less-well-off members and social inequalities, whereby

> The man of genius is . . . buried in a country parsonage of eight-score pounds a year; while the other . . . an impenetrable blockhead at school . . . with the bare abilities of a common scrivener, has got an estate of above a hundred thousand pounds . . . one of the best benefices in the west of *England*, by setting a country gentleman's affairs in some method, and giving him an exact survey of his estate.[29]

58 William Cole, attributed. Gothic Temple, Blecheley Parsonage, Buckinghamshire, elevation, 1753. Pen and ink. © The British Library Board, Collections of Various Kinds, Add. MS 5834, f. 178v.

The press reported the plight of a clergyman at Brandon, Suffolk, who had twenty-eight children and was living on an annual income of £65 'for the service of two churches, nine miles apart, and the teaching a free school',[30] and there was the tragic circumstances of the Revd William Dodd (pl. 59), proprietor of the Charlotte Street Chapel, Pimlico, and editor of the prestigious *Christian Magazine*, who was executed in 1777 for forging a bond of £4,200 in the name of the 5th Earl of Chesterfield, his former pupil.[31] Added to this were the evils of pluralism, where clergymen accepted the livings of more parishes than could be adequately cared for in order to boost private incomes, which bred the 'very hurtful tendency's' of absenteeism (pl. 60).[32] Young clergymen were frequently dependent on the goodwill of their patrons:

> So shall you ne'er have cause to weep
> An empty church, a scatter'd sheep;
> Nor forc'd upon a thankless town,
> With indignation quit your gown.

59a John Russell. *Revd William Dodd*, with a plan of the Charlotte Street Chapel, Pimlico, London, 1769. Oil on canvas. National Portrait Gallery, London, no. 251.

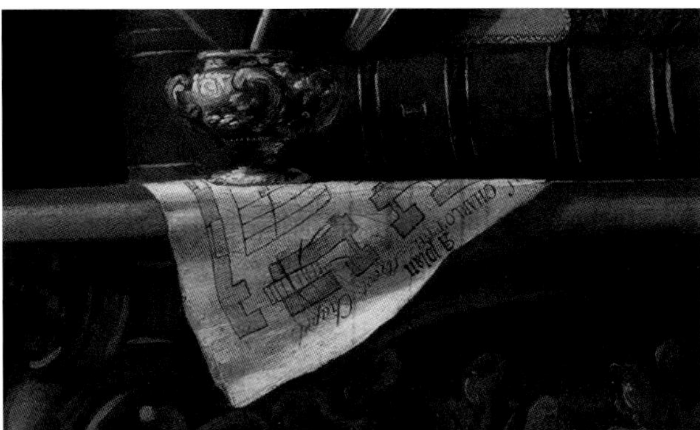

59b John Russell. *Revd William Dodd*, detail of pl. 58a showing the plan of the Charlotte Street Chapel, Pimlico, London.

Support all parties, while in place,
And all abandon – in disgrace.
To fav'rite courtiers homage render,
And canonize our Faith's Defender.
By arts like these, and not devotion,
You'll gain a priest's first wish-promotion:
The Thane will recommend your plea,
And grant you the next vacant see.[33]

60 Anonymous. 'The Pluralist', 1 August 1744, detail. Engraving.

It was to curb such unseemly behaviour, as well as deal with other parish matters, that the Anglican Church was regulated by a hierarchal diocesan government filtering down from archbishops, bishops and archdeacons to vicars, churchwardens and vestrymen.[34] The Scottish equivalent was the General Assembly of the Kirk (pl. 61).[35] Thus, the Vestry of St Thomas, Southwark, attached to the famous hospital, ordered its wardens not to 'use the Church yard to Dry their Clothes, or . . . suffer any other Person to do the same and whosoever Shall Come Upon the . . . yard for that purpose without leave from the Vestry shall be prosecuted at Law'.[36] Nor does Ned Ward's *The London Spy* paint a pretty picture:

> dignified with the office . . . of . . . Churchwarden, by the very conceit of this he is so puffed up that during the possession of the poor-box he reckons himself as great as the Pope, and measures a foot more in the waist upon his first entrance into this parochial authority than he did in seven years before he was chosen to it.[37]

There were inevitable tensions. The *Gentleman's Magazine* reported a 'disturbance' at the Berkeley Chapel, Mayfair (pl. 1), when the parishioners 'desired a stranger [an itinerant] to preach, without acquainting Mr *K* [who] resented it, and some severe altercation passed unbecoming gentlemen of truly christian meekness' – a case of double-booking![38] The clergy occasionally became embroiled in building disputes. For example, the 3rd Earl of Lonsdale, lord of the manor of Whitehaven, Cumberland, recounted that in 1749 'some Persons . . . preached to great Numbers of People in the Markett place & elsewhere in the Neighbourhood who seldom or never went to Church, yet would by degrees have been brought to attend the Worship of God, if there were Conveniencies for them'. When a subscription was

> very far advanced for . . . Building a new Church . . . several Clergymen of Distinction & great worth . . . thought it was very commendable & might do a great deal of good in so populous a Town, where great Numbers had not an Opportunity of attending Divine Service for want of Room . . . As for what some may suggest that . . . a new Church may be an hindrance to the present Ministers [of Holy Trinity and St Nicholas] in their Incomes, I am perswaded they would lose more if it was attempted to be hindered by their, or their Intimate Friends making an Opposition to it, than if they let those that want a new church go on with it without shewing a Dislike to it on their Part.[39]

Sometimes these disputes were made public. We have already noted the case of Kirriemuir (p. 58). Here are two others. The decrepit state of medieval All Saints, Derby (now the cathedral), compelled some parishioners to absent themselves from worship, others 'so much frightened at every crack of Wind (which shook the whole Fabrick) as to run out of the Church for their Security', and the worthy vicar, Dr Michael Hutchinson, to promote James Gibbs's ambitious scheme for rebuilding all but the splendid Perpendicular west tower (pl. 423). The parsimonious Corporation held the contrary view that 'a Wall run up against the Chancel, at about a Hundred Pounds charge, would have secured [the old fabric] for a great many years' and '*catechiz'd*' Hutchinson for daring to allocate £3,000, raised by public subscription, for the new project. He retorted by asking if it would prefer him to build '*a paltry Church at that Price, and . . . put the rest into his own Pocket?*' The Corporation dallied and the determined vicar resolved the dispute in pre-dawn of 18 February 1723 by secretly ordering workmen to demolish the building so that, according to the astonished mayor, 'there was no Way left, but for every one to lend his helping Hand' towards the renewal.[40] In 1748 the Revd Sir Gilbert Williams, the vicar of St Mary, Islington, London, was taken to court for not repairing the dilapidated medieval chancel, which was in danger of collapse, where 'Articles were Exhibited against him' to effect that the space 'commonly called the Vicars Chancell, and . . . of right belonging to him . . . for time immemorial . . . have reced the profits arising from the Burials and Pews', but he 'Refuses or Neglects' to spend £34 13s. 0d. for a 'Substantial Repair' (according to an estimate calculated by 'able and Experienced Workmen'). In 1751 it was decided to rebuild the entire church with funds raised on a rate of 5d. in the pound among parishioners and the issue returned as to whose 'right it is to keep the Chancell in Repair', with a resolution that Williams 'be Compelled to Repair . . . in a Durable Manner, and . . . be condemned in promoters Costs'.[41] Vicars and their churchwardens, annual appointees who controlled parochial matters such as overseeing the poor, managing parish properties, collecting rents, allocating pews and maintaining the fabric, together took on the demanding business of fund-raising.

61 David Allen. 'The General Assembly of the Kirk of Scotland', Edinburgh, Midlothian, Scotland, 1787. Pen and ink and wash. © The British Library Board, K. Top. XLIX-68-g-2.

62 G. Scotin. 'The Monument of the Lateworthy, Great, Good, Pious, and Charitable Edward Colston Esqr.', All Saints, Bristol, Somerset, 1751. Engraving. City of Bristol Museum and Art Gallery. James Gibbs architect, Michael Sidnell mason, John Michael Rysbrack sculptor, 1728–29.

Five

FUND-RAISING AND OTHER PUBLIC AFFAIRS

Since tho'it was by computation found
The Pile would cost them thirteen hundred pound
Toby [Bowles] That lump of magistracy was loth to spend so much on heaven.
But gave his vote to have it done for seven.
Accordingly the drunken Corporation,
Who prized their liquor more than their salvation,
Decreed that out of reverence to the chair,
Seven should be given to God, and six elsewhere[1]

This witty poem satirises the 'impious and remorseless town' of Deal in Kent 'Peopled by . . . savages of human kind [practising] fraud, oppression, theft and rapine', a 'Sodom [and] Nineveian ground [where] spotless souls' attempted to stem the 'tides of vice [and save] miscreants against their will [by] an honest scheme [to] make religion get the start of trade [and] bring them all to heaven a shorter way [by building] a place of worship nearer home . . . To which none could plead weariness to come'.

Church building in the eighteenth century could be an expensive business. While no general trend emerges, since particular circumstances varied widely from example to example (see Appendix B), clearly more was spent on new builds in the metropolis (£33,661 16s. 7¾d. at St Martin-in-the-Fields; £40,602 0s. 6d. at Christ Church, Spitalfields, pls 416, 368) compared to the provinces (ranging from a modest effort like St Andrew-by-the-Green, Glasgow, at £1,110 to an ambitious one like All Saints, Newcastle upon Tyne, at £27,000; pls 497, 673). To achieve these sums often meant overcoming great difficulties. Supported by an Act of Parliament 'for the more easy Recovery of Monies for Repairing of Churches' passed in 1702–3, funding building work was largely in the hands of the local vicar, his churchwardens and the lay proprietor, usually the lord of the manor.[2] Thus, Edward Harley, 2nd Earl of Oxford, the leading landowner in St Marylebone, London, was applied to for 'Directions' on contacting 'persons of Quality & Distinction to Communicate to them the Designs [and] touching on the proper method of raising money' for the new parish church.[3] One of the chief aims of periodic Visitations made by bishops and archdeacons through their dioceses was to determine from vicars if 'any Lands or Tenements had been left for the Repair of your Church?'[4] In the case of Wendlebury, Oxfordshire, after twenty months of campaigning the parishioners, unable to raise the required £200 'without utterly distressing themselves', asked: 'Whether the constant experience of the ill success of these collections upon Briefs be not a matter of sufficient importance to move it to his Majesty or to the houses of Parliament, that an annual fund be established to supply the deficiencies . . . Or rather such a fund as might answer every demand of this kind without applying for Briefs at all?'[5] A Brief is written consent from a bishop or senior ecclesiastical official authorising collections of funds for good causes, including repairs and rebuilding programmes, of which many were issued throughout the century across Britain,[6] though the often miserly sums raised challenge ideas of eighteenth-century charitable instincts spreading very far beyond the intended geographical boundaries, as we will see.

The most common method of fund-raising was by imposing an annual rate on congregants. In preparation for building All Saints, Southampton, Hampshire, the parish treasurer calculated generating £268 15s. 0d., together with letting twenty-six houses on an average rent of £50 each, which would accrue £48 15s. 0d., thirty-one pews at £1 each, and 'Catecombs' at more than 30 guineas. This, he concluded, was the 'very best & most advantageous Money I ever have, or even can lay out were I to live to the Age of Methusalah'. These reckonings in turn would impact on the church's appearance, since a 9d. rate allowed for a building without a portico costing £500, provided catacombs were sold for £600, or an additional £1,200 if 'a Portico is wanted'. Revenue was also anticipated from the sale of material from the demolished medieval fabric, which the architect reckoned should be disposed of either

> by auction to the best bidder as it stands, or to the contractor who may offer for the whole in one sum, for no person who offers for part of the work only can take it because he can only use that part of the materials belonging to his own trade, & the materials being of several sorts belong to several trades.[7]

The *Gentleman's Magazine* was of the opinion that Hackney parish church in London, catering to an approximate population of 9,500 and attracting annual rentals of £33,000 in 1795, 'is at liberty to raise a rate adequate to its wants' (6d.), though the trustees advertised in the press their willingness to 'receive proposals from persons desirous of advancing any sum not exceeding 5000 l. either on annuities for an absolute term, not less than seventy or more than 99 years, or on Bonds of 100 l. each, redeemable by lot, on six months notice, or on annuities for life', with payment secured by an annual 'Parochial Rate'.[8]

Funding also attracted generous individual benefactions. Holy Trinity, Leeds, was launched by private bequests of £1,000 each from a local philanthropist and Lady Elizabeth Hastings, 'Desiring to promote & set forward so pious an undertaking for the Glory of God & the Good of mankind'. These were encouraged by impassioned sermons demonstrating the holiness of munificent contributions and what is 'conducive to the temporal as well as spiritual welfare of the people', which attracted 390 voluntary subscribers, ranging from large sums given by wealthy merchants and local aristocrats (among them Lord Burlington), smaller amounts from craftsmen active in local building trades, some of whom subsequently successfully attracted building contracts, to hundreds of ordinary folk, some giving as little as 5s.[9] Rare printed subscriptions for completing the tower of St Paul, Sheffield, in the years 1769–72 listing 469 contributors realised a total of £590 3s. 6d.[10]

One of the interesting aspects of this method was the wide participation of subscribers across England. St Philip, Birmingham, attracted gifts from as far afield as London, Sheffield in Yorkshire and Bristol in Somerset, as well as the universities of Cambridge and Oxford. George I gave £600 (p. iii).[11] These had significant architectural repercussions (pl. 12). A loquacious epistle of 1766 to George III, who gave permission to build the German Lutheran church in The Savoy, London, designed by the Royal Architect, Sir William Chambers, recorded that although available money was

> far from being sufficient to defray the Expences . . . yet the Committee did not scruple to begin the Work in the Name of God, and trust that He whose Worship and Glory is thereby intended, will raise them Friends, and Benefactors, who from that noble and exalted Principal of Charity which is the greatest of all moral Virtues, and the first Fruit of true and living Faith, will enable them to finish it in due Time . . . It cannot be said, that the Parallel between the Churches in our Days, and the Tabernacles of old or the Temple of the Jews at Jerusalem, does not hold good in every particular; yet the whole Scripture being designed for an Encouragement of Faith, Love, and all manner of good Works, to the End of the World, it will not be improper to observe that the great God of Heaven and Earth, did not think it a Diminution of his Glory to have these Places of divine Worship erected by the free Gifts and Voluntary Contributions of his People. So far from it that he rather greatly advance his Honour, by inclining and making their hearts willing to such a Degree, that their Offerings even surpassed their Wants. Low therefore as the Ebb of Religion seems now to be; yet we have no reason to doubt that a great Remnant still is left, who have the Worship and Glory of God and their Redeemer at heart, and who will not grudge to bestow a small part of their Abundance, to promote the Interest of his Kingdom upon Earth, and the Salvation of immortal Souls.[12]

In Ireland the leading benefactors were prominent churchmen: Richard Robinson, Archbishop of Armagh, and Frederick Hervey, the Earl Bishop of Derry (of Ickworth House fame), who between them were responsible for erecting three dozen new churches during the second half of the century.[13] In an exceptional case, that of the 'Great, Good, Pious, and Charitable' Edward Colston of Bristol, a detailed list of public charities and benefactions, including a total of £1,070 bequeathed towards repairing and beautifying ten local churches, is presented on a pair of panels framed in an aedicule rising over his reclining tomb figure carved by Michael Rysbrack to James Gibbs's design. Its engraved representation is flanked by allegorical groups representing Charity (pl. 62).

Such operations did not always run smoothly. During the rebuilding of medieval St Botolph, Lincoln, in 1723 it was claimed that the parish book dating back to Elizabeth's reign was

> Clandestinely Taken Away or Mislaid, On Purpose to Asperse the Chief Promoters and Rebuilders . . . thereby Insinuating into the Minds of Well Meaning Parishioners, yt Noe Fair Accound of their Lays Raised for that Purpose, Have been Yett Given as the Laws Direct; and that the . . . Book is on purpose Fraudenly Kept Back by the Churchwardens, & only pretend to be lost to prevent Further Inspection.[14]

Engravings depicting the proposed church were occasionally produced to stimulate fund-raising, as in the case of All Saints, Oxford (pl. 440), which in turn served as a model for St Ann, Manchester (pl. 444), and of All Saints, Derby (pl. 423), where a nationwide subscription launched in 1722–3 to 'Carrying on soe good [and] necessary a worke' attracted 150 benefactors, ranging from the mayor (£120) and the Duke of Devonshire of nearby Chatsworth (£105) to Sir Isaac Newton and a Mr Lloyd of Covent Garden (£5 5s. od each); it raised a total of £4,162 13s. 6d. The *Weekly Journal; or, Saturday's Post* reported its 'rebuilding at the charge of several Persons of Distinction'. The vicar, Michael Hutchinson, who, according to the epitaph on his monument in the church, 'from a pious zeal, and unwearied application' issued an imposing copper plate of the plan and south elevation engraved by Heinrich Hulsbergh, who cut 300 plates, for which he received £12 17s. 8d., and which the architect, Gibbs, subsequently included in *A Book of Architecture* (1728).[15] It is worth mentioning here that some churches were venues for fund-raising in support of other civic institutions. For example, in 1782 a sum of £144 1s. 8½d. was collected in sixteen Leeds houses of worship for the benefit of the new General Infirmary.[16]

The business of fund-raising could be frustrating. At Bampton, Westmorland, which was 'in a Slovenly pickle; dark, black . . . ill-seated', the bid in 1723 to raise £782 16s. 10d. for rebuilding proved too low to attract a Brief – the bottom line then being drawn at £1,000, so the Vestry was 'forced to drop the Design to a more favourable Time, if ever that Day might dawn upon us. Thus we were no sooner out of the Port, than . . . driven in again to lay by, & watch [for] a more prosperous Gale . . . A long Interval was spent between Darkness & Despair'.[17] In 1724 the irascible Sarah, Duchess of Marlborough, resident of The Mall, refused to pay duties for building nearby St Martin-in-the-Fields, and even 'Denyed Entrance' to the collectors, Cibott and Phipps, who had to call in the under-sheriff for 'Assistance'.[18] Subscriptions for Francis Smith's new Palladian church of St Mary, Monmouth, still unpaid seven years after completion, were categorised under 'Hopeful', £32 11s. od., and 'Desperate' or 'Hopeless', £51 9s. od.[19] At Goadby, Leicestershire, in 1752–3 William Woodcock, churchwarden, brought a case against the vicar, John Whittingham, in connection with his annual tithes and profits of £80, which the previous minister had always used to maintain the chancel, yet it had been 'out of repair in Severall parts' for three years. The Ecclesiastical Court decided in favour of the latter on the grounds that Goadby was only a chapel of 'Appendant-Ease' and not a rectory, as the wardens had 'idly dreamt'.[20] Finally, the fascinating and perhaps unique collection book of 1776–7 of Henry Kempson, secretary to the trustees for building St Paul, Birmingham, reveals a barrage of disappointments: Richard Sharp 'denies Subscribing'; Winstanley 'says he was deceived he subscribing only on Condition the work was to be done by Towns people'; Reynolds hopes 'it will not be a Methodist place'; Ford 'thinks to pay his in Ironwork'; Smith 'is afraid it should not be built so will stay a little longer to see'; Rogers is 'afraid it will never be finished'; Brown and Skinner 'were drawn in by being told their Subscriptions . . . would never be wanted'; Joseph Morris 'repents & thinks he shall revolt'; James Dallaway 'says his Circumstances are so altered since he subscribed that he cannot afford to pay it'; Sorrell 'can't afford now'; Joseph Elkin 'has many losses & can't afford to pay'; Joseph Bigs was 'out, the Wife says he is not in Circumstances to pay but it seems otherwise'; Bonington was 'never at home'; Butler 'is dead'.[21]

A further, lucrative form of fund-raising was musical performances.

> Light Quirks of Musick, broken and uneven,
> Make the Soul dance upon a Jig to Heaven.[22]

Among the most celebrated were George Frederick Handel's promotions to complete the London Foundling Hospital, held in its chapel, beginning in 1749, when he conducted *Messiah*. It was repeated in 1750 to celebrate the installation of the organ, charging a half-guinea per person and attracting an audience of 1,000, with many turned away, despite prohibiting the wearing of swords and hoops, grossing £728 3s. 6d.; again in 1751, with the composer playing an organ voluntary, which raised £600 in April and 700 guineas in May, attracting 'above 500 coaches besides chairs, &c.'; yet again in 1752, when 1,200 tickets were sold at 10s. 6d. each, the 'most Noble and grand Audience . . .

expressed the greatest satisfaction at the exquisiteness of the composition [and] the completeness of the Performance'. *Messiah* was performed a few months after Handel's death in 1759, having bequeathed a copy of the 'Sacred Oratorio' to the hospital.[23]

In 1767 *Messiah* raised £500 at All Saints, Wakefield, 'to the great delight and satisfaction of the most crowded and polite audience ever seen in this Country'. In the following year at St Philip, Birmingham, it 'met with the most distinguished Applause. The Concourse of Nobility and Gentry . . . a most Splendid Appearance', reaping £800. In 1769 the new organ at Beverley Minster was launched with *Judas Maccabaeus*. The *Te Deum* and 'other pieces of sacred music' played in St Mary, Oxford, in 1774 on the anniversary of the foundation of the Radcliffe Infirmary brought 'very considerable collections. . . . at the church door'.[24] The *Te Deum*, *Coronation Anthems* and works by William Boyce were 'performed to a Crowded and respectable Company with universal approbation' at St Paul, Birmingham, in 1778, raising £800. During the Musical Festival of 1791 the church was the venue for excerpts from 'A Grand Selection of Sacred Music' – *Joshua*, *Saul*, *Israel in Egypt*, *Samson*, *Athalia*, *Theodore*, *Judas Maccabaeus*, *Jephtha* and the *Coronation Anthems* – to pay for Benjamin West's dramatic painted glass in the chancel (pl. 98).[25]

Handel was also a popular choice for special, private musical occasions having nothing to do with finances. In the chapel of the 'Princ'ly' Duke of Chandos's palatial mansion at Cannons near London, where he found employment from 1717, the eleven *Chandos Anthems* were first performed.[26] Gibbs's fabulously opulent room (pl. 380) was described by Defoe in its heyday as 'a singularity, not only in its building, and the beauty of its workmanship, but in . . . that the Duke maintains there a full choir, and has the worship perform'd there with the best musick, after the manner of the Chappel Royal, which is not done in any other noble man's chappel in Britain'.[27] The *Te Deum* and *Jubilate* performed at the Feast of the Sons of the Clergy in St Paul's Cathedral, London, in 1733 by 'a much greater Number of Voices and Instruments than usual' solicited a fifty-seven-line ode, which enthused on

The Thoughts of Men, in Godlike Sounds he sung,
And voic'd Devotion, for an Angel's Tongue . . .
Thou Soul of HANDEL! – – through what shining Way,
Lost to our Earth, since David's long past Day . . .
Ne'er did Religion's languid Fire,
Burn fainter – – never more require
The Aid of such a fam'd Enliv'ner's Care:
Thy Pow'r can *force* the stubborn Heart to feel,
And rouze the Luke-warm Doubter into *zeal* . . .
Inspire Content, and Peace, in each proud Breast,
Bid the unwilling Land be blest.[28]

An 'Anthem composed and set to music by Mr Handel' was performed on the occasion of the marriage of Princess Mary to Frederick of Hesse-Cassel in the Royal Chapel at St James's Palace in 1740. This had previously been the venue of the nuptials of Frederick, Prince of Wales to Princess Augusta in 1736, accompanied by 'a fine Anthem performed by a great number of voices and instruments', and in 1725 of a service described by César de Saussure as 'entirely musical, some of the laymen having superb voices' and featuring 'a delightful symphony, and what is not sung is intoned by the clergy'.[29] Handelmania reached a peak with the Westminster Abbey Commemoration of 1784 (frontispiece and pl. 250).[30] During the season of 1787, which again attracted the royal family, most of the nobility, foreign ministers, clergy, 'many persons of distinction . . . and above 2000 of the Commonalty not inferior, in dress and appearance, to the Gentry of any nation', heard 'sublime choruses and some 800 performers!'. Queen Charlotte was 'so much enraptured, as to join in'.[31] Furthermore, the *Gentleman's Magazine* reported in 1771 that a rehearsal at St George, Hanover Square, with a 'very large [and] excellent . . . Band' of fifty 'eminent masters . . . the vocal by the Gentlemen of his Majesty's Chapel Royal, the Choirs of St Paul's [and] Westminster abbey' conducted by Dr William Boyce 'gave the utmost satisfaction to a very polite audience', raising £140 16s. 0d., though a further performance at St Paul's managed only £125 16s. 9d., compared to previous years, where it ranged from £157 13s. 3d. to £223 9s. 3d.[32]

It should be noted that routinely for church services the parish clerk led verses of psalms or hymns and congregational responses. Small choirs occupying west galleries accompanied by instruments became widespread late in the century, but they were of a fairly low musical standard. They were made up of local singers instructed by itinerant singing masters and using a lead singer, generally a clerk assisting the vicar, or charity children or young men's religious associations able to learn the psalms.[33]

Singers were sometimes accompanied by an organ. The *Leeds Mercury* of 19 September 1769 assured its readers that in a church the 'Band will consist of the best Performers, Vocal and Instrumental, that can be procured, [with] an organ . . . erected for that Purpose', while Smollett's Humphrey Clinker observed that the

> good people of Edinburgh no longer think dirt and cobwebs essential to the house of God. – Some of their churches have admitted such ornaments as would have excited sedition, even in England, a little more than a century ago; and psalmody is here practised and taught by a professor from the cathedral of Durham: – I should not be surprised, in a few years, to hear it accompanied with an organ.[34]

It was believed that organs aided in 'promoting the Glory & Worship of the Almighty and Raising the Devotions of Pious Christians by Harmoniously praising his Holy Name with Psalms & Hymns'.[35] These instruments varied in quality and appearance. The *Gentleman's Magazine* noted in 1797 a recommendation to install '*Box-Organs*, as helps to Singing, in our Village-Churches', while expressing concern that they 'might diminish the solemnity of the service'.[36] A rare perspective of the gallery erected in 1719 in Stockton-on-Tees (pl. 63), presumably drawn early in the following century to record pew allocations, shows the modest instrument purchased by subscription in 1750 for £250 12s. 0d. from Thomas Griffin of Fenchurch Street, London, housed in a case made by John Newham Jr.[37]

Though a well-documented subject in its own right and too extensive to examine in detail here, something should be said about organ case design and construction as revealed in parish documents.[38] Early eighteenth-century forms favoured the flamboyant treatment renowned in the Wren-Gibbons cases at St Paul's Cathedral (pl. 305),[39] for example, that dominating Bath Abbey (pl. 64), which was 'thought by very good judges to be one of the best in Europe',[40] crowned by over-life-size statues of *King David* playing the harp and two *Evangelists*, as depicted in an engraving 'Done by the Encouragement and Subscription of the Nobility, Ladies and Gentlemen, and the Principal Inhabitants', a prime example of church art uniting the ambitions of locals and visitors alike.[41] Johann Snetzler, an immigrant Swiss who became the leading builder in Britain between the 1760s and 1780s, supplied an organ to All Saints, Rotherham, Yorkshire (1775–7), which is unusually well documented in letters and bills and offers insights into his working practice, though neither instrument nor case survive. Between 1760 and 1778 a local architect, John Platt Jr, supervised the construction of a new west gallery designed to contain the 4 ton organ, costing £678 0s. 11d. In June 1776 Snetzler recommended a wainscot case 'in the Gottick taste' (to suit the medieval church), which would be finished in twelve months ('the shortest time it can be done in'); in November he responded to the churchwardens' offer that 'if any money should be wanted you would collect some from the Subscribers . . . and remitt it to me' by explaining that 'that is not my Method of doing business. I have generaly two or three of the most reputable & substancial of the subscribers to enter into an obligation, to pay me the money agreed for, on the delivery of the organ', which was ready to be crated in October 1777.[42] The appearance of a new organ in church was an occasion for jubilation. When James Wyatt's and Samuel Green's creation, first heard at the Handel Commemoration in Westminster Abbey in 1784 (frontispiece), arrived at its final destination over the choirscreen at Canterbury Cathedral, it

> produced that happy effect so long wished by every admirer of that ancient and magnificent structure. The ornamental parts . . . all in true Gothic taste, surmounted with spires, embellished with pointed arches, and occupying . . . the whole of the grand arch under Bell Harry Steeple, gave satisfaction . . . to every eye; but, when the musical powers of the instrument were displayed, the auditors, who . . . were about 2000, were struck with astonishment . . . by its superior excellence.[43]

Occasionally, church bands were supplemented by additional instruments. A base viol purchased for £3 17s. 0d. for Whitkirk near Leeds was 'for the sole and proper Use of the Singers, so long as there shall continue above two entered to be instructed . . . by a

63 Anonymous. View of the west gallery with the organ, Stockton-on-Tees parish church, County Durham, *c*.1827. Pen and ink and wash. Durham Record Office, EP/Sto 38. Pews 1719, Thomas Griffin organ maker, 1750.

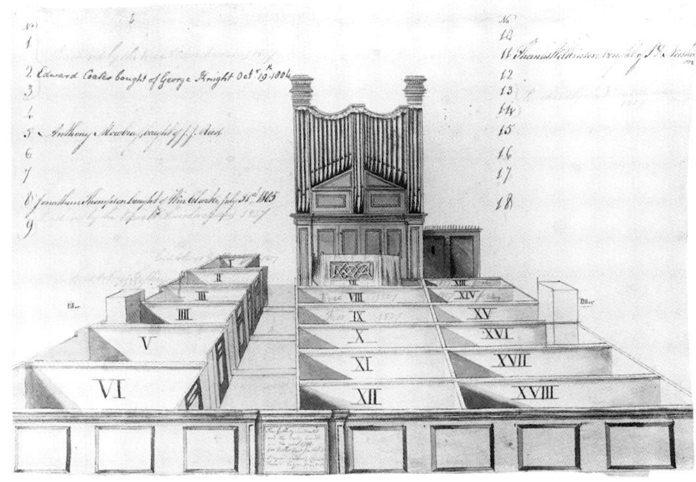

64 James Vertue. 'A Perspective View of The Abbey Church of St. Peter and Paul at Bath [Somerset]', 1 October 1750. Engraving. © The British Library Board, K. Top. XXXVII.27-h. Abraham Jordan organ maker, 1708, altarpiece, 1725–26.

Master of this Church'; it was given to two local joiners 'to take Care of, and to have always ready in good and sufficient Repair [and] not lend [it] to any one under any Pretence whatever'.[44]

However, there was also a downside. Some traditionalists regarded musical performance in church with the same suspicion as its nefarious association with attendance at the playhouse and other public places of entertainment, or, as Pope warned, to 'Load some vain Church with old Theatric state' (a view that would be taken to extremes by Evangelical Victorians).[45] Thus, Ned Ward's description of a 'public music-room', looking 'so far above the use it's now converted to that the seats are more like pews than boxes; and the upper end, being divided by a rail, looks more like a chancel than a music box. I could not but imagine it was built for a fanatic meeting-house but they have forever destroyed the sanctity of the place by putting an organ in it'.[46] In 1735 a temporary playhouse was erected in York Minster Yard without consent of either the dean and chapter or the Justices of the Peace by Thomas Korogan and his 'Company of Actors . . . reputed papists [which] tends greatly to corrupt the honest and industrious to promote Extravagance Idleness and many other Disorders'.[47] *The Spectator* ridiculed psalmody by concocting a country clergyman's letter recounting 'some little indecencies which cannot so properly be exposed from the pulpit', including a London widow who 'appears every *Sunday* at church with many fashionable extravagancies, to the great astonishment of my congregation', most offensively 'her theatrical manner of singing the psalms [introducing] above fifty *Italian* airs into the hundredth psalm'. 'I AM very far from being an enemy of church music: but fear this abuse of it may make my parish ridiculous, who already look on the singing psalms as an entertainment, and not part of their devotion.'

Furthermore,

> a great many of our church-musicians being related to the theatre . . . have, in imitation . . . Introduced in their farewel voluntaries a sort of music quite foreign to the design of church-services, to the great prejudice of well disposed people . . . I have found by experience a great deal of mischief; for when the preacher has . . . with great piety and art . . . handled his subject . . . and . . . found . . . in the rest of the pew good thoughts and dispositions, they have been all in a moment dissipated by a merry jig from the organ loft . . . Pray, Sir, do what you can to put a stop to those growing evils.[48]

The diarist George Vertue also observed that 'all over England (except great cities) in the parish Churches the Psalms . . . are ill sung & out of Tune. Time. &c. & often by the Ignorance of the Clerks. so wretchedly performd that it is a misery to hear them'.[49] Torrington found singing in Manchester parish church 'too bad to tempt my continuance', while Addison painted a witty picture of opera-going where the fashion 'so prevails' among audiences of singing along with the performers that the latter 'sometimes . . . do no more in a celebrated song, than the clerk of a parish church, who serves only to raise the psalm, and is afterwards drowned in the music of the congregation'.[50] Nonetheless, a correspondent to the *Grub-street Journal* believed

> *Church-musick* . . . capable of raising the noblest hints in the mind, and filling it with the most sublime and worthy conceptions [and] by this means our pleasure and duty might be made to accompany one another; our virtue would be improved in proportion to our delight and a more vigorous and lively devotion created in the heart, than the best form of words without its assistance could effect.[51]

The impact of musical performance in church is summed up by the hyper-critical Torrington in 1789 when,

> tho the Psalmody . . . was on the decline, yet was it tolerably supported by 2 Bassoons, a Clarinet, and a german Flute. – Nothing shou'd be more encouraged as drawing both Young and Old to Church, than Church Melody, tho' the Profligacy and Refinement of the age has abandon'd and ridiculed it: But were I a Squire of a country Village I wou'd offer such Premiums and Encouragement, (of little cost to myself) as wou'd quickly rear an ambitious, and laudable desire of Psalm-Singing, and put forth a little Chorus of Children; than which nothing is more Elevating and Grateful and Sublime, hearing Innocence exert their little Voices in praise of their Creator. For let Fashion say what it can, Every Ear is more gratified by a chorus of youth, than by the most violent Exertions of Taste.[52]

65 William Hogarth, *The Wedding of Stephen Beckingham and Mary Cox*, 1729–30. Oil on canvas. The Metropolitan Museum of Art, New York, inv. no. 36.111.

Six

FROM THE CRADLE TO THE GRAVE

EPIGRAMS, from the *Bath Journal*

In crowds the *ladies* throng, where *Pleasure* calls,
To *gaming-rooms*, to *concerts*, and to *balls*.
BUT NONE TO CHURCH! – *What for*? No *men* are there.
Must *Belles* on one another only stare?
The REPLY.
BUT *none to Church!* – 'tis false! your pious fools,
Polish'd *no higher* than by *bible rules*,
Lame, *Old*, and *Ugly*, thither run in sholes;
– THEY'VE nothing else to do *but mind their souls*.
ANOTHER.
WE *Belles not go to church*! – What then? – Pray tell;
We *play at Cards on* SUNDAY'S, – that's as well.[1]

The range of activities connected with churchgoing – divine worship, musical concerts, weddings, baptisms, catechisms, funerals and a variety of commemorations from tombs and catacombs to mausoleums – is an index to Georgian daily life. James Boswell, who 'took a whim to go through all the churches and chapels in London . . . one each Sunday' during 1762–3, recorded on 21 November 1762: 'went to Mayfair Chapel . . . heard prayers and an excellent sermon . . . on the comforts of piety . . . I thought that GOD really designed us to be happy . . . I have now and then flashes of devotion and it will one day burn with a steady flame'; on 28 November: 'to St James's Church . . . In the midst of divine service I was laying plans for having women, and yet . . . had the most sincere feelings of religion . . . I am . . . given . . . to the most brilliant and showy method of public worship'; on 5 December: 'to St George's Church . . . I was upon honour much disposed to be a Christian. Yet I was rather cold in my devotion. The Duchess of Grafton attracted my eyes rather too much'; on Christmas Day: to St Paul's Cathedral, 'in that magnificent temple fervently adorned the GOD of goodness and mercy'; on 16 January 1763: 'I heard service and sermon in the New Church in the Strand, which insensibly relieved me from my cloudy spirits'; on 10 April: 'to the Temple Church and heard a very good sermon [which] with the music and the good building put me in a very devout frame, and . . . my mind was left in a pleasing calm state'; on 17 April: 'to St Bride's . . . where the parson was so very heavy and drawling that my friend tired, and we came away before the sermon . . . rather unsettled and in bad humour'; on 8 May at Audley Chapel, 'so dissipated that I could not fix my attention, so I came out . . . then stepped in to a Romish Chapel and was filled with most romantic ideas'; a week later: 'to Dr Fordyce's meeting in Monkwell Street . . . Blair's New Kirk delivery and the Dissenters roaring out the Psalms sitting on their backsides . . . in short the whole vulgar idea of the Presbyterian worship, made me very gloomy. I therefore hastened . . . to St Paul's . . . and had my mind set right again'; on 10 July: 'to Bow Church, the true centrical temple for the bluff citizens. I had many comfortable ideas.'[2]

Boswell's extravagantly ecumenical church crawl exposed some of the foibles of churchgoing. There was the predicament of disparities in attendance: Leeds parish church was 'monthly fill'd . . . twice round with devout Communicants (one of the most blessed Prospects this World affords)' and 'the most comfortable

Sight a pious Christian can behold',[3] whereas London churches, while 'beautiful [and] an honour to the taste of the people . . . *within* . . . are not quite so much attended as in Birmingham', observed a local historian, who 'attended divine service' at St Mary Aldermary, where 'the Bishop of L – preached, almost to an empty church'.[4] James Paterson's remarkable volume entitled *Pietas Londinensis; or, The Present Ecclesiastical State of London; Containing An Account of all the Churches, and Chapels of Ease, in and about the Cities of London and Westminster; of the set Times of their publick Prayers, Sacraments, and Sermons . . . To which is added, A Postscript, recommending the Duty of publick Prayer* (1714) took an

> Opportunity to allure and perswade all good Christians, and more especially those *lazy*, *luke-warm*, and *indifferent Professors*, or *nominal Christians*, to frequent the *House* of *Prayer*, and to love and affect that Exercise, which is the most necessary Part of all Publick Duties . . . Frequency in Prayer is an principal means to . . . transform the Mind into Holiness.[5]

Defoe's *Augusta Triumphans; or, The Way to make London the most Flourishing City in the Universe* (1728) complained that the Sabbath

> is not kept with due solemnity; masters and mistresses of families are too remiss in the care of the souls committed to their charge. Family prayer is neglected; and, to the shame of scoffers . . . too much ridiculed. All ages and sexes, if in health, should be obliged to attend publick worship . . . they would edify by what they should hear, and many wicked acts would be stifled in their infancy . . . Our common people make it a day of debauch, and get so drunk . . . they cannot work for a day or two following.[6]

'I am sexton of the parish of *Covent-Garden* . . . as I was tolling into prayers at eleven . . . crowds of people of quality hastened to assemble at a puppet-show.'[7] For those 'truly Devout and Religious, who had rather frequent the House of God, than loyter in the Tents of Wickedness',[8] regular worship was crucial: 'country-people would soon degenerate into a kind of savages and barbarians, were there not such frequent returns of a stated time, in which the whole village meet together with their best faces, and in their cleanliest habits, to . . . hear their duties explained to them, and join together in adoration of the Supreme Being'.[9] The Sabbath was sacrosanct: '*Sunday* Debauches are Abuses that call loud for Amendment . . . Instead of a Day of Rest, we make it a Day of Labour, by toiling in the Devil's Vineyard; and but too many surfeit themselves with the Fruits of Gluttony, Drunkenness, and Uncleanness.'[10]

Proper rules of behaviour were announced in the popular press:

> 1. All Persons . . . come in good Time, and seat themselves quietly before the Service begins . . . 2. they shall be as careful of their Behaviour . . . if they were to meet in any other Place . . . 3. during any Part of the Sermon, no body to *talk*, *laugh*, or do any Thing else that may disturb *scrupulous Consciences* who are attentive to it.[11]

For children:

> Decently walk to thy Seat . . . run not, nor go wantonly . . . Shift not Seats . . . Talk not . . . Fix thine eyes upon the Minister; Let it not wildly wander to gaze upon any Person or Thing . . . Be not hasty to run out of the Church when the Worship is ended, as if thou wert weary of being there . . . Walk decently and soberly home, without hast or wanton-ness.[12]

Reality was otherwise. *The Spectator* attacked 'persons that have behaved themselves irreverently at church [and those who] are very zealous and punctual to perform an ejaculation that is only preparatory to the service of the church, and yet neglect to join in the service itself', like the man who 'bows to all his acquaintances, sits down, takes a pinch of snuff . . . perhaps a nap and spends the remaining time in surveying the congregation'. 'We have in *England* a particular bashfulness in every thing that regards religion. A well-bred man is obliged to conceal any serious sentiment of this nature, and very often to appear a greater libertine than he is, that he may keep himself in countenance among the men of mode.' Moreover,

> the ceremonies, bows, curtsies, whispering, smiles, winks, nods, with other familiar acts of salutation, which take up . . . so much time, that might be better employed, and which seem so utterly inconsistent with the duty and true intent of our entering into those religious assemblies . . . I CANNOT help . . . remarking on the excellent memories of those devotionists, who, upon returning from church, shall give a particular account how two or three hundred people were dressed.[13]

Divine worship provided ideal opportunities to show off wealth and taste. In a Cornish church,

> in the midst of the service, a lady who is the chief woman of the place, and had passed the winter at *London* . . . entered . . . in a little head dress, and a hooped petticoat. The people, who were wonderfully startled at such a sight . . . rose up. Some stared at the prodigious bottom, and some at the little top of this strange dress.

Elsewhere, 'several females . . . came to church with their heads dressed wholly in ribbons, and looked like so many victims ready to be sacrificed'.[14] A correspondent to the *Universal Spectator* in 1734 also 'found *Churches* were for People to shew their *fine Cloaths* in, their *Diamonds*, *Rings*, *Toupees*, and *Snuff-Boxes*; every thing but their *Devotion*: Here some whisper, nod, bow, ogle, kneel, and laugh; others look about, frown, are concern'd, affronted with their Gallants, seem *serious* with their *Lovers*, and trifling with their *God*.'[15] This was perceived as part of the process of enhancing one's prospects. There was young Jenny Simper, who had her 'fortune to make . . . for which reason I came constantly to church to hear divine service, and make conquests'.[16] She presumably differed from 'the fair penitents [who] pray in their patches, sue for pardon in their paint, and see their heaven in man', attending St Martin-in-the-Fields.[17] Of course, both might lead to marriage.[18]

William Hogarth's portrayal of the wedding in 1729–30 of Stephen Beckingham and Mary Cox (pl. 65), with cloud-borne *putti* spilling a cornucopia of fruit and flowers over the happy couple, takes place in an appropriately St Martin-in-the-Fields-like interior.[19] The artist tried unsuccessfully to 'make a draught' of the celebrated dynastic alliance between George II's eldest daughter, Anne, and Prince William of Nassau and Orange on 14 March 1734 in order to 'paint it & make a print for the public'. Despite royal approval, he was 'deprived . . . of persuing . . . any such design', thereby securing the advantage to his rival William Kent, who was in charge of the temporary adornment, which cost £3,980, and who issued the splendid print engraved by Jacques Rigaud (pl. 66). Inigo Jones's Queen's Chapel, St James's Palace (1623–5), was fitted up, the diarist George Vertue recording 'the great preparations, & public discours all over the Nation' regarding 'the particular decoration',[20] which included hanging the windows and temporary galleries with gold-fringed crimson velvet, and the nuptial platform approached by a richly patterned carpet illuminated by chandeliers, with extra artificial light provided by wall sconces, which Lord Hervey admired for being in 'an extremely good taste'.[21] Kent transformed the room from its archetypal Palladian ambience to one having rich associations with Roman baroque church interiors, which had undergone similar temporary refashioning during the years of his Italian sojourn.[22] It was for this gorgeous event that Handel composed the celebratory serenata *Parnasso in Festa*, performed at the King's Theatre, Haymarket, in which Apollo sang of 'the god of wedded love and faith to praise, today with cheerful hearts your voices raise . . . Whilst the heavens around display their brightest splendour on this happy day.'[23] Of course, these were a far cry from the modest affairs of ordinary parish weddings, of which few could have been as melodramatic as that between Michael Thomas and Ann Bradley held at St Olave, Southwark, on 5 November 1770, which was interrupted by a press gang and from the ensuing fray the 'poor black, with his [white] bride' narrowly made their escape.[24]

Post-Reformation baptism followed the order set out in the Book of Common Prayer (1552) with immersion in a font (pl. 67a). An occasion when the minister came into close personal contact with his parishioners, it was an important symbol of the pastoral authority of the parish church, so that 'ancestral' fonts, largely spared the worst excesses of iconoclasm, tended to survive even when churches underwent major renewal or entire rebuilding, including in non-medieval styles. A particularly spectacular example is the large twelfth-century font at Beverley Minster, which received a stupendously carved wood baroque cover in 1726.[25]

New fonts generally followed fashion, like the churches themselves. During the baroque this was set by the London New Churches, typically at St George, Hanover Square, which is made of 'Statuary & Black & Yellow Marble [with an] Octangular Cover of Wains[cot]t . . . formed with an Ogee having Ribs of Lime tree on Every Angle and a Carved Dove at the Top', costing £15 12s. 11d.[26] Some derived from pattern books, the earliest specimens probably being the set published as plate 146 in Gibbs's *A Book of Architecture* (1728): 'Cisterns rais'd upon Pedestals, which may also serve as Fonts'.[27] During the early neoclassical period they tended towards individuality, such as the gothic compound colonnetted form at Hartwell (pl. 67b) designed by Henry Keene, then employed as surveyor to the fabric of Westminster Abbey, and the deliciously Piranesian fantasy at West Wycombe, Buckinghamshire, with its 'inimitable workmanship; four carved doves [which] seem to be drinking out of it, one dove . . . going up by the side, and a serpent following it; and the bason . . . with the cover . . . of solid gold' (actually

66 Jacques Rigaud after William Kent. 'The Marriage of Princess Anne and Prince William of Nassau and Orange in the Queen's Chapel, St James's Palace, Westminster, 14 March 1734'. Engraving. © The British Library Board, K. Top. XXVI-2-f. Inigo Jones architect, 1616–35, temporary decorations by Kent, 1734.

67a Bernard Picart. 'Le Baptême des Reformés', dated 1732, in *Ceremonies et Coutumes Religieuse De Tous Les Peuples Du Mond*, vol. III, 'Dissertation sur le Religion des Protestans', fig. 19, 1733. Engraving. Author's collection.

67b (*right*) Henry Keene. Font dated 1756 in St Mary, Hartwell, Buckinghamshire, untraced. English Heritage (National Monuments Record), A44/4418.

68 Designer unknown. Funeral ticket of Mrs Mary Thomas, undated. Engraving, pen and ink. City of Westminster Archives, Ashbridge 222/441.

silver gilt), signifying Redemption through baptism.[28] At Stapleford, Leicestershire, the marble font could be screwed to the floor 'when wanted, but not to be stationary', while at St George, Hanover Square, it was stored under the altar, run on castors and pulled out when required, which reminded *The Ecclesiologist* of a wine cooler![29]

Death dramatically transformed churches into the 'Silent Mansions of the Dead'.[30]

> Behold Sir Balaam . . .
> His Compting-house employ'd the Sunday-morn;
> Seldom at Church ('twas such a busy life)
> But duly sent his family and wife.
> There (so the Dev'l ordain'd) one Christmas-tide
> My good old Lady catch'd a cold, and dy'd[31]

Protestant funeral cortèges were melancholic affairs (pl. 68), with church interiors often temporarily painted or draped in black.[32] From the Revd Robert Blair's *The Grave* (1743):

> The gloomy Isles
> Black-plaster'd, and hung round with Shreds of
> 'Scutcheons.
> And tatter'd Coats of Arms

This reflected not only Restoration court fashions but also Continental practice as recorded in engravings.[33] In 1789 'funeral offices' for Carlo III of Spain were performed in the York Street Chapel, London,

> with very great solemnity. The whole . . . hung with black; the sconces and armorial bearings of the Crown . . . placed round the chapel, and in the centre a magnificent canopy, with Royal Crown and Sceptre . . . in a style of solemnity and elegance truly attractive. There was a great concourse of nobility and gentry.[34]

For Queen Caroline's funeral in 1737 at Westminster Abbey, the royal mausoleum, the route from the north door was 'lined throughout on the Floor . . . Sides, and over head, with Black Bays [baize]'.[35] In 1751 the 'bowels of [Frederick Prince of Wales] in an urn cover'd with crimson velvet, were brought from *Leicester House* in a coach . . . carried by 4 yeomen to Henry VII's chapel', attended by two dukes, one earl and five other aristocrats, members of the royal household, with the coffin 'Covered with a black velvet pall . . . under a canopy of black velvet borne by 8 of his R.H.'s gentlemen' and accompanied by the dean, prebendaries and gentlemen of the choir 'carrying wax tapers [with] two drums beating a dead march during the service'.[36] The prince's father, George II, who died nine years later, was transported from Kensington Palace to the House of Lords and thence to the abbey in a coffin 'covered with a large Pall of Purple Velvet . . . lined with Purple Silk, with a fine Holland Sheet, adorned with ten large Escutcheons . . . painted on Sattin . . . under a Canopy of Purple Velvet'.[37]

The abbey was also the scene of the most eminent British funerals.

> O THOU! the noblest of our antient piles!
> Rich in thy 'fretted roofs' and 'long-drawn ailes!'
> But chief as mansion of th' illustrious dead[38]

Before burial there, John Sheffield, Duke of Buckingham (died 1721), lay in state in his St James's Park mansion 'in a very magnificent Manner . . . in a Room of State hung with Velvet, within an Alcove, and a Canopy, with Feathers . . . Coronet, Cap . . . Cushion, and all the Trophies of Honour fix'd round him'. These trappings were subsequently permanently expressed in his opulent marble monument carved by Peter Scheemakers and Laurent Delvaux, one of the showpieces of Henry VII's Chapel.[39] State funerals drew huge crowds. The black velvet palled and canopied coffin of William Pitt, 1st Earl of Chatham, who famously expired following the Parliamentary debate in 1788 on the future of the American colonies, was led by the High Constable of Westminster in mourning cloak preceding a 'Cavalcade comprising six Earls, 70 poor men carrying black staves and a "Gentleman Usher" bearing a black velvet cushion on a black silk carpet'; Horace Walpole warned Lady Ossory against attending because it would attract 'a mob very unfit for you'.[40] For Elizabeth, Duchess of Northumberland the

> crowd . . . was so great . . . that the . . . Bishop of Rochester and the gentlemen and boys of the choir could not perform the service . . . The old Gothic screen . . . to St Edmund's Chapel . . . by the number of people climbing upon it, fell down . . . The Bishop . . . narrowly escaped being dangerously hurt . . . considerable damage was done to the monuments.[41]

For the funeral of the actor David Garrick, thirty-four family coaches, with drivers and footmen wearing 'black silk hatbands and gloves' and a huge entourage of mourners, among whom were Richard Brinsley Sheridan, Edmund Burke, Samuel Johnson, Joshua Reynolds and Robert Adam, followed the crimson velvet coffin with 'silver gilt nails and plate'. They processed from the Adelphi terrace to the abbey, the streets crowded with innumerable spectators, and 'so many carriages . . . that they were not passable'. The funeral cost £1,500, with the dean and chapter remunerated a fee of 100 guineas.[42]

This dependence on burial charges could lead to extravagant installations for complete nobodies, reaching a crescendo in the eighteenth century and regarded by some as 'pestilential'. Goldsmith ridiculed this practice in *The Citizen of the World* (1760–61): 'There no intruders by the influence of friends or fortune, presume to mix their unhallowed ashes with philosophers, heroes, and poets. Nothing but true merit has a place in that awful sanctuary'. Hardly! The 'gentleman was rich . . . so he paid his money for a fine monument'.[43] 'I don't think England', observed Maximilien de Lazowski (travelling companion of the La Rochefoucauld brothers in 1785), 'has an equal in the world for the great importance it assigns to epitaphs, or where funeral monuments are so multiplied, and carved at such expense. When the merest gentleman dies, he is carried at great cost to the tomb of his ancestors.'[44] Moreover, in 1755 *The Connoisseur* and the *London Magazine* jointly warned against their inherent paganism:

> If Socrates, or any other of the ancient philosophers would revive again, and be admitted into Westminster Abbey, he would be induced to fancy himself in a Pantheon of the heathen gods. The modern taste, (not content with introducing Roman temples into our churches, and representing the virtues under allegorical images) has ransacked all the fabulous accounts of the heathen theology to strike out new embellishments for our Christian monuments.

'If there is not a stop put to this taste, we may soon expect to see our churches, instead of being dedicated to the service of religion, set apart for the reception of the heathen gods.'[45]

This coincided with the building's rise as a major tourist attraction (pl. 6).

Next, to the Abbey let's repair,
The Man dismiss'd, they walk around,
Many new Monuments they found,
In all Art's, Workmanship compleat.
Grand, and magnificently neat.[46]

In a long poem published in John Dart's de luxe, large-format, two-volume *Westmonasterium; or, The history and Antiquities of The Abbey Church of St Peters Westminster* (1723), the author waxed romantically on

Where LOVES no more, but MARBLE Angels moan,
And little *Cherubs* seem to sob in Stone.

Where thro' the painted Glass the Beams invade,
With rich strain'd Light, and cast a painted Shade;
Gild dusty Tombs, flow o'er the mould'ring Train,
And spread, like Funeral Lamps, their Light in vain

Where the nice Statuary's Skill is *shown*
In living Sculpture and the figur'd *Stone*,
With vast expensive Pride adorn'd the Place,
Fit to contain the Ashes of his Race.[47]

As hinted earlier, monuments themselves became a useful source of abbey revenue. Not only did the authorities impose funeral fees – £74 18s. 0d. for Buckingham in 1721 – but charged visitors 'Three-pence to see the Tombs'.[48] De Saussure reported that 'By giving sixpence to a guardian we shall be shown all the objects of interest', but added: 'Our conductor, holding a stick in his hand, and speaking so quickly that I had much difficulty in understanding him', and concluded: 'I think we have sojourned long enough among the dead and their tombs.'[49] Nevertheless, on 1 May 1737 'Great Numbers of People went . . . to see a Monument in Memory of Mr *John Gay*, open'd in the Poets Corner'.[50] Even greater success attended William Shakespeare's posthumous tomb of 1743, which 'excites an awful admiration in the beholder' and 'tossd' the sculptor, Peter Scheemakers, 'on the summit of the wheel'.[51]

Refined tastes condemned the abbey's haphazard distribution of monuments. In *An Essay on Design* (1749), the architect John Gwynn, while conceding that 'some [are] finely executed, [they] neither add Beauty to, nor receive it from, the Place that contains them . . . Most . . . are only stuck against Parts of the Structure . . . hide and deform particular Members of the original Whole [and] appear only like a great Stock in the Work-shop of a Statuary', which was contrary to 'Our Gothic Structures, bad as we esteem them . . . are yet generally compleat, according to the original Idea of their . . . Architects [since] nothing should be crouded in, that was not Part of . . . the Builder's Original Design'. The exceptions are William Kent's pair of carefully positioned monuments to Sir Isaac Newton and James, Earl of Stanhope attached to the eighteenth-century choirscreen (pl. 290). Gwynn promoted the idea of such sculpture filling up 'Vacancies', and asked: 'Would not an elegant Pile, judiciously and purposely designed for a Repository to the Monuments of the Great, be a national Ornament, and Incentive to Emulation, a kind of Temple of Honour, in which the Noble-minded would endeavour to procure a Place by the Practice of Virtue?'[52]

These ideas were taken to impracticable extremes in the Revd William Hanbury's megalomaniac proposal for creating in the rural wilderness of Church Langton, Leicestershire, a colossal church with floors paved in the 'finest Marble, Porphery, and Jaspar . . . so constructed, that it may in magnificence and grandeur, exceed all others; and become not only the Principal ornament of the Country, but an Honour to the Island'. The exterior and interior were to be overwhelmed with figurative sculpture: 'suitable Statues of Saints, with short inscriptions on the . . . Pedistals . . . properly arranged along the Walls on both sides . . . round the body [and] the great Transept' (as well as on the exterior), together with 'suitable Monuments' to the 'Trustees and Visitors in spaces behind the high altar called the *Sanctum Sanctorum*'. Unsurprisingly, nothing was built.[53] On the other hand, Hawksmoor's unrealised scheme for a flamboyant multi-figured tomb to John Churchill, Duke of Marlborough, in Blenheim Palace chapel (pl. 69) demonstrates the great care taken in integrating sculpture and architecture, which contrasts with the usual haphazard arrangements found in Westminster Abbey and most parish churches.[54]

Humphrey Clinker was appalled that in British churches 'in general, we breathe a gross stagnated air, surcharged with damps from vaults, tombs, and charnal-houses . . . so many magazines of rheums, created for the benefit of the medical faculty' and that 'more bodies are lost, than souls saved, by going to church . . . The practice of burying in churches was the effect of ignorant superstitions, influenced by knavish priests, who pretended that the devil could have no power over the defunct if he was interred in holy ground.'[55] Some authorities took preventative measures. At St Stephen

69 Nicholas Hawksmoor. Design for the monument of John Churchill, 1st Duke of Marlborough, Blenheim Palace chapel, Oxfordshire, *c.*1722, unexecuted. The Bodleian Library, University of Oxford, MS. Top. Oxon. A37, f. 135.

Walbrook in 1777 the Vestry would not 'permit any Bust Statue Monument or painting whatsoever to be brought into the Church to be put up . . . taken down . . . or . . . carried out . . . with[ou]t. a Faculty or the Leave of the Church Wardens'.[56] Hawksmoor and Gibbs, as New Churches co-surveyors, favoured the vaulting option

> as Extreamly Beautifull as well as Convenient . . . for keeping the pavement drye, for preservation of the Pews, for securing of the fabrick . . . If it is not vaulted the Paving will never lye even, there being so vast a number of Corps buryed, the pews will always be in a Rotten and Damp Condition, the walls . . . underminded wth. Sepulchres &c. Notwithstanding all the good wishes and Care to the Contrary.[57]

As Westminster Abbey filled up with tombs (130 erected between 1700 and 1800, compared to approximately 125 before 1700 stretching back into the middle ages), provision was made for creating additional burial vaults.[58] The Vestry of Kentish Town Chapel, London, concluded that

> the Expence attending the Repairs of the Church . . . having been so great as to admit of no diminution of the Debt owing to the Trustees . . . And . . . their being a very spacious dry Vault . . . well adapted for the purpose of the Interment of the Dead, which will contain a good number of Corpses . . . that as an inducement for burying . . . the ffees ought to be moderate and . . . not to exceed five Guineas for . . . each person of the age of 12 years and upwards . . . for Children under [that age] four Guineas only.

From this the vicar reaped 10s., the sexton 5s. and the clerk 2s., with the residue 'applied towards the Discharge of the Debt'.[59]

Yet, there were problems. In 1773 Lord Bertie commented on the 'impropriety of interring in . . . Vaults . . . without . . . Leaden Coffins' and the use of 'Air-holes to let fresh Air into the . . . Vaults, which instead . . . let out the Stench . . . into the Street much to the Annoyance of the whole Neighbourhood and public in General'.[60] The same criticism was levelled against churchyard burials. Thomas Grey, grave-digger to St George, Hanover Square parish, testified to Parliament that 'for want of Room, they were forced to bury the Dead within 3 Feet of the Surface; and that he had frequent Complaints . . . by the Neighbours, in warm Weather, of noisome Smells'.[61] A petition from Sowerby to the Archbishop of York complained grimly that the

70 James Gibbs. Mausoleum to Marwood William Turner, Kirkleatham, Yorkshire, 1740, attached to St Cuthbert, 1756–9, John Carr architect. English Heritage (National Monuments Record) AA53/12873.

burial ground 'is so small that many of the dead are buried in the Isles and under the seats . . . and the Corpses of persons lately buried in the Chapel Yard are frequently mangled in digging to make Room for others; to the great detriment and Nuisance of the Living'.[62]

This problem taxed the New Churches Commissioners as early as 1712. Wren hoped 'all Burials in Churches might be disallowed' on the grounds that the practice was 'unwholesom [and] the Pavements can never be kept even, nor Pews upright', while the yard 'also is inconvenient, because the Ground being continually raised by the Graves, occasions, in Time, a Descent by Steps into the Church, which renders it damp, and the Walls green'.[63] Vanbrugh, too, pressed for churches to be 'free'd from that Inhumane custome of being made Burial Places for the Dead. a Custome in which there is something so very barbarous in it self besides the many ill consequences that attend it; that one cannot enough wonder how it ever has prevail'd amongst the civiliz'd part of mankind'.[64] Both architects recommended 'Cemeteries seated in the Out-skirts of

71 Nicholas Hawksmoor and Daniel Garrett. Mausoleum, Castle Howard, Yorkshire, 1729–42.

the Town . . . inclosed with a strong Brick Wall . . . having a Walk round, and two cross Walks, decently planted with Yew-trees . . . In these Places beautiful Monuments may be erected.'[65] Vanbrugh particularly believed that the

> Richer sort of People, will think their Friends and Relations more decently inter'd in those distinguished Places, than they commonly are in the Ailes and under Pews in Churches; And will think them more honourably remember'd by Lofty and Noble Mausoleums, erected over them in Freestone (which no doubt will soon come into Practice,) than by little Tawdry Monuments of Marble, stuck up against Walls and Pillars.

This reflects out-of-town garden cemeteries of the type he had seen at Surat during a visit to India in the years 1683–5, and which was to become modish in the nineteenth century.[66]

Hawksmoor's celebrated Mausoleum to the Earl of Carlisle at Castle Howard, modelled on the so-called Tomb of Gallienus, Rome, and built at a staggering cost of £78,240, was deemed 'of such architectural excellence and beauty, as to make the beholder almost wish to be an inhabitant' (pl. 71).[67] One of its astonishing peculiarities is the anachronistic combination of a rotunda, serving as the family mortuary chapel, encircled by monumental free-standing columns echoed by internal three-quarter columns embedded in elliptical recesses in the walls – in effect an open double colonnade with its inner intercolumniation augmented by structural masonry – rising over a basement vault with a central, gothic-ribbed dome, as if some surviving but ruined Antique pagan Roman structure had been reclaimed for Christian usage, reinforcing the poignancy of death and resurrection.

Gibbs, too, subscribed to this tradition in the Mausoleum at Kirkleatham, Yorkshire (pl. 70), erected 'TO THE MEMORY OF MARWOOD WILLIAM TURNER, ESQUIRE THE BEST OF SONS', who died young at Lyon in 1739 while on the Grand Tour. This striking structure was inspired by reconstructions of the long-vanished Mausoleum of King Mausolus and Queen Artemisia at Halicarnassus, Asia Minor (fourth century BC).[68] Finally, to avoid taking the whole business too seriously here is an inscription on the pedestal of a proud figure pointing to the newly built chapel at Casewick, Lincolnshire:

> This is the statue of Sir *John Trollop*,
> Who caused yonder stones to roll up;
> And when to Heav'n God calls his soul up,
> His body is to fill this hole up[69]

72 William Milton, attributed. View towards the chancel of Redland Chapel, Bristol, Somerset, *c.*1750. Pen and ink and wash. © The British Library Board, K. Top. XIII.95a. John Strahan, William Halfpenny and Thomas Paty architects, 1740–43.

Seven

THROUGH THE WEST DOOR

Churches are, of all public monuments those which attest most certainly to the state of art of the time of their construction, the taste and the knowledge of the people . . . who erected them, the opulence and the degree of industry of the century that saw their completion.[1]

What did the eighteenth-century Anglican church interior look like? What were its distinctive features? A contemporary view of the Cossins family's Redland Chapel, Bristol (pl. 72), reveals that the service was directed exclusively towards the pulpit and communion table, the Word and the Sacrament. The inscription tacked to the back of the pews alludes to

So neat a Temple, fraught with every Grace,
Jehovah, makes, no doubt, his dwelling place
From this fair Altar may thy Incense rise,
And gain a Seat for thee above the Skies[2]

Certainly it bore little resemblance to the Continental Catholic church either in planning, with its obsessions for domical crossings, or with its elaborate, monumental altarpieces and its richly painted and sculpted religious imagery engulfing the spaces. Such interiors were familiar to the British through engravings such as Andrea Pozzo's widely distributed treatises (pl. 73), as well as first hand. 'I need not tell you', wrote Smollett from Italy in 1765, 'that the churches here are magnificent, and adorned not only with pillars of oriental granite, porphyry, jasper, verde antico, and other precious stones; but also with capital pieces of painting by the most eminent masters.'[3] In Britain, Post-Reformation removal of the chancel screen to reveal the communion service to congregants assembled in the body, and the advancement of the pulpit into this public arena, sometimes with the chancel space reduced to a minimum (pl. 74), made Anglican churches architecturally less pretentious and functionally more straightforward. They are epitomised by Wren's recommendation of 1711 for the ideal New Churches pattern of St James, Westminster (pl. 478), where a rectangular body of 60 by 90 feet is 'very broad and the middle Nave arched up [with] the whole Roof . . . upon . . . Pillars, as do also the Galleries', large enough to hold 2,000 and 'fitted for Auditories . . . that all who are present can . . . hear the Service, and both . . . hear distinctly, and see the Preacher – unlike the *Romanists* [who] may build larger Churches, it is enough if they hear the Murmur of the Mass, and see the Elevation of the Host'.[4] The internally unobstructed rectangular box of St Nicholas, Bristol, represented the ideal solution: 'light . . . airy . . . open . . . well calculated for the audience all to see and hear the preacher'.[5]

The crucial issue of acoustics, of making the Word manifest, preoccupied architects, clergymen and above all worshippers. When Ralph Thoresby, the Leeds antiquary, attended St Paul's Cathedral he found the experience 'very unprofitable [due to the] confused reading (two at the same time, the gospel or lessons) singing prayers and organs . . . the continuous noise and hurry of persons'.[6] Thomas Campbell, an Irish clergyman, visiting the barn-like space of the Foundling Hospital chapel (pl. 35), complained that he had 'hoped to hear the Charity girl who performed . . . at the Oratorio but the distance was so great I could not distinguish her voice'; a few years later it was proposed to reposition the pulpit and reader's desk closer to the east gallery so that the 'Congregation would hear much better'.[7] Some churches were ill equipped. Aynho (pl. 111), though 'a neat Structure without Pillars', was 'not well built for the advantage of Hearing'.[8]

Gibbs explained that the body of his church in the Strand (pls 378–9) 'consists of two Orders, in the upper of which the Lights are placed; the Walls of the lower, being solid to keep out Noises from the Street, is

73 Andrea Pozzo. Section of 'Vestigium Templi rotundi' in *Perspectiva Pictorum et Architectorum*, 1693–1700 (Augsburg, 1709 edition, fig. 89). Engraving. Author's collection.

74 Kenton Couse. Design for a 'Section of the Church from West to East', Holy Trinity, Clapham, London, 1774. Pen and ink and wash. London Borough of Lambeth, Archives Department, LP 22/713/ Hol. T. 8k.

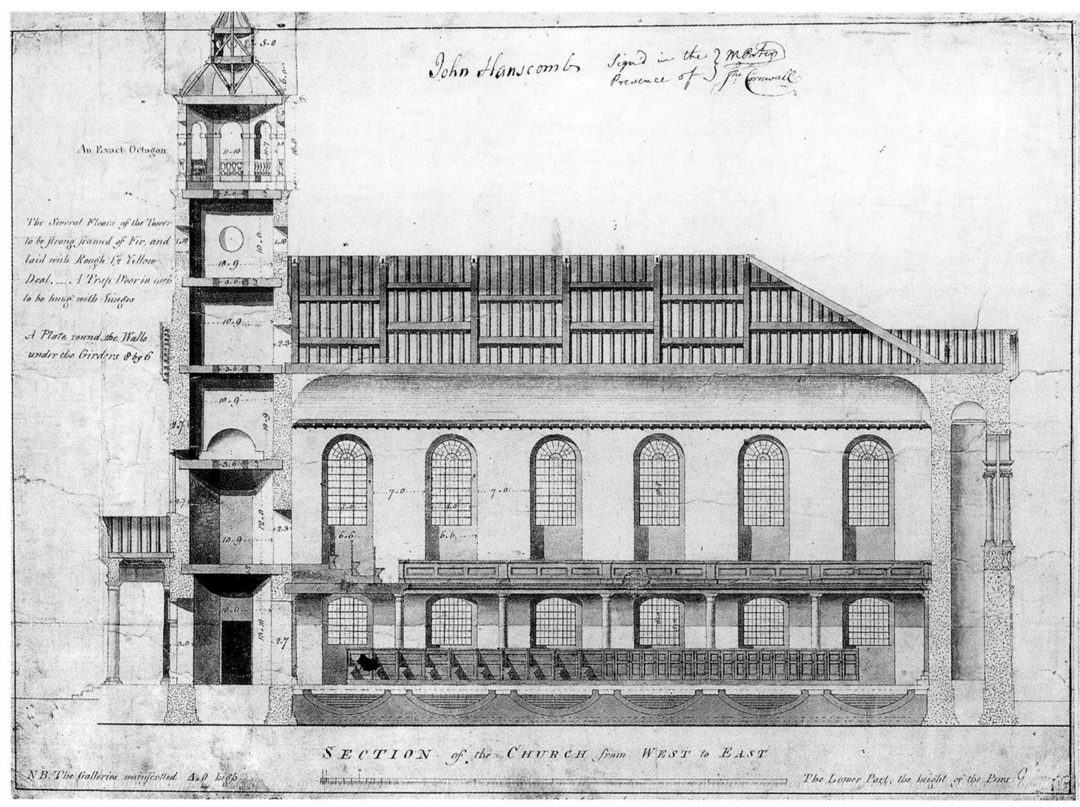

adorned with Niches',[9] whereas at St Leonard, Eastcheap, the Revd Townley sought 'a remedy to the noise of carriages during divine service . . . either by removing the church, or shutting up Grace and Fenchurch streets'. The church eventually vanished.[10] Another option was to reduce the chancel, which in the case of Settrington, Yorkshire, was 'unnecessarily large [and] would be much more convenient for the hearing of the Minister from the Communion Table if . . . Shortned by taking down . . . the East end five Yards and one foot and bringing the East end and window so much forward'.[11] Waltham Abbey, Essex, was 'beautifully cieled, which is a great Advantage to the Congregation in hearing the Voice of the Preacher . . . formerly lost for want thereof'.[12]

At St Paul, Liverpool, the octangular rotunda arrangement of the 'dark grey . . . rude gigantic' columns caused grave acoustical problems: the

> open dome renders the voice extremely indistinct, and in some parts almost unintelligible. Several attempts have been made to remedy this inconvenience; particularly by spreading oiled paper over the bottom of the concave, like parchment upon the head of a drum, but the ears of the audience are not so much benefited, as their sight is offended by this contrivance.[13]

The interior was condemned as 'a positive satire on all order and design . . . neither calculated to hear nor to see', the massive stone columns 'so thick and abundant' that they concealed one half of the congregation from the other; the minister was 'seen by few', the reader's voice 'so lost and unintelligible' due to the lowness of the cupola, 'which like a vortex swallowed all sound', while additional chancel columns added to the 'gloomy horrors of the spot [and] have a chilled and damp effect on the whole auditory'.[14] At St Chad, Shrewsbury (pl. 681), the combined pulpit and desk was positioned strategically in a central arena within the rotunda body so that the minister was conspicuous to the entire congregation. For the same reason the gallery and roof are supported by extravagantly tall, slim, cast-iron columns, the results of heated discussions between the architect, George Steuart, and the building committee on how to solve the problems of seating and echo in a space that needed to be large enough to accommodate some 1,200 souls. When, in 1789, the committee concluded that in the circular design 'the Echo . . . will be very great' and suggested that 'the oblong plan . . . first Approved [of unrecorded appearance] wod . . . be preferable to the present . . . plan in all respects', Steuart pointed out that the 'Manner of the Chancel . . . Columns, Gallery and flat Ceiling all contribute to destroy Echo' and persuaded them that the rectangular design 'is no less liable to Echo which is Ocasioned by the Compact and close finishing where there is not Objects to break and divide the Sound [while the] Oblong removes half the hearers a great way from the preacher'.[15] When asked 'Whether he has had Experience in Churches of this (circular) construction that have been free of Echo', Steuart cited the Countess of Huntingdon's Spa Fields Chapel, Islington, accommodating 800, where 'the preacher [is] Wonderfully well heard', and St Andrew, George Street, Edinburgh (pl. 672), of 'an Oval Shape . . . much Approved'.[16]

Auditory restriction was particularly worrying in the context of increasing competition from the Methodists, its leader John Wesley observing that the Norfolk Street Chapel, Sheffield, Yorkshire (1780, demolished), 'was much crowded, though one of the largest in England; but all could hear distinctly'.[17] Since the problem was blatantly obvious at St Alphage, Cripplegate – contrary to custom the pulpit was attached to the west wall while the congregation faced east towards the altar – it is hardly surprising that so much attention was devoted to the design and position of this item of furniture.[18]

Swift's satirical description in *A Tale of a Tub* (1704) of pulpits as 'Oratorial Machines' strikes irrefutably at their essence.[19] Wren calculated that a 'moderate Voice may be heard 50 Feet distant before the Preacher, 30 Feet on each Side, and 20 behind the Pulpit, and not this, unless the Pronunciation be distinct and equal, without losing the Voice at the last Word of the Sentence, which is commonly emphatical, and if obscur'd spoils the whole Sense'.[20] Maximum impact was achieved by elevating the 'tub' on a stem to facilitate preaching at both floor and gallery levels (pl. 563). Sometimes considerable skill was employed in making final adjustments: at Sunningdale, Berkshire, the churchwardens were ordered to 'putt up a Sounding Board . . . and Rayse the pulpit 6 or 8 inches as shall be adjudged proper'.[21]

From the evidence of surviving drawings and published patterns there is good reason to conclude that architects largely took on responsibility for designing pulpits, with carvers sometimes contributing decorative flourishes, as in the case of the collaboration between Nicholas Hawksmoor and Grinling Gibbons at St Alfege, Greenwich (pl. 129), a wainscoted tub inlaid with 'many Small Figures' supported on a hexagonal stem, the 'Tipe', or sounding board, rising on fluted columns forming an arch. The 71-year-old Gibbons carved 'Raffled Leaf, Husk, & Berrys . . . Grotesque Faces [and] Scrolls . . . wth. Leaves to cover the Irons

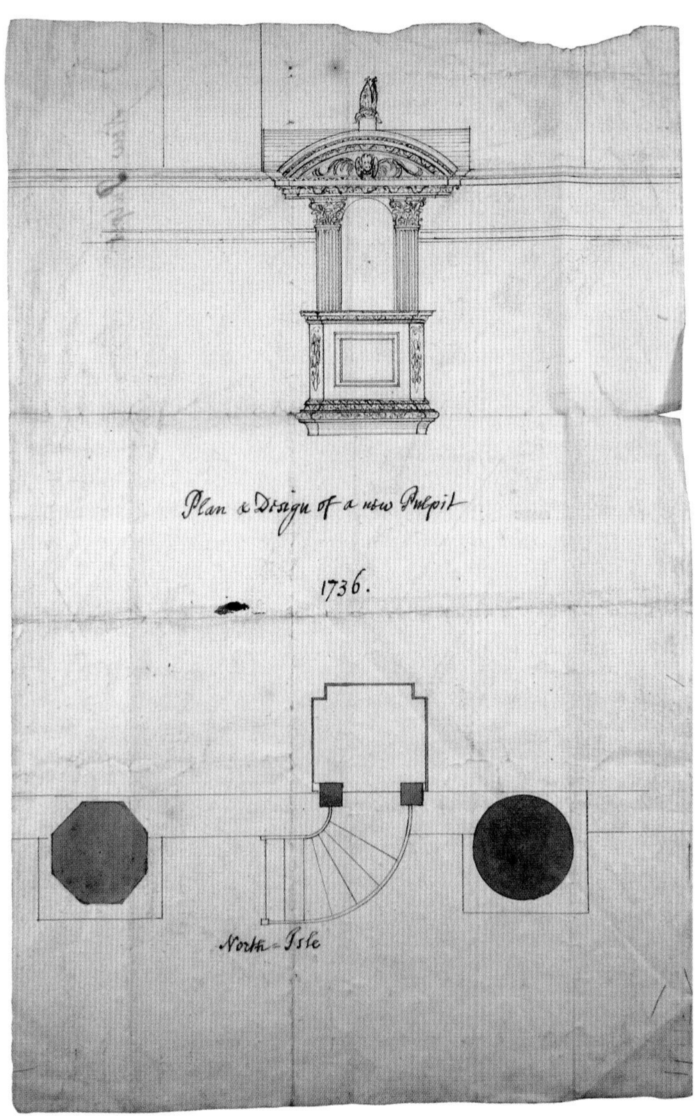

75 John James, attributed. 'Plan & Design of a new Pulpit' for Canterbury Cathedral, Kent, 1736. Pen and ink and wash. Canterbury Cathedral Archives, Dcc/Fabric 5/16.

76 Designer and maker unknown. Pulpit, undated, Stockton-on-Tees parish church, County Durham. Oak. English Heritage (National Monuments Record), A44/14119.

which bear the Pulpit'. The cost was £222 19s. 16d. Destroyed in the Second World War, this was the most splendid and architectonic of the eleven pulpits fashioned between 1717 and 1723 for the New Churches, as well as the best-documented Georgian example.[22] Hawksmoor's influence is apparent in the pulpit erected at St George, Hanover Square (pl. 432), by John James, a Greenwich resident, carpenter by training and Hawksmoor's co-surveyor at St Alfege, and one proposed but never executed for Canterbury Cathedral in 1736 (pl. 75), where James was then in charge of construction.[23] That metropolitan pulpit forms found favour in the provinces is further suggested by strong similarities between George Dance Sr's idiosyncratic

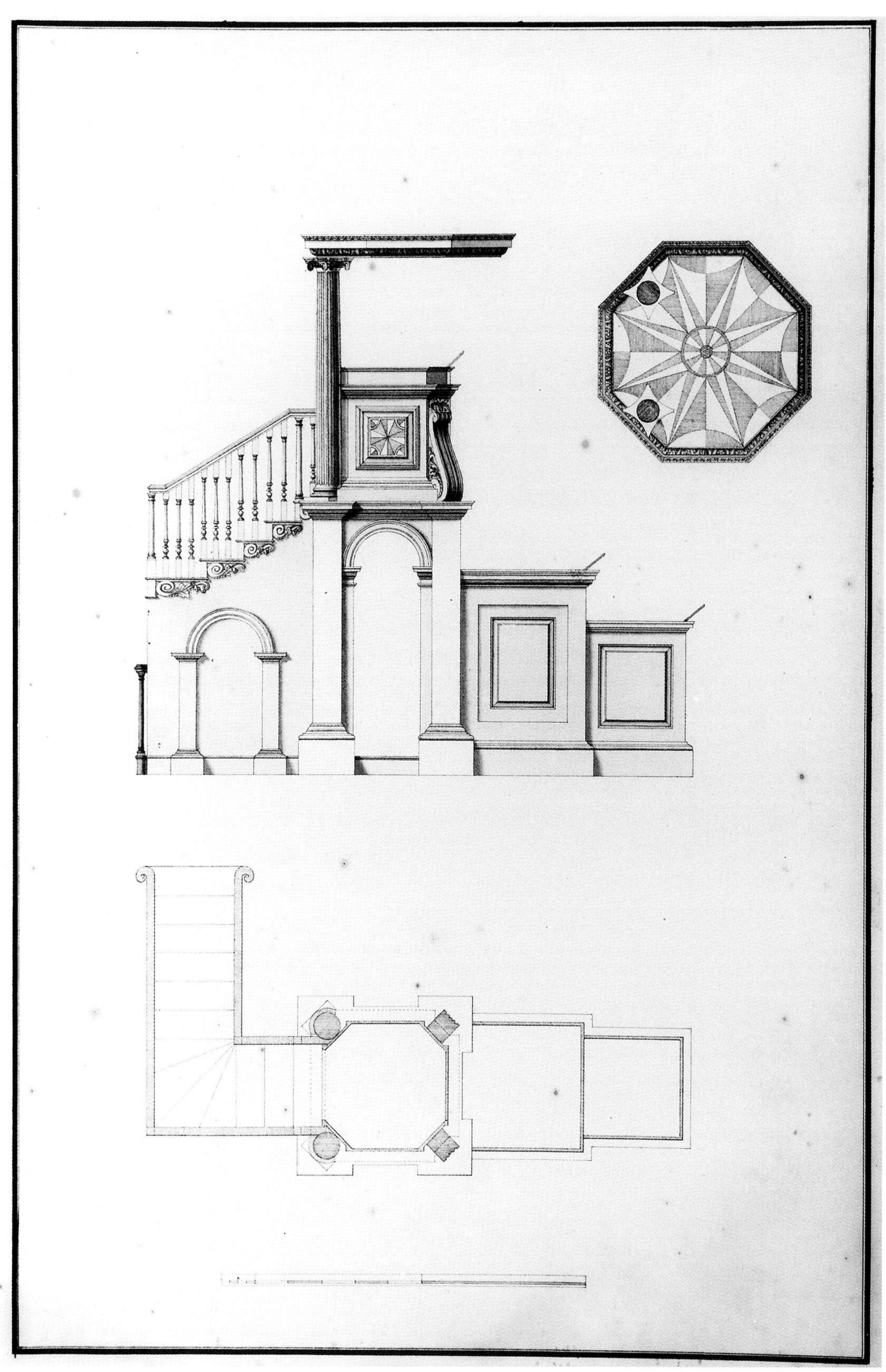

77 George Dance Sr. Design for a pulpit and desk, St Matthew, Bethnal Green, London, 1743–46. Pen and ink and wash. Sir John Soane's Museum, London, 15/9.

77a George Dance Sr. Design for a pulpit and desk, St Matthew, Bethnal Green, London, 1743–46, detail of pl. 77.

design for St Matthew, Bethnal Green (pl. 77), with its scrolled consoles and fluted Ionic columns, and the structure at Stockton-on-Tees, County Durham (pl. 76), a port town with strong mercantile links to the City of London, where Dance served as the influential clerk of the works.[24] James 'Athenian' Stuart and William Newton created a neoclassical masterpiece for Greenwich Hospital chapel (pls 648, 651). Gothic designs were preferred by Robert Adam for Croome d'Abitot, Worcestershire (pls 174, 177), and by Henry Keene for Westminster Abbey (1775, now at Trottiscliffe, Kent), with its tester carried exotically on a palm tree (pl. 213). It is worth noting that the more flamboyant examples of Continental Catholic pulpits, while entrancing English tourists – Sir James Thornhill's son, visiting Bruges Cathedral in 1726, marvelled at the 'fine pulpit which is supported by three figures as big as life neatly Carv'd . . . the top . . . made in form of a glory . . . gilded, with a dove in the center, the whole . . . well design'd & executed' – understandably were never imitated in Britain.[25]

Determining a pulpit's most advantageous location could be hit or miss. At the Reformation, as already mentioned, they had been released from behind the choirscreen and brought closer to the congregation, with the tester, or sounding board, amplifying the preacher's voice, thus acquiring a more central role in worship. Sometimes they were double- or triple-deckered by the additions of reader's and clerk's desks, towering above the congregation. In the eighteenth century there was a short-lived enthusiasm for placement well into one side of the nave, or directly in front of the chancel (pl. 45).[26] The position of the pulpit in the middle aisle of St Mary, Islington, proved 'inconvenient' since this allowed 'very little Room' for people to pass and 'greatly intercepted' the altar, though it was never moved,[27] while the Vestry of St Michael, Bristol, agreed that 'in consideration of the Impropriety of the Situation' to erect a 'temporary' one in the middle aisle 'for a trial whether that direction shall be judg'd more eligible'.[28] At St Mary-le-Strand the joiner, obliged to make a 'Pair of New Twisting Rails to the Stairs . . . in lieu of those Disliked by Mr Gibs', also dismantled the recently completed ensemble of pulpit, reader's and clerk's desks and repositioned it 'nearer the West end', closer to the congregation.[29] A practical if novel solution was to propel the furniture complete with minister around the church, as John Wesley witnessed in 1781 in the octangular Shrewsbury Hospital chapel, Sheffield: 'It rolls upon wheels; and is shifted once a quarter, that all the pews may face it in their turns.' He speculated that this was the 'first contrivance of the kind in Europe',[30] though in the years 1724–6 John Bedell had charged £12 for 'Pulpitt Wheels' for Beverley Minster, which were installed by George Best for 8s. 6d., and an account of 1774 for St Paul, Liverpool, mentions a 'movable pulpit [with] a stair-case in the centre, unseen by the congregation by which the preacher gradually ascends to public view'.[31]

It goes without saying that performing ministers were subjected to both criticism and ridicule. Swift believed the 'Two principal Qualification of a Phanatic Preacher are, his Inward Light, and his Head full of Maggots; and the Two different Fates of his Writing are, to be burnt or worm-eaten.'[32]

> I Went to M–r–d–n one Sabbath even,
> To hear the priest direct the way to heav'n;
> I heard, but could not see; the stately pew,
> And lofty pulpit, hid him from our view;
> With heavenly truths he charms our listning ears,
> The truths we hear; the preacher ne'er appears;
> Then laugh no more when Homer's tripods walk,
> Since now our desks can pray, and pulpits talk.[33]

In 1775 Dr Thomas Campbell 'stepped in to St Martin-in-the-Field', but 'cd: get no farther than the door; such a crowd I never saw under one roof', since the Revd Richard Harrison was

> in the pulpit . . . No bombast-player in Tom Thumb or Chrononhoton & ever so roared & so bellowed

as he did – & his manner was as lifeless as his manner was Hyper-tragic . . . it was those ways . . . which made his pass for a fine preacher. And this is a strong example, what action in the pulpit can achieve.[34]

Campbell also reported on 'the most meagre . . . discourse . . . on our Saviours temptation' at Temple Church – 'a most beautiful Gothic structure – where the minister stood, like Gulliver stuck in the marrow bone . . . without grace or emphasis . . . in slow cadence', followed the same evening at Westminster, where the sermon was 'still duller & as ill delivered'. At St Clement's he was 'wofully disappointed' with the Revd Burrows, 'His matter is cold, his manner hot, his voice weak, & his action affected'. Ill-fated Dr Dodd (pl. 59) 'leans too much upon his notes [and] mises the action of an extempore delivery, which makes a jaring jumble'.[35] Nor was Campbell alone disenchanted with preaching techniques. The anonymous 'O' complained that 'Our preachers stand stock still in the pulpit, and will not so much as move a finger to set off the best sermon in the world.'[36]

So, when one crop-sick parson, in a doze
Is reading morning-service through his nose,
Another in the pulpit straight appears,
Claiming the tired-out congregation's ears,
And with a duller sermon ends their prayr's.[37]

The following advice appeared in the *Gentleman's Magazine*: 'Directions how to make and preach a Sermon that shall please', 'Hints to the Clergy', 'Art of Preaching', 'Hints to the Clergy on their Delivery', 'Fragments of a Rhapsody on the Art of Preaching', 'Hints to the Clergy, relative to their Conduct in the Pulpit'.[38]

Petrus Apo
Johannes Apo
Jacobus Apo

Eight

THE BATTLE BETWEEN DECORATION AND ADORATION

Th' *Almighty Architect* forms in Mankind
The Heart, and nobler Organs of the Soul,
In the first place; so here first built we find
The sacred *Choire*, that animates the Whole.[1]

The Frenchman André Rouquet, in *The Present State of the Arts in England* (1755), could be excused for concluding that Protestantism 'does not avail itself of the assistance of painting to inspire devotion', but disingenuous in claiming that 'their churches at the most are adorned with an altar-piece, which no body takes notice of'.[2] In fact, the altar, together with the pulpit, were the focal points of Anglican worship, as the quote opening this chapter makes perfectly clear. Edward Hatton's *A New View of London* (1708), promoted as 'a more particular Description . . . than . . . hitherto . . . known . . . of any City in the World', devotes 490 pages to churches with special attention to altarpieces. For example: Wren's St Bride is 'beautiful and magnificent', its columns 'painted Flake-stone colour', with 'a handsome . . . Window, adorned with a neat Scarlet-silk Curtain edged with Gold Fringe' and over a 'painted *Nebulous* and above the Clouds appears (from within a large Crimson Velvet Festoon painted Curtain) a Celestial Choir, or a Representation of the Church Triumphant, in the Vision and Presence of a Glory in the shape of a Dove, all finely painted, the Enrichments are gilt'; alas, all now vanished.[3] Some idea of their impact is preserved in the vivid colours of eighteenth-century painted glass (pl. 78) and in a wonderful sampler embroidered by young Elizabeth Hewett in 1732 (pl. 79), with its depiction of Moses and Aaron flanking the Decalogue (the recitation of the Ten Commandments as revealed on Mount Sinai had been introduced into the Communion office in the 1552 Book of Common Prayer) and Christ's Ascension and a trumpeting Gabriel in the spandrels.

Altarpieces are particularly accurate fashion barometers. The richly sophisticated structure at All Saints, Oxford (pl. 80), was erected in 1718 while Nicholas Hawksmoor was involved in completing Henry Aldrich's building and employing the decorative vocabulary of St Paul's Cathedral choir, which had been built during the years (1691–1712) when he assisted Wren in preparing working drawings.[4] It was similar to the ones Hawksmoor used in the New Churches: that at St Mary Woolnoth, for example, is composed of Corinthian columns 'fill'd with wreathes . . . surrounded wth. Chaplets of Leaves . . . Tables for Commandments . . . crown'd with a large . . . Canopy wth . . . Cherubs Heads . . . & other Enrichments', costing £215.[5] At the height of Palladian taste, John Joshua Kirby, who rose to become drawing master to the future George III, designed one for Hadleigh, Suffolk (pl. 81). It is described in considerable detail in the contract as composed of an

> Entablature with a Compass pediment in the Middle . . . the under part . . . finished with a plain Dado . . . frame worke & pannells . . . large Mouldings . . . carved for the Lords prayer Decalogue Cred . . . figures of Moses & Aaron . . . under each . . . a festoon . . . the Entablature . . . continued the whole

78 *(facing page)* William Peckitt. *St Peter, St John the Evangelist and St James*, formerly in St John Deansgate, Manchester, Lancashire, 1769, now in St Anne, Manchester. Enamel paint on glass.

79 Elizabeth Hewett. Sampler depicting a high altar with Decalogue, Moses and Aaron and angels, dated 1732. Linen plain weave with silk embroidery. Philadelphia Museum of Art, Bequest of Mrs. William R. Mercer 1960-60-11.

80 Michael Burghers. 'A Prospect of the Altar piece of All Saints Church in Oxford', 1718. Engraving. © The British Library Board, K.Top. XXXIII.26-c. Nicholas Hawksmoor, attributed.

> width of the Altar . . . inriched with [Doric] Modillion Tryglyphs . . . wrought of the best Wainscott

by the Ipswich joiner Josiah Harris. The contract further specified that Kirby 'in a Workmanlike manner to the best of his skill & ability [should] Draw & paint . . . the figures . . . in their proper or usual Coloures & Ornaments . . . gild the . . . pannells . . . write . . . with Black . . . paint a Glory with Cherubims in the . . . Pediment . . . together with seven Vases', at a cost of £15 15s. 0d., the total charge being £52 10s. 0d. The structure was later removed.[6] Other styles were also catered for. John Carter, who was later to emerge as one of the most vocal exponents of medievalism, published in 1778 a 'Gothic ALTAR-PIECE' as a demonstration of the application of an 'exceedingly light, delicate and rich abundance of little, whimsical, wild and chimerical ornaments'.[7] In 1785 John Butler erected an 'elegant superb altarpiece in stucco plaister' at Martock, Somerset (designer unknown, since destroyed), 'as a testimony of his regard and affection for the church and place of his nativity'. Its triumphal form, imitating

81 John Joseph Kirby. Design for the altarpiece, St Mary, Hadleigh, Suffolk, 1744. Pen and ink and wash. Centre for Kentish Studies, U23 Q3/1.

Robert Adam's monument to Elizabeth, Duchess of Northumberland (1778), among the grandest in Westminster Abbey, epitomises provincial aspirations.[8]

However, comparatively few eighteenth-century altarpieces survive completely intact, as depicted in Miss Hewett's sampler (pl. 79), with its tripartite columnar structure, draped table laid with silver-gilt chalice, paten and candlesticks, altar rails and black and white marble paving, perhaps a true record of her local (unidentified) church. The choice of silks may even reflect the actual colour scheme.[9]

The appropriateness of elaborate painted imagery was among the chief religious debates in eighteenth-century England.

Q. *What is a 16th Error of the Papists?*
A. Their worshipping of Images.
Q. *What is the* Protestant's *Belief?*
A. That it is not lawful to make Images of GOD;
nor to direct our Worship to an Image,
or by the help of an Image;
or to give religious Worship to any Creature.[10]

Joseph Trapp, a preacher attached to St Martin-in-the-Fields, supported unreservedly the contentious decision taken by Christopher Vane, Lord Barnard of Fairlawn, Kent, in 1722 to embellish with uncommon pictorial lavishness the newly built parish church at nearby Shipbourne (both the house and church were designed by the Catholic James Gibbs). Trapp's un-puritanical consecration sermon of 1723 carefully reasoned that

> It might be . . . objected by Some *that Parish-Churches, at least in obscure Country-Villages, should not be* fine, *and* splendid. *But They seem not to consider, that the Almighty Author of our Being is no less the GOD of the Country as well as of the* City, *than of the* Valleys *as well as of the* Hills [from I Kings 20:28]. *If there be any Difference; the Advantage is rather on This Side. How delightful is it to see such a beauteous sacred Edifice, encompass'd with Fields, Trees, and Meadows; The Artificial Gilding of That and the Natural Verdure of These casting a mutual Lustre upon Each other, and Both upon the Creator! This Contraste is thought proper, when Houses are built for Men: And why should it not be so, when they are built for* God? *If Any look with a* malignant Eye *upon This pious and Charitable Work . . . let him seriously reflect upon That of the Psalmist, the one Part applicable to* [Lord Barnard], *the other to Himself* [Psalms 112:9–10].

Trapp believed

> that in the Building, Finishing, and Preserving of [churches], *Decency* at least is necessary; and even *Magnificence* highly commendable. God is *honour'd* by the *Stateliness* and *Elegancy of Houses* dedicated to his . . . *Service* [which] is apt to assist our Devotions; by filling us with awful and reverential Thoughts of the Divine Majesty . . . the distinguishing Habits of Those who minister in holy Things, the sacred Utensils, Church-Musick, Paintings, Gilding, Carvings, and all Ornaments whatsoever. In all which, the Medium should be kept between too much Plainness and Simplicity on the one Extreme; and too much Lightness, Gayety, and Gaudiness on the other. Much more should the Middle be maintain'd between no Ornaments, Beauty, nor even Decency at all, the Extremes of some Protestants in our Country; and extravagant, immoderate Ornaments, superstitious Foppery, and gross Idolatry, the Extreme of the Papists in all Countries, where their most corrupt Religion prevails . . . And if Some will be so perverse as not to distinguish between *Decoration* and *Adoration*; we are sorry for it, but cannot help it.[11]

What could be plainer?

Many of these ideas had been anticipated by, perhaps even derived from, James Lacy's published *Sermon Preach'd at the Consecration of a Church in the Parish of Castle-Ton, near Sherborne, Dorset. September 7. 1715* (London, 1715), which stressed that once early Christianity had been established churchmen

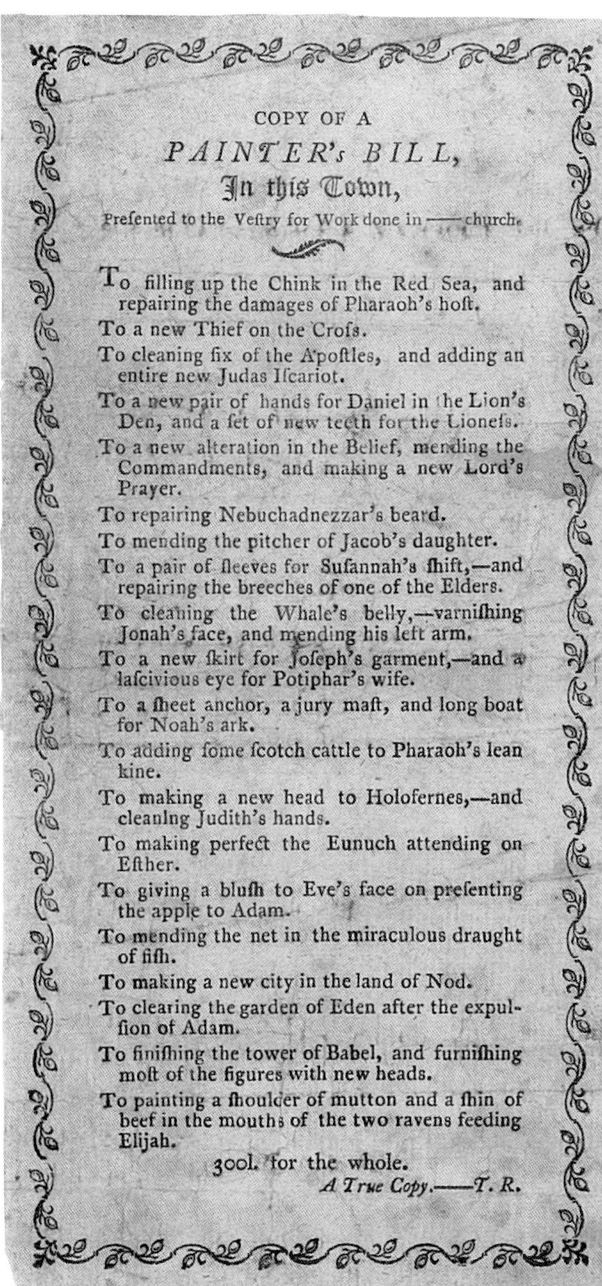

COPY OF A

PAINTER's BILL,

In this Town,

Preſented to the Veſtry for Work done in ——church.

To filling up the Chink in the Red Sea, and repairing the damages of Pharaoh's hoſt.

To a new Thief on the Croſs.

To cleaning ſix of the Apoſtles, and adding an entire new Judas Iſcariot.

To a new pair of hands for Daniel in the Lion's Den, and a ſet of new teeth for the Lioneſs.

To a new alteration in the Belief, mending the Commandments, and making a new Lord's Prayer.

To repairing Nebuchadnezzar's beard.

To mending the pitcher of Jacob's daughter.

To a pair of ſleeves for Suſannah's ſhift,—and repairing the breeches of one of the Elders.

To cleaning the Whale's belly,—varniſhing Jonah's face, and mending his left arm.

To a new ſkirt for Joſeph's garment,—and a laſcivious eye for Potiphar's wife.

To a ſheet anchor, a jury maſt, and long boat for Noah's ark.

To adding ſome ſcotch cattle to Pharaoh's lean kine.

To making a new head to Holofernes,—and cleanlng Judith's hands.

To making perfect the Eunuch attending on Eſther.

To giving a bluſh to Eve's face on preſenting the apple to Adam.

To mending the net in the miraculous draught of fiſh.

To making a new city in the land of Nod.

To clearing the garden of Eden after the expulſion of Adam.

To finiſhing the tower of Babel, and furniſhing moſt of the figures with new heads.

To painting a ſhoulder of mutton and a ſhin of beef in the mouths of the two ravens feeding Elijah.

300l. for the whole.

A True Copy.——T. R.

82 'T. R.', 'Copy of a Painter's Bill In this Town Presented to the Vestry for Work done in ___ Church', undated, reproduced actual size. Engraving. Author's collection.

spared *no* Cost, and thought nothing too *dear*, not only to *Build*, but to *Beautify* and *Adorn* those *Sacred Edifices*. Expences of that Nature went under the Name of *Piety* and *Devotion*, and none counted *That* Waste, which was expended about so *Religious* a Work . . . *Are not such Places more apt to excite Devotion, than Places of common Use?* . . . and strikes a kind of Awe into our Thoughts, when we reflect upon that *Sacred Majesty* we . . . converse with there. And the *Beauty* and *Comeliness* of it, not only takes our Eye, and pleases it, but carrieth also its *Profit* along with it, *enlivens* our *Devotion*, rouses it when it *slumbers*, and *recalls* it when it *wanders* . . . as the *Soul* receives Impressions through the *Senses*, to the *Devotion* of it may be heightened by the *Loftiness*, the *Beauty* and *Ornaments* of the *Temple*.

Lacy applauded: 'That we have *Comliness* without affected *Gaudiness*; *Gravity* without *Morosity*; no *Ornaments*, no *Usages* administring to *Superstition* or *Idolatry*.'[12] Interestingly, this was also the policy pursued by Zachariah Pearce, Chaplain in Ordinary to His Majesty and vicar of St Martin-in-the-Fields, the royal parish church, in his consecration sermon of the church in 1726 (pls 416–17), describing it as a

> Stately Fabrick . . . eminent among all other Parochial Ones for the Beauty and Grandeur of its Structure, and for the innocent Richness and Propriety of its Ornament; exhibiting nothing that is either Idolatrous or Superstitious, nothing that can mislead true Piety, or that tends to abate its Vigour; having nothing calculated to affect the Fancy more than the Heart, nothing fitted to raise the Mind upwards so much as in Devotion.[13]

It is a mark of the success of Gibbs's ability to subsume his Catholic tendencies in the creation of this Protestant masterpiece. Shipbourne also represented a notable pioneer manifestation of enlightened Georgian attitudes towards Protestant decoration and the proliferation of religious subject matter in churches. This was satirised in an undated and clearly spurious Georgian painter's bill (pl. 82).[14]

Sir James Thornhill's decoration of St Paul's Cathedral dome (1709–21), 'confined to the Scripturall History taken from the Acts of the Apostles', was the triumphant outcome of a competition with rival foreign Catholic artists – John Talman reported from Rome hearing that 'two very pitifull painters are Setting out for England to paint the Cupola', each no more than 'a Scene painter' – with one committeeman reputed to have insisted that the winner 'be a Protestant [and] an Englishman'.[15] In 1755 the British public was treated to an astonishing proposal conveyed in a magnificent engraving measuring 25 by 34 inches, dedicated to George, Prince of Wales, priced 12s. (pl. 83), for radically transforming the internal appearance of the national cathedral by means of a dazzling programme of painting and sculpture on the dual themes of religious renewal and military prowess. The scheme's co-authors, the architect John Gwynn and the engraver Samuel Wale, envisaged it as 'promoting the advance-

To his Royal Highness George Prince of Wales,
This SECTION of St. Paul's Cathedral, decorated agreeably to the original INTENTION of Sr. Christopher Wren;
Is, with all humility, inscribed, by his Royal Highness's most devoted, and most Obedient humble Servants.

83 (*facing page, and details above left and right*) Edward Rooker after John Gwynn and Samuel Wale. 'Section of St. Paul's Cathedral; decorated agreeably to the original Intention of Sir. Christopher Wren', showing dome and transept towards chancel, 27 May 1755. Engraving. © The British Library Board, K. Top. 23-36-e.

ment of grandeur and elegance' in public buildings – the Cathedral as Public Museum.[16] They also claimed it represented the crossing and choir 'decorated agreeably to the original INTENTION of . . . Wren', though contemporary evidence to support this is vague and should be regarded with caution.[17] More likely it was a response to the notion that the cathedral 'deserves particular Attention [as] the finest Out-side of any Church in the World, and might be the finest In-side also, if the Religion of the Country allow'd *Altars* with *Statues*, and paintings at every Pillar, as in *Italy*'.[18] An overly ambitious failure exiled to art historical limbo, the scheme of 1755 has never succeeded in finding a deservedly secure place in recent discussions of Georgian architecture, let alone of painting or of sculpture.[19] Thornhill's celebrated dome decoration was to be preserved, while the empty niches encircling the drum were to be filled with single statues and the bare walls of the Whispering Gallery with narratives, including a clearly identifiable *Stoning of St Stephen*, together with emblematic figures and New Testament inscriptions in the pendentives. This resembles current Continental practice.[20]

Below this the decoration is wholly unexpected in the Anglican context. The surfaces of the crossing,

84 William Talman, Grinling Gibbons, Caius Gabriel Cibber, Louis Laguerre and Antonio Verrio. Chatsworth House chapel towards the high altar, Derbyshire, 1687–1704. © Chatsworth Settlement Trust.

transepts and choir, which had remained unembellished since the completion of the fabric in the 1710s, were to be overwhelmed by a riot of exuberant paintings and sculpture: a Veronesian *Last Supper* revealed by *putti* drawing drapery up into the figure-infested entablature, filling the middle window of the choir and perhaps intended to be painted on glass.[21] The vaulting and upper crossing arches feature elaborate sculpture groups depicting *Christ's Resurrection* and two *Evangelists*; the clerestory windows have further seated figures, drapery, festooned *putti*, large and small paintings depicting the *Garden of Gethsemane*, the *Good Samaritan* and again *St Stephen's Stoning* filling the intercolumniation. In Wren's transept recesses are free-standing, secular monuments honouring unidentified military heroes, one incorporating cannon, presumably memorialising the war between Britain and France during the preceding decade.[22]

Utterly anathema to English Protestant sensibilities – the July 1755 issue of *The Connoisseur* observed: 'Should anyone propose to take down from St Paul's Cathedral those paintings by . . . Thornhill . . . and in their place to set up Titian's pictures of the amours of ancient gods, everyone would be shocked at the impiety of the proposal. Nor is the fashion of introducing heathen deities into our monuments much less absurd' – this extraordinary programme, nearly verging on the papistic, was doomed to failure. Nonetheless, this was not quite the end of the story. In 1773 Sir Joshua Reynolds, President of the Royal Academy, generously offered the services gratis of his fellow academicians to adorn the 'too plain' interior of St Paul's Cathedral in an attempt to argue a case that the 'art of painting would never grow up to maturity and perfection, unless it could be introduced into churches, as in foreign countries'. His appeal fell on deaf ears, the Bishop of London and the Archbishop of Canterbury claiming that 'it would occasion a great noise and clamour . . . as an artful intrusion of popery'. When the R. A. again broached the subject to the dean and chapter in 1796 its letter went unanswered.[23]

Sumptuous pictorial programmes, however, were acceptable in the private sector, with precedents set in the late seventeenth century in the King's Chapel, Windsor (1680–82, destroyed), and at Chatsworth, Derbyshire (pl. 84). The latter was described by Celia Fiennes in 1697 as a 'very lofty' (48 by 27 foot) double-storey room with

> 4 large pillars of black marble two at the altar 2 just at the bottom to support the gallery for the Duke and Duches [of Devonshire] to sitt in; the pillars are 14 foote and so bigg that I could not compass one with my arms . . . and so finely polish'd like a looking-glass; the pavement is black and white marble vein'd lay'd longways in large stones all of the same.[24]

Its most striking architectural feature is the elaborately carved, apsidal-shaped marble and alabaster altarpiece resplendent with Ionic and Corinthian pilasters, statues of Faith and Justice, a coat of arms with '3 Cherubim Heads Leather worke . . . 2 double ffestoons hanging from . . . the Urnes . . . Sheets of Drapery hanging . . . 17 ft. long on the Sweep, tied up in a Knot', 'a Dove in Glory in the Rayes 21 in. diameter . . . branches of Olives . . . Wheat-eares . . . Beads . . . ruffled Leaves . . . Lace . . . Egg and Husks . . . Eggs and Ankers . . . 37 Panels with Roses' engulfing Antonio Verrio's *Christ and the Doubting St Thomas*, 'a most excellent & masterly peice . . . not improperly esteem'd the best of his workes' in an octagonal, black marble frame.[25] This

85 Sebastiano Ricci. Oil sketch for the *Baptism of Christ*, north wall of Bulstrode House chapel, Buckinghamshire, 1712–14, demolished 1862. Metropolitan Museum of Art, New York.

architectural and decorative exuberance is reflected in five early Georgian interiors, two long vanished.

Henry Bentinck, 1st Duke and 2nd Earl of Portland's chapel at Bulstrode House, Buckinghamshire (1712–14), a cedar-lined room measuring 24 by 42 feet located at the end of the picture gallery, apparently had no striking architectural presence and relied entirely on its sumptuous baroque effect from large-scale frescoes covering the upper walls and ceiling executed by the great Venetian painter Sebastiano Ricci, admired for their 'Noble free invention. great force of lights & shade. with variety & freedom. in the composition of the parts'.[26] Destroyed when the house was demolished in 1862, the appearance of the interior, except for the *Annunciation* over the west gallery, can be reconstructed from surviving oil sketches. An oval *Ascension of Christ* (Shipley Art Gallery, Gateshead, Co. Durham) covered the ceiling, while on the north and south walls respectively were the *Baptism of Christ*, set on the River Jordan under a sky streaked with sunlit clouds (pl. 85), and the *Last Supper* (National Gallery of Art, Washington, DC), in which the artist himself appears 'in a Modern habit comeing into the room'.[27] Both are framed within *trompe-l'œil* proscenium arches, as if enacting biblical tableaux, with cartouches carrying relevant scriptural texts, angels and gilt statues of the Four Evangelists standing on *putti*-enhanced brackets, all accurately casting shadows as if illuminated from the real east windows above the altarpiece, which contained William Price's richly painted glass depicting the *Stoning of St Stephen* (lost) and *Conversion of St Paul* (now in St Andrew-by-the-Wardrobe, London). The architect is unrecorded, but perhaps not coincidentally four other similar interiors – at Cannons, Whitchurch, Wimpole and Great Witley – were created by James Gibbs, a Scots Catholic trained in Rome between 1703 and 1708.

The chapel attached to Cannons House near London (1716–20), built for James Brydges, Earl of Caernarvon (later 1st Duke of Chandos), Paymaster to the Troops, a person of immense wealth and extravagant taste, the 'Princely Chandos', was intended to emulate 'a grand *Versailles*'.[28] Components itemised in the demolition sale catalogue of 1747, some still surviving in their rein-

stated locations, together with contemporary descriptions and the architect's presentation drawings (pl. 380), reveal a plain brick and stone, single-cell, 25 by 70 foot rectangle, internally richly articulated by full-height paired fluted Corinthian pilasters, an elaborate, canopied family pew raised over the west lobby, a monumental tripartite Serliana surmounting the eastern altarpiece and a flat ceiling containing three large, polylobed oil paintings depicting the *Nativity*, *Crucifixion* and *Annunciation*, with ten smaller roundels of *putti* holding emblems of the Passion, by the Venetian-born Antonio Bellucci, then working in England, enframed within gilt plasterwork by Gibbs's favourite Swiss *stuccatore* Giovanni Bagutti. This powerfully Italianate space was set ablaze with jewel-like colours flooding through Joshua Price's ten large painted glass windows depicting the *Annunciation*, *Visitation*, *Adoration of the Shepherds*, *Adoration of the Magi*, *Miraculous Draught of Fishes*, *Healing the Lame*, *Resurrection*, *Supper at Emmaus*, *Worship of the Golden Calf* and *Baptism of Christ* (pl. 86), based on cartoons attributed to both Sebastiano Ricci and Francesco Sleter.[29] The windows and canvases were reinstated by Gibbs at Great Witley, Worcestershire (pl. 90); the plasterwork, which is not listed in the sale catalogue, does not seem to have survived demolition, but some notion of its appearance is perhaps reflected in a contemporary, rejected scheme for St Martin-in-the-Fields (pl. 126).

At nearby Whitchurch Gibbs simultaneously completed the interior of the parish church (1713–15) by John James, whom he had recently replaced in Brydges's affections. The modest 43 by 95 foot rectangle was expanded visually by covering the walls and ceiling with illusionist paintings by Louis Laguerre and Francesco Sleter of statues of *Virtues*, set in robustly baroque niches, and grisaille panels depicting the *Life of Christ*; the coved family pew is canopied by Bellucci's colourful *Transfiguration* (pl. 87). Brydges's 'favourite Hands . . . rais'd a PILE to Heaven . . . in a most Beautiful manner', rhapsodised Charles Gildon in *Canons; or, The Vision* (1717).[30]

The lateral subdivision of the segmental arched ceiling by coffered and rosetted bands, a leitmotif of Gibbs's St Mary-le-Strand (pl. 379), reappeared again in

86 (*above left*) Joshua Price. *Baptism of Christ*, detail, 1716–20. Enamel paint on glass. Removed from Cannons House chapel, Middlesex, 1747, now in St Michael, Great Witley, Worcestershire.

87 (*left*) John James, James Gibbs, Antonio Bellucci, Louis Laguerre and Francesco Sleter. Interior towards west gallery, St. Lawrence, Whitchurch, Middlesex, 1714–20.

88 James Gibbs. Plan and section design for Wimpole Hall chapel, Cambridgeshire, 1719. Pen and ink and wash. Sir John Soane's Museum, London, Folio II Misc. Wren Box no. 19.

his preliminary study for Wimpole Hall chapel in 1719 for Edward Harley, 2nd Earl of Oxford (pl. 88). Here they spring from paired fluted Ionic pilasters raised on wainscot panelling. The blind arches above the rectangular windows are decorated with shells, in the manner of Borromini's 'Conchiglia' in San Carlo alle Quattro Fontane in Rome (pl. 363).[31] Fenestrated along both long walls, the room would have been light-filled, precisely defining the dominantly architectural grid, but the decision to build service rooms in the courtyard to the north of the chapel wing released its now solid inner wall for a gorgeously festive treatment, in which Thornhill's over-life-size grisaille statues of the four *Church Fathers*, an iconography apparently based on Tournai Cathedral, which the artist had visited, are framed by repeated *trompe-l'œil* Serliana, each containing a shell-capped niche, with the paired columns crowned by seated *amorini* (pl. 89).[32] In a preliminary sketch the western end of the wall at gallery level features a peeping figure drawing aside drapery, perhaps Thornhill himself imitating Ricci at Bulstrode (pl. 85).

89 James Gibbs and Sir James Thornhill. Interior towards altar of Wimpole Hall Chapel, 1719–24. The National Trust.

As executed, the gallery niches contain feigned urns with reliefs of the *Baptism of Christ* and the *Last Supper*, repeating Bulstrode's iconography. The coved ceiling is occupied relentlessly with bright blue and gilt rosetted octagonal coffers, prompting a French visitor in 1728 to observe that the 'colours are not perfectly chosen . . . they look like illuminations'.[33] On the east wall the architect's previously proposed plain altarpiece was transformed into the painter's dramatic tableau of the *Virgin and Child with the Adoration of the Magi* set within an illusionist equivalent of Cannons's Serliana, hung with red velvet curtains drawn up by flying *amorini*, as if the biblical action is being performed within a theatre proscenium, with the central figures standing impossibly forward of one of the contorted columns. This was the last of the English private chapels dominated by *trompe-l'œil* figurative painting. Henceforth, an architectural language became increasingly de rigueur.

90 James Gibbs. Interior towards chancel, Witley chapel, Worcestershire, 1733–47.

Chandos's death in 1744 without a male heir sealed Cannons's fate. In 1747 Samuel Gale wrote his friend the Revd William Stukeley:

> Yesterday I went . . . to visit the . . . noble palace . . . which, alas! is now to be sold purely to be demolished for the sake of the beautifull materials . . . I see vast havock amongst vases, statues . . . the tearing down of the fine painted ceilings . . . the noble stuckos & gilding, which . . . will be in a few days dissipated to the 4 quarters of the isleand; the chapel . . . will be last destroyed. Alas! I lament the fate of the glorious painted windows . . . casting a dim religious lighte, & the well tuned organ now struck dumb . . . Such is the sad vicissitude of human grandeur. Half a century has seen a great estate raised & reduced to nothing.

Stukeley replied:

> Your account . . . was a perfect tragi-comedy, & your peroration from the pulpit drew tears from the nodding marble pillasters, from the painted figures on the ceiling. When our nobility are become so wicked as to cast off all religion, we expect they will in turn become thus forlorn, cast out of the hand of providence, who raised 'em to dignity on purpose to set good examples to the world.[34]

The dispersal is recorded in copies of the sale catalogues annotated with buyers' names, which identifies items now at Holy Trinity, Gosport, Hampshire, and Fawley, Buckinghamshire.[35]

But it was at Great Witley, Worcestershire, an earlier mansion remodelled from 1733 for Thomas, 1st Lord Foley, a former Commissioner for Building Fifty New Churches and relative of the Harleys of Wimpole, and his heirs, that Gibbs brilliantly recycled Cannons's cast-offs. His three-by-five-bay brick and stone-trimmed structure (1733–5, recast in stone *circa* 1860), linked at the east end by a passage to the picture gallery of the great house (now a ruin), is the most spectacular ecclesiastical interior of the 1740s (pl. 90). This advanced expression of late baroque moving towards rococo is unique in England, yet an anachronism, since by that date no heavyweight religious painters capable of working on an heroic scale, either foreign or native, were practising in England, and such sumptuous display could be fabricated only by adapting ostentatious though bargain-priced jetsam:[36] thus, the punctuations of Joshua Price's painted pictorial windows purchased

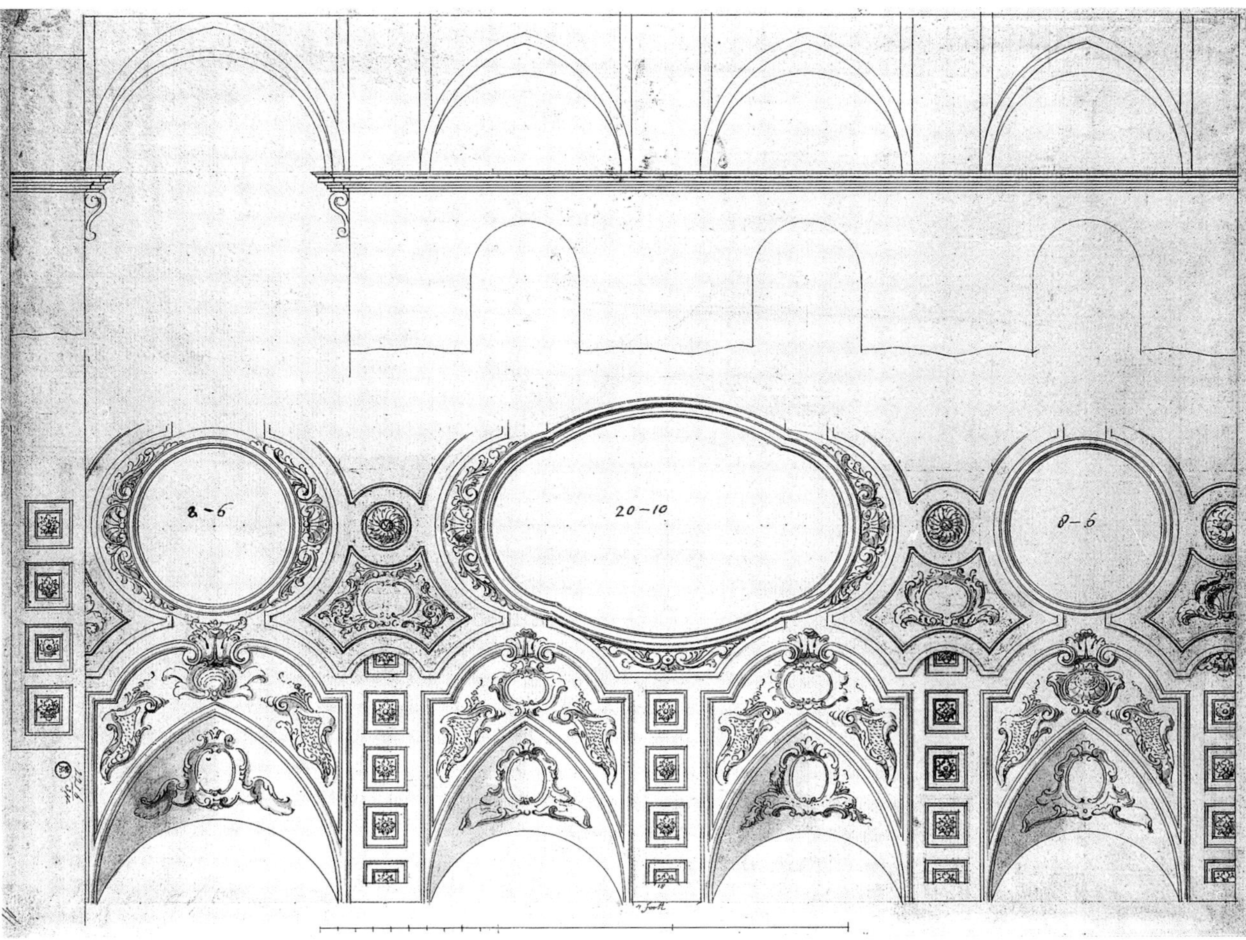

91 James Gibbs. Design for a new ceiling, Witley chapel (St Michael), Great Witley, Worcestershire, 1747. Pen and ink and wash. Victoria and Albert Museum, 2216-34.

from Cannons for £278 5s. 6d., which, in order to fit their new, longer openings, required bands of foliage painted by his son William Price inserted at their bottoms (pl. 86). Gibbs's sole surviving preparatory drawing (pl. 91) indicates (in the linear upper register) his original structure of 1735, with plain walls and ceilings and minimum architectural detailing, while beneath, embellished with wash, his later proposal (datable not earlier than Chandos's death in 1744) for inserting a segmental membrane below the still existing flat ceiling, with empty spaces awaiting Bellucci's thirteen oils on canvas. These are unlisted in the 1747 sale catalogue, which suggests that they were previously negotiated by private treaty. Since Cannons's elaborate plasterwork, of unknown appearance, could not be safely removed intact, Gibbs offered a new, more up-to-date ornamental programme. His signature bands of rosetted coffering are now interrupted on their course across the ceiling by a shallow overlay of isolated single rosettes, shells, foliage and cartouches, of a type already employed at St Martin-in-the-Fields and published as 'Compartments for Monumental Inscriptions' in plates 128–35 of *A Book of Architecture* (1728), now treated more playfully in a manner difficult to reconcile with a date contemporary with Cannons but closer in spirit to Roman work of the 1740s.[37] What makes Witley's ceiling special is Lady Luxborough's observation in 1751 that the ornaments are 'a sort of stucco-paper [papier mâché] . . . stamped so deep as to project considerably and . . . very thick and strong . . . the ornaments are all detached, and put on separately . . . and when finished, cannot . . . be known from fretwork'. They proved 'quite as beautiful, and more durable, than either wood or stucco; and for ceilings infinitely preferable, especially as they may be moved, being only fastened with tacks'. The decorations continue on the walls and window splays, as noted by Richard Pococke in 1756. When William Shenstone visited in 1762 he praised the

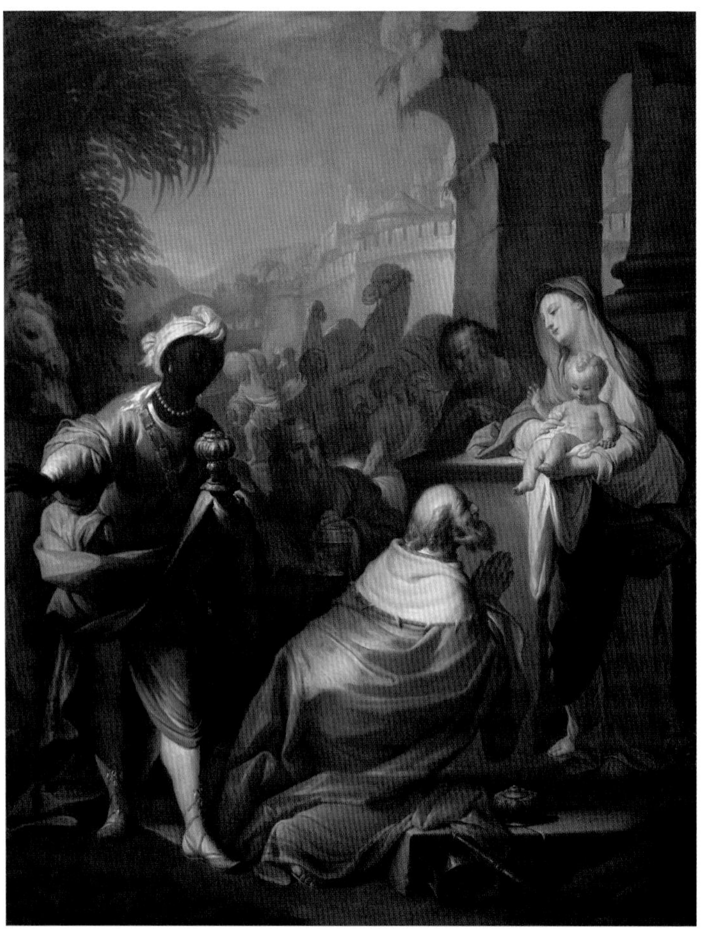

92 Andrea Casali. *Adoration of the Magi*, altarpiece from the Foundling Hospital chapel, London, 1750. Oil on canvas. The Foundling Museum, London.

'very superb and elegant . . . gilt Stucco-Ornaments . . . the best painted Windows I ever saw . . . the Organ perfectly neat, and good, in Proportion to its Size', as well as 'the middle Aisle rendered comfortable by Iron Stoves, in the Shape of Urns'; in short, 'it is perfect Luxury to say one's Prayers in it'.[38]

Most altar paintings were Continental imports, either originals or good copies (both acceptable to Georgian taste), part of an increasing growth in Old Master collecting trends, frequently presented by local landowners in their role as lords of the manor, or alumni in the cases of College chapels. At Cambridge, Maratta's *Annunciation* (Gonville and Caius), Jouvenet's and Stella's *Presentation in the Temple* (Jesus and Trinity), Barocci's *Entombment* (Pembroke), Pittoni's *Nativity* (Sidney Sussex), the last acquired in Venice in 1783 for 20 guineas; a *Deposition* attributed to either Raphael or Daniele da Volterra was gifted to King's in preference to Romney's *Mater Dolorosa*; at Oxford, a *Resurrection* after Rubens (Pembroke), *Salvator Mundi* after Dolce (University) and so on.[39] A picture with an unusually interesting provenance, Andrea Procaccini's *Transfiguration*, presented to St James, Whitehaven, Cumberland, by Sir James Lowther, had previously been part of a multiple altarpiece in the chapel of the Escorial, heralded in George Thompson's *A Description of the Royal Palace, and Monastery of St Lawrence, Called The Escurial; and of the Chapel Royal of the Pantheon* (1760; the engraved plate dedicated to Lowther) as a 'celebrated work . . . executed in the finest taste [which] strikes the beholder with veneration and astonishment'.[40]

Continental painters practising in Britain also attracted major commissions. One of the earliest and most showy was Sebastiano Ricci's *Resurrection* in the apse of Wren's chapel at Chelsea Hospital, which Vertue considered 'finely painted . . . according to most impartial Judges in a better & more masterly Stile than any painter now living'.[41] At Emmanuel College, Cambridge, Giacomo Amiconi's delicately coloured *Return of the Prodigal Son* is set within a feigned Tuscan colonnade that extends the real space of the room into an idyllic landscape. But his rococo style was not universally admired, and he returned to Italy in 1739.[42] Nor was a sweetly coloured *Adoration of the Magi* by Andrea Casali (pl. 92), who had a reputation for painting 'more in two hours yn any other of his Profession can in a whole day',[43] which he offered gratis as an altarpiece to the Foundling Hospital chapel and was given a frame designed by its architect, Theodore Jacobsen, and carved by the renowned cabinetmaker John Linnell. It was 'tho't to be not strong enough, by some & of a pale weakly colouring', so survived *in situ* only until 1801.[44] The impact of Anton Raphael Mengs's *Noli me tangere* (All Souls, Oxford, now Ashmolean Museum), commissioned from the painter in Rome in 1771, was described by one visitor, who was 'emotionally moved' by the depiction of Mary Magdalene at the moment she suddenly sees the dead Jesus standing before her, her face lit up with 'all the human passions – pain, joy, grief'.[45]

Conservative Anglicans may well have felt their worst fears realised, and certainly one of the compelling features of all these pictures was their vulnerability as fodder for anti-Catholic propaganda. Protestant suspicion of lingering Catholic presence in church art remained potent through the eighteenth century. Swift, in *A Tale of a Tub* (1704), contrasted Papists, with their fondness for '*lofty Ornaments*' and '*Pictures . . . of God like an old Man, of the Virgin* Mary, *and our Saviour as a Child*', and Dissenters, who '*feared* no Colour, but mortally *hated* all, and, upon that Account, bore a cruel Aversion to *Painters*', and who '*quarrel at the most inno-*

cent Decency and Ornament, and deface the Statues and Paintings on all the Churches in England'.[46] Bishop Fleetwood's *A Letter to an Inhabitant of the Parish of St Andrew's Holbourn, about New Ceremonies in the Church* (1717) refers to 'Picture, Images or Statue of a Saint' as instances of 'the most corrupt Practices of the Church of Rome'.[47] A regular reader of the *Gentleman's Magazine* wrote in 1781, a year after the infamous anti-Catholic Gordon Riots in London, of 'former times, when this country was the seat of ignorance and popery [and] it was common to decorate churches with figures of Saints, and . . . the Deity . . . What a pity it is, all such representations are not defaced.'[48] While it is true that English travellers abroad might be struck by the paintings, sculpture and other glamorous ornaments of Continental churches, which 'surpass imagination', they also admitted that 'the bigotry of the people is so great that what we admire we cannot like', and regretted 'the bestowing so much industry and art upon so silly subjects as the life and actions of one enthusiastic and the fabulous martyrdom of a bigot. Corporal and ridiculous representation of the Deity serve to corrupt and debauch our idea of him'.[49] By contrast, London churches were regarded as 'rather convenient than fine, not adorned with pomp and pageantry as in Popish countries; but, like the true Protestant plainness, they have made very little of ornament either within them or without'.[50] Picture-wise, one of the least offensive, least papistic images were figures of Moses and Aaron, prophets closely associated with the Decalogue of the high altar (pl. 79).

Perhaps too much was made of such Anglican rectitude, however, and certainly an otherwise discerning French observer of English attitudes, André Rouquet, was mistaken in asserting, as noted earlier, that here 'religion does not avail itself of the assistance of painting to inspire devotion; their churches at the most are adorned with an altar-piece, which nobody takes notice of'.[51] In fact, the century witnessed a series of vituperative controversies about religious imagery in churches. The earliest major incident concerned James Fellowes's *Last Supper* in St Mary Matfelon, Whitechapel, London (pl. 93). Here the foreground figure of Judas '*in a Priest's Gown . . . and other Appearances of a dignify'd* Clergy-man *of the* Church of England', a correspondent to the *Daily Courant* alleged, blatantly portrayed Dr White Kennet, the devoutly Protestant bishop of Peterborough, and cynically suggested that 'It is perhaps the Interest of your Door-Keepers to have your Church made a *Theatre*, or such like Place of crowding to see a Sight . . . till Thousands of People come and believe their own Eyes, and till an universal Horror calls for the Removal or Amendment oft.' The Bishop of London promptly ordered the picture removed, provoking no-nonsense pamphleteering in which the parishioners expressed amazement 'at such an unexpected Blast [and] the great Damage the Picture . . . wou'd sustain by being torn down', but agreeing to an alternative solution to 'put a *Beard upon* Judas, *and alter his Complexion*'. The commissioning rector, Robert Welton, preaching a sermon entitled *Church-Ornament without Idolatry Vindicated* (1714), claimed that the painting was part of a programme

> *to Beautify . . . the* House of God [and] *such an Accompolishment to all the rest, that some* Dissenters *. . . did declare, that* [it] was worth all that had been done before: *And upon the Universal Assembly of the whole Parish, I receive'd their publick Acknowledgments for . . . Erecting . . . it* [whereupon] *the* STRATAGEM *about* Judas *was concerted* [and] *mischievous Practices were on Foot against us . . .* Forgeries *and* Falshoods, according to the usual Custom of a restless Faction, our ALTAR – PIECE *was become the publick Discourse.*

He dreaded the consequences, the

> *Wound . . . and a Stifling of that publick Spirit, that has, of late, ran so Gloriously thro' the Nation, of beautifying and Adorning our . . . Churches; and upon which Account, my Church, my People, and my Self, are become a By-Word, and the Reproach of the very Scum of a* Whigg. Faction . . . *O! How do the Enemies of* God *Blaspheme and Triumph upon this Occasion!*

They were '*stagger'd at the Blow . . . as if we have been committing Idolatry, or Setting up Image-Worship, at the same Time we were Erecting one of the most proper Ornaments in our Church that Religious Devotion cou'd invent*', and asked 'shall we Rifle the House of God of its most becoming Ornaments, because others abuse them by a superstitious Devotion to 'em?'.[52]

The widely publicised Whitechapel controversy may have contributed to the presence of a similarly composed *Last Supper* that formed the centrepiece of the remodelled medieval chancel of St Peter, Leeds (pl. 94). Sometime between 1709 and 1712 the entire east wall, its great window having been blocked up and plastered over, was embellished with subject pictures taken from the Old and New Testaments painted in fresco by a French émigré named Jacques (or James) Parmentier (destroyed in 1839). The upper wall and ceiling consisted of '*Moses and Aaron giving the Ten Commandments surrounded by angels and cherubs amidst Thunder and Lightning at the ending of the thick Clouds*'. The ensemble was described in an 88-line poem in 1738:

93 James Fellowes. 'A Representation of the Altar-Piece lately Set up in White-Chappel Church [St Mary, London]', 1714. Engraving. © The British Library Board, K. Top. XXIII-28-2.

Nor less devoted th' apostolic twelve
Attend the solemn feast . . .
. . . Over those,
Illumin'd Moses shews th' eternal laws,
Spoke by almighty voice in thunder peals.
On th' other hand, clad in his gorgeous robes
Selected Aaron bears the golden urn
Whence grateful odours fum'd; and more aloof
Cherub and seraphim on golden wing
Glow in the sunshine of celestial day.[53]

Another controversy, politically motivated, erupted in 1725 over William Kent's altar painting in St Clement Danes depicting a non-scriptural subject, *St Cecilia and a Heavenly Host of Musicians* (destroyed in 1941 by enemy bombing). In *A Letter From a Parishioner . . . To the . . . Bishop of London, Occasion'd by His Lordship's causing the Picture . . . to be taken down. With Some Observations on the Use and Abuse of Church Painting in General, and of that Picture in Particular* (1725), it was claimed to be a portrait of Princess Sobieski, the Pretender's wife, with family members. The anonymous author praised the cleric's timely injunction in removing

> that ridiculous, superstitious Piece of *Popish Foppery* [which] gain'd you the *Applause* and good *Will* of all *honest Men*, who were *scandalized* to see that *holy Place* defiled with so *vile* and *impertinent* a *Representation* [hung] to *affront* our *most gracious Sovereign* [with] the *unknown Resemblance* of a Person, who is the Wife of *his utter Enemy*, and *Pensioner* to the *Whore of* Babylon . . . unfit for so *sacred a Place* . . . too awful to be made the Receptacle of *such Trumpery.* No *Wonder* our Church has been throng'd with Spectators to the great Hinderance of *Divine Worship*; the *Altar Piece* of *Whitechapel* is yet *fresh* in *every one's* Memory [such images] *drawing away* the *Eyes*, and sometimes the *Hearts* of *wanton* and *unsteady Persons . . . indolent, unthinking* Wretches . . . *gasping* and *gazing* . . . at every Object, *Pictures especially*, and have no Regard to the Solemnity of the *Place* or *Occasion*; they come there but for *Fashion* or *Customs sake*, and rather than find no Employment, will Turn over the . . . Pictures in their *Common Prayer* Books all the Time of divine Service. This is *the Abuse* of Pictures in Churches.[54]

A correspondent to the popular press in 1735 found that the newly installed altarpiece in St James, Clerkenwell, depicting the *Holy Family* flanked by *Moses* and *Aaron*, 'gave me great Offence, as I find it does many . . . which in my Judgment, is the Reproach of Protestantism, and very near ally'd to Images, which we so justly condemn in the Church of *Rome*. And as such Fopperies are now growing upon us'. He called on the Bishop of London for its removal and

> not suffer any of the Kind, either there, or in any other Church, within your Jurisdiction . . . Pictures (however dignify'd or distinguished) naturally tend to great Superstition, and to take Peoples Minds from what should be the Subject of their Thoughts during . . . divine Service . . . put a stop to this growing Evil . . . if People will have Ornaments . . . the

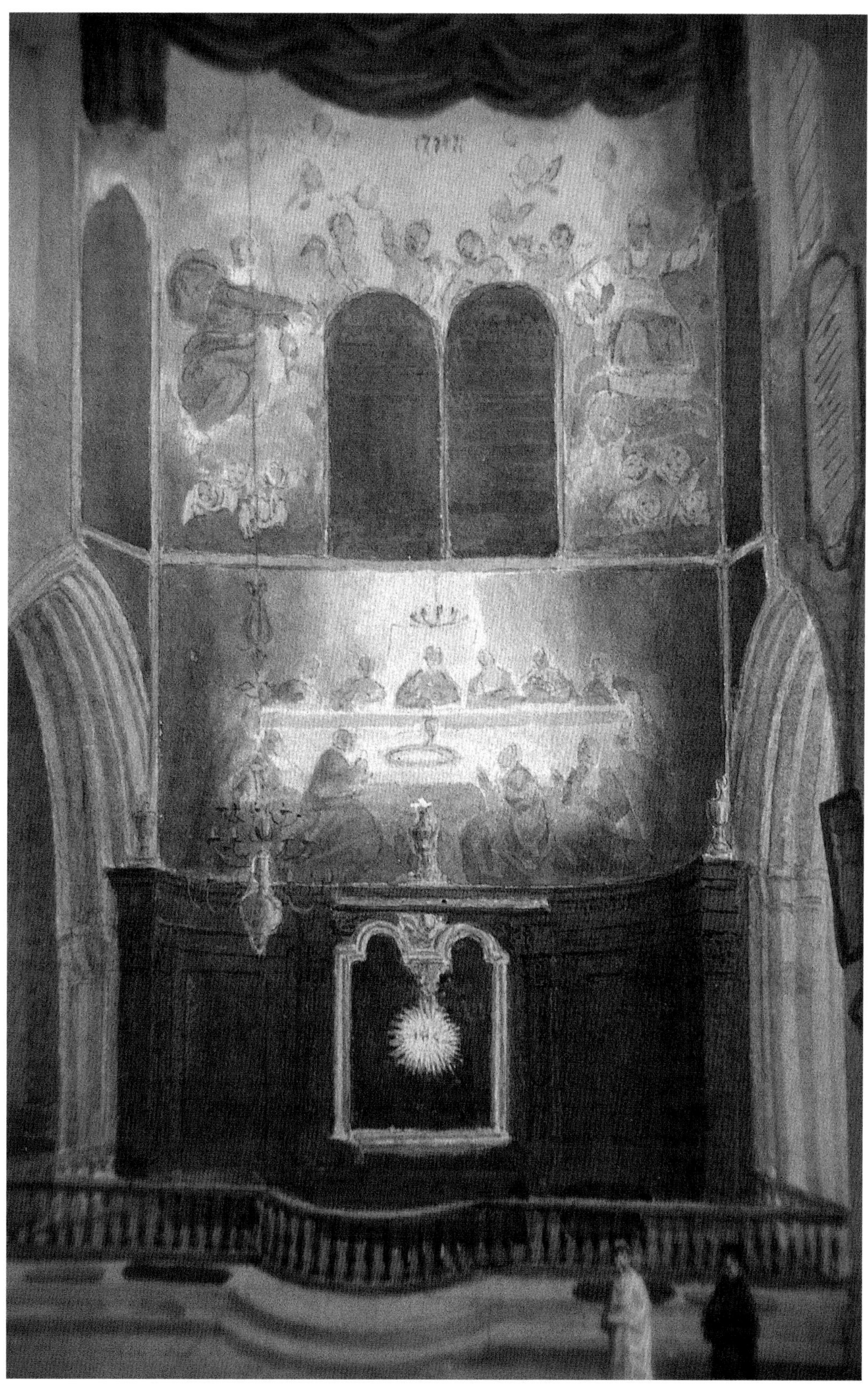

94 Joseph or John Rhodes. 'View of the Altar from the Centre of the Chancel Showing Reredos with Paintings Above', St Peter, Leeds, Yorkshire, *c.*1838, detail. Watercolour. Leeds Library and Information Service, F5 759.2 R 346, no. 4. Altarpiece, carved wood, attributed to William Etty, *c.*1715; James Parmentier, *The Last Supper* and *Moses and Aaron giving the Ten Commandments surrounded by Angels and Cherubs amidst Thunder and Lightning at the Rending of the Thick Clouds*, fresco, 1709–12, destroyed *c.*1838.

95 Sir James Thornhill. Oil sketch for the *Last Supper* altarpiece, for St Mary, Weymouth, Dorset, *c.*1719–20. Yale Center for British Art, New Haven, Paul Mellon Collection.

> Commandments, with the Creed, and the Lord's Prayer, are only what they should be indulg'd.[55]

These attitudes explain the authorities' rejection of the Royal Academy's proposal for St Paul's embellishment described earlier in this chapter.

Censure of popery in paintings was partly countered by preference for native Protestant artists, of whom the most prominent were Sir James Thornhill and his son-in-law, William Hogarth. Apart from St Paul's dome and Wimpole Hall chapel (pls 83, 89), the former's finest religious endeavour is the *Last Supper* at Weymouth (1721), which, as MP for the town, he painted gratis, and for which a beautifully rendered oil sketch also survives (pl. 95). 'Great attention is differently expressed in every face. In Judas you see a lurking, ill-natured, mischievous villan', remarked one visitor.[56] Hogarth's most notable achievement in this field is the 17-foot-square triptych of the *Ascension*, *Sealing of the Sepulchre* and *Three Marys Visiting the Sepulchre* painted for St Mary Redcliffe, Bristol (now in St Nicholas), costing £525 in 1755, a robust, colourful composition inspired by Raphael's *Transfiguration* in San Pietro in Montorio, Rome (now in Pinacoteca Vaticana).[57] The Revd John Penrose described the impact of the Hogarth as 'extremely fine and had a wonderful Effect upon us', though not above criticism, while an Irish cleric thought it 'shines in all its Lustre. Who cd. Imagine yt. so Humorous & Burlesque a pencil as Hogarths shd. wthout the Greatest violence to his Naturall Genius be confined to such a Grave & serious Subject & to Arrive at Excellence in Both'.[58]

More ambitious projects, however, most notably the radical scheme of 1779 by Sir William Chambers, Comptroller of the King's Works, collaborating with the London-based American painter Benjamin West, to transform the King's Chapel, Windsor (pl. 96), failed to materialise, despite the latter's tremendous reputation as a religious painter:

> dost thou know of an Artist, whose name
> May be written with thine in the annals of Fame,
> May a Man, most esteem'd, and of a Painter,
> the best?
> Apelles reply'd without pause 'There is WEST'[59]

This entailed replacing Verrio's narrative sweep of 1675–84 in the upper register of the north wall with five tableaux on the theme of *Revealed Religion* separated by foliated pilasters supported on pairs of draped female figures holding emblematic shields, and nine further panels in the attic flanked by single standing figures. The spandrels of Hugh May's south windows are embellished with elegant angels drawing back painted curtains. The vocabulary derives from Chambers's Franco-Italian experience, which West, who travelled in Italy between 1760 and 1763, would have shared.[60] The ceiling arrangement looks back to Inigo Jones's compartmentalised Banqueting House, Whitehall (pl. 545). Into all the voids West, advised by an ecclesiastical committee, proposed inserting an extraordinary series of high-minded morality subjects on the themes of the Mosaical, Antediluvian, Patriarchal, Revelation and Gospel Dispensations inspired by Raphael, Rubens and Poussin. West regarded this as the 'greatest work of my life'.[61] Though a private enterprise, it enjoyed wide public exposure unrivalled in its day, through the exhibition of several dozen sketches and oil paintings at the Royal Academy of Arts in London, and for which he received some £20,000. Nonetheless, George III lost interest, perhaps exacerbated by the painter's undisguised, anti-royalist sympathies in the wake of the colonial war, and the programme was finally abandoned in 1801.[62] West, however, scored a resounding success at Greenwich Hospital chapel (pl. 649) with his magnificent altar painting depicting the shipwreck of St Paul (1782–95). It formed the centrepiece of an elaborate pictorial programme, both painted and sculpted, integrated into the exquisite neoclassical architecture based on the life of Christ and biblical figures, the iconography of which was determined by the governors and, like its medieval predecessors, directed mainly at an illiterate congregation. Contemporaries reckoned it 'cannot fail to having a proper effect on the minds of seafaring men'.[63]

96 Sir William Chambers and Benjamin West. Design for *Revealed Religion* for the redecoration of the King's Chapel, Windsor Castle, Berkshire, 1779, unrealised. Pencil, pen and ink and gouache, watercolour. Yale Center for British Art, New Haven, Paul Mellon Collection.

West's great east window of St George's Chapel, Windsor (1792), the *Last Supper*, with its soft colours and natural rendering of clouds, was hailed as a 'complete memorial of the revival of the art of staining Glass' in contrast to its western brethren, 'full of antient Glass', with its 'ill shaped, scarcely intelligible' figures that have 'no appearance of a painting'.[64] He was, with Reynolds, responsible for completing this transformation of glass painting from the medieval tradition of static, compartmented figures rendered in staining techniques to expansive, dramatic Georgian tableaux executed in enamel colours using brushes. In James Wyatt's great west window of 1777–81 at New College chapel, Oxford (pl. 97), the glass painter Thomas Jervais undertook an ambitious ensemble of twelve panels consisting of a beautiful *Nativity* in the style of Correggio, with Mrs Brinsley Sheridan posing as the Virgin in the large central panel, where the mullions and tracery were abandoned in order to treat the subject as a monumental 10 by 18 foot easel picture. To the left are Reynolds and Jervais portrayed as shepherds, a poignant association, while the lower range contains a central group of Charity with single figures of Virtues and Graces, including Fortitude (third from the left) based on the antique statue of the Cesi *Juno*.[65] Thomas Warton's long panegyric *Verses on Sir Joshua Reynold's Painted Window at New College, Oxford* (1782), an indication of its popularity, speaks of

> hues romantic tinged the gorgeous pane,
> To fill with holy light the wondrous fane

> Thy powerful hand has broke the Gothic chain,
> And brought my bosom back to truth again:
> To truth, by no peculiar taste confined,
> Whose universal pattern strikes mankind

97 Thomas Jervais after Sir Joshua Reynolds. 'The much admired PAINTED WINDOW OF NEW COLLEGE CHAPEL, OXFORD', 1816. Coloured engraving. © The British Library Board. Executed 1777–85.

Reynolds, 'tis thine, from the broad window's
  height,
To add new lustre to religious light
Not of its pomp to strip this ancient shrine,
But bid that pomp with purer radiance shine:
With arts unknown before, to reconcile
The willing Graces to the Gothic pile.[66]

The *Gentleman's Magazine* reported the king and queen spending the whole occasion of an organ salute in 1785 'contemplating the painted glass'. Though Walpole, granted a studio preview, praised the 'glorious' *Nativity* as seen in a 'darkened . . . room . . . the sun shining through the transparencies, [which] realizes the illumination that is supposed to be diffused from the glory, and has a magic effect', he contradicted this in other correspondence: '[James] Essex agreed with me that Jarvis's windows . . . will not succeed. Most of his colours are opaque, and their great beauty depending on a spot of light for sun or moon, is an imposition';

98 Benjamin West. Oil study for triptych of the *Conversion of St Paul*, *St Paul persecuting the Christians* and *Ananias restoring St Paul's Sight*, 1786. Dallas Museum of Fine Art, Texas. Francis Eginton, 1791, enamel paint on glass in St Paul, Birmingham, Warwickshire.

'I . . . foretold their miscarrage. The old and the new are as mismatched as an orange and a lemon . . . Sir Joshua's washy Virtues make the Nativity a dark spot from the darkness of the Shepherd . . . from most of Jarvis' colours being transparent.'[67] Torrington preferred 'the old high-coloured paintings, and their strong steady shades, to these new and elegant-esteem'd compositions . . . these twisting emblematical figures appear to me

99 William Peckitt. *Virgin and Child with St John and Angels*, 1772, St Bartholomew, Binley, Warwickshire. Enamel paint on glass.

half-dress'd, languishing harlots'.[68] Reynolds, too, is said to have been disappointed.[69]

The Georgians regarded painted glass as fundamental to the success of medieval church interiors. Torrington complained that their removal from St George, Doncaster, Yorkshire, where they served as an 'obstruction of the sun, and for meditation' rendered the building 'like a greenhouse', while their 'total want' at Worcester Cathedral confirmed them 'so necessary for church grandeur to cast a dim religious light'.[70]

The new innovative pictorial windows have the advantage, particularly when placed strategically at the east end of the chancel, where they served as surrogate altarpieces, over both their oil equivalents and small, irregular, leaded panes of medieval glass, of representing the image as a monumental, uninterrupted tableau infused with a theatrical, almost miraculous illumination.[71] Nowhere is this more powerfully felt than in the surviving masterpiece of the Birmingham artist Francis Eginton, who was particularly admired for figures 'softened by that gradation of tints and chaste colouring unknown to the ancients in the art of glass painting'.[72] In 1785 the parishioners of the recently built St Paul, Birmingham, commissioned a grand 17 by 18 foot east window designed by West on the New Testament subject of the apostle's life, for which a series of dazzling oil sketches were exhibited at the Royal Academy (pl. 98). West later described the impact of 'the wonderfull working powers . . . made manifest to the World' in the finished window, 'chear the sight of those unborn that Generations yet to come may know the goodly things that were done, in the days of our good King Azakiah'. In 1791 the press called for subscriptions towards its cost of 400 guineas in order to secure 'a performance which must stamp the highest credit on the eminent ability of the Artists, and reflect honour on the town', and Eginton publicly thanked his supporters and hoped they 'will candidly allow the Difficulties attendant on the Execution of his Work to apologize for its Imperfections'.[73] His other major work, *Evangelical Faith* (1794) at St Alkmund, Shrewsbury (pl. 232), is discussed in chapter 16.

The other master of modern realism, yet retaining an esteem for the medieval tradition, who enjoyed a national reputation, was William Peckitt of York, whose obituary in 1795 spoke of 'the many ingenious and noble designs [that] . . . has distinguished and immortalized his name'.[74] His gracefully rendered chancel window at Binley, Warwickshire (pl. 99), is a faithful copy of Andrea del Sarto's *Madonna of Humility with the Infant Christ, St John the Baptist and Angels* (the so-called *Corsini Madonna*), of which several versions, as well as an engraving, were known in England in the eighteenth century.[75] Of the trilogy of single saintly figures (pl. 78), each standing within an ogee arch, originally installed over the altar in St John Deansgate, Manchester, two replicated those in Peckitt's largest endeavour, the west window of Exeter Cathedral, executed in 1766 (pl. 100), which in turn derived from Thornhill's Westminster Abbey north transept rose of 1721.[76]

The installation of painted glass, including reinstating ancient panels, though a thriving trade in England,[77] was not without troubles. A sensational case surrounded St Margaret, Westminster, in the late 1750s, when the churchwardens purchased a magnificent 12-foot-high, five-light, sixteenth-century Netherlandish window depicting the *Crucifixion of Christ*, going cheap at £420, and installed it without applying for a faculty (pl. 247). The dean and chapter of Westminster brought a case against the wardens in the Ecclesiastical Court, which

100 Robert Pranker after William Peckitt. *The Great West Window*, Exeter Cathedral, Devon, undated. Coloured engraving. © The British Library Board, K. Top. xi.69-p. Enamel paint on glass, 1766, removed 1904, since vanished.

included a charge of introducing an idolatrous image into the church. The Revd Thomas Wilson, the minister who instigated the purchase, published an influential 143-page tract, *The Ornaments of Churches Considered* (1761), on the grounds that the controversy rendered it 'a Topick of popular Discourse . . . in many . . . Parts of the Kingdom'. He pointed out that the window's COLOURING . . . EXPRESSION, and . . . GENERAL BEAUTY . . . were universally admired . . . and . . . the greatest Propriety was deemed to arise for placing it over the Communion Table [which would] crown all . . . other Efforts in beautifying this Church. [A] strong Argument for Public Worship [is that] since those who perhaps in their lonely Hours would never lift

> their Thought to the Author of their Existence, are forcibly drawn by an Impulse they can scarcely disobey, into a Train of serious and awful Ideas [and] the Question is . . . what Objects are the most proper to excite that Spirit and Truth which are the Essence of Religion.

One objection to their use as church ornament was the

> Tendency . . . to introduce Superstition and Popery [and] It is certainly true, that every Approach . . . towards a proper Dignity in the Worship of God, is also a Step towards a vicious Excess; [the] great Argument against admitting . . . Painting and Sculpture . . . into our Churches, is drawn from the Danger of Idolatry.

The author, Archdeacon William Hole, concluded that since

> Churches are always to hold a certain Proportion and Superiority in Magnificence to other Edifices . . . Painting and Sculpture, considered merely as Ornaments, should not be excluded . . . historical Pictures in which the Life and Actions of our Blessed Saviour were related . . . would be an auxiliary Method of conveying part of those Truths . . . Painting would then be employed as every Art and Science ought, in the Promotion of Virtue, and deserve the distinguishing Title of *The Handmaid of Religion*.

He also confessed a further motive: 'the Hope of their one Day appearing with all their Lustre in an Island, whose Heroes, Philosophers, and Poets, have done Honour to Humanity, whilst her Painters and Sculptors have scarce ever attained to Mediocrity'. The case against St Margaret's was duly dropped.[78]

The achievement of these church windows was summed up in the Revd Samuel Parr's assessment of improvements made in 1794 to Hatton church, Warwickshire, which included the installation of Eginton's *Crucifixion with SS Peter and Paul*, flanked by an *Agony in the Garden* and an *Ascension*:

> I anxiously hope, that after my Decease all future Ministers and Church Wardens . . . remembering my well meant labours . . . will conscientiously take care to preserve the . . . chancel Windows, from . . . Injury . . . that every fifth year, in conformity to . . . Egintons positive instructions . . . they will have fresh putty applied by a Skilful Glazier . . . order fresh small nails . . . for securing all the . . . panes . . . the iron lattice work . . . inspected [and] repaired

as well as general improvements that were

> not . . . directed towards unprofitable and ostentatious decoration of a mere building, but . . . intended for proofs of my sincere good-will towards the interests and . . . honour of the Church of England, and as encouragement for the parishioners . . . and their Successors, to be constant in their attendance upon divine worship, and to avail themselves of all the numerous and powerful aids that the discipline and Common Prayer of that Church affords, for the exercise of rational and truly Christian devotion [and] preserve them from the dangerous influence of fanaticism, bigotry, and Superstition, and to diffuse among them by precept, and . . . example, a spirit of civilization, peace, amity, and good neighbourhood.[79]

Part Two

CHURCH BUILDING

Drawn by B. F. Scott.
Engraved by John Scott.
St. PAUL'S. COVENT-GARDEN.
As it appeared on Fire, at eight O'Clock, on Thursday Evening 17th. Sepr. 1795.
Was Built by that Celebrated Architect Inigo Jones, in 1640 by the direction And at the Expence of the Earl of Bedford, Ancestor of the present Duke, to whom th ad was granted by Edward VI. in 1552. This Structure was Erected as a Chapel of Ease to St. Martins in the Fields _ and remarkable for its Majestic Simplicity, which never fail'd to Attract the Eye of the Curious _ It was seperated from St. Martins, Constituted an Independant Parish and confirmed in 1660 _ When the Patronage was vested in the Earl of Bedford, and remained as it came from the Hands of the Original Architect _ until the above Accident which happen'd while Repairing.
Published 5th. Novr. 1795 by LAURIE & WHITTLE. 53 Fleet Street London.

101 John Scott after B. F. Scott. 'St. Paul's Covent Garden. As it appeared on Fire at eight O'Clock on Thursday Evening 17th. Septr. 1795'. Coloured engraving. © The British Library Board, K. Top. 242.1-d.

Nine

THE 'FATE OF SUBLUNARY THINGS'[1]

Shame to our Country, and a Scandal to Christianity that in many Towns where there is a prodigious Encrease in the Number of Houses and Inhabitants so little Care should be taken for the building of Churches, that Five Parts in Six of the People are absolutely hindered from hearing divine Service . . . A Neglect of Religion, so ignominious . . . that it can hardly be equalled in any civilized Age or Country[2]

There were many reasons to promote the building of new churches, not least of all to rectify the martyrdom of destruction suffered by existing fabrics resulting from malevolent acts of Nature or the foibles of human error (pl. 101). More optimistically new builds demonstrated 'such a Regard to Religion, that it is hoped, from such virtuous Beginnings [of George II's] Auspicious Reign will be attended with the Encouragement of Religion, to the Extirpation of Vice and Immorality', as in the case of St Luke, Old Street, and St John, Horselydown (pls 433, 435), both begun in 1727.[3] It was felt to be an act of piety that 'such Increasing of the Number . . . should be made for the better Instruction of the Inhabitants in the true Christian Religion, as professed in the Church of *England* . . . a Work, declared by Parliament to be so much for the Honour of God, the spiritual Welfare of the Subjects of this Rhelm, and the Interest of the established Church'.[4] New, improved places of worship were linked with the amelioration of disfranchised members of society. A satirical poem, *Deal in an Uproar* (1709), concerning the 'Sodom' and 'Nineveian' Kent fishing port, an 'impious and remorseless town [peopled by] savages of human kind [practising] fraud, oppression, theft and rapine', refers to sincere attempts to 'stemming tides of vice [and] saving miscreants against their will' with an 'honest scheme'

to make religion get the start of trade,
And since the church from thence too distant lay,
To bring them all to heaven a shorter way
And build a place of worship nearer home
To which none could plead weariness to come.[5]

The result is plain but handsome St George's Chapel (pls 525–6). In 1711 the New Churches Commissioners were petitioned by 12,000 souls of Deptford, the majority 'Seamen, or Workmen and Labourers in her Majesty's Dock-yard . . . many of which live in One House, and so are rated only as One Family', or 'Butchers, Victualers, and others . . . exposed to the Losses and Hazards of . . . the Seae Service'. Lately the Thames-side town had been 'very much impoverished by the Length and Extensiveness of the War [with France], The great Storm, The number of persons killed or taken Prisoners, and other Difficulties', so that the inhabitants 'cannot possibly be accommodated' in the recently rebuilt parish church of St Nicholas.[6] This resulted in the spectacular St Paul (pl. 362). The Leeds antiquary Ralph Thoresby remarked:

> how comfortable it is to consider, that many poor Creatures, who would otherwise, it is to be feared, go prayerless to Bed (and perhaps into Eternity too) . . . have . . . the happy Opportunity of offering up their Prayers and Praises to the Almighty in this holy Temple [St Peter's parish church, Leeds]; the good Effects . . . visible, in the considerable Increase of Communicants at the most solemn Christian Institution; many of whom being of tender Years, afford a comfortable Prospect of a rising Generation![7]

The rector of Lower Heyford, Oxfordshire, reported that his church

> wants whitewashing. The Pavement . . . is very bad . . . The Church Ways intolerable . . . I have acquainted my Parish with all the Things . . . I complain of . . . and beg'd of Them, that They might be reform'd: but all my Intreaties, and even Threats . . . have been to no Purpose. I believe . . . it is not a dis-

regard to Decency, but Poverty is the occasion of These Things, every Penny comes with extreem Difficulty from them.[8]

It might be a matter of providing convenience and accessibility for remote congregations. Enlarging Coleford Chapel, Gloucestershire, which was 'a Great Distance' from the parish church,

> will not only be of Great Advantage to Aged and Infirm Persons . . . and to a great Number of Miners . . . to Offer up their Religious Service to Almighty God, who working hard all the Week . . . are not Easily prevailed upon to Travell so far . . . upon the Lords Day but will also probably [attract] Unsteady people from falling away from the Established Church, which many will otherwise be in Great Danger of Doing . . .

alluding ominously to 'a Congregation of protestant Dissenters meeting every Lords day in the . . . Town'.[9] Wednesfield, Staffordshire, was erected to accommodate 'chiefly . . . Persons employed in the Iron Manufactories' who found it 'very troblesome and inconvenient' to travel the two miles into Wolverhampton when the road was 'very deep and dirty in the Winter Season'.[10] Finsthwaite, Lancashire, was built in 1724 at the parishioners' expense because of 'the great Distance from the Parish Church and the Roughness of the Country', and Allonby, Cumberland, in 1745 by the prebend of St Paul's Cathedral on behalf of the inhabitants 'who are almost deprived of the benefits of all public worship by reason of their great distence from their . . . parish church'.[11] Anthony Benson left £600 towards a new chapel at Cockermouth in the same county, because it was 'remote . . . and . . . abounding with quakers'.[12] Even in London there were parishes of 'very large extent, and extremely populous, Containing thirty or forty Thousand Souls, many of them at too great distance from the Parish Church', which encouraged parochial subdivision and the creation of new, smaller parishes and chapels of ease.[13] Thus, the inhabitants of Kew, Surrey, living a 'very great distance' from the parish church at Kingston and 'hindered from resorting so frequently as they ought to the publique worship of God which they esteem a most grevious calamity', erected a handsome chapel on Kew Green with royal aid.[14]

Other churches were ill-situated. Of old, waterlogged St John, Wapping, on the low-lying edge of the Thames, appalled parishioners testified to Parliament that 'going into the Church is as bad as going into a Vault'; 'many other Inhabitants have been intimidated from attending divine Worship'; another 'sat at one End . . . where the Graves in the . . . yard were over his Head and that he was taken very ill . . . and . . . not able to follow his Business for a Fortnight'; yet another

> often found the Church cold and damp . . . the . . . yard . . . so full of Corps, that some lay partly above Ground; and . . . found the Stench so great . . . they bury Five or Six . . . upon one another . . . People complain, in the Summer time . . . they have not been able to bear their Windows open, the Stench has been so great . . . the Coffins . . . lie above Ground in many Places . . . the Ground . . . so full that they can't be put lower.

In 1758 they got a new but 'very mean' church costing only £1,600, consisting of a 'plain body, a tower which scarcely deserves the name, and a spire that might be taken for a lengthened chimney'.[15]

The compulsion to improve is reflected in two crucial questions appearing in episcopal Visitations: 'Is your Church or Chapel in good and sufficient Repair, as to the Roof, Walls, Windows, Doors, Floors and Seats?' and 'Are all Things kept in such Decent Sort as becometh the *House of* GOD?'[16] – the dual activities of repair and maintenance. During his Cumbrian peregrinations in 1703 the ever industrious Bishop Nicolson found Ireby church 'has been lately a little brush'd up, in expectation of my comeing to see it. But 'tis still very Tawdry'; Kirkbridge was

> in so scandalous and nasty a Condition. Every thing, to the highest Degree imaginable, out of Order. The Roof of the Quire comeing down, the Communion-Table rotten, the Reading Desk so inconvenient that 'twas impossible to kneel in it, the Pulpit inaccessible, no Seat, nor pavement in the Quire, &C. So ill an example in a Rich Parson (who is, in Effect, the Lord of the Mannor as well as the Rector of the Parish) cannot but beget a proportionable Slovenlyness in the Parishioners; who have their Seats tatter'd, the Floor all in holes, no Surplice, no Common-prayerbook, a very few fragments of an old Bible, &c . . . In short – The whole look'd more like a Pigsty than the House of God.[17]

Of Bitterley, Shropshire, it was reported in 1793 that the

> Steeple will become ruinous, if not attended to . . . the floor of the Nave is already too bad for safety or decency. The desks . . . infirm . . . the pews . . . rather unseemly . . . the whole . . . susceptible of great improvement . . . the longer repairs of any kind are delayed the more burthensome they become.

In the following year Thomas Telford surveyed the fabric and reported on the 'extremely dangerous . . . State . . . & . . . nothing short of taking down & rebuilding would be advisable'. There is no evidence, however, that anything was done, and the medieval wreck was not restored until 1876–80.[18]

As already hinted in chapter 2, there were serious threats from the Dissenters. With increased proselytising it was an easy matter to convince Anglican authorities to initiate improvements and new-builds. The parishioners of Fenny Stratford, Buckinghamshire, claimed that

> taking Advantage of . . . our un-happy Circumstances, [the sect] . . . erected in our Town a Meeting House or Conventicle, to promote Schism, and Separation from the true Religion, by Law establish'd. –– But as this prov'd very disagreeable and unacceptable to us, as Means were at length found to purchase, buy off, and pull down the . . . Building.

Moreover,

> the want of a CHURCH or CHAPEL has been a great detriment to the *Trade* and *Morals* of our *Town*: Travellers used it as a Reason to avoid resting here on the *Sabbath-day*; and it affords the *Inhabitants* an opportunity to profane it [so] out of a passionate Desire to put a stop to this Evil, and take away so just a Reproach; the better Sort among us were . . . excited to make a Collection to the utmost of our Abilities for the Structure of a CHAPEL: which . . . has . . . been carried on with so much Vigour; that in the space of *four Years*, it has been almost completed [pl. 142].[19]

In Yorkshire, one of the birthplaces of Nonconformity, the local press reported from Hunslet near Leeds that

> a certain *Culamite*, who was to have officiated in the Absence of our Curate, being refus'd Admittance into the Chapel . . . and being religiously flatulent, found it necessary to mount a Table under the Pear-Tree . . . and . . . for one Hour and a Half, discharged himself of a large Quantity of Methodistical Rant.[20]

In 1767 the owner of nearby Kippax Park informed the Archbishop of York that a local family connected by marriage to the Countess of Huntingdon (of Connexion fame) 'enters most zealously . . . into her Pious design and labours for the Reformation of the Church, Clergy and People. To render the former . . . odious . . . appears to be . . . an essential step towards this end' and so secured the living for Mr Crooke, the incumbent curate of Hunslet,

> a man whose only recommendation is his most shameful and scandalous Behaviour in the Church . . . joined to his being devoted to the Methodists, having no other ways to distinguish himself . . . By these means . . . the . . . Pulpit [is] opened to every Methodist in the Kingdom . . . The whole train with their mob at their heels, and the People . . . crouded out of the Church. Kippax may be called their Metropolis . . . one of these Chaplains a bold noisy boisterous man, was said to have been a Romish priest . . . convert.

Not only that, but 'among the Irreverent Irregular Doings . . . in our Church . . . I have heard such variety of Blasphemous, Ridiculous, absurd, noisy, bold boisterous nonsense as Bedlam alone can equal; allways extempore, so that if one could pick up . . . any thing they hear uttered, out of their incoherent Jumble, They would flatly deny it'.[21] In the following decade John Wesley reported preaching on Birstall hill 'to the largest congregation that ever was seen there . . . twelve or fourteen thousand' and 'some thousands more at Leeds'.[22] At Whitehaven, Cumberland, a thriving commercial port on the Irish Sea,

> great Numbers . . . are put under a Necessity either of staying at Home, and Neglecting the Publick Worship of Almighty God, or of Going to other Churches . . . at a great Distance and with much Inconveniency. And several others may be induced . . . to resort to the places of Worship amongst those that Disent from the Church of England.[23]

Finally, in the case for a new, much larger church for Hackney, an Anglican correspondent to the *Gentleman's Magazine* pointed out that there were already two Meetings and two Methodist chapels in the parish, and since 'Non-conformists are seldom deficient in zeal, it is no unusual thing with them to wait upon strangers, and offer them the best accommodation, &c. upon the first coming among us.' Within a few years the parish counter-attacked by replacing its medieval church on an ambitious, classically avant-garde scale (pls 712–13).[24]

The presence of such seemingly unsavoury establishments became a sure means of securing rebuilding funds for the Fifty New Churches programme that operated between 1711 and 1733. Among the sites considered for St Anne, Limehouse, was one located between Anabaptist and Presbyterian Meetings, which 'will be more likely to do good to Souls and may be an effectuall means to recover many erroneous Christians and bring them into the Pale of the Established Church', while a petition stressed the lack of

102 Artist unknown. View of Honiley House and St John Baptist, Warwickshire, undated. Pen and ink and wash. Stratford-upon-Avon Record Office, DR 272, f. 15. Church attributed to Christopher Wren Jr., 1723.

> Sufficient Room . . . to Contain the Inhabitants . . . who would otherwise Resort [to the parish church] whereby many of the . . . poorer Sort are Tempted to become Loose and Irreligious and not going to Church at all or of being Seduced to Resort to Meeting Houses of which there are a great Number . . . of Different persuasions.

Another expressed 'great Grief and fear' that a recently completed Meeting 'will not be the only one that will be erected' and believed a new church 'would effectually putt a stop to so growing an Evil'.[25] The population of Bermondsey parish pressed for a new fabric on grounds that 'Dissenters gain greatly upon us under this Misfortune [of delays in construction]; and to encourage Proselites have very lately Erected a New Meeting house very near the Ground Devoted for the New Church'.[26] Ned Ward rhapsodised:

> to see Paul's Church as empty as a Saturday's 'Change
> and the meeting-house as full as Westminster Hall[27]

Beyond London a substantial and important building initiative was in the hands of the gentry and aristocracy in their capacity as lords of the manor. The Bishop of Lincoln's endorsement of Sir John Delaval's rebuilding of nearby Doddington parish church at his own expense (pl. 215) was based not only on his 'good intention' but a 'wish' that his example would be 'follow'd by others', since many country churches were in a 'very decay'd state'.[28] The owner of Honiley, Warwickshire, proudly inscribed over the west door of the church adjacent to his residence, a perfect ensemble (pl. 102), 'AD GLORIAM DEI JOHANNES SANDERS: ARM: PROPIIS SUMPTIBUS HANC ECCLES AEDIFICAVIT ANNO SALUTIS: MDCCXXIII' ('To the Glory of God John Sanders Esq., At His Own Expense Built This Church In the Year of Salvation 1723').[29] Sir Lionel Lyde was wholly responsible for the exquisite, pioneer Greek Revival Ayot St Lawrence, Hertfordshire (pl. 643). Henry, 6th Earl of Gainsborough rebuilt Kinoulton, Nottinghamshire, in the years 1790–92 in an unspectacular, conservative style to the design of the little-known, London-born architect W. D. Legg, at a cost of £1,432 10s. 0d. (pl. 103).[30] The churchwardens of St Paul, Bedford, applied to the Duchess of Bedford at Woburn in 1772 to solicit her assistance in executing a scheme by George Dance Jr, the City of London surveyor, for 'improving and beautifying [the] meen

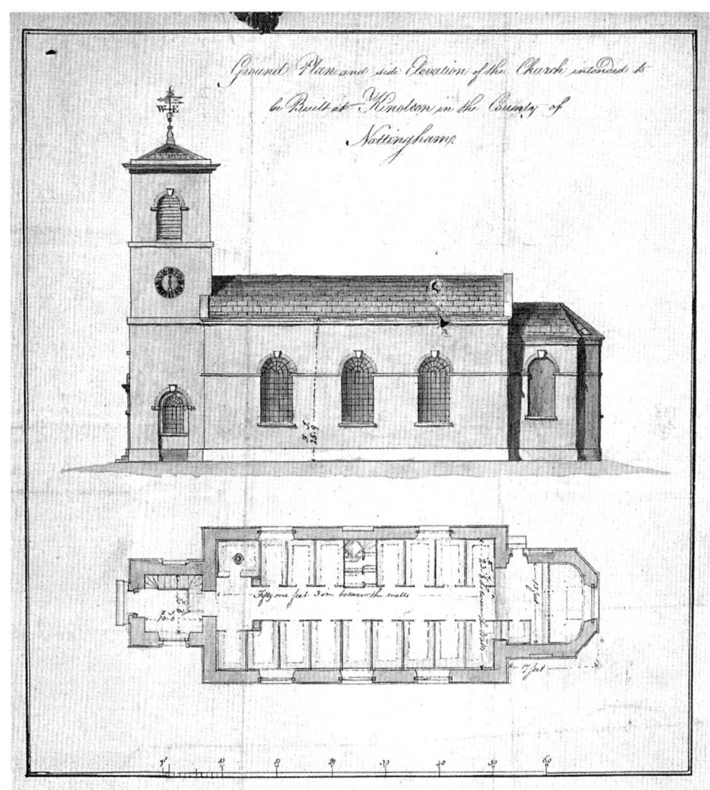

103 William Daniel Legg. 'Ground Plan and side elevation of the Church intended to be Built at Kinoulton', Nottinghamshire, 1790. Pen and ink and coloured wash. Borthwick Institute, York University, Fac.1792/1b.

appearance' of the interior, estimated to cost £900, which was 'too great for the Parishioners only', expressing how 'pleased' they would be in Her Grace's 'Concurrance . . . in our Intentions', which would 'give a Sanction and encouragement for the design . . . and animate those to whome we intend to apply'.[31]

Above all, it was the necessity of replacing damaged or destroyed fabrics that propelled the majority of building programmes.

> The sounds direct my eye along the vale
> To where the venerable structure rears
> Its elevated spire, which long has brav'd
> The pelting fury of the brumal storms[32]

The greatest cause of destruction lay in the vicissitudes of Nature – storms, floods, 'God's dreadful visitation by fire'.[33] Defoe reported, almost unbelievably, that the prosperous town of Dunwich on the Suffolk coast of the North Sea, which was 'in danger of being swallowed up . . . once had fifty churches . . . I saw but one left, and that not half full of people . . . owing to nothing but the fate of things', conjuring an apocalyptic vision of 'the decay of publick things, things of the most durable nature' likened to the 'ruins of Carthage, of the great city of Jerusalem, or of ancient Rome . . . Nineveh . . . Babylon . . . great Persepolis'.[34] Churchgoers were rightly fearful of such unpredictable phenomena, as is clear from the *Gentleman's Magazine* account of an incident one noon in July 1768 at Selkirk, Scotland, when

> the clouds began to thicken, and the darkness came on so fast . . . that the Service . . . was interrupted, and the people . . . thrown into the greatest consternation . . . lightning began to flash, and . . . thunder to roll in so dreadful a manner, that no man living ever heard the like. The whole country was alarmed, and verily believed the day of judgment was come.[35]

These events evoked biblical-like language in the popular press: a fire fanned by high winds reducing the church at Tunbridge Wells, Kent, to 'a heap of ruins' was reckoned more fierce than the 'fiery furnace into which Shadrack and his companions were cast'.[36]

In Defoe's vivid account of the events of 26 April 1703, *The Great Storm; or, A Collection of the Most Remarkable Casualities and Disasters which Happened in the Late Dreadful Tempest, Both by Sea and Land* (1704), 'the air was . . . full of meteors and vaporous fire, and in some places both the thundering and unusual flashes of lightning, to the great terror of the inhabitants', during which stone, brick and tiles 'flew with such force, and so thick into the streets'. In Somerset, the battlements of Batcombe were blown down and 'a great deal of damage done', and the tower of Compton Bishop was 'much shattered . . . the leads . . . taken clear away, and laid flat in the churchyard', while at Fairford, Gloucestershire, 'a large and noble structure', the 'winds were [so] strong and boisterous [that] they unbedded 3 sheets of lead upon the . . . roof, and rolled them up like so much paper', while the celebrated twenty-eight windows filled with splendid renaissance painted glass, which 'equal . . . if not exceed, any parochial church in England . . . felt the fury of the winds'.[37] More than a dozen other churches were similarly affected, including the unfortunate Flixton in Suffolk, which, having had its roof blown off, remained in ruins, its walls used to build stables and the font 'having been split asunder' to support the 'two ends of a hog-trough'.[38] During a 'violent storm and hurricane' the turrets and battlements of Glasgow Cathedral were 'throun doun . . . broke throu and damnified the roof . . . and several other parts of the church chattered and disordered and the top of the speir made to decline and bow doun'.[39] During Sunday service at Keverne, Cornwall, 'lightning

104 T. Jefferys. 'A South West Prospect of the Parish Church of Husbands Bosworth, as it was Damaged by a Dreadful Storm on July the 6th. 1755', Leicestershire. © The British Library Board, K. Top. XIX.13

shivered the steeple . . . threw it upon the body', striking the congregation with 'astonishment . . . Many had their cloaths singed by the fierceness of the lightning, and some their watches melted.'[40] A first-hand account of the conflagration of 4 June 1731 that devastated the prosperous market town of Blandford Forum, Dorset, spoke of the 'Fury of the Flames', entrapping the church and melting the lead roof; the 'Stones split and flew . . . the Bells . . . dissolved and ran down in Streams', some citizens sheltering within, others 'behind the Tomb-Stones'.[41]

On occasions, storms were so stupendously spectacular that they were commemorated in popular prints, as in the case of Husbands Bosworth, Leicestershire (pl. 104), 'Damaged by a Dreadful Storm' on 6 July 1755, where the dramatic image is confirmed by the accompanying description of

> Hail and Rain attended with terrible Thunder & Lightning as has not had its equal in the memory of Man . . . stones were struck out of the Walls within side, the Pavement in some places raised an Inch above their former level, the Bells displaced, their Frames and Wheels oddly splintered, the spire . . . very much shatter'd, a large Chasm opened in it, about twelve Yards in length & one in breadth, from whence many heavy Stones were forced to a very great distance; Globes of Fire were seen in the Air, Flashes of Lightning in a terrible manner ran along the Streets, and a great Smoke and Sulpherous smell issued from the Apperture of the Spire, and what is remarkably providential several hundred weight of Stones fell about & upon the Grave where the Minister (and a large Congregation attending) had just before buried a Corps.[42]

During the eighteenth century the more frequent appearance of lightning in landscape painting may well have been prompted by such reportage engravings. A print of St Paul, Covent Garden, aflame in 1795 was issued within weeks of the disaster (pl. 101). A fire in the turret believed to have broken out as a result of a plumber leaving charcoal burning overnight 'raged with such violence as to render every effort to subdue it fruitless, and which in the end destroyed the whole . . . leaving only . . . the bare Walls of that beautiful Edifice'; a later account conjured up 'a grand scene, projected before a background of liquid fire'. It was claimed the flames spread through an impropriety of the Water Offices 'turning off the Mains during the Night in order to obtain a more ample quantity . . . for their private emolument'.[43]

Sometimes it was a matter of quick-wittedness. When during a 'very great storm' lightning struck Salisbury Cathedral's lofty steeple, its surveyor, Francis Price, with help from workmen and townspeople, quelled the flames, otherwise 'all the assistance on earth could not have prevented the total destruction of this pile'.[44]

Vestries tried various solutions to protect their buildings, from window shutters – installed at Cardington, Shropshire, because the wind was 'so violent as to break the glass'[45] – to fire engines. Careless workmen leaving a chafing dish of hot coals unattended during roofing repairs at York Minster in 1753 caused a blaze that spread with 'great Rapidity' and the fabric was saved only by the public, who 'ran from all Quarters to assist', using a 'Number of Water Engines'. In the following year a further engine and buckets were purchased in London for £24 17s. 0d., though this would not prevent Jonathan Martin, the notorious pyromaniac, gutting the Minster in 1829.[46] At Holy Trinity, Sunderland, County Durham, Edward Hill received 6 guineas for 'cleaning & keeping the Fire Engin in repair & playing it off at least Four times in a Year [and was with] his Servants ready to draw out & . . . Working it in case of any Accident by Fire'.[47] The maleficence of metal fixtures, particularly vanes, clock dials and chandeliers, was remedied by installing Benjamin Franklin's lightning conductors.[48] Vestries also took out insurance policies (pl. 105).

Nor should the destructive force of violent earthquakes be forgotten. On 29 December 1768 one struck the tower of Byton, Herefordshire, which 'split in many places . . . Men and women, with their children, ran towards the church, as to a place of safety, but . . . were prevented entering by the very ruinous condition'.[49] The Revd William Stukeley was left in no doubt that another in London was 'a warning judgment of God to the growing impiety and profaneness of the age!'.[50]

The terror of structural collapse created mayhem. In 1718 the 1,300-year-old St Mary Magdalene, Woolwich,

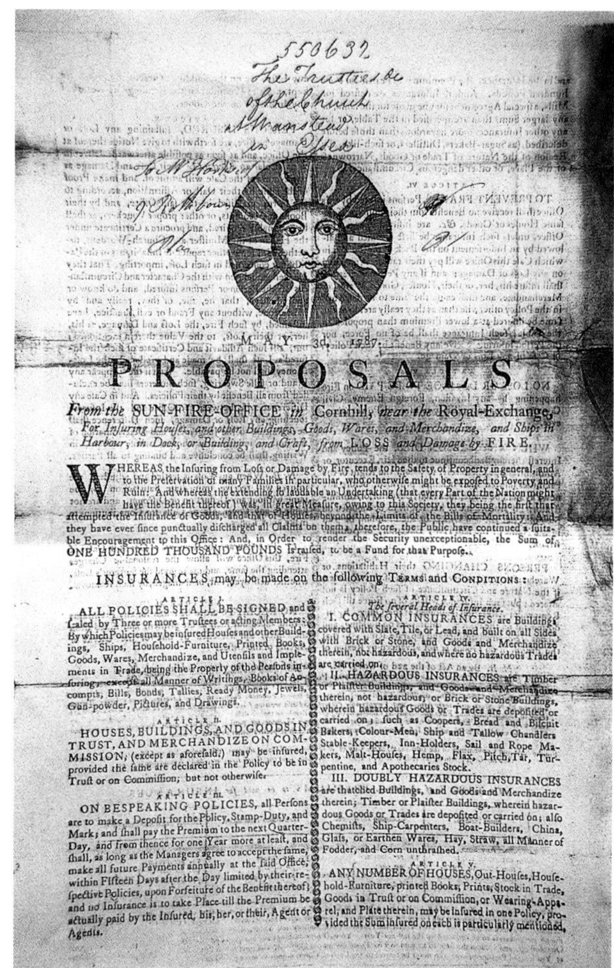

MAY 3d, 1787.

PROPOSALS

From the SUN-FIRE-OFFICE in Cornhill, near the Royal-Exchange,
For Insuring Houses, and other Buildings, Goods, Wares, and Merchandize, and Ships in Harbour, in Dock, or Building, and Craft, from LOSS and Damage by FIRE.

WHEREAS the Insuring from Loss or Damage by Fire, tends to the Safety of Property in general, and to the Preservation of many Families in particular, who otherwise might be exposed to Poverty and Ruin: And whereas the extending so laudable an Undertaking (that every Part of the Nation might have the Benefit thereof) was, in great Measure, owing to this Society, they being the first that attempted the Insurance of Goods, and that of Houses, beyond the Limits of the Bills of Mortality: And they have ever since punctually discharged all Claims on them, therefore, the Public have continued a suitable Encouragement to this Office: And, in Order to render the Security unexceptionable, the Sum of ONE HUNDRED THOUSAND POUNDS is raised, to be a Fund for that Purpose.

INSURANCES may be made on the following TERMS and CONDITIONS:

ARTICLE I.

ALL POLICIES SHALL BE SIGNED and sealed by Three or more Trustees or acting Members: By which Policies may be insured Houses and other Buildings, Ships, Household-Furniture, Printed Books, Goods, Wares, Merchandize, and Utensils and Implements in Trade, being the Property of the Persons insuring, except all Manner of Writings, Books of Accompts, Bills, Bonds, Tallies, Ready Money, Jewels, Gun-powder, Pictures, and Drawings.

ARTICLE II.

HOUSES, BUILDINGS, AND GOODS IN TRUST, AND MERCHANDIZE ON COMMISSION, (except as aforesaid.) may be insured, provided the same are declared in the Policy to be in Trust or on Commission; but not otherwise.

ARTICLE III.

ON BESPEAKING POLICIES, all Persons are to make a Deposit for the Policy, Stamp-Duty, and Mark; and shall pay the Premium to the next Quarter-Day, and from thence for one Year more at least, and shall, as long as the Managers agree to accept the same, make all future Payments annually at the said Office, within Fifteen Days after the Day limited by their respective Policies, upon Forfeiture of the Benefit thereof; and no Insurance is to take Place till the Premium be actually paid by the Insured, his, her, or their, Agent or Agents.

ARTICLE IV.

The several Heads of Insurance.

I. COMMON INSURANCES are Buildings covered with Slate, Tile, or Lead, and built on all Sides with Brick or Stone, and Goods and Merchandize therein, not hazardous, and where no hazardous Trades are carried on.

II. HAZARDOUS INSURANCES are Timber or Plaister Buildings, and Goods and Merchandize therein, not hazardous, or Brick or Stone Buildings, wherein hazardous Goods or Trades are deposited or carried on; such as Coopers, Bread and Biscuit Bakers, Colour-Men, Ship and Tallow Chandlers Stable-Keepers, Inn-Holders, Sail and Rope Makers, Malt-Houses, Hemp, Flax, Pitch, Tar, Turpentine, and Apothecaries Stock.

III. DOUBLY HAZARDOUS INSURANCES are thatched Buildings, and Goods and Merchandize therein; Timber or Plaister Buildings, wherein hazardous Goods or Trades are deposited or carried on; also Chemists, Ship-Carpenters, Boat-Builders, China, Glass, or Earthen Wares, Hay, Straw, all Manner of Fodder, and Corn unthrashed.

ARTICLE V.

ANY NUMBER OF HOUSES, Out-Houses, Household-Furniture, printed Books, Prints, Stock in Trade, Goods in Trust or on Commission, or Wearing-Apparel, and Plate therein, may be insured in one Policy, provided the Sum insured on each is particularly mentioned,

105 Sun-Office, London. 'Proposal' 550632 for annual insurance against fire damages not exceeding £4,000, for St Mary, Wanstead, Essex, addressed to Thomas Hardwick Jr., architect, 20 November 1788. Engraving. Essex Record Office, D/P/292/28/5.

'rotten and mouldering', began to sink and gave 'such a crack when it was full' that the congregation was 'put . . . into a very great consternation [and] many were trampled under foot and hurt in crowding to get out'.[51] At the opening of a new Methodist Meeting House at Colne, Lancashire, in 1777, 'just as Mr Wesley entered the pulpit, one of the galleries gave way, by which accident eight or ten persons had their limbs broken, more than forty were bruised, some of them, it is feared, mortally'.[52] The local press and monthly news compendiums revelled in reporting such sensationalism. According to the *Oxford Journal* on 14 December 1790: the arches of Banbury tower 'gave way, which occasioned a Chasm from the bottom to the top, and instantly the whole . . . became cracked, and shivered in a variety of directions, admitting the light through each,

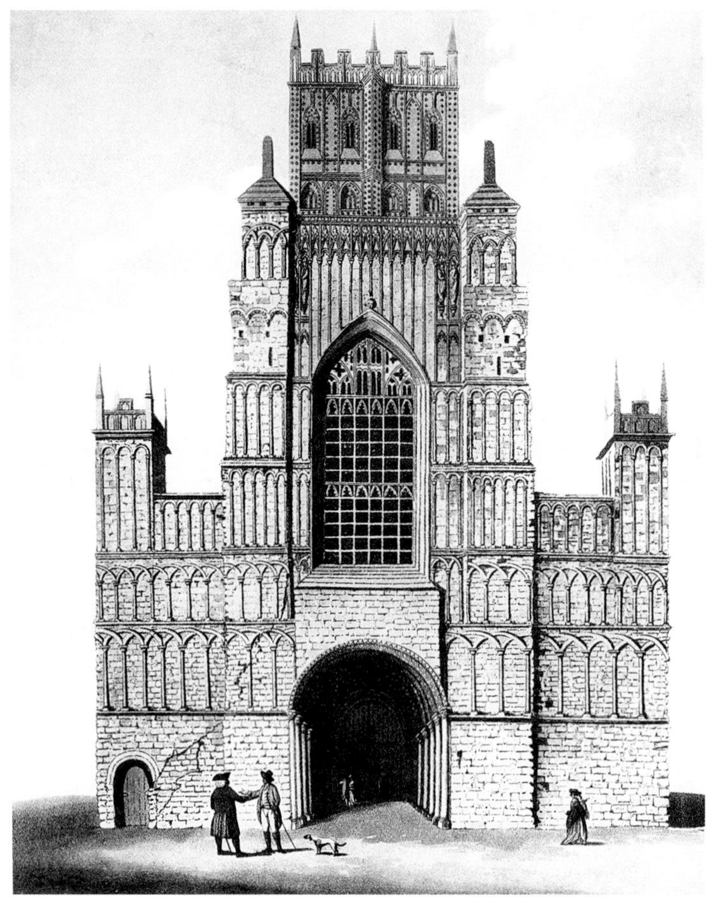

but yet preserving a perpendicular Fall, even in its pinaccles'.[53] No accounts of catastrophes were more sensational than those appearing in the *Gentleman's Magazine*. Structural faults in the masonry of the romanesque west front of Hereford Cathedral detected in 1763 remained precarious when they were described by James Wathen on 17 April 1786 as 'settling of the walls and arches from their perpendicular . . . to which very little attention had been paid or . . . assistance given' (pl. 106). Three days later the *Hereford Journal* reported the collapse of '*all that beautiful* and *magnificent structure* . . . now a heap of rubbish', while a dramatic eyewitness account of a person who travelled to see the 'sacerdotal shame' recorded the 'tremendous . . . glorious *clash* it made' (pl. 107). The *Gentleman's Magazine* blamed the 'barbarous indolence of the chapter', though

106 (*left*) J. Middiman and F. Jukes after James Wathen. 'View of the West Tower and Front of Hereford Cathedral taken on the Morning of the 17th of April 1786 (on which Day the Tower fell)', 12 April 1788. Engraving. © The British Library Board, K.Top. XVI.19-g.

107 (*below*) James Wathen. 'View of the Ruins of the West Tower & Front of Hereford Cathedral, taken April 18. 1786 (being the day after the Tower fell)', 12 April 1788. Engraving. © The British Library Board, K.Top. XV.19-h.

this was apparently unfounded. A later commentator described it as 'the most remarkable event of modern times in the history of English cathedrals'.[54] Then, in July 1788, as reported in the *Shrewsbury Chronicle and Shropshire, Montgomeryshire, Denbighshire, Merionethshire, Flintshire, &c. General Advertiser*, St Chad, Shrewsbury, 'suddenly fell down, to the great astonishment of the inhabitants . . . the four massy pillars which support the tower, were only case with rubble . . . How very providential that this dreadful catastrophe did not happen . . . when the congregation was assembled for divine worship.'[55] The rigmaroles at Hereford and Shrewsbury set the region's nerves on edge, so that at Madeley, Shropshire, in 1794 the

> noise made by the fall of a person . . . seized with a fit, excited an universal apprehension that the building was giving way . . . confusion, distress and terror . . . ensued . . . great numbers were much hurt by jumping out of the windows, or being jammed in the doorways, whilst the shrieks of Women and Children left behind increased the horror of the Scene.[56]

Such incidents were caused not only by neglect but also by poor construction and 'the mere tyranny of time'.[57] Ancient Blidworth, Nottinghamshire, 'fell . . . by means of an unskillful or foolhardy Workmen, who, in making a Vault, undermined one of the main Pillars [and the] unhappy Workman [was] buried in the Ruins . . . tho, it must be confess'd, the Church was in a very ruinous Condition before' and the 'Timber . . . appears . . . so decay'd and rotten that . . . it could not have stood long without this Accident'.[58] Fornham, Suffolk, was consumed by fire in 1773, 'occasioned by the inadvertency of a man shooting at jack-daws'.[59] By 1792 St Mary, Elmsthorpe, Leicestershire, its roof having collapsed after thieves stripped off the lead, was 'occasionally made a garden, and used as a penn for cattle'.[60] Finally, in 1800 Chelmsford parish church in Essex collapsed when workmen digging a vault undermined two of the nave pillars, as recorded in a pair of engravings. It was reckoned this 'will be timely warnings to the inhabitants and incumbents . . . how they trust . . . country or inexperienced workmen'. Indeed, during subsequent repair work the bricklayer was found guilty of stealing lead and sentenced to fourteen years transportation. Moreover, John Johnson, the 'able and experienced Architect' appointed surveyor to undertake the restoration, was accused of knowing nothing of such business and 'So Base as to Call the [local] Tradesmen . . . a Sett of D_m'd Villions'.[61]

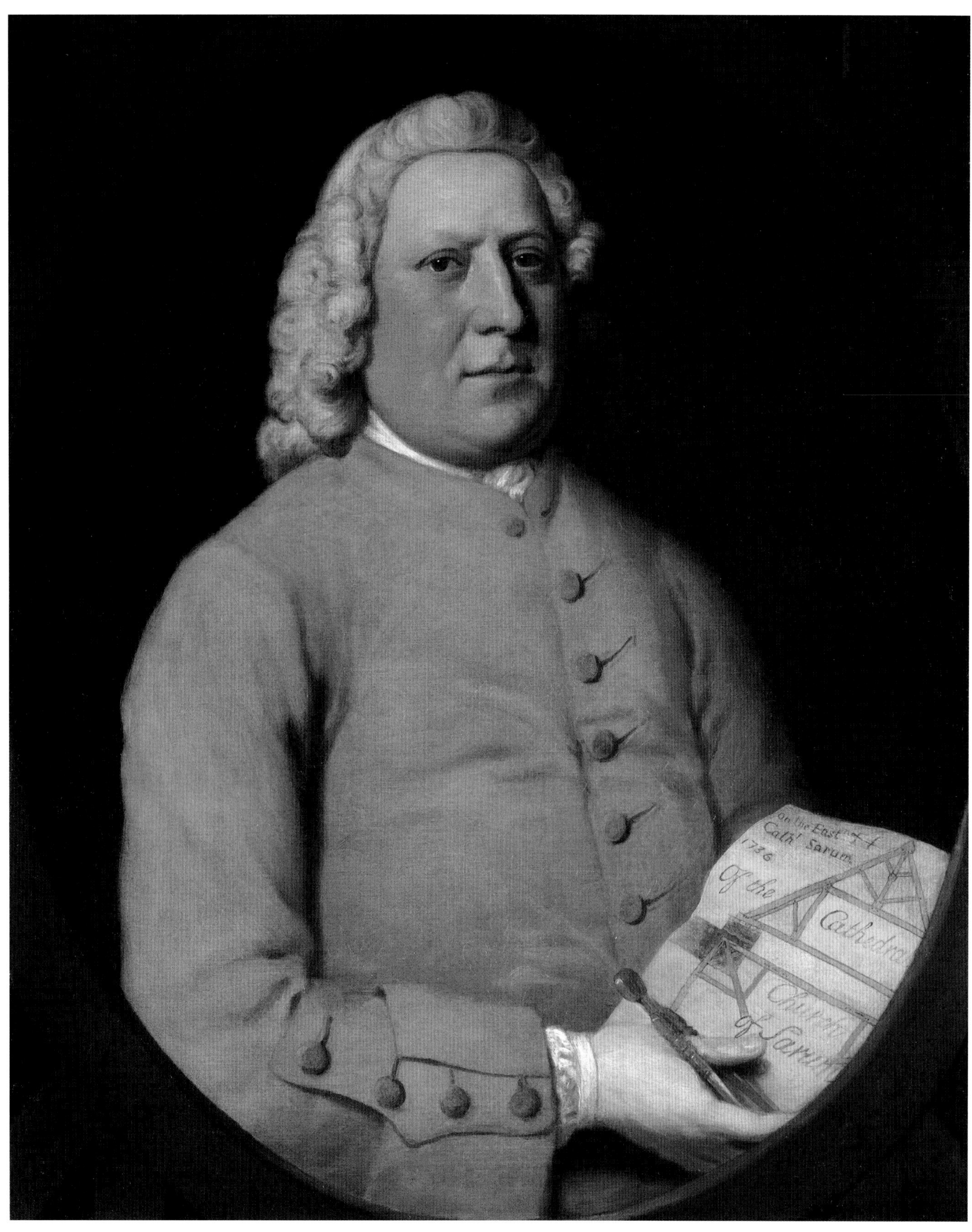

108 George Beare, *Francis Price*, 1747. Oil on canvas. National Portrait Gallery, London, inv. no. 1960.

Ten

ARCHITECTS AND BUILDERS

Of all buildings churches give architects the best opportunity to display the marvels of their art[1]

– a sentiment confirmed in the noble, business-like countenance of Francis Price, responsible for repairing the timber framework of Salisbury Cathedral's medieval roof, thereby preserving the great fabric, compellingly captured by the portraitist George Beare (pl. 108). It is of some import that Richard Neve's *The City and Country Purchaser, and Builder's Dictionary; or, The Compleat Builders Guide*, first published in 1703, describes two categories of architects. The '*Divine Architect of this World*' (God) who vouchsafed through biblical texts to 'give necessary *Precepts* and *Rules* concerning some *Buildings*', including the Ark of the Covenant, the Tabernacle and Altar, and Solomon's Temple at Jerusalem, the '*Ominiscient Architect*' who directed 'Men to Build by Design . . . a *Prototype, Model, Draught*, or *Pattern*' and also provided dimensions and selected materials. The other architect was the 'Master workman [or "Surveyor"] in a Building' who 'designs the Model, or draws the Plot, or Draught of the whole Fabrick; whose Business it is to consider of the whole Manner, and Method of the Building', showing 'respect to its due *Situation, Contrivance, Receipt, Strength, Beauty, Form* and *Materials*'.[2]

This latter, terrestrial *Doppelgänger* – eventually to evolve into the modern concept of an independent professional architect concerned exclusively with design issues – then still maintained close ties with hands-on practitioners in the building trades, as evident in the late Stuart London City Churches, where cooperation existed between Sir Christopher Wren in his supervisory role as Surveyor of the King's Works and his executive teams of craftsmen, who might be adept equally at design and construction. This was the case, for example, with John James, trained as a master carpenter, who rose to the more creative and prestigious position of Wren's assistant surveyor and ultimately surveyor of St Paul's Cathedral, surveyor of the fabric of Westminster Abbey and surveyor to the Commissioners for Building Fifty New Churches, while continuing to involve himself in practical carpentry. Where at this period ecclesiastical buildings differed substantially from their secular counterparts can be seen in the structure of the New Churches programme of 1711 in London, where conceptual drawings were firmly under the control of the Commissioners' appointed architects (designated as co-surveyors): Thomas Archer (an 'amateur' architect), John James, James Gibbs (the first Briton to receive a professional architectural training abroad, with Carlo Fontana, the papal architect in Rome) and Nicholas Hawksmoor (Wren's long-time assistant). Craftsmen's designs, when supplied, were restricted to embellishments and furnishings. From around 1730 craftsmen began to capitulate to architects in this crucial inaugural stage, at the same time increasingly relying on ideas sourced from pattern books, particularly in the provinces, such as Gibbs's *A Book of Architecture* (1728, 1739), with 34 of its 150 plates devoted to his churches and their 'proper Ornaments'. This aimed at appealing to 'such Gentlemen as might be concerned in Building, especially in the remote parts of the Country, where little or no assistance for Designs can be procured . . . which may be executed by any Workman who understands Lines'.[3] In turn, architects increasingly operated exclusively within the supervisory arena of the contract system, as evident by the presence of these often highly detailed technical memoranda in a majority of churches recorded in the Documents (CD-ROM), so that in 1788 John Soane could claim prophetically that the 'business of the Architect is to make the designs and estimates, to direct the works . . . he is the intermediate agent between the employer . . . and the mechanic'.[4] Their relationship, however, was not always unambiguous, and they were sometimes in conflict with Vestries at the mercy of wildly desperate assessments of the fragile conditions of their churches. A Parliamentary committee dealing with All Saints, Gainsborough, Lincolnshire, for example, reported that Edward Goddard, mason, spent only three hours surveying the medieval fabric in a haphazard, roughshod manner, including examining the internal pillars by standing 'upon one of the Seats', from which he concluded that it could be repaired 'to stand for many Years' at a cost of £200 to £400, though he 'made no Computation, to justify his Opinion'. Whereas Francis Smith of Warwick (the subsequent architect of the new church) and Francis Bickerton, who had worked on repairs to York Minster, both 'Professed Surveyors . . . of unquestionable Credit', made thorough, realistic surveys, concluding that 'there is no computing how long a Building in those Circumstances may possibly stand, the precise Time of . . . falling . . . always uncertain . . . depending upon many Contingency's' but which 'generally are very sudden & surprising'.[5]

Another episode involving Faversham, Kent, demonstrates the problems of controlling operations from afar. The architect for remodelling the medieval fabric, George Dance Sr, clerk of works of the City of London and a leading ecclesiastical designer, apologised to the building committee in 1754 for not delivering the builders' contracts personally, because he was 'so much Engaged in many very material transactions at this time, that it is next to impossible'. While his scheme was approved because 'it will not only add Great Beauty . . . but make that Convenient Room which is wanting for all the Parishioners', Dance was left defending it vigorously against opposing proposals by local builders, who, he claimed, 'imagine themselves equal to a Task they are perhaps unfit for'. He presented a 'long Epistle' about the committee 'approving the Crude Scheme' sent to him for comment, having 'absolutely rejected mine, the two Designs being in almost every respect diametrically opposite'. The rival scheme was 'greatly liked by the Parishioners [because] they thoroughly understand it, and will please themselves in pursuing it; I wish to God I had reason to congratulate them upon it, and to agree with them that it will lessen the Expence; but I am no friend to more unmeaning complaisance.' Dance goes on: 'as it is very disagreeable, I would decline saying any thing further . . . only as you desire my opinion . . . good manners obliges me to it, and therefore I will give it without the least partiality or disguise'. The roof was 'one of the most Rickety things I ever saw . . . treble the Expence of mine',

> the whole Nave . . . extremely dolefull and gloomy . . . and upon the whole, I cannot, without violence to my reason, approve of this Scheme, nor can I think of a better and more reasonable one, than what I have already sent you, which will be lightsome, Airy, and commodious, and may be executed at a moderate Expence.

In other words, from 'Practice, Experience, and the . . . Rules of Architecture . . . the whole will be right, safe, and secure', whereas the other, if executed, 'will shock People when they see its bad effect'.[6]

Such controversies were partly exacerbated by general suspicions about the virtues of architects. For example, the *Grub-street Journal* condemned James's proposals for improving St Margaret, Westminster, as 'no very honest design of putting the inhabitants to . . . great . . . unnecessary Expence . . . to make work for them [the architects]'.[7] Or Dean Bullock's insightful observations on Matthew Brettingham's restoration of Norwich Cathedral:

> I am throughly Sensible, that in pushing on . . . repairs of a long neglected [fabric], it is a very easy matter to give offence, this Brettingham is a grievous burthen . . . we pay him needlessly for wt we could do as well, & as cheap without him . . . the Truth is . . . he has too much skill in forwarding a work wch we have no inclination to, & . . . we are sick of him . . . [though] we have had things done not only in a better mannr. but at a Cheapr Rate by his assistance . . . but the pavement is a plain jobb, wch surely might be contracted for without. the assistance of a Surveyor.

Yet, the surveyor's lower estimate did help secure more advantageous building contracts, so that 'I shou'd wrong my own judgment if I did not support him as far as I am able [and] Espous'd [him] wh some warmth'. Work on the west 'Turrets' proceeded.[8]

Nor was it always an easy matter to appoint a suitable architect. This from a verbatim account of a London surveyor, Richard Norris, in his testimony to a House of Commons committee in 1790 regarding his proposal for rebuilding Hackney parish church to accommodate 1,800 worshippers and costing £10,000: 'Q: "Have you been frequently concerned in large Buildings?" A: "Not very big Buildings." Q: "Did you ever Plan or design [a church] before?" A: "I don't remember that I did." Q: "Did you ever build a Church?" A: "No" '.[9] Not surprisingly, the Vestry preferred his rival James Spiller, a pupil of James Wyatt and an associate of John Soane. The secrecy demanded for open architectural competition further fuelled misgivings: in 1758 ten unnamed but mottoed designs (all unfortunately untraced) were submitted for the Magdalene House, Southwark, an institution for repentant prostitutes, tagged sanctimoniously: 'There is more Joy in Heaven over one Sinner that repenteth, than over Ninety and nine just Persons that need no Repentance', 'No complaining no begging in the Streets', 'A Well Wisher to the Charity', 'Pro Patria', 'Evils may be more easily prevented than cured'. None was deemed to 'have sufficient Merit to intitle them to the Premium' and the project was temporarily abandoned.[10]

Or, take the case of St Botolph, Bishopsgate. The new church of 1724–8 (pl. 572) was criticised by contemporary commentators for the 'very disagreeable . . . forms' of the doors, with their 'intolerably bad' architraves, the inelegant lack of height in the tower and in placing a window in the middle of the street front, an 'error of the first magnitude'.[11] The building has also been dismissed by modern historians as the eccentric, clumsy endeavours of an obscure City architect named James Gould, whose authorship of St Botolph has been a matter of dispute, largely due to its contentious building history. In May 1724 seven architects submitted rival designs, none of which has survived, ranging from John James and Edward Oakley (who was subsequently appointed measurer) to locals such as the father and son team of Giles and George Dance (the latter having married Gould's daughter in 1719). During construction the Dances, Thomas Dunn (employed at Christ Church, Spitalfields, St Mary Woolnoth and St George, Hanover Square) and John Townsend (at St Mary-le-Strand) served as masons. From the outset there were tensions. The accuracy of Gould's specifications was questioned, while Oakley's report of 1726 noted differences in bonding methods. Significantly, the masons explained that they had removed or modified window and door detailing to 'make the work more Beautifull' and

> Consider'd wth The Utmost Care the Benefitt, and Advantage of the Building for Which Reason, Wee could not Omitt this opportunity of Performing, what We thought so Materiall and Necessary, Towards The Increase both of Strength, and Beauty to the Worke, Notwithstanding it was A Considerable Addition of Charge to us . . . we flatter ourselves that the Justness of Our Intentions . . . will give . . . Intire Satisfaction.[12]

In other words the builders, and most likely specifically George Dance, who was soon to emerge as one of the leading City Churches architects, took audacious aesthetic liberties to improve what was regarded as Gould's faulty design. I will have more to say about this uncommonly interesting church in chapter 25.

Even the eminent Sir Christopher Wren was not immune. A celebrated series of controversies chronicled in printed broadsheets concerned choice of material to cover the vast 30,000-foot surface of St Paul's Cathedral dome (pl. 2). A Parliamentary committee considering two proposals submitted in 1707, one for 170 tons of the 'best Sort . . . of *Derbyshire* Lead' costing £2,500, which the architect favoured, and another the 'finest *British* Copper' at £3,050, which he dismissed on grounds that its colour did not harmonise with the Portland stonework and tarnished to an ugly black, nevertheless decided to encourage the copper-works industry by employing it on the lantern and west towers.[13] The anonymous author of *The Cupulo* wrote, inaccurately turning the story topsy-turvy,

> Of mountain bulk, and of stupendous size
> Its eminence aspiring to the skies
> Ev'n KIRK resolv'd that since the dome was built,
> It ought in conscience to be double gilt[14]

This prompted Defoe to claim that Wren sanctioned the dome covered in 'copper double gilded with gold; but he was over-ruled . . . and the city thereby, deprived of the most glorious sight that the world ever saw, since the temple of Solomon'.[15]

Wren's longevity and his degenerating draughting talent exposed by his shaky signature on a Westminster Abbey study (drawn by his assistant William Dickinson) dated 1719, when he was 87 years old (pl. 151), is symptomatic of the difficulties suffered by architects in old age or sickness. As early as 1724 the 62-year-old Nicholas Hawksmoor, who had just succeeded Wren as abbey surveyor, was described as a 'Sick Lame man'; early in the following year James was recommended for the post of under-surveyor partly on grounds that his boss was 'rendred almost incapable of attending . . . Duty, thro' . . . frequent . . . violent Fits of . . . Gout' and 'very often confined to his House', and in 1727 the architect apologised for not being 'strong enough to venture out having had much of my old Enemy ye Gout', though he continued to serve effectively until his death in 1736.[16] In any case, he had an independent streak that did not always suit clients, as Henry Cheere's memorably grumpy portrait bust makes all too clear. At St George, Bloomsbury, Hawksmoor was admonished for incurring additional expenses in steeple decorations without the Commissioners' consent, for which he would be personally held responsible in the future.[17]

There was the occasional lawsuit. In 1773 Stephen Wright, master mason in HM Office of Works, was called in by the Duke of Newcastle to comment on Fuller White's remodelling of St Swithin, Baumber, Lincolnshire, then the subject of adjudication between client and architect. A carpenter by trade, White had been given the job in order to 'save the Expence of full Commission to a Regular Surveyor Whose duty is to draw designs, see they are perform'd in a Substantial & Workmanlike manner, Adjust measuremts, & make out or revise all Artificers Bills &c'. Yet the duke had cause for regret because White had failed to deliver accounts, 'notwithstanding repeated Solicitations, Orders, & Threats, without any Obediance being paid . . . which created strong Suspicions of very bad designs, by such unwarranted delays, which wrought his dismission, & . . . a Procecution to force him to an Acct'. Indeed, this lack of diligence is born out by White's surviving flimsy work there.[18] Nor was this an isolated incident. The trustees for rebuilding St Alkmund, Shrewsbury, were obliged to inform its surveyors that it had come to their attention that they 'very seldom or never attended to inspect the Building' and instructed them to do so now regarding the contractors who were erecting the timber roof.[19] These were not the only hazards facing architects. Shortly after Joseph Dixon won the competition for rebuilding St Mary, Battersea, 'some evil minded Person had industriously reported' that in the architect's capacity as a churchwarden he 'had embezzled or made an improper Use of . . . Parish Money', but the Vestry was 'thoroughly satisfied that the same is false and without the least foundation'.[20]

Normally, conditions of employment of a professional architect were clearly set out in the contract. At St Botolph, Aldgate, for example, George Dance was obliged 'to see and approve of all the several Materials before they shall be respectively used', 'draw as many plans or Designs . . . as the Trustees shall direct for their approbation [and] attend from time to time . . . to see the Work compleatly and in a Workmanlike manner performed according to such Agreements . . . made with the Workmen'. If he failed the trustees were empowered 'to discharge him' and pay him 'according to the proporcons of the Mony . . . expended . . . at that time', with the fee set at 3 per cent on the total building cost.[21]

Even then the course of construction did not always run smoothly. Take the complicated, protracted machinations surrounding All Saints, Southampton, the only notable new church built in the town in the eighteenth century. On the basis of his design the young, precocious Willey Reveley was appointed architect in 1791, but over the next two years followed a sequence of contradictory adjustments to the proposal made either on his own cognizance or from interference by a woefully inexperienced building committee, whose 'resolutions are so opposite in their tendencys that they thwart each other', complained Reveley, so that the work 'is a sort of battle dore & shuttle cock'.[22] This was compounded by bitter behind-the-scenes recriminations. The call for designs in 1790 attracted no less than seven contenders, including his eminent London rival George Byfield, whose offering (untraced) was at first well received, then rejected in favour of Reveley's because it did not have 'all the Convenience & Size . . . the Committee . . . thought it had' and was also 'the dearest', and despite lowering his estimate was condemned for exemplifying those 'Cheap Churches . . . with Bad Materials & . . . Work . . . put in the room of the very best'. Shortly afterwards the public was alerted in two printed handbills to a 'scene of Masonic Buffoonery' in which 'an Old Mummy' (the committee's president) was accused of favouring Reveley's scheme, '*a sandy uncemented pile of his own decrepitude . . . without one struggle*', thereby supporting '*the Millstone of exorbitant Expence fixed by a Gordian Knot*' around the parishioners' necks, while rejecting '*a Plan which, for the beauty of its architecture, and the moderation of its estimate, was highly deserving of preference*'. '*Is the Temple of the Almighty to be erected in the bread of the poor and hungry?*' asked the anonymous pamphleteer, perhaps incited by recent revolutionary events in France and the publication of Tom Paine's *The Rights of Man*. But he did not stop there. '*The present plan . . . is either the chimera of an infatuated brain, or the design of a wicked heart conscious of its own depravity.*' The committee condemned these pieces of pomposity for 'Scurrility & Personal Abuse . . . scarcely ever equalled [and] nothing but a violent illiberal Attack on the Majority of the Trustees done with a View to harass & vex them & . . . serve only to cause Animosities & Disturbance in the Parish'.[23] Nothing more was heard from either the author or Byfield, but the bickering continued. In 1792 the parties debated over the merits of undertaking construction 'by *measure & value* on the lowest offers', which Reveley believed the 'most advantageous . . . mode of proceeding . . . where the least uncertainty remains, & . . . economy is the leading feature' (as was the case here due to difficulties in resolving major aspects of the design, particularly the form of the portico, the position of the steeple and the choice of materials). He reckoned 'more offers will be made on these terms' and also it

> admits of retracting any orders . . . that might render the church too expensive . . . admits of any alteration whatever during the work, a liberty the most pretious both as economical & rendering every part more compleat . . . produces the best work because the moment any contractor fails in his engagement you may turn him off & take another . . .

and, finally, 'prevents all disputes whatever'. Reveley, however, found the committee's 'resolutions . . . so opposite in their tendencys that they thwart each other. It is impossible to advertise [in the press for builders' proposals and estimates] because the alterations necessary will require something to execute [and] they seem now aiming at useless Expence entirely.' Moreover, 'how can any advertizement be inserted when the designs are daily undergoing the most material alterations', and he pointed out that 'the very act of going to law [in the event of disputes] is a greater loss of money & more especially of time than any penalty can repair'. 'I should think it much better to be more settled in the design . . . before advertisement is thought of . . . but the manner in which the Committee has regularly treated my advice, makes me entirely free from responsibility either for the contents of people or Expence.' In the following year (1793) G. G. Hookey, a local builder who contracted for construction for an estimated £7,750, complained of 'an unwarrantable Attack on my Character' because the committee had 'Cause of Discontent' for his firing the foreman, retorting that this was an 'Interference [and] Intermeddling with his Right [which] tends to enslave his Mind and endanger his property' (that is, his responsibilities for overseeing operations). Reveley, who felt that he had been 'drawn into a long train of disputes', told Hookey that he disapproved of 'turning off your foreman and letting out the work to task' which was 'a contradiction to my advice' and where 'no improvement . . . can be expected'. In turn, he informed the committee that

> If . . . Hookey is to keep up a constant display of his rights in opposition to mine, the work will never proceed at all but by my suffering him to go on well or ill as he pleases, and . . . not make it a point of honour to do as I direct him . . . his determined resistance to my orders and to try his strength with me in the parish are not only extremely disagreeable to me as personalities, but give me just cause to apprehend that he will on frequent occasions dispute points, in which case . . . prejudice to the work and to the interest of the parish must insue.

There was one final hiccup. In 1796, following the building's completion (pls 659, 661), Reveley complained that 'the delay of the trustees in paying my bill is cruel & undeserved', which 'irritated' him since he was 'on the eve of an expensive journey & having more than £1000 due . . . from various persons I have not five pounds in the house'. The next year he still daily felt 'want of money' due to the 'scarcity of business & the difficulty of obtaining payment' (presumably resulting from the war with France), which was finally received only in December 1798, six months before his untimely death on 6 July 1799, age 39.[24]

The impact on architectural prosperity in Britain of the Continental wars that erupted following the French Revolution in 1789 is variously demonstrated. On 1 February 1793 France declared hostilities against Britain and the Dutch Republic. In October the Vestry of St Michael, Madeley, Shropshire, deemed it 'impracticable from the loss of trade, by diminution of demand thro' the War &c. to build two churches' in its fast-growing parish, and only one was realised, of predictably geometric austerity (pl. 693).[25] In November it was noted in connection with All Saints, Southampton, that timber bought since the outbreak of war had risen by 1s. 6d. per foot.[26] St Alkmund, Shrewsbury parish, towards the completion of the new church in 1794 (pl. 231), sought Parliamentary powers to borrow £3,000, which was 'extremely material . . . to avoid every unnecessary Expence'.[27] At St John, Hackney, in February 1797, four months after Spain declared war on Britain, the tower's construction was postponed due to the 'present state of Public Affairs' to a 'future period, when a design more suitable . . . may be executed at a much less Expence, than the present high price of every Article, both . . . Materials and wages' (pl. 712).[28]

Architects could also be generous towards their rivals. In 1776 Samuel Wyatt and George Gibson travelled from London to Birmingham to comment on a design made for St Paul's parish church by Roger Eykyn of Wolverhampton; they rendezvoused at the Hen and Chicken.[29] Moreover, they occasionally served as arbitrators in building disputes, provision for which might be written into the contract. The trouble at Tetbury, Gloucestershire, concerning attempts to preserve the decayed medieval fabric, work of considerable substance, is a classic example of imperspicuity. From the 1730s a succession of architects and builders surveying the structure discovered 'very lean Mortar . . . made with ordinary sand and little Lime . . . very bad . . . rotten . . . scanty . . . Brittle' timber, even 'Sappy young Stuff unfit for Building . . . pieces let in artificially to deceive . . . daub'd over with Dirt or Cow Dung', repairs 'in many places . . . only mended or Slop't with Mortar' and 'outside . . . white wash'd to deceive any future Judgment . . . Peck't or how'd out in patches . . . loose stones put in an insupportable manner . . . rather than repairing . . . so meanly perform'd that the money laid out is but little better than Sunk'. Some of these men were found unreliable. William Killigrew and a Mr Tomkinson were reputed to live 'so hellish a Life . . . gott Rockey every Night constant'. Such bungling was confirmed when the 'Eminent Architect' James Gibbs was called in as 'Umpire' after much negotiation about a proper fee, though it transpired that he had 'not viewdd the Roof in Person but trusted a Report' submitted by John Townesend, a master-builder based at Oxford.[30] The church was finally demolished and rebuilt in the years 1775–8 (pl. 225).

In building operations, both working and presentation drawings were pivotal, and a number appear in this book, some published for the first time. All are invaluable as evidence of the designer's (whether architect or builder) intentions, or as surviving records of the appearance of lost buildings. They range from the graceless, such as that for Horwich, Lancashire (1776–82; pl. 499), rendered by an unknown hand for an inexpensive structure (costing £1,006 17s. 1d.) catering to cottagers, labourers and workers in cotton manufacturing, to the dazzlingly sophisticated, like the set prepared by Thomas Ivory for the Governors of the King's Hospital, or Blue Coat School, Dublin, bound in morocco leather for presentation to George III, also dating to 1776 (pl. 622). Some drawings were rendered as large as life to be used on site as templates during construction; unsurprisingly, few have survived.[31] When Dance Sr reported to the Aldgate trustees in 1744 on the completion of the church he felt it was 'Incumbent upon me to take Notice That the Work has not been Performed Strictly Comformable to the Drawings and Particulars Signed and Agreed to by the Contractors' (pl. 554).[32] The accounts for building St Mary Magdalene, Bridgnorth, Shropshire, record the fee of £147 10s. 8d. for work undertaken between 1792 and 1798 by the architect Thomas Telford, including 'Reports Journeys, attending the Meetings of the Trustees and all the occasional Inspections . . . while the Building was carrying on . . . Nine days attending the taking the Dimensions of the whole Church . . . and making out Comparative Statements of the Variations of the Several Works', as well as 'drawing Plans', about which he wrote to the trustees' attorney: 'I have not neglected the working Drawings . . . nor will you be surprised at the time they require when you have seen the number that are necessary – they are now . . . nearly completed and would have been wholly so, had not my drawing Clerk been taken ill.'[33]

Architectural draughting was more widespread than might be imagined, though performances varied considerably. It had already reached a technically ambitious standard in London by the early decades of the eighteenth century. Even architects not among the first rank, like Kenton Couse, drew with affectionate precision (pl. 74). Some incorporated alternative ideas on attached flaps (pl. 278), a practice hardly ever employed in the provinces.[34] Provincial drawings are appealing just because they lack such cosmopolitan refinements (pl. 726), though not necessarily invention. By the 1710s draughtsmanship had begun to improve substantially. Nowhere is this more compelling than in the work of one of the leading Lancashire architects, Henry Sephton, about whom nothing is known as to how he learned his art.[35] A sheet for the main elevation of Ince Blundell Hall near Liverpool (*circa* 1720), his major country house, signed confidently 'Henry Sephton Invent & Delin', is in the manner of Colen Campbell's *Vitruvius Britannicus* (1715), which includes engravings of Blenheim Palace and Buckingham House, London, Sephton's compositional sources, and also recalls his meticulous rendering of brickwork.[36] His earliest dated surviving work, St Aidan, Billinge, Lancashire (pl. 299), is intriguing in terms of its individualistic and sophisticated presentation drawings attached to a building contract of 11 December 1716 (pl. 300). The plans and orthogonal elevations, which he termed 'Prospects', are delicately rendered in pen and ink on vellum, individually framed like illuminated miniatures, with the porch, tower and chancel shaded and casting shadows. I know of no comparable example in Georgian architectural drawings.[37] Yet more novel is the companion study for the interior (pl. 110), this time on paper, a rare one-point perspective with the viewpoint taken above the cornice line and the roof removed to allow the viewer to look down into the body and chancel with the walls shaded and column bases casting short shadows, while one complete section of roof trusses is seen head-on. Perhaps Sephton had consulted John Moxon's popular *Practical Perspective; or, Perspective made easie* (1670), 'Useful for . . . Architects . . . that are any waies inclined to Speculatory Ingenuity', or Robert Pricke's *Perspective Practical; or, A Plain and Easie Method Of true and lively Respresenting all Things to the Eye at a distance, by the Exact Rules of Art As . . . Churches* (1673; pl. 109). Indeed, the schematic rendering of shadows subscribes to engraving conventions.

109 Robert Pricke. 'A Vault like a Scallop-shell may serve for the hollow of a Church' in *Perspective Practical*, 1672, p. 74. Engraving.

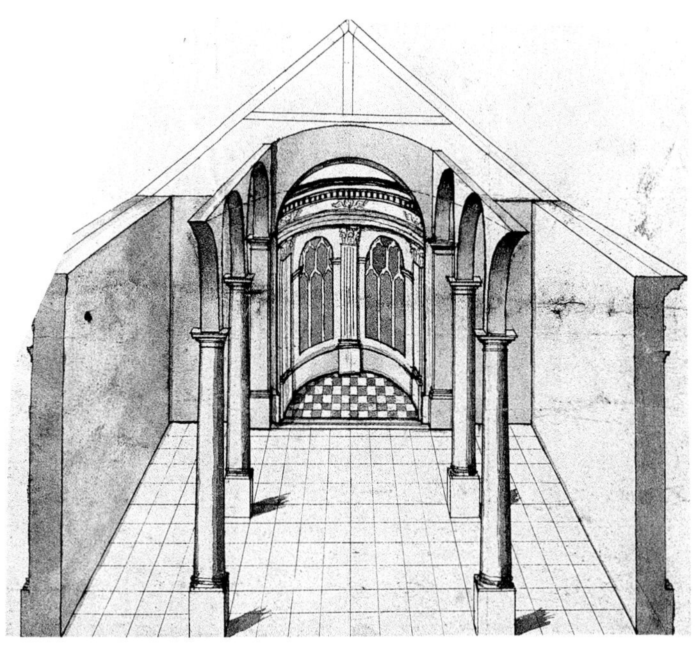

110 Henry Sephton. Design for the interior towards the chancel, St Aidan, Billinge, Lancashire, 1716. Pen and ink and wash on parchment. Wigan Archives Service, WLCT, D/DZ A13/18.

111 Edward Wing. Design for 'A Section of ye. East end of Aynho Church with a Prospect of the Chancell' (St Michael), Northamptonshire, 1723–5. Pen and ink and wash. Northamptonshire Record Office, faculty Reg. 1, f. 184

A copy of the latter pattern book, now belonging to the British Architectural Library, is inscribed 'Richard Trubshaw his Book June 16th 1727 Cost me 5 shillings att Daventry' (Northamptonshire). Trubshaw, based in Staffordshire and responsible for a group of Palladian churches in the Midlands, as a young man had worked in Oxford in 1715, where he purchased a copy of *Vitruvius Britannicus*, on which his repertory largely depended.[38] Gibbs's highly influential *A Book of Architecture* (1728, 1739), with its many ecclesiastical designs, attracted a long list of provincial subscribers, including the Scots architects William Adam and Alexander McGill, William Etty of York, William Townesend of Oxford and the Bath bookseller Leake.[39] Perhaps this was the milieu in which Sephton moved.

Sephton's exact contemporary Edward Wing, an architect-builder practising in Buckinghamshire, was denounced for his

> idle manner [which is] the amazement of all people who had any judgment . . . it being usual with him and his men to drink . . . more hours, than work and when at work it went on so slowly, that the going up . . . was to fenny stratford people become like the birth of the Mountains in the fable . . . but at length the mighty mouse appear'd up went some part . . . tho' in a very odd manner . . . their work not being . . . worth twelve pounds a man by the day.

He was covetous of his drawings, having submitted a 'Design of a Cupula . . . projected on a hexagon', but hoped it 'will not be Employ'd as Instruments for any other man to Work by'.[40] Drawings for Aynho, Northamptonshire, for which he charged £1 10s. 0d., include a wonderfully adventurous scenographic view (pl. 111), which he, too, called a 'Prospect', showing the roof trusses head-on but the chancel more conventionally than Sephton at eye-level one-point perspective, presumably in order to demonstrate how the side walls could be punctured by openings to illuminate further the communion table.[41]

Later in the century more skilfully rendered publications were available. Thomas Malton's beautifully illustrated *A Compleat Treatise on Perspective in Theory and Practice; on the True Principles of Dr Brook Taylor* (1779; pl. 496) emphasised that 'no pains has been spared to make the Work known, in almost every City and chief Town in England, which the Author has visited'. It attracted an impressive list of subscribers, including many church architects, among them the Adam brothers, William Chambers, Kenton Couse, James Gandon, William Hillyer, John Hobcroft, Henry Keene, William Newton, H. G. Oldfield, George Steuart, James 'Athenian' Stuart, John Woolfe and James Wyatt (whom we shall meet later in the present publication), as well as the Archbishop of Armagh, Primate of Ireland, and assorted builders. In the preface Malton observed that

> In every Age . . . where the Polite Arts are cultivated and encouraged, Emulation, and a desire of Fame, inspired the Breasts of the rising Generations; the ingenious Mechanics catches the ardent and laudable Flame . . . the People are necessarily enriched, and the State becomes potent and formidable. Architecture rears her stately Domes and lofty Turrets to the Skies . . . Perspective is allowed by all, who are well acquainted with it, to be the Basis of all the Polite Arts which have their foundation in Drawing . . . An Architect . . . would be better able to judge of the effect it would produce, and convey a just Idea of it to others, before the Design is executed.[42]

Some notion of fees charged for drawings can be gathered from building accounts: Gibbs received £10 10s. 0d. for Wimpole Hall chapel in 1719 and a further £1 1s. 0d. for each of two other studies in 1721 (pl. 88); Robert Morris was paid 8 guineas for a set for the Octagon Chapel, Norwich, in 1754 (pls 509, 582); Adam charged £15 15s. 0d. for the high altar of King's College chapel, Cambridge, with £26 5s. 0d. for a gothic alternative in 1768–9 (pls 328–9).[43]

Occasionally, architects also presented clients with wooden models. Parish records frequently refer ambiguously to 'models', which may signify either drawings or three-dimensional objects. The 'modell of a new Steeple' for Burton Overy, Leicestershire, however, is clearly the 'Model . . . drawn [by my] surveyor', Henry Dormer (pl. 304).[44] *The Builder's Dictionary* (1734) explicitly recommended 'for the better con-ducting and executing some great Work, and to give an Idea of the Effect it will have in large . . . In all large Buildings it is much the surest way to make a *Model* on Relievo, and not to trust to a bare Design or Draught.'[45] John Evelyn's English edition of R. Fréart's *A Parallel Of The Ancient Architecture With The Modern* quoted Henry Wotton's wise advice that the 'bigger' models are the 'better . . . in a Fabrick of some Forty or Fifty Thousand Pounds Charge, I wish Thirty Pounds at least laid out before-hand in an exact Model; for a little Misery in the Premises, may easily breed some Absurdity of greater Charge in the Conclusion'. The most celebrated example is Wren's 21 by 13 foot-high oak and pear wood Great Model in the form of a domed Greek cross for St Paul's Cathedral (1673–4).[46]

The call on 18 June 1712 by the New Churches Commissioners for 'proper Modells', resulting in thirteen specimens, was the largest concentration produced during the eighteenth century. Their purpose was made emphatic in a resolution that 'no church shall be begun untill a plan, or Modell, and an Estimate be made . . . And that when . . . agreed upon; It shall not be altered, without the directions of the [Commissioners]; and an Agreement made for the charge of Such Alteracon'.[47] Though only two have survived (both for Gibbs's St Mary-le-Strand), all their plans and several elevations were recorded in the nineteenth century (pls 7, 369, 405–6, 410). One of the two intact Strand models (pl. 112) was returned to Gibbs following his dismissal as surveyor in 1716 to enable him unofficially 'to perfect' the church, which was completed in 1724.[48] Of all the surveyors Gibbs used models most effectively to resolve design issues. That for his masterpiece, St Martin-in-the-Fields, for example, features a preliminary study on paper pasted to the inner side of the removable roof, and alternative exterior wall treatments (pl. 113). In addition, numbers of dependent models were prepared for the New Churches, now all vanished: the tower and vaulting for Christ Church, Spitalfields;[49] 'the Fronts of the Gallerys . . . Pulpit [and] West Door' for St Anne, Limehouse;[50] a 'Model of a twisted Column (of the Corinthian Order) for the better Instruction of the Joiners' at £5, supplied by Hawksmoor for the high altar of Thomas Archer's St John, Westminster,[51] and so on. During building operations (1712–34) all the models were displayed on metal shelves in the Commissioners' Lincoln's Inn Fields headquarters, subsequently in Old Palace Yard, Westminster, and finally in Henry V's chantry in the abbey until their removal and later disappearance, perhaps the greatest single loss sustained by British eighteenth-century architectural history.[52]

The practice spread quickly.[53] The 'proper & Convenient Modell & Design' proposed *circa* 1720 for Penrith (untraced) was clearly a wooden object (since 5s. was spent on 'Painting the Church Model'); it was made by William Etty, who had close ties with John Vanbrugh, one of the New Churches Commissioners.[54] Etty's model for Holy Trinity, Leeds, also lost but recorded in a contemporary engraving (pl. 419), was presented in 1723 for approval by the Archbishop of York (previously one of the New Churches Commissioners), as well as for the 'Workmen to go by'.[55] Fine models associated with St Giles-in-the-Fields, St John, Hampstead, and St Nicholas, Warwick, remain *in situ*.[56] Normally discarded after their purposes were no longer required, that any of these ephemera should have survived into the present day is something of a miracle.[57]

What about architects' fees for supervising building operations? George Steuart's expenses connected with St Chad, Shrewsbury, included travel, waiting on the building committee 'to take instructions for Designs' and making 'Several', attending meetings with a 'Book of Working Instructions' and 'Sett out the building make contracts and Arangements for the work', etc., for which he demanded either 3 per cent on the total cost of the contract at £14,430 14s. 6d., based on his presentation and working drawings (all vanished), or 5 per cent 'if it was their wish that I should Superintend the Work'. This was a standard rate. But in 1791 the committee insisted on the 3 per cent rate on 'his Original Estimate', despite an increase in costs, plus 40 guineas for additional journeys, otherwise they would 'consider him from this time no longer in their employ [since] they are Unanimous in their Opinion that his Expectations are too enormous to be complied with'. Steuart, who had provided a spectacular design (pls 679–81), replied in a lengthy, carefully considered letter that he had

> some difficulty in my Mind, as to the propriety of an Answer . . . there are certain rules established in every profession for the direction of the practitioners in the transaction of their Business; And which it is the Duty of every Member . . . to Support. I hope, therefore, when I Accept of whatever reward the Committee may deem my Attention to The building . . . deserves; it will not be considered as a precedent in the Conduct of any future Work.

He goes on:

> I am extremely Sorry if any Misconduct on my part has Occasioned the Commissioners to think my exertions not equally Worthy of the same Notice at this Advanced State of the Building as at the beginning. If it were but known the time I have already expended in the preparations of the Drawings, the Money paid to my Clerks for the Execution of them, the time and Expence I shall be at for Near two Years more in Adjusting the Accounts with every Contractor; then I trust my Original Expectations of the customary pay of Gentlemen employ'd in the Way of My profession woud not be thought to deserve the Title bestowed upon it in the resolution [which] I cheerfully Subscribe to . . . And they may be Assured, that however Small the reward . . . I shall pursue the execution of the Building with the same Unremitting Assiduity I trust I have hitherto done.

112 James Gibbs. Model for St Mary-le-Strand, London, 1714. Pearwood and boxwood. RIBA Library Drawings Collection, on loan from the Trustees of Burghley House.

113 James Gibbs. Model for St Martin-in-the-Fields, London, 1721. Pine, mahogany and pen and ink on paper. RIBA Library Drawings Collection, on loan from the Vestry of St Martin-in-the-Fields.

In 1794 the trustees refused to 'recede' from their original decision to permit only 3 per cent on the original estimate or 'any farther Sum for his Trouble as the Architect'.[58] By contrast, it appears that the building committee of All Saints, Southampton, was so uncertain about procedures that it was obliged to borrow William Paty's detailed contract of 1786 for constructing Christ Church, Bristol, where he and other family members were employed as both architects and builders.[59]

Inevitably, distinctions between architect and builder were not always clear-cut. Architects required a degree of technical familiarity to supervise building operations successfully. Gibbs was ordered to direct that materials salvaged from the old demolished St Martin-in-the-Fields could be reused only as he gave 'Express leave', and to sanction only a 'proper method' to secure the outer walls from the 'Extraordinary pressure' of the earth and buried coffins.[60]

The cantankerous, gout-ridden Hawksmoor uncharitably referred to 'Workmen advanc'd to . . . Architects' as a term of derision,[61] yet there are cases of mutual respect and friendship between the two professions. For example, Francis Smith, the chief early Georgian Warwick architect, recommended Thomas Woodward Sr for rebuilding the tower of Blockley, Gloucestershire, on grounds that he estimated a 'Cheap rate as . . . can be done by any Man in England that will do it well' and deserves 'every penny'.[62] Some rose to national prominence, like Francis Price proudly holding a draughting instrument and his celebrated design for repairing the timber framework of Salisbury Cathedral (pl. 108).

While there is no substantive evidence that women rose into the architectural profession, plenty served in the building trades.[63] They were often builders' widows, as in the case of Elizabeth Gregory, a carpenter who received £170 between 1707 and 1715 for

> making Ladders . . . altering & making good . . . Plumbers Moulds . . . making & putting up Window frames . . . Drawing-boards for . . . Masons Glaziers & Smiths . . . striking . . . Centers to . . . 4 Ribbs on . . . flatts of the South Cross . . . Shedds for . . . Masons . . . Putting up a Rayle under the North Window . . . makeing a Module of a Section of . . . Rt Wainscot for the Cross . . . tower & Spire

of Westminster Abbey[64] or Widow Harris, who was 'Implored to doe the Smith's Work' at St Mary-le-Bow in 1705.[65] Elizabeth Mines's rejected estimate for plastering St John, Westminster, in 1744 forced her to accept Thomas Clark as a partner.[66] Mrs Crowley and Company was paid £10 5s. 6d. for 'an Iron Circle' for the dome of Gibside Chapel, County Durham, in 1768.[67] Mrs Philip Lloyd, wife of the dean of Norwich Cathedral, painted glass in the east window (1777–80), which was the subject of a sonnet praising 'female piety and art' published in the *Gentleman's Magazine*.[68] Mrs Drew received 2 guineas for 'a large Majesty Escutcheon painted upon Silk hanging on the pulpitt Cloth' at St Margaret, Westminster, to mark the death of Queen Caroline in 1737.[69] The aristocratic Elizabeth Creed painted altarpieces for Aston, Barnwell, Tichmersh and Woodford in Northamptonshire.[70]

Parish records offer invaluable glimpses into the working lives and aspirations of builders and craftspeople. A substantial part of the Index has been devoted to identifying hundreds of men and women, some celebrated, many others now obscure, grouped by designated trades, but also those unspecified, all in the hope of shedding further light on their business activities, technical virtuosities, fees and achievements, their plights and fates, as we shall see shortly. But also their triumphs. John Simpson, the 'proper person' hired as 'Superintendant of the Works' during the construction of St Chad, Shrewsbury, is honoured in the church by an epitaph that reads: 'In His professional capacity Diligence, Accuracy and Irreproachable Integrity Insured His Esteem and Confidence Wherever He Was Employed And Lasting Monuments of His Skill and Ability Will Be Found in The Building of This Church Which He Superintended.'[71] At the close of work on St Mary, Battersea, the foreman received 4 guineas 'as a gratuity for his Sobriety good Behaviour and Diligence',[72] while on a similar occasion at Hereford Cathedral the fifty-nine-strong workforce was treated to a celebratory dinner costing a total of £2 19s. 10d., with an additional £3 7s. 0d. spent on 'Drink'.[73] On the other hand, unwarranted jubilation at completing the steeple of St Mary-le-Strand compelled the New Churches Commissioners to condemn the builders as 'guilty of great disorder'.[74] That Simpson was commemorated by a handsome marble monument featuring Sir Francis Chantrey's fine portrait bust suggests that the upper echelons of the trade were highly regarded in polite society.[75] Nor was it uncommon for local craftsmen to donate items of furnishings as part of their obligation towards parish rebuilding programmes. St Leonard, Shoreditch, was a typical example.[76]

Nevertheless, the status of others could be precarious. Take the well-documented case of John Lee, contracted in 1745 to undertake bricklaying at the prestigious St John, Hampstead (pl. 262), which was to be performed in a 'good Substantial . . . Workmanlike manner' using 'hard sound and even Coloured Waltham Green Gray Stocks' costing £840, where conditions imposed by the building committee were rigorous and sometimes harsh. This allowed 'Inspectors' access to the site in pursuit of practices 'not agreeable' to the architect's 'proposals . . . or . . . intent', requiring removal of the offending materials at Lee's expense. He was obliged to forfeit 12s. 'for every hundred of lime' if found to have used 'Samell or Bad bricks', £5 'for every Thousand of Bricks' if work was delayed. Should he 'Neglect to carry on . . . for the space of ten Days', except 'occasioned by bad weather or Non Payment of . . . money' due, the committee had 'full power [and] free liberty to Employ any other Workman', deducting fees 'without being Deemed Guilty of any breach' of contract. Moreover, the committee enjoyed the prerogative at any time 'to alter any thing in the Design . . . by adding . . . or diminishing', which 'shall not be esteemed a Variation from the Agreement . . . only paying or Allowing such reasonable Price or making such . . . allowances for such Alterations . . . agreed upon'.[77] A potential recipe for disaster. A few years later, when stonework was in danger of falling due to 'very insufficient bearings', the mason Sanders Oliver refused to 'make . . . satisfaction' for having 'notoriously . . . broke' his contract by selecting Purbeck instead of Portland stone; the committee considered legal action but on 'very carefully' reading Oliver's proposals was 'Generously advised not to proceed against him'.[78]

The Bishop of Ossory proposed to stimulate Kilkenny Cathedral's beautification by having 'one piece of every kind of carved work', including stalls for the chapter house and choir, made in England and transported via Bristol, thence by boat across the Irish Sea as a 'pattern for the Carver' to replicate, since he 'can afford to work cheaper' in Ireland. The bishop insisted that the craftsman 'must be a sober man, live in my house . . . not be above eating at the servants' table, & . . . keep out of other company otherwise he will be undone'.[79] London-born Charles Evans, clerk of the works for remodelling medieval Stoke Gifford, Gloucestershire, wrote to the client, Elizabeth, Dowager Duchess of Beaufort, of the

> difficulty with your Carpenter Mr: Grace . . . and his Man [who] did express some discontent . . . about their low Wages [which] I confess . . . is very low, but I do presume they work accordingly, and as for their Merit in Business . . . lies in a very narrow compass. As to my Man Rhind, who . . . is an Orderly Person and a very good Workman, & I hope he behaves as such, the Distance he lives from his work is certainly inconvenient and will take up some time in going to and from his Meals, he being a decent Person will not carry his Victuals with him. If your Grace thought fit to let him eat in the House, this inconvenience would be removed.

Evans added that in Rhind's 'capacity rather as a Director [that is, a site manager] than a Workman, I cannot charge your Grace less than Twenty Shillings pr week for him, exclusive of his Lodging'.[80] The prestige sometimes enjoyed by master craftsmen in parish life is vividly demonstrated in the autobiography of Thomas Johnson, a leading English rococo designer, carver and gilder, who was appointed clerk of the Bedford Chapel, Bloomsbury, in 1769 by promising to gift a carved and gilt altarpiece, and undertake carving the pulpit and clock. For the opening in 1771, on finishing off the new organ case with a crowning ornament, he stepped back to see how it looked, 'slipt of the scaffold, and fell with my side on the top of a pew [and] broke two of my ribs'.[81]

Parish records also reveal an *esprit de corps* among the various trades, particularly in the cases of large-scale operations such as the London New Churches and their progeny, where craftsmen freely moved from one job to another. Carpenters made 'molds', 'Templets' and 'Rules' for the 'Plaisterers use'.[82] They devoted two days to 'moveing Mr [Giovanni] Bagutty's Scaffold Board' and 'making a Scaffold . . . to Work the Ornamt. on Earth Side of Organ', a sure means of following the great Swiss decorative plasterer's progress across the vault of St Martin-in-the-Fields (pl. 417), and also supplied 'Templets for the Smith to work the Great Semicircular Windows' at St Mary Woolnoth (pl. 373).[83] At St Mary-le-Strand the masons drew 'Flowers on the Cieling as a pattern for the Plaisterer's Work' (pl. 379) and produced templates for the smiths 'to work the Ironwork of the round stairs'.[84] This sort of co-operation continued throughout the century, as evident in 1769 at Westminster Abbey, where the carpenters supplied an 'outside Mold for the Smith to make Iron work by & a drawing board [from] 80 feet Inch deal', while in 1789 at St Mary, Paddington, the bricklayer's scaffold was placed at the disposal of 'all the other Tradesmen provided they do not hinder or impede in his Business'.[85] On rare occasions craftsmen were singled out for public accolade, as in this notice, which appeared in the *St James's Evening Post* on 8 February 1717:

> There is to be seen the most Masterly piece of Carpenters worke, it being for the Roof of that Magnificent and beautiful Church at Westminster

> [Thomas Archer's St John, Smith Square] to the praise of that Most Ingenious young Man Mr John Grove Master Carpenter . . . All Judicious persons that has seen his Performance will agree that he has shown himself a great Master; and for his age the World Cannot parralel he deserves to be incurraged by all lovers of Art.[86]

Grove died in 1723 and his timberwork was destroyed in a fire in 1742.

A craftsman's vocation could also be fraught with uncertainties. Though by their very nature the trades were often family-orientated, passing down from generation to generation, in one case when the New Churches Commissioners considered renewing a contract on the following presumption – 'A.B. is since dead and his Ex[ecut]ors have Assigned the . . . Contract and all beneffitt . . . to his Son who is a Mason and follows the Business his Father did . . . the Son insists he is Entitled' – they concluded they were not obliged to do so.[87] Or, take the case of a bricklayer's contract at Hampstead parish church which specified that should his materials prove faulty or contrary to the 'intent of the meaning' he would be banned from proceeding further, the offence 'carried off the Premises at his own Expence', or in an era without the benefits of health insurance, should he 'Neglect to carry on . . . for the space of ten Days . . . unless occasioned by bad weather or Non Payment of . . . money' the client had 'free liberty to Employ any other . . . Workmen', deducting the costs from the agreed fee 'without being Deemed Guilty of a breach' of faith'.[88] This might explain the participation of wives and widows in the business.

Complaints of 'the difficulty of getting . . . repairs done by proper Workmen, and the great Expence of every small Job, and the too frequent and notorious Imposition . . . in their Bills . . . whereby small defects are too much neglected to be repaired' came from Grimoldby, Lincolnshire.[89] Richard Dyche, the mason at Saffron Walden, Essex, was reprimanded for being 'retarded and neglected in a shameful and unreasonable manner . . . so as [not] to give satisfaction to your employers and bring credit to yourself'. This led him to prosecute the client, Lord Howard, for recovery of his contract fee, which was finally secured only by his widow.[90] Joshuah Fletcher, the mason at St George, Hanover Square (pl. 1), ran into trouble during 1723–4 on account of being 'very negligent and unfaithful in the discharge of his duty, employing very few hands to expedite the work and often employing [them] to other uses and purposes'. This resulted in the stonework progressing 'so slowly that the Portico and inside of the Church will not be Finished by Christmas', which the joiners 'Adjudge to be through perverseness'. Fletcher, hearing that the Commissioners were 'very Uneasy About my precedings', claimed that he had been carrying on 'with All the Diligence . . . I could Or Any Man that had Labour'd under the Difficultys . . . I have gone through'. He had begun 'with all Expedition [and] Encouraged . . . to Lay down my Stone in the Square but was Soon disturbed . . . forced to bring it out Again [which] gave Offense to Some Other Gentlemen who Obliged me to Remove it off their Ground till by Degrees I was not Suffered to Work their at All'. In 1725 he wrote 'signifying . . . he is willing to quit . . . if it be the pleasure of the Board [since] I have been in a declining Condition for a Long time, & yet have taken due Care to provide Materials, & give proper Orders to proceed with all possible Expedition'. He added: 'I think it Very Hard that my Business shou'd be disposed of to Other people before I am dead . . . & if it should please God to raise me Again, I cou'd As Soon finish it as the Persons Yr Hons. Have thought fitt to Employ [Edward Strong and Christopher Cass]. But My Lds it is very Hard to bury me before I am dead.'[91]

Others found themselves on the wrong side of the law. In 1711 Richard Jenning, master carpenter, who had supervised the complex construction of St Paul's Cathedral dome, despite being esteemed by Wren as 'very honest, Diligent and Faithful in all the Trusts he has had', was dismissed on the grounds of

> Goods and Materials . . . much embezel'd by him . . . great Quantities of Timber, Boards, Nails, Ropes &c were by his direction, or those acting under him, conveyed away [while] several Workmen, after they had answered their Call, were set to work by him in other Churches and Places, and some . . . employed . . . to make Models for other Churches, Presses, Window-Cases &c . . .

using Cathedral resources. This incident was the subject of the pamphlet *Frauds and Abuses at St Paul's* (1712).[92] Peter Patrick and Robert Brumfield, labourers at St Mary Woolnoth, were prosecuted for having 'stolen some Iron and Lead'.[93] Some builders as well as architects mismanaged funds. William Lumby of Lincoln, who was unable to pay his team for work at nearby Doddington church, managed to evade the 'Bailys' (bailiffs) for a month.[94] William Wilson, 'a Bankrupt [and] Prisoner in Ludgate where he has been for a year past and upwards', failed in his petition to be reinstated as bricklayer at St Luke, Old Street.[95] 'Domus Dei' (a motto name assumed for competitive purposes), who submitted an unsuccessful scheme for All Saints,

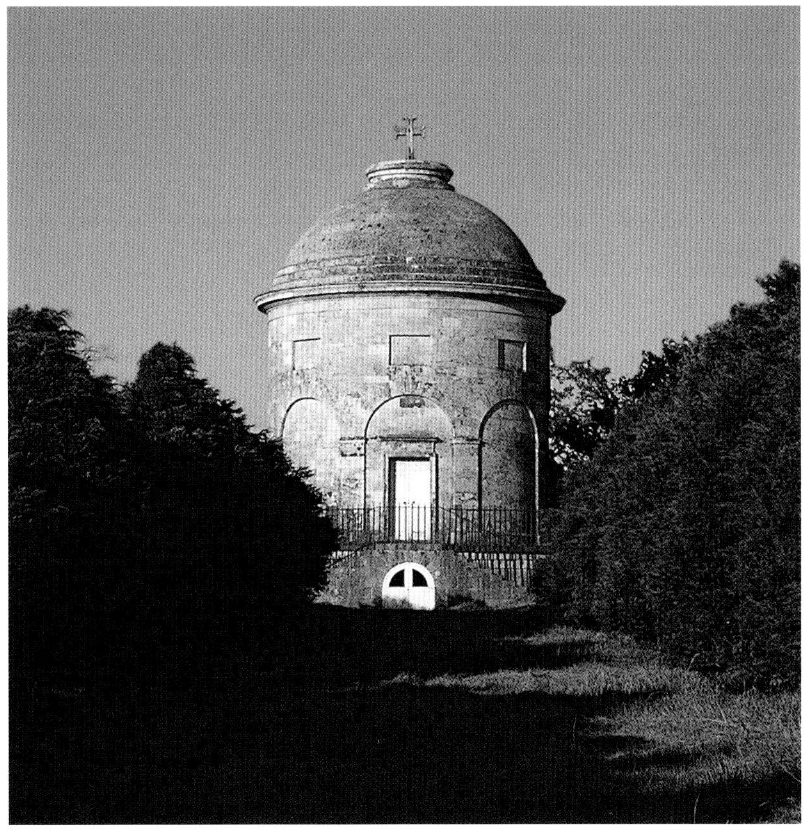

114 Thomas Atkinson. Constable Mausoleum, Halsham, Yorkshire, exterior, 1792–1804.

Southampton, a desperate Londoner whose current address in 1790 was given as King's Bench Prison, Southwark, where he was in 'confinement for Debt', explained that it was 'not in his power wholly to comply with the Terms of the Advertisement, his situation precluding him from engaging as a Builder'. He added that 'If the Design should be approved of the Author apprehended a very moderate Profit', but if not he 'shall esteem it a favour if they returned the *numbered* Papers in a Deal Case'; thereupon he vanished into obscurity.[96] A letter from Thomas Silk, plasterer, contained 'particulars of my demand' for work done at Wanstead, Essex, with an observation that

> it is not my Opinion but, that of the most respectable of the Trade – Architects cannot have such general judgment as to over thrown such respectable Evidence – Ruin'd and having suffered 41 Months imprisonment I trust, & considering that the Work is done in the very best manner that the Gentn Trustees will not hesitate to order me immediate payment.[97]

Then there was the anguishing matter of the Constable Mausoleum at Halsham, Yorkshire, revealed in a remarkable series of letters covering the years 1792 to 1798. The distinguished York architect Thomas Atkinson contracted to build this circular domed structure (pl. 114) for £3,300 in 1792 and complete it within four years, assuring the client, Edward Constable of Burton Constable, that 'though you may think me tedious, I will venture that displeasure, rather than slite by hurry the Jobb that I intend to speak to my character as a work = man for centurys to come'. However, the operation extended overtime, with John Atkinson, Thomas's son and assistant, explaining to Constable that the latter's disappointment 'has given me extreme uneasiness because I know your complaints to be just and beyond my Power to remedy' and it has 'weigh heavy on my fathers Spirit, now that he sees the utter impossibility of fullfilling his promise'. The problem lay in 'the hardness of the black marble' lining and 'the consequent extreme difficulty of working it, [which] have greatly exceeded any Idea either he or I had formed, and here he had no experience to guide him in his computation . . . for such a piece of work I believe in black marble, was never executed in this, or any other Kingdom'. John Platt Jr,

> the proprietor of the Marble works at Ashford [Derbyshire] declares in all his business he never met its equal for extreme dificulty and tediousness: – being circular it baffles the mechanism of their Machines, and obliges them to do by hand in a Week, what, if it were in a direct line, with their Engines might be done in two days.

Up to thirteen 'Men are constantly employ'd . . . More good hands we can not procure, bad ones we dare not make use of: – but they are tired out, and notwithstanding they have frequently raisd their Wages . . . are worse to keep to it than cowards to a battery of Cannon.' Atkinson Jr goes on: 'Believe me this is strictly true, and no Fabrication invented merely to excuse a culpable Neglect . . . My father, tho to my (perhaps partial) Eyes, one of the worthiest of Men, is also the most unaccountable.' By 1796 the Atkinsons were 'really in the greatest distress for want of Money'. In the following year they experienced the 'greatest difficulty [procuring] cash to pay weekly wages' and asked Constable for a loan of £200, John finding it 'painfull . . . in justice to myself, and my future hopes, to be oblig'd to throw some share of blame on a tender Parent [who] regrets the Folly of his first delays severely'. But the client reported that since work had commenced 'the Father has only been there thrice – four times at Most. The son never – as his Father would not permit him to see it.' This was apparently due to both being 'very ill and confin'd to . . . bed'. Constable was also asked to advance Platt £100, which was declined; as a result, Atkinson Sr claimed that both he and the quarry owner faced arrest, the former being warned that 'Silence [in] frankly and confidently [communicating] the truth . . . will receive the worst constructions and will be the signal for legal and compulsory measures.' The 'Intimacy & very great regard & Friendp. [over] many years' in which Platt regarded Atkinson led him to offer to 'do any thing in my Power to serve him [and] not suffer any delay on my Part . . . to forward the Work'. Then, on 4 May 1798, at the age of 70 and insolvent, having been 'seized with a Fitt abt. a Fortnight ago', Thomas 'dropt down Dead . . . near his own Door', leaving his family 'completely Beggars [with] one farthing left to divide' between them. Constable felt that 'Young Atkinson's Conduct . . . unaccountable in the Extreme [and] the best way will be to shake him off at once & for Ever'.[98]

There were worst tragedies. At St Paul's Cathedral Richard Staples, labourer, was 'killed by the fall of a Great Stone from the top of the Work'; his widow received £5 compensation; John Mullins, another labourer, was also killed, his widow receiving £10. Later, a mason named Thomas Copson, 'formerly maimed' while on the job, was re-employed, and 'a poore Boy belonging to the Plasterers . . . who fell a great way from the Cupola, & was very much hurt' was awarded £3.[99] In 1722 'a poor Labourer who had the misfortune to have his skull broken in pulling down the Old Steeple' of St Martin-in-the-Fields received 5 guineas 'towards his releif out of his Majesties bounty money', while William Rawlins, 'a day labourer who accidentally lost the Use of his Arm by a Stone falling on him', got 2 guineas; the following year Amos Ford, labourer, received 1 guinea 'for Charity . . . having spoiled one of his ffingers by the fall of a Stone' and 30 shillings went to Samuel Marcy, 'who fell dowe and broke two Ribbs'.[100] John Dawson, mason's assistant, 'ffalling Downe Whilst at Worke [and] very much Bruised', received £2 2s. 0s. compensation 'Towards . . . his Lameness and Sickness, not Able To Work' at St Botolph, Bishopsgate.[101] Collapsing scaffolds at Lady Glenorchy's chapel, Edinburgh, killed its architect, John Dove, and his foreman in 1773.[102]

The *Gentleman's Magazine* revelled in such incidents. At Kirkby Stephens, Westmorland, during dismantling the old fabric, a nail that the carpenter

> had not perceived caught hold of his cloaths, and the piece of timber, being heavy, drew him after it from a window 15 yards high, and dash'd his brains out against some of the pieces he had thrown out before, an accident . . . the more regrettable as it happened on a *Saturday* night, when the man had just compleated his job, and was in haste to return with his money to his wife and family.[103]

During repairs to the hurricane-damaged spire of medieval St Dionysius, Market Harborough, Leicestershire, a mason named Jackson

> had a hair-breadth escape . . . Coming down . . . from his work [when] one of the crockets broke with him, and he fell near twelve feet, but luckily was caught by a scaffold . . . his body was nearly balanced half off . . . His fright was so great, that he recovered himself with great difficulty, but received no further hurt.[104]

During James Wyatt's restoration of Hereford Cathedral in 1790 a 'very dreadful accident happened' in dismantling the vaulting. Instead of suspending a hanging platform from the timbers above,

> by the advice of the director, sixteen workmen stood on the top, and, upon . . . moving . . . a single stone,

the whole . . . sunk . . . A few . . . were fortunate enough to jump upon a part that continued firm, while some clung to the side walls; one man took hold of a rope . . . and was saved; another, after holding by a piece of timber for a few minutes, dropped, and was dashed to pieces; and a third was buried under the ruins of the scaffolding . . .

Five men were taken to the infirmary, much hurt; two . . . lay dead in one of the aisles; another is since dead; and whether the other will recover, is at present doubtful . . . Perhaps if Mr. Wyatt had been present, no life would have been lost.[105]

In 1794 at Banbury, as workmen were drawing up a large cornice stone, the tackle suddenly gave way; one man miraculously escaped by grasping a rope, though two others were dashed to the ground. One died of a fractured skull, broken jaw and thigh, the fall so forceful that his watch was driven into his belly; the other survived but never again spoke and his insides were mortified so he had little hope of recovery. A grizzly business.[106]

115 Matthew Skinner. 'The South View of Islington Church & Steeple, with Scaffolding & Wicker-work' (St Mary), 18 February 1788. Engraving. Islington Local History Centre, Y59J 85 St Mar PC. Lancelot Dowbiggin architect, 1751–4.

Eleven

ON BUILDING AND MAINTENANCE

Breastsomers of fir over the Columns . . . in two flitches

a Teagle to hoist up . . . Stones

Wicker-work . . . Scaffold

– the latter as employed by the aptly named Thomas Birch, basket maker, at St Mary, Islington, in London (pl. 115).[1] A host of contemporary documents – parish vestry minutes, churchwardens' accounts, builders' proposals, contracts and bills, with their idiomatic spelling and occasionally obscure vocabulary (see Glossary, pp. 739–45), shed invaluable aesthetic, technological and financial light on every aspect of construction, from brick, stone, wood, iron and plaster work to carving, glazing, painting and colouring, paving and other floor treatments, which are fundamental to an understanding of the complex business of church building, as well as the maintenance of fabrics. Those dealing with the London New Churches are unrivalled in the eighteenth century.[2]

Central to this activity was the formal contract between client, designer and builders, expressed straightforwardly at Redland Chapel, Bristol (pls 72, 437), where the architect, William Halfpenny, agreed 'to Give proper Directions as is Usuall' to the 'Directers of Buildings, to all the Workmen [to] Work in a Workmanlike Manner . . . Make proper Use of the Materials without Waste [to] See the Whole Compleated', visiting the site on six days a week, forfeiting 3s. 6d. every day neglected and to 'Measure all the Work'.[3] At Bridgnorth, Shropshire, there is a direct relationship between the lengthy, detailed contract and the impressive sophistication of the building (pls 662–4).[4] At St Thomas, Bristol, the division of labour was made explicit in the press advertisement call for 'Persons willing to contract for each distinct branch of the work' rather than a general contractor.[5]

A range of ingenious machinery was devised to aid the various trades. The most remarkable was Nicholas Hawksmoor's and William Thornton's temporary timber framework erected against the north transept face of medieval Beverley Minster to screw it back to perpendicular, applauded in a pair of contemporary engravings (pls 137–8), which saved the building from probable destruction. A 'Lumber Room' was later erected for the wood and stone 'lying dispersed about the Church Yard . . . to preserve them from being embezzled'.[6] Among the items stored would have been hoists: Christopher Cass, mason, supplied 423½ tons for hoisting from a height of 100 to 184 feet at St Luke, Old Street, London.[7] The sum of £4 14s. 0d. was spent on 'long Rops, Tackel falls, Small lines, Machines &c' for raising stone and other materials at Norwich Cathedral; at Durham it was ordered that 'Scaffolding . . . must be very considerable and . . . connected with the utmost care in the lofty situation of the pinacles', employing 'wheel and pinion' as the 'most handy method' of lifting items, while where the 'weights being not great, one horse fixed to the upright shaft with a mechanical advantage in power of . . . 6 to 1' was preferred.[8] The relief on the base of Gibbs's design of 1714 for the Strand Column features a rare representation of an operating crane (pl. 377). The erecting, dismantling and re-erecting of scaffolding in the interior of St Paul's Cathedral during the years 1719–21 trace the progress of Thornhill's painting of the crossing dome; in preparation for restoring them half a century later, the Italian painter Spiridone Roma devised a small, more effective scaffold independent of the structure, which, however,

116 Samuel Hieronymus Grimm. View of north elevation of St Swithin, Walcot, Bath, Somerset, detail, August 1790. Pen and ink and wash. © The British Library Board, Kaye Collection, x, Add. MSS 15546, f. 132. John Palmer architect, 1787–92.

proved too expensive to install.[9] The cost of scaffolding of a standard type recorded by Grimm in use at Bath (pl. 116) ranged from 2s. 1d. for 'three Men [working for] 4 hours Each' at St John, Briggate, Leeds,[10] to 3s. for a 'plaisterer and boy ¾ of a day Each fetching down and building Scaffold' at Westminster Abbey,[11] £7 for one measuring 40 by 17 feet with 'Four Stages One over the other for the Painters use at the Altar' of St Alfege, Greenwich,[12] to a range of charges at Holy Trinity, Much Wenlock, Shropshire: 'Four Large Poles' 27 by 9 feet at 16s. each, '4 Standarts' 32 by 9 feet at £1 16s. 0d. each, fifty 'Ordinary Poles', totalling 16 feet at 1s. each, £2 10s. 0d., two 45-foot ladders at £2 4s. 0d. and 200 hundredweight of cord at 5d. per pound at £4 8s. 4d.[13] At Lincoln Cathedral the impracticable cost of keeping the lofty central and western spires in repair (pl. 157) by erecting scaffolds every time a sheet of lead was blown off was in principle solved by Gibbs's recommendation in 1725 to replace them with 'small cupelettes of stone', but bizarrely this led to town riots and the speedy abandonment of the scheme.[14]

Hawksmoor supplied an 'Augar for Boreing Ground' to the New Churches Commissioners in their search for geologically appropriate building sites.[15] Laying secure foundations involved 'Trussels for the Men to stand on, and Beetles [heavy mallets] to drive down the piles';

> three Bricks for four courses . . . thence two Brick & half to the Levell of the Floor . . . All . . . well Burnt Stocks . . . even throughout and flushed with Mortar . . . made of good Sand and Lime not less than two hundred to a Rod of Brick Work and . . . well beaten.[16]

Both brick making and laying were complex operations, as the twenty-eight-page entry in *The Builder's Dictionary; or, Gentleman and Architect's Companion* (1734), approved by Gibbs, James and Hawksmoor, makes clear. Cast in moulds – 2s. 6d. was charged for 'making [and] plateing [a] Brick Mold' for Church Minshull, Cheshire,[17] and 5s. for 'fixing up Screeds for a Guide for the Bricklayers' at Beverley. David Fisher received £51 for water carriage of 146,000 bricks to the Minster there.[18] Robert Charlesworth was paid £2 10s. 0d. for 'a Trial to make Bricks' for Walton on the Wolds, Leicestershire.[19] The cost of bricks, sometimes supplied to the same building by several manufacturers, varied according to type and quality. At St Philip, Birmingham, there were 17,000 from Richard Banckes at £8 12s. 10d., 16,500 from James Ellis at £8 3s. 0d., 567,650 from Steven Ellitt & Co. totalling £198 13s. 7d., 282,850 from Thomas Fowler at £105 6s. 8d., 10,000 from Joseph Hands at £5, 22,000 from John Shaw at £10, 15,500 from Edmund Stevens at £7 17s. 3d., altogether 931,500, none of which was exposed to view in this wholly stone-faced building. Richard Pinly & Co. charged £5 7s. 0d. for building two brick kilns.[20] At the Wesleyan Chapel, Sheffield, in 1779 Cadman and Roberts charged £31 14s. 4d. for 71,280 bricks, the aptly named Thomas Holy £4 11s. 6d. for 6,100 stock bricks, £7 16s. 7d. for 15,666 'Common Stock' and £1 3s. 3d. for 3,100 'Ruff'.[21] The bricklayers' contract for St John, Hampstead, is uncommonly well detailed.[22]

The New Churches programme was plagued by scandal. In 1713, as construction got under way, two rival brickmakers offered differing formulas. Richard Waterman proposed making bricks from 'naturall Earth without the use of any Spanish' (that is, 'Sea Cole Ashes – After the Unfamous way of the City of London'[23]) and burnt 'with no other fireing butt wood or Coales', which he proposed performing 'in the best maner' and delivering 'any place att the Waterside between Brentford and Deptford' (that is, across much of Greater London) at 14s. per 1,000. Thomas Atkins reported 'a great Quantity of Extraordinary good Earth for making

. . . Bricks at Kentish Town . . . using . . . 6 Loads of Spanish to Each hundred Thousand', the Spanish 'only to keep the . . . Earth when made into Bricks from Sheering or Cracking', which produced 'Extraordinary Strong Bricks fit for bearing any Weight' and could be supplied at 12s. per 100. The Commissioners opted for the non-Spanish version.[24] Almost immediately there were difficulties. At St John, Smith Square, Westminster, 'for want of some trusty Person to overlook the Work', the Commissioners were 'abused by the Bricklayer [as] Most part of the Bricks used . . . are the worst . . . ever saw and . . . not worth nine shillings p thousand, so that the foundation, which ought to be good and Sollid, will prove but a very sorry one'. The problem was serious because the site, lying close by the Thames, was proving waterlogged and structurally potentially dangerous. The surveyors reported that the bricks were 'well banded and filld wth. Mortar' but questioned mixing them with 'Samel, or Soft Bricks', which though 'in Soe great a Mass . . . can doe noe Harm' should be 'Sorted and Destroyed'. They warned that the foundation 'will certanly bear any Necessary fabrick, altho it may be Oppress'd by too Vast An Edifice'. As we shall see later, this proved close to the truth. Thomas Hues's and William Tufnell's contract specified 'well Temper'd . . . Mortar . . . beaten wth: wooden Beaters', allowing 200 pecks of lime to two loads of Fulham sand per rod, 'Sound Bricks hard and Well Burn't, removing those that were semel, Shatter'd or Shaken in the making or Burning'.[25]

Success was equated with superior-quality material as well as design, particularly when exposed externally, and the architectural forms themselves are elegantly precise. A fine example is St Mary, Paddington (pl. 117). The contract called for

> good sound square well burned brick of a full Gage . . . the Groins . . . properly cut and rubbed . . . Niche heads & Arches . . . neatly cut and set in Puttey . . . all the Walls . . . kept perfectly level and perpendicular . . . All the Mortar . . . of the best Chalk Lime well burnt . . . the Sand clean . . . of a sharp grit got from out of the . . . Thames above Westminster Bridge the Lime slacked quick the whole screan'd fine and well chaffed.[26]

Complaints of 'improper Materials such as Old Mortar and Rubbish . . . worked without proper Bond' used to fill up the core 'faced only with sound Brickwork to the prejudice of the Building and contrary to the Contract' were dismissed by the architect, John Plaw, as 'totally groundless'; nevertheless, the bricklayer, William Jarratt, duly 'absconded'.[27] Nor did such punctilious care prevent serious technical embarrassment. The daring internal choreographic construction (pl. 698) cocooned in its thin, fragile brick skin was jeopardised by the 'Several Sinkings of the Arches' resulting from the collapse of the central ceiling, crushing the slender supporting wooden columns. Reckoning these had 'received a great quantity of root . . . so as to reduce their power of Resistance', Plaw recommended a partial rebuilding, despite claims that the cause was insufficient 'Buttments', which sunk the structure 'below their proper Horizon'. He produced 'a Design for remedying the Defects' where the builder agreed to 'take the whole Burthen of the Expence upon himself' if compensated by £100, while the architect, in fear of loosing the commission, 'apologized . . . for all the past Misconduct and said he was willing to do any Thing in future to oblige'.[28]

Plaw's contemporary, Willey Reveley, also in thrall of simple, pure late neoclassical forms, specified in his masterpiece, All Saints, Southampton (pl. 659), that the brick engaged columns of the front were to be 'worked and rubbed perfectly true and smooth . . . joined only with very liquid mortar perfectly free from grits and ground . . . No tooling to be left . . . but the whole shaft . . . rubbed with sand and water and worked as true if turned in a lathe out of one piece'.[29]

The New Churches papers are especially informative about the range and detailing of masonry work. At Hawksmoor's St Mary Woolnoth, Thomas Dunn charged £4 10s. 0d. for 'Two keystones with 3 Cherubs Heads in Each' (pl. 118).[30] Edward Strong charged £200 for two lions and unicorns, each 10 foot 3 inches high, £90 for the crowning 11-foot-high statue of George I, £120 for '4 Festoons' 10 feet long and '4 Crowns' at £7 each on the tower of St George, Bloomsbury (pl. 409).[31] Embellishments to St Mary-le-Strand included 'Timpans of pedaments over windows wth. Cherubs heads and Festoons' (pl. 119),[32] while the tower of St Alfege, Greenwich (pl. 543), featured '21½ Faces of Ionick Capitals' costing £42 13s. 4d., '8 Capitals to ¾ . . . Corinthian . . . Columns' at £64, with '48 Flowers . . . between', £3 12s. 0d., '8 Vauses on the Cornice . . . with Rafled leaves & a flame at Top', £38, and four others 6 feet high with 'Drapery, shels & pine apple' at £34.[33] This repertory is reflected in the provinces. At Holy Trinity, Leeds, which was promoted by Yorkshiremen knowledgeable about London fashions (Ralph Thoresby had visited St Alfege during its building campaign, while Archbishop Dawes had served as a New Churches Commissioner), John Pate carved nine window 'Scrowls' in a Gibbsian manner for £2 14s. 0d. (pl. 120).[34]

117 John Plaw. Detail of brickwork, St Mary, Paddington, London, 1788–93.

118 Nicholas Hawksmoor. Keystone of window, St Mary Woolnoth, London, 1716–24.

Various artificial treatments were popular, most notably roughcasting – the mason Thomas Innes's charge of £16 3s. 0d. for 'Ruff casting' Cumnor parish church, Berkshire, in 1751 is typical,[35] and 'Adamattic Composition' as proposed for St Sepulchre, Newgate, London, in 1778, which would be 'equally Durable' as rebuilding and buttressing the tower.[36] The most famous was Coade Stone, manufactured in London from 1769 by the partnership of Mrs Eleanor Coade and John Sealy using clay, wasted ceramics and other then-secret ingredients cast in moulds designed by architects like Robert Adam and sculptors like John Bacon largely in the fashionable neoclassical styles. In 1788 Thomas Hardwick Jr, in respect of his church at Wanstead, Essex, reported that 'Capitals of the Columns in Coade's Manufactory may be had for 5 Gns. Each; Those of Plaister 4 Gns. Each – But the former being judged to be much more durable, Agreed to give the Preference to Coade's'. In the following year he reported that the 'Capitals are in great Forwardness: They are formed, & wait only to be put into the Fire'. The bill specified 'Ornamental Stone Manufactory Lambeth . . . 10 Corinthian Caps Dia 1 ft: 3 in High', £52 10s. 0d., '454 feet . . . deal in 5 large packr Cases', £6 12s. 5d., '55 feet ffir scantling [planks] for Stays & inside Ledge', 9s. 2d., 'Package & Deliver . . . to the lighter', 17s. 6d., 'lighterage to Wanstead & Expence of Lighterman', £1 15s. 6d., 'Expences there & back Beer &c.', 4s. 8d., 'Going To Stratford Lebow with twoo Carts for the Tops of the Columns, they not being able to Get them out of the Boat', 19s. 9d., 'Mason & Labourer 7½ Ds Setting Capl.', £2 8s. 9d., 'Cramps . . . Beer . . . Lodging . . . Cleaning off work letting in Leaves &c and Carv.', £1 1s. 6d.[37] The surface could be painted to blend in with the surrounding architecture.[38]

A Treatise on Carpentry (1733, with an enlarged edition of 1735 retitled *The British Carpenter*) by Francis Price (pl. 108) was the first comprehensive work on the

119 James Gibbs. Window, St Mary-le-Strand, London, 1714–17.

120 William Etty. South elevation, Holy Trinity, Leeds, Yorkshire, 1723–27.

subject in English, with instructions on roof and spire construction 'founded on a serious Perusal of some of the most celebrated ones in London'.[39] Some of these found their way into popular pattern books, such as Batty Langley's *The City and Country Builder's, and Workman's Treasury of Designs* (1740) and *The Builder's Jewel* (1741; both republished in numerous editions).[40] Thence into actuality, as in the case of Christ Church, Southwark, a plain Palladian box of 75 by 51 feet, the single-span flat ceiling hung from a standard system of principal rafters, tie beams, struts and king post (pl. 121). Two bulwarks of HM Office of Works, Kenton Couse and John Vardy, displayed exceptional aptitudes; the latter's drawings for remodelling medieval Allerton Mauleverer, Yorkshire (pl. 326), are accompanied by a lengthy and detailed carpentry and joinery contract.[41]

A variety of imported, mainly Baltic timbers were employed. For Allerton, 'Mememel of the best quality free from strakes & large knots No American pine on any account the floor boards'; for Paddington,

> All . . . of the very best Riga . . . free from Sap or Vein and not suffered to be used if Foxey or unsound . . . Moldings . . . struck solid out of Dantzig Plank . . . Pewing . . . capped with Honduras Mahogany . . . front Doors . . . of the best Christiana Yello Deal.[42]

Prices for St Chad, Shrewsbury, ranged from 'Dantzig . . . perfectly sound, sawed and delivered' at 19s. 9d. per cubic foot, 'Peterburgh Fir Plank', £36 per 100, 'Best christian white Plank', £23 per 100, 'Riga wainscot', 7½d. per foot, as well as 'English Oak . . . all perfectly sound', at 1s. 4d.[43] For Salisbury Cathedral, 'Sawyers 6 Shillings pr: Tunn for Square . . . Stuff', '268ft. Run: of new Beams dovetail'd at key'd to old Beams', £5 0s. 6d., '153 Cleets nailed under . . . rafters and . . . Purloyns at 2d each', £1 5s. 6d. (pl. 143).[44] Political events invari-

121 James Horne. Design for 'Section of the East End of Christ Church', Southwark, London, 1738. Pen and ink and wash. © The British Library Board, K.Top. XXVII-5-f.

ably affected prices. For example, in March 1791 Russia acquired Ochakov from Turkey, and six months later James Spiller, architect of St John, Hackney, was ordered to prepare 'Specifications ready to advertize immediately as the negotiations with Russia are now determined which occasioned the deferring the contracting for building a new church'.[45]

Professional altercations aroused by timber construction are testified in two incidents. A dispute flared up at St Botolph, Bishopsgate, in 1726–7 when it was reported that the stock was in a 'Great part . . . Unsound Doaty [decayed] Timber . . . by no means Proper . . . for the Purpose' of framing the roof, and needed exchanging for 'Good Sound Oak', with the carpenters compelled to 'Gett . . . Fresh Timber . . . forward Withal Expedition', and if not executed within three months 'They will Owne Themselves To Be Guilty of A Great Neglect'.[46] In 1742 John Wood Sr publicly condemned a rival's awkward roof design for St Michael Extra Muros, Bath, as 'a Piece of Work of a very uncommon kind; for the Building is span'd at twice the Weight of the whole Covering towards the Center of its Beams; and to make a Lodgment for Dirt and Snow directly over the very Middle of the Church! Thus one Absurdity, or rather Iniquity accompanies another', adding 'a Timber Floor and an M Roof . . . are artful Contrivances, for the Benefit of Trade, as the knavish Sort of Workmen term it; and Time will demonstrate it in this Structure'.[47]

Roofing treatments were sometimes complex issues. Though Wren complained in 1712 that English tiles 'are ill made . . . an excellent Tile may . . . be very durable [but] our Artisans are not yet instructed in it',[48] native varieties became increasingly popular. A 'specimen of Clay or Pantile' manufactured at Broseley, Shropshire, in 1752, priced at 30s. per 1,000, claimed the 'best and most durable sort', was considered in opposition to 'Cornish Tyle' called 'Denny Ball Scantile', for Kingswood, Bristol.[49] For All Saints, Southampton, Willey Reveley recommended copper as 'the best of All roofs, and the cheapest' but discovered it was 'more expensive than was imagined' and used it only on the dome of the tower at 'not less than 14 oz to the foot [with] the seams . . . turned in a neat and workmanlike manner'. The building committee preferred Westmorland slate for the main roof. Reveley opted for 'Patent Slate . . . as being much lighter . . . laying flatter and much less . . . expensive' but eventually agreed on 'the best Welsh slates, well bedded in cement and screwed to the rafters and executed in every respect agreeable to the patent granted by Mr Wyatt'.[50] Westmorland slate was the most widely used. A Mr Dover received £132 for supplying 44 tons at £3 per ton for St Olave, Southwark; John Westcott, '20 Square 55 feet . . . Naild on Boards wth: 8d & 6d Clout Nails painted at 65 sh pr Sqr: – Carriage from London . . . Mens time . . . & home . . . Lodgings', £66 15s. 9d. for Hartwell, Buckinghamshire; at Banbury, Oxfordshire, the 'very best large green Westmorland Slating of the first quality of those for the London Market with strong Copper Nails proportioned to the Weight of the Slate'.[51]

The relative merits of slate and lead were much debated. Part of the attraction of lead lay in its low melting point, which meant that it could be re-cast as necessary. At Faversham, Kent, it was claimed that substituting slate for lead 'will greatly lighten' the roof.[52] Wren patriotically recommended it for the New Churches as 'certainly the best and lightest Covering, and being of our own Growth and Manufacture, and lasting, if properly laid, for many hundred years, is, without question, the most preferable'.[53] It had the further advantage of pliability: at Hartwell, William Chapman fashioned '144 Feet 8 in: of Gothic Pipe . . . in . . . 3 Shafts' and '4 Gothic Cistron Heads'.[54] It also enjoyed ancient canonical authority: Eusebius related in connection with the Holy Sepulchre, Jerusalem, that Constantine 'covered the outward part of the Roof with lead, in regard that was the strongest defence against winter showers'.[55] Yet lead was also vulnerable. John James reported that the material at St George, Wapping, was better than at St Anne, Limehouse, 'tho the Summer may shew the Contrary', while at Christ Church, Spitalfields, sections on the south side split 'wholly owing to the violent heat of the sun reflected by the stone wall on that side, and not . . . to the fault of the Plumbers work'.[56] It suffered from ubiquitous theft: the *Leeds Mercury* reported on 17 December 1782: 'Friday night a considerable quantity of lead was sawed off the water-spouts belong[ing] to Holy Trinity . . . and carried off'.

Prices fluctuated almost daily. On 27 April 1721 at Spitalfields it had 'much risen since the Plumers Work . . . was contracted', as a result 18d. per 100 had to be allowed beyond the former estimate, but on 3 May this was 'set aside' with an announcement that the 'Price . . . is sinking' and the plumber was offered 15s.; moreover, since the 'Boards have been a great while expos'd to the weather and may be subject to the worm' they were ordered to be covered with 'Pitch and Tarr before the Lead be Layd on'.[57] The material required regular maintenance. A Mr Sharpe received 3 guineas annually 'to keep the lead on the roof [of St Paul, Sheffield] in repair, and to relay at least five fresh sheets . . . each year in a workmanlike manner'.[58] Regarding Lincoln Cathedral, James Essex recommended that it was 'absolutely necessary to keep . . . Gutters & Spouts clean & free from weeds . . . at least 5 or 6 Times a year . . . especially at the Time . . . Birds are building, & after great Rains, or much Snow; which should never be suffered to freeze the Spouts'.[59]

The Documents section of the present publication (CD-ROM) reveals a surprising abundance of constructional and decorative ironwork throughout the century, its relatively recent origins lying in columns supporting new galleries added when Wren adopted the House of Commons for Scottish members at the time of the Act of Union in 1707, and those supporting the west gallery of St Magnus Martyr, London, in 1712.[60] It was employed extensively in the London New Churches. At St Alfege, Greenwich, for example, two 3-inch-square 'Iron pillars' supporting the west gallery cost £13 1s. 0d., 'Iron Brackets wrought with Scroll work' for the east gallery, £22 16s. 0d., 13 yards 2 feet of iron gallery fronts 'finely wrought wth. Scroll Work', £34 3s. 4d., '152 Squares of Iron for Stiffening the Fronts and Partition of the Pews', £3 16s. 0d., and so on (pl. 129), none of which survived the Blitz of 1941.[61] At St Mary-le-Strand the smith was paid £1,080 8s. 8d. for '38 Pillasters & 34 Bayes of Iron fence round the Church' and £7 11s. 0d. for 'a Fronticepice of Scrolls & chas'd Work in the Gates at the West End'.[62] Another smith received £61 5s. 0d. for '35 Foot Run. in an Altar Rail of Scrollwork consisting of Six framed Pillars, two Gates . . . wth 32 Pannels all Fram'd Work' in St George, Hanover Square.[63] Gibbs designed exceptionally bold cast-iron baluster fencing to enclose the portico and churchyard of St Martin-in-the-Fields (pl. 122).[64]

Outside London, the masters of wrought iron continuing to work in the fashionable baroque of the Frenchman Jean Tijou, Wren's chief smith at St Paul's Cathedral,[65] included Robert Bakewell, who at All Saints, Derby, was paid £157 10s. 0d. for executing to

122 James Gibbs. Cast iron churchyard fence, St Martin-in-the-Fields, London, 1720–27.

Gibbs's design a group of magnificent screens and gates enclosing the chancel.[66] His principal rivals were William Edney of Bristol, creator of the gorgeous screen in St Mary Redcliffe,[67] and the Welshmen Hugh and Robert Davies.[68] In Yorkshire the trade was dominated by Maurice Tobin and Son, Leeds whitesmiths, who supplied metal gates, hinges, knobs, latches, locks, plates and sash pulleys to St John, Briggate, and Horsforth Chapel.[69]

Architectural ironwork particularly thrived in the Salopian heartland around Coalbrookdale, site of Abraham Darby's pioneering Ironbridge (1775–9), designed by one of the county's leading church architects, Thomas Farnolls Pritchard.[70] An early account relating to St Luke, Hodnet (1732–6), itemises John Ray's bills for 153 feet 2 inches of 'Iron for pillers & bars for . . . Windows' at £1 9s. 11d. and '246 pounds . . . for the Windows' at £2 7s. 4d.[71] By the 1790s this activity had increased impressively. Two or three churches imaginatively adapted cast iron to the gothic fashion. When All Saints, Wellington, an uncommonly sophisticated Soanian classical design with medieval detailing by George Steuart, was consecrated in 1790 the *Shrewsbury Chronicle* reported that the officiating Bishop of Lichfield and Coventry 'particularly noticed the Cast-Iron Pillars (by which the Galleries and Roof are supported), which he said gave a superior Lightness to anything of the kind he had ever seen' (pl. 337).[72] More committed to the medieval is Carline and Tilley's St Alkmund, Shrewsbury (pls 231, 233), which originally had thirteen large cast-iron-frame windows; those along the body had their upper sections louvred to cut the glare of sunlight, while the extreme thinness of the tracery of the chancel window reduced the supporting structure to a minimum in order to maximise the pictorial impact of Francis Eginton's painted glass of *Evangelical Faith* (pl. 232).[73] Some of the original windows were replaced by heavy Victorian stone mullions, but at Adderley, Shropshire, a similar set survives complete (pl. 123).[74]

123 Richard Baker. Cast-iron window frame, St Peter, Adderley, Shropshire, detail, 1793–1801.

Work at St Chad, Shrewsbury, is particular well documented. In 1790 John Fradgley, blacksmith, executed 'all the Iron Work . . . in a proper Workmanlike manner . . . with diligence and Dispatch', including

> Masons Cramps of all sizes Bars and Chains for Ties and Apertines . . . Screw Bolts with proper Nuts Straps Staples and Dog Nails . . . for the Roof Gallery and other Parts . . . in Case any bad or insufficient Iron . . . shall be found . . . not . . . properly wrought . . . returned and good . . . found.

In 1791, in response to a call in the *Shrewsbury Chronicle* for proposals for 'Cast-Iron Sashes', Messrs Underwood & Co. of High Holborn, London, submitted an estimate for 'patent Metal' sashes at 2s. 3d. per foot, including all expenses except transport. Their contract specified 'Sixteen Circular head Wrought Iron and Metal Sashes' 16 by 6 feet 'hung on Steel Centre with Brass Knobs and Latches agreeable to the . . . pattern . . . furnished by George Steuart' (the architect) costing £250.[75]

Weathervanes became a specialist manufactory. The *Gentleman's Magazine* reported of Salisbury Cathedral in 1759 that the decayed oak 'fane' of 1673 was blown down, and three years later announced the erection of a 'new construction' of gilt copper measuring 7 feet, which 'runs on four wheels, and will turn with the gentlest gale that blows'.[76] At Maldon, Essex, 'one made big enough for Salisbury' consisted of 'a pine Tulip at top a Crown & ball; then star . . . of lead to hold it on', which when 'hoisted up down it tumbled being so ponderous'; therefore, it was 'agreed to Lop off the Crown & other things & up it went again'.[77]

There was also a wide variety of small, inexpensive metal items: '1 Large Bright plate for the Bolts of the Communion Rail' at St George's Chapel, Queen's Square, London,[78] at St Thomas, Southwark, an 'Iron Rail, for the Vestry pew to hang hats . . . Brass pins for the rest', and at St Michael Paternoster 'Iron racks for the Conveniency of hanging . . . Hatts in the Common Council Men's Pew'.[79] There were '135 Pair of Pew-hinges home made according to the Pattern', costing £13 10s. 0d., and £2 16s. 0d. for '42 Pair of Smoothfeild Strong Butt-hinges for Flaps of the Seats' supplied to St Alfege, Greenwich.[80] 'Iron Plates' were inserted into the gallery column heads 'to keep the posts from eating into the Bressumer' at St John, Westminster.[81]

Iron was especially beneficial in securing roof timbers and masonry walls. At Stone, Staffordshire, 'four principall Beams [were] Strapt . . . to the King post with Iron Straps Bolts and Cotters'.[82] James Donaldson, a clerk in Robert Mylne's office, prepared 'Patterns or Modells of the intended Iron Work for the Roof' of Greenwich Hospital chapel, including 'nut & Screw 1–11 between the plates', '2 broad bands with neck & Screw of each', 'a plate & caulhinge at each end with holes for the . . . long bolts', each illustrated by a simple diagram.[83] Screw-threaded nuts and bolts tightened the transept roof joints of Lincoln Cathedral.[84] At Canterbury Cathedral George Dance Sr proposed rebuilding the south transept gable, introducing 'cramps every third course' and 'two iron chains in a proper manner . . . at the bottom and . . . immediately over the circular window with proper collars let into blocks'.[85] Francis Price's book devoted to Salisbury is a remarkable visual record of iron's use in repairing great medieval cathedrals (pl. 124).

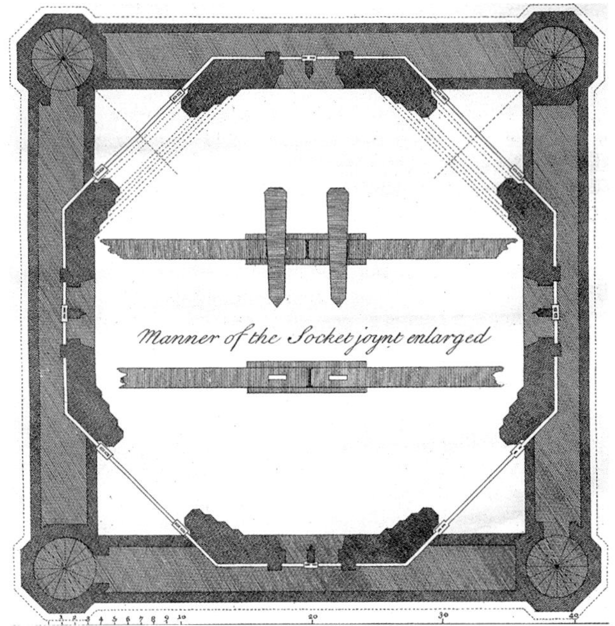

124 Paul Fourdrinier after Francis Price. 'A Plan, . . . of the Spire, with the Bandage lately added to strengthen it' and 'Manner of the Socket joynt enlarged', 1748, in F. Price, *A Series Of particular and useful Observations . . . upon . . . the Cathedral Church of Salisbury (Wiltshire)*, 1753, pl. 8, detail. Engraving. Author's collection.

Finally, there is the strange incident hinting at the possibilities of sinister activity exposed in an anonymous pamphlet entitled *Screw-Plot Discover'd; or, St Paul's Preserved* (1710).

> Of Treasons that were hatch'd in Hell
> How after all the Screws were stole
> And all the timber work round *Pauls*,
> Was loosen'd so (I pray you mind)
> As might Effect what they design'd,
> A lusty Man, as some folks tell,

125 William Smith Jr and John Wright. Ceiling, Stoneleigh Abbey chapel, Warwickshire, 1744.

Who was, at time prefix'd, 'tis said,
To pull the Church down on his Head
And . . . he that held the Rope
Must be the Dev'l or the Pope.[86]

This fantastical episode, described more explicitly in the *Gentleman's Magazine* as 'that ingenious Alarm to the Kingdom, that the *Whigs* had contrived to *kill the Queen* by stealing the Screws out of the Timber . . . by which the *Roof* of that famous Cathedral was to have fallen upon her Head, on the Day of Thanksgiving', citing the popular press, which claimed that 'some evil designing Persons have unscrewed and taken away several Iron Bolts out of the . . . West Roof', could hope to have succeeded only with the unlikely complicity of either the cathedral authorities or its architect or the builders. The pamphleteering was probably politically motivated, perhaps provoked by the impeachment of the anti-Whig Dr Henry Sacheverell for preaching on 'The Perils of False Brethren in Church and State' at St Paul's on 5 November 1709.[87]

Plastering internal walls and ceilings was divided between plain and ornamental work. At Banbury the Oxford plasterer William Roberts contracted for 'Plain floated and set ceilings three Coats finished in Bristol lime and white hair [on] lath . . . of heart riga fir nailed with wrought iron nails' at 1s. 4d. per yard, the walls 'stuccoed floated with hard washed dressed sand' at 1s. 7d., 'circular plain mouldings . . . to cornice round the Dome', 1s. per foot, and 'straight ones', 10d.[88] Formulas included Wren's recommendation of 'a Rendering as hard as Stone . . . composed of Cockle-shell-lime well beaten with Sand; the more Labour in the beating, the better and stronger the Mortar', which he used in St Paul's Cathedral vaulting and preferred to the 'constant Practice [of] Chalk-lime . . . well mixed with good Sand [which] is not amiss, though much worse than hard Stone-lime'.[89] At St Paul, Deptford, the

> first Coat [was] to be . . . laid and Scratched in order to make good key for the Second which is to be try'd with a ten or twelve foot rule, & floated, Both . . . of Good Stuff, well turn'd up and wrought in the best manner and finished with a good Coat of white haird Stuff. . . hard finishing . . . done in the best manner with two Coats of hard Stone Lime and Sharpe sand well wrought and beat up . . . All the Work to have no more than one Load of Sand to One hundred of Lime, and not less than ten Bushells of Good black hair . . . The Sand to be good Sharp Pit sand and not the white Sand dug up on black heath.[90]

Plaster was sometimes regarded as a cheap substitute for stone.[91]

The late baroque repertory is unusually well represented in the London New Churches. At St George, Bloomsbury, for example, 'Foliage with mitres, Cherubs Heads &c in the Ceiling of the Altar with an Enriched ovolo round . . . A Shell over the Nich . . . Enriched Ovolo & Oak Leaves' is precisely what was executed (pl. 376).[92] Among outstanding provincial reflections is the chapel in Stoneleigh Abbey, Warwickshire (pl. 125), designed by William Smith Jr, and executed by John Wright. He was paid £296 11s. 11d. in 1744 for modelling 'Beams enrich'd with Shells of Leatherwork', 'Vetruvian Scrowle . . . fully enrich'd', 'a Center pannel . . . with . . . I:H:S a Blaze & Blunt Rays with Nine Cherub heads in ye Clouds', 'Two End pannells one with a large figure of Hope an Angel attending with ye Anchor & 2 Boys', the other with 'Two Angels sounding ye Resurrection & four . . . figures . . . coming out of their Graves the scene a Church Yard', and so on. Thomas Roberts of Oxford's spectacular Perpendicular decoration at Hartwell (pls 169–70), for which he was paid £576 in 1755, included the 'great Stucco Cieling . . . finished with Gothick Moldings' with multi-shaft columns 'Enrich'd [with] double Capitals, plain Bases and double Annulits', £56, windows with 'OG Arches to the heads, ornamented with Moldings & foliage leaves', arches with 'sofits wrot: in many Gothick pannels', 'All the Ornaments and Moldings . . . cast in Solid Alabaster [plaster using] Lime Bristol', a durable material that escaped the ele-

126 James Gibbs, perhaps with Carlo Giuseppe Artari and Giovanni Bagutti. Design for the 'Ceiling for ye New Church of St Martin'-in-the-Fields, London (east is to left), undated. Pen and ink and wash. Ashmolean Museum, Oxford, IV.31.

ments but not the destructive hand of neglect and the demolition crew in the 1940s.[93]

For late classicism there is the detailed evidence of two major churches. Great Badminton, Gloucestershire (pl. 505), features 'Dentil & small O.G enrich'd . . . Ovolo', 'circular Goloso', 'Flowers with Water Leaf', 'Rich raffled Flowers' etc., the bill totalling £337 1s. 8d.[94] Some notion of the labour intensity of such work is gained from Joseph Rose's bill for operations at Amersham, Buckinghamshire (1781–5), which entailed 'Sundry Plasterers 269 days a 3/6', totalling £47 1s. 6d., and 'Labourers . . . 98½ days' at £7 15s. 6d.[95]

Figurative and pictorial subjects rendered in plaster represented an acceptable equivalent to the lavishly painted interiors of Continental Catholic churches, which both abhorred and titillated British travellers. Joseph Addison observed that the 'Custom' of treating interiors 'extremely magnificent . . . spoils the Beauty of . . . *Roman* Catholic Churches, and often covers the Walls with wretched Daubings, impertinent Inscriptions', etc.[96] Yet, it is telling that an extreme expression of this treatment in England in a proposal for St Martin-in-the-Fields (pl. 126), by the Catholic, Roman-trained Gibbs, in which the ceiling is subdivided into elaborately framed cartouches and polylobes resplendent with religious imagery (perhaps episodes from the life of the patron saint), *putti* and the Holy Ghost in clouds above the altar, which would have been entrusted to his favourite Ticinese *stuccatori*, Carlo Giuseppe Artari and Giovanni Bagutti, 'the best Fret-workers that ever came into *England*', was rejected by the building committee in favour of a more restrained, geometrical, non-pictorial solution with a few, concentrated areas of fancy but inoffensive *putti* heads, cartouches and foliage.[97] Sefferin Alken's *Christ at Emmaus* altarpiece executed in polychrome plaster (pl. 127), a near-replica of Titian's *Supper at Emmaus*, available in a Mortlake Tapestry version (*circa* 1625) hanging in St John's College, Oxford, and William Collins's *Annunciation of the Virgin* altarpiece at Warwick (pl. 128), are rarities in the Anglican sphere.[98]

Occasionally, things went wrong, as in the case of Thomas Betson, who won the competition to plaster the interior of St John, Westminster, in 1744 (following a devastating fire) with the lowest estimate, £267, 'Provided he gives Security for the due Performance . . . to the Satisfaction of the Churchwardens in the Penalty' of £500. It transpired that 'having been ill of

127 (*above*) Sefferin Alken. *Christ at Emmaus* altarpiece, St Margaret, Westminster, London, 1758–59. Polychrome plaster.

128 (*left*) William Collins. *Annunciation of the Virgin* altarpiece, plaster and wood canopy by Timothy Lightoler, Beauchamp Chapel, St Mary, Warwick, Warwickshire, *c.*1760.

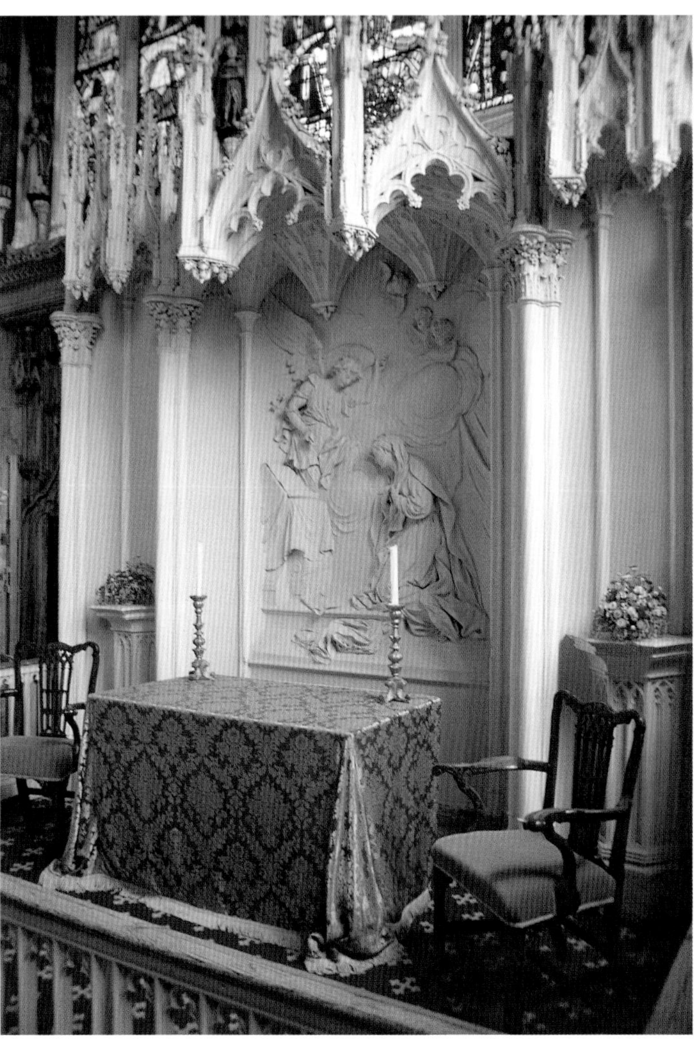

the Gout, The persons he had employ'd to measure the Work . . . had made several Mistakes' so he 'refused to give Security' and the job was offered to Clark, the next lowest (£386), who also 'made several Mistakes in computing the Work', so the contract finally passed to Mrs Elizabeth Mines (£452), who gave a security of £900.[99]

Carvers were among the elite craftsmen involved in church interiors. The most celebrated was the Dutch-born Grinling Gibbons, who in 1719, two years before his death, executed the six Corinthian capitals and other decorative elements of Hawksmoor's bold altar screen in St Alfege, Greenwich (pl. 129).[100] John Webster of London petitioned the New Churches Commis-sioners in 1716, 'having been Bred a Carver & followed the Art & Mystery for Twenty Three years Past In which Time he has had the Honour to be Employed in the Kings Palaces . . . and Knowing Himself to be Compleatly Qualified (in All Respects) for An Admittance into your Honours Service'.[101]

For wainscot panelling cedar wood was especially coveted. Zacharias Conrad von Uffenbach, a German traveller, described in 1710 the effect on entering the late seventeenth-century interior of Trinity College chapel, Oxford, as not only presenting 'an incomparable appearance, but also gives off a thoroughly agreeable and excellent perfume', adding: 'This need not cause surprise, since cedar . . . is neither rare nor costly here, for it grows luxuriantly in Ireland and is shipped over at a trifling expense.'[102] In 1722 Francis Nicholson, Governor of South Carolina, presented cedar planks to St Martin-in-the-Fields.[103]

While most modest-sized churches featured naked floor boards, sometimes covered by rush matting (p. vi), the desirability attached to strong, permanent paving is aptly demonstrated at St John, Hampstead, where soon after completion rising damp had to be rectified by installing 1,977 feet of Newcastle stone under the pews.[104] Parish churches favoured the repeated geometrical patterns of contrasting marbles concentrated in the chancel, as displayed in Thomas Eayre's plan for Stoke Doyle, Northamptonshire, for which the estimate on 550 feet of pavement laid at 2d. per foot amounted to £4 11s. 8d. (pl. 130).[105] The fashion can be traced back to the seventeenth century, perhaps the earliest recorded example being the pavement before Inigo Jones's Winchester Cathedral screen (pl. 316).[106]

Large-scale renewal in cathedrals was normally prompted by old deteriorating flags resulting from the long-established custom of internal rather than churchyard burial.[107] Because the floor of Canterbury in 1768 was 'very bad [and] no ways becoming such a Building',

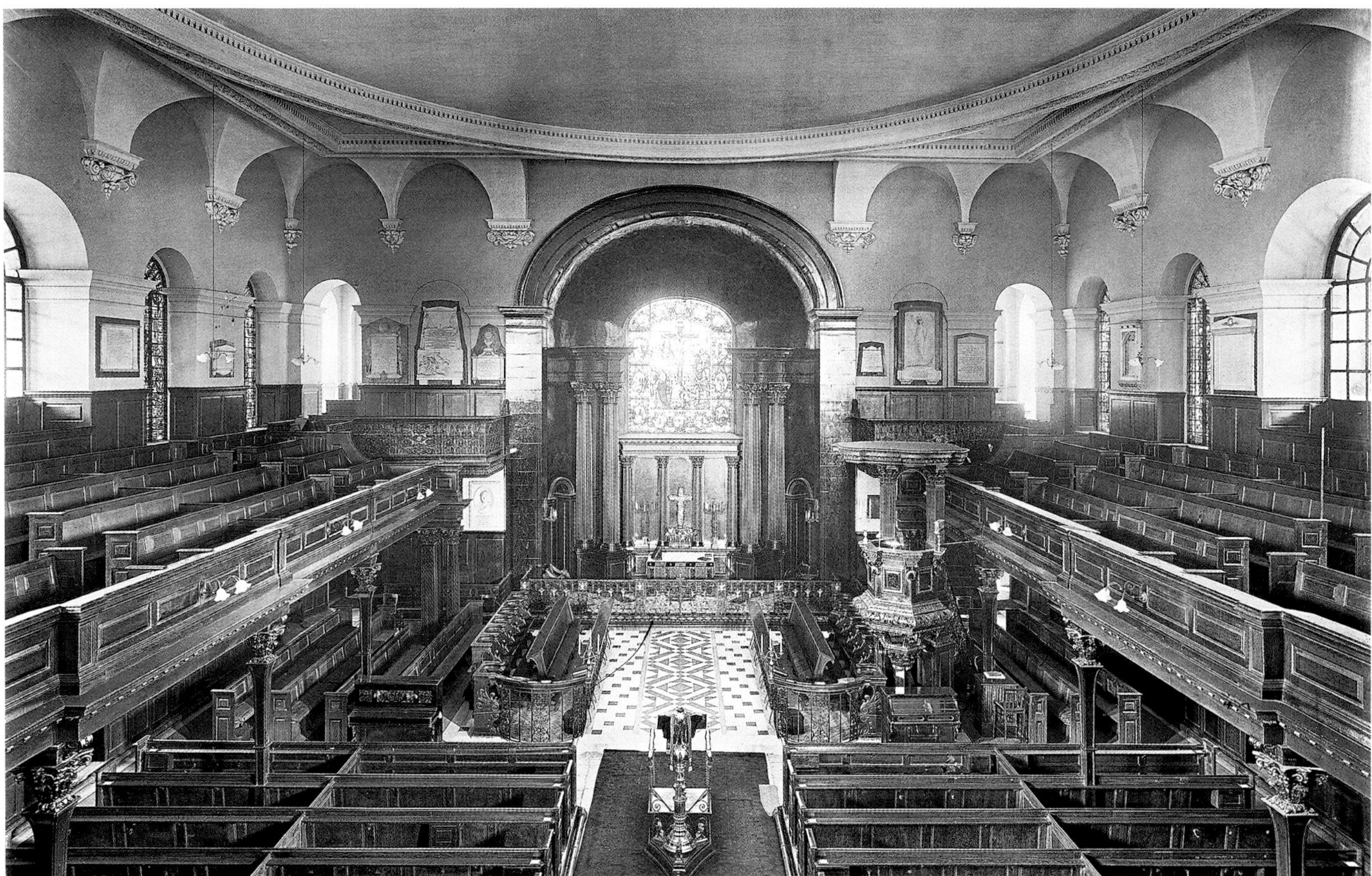

129 Nicholas Hawksmoor. Interior towards chancel, St Alfege, Greenwich, London, 1712–26, pre-1941 Blitz photograph. English Heritage (National Monuments Record), DD75/00044.

its surveyor, Robert Mylne, then acting in the same capacity at St Paul's, advised re-laying the nave with 7,100 feet of 'new purbeck' at 9d. per foot, estimated at £266 5s. 0d., and resetting 'old paving and . . . Grave or Monumentall Stones new Worked on the face [and] new jointed', which included 'Carrying the Rubbish and Soil to make . . . extra Height [and] filling up the parts to answer the new Levell', totalling £405.[108] At York in 1734–5 Lord Burlington and William Kent covered all but the eastern end of the choir, which involved 10,592 feet of black marble and 23,711 feet of 'white stone' laid on 34,304 feet of brick, totalling £1,619 10s. 5d., which survives virtually intact. In Drake's engraving (pl. 131) the contrast between unreformed, haphazard and new, geometric paving is telling. The project ran into financial difficulties because the masons complained to the dean and chapter that 'by a misfortune of agreeing to take up the Old floor and Carrying out, Leavelling the floore & Raising the graves and the Expence of carrying part of the Earth out of . . . town which we did not Expect', together with £40 'Allowd for Saws[,] we have Suffer'd the Loss of 58 pounds [but] hope you will not stick to . . . and not let us be loosers – When this is allow'd by the Misfortune of the quarry and Other misfortunes [including] Altering the designe after the Stones were got . . . we shall be loosers' by £73 6s. 6½d.[109]

The proposals for repaving Lincoln Cathedral during 1778–9 are particularly interesting for the fulsome documentation and unusually meticulous care taken. James Essex, the architect in charge, recommended removing the old floor, ramming and levelling it with 'dry Rubish [and] sand fit for the reception of the new floor . . . done with the best stone of it's kind sound and free from vents or cracks'. Various tenders were received, ranging from 'Leeds paving . . . the best in the Kingdom . . . not being liable to rise in flakes or Shill', laid in 'Random lengths' priced at 4s. 9d. per yard (rejected as 'a bad Colour'), to Roche Abbey at 8s. 6d., which 'will always retain remarkable whiteness & forms a great Qntrast . . . with black Marble Dotts', 'Sheffield Blue' to Hopton, 'a fine Colour . . . the best . . . in

130 Thomas Eayre. 'The Ground Plot' design for St Rumbald, Stoke Doyle, Northamptonshire, 1723. Pen and ink and wash. Shropshire Records and Research Centre, 6000/17810.

131 Richard Boyle, 3rd Earl of Burlington and William Kent. 'The ichnography of the Cathedral church of York, with the new Pavement', in Francis Drake, *Eboracum: or the History and Antiquities of the City of York*, 1736, pl. 5. Leeds Library and Information Service. Executed 1731–5.

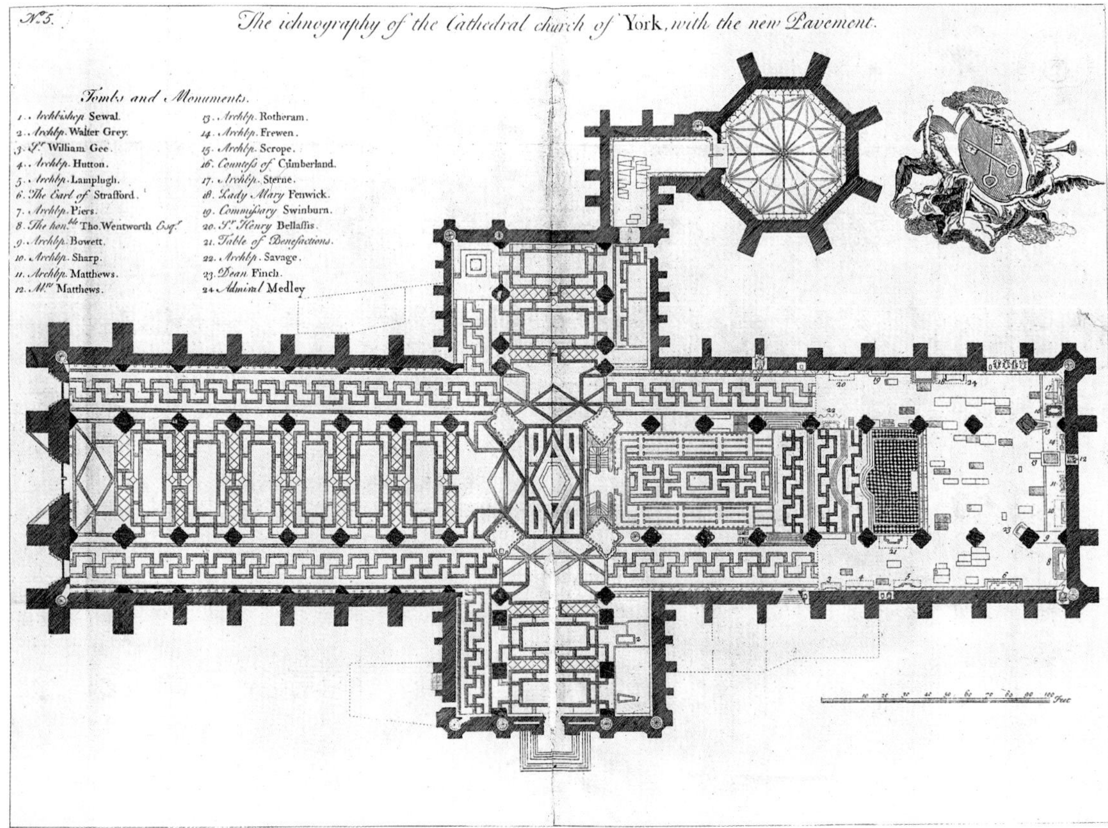

Quality . . . produced', Woodhouse 'the best and Cheapest . . . that will indure ages . . . hard Compact . . . & very good Colour' laid at 4s. 6d. per yard, to Newton 'very handsom . . . & better Colour . . . but not quite so hard', as well as Portland at 1s. 8d., and 'Yorkshire Cromwell Bottom the best Grit Stone in the Country' at 8d. The local masons, John Hayward and William Lumby, specified 2,584 yards of 'Best Lincoln Stone' costing £710 12s. 0d. and 1,694 yards of Hopton with black marble dots at £1,016 8s. 0d., employing sixteen workmen for twelve months. John Platt II of Rotherham, proprietor of 'Marble Quarries & Machines' in Derbyshire (whom we have already met in connection with work at Halsham Mausoleum, pp. 155–6), specified 'Bird-Eye' grey and black marble following an 'ingenious Design' (untraced), which 'would having a Striking Effect; but the Execution . . . very expensive'. Essex did not think it would 'save any thing by contracting for the materials at the pitts as they will loose more by waste than they will save in the price' and in a change of mind favoured boarding rather than stone within the altar railing 'covered with a carpet', which 'will be much warmer & handsome'.[110]

There were effective alternative floor treatments. At Ettington, Warwickshire, there was a choice between stone and 'neat brick Quarries'.[111] Litchfield Cathedral choir was paved with 'Alabaster and Canal Coal intermixt'.[112] Nathaniel Smith was paid £22 4s. 0d. for 'Painted Cloth . . . in squares. to Imitate Portland & Breming Stone Pavement . . . Containing 53 Square Yards [and] 111 Square Yards at 4d. a Yard' at Audley End, Essex; that is, a precursor to linoleum.[113]

The Builder's Dictionary (1734) devoted thirteen pages to the glazing trade, describing the material as 'an artificial Concrete of Salt, Sand, or Stones . . . *fusible* by a strong Fire . . . tenacious and coherent . . . does not waste or consume in the Fire . . . where . . . red-hot . . . is ductile, and capable of being fashion'd into any Form . . . admits of Polishing', and identified the 'Sorts' of native manufacture as Ratcliff Crown from London, 'the best and clearest . . . of a light Sky-blue Colour'; Newcastle, 'mostly used in England . . . of an Ash Colour, and subject to Specks, Streaks, and other Blemishes . . . frequently warp'd and crooked'; and Bristol, of which 'very little . . . comes to *London*, by reason they have not the Convenience of sending it by Sea, as they have from *Newcastle* by Coal Ships; though . . . as cheap, and better than *Newcastle*'. In addition, Stourbridge, Worcestershire, was 'famous for its glass manufacture . . . coloured in the liquid in all the capital colours in their several shades . . . a secret which they have here'.[114] A total of 85 feet of 'best Ratcliffe Crown Glass to new Sashes in large Squares at 16d. p Ft', priced at £5 14s. 0d., was supplied to the Jerusalem Chamber, Westminster Abbey, and the same to Banbury, 'in broad Lead the Square not larger than eight inches by six . . . tied with strong bands to the Iron work Soldered together or properly pinned into the Casement' at 1s. per foot.[115] William Ransome was directed to 'make a New pattern of the Comon New Castle Glass, to the Satisfaction of the Surveyors' for St Alfege, Greenwich, and there contracted for the glass 'Sett in Strong lead . . . the Vice being Set for that purpose, the Glass . . . Cutt into Squares of about 9 by 6 Inches, well ly'd, Solder'd, and Cemented with good bandings to the Iron Barrs', 1,892 feet costing £55 3s. 8d.[116] At All Saints, Southampton, 'all the sashes with newcastle crown . . . free from waves or blisters . . . no crooked glass . . . and all panes that break without a blow from the glass being stained by brads within one year from the finishing . . . to be replaced at the contractors expence', 1,609 feet estimated at £100 11s. 3d.[117] Thomas Stroud estimated for '24 Windows [containing] 1320 p. of Glazing' at St Paul, Bristol, 'If the largest Size Squares . . . 9½ pr: Foot', £52 5s. 0d., or the 'smallest size . . . 8½', £46 15s. 0d., 'compleated in a good Workmanlike manner, with the best Materials [including] good Bristol Crown Glass'.[118]

The technology grew increasingly sophisticated. 'With a view to ventilation' at St James, Manchester, 'the windows (which are large) are hung on a particular Manner, so that they will set, on the outside and inside, to an angle, and are balanced so as to remain in any diagonal position which may be deemed necessary for the admission of air'.[119] St Mary Magdalene, Bridgnorth, Shropshire (pl. 662), was 'Glazed in narrow Lead with . . . best Bristol Crown Glass each window to have a part about three feet by two feet made in a distinct frame and fixed on Centres so as to open and shut by a Chord and Pulley . . . and the whole made to exclude the rain effectually'.[120] All Saints, Southampton, had the 'lower range . . . hung on pivots of iron let into brass sockets and plates, those in the flanks of the altar to have the lower half fixed and the upper to pull down and those on the flanks of the church . . . double hung with brass pulleys and patent sash-lines and leaden weights'.[121]

Despite the impression given by 'An Admirer of propriety in Church decoration' writing in the *Gentleman's Magazine* in 1807 that

> Nothing gives me greater pleasure, than to see our churches kept in a clean decent order, as far as plain *painting* goes; but I dislike *glaring colours, excess of*

> *gilding, painted pannels, crimson pulpit cloths with rich gold fringe, and such tawdry decoration*, which, in my humble opinion, are more appropriate for a theatre than for a building dedicated to the service of God[,]

nothing could be further from actual practices.[122] In keeping with the often riotous taste of fashionable domestic interiors and dress, ebullient colour schemes penetrated parish churches more frequently than might be supposed, a trend already observed in the case of furnishing textiles and painted glass. The Bishop of Carlisle, visiting Bridekirk, Cumberland, in 1703, noted that the reading desk and vicar's pew had been 'lately painted and adorned (almost to a Tawdryness)'.[123] Though the study of church colouring has not been pursued with the same methodical, scientific rigour devoted to the domestic sphere,[124] and despite frequent exasperatingly vague references to 'plain Colour', 'fair Colour', 'decent Colour', 'light Colour', 'any Common Colour as shall be directed' and so on, without specifying the precise hue, systematic scrutiny of eighteenth-century accounts proves surprisingly informative, and certain tastes and trends emerge.

132 Artist unknown. Interior of St John, Chester, Cheshire, *c.*1830. Watercolour. Grosvenor Museum, Chester, 164.A.1972.

By far the most widely preferred treatment early on was white paint or whitewashing, the latter a mixture of water and slaked lime, which was inexpensive, easy to apply and had the advantage of destroying harmful insects.[125] White carried the powerful religious connotation of the ideal of Christian perfection reinforced by the authority of celebrated renaissance writers. Alberti's Seventh Book (concerned with 'Ornament to Sacred Buildings') of *De Re Aedificatoria*, first published in 1486, stated that 'Purity and Simplicity of Colour, as of Life, must be most pleasing to the Divine Being; and . . . it is not proper to have any Thing in a Church that may be likely to draw off Men's Thoughts from Devotion and fix them upon the Pleasure and Delight of the Senses.'[126] Palladio concurred in *I quattro libri d'architettura* (1560) that 'none is more suteable to Temples [by which he meant pagan temples as well as Christian churches] than white; by reason that the purity of this color, express'd in the purity of Life, is highly grateful to GOD'.[127]

Yet, the results were not always satisfactory. Defoe commented that Salisbury Cathedral was 'certainly hurt by . . . white washing . . . wherein [the chapter] very stupidly, have everywhere drawn black lines to imitate joints in stone'.[128] Having the pillars of York Minster's south crossing aisle 'washed over . . . made [them] undistinguishable', and it was lamented that while the technique applied to Westminster Abbey was intended to 'preserve the ancient Gothic grandeur [and] all the venerable majesty of its former state, yet the beautiful carving which it was once adorned is irretrievably lost'.[129] Horace Walpole claimed that by the 'coarsely daubed' whiting at Canterbury 'gloom is so totally destroyed' and he was 'shocked at the nudity of the whole'.[130] The 'effect and solemnity' of Hereford Cathedral were 'much injured by its being painted a dead white',[131] as demonstrated in a rare view of romanesque St John, Chester, which was whitewashed in 1788 at a cost of 7 guineas (pl. 132).[132]

> On *seeing* HAUGHAM ABBEY, *a fine old Ruin near Shrewsbury, white-washed.*
>
> HOW awful once thy antient face,
> How spoilt by vain renewing,
> Of old thy gravity was grace,
> Now spruceness thy undoing.
>
> Thou who wast once a rev'rend sage,
> Alike in fact and show,
> Art now ridiculous in age,
> And look'd a batter'd beau.[133]

Stone colour had notable precedents, as favoured by Wren for St Paul's Cathedral and the City Churches.[134]

St Botolph, Aldgate, had 'Wainscot, painted fake stone Colour'.[135] Isaac Mansfield charged £4 14s. 5d. for applying 378 yards on the walls of Christ Church, Spitalfields.[136] Palladian St Giles-in-the-Fields had a 'stone finishing troweld smooth'.[137] At Kirkleatham Hospital chapel, Yorkshire, a Mr Carpenter was paid £27 2s. 11d. for paintwork in which pigment was mixed with sand to produce a convincingly authentic texture (pl. 503).[138] What exactly stone colour was is a matter of conjecture. Formulas refer to a light grey made of white lead mixed in oil with small amounts of Prussian blue, spruce yellow and umber,[139] presumably allowing the painter to harmonise with the specimen stonework. At medieval Burton Agnes, Yorkshire, a beautification programme specified plastering the walls 'like Stone of the Colour of the pillars'; at Banbury, 'the same as the Stone Columns now are or as near . . . as may be'; at St Michael, Cornhill, it was 'Portland stone colour'.[140]

Faux marble was favoured for major architectural features: at Westminster Abbey 454 yards of paintwork on Wren's high altar 'in imitaton of Sussex Marble' cost £34 1s. 0d., and 560 yards of the same on the ribs of the north transept vault at £51 6s. 8d.[141] St Martin-in-the-Fields was charged 3s. for 'mending the Marble Painting to the Organ Case'.[142] St Michael, Cornhill, instructed its craftsmen to 'make different Specimens of the Manner in which it would be proper to Paint the Pillars'; the 'unanimous Opinion [was] in Imitation of white veined Marble plain and fluted according to one of the Specimens'.[143] The Corinthian altarpiece at Rendlesham, Suffolk, was 'painted as Siena marble'.[144] Imitation wood graining was also popular. At Banbury the entablature, architraves and organ case were 'grained . . . in imitation of Wainscott', that is, oak.[145]

More audacious, recherché colouring was sometimes favoured: red, ultramarine, olive, yellow ochre, umber, Prussian blue, 'Vernice' green, French grey, straw. The bill of the plasterer, Joseph Rose, for St Mary, Amersham, itemised 'Blue Black . . . Spanish Brown . . . Turkey Umber and Spruce Ochre'.[146] Thomas Hardwick Jr's beautifully rendered presentation drawings for St James, Hampstead Road, London (pl. 133), in contradiction to painting the interior in 'Stone or any Common Colour', shows a luminous yellow ochre, a slightly richer tone of which appears in his Italian journal demonstrating the 'manner of finishing one of the rooms in the [ancient Roman] house discovered in 1771 near the Villa Negroni at Rome'.[147]

Expensive gilding provided additional glamour: '3150 Leaves of Gold & laying on at 13*s* p. hundred' costing £20 9s. 0d. was supplied for Westminster Abbey crossing lantern; at Roman Catholic Lulworth Castle chapel 36 feet of 'Impost with Flutes & pateras', 110 feet 3 inches of 'Eliptical fluted Mouldings', 82 feet of 'Astragal at foot of Frize', all 'gilt in Burnished Gold', totalled £50.[148] This treatment tended to concentrate on altarpieces. At St Paul, Deptford, the painter Henry Turner charged £189 for '94½ yrds of Painting and Guilding about the Altar Containing the Fluting of the Columns & Pilasters, the Enrichments of their Bases & Capitals wth Guilding and Ornaments in the Soffits, together wth a Large Curtain, Cherubs Heads and a Glory in the Spherical Arch', while at All Saints, Southampton, 'Gilding to Railing and Gilders time', for sixteen days, cost £3 12s. 0d., using '24 Books of Gold' at 2s. 6d. each, £3.[149] Yet, because of suspicion of what was regarded as Catholic over-indulgence, its application in Britain was relatively restrained. John James advised the dean and chapter of Rochester Cathedral that the ornamental part of the crossing vault would 'very well bear Guilding in the Ovolos of the Bed-moldings, and the Small fflowers of the Goloss in the square Soffite, as also the Edges of the Oak-leaves in the Circular Soffite', though this would render it 'more rich than any part of the Ceiling of the Choir wch: I think should not be'. He preferred gilding only the 'four fflowers upon the Corners of the outer Square, and perhaps the Pendent piece in the Center . . . (the fluting of it at least)'.[150] For the altarpiece of King's College chapel, Cambridge, it was reckoned 'Beauty . . . should consist in its Plainness & Simplicity; by which . . . it is not meant to exclude all the Ornaments . . . but only to avoid all Gilding & Finery, which every Body condemns'.[151]

> You set the Hassock and you dust the Pew;
> Nor with less Care you rub the shining Board,
> Where Widows worship and Spadille's ador'd[152]

The impulse towards church maintenance, the chore of diligent workers like Goody Biddice, the heroine of the above rhyme, has its origin in early Christianity. Eusebius, the fourth-century bishop of Caesarea and author of the influential *Ecclesiastical History* (reprinted with annotations in the early eighteenth century), recounted that in St Jerome's panegyric on Nepotian 'that he took care to have every thing neat and clean about the church, the altar bright, the walls whited, the pavement swept . . . and the vessels shining . . . These were but small things . . . but a pious mind devoted to Christ is intent upon things great and small, and neglects nothing.'[153] By the eighteenth century numbers of old fabrics had fallen into disreputable states. Glasgow Cathedral, reported the *Gentleman's*

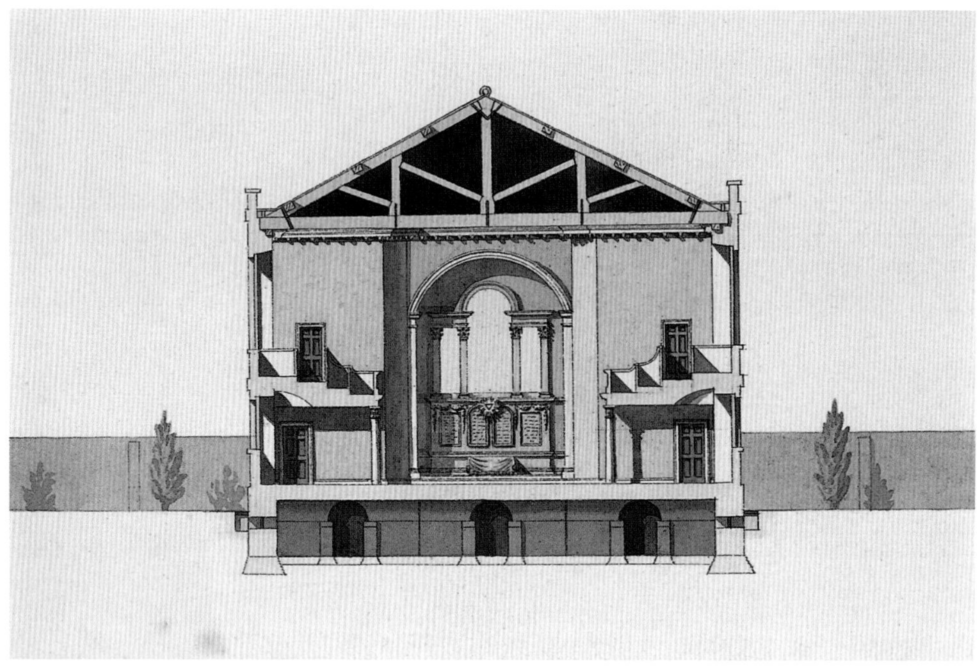

133 Thomas Hardwick Jr. Design for the interior towards the chancel, St James, Hampstead, London, 1790. Pen and ink and coloured wash. City of Westminster Archives Centre, D1715, f. 523.

Magazine in 1766, 'is an old majestic Gothic structure . . . but within, it is miserably kept (as all their churches are) the roof quite out of repair, the pavement broken, and the walls covered with mould and dirt'.[154] Torrington found South Kyme, Lincolnshire, a 'most venerable looking church . . . of such beautiful antiquity [but] Within, the filth and ruin would beggar all description! The roof falling in! – A dirty floor! An altar table that a pauper would not feed from!!'[155] Guestling, Sussex, was 'kept in very bad order, and claims not the least pretension to neatness'.[156] These were the results of neglect: the 'Plough and Rubbish' were ordered 'removed out' of Diseworth, Leicestershire; the 'space under the belfry' at Lydbury North, Shropshire, was 'indecent' and the 'rubbish must be removed'.[157] Vandalism was also to blame: at Hawksmoor's recently completed Limehouse and Wapping churches 'great Damages done . . . by pilforing people' prompted discussion of 'the best means to prevent the Damage'; the prevention officer at Lincoln Cathedral was ordered to 'see that Boys do no mischief . . . by breaking Windows', while at Cossington, Leicestershire, the 'Lattice gates [were] fixed at the South & north doors sufficient to keep out Children and cattle in order that the doors may be occasionlly opened to air the church'.[158] There were oddities like avian instructions: at Queniborough, Leicestershire, the Vestry ordered: 'Care to be taken to keep out the Birds which make the Chancel filthy', a problem solved at St Leonard, Colchester, where the authorities paid James Hawkins 4d. for 'ox vomet &c to destroy the birds'.[159] At Abberley, Worcestershire, 'Cromwell's soldiers . . . broke most of the painted glass, tore away the brass, iron, and lead, from many monuments, and introduced that ruin and filth into country churches which hath remained, and in many encreased, ever since [and now] is very damp and dirty . . . the more inexcusable' since the fabric 'might be made wholesome at a small expence'. There were 'some easy remedies': 'Casements ought . . . to be made to all church-windows, which should be opened every fine day',

> Narrow slits should be cut in all the . . . Doors, that the putrid air within, arising from dead bodies, and other offensive matter, might be constantly ventilated . . . frequently sweeping, white-washing, and painting, would make the publick service of GOD more decently, and more frequently attended; and many good people would be saved from colds, rheumatisms, palsies, and a hundred other disorders.[160]

Maintenance of the nave and tower was one of the responsibilities of churchwardens and vergers, while the incumbent or patron of the living, usually the leading local landowner, dealt with the chancel. The dean and

134 Samuel Scott. View from the north-west, St Mary, Twickenham under scaffolding, undated. Watercolour. Ashmolean Museum, Oxford. John James architect, 1714–15.

chapter of Chester Cathedral 'thought proper' that the latter 'be admonished To keep the stalls wainscote [and] floor in the Choir and broad Isle clean'.[161] Private patrons were also encouraged. Sir Michael Warton left Beverley Minster, Yorkshire, £4,000 in his will of 1725, to be applied in keeping it in 'perpetual repair'.[162] An interesting regime existed at Hampstead parish church, where Abraham Armstrong was employed 'to keep Clean & open' the pews, pulpit, reading desk and vestry, 'for which he is to be allow'd all the Gratuity's that may arise from . . . Inhabitants or Strangers', as well as 20s. for 'Mops Brooms Brushes & other necessarys', with the widows Mary Garnor 'to keep Clean & open the Pews in the North Gallery & half the West End' and Mary Ayres on the south and other half of the west sides, both under the same terms.[163] From time to time the authorities attempted to evade responsibilities. Bishop Nicolson of Carlisle complained of Ireby in 1703: 'The Quire has been lately a little brush'd up, in expectation of my comeing to see it. But 'tis still very Tawdry, and unbecoming the wealthy Abillities and Pretended Zeal of [the] clerk of the Committees in the House of Lords.'[164]

At Salcombe, Devon, a chapel was set aside to 'hold materials for repairing the church'.[165] These included scaffolding: a Dr Dove offered a scheme for 'moving Scaffold for . . . Cleaning & repairing the Stone Roof' at Norwich Cathedral,[166] an operation recorded in a view of Twickenham parish church by Samuel Scott, who lived opposite (pl. 134). At Westminster Abbey the carpenter supplied a 'platform close on the Gangway Westward over the Choir to keep Rain and Dust from falling into the Church'.[167]

During the refurbishment of St James, Piccadilly, in 1789 the pews, clock and organ were protected by paper and matting.[168] There was also a range of cleaning equipment: Thomas Surr, a glass dealer from York, provided the Minster with '1 Largest Sweeping Brush' 4s. 6d., '2 Large Whiteng Brushes' 2s., '4 Best Whitening Brushes' 4s., '1Best Mop' 1s., '1 Dustg Brush' 10d., '1 Large Hand Brush' 10s., and '1 Dust Basket' 1s.[169]

For the maintenance of steeples, Wren cleverly recommended at Westminster Abbey using the crockets, or 'Calceolus flower' as he called it, as 'a proper Form to help Workmen to ascend on the Outside to amend any Defects, without raising large Scaffolds upon every slight Occasion' (pl. 153).[170] The work was generally entrusted to specialist steeple keepers. A London mason, William Staines invented an innovative system of basketwork scaffolding, first used at St Bride, Fleet Street, in 1764, after Wren's lovely structure was struck by lightning.[171] The contraption was employed again at St Mary, Islington, in 1787. In the previous year it was reported that since its erection in 1751–4 (pl. 489),

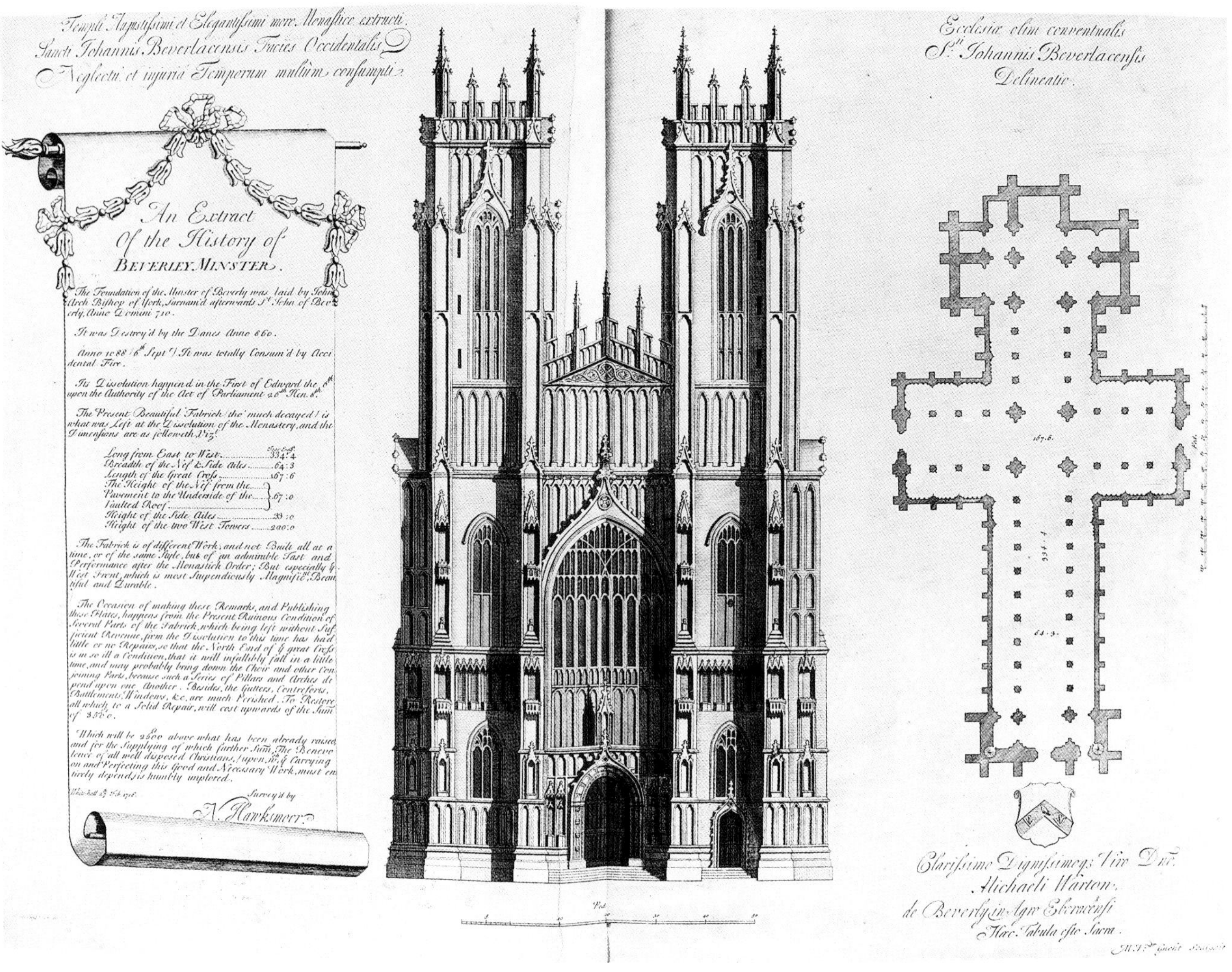

135 Michael van der Gucht after Nicholas Hawksmoor. 'Templi Augustissimi et Elegantissimi more Monastice extructi Santi Johannis Beverlacenis Facies Occidentalis Neglectu. et injuria Temporum mulium confumpti', 27 February 1716/17. Engraving. The Hepworth, Wakefield, Gott Collection, III, f. 5.

> various and Unequal pressures . . . the natural Consequence of its form and figure does not seem to have been put to right . . . The Tower . . . settled . . . more than the other Walls . . . from thence arises, considerable fractures . . . the Ring of Bells . . . contribute . . . to increase that . . . Weakness.

The surveyor, Robert Mylne, suggested inserting 'four Iron types or Chain barrs . . . thro: the Walls . . . with plates and Screws on the outside . . . in the fashion of *Patera's* . . . Screwed up tight on the outside'. An ingenious alternative remedy, however, was employed by Thomas Birch, who issued an explanatory engraving (pl. 115) demonstrating the 'Scaffold & Wicker-work . . . entirely formed of Willow, Hazel & other Stick [with] a Staircase in a Spiral line . . . avoiding the dangerous method of Scaffolds, by which the ascent was as easy and safe as the Stairs of a Dwelling-house'. So much so that Birch went public by displaying his 'simple and secure Invention' to the 'Curious' between 10 and 12 a.m. and 3 and 7 p.m. every day, admittance 6d., reaping from £2 to £4 daily, thereby supplementing a modest service fee of £20.[172]

The battle to preserve the structurally more complex, 295-foot-high Perpendicular west tower of St Michael, Coventry, is especially instructive. By 1789 it had deteriorated into a 'dangerous state' when John Cheshire, who had 'lately given several proofs of his abilities in the erection of . . . new spires', approved 'an easy method of securing [the present] *chef-d'oeuvre* of the kind . . . as cheap and practicable'. Nothing further was done until 1793, when the proposal by James Wyatt

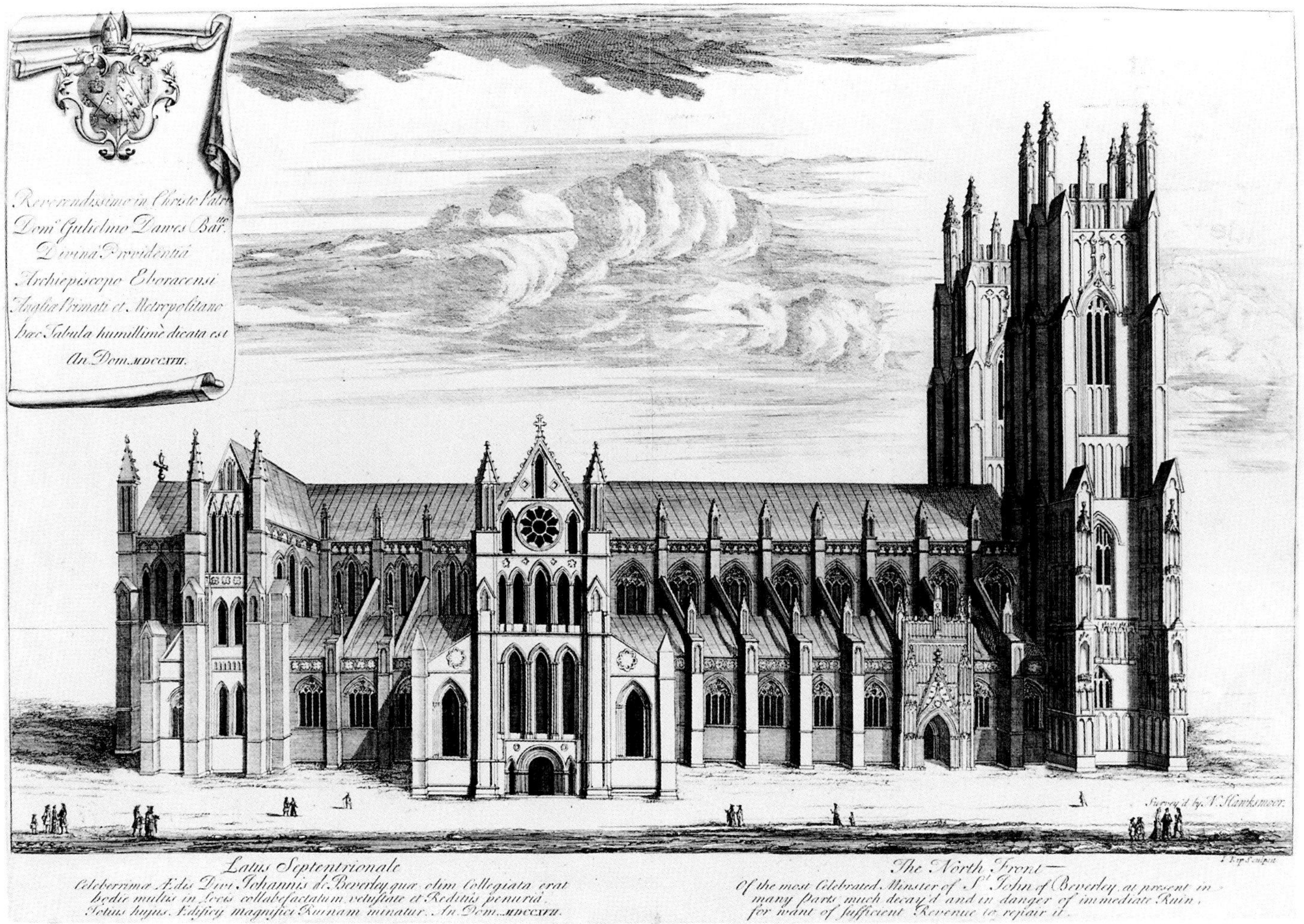

136 Jan Kip after Nicholas Hawksmoor. 'The North Front', Beverley Minster, Yorkshire, 1717. Engraving. The Hepworth, Wakefield, Gott Collection, VIII, f. 6.

and Joseph Potter, who had supervised the former's alterations at Lichfield and Hereford cathedrals (1788–93), was approved, which involved re-hanging the bells, the cause of the structural decay, in a timber frame within the stone carcass. A member of the restoration committee, Sir Roger Newdigate of nearby Arbury, a notable amateur architect and gothic advocate, offered alternative solutions of either re-siting the bells in a separate building (perhaps recalling the example of Salisbury Cathedral) or the more complicated and perhaps dubious idea of lining the tower's interior with large blocks of rough ashlar freestone,

> bedded & jointed together . . . each course . . . filled with . . . putty, which will restore . . . the connexion of the old walls where the mortar has been loosened or shaken out, & . . . enable the workmen who . . . renew the ornaments of the outside to cut out the rotten . . . parts without danger [and] the inside walls to be connected with the old walls, & . . . take its share of the weight [with] ties at the angles of the new wall . . . to keep it from spreading.

When the Wyatt-Potter programme was pursued, Newdigate protested, then resigned, 'fully convinced that, instead of retarding it, will most assuredly accelerate the destruction of . . . that wonderful edifice, which has not its equal on the globe'.[173] Significantly, the restored structure, which cost £2,649 4s. 9¼d., alone survived the devastating Blitz of 1940.

Pollution was also problematic, particularly in London. The ornately carved St Paul's Cathedral was espe-

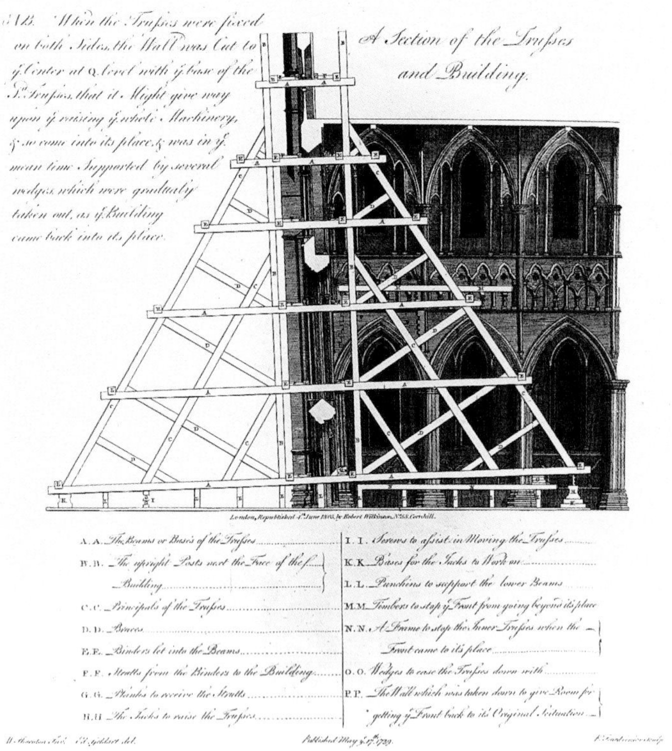

137 Paul Fourdrinier after William Thornton and Edward Geldart. 'A Section of the Trusses and Building', Beverley Minster, Yorkshire, 17 May 1739. Engraving. The Hepworth, Wakefield, Gott Collection, VIII, f. 16.

cially vulnerable. Abbé Fougeroux observed as early as 1728 that the Portland stone 'would retain its whiteness and its polish were it not for this accursed smoke which is so corrosive that it eats away the other kinds of stone and blackens this kind almost all over', while some fifty years later the 'atmosphere . . . is . . . heavy, impregnated so strongly with coal that the lower part . . . & the other churches are blackened prodigiously'.[174] Colen Campbell's St Paul's-inspired '*new Design for a Church in* Lincoln's-inn Fields' (1712) was 'dress'd very plain, as most proper for the sulphurous Air of the City' (pl. 515).[175]

In the case of old buildings drastic measures had to be taken. At Durham Cathedral in 1786 'Stones that are moulder'd away in part by the Weather and the ravages of Time are pick'd out, and in their room New ones are substituted, while those that are found good & sound are rendered in apparent unison with the rest by a general polish.'[176] So, too, at Canterbury, where 'small Columns round the inside . . . of a particular species of Purbeck . . . scaled . . . and grown sandy inwardly' could be preserved by scraping off the loose surfaces and 'Oil them all over [with] boiled Linseed Oil', necessary conservation since in many places they supported 'very heavy and Essential parts of the Structure'.[177] To sustain the onslaught of the elements roofs needed to be kept in good repair. At Hereford Cathedral Barnaby Sayse received £2 10s. 0d. in 1704 for 'sweeping and cleaning'; at Chesterfield 8d. was spent in 1770 towards 'preventing Rain getting to the Organ'; at St Paul, Covent Garden, the slater contracted in 1797 'to keep the Slating . . . in Repair for twenty years' for 2 guineas per annum.[178] At Longdon, Worcestershire, William Justin, a local bricklayer, was instructed to 'preserve maintain and keep [the fabric] . . . in a good substantial and decent manner . . . Wind and Water Tite' by covering the roof with 'blue slate', as well as keeping timbers and plastering 'in perfect good order', painting the doors every three years and generally look after the church for twenty-one years, at an annual salary of £1 1s. 0d., though he was 'not to be accountable for . . . Damage done [by] Fire . . . Thunder or Lightning by the fall of the Tower, or . . . wilful damage by a Mob, or by any other unlawful proceeding'.[179] Occasionally, the Vestry sought practical expertise advice. Willey Reveley recommended for All Saints, Southampton, that

> no leakage in the slating should ever remain unstopped as the mischief is always great & may be prevented by a little care . . . in wet seasons . . . let the crack be plastered with lime & hair within side & remain so till a proper season . . . will permit new slates . . . The painting of the external woodwork should be repeated whenever it begins to rub off like chaulk upon the finger, or any appearance of Rust comes upon the iron work . . . If the snow is to be thrown off . . . let it be done with wooden shovels without the least iron about them otherwise the gutters & slating will be entirely cut to pieces I recommend shovels of deal only.

Though he added: 'no leakage will be found from any quantity of snow because I have purposely contrived the roof to clear itself'.[180] James Hawkins charged 2s. 6d. for 'Cleaning the snow from the . . . Leads and . . . the ice from the Church' of St Leonard, Colchester.[181] Of the walls at Cossington, Leicestershire, the Vestry ordered 'the Nettles and Weeds growing out of the fabrick between the stones be pulled out [and] a long brush and short Ladder be provided to sweep and keep clean the walls'.[182] Mr Ellison agreed to repair the chancel window at Bedlington, Northumberland, for £2 4s. 0d. on condition of 'Upholding it for 30. Yeares'; Okey Goodman contracted to keep windows in Billinghay, Lincolnshire, 'in good and sufficient repair' for

10
20
30
40
50
A Representation or View of the North Front of ye Great Crofs Isle
of Beverly Minster which over hung four foot beyond its Base &
was brought back into its place, by means of ye Timber Framing here Describ'd
Published May ye 17th 1739

138 Paul Fourdrinier after William Thornton and Edward Geldart. 'A Representation or View of the North Front of ye Great Cross Isle of Beverley Minster', Yorkshire, 17 May 1739. Engraving. The Hepworth, Wakefield, Gott Collection, VIII, f. 15.

seven years at 5s. annually; Richard Empson Jr at Beverley for seven years at £18, 'he finding all Glass, Lead, Solder, Labour and all other incidental . . . expences'.[183]

While the Bishop of Ossory, commenting on Kilkenny Cathedral in 1756, conceded that the 'stucco . . . w'd be broken to pieces in cleaning . . . for we [the Irish] are not the most careful people in the world',[184] throughout England considerable efforts were made to look after church interiors. Francis Cundall supplied 'halfe a yard of Sark woll to wash down the Green walls' at Ripon Minster; the sculptor Francis Bird cleaned the altar at All Hallows, Thames Street, London, and charged £1 4s. 0d. for '8 Days work in Cleaning . . . and Polishing the . . . Font'; at St Paul, Covent Garden, monuments were covered with 'deal boards to prevent [them] being defaced' during building repairs in 1787.[185] At Christ Church, Spitalfields, a wide range of cleaning equipment was provided, including baskets, shovels, pails, scrubbing, wainscot, pulpit and hearth brushes, 'Thrumb Mops Ragg Mops Brooms', altogether costing 10s.[186] At St Paul's Cathedral a 'Rat-Catcher' charged £1 1s. 6d. for 'clearing the Choir from Ratts' in 1700, and four years later the mason Edward Strong was employed for sixteen days 'Cleansing Marble Bases & Pillars under Organ Gallery, agst the Queen's coming'.[187]

The outstanding campaign from a structural standpoint centred on Beverley Minster (*circa* 1230–1450). Surveys carried out in 1717 by Nicholas Hawksmoor and Thomas Thackeray, a local master mason, evoked a 'Beautiful Fabrick . . . of different Work, and not Built at a time, or of the same Style, but of an admirable Tast and Performance after the Monastick Order . . . especially the West Front, which is most Stupendiously Magnificent, Beautiful and Durable' (pl. 135). It revealed that since the Reformation the fabric had had 'little or no Repairs, so that the North End of the Great Cross is in so ill a Condition, that it will infallibly fall in a little time, and may probably bring down the Choir and other Conjoining Parts, because such a Series of Pillars and Arches depend upon one Another'. A sum of £3,500 was reckoned to 'Restore [it] to a Solid Repair'. Thackeray's further, more technical and alarming report confirmed a 'great deal' of mortar and plaster falling off the north transept (pl. 136), exposing a gap between the outer wall and vaulting, leaving the roof unsupported, hanging 'as it were by its Selfe'. Moreover, the east side was 'flown out' in the 'low Isle' with three ribs supporting the roof 'intirely perished' 4 feet before reaching the bottom, the wall above the battlement, instead of supporting the main roof, was 'flown . . . four Inches' from it, also many cracks in the arches and walls 'fill'd up with Mortor Some Years agoe', fuelling 'fear if Some care be not imediately taken . . . the North Isle will fall which may occasion the Ruine of the whole Minster'. In 1718 four hundred engravings of plates 135 and 136 were issued, directing attention to the impending disaster. In the following year the York joiner-architect William Thornton contrived an ingenious 'Engine' for sandwiching the outer and inner transept walls in temporary scaffolding (pls 137–8) and by means of wedges screwing it back to perpendicular; then the old vaulting was replaced by a lightweight laminated wood and plaster structure.[188] John Carter described this stupendous achievement, unique in the history of Georgian architectural engineering, as 'magic efforts'.[189]

Part Three

THE MEDIEVAL TRADITIONS

139 Francis Place. View from the south-west, York Minster, *c.*1705. Pen and ink and wash. York Museum Trust (Art Gallery), R1756.

Twelve

'RABIES GOTHORUM'[1]

Q. Why was Gothic architecture, chiefly preferred for church buildings?

A. Because it was thought to be better suited to the purposes of devotion, striking the imagination with a religious dignity, and holy awe, so as to dispose the mind to the worship of the deity.[2]

Pre-eminent among these structures are the great cathedrals (pl. 139). Not everyone, of course, agreed with the Revd Reeve's catechism. James Ralph, writing in 1734 of St Edward's Chapel, Westminster Abbey, which contained some of its greatest medieval treasures, thought it 'has nothing remarkable . . . but certain Gothique antiquities, which are made sacred by tradition only, and serve to excite a stupid admiration in the vulgar'.[3] Worship as much as style motivated the use of gothic, and a substantial body of opinion by churchmen and antiquaries, deeply rooted in seventeenth-century ideals, believed that past churches were better, and that alterations should be made with excessive care and reverence, while admonishing the architectural godlessness of the modern age. For convenience and clarity I have divided Part Three into seven chapters, dealing with the nature of eighteenth-century gothic; the campaigns to preserve, repair and enhance ancient churches and cathedrals, with the latter often providing architectural and decorative incentives lower down the ecclesiastical hierarchy. This is followed by considerations of gothic's origins in Wren's circle, its transitional phases during the 1730s and 1740s, the reassertion of 'true Gothic taste' from the 1750s to the 1770s, and its final decades. The phenomenon of stylistic mixture – what Horace Walpole, that champion of gothic, disparaged as 'the bastard breed'[4] – forms a distinctly separate, authentic and significant yet much neglected expression in its own right. Finally, there is the largely forgotten resurrection of romanesque.[5]

Until the rise of antiquarian scrutiny during the second half of the eighteenth century, the lack of not only an accurate understanding of the origins and historical development of medieval architecture but also a generally accepted terminology to distinguish its stylistic phases (which was codified only in Thomas Rickman's *An Attempt to discriminate the Styles of English Architecture from the Conquest to the Reformation*, 1817) made it difficult to define gothic precisely. Typical was the Revd Francis Peck, who claimed that 'by a nice examination of the different modes in the fabric [of medieval churches] the different ages when they were in use may be pretty nearly ascertained', yet admitted he could not say 'which ought to be reckoned first in point of antiquity. For I do not pretend to range them.'[6] There were, however, several early attempts, notably by Sir Christopher Wren. Of pre-Fire (1666) St Paul's Cathedral, he accurately reckoned the thirteenth-century choir as 'a more modern *Gothick*-stile, not with Round [romanesque] . . . but *sharp-headed Arches*',[7] while his report of 31 August 1668 on the 'State of the Cathedral' at Salisbury, Wiltshire (begun 1220), commends the fabric as 'one of the best patternes of Architecture in that age wherein it was built . . . for many things, beyond what I find in divers Gothick Fabricks of later date'. In particular, the 'Windowes are not made too great, nor yet the light obstructed with many mullions, & transomes of Tracery-worke which was the ill fashion of the next following Age'.[8] But it was Wren's report of 1713 on Westminster Abbey (begun 1245), for which he was then serving as surveyor, that offered unusually perceptive observations on 'the Modes of Building . . . of 500 Years, or, more' based on examination of the 'Records' (which still remain in the Muniments) – an early instance of the architect as architectural historian. Recognising 'the *Gothick* Manner of Architecture (so the *Italians* called what was not after the Roman Style)', he thought 'it should with more Reason be called the *Saracen* Style', which the English 'borrowed . . . out of . . . *Arabick* Books . . . The *Crusado* gave us an Idea of this Form; after which King *Henry* [III, reigned 1216–72] built his Church', while the choir vault, 'finished 23 Years after his Decease, in the Reign of . . . *Edward* the First' (1272–1307) and 'more adorned and gilded, is without due Care in the Masonry, and is the worst performed of all done before'. Wren then pursued further his themes of the '*Saracen* Mode of Building seen in the East, [which] soon spread over *Europe*, and particularly in *France* [where] Nothing was thought magnificent that was not high beyond Measure, with the Flutter of Arch-buttresses, so we call the sloping Arches that poise the high Vaulting of the Nave'.[9]

By the seventeenth century, when the word gothic came into common usage, it was synonymous with the notion of the destruction of the classical rules of art by uncivilised northern invaders of the Roman Empire and therefore a ubiquitous term of disparagement: 'mostruosi & barbari'.[10] Wren himself described the '*Goths* [as] rather Destroyers than Builders' (hence his preference for the term '*Saracen*').[11] His friend John Evelyn wrote contemporaneously of 'a certain fantastical and licentious Manner of Building' and 'Congestions of heavy, dark, melancholy and *Monkish Piles*, without any just Proportions, Use or Beauty . . . the Irruption and Swarms of those truculent People from the *North* . . . over-running the Civilized World [found on] vast and gigantic Buildings . . . but not worthy of the Name of *Architecture*'; rather a 'Barbarity . . . we may look upon as purely *Gothic*, who consider nothing with *Reason*'.[12] The intellectual Roger North condemned gothic as an instance where 'nothing insnares weak judgment like ignorance pretending to art'.[13]

These jaundiced views spilled over into the eighteenth century. Addison advised Grand Tourists visiting Siena that

> There is nothing in this City so extraordinary as the Cathedral [1250–1400], which a Man may view with Pleasure after he has seen St *Peter's* [in Rome], though it is quite of another Make, and can only be looked upon as one of the Master-pieces of *Gothic* Architecture. When a Man sees the prodigious Pains and Expence that our Forefathers have been at in these barbarous Buildings, one cannot but fancy to himself what Miracles of Architecture they would have left us, had they only been instructed in the right way.

Moreover, 'nothing in the World can make a prettier Shew to those, who prefer false Beauties, and affected Ornaments, to a noble and majestic Simplicity'.[14] Peck wrote of 'the barbarousness of . . . all our old churches in Gothic . . . & the many rudenesses it is it self charged with'.[15] Sir John Clerk of Penicuik wrote to Roger Gale, a fellow member of the Society of Antiquaries of London, in 1736 that gothic was

> to be only the degeneracy of Greek and Roman Arts and Sciences. In this view I myself have admired the laborious Dullness and Stupidity which appear in all the Gothic contrivances of any kind. These Barbarians had the originals in perfection and yet could discover no beauties for their imitation, but Goths will always have a Gothick taste.[16]

It followed that gothic was proscribed in some circles. Evelyn catalogued its misdemeanours: 'slender and misquine *Pillars*, or rather Bundles of *Staves*, and other incongruous Props to support incumbent Weights, and pondrous arched Roofs . . . trite and busy Carvings . . . such as rather glut the Eye', citing Henry VII's Chapel (1503–12) at Westminster Abbey with

> its sharp *Angles*, *Jetties*, narrow *Lights*, lame *Statues*, *Lace*, and other *Cut-work* and *Crinkle Crankle* . . . clumsy Buttresses, Towers, sharp-pointed Arches [and] Doors . . . without Proportion; nonsensical Insertion of various Marbles Impertinently placed; Turrets and Pinacles thick set with *Monkies* and Chymaeras (and abundance of busy Work and other Incongruities).[17]

Setting out a case for the appropriateness of classicism for churches, North believed that

> It is necessary a fabrick should be strong, and where ever weakness appears, there is a fault; and that was so much affected by the Gothick architects in shew that it carryed them into the worst of faults, real weakness. Wee see in our ancient churches, a world of contrivance in leading the ribbs of a massy roof into one threadd, and so in vast length, and strange smallness downe to the bottom; as if the whole seem to stand upon knitting pins or so as every one should conclude impossible to stand on the seeming support. This, if the gimcrack were not discerned to be a meer shew, and not the true support of the fabrick, must instead of secure injoyment terrifie the people, least it should fall on their heads.

Moreover, the

> perpetuall breaking a surface, with carving sett offs, and small members, this is conspicuous in Henry VII's chappell . . . which is so full of it as to be spoyled, and it is as easy to examine the parts of a mist as of

> that . . . A clutter is alwais faulty, because it torments the sence to comprehend it . . . carving for carving sake, without such use, is an impertinence, like babble in company, of no profit. More cost more worship, is not a law of architecture . . . Therefore the gothick way of making wonderment at the stupendious weight borne upon thredds . . . is one of the worst of faults. Magick and trick will not serve in building, where lives depend; those are fitter for theater, and puppet-show, where men come to be cheated a few hours with a vain shew of what is not.

North concluded that 'nothing insures weak judgment like ignorance pretending to art. And of this sort the Gothick way hath much.'[18] Wren observed that 'the Flutter of Arch-buttresses are the first Thing that occasion the Ruin of Cathedrals, being so much exposed to the Air and Weather . . . and if they give Way, the Vault must spread',[19] and while the French theorist Abbé Laugier, in his influential *Essai sur l'Architecture* (1753), recognised that flying buttresses 'prevented the walls from moving aside [and] unfortunately are unavoidable', nevertheless concluded that they 'make the outside of our churches unsightly'.[20]

The most persuasive criticism was directed towards the excesses of gothic ornament. A Grand Tourist confronted by Milan Cathedral in 1776 (pl. 330) observed:

> It is not to be wished that any more . . . should be thrown away upon such a building . . . yet the whole edifice offers in its immensity a view of magnificence, & in its several parts a high finishing frequently adorned with elegance. The profusion of ornament is even ridiculous. The immense number of statues which the eye discovers, both within, & without, is too much for it to rest upon with pleasure, or to examine with any attention . . . It is impossible to view this lavishing of ornament without a species of indignation.[21]

Pope described his fictitious Temple of Fame

> Of Gothic structure was the northern side,
> O'er wrought with ornaments of barb'rous pride[22]

Richard Neve's *The City and Country Purchaser, and Builder's Dictionary* (1726 and 1736 editions) condemned gothic's 'incorrect Profiles . . . whimsical decoration . . . wild and chimerical Ornaments'.[23] On the other hand, the antiquary William Stukeley praised York Minster in 1740 (pl. 139) for its 'astonishing beauty', producing 'an effect superior . . . to any building upon earth. I cannot persuade myself to except even S. Peter's at Rome', while the chapter house was 'grand and beautiful beyond imagination. I must needs prefer it to the Pantheon itself; assuredly, in regard to the effect it produces, superior.'[24]

Yet there was an inherent problem. In 1738 John James, who had succeeded Nicholas Hawksmoor as Westminster Abbey surveyor, perhaps taking a hint from North's difficulty in deciphering gothic forms as those of the 'parts of a mist' (noted above), complained of conflicts in the latter's still incomplete remodelled west front (pl. 154):

> this Work being of Such a Nature that tis impossible to measure it with any exactness 'till performed. In plain [classical] Work a Computation may be made to almost an exactness, by reason of the certainty of measure beforehand [as demonstrated in pattern books devoted to the classical orders], but in Works so complicated as the window-heads and the windings and turnings of so many Gothick Ornaments tis impossible to measure them from Drawings; and a thing of no small difficulty to measure them when wrought.[25]

Gothic architecture signified at least for some the absence of rules, hence its inferiority to the classical style. Its repertory, however, could not be universally judged in this manner. While Exeter Cathedral, which had been constructed over 437 years, was admired for its unusual continuity of style – according to one early Georgian commentator, it was 'so uniformly compact, as if the whole was built by one Man . . . done in an instant of time'[26] – this failed to appreciate the 'natural' growth of such large buildings over lengthy construction histories. For example, *England Displayed* (1769) fulminated against Lincoln Cathedral's lack of the 'least affinity' of its parts, the 'shameful disregard to the design' by the disposition of its 'chief ornament . . . so irregularly varied that all . . . connexion and harmony are destroyed', having the effect of 'pieces of different structures patched up together'.[27]

By the end of the century Uvedale Price was hailing 'the outline of the summit [of] Gothic architecture [which] presents such a variety of forms, of turrets and pinnacles, some open, some fretted and variously enriched, that even where there is an exact correspondence of parts, it is often disguised by an appearance of splendid confusion and irregularity' and the 'extreme richness and intricacy' of window tracery as 'the triumph of the picturesque'.[28] This largely depended on pursuing successful preservation policies.[29]

> Let Weeping Magdalen cease her Tear,
> And with a Smile clear up her Eye,

This litle Chappell Standing here,
Made Sacred to her Memory:
Neglected late in rubbish lay,
Ore grown with mosse and mouldering dust:
Is now rebuilt Sprightly and gay
Like a young Phonix from her nest.
Devotions warmth did soe inspire
With holy zeal, each generous heart,
That all concern'd, with glad desire,
Pursu'd the work, and did impart
Each one their Share; with Such good will
And with Intentions large as free;
Still to give more, and more untill,
They brought it to what now you see.
Neither too gaudy, nor too great,
But decent as the house of prayer;
Designed to be clean and neat,
As hearts should be, that cometh here.
And if posterity list to know,
To what Amount the Cost did come
This Book to aftertimes will show
Each Severall & the Totall Sume.
And now since finish'd, let us pray,
That God will blesse and oren't again,
And that his Gracious presence may
Dwell there always, Soe be't Amen.[30]

The printed *Articles To be Enquired of in the Visitation of . . . Edmund Pyle . . . Archdeacon of York* (1762) asked, among other things, 'Is your Church or Chapel in good and sufficient Repair, as to the Roof, Walls, Windows, Doors. Floors and Seats? Are all Things kept in such Decent Sort as becometh the *House of* GOD?', 'Have you any Charities or Benefactions left to your Parish towards . . . repairing and maintaining', 'Are your . . . rates regularly made, confirm'd and gathered, as often as needful, for the Repairs of the Church?'.[31] Grass-roots responses reflect both simple cases of repairs to fabrics and special interests in, or, contra-wise, hostilities to gothic. From the bishop's visitations through Cumberland and Westmorland (Cumbria) during 1703–4 we learn that the body of Aiketon was 'well roof'd and floor'd . . . I wish the Quire may be put (as is promis'd) into as good or better a Condition . . . There's a good pavement . . . but lyes disjointed, and shews it has a heedless owner'; the choir of Barton was

> very well repair'd lately . . . On the north . . . is a long and nasty Isle . . . 'Tis hoped this will also be shortly put into a more comely condition . . . The Body . . . is (this very year) put into a very decent Order, at a great and cheerful expense of the whole parish.[32]

At the other end of the century Archdeacon Joseph Plymley of Shropshire reminded Bitterley's church-wardens 'that the [midsummer] season is approaching wherein [the fabric] may be conveniently repaired', since he

> fears the Steeple will become ruinous, if not attended to; & that the floor of the Nave is already too bad for safety or decency . . . Indeed the whole . . . Fabric is susceptible of great improvement . . . The great respectability of the Parish . . . makes [me] confident that this necessary work will be properly gone thro' with.[33]

As the medieval message became more firmly established, the high aspirations of architects and their clients soared. For example, the Vestry of Saffron Walden, Essex, in a desire for 'keeping up the Original Grandeur of this Building', wrote to their patron in 1790 that the

> unsafe . . . Fabrick of this ancient Church is justly deemed a magnificent Relick of Gothic Architecture, and standing as an Elegant Monument of Antiquity in a stile superior to anything of the kind in the Country [had become a] heavy burthen on the Parishioners, either to keep up, as it now is, or to restore to its pristine Beauty and Order, for the sake of the Elegance of the Building itself, or to transmit it to Posterity by way of Ornament only, yet . . . would feel great Reluctance to have it reduced, or that any New Building should be raised out of its Ruins, merely to save an expence to those who cannot, or to others who may be unwilling to bear the estimated charge or any enlargement of it.[34]

This exposed the crux of the problem.

At the same time, what the antiquary John Carter, writing in the *Gentleman's Magazine*, identified as the dubious practice of 'Architectural Innovation', or 'modernization' of medieval churches, was also called into question by a wider, more vocal readership. In 1802 'A LONDON CURATE', accompanying 'an intelligent Antiquary', visited ancient St Katherine By the Tower, London, which had recently 'undergone a *repair*'. Correctly fearing that it 'might have been *beautified*', the cleric begged 'An Architect, to whom all true Antiquaries are under great obligation' (Carter himself) not to visit. But doing so he 'hardly recognized' the former building, where

> a fine opportunity of restoring the original façade has been lost. [Its] great West window . . . obscured by an extraneous building erected against it [and which [a] scientific architectural Antiquary would

> have removed . . . and . . . replaced the tracery [was instead] cut away . . . and a new one, of an uncommonly sharply-pointed arch introduced . . . *as occurs in no part* of the original edifice. Little white finials are put on the top here and there; the whole front is thickly incrusted with a pebbled rough-cast coat.

Of the pews, 'our eyes were agonized by the fiery red colour . . . imitating mahogany'. The organ was in a '*Gothic taste* [that] matches not with the species of Gothic of the remaining structure'. The clerestory windows 'have had many tricks played with them'. The chancel window was 'the most ugly ill-devised window that ever disgraced an *innovating architect*, or *botcher of buildings* rather, [having] most cruelly and most wantonly destroyed [the] delicate Gothic ornament' of the original, the '*innovator* . . . tinctured [the stalls] of a flat *reddish chocolate colour*; which [is] frightful [and] stuck little pinnacles upon the tops of the clustered columns of the choir . . . *knotty points* . . . twice the size of a rolling-pin, and . . . made of plaster . . . things . . . never put in such places before'. The '*outside* of the choir . . . resembled a prison', the original Caen stone replaced by 'excellent *brick work*!'.[35]

The eighteenth century was obsessed with the ideal, if not always the reality, of preserving ancient places of worship. Of the great cathedrals only Wells, admired throughout the century as 'a fine regular Old Building', the 'whole fabrick of . . . excellent masonry, and adorned in good Gothick taste . . . very elegant, and neatly kept', had been spared the restorer's hand.[36] At Carlisle, however, a quite different situation was encountered, a much more typical case of eighteenth-century attitudes to cathedral repair. The fabric, which had been badly damaged in the Civil War, when Cromwell's troops tore down most of the western nave, was, according to Brown Willis's assessment of 1727, 'very meanly built, with small Windows, darkish and narrow; and the Roof lies low, like a common Parish-Church'. Only its choir was refurbished in 1765 (pl. 199), but the general external fabric remains stunted and crudely buttressed to this day.[37]

By contrast, the majority of these magnificent fabrics – Bath, Beverley, Canterbury, Durham, Ely, Gloucester, Hereford, Lichfield, Lincoln, Peterborough, Rochester, Salisbury, Selby, St David's, Westminster Abbey, Winchester, Worcester and York – due to their great antiquity, colossal size and both structural and decorative complexity, not only compounded problems of renewal but also sustained continuous operations throughout the whole eighteenth century (and, of course, centuries before and after). This involved generations of architects and craftsmen often working in the forefront of architectural and engineering innovations (as we have seen at Beverley and will do so later in Part Three, in chapters 13–16). Much in the public eye and generally profusely documented, they make uncommonly invigorating study.

Some questioned the benefits of restoration: 'I have very rarely, or as seldom found a new Building joined with any tolerable Decency or Advantage to an old one, as a young and beautiful *Virgin* to an old, decayed, and doating *Husband*', wrote John Evelyn. 'I might almost affirm as much concerning *Repairs*, where there are great Dilapidations; since by that time they have calculated all Expences of pulling down and patching up, they might have built entirely new from the Ground, with the same, and oftentimes with less Charge, but with abundance more Beauty and Conveniency.'[38] Thomas Telford believed that connecting medieval St Mary Magdalene, Bridgnorth, Somerset, with 'new Work . . . ought to be totally abandoned, as unpracticable . . . leading to a train of unlimited expenses'. It was replaced by a wholly classical building (pl. 662).[39]

Nonetheless, precautions were taken. At Normanby-on-the-Hill, Lincolnshire, a faculty recommended that the old, lead-covered wooden spire, which 'by length of time [had] become very much decayed . . . if repaired . . . would . . . in a Short time cause [it] to fall down unless supported by a great Expence' and therefore 'must be taken down'.[40] The chancel of St Gregory, Fledborough, Nottinghamshire, 'a very Ancient and large Structure . . . being very lofty and much exposed to the Winds and storms is often damaged'. By 1764 it was much out of repair, despite the rectors spending 'several Sums . . . in . . . Upholding' it, and 'by the violence of the late high Winds a great part of the Roof is blown off . . . so that it cannot be repaired but with difficulty and great expence'. The petitioners to the Archbishop of York came up with an expedient if hardly ideal solution. The Duke of Kingston as lord of the manor and owner of an adjoining south aisle, 'having been a long time useless and . . . ruinous [was] willing to take down and at his own Expence . . . rebuilt the South Wall', reducing the chancel by two-thirds but retaining its present width, which would make 'a handsome building and keep the Church more warm and healthy'. Since the parish consisted of only eight dwellings, 'it would still remain full large enough for the Celebration of divine Service'.[41] At Horsenden, Buckinghamshire, the patron literally cut his losses by demolishing the 'very ancient' body, which was 'unfitt for divine Service' and rebuilding the west tower in its medieval form, but attached to the front of the still

140 P. Mazell after Jan Wyck. 'Inside of the Chappel Royal of Holyroodhouse', Edinburgh, Scotland, in John Slezer, *Theatrum Scotiae*, 1693. Engraving. © The British Library Board, K. Top. 49-68.h.6. James Smith architect, 1688, ruined 1768.

'strong & Substantial' chancel.[42] Occasionally, improvements were over-zealous, as at St Nicholas, Newcastle upon Tyne, where two local architects, William Newton and David Stephenson, converted the large medieval fabric 'into a kind of cathedral . . . with great taste and elegance', though 'the antiquary must for ever lament the alteration, as almost all the ancient funeral monuments have been destroyed'.[43]

Restorations could go disastrously wrong. In rebuilding the tower of St Peter, St Albans, Hertfordshire, in 1756 'essential injury' was done to the building by 'violating the principles on which it had been originally constructed' (the builders failed to carry the four great piers supporting it up to the floor but 'contented themselves with an outside easing, filled only with rubble'). In 1785 a carpenter employed to make repairs 'introduced one of his friends in the character of a surveyor' and together set the piers on '*wooden legs* . . . dragged from London (where probably they had been lying upon the mud in the . . . Thames) . . . surrounded them with brick-work . . . walled round, and covered with plaster . . . so as to make them look like strong massy columns', charging £2,790.[44] Some campaigns had chequered histories, as in the brief life of the Chapel Royal at Holyrood Palace, Edinburgh. The medieval abbey was converted in 1687 into a chapel for James VII's revived Order of the Thistle (pl. 140), but in the following year it was wrecked by Protestant mobs. Henceforth, this 'elegant & noble structure' was tainted by being 'in a poor nasty condition [with] it's Pavement gone', becoming 'an antient, very venerable, but declining fabrick, now only used as a burying-place for persons of quality', 'the whole full of dirt and rubbish' resembling 'a dog kennel'. Around 1754 the 6th Duke of Hamilton, hereditary keeper of the palace, instructed the Edinburgh architect John Douglas to survey and report on the chapel's 'Ruinous Condition' with a view to restoration, but the duke, who approved the scheme, died before implementing the contract, and it was not until 1757–8 that work began. Douglas and a local mason named James Mcpherson had submitted alternative estimates ranging from £893 7s. 8d. to £1,124 13s. 2d., to include both materials and workmanship, which entailed taking down the slate roof, erecting walls 1 foot 4 inches thick at 2-feet intervals, 'to raise and frame the Reverse of the Arch . . . to admit . . . a proper pitch . . . to Cover the Whole of the Roofs with hewen Stone', replacing 9,991 feet of stone paving at 6d. per foot, pointing the whole of the external ashlar and harling the 'Rubble . . . where there is no Ashler', and using 'Rubble . . . in making up the windows where the Stone Roof of the Isles is to join to the side walls of the Main body'. Ten years later, however, the new stone vault together with the clerestory and north wall collapsed, though a later visitor reported that 'some beautiful Gothic arches are yet standing'.[45]

Of those who played leading roles in the preservation and restoration of medieval churches, Francis Drake, Andrew Ducarel, James Gibbs, Charles Lyttelton, Francis Peck, William Stukeley, John Talman, George Vertue and Browne Willis were members of the Society of Antiquaries of London (founded 1707). Stukeley also belonged to a fellow organisation, the Gentlemen's Society of Spalding in Lincolnshire (founded 1709–10).[46] Willis (1682–1760) is most topical. Educated at Westminster School, within the abbey precinct, and at Christ Church, Oxford, memorable for its outstanding medieval and post-medieval gothic buildings, he settled in Buckinghamshire, served as MP in 1705 and shortly afterwards launched a lifelong study of antiquities, church building and repairs.[47] He visited all the English and Welsh cathedrals and wrote the three-volume *Survey of the Cathedrals* (1717–30). In the preface to the 1742 edition he warned

> how the neglect of . . . Repairs of Cathedrals, and the perverting to private and selfish Use the Benefactions appropriated to the Support of these venerable Edifices, without any Dread of Sacrilege, or Regard to those Statutes most solemny sworn to . . . *seeing* how these Causes have produced the deplorable Effects of Ruin and Destruction of some of our Cathedrals; all . . . Church Dignitaries may be . . . awakened, and deterred from either doing, or omitting, what must necessarily be attended with the like Consequences.

In letters of 1736–7 to his friend, Bishop Sherlock of Salisbury, then directing major repairs to the cathedral, Willis wrote of the 'unspeakable pleasure I hear the noble things Your Ldshipp is doing . . . & how that magnificent Fabrick will owe its preservation to yr care & generosity', and pressed for the publication of a 'History of . . . the Fine Fabrick . . . in draughts' to record 'the Beautys communicated to the World under yr . . . Patronage'.[48] This eventually led to Francis Price's pioneer *A Series of particular and useful Observations, Made with great Diligence and Care, upon that Admirable Structure, The Cathedral-Church of Salisbury* (1753). Between 1736 and 1742 Willis collected money to rescue the tower of Stony Stratford, Buckinghamshire, following the church's destruction by fire. In a letter of 1742 to Sherlock he sought approval for his 'attempt in preserving the steeple', which would have been 'down had not immediate care been taken', and doubted that the body 'will not be built up again [as a] great ornament to the town & Landmark to the Country'.[49] In 1737 Willis appealed poetically to Viscount Cobham of Stowe to restore the tower of nearby Buckingham parish church:

> Oh, look on it as first it looked on you,
> Exalt again its Spire to crown your view,
> And ancient Magisterial Rights renew.[50]

In 1755–6 he rose to the defence of Bow Brickhill, also in Buckinghamshire, whose parishioners were attempting to prevent its demolition, informing the archdeacon that he had viewed the 'pretty good building [and] cannot be Passive . . . as I have had a Zeal in all places to which I bore any Relation to promote the ornamenting of churches'. He contributed £30 towards the £79 required to make the repairs by 'Two very experienced workmen'.[51]

But it was work on his own parish church at Fenny Stratford between 1724 and 1730 that provides the clearest ideas of Willis's architectural activities. Here his preference for gothic was rooted in his intention for the building to serve as a memorial to his grandfather.[52] This included the introduction of old painted glass and a compartmented ceiling decorated with subscribers' arms in the manner of the Arts End of the Bodleian Library, Oxford (*circa* 1612), his Alma Mater. The design, engraved as part of a printed petition for raising funds (pl. 141), also featured thirteenth-century Y- and intersecting tracery, battlements and pinnacles alongside Tuscan pilasters, round-headed doors and windows.

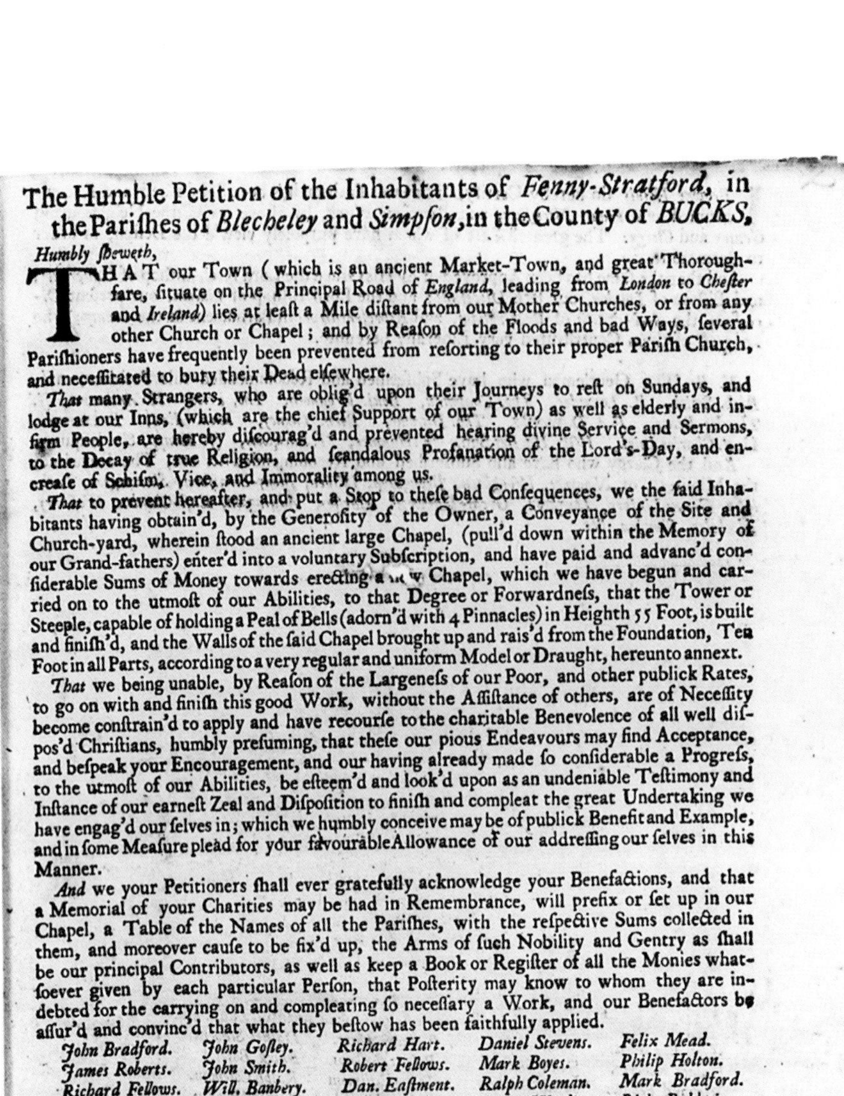

The Humble Petition of the Inhabitants of *Fenny-Stratford,* in the Pariſhes of *Blecheley* and *Simpſon,* in the County of *BUCKS,*

Humbly ſheweth,

THAT our Town (which is an ancient Market-Town, and great Thorough-fare, ſituate on the Principal Road of *England,* leading from *London* to *Cheſter* and *Ireland*) lies at leaſt a Mile diſtant from our Mother Churches, or from any other Church or Chapel; and by Reaſon of the Floods and bad Ways, ſeveral Pariſhioners have frequently been prevented from reſorting to their proper Pariſh Church, and neceſſitated to bury their Dead elſewhere.

That many Strangers, who are oblig'd upon their Journeys to reſt on Sundays, and lodge at our Inns, (which are the chief Support of our Town) as well as elderly and infirm People, are hereby diſcourag'd and prevented hearing divine Service and Sermons, to the Decay of true Religion, and ſcandalous Profanation of the Lord's-Day, and encreaſe of Schiſm, Vice, and Immorality among us.

That to prevent hereafter, and put a Stop to theſe bad Conſequences, we the ſaid Inhabitants having obtain'd, by the Generoſity of the Owner, a Conveyance of the Site and Church-yard, wherein ſtood an ancient large Chapel, (pull'd down within the Memory of our Grand-fathers) enter'd into a voluntary Subſcription, and have paid and advanc'd conſiderable Sums of Money towards erecting a new Chapel, which we have begun and carried on to the utmoſt of our Abilities, to that Degree or Forwardneſs, that the Tower or Steeple, capable of holding a Peal of Bells (adorn'd with 4 Pinnacles) in Heighth 55 Foot, is built and finiſh'd, and the Walls of the ſaid Chapel brought up and rais'd from the Foundation, Ten Foot in all Parts, according to a very regular and uniform Model or Draught, hereunto annext.

That we being unable, by Reaſon of the Largeneſs of our Poor, and other publick Rates, to go on with and finiſh this good Work, without the Aſſiſtance of others, are of Neceſſity become conſtrain'd to apply and have recourſe to the charitable Benevolence of all well diſpos'd Chriſtians, humbly preſuming, that theſe our pious Endeavours may find Acceptance, and beſpeak your Encouragement, and our having already made ſo conſiderable a Progreſs, to the utmoſt of our Abilities, be eſteem'd and look'd upon as an undeniable Teſtimony and Inſtance of our earneſt Zeal and Diſpoſition to finiſh and compleat the great Undertaking we have engag'd our ſelves in; which we humbly conceive may be of publick Benefit and Example, and in ſome Meaſure plead for your favourable Allowance of our addreſſing our ſelves in this Manner.

And we your Petitioners ſhall ever gratefully acknowledge your Benefactions, and that a Memorial of your Charities may be had in Remembrance, will prefix or ſet up in our Chapel, a Table of the Names of all the Pariſhes, with the reſpective Sums collected in them, and moreover cauſe to be fix'd up, the Arms of ſuch Nobility and Gentry as ſhall be our principal Contributors, as well as keep a Book or Regiſter of all the Monies whatſoever given by each particular Perſon, that Poſterity may know to whom they are indebted for the carrying on and compleating ſo neceſſary a Work, and our Benefactors be aſſur'd and convinc'd that what they beſtow has been faithfully applied.

John Bradford.	*John Goſley.*	*Richard Hart.*	*Daniel Stevens.*	*Felix Mead.*
James Roberts.	*John Smith.*	*Robert Fellows.*	*Mark Boyes.*	*Philip Holton.*
Richard Fellows.	*Will. Banbery.*	*Dan. Eaſtment.*	*Ralph Coleman.*	*Mark Bradford.*
Jonathan Daniel.	*Ethelbert Searle.*	*Joſeph Hinchley.*	*James Woodin.*	*Rich. Baldwin.*
George Bradford.	*Edw. Chandler.*	*Benj. Etheridge.*	*John London.*	*Will. Bowman* &c.

141 G. Hurlett after J. Gosley. 'The North East Prospect of St. Martins Chapel att Fenny Stratford', Buckinghamshire. The Bodleian Library, University of Oxford, MS Willis 52b, f. 2r. Edward Wing architect, 1724–30.

Willis experienced frustrating difficulties with his architect, Edward Wing, and dismissed him on grounds of mismanagement in 1728, leaving its completion to a local joiner, John Symonds (pl. 142).

The rehabilitation of medieval towers and spires forms an interesting sub-category of this story. Their importance was aptly expressed in *England Displayed* (1769), where York's pre-eminence over Lincoln as among 'all other Gothic churches, not only in this kingdom, but throughout Europe' (pls 139, 157) was faulted only in its crossing tower lacking great height, though noting 'a tradition . . . that a wooden spire was once intended to have been raised', in which case it would have exceeded even Salisbury.[53] Salisbury itself (pl. 143) 'is a glaring Building, and resembles a great Lanthorn . . . its Spire . . . wonderful, running up pyramidically of free Stone to a Point . . . 410 Foot high'.[54] It represented the Georgian standard of consummate loftiness. Swift's Brobdingnag, peopled by 'a race of giants as tall as an ordinary Church Steeple', has as its most impressive landmark a 'Temple . . . Tower . . . reckoned the highest in the Kingdom . . . Three Thousand Foot high . . . yet allowing the Difference between the Size of those People and us, the Steeple at *Salisbury* is higher in Proportion'.[55] Steeples, of course, were the loftiest, architecturally most distinctive feature in both urban and rural landscapes. Celia Fiennes on her northern journey of 1697 observed of Grantham's 281-foot-high structure in low-lying Lincolnshire: ''tis a long tyme when you see a great part [of it] ere you come to see the Church or town'.[56] This is true even today. They were the chief expression of the Georgian idea of churches as 'parochial fortresses',[57] their heavenwardness offering a religious reverence and awe that classical forms could not achieve nearly so well. Francis Peck believed that while 'Our old parish churches . . . do not often present us with any thing so vastly fine [as King's College chapel, Cambridge], sometimes we meet with a steeple . . . remarkably sweet & pretty'.[58] Opinions differed as to their relative merits. Stukeley reckoned that Wrexham possessed 'the finest tower-steeple I ever saw, except Boston'; it was 'one of the wonders of Wales . . . finished with exquisite taste', whereas Defoe was 'greatly disappointed they must be much mistaken, who tells us 'tis the finest in England . . . the work is mean, the statues . . . in dejected postures, without any fancy or spirit . . . and . . . Time has made [the] reddish crumbling . . . stone . . . look gross and rough'.[59]

Though a long list could be made of medieval towers and spires lost in the eighteenth century, the Georgians also pursued their repair with special vigour and their treatment epitomises preservationist policies. Responding to damage to St Cuthbert, Darlington, County Durham, sustained in 1750 when 'most terrible Claps of Thunder, and Flashes of Lightening, ever known in the Memory of Man . . . split [the crossing spire] from Top to Bottom', £105 was spent two years later dismantling and carefully reconstructing 45 feet of the original structure, which still survives intact.[60] In the 1790s Daniel Hodkin, a Chesterfield architect, wrote to the parish churchwardens pleading with almost evangelical intensity that their famously twisted medieval spire (pl. 144)

142 Edward Wing. West front, St Martin, Fenny Stratford, Buckinghamshire, 1724–30.

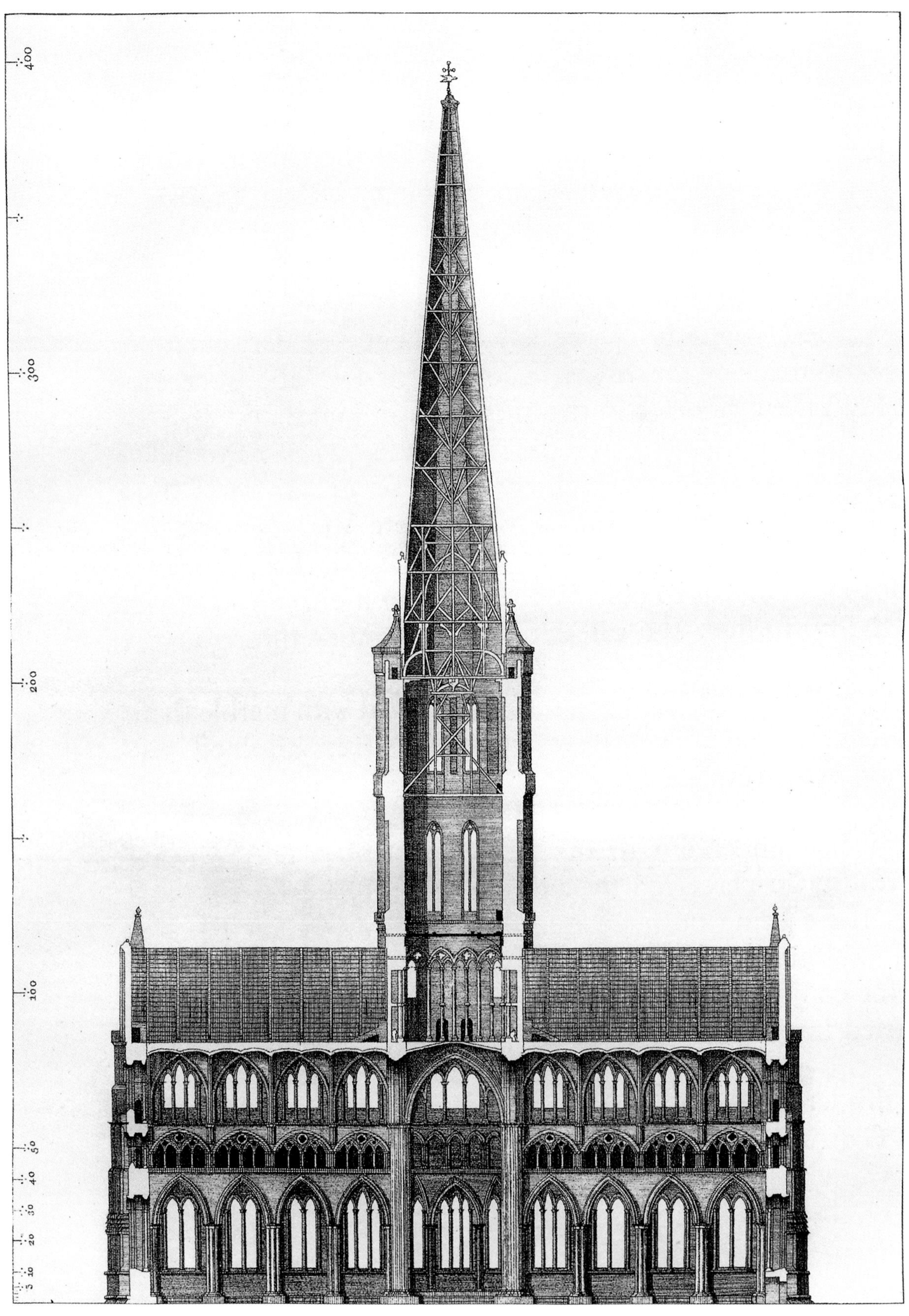

143 Paul Fourdrinier after Francis Price. 'A Section of the Church, with the Tower and Spire: Shewing the Critical Mechanism of the whole Structure', 1738, in F. Price, *A Series Of particular and useful Observations . . . upon . . . the Cathedral Church of Salisbury (Wiltshire)*, 1753, pl. 6. Engraving. Author's collection.

> will remain in an unfinished state if the four pinnacles are not put on, and you will always wish they had been done when you see the effect so much different . . . I cannot take leave without a repetition of begging of you to raise your spirits and say with one voice we will have them done and look so respectful as any of our neighbours.[61]

The nationwide impetus for these improvements was provided by maintenance operations on what Celia Fiennes called the 'Dagger' spire of Salisbury Cathedral (pl. 143).[62] Wren's report of 1668 to Bishop Ward of his comprehensive structural survey found it 'seeming to threaten no inconsiderable decayes' and 'enumerated . . . the particular defects . . . so proper remedies may be applied to restore it, where age, injuries of weather or the neglect . . . in times of trouble, have occasioned weaknesse, & tendencys, towards Ruine'. The four crossing piers, measuring little more than those of the aisles, supported the unbuttressed 410-foot-high tower, rising a further 150 feet into a spire of only 7 inches thickness (from this Wren concluded that it must have been an afterthought). The lofty structure was now between 3¼ and 5½ inches out of perpendicular, which could be remedied by securing the walls with 'many large bandes of Iron within and without', though this was 'against the Rules of good Architecture . . . because Iron is corruptible by rust [and] fallacious' and 'so great a pyle . . . once overpoysed, all Bandage of Iron will be as Pack thread'. The 'diverse long cracks' in the spire occasioned by 'stormes of Lightning' could be healed with 'hard Stone set dry and well wedged up . . . with Tiles & Oystershells' or by securing the vault with 'little Cedar pinnes . . . old Sugar Chests which is a kind of Cypresse in the Barbadoes would doe as well'.[63] These haphazard, far from state-of-the-art solutions were revived as a topic of interest with the reprint of the Report in Richard Rawlinson's *The History and Antiquities of the Cathedral Church of Salisbury, and the Abbey of Bath* (1719) and again partially in *Parentalia* (1750), but most memorably in Francis Price's *Series of particular and useful Observations . . . upon . . . The Cathedral-Church of Salisbury* (1753), which sold for 7s. 6d. and was 'Calculated For the Use and Amusement of Gentlemen, and other curious Persons, as well as for the Assistance of such Artists as may be employed in Buildings of that Kind: By all which they will be able to form a right Judgment upon this, or any ancient Structure, either in the Gothick or other Stiles of Building'. It reveals a deep appreciation for medieval constructional skills more often associated with post-Georgian assessments. Price discovered that while the crossing tower and spire 'contribute to the grandeur and dignity of the whole . . . with this additional and extraordinary beauty . . . come some deformities, by means of the application of various braces of stone, &c . . . which detract much from the delicate appearance of the building'. The 'architect . . . was not without his jealousies and fears', and he added 'a most excellent bandage of iron to the upper part of the arcade . . . perhaps, the best piece of smith's work, as also the most excellent mechanism of any thing in Europe of its age'. Others would be made 'as time should require, partic-

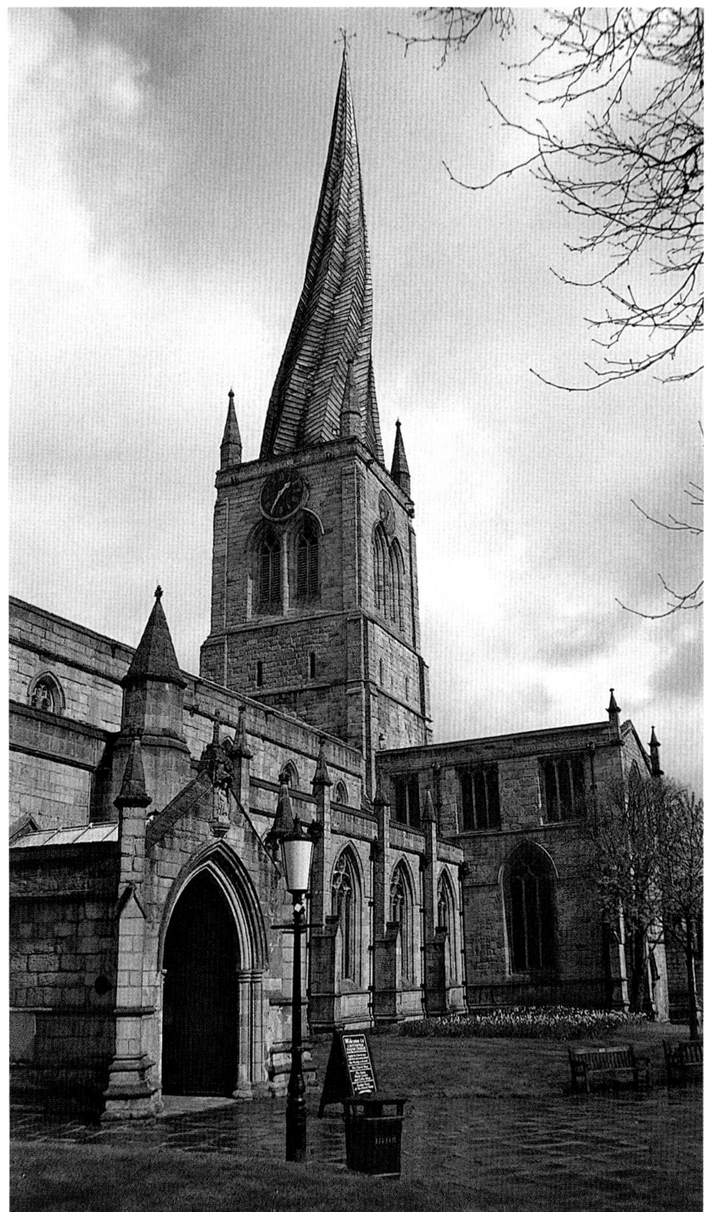

144 View from the south west, St Mary and All Saints (now the Cathedral), Chesterfield, Derbyshire, 1325–50.

ularly those which . . . hoop the spire together [and] though entirely covered . . . by sheet lead . . . rust and swell to a prodigious degree'. While four sides of the octagonal spire stand on the tower's inside walls, the others are supported by un-buttressed arches, of which Price could not 'help taking notice of the lively imagination of the architect, and his extraordinary care to preserve and adorn this part'. It was an 'admirably conceived . . . grandeur of finishing the tower'. Price concluded from this that 'Notwithstanding these apparent dangers, and the improbability of its duration, the work has stood safe near five centuries, and may yet, by diligent care and application [as well as keeping] all these connections in good repair . . . stand many more'.[64] But it was also pointed out that originally the structure, '*twice the Height of the Monument in* London, and *reckoned* the *highest in* England . . . *is too weak to carry Bells, and therefore a Belfry* [was] *erected at a little Distance from the Church*'.[65] Price, who served as surveyor from 1737 until his death in 1753, devoted those years to the fabric's well-being, particularly the vast, complex structure of the roofs, assisted by the London architect John James, then surveyor to the fabric of Westminster Abbey.

The Wren-Price surveys proved pivotal. Price himself turned to the needle form as a model demonstrating the rules for shaping three specimens illustrated in his *The British Carpenter* (1735).[66] A scheme for the new spire at Stratford-upon-Avon, Warwickshire, by Timothy Lightoler, 'a person reckon'd to have great judgment in Works of such kind', more or less reconstituting the old structure, was sent to James West of Alscot Park, a medieval enthusiast, in hope of raising £250 'sufficient to compleat the proposed Design [of] so ornamental & laudable a work'. It was described as having a 20-foot octagonal base and a 'Pyramid . . . carved up . . . 81 feet [of] beautiful Warwick squar'd Stone, as high again as the . . . old baubling Spire [which] really will have a very fine effect'.[67]

Proposals for repairing the spire of Shottesbrooke, Berkshire, struck by lightning on 20 July 1757, were received from an unnamed London stonemason estimated at £900, from another based at Bath for £600 and from the Oxford mason John Townesend for £300, which was accepted on the basis of its cheapness. Of these widely differing prices, Thomas Rickman later remarked that 'there are Traders in Warwickshire called Steeple Menders, which probably would account for the low price of the Oxford offer'.[68] The most celebrated of this specialist breed were John Cheshire, a master mason of Over Whitacre, Warwickshire, and Nathaniel Wilkinson, his Worcester rival, who served in that capacity at the cathedral. Both were members of families who plied the same trade.[69] Wilkinson's grandfather, Thomas, had been responsible for dismantling the spire of Ripple in 1713, where his detailed account described the structure as 'very ruinous [and] Cannot be supported & repaired but Must necessarily be pulled down or else it will Quickly fall & endanger the fabric'. He claimed 'all Timber c Materialls . . . for his Owne Use, Except the weather Cocke' and agreed to 'Make Good all Such Damage att his owne Charge'. He then rebuilt the tower to the 'same height' and added an additional 5 yards in the 'best Sort of Stone', complete with 'railes c bannisters flower potts fannes c other Handsome Ornaments'. Thomas was obliged to revise his original estimate of £160 for this and other repairs to the fabric, which required 190 tons of stone at 7s. 6d. per ton, because 'having Consider'd the Work I Find . . . I Cannot afford to Compleat it, under . . . £172 . . . Taking all and Finding all, at which I Can propose but very Slender Proffitt'.[70] This is the background to Nathaniel Wilkinson, who erected soaring spires in Herefordshire, Gloucestershire and Gwent, and the 'wondrous taper-ribbed Spire' of St Andrew, Worcester, rising 155 feet from a 90-foot-tall tower, all that survives today of the medieval church (pl. 145). It was praised in 1764 as the 'chief ornament of . . . the whole city . . . the whole kingdom [and a] challenge [to] the whole world to equal', and though Salisbury's was 'much higher [it] ends abrupt' whereas this 'carries on [in a] most gradual and exact diminution . . . to a very small termination . . . concluded with a Corinthian capital'.[71]

Cheshire was the subject of a rare extended accolade by 'Gothicus' in the *Gentleman's Magazine* in 1789:

> As no country in Europe presents to view nobler edifices in the Gothic order than . . . our own, we may readily conclude, that . . . English architects excelled the foreigners of those days, and . . . our work-men surpassed all others in the boldness and magnificence of their structures. In order to shew that no encouragement is still wanting, and the same spirit for execution yet exists . . . there is . . . a person, whose skill . . . seems to approach the art of remoter times . . . This ingenious man has lately given several proofs of his abilities in the erection of some new spires, and the re-building of churches. His executions are bold and accurate in this particular style . . . From . . . conversations . . . I have had with him . . . I can . . . pronounce, that he is capable to execute any edifice in the Gothic taste, even after the most ornamented and composite design . . . Hitherto his abilities have been confined to the re-building of

> some ruinated spires, or new modeling ill-proportioned ones.

St Michael, Coventry, is singled out as

> most admirable . . . a singular model, unimitated . . . and, though . . . not rising to that of Salisbury . . . yet . . . is more striking and pleasing to the eye . . . so rich and beautiful, so light and graceful, nothing can be . . . added or removed, to make it more noble or surprising . . . a *chef-d'oeuvre* of the kind.[72]

The practicalities of maintaining medieval towers are well attested at St Sepulchre, London. It had been renovated in 1671 and again in 1713–14. In 1778 Thomas Clark and James Steer, surveyors, reported on the cost of repairs 'in the Different Modes', observing that while the foundation was 'Sufficiently permanent to Stand many Years & to bear Casing yet they Cannot recommend the Casing With Stone not only on Account of the great Augmentation it will be to the Bulk . . . & of the Additional Weight but also on Account of the Enormous Expence', £1,600. However, 'if it were . . . only Repaird & pointed the Eight Buttresses will require Rebuilding which if done with portland Stone will with the necessary Repairs to the two Windows & other parts . . . Including . . . Gilding . . . the Dial of the Clock' cost £610. Furthermore (and to modern thinking conservationally incorrect), they proposed repairing and covering the whole tower 'with the Adamattic Composition' for £570. The Vestry decided to repair the masonry 'in such manner only as to Secure [it] from any Extraordinary Damage by Weather. to which in its present State it is Liable', which Clark and Steere suggested doing 'Effectually' by taking down 'the Front part of all the Buttresses as low as . . . the Leads . . . & rebuild [by] Introducing new portland Stone every other Course . . . properly Cramp'd' at a cost of £393. They were ordered to remove 'only . . . the Loose Stones as cannot be fastened [and] if the Cavittys . . . are of such a Size as to Admit the Lodgements of . . . Water as may be prejudicial to the Building [then] replace with New Stone'.[73]

Critical to the activities of preservation were topographical views – the present book illustrates a wide range of examples.[74] Miles Gale, the rector of St Andrew, Keighley, Yorkshire, was by no means alone when, in 1713, he measured and drew his church 'as a standing Monument to continue its memory to future generations'.[75] This was perhaps also the intention of the Boston carpenter John Sherlock Jr in 1711 in meticulously recording the plan and elevation of early fourteenth-century St Botolph (pl. 146), with its 272-foot-high 'Stump . . . the highest . . . and noblest in Europe, flattering a weary traveller with its astonishing aspect even at ten miles distance'.[76] It may relate, however, to a Parliamentary petition of 1709 seeking

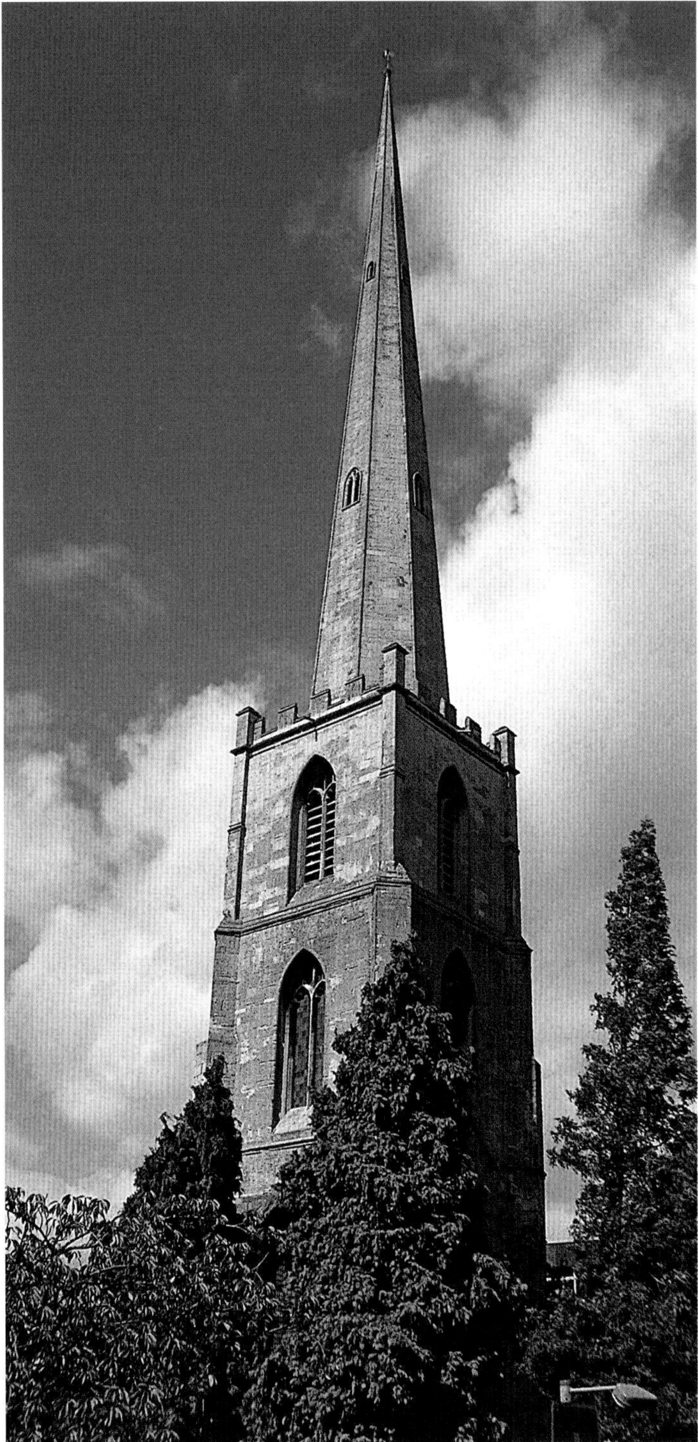

145 Medieval spire, St Andrew, Worcester, Worcestershire, repaired by Nathaniel Wilkinson, 1751.

146 'The Geometrical Plan & South prospect of St. Botolph's att Boston in ye County of Lincoln Taken and Drawn by John Sherlock junr Carpenter of Boston 1711'. Pen and ink. The Bodleian Library, University of Oxford, Gough Maps 16, f. 26.

help in raising funds 'to preserve the Foundation . . . to keep off a violent ebbing and flowing Water' as well as 'keeping [the fabric] in repair'.[77]

As an essential part of its preservationist policy the Society of Antiquaries of London issued a wide range of single engravings, bound collections under the title of *Vetusta Monumenta* and magnificently illustrated volumes devoted to individual cathedrals. John Carter, an inexhaustible, outspoken and sometimes irritating advocate for the supremacy of medieval architecture, who was appointed its 'official war artist' in 1784, was to play a central role in the development of gothic ideas in the eighteenth century, the subject of the following chapters.

147 Nicholas Hawksmoor. Design for the west towers, Westminster Abbey, London, 1735. Pen and ink and wash. Westminster Abbey Muniments, Hawksmoor no. 17.

Thirteen

THE BEGINNINGS OF EIGHTEENTH-CENTURY GOTHIC

I wish I had the honor to know, whether they are Gentlemen-Connoissieus, Criticks or Workmen advanc'd to the degree of Architects, be that as it will I dare pronounce they are not enough skill'd in masonry, and the Styles of Building; if they will object, that the new works and repairs, are not conformable and pursuant to the Old . . . It appears to me that they do not rightly understand that word (Gothick)[1]

The first four decades of the century were dominated by the powerful presence and imaginative explorations of gothic created by Nicholas Hawksmoor, working both independently (pl. 147) and in collaboration with Sir Christopher Wren, and an unsung hero of this enduring style, William Dickinson. Their ideas filtered down to a variety of parish churches in London and beyond, creating some singularly stylistically unadulterated churches (see chapters 13 to 16), others hybrids often of such unusual inventiveness that they can be fully understood only as a separate though interconnected development (see chapter 17). But to make sense of these achievements we should begin a few years before 1700 in the ancient Midland town of Warwick, which underwent an unexpected and spectacular transformation.

On 5 September 1694 a 'sudden, outrageous, and most dreadful Fire . . . driven by the Violence and Fury of a tempestuous Wind' – 'CONFLAGRATIONE STUPENDA' – consumed much of this prosperous centre, including the entire western part of the huge parish church, leaving the fourteenth-century chancel and its flanks, including the fifteenth-century Beauchamp Chapel, miraculously untouched. On 26 February following the rebuilding committee appointed by an Act of Parliament sent a 'draught' of the bruised and confused building (a version of pl. 149) to London to solicit Wren's expertise.[2] The preparatory drawings and some design work were entrusted to Wren's 'gentleman', Hawksmoor, a poignant moment with the senior genius moving towards the end of an eminent career as a church designer and the younger one, already in full control of his draughting skills, at the beginning of his. Here (pl. 148) the traditional medieval arrangement of nave, transepts, aisles and clerestory was preserved, with the damaged jumble of gothic nave, romanesque west tower and porch reordered and crowned by an ambitious spire reminiscent of the early fourteenth-century structure of St Mary, Oxford, carried on flying buttresses owing something to fifteenth-century Louth, Lincolnshire, and Wren's St Dunstan-in-the-East (1695–1701).[3] An ogee-domed enclosure rises over and theatrically top-lights the south and north transepts. These Tudor gothic structures, based on the buttress terminals of Henry VII's Chapel at Westminster Abbey (pl. 153) and employed by Wren in the upper stage of Tom Tower, Christ Church, Oxford (1681–2), was an equivalent of the classical dome, but its octagonal rather than round form underscores this affinity. We will meet with it again. In another drawing similar, slimmer structures surmount the western corners of the side aisles, a picturesque novelty Hawksmoor later reinterpreted with Roman *gravitas* at St George-in-the-East (pl. 371).[4] The most notable aspects of the Warwick proposals were their use of authentic gothic vocabulary and an assertion of stylistic homogeneity. Nevertheless, they were promptly rejected in favour of a radically different approach by a local architect, which will be discussed in chapter 17. Soon afterwards, Wren and his office turned their attention to more rewarding endeavours.

When James Paterson published *Pietas Londinensis; or, The Present Ecclesiastical State of London* in 1714 he noted

148 Nicholas Hawksmoor. Design for the reconstruction of St Mary, Warwick, Warwickshire, south elevation, 1694. Pencil. All Soul's College, University of Oxford, IV.45.

149 Artist unknown. South view of St Mary, Warwick, Warwickshire, fourteenth–fifteenth century, prior to the 1694 fire. Pen and ink and wash. Birmingham City Archives, Local Studies, Aylesford, II, f.229.

Westmonast: ecclesiæ
conv: facies aquilonalis.
The North Prospect of the Conventuall
Church of Westmynster.
Contra injuriam
Temporum
P
Guil: Bromley Ar:

150 Wenzel Hollar. 'The North Prospect of the Conventuall Church of Westmynster', London, in Daniel King, *The Cathedrall and Conventuall Churches of England and Wales*, 1672, pl. 18. Engraving.

that the abbey church of St Peter, Westminster, left unfinished at the end of the middle ages, had become partly 'destroyed by the Teeth of Devouring Time' (pl. 150).[5] As the English national church, with a uniquely unassailable position as the focus of both coronations and royal burials located adjacent to the Houses of Parliament, it had survived the worst ravages of both the dissolution of the monasteries at the Reformation and the Civil War a century later.

Hail! Sacred Fane! Whose venerable Pile
Guards all the faded glories of our isle;
Beneath whose ample arches dusky shade,
Kings, princes, conquerors in dust are laid;
Within thy womb what crouds of heroes sleep?
While o'er the mighty dead the marbles weep.
Here kings enthron'd survey their fate beneath;
How near the seats of empire and of death![6]

Nonetheless, it required major improvements. Writing at the end of his life Hawksmoor thought Wren, who had been appointed surveyor in 1699, had spent money wisely towards 'preserving a noble Fabrick in which almost all our Kings and the greatest of Families of the Kingdom lie interred, from falling down [and that] if violence do's not happen will stand 1000 years'.[7] It held a distinct and special position among the older architect's ecclesiastical œuvre as a specimen of 'Gothick . . . far removed from the Manner and Proportions of the *Antique*' that characterised 'many of [his] newest Churches' in London.[8] Indeed, Wren stressed to the dean and chapter in 1713 that for his 'new Additions I have prepared perfect Draughts and Models, such as I conceive may agree with the original Scheme of the old Architect, without any modern Mixtures to shew my own Inventions' and which are 'still in the *Gothick* Form, and of a Style with the rest of the Structure, which I would strictly adhere to [since] to deviate from the old Form, would be to run into a disagreeable Mixture, which no Person of a good Taste could relish'.[9] Unsteady handed (as confirmed by the octogenarian's shaky signature on pl. 151), Wren relied on his draughtsman, measurer since 1696 and deputy surveyor from 1711, William Dickinson. A 'celebrated Architect' in his own right, he was also a highly accomplished and resourceful medievalist,[10] and at the abbey was responsible for all the meticulously rendered working and presentation drawings before Hawksmoor's appearance there in 1723.

Reparations began modestly in 1700 with work on windows, buttresses, vaulting and so on, including renewing the 'tender . . . embroidery Work' of the Perpendicular fan vaulting of Henry VII's Chapel beyond the choir, which 'looks so far exceeding human excellence that a man would think it was knit together by the fingers of angels, pursuant to the directions of Omnipotence'.[11] The chapel exterior had become 'so eaten up by our Weather, that it begs for some Compassion [because] it is the regal Sepulture'; according to Wren, it was 'the unhappy Choice' of Reigate stone which in its decay and falling off 'perpetually in

151 Sir Christopher Wren and William Dickinson. Approved design for remodelling north transept front, Westminster Abbey, London, 20 May 1719. Pen and ink and wash. Westminster Abbey Muniments, (P) 900–900A, flap down showing existing medieval structure (right), proposed reorganization (left).

great Scales' rendered the building 'disfigure'd in the highest Degree'. His remedy was to invest the walls with 'a better Stone' transported by barge from the Burford quarries in Oxfordshire, though here a shortcoming lay in mismatched old and new materials, which, according to a later commentator, produced an 'offensive . . . sort of patch-work'.[12] By 1716 at the latest the essential requirements were identified: completing the north transept front, the crossing spire and the west tower, a programme that began in 1719 and took twenty-six years to complete.

On 20 May 1719 Wren and the building subcommittee approved a scheme for remodelling the north transept front facing King Street (present-day Parliament Square), traditionally regarded as the 'principal Entrance', into what he had referred to in 1713 as 'its proper Shape first intended' (pl. 151). This was presented as a before and after study defined by an irregular flap extending from the peak of the gable along its left slope, taking in the whole of that side of the elevation, including the bands of quatrefoil and the arcades above and below the rose window and also above the middle and smaller eastern arched porticoes, as evident in the obviously different architectural treatments. The earlier, stunted, right-hand portion had been, according to Wren, 'indiscreetly tamper'd with some Years since, by patching on a little *Dorick* Passage before the great Window . . . cropping off the Pyramids [pinnacles], and covering the Stair-cases [far right] with very improper Roofs of Timber and Lead, which can never agree with the other Parts of the Design'. On the improved portion Wren insisted that the outer staircase structures 'be new ashlar'd, and Pyramids set upon them *conformable to the old-Style, to make the Whole of a Piece*' (my italics). It seems more than likely, though there is no documentary evidence, that he turned to French gothic examples (which had influenced the rebuilding of the original romanesque abbey beginning in the thirteenth century),[13] in particular, the south transept of Beauvais Cathedral (pl. 152), a colossal wonder whose choir famously collapsed in 1284, followed by the lantern tower in 1573, and which Wren might well have paused to examine on his way to Paris in 1665–6, at a time he was grappling with the difficult logistics of his pre-Fire design for restoring medieval St Paul's Cathedral.[14] This association is insinuated in Wren's report of 1713, where he refers to the French gothic fashion that the English 'affected to imitate', in which 'Nothing was thought magnificent that was not high beyond Measure'.[15]

Construction on the abbey front moved apace. During 1719–20 the decayed stonework was replaced and the staircase windows gothicised. Dickinson measured from the foundation to the top of the first stage of arcades above the ogee-arched portico, including 'Masoning and Carving 33 Gothick Capitalls'. Then work went on into late 1721 from there to the next stage of the 'Gothick Arcade' below the rose window,

152 South transept front, Beauvais Cathedral, France, *c.*1500–50s.

including the 'Crockett heads [of the] two lower Neeches', the pair of buttresses flanking the rose and 'Gothick Cornice', the 'great North Rose . . . and the whole heads of Neeches and Windows, looking into the Church', including 'carving 30 Gothick Capitals . . . 55 small Crockets . . . 4 Gothick Capitals to . . . 2 Neeches [and] 20 Crockets'. During 1723 Dickinson designed and installed an 'Iron Fence after the Gothick manner' in front of the portico (which survived into the age of photography). In September it was estimated that £1,300 4s. 0d. would be needed to complete the gable end, the four great pinnacles, 'Tracery work . . .

153 Sir Christopher Wren and William Dickinson. Design for the crossing tower and spire, with one bay of King Henry VII's Chapel, Westminster Abbey, 1715. Pen and ink and wash. Westminster Abbey Muniments (P) 913.

224 Crockets with Branches' and so forth. Meanwhile, the 'great Rose Window', which Wren reported had been 'some Years since, before I was concerned . . . patched up . . . upheld, and stopt up . . . with Plaister . . . to prevent further Ruin', was refashioned. On 22 May 1721 Dickinson prepared a 'plainer' pattern for Portland stone mullions, differently detailed to the scheme of 1719, which were filled with '16 large Figures 7ft. high of . . . Apostles and Evangelists' and a 'Glory in the Middle' totalling 738 feet of glass, to designs by Sir James Thornhill. According to a contemporary press report, these were 'curiously painted after the Antique [that is, medieval] fashion' by Joshua Price, 'who is reckoned the only artist in England capable of doing it'.[16] This was his most ambitious as well as his last work (he died in September 1721); the glass was swept away by the Victorians.

After nearly half a millennium Wren courageously attempted to resurrect the crossing tower, identifying in 1713 the medieval builders' 'original Intention . . . the Beginnings of which appear on the Corners . . . but left off before it rose so high as the Ridge of the Roof'. But first a serious engineering flaw required rectifying: the theft of 'Iron . . . hooked on from Pillar to Pillar' tying the crossing piers 'every Way' had progressively swayed the four massive supports inward, cracking their arches, so could not 'prove a sufficient Butment to stand against the Pressure of so many Arches, unless they were very much bigger than the other Piers; but that could not be without cumbering up the principal Part of the Church' (the nave vista). This was remedied by adding 'more Weight upon them . . . by building a Tower according to the original Intention of the Architect'. There was, however, no indisputable evidence of what had been intended, forcing the team to look elsewhere for appropriate sources, which produced a series of alternative solutions. Some were presented as flaps attached to earlier proposals, revealing how their ideas shifted to and fro over several years. One recalls the massive rectangular base of Bell Harry tower at Canterbury Cathedral (completed in 1498, contemporary with Westminster's nave vaulting and great west window).[17]

A group (pl. 153) based on Salisbury's spire (pl. 143) subsequently emerged as an oak and pear wood model crafted in 1715–16 by Elizabeth Gregory. Wren emphasised that while retaining the '*Gothick* Form' he 'varied a little' by making twelve rather than eight sides. Its more elaborate treatment, with repetitive, diminishing lucarne and bands, suggest he had in mind the stupendous triplex of Lichfield Cathedral, a source perhaps confirmed by the subsequent decision to develop spires atop the abbey's twin western towers.[18] Wren's 'Gothick Manner of Architecture' was fundamental to his idea of the cathedral, having observed that Salisbury's builders carried 'all their Mouldings perpendicular [and the] spire . . . to great Height . . . therefore the Pride of their Works was in Pinacles and Steeples'.[19] The gothic exclusivity of the Wren-Dickinson partnership was a remarkable achievement for its time, but, as we shall see, one that gradually lessened over the next decades in the hands of others. This inaugural phase of improvements ended with Wren's death on 25 February 1723. He was succeeded as surveyor by the 61-year-old Hawksmoor; Dickinson's role as both draughtsman and co-designer correspondingly diminished: his will described him as 'Weak in body', though of sound mind,[20] and with his own demise on 24 January 1725 the under-surveyorship passed briefly to Thomas Hinton, who was strictly a builder. The chapter had been thrown into turmoil in 1722 with the arrest and exile of the Jacobite Dean Atterbury and his replacement by the ineffectual (building-wise) Samuel Bradford. Moreover, though the dean and chapter placed 'especiall Trust and Confidence in [Hawksmoor's] Ability Skill and fidelity' by conferring 'full power and Authority . . . to be one of the Sub-Comissioners for the Management and Carrying on the Works',[21] it emerged, as we have seen, that Hawksmoor's gout debilitated his on-site performance (p. 143).

Despite restrictions imposed by diminishing funds during 1724–5 and orders for workmen to proceed in repairing the crossing up to the battlement stage, but 'not to carry the Work farther . . . and to desist from going so far if the old Stone will not hold out to do it',[22] this ambivalent transitional period proved to be perhaps the most dynamic moment in design terms. Hawksmoor turned his attention to resolving the crossing issue (see chapter 17) and the daunting task of completing the west front. The abbey was not unique among major gothic structures in this respect: there are the celebrated examples of Saint Denis and the cathedrals of Toul, Cologne and Strasbourg.[23] Begun *circa* 1338 (in fact, a recasting of Edward the Confessor's romanesque masonry), construction had stopped in 1534 with the west front, in Wren's words, 'left imperfect' by one tower 'much higher than the other, though still too low for Bells, which are stifled by the Height of the Roof above them' (pl. 154). It was 'hoped in good Time, [this] will be as well adorned [with] nothing more properly then a lofty Spire'. Nothing more was done until after the appointment of Joseph Wilcocks as dean in 1731. Taking his hint from Wren's recommendation of 1713 that both towers 'ought certainly to be carried to an equal Height . . . still continuing the *Gothick* Manner in the Stone-work, and Tracery', while 'the great West-window is also too feeble [and] crazy [and] Something must be done to strengthen [it] and the Gabel-end of the Roof [which is] Weather-boards painted . . . but ought . . . to be of Stone', Hawksmoor embarked on his gothic masterpiece. An early design (pl. 155) developed an idea already tested successfully at All Soul's College, Oxford (1715),[24] of spanning the central recessed window bays of each tower at high level with quirky ogee gothic bridge-arches, surmounted by a continuous range of panelled battlements, which not only finished off the top stage but also camouflaged the awkwardly protruding nave roof gable. A medieval solution that Hawksmoor knew first hand and considered 'has an agreeable effect' is Beverley Minster (pl. 135), where he had been working since 1716.[25] By 1734 it was decided to leave the gable exposed and explore crowning the towers with spires (pl. 147), recalling his abortive design for Warwick (pl. 148). In the following year the *Grub-street Journal* commended the elevation's 'beautiful height which strikes the first impression on the eye of the beholder' and applauded

> the able hand of . . . HAWKSMORE [and] the prudent proceedings of this great artist, in his . . . masterly and elegant method of repairing . . . how he has judiciously made new the weatherings and windows; how he puts in new stone where the old is found to be infirm, and sculpts down the sound, &c. so that when 'tis compleated, 'twill appear with equal beauty, as the first day it was erected.[26]

Work continued for another ten years, largely under the direction of Hawksmoor's successor, John James, who vigorously (though not exclusively) pursued a medieval vocabulary, as we see in Canaletto's famous view (pl. 261), where the modernity of the upper regions is evident only on close scrutiny. The 'solemn and majestic manner, wherein all the parts will have a just connection, and true affinity to each other' had been fulfilled.[27] Yet, on close inspection this deceptively homogeneous composition exposes an eclectic ensemble, a sort of architectural equivalent to geological stratification.

Beginning with the entrance porch of 1338–43 and concurrent recasting of the lower section of romanesque buttresses but still in thirteenth-century style, the reworked central window of 1491–5 was flanked by early fifteenth-century quatrefoil panels and on the north tower a window of 1513, which Hawksmoor replicated on the south but with differently detailed spandrels. Above there was entirely new work incorporating some blatantly un-gothic details in the baroque hoods of the circular openings, with their cherubim and festoons.[28] He was not alone in the Europe of his day

154 Nicholas Hawksmoor. Design for 'The West Front and the . . . Great window as, now in a Sad Ruinous and unfinished Condition. Ano 1731', Westminster Abbey, London. Pen and ink and wash. Westminster Abbey Muniments, Hawksmoor no. 6.

155 Nicholas Hawksmoor. 'Sketch proposed of The West front of ye Collt. Church of Westminster completed &c', Westminster Abbey, London, 1731. Pen and ink and wash. Westminster Abbey Muniments, Hawksmoor no. 7.

in creating such a convincing and at the same time somewhat inaccurate, twin-towered façade. In France between 1707 and 1709 there is Saint Pierre, Corbie, and the unrealised Sainte Croix, Orleans (pl. 156).[29]

Hawksmoor identified medieval precursors for this treatment in a letter dated 18 March 1735 to Dean Wilcocks, confidently placing his proposed façade within the context of three major English medieval cathedrals, probably relying on Daniel King's engravings of 1672. Ripon, Yorkshire, 'had 2 spires . . . but they were blowd doune by a Tempest' and not reinstated.[30] Of the twin western and taller crossing towers of

156 (*right*) Robert de Cotte and Guillaume Henault. Design for west front, St Croix Cathedral, Orleans, France, 1708–09. Pen and ink and wash. Bibliotheque Nationale, Paris, Topographie Va19, f. 144 (from Germann, 1972, pl. 2).

157 Joseph Baker. *View of Lincoln Cathedral from the West*, 1742. Oil on canvas. The Collection, Lincoln.

Lichfield, the latter had collapsed during the Civil War siege of 1646 but was rebuilt in the years 1661–9.[31] One of the lead-covered broach spires of Durham 'was thrown downe by a Storm and the Church pulld down the other, (they being poor) and sold the Materialls'.[32] The '2 spires' at Lincoln (pl. 157) were the subject of a sensational controversy in the 1720s concerning their removal, which caused the townsfolk to riot (described on p. 304). Though Hawksmoor was not involved he probably heard about the incident from John James, one of the participants.[33] Hawksmoor might also have cited the spire of Rochester Cathedral, damaged in the Great Storm of 1703, immediately restored, followed by further repairs in 1716 under Dickinson's supervision,[34] and Canterbury, where Hawksmoor was fitting out the interior around 1704, contemporary with proposals to restore the north-west tower according to a survey conducted by unnamed 'able and skilful Workmen from London'.[35] It had been 'much shaken' in 1703 and became 'too weak to bear the Spire . . . by reason of the vast weight and hight . . . which should it fall would greatly endanger . . . the Roofe of the Body'. In 1705 the dean and chapter ordered its removal and making 'Good the Tower . . . as we have opportunity in such manner as shall be found best for the safety and ornament of the . . . Church'.[36]

By the close of this phase of Westminster Abbey's repair and restitution programme the 'new Ornaments [and] stately Towers . . . erected in a masterly Manner' were, in the words of a Georgian guidebook, 'thought to exceed in Point of Workmanship any Part and the ancient Building, is now render'd more complete than ever'.[37]

Unsurprisingly, one of the first medieval parish churches to benefit from these achievements was St Margaret, standing in the abbey's shadow (pl. 261),

158 John Talman. Plan and elevations design for All Souls College Chapel, Oxford, detail, *c.*1708. Pen and ink and wash. Worcester College Library, University of Oxford, no. 40.

which underwent three distinct campaigns of rehabilitation (in 1734–9, 1757–63 and 1798–1803), each unusually well documented and together representing a model of Georgian improvement to an ancient fabric. Though governed by an independent Vestry, the building was under the somewhat heavy-handed control of the abbey's dean and chapter, so that, for instance, during delicate financial negotiations in 1734 Hawksmoor wickedly advised the dean: 'let us fence against the people of St Margets, who have Sadly maim'd and deformed their Steeple; to move compassion, when they beg for Mony, to Restore it', while in 1761, as we have seen in chapter 8, they railed virulently against the churchwardens' installation of the great *Crucifixion* window in the chancel. At the same time, as the official place of worship of members of the House of Commons (since 1614), Parliament 'exercised its Munificence by Grants' for repairs and improvements (delegating more than £10,000 during the eighteenth century), with the Speaker enjoying the use of a magnificent private pew, so that it was regarded as 'in some measure a national church'.[38]

The first phase of repairs under James, partnered with Thomas Hinton, then also serving as the abbey under-surveyor, centred on remodelling the north-west tower (1734–6), which more appropriately belongs to chapter 17, dealing with the mixture of gothic and classical, but pertinently was to feature a spire, though none was erected. In 1735 James reported on the 'dangerous condition' of the body's roof, repairs to which entailed installing ceiling panels finished with 'small Moldings and Ornaments' estimated to cost £450. This work, however, was not free of the difficulties often attending restoration, the architect reporting that on opening the roof he found it 'very bad' and recommended an 'absolute necessity of new Framing the whole and putting in every Beam intirely new . . . which with some decorations . . . more than first intended has made the Work exceed the Estimation'.[39]

Outside the capital, the earliest and most exuberant gothic activity was promoted by John Talman, an inquisitive connoisseur-architect and first director of the Society of Antiquaries of London. Recent research has revealed his shared aspirations with fellow Catholics for a return to the true Christian religion outlawed by what they regarded as the illegitimate reign of post-Reformation Protestantism. This manifested itself in a substantial output of accurately detailed record drawings executed by himself or by commissioned Continental artists of early Christian and medieval buildings and liturgical objects seen during his extensive travels in Italy between 1709 and 1723, which represent a remarkably early expression of reawakened gothic.[40] In 1708 or early 1709 he offered All Souls College, Oxford, then about to launch a major remodelling programme of the fabric (founded in the fifteenth century by Henry Chicheley, who as Archbishop of Canterbury is commemorated by a splendid tomb in the cathedral, pl. 275), a 'small performance' of the hall and chapel with 'some but imperfect additions . . . to render it more ornamental', which was 'unlike any other in Oxon & pretty much after the Italian Gothick' (pl. 158). The flamboyant mélange of clerical statues, crockets, pinnacled buttresses and battlements, 'noble fret [and] Acroteres of Hard metal or brass gilded' (according to the accompanying description), probably derived from the fourteenth-century cathedrals of Orvieto and Milan (pl. 330).[41] It may have been this scheme that William Stukeley referred to as being 'in the anachronism of the Gothic degenerate taste'.[42] The job went to Hawksmoor in 1715, who condemned the rival offering as 'new fantasticall perishable Trash . . . utterly destroying or barbarously altered or mangleing it, [which] wou'd be useing the founder Cruelly' and, as at Westminster Abbey, he called for 'the preservation of Antient durable Publick Buildings, that are Strong and usefull' and that 'whatever is good in its kinde ought to be preserv'd in respect to antiquity, as well as our present advantage, for

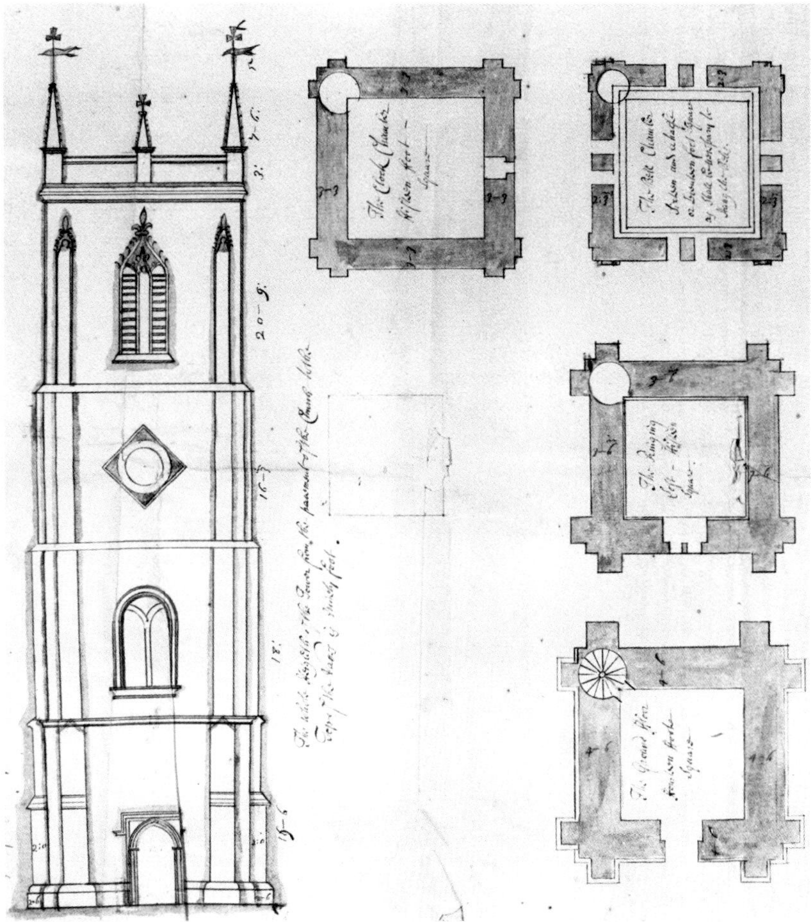

159 William Kempster. Plans and elevation design for the tower, SS Peter and Paul, Blockley, Worcestershire, 1725. Pen and ink and wash. Worcestershire Record Office, 705:66, BA228/78.

destruction can be profitable to none but Such as Live by it'.[43]

Nothing so sophisticated yet uncomfortably Continental was ever again attempted in England (except perhaps the gothic work of James Adams, pl. 329); other work was modestly parochial, though not without interest. This includes a fascinating group of West Country towers that throw special light on the elusive boundary between so-called gothic survival and revival. At Dursley, Gloucestershire, the old structure, which collapsed in 1699, damaging the west end of the church and killing several people, was replaced by a new build (1708–9) designed by Thomas Sumsion, 'one of the last English master masons to carry on an authentic medieval tradition'. His model was the richly detailed fifteenth-century church in his nearby home town of Colerne, Wiltshire, with the openwork battlements and pinnacles inspired by Gloucester Cathedral, whose 'stately Tower [was] justly esteemed a most admi-rable Piece of Architecture'.[44] A later manifestation of this type is the 'new Tower' erected at Blockley, Gloucestershire, in the years 1724–8 'according to the Draught given in by [William] Kempster' (pl. 159). Thomas Woodward Sr's estimate of £500 was 'at as Cheap a rate as it . . . can be done by any Man in England that will do it well', who, in the opinion of Francis Smith, a leading Midlands builder-architect, should be 'Encour-aged to do his work well and . . . deserve every penny he has charged'. The participants are particularly poignant in that Smith had been one of the executants of St Mary, Warwick (pls 270–71); Kempster's brother, Christopher, had assisted Wren in completing Tom Tower, Oxford (1681–2); and Blockley's upper-storey, three-light windows correspond to those on the fifteenth-century parish church of Chipping Campden, only 5 miles away and Woodward's home town.[45]

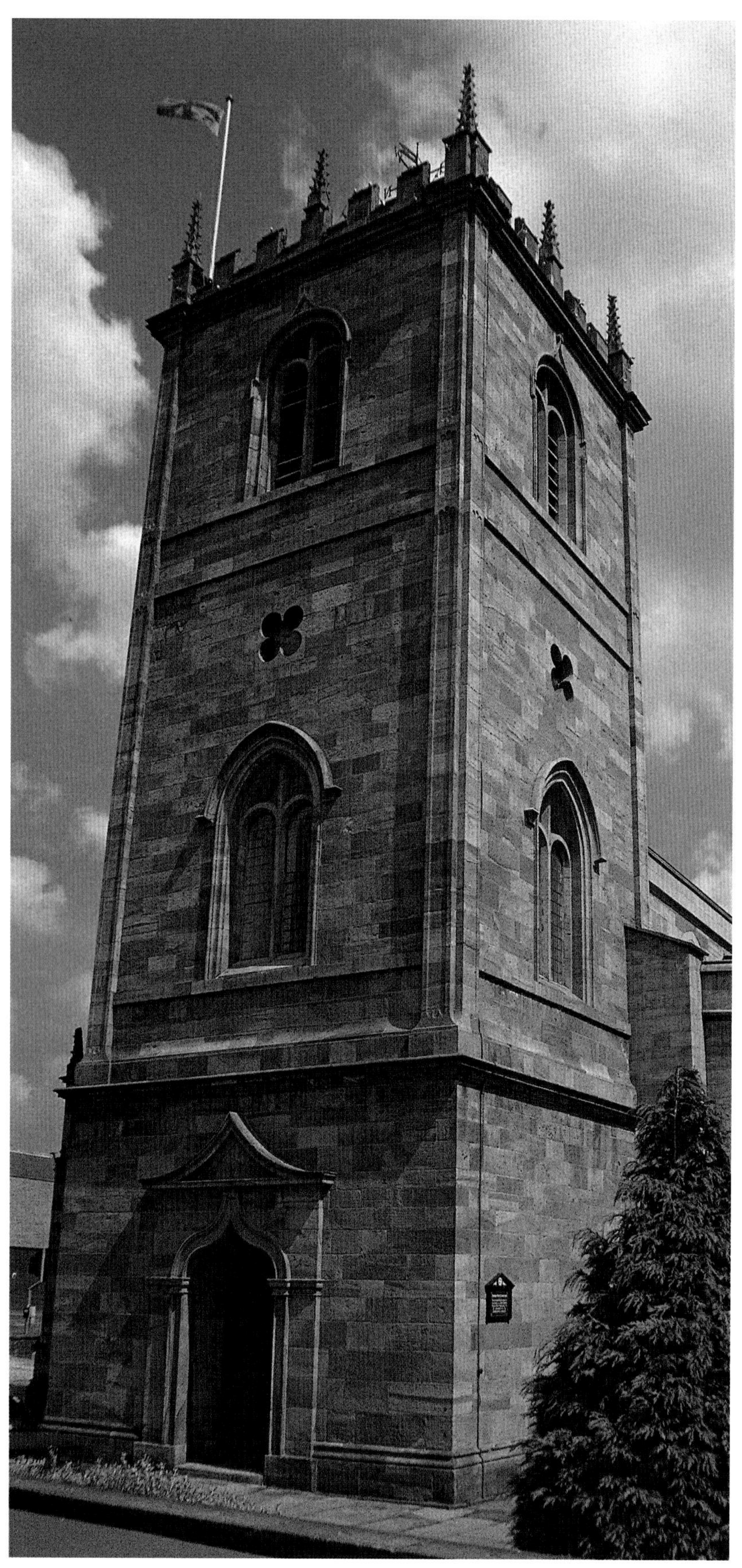

160 John Carr. West elevation, All Saints, Dewsbury, Yorkshire, 1764–66.

Fourteen

GOTHIC IN TRANSITION

> A few years ago everything was Gothic; our houses, our beds, our bookcases and our couches were all copied from some parts or other of our old Cathedrals[1]

At the time Hawksmoor was completing his work at Westminster Abbey (he died in post in 1736), gothic church design reached a major juncture in its progress through the century. In the 1730s the earliest published critical writings in English on the subject appeared, coinciding with and in some measure influenced by a significant change in the interpretation of the style as it came to be dominated by the next generation of architects, the oldest of whom was William Kent, born in 1685, and which included Batty Langley, Henry Keene, William Robinson, Timothy Lightoler, William Halfpenny, John Carr (pl. 160), James Bridges and John Wing Jr. The tone was set in 1735 by the elderly Hawksmoor responding to accusations made by James Ralph in *A Critical Review of the Publick Buildings, Statues and Ornaments in, and about London and Westminster* (1734) that his 'new works and repairs' at the abbey 'are not conformable and pursuant to the Old'. This solicited the reply: 'Mr Rafe . . . who mistaking the whole History of Building and . . . most of the Terms of Art makes use of the word Gothick to signife every thing that displeases him, as the Greeks and Romans calld every Nation Barbarous, that, were not in their way of Police and Education'. He was the victim of the purported Burlington-Palladian circle's general attack on the baroque and the lack of a strict classical interpretation of antique models, rudely vocalised by Ralph, though not necessarily sponsored by the Architect Earl, made manifest in Hawksmoor's ejection in 1730 from the competition to rebuild St Giles-in-the-Fields (successfully secured by Henry Flitcroft, 'Burlington Harry'), and his dismissal in 1735 as clerk of the works at Greenwich Hospital (through the machinations of Thomas Ripley, whom Hawksmoor charged with possessing 'power from his great Friends to Destroy me at Greenwich').[2] At Westminster the more erudite Hawksmoor associated 'the manner of Building . . . in Henry the 3rds, time . . . with sharp pointed Arches, and the Pillars dress'd with small Torus's, instead of Fluteings, or Channelling, us'd by the Greeks', the west front being in

> a more Modern Style and is what the ingenious Masons, call Tracery . . . I do assure you that I have pursued the Tracery manner . . . in . . . rebuilding that great [west] window. In restoreing (the perish'd Canopys) in cleaning and repairing the broken part of the front . . . Barrs of Architecture, Moldings, Arcketts and Ornaments, with all the exactness I could, or where it was reasonable . . . If I have in any case departed from what the work was Originally; or intended; it was only where it was irrationall and impracticable to follow, for example the Cornices were so small that they could not . . . throw off the Rain . . . I have given them a greater projection to preserve the under work, but still kept to the Gothick manner [to] protect the work for ever.[3]

Langley, Ralph's nemesis, responding in the *Grub-street Journal* (1734–5), under the pseudonym Hiram, legendary architect of the Temple at Jerusalem, praised the west front, including Hawksmoor's proposed spires, for rising 'in a solemn and majestic manner, wherein all the parts will have a just connection, and true affinity to each other'. It was 'much more grand and magnificent than the *chapel* of HENRY VII', as well as Salisbury's '*Gothique*' tower and spire, Boston 'Stump' and York's west front, possessing 'beauties and grandeur, not to be condemned by the most exquisite judge [but] are the admiration of all judges', and other endearments associated with Englishness and the mason tradition.[4] Langley was reacting against a generally unfavourable perception of gothic, which was used as a Ralphian,

161 (*above*) Batty and Thomas Langley. 'Arcades for Piazza's', detail, in B. Langley, *Ancient Architecture Restored and Improved*, 1742, XXIX. Engraving.

162 (*left*) Samuel Hieronymus Grimm. Lord Mayor's Chapel, Bristol, Somerset, September 1789, with James Paty's porch, 1777–8, detail, removed 1888. Pen and ink and wash. © The British Library Board, Kaye Collection, IV, Add. MS 15540, f. 157.

anti-classical term of abuse and detestation. *The Builder's Dictionary* (1734) characterised it as an 'Abundance of little, whimsical, wild, and chimerical Ornaments . . . very incorrect . . . Profiles . . . Every Thing . . . cramm'd with Windows, Roses, Crosses, Figures, &c . . . huge Vaults raised on Slender Pillars, which one would expect every Minute to tumble down'.[5] Langley formalised his ideas in *Ancient Architecture, Restored, and Improved, by a Great Variety of Grand and useful Designs, Entirely new In the Gothic Mode . . . Exceeding every Thing thats Extant*, published in 1742 (and again in 1747, retitled *Gothic Architecture, Improved By Rules and Proportions*) and dedicated to the dean and chapter of Westminster. Here, the abbey's '*Venerable* and *August Pile*' (represented in the first two plates by measured columns erected during the reigns of Henry III and Edward I) was proclaimed 'the most *Magnificent* in this Kingdom (and the most inimitable Structure in the World)'. He sought to systematise gothic by the same rigours applied by theoreticians of the antique orders; indeed, to exceed classicism by claiming that whereas gothic 'modes of building have been and are condemned by many, on a supposition that their principal parts have been put together without rules or proportions', the abbey columns 'prove that such is a want of judgment' and that their 'beautiful proportions and geometrical rules . . . are not excelled (if equalled) in any part of the Grecian or Roman Orders'.[6] Invented gothic columns and entablatures were treated in the same analytical manner as their classical counterparts. Remarkably, the book remained popular well into the era of archaeological authenticity. John Carr, a leading neoclassical architect practising in the north, acquired a hand-drawn copy of *Ancient Architecture, Restored, and Improved* in 1770 (only one year before the publication of James Bentham's groundbreaking *History and Antiquities of . . . Ely*, to which he was not a subscriber).[7] In 1777 James Paty Jr turned to plate XXXIX (pl. 161) as a model for a porch addition (removed 1888) to the Lord Mayor's chapel, College Green, Bristol (pl. 162), by then hopelessly old-fashioned.[8]

The pivotal, pioneer figure in the re-emergence of gothic-style ecclesiastical furnishings in the early eighteenth century was the decorative painter turned architect William Kent. So little research has been undertaken on this aspect of his versatile artistic career that it is still unclear how he became enamoured with gothic. On to a standard medieval bowl and stem-form pulpit, as well as the archbishop's throne and choir-stalls at York Minster, dating between 1737 and 1741, now destroyed (pl. 163),[9] he applied a plethora of gothic trefoils and quatrefoils, crocketed pinnacles, pendants, bosses, tierceron vaulting and the like, carved in oak, based on authentic medieval work elsewhere in the fabric. Both testers were modelled on the celebrated fifteenth-century flying buttresses and spire of St Nicholas, Newcastle upon Tyne.[10] A contemporary commented that the pieces were 'in the *Gothick* Taste, suitable to the rest of the Building, and have a fine and beautiful Effect'.[11] While the Minster itself may well have dictated this obviously suitable stylistic choice, it is notable that Kent's contemporary beautification of the interior under Burlington's direction consisted of a wholly classical re-pavement of the building (pl. 131).

Despite the absence of conclusive documentary evidence in the case of Shobdon church, Herefordshire (pls 164–5), which has long puzzled architectural historians, there are good reasons to believe that Kent, perhaps with the involvement of Richard Bateman (the estate manager acting on behalf of the absentee owner, his nephew Viscount Bateman), a member of Horace Walpole's Strawberry Hill Committee of Taste, was the principal designer. The Revd Richard Pococke, visiting in 1756, the year of its completion, described this playfully charming, homogeneous church as 'rebuilt . . . in the Gothic style, and . . . very finely finished within

163 View of the pulpit and choir stalls of York Minster, York, in J. Hildyard, *An Accurate Description and History of the Metropolitan and Cathedral Churches of Canterbury and York*, 1755, pl. 105, detail. William Kent architect, 1737–41. A section of the medieval screen on the right.

. . . in the same style, every part being embellished with Gothic ornaments'.[12] The recent publication of John Vardy's *Some Designs of Mr Inigo Jones and Mr Wm Kent* (1744), which also illustrates the latter's gothic work at York, Westminster Hall and Gloucester Cathedral (1739 and 1741), would have held the viscount in good stead. In 1746, while Kent was still alive (he died in 1748), Bateman had 'a mind to have a design made' in London, but received only 'plans' (untraced), in February 1749, perhaps ones left behind by Kent. The client was 'impatient' to have them 'altered' in preparation for building, though construction did not begin until 1752–3. The 'architect' mentioned in early 1750, presumably acting as executant, may well have been Kent's colleague Henry Flitcroft, who had internally remodelled the classical mansion at Shobdon (1746–8).[13] While involved as both an arbiter in disputes and archi-

164 William Kent and John, 2nd Viscount Bateman, attributed. View from south-west, St John Evangelist, Shobdon, Herefordshire, 1748–56.

tect in charge of alterations between 1749 and 1752 at medieval St Mary, Tetbury, Gloucestershire, less than a day's journey to the south-east, Flitcroft's proclivity towards gothic is uncertain. St Andrew, Wimpole, Cambridgeshire (1749), except for the retained medieval north chapel, is a Palladian box (pl. 569), although his rebuilt body at Stoke Edith, Herefordshire (1740–41), in an equally plain Palladian manner (pl. 567), not only preserves the medieval tower but was also to involve, on the new, unfenestrated park elevation facing towards the mansion, 'dressing up the recess in the Gothic Manner' (the 'Sketches' for which are untraced), which may or may not have been executed.[14]

Shobdon is a mimetic Kentian concoction (pl. 164). The unusual two- and three-light plate tracery windows with quatrefoils duplicate those in his remodelling of fifteenth-century Esher Place, Surrey (*circa* 1733). The church interior is a remarkably intact gothic fairytale (pl. 165), its pulpit a version of that at York (pl. 163),

165 William Kent and John, 2nd Viscount Bateman, attributed. Interior towards chancel, St John Evangelist, Shobdon, Herefordshire, 1748–56. English Heritage (National Monuments Record, BB87/10396).

166 James Cole. Geoffrey Chaucer's tomb, 1555, in John Dart, *Westmonasterium. Or The history and Antiquities of The Abbey Church of St. Peters Westminster*, vol. I, 1723, pl. VII, detail. Engraving. Henry Moore Institute Library, Leeds.

tempered above all by the experience of quarrying Westminster Abbey and John Dart's beautifully illustrated *Westmonasterium* (1723). The triple ogee arches with crockets and rosette drops separating the chancel and transepts from the body recall numerous abbey tombs (pl. 166). Supported on compound, ringed piers, they give this expansive eastern area the ambience of a semi-independent family burial place (originally no monuments were permitted in the church), reinforced by the presence in the transepts of fish-tailed panels, or *tabula ansata*, with their sepulchral association in antiquity. The guilloche-like altar rail and pew fronts, while based on French renaissance sources (see p. 316), achieve a sort of gothic legitimacy by having already appeared as the crowning balustrade of Hawksmoor's Westminster Abbey west front, completed in 1745 (pl. 261). In addition, Batty Langley's rich repository of patterns in *Ancient Architecture* (1742) provided the patterns for the chimneypiece in the Bateman pew within the short south transept, as well as the external ogee door and trilobed window resting on a straight hood mould inserted into the earlier (*circa* 1730) west tower.[15]

Exactly contemporary with Shobdon and also surviving intact is the chapel refitted in the medieval south wing of Hartlebury Castle, Worcestershire (pl. 167), the glamorous episcopal residence of Bishop Maddox, designed by the 22-year-old Henry Keene, already in post as Westminster Abbey 'College Surveyor', responsible for the dean and chapter's urban property and other estates. The oak entrance screen merges features from Kent and Langley.[16] He also harvested authentic gothic details from the abbey; for example, the fan vault is a simplified, stucco version of Henry VII's Chapel, 'the wonder of the entire world'.[17] Later, in remodelling University College Hall, Oxford (1766), he took off 'casts in plaister' and had 'leaves all carv'd from these exactly, only of different sizes'.[18]

Keene quickly became an experienced interpreter of period medieval vocabulary. In 1750 the dean and chapter of Worcester recommended that he be 'applied to for a draught of a proper Ornamental Portico in the Gothick Stile . . . to be erected over the great Gate of the Cathedral instead of a mean, deformed covering now . . . falling into Ruines'. When Walpole visited in 1753 he remarked that 'Gothicism and the restoration of that architecture, and not the bastard breed [Kent and Langley], spreads extremely in this part of the world.'[19]

In 1752, the year Keene rose to the surveyorship to the dean and chapter of Westminster Abbey, he began work on Sir William Lee's chapel at Hartwell, Buckinghamshire. Today reduced through neglect to a pathetic shell, this stunning masterpiece has been misinterpreted by modern historians as a creation of those 'carefree days' of rococo gothic and 'a classical design in fancy dress' by an architect who 'had no real understanding of Gothic'.[20] To the contrary, vividly detailed but only recently noticed building accounts reveal a courageously avant-garde venture in promoting an exclusively gothic style for an entirely new church. These bills, which identify Keene's team of talented craftsmen, including his joiner-father, Henry Sr, and the distinguished Oxford plasterer Thomas Roberts, are resplendent with specifications for 'Gothick Arches' and 'Niches', 'Molded hollow on framing to Gothick pannels . . . & heads', 'Gothick Groined Bracketing', 'Gothick Enricht Cornice with Small Arches and Ornaments', 'Gothic Pipe [and] Cistron Heads', 'Raffled Leafs [and] Pinnacles', 'Gothick Capitals', '86 Gothick Roses', 'Crown Glass in broad lead, cutt in Gothic Figures', '144 Crocketes on . . . Pinikells' and so on.[21]

This is hardly surprising, since, apart from Keene himself, a most committed gothicist, the client's uncle, Sir George Lee, who contributed to the building costs, which totalled £2,443, had been an undergraduate at Christ Church, Oxford, with its memorable Perpendicular fan-vaulted staircase (1638) and the sixteenth-century Tom Tower, to which Wren added a splendid crown (1681–2).[22] The accounts further reveal that following the success in 1752 in securing a faculty to

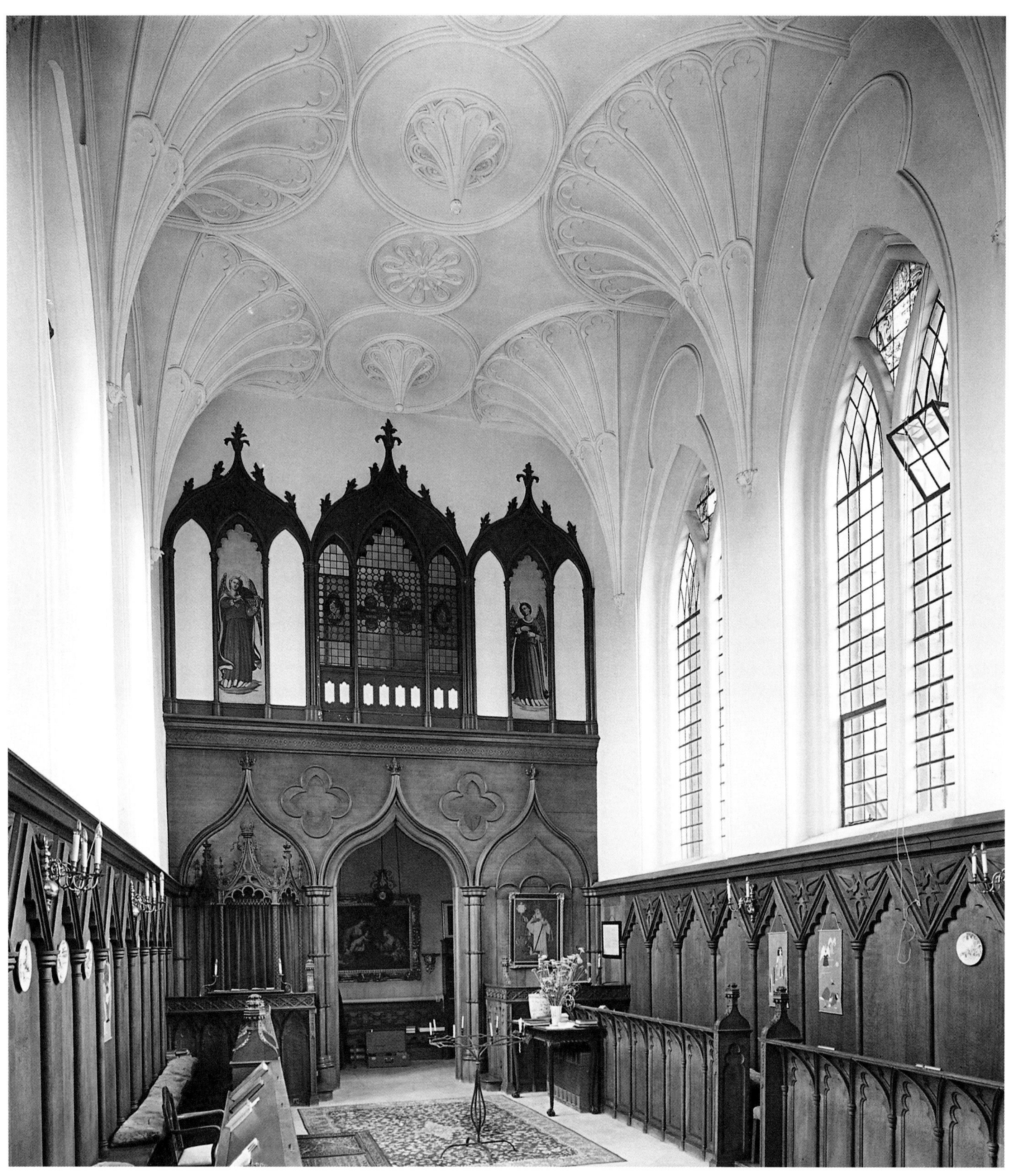

167 Henry Keene. Interior towards entrance, Hartlebury Castle chapel, Worcestershire, 1748–50. English Heritage (National Monuments Record, BB83/5036).

168 (*left*) Henry Keene. South elevation, Hartwell House Chapel, Buckinghamshire, 1752–5. English Heritage (National Monuments Record, A44/4408, photographed 1943 prior to internal collapse 1948–51).

169 (*below left*) Henry Keene. Interior towards north, Hartwell House Chapel, Buckinghamshire, 1752–5. English Heritage (National Monuments Record, CC44/434, photographed 1943 prior to collapse 1948–51).

170 (*below right*) Henry Keene. Ceiling, Hartwell House Chapel, Buckinghamshire, 1752–5. English Heritage (National Monuments Record, A44/4416, photographed 1943 prior to collapse 1948–51).

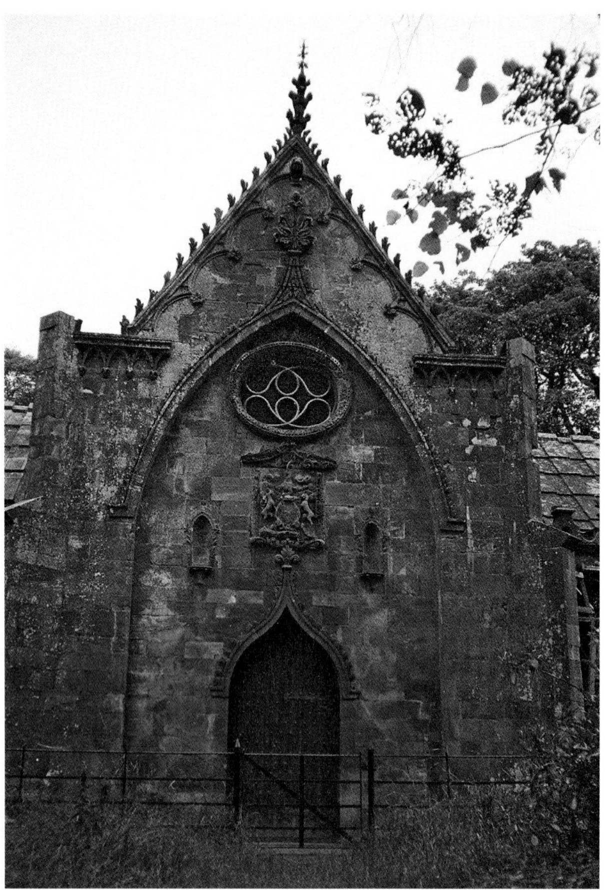

demolish the decayed fifteenth-century parish church and relocate it as a free-standing structure close to and within view of the Jacobean mansion, which, except for its function and size, served virtually as a garden pavilion, Keene supplied two alternative designs, as well as 'several Extraordinary drawings . . . occasion'd by Alterations, & Additions . . . more than was intended' in the (untraced) contract. Of these only the presentation set of a preliminary proposal has survived: an awkward, timidly towered and battlemented, ill-lit, bald cruciform building with its canted crossing forming an incipient octagon. The slightly earlier Shobdon comes to mind (pl. 164). Then early in 1753 Keene made a leap of architectural faith from this undemonstrative design to the inspired originality and rich detailing of the executed building (pl. 168). Here the congregational space was reformed into a regular, 16-foot-sided octagon, 64 feet high, anchored between nearly identical projecting

171 (*left*) Robert and James Adam. Entrance front of mausoleum church, Yester, Lothian, Scotland, 1753–54. Royal Commission on the Ancient and Historical Monuments of Scotland Enterprises, EL/5959.

172 (*below*) Artist unknown. 'A Perspective View of the Outside of Roslin Chapel', Lothian, Scotland, undated. Pen and ink and wash. © The British Library Board, K.Top. XLIX-79-f.

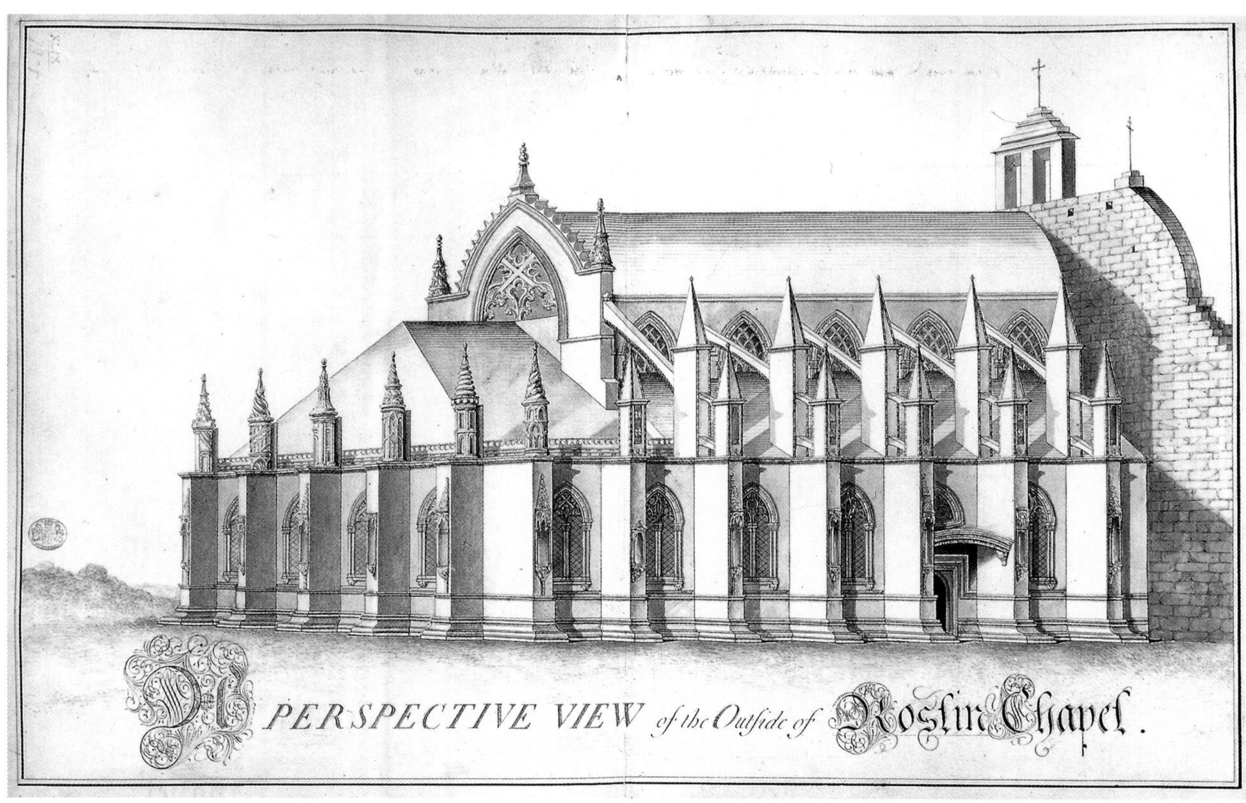

towers, 88 feet high, signalling entrance lobby and chancel, with two additional side doors leading directly into the body used by members of the household and other parishioners. This stands out as the earliest octagonal church erected in the gothic style; its generic model was the chapter house of Westminster Abbey. The broad north and south elevations are an uncanny foretaste of J. H. Müntz's so-called Gothic Cathedral at Kew.[23] The radically new element at Hartwell in its heyday was its ornamental exuberance, quarried largely from Westminster: the shallow, trilobe-ended panels on the towers' clasping buttresses from the abbey's west front (pl. 261); the quatrefoils clustered in threes and fives as the window aprons found in numerous medieval tomb chests (pl. 166); the pierced quatrefoils of the attic windows and parapets, a Keene *leitmotif*, which also proliferated there; the lozenge-shaped transoms in the main windows (pl. 169); the 'sofits wrot: in many Gothick pannels' in the internal west and east arches from the Islip chapel; and above all Robert's spectacular 'Stucco Ceiling . . . compleatly finished with Gothick Moldings and ornaments . . . cast in Solid Alabaster' (pl. 170), including fans of repeated radiating cusps, mouchettes and rosetted quatrefoils, with a smaller version covering the chancel, like some exquisite starry sky, clearly inspired by Henry VII's Chapel.[24] Keene was not alone in admiring Perpendicular fan vaulting. Visiting Gloucester Cathedral in September 1753, Walpole confessed: 'of all delight, is . . . the . . . cloister [1351–77]. It is the very thing that you would build, when you extracted all the quintessence of trefoils, arches, and lightness'.[25] Nor was Westminster Keene's only source of authentic inspiration. In the treatment of the crocketed ogee arches and windows and the inscription compartment frames of the body (pl. 169), he must have had in mind Chichester market cross of 1501, which had undergone repairs in 1746 by William Ride, who also drew the structure for an engraving issued by the Society of Antiquaries of London in 1749.[26] There is an additional surprising element to Hartwell, to which I shall return in chapter 18.

The youngest and least likely yet most remarkable of the generation of transitional gothic architects to emerge in mid-century was Robert Adam. Son of William Adam (who had supervised the construction of Roger Morris's Inveraray Castle, 1745–8, the outstanding gothic-style domestic achievement of the period in Scotland), Robert and his brother John created a mausoleum church at Yester, Lothian, for the 4th Marquess of Tweedale in 1753–4. They truncated the disused medieval church and added a new front (pl. 171) in the eccentric form of a cusped and crocketed gable crowning a large pointed relieving arch enclosing an ogee door and circular mullion window.[27] Though the repertory is familiar from Langley's *Ancient Architecture* (1742), its direct and explicitly antiquarian source is the extravagantly enriched, unfinished fifteenth-century chapel at Rosslyn, near Edinburgh (pl. 172). This 'most noble Gothic structure, exceeded by few', had, reported Stukeley in 1739, 'laid open to the weather . . . since the Reformation [but] made as beautiful and stately as most of that sort . . . in the kingdome' under the direction of Sir John Clerk of Penicuik, the Adams' friend and fellow member of the Society of Antiquaries of London, who was also William Adam's sometime country house collaborator.[28] Robert's next church work, on returning from four years study in Italy in 1758, was an unrealised scheme to complete the west tower of Perpendicular Harewood parish church (pl. 173) for Edwin Lascelles, a recent social upstart among the Yorkshire landed gentry looking to establish a local foothold (which Adam and others succeeded in achieving in creating his grand Palladian mansion). The nearby medieval church suffered from a lack of elevation, which Adam proposed to remedy by the addition (rendered in pencil on his sketch) of a delicately detailed top stage of tracery, crockets and cusps, repeated as filigree along the starkly straight cornice of the sloping side aisles.[29]

173 Robert Adam. Design for 'finishing…the top of the Steeple in the Gothick taste', All Saints, Harwood, Yorkshire, detail, 23 April 1759. Pencil, pen and ink. Sir John Soane's Museum, London, AD 21/148.

In 1761 Adam assumed responsibility for completing Croome D'Abitot church, Worcestershire (consecrated June 1763), from Lancelot Brown, who in 1758 had designed the sedate, boxy gothic carcass with a characteristically Perpendicular tower.[30] The interior (pl. 174),

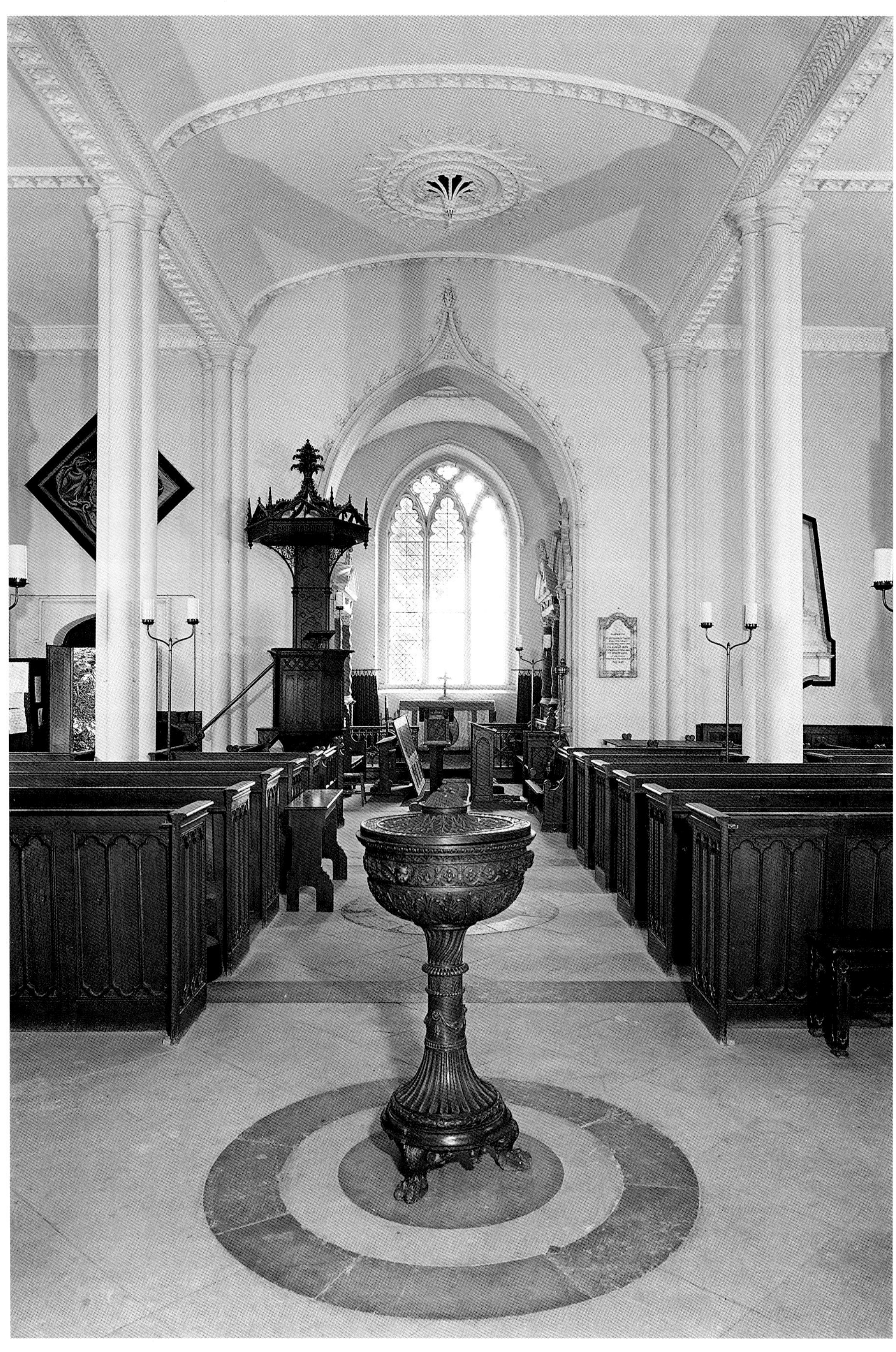

174 Lancelot 'Capability' Brown and Robert Adam. Interior towards chancel, St Mary Magdalen, Croome D'Abitot, Worcestershire, 1758–64. English Heritage (National Monuments Record, BB74/161).

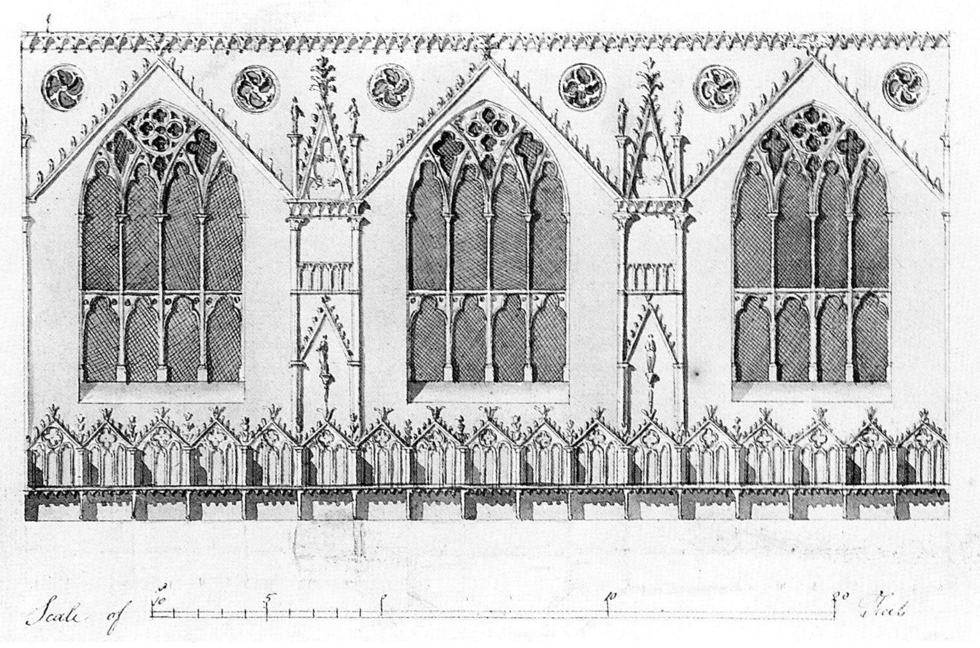

175 Robert Adam. 'Design of the Manner of Finishing of the Side Stalls of the Church at Croome', Croome d'Abitot, Worcestershire, detail, 1761. Pen and ink and wash. Sir John Soane's Museum, London, AD 50/15.

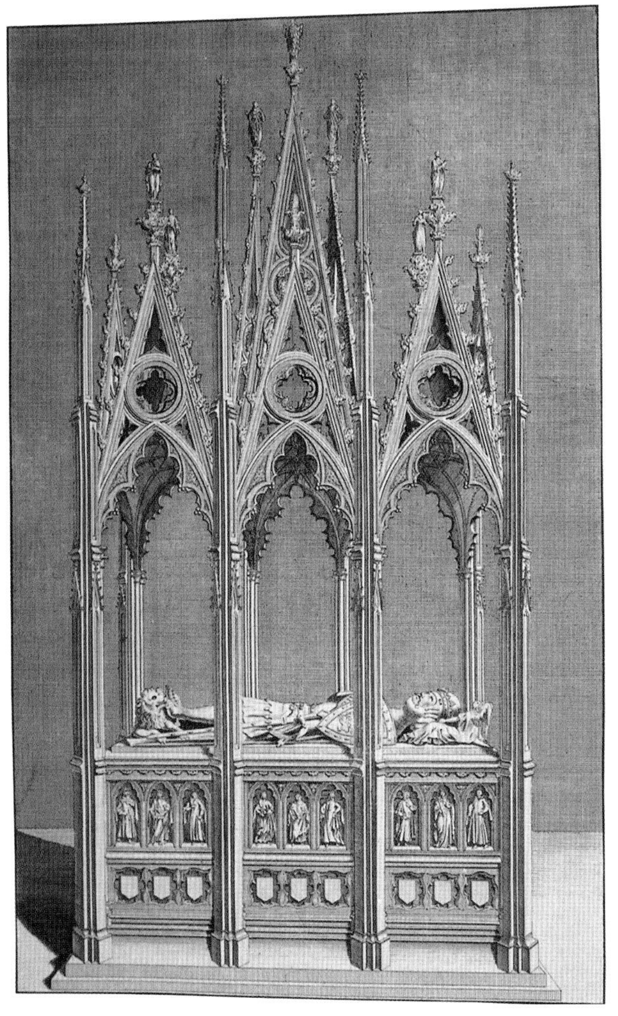

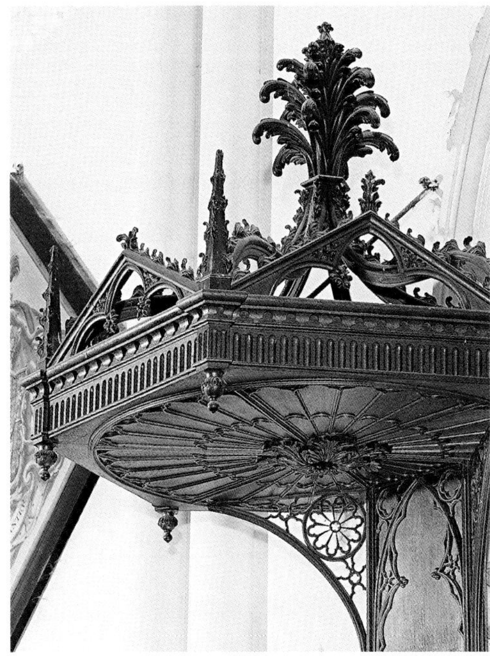

177 (*above*) Robert Adam. Pulpit sounding board, wood, St Mary Magdalen, Croome d'Abitot, Worcetershire, 1760. English Heritage (National Monuments Record, BB74/174).

176 (*left*) James Cole. John of Etham, Earl of Cornwall's tomb, after 1339, canopy destroyed 1776, in John Dart, *Westmonasterium, or The History and Antiquities of The Abbey Church of St. Peters Westminster*, vol. I, pl. 106, 1723. Engraving. Henry Moore Institute Library, Leeds

where slender colonnette piers divide the elliptical vaulted nave from nearly full-height, flat-ceiling aisles, is less spatially dramatic than Shobdon (pl. 165). An early proposal for the interior (pl. 175) shows Adam's suggested enhancement of the side walls by ranges of repetitive, triangular-headed stalls in the manner of Hartlebury (pl. 167), big thirteenth-century-style windows with intersecting cusped tracery,[31] framed by crocketed gables, quatrefoil soffits and steeply triangular-topped piers familiar from Westminster Abbey tombs (pl. 176). The most exquisite ornament is concentrated on the pulpit and tester (pl. 177), the final flowering of its Kentian forebear (pl. 163).[32]

Though Kent, Keene and Adam represent the bedrock of mid-eighteenth-century ecclesiastical gothic, there was also a flurry of earnest activity among architects who experimented only occasionally with the genre but nevertheless deserve places in this history.

In 1746 George Dance Sr, clerk of the works to the City of London and among its leading classical church architects, informed the dean and chapter of Canterbury Cathedral that its romanesque south-east transept gable (pl. 209) required immediate repair to prevent imminent collapse. He recommended removing the weatherboarding and other timberwork blighting the exterior, and rebuilding the internal stone wall, columns and arches as shown in his presentation drawing (pl. 178), which entailed inserting an elaborate system of iron chains and cramps so that it would be 'well secured from flying out' and never 'inclining from their true Situation', though nothing was undertaken.[33] Possible models for this curious solution are not easily identified: the rose recalls one of the 'Windows for Attic Storys' published in plate XXXIV in Langley's *Gothic Architecture, Improved* (1747), while the irregular glissade of slender compound piers linked by lancet, ogee and elliptical arches may originate in actual medieval work, such as the overdoors of the entrance into Salisbury Cathedral's chapter house.[34]

In 1753–4 William Robinson, clerk of the works at Greenwich Hospital, who was responsible for early transformations at Strawberry Hill in the late 1740s that were condemned for not being 'truly Gothic',[35] provided designs (untraced) for a new church at Stone, Staffordshire (pl. 179). The documents devote much discussion about the niceties of construction but little about stylistic matters. Similar to Shobdon with its isolated hoods (pl. 164) and to Croome with its traditional tripartite planning, but sidelined as a 'miserable Gothic-like church', it must have been a rural novelty when completed.[36] William Baker, a Midland architect employed at Stone as clerk of the works, made frequent journeys the few miles to Seighford, where, between 1754 and 1757, he refashioned the tower and part of the medieval body in a similar gothic manner (pl. 180),[37] a strange, clumsy work with vestigial recessed panelled outer bays perhaps owing something to the then fifty-year-old St Mary, Warwick (pl. 270).

The creator of the splendid gothic altarpiece at Warwick (pl. 128), Timothy Lightoler, favoured Stone's uncompromisingly rigid, symmetrical preaching box form for St John, Manchester (1768–70, demolished 1931; pl. 181), and its twin, St John, Liverpool, erected posthumously in the years 1775–83 (demolished 1898). Both were large, utilitarian buildings given a dash of fashion by fourteenth-century-style ogee-framed windows and doors, flat cusp-panelled lierne rib vaults and crocket-pinnacled buttresses gleaned from Langley's now ubiquitous *Ancient Architecture, Restored, and Improved* (1742).[38]

178 George Dance Sr. 'Survey of the Upper Cross Isle' and section design for remodelling internal south end of south-east transept, Canterbury Cathedral, Kent, 1746–7. Pencil, pen and ink and wash. Canterbury Cathedral Archives, Dcc/Fabric 5/20.

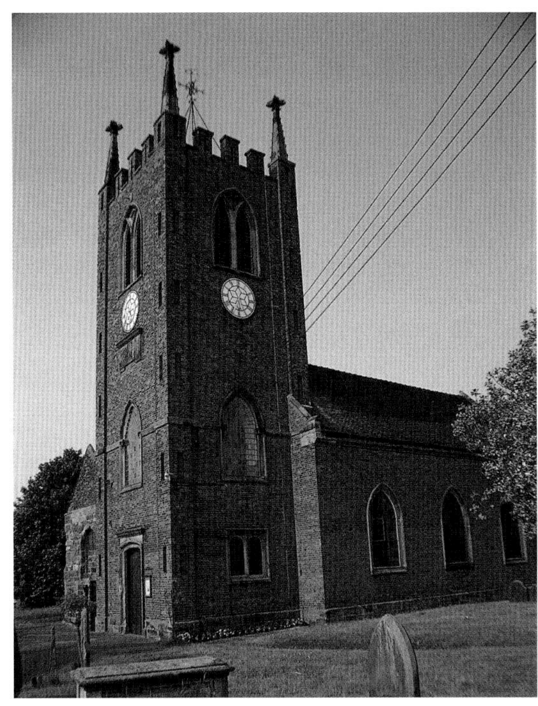

180 William Baker. South-west view, St Chad, Seighford, Staffordshire, 1754–7.

179 (*left*) William Robinson. North-west view, St Michael, Stone, Staffordshire, 1753–9.

A similar vocabulary invests the Countess of Huntingdon's Connexion Chapel, Bath (1765; pl. 182), the sect's first attempt in the fashionable spa to evangelise the upper ranks of society, which helps to explain the stylistic choice, at that date still a local oddity apart from the abbey. Its model is a Langleian domestic offspring by the Bristol-based architects William and John Halfpenny (pl. 183), who advocated:

> As there is nothing more acceptable and advantagious to the Public in general than Invention and Variety of Construction . . . we have endeavoured . . . to oblige with several new Designs . . . in the *Gothic* . . . Manner, with Intent to advance . . . that noble Science, in Compliance to that present Taste [where] if Gracefulness and true Symmetry are found in the Structure, they will be sufficient Bars to any false or frivolous Aspersions.[39]

Walpole described the chapel, which incorporated the countess's residence, a canted-bayed, ogee-windowed and embattled structure camouflaging the austere worship unit from the street and pedestrian inquisitiveness, as 'very neat, with true Gothic windows (yet I am not converted); but I am glad to see that luxury is creeping in upon them before persecution: they have very neat mahogany stands for branches [candelabras], and brackets of the same in taste'.[40] The compound represented a new experiment in Nonconformist layout, a hierarchal distribution of purpose and space with candid expressions of feminism that did not go unnoticed by early visitors. 'The Chapel is exceeding Decent', reported the Revd John Penrose in 1766, the year of its completion, with the communion table railed within an eastern alcove, flanked on each side by a vestry and a 'little Room' for Lady Huntingdon and her 'Friends'. Four steps ascend to a western gallery within a 'handsome Iron Rail'; to the south is the reader's stand in the form of a 'white Eagle', to the north the clerk's desk, while behind and raised three steps higher is the 'Preacher's Eagle'. Behind each was a scarlet damask-covered chair. Within the railed area 'sat several Ladies', with the congregation occupying 'Forms' (benches).

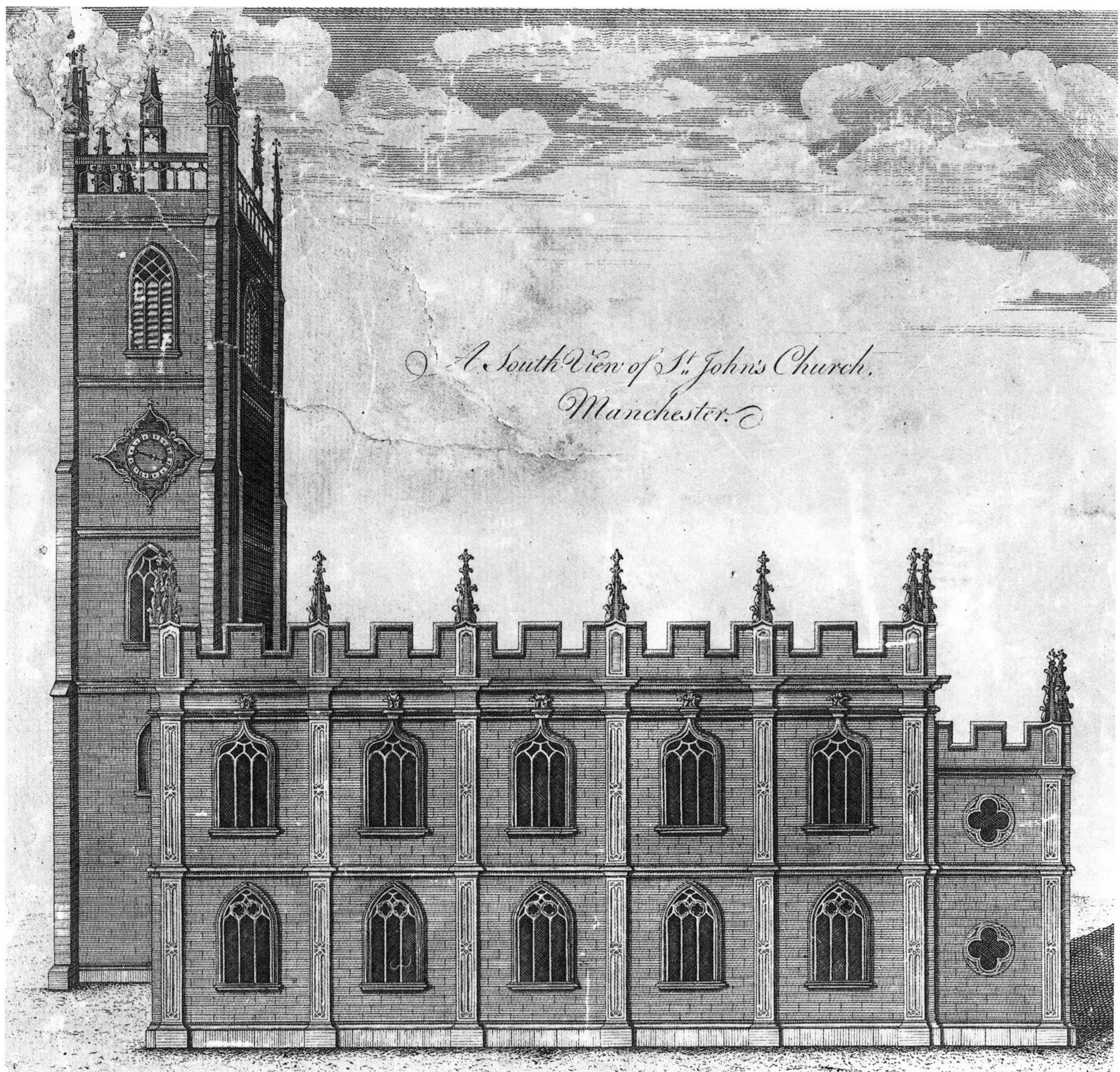

181 Oldham and Bottomley. 'A South View of St. John's Church, Manchester', Lancashire, undated. Engraving. Manchester Local Studies Unit Archives, 65277. Timothy Lightoler architect, 1768–70, demolished 1931.

Each congregant was presented with a 'Message-Card' inscribed: 'Strait is the Gate and narrow is the Way, which leadeth into Life and few there be that find it.'[41]

A contemporary provincial architect also enamoured with adapting published secular patterns for houses of worship was John Carr (pls 31–2), a resident of York, who played a prominent role in municipal life – serving as Lord Mayor in 1770 and 1785 – and practised in the shadow of the cathedral (pl. 139). The 'richness and extent of Yorkshire quite charmed me. – Oh! What quarries for working in Gothic!' enthused Horace Walpole.[42] Carr's earliest church, St James, Ravenfield (pl. 185), with its fundamental components of rectangular body, polygonal chancel and hesitantly advancing west tower, its awkwardly distributed quatrefoil and Y-tracery windows, and its hint of classicism in the triangular pedimented frontispiece, shows no predilection for quarrying authentic medieval vocabulary, or even an awareness of John Hildyard's magisterial and exactly contemporary *An Accurate Description and History of the*

182 Architect unknown. Street elevation, Countess of Huntingdon's Connexion Chapel (now Building of Bath Museum), Bath, Somerset, 1765.

183 William and John Halfpenny. 'Elevation of a Design for a House' in W. Halfpenny, *Chinese and Gothic Architecture Properly Ornamented*, 1752, pl. 11, no. 1, detail. Engraving.

Metropolitan and Cathedral Churches of Canterbury and York (1755).[43] Nine years later Carr embarked on the largest, most accomplished of his gothic churches, All Saints, Dewsbury (pls 160, 186), a 'ruinous shaken decayed' structure of Saxon origin.[44] This involved removing the side walls to widen the body, re-erecting these and the west tower in a sedate gothic relying on the beauty of elegantly shaped ogee doors and mullion windows set in expanses of plain, sharply cut stonework.

More convincingly gothic, lying at the end of this transitional phase, is the work of James Bridges, active in Bristol between 1757 and 1763, and John Wing Jr, a member of a well-established East Midlands masonry dynasty. Neither was fond of relying on standard pattern books.

During the years 1758–61 Bridges remodelled ruinous medieval St Werburgh, Bristol (demolished 1878), which featured internal 'fluted Gothic . . . pillars and arches', the carpenter's contract specifying extensive reuse of 'old stuff . . . work'd up again, as far as shall Prove to be good & sound'.[45] Then he newly built St Nicholas (pl. 184), begun in 1762 and completed within five years, following his departure for the West Indies in 1763, by Thomas Paty, who described it as being 'in the plainest Manner, and upon the most frugal Plan'. A seven-bay rectangle with large, repetitive, Perpendicular windows – which Bridges enigmatically claimed he based on an unidentified '*Plan I saw executed, when on* my travels through . . . *Pensilvania*'[46] – it bears a strong resemblance to local medieval churches.[47] The church was an impressive stylistic achievement for its time, only the effete slenderness of the dividing buttress strips and the now-destroyed internal rococo plasterwork (Paty's contribution) betray its Georgian date.

184 James Bridges and Thomas Paty. North elevation, St Nicholas, Bristol, Somerset, 1760–67.

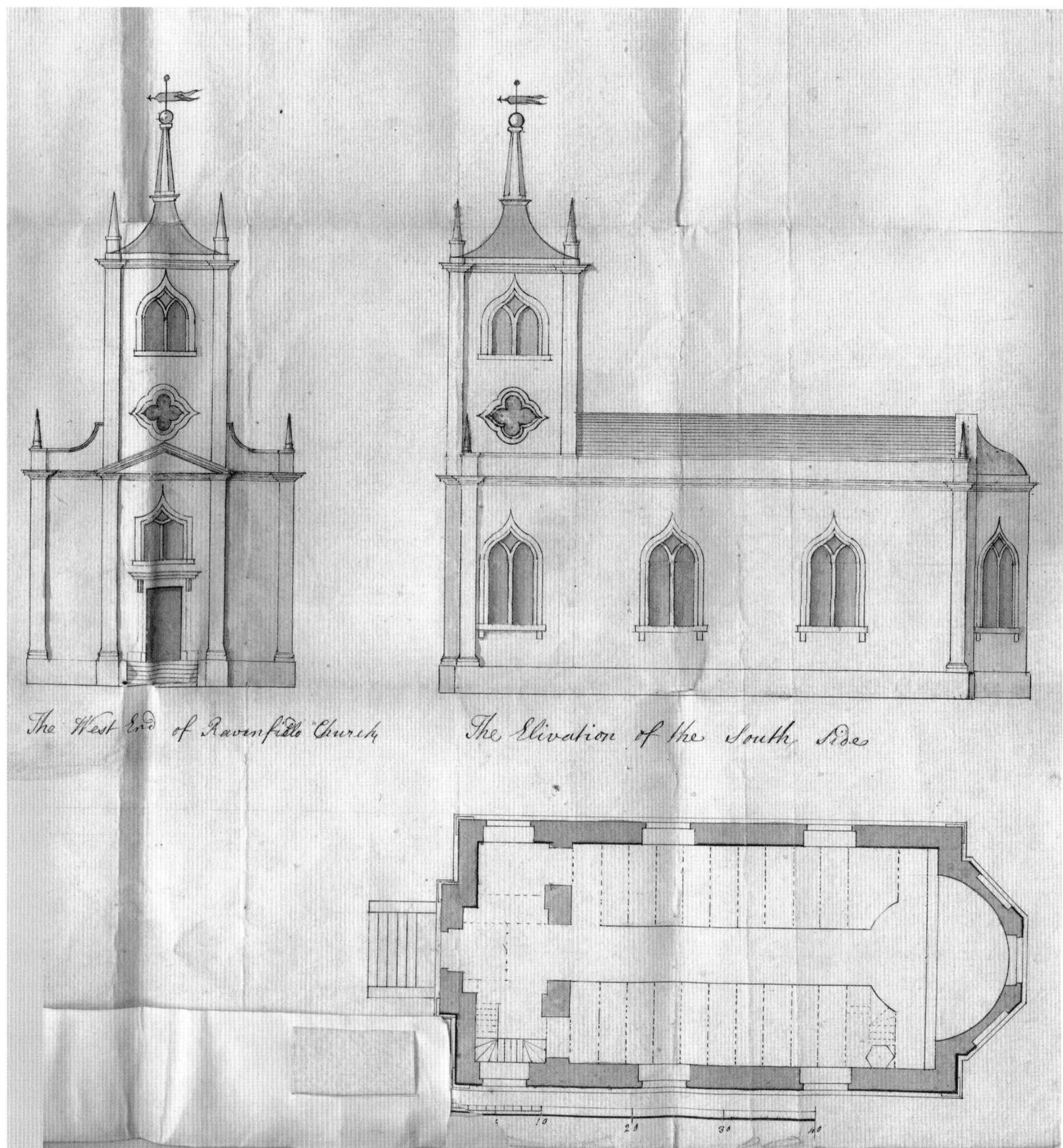

185 John Carr. Design for 'The West End of Ravenfield Church' (St. James) and 'The Elivation of the South Side', Yorkshire, 1755–56. Pen and ink and wash. Rotherham Metropolitan Borough Council, 63-B/8/1/5/37.

The repetitious window pattern of Wing's King's Norton, Leicestershire (pl. 187), is mitigated by a rich treatment of dividing buttresses and pinnacles tied at the parapet by bands of openwork quatrefoils of a type so admired at King's College chapel, Cambridge, and also employed by Keene at Hartwell (pl. 168). The flowing tracery of the central light of the east window derives from the chapter house vestibule at York.[48] Twin, ogee-headed bell openings, recorded in the architect's design for the 156-foot-high west tower, subscribe to familiar Perpendicular motifs,[49] while the lucarne spire (destroyed by lightning in 1850), with short buttresses flying from the corner pinnacles, recall Thaxted, Essex, which surely not coincidentally was undergoing

186 John Carr. North elevation detail, All Saints, Dewsbury, Yorkshire, 1764–66.

repairs in 1757.[50] King's Norton, despite Wing's or his client's unaccountable preference for wholly classical internal furnishings (pl. 188), was hailed as 'one of the compleatest churches . . . of its size [in the country], built in a very handsome manner of stone in the style of a Cathedral'.[51] Perhaps no other new rural church anticipated so convincingly the rising spirit of gothic authenticity that was emerging in the 1760s.

187 (*above right*) John Wing Sr. South-east view, St John Baptist, King's Norton, Leicestershire, 1757–61.

188 (*right*) John Wing Sr. Pulpit and desk, St John Baptist, King's Norton, Leicestershire, 1757–61.

189 Artist unknown. 'Chapel in the Garden at Strawberry Hill -Twickenham', Middlesex, *c.*1785. Pen and ink and watercolour. The Lewis Walpole Library, Yale University, 49.3678. John Chute, Thomas Gayfere Sr, architects, 1771–73.

Fifteen

A NEW SPIRIT OF 'TRUEST GOTHIC TASTE'

Bentham and Essex . . . were the first
who exhibited any thing like precision or true taste
in the restorations which they superintended or made[1]

Around mid-century two new ideas emerged to help propel ecclesiastical gothic into its next important phase. One entailed the (now discredited) systematising of its vocabulary along classical lines hinted at in 1742 by Batty Langley, who claimed that 'by strict Researches . . . I have discovered many of the Rules, by which [gothic's] principal Parts are proportioned and adorned [by which the] whole Result commands the *Admiration* and *Attention* of all Beholders'.[2] This eventually led in the early nineteenth century to a more careful identification of the different styles and their accurate chronology. The other, and practically more important, was recognition of the benefits of the pictorial sources produced by both professional and amateur artists that began to swamp the market, of which numerous examples appear in this book. This phase saw the emergence of a crucial player – Horace Walpole – and an iconic building – the Chapel in the Wood (sometimes called the Chapel in the Garden) at Strawberry Hill, his celebrated Twickenham villa (pl. 189).

Though Browne Willis observed of Francis Place's 'most accurate' views of York Minster (pl. 139) that 'every thing of this Church is so very magnificent, that it deserves a particular Representation; for Words cannot express the Beauty and Elegance of the Architecture',[3] a rapport between picture and text is demonstrable. Take the example of King's College chapel, Cambridge (pl. 190). Appreciation gradually shifted from uncritical wonderment – 'the finest building I have heard off'[4] – to enquiring stylistic and constructional analysis – 'the longest and largest Room, without Pillars to support its Roof, that, perhaps, is in the World [with] one continued Vault of Free-Stone, and the Stones prodigiously large, supported only by Buttresses without', 'amazing, not so much for the greatness of the work, though truly great, as for a lightness and elegancy beyond any Gothic structure in my knowledge', sometimes placing it in a wider European

190 William Stukeley. View of interior towards chancel of King's College Chapel, Cambridge, Cambridgeshire, undated. Engraving. The Bodleian Library, University of Oxford, 207E. Reginald Ely architect, 1446–1515.

context: the 'noblest and best piece of Gothic Architecture in the world except the great church at Milan', 'the Sainte Chapelle [in Paris] put me in Mind of our magnificent chapel of King's College'.[5] Thomas Sandby 'made a general sketch . . . for the use of the lectures he reads on architecture at the Royal Academy', where he served as the first Professor of Architecture. Françoise de la Rochefoucauld found it

> utterly beautiful; vast and raised to a prodigious height, the vault is borne aloft solely by the two side-walls and without the aid of a single pillar, which is perhaps unique for this type of building . . . a most difficult feat of construction [while the roof] timber-work . . . is prodigiously light and admired by the experts who come to see it from afar.[6]

John Soane, in *Plans Elevations and Sections of Buildings* (1788), characterised gothic architecture not as 'those barbarous jumbles of undefined forms in modern imitations . . . but the light and elegant examples in many of our cathedrals, [and] churches . . . which are so well calculated to excite solemn, serious and contemplative ideas, that it is almost impossible to enter such edifices without feeling the deepest awe and reverence', and he described King's as 'a glorious example of the wonderful perfection of Gothic architecture; there is a boldness and mathematical knowledge peculiar to this edifice, which claims our earnest attention and admiration, which excites us to the pursuit of geometrical knowledge, and reminds us of the high opinion the ancients had of geometry'. In the last years of the century William Wilkins Jr prepared 'the most accurate drawings [showing] measurements of every part . . . externally and internally' and devoted much time 'in the study of the principals of its construction'.[7]

One of the avowed aims of the Society of Antiquaries of London was 'to collect and print . . . at their own charge . . . all Accounts of antient Monuments that come to their hands, whether Ecclesiastical or Civil [including] abbeys, churches and whatever may properly belong to the History of Brittish Antiquitys'.[8] It also sponsored the series entitled *Vetusta Monumenta*, published in seven volumes from 1748, and in 1792 launched a programme of commissioning accurately rendered drawings 'of the different Cathedrals and other religious Houses in the Kingdom' from the talented draughtsman John Carter.[9] A Society member, the Lincolnshire antiquary William Stukeley produced charmingly naive drawings and engravings of medieval churches for publication in *Itinerarium Curiosum; or, An Account of the Antiquities, and Remarkable Curiosities in Nature or Art, Observed in Travels Through Great Britain* (1724, 2nd edn, 1776). Later there were Thomas Lyus, Francis Grosse and Samuel Hieronymus Grimm (pls 42, 44a–b, 116, 162), and J. M. W. Turner (pls 205, 254).[10]

Browne Willis's three-volume *Survey of the Cathedrals*, devoted to Bangor, Llandaff, St Asaph and St David in Wales (1717–21), York, Durham, Carlisle, Chester, Man, Lichfield. Hereford, Worcester, Gloucester and Bristol (1727), and Lincoln, Ely, Oxford and Peterborough (1730), are each illustrated with 'Curious Draughts . . . newly taken to rectify the erroneous Representations' in Sir William Dugdale's *Monasticon Anglicanum* (1655–73) and 'other Authors'.[11] They arose from Willis's 'zeal . . . to have the Antiquities' of Lincoln Cathedral, his own diocese, published when 'no one else would attempt it'. Though Hereford was 'meanly engraven', 'the Pinnacle-work' on Gloucester tower 'not sufficiently expressive of the Beauty and Tenderness of the Original' and Bristol 'not put in good Perspective', nevertheless he believed 'the Architecture will be sufficiently understood, and these Draughts being done in a more exact Manner than any of the common Prints, which they will be found in several respects to differ from, and to excel'.[12] These set precedents for publications such as Robert West's and William Henry Toms's two-volume *Perspective Views of all the Ancient Churches, and other Buildings, In the Cities of London, and Westminster, and Parts adjacent* (1736–9), which dealt with pre-Fire survivals and incorporated brief histories within each plate.[13]

In the Revd John Dart's *Westmonasterium; or, The history and Antiquities of The Abbey Church of St Peters Westminster* (1723), the images are almost exclusively devoted to tombs (pls 166, 176), but his companion *The History and Antiquities of The Cathedral Church of Canterbury* (1726) was supplemented with 'other Things remarkable', including a detailed survey of the fabric and a history based on original, cited documents together with 'several Prospects . . . Engraven by the Best Hands' (pls 209, 275), the first presented in large format. Here he stressed the fabric's 'venerable Grandeur . . . striking a distant Awe upon the Beholder', the 'lofty and curious . . . Middle-Tower [which] has a very majestick and noble Appearance . . . curiously Carv'd . . . and well enlighten'd with stately Windows'; 'Entring the Church, we are suddenly struck after an awful and solemn manner, at the Grandeur and Spaciousness of the . . . Nave', the 'Cross-Isle of the same Age or somewhat older then the Nave', while the 'beautiful . . . Choir . . . though . . . now 600 Years [old] shews no sign of decay, but is majestically Noble' and so on.[14] The book attracted 397 subscribers, including the archbishops of Canterbury and York and twenty-four bishops whose cathedrals were to undergo restoration during the century, as well as such luminaries as Christopher Wren Jr (then compiling *Parentalia*), Roger Gale, John Talman and Edward Stanton, master mason to Westminster Abbey. Each subscriber was designated by name and coat of arms, a clever promotional ploy. In *Academia Tertia Anglicana; or, The Antiquarian Annals of Stamford* (1727), the Revd Francis Peck, citing 'several [churches] which I have seen in draughts', professed ignorance of their architectural niceties yet commented that it

> may be said for some Gothic buildings, that they abound with as much variety, & some times strike the eye as agreeably, as the finest pieces of the more regular [classical] orders. Thus, if we consider the best buildings we have of this kind in England, there is something vastly great & magnificent, & something also vastly beautiful in the composure . . .

exemplified by the internally 'neat structure with pillars' of Westminster Abbey and the Temple Church in London and of Lincoln Cathedral. 'Some think their beautiful, taper, pillars far exceed the modern bulky supporters of [Wren's] S. Pauls, which . . . have little else but the fluting & capitals of the Corinthian order to recommend them'; of 'a structure without pillars, nothing hardly equals Kings college chapel in Cambridge'. Parish churches 'were often built *very like,* & always *something like* one another', though each 'had something peculiar in the way of architecture'.[15] On a popular level gothic churches featured regularly in the *Gentleman's Magazine* from its inception in 1731. The issue of June 1789, for example, published a vignette of what 'Murtagh McWhiskey' claimed was the first view of the west front of St Patrick, Dublin, 'ever given to the publick . . . unless locked up in some great gentleman's study'.[16] More interestingly, it devoted increasingly more space to French examples, particularly less well-known buildings.[17]

This was symptomatic of a general British enthusiasm for Continental gothic and awareness of its promotion especially by French theorists, most notably Abbé de Cordemoy's *Traité d'Architecture* (1714) and Marc-Antoine Laugier's *Essai sur l'Architecture* (1753).[18] In 1710 John Talman, having himself previously recorded such buildings in Italy, pressed a Florentine contact to send 'the finished view of Santa Croce . . . done exactly'.[19] In 1749 the Revd Jeremiah Milles (later President of the Society of Antiquaries of London) showed his fellow members 'a very noble Design in Gothick Architecture made for the West-end of the Cathedral Church of Cologne . . . but never put in execution'.[20] Already attracted to European gothic, in 1739 in Paris Horace Walpole concluded that Saint Denis 'excels Westminster; for the windows are all painted in mosaic', then in 1766 he visited the Sainte-Chapelle, which 'answered my expectations'.[21] By the time Edward Dewes progressed on the Grand Tour in 1776 he felt comfortable in devoting as much attention to medieval buildings as classical ones: St Bavo, Ghent, was 'the finest church I ever saw: The greatest part of the inside done with marble', the cathedrals of Cologne, 'not yet finish'd . . . a good deal the look of Gloucester', Metz, 'a noble piece of building, tho more curious withoutside than within . . . very lofty, not extraordinary fine [but with] fine painted glass', Strasbourg, 'very lofty . . . the outside is the most curious, particularly the spire is very fine . . . all open & carved up to the top', Paris, 'the outside very full of images . . . the inside large & lofty'. Above all Milan (pl. 330):

> I thought no church could come up to Ghend but now it puzells me to tell which is the neatest . . . the finest & largest building ever seen . . . walk'd up to the top . . . which is the greatest curiosity of all, the highest spire was finish'd but last year with a brazen [bronze] image at the top representing the Virgin Mary . . . it is not only the beauties of the pinacles which are worth going 100 miles to see . . . returnd home expecting never to see such another building after I leave Milan.[22]

Perhaps most significantly, the supremacy of the great English cathedrals within the gothic hierarchy was reaffirmed by mid-century. *Parentalia* (1750) included Wren's account of pre-Fire medieval St Paul's, identifying its chapter house as 'of a more elegant *Gothick* Manner' than the body, which featured 'the usual Proportion of Spires in *Gothick* Fabricks', together with the text of Wren's survey of Salisbury of 1668, 'justly esteemed one of the best Patterns of *Gothick-building*', with a detailed critical structural analysis, as well as his Westminster Abbey report of 1713, in both cases accompanied by illustrations.[23] The Salisbury report was republished in Francis Price's *A Series of particular and useful Observations, Made with great Diligence and Care, upon that Admirable Structure, The Cathedral-Church of Salisbury* (1753), together with Price's own assessment of the fabric supported by thirteen engravings prepared by the author between 1738 and 1748 and entrusted to the excellent London-based French engraver Paul Fourdrinier, whose work Vertue admired for 'neatness & beauty' (pls 124, 143, 222).[24] It attracted 294 subscribers and marked the first serious attempt to describe and analyse the structure of a major gothic building.[25]

Henceforth the promotion of gothic became the providence of mainstream non-architectural literature. In *The Analysis of Beauty* (1753), William Hogarth observed:

> there is . . . such a consistency of parts altogether in a good gothic taste, and such propriety relative to the gloomy ideas, they were then calculated to convey, that they have at length acquired an establish'd and distinct character in building. It would be look'd upon as an impropriety and as a kind of profanation to build places of mirth and entertainment in the same taste.[26]

The 1762 edition of Defoe's *A Tour Through the Whole Island of Great Britain* included a structural appreciation of '*Gothic* Architecture' that had not featured in earlier editions. This

> admits of an extravagant Airiness and Lightness. In that Sort of Building the Designer is bound down to no Rules of Proportion but what his own Fancy suggests; whereas, in the other [classicism], Dimensions so universally followed, cannot be deviated from . . . But where is that Exactness observed in any *Gothic* Structure? It must be allowed, there are some of those Buildings, that, in the Whole, look very august and venerable. Yet, let any one view the vast Buttresses round the Outside of *Westminster-Abbey*, and see what a Croud of Lines and Breaks they occasion in the Perspective, and they will then easily account for the Lightness of the Inside of that Church; for those Buttresses, by extending so far out, support the whole Structure, more than its Walls or Pillars.[27]

This is a refutation of the Langleyian view that opened this chapter. The public edition of *A Description of the Villa . . . At Strawberry Hill* (1784), distinct from its earlier manifestation as a visitors' guide, was intended as a vehicle for 'exhibiting specimens of Gothic architecture, as collected from standards in cathedrals and chapel-tombs . . . shewing how they may be applied to chimney-pieces, ceilings, windows, balustrades, loggias, &c. The general disuse of Gothic architecture, and the decay and alterations so frequently made in churches', Walpole reckoned, 'give prints a chance of being the sole preservatives of that style.'[28] It is with this rich visual and written tradition that we may now turn to the seminal contributions of Walpole and his circle.

In the early 1750s Horace began altering and enlarging his recently acquired, nondescript residence at Twickenham on the Thames, progressing from Langleyian to authentic gothic in what would become two decades later the celebrated villa of Strawberry Hill. Its crucial feature was the domestication of ecclesiastical motifs.[29] Walpole turned for advice to two knowledgeable friends: the antiquary Richard Bentley and John Chute. In 1752 Bentley had fashioned a 'fictitious steeple' for Nicholas Hardinge (died 1758) of Kingston upon Thames (pl. 191). An unrealised spired octagon with cusped arches, quatrefoils, mouchettes and crocketed pinnacles rising from a flying-buttressed base, it was almost certainly intended to replace the dour gothic tower over the crossing of the medieval parish church erected in 1708 to a design by John Yeomans

191 Richard Bentley. 'Design for a fictitious steeple for Nich. Harding Esr at Kingston', All Saints, Kingston-upon-Thames, Surrey, 1752. Pen and ink and wash. The Lewis Walpole Library, Yale University, Bentley Album 40.

192 James Peller Malcolm. South-east view with John Yeoman's 1708 crossing tower, All Saints, Kingston-upon-Thames, Surrey, September 1798, in Manning and Bray, vol. 1, 1804, facing p. 369, detail. Engraving.

promoted by the vicar, Gideon Hardinge, probably Nicholas's father (pl. 192).[30]

In 1754 Walpole initiated the remodelling of the old chapel at The Vyne, the Hampshire Tudor mansion recently inherited by his other collaborator, John Chute, 'an Exquisite Architect . . . of the purest taste both in the Grecian & Gothic styles'.[31] In the following year Walpole wrote of 'the most heavenly chapel in the world', with an

> Antichapel. To be finish'd as the End is . . . Windows . . . painted . . . with the pedigree. The Chapel [with] 3 pictures under the Windows, of the Lord's Supper, Christ in the Garden & Christ walking on the Sea. The 4 Evangelists in the long pannels on each side. A rich purple & silver altar cloth, with handsome old embossed plate. A brass Eagle for a reading desk. The walls above . . . painted in a Gothic pattern: & a Closet with a Screen in the same Pattern.[32]

In 1756 a mutual friend, the poet Thomas Gray, asked Walpole to bring down on his next visit a print of the fifteenth-century St George's Chapel, Windsor, in preparation for creating the adjacent Tomb Chamber. When Chute rejected Bentley's columbarium scheme, with features inspired by Langley's *Gothic Architecture, Improved* (1747), the frustrated Walpole was 'done advising [because he] will never do anything'.[33] Subsequently, the Greek-born painter Spiridone Roma supplied a magnificent pair of large *trompe-l'œil* canvases for the chapel's upper south and north walls (pl. 193), depicting arcades, windows and fan vaulting based on Gloucester Cathedral cloisters. Thomas Carter Jr, perhaps reflecting Chute's intentions, carved the exquisite white marble effigy of Chaloner Chute (died 1659), who is posed reclining on a neoclassical tomb chest embellished with fluted Ionic columns and coats of arms in cartouches, an intriguing amalgam of various seventeenth-century English sepulchral sources probably supplied by the learned client (pl. 194).[34] It is illuminated by John Rowell's vibrantly coloured painted glass (1730–31) depicting the *Adoration of the Magi* after Van Dyck, which Chute acquired in 1756. A later visitor praised the 'very handsome anti-chapel, of wainscot, studded . . . with gold, and carved with delicate gothic ornaments', and the chapel 'glazed with most rich painted glass in compleat preservation . . . The seats . . . carved into many very grotesque forms . . . is so beautiful, that I feel my inability to do it justice', the Tomb Chamber 'door and wainscot . . . ornamented with very delicate gothic carve-work . . . more beautiful in its kind, than any thing I have ever the fortune of seeing'.[35]

Having already created a small gothic oratory within the Twickenham villa, in 1768 Walpole commissioned Chute to design the octagonal Chapel in the Woods on the estate's perimeter, with blue and gilt fan vaulting, to which Thomas Gayfere Sr, master mason at Westminster Abbey, contributed an exquisitely detailed Portland stone front (pl. 189) copied from the left-hand section of the early sixteenth-century Bishop Audley's chantry chapel in Salisbury Cathedral (pl. 195).[36] This was apparently the first Georgian example of a freestanding building quoting a medieval structure verbatim, though its novelty goes far beyond this pioneer expression of eighteenth-century antiquarianism. Walpole had conceived the chapel not only as a place of religious meditation but also as a repository of 'valuable pieces of antiquity'. In 1771 he reported to William Cole, a member of his 'Committee of Taste', of his acquisitions of a medieval painted window with portraits of Henry III and his queen from Bexhill, Sussex, 'a magnificent shrine' to the early Christian martyrs Simplicius, Faustina and Beatrix, and the so-called shrine of Capoccio (1256), procured from Santa Maria Maggiore in Rome with the assistance of William Hamilton, which held special fascination since the recipient believed it to be the work of one Peter Cavalini and that he had also fashioned Edward the

193 Spiridione Roma. Painted decoration on north wall of chapel, The Vyne, Hampshire, 1769–71. Oil on canvas. The National Trust.

Confessor's shrine in Westminster Abbey. During the years 1772–4 Walpole added Donatello's head of *St John the Baptist*, a present from his friend Sir Horace Mann, the British resident in Florence, together with an altarpiece in the style of the Carracci pillaged from St Edmundsbury, Suffolk, a crucifix inlaid with mother-of-pearl bought at the Richard Bateman sale in 1774, a bronze crucifix and a faience statue of an 'ancient king of France', among other artefacts. Walpole found it 'very extraordinary . . . I should happen to be master of these curiosities', which gave the interior a 'genuine air of antiquity' and, quoting Milton's *Paradise Lost*, thought it 'more gorgeous than the spoils Of Ormus and Ind'.[37] Perhaps he was inspired by the celebrated example of Vespasian's Temple of Peace in Rome (AD 71–5, destroyed in antiquity and mistakenly associated by Palladio with the adjacent Basilica of Maxentius/Constantine), described in *I quattro libri d'architettura* as the place where the emperor 'preserved all the vessels, and ornaments . . . of the temple of *Jerusalem*', spoils of the city destroyed by his son Titus.[38] In the process of achieving antiquarian authenticity, however, Walpole was not above butchering the Carracci altarpiece by sawing it into panels to 'aptly accompany the shrine'. Nevertheless, he hailed the chapel as 'exquisitely performed in the truest Gothic taste'.[39] The interior also owes much to Henry Keene's earlier Hartwell House chapel (pls 168–70).

194 Thomas Carter Jr. Monument to Chaloner Chute, marble, 1775–81, John Rowell, *Adoration of the Magi*, enamel paint on glass, in Tomb Chamber, The Vyne, Hampshire, 1730–31. English Heritage (National Monuments Record, BB70/07139).

To this group of mid-eighteenth-century endeavours also belongs an unsigned, undated and not to say puzzling plan for a new gothic church at Glynde, Sussex (pl. 196), for Richard Trevor, Bishop of Durham, proposed by his brother, Robert Hampden Trevor, an amateur architect with political affinities to the Walpoles. The design must date before Sir Thomas Robinson's Palladian offering was approved in 1763 (pl. 536).[40] The plan is a coaxial, multi-vista complex measuring overall 70 by 85 feet composed of seven inter-

195 Chantrey Chapel of Bishop Audley (d. 1524), Salisbury Cathedral, Wiltshire. English Heritage (National Monuments Record, BB71/03286).

locking, sexpartite-vaulted hexagonal chambers, the outer ring illuminated by three-light windows, approached through a projecting porch-cum-bell-tower aligned to the railed high altar. With no further evidence of the circumstances of its making or the elevational treatment of this unorthodox creation, unprecedented in British architecture, one may speculate that it has an origin in the gotho-baroque Nieuwe Kerk (1649–56) in The Hague, where R. H. Trevor served in various senior political offices between 1734 and 1746.[41] Glynde also calls to mind the layout of the eastern sanctuary and its surrounding chapels at Westminster Abbey, though now treated as a free-standing structure. Pertinently, in 1734 James Ralph had suggested, admittedly with no prospect of realisation, demolishing adjacent St Margaret's parish church in order to bring Henry VII's 'fine chapel [lying beyond the sanctuary] . . . in to play . . . as one of the most expensive remains of the ancient *English* taste and magnificence', having it 'entirely detach'd from the *Abbey* . . . with a sumptuous front' added to the east end facing Old Palace Yard and the Houses of Parliament.[42]

John Hobcraft, a London carpenter and builder who was Chute's assistant at gothic Donnington Grove, Berkshire, and Robert Adam's at Croome D'Abitot (pl. 177), independently fitted out the exquisite country chapel at Audley End, Essex, with 'clustered columns, pointed arches, and fan groined tracery . . . in imitation of a cathedral' (pl. 197).[43] The rectangular, arcaded body, 51 by 27 by 21 feet high, with the Griffin family pew at one end, faces towards the chancel illuminated by William Peckitt's 100-foot-square, vividly coloured window depicting the *Last Supper* (pl. 198). A broader, higher, central area housing a raised chair (copied from Adam's at Croome) (pl. 197a) and lectern overlooked a transept-like recess lit by Peckitt's *Offering of the Eastern Magi* (later removed and lost). The fan vaulting of the west end derives from Gloucester Cathedral cloisters, which, as we have seen, Roma also made splendid use of at The Vyne (pl. 193). Delicate Perpendicular plasterwork proliferates. Hobcraft's room is perhaps a reflection of the fifteenth-century gatehouse of St John's Abbey, Colchester, Essex, the subject of an

196 Robert Hampden Trevor. 'A Plan for Glynde Church', Sussex, detail, undated. Pen and ink and wash. RIBA Library Drawings Collection, G3/49.

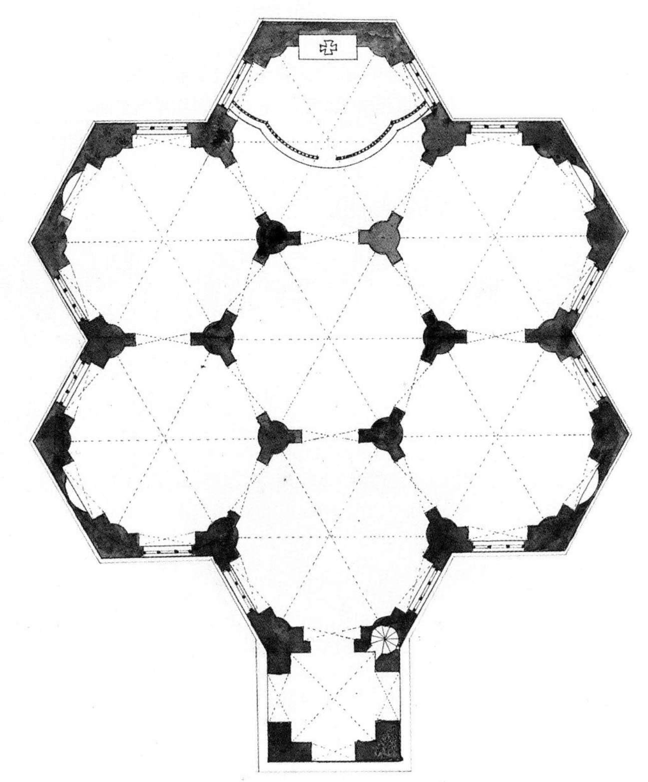

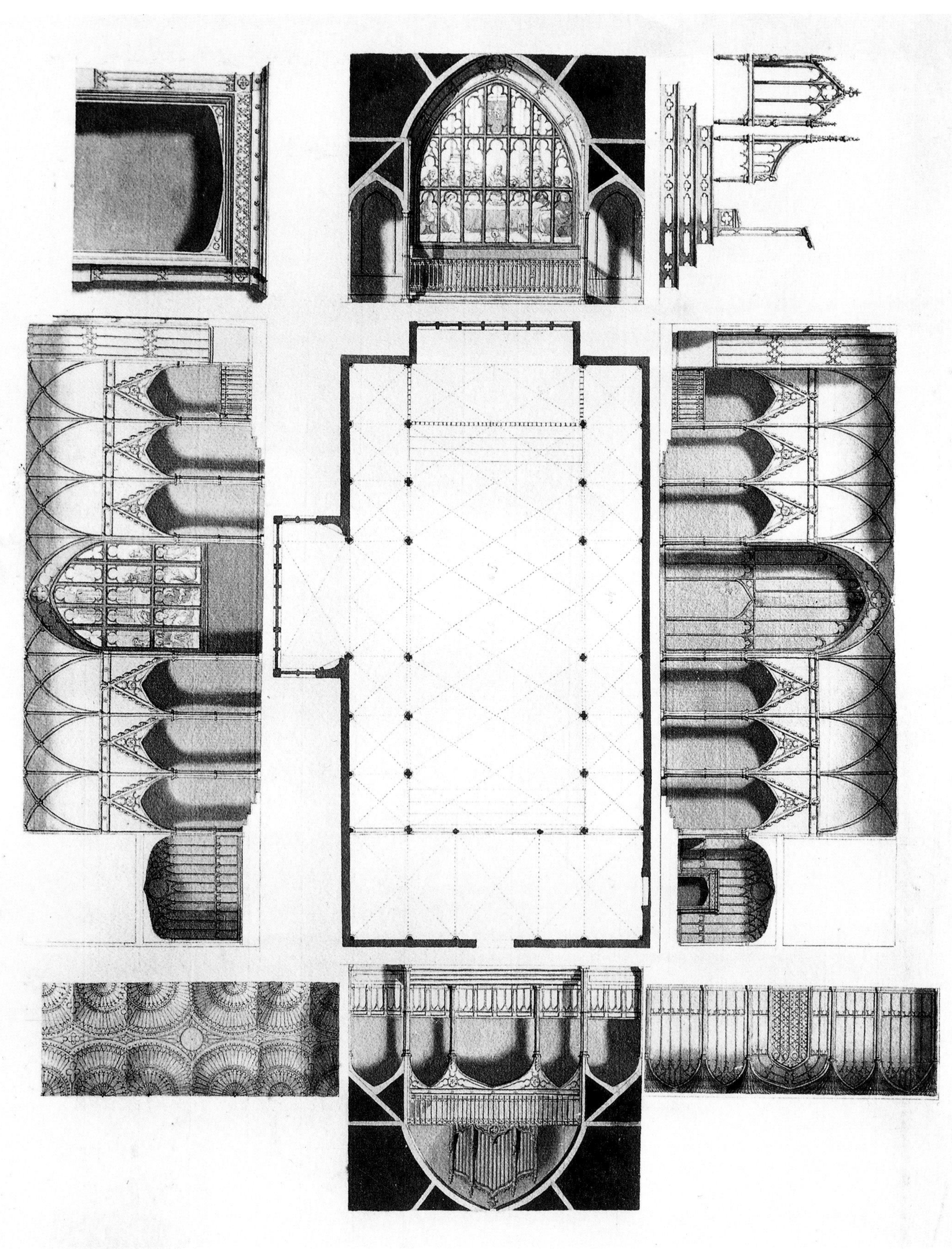

197 John Hobcroft. Plan, elevation, sections design for Audley End chapel, Essex, 1768. Pen and ink and wash. English Heritage (National Monuments Record, AL 0515/002/01).

197a John Hobcroft. Plan, elevation, sections design for Audley End chapel, Essex, detail of pl. 197, showing the raised chair.

engraving promoted by the Society of Antiquaries and published in 1768, the very year he began work at Audley End.[44]

Though Cole's claim that the chapel's designer was the Cambridge joiner James Essex, who had 'as Stedy good Hands, as Aney In England',[45] and who was employed as a craftsmen at Audley End, cannot be sustained by the documents, it was Essex's decisive role as architect at King's College chapel, Cambridge, and the cathedrals at Ely and Lincoln that confirms him as the real hero of this coming of age of Georgian church gothic.

The exploitation of authentic gothic for churches reached its first hiatus with the publication in 1771 of

198 (*below*) John Hobcroft. View towards communion table with William Peckitt, *The Last Supper*, enamel paint on glass, Audley End chapel, Essex, 1770–71. English Heritage (National Monuments Record, J880/77)

the *History and Antiquities of the Conventual and Cathedral Church of Ely From the Foundation of the Monastery, A.D. 673 To the Year 1771* by James Bentham, a former minor canon there and Fellow of the Society of Antiquaries. It includes his reflections on 'the particular modes of Building used . . . the state of Architecture at different periods [and] the History of what is called Gothic Architecture in this Kingdom; its origin [and] progress [employing] a variety of ancient Charters, and other authentic Writings [which] must afford an agreeable and useful entertainment to every curious and inquisitive mind'. Bentham argued that there 'is not perhaps, any one Fabrick in this Kingdom that exhibits a larger, more elegant, or a more magnificent display of what is called *Gothic* Architecture . . . or what will better illustrate the History of this kind of Building in England'. He believed that

> These things, if set in their proper light, might afford matter sufficient for a whole Volume: and it would be a subject well worth the attention of an Antiquarian, to investigate the Origin and Progress of Architecture in our Country; to note the various Modes of Building in different Ages; to observe the transitions from one Style to another; and the gradual advances towards Perfection, from examples that are still remaining.[46]

While the text in fact largely deals with the Saxon and Norman fabrics, most of the splendid engravings are devoted to gothic portions of the building. Bentham was assisted by a formidable triumvirate comprising Essex, Cole and Gray, all three based in Cambridge. To make the circle complete, in a letter to Gray of 1769, Walpole (who employed Essex at Strawberry Hill from 1776) advised giving 'a series of plates . . . from the conclusion of Saxon architecture . . . till the beautiful Gothic was arrived at its perfection; then how it decreased in Henry the Eight's reign' (with the arrival of the renaissance). Cole himself would 'ascertain the chronological period of each building . . . for you know the great delicacy and richness of Gothic ornaments was exhausted on small chapels, oratories and tombs' (the concept behind the Chapel in the Woods, pl. 189). 'For my own part', Walpole went on,

> I should wish to have added detached samples of the various patterns of ornaments, which would not be a great many, as excepting pinnacles, there is scarce one which does not branch from the trefoil; quatrefoil, cinquefoil, etc. being but various modifications of it. I believe almost all the ramifications of windows are so: and of them there should be samples too.

This section did not make its way into the publication.

Most telling in Walpole's 1769 letter is his judgement of Essex's contribution of 'observations on the art, proportions and methods of building, and the reasons deserved by Gothic architects for what they did. This would show what great men they were, and how they raised such aerial or stupendous masses, though unassisted by half the lights now enjoyed by their successors'; this Essex 'can do better than anybody, and is perhaps the only person who can do it'.[47] He was the most authoritative and sensitive of the later generation of Georgian gothicists and the leading cathedral restorer of the age. Colvin (confirming Walpole's opinion) has rightly observed that

> it is as a Gothic architect that he is chiefly remarkable: for, unlike his contemporaries, who regarded Gothic merely as a decorative style . . . Essex fully appreciated its structural character and had an archaeologist's knowledge of its detail. He was, in fact, the first practising architect to take an antiquarian interest in medieval architecture, and his knowledge of Gothic construction remained unique until the ecclesiological movement of the early nineteenth century . . . At Ely and Lincoln he carried out technically skilful and for the most part aesthetically judicious restorations in a manner that was unique in the eighteenth century.[48]

Nor was he indiscriminately reverential towards gothic: 'we are not to imagine everything done in the past was good architecture any more than in the present age'; he had no time for

> the ridiculous imitations frequently made by our modern builders, who, mistaking the principles of pure architecture, think they have produced something in the Gothic style when they have collected together a jumble of discordant parts of old buildings which have no relation to each other and support a string of pointed arches by a row of broom-sticks instead of pillars.[49]

This was surely a disguised assault on Langley and his minions, and demonstrated a genuine understanding of medieval structures: 'As the Gothic Architects endeavoured, in all their Works, to surprise by an apparent weakness, so they often made them weak in Reality, when they only intended them to be so in Appearance.' Essex was also undoctrinaire:

> In Repairing . . . Ornaments . . . some regard should be had to . . . Uniformity of . . . work . . . but it is not necessary to restore every ornamt that is broken, for as there generally is a Superfluity of ornament in Gothic Architecture . . . uniformity will often be

better preserv'd by takg: away a remaing: part, than by restorg: that which was lost, and this may be done sometimes without offence to the most Judicious Eye. and very often it will be an improvement to the beauty of the work rather than a defect, so that by observg: this rule much time & expence may be saved in beautifying . . . for when the proportions of the parts are just the ornaments will never be missed, & when they are not, too great a profusion of ornaments will disgust the admirers of Simplicity & proportion without concealg: the want of it.[50]

Yet, almost Pugin-like, he strove to think into the mind of the medieval builder: restoring Lincoln's great crossing tower 'as near as I could agreeable to the Ideas of the Architect who built [it, and] tracing the original state of [the internal west end] and if possible restore it to the state which the builders intended it'.[51] Above all, Essex was, in the words of Cole in a letter to Walpole, committed to the exclusivity of gothic rather than 'the motley manner of those usually given for Gothic even by some of the best modern architects'[52] – hardly a disguised condemnation of the Adam brothers, at that time Essex's rivals in the commission for designing a new altarpiece in King's College chapel, who predictably submitted alternative gothic and classical schemes, as we shall see in chapter 17.

This was Essex's first such foray, one of the pivotal episodes in his deft manipulation to establish an authentic approach to interpreting a contemporary church gothic. Though a circuitous, protracted history, it is particularly instructive for being so well documented and of such special concern to Walpole and his circle, at the completion of which the distinguished medievalist confessed that Essex's achievement was 'more beautiful than Strawberry Hill [and] penetrated me with a visionary longing to be a monk' in the chapel.[53] Despite universal admiration for King's as 'one of the finest buildings in Europe . . . after the Gothick manner', criticism was levelled at the 'meanness of the [old] altar-piece . . . only a little wooden screne wth 2 or three strips of silk [erected in 1633, which] takes of very much from its beauty'. This had prompted the College provost in 1709 to bequest £150 towards a replacement, topped up in 1718 to £304 and reaching £1,000 by 1742.[54] In 1756 Essex launched a campaign of recording the chapel (the College was his Alma Mater) in measured drawings for publication (perhaps inspired by Francis Price's book of 1753 on Salisbury Cathedral, to which Essex's mentor, the distinguished Cambridge architect Sir James Burrough, subscribed), which never materialised. In 1759 he drew, and perhaps also contributed to, Burrough's design for a new altarpiece. The latter recommended construction in either wood or stone 'corresponding to the rest of the Chapel'. The College agent took the schemes, which included gothic and classical alternatives, to London to solicit observations from 'competent Judges', all of whom favoured the use of stone and agreed that it 'must be in the Gothick Style'. James 'Athenian' Stuart was 'particularly . . . of this Opinion', remarkable since 'he is well known to disapprove entirely of the present fashionable Taste for Gothic Architecture'. Charles Lyttelton, Dean of Exeter, who had spent several days at King's in 1757 'viewing the wonderful piece of Gothick Architecture', had consulted his friend and 'exceeding good Judge' Sanderson Miller.[55] They concluded that the 'Beauty of the Altarpiece should consist in . . . Plainness & Simplicity' and while not excluding 'all . . . Ornament [should] avoid all Gilding & Finery', of which Burrough proposed 'to have a great deal [but] which every Body condemns'. Indeed, 'among the several Gentlemen & Artists [the agent] talked with . . . don't find One who entirely approves of it'. Miller 'thinks [it] will admit . . . Alterations' and recommended smaller turrets and a 'Break . . . rather than a strait Line through the whole Length'. Everyone enquired whether the College was 'tied down to this Plan' and suggested that it would be better to solicit designs from 'Architects of the most approved Taste now in England . . . since private Regards ought always to give way to a Matter of Public Concern'. Ironically, Stuart was regarded as the 'ablest Person',[56] and pertinently in 1771 he was to produce a heroic gothic design for the east end of St George's Chapel, Windsor (pl. 259).

One of the first to reap the rewards of this debate was Lyttelton, who on his elevation to the bishopric of Carlisle in 1764 initiated a similar regime of improvement to the cathedral's faded choir under the direction of his nephew, Thomas Pitt (later 1st Baron Camelford), an amateur architect educated at Clare College, Cambridge (1754–9), who from 1762 was Walpole's Twickenham neighbour and friend. Horace recommended him as able to 'sketch the Gothic part . . . better than anyone'.[57] Completed in 1765, with the detailing of the wooden screen and railing tamely repetitive (pl. 199), it was the earliest realised Georgian gothic altar in an English cathedral.[58]

By 1765 Essex's own altarpiece offering was well received by the College authorities, but his £1,500 building estimate, which specified using stone, was considered too costly, and Stuart remained an option for producing a 'new plan – that we may have His Judgment and Character for knowledge in such things,

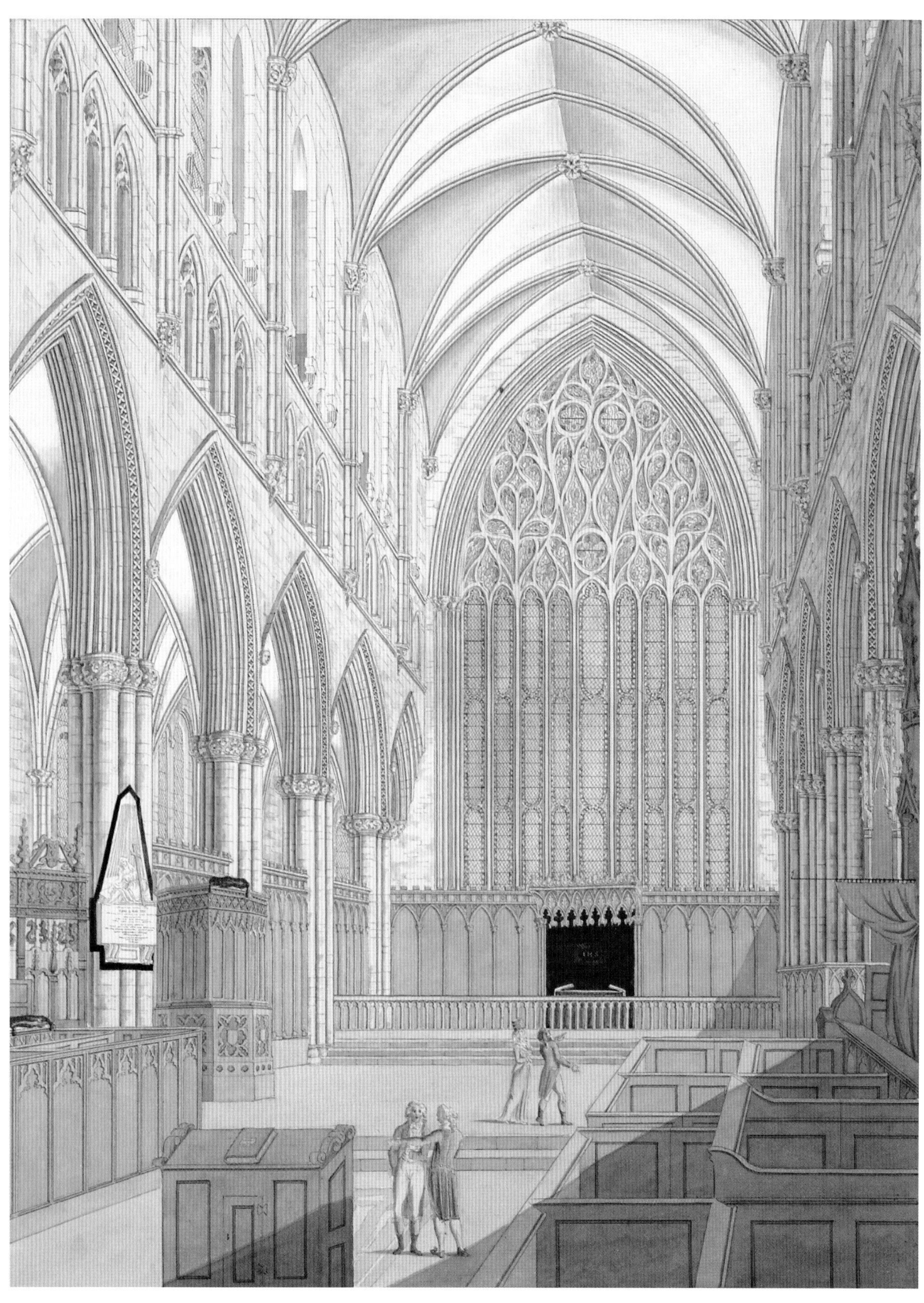

199 Robert Carlyle Sr. 'The Choir of Carlisle Cathedral', Cumberland, 1792. Watercolour. Tullie House, Carlisle, CALMG: 1970.80.2. Thomas Pitt's refurbishment, 1765, dismantled 1856.

– to justify us to the World'.[59] The story then briefly took an unexpected turn with the appearance of James Adam, who submitted contrasting gothic and classical schemes (1767–70), more appropriately described in chapter 17, and it was not until Essex's revised design was approved in 1770 that work began in earnest. Cole remarked on 'how able [the architect is] to have the whole management of it', and to Walpole that Essex's 'love of Gothic architecture . . . will thrive well in his hands'.[60] This scheme (pl. 200) was more subdued and low lying than either Burrough's or Adam's, complying with the College's obstinate requirement of exposing the whole of the stained-glass east window. It is not far removed from the Carlisle altarpiece (pl. 199), though more vigorously detailed, as revealed in the mason's bill of 1775.[61] The result was triumphant: 'so justly esteemed by connoisseurs [for] corresponding to the simplicity and magnificence of the building . . . a most perfect monument of Gothic architecture', crowed the *Cambridge Chronicle* on 25 March 1775.

Meanwhile, Cole was encouraging the promotion of Essex's history of gothic architecture, in abeyance since 1756, which lamented that no style was 'so little observed, and less understood . . . though it is not by any means so barbarous and inelegant as is generally supposed [nor] deserve so much ridicule as the present Age are pleased to bestow upon them', recommending that 'some time must be spent in measuring their parts comparing them with each other'.[62] These ideas were to bear fruit in his great improvement programmes at Ely and Lincoln, the first cathedrals to undergo more than cursory internal alterations. The affiliation between these activities is manifest in a report of 1759 concerning Burrough's King's altarpiece in which Essex is mentioned as having 'just planned an Altarpiece for . . . Lincoln'.[63]

Soaring above its lofty hilltop, Romano-gothic Lincoln received a mixed critical reception during the eighteenth century (pl. 157). Stukeley, Willis, Burlington and Walpole gave unqualified praise; others worried about its lack of internal beauty and decrepit condition, what one guidebook called its 'wrinkled Majesty'.[64] The fabric's welfare was in Essex's authoritative hands from 1755 to his death in 1784 and, thus, represents a microcosm of his achievements as the paramount gothicist. He began by recommending spending £15,000 on various repairs and a programme to 'beautify the Inside . . . by dressing, Cleaning and new polishing the Walls, Columns, and Arches'. By 1766 he had created a new choir enclosure, executed by a virtuoso Nonconformist stone carver named James Pink, who proudly inscribed his name on its south-west corner

200 James Essex. Design for altar screen, King's College Chapel, Cambridge, Cambridgeshire, 1771. Pen and ink and wash. © The British Library Board, Add. MSS, 42569, f. 7.

(pl. 201). Its high altar is based closely on Bishop de Luda's tomb at Ely (he had served as prebendary of York and Lincoln previous to ascending to the bishopric in 1290) (pl. 202).[65] This represents a stylistically undisturbed continuity over centuries, the likes of which had not been seen before in an English cathedral in the eighteenth century, which understandably accounts for its miraculous survival against almost ubiquitous Victorian prejudices. Interestingly, during the ensuing negotiations for selecting a design and appropriate stone for repaving the interior (1778–9), Essex observed that 'when the Altar was set farther back' than its medieval position the dean and chapter 'thought it necessary to raise the floor higher . . . thinking the Reader would not be so well heard without it'. He suggested modifications to the steps and rails; in 1783 that the former be 'square without mouldings on the front . . . moulded steps being too modern for that place', and the seats 'made in a Stile more agreeable to the Stalls'.[66]

In 1774–5 Essex tackled the problem of the crossing tower, having concluded that its upper part was 'not designed by the Architect . . . to bear a Spire of Stone

201 (*above*) Samuel Hieronymus Grimm. Lincoln Cathedral interior towards choir, 1786. Pen and ink and wash. © The British Library Board, Kaye Collection, v, Add. MS 15541, f. 72. James Essex architect, 1765–66.

202 (*left*) P. S. Lamborn. Tomb of Bishop de Luda (d 1298), Ely Cathedral, Cambridgeshire, in Bentham, II, 1771, pl. XVII. Engraving. Author's collection.

[and was] incapable of supporting one', and though a lead-covered timber structure 'might be built [its height] in proportion to the Diameter and height of the Tower . . . would greatly exceed the highest . . . in England, and . . . too high for a situation so expos'd'. Providing no evidence on which the reconstruction was based, he offered a less ambitious design (untraced) featuring 'four Spires and open Battlements . . . made . . . as near as I could agreeable to the Ideas of the Architect who built the Tower'. The western, lead-covered timber spires were 'very sound, and may last a great many Years when the [supporting] Stonework . . . is properly repair'd' and when requiring rebuilding in '50 or 60 Years . . . may be made of Stone'.[67] In

203 William Lumby after James Essex. Design for 'hiding the Beam' between the east transept and Angel Choir, Lincoln Cathedral, Lincolnshire, 1779, with flap. Pen and ink. Lincolnshire Archives, D&C/A/4/15.

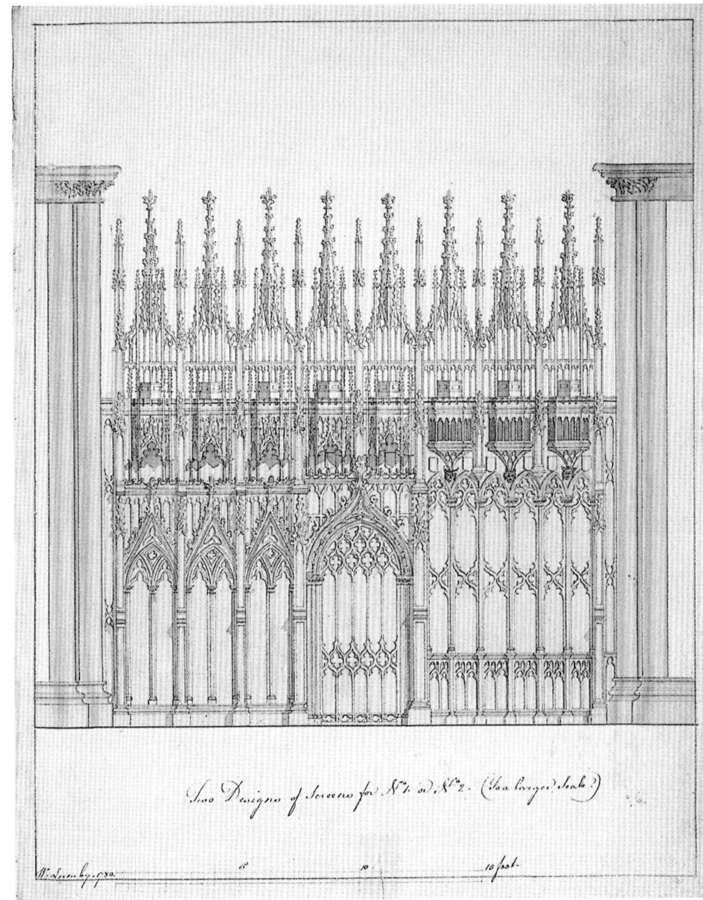

204 William Lumby after James Essex. 'Two Designs of Screens for No 1. Or No. 2. To a larger Scale', Lincoln Cathedral, Lincolnshire, 1780. Pen and ink. Lincolnshire Archives, D&C/A/4/15.

1775–6 he rectified James Gibbs's now fifty-year-old insertion of round-headed arches in the internal western bays, and recounted in a detailed structural analysis: 'tracing the original state . . . and if possible restore it to the state . . . the builders intended . . . to hinder the weight of the . . . towers from squeezing the peers further'. This entailed cutting foliated colonnettes into their inner angles and instructing William Lumby, a local master carpenter acting as his clerk of the works and draughtsman, to leave 'a few Inches more . . . between the point of the Arch & foot of the Cornice if it can be done without hurting the View of the Window'. He also proposed creating 'a vestibule, with a Gothic Ceiling of stucco'.[68] From 1778 to 1780 Essex concentrated on repairing the interior, including repaving the entire building, a technically demanding operation and in the present context pertinent for the reference made by Thomas Atkinson of York, one of the tenderers for supplying material, to the quality of Portland stone as recommended by Thomas Gayfere, master mason to Westminster Abbey, further evidence of the close-knit nature of these committed gothicists. In 1779 Essex, utilising Lumby as draughtsman, prepared designs for 'hiding the Beam' between the east transept and the Angel Choir (pl. 203), and in the next year a richly ornamented screen (pl. 204), based on the medieval Longland and Burghersh chantries.[69] In a final gesture in 1783 he advised the dean and chapter that opening the choristers' vestry and the space opposite would 'add much to the beauty' of the building. On retirement in the next year he was presented with a silver salver 'in token of respect for his Abilities'.[70]

In 1756 Bishop Lyttelton of Carlisle reported that Ely, though 'the fifth largest Church in the Kingdom',

205 Joseph Mallord William Turner, Interior of Ely Cathedral Looking Towards the North Transept and Chancel, Cambridgeshire, 1797, showing James Essex's 1768–70 remodelling. Watercolour. Aberdeen Art Gallery and Museums Collection, ABDAG 003016.

was in a 'slovenly condition [and] Far inferior to every other Cathedral except Carlisle'.[71] Essex's pessimistic survey of the following year centred on the 'Great Octagon Tower' (1322–40), which, despite being 'much assisted' by additional timberwork and iron ties, still supported a useless spire that is 'of much Diservice [and in] bad Repair'. Yet its loss would be 'a great Mistake . . . more detrimental to the Strength than the Ornament of the Building . . . a Work of the greatest Importance [and its] Neglect . . . may be attended with the Destruction of the Church, & the Loss of many Lives'. The 'greatest Care is required to preserve it in the State it ought to be'.[72] The lantern he rebuilt pinnacled but no longer sporting flying buttresses, dominated by large thirteenth-century-style windows, which flooded light into the central crossing (pl. 205). This vast though cluttered space was the subject of a report in 1759 that advised shifting the choir-stalls eastward deeper into the presbytery, an area that had lost its importance with the destruction of St Etheldreda's shrine, releasing the crossing as a post-Reformation preaching auditory.[73] Browne Willis mentioned in 1730 the late seventeenth-century Bishop Gunning's fondness for such clearance, and he himself endorsed the idea because it would add 'vastly to the Beauty of the Church'.[74] But the idea broke radically with previous English arrangements: of the dozen cathedrals featured in Willis's *Surveys* of 1727 and 1730, for example, only Bristol dispensed with this precedent. Essex's argument, wholly grounded in aesthetic rather than constructional requirements, was based on an impassioned plea that 'no Man of Taste' could deny the choir's relocation, 'considering how much it would have added to the Magnificence & Beauty of the Building', since its present situation 'destroys . . . the greatest Beauties of the Dome', whereas removing 'all that Confusion & Littleness which . . . fills the Arch [would create the] fine Effect [of aisles] open from End to End' and the exposure 'at one View' of the crossing and the new choir 'placed where it ought to be'. He also attacked the 'deficient . . . Judgement [of those] not worthy to be called an Architect [who] have no Conception of any Thing being grand which is not gaudy, nor beautiful that is not little & trifling'.[75]

Essex's reordering represented the most radical, innovative transformation of a great medieval internal space during the long eighteenth century. Yet, it was rooted in an unexpected historical precedent. He cited Wren's 'magnificent Dome of St Paul's London; whose greatest Beauty consists, in having the space it occupies, free & open'.[76] (The pertinent association here is that the latter's uncle, Matthew Wren, had served as Bishop of Ely.)[77] In this respect Essex was imposing the baroque craze for grand domical spaces and uninterrupted vistas (537 feet west to east) on to the medieval pattern (pl. 206). As in the case of Trevor's centralised Glynde scheme (pl. 196), Essex appears to have looked back to Langley's suggested remodelling of the London cathedral proposed in the *Grub-street Journal* in 1734, which involved removing the elaborate choirscreen and organ since

> they are both a nusance, and spoil the nobleness of the grand view: and in lieu . . . erect a light and airy frontis-piece of curious open iron-work, which would admit a clear view throughout . . . together with a magnificent *altar raised in . . . a magnificent alcove* [terminating the choir] with all the august majesty that could be desired.[78]

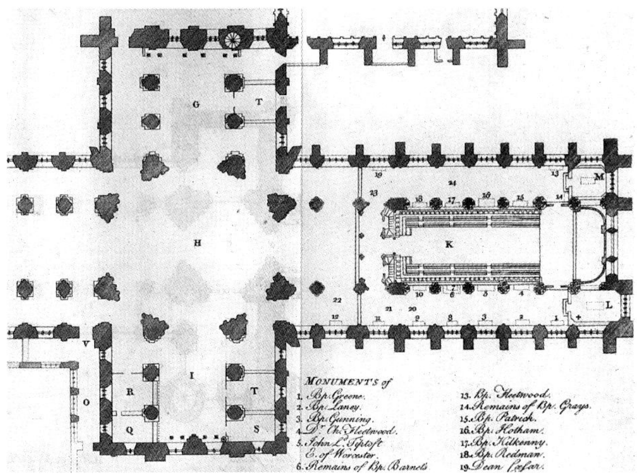

206 'A Plan of the Cathedral Church of Ely, with the Choir as proposed to be removed to the East End, 1768', in Bentham, II, 1771, pl. XL, detail. Engraving. Author's collection.

Essex's improvements were finally realised in 1768 with the chapter's decision to pave the choir in Portland stone and black marble, and enclose it across the third pier beyond the crossing by a screen of his own design (pl. 207).[79] Perhaps recalling Sanderson Miller's advice in 1759 regarding King's College chapel altarpiece that its 'Beauty . . . should consist in . . . Plainness & Simplicity [and] avoid all Gilding & Finery, which every Body condemns',[80] such as the riotous Continental gothic of James Adam's abortive design of 1768 (pl. 329), the architecture of Ely's screen is anchored in its early fourteenth-century de Luda tomb (pl. 202). Essex also reinstated the carefully repaired medieval stalls, but thought better of surmounting the altar with an organ and instead, in 1769, under Walpole's direction, com-

207 James Essex. Design for 'The East End of the Choir and Altar', Ely Cathedral, Cambridgeshire, October 1768. Pen and ink and wash. Fitzwilliam Museum, Cambridge, 1124b.

missioned a new east window from the Irish glass painter James Pearson, who produced a delicate ensemble of the *Nativity with the Four Evangelists*, his earliest recorded work (removed in 1857).[81]

Bentham was unequivocal in his praise of Essex's achievement in preserving Ely's quintessence, no one 'Fabrick in this Kingdom that exhibit's a larger, more elegant, or a more magnificent display of . . . *Gothic* Architecture . . . worthy of that Taste and spirit of Improvement, which so eminently distinguish this Age and Country'.[82] His repair and restoration of Winchester Cathedral (1775–82) reveals an unrivalled knowledge of the intimacies of gothic construction.[83]

Essex's last gothic work, the octagonal west tower and spire and perhaps also the castellated west front of Debden, Essex (pl. 208), erected posthumously in 1786 but referred to in an inscription in the vestry as 'from the Design of the ingenious Mr Essex', confirms his equally sensitive handling of small-scale parish churches.[84] Cole endorsed this achievement by acknowledging: 'he knowing more of Gothic Architecture than any one I have heard talk of it; by his Works of this Sort, will convince the World that many People, who have wrote on the Subject are but Dabblers in the Science, & know not what they are about'.[85] This enlightened approach and scrupulous attention to authentic detailing, a forerunner of Victorian attitudes, profoundly influenced the rehabilitation policies of other architects.

Robert Mylne, surveyor of St Paul's Cathedral from 1766 and of Canterbury Cathedral from the following year, an appointment secured under Archbishop Thomas Secker, a subscriber to Bentham's book, produced an eight-page report on the latter fabric in 1768, itemising 'defects' requiring immediate remedy (pl. 209).

208 Artist unknown. South west view, St Mary, Debden, Essex, detail, 179?. Watercolour. Debden Hall Album. English Heritage (National Monuments Record, BB85/3315). James Essex architect, 1786 spire, removed 1930.

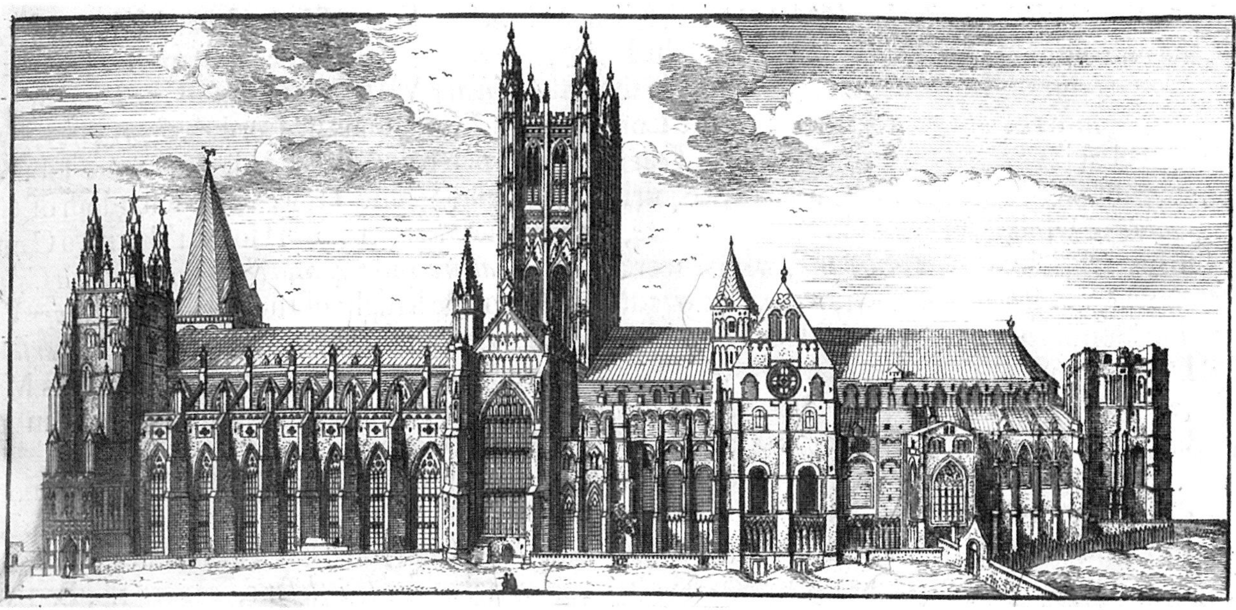

209 James Cole. South view of Canterbury Cathedral, in John Dart, *The History and Antiquities of the Cathedral Church of Canterbury*, 1726, p. 39. Engraving. Author's collection.

These included the eastern transepts and choir with their 'impudent' timber construction and 'wet, wasted ends' in the eaves, which exert 'a great lateral pressure against the . . . Walls', also the south transept window (which George Dance Sr had attempted to repair in 1751). Mylne proposed safeguarding it by inserting columns in order to 'discharge the Weight [and] preserve its true figure'. The 'great defects' in the romanesque north-west tower, which 'are not so old as the original construction' since the upper, gothic stage was 'of a different taste and design [and] of better Workmanship', could be ameliorated by restoring the buttresses or tying the corner 'Diagonal-wise [and] finished with Pinnacles of the same design and . . . size of its corresponding Tower', thus adding 'greatly to the Beauty of the Principall Front and Uniformity of the Building' (a solution achieved only with the tower's rebuilding in the years 1832–41). Finally, he urged removing the recently erected south porch because it was a 'blemish [and] no preservation against the Cold' and instead install an internal screen with spring doors. A second report (1770), confirming that much of the above work had been executed, discussed replacing the wooden south-east transept gable for stone to relieve the 'perpendicular pressure on the Round Windows' and removing the ruinous spire over the south-west corner staircase of the crossing to 'make both Corners of that front uniform', as he had hoped to do on the west front. Here is evidence of the imposition of the classical discipline of symmetry (by an architect very much of that persuasion) on medieval buildings that had grown irregularly over a lengthy period of stylistic and constructional changes.[86]

Also in 1770, John Carr, coming to the end of the gothic phase of his church work, submitted a nineteen-page report on the condition of York Minster, its specificity and systematic comprehensiveness evidence of an increasing professionalism in dealing with the complex business of cathedral restoration (pl. 139). His approach differed from Essex in several respects. Largely avoiding aesthetic issues (except in pressing for the removal of 'those ugly Walls on the North side . . . which hide so much of the Base of this Noble Structure') and internal improvements, since 'In viewing . . . the Building I did not observe any material defects' apart from repairs to several pillar bases, wall benches, marble columns and hole-ridden vaulting, he concentrated on remedying deteriorating exterior features. In the case of 'an ugly decay'd Wood Window, which ought to be Stone' he was not beyond recommending 'filling . . . the Decay'd places . . . with coarse Plaister to keep out the Wet [or] a good Coat of Plaister [to prevent it] from further decay'. An invaluable feature of Carr's report is the subsequent annotations of work either 'done' or 'not done', with nineteen out of twenty-seven categories successfully accomplished by 1797.[87]

At the same time he carried out major repairs to St Peter (now the cathedral), Sheffield. A visitor in 1735

210 John Carr. Design for 'The East Elevation', St Peter, Sheffield, Yorkshire, detail, 1771. Pen and ink and wash. Sheffield Archives, ACM Ebu 252-4.

described the medieval building as 'large . . . but irregular [with the interior] crowded and darkened with old Lofts and Pews like a Scotch Kirk'. Apart from renovations to the crossing tower in 1722, nothing substantial was done until 1771–4, when Carr remodelled the chancel exterior by providing a 'proper Cornice . . . under all the Battlements . . . new Parapet [and] Pinnacles . . . where necessary' and the east window 'wholly new Worked [and] such old Materials . . . found useful . . . applied in the intended New Work' (pl. 210).[88] His design reveals a characteristic combination of Langleyian and more authentic gothic detailing.

Carr returned to York for a second bout of rehabilitation in 1794–5, concentrating on the nave roof and vaulting, which entailed replacing the lead on the southern slope with 'best blue Westmorland Slate' and infilling the liernes with lath and plaster (pl. 211). He had power to decide from whom materials were purchased to ensure that 'those only of the properest quality begot [with] preference . . . given to the Workmen employed about the Church, and the Tradesmen who usually provide the different Articles wanted', as in medieval times.[89] His management of such a stupendous operation had links with Essex's more innovatory programmes: the long rivalry existing between York and Lincoln,[90] associations with William Mason, a York canon and close friend of Horace Walpole, and Joseph Halfpenny, author of *Gothic Ornaments in the Cathedral Church of York* (1795), to which Carr subscribed; in the introduction Halfpenny advised: 'A Careful perusal of Mr Bentham's History of . . . Ely . . . will enable any person to obtain a competent Knowledge of the Principles of Gothic Architecture'. Carr was by no means alone in this heroic pursuit.

Between 1767 and 1775, at the height of Essex's Ely and Lincoln restorations, the Revd William Hanbury pursued an astonishing, visionary scheme (which had no chance of being realised), to create a cathedral-like collegiate church complex in his Leicestershire village of Church Langton, some 50 miles west of Ely and within Essex's heartland. These ambitions were understandable since Hanbury had received the living in 1749 after being ordained by the Bishop of Lincoln. Never progressing beyond the drawing board (the sole 'Ichnography or Platforme' presented on 1 March 1773 is untraced), it is hardly curious that it has escaped the attention of architectural historians, and while undue significance should not be placed on this hare-brain scheme, it does deserve serious scrutiny as an expression of Georgian aspirations.[91]

On 1 March 1773 Hanbury referred to

> Directions . . . sufficient to inform the ingenious Architect [unnamed] how the Founder could wish to have his Church built, direct his Judgment, inspire him with suitable Ideas for his great and Immortal Employment, induce him to exert his whole powers to unite Piety and Grandeur, and in every respect to complete it in the most august and finished taste.

He intended to 'invite the most able and expert Artists to exhibit models . . . pay them well for their trouble, and appoint a Committee of approved Judges to assist . . . in determining upon the best'. Perhaps he aspired to imitate Walpole's Committee of Taste, with James Essex's participation. However, William Woty's verse published in 1773 for the benefit of the charity,

> On yon proud eminence where LANGTON stands,
> That yield a prospect of the richest lands,
> There shall the grand Collegiate Church arise;
> Gothic the style, and tending to excite
> Free-thinkers to a sense of what is right;
> With length'ning ailes, and windows that impart
> A gloomy steady light to chear the heart,
> Such as affect the soul, and which I see
> With joy, celestial Westminster! in thee[,][92]

suggests that he may have favoured the current abbey surveyor, Henry Keene, who was also employed over a twenty-year period at Magdalen College, Oxford,

211 Joseph Halfpenny. 'Groinings of the inner Roof, as they appeared, before the spaces were closed with lath and plaster', York Minster, Yorkshire, 1796. Watercolour. York Museums Trust (Art Gallery), R 1784.

Hanbury's Alma Mater.[93] An annual salary of £100 for a 'Resident Surveyor' earmarked in 1775, with a note that 'this Office indicates the Artists Business, and the Diligence of Mr: Price of Salisbury affords a laudable patern for him to copy after' (Francis Price, author of *Series of particular and useful Observations . . . upon . . . The Cathedral-Church of Salisbury*, 1753), perhaps hints at what sort of model Hanbury had in mind. Moreover, during this time he had undertaken several architectural tours 'throughout all England for various Observations'. In 1771 he travelled to Peterborough, Croyland and Boston examining 'every thing that was curious in Lincolnshire and the Adjacent parts', then to Lichfield and 'whatever was curious in and about Staffordshire'. In 1772 he went to London, Rochester, Canterbury, Southwell ('to view the Collegiate Church'), Lincoln, Beverley ('most highly delighted with that most elegant Collegiate Church . . . inferior in nothing except size, to any Cathedral in Yorkshire'), then to York ('staid a month, constantly attending divine service'), Chichester and Salisbury, Wells, Bath, Bristol, Gloucester and Tewkesbury.[94] This diversity of interests helps to explain the scheme's grandiosity and architectural cacophony, of which the church – measuring internally 660 by 300 feet at the 'Great Transept' by 453 feet to the top of the central tower, with the nave vault rising 153 feet (compared to Salisbury's 452 by 205 by 400 and 84 feet), with 90-foot-high pillars – is the centrepiece of a vast building complex (described on pp. 17–18). Calculated sixteen years in the making and costing £400,273, it conjures up nothing less than John Carter's megalomaniac illustration to 'The Death of Matilda' from Walpole's gothic novel *The Castle of Otranto* (pl. 212). The cross-plan church, dedicated (like Westminster) to St Peter, was to be 'so constructed, that it may in magnificence and grandeur, exceed all others; and become not only the Principal ornament of the Country, but an Honour to the Island'.

212 John Carter. 'The Death of Matilda' 1791, from Horace Walpole, *The Castle of Otranto*, 1764. Watercolour. RIBA Library Drawings Collection.

The 'most Noble and uniform' entrances on the west, north and south sides, were each surmounted by a pair of 318-foot-high towers, and 'every termination of view . . . enriched with all Elegance, grace, and such profusion of Decorations, as the keenest Genius, and most luxurious Imagination can suggest'. There would be marble floors and pillars, 'the finest Marble, Porphery, and Jaspar' in the choir and high altar, the 'whole . . . vaulted with Stone curiously wrought, gilt, and painted', the columns 'light, free and easy, contrived to assist the view and enrich it with Symmetry and Beauty', the windows 'the grandest that can be devised [with] the grandest painted Window' at the east end. During divine service ministers would 'descend . . . into the Lower Transept . . . pass along the South . . . East . . . Ayle . . . re-enter the Choir above the Stalls . . . and advance to the . . . High Altar'. Beyond this the Sanc-tum Sanctorum and Lady Chapel would house 'suitable Monuments' to Hanbury and his family ('in a dry, light, airy Room' of their own), as well as the professors and trustees, who 'with good fidelity preside over the Charity Twelve years' and on which an astonishing £1,000 each would be spent (an unprecedented sum at the time). Throughout the building there would be no less than 100 'suitable Statues of Saints' carved of the 'finest Freestone', including 'Female British Saints', with further figures placed along the external battlements and in niches. Female inmates of the adjacent hospital would occupy galleries placed between the nave piers and on each side of the choir, with pews and stalls of 'the finest grained Mehogany'. It is as if Carter's Walpolian fantasy was to become reality. As in the cases of Lincoln and Ely considerable attention was paid to selecting 'good Building Stone from several of the most noted Quarries' based on samples, and Hanbury planned petitioning Parliament 'to form a Navagable Canal from Stamford to [Market] Harborough, thence to the Oxford Cut, for . . . bringing up Materials'. Remarkably for the time, the use of structural and decorative plasterwork was not contemplated. In his quest for perfection Hanbury insisted that his

> Ingenious Architect . . . have a strict regard to the Foundations, pillars and adjacent part of the Tower, that by building them large enough, and causing them by proper Arches &c: to unite in one Common Strength for its support, it may be properly raised to the desired height, without danger of any . . . giving way a circumstance which has too often happened in Buildings of this nature.

However, 'If any of the Parts should give way like those of York Peterborough Ely &c: the Building is not to be left unfinished, as the Lantern Towers of those Cathedrals: but the whole shall be taken Down to the bottom, and a better and more substantial under part constituted', Hanbury adding: 'All necessary precautions to be taken, in order to prevent bad effects from Lightening &c:'. The tours described above proved useful. For example,

> The upper Transept is designed to strengthen the Building and throw light into the Choir: – All large Cathedrals afford instances how usefull and ornamental such kind of Transept is to the upper parts of them: – That of York extends little or nothing beyond the breadth of the Church, and it is left to the ingenious Architect to contrive this to be somewhat similar to that of York, or project on both sides like . . . Lincoln and others.

Behind this utterly impracticable vision, abandoned at Hanbury's death in 1778, may have been the inspiring resurrectional notion expressed by Walter Harrison in *A New Universal History, Description and Survey of the Cities of London and Westminster* (1775), that Westminster Abbey had recently been 'rescued from that ruin into which it was falling . . . and the havock . . . during the unhappy civil commotion that defaced the ancient beauty of all religious houses in this Kingdom, can never be recovered; yet it has'.[95]

Meanwhile, Henry Keene was carrying out extensive internal refurbishment of the abbey. He had succeeded to the surveyorship in 1752 but did not begin major improvements until 1769, probably following his architectural tour of the Netherlands.[96] This began with refitting the Jerusalem Chamber adjacent to the southwest tower. Unlike previous surveyors after Wren and Dickinson, he was committed to a wholly medieval repertory, as the workmen's bill of 1769 confirms: 'figured Gothic pannells . . . nailed in Gothic figures wth Gothic rose headed nails . . . Gothic Archt Cieling . . . Gothic Shields . . . Cornice with Gothic bands . . . Gothic bracketting to Cieling in ribs . . . Gothic figurd Sashes . . . Circular Sofites in Gothic figured pannels', etc. Among the craftsmen was the abbey's master mason, Thomas Gayfere Sr, who was also employed at Strawberry Hill, as we have seen. All this has been swept away without pictorial record, but its richness must have been an echo of Keene's church at Hartwell (pls 168–70). In 1773 he, Essex and James Wyatt (soon to succeed as surveyor) reported on the propriety of moving the choir eastward, as had just been done at Ely, and in the following year Keene contracted to install a 'new Choir [making] use of such parts of the present Choir as are found fit and proper' (pl. 213),

213 J. Bluck after F. Mackenzie. View of the Choir and Presbytery, Westminster Abbey, London, 1 November 1811, in R. Ackermann and W. Combe, *The History of the Abbey of St Peter's Westminster*, II, 1812. WAM. Henry Keene architect, 1774, dismantled 1847.

together with a new pulpit (banished in 1824 to Trottiscliffe, Kent). This is an offspring of Kent's at York (pl. 163), but with relief panels reflecting the abbey's transparent roses and a tester supported by a flamboyantly carved palm tree, symbol of eternal life and resurrection. In 1775 the dean, having failed to move the choir on the opposition of his chapter, consulted Walpole about a design for a new altarpiece, which the latter recommended in the form of 'an octagon canopy of open arches, like Chichester Cross . . . elevated on a flight of steps, with the altar in the middle, and semicircular arches to join the [prebendary] stalls, so that the Confessor's chapel and tomb [on a raised position behind] may be seen through in perspective', for which he sent a plan to William Mason of York, who proved correct in thinking that the scheme 'will never be executed'.[97] Implementing such a scenographic invention would have meant removing Wren's grand though by now stylistically anachronistic classical altarpiece, which in fact was not done until 1820. This interlude of improvement ended with Keene's death on 8 January 1776.[98]

Experiments into avant-garde gothic at the great cathedrals described in this chapter inevitably filtered down to smaller parish churches across the country during the 1760s and 1770s. This is epitomised at Bishopthorpe, adjacent to the palace of Robert Hay Drummond, Archbishop of York, on the outskirts of the city, designed by Thomas Atkinson, about which hardly anything is now known. The surviving but ruined west front (pl. 214) is notable for its close imitation of a single medieval elevation (which it shares with the slightly later chapel at Strawberry Hill, pl. 189), in this case the symmetrically arranged grouping of the delicately ornamented door, window, niches, crocketed buttresses and prominently battlemented and pinnacled central gable of York Minster (pl. 139).[99] In 1778 Atkinson revived his ogee porch on Bishopthorpe Palace (1766–9) to reinvigorate medieval All Saints, Pavement, York, in a proposal to replace the independent baroque market cross of 1672 to the east of the church by an attached arcade (pl. 39).[100]

Between 1770 and 1775 the Lincoln master carpenter Thomas Lumby and his son William, who solicited Essex's endorsement as a person 'so good a judge of the work that is wanting' at Lincoln Cathedral, while what 'he has done there under my direction, convinces me that he may be trusted with the execution of any thing that may be wanting',[101] independently remodelled the medieval church at nearby Doddington (pl. 215). Its two distinctive features, the quatrefoil circular window in the tower and the ogee arched porch with flanking niches (pl. 216), owe something of their form and ornamental vitality to the thirteenth-century cinquefoil inserted into the top of the central recess of the cathedral's west front (pl. 157) and to Essex's high altar at Ely (pl. 207).

214 Thomas Atkinson. West front, St Andrew, Bishopthorpe, Yorkshire, 1776, body demolished 1899.

The climax of Robert Adam's suite of principal apartments in the refashioned medieval keep of Alnwick Castle, Northumberland, was the chapel (1773–80, destroyed *circa* 1854), a voluptuously unrivalled gothic (as he was also doing in a classical idiom in the 1st Duke of Northumberland's London residence in the Strand and at Syon). Its 'almost pontifical blaze of ornament and gilding' bothered some visitors: the

> *light* gothic ornaments . . . in *plaister* . . . painted in *gay* colours, seemed . . . trumpery . . . Never . . . seen . . . so much to admire so much to condemn . . . to see the *House of prayer*, turned into the *House of ostentation of the Percy family* filled me with indignation.

The inclusion of a large marble 'Gothic sarcophagus' containing the remains of Duchess Elizabeth (who died on 5 December 1776) was particularly suspect.[102] But this misunderstood the duke's desire to pay tribute to his beloved wife by creating a mausoleum-cum-chapel in the mode of the Tomb Chamber at The Vyne (pl. 194), which Adam is likely to have known since he had

215 (*top*) William Lumby. South-west view, St Peter, Dodington, Lincolnshire, 1770–75.

216 (*above*) William Lumby. West door, St Peter, Dodington, Lincolnshire, 1770–75.

decorated the Round Drawing Room at Strawberry Hill (1766–9), employing motifs derived from the rose window of Old St Paul's Cathedral and Edward the Confessor's tomb in Westminster Abbey.[103] Such historicism also informed Alnwick chapel, for Francis Grose in 1775 praised

> the highest display of Gothic ornament in the greatest beauty . . . and the several parts . . . have been designed after the most perfect models of Gothic excellence. The great east window is taken from one of the finest in York minster. The ceiling is borrowed from that of King's college, in Cambridge; and the walls are painted after the great church in Milan.[104]

Furthermore, it was part of an elaborate medieval aura surrounding the castle, epitomised in the Bishop of Dromore's poem *The Hermit of Warkworth: A Northumberland Ballad* (1775), dedicated to Duchess Elizabeth, a long account of medieval daring-do, citing ancient texts in the pedantic antiquarian tradition and eulogising a tiny chapel 'still intire [and] very beautifully designed and executed [with] all the decorations of a compleat Gothic Church or Cathedral in miniature [including] a small Tomb' incorporating a female effigy, with adjoining sacristy and vestry containing an altar where Mass was celebrated.[105]

James Plumptre visited the castle chapel in 1799, and his impressions, including the understandable confusion created by the deceptive orientation of the space, were probably typical:

> the first glimpse presented a thousand pleasing ideas to my mind . . . a spacious oblong apartment, lying East and West, with a large gothic window of painted glass at the E. end, representing some interesting story in sacred history, a handsome altar of marble under it, the roof of beautiful gothic, the sides embellished with paintings of scriptural history, and a marble floor inlaid. I entered and walked towards the E. window (as I imagined) to inspect the painting, when lo! The Percy arms presented themselves . . . I cast my eyes down to look at the Altar, when I beheld a white marble sarcophagus . . . Shocked at seeing a tomb instead of an altar, I . . . was informed that it was [in fact] the S. window, the chapel lying n. & s. Upon the floor lay a painted floor cloth . . . the walls . . . painted with *genealogies of the Percys up to Charlemagne*!!! [pl. 217] Three Chandiliers hung from the ceiling. The [actual and liturgical] E. window is on the left of the entrance, and is small, with a chair and reading desk before it. Opposite . . . is a circular recess [the castle tower], with a

Design for finishing the Pannells in the Chapel at Alnwick, containing the
Pedigree of the Family, proposed to be partly done in Stucco & partly
in Painting
Feet

217 Robert Adam. 'Design for finishing the Pannells in the Chapel at Alnwick, containing the Pedigree of the Family, proposed to be partly done in Stucco & partly in Painting', Northumberland, 1777. Pen and ink and coloured wash. Sir John Soane's Museum, AD 39/19.

A
B
Design of a Carpet for the Chapel at Alnwick Castle, in two different ways.
one full half of the Original finished

218 Robert Adam. 'Design for a Carpet for the Chapel at Alnwick Castle in two different ways one full half of the original finished', Northumberland, 1780. Pen and ink and coloured wash. Sir John Soane's Museum, AD 17/202.

> window; here the family sit on chairs with the Percy arms on the back.[106]

The east window was a variation on the flamboyant fourteenth-century fenestration of York Minster: Grose, who saw the room in 1775 in the progress of decoration, reckoned the 'painted glass will be in stile superior to any thing that has yet been attempted, and worthy of the present more improved state of the arts'. The patterned carpet (pl. 218) in the round family pew opposite the polylobed pointed-arch entrance almost certainly echoed, in the familiar Adam practice, the 'transcendent beauty' of the circular ceiling directly above supported by 'six Gothic columns'. The room itself had 'three chandeliers, each holding twelve candels . . . of beautiful, light and elegant forms, made in composition by Mr Smith of Bond Street and richly gilt', together with twenty-four stools of white and gilt frames upholstered in green silk, and nine gold and white wheel-back chairs with cane seats and green velvet cushions.[107]

The cause of revived ecclesiastical gothic received a further popular perk with the publication of *The Builder's Magazine* (1774–8, with many later editions), which was intended 'to take the pupil by the hand and lead him through every branch of Architecture', illustrated with designs invented and drawn by John Carter, an architect and draughtsman, whom we will meet again in the 1790s as an irrepressible gothocentric promoter of medieval buildings.[108] The *Magazine* offered a balanced orthodox perception of gothic as

> exceedingly light, delicate and rich. The abundance of little, whimsical, wild, and chimerical ornaments, are its most unusual characters . . . All the ancient cathedrals are of this kind. It is not to be doubted, but that the inventors of the Gothic architecture thought they had far surpassed the Greek architects. A Greek building has not one ornament, but what adds beauty to the whole. No daring out-of-the-way strokes, nothing quaint to impose on the eye. The proportions are so just, that nothing appears very grand of itself, although the whole is striking and noble. On the contrary, in the Gothic architecture, we see large vaults raised on slender pillars, which one would expect every minute to tumble down, though they will stand for many ages. Every thing is crammed with windows, roses, crosses, figures, &c.

219 J. Royce after John Carter. 'Elevation of a Design for a Church', 1 January 1777, in 'A Society of Architects', *The Builder's Magazine*, 1774, pl. CX. Engraving. Author's collection.

Moreover,

> Gothic architecture has, for these few years past, fallen greatly under the censure of the immoderate admirers of Grecian architecture, yet if we candidly consider, we shall find both styles have their separate beauties and use. The Grecian taste certainly best suits . . . publick buildings . . . but for religious structures, Gothic, undoubtedly, ought to be preferred . . . Therefore condemn not Gothic entirely, but as occasion serves and the subject requires, give preference to it.[109]

Of the publication's 185 engraved plates, most are French-inspired avant-garde neoclassical essays, with only thirteen in the gothic style, of which six are devoted to ecclesiastical subjects. Inevitably, this youthful stage of Carter's career has been largely marginalised by modern writers. One scheme, however, is of particular interest to the present study, a 'Design for a CHURCH' dated between 1 January and 1 July 1777, uniquely represented by seven plates comprising a plan, two elevations, three sections, an east window, a west door and a roof structure.[110] The plan and elevation (pl. 219) are remarkable, for their date probably unprecedented since medieval times: a Latin cross, measuring overall 130 by 196 feet, soaring 128 feet, with thick, multi-shaft, cathedral-like crossing piers (inspired by Exeter Cathedral) and a substantial chancel raised on two steps and dominated by a five-arched reredos, flanked by a sacristy 'where the utensils, the ornaments of the church, ministers vestments, &c. are kept', a thoroughly un-Protestant facility that did not reappear in England until the early nineteenth-century post-Catholic Emancipation.[111] Carter's elevation treatment is uncommonly authentic-looking and its immediate impact is discernible at Moreton, Dorset (pls 220–21), with its curvilinear, mouchette, thirteenth-century style windows and quatrefoil bands. The bold, semicircular sanctuary facing towards the family residence (in classical style) suggests its possible dual function as a mausoleum church. The exquisite rococo wall monument in the family pew dedicated to Mary Frampton (died 1762), of a 'Chearfulness and Sweetness of Temper . . . pleasing Form [and] very ample Fortune' (according to the inscription), was carved by P. M. Vangelder under

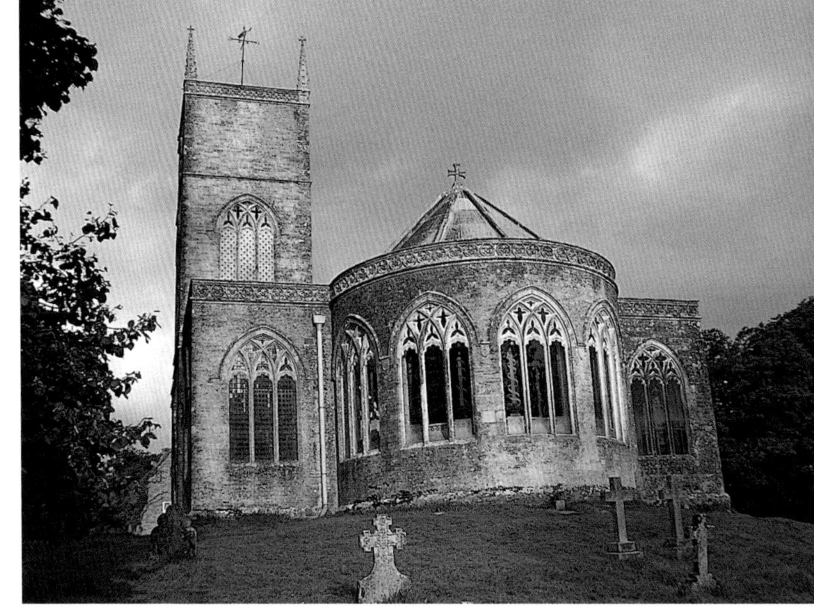

220 (*right, above*) John Carter, attributed. West front, St Nicholas, Moreton, Dorset, 1776.

221 (*right*) John Carter, attributed. South elevation, St Nicholas, Moreton, Dorset, 1776.

the direction of Carter's cousin, Thomas Carter Jr, who also was responsible for the Chaloner Chute tomb in The Vyne (pl. 194). It is likely that John Carter designed the church.[112]

In the mid-1770s Salisbury Cathedral resurfaced as an influential model, coinciding with the second edition of Francis Price's celebrated publication of 1753. The crucial image now is of St Mary's Chapel (pl. 222), with its hall arrangement, where all three aisles are equal height, separated by slim, free-standing clustered columns. Its principal benefit is to open up the congregational space for the minimum interruption of sight lines, one of the chief aims of Protestant architecture, where the pulpit is the central focus. An early

222 (*left*) Paul Fourdrinier after Francis Price. 'A Perspective View of the termination of the Isles', 1747, in F. Price, *A Series Of particular and useful Observations . . . upon . . . the Cathedral Church of Salisbury* (Wiltshire), 1753, pl. 12. Engraving. Author's collection.

223 (*below*) Thomas Johnson. Interior towards west, St Nicholas, Warwick, Warwickshire, 1775–80. English Heritage (National Monuments Record, A42/9581).

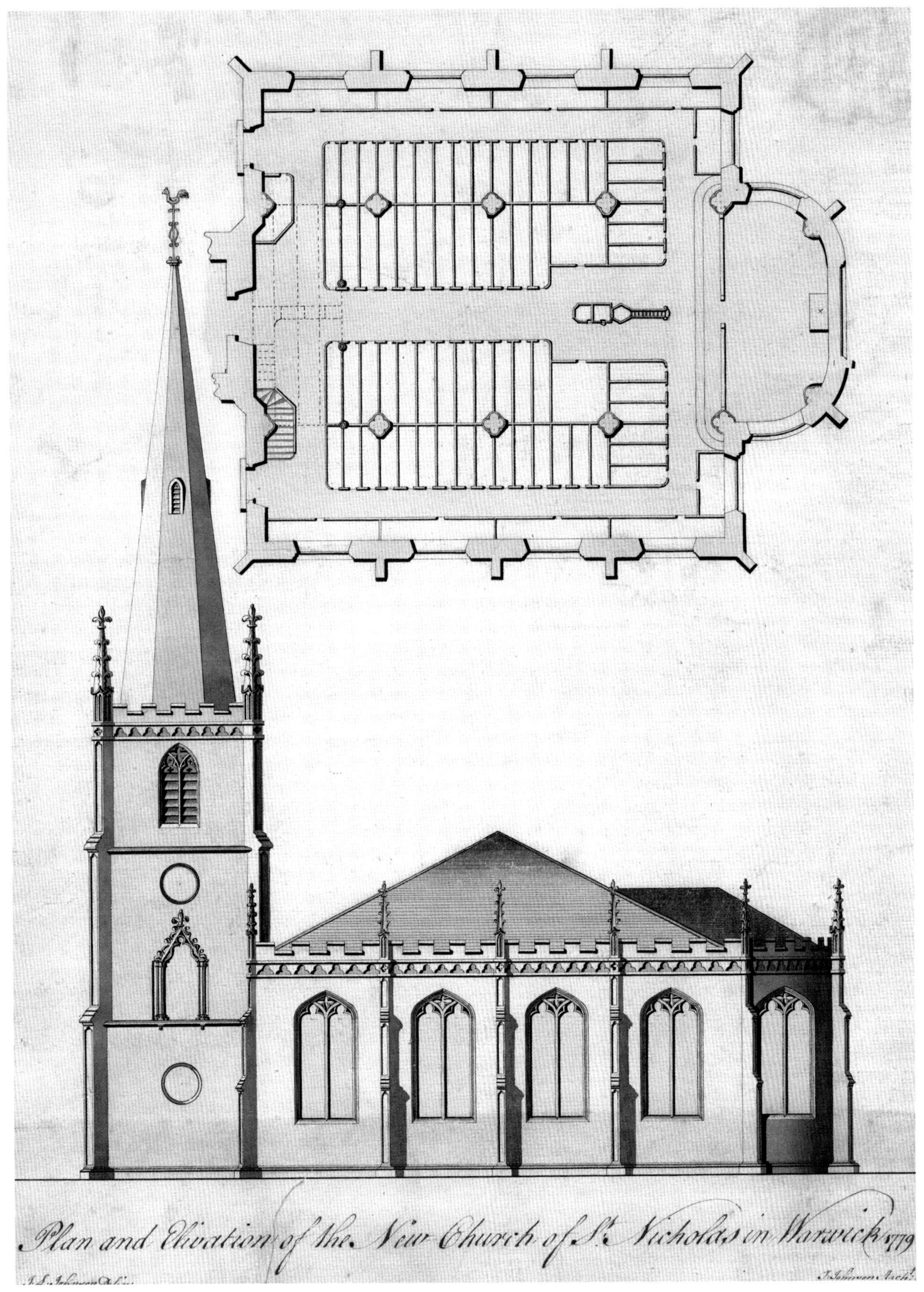

224 John Lees Johnson. 'Plan and Elevation of the New Church of St. Nicholas in Warwick. 1779', Warwickshire. Pen and ink and coloured wash. Warwickshire Record Office, DR92/28. Job Collins and Thomas Johnson architects, 1748–82.

225 Francis Hiorne. Interior towards chancel, St Mary, Tetbury, Gloucestershire, 1775–81. English Heritage (National Monuments Record, BB49/3005).

post-medieval manifestation of this is St Mary, Warwick (pl. 271).[113]

Interestingly, this solution was developed in the late eighteenth century by two local architects. St Nicholas, Warwick (pl. 223), for which both a beautifully rendered presentation drawing (pl. 224) and an impressive wooden model survive, was designed jointly by Job Collins, a local mason apprenticed to John Dunkley, presumably a relative of Samuel Dunkley, who worked at St Mary (pl. 274), and Thomas Johnson, whose masterpiece is the pioneer Greek revival County Gaol (1779–82).[114] His compatriot Francis Hiorne turned to Salisbury as the basis for perhaps the most important church gothic essay of the period, Tetbury, Gloucestershire (pl. 225). The failure to preserve the decayed medieval fabric between 1729 and 1753 (see Docs 532–7), exacerbated in 1770 when a great part 'undermined by . . . floods . . . tumbled down [and] crushed [it] to pieces', led to a complete rebuilding of the body to an entirely different design. This soaring space lit by huge Perpendicular windows, with low-level outer chapels in the manner of King's College chapel, Cambridge, is a tour de force of daring technology in which extravagantly tall, slender, free-standing columns constructed entirely of wood (rather than of cast iron, as sometimes claimed) are hung from (rather than support) timber sexpartite vaulting tied by 'Iron Bolts and Stirrups [to a] strong Roof of Oak Timber', as specified in the contract of 25 May 1776.[115] The interior, so prophetic of some of the Six Hundred New Churches of 1818–56,[116] gave William Mason of York 'the very highest opinion of [Hiorne's] Gothic taste'.[117]

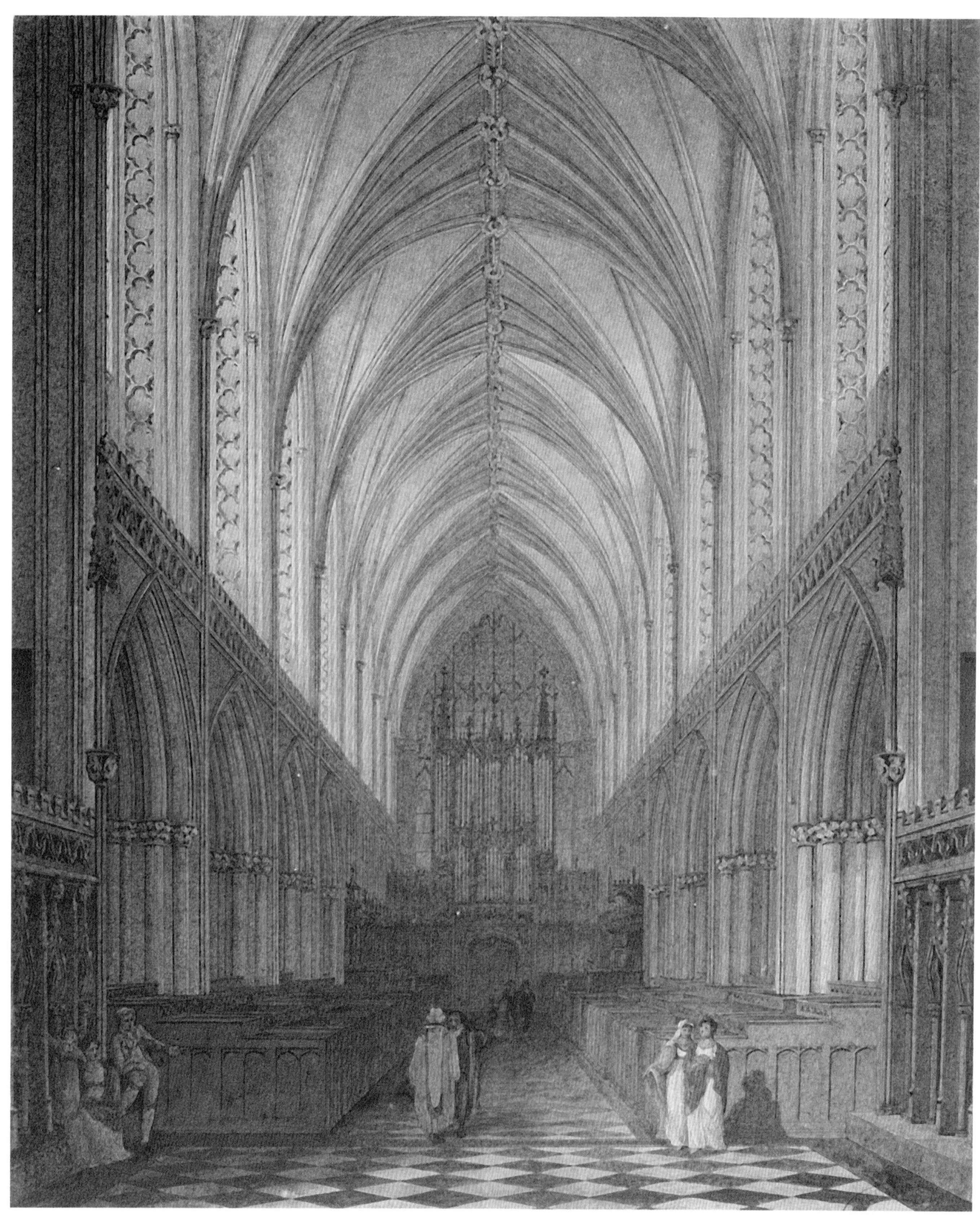

226 Artist unknown. 'The Choir of Lichfield Cathedral looking from the Altar towards the Organ', Staffordshire, undated. Watercolour. Staffordshire Record Office, Staffordshire Views, VI, f. 85. James Wyatt architect, 1783–95.

Sixteen

'ANCIENT GOTHIC IN ALL ITS RICHEST ORNAMENTS'

The Cathedral . . . should in its . . . appearance bear the character of the aera in which it was built[1]

This chapter explores the careers of some of the leading gothic church designers practising between 1780 and 1800, including George Richardson, Henry Emlyn, Carline and Tilley, George Dance Jr, James Adam, John Nash, S. P. Cockerell, John Carter and, above all, James Wyatt (pl. 226).

Lord Torrington, visiting remote St Asaph's Cathedral, Clwyd, Wales, in 1784, two years after £2,800 had been spent on improvements, praised the dean and chapter for maintaining it 'in the nicest order', the chancel window having been 'built after the model of that beautiful one at the west end of Tintern Abbey, and the stalls . . . clean and well cushion'd. I feel a pleasure in seeing any of our churches resume their papistical grandeur, and emerge from the devastation of fanatics and sectaries.'[2] The architect in charge, Joseph Turner – his monument at Hawarden praises his 'many Splendid & Publick Works [as] a lasting Memorial of his Taste and Abilities' – was capable of designing with consummate ease and skill in a completely convincing gothic idiom, as demonstrated in his accomplished drawing for the east window and altarpiece (pl. 227).[3] This was largely due to a momentum during the 1780s in critical writings on gothic that found a popular outlet in the *Gentleman's Magazine*. For instance, responding to a review by 'Ruben D'Moundt' in 1782 of an article in *The Bibliotheca Topographica Britannica*, readers were referred to Bentham's *Ely* as offering a history of gothic on the 'irrefragable authority' of James Essex and Thomas Gray, 'whose judgements no man of real science will call in question'.[4] This increasingly encouraged clients and their architects to embrace the style wholeheartedly.

The Revd Robert Sherard, 4th Earl of Harborough, who had links with Salisbury, commissioned George Richardson, a member of the Adam circle, to design two churches in a particularly sophisticated gothic that imposed a neoclassical discipline of 'Squares, Circles, Octagons, &c . . . essential Ingredients' in the repertory of his influential *Book of Ceilings, Composed in the Style of the Antique Grotesque* (1774–6). Teigh, Rutland, of 1782–94 (pl. 228), is informed by a quiet exterior preserving the plain medieval tower. At Stapleford, Leicestershire (pl. 229), in the grounds of Sherard's estate, the completely new church, with more stately proportions, is carefully integrated by continuous, repetitive, delicate Perpendicular decorations, surrounding both tower and body. The aristocratic, luxuriously appointed interior was vividly brought to life by the county historian, John Nichols, in 1785:

> The inside . . . is . . . beautifully elegant; and . . . very handsomely paved . . . The ascent from the nave to the chancel is by three steps; and one more step leads to the altar . . . beautifully formed of marble, with borders of black, statuary, and dove colour. In the centre is a neat tablet, with the emblems of Hope and Eternity, an anchor suspended on an encircled serpent; and at the top a handsome urn.[5]

An insurgence of innovative technology and promotion of new materials marked these final decades. At St George's Chapel, Windsor Castle, the Coade manufactory based at Lambeth in south London supplied an artificial 'stone' cast from moulds, which had the long-term benefits of remaining permanently crisp and unblemished.[6] Normally confined to decorative embel-

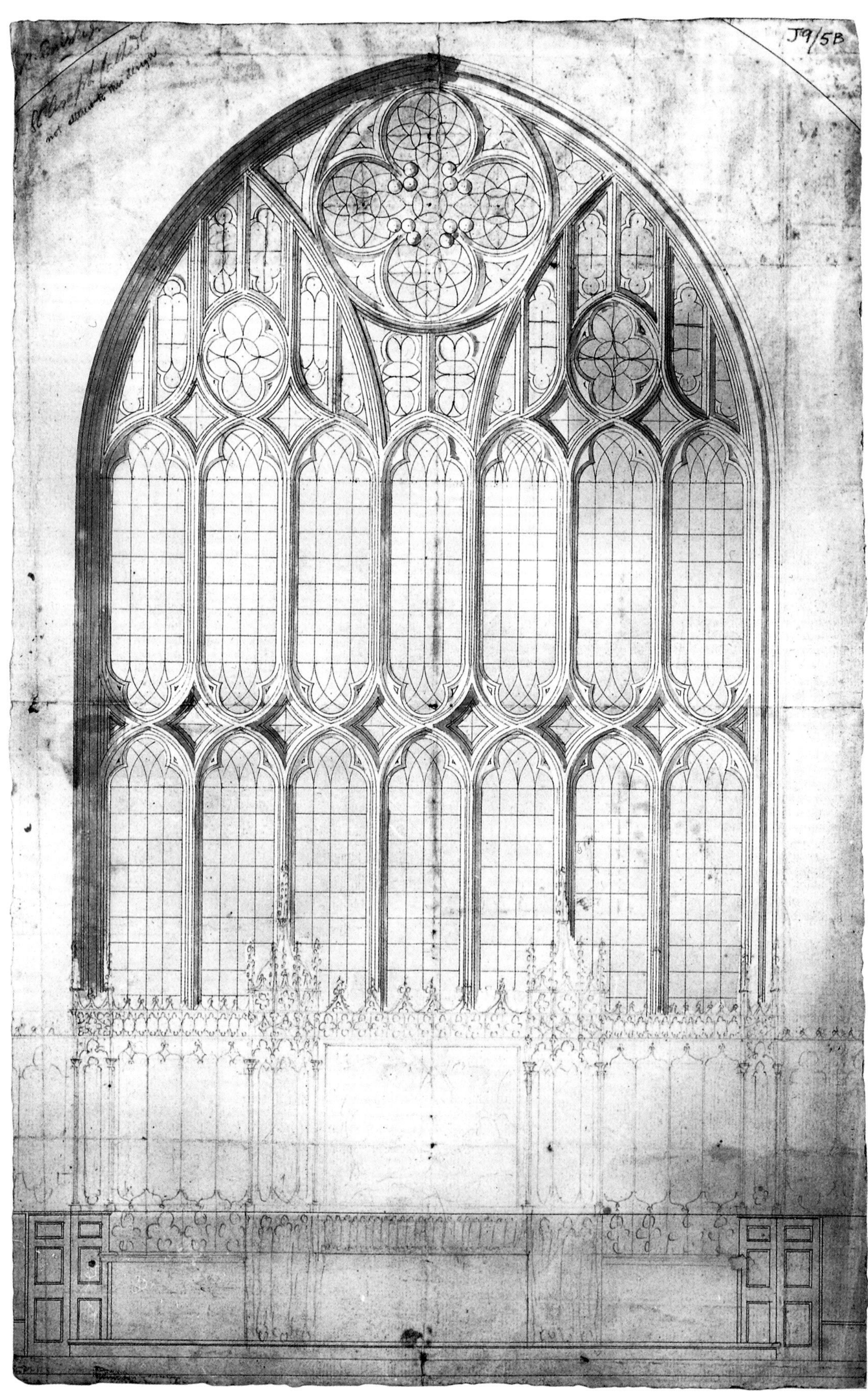

227 Joseph Turner. 'Design for East window and Alterpiece for St Asaph Cathedral 1782', Clwyd, Wales. Pencil, pen and ink and wash. RIBA Library Drawings Collection, J9/5B.

228 (*top*) George Richardson. South elevation, Holy Trinity, Teigh, Rutland, 1782–94.

229 (*above*) George Richardson. West front and tower, St Mary Magdalen, Stapleford, Leicestershire, 1783.

lishments,[7] at Windsor it was employed on a hitherto unprecedented large and splendid scale by a local architect and builder, Henry Emlyn, who prepared meticulously rendered drawings and superintended the 'princely work'. This included an organ gallery supported on extremely slender columns with fan vaulting copying the medieval structure in the aisles (pl. 230).

230 Henry Emlyn. Organ gallery, St George's Chapel, Windsor, Berkshire, 1786–92.

The material was also used for the new pulpit and font, the Sovereign's and Prince of Wales's stalls, each with equally elaborate canopies and seat backs modelled with scenes depicting the royal couple travelling by carriage to St Paul's Cathedral to attend divine service, Mrs Nicholson's attempted assassination of the king, and the queen's bounty to schoolchildren, executed in a fifteenth-century style, the equivalent to the currently fashionable taste for modern history painting. The *Gentleman's Magazine* reported on Benjamin West's 'much admired' *Last Supper* altarpiece and Thomas Jervis's spectacular, 11-foot-high east window depicting *Christ's Resurrection* flanked by *St Peter* and *St John* and the *Three Marys Going to the Sepulchre*, comprising approximately seventy over-life-size figures, West's first attempt at designing for painted glass, which was praised for being rendered in a 'masterly manner [and] beauti-

231 John Carline II and John Tilley. South elevation showing original cast-iron window mullions, St Alkmund, Shrewsbury, Shropshire, 1792–5. Shropshire Records and Research Centre, B3814, photographed 1891 prior to partial remodelling.

fully striking, [vying] in workmanship with the first in Europe' (pl. 18).[8] By then, however, West's favour with George III was waning and the critics pounced. Walpole thought his *Resurrection* 'too sombre' for the subject, Christ 'a poor figure scrambling to heaven in a fright, as if in dread of being again buried alive; and not ascending calmly in secure dignity', while Judas in the *Last Supper* altarpiece was 'so gigantic, that he seems more likely to burst by his bulk than through guilt'.[9] A fellow artist, Richard Westall, found the west window *Crucifixion* (1796) 'the strangest thing He ever saw. All sorts of shapes are introduced, & every incident . . . described in Scriptures . . . forming altogether a most absurd jumble'. But as an architectural and decorative ensemble the refurbished chapel was a triumph, the *Gentleman's Magazine* again lauding the restoration of the choir 'to its pristine beauty' and Emlyn 'an uncommon genius of that place, to whose taste, judgement, and execution, posterity will be much indebted . . . an everlasting monument to [his] memory . . . it will remain and excite praise when he shall be no more'.[10]

St Alkmund, Shrewsbury (pl. 231), by John Carline II and his partner John Tilley, offered a new way into the gothic past through the invention of architectural iron-work, the bi-product of the early establishment of the Industrial Revolution in Shropshire, of which Shrewsbury is the county town, centred at the heart of manufacture at Coalbrookdale, where the Shrewsbury architect Thomas Farnolls Pritchard had designed the world-pioneering Iron Bridge in the years 1777–9.[11]

Much is known about the designing and construction of St Alkmund, which is notable not only for its

232 Francis Eginton. *Evangelical Faith*, 1795, St Alkmund, Shrewsbury, Shropshire. Enamel paint on glass. © R. J. L. Smith.

233 John Carline II and John Tilley. Interior towards chancel with original altarpiece and Francis Eginton's *Evangelical Faith*, enamel paint on glass, St Alkmund, Shrewsbury, Shropshire, 1792–5. Shropshire Records and Research Centre, B4766 (from Birmingham City Archives glass negative), photographed 1891, prior to partial remodelling.

exclusively medieval detailing but also for its impressive use of iron technology, including cramps fixed to the ends of beams to halt bulging walls, timber wall plates secured by 'strong wrought Iron Straps and screwpins', cast-iron pillars supporting galleries, door hinges, locks and, most memorably, the thirteen large Perpendicular lancet windows with gothic 'cast Iron muntins and sash frames with one Casement in each' (four of which survived Victorian refenestration and at the time of writing are undergoing restoration). Pertinently, the rebuilding drawings (untraced) were on display for workmen to examine at Messrs Lloyds, Ironmongers in the town in 1793.[12] Nor may it be coincidental that in the same year Joseph Bottomley published *A Book of Designs*, which illustrated similar 'Gothic Windows for Chapels'.[13] While iron had been employed in sash construction in the county at least since the 1730s,[14] St Alkmund was on an unprecedented grand scale, paralleling the promotion of Coade at Windsor. Why this should have been so becomes apparent in the interior (pl. 233), a plain, aisleless preaching box originally fitted out with an altarpiece, pulpit, desk and a pair of chandeliers, all in gothic style, illuminated by large expanses of clear glass, louvred in their upper sections to provide both ventilation and protection from direct sunlight. This concentrated worshippers' attention on the shallow chancel, overwhelmed by Francis Eginton's dramatic painted glass depicting the lone figure of Evangelical Faith (pl. 232) kneeling on the Cross, eyes heavenward and arms rapturously extended towards a celestial crown appearing in the bright effulgence amid parting clouds, the equivalent of a grand painted altarpiece.[15] Carline's encouragement that it 'will certainly be a very great ornament to the Church', its modest cost of £110 worth 'more than four times that sum in appearance, and solemnity', came less than a fortnight after his recommendation to use 'cast Iron mutins and sash frames'. Recent restoration work has revealed traces of gilt on the interior framework, which would have introduced a softer, lucent tone, combined with morning sunlight flooding through the skeletal structure to create a continuous pictorial surface, merging tracery and painted glass to create the effect of an altarpiece in a gilded frame, rather than the fragmented treatment of tradi-

234 S. Porter after J. Murphy. 'West Elevation of the Church', Sta. Maria Da Vitoria, in James Murphy, *Plans Elevations Sections and Views of the Church of Batalha, in the Province of Estremadura in Portugal, with the History and Description by Fr. Luis de Sousa; with remarks. To which is prefixed an Introductory Discourse on the Principles of Gothic Architecture by James Murphy Archt.*, 1795. Engraving. Sir John Soane's Museum, London.

235 James Wyatt, attributed. South elevation design for a church, undated. Pen and ink and coloured wash. RIBA Drawings Collection.

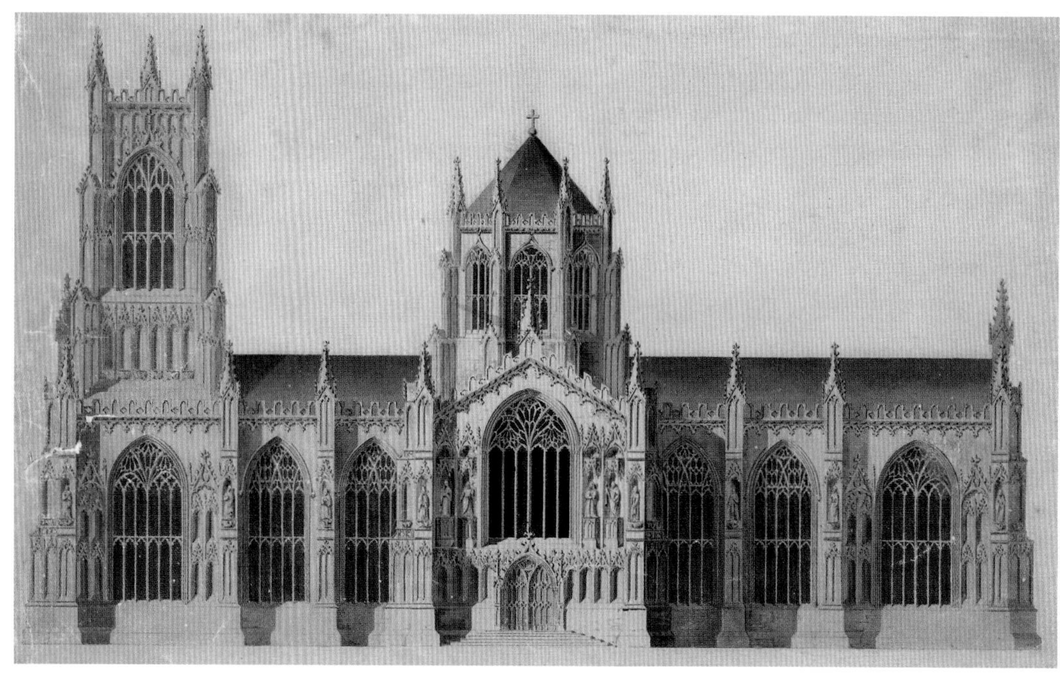

tional medieval painted glass. The parishioners 'quickened by so lively an Invitation to the Altar . . . unanimously approved'.[16]

The 1790s also witnessed innovative thinking on church planning beyond the traditional rectangular box, and introducing Picturesque vocabulary such as castellation, as well as exquisitely refined Continental-inspired decoration.

In 1760 the amateur architect Thomas Pitt, who was soon to be involved in refurbishing Carlisle Cathedral choir (pl. 199), visited the Capelas Imperfeitas at Batalha in Portugal, a unique medieval, English Decorated-style church-mausoleum, which, according to the Cambridge antiquary William Cole, who translated Pitt's (now lost) notes in 1772, he proclaimed 'the most elaborate & exquisite Gothic Architecture I ever saw'.[17] This spectacular Manueline monument was 'very little known' in Britain until the appearance of James Murphy's *Plans Elevations Sections and Views of the Church of Batalha* (London, 1795), where it was recommended to readers because 'the excellence of its architecture justly entitles it to rank with the most celebrated Gothic edifices of Europe'. The author had visited the building in 1789 'full of excitement', and in 1793, in preparation for publication, William Conyngham FSA had sketched it for engraving (pl. 234).[18] An undated scheme for an unidentified, cathedral-size church attributed to James Wyatt is best understood as the fruition of this pioneer study (pl. 235).[19] Yet the sudden proliferation of gothic octagons ringed by chapel-like recesses before 1795 can be explained only by Batalha's earlier familiarity among British cognoscenti and architects (pl. 236).

George Dance Jr, who was to subscribe to the book, employed the arrangement to striking effect at St Bartholomew-the-Less, Smithfield (pl. 237), begun in 1789, the year Murphy had visited Portugal.[20] Dance demolished the chancel of the medieval church, preserved its outer walls and south-west tower, refashioned the north aisle into a separate vestry and created within the remaining 40-foot-square nave an elegant, lierne-vaulted, pyramidal-roofed octagon, lit by lunettes within the vaulted ceiling filled with yellow, blue, lavender and pink geometric glass. While an instance of his interest in atmospheric lighting via high-placed windows and vaulted spaces (prevalent in his classical buildings), it was perhaps also a response to Murphy's advocacy of the notion that 'It is in vain that we attempt to restore Gothic Architecture, without the admission of stained glass; especially in Churches, where a degree of obscurity is perfectly consonant with the tombs.'[21]

Thomas Hardwick Jr's charmingly bijou octagonal Greek-cross 'Church designed for Thos. Johnes' (pl. 238), otherwise undocumented, is very likely an unrealised scheme for Eglwys Newydd at Hafod, Cardiganshire, which the client inherited in 1783. Perhaps not coincidentally, the painter Thomas Jones, Hardwick's travelling companion in France and Italy during 1776–8, exhibited views of Hafod in 1786 and 1788.[22]

At St George's Episcopal Chapel, Edinburgh (pl. 239), internal difficulties of adapting the form for Protestant usage prompted the building committee to question the architect, James Adam, 'concerning the want of light' and observe of one of his (now lost) drawings that the gallery front obstructed the line from an upper window to the opposite angle, shutting out daylight from the rear pews and a considerable part of the interior and casting much of it in darkness. Adding that 'letting in the light of the two North windows would confound & . . . put out all the rest' and that

> the corners of . . . the division . . . *must* come down to let in the light of the North window, [and] allowing Campbell and Wright, to judge more scientifically than you that the passages between the pillars in the gallery are too *narrow* . . . The pews below are differently arranged upon *paper* for your examination.

The annotation ends with the writer confessing: 'I never dispute or trifle with men of True genius & taste in any profession especially in that where one great Master stands alone.'[23]

Among the distinctive features of Adam's Edinburgh chapel are the castellated and bartisaned treatments of the front, motifs he repeated in the Barony Church, Glasgow (pl. 240), with its carefully arranged pyramidal composition, which is close in spirit to the Picturesque Scottish baronial villas of his more famous late brother, Robert.[24] A contemporary described the Barony as a

> beautiful design upon a modern plan [which] cannot properly be denominated either Grecian or Gothic [but] of the mixed kind, a species which . . . characterises the productions of the Adams . . . in this country, and which, from being managed with taste, often, as in the present instance, produces a very good effect. The design, has, however, not got sufficient justice, in being constructed with rubble instead of ashler work.[25]

The young John Nash pursued a similar vocabulary in his restoration of romanesque St David's Cathedral, Pembrokeshire, between 1789 and 1795 (pl. 241). In an audacious operation, a sort of latter-day Beverley Minster (pls 137–8), the bulging west front was braced by flying buttresses anchored by brutal octagonal-topped piers, while the upper wall was rebuilt in a castellated gable form with the original 'Saxon' arcade replaced by a single large window with gothic tracery salvaged from the ruins of nearby St Mary's College chapel. Nash exhibited a set of before and after views at the Society of Antiquaries of London on 5 March 1795 as a demonstration of the fabric's return to 'its restored state according to the Judgment of the Artist', qualifying the term 'because I did not think myself at liberty to change any part of the original forms but

236 (*right*) 'The Entrance of the Mausoleum of Emanuel the Great of Portugal', Sta. Maria Da Vitoria, in James Murphy, *Plans Elevations Sections and Views of the Church of Batalha, in the Province of Estremadura in Portugal, with the History and Description by Fr. Luis de Sousa; with remarks. To which is prefixed an Introductory Discourse on the Principles of Gothic Architecture by James Murphy Archt.*, 1795, detail. Engraving. Sir John Soane's Museum, London.

237 (*below*) George Dance Jr. Design for remodelling the interior, St Bartholomew-the-Less, London, 1789. Pen and ink and coloured wash. Sir John Soane's Museum, London, Dance 4.9.13.

238 Thomas Hardwick Jr. 'Church designed for Thos. Johnes', signed 'T. H.', probably Eglwys Newydd, Haford, Cardiganshire, Wales, detail, undated. Pen and ink and wash. Private collection. Courtauld Institute of Art, 783/12(36).

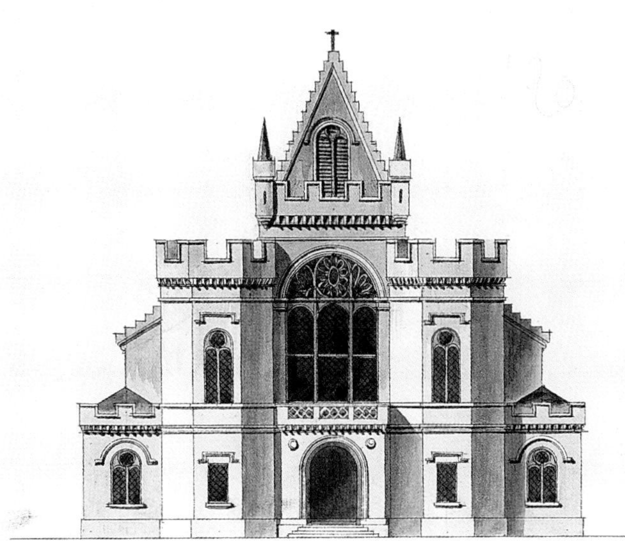

240 James Adam. Design for 'Elevation of the West front of the Barony Church Glasgow', Strathclyde, Scotland, detail, 12 January 1793. Pen and ink and wash. Sir John Soane's Museum, London, AD 37/120. Demolished 1890.

239 Front elevation, St George's Episcopal Chapel, Edinburgh, Midlothian, Scotland, in Shepherd 1829a, detail. Engraving. James Adam architect, 1792–93, altered 1934.

merely to reinstate them and where the original forms could not be ascertained, I have every where copied from other parts of the building, coeval in date with the part wanting'. He esteemed himself 'happy if he can in any way forward the magnificent & laudable purpose of the Society respecting the remains of Saxon & Gothic buildings in this Kingdom'.[26] Nonetheless, the eccentric and clumsy results were not well received. Sir Richard Colt Hoare thought the reworked façade 'presents no fine specimen of architecture'; that it was 'beneath criticism; such an heterogeneous mixture

241 John Nash. Remodelled west front, St David's Cathedral, Pembrokeshire, Wales, 1790–91, photograph prior to remodelling in 1862. From Evans and Worsley 1981, pl. 23.

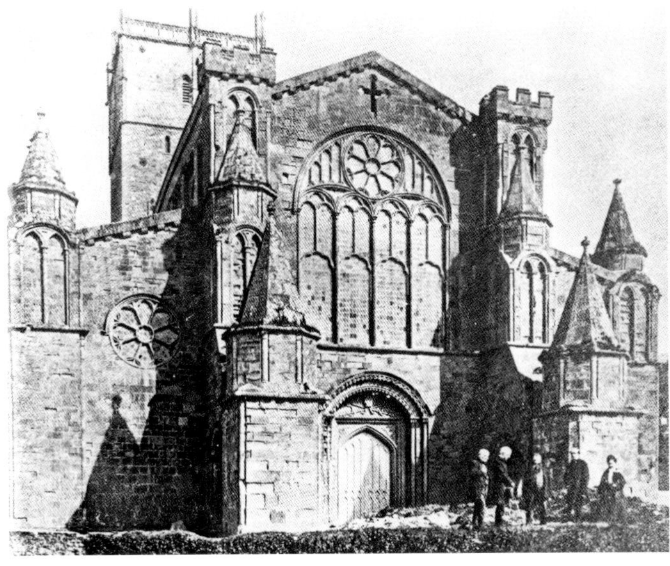

242 William Watts. South-west view, All Saints Chapel, Bath, Somerset, detail, 1794. Engraving. John Palmer architect, 1789–97, demolished 1942.

of Saxon, Gothic and castellated . . . I never before beheld'.[27]

The aristocratic All Saints Chapel, Bath (pl. 242), by John Palmer, a private development on the grassy slopes below Lansdown Crescent, was a 'Gothick edifice in a very neat tasty stile embellished with turrets and niches'.[28] Measuring 64 by 46 feet, it featured

> four recesses for stoves [and a gallery] all round . . . forming an oval . . . supported by eight light Gothic pillars, which rising to the roof branch off into ribs . . . The middle part of the ceiling . . . also oval . . . rises six feet higher, and . . . enriched with appropriate ornaments in Stucco.[29]

Among the glories of York Minster (pl. 139), Arthur Young was most struck by its 'lightness', the abundant 'surprisingly light' stone carving and 'uncommonly light' framework of the west and east windows, while others found the 'elegance and lightness [of] its pillars, Windows, Arches, & roof . . . beyond comparison'.[30] In the closing years of the century a tendency towards delicate, overly refined gothic decoration, even in the unlikely context of rude, rustic materials, produced the celebrated diminutive 'Willow Cathedral' erected by Sir James Hall in his garden in 1792 (pl. 243), an account of which was presented to the Royal Society of Edinburgh in 1797.[31] In *Essay on the Origin, History and Principles of Gothic Architecture* (1813), he argued for the sources of columns, crockets, cusps and window tracery not in grand architecture but in Nature: bundled rods, willow-poles, bark. He traced the predecessors to familiar gothic stone-constructed buildings in historical references to wickerwork structures erected at Durham and Glastonbury, illustrating a structure similar to plate 243 but with the crossing tower based closely on the fifteenth-century crown of St Nicholas, Newcastle upon Tyne.[32]

Hallian rusticity was achieved in flint and freestone at St Margaret, Thorpe Market, Norfolk (pls 244–5), designed by Henry Wood of London, vividly described in Edmund Bartell Jr's *Observations upon the Town of Cromer, Considered as A Watering Place, and the Picturesque Scenery in its Neighbourhood* (1800). It was in

> a peculiar stile [which] attracts many spectators for its novelty . . . simple and elegant . . . the points of the gables terminated by a stone cross after the monkish fashion. The inside . . . finished with extreme neatness and in parts with a considerable degree of taste. The chancel . . . and . . . west end divided from the body . . . by [a] light gothic wainscot screen [woodwork with iron diapering] decorated with modern glass paintings [depicting] the Dove sent forth from the Ark [flanked by] Moses and Aaron . . . the King's Arms, well painted upon copper . . .

flanked by the family arms in painted glass.

> The greatest defect . . . is in the disposition of the stained-glass in the windows, which instead of being concentrated in such a manner as to throw that devotional gloom into the church which produces such an evident effect upon the mind, and which appears to me to have been the original intention of stained or painted glass, is scattered over the whole window in small pieces, greens, purples, reds and yellows, regularly intermixed with white, giving to the whole an appearance of too much gaiety, independent of the unpleasant manner in which, in a day when the sun is bright, the different colours . . . are reflected over the church and upon the . . . congregation. Whoever has seen King's College Chapel or any other building where there is a profusion of painted glass and where the other parts are fitted up with Norway oak, the colour of which is dark brown, must have perceived a visible effect produced by the solemnity of its appearance. In all churches having any claim to antiquity the light appears to have been sparingly introduced, and to me it has always a very pleasing effect.

243 Alexander Carse. Design for the 'Willow Cathedral', *c.*1794. Watercolour. RIBA Library Drawings Collection, H3/1, f. 12. Sir James Hall architect, 1792.

Yet, these few defects 'are so well counterbalanced by its . . . numerous beauties . . . that it cannot fail to be in a high degree worthy the attention of the curious'.[33] It should be noted that the exterior, with its prominent corner turrets, is a pared-down, miniature version of King's.

Let us now look more closely at some of the better documented buildings in these categories by three of the leading advocates of the period: Samuel Pepys, Cockerell, John Carter and James Wyatt.

The long hiatus following the partial remodelling of St Margaret, Westminster, in the 1750s (Doc. 268, pp. 913–17) was finally interrupted in 1798, when extensive improvements were undertaken by Cockerell, one of the most imaginative yet today least appreciated church designers of the decade. (See also St Martin Outwich, London, and both Banbury, Oxfordshire, and Tickencote, Rutland.)

Cockerell's surveys of St Margaret of 1798–9 are models of their kind – systematic, thorough, honest, highly professional and indicative of the sort of training received by his own pupils, among them his brilliantly talented son, Charles Robert Cockerell, and the Yorkshireman Benjamin Henry Latrobe, who became a leading architect in America. The surveys revealed the general fabric 'very much in want of Repair', a particularly pressing problem not only because he was 'apprehensive of . . . more serious Mischiefs' but also because the parish had of 'late years greatly encreased by additional Poor, particularly the Wives and Children of Soldiers', the direct result of the current war with France.[34] Apart from a raft of incidental repairs he concentrated on the principal issues of improvement. About 70 feet of the upper south and north nave walls, filled with rubble and faced with tiles, brick, stucco and the like, together with the cornice and parapet, were taken down and rebuilt using a combination of 'sound' old and 'rich' new materials covered with Portland stone with 'proper Bond . . . thoroughly cramped & plugged . . . with Copper or other incorrosible Fastnings'. Most of the mutilated window frames were renewed with Portland stone and 'new Crown Glass in very strong lead of a larger Character'. The 'much sunk' side aisle roofs, where the 'Oak or Chestnut anciently not ceiled

244 Henry Wood. South-west view, St Margaret, Thorpe Market, Norfolk, 1796. English Heritage (National Monuments Record, AA78/2809).

245 Henry Wood. Interior towards chancel, St Margaret, Thorpe Market, Norfolk, 1796. English Heritage (National Monuments Record, AA78/2807).

over . . . covered with lead . . . assisted by additional Timber . . . Iron Straps & bolts' made them 'very weak', were remedied by relaying a 'very strong flat Roof of Riga or Dantzick fir' and inserting 'very strong wrought Iron ties . . . 40 feet long, over the heads of the Gothic Arches . . . faced with Stone'. Finding the dormers increased the roof's weakness and gave a 'very ill effect to the Appearance of the Church'; the only way to light the rear of the galleries was to increase the window heights. The chancel, which since Couse's remodelling had 'settled considerably outward, and drawn with it the Arches', was 'now so weak, as to be . . . agitated by the ringing of . . . Bells'; the resulting void occasioned 'great coldness' and weakened the preacher's voice. The dirty altar and other decorations distracted the congregation's attention and its 'general Character . . . do not correspond with the Simplicity & Stile of the Building'. These debilities were repaired and the high altar remodelled to make it 'Calm tho' rich . . . pure and uniform [and] harmonized with the general Style & Character of the rest'. The 'dressings & Decoration' were removed, carefully sorted and reinstated in a narrow bay separating the chancel and nave; the stucco covering the chancel masonry was decorated 'moderately in . . . Character with the rest of the Altar'. Throughout, special emphasis was given to preservation rather than replacement. For example, the ornaments of the recently reworked west porch had collapsed, but the 'plain & useful parts . . . sound . . . more simple & in a better Character by this mutilation' were left untouched.[35] These improvements (swept away in 1876–7), while proffered as technical expediencies, disguised a highly sophisticated decorative treatment recorded in a pair of beautifully engraved views of 1804.

Plate 246 reveals that a wainscot-panelled Speaker's Seat replaced James's pompous, inappropriately baroque throne; the west gallery organ was recased and a new hexagonal pulpit installed, raised on a central stem and supported by three pinnacled flying buttresses (reminiscent of the exterior of nearby Henry VII's Chapel). The canopied reader's desk was crafted by Edward Wyatt, carver and gilder to the Office of Works and nephew of James Wyatt. Described as comprising a 'load of work laid over them in the pointed-arch manner . . . the formation of which is altogether new and fanciful', the ensemble was among the most splendid late Georgian furniture.[36]

Plate 247 shows how the transition from nave to chancel was achieved by inserting a slender bay of delicate clasping buttresses and gabled canopies rising in tiers and holding what appears to be Andrea Casali's *trompe-l'œil* statues of *St Peter* and *St Paul* salvaged from Couse's scheme. Similar work, perhaps inspired by medieval monuments in the abbey (pl. 166), surround Alken's altar relief. Slender clustered piers soar into a lierne vault, the centre of which was finished with a large circular opening, in the manner of Hawksmoor's Westminster Abbey crossing (pl. 284), but with the addition of 'painted clouds on its concavity . . . to shew . . . an imaginary view of the realms above'.[37] Cockerell intended to 'Correct the Motley Character of the present . . . East end into a lofty Groined Arch, conformable to the general Stile of Building of the Church, with suitable but simple Decorations; and keep the whole in an Unity of Character, to give Grandeur & Effect to the rich painted Window' retained from the earlier remodelling.

Early purists were highly critical. The alterations were

> of the ridiculous kind [and] of a serious nature . . . so far as obliterating the original excellent design [which] have felt the ruthless blows of the Artificer's hammer, whose architectural wounds have been seared up with professional fancies, which will . . . be the continued butt of contempt, mingled with regret and sorrow.

The original 'extremely beautiful' north windows, which had survived the 'new creation [of the previous remodelled] Fantastic Order [are] now no more', one intended 'as a proof how the old ones are to be considered as deformed, and the work of the present day more refined and elegant', yet 'I never saw an antient window after [this] design'. Furthermore, 'Common house parapets have been given to each story; and an open porch on the South front, a true Fantastic Batty Langlean design, has had its sides filled-in, with two pointed door-ways . . . such a feature . . . only . . . met with in the Roman and Grecian styles.' The west gallery was 'a modern decoration from Coade's manufactory, containing the royal arms'; the ribs of the nave ceiling were 'half a *straight curved* line (this must be seen to be understood) and half a pedimental one', for which the only model was 'some low . . . passages . . . seen in our colleges', while the abbey-like chancel on this parochial scale was 'not to be approved of'.[38]

The author of this diatribe was John Carter, of *The Builder's Magazine* fame, who had made choir improvements at Canterbury, 'performed in the strictest attention to the original work', but also an altarpiece in Peterborough Cathedral, which Torrington condemned for the 'meanness of the fitting up'.[39] As a practising architect, his fullest energies were devoted to a new Roman Catholic chapel at Winchester, Hampshire, in 1792, courageously erected less than two years after the

246 George Hawkins after Joseph Kay. 'Interior of St. Margaret's Church, Westminster, as seen from the East End', 4 June 1804. Engraving. City of Westminster Archives Centre, E131(8). Samuel Pepys Cockerell architect, 1798–1803.

247 George Hawkins after Joseph Kay. 'Interior View of the Chancel of St Margaret's Church, Westminster', 23 April 1804. Engraving. City of Westminster Archives Centre, E131(7). Samuel Pepys Cockerell architect, 1798–1803.

Pl. 248

Inside View OF THE Altar End.

Outside View of ST. PETER'S CHAPEL, Winton.

NORMAN DOORWAY LEADING TO THE CHAPEL, FROM ST PETER'S STREET.

248 J. Passe after James Cave. 'Outside View of St. Peter's Chapel, Winton. Inside View of the Altar End. Norman Doorway Leading to the Chapel, from St. Peter's Street', Winchester, Hampshire. 1 November 1798, in John Milner, *History Civic and Ecclesiastical, & Survey of the Antiquities, of Winchester*, vol. II, 1801, following p. 240. Engraving. Author's collection. John Carter architect, 1792, remodelled 1888 and later.

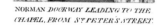

architecturally destructive anti-Dissenter 'Church and King' riots in Birmingham (see chapter 2).

The client, the Revd John Milner, vicar-apostolic of the western district of England, was the author of the two-volume *History Civil and Ecclesiastical, & Survey of the Antiquities, of Winchester* (1798–1801), which includes a detailed description and engraved views of the chapel in its heyday (pl. 248), internally entirely swept away in a later remodelling that left only a nondescript shell. It was the faith's first public place of worship to adopt gothic, redolent of associations with England's medieval past, a hallmark of Catholic church architecture that gained national currency only with Pugin's aggressive proselytising from the 1830s.[40]

Milner played a crucial role in determining the iconography and selecting the historical sources, and despite his apology for 'a departure' from Carter's drawings (untraced) 'through the inattention of the workmen, and . . . from motives of economy', the building was a decorative triumph.[41] Milner began by explaining his reasons for dismissing the 'modern style' favoured by other chapels, which were 'in general square chambers, with small sashed windows and fashionable [that is, classical] decoration, hardly to be distinguished . . . from common assembly-rooms', and instead 'to imitate the models . . . left us by our religious ancestors, who applied themselves with such ardour and unrivalled success to the cultivation and perfection of ecclesiastical architecture [by] the inventors of the Gothic style . . . and of its corresponding decorations in the middle ages', which were 'closely followed in the present oratory'.[42] The 75 by 35 foot stucco-coated block featured 'shelving buttresses' and a (now-lost) 'parapet with open quatrefoils and crocketed pinnacles, terminating in gilt crosses'. The model was King's College chapel, Cambridge, which John Soane had recently praised as

> light and elegant . . . a glorious example of the wonderful perfection of Gothic architecture; there is a boldness and mathematical knowledge peculiar to this edifice, which calms our earnest attention and admiration, which excites us to the pursuit of geometrical knowledge, and reminds us of the high opinion the ancients had of geometry.[43]

The interior of the Winchester chapel was jewel-like. Against a grid of slender half-columns attached to the side walls rising to a delicate cross vault washed by a chaste palette of 'French grey' on walls and ceiling and 'straw colour' on columns and ribs, with painted and gilt bosses of the implements of the Passion, were reflected vibrant yellow, blue and umber colours of the

249 Butter Cross, Winchester, Hampshire, detail, fifteenth century.

five, three-light windows, 'richly painted, with alternate quatrefoils and croix pates', and many ovals with 'figures of the most renowned saints or kings'. Painted glass in the overdoors depicted the 'mutual relation of the old and new law' redolent with Catholic imagery, including the *Blessed Trinity*,

> the tables of the law, surrounded with dark clouds and rays of lightning, with other objects of terror . . . the Divine Messiah at full length, resting on a cross, and in the attitude of preaching . . . the mystical dove shedding his rays . . . a crown, an olive, and a palm branch [and] the most illustrious personages belonging to the two covenants.

The quatrefoil window in the west gallery was painted by Francis Eginton with emblems of the Blessed Trinity flanked by the *Doctors of the Church* and emblems of Faith, Hope and Charity. On the west and north walls framed in ogee arches echoing the windows were *chiaroscuro* paintings on canvas by 'the ingenious and indefatigable painter' William Cave Sr, a local Catholic, depicting episodes from the New Testament copied from various Old Masters (Raphael, Lemoine, Poussin and Holbein).

The focus of the room was Cave's altarpiece after Raphael's *Transfiguration* (in the Vatican), 'allowed to be the first picture, in point of merit, extant', enclosed in a 16-foot-high cinquefoil arch painted white with gilt ornaments and buttresses with pomegranate pinnacles, the whole crowned by a lily and quatrefoil filled with 'the luminous dove', 'a transparent painting upon glass . . . which, by means of light that is let in upon it from behind, produces a surprising and pleasing effect'. The flanking doors were 'rich with Gothic carvings', including emblems of the Four Evangelists and gilt cherubs supporting the canopies, with a range of blind arches above and figures of *St Peter* and *St Paul* 'painted in light and shade, to imitate sculpture'. At the top of the wall was 'a closed embattlement' with angels in the act of adoration and *trompe-l'œil* statues of *St Swithin* and *St Birinus*, the chapel's patrons, with small compartments immediately below painted with 'the most remarkable incidents in the histories of these two holy personages'.

The furnishings, mostly painted white and gilt, were equally splendid. The 'peculiarly rich and elaborate' tabernacle on the altar was 'a model of the west end of York Minster, but with such variations as the nature and use . . . require', with the door carved with emblems of the Passion and the towers containing canopied niches holding 'gilt emblematic statues . . . of Faith, Hope, the Love of God, and the Love of our Neighbours', surmounted by a Cross 'covered with stones of cut glass' and an 'exceedingly well wrought' ivory of *Christ*. Six candlesticks stood on a carved gothic fascia. There was also a hanging lamp 'richly sculptured, gilt and painted, with a number of angels supporting the several emblems of our Saviour's passion'. The *Deposition* on the altar frontal, copied from the 'celebrated picture of Domenichino, in the possession of lord Arundell' and side panels depicting 'Calvary with the three vacant crosses [and] the garden and sepulchre in which our Lord was buried [were] painted in chiaro obscuro, to represent carving'. Nearby were small credences 'copied from similar tables still existing in certain chantries in [Winchester] cathedral', above which were carved and gilt 'emblematic devices' of hearts surrounded by a spear and transfigured by a sword, 'surrounded with rays of glory'. The priest's seat was copied from Edward I's Coronation Chair in Westminster Abbey. Two 'gorgeous lamp pedestals' standing outside the altar railings were 'borrowed' from the fifteenth-century Butter Cross in Winchester High Street (pl. 249).[44] Despite this heartfelt commitment to the Pre-Reformation past, the chapel by no means epitomised 'revived . . . antient Gothic in all its richest ornaments, and fascinating charms'.[45] This was regarded as being the prerogative of the 'ingenious Mr James Wyatt'.

By the time Wyatt succeeded to the Westminster Abbey surveyorship in 1776 no further structural improvements were required and his most notable achievement was masterminding the temporary decorations for the Handel Commemoration staged between 26 May and 5 June 1784. In *An Account of the Musical Performances* (1785), Charles Burney lauded these as 'one of the grandest and most magnificent spectacles which imagination can delineate', where the architect's 'genius in *Gothic* . . . so wonderfully corresponded with the style of architecture of this venerable and beautiful structure, that there was nothing visible . . . which did not harmonize with the principal tone of the building, and which may not, metaphorically, have been said to be in *perfect tune* with it' (frontispiece and pl. 250). He described the organ in its gothic case (built for Canterbury Cathedral but temporarily sidetracked for the occasion), the orchestra hung with 'festoons of crimson morine' and at the east end the royal box 'in a beautiful Gothic style . . . richly decorated and furnished with crimson satin, fringed with gold'. Among an audience of some 3,000, Betsy Sheridan, sister of the playwright, noted the bishops' seats 'adorn'd with Purple' and a band of 600 performing *Esther*, *The Dettingen Te Deum*, a selection from the *Funeral Anthems* and the oratorios including *Messiah*, 'so truly great that my whole frame thrill'd'.[46] The place of worship had been secularised and transformed briefly into a combination of theatre and throne-room. Wyatt repeated some features of the royal box in an unrealised bishop's throne designed for Lichfield (pl. 251), and it was adapted by Edward Glanvill for the Handel Commemoration of 1792 held next door in St Margaret's (pl. 252).[47]

These temporary celebrations, however successful, were subordinated to the core of Wyatt's ecclesiastical activities, which lay in cathedral improvements, concentrated at Lichfield, Salisbury, Hereford and Durham, as well as at two Oxford colleges, covering the crucial years between 1781 and 1805. Unfortunately for him, these works coincided with the eruption of his archenemy John Carter's public rant in the *Gentleman's Magazine* and in the Society of Antiquaries of London against his restoration methods, one of the turning points in the evolution of the gothic style, with the

250 W. and J. Walker after J. Dixon. 'View of the magnificent Box erected for their Majesties, in Westminster Abbey, under the Direction of Mr. James Wyatt, at the Commemoration of Handel', 30 June 1784, from *The European Magazine*. Engraving. The Bodleian Library, University of Oxford, Gough Maps 23, f. 10b.

result that for the first time we gain a fuller, many-sided but also more biased view of Wyatt's achievement in this genre. Carter, 'prompt, and ready to come forward in vindication of our National Architecture', wrote of fears of destruction of the 'remains of antient architectural splendour; which . . . should be venerated, and meet with . . . warmest protection . . . instead of which, a more than barbarous joy seems to possess the souls of these innovators at this (unfortunately for the world) innovating day!'[48]

In 1781 Wyatt surveyed 'much mutilated' Lichfield Cathedral, a victim of Civil War bombardment, and between 1783 and 1795 made designs for combining the existing choir and Lady Chapel into a single, uniform

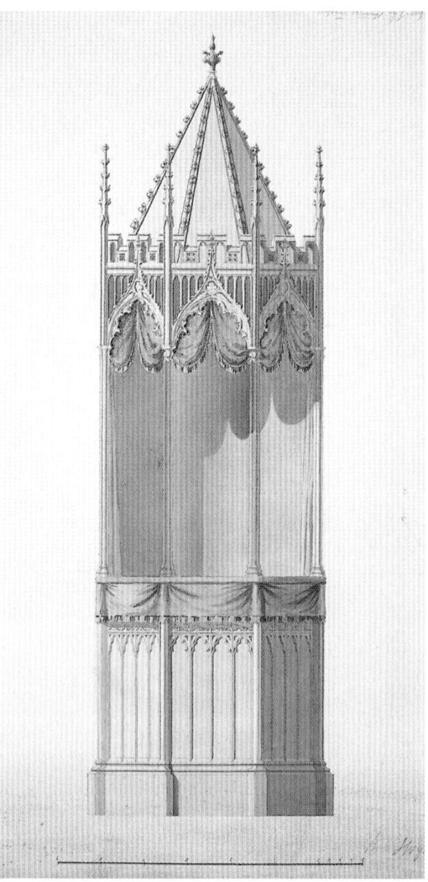

251 James Wyatt. Elevation design for the Bishop's throne, *c.*1787, Lichfield Cathedral, Staffordshire. Pen and ink and coloured wash. Staffordshire Record Office, M.1064/17.

'Grand Choir' (pl. 226). This featured a reredos incorporating fragments from its medieval predecessors and a new east window of the *Resurrection* painted by Francis Eginton after Joshua Reynolds. Some were quick to condemn:

> Every method of confusion is introduced; the periods of the Gothic architecture are cruelly confounded . . . the South transept buttressed up . . . with two such masses of stone-work as would disgrace the clumsiest country mason. Having seen how well the North transept of Beverley minster was restored 80 years ago . . . I am the more surprised at such oukward management in the improved state of mechanics among us.[49]

The 'choir skreen . . . is a patchwork of old and modern Gothic'.[50] Carter offered a gloomy assessment: lead roof covering that gave 'an air of dignity' replaced by 'common house slating'; hijacked parapets, battlements and pinnacles reducing the roof 'to a dripping eve's finishing, like the coverings of a barn, or any other outhouse repository'; loss of 'high enrichments [and] *minutiae* of our antient architecture' on the north and south transepts; renewed window mullions 'displaying more the art of invention, than the pride of being thought good copyists'; the choir entrance 'entirely shut out from the nave by the new screen and the *glazier's work* . . . of fresh manufacture, and . . . remnants of the demolished . . . screen' (Carter recalling 'the divine beauties of that superb decoration'); the east window blocked up to give greater prominence to Eginton's work so that 'a theatric glare of light may be thrown on a modern painting on glass; and . . . the Communion-table . . . thrown into darkness and insignificance'.[51] This was just the beginning of Wyatt's Calvary.

On 2 June 1788, in answer to the dramatic collapse of the romanesque west tower of Hereford Cathedral two years earlier (pl. 107), Wyatt recommended removing the unsafe central spire, raising the tower several feet, taking down the 'much injured' nave and aisles, rebuilding the west end 'to the original extent [but] adding flying buttresses to support the Walls' and erecting internally 'new Groins of Bracketing, Lath and Plaister', solutions alien to parts of the medieval fabric yet 'necessary . . . to reinstate the whole in the most perfect manner that the nature of the building will admit' and to ensure 'the future preservation of so noble a pile of Building'. The scheme received broad approval but its implementation was troubled by controversy over reducing the original dimensions. Bishop Beauclerk opposed the idea suggested by the dean and chapter in 1786 of 'contracting the West end' and making the transepts 'nearly equidistant' so that the 'great Tower . . . will stand in the Center of the whole Building', producing a 'more uniform' ensemble. Instead, he ordered a new design 'to cover the whole site according to its ancient Dimensions'. Anthony Keck and Thomas Hardwick Sr prepared designs.[52] Before a decision was taken, Beauclerk died and his successor, John Butler, commissioned Wyatt to add what the local press described as a 'new part . . . to this venerable structure [which] is plain and elegant, and will prove a support and ornament to the present building' (pl. 253). No doubt uncomfortable working with romanesque, he produced a front based on fourteenth-century Winchester Cathedral, but during construction, when collapsing scaffolding killed a workman, the surviving side walls of the nave spread outward further, confirming that this entire section required rebuilding. A 'considerable addition' to the crossing tower was proposed in 1793, 'in lieu of the Spire [as] essential . . . to the dignity of the Building, as well as ornamental to the

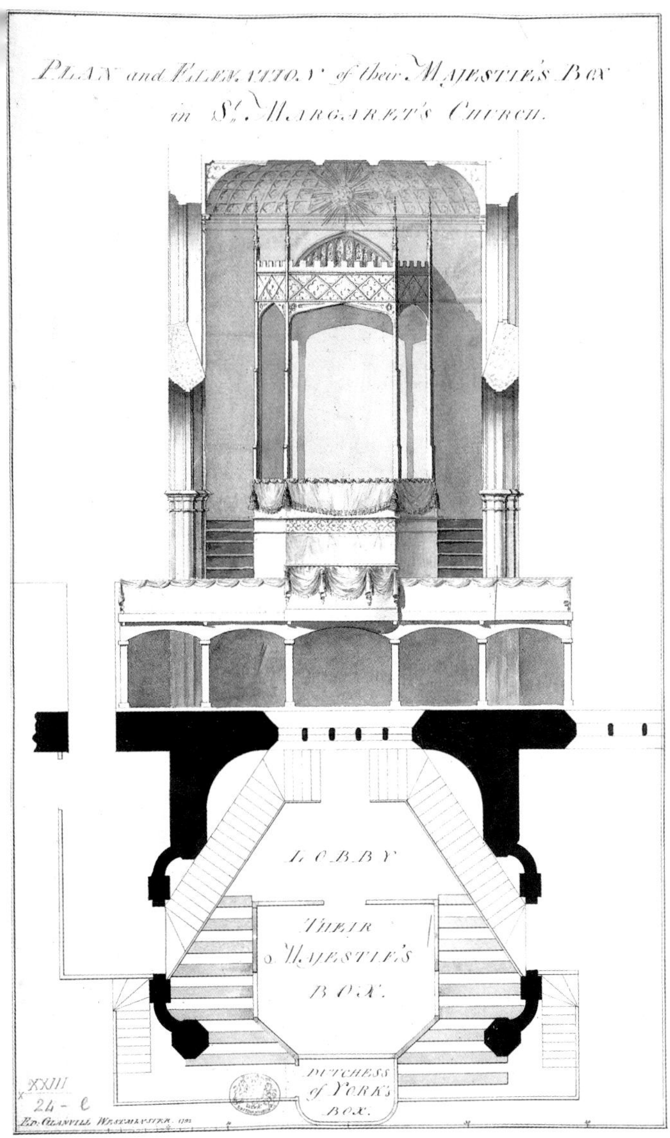

252 Edward Glanvill. 'Plan and Elevation of their Majestie's Box in St. Margaret's Church', Westminster, London, 1792. Pen and ink and wash. © The British Library Board, K.Top. XXIII-24-e.

surrounding country'. Buttresses were erected to counteract the spreading south transept walls.[53]

The restoration was mercilessly condemned in the *Gentleman's Magazine*. 'The nave looks *neat* and *nice*, but all its grandeur and antiquity is . . . no more. The proposed addition to the tower is so flat that it will not be adopted, and it had been well if none of the plans and projects had been carried into execution.' 'Wyat endeavoured very much to lengthen the choir . . . as he has done at Lichfield: had he succeeded it would have been all seeing and no *hearing* . . . but what is going to be done very shortly within must violate every rule of propriety, and of respect for the skill and taste of our forefathers': the north transept was to be closed off. This was an 'act of folly and want of taste in the chapter'.[54]

Wyatt's activities at Salisbury (1787–92) further opened the Pandora's box of vituperative public debate and famously his harsh condemnation as a 'Destroyer'. The cathedral, begun in 1220 and completed within sixty years in an exclusively Early English style, enjoyed a reputation for displaying 'uniform' design, still a '*tout ensemble* . . . perfect in its kind for 500 years from its first erection' (pl. 143).[55] The demolition in 1790 of the unique free-standing belfry (though long considered 'neither useful nor ornamental') on grounds that it would 'give a beautiful view of the church from the High-street', sparked a controversy unprecedented in its press exposure.[56]

Richard Gough, Director of the Society of Antiquaries of London, had earlier, in 1789, alerted readers of the *Gentleman's Magazine* to the 'rage of reformation' that prompted clearing the Lady Chapel of monuments to open the space into the choir 'under pretence of giving *uniformity*' to the vast interior, and the destruction of two side chapels and 'curious paintings' on the choir and transept vaults '*scraped* off and covered . . . with a uniform wash'. This was done partly to neutralise irregularities created by the insertion of a south window to light the high altar.[57] Defending Wyatt's alterations, an 'Enthusiastic Admirer' countered Gough's

253 Artist unknown. South-west view, St Ethelbert's Cathedral, Hereford, Herefordshire, detail, *c.*1840. Watercolour. The Dean and Chapter of Hereford and the Hereford Mappa Mundi Trust.

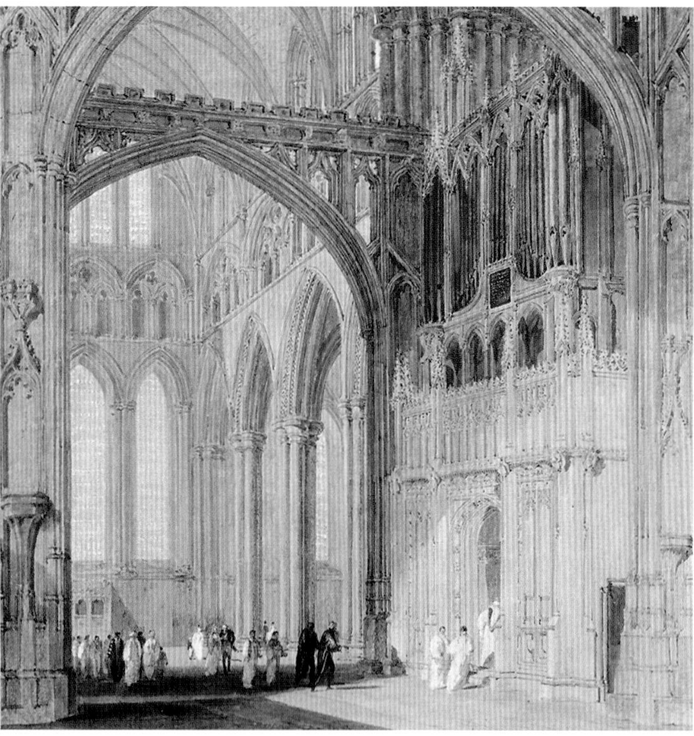

254 Joseph Mallord William Turner. *View of the Great Crossing, North Transept, Choir Screen and Organ* (Salisbury Cathedral, Wiltshire), detail, *c.*1802. Watercolour. © Salisbury and South Wiltshire Museum. James Wyatt architect, screen and organ, 1787–92.

'spleen . . . vented against' the scheme on grounds that the building will be 'rendered infinitely more beautiful' since there was 'nothing . . . more discordant' than the chapels 'erected at different periods . . . 200 years subsequent' to finishing the main fabric, while the whitewash 'will give harmony, propriety, and effect' to an interior 'reduced to an unreasonable condition [by] the madness of Cromwell's adherents'. Gough counterblasted that 'were an architect of the 18th century to determine on . . . propriety, conformity, or correspondence of the parts of a building, of four preceeding centuries, we might sacrifice every part of the most beautiful of our public structures to his ideas of elegance'.[58] 'Philagothos' then asked if the cathedral must remain 'with heaps of chaotic deformity, because the culpable negligence of past times . . . allowed . . . irregular and indecent interments? Or . . . accounted impious to lop off the excrescences which ignorance and vanity had attached to . . . the most beautiful structure, and to restore it to its primitive simplicity and elegance!'[59]

This suggests that Wyatt and Bishop Shute Barrington were aiming to fulfil the beau idéal of the building as the pristine architecture presented in Francis Price's much-lauded *A Series of particular and useful Observations, Made with great Diligence and Care, upon that Admirable Structure, The Cathedral-Church of Salisbury* (1753) with its unsullied engravings, the 1774 edition of which Wyatt owned and is today preserved in the cathedral library. Interestingly, his replacement of the medieval pulpitum by a spectacular screen and organ, immortalised by Turner (pl. 254), was not criticised (though both were swept away in 1863).

In 1789 Wyatt restored the medieval altarpiece at New College chapel, Oxford, mutilated during the Reformation and hidden under a layer of plaster until 'an elegant specimen' was rediscovered in 1779 and the whole 'Gothic work' was exposed 'with great care . . . up to the cieling'.[60] This entailed commissioning from Richard Westmacott Sr five marble reliefs depicting the *Salutation of the Virgin*, *Nativity*, *Descent from the Cross*, *Resurrection* and *Ascension* (still *in situ*) to replace the destroyed images of the same subjects.[61] The architect's most interesting work here was his involvement in producing painted glass windows redolent of the middle ages. When he assumed direction for the latter commission it had already undergone three distinct programmes of window renewal, in 1735–40, 1765 and 1772–4. The College criticised the last because the niches were 'not of that pure Gothic I would wish, having too much resemblance to those grotesque designs which should never be admitted into any serious composition'.[62] Within four years the west window was replaced with a *Nativity* after Correggio flanked by tiers of *Virtues* and *Graces* painted by Thomas Jervais after cartoons by Sir Joshua Reynolds, which proved even more controversial (pl. 97). A correspondent to the *Gentleman's Magazine* praised 'the restoration of its antient splendour, set like an antique jewel in a precious case of modern workmanship, under the direction of the ingenious Mr Wyatt, whose . . . skill and judgement in regard to Gothic architecture are as truly unequalled by any artist since the introduction of the Grecian and Roman orders into this country'.[63] Nonetheless, 'A FRIEND OF J. CARTER' censured the 'central points in Mr W's new roofs [as] too flat, and the ramifications too few and plain for the manner he professes to imitate'.[64]

Between 1790 and 1792 the architect proposed replacing the classical fittings in Magdalen College chapel, Oxford, with elaborately detailed Perpendicular stalls, canopied niches suspended from angelic corbels between the windows, a new plaster lierne vault 'in the manner' of New College and a reredos covering the entire east wall, obliterating Isaac Fuller's seventeenth-century *Last Judgement* mural. Of three alternative

255 James Wyatt. Design for the reredos, Magdalen College Chapel, Oxford, Oxfordshire, 1792. Pencil, ink and watercolour. College archives, FA5/3/1AD/4.

designs for the last, all retaining a Spanish baroque painting of *Christ Carrying the Cross* presented in 1745, one (pl. 255) was closely modelled on William Waynflete's chantry chapel in Winchester Cathedral, an apt choice because this famous bishop (died 1486) had founded the College (pl. 256). Restoring the old glass in the west window, chronicled in a group of letters written between 1793 and 1796 to the College by Francis Eginton, involved 'making a sketch conformable to . . . Wyatt's Plan', preparing a 'Compleat Model' and drawing a 'Correct Cartoon of every compartment the full size of the Glass with all the lost Figures restored according to the Original Design'. The artist reckoned this

> one of the grandest compositions I ever saw [with] the effect [answering] your highest expectation. I have repainted every part and instead of the cold tint which pervaded the whole of this and every other window I have seen in claro obscuro, I have defus'd a general warm tint throughout, which gives harmony to the colouring and will produce a soft and pleasant light in the chapel . . . for nothing is so destructive to the effect of painted Glass as too great a quantity of unmodified light being admitted into the . . . Room.

In the context of late Georgian taste it is not difficult to appreciate Eginton's popularity among both clients and architects.[65]

Anti-Wyatt ferocity regarding restoration reached its climax at Durham Cathedral beginning in 1794, yet ironically here he was not wholly to blame, as close scrutiny of the documents reveal.[66] The 'Exceeding Ruinous [and] indifferent appearance' of the stupendous cathedral[67] had been prone to improvements

256 J. Passe after James Cave. 'South East View of Bishop Waynflete's Chantry in Winchester Cathedral', Hampshire, 1 March 1809, in Milner, 1809, vol. II, opposite p. 60. Engraving. Author's collection. Erected 1366–1404

257 James Wyatt. Design for remodelling the exterior of the Nine Altars Chapel, Durham Cathedral, County Durham, 1795. Pen and ink and wash. Dean and Chapter Library, no. 12.

throughout the century and suffered from a lack of professional expertise and a predilection for local patronisation. Bishop Trevor wrote to Sanderson Miller in 1751, for example, seeking the name of an appropriate carver, since he was 'afraid our People of Durham do not much understand this kind of Antique Work'. Significantly, despite the overwhelming presence of romanesque, all the new work was in the gothic style.

In 1770 Thomas Wright of Durham proposed replacing the lead needle spires with 'Minarets' (crocketed pinnacles) on the crossing and west towers. In 1777 another local, John Wooler, with a view to 'restoring the whole into as complete a State of Repair as the structure itself may require', discovered a 'Rent' in the nave vault, but since it was probably 'of a pretty long standing . . . its future Stability may not be necessary . . . entered into for the present'. He recommended it 'filled up . . . with comon plaister of Lime & Hair', some of the external walls rebuilt 'with the best Stone . . . in as regular and uniform a Manner as can well be done, and . . . Capp . . . them with . . . proper Pinacles'. To remedy the 'almost universal . . . wasting Condition of the Stones . . . it will be necessary to chip or pare off . . . 3 Inches . . . to bring [it] to a tolerable even or Streight Surface [and fill up the joints] with a proper Mortar, struck in with the Chips or Splinters of flints and Gallets', in this way resisting 'the Ravages of Time for Centurys to come'. The modern conservator's nightmare. In 1779 Wooler tackled repairing the Nine Altars Chapel at the east end, prescribing a partial deconstruction and replacement with a 'jamfering Basis . . . as nearly as may be the same as that of the Eastern Shaft . . . Beads, Staffes, and Casses in every respect the same'. It was this somewhat haphazardly repaired, shabby-looking fabric that Wyatt inherited in 1794, and where he concentrated on making several major improvements.

The unfinished, irregular exterior of the Nine Altars Chapel was largely rethought, with the pinnacles and roof gable enriched, the windows restructured and the medieval painted glass replaced by plain glazing, creating a balanced, symmetrical but characteristically joyless composition (pl. 257). Wyatt also proposed embellishing the corners of the crossing tower of 1490 with statued niches and crowning it with a new flying buttressed octagonal lantern and needle spire reminiscent of the Capelas Imperfeitas, providentially published in 1795 in Murphy's *Plans Elevations Sections and Views of the Church of Batalha*. Stylistically inappropriate, this was not realised. Inside, he suggested, again unsuccessfully, combining the choirscreen and organ (the latter replacing the baroque case of 1683) in a single, splendid gothic structure (pl. 258). Its flanks were modelled on the exquisite fourteenth-century Neville screen standing behind the communion table.[68] Wyatt would have been familiar with similar ogee-domed canopies at Westminster Abbey (pl. 153). A new, Lincoln-inspired altar-screen, elevated and transparent in a manner envisaged by Walpole for the abbey in 1775, repeated motifs already employed at Magdalen College (pl. 255).[69]

In 1795 the dean and chapter resolved to raze the romanesque chapter house, which Wyatt had 'pronounced . . . ruinous', and replace it with 'a new room . . . erected on the same Scite according to the Plan given in by Mr Morpeth' (successor to Nicholson, who had died in 1793). Bishop Barrington also approved Wyatt's scheme for erecting a 'New Terrace' in front of the cathedral overlooking the River Wear, which would have entailed the wholesale demolition of the magnificent twelfth-century Galilee Chapel (which Wooler had specified in 1777 as having 'Defects in the Foundation [and] ought to be restor'd'). Since the building housed the Venerable Bede's tomb and attracted penitents, the dean mercifully reversed his order.

258 James Wyatt. Design for the 'Elevation of the Organ Screen towards the Nave', Durham Cathedral, County Durham, 26 September 1795. Pen and ink and wash. Dean and Chapter Library, no. 9.

Elsewhere, things were not going well for Wyatt. Was this to be his Waterloo? During 1795–6 he 'completely renewed' the roof and east window as well as making 'other repairs' to the early seventeenth-century pseudo-gothic chapel of Lincoln's Inn, London, which 'enraged' the client on account of the inflated cost of £7,000, which he claimed might have been done for £1,500.[70]

It was at this propitious moment that Carter pounced. A vociferous critic of modern misuses of authentic gothic and a staunch advocate of minimum interference in historic fabrics, he subscribed to the notion of the natural growth of great medieval buildings and approved the 'blending together of [romanesque and gothic] species of architecture [as] a happy and picturesque effect', expounding in an unrelenting barrage of articles entitled 'On the Pursuit of Architectural Innovation' published in monthly issues of the *Gentleman's Magazine* between 1797 and 1817.[71]

Carter himself had not been free of censure. Torrington attacked his 'miserably-fancied' choirscreen and the 'meanness' of his altar at Peterborough Cathedral (1780), while Plumptre thought the fittings 'in a modern way . . . by no means tallies with the antique grandeur [of this] most magnificent' building.[72] Nor could Carter have easily criticised Wyatt's proposed replacement of Durham's old choirscreen since he himself condemned its mannerist 'enrichments . . . so peculiar to the reign of Charles II [as a] disgusting piece of perverted skill'.[73]

Meanwhile, Carter's reputation as a talented architectural illustrator and a serious medievalist steadily grew. He published *Specimens of the Ancient Sculpture and Painting* (1780–94), *Views of Ancient Buildings in England* (six volumes, 1786–93), *The Ancient Architecture of England* (1795–1814), *Plans, Elevations, Sections and Specimens of the Architecture and Ornaments of . . . St Stephen's Chapel, Westminster* (1795), followed by Exeter Cathedral (1797) and Bath Abbey (1798), as well as various publications with Richard Gough and the Society of Antiquaries' *Vetusta Monumenta*. Carter was elected a Fellow in 1795, hailed as 'Antiquity's most resolute friend',[74] and in the same year, in preparation for producing detailed drawings for the Society, visited Durham and was 'much dissatisfied with alterations making by Wyatt . . . who', according to the diarist Farington, 'instead of restoring, which is all that Carter thinks ought to be done, is introducing parts quite out of character'.[75] He then attacked the so-called 'improvements' publicly in the *Gentleman's Magazine*. The (premature) reports of the chapter house's destruction was ridiculed as having been 'declared an uncomfortable place of no interest . . . in a dangerous state of decay' and thus replaced by a 'modern chamber, with every *elegant* and fashionable assortment of luxurious furniture . . . an elegant drawing room [by an] Architect . . . in the race for glorious change'. Carter asked: 'Why cut from an aged trunk the chief stem which gives life to the still flourishing foliage of its wide extending branches?'[76] The pinnacles of the Nine Altars Chapel sprouted 'spires entirely unlike their first work'.[77] Merging choir and Lady Chapel produced a 'dreary continuation' of space, the 'innovating pranks played with the sacred repositories' resulting in the 'most glaring conspicuous . . . confusion in architectural modes'.[78] Fortunately, the medieval altar screen 'endures still', unlike those replaced by Wyatt at Lichfield and Salisbury.[79] Carter concluded: 'Our Cathedrals, according to the new system, are either to be new decorated, new arranged (not through worldly motives or new principles), or left to their *just* deserts, neglect; decay and ruin of course succeeding. The end with some is then gained.'[80]

Animosity spilled over into another celebrated medieval monument, St Stephen's Chapel in the Palace of Westminster (destroyed by fire in 1834), which Carter had first recorded in drawings for the Society of Antiquaries in 1791 but was hindered by the 'incumbrance of modern brick walls, cielings, galleries, partitions, benches, &c.'.[81] After the removal of modern wainscot in 1800, he was, despite several attempts, refused entry on Wyatt's orders, in his position as Surveyor of the King's Works, and in revenge for this humiliation Carter aired his grievances in print, recounting how in 1797 'the ingenious Architect' had been 'black-balled' from membership to the much-coveted Society.[82] John Milner was prevented from reading to members his 'Dissertation on the modern Style of altering antient Cathedrals', which exposed Wyatt's architectural misdemeanours, by friends 'fearful for that gentleman's fame as an architect, and . . . that this description of the destruction committed by him in Salisbury cathedral . . . would . . . incapacitate him from having the honour to enjoy a seat among them'.[83]

Nevertheless, his election was postponed by only a few months. In 1806 the Durham Cathedral chapter resolved that William Atkinson and John Bernasconi estimate the expense of completing the central tower, including 'Battlements & Figures', as well as, surely for Carter, the perfidiousness of 'producing the Effect of Roughness & the Appearance of Antiquity and . . . such opinion as can be supported by experiment . . . as to the Probability of the Duration of the Cement'.[84]

Some of Carter's enmity was focused on Wyatt's false principle of imposing classical discipline on medieval buildings. At Salisbury the notion of creating 'a regular uniform design of one pure style of Architecture pervading every part [while] certainly to be admired, as most creditable to the Architect, who has conformed to those rules laid down in the examples of the Roman and Grecian schools', ought nevertheless to be proscribed in the face of 'that indescribable delight received from the beautiful irregularity conspicuous on our other Cathedrals [which] has . . . its consequent charms, equal, if not superior to the squared precepts of regular design'.[85] This led to debates on the relative merits of classical and gothic for churches. 'Jack Prancer' expounded in the *Gentleman's Magazine* 'the *superior* elegance, richness, grace, and propriety, of the Gothic architecture over the ridiculous and contemptible *plainness* and *simplicity* of the Grecian', whereas 'Will Prancer' praised St Paul's Cathedral,

> which some Gothic *deluded* admirers have dared to term a huge religious 'bird-cage'; for . . . the first column lets us know . . . what every other part of the structure consists of. Not so our old Gothic cathedrals [where we] run over the *silly, endless, fantastic* varieties, which at every step stands to *obstruct* our perambulations. Oh! the waste of paper and time that such *savage* piles have occasioned, turning the heads of superannuated Antiquaries, who fondly imagine that by such labours they do their country service![86]

In truth, until the succession of gothic styles was widely understood, both admirers and critics of medieval churches had few ways of conceptualising them as the work of different times, which overlapped with what were regarded as positive or negative features about gothic buildings: variety, movement, richness versus chaos, disorder, confusion.

Gothic in eighteenth-century Britain, neither so simplistic nor unilinear as the evidence presented in chapters 12 to 16 might suggest, in practice involved two concurrent streams: Carter's beloved, unadulterated medievalism and a mixture of gothic and classical. Of the latter, 'Indoctus' pointed out in a letter to the *Gentleman's Magazine*, supporting Wyatt's improvements at Salisbury, that 'there are few Gothic churches part of which has not been taken away, and . . . supplied in a dissimilar style . . . Saxon united with . . . Gothick, and . . . Grecian . . . sometimes . . . all injudiciously jumbled together'. At Winchester the nave and choir are separated by

> a very handsome Grecian skreen . . . by Inigo Jones . . . a beautiful Gothic altar-piece is decorated by a canopy and festoons in the Grecian style. Of all the separate parts who does not admire the excellence? But who does not . . . perceive their disagreement? . . . the efforts of our modern artists tend to clean . . . Gothic architecture . . . from its corruptions . . . Our modern Palladio, Mr. Wyatt, is now busy in dispelling this great absurdity, which is something like mixing the Greek and Gothic mythology in poetry.[87]

Carter himself experienced difficulty in evaluating this mixture, evident, for example, in how ill informed he was when ululating against the 'truly-ridiculous jumble of Roman and Grecian decoration intruded on the upper part' of Westminster Abbey's west towers by 'Wren [whose] performances evince how much that architect despised his country's native architecture, [and] makes us turn over our eyes . . . with disgust and regret',[88] where, in fact, this stylistic hybridity was a tendency of Wren's brilliantly wayward disciple, Nicholas Hawksmoor (pl. 261).

The dilemma that this posed for architects, particularly those most committed to the cause of ecclesiastical classicism, is well demonstrated in the case of James Stuart, pioneer Greek revivalist and co-author of the influential *Antiquities of Athens* (volume I, 1762), who otherwise did not dabble in the Middle Ages, except in insisting on gothic for the altarpiece of King's College chapel (p. 241). Commissioned in 1771 to remodel the east end of medieval St George's Chapel, Windsor, he offered improbably and perhaps even diffidently a spectacular gothic cacophony (pl. 259), a broadened, undisciplined version of Hawksmoor's study for the west front of Westminster Abbey, but with none of its avant-garde originality (pl. 155). His presentation drawing is dramatically rendered in jewel-like colours against a black background to emphasise the desired gloomy ecclesiastical ambience. Inexplicably, this was rejected in favour of a classical alternative (appearance unrecorded), but then in 1785 this structure was removed by royal command in favour of a more authentic gothic ensemble designed by Thomas Sandby and executed by Henry Emlyn (pl. 18).[89]

An equally disconcerting yet inevitable outcome was the rejection of Carter's striking design dated 1 August 1778 for the Westminster Abbey monument to William Pitt, 1st Earl of Chatham (pl. 260). This depicted his final appearance in the House of Lords four months earlier, on 2 April, when he collapsed during a crucial debate on the American war, precipitating his death

259 James Stuart. 'A Design for The east end of St. Georges Chapel', Windsor Castle, Berkshire, 1771. Pen and ink and gouache. Chapter Archives and Library, Windsor, F. 21, by permission of the Dean and Chapter of Windsor.

within a month.[90] Carter shows the statesman 'in his last sickness' flanked by Lord Camden and Britannia 'weeping over her dying son', dressed in a combination of contemporary clothes and classical drapery, arranged frieze-like and raised on a gothic tomb chest set against a tripartite screen modelled on the fourteenth-century tomb of John of Eltham.[91] This marked an unprecedented treatment, the first reappearance in abbey tombs of gothic motifs since the end of the middle ages. The dean and chapter, however, favoured John Bacon's wholly classical scheme of 1779, in keeping with current stylistic preferences throughout the building.[92]

260 Royce after John Carter. 'Design for a Monument, to the Memory of William Pitt, Earl of Chatham', Westminster Abbey, London, in 'A Society of Architects', *The Builder's Magazine*, 1774–8, pl. CLXXX. Engraving. Author's collection.

261 Antonio Canaletto. *Westminster Abbey with a procession of the Knights of the Order of Bath*, with St Margaret's church in the background, London, 26 June 1749. Oil on canvas. Westminster Abbey Library.

Seventeen

THE 'BASTARD BREED'

Architecture owes all that is perfect to the Greeks . . . The barbarism of succeeding centuries . . . called forth a new system . . . in which neglected proportions and ornament childishly crowded produced nothing but stones in fretwork, shapeless masses and a grotesque extravagance . . . Let us admit, however . . . this architecture had its beauty . . . bold outline . . . delicate chiselling and . . . untrammeled grandeur . . . We have halted between two styles, and the result is a new kind of architecture that is only half antique and may make us regret having abandoned Gothic architecture altogether.[1]

A sort of Medley, neither Gothic, nor anything else[2]

What! is the Grecian temple better calculated to inspire devotion in a Christian than in a Gothic cathedral?[3]

The quandary that Georgians found themselves in the face of stylistic schizophrenia voiced in the above quotes, memorably expressed in Hawksmoor's completion of the west front of Westminster Abbey (pl. 261), is epitomised in the following fiction entitled 'A Ramble on the Heath' by Ephraim Hardcastle (the nom de plume of W. H. Pyne) published in *Wine and Walnuts; or, After-Dinner Chit-Chat* (1823). Readers were invited to eavesdrop on a conversation of assorted celebrities – Garrick, Reynolds, Sterne, the antiquary Andrew Ducarel and others – discussing the Palladian church of St John, Hampstead, with its idiosyncratic skyline of battlements, pinnacles and needle spire (pl. 262). 'Why, that's Burlington Harry, sure, trudging up the path', referring to Henry Flitcroft, who had 'studied in the Burlington school' and had submitted an unsuccessful scheme for St John's. 'What do you think of my church, Mister Gainsborough?', he asked. The painter replied: 'I would proclaim that he who build a church, should erect it in the old English architecture, and fail not, or lose his ears. Why did you not make a Gothic church?' Flitcroft: 'For two good reasons . . . First, because we had not money enough – and, secondly . . . because – because – because I have no opinion of Gothic.' Gainsborough: 'Burlington had a contempt for Gothic; *ergo*, the Burlington school have a contempt for Gothic.' This was followed by much laughter: 'Ha Ha!'[4]

Here a distinction needs to be made between, on the one hand, the enhancement of ancient medieval fabrics by implanting alien classical elements as part of the natural growth of buildings and on the other the vicissitudes of fashion over a broad period of stylistic change, endemic in Christian architecture throughout the Western world. An excellent example was the resurrection of Wren's monumental baroque altarpiece originally created in 1685–6 for James II's Roman Catholic chapel at Whitehall, which had been dismantled following the monarch's fall in 1688 and stored elsewhere, thus surviving the conflagration that almost totally destroyed the palace in 1698, and subsequently gifted by Queen Anne to Westminster Abbey, where it was re-erected between 1707 and 1709 (pl. 213).[5] The marble structure stretched some 30 feet from pier to pier at the entrance to Edward the Confessor's chapel at the east end of the presbytery and rose about 50 feet into the vaulting. Craftsmen's accounts reveal how Wren freshened and adapted its papistical form for Protestant national worship. The pair of crowning angels carved by Arnold Quellin and Grinling Gibbons embellished with silver and burnished gold were pro-

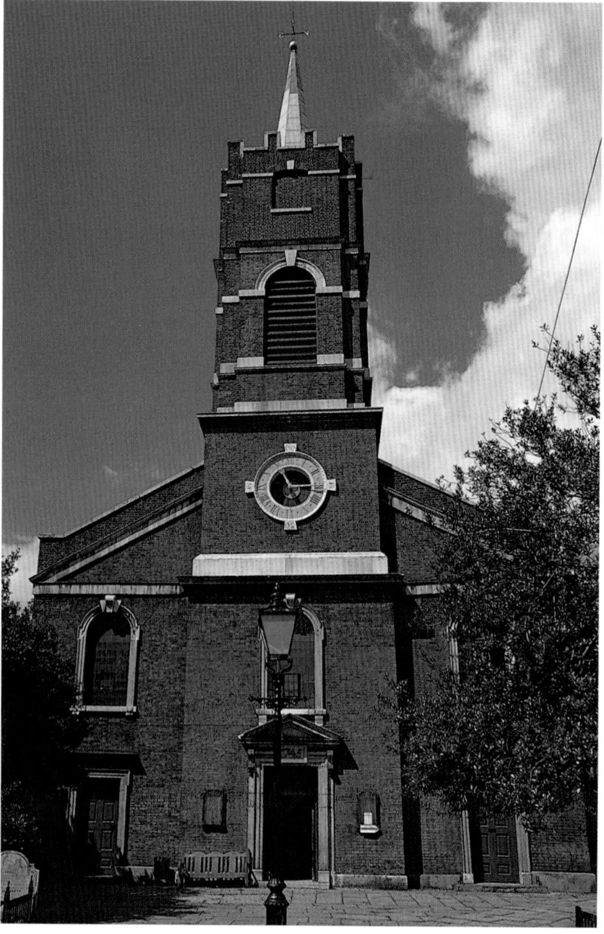

262 John Sanderson and Samuel Steemson. Entrance front and tower, St John, Hampstead, London, 1745–84.

vided with 'new lawrells . . . palms & . . . fingurs', the three crowning 'boys' (*putti*) with a palm branch and an Old Testament. The large white marble panel dominating the upper tier was sawed, polished and inscribed with 'Sentences . . . att Several times being Altered', its Glory and foliage enriched by 200 sheets of gold leaf, five capitals and 540 feet of marble 'new mended [and] polished', and so on.[6]

While inevitably attracting suspicion,[7] it also made an important early impact. Wren's deputy, William Dickinson, who measured the completed structure in 1710, proposed (but did not realise) a similar fixture in 1718 for Great Waltham, Essex, which was to feature Corinthian columns, a modillion cornice, circular pediments, palms, cherubim and seraphim heads, at a cost of £100 11s. 0d.[8] This may have involved Edward Tufnell, one of the masons responsible for reinstating the Whitehall altar,[9] and in turn in 1726 his 'Magnificent Altar-Piece', constructed of black, purple and gold veined marble, its Serliana framing Jan van Diest's *Adoration of the Magi*, was erected in Bath Abbey (pl. 64).[10]

On the other hand, to return to our main theme, are the many wilful mixtures of these two seemingly incompatible mainstream styles simultaneously cohabiting in one building, a treatment that preoccupied John Gwynn in *London and Westminster Improved* (1766),[11] that so upset Abbé Laugier (in the quote opening this chapter) and that Horace Walpole unkindly ridiculed as the 'bastard breed', about which the former alternative explanation fails to account for the 'well-meant fury' (in the poet Thomas Gray's phrase) tormenting the British.[12]

This collision, in the words of the architect James Essex, begot a 'variety of fantastical figures . . . in which the Grecian and Gothic ornament were . . . absurdly mixed together'.[13] Laugier's 'new kind of architecture', which the British called 'Modern Architecture', that is,

> what is far remov'd from the Manner and Proportion of the *Antique*, having its Ornaments wild and chimerical, and its Profiles incorrect . . . only applicable to such Architecture as partakes of the Gothick, retaining somewhat of its Delicacy and Solidity; and partly of the Antique, whence it borrows Members and Ornaments, without any Proportion or Judgment.[14]

George Vertue correctly identified its origins 'in Italy & other Places beyond [the] Seas [where it] . . . revived the fine tast of antient Building . . . passing thro' France or Germany . . . into England [and] in its way had a mixture of their Gothesisms with it'.[15] Alert if not always sympathetic British travellers specified particular Continental antecedents. For example, Edward Wright, who visited Milan in the early 1720s, reported that the 'famous *Dome*, so much talk'd of, disappoints one a little at first sight, the Front being not half finish'd . . . tho' it was begun . . . 1387', and he explained that the

> Architecture is *Gothick* . . . And for Ornaments, it is indeed surprizing . . . the late Directors . . . have studied a Refinement in the Taste of Architecture, by making the Pilasters, Door-cases, and such Window-cases as are done, somewhat in the *Greek* Way instead of *Gothick*: But it seems not to have so good an Effect as they propos'd; for the Work is now not of a piece . . . ('tis about a hundred Years . . . that it has not been touch'd) and are at work on other parts, which they go on with in the *Gothick* Way, suitable to the rest, but in a very slow Manner.[16]

This blending and compressing of the historical progress is encapsulated in the young Robert Adam's

Piranesian fantasy (pl. 263) drawn at Coblenz (Koblenz) in 1757, during his return journey from Rome, in which the lower storeys of the thirteenth-century St Kastor Cathedral were reworked as a romanesque-gothic-Palladian medley.[17]

The most celebrated English example from the past was Inigo Jones's partial external classical envelopment of pre-Fire medieval St Paul's Cathedral (demolished after 1666), first published, in engraved form, in 1727 (pl. 324).[18] The exalted reputation of this lost masterpiece, together with the Corinthian choirscreen (1637–8) in Winchester Cathedral (pl. 316), and a belief, spurious as it happened, that he designed Lincoln's Inn chapel, with its classical interlopers (pl. 264) – Vertue's engraving of 1751, made under the auspices of the Society of Antiquaries, lauded the 'Skill of that famous Architect . . . shewn . . . in this particular Structure, having . . . adapted the old Gothic way of Building to the Manner of the Tuscan Order' – bestowed legitimacy on the choice of a hybrid solution for church architecture.[19] Germane to this is the similar classicisation of the short-lived Chapel Royal, Holyrood House, Edinburgh, of 1688 (pl. 140).

The issue of what Farington described as a 'Mixture of Gothic & Roman Manner' and Carter called 'medley work'[20] centred on the conflicting sentiments held by viewers about the rival styles. The *Gentleman's Magazine* in 1758 noted a general consensus that 'there is an awful solemnity in [gothic] structures, that makes a more lasting impression on the mind, than all the studied exactness of the Grecian models',[21] and Walpole believed: 'it is difficult for the noblest Grecian temple to convey half so many impressions to the mind as a cathedral does of the best Gothic taste . . . One must have taste to be sensible of the beauties of Grecian architecture; one only wants passion to feel Gothic.'[22]

By contrast, John Evelyn's *A Parallel Of the Antient Architecture With The Modern* (four editions issued between 1664 and 1733 of Fréart's French publication of 1650) invited readers to 'compare . . . judiciously, without Partiality and Prejudice, and then pronounce which of the two *Manners* strikes the Understanding as well as the Eye with the more Majesty and solemn Greatness', giving the example of a medieval cathedral 'where . . . abundance of busy Work and other Incongruities dissipate and break the Angles of the Sight, and so confound it, that one cannot consider it with any Steadiness, where to begin or end', contrasted to 'that noble *Air* and *Grandeur*, bold and graceful Manner which the *Ancients* had so well and judiciously established' instanced by the 'glorious . . . *Cupola, Portico, Colonades*' of Wren's St Paul's.[23] In repairing the fire-damaged structure Wren initially considered taking

> a middle Way . . . to neglect nothing that may conduce to a decent uniform Beauty, or durable Firmness in the Fabrick [which] will be as easy to perform . . . after a good Roman Manner, as to follow the *Gothick* Rudeness of the old Design . . . I cannot propose a better Remedy, than by cutting off the inner Corners of the Cross, to reduce this middle Part into a spacious *Dome*.

That is, interlocking the Latin cross of Ely Cathedral with its great octagonal crossing (pl. 206), but now domed rather than towered and surmounted by a '*Lantern* with a spiring Top'.[24] In opting ultimately for total demolition and rebuilding in a comprehensively classical idiom (pl. 2), Wren was warning against the aberration of stylistic hybridism (just as he single-mindedly favoured unadulterated gothic at Westminster Abbey, as we have seen in chapter 13). Other observers

263 Robert Adam. 'Fabrique Gothique desinee en descendant Le Rhin I dee prise d'une Eglise sur le Cote de Dit Fleuve. 1 Decemr 1757...Coblentz', detail. Pen and ink. Sir John Soane's Museum, London, AD 54/IV/2. Fantasy on east end of St Kastor, Koblenz, Germany, thirteenth century.

264 George Vertue. 'Lincoln's Inn Chappel . . . erected from a Plan of...Inigo Jones', London, 1751. Engraving. © The British Library Board, Crace Collection, 1880, 1113.4361. John Clarke architect, 1619–23.

concurred. 'Gothick is . . . best adapted . . . to places of devotion . . . the architect should study, but never blend, both styles . . . in the same design or original building', responded 'Architectus' to Jones's re-casing of St Paul's.[25] The precise manner in which these notions were implemented, astonishing in their variety and invention and far from merely erratic expressions of provincial waywardness, is best determined in the actual works of individual architects.

An iconic classical motif, the Serliana (or so-called Palladian or Venetian triple-light window, with a wide central arch and flat-headed flanks), originally published in Sebastiano Serlio's *Tutte l'opere d'architettura et prospetiva* (1573), perhaps carrying a Trinitarian message, was introduced to English ecclesiastical buildings by Inigo Jones in the Queen's Chapel, St James's, in 1623–5 (pl. 552), and occasionally featured in later Stuart metropolitan churches.[26] It may have first appeared outside London in a rudimentary form at Holy Trinity, Berwick-upon-Tweed, Northumberland, designed in the years 1650–53 by John Young, a London mason (pl. 265), perhaps as part of the repairs and beautification of the walls and roof in 1688, including the present Serliana. The Court Order for Berwick specifying construction was approved by Wren in his capacity as Surveyor of the King's Works and executed by his York representative, John Etty.[27] Between 1695 and 1699 Etty supplied large quantities of timber for the construction of the crossing dome and the nave and aisle roofs of St Paul's Cathedral.[28] Very likely he was familiar with Wren's variant window in which the area of the outer arch was also glazed, employed most impressively at St Bride, Fleet Street, with its body 'strong, pleasant, well built . . . and very regular, all the Apertures, &c. on one side answering exactly to those on the other' (pl. 266).[29] John's son, William Etty, who served as clerk of the works at Castle Howard under Vanbrugh and Hawksmoor from 1701, and in 1703 travelled to London to consult with them, provided further opportunities to study the City Churches first hand.[30] The open Serliana enjoyed special popularity in the north of England, appearing in three important buildings from the early decades of the eighteenth century, most notably at Stockton-on-Tees, County Durham (pl. 482), ascribed to Wren but more likely William Etty's creation (see pp. 446–7). The other two, both remodellings of medieval fabrics, are more immediately relevant.

Following the collapse of Selby Abbey's romanesque crossing tower in 1690, destroying the south transept and the westernmost south choir bays, the tower was rebuilt in a boxy, classical form resembling Wren's St Mary, Ingestre, Staffordshire (1673–7).[31] The new choir

265 John Young and perhaps John Etty. South elevation, Holy Trinity, Berwick-on-Tweed, Northumberland, 1648–53, 1688

windows were brutally alien (pl. 267): a pair of round-headed tripartite mullions set within round arched frames, as in Ingestre's chancel, and a lone triple light composed of a central arch and cross transom inserted into a pointed relieving arch, all three with central vertical braces implying a structural rather than a purely decorative function. (Note, too, the crudely abandoned tracery parapet.) Perhaps this is the Ettys' work.

William Etty alone may have been involved with the capricious refashioning of the east end of St Hilda, Hartlepool, County Durham (1719–24, rebuilt 1870), begun the same year he designed nearby Holy Trinity, Sunderland (pls 461–2), and was appointed Vanbrugh's clerk of the works at Seaton Delaval, a further stop along the eastern coast. Having postponed the initial scheme to replace the decayed fabric, in 1724 the Hartlepool Vestry conceded the 'Unavoidable Necessity to Come to Some new Resolution . . . to Shorten the Chancell . . . make . . . flatt Roofs [which] in the opinion of men of Judgment as well as our Own [would make the church] Decent and Commodious, for the public Worship of God'. This involved abandoning repairs to the windows after the same form 'they now are . . . in respect to the glory of the antiquity' of the building in favour of what was later described as 'refitted with a sort of Venetian window in imitation of the Gothic'. That is, a repetition of the Selby clerestory window, which Grimm's later views show filling the five easternmost bays of the north and south aisles as well as the east end (pls 268–9), where it is framed externally by delicately panelled pilasters (as

266 (*right*) William Henry Toms. 'St: Brigit, alias St: Brides: Church', Fleet Street, London, in Maitland, 1756, p. 395, pl. 7. Engraving. Author's collection. Sir Christopher Wren architect, 1671–1703.

269 (*facing page, bottom*) Samuel Hieronymus Grimm. Interior towards chancel, St Hilda, Hartlepool, County Durham, undated. Pen and ink. © The British Library Board, Kaye Collection, III, Add. MS 15539, f. 148. (?)William Etty remodelled east end, 1719–24, rebuilt 1870.

at Stockton, pl. 482) and lights a distinctly Etty-like reredos.[32]

The decision in 1695, a year after the disastrous Warwick fire, to reject Wren's and Hawksmoor's predictably unadulterated gothic design for rebuilding St Mary (pl. 148) in favour of a strikingly individual solution by Sir William Wilson, an 'ingenious gentleman' architect from Leicestershire, entailed radically rethinking the orthodox arrangement of nave with clerestory and subsidiary side aisles (conforming to the height of the surviving eastern chapels flanking the chancel, pl. 149) as a hall church of three equal-height, rib-vaulted spaces separated by tall, colonnette piers (pls 270–71). Their acanthus leaf, egg-and-dart and bead-and-reel

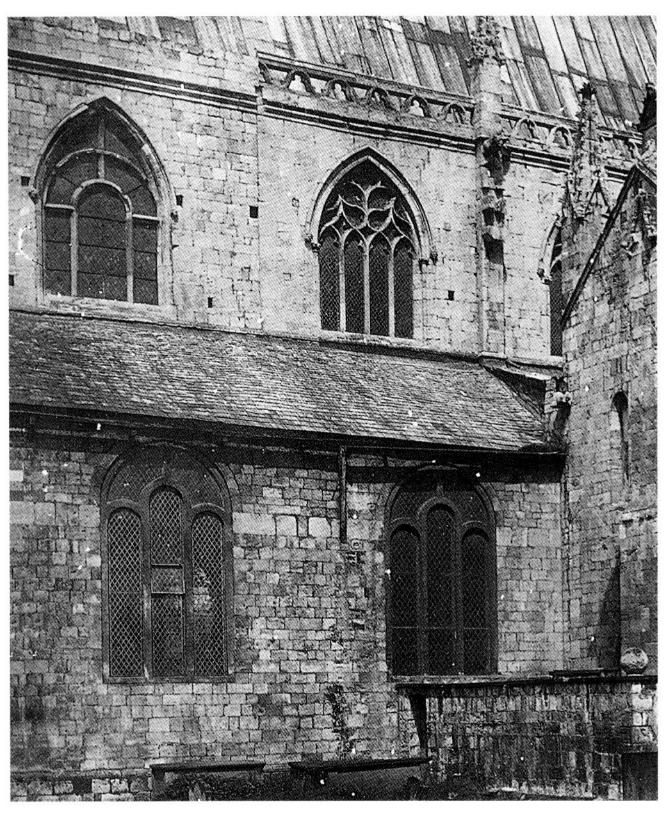

267 (*left*) South choir aisle, Selby Abbey, Yorkshire, as remodelled by John and (?)William Etty after 1690, detail. North Yorkshire County Council, Selby Library. Remodelled 1889.

268 (*below*) Samuel Hieronymus Grimm. South-west view, St Hilda, Hartlepool, County Durham, undated, detail. Pen and ink. © The British Library Board, Kaye Collection, III, Add. MS 15539, f. 146. (?)William Etty remodelled east end, 1719–24, rebuilt 1870.

270 *(above left)* Sir William Wilson. South elevation and west tower, St Mary, Warwick, Warwickshire, 1695–1706.

271 *(above right)* Sir William Wilson. Interior towards south-west, St Mary, Warwick, Warwickshire, 1695–1706. English Heritage (National Monuments Record, A42/9543).

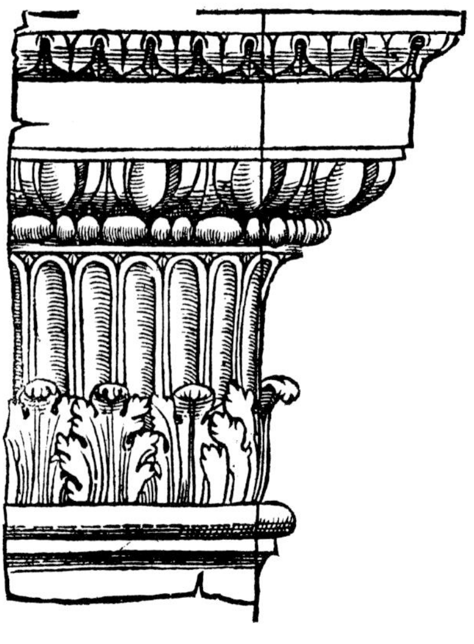

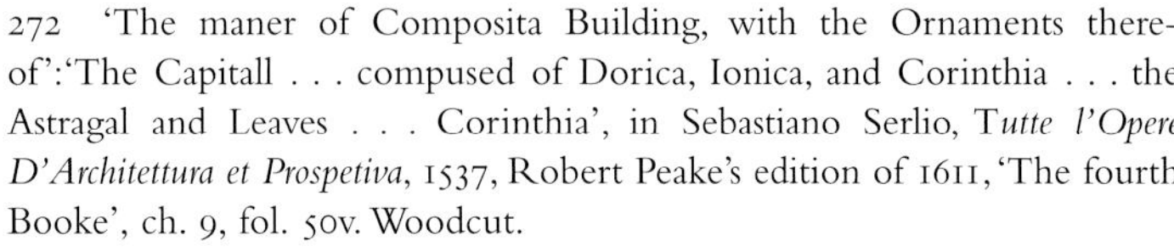

272 'The maner of Composita Building, with the Ornaments thereof': 'The Capitall . . . compused of Dorica, Ionica, and Corinthia . . . the Astragal and Leaves . . . Corinthia', in Sebastiano Serlio, T*utte l'Opere D'Architettura et Prospetiva*, 1537, Robert Peake's edition of 1611, 'The fourth Booke', ch. 9, fol. 50v. Woodcut.

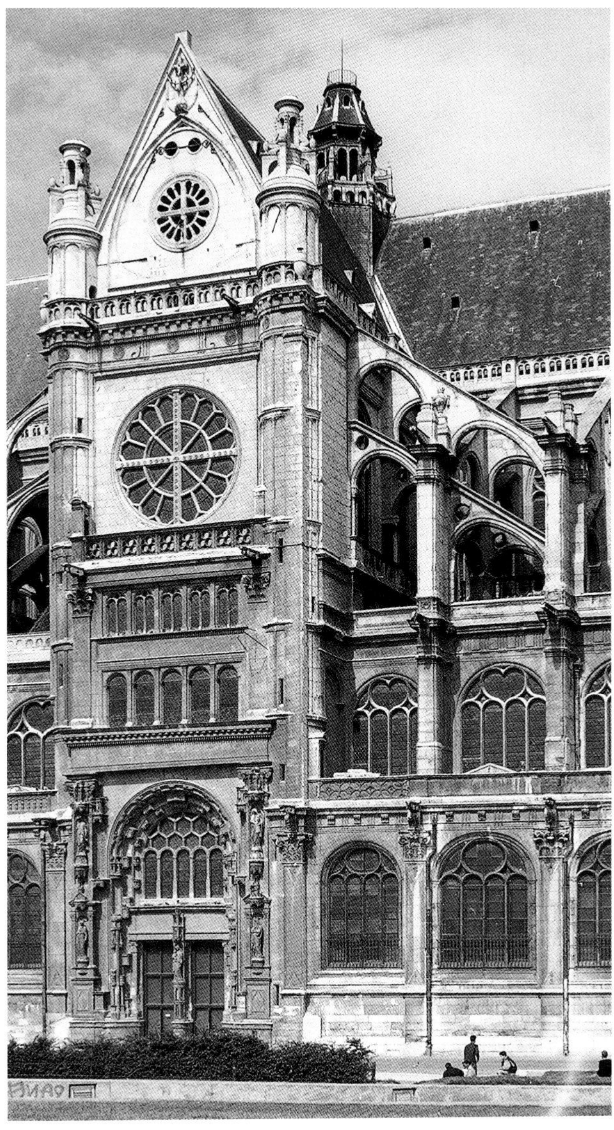

273 Architect unknown. North elevation, St Eustache, Paris, France, 1532–1640. Courtauld Institute of Art, A93/214.

detailing derived from antique sources in Serlio's *Tutte l'opere* (pl. 272), about which the author observed poignantly: 'Since the ancient Romans made different mixtures, I will choose some of the better known and also better conceived so that the architect with his own good judgement may, depending on the situation, make a choice of that which will be most suitable for him.'[33] Wilson's most demonstrative features are the classically pedimented, gable-ended transepts, the late gothic Flamboyant tracery filling the huge pointed-arch windows lighting the body and the Tuscan-crowned buttresses separating them, leaving little doubt that he had turned for his model to Saint Eustache, Paris (pl. 273), a celebrated French example on the cusp of stylistic change (unsympathetically though aptly described by Viollet-le-Duc as 'a kind of gothic skeleton clothed in Roman rags').[34] However, how Wilson would have gained knowledge of this building remains a mystery.[35]

One further remarkable feature of St Mary's should be mentioned. The internal transition from the old to the new parts of the building at the demarcation of fire damage, a 'portall' installed across the Beauchamp Chapel's west end in 1704 (pl. 274) by Samuel Dunckley, a local master mason, repeats medieval motifs from the door surround leading from that space into the smaller medieval Dean's Chapel adjacent to the chancel. Compared with authentic fifteenth-century work, Dunckley's carving looks mechanical and lacklustre (a forerunner of Batty Langley's mid-Georgian pattern book repertory), yet it must have been this addition that prompted a later visitor to proclaim the new building 'well according with the old chancel'.[36]

274 Samuel Duckley. Entrance to Beauchamp chapel, 1704, St Mary, Warwick, Warwickshire. English Heritage (National Monuments Record, AAA70/54).

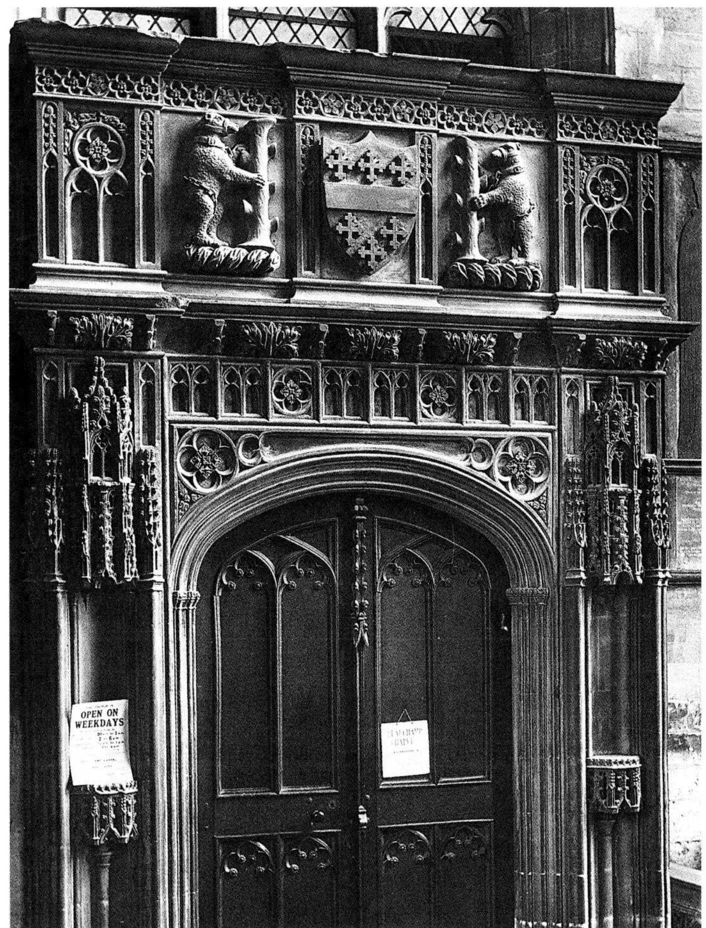

275 James Cole. Interior towards south transept with Archbishop Tenison's throne in background right, Canterbury Cathedral, Kent, in Dart 1726, p. 159, detail. Engraving. Author's collection. Nicholas Hawksmoor architect, 1704, now dismantled.

This was to be the special achievement of Nicholas Hawksmoor, who his obituarist (said to have been his son-in-law, Nathaniel Blackerby) claimed was 'perfectly skill'd in the History of Architecture, and could give an exact Account of all the famous Buildings, both Antient and Modern, in every Part of the World; to which his excellent Memory . . . greatly contributed'.[37] He broadened the scope of gothic as a continuum originating or growing out of fragments of classical antiquity, a perception that, however garbled, justified the pluralism of his style, equitably combining and interchanging *all'antica* and medieval forms.[38] Whereas Wren at Westminster Abbey advocated preserving continuity 'with the original Scheme of the old Architect, without any modern Mixtures to shew my own Inventions', as we have seen in respect to his report of 1713 (p. 203), Hawksmoor was exhilarated by the possibilities of hybridism. Some hint of this is already present in Archbishop Tenison's baroque throne in Canterbury Cathedral (pl. 275), standing regally at the entrance to the south-east transept among a jumble of elaborately gothic tombs, described by a later visitor as 'a Nitch, haveing on each side three Corinthian Pillars making a Triangle [plan], from the top of the Cornice on the Pillar nearest the Seat, springs an Arch . . . extremely whimsical'.[39] The imitation textile panels hanging from the crown recall Bernini's Baldacchino (1624–35) in St Peter, Rome.[40] Yet Hawksmoor even broke with this spectacular icon by consolidating his columns in tight groups of three in the later manner of Andrea Pozzo's *Perspectiva Pictorum et Architectorum* (1693).[41] The carving was executed by Grinling Gibbons, who had undertaken the bishop's throne and organ case in St Paul's Cathedral in 1697, and later Hawksmoor's high altar at St Alfege, Greenwich, which had similar diagonal groupings of monumental Corinthian columns (pl. 129).[42]

A version of the ogee domes that Wren and Hawksmoor had failed to realise at Warwick (pl. 148) was erected over the central crossing of Beverley Minster in 1721–3 (pl. 276). Removed in 1824, in views it appears to have been irresolute and vapid, although the Yorkshire historian Thomas Gent recalled seeing the structure 'at a Distance, on a Summer's Day, with its beautiful Dome, and a Ball, gilt with Gold, glittering by the refulgent Beams of the Sun'.[43] An anonymous, undated but early eighteenth-century perspective of the building may represent an unrealised scheme for replacing this unsatisfactory, low-lying feature by a more prominent gothic buttressed octagon with an ogee dome (perhaps reusing the existing lead-covered wooden structure) crowned by a spire, a hybrid form without medieval precedent popular in the eighteenth century, which became an architectural cause célèbre.[44] At Lincoln in 1725 Gibbs recommended a measure to secure the romanesque west towers 'against an utter desolation', replacing the lead-covered wooden spires (pl. 157) with 'lanthorns of stone put up upon the corners, and the middle part flatted [which would] ease the towers very much, and be more graceful than the present spires, for it is evident [that they] being of a considerable height makes them more lyable to be shaken with the winds'.[45] This proposal was opposed by John James, who regarded the spires as 'a very great burthen', their 'very ill effect . . . resembling so many extinguishers set upon great candles'. He himself favoured 'thin peramidal acroteria [pedestals], after the Gothick manner'. A microcosm of the stylistic battle. Only when a 500-strong local mob rioted against both schemes did the dean and chapter wisely abandon the project.[46] Nonetheless, at Salisbury, which had 'the peculiar good fortune of being perfect; for there are few Gothic churches part of which has not been taken

276 H. Overton after J. Hoole. 'The North East Prospect of Beverley Minster in York Shire', detail, 1737. Engraving. English Heritage (National Monuments Record, BB007255, courtesy Beverley Art Gallery). Nicholas Hawksmoor architect, crossing dome, 1721–3, removed 1824.

277 Paul Fourdrinier after Francis Price. 'Belfry: with a Scheme for a Roof, when the Spire stands in need of being renewed', 1746, in F. Price, *A Series Of particular and usefulObservations . . . upon . . . the Cathedral Church of Salisbury* (Wiltshire), 1753, pl. 10, detail. Author's collection.

away, and sometimes supplied in a dissimilar style',[47] Francis Price listed in an estimate of 1736 for repairs 'four Spireing pinacls [which] seem to threaten falling', accompanied surprisingly by a 'sketch of the supposed covering instead of the Pinacles' in the shape of a Palladian ball on a socle-crowned octagonal dome, which, however, was not executed.[48] Furthermore, he published a 'Scheme for a Roof' on the free-standing belfry 'when the Spire stands in need of being renewed' in the form of a four-sided dome on drum, which is without medieval precedent (pl. 277). In any case, the entire structure was subsequently razed.[49]

Beverley's dome was a trial run for resolving the same problem at Westminster Abbey, where no more than the crossing podium had been completed by the medieval builders and Wren had been keen to consummate their unfulfilled intention of erecting a soaring needle spire in the manner of Salisbury. He advised the dean and chapter that it 'will give a proper Grace to the whole Fabrick [though varying] a little from the usual Form, in giving twelve Sides . . . instead of eight'.[50] This resulted in one of the most memorable if unfulfilled episodes in Georgian architecture, revealed only with the recent discovery of a cache of drawings

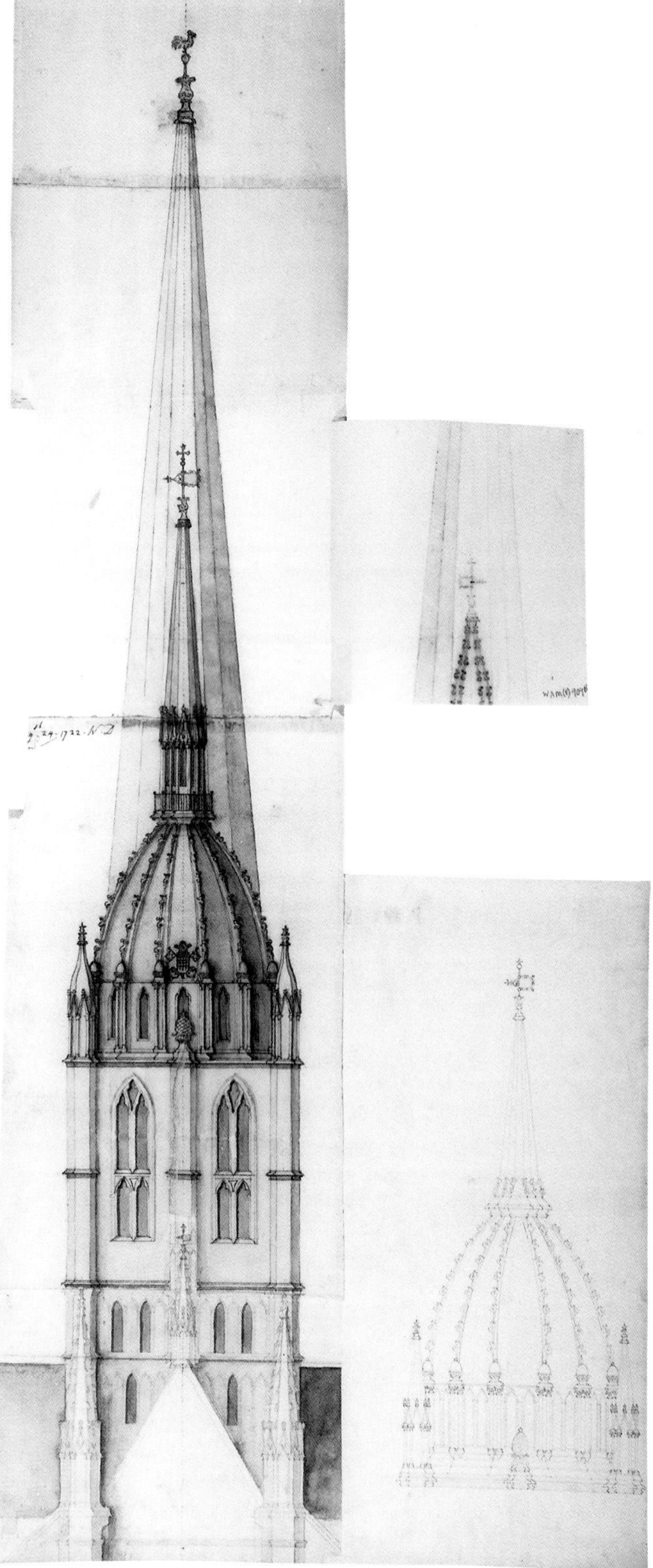

278 William Dickinson. Design for the crossing tower with alternative dome and spires, Westminster Abbey, London, detail, 1713. Pencil, pen and ink and wash. Westminster Abbey Muniments, (P)909A. Sir Christopher Wren architect.

by William Dickinson (Wren's under-surveyor between 1711 and 1725 and partly reflecting his own ideas) and Hawksmoor (who succeeded to the surveyorship on Wren's death in 1723, then on his own following Dickinson's death two years later). Both architects employed a flap format to present alternative solutions. One (pl. 278) shows the ghost of Wren's imagined spire rising behind Dickinson's full-bodied dome richly articulated with pineapples (an ancient symbol of fertility), pinnacles and ranks of crocketed ribs, a monumentalised echo of the buttresses surrounding the adjacent Henry VII's Chapel (pl. 153). The pineapple crowning the central buttress also appears on Dickinson's 1712 embellishment of Wren's St Christopher-le-Stocks (pl. 479). In 1724 Dickinson made estimates to

> secure and stiffen the 4 legs or pillars to the middle tower . . . erect a middle Tower . . . stone vaulting [and] a Dome and Lanthorn upon the same . . . Raise . . . a new Octagon Tower [85 foot high to the] top of the pinicalles [and a] new Gothick Spire . . . wth: all it's proper Ornaments.[51]

Spherical terminals had a particular association with the abbey:

> . . . the Beauties of the Eastern *Dome*
> Where *Gothick* Tow'rs irregular, deride
> The juster Order of *Corinthian* Pride
> . . . Domes and Marble Turrets strike my Eyes,
> and shooting Spires co-equal with the Skies[52]

Then it was Hawksmoor's turn to develop this idea. His vigorous studies were copies of Daniel King's engravings in *The Cathedralls and Conventuall Churches of England and Wales* (pl. 150) amended to incorporate his own domical solutions (as well as the completion of the west towers). One (pl. 279) features a crocket-ribbed octagon rising from a polygonal drum enriched by buttresses suspended from corbels and quatrefoil panels, with ogee-domed half-octagonal *tempietti* inspired by Brunelleschi's *tribune morte* (1420–36), lying within the gothic zone of the Florentine cathedral dome (pl. 280).[53]

While Hawksmoor is not recorded as having travelled abroad, his historical prowess, as noted above, and his cosmopolitan architectural library, as well as his prints and drawings collection, would have served him well.[54] It is, therefore, entirely plausible that he was familiar second-hand not only with this celebrated Italian example but also with Bayeux Cathedral in Normandy (pl. 281), where the incomplete fifteenth-century octagonal tower received a baroque dome with

279 (*above*) Nicholas Hawksmoor. Design for 'The North Front of...Westminster With ye 2 West Towers and the middle Lantern as intended', London, 1724. Pen and ink and wash. Westminster Abbey Muniments, Hawksmoor no. 4, flap down.

280 (*left*) Bernardo Sansone Sgrilli after Giovan Battista Nelli. North elevation of Florence Duomo, detail of drum of dome, 'Alzata Esteriore del Medesimo Tempio', in Nelli 1733, pl. VI, detail. Engraving. Filippo Brunelleschi architect, 1417–34.

lantern in 1714.[55] An evocative reflection of this flamboyant form is the fantastical church portrayed in Canaletto's *English Landscape Capriccio* (pl. 282) painted for Hawksmoor's client, Thomas, 5th Baron King of Ockham Park, Surrey, which is clearly identifiable by its distinctive multi-light east window as the thirteenth-century parish church of All Saints, and may even represent an otherwise unrecorded and unrealised scheme by him.[56]

Hawksmoor also explored a simpler, more disciplined, wholly gothic, Beverley-like ogee alternative (pl. 283), featuring an elaborate internal Perpendicular vault (pl. 284) based closely on authentic medieval examples.[57] Nothing came of these proposals, though their rationale was expressed in Dickinson's encouragement to the dean and chapter in 1724 'to Compleat the whole' of the recently deceased Wren's restoration on the grounds that

> as the Metroppolis . . . is finish'd: wth: a Noble Church & Dome after the Italian manner, in Honour of St: Paul, & wee Question not but that St: Peter

281 Bayeaux Cathedral, France, thirteenth century, with Jacques Moussard's crossing dome, 1714, replaced 1855. From Denslagen 1994, pl. 49.

282 Antonio Canaletto. *English Landscape Capricco*, detail, *c.*1754. Oil on canvas. National Gallery of Art, Washington DC, Paul Mellon Collection, acc. no. 1964.2.2.

> will come in for his share to have a Gothick Tower & Spire of Stone Erected in the Middle together wth: . . . two Towers at the West and all wch: when finished in Workmanlike manner will without doubt give a great Grace & a Decent finishing to so Noble and Ancient a City.[58]

These aspirations are no more than adequately represented in Fabris's imaginary view of the building as it would look at this stage in its evolution, with the completed west towers spired but a woefully anti-climactic crossing tower (pl. 285).

In 1726 Hawksmoor, perhaps with Borromini in mind (pl. 363), designed a blatantly Continental baroque high altar for York Minster (pl. 286), positioned forward of the fifteenth-century gothic screen separating the choir and Lady Chapel. This huge, triumphal, semi-transparent structure, according to his instructions accompanying the presentation drawing, was to have its rear elevation 'wrought fair [so as to be] seen through the Stone Screen' and beyond to the great eastern window resplendent with fifteenth-century painted glass (pl. 317).[59] Nothing approaching such a monumental, Jesuitically scenographic solecism outside London had ever been suggested for a major medieval building, and its inevitable doom was rightly attributed by the renowned local historian, Francis Drake, to 'all of the regular [Corinthian] orders [which] by no means suit a *Gothick* cathedral'.[60]

Hawksmoor fared better at Beverley with the choirscreen made of Roche Abbey stone (pl. 287),

285 (*facing page bottom*) Pietro Fabris. *Imaginary View of Westminster Abbey from the North*, *c.*1734–40, purported to have been completed according to Sir Christopher Wren and Nicholas Hawksmoor, with St Margaret parish church on left, as remodelled by John James, 1734–5. Oil on canvas. Westminster Abbey Muniments.

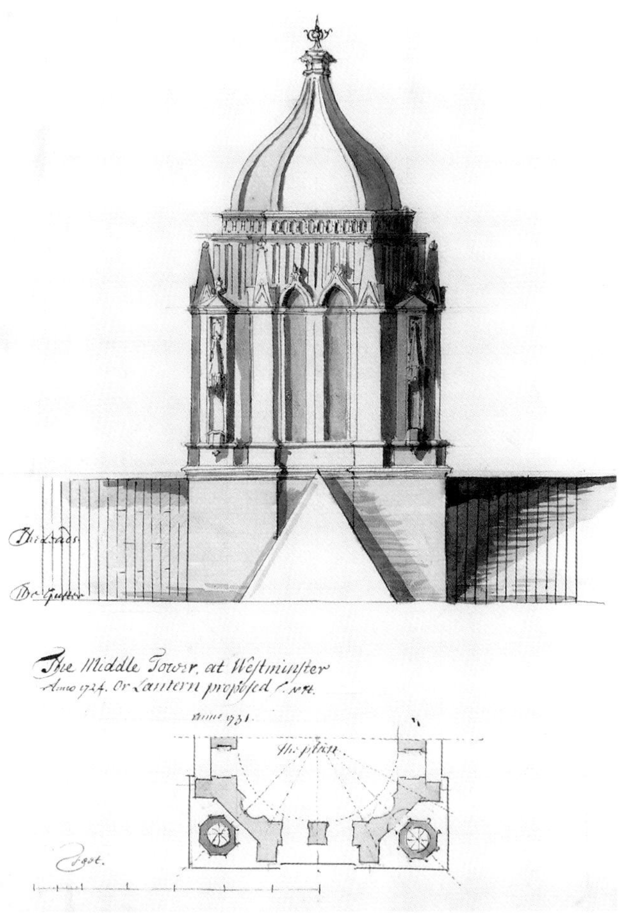

283 (*left*) Nicholas Hawksmoor. Design for 'The Middle Tower, at Westminster Anno 1724. Or Lantern proposed', with plan, Westminster Abbey, London, 1731. Pen and ink and wash. Westminster Abbey Muniments, Hawksmoor no. 5.

284 (*below*) Nicholas Hawksmoor. Design for 'The Ceiling of the Lantern', Westminster Abbey, London, 1724. Pen and ink and wash. Westminster Abbey Muniments, Hawksmoor no. 10.

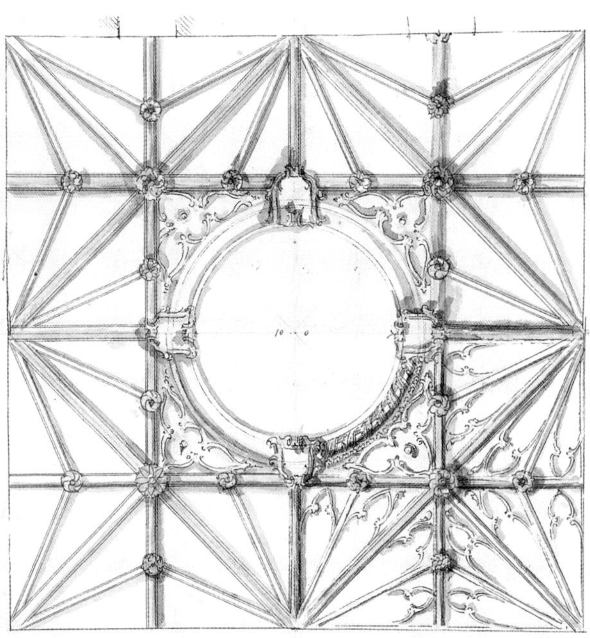

286 Nicholas Hawksmoor. Plan and elevation design for 'The Corinthian Altar . . . at York . . . by Nicholas Hawksmoor', York Minster, Yorkshire, 1726. Pen and ink and wash. © The British Library Board, K.Top. XLV.7.ff.2.

'curiously carv'd imitating wth elegance the Gothic manner', in an attempt to blend with the celebrated nearby fourteenth-century Percy tomb.[61] The ogee cusped arches, niches and castellation recall the fifteenth-century Archbishop Chicheley's tomb at Canterbury (pl. 275), but predictably the structure incorporated Corinthian capped colonnettes, reinforcing what is after all a subliminal Serliana. In 1733 the historian Thomas Gent noted the otherwise undocumented internal west doors (pl. 288), their 'large Effigies of the Four Evangelists . . . with . . . proper Emblems beneath' framed by swirls of trumpeting angels, cherubs' heads, flowered swags and heart-shaped tracery derived from York's great west window (pl. 139).[62] A visitor to Beverley in 1734 remarked that the doors were 'new cased after the *Gothick* Fashion' and confessed that the whole building was now 'so grand, that . . . I hardly know its Equal, since it appears not only with the Majesty and Solemnity peculiar to the *Gothick* Architecture, but likewise (being so well repaired) with all the Beauty and Elegance of the Modern, like a new Fabrick built after the old Fashion'.[63]

Hawksmoor's wooden galleries supported on fluted Doric columns with full entablatures inserted between but detached from the nave arches at Beverley in 1725 (removed in 1825 because considered insensitive)[64] anticipated his low, flanking Corinthian arcades anchoring the York altarpiece to the north and south choir piers (pl. 286). In turn, both Yorkshire minsters served as springboards for his final Westminster Abbey improvements, in particular the new screen across the western end of the choir. The proposed classical version

287 Nicholas Hawksmoor. Choir screen, Beverley Minster, Yorkshire, *c.*1729–31, dismantled 1877.

288 Nicholas Hawksmoor, attributed. Internal west door, Beverley Minster, Yorkshire, by 1733.

(pl. 289) was intended as a reflection of the Whitehall altarpiece at the opposite end of the choir (pl. 213). A narrow section of masonry inserted between the structure and piers preserved the integrity of the Doric order. The preferred 'Gothick Design' (pl. 290) has embellishment concentrated around the central ogee arch and vaulted passage into the choir, an echo of the external medieval west door (pl. 154). A pair of Tijou-like wrought-iron gates with 'Scroul Work, chased work and Foliage' was supplied in 1729.[65] One of the perks of this arrangement was to free the walls as settings for Michael Rysbrack's heroic tombs to Sir Isaac Newton (1731) and Lord Stanhope (1733), though accommodation of their obelisk tops within awkwardly projecting attics suggests that the authorities had not originally envisaged the screen as such a backdrop (their present gothic surrounds are Victorian additions). The only other internal improvement Hawksmoor realised was to replicate the elaborate sixteenth-century choir-stalls to accommodate extra seating for Knights of the Bath, whose Order had been restored by George I in 1725, which remain intact. Thus, progressing along the abbey's central axis alert visitors encountered a carefully orchestrated sequence of stylistically contrasting landmarks: gothic west porch set in romanesque masonry, gothic choirscreen with Roman-inspired tombs, baroque gates, gothic stalls, classical high altar.

While Hawksmoor struggled to resolve the forms of both the crossing and western towers, he was also concerned with comparable gothic structures elsewhere. In 1713 at King's College, Cambridge, as a solution to preserving the integrity of the chapel, 'deservedly . . . one of the finest Gothic buildings in the world', he had suggested erecting a soaring, free-standing tower to the west, its steeple Borrominiesque in its contrasting concaves and convexes hinged on projecting pilasters.[66] In 1717–18 he designed the spectacular twin-towered All Souls College, Oxford.[67] Between then and 1722, following a false start due to lack of funds, the tower of St Michael Cornhill, London, was completed (pl. 291). Here Hawksmoor concentrated his now-familiar robust detailing on the two upper stages, idiosyncratically

289 Nicholas Hawksmoor. Design for 'The Skreen at ye choir at Westminster' Abbey, London, 1728. Pen and ink and wash. Westminster Abbey Muniments, Langley Collection, Box II.8.(1)

290 'Entrance into the Choir' with John Michael Rysbrack's monuments to Sir Isaac Newton and James, 1st Earl of Stanhope, 1731–3, ironwork gate 1720, and in background Sir Christopher Wren's high altar, 1685–6, in Ackermann 1812, vol. II, pl. 20. Engraving. Westminster Abbey Muniments, Box 98.

extending the middle pinnacles' bases downward as pilasters separating the belfry openings in the manner of Wren's St Alban, Wood Street.[68] James Ralph considered the tower 'tho' in the Gothique stile . . . undoubtedly a very magnificent pile . . . and deserves very justly to be esteemed the finest thing of that sort in *London*'.[69] Yet, it is the stylistic anomaly that was the very point of the mid-Georgian architectural commentator Thomas Osborne's concerns: 'The architect will see here a very high degree of Gothick decoration: he will know it is improperly connected with the plain part below; and he will understand that he may employ either as he shall have ocasion; though not both in one building.'[70]

291 (*right*) John Le Keux after Robert William Billings. West tower, St Michael, Cornhill, London, 1 January 1838, in Godwin 1838, vol. 1, detail. Engraving. Nicholas Hawksmoor architect, 1715–22.

292 (*below left*) Architect unknown. North-west view, St Nicholas, Ingrave, Essex, 1734–6.

293 (*below right*) John Wing Sr. South-west view, St Peter, Gaulby, Leicestershire, 1741.

However, two churches, both insufficiently documented, show its influence. Ingrave, Essex (pl. 292), was built on virgin ground in 1734–5 for the inhabitants of the recently consolidated parishes of Ingrave and Thorndon by Robert James, 8th Lord Petre, the Roman Catholic lord of the manor, who possessed a substantial architectural library and may have acted as his own designer.[71] The austere, red brick classical body ornamented only with a continuous dentile cornice (reminiscent of Deal, pls 525–6) is screened by an unusually powerful monolithic astylar tower with its medieval-inspired polygonal turrets projecting from the slender side elevations and a Cornhill-like arcaded frieze across the crown.[72] The classical tower of Gaulby, Leicestershire (pl. 293), is 'overcharged with whimsical decorations', while its elongated corner pinnacles and shorter intermediary accents subscribe to a familiar late gothic arrangement favoured in the eighteenth century; the former's weird shape, combining fluted and foliated scrolled octagonal shafts surmounted by pagoda-like crowns, is without parallel and their model remains enigmatic, perhaps no more than the architect's fancy.[73]

The ambiguities of certain Hawksmoor churches were fiercely debated in the popular press. In 1734 Ralph attacked Christ Church, Spitalfields (pl. 368), as among his 'mere Gothique heaps of stone, without form or order; and meet with contempt from the best and worst tastes alike . . . built at a monstrous expence, and yet is, beyond question one of the most absurd piles in *Europe*'.[74] He was employing 'Gothique' as synonymous with barbaric, as a term of derision rather than defining an historical style. His intentions were misunderstood by Batty Langley, who in the *Grub-street Journal* of the same year counter-blasted: 'With what blindness, stupidity, and ill-nature, are these words thrown out! For [the churches are] not . . . in the *Gothique* stile [yet] have their beauties and grandeur [and] are the admiration of all judges.' Furthermore, the 'stile or mode' of Hawksmoor's companion churches, St Anne, Limehouse (pl. 370), and St George, Wapping (pl. 371), are 'a mean, between the Greek and Gothique architecture . . . first invented and practiced by . . . HAWKSMOOR'. Langley considered Spitalfields 'vastly different from *Gothic*', though believed 'had more care been taken in the gradual diminution of its spire, it would have had a much better figure [which] is a real fault'.[75] Here, too, Langley failed to grasp this extraordinary structure, which Hawksmoor intentionally designed in a medieval broach form (a tapering octagon on a square with the intersection producing half-pyramids at the corners). The model was probably the lost spire on Ripon Minster (pl. 294), which he mentioned

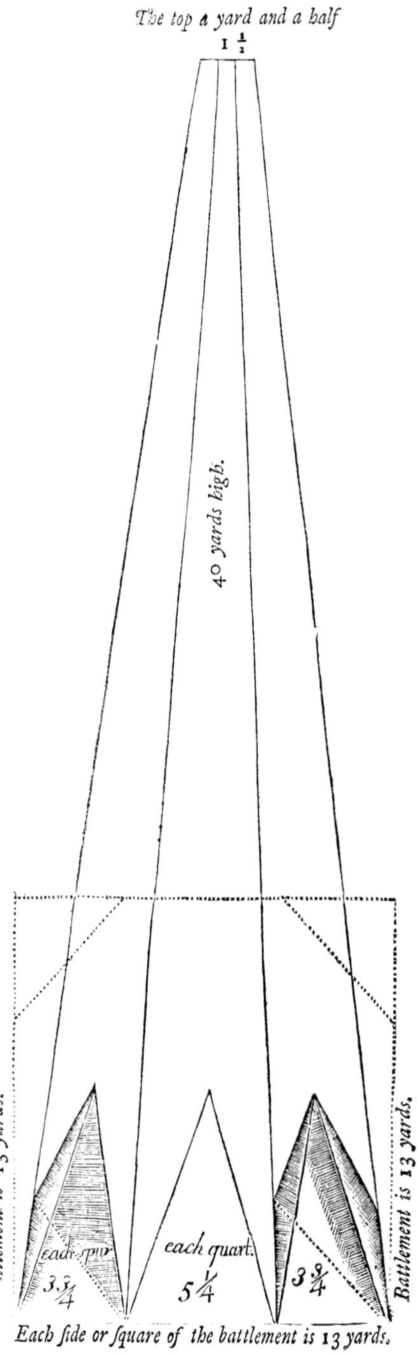

294 'St. Wilfrid's steeple', Ripon Minster, Yorkshire, in Drake 1736, Appendix following Book II, Chapter IV, p. xcv. Engraving.

in his letter of 1735 to the dean of Westminster.[76] Was it coincidental that during 1725–7, when the final shape of Spitalfields was determined, Alderman John Aislabie, who as mayor of Ripon in 1702 had erected in the marketplace the earliest monumental obelisk in England, to Hawksmoor's design, towards the cost of which the diocese contributed, had in 1724 also given

£200 towards mending and dressing the minster windows, re-leading the roofs and repairing the fire- and storm-damaged, lead-covered wooden spire atop the crossing known as St Wilfrid's Steeple?[77]

Hawksmoor's final and most revealing excursion into hybridism (apart from Westminster Abbey's west towers, begun in 1734)[78] was his rejected scheme of 1730 for rebuilding the decayed medieval church of St Giles-in-the-Fields, London. He had first submitted a proposal in 1711 as part of the Fifty New Churches commission, but despite the parish's 'unsupportable burthen [of maintaining] so old and crazy a church in repair and decent order', nothing was done for another nineteen years, when the architect, then approaching 70, prepared at least twenty-five drawings representing two alternative solutions for a new church, to cost £8,000 (pl. 295).[79] Its medieval foundations and the entire structure

295 (*right*) Nicholas Hawksmoor. Design for 'The West Front', St Giles-in-the-Fields, London, 1730. Pen and ink and wash. © The British Library Board, MS 15505, ff. 11v–12.

296 (*below*) Nicholas Hawksmoor. Design for 'The South Front', St Giles-in-the-Fields, London, 1730. Pen and ink and wash. © The British Library Board, MS 15506, ff. 13v–14.

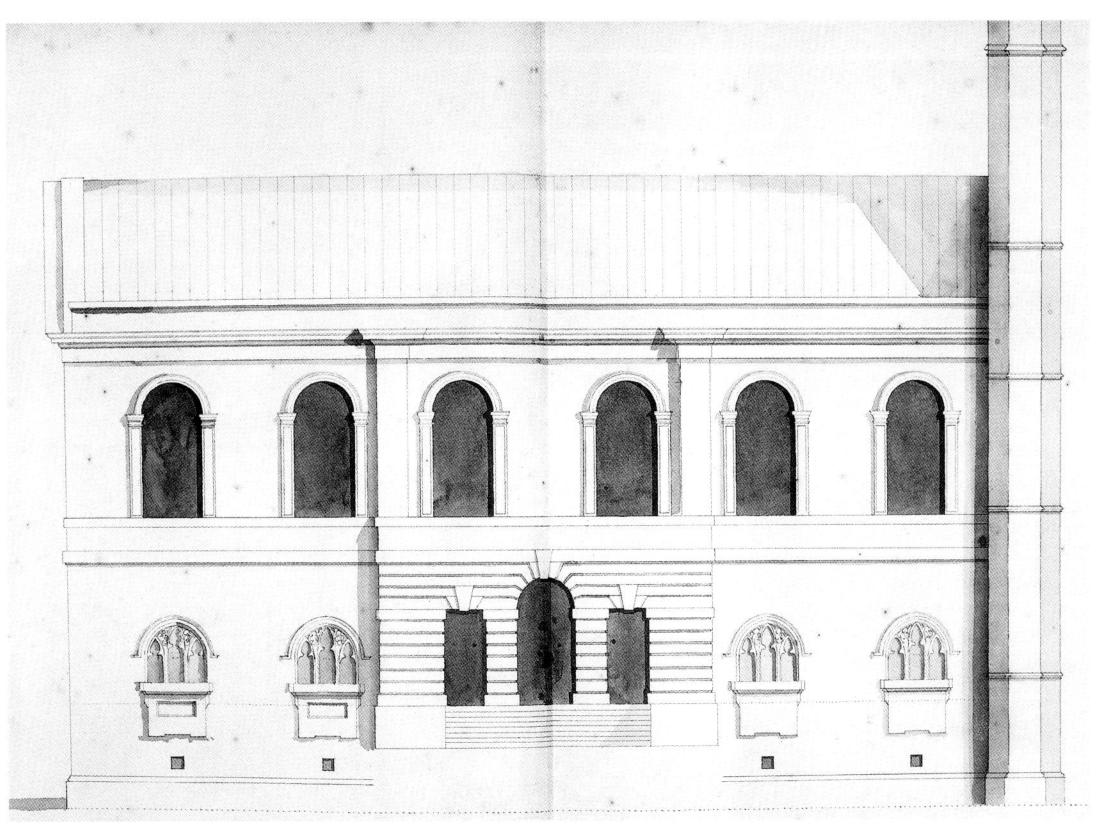

297 John James. Medieval north-west tower, St Margaret, Westminster, London, detail, remodelled 1734–5.

298 Tomb of George Fascet, Abbot of Westminster (d. *c.*1500) in Dart 1723, vol. I, p. 191 (top detail) and 'The Dorick Entablature in Perspective', in James 1707, fig. 27 (bottom detail). Engravings.

of the north-west tower, including polygonal corners, were preserved. Classical motifs invaded its lower stages and crowning balustrades, a repeated guilloche, a telling motif (later used at Westminster, pl. 261) derived from the Château Verneuil and illustrated in J. A. du Cerceau's *Les Plus Excellents Bastiments de France* (1576–9).[80] The reworked top stage, as at Cornhill (pl. 291), is marked by the now-familiar arched frieze. The ensemble also resembles Ingrave (pl. 292). The long elevations of the body (pl. 296), with their projecting entrance porches, explore several alternative fenestrations from square and elliptical blocked surrounds to pointed hoods with presumably reused fragments of surviving gothic tracery supported on oversized classical aprons. The message seems manifest: an ancient church (founded 1101, rebuilt 1623) resurrected for Georgian worship.[81]

Hawksmoor was not alone in manipulating diverse architectural motifs in eccentrically individualistic ways. Having early on committed himself to 'the greatest plainness' in the manner of 'our famous Mr Inigo Jones',[82] John James was frankly flummoxed by Hawksmoor's frenzied neo-medieval ornament on Westminster Abbey's west towers (pl. 261), which as his successor as surveyor he was responsible for completing between 1735 and 1745. He explained to the dean and chapter the inherent impossibility of measuring work from drawings 'with any exactness 'til performed . . . and a thing of no small difficulty . . . when wrought [since in] plain Work' based on established classical rules 'a Computation may be made to almost an exactness', whereas this was not the case in complicated forms such as window heads and the 'windings and turnings of so many Gothick Ornaments'.[83]

In 1734–5 at St Margaret, Westminster, standing in the abbey's very shadow, James offered an alternative, elemental hybrid that a later detractor condemned as an 'unaccountable medley of ancient and modern', yet one hardly lacking in originality.[84] In his partly rebuilt north-west tower (pls 261, 285, 297) repetitive quatrefoils recalling decoration on innumerable medieval tomb chests scattered throughout the abbey (pl. 298), now unmoulded as if stamped from a pastry-cutter, are juxtaposed with single Roman Doric triglyphs as typically presented in contemporary architectural treatises, while bands of recessed diamonds and dashes and blind cross-shaped arrow loops devoid of all military prowess owe nothing to Hawksmoor. It is intriguing that Hawksmoor had recently placed two isolated, oversized triglyphs on the external eastern pedimental angles of the clerestory of Christ Church, Spitalfields (completed 1729).[85] In the *Grub-street Journal* Langley damned the 'shameful demolition of the tower [as] a very indiscreet action, if not a designed abuse on the inhabitants' by an architect who was neither 'well chosen, nor understood what he was about'; nor did he approve of a scheme to add a spire, condemning it as a piece of churchwarden vanity, a 'movement to perpetuate their memory to posterity'.[86] James himself was not insensible of the benefits of preservation: in rebuilding the broach spire of St Michael, Southampton, in 1732 he had stipulated that in dismantling the structure 'someone should be employed to take the exact size of everything that the same may be built again', which was done.[87]

Under similar circumstances James Gibbs's approaches towards preservation and stylistic mixture were more subtle. In choosing to rebuild the decrepit medieval body of All Saints, Derby, in a classical idiom while conserving its majestic, richly decorated Perpendicular tower (pl. 423) on grounds that the latter's 'plainness . . . renders it more suitable to the old Steeple',[88] he carefully aligned the two foundation platforms, the old canopied niches and string-course with the new window sills and Tuscan capitals, while the body's entablature, balustrade and vases fit comfortably opposite the blank wall between the string-course and the quatrefoil frieze above it.[89]

Elsewhere beyond London, hybridism thrived with unparalleled vigour in churches designed by celebrated metropolitan architects, among them the Adam brothers in Cambridge, Burlington, Kent and Vardy in Yorkshire, George Dance Sr in Kent, and Robert Taylor in Surrey and Oxfordshire, but also by provincials such as Sir James Burrough, William Lumby, George Steuart, the Woodward brothers, George Richardson and, above all, in the fertile imagination of the frustratingly enigmatic Henry Sephton.

A leading Lancashire builder-architect, though now little remembered, Sephton was among the most original provincial church designers of the early eighteenth century in Britain, adapting fashionable classical forms in daring new ways, which makes the absence of information about his early life and professional training all the more distressing. He is first heard of in 1714–15 in connection with surveying the medieval steeple of Prescot, near Liverpool, which he rebuilt four-square with full Doric angle pilasters and vases crowned by an octagonal spire with lucarne. The building accounts reveal that in 1659–60 a mason named Daniel Sephton was paid 1s. for setting and pointing the steeple of 1610, while between 1722 and 1759 other Sephtons – Thomas, William, John and Peter, members of a local dynasty working in the building trades – were involved in repairs to the fabric.[90] In 1716 Henry was described as a mason resident at Billinge, 7 miles north-east of Prescot, where he was proprietor of a quarry.[91]

St Aidan, Billinge, Lancashire (1716–18), a rebuilding of a sixteenth-century chapel (of unknown appearance) is his masterpiece, surviving intact except for a remodelling of the east end in 1908, which involved moving the chancel and interpolating transepts between it and the body (pl. 299). The building contract of 1716, accompanied by two remarkable drawings (pls 110, 300), specify a structure measuring 77 by 44 feet and constructed entirely of local Grindle stone supplied from Sephton's 'Delf'. The side elevations were to be 'Strengthn'd And Adorn'd by five Dorick Pilasters [with] a Stone battlement . . . finish'd with Urns upon Every Pilaster', the west front featuring 'four Dorick pilasters . . . One Large Door in the Tower . . . supported with Two Dorick pillars And . . . Ionick pilasters' surmounted by a tempietto-like 'Cupola' and the 'East End of the Alcove [chancel] rail'd and banister'd'.[92] Here Sephton flirted with ambiguity and contradiction with consummate skill. The implication of a full-width west pediment is subverted by corner breaks crowned by urns and a frontispiece shooting through the apex of what after all is a gable. The full Doric order enwrapping the body, complete with metopes and triglyphs in the western frieze, hints at a pseudoperipteral temple framework not far removed from Hawksmoor's contemporary St Alfege, Greenwich (pl. 403), but here introducing Wrenian lugged window surrounds 'Supported With Mullions of Stone And [Reticulated] Tracery'. Can Sephton have reused fragments from the former chapel, as Hawksmoor apparently had considered doing at St Giles-in-the-Fields (pl. 296)? May he have seen Wilson's distinctive window mullions at St Mary, Warwick (pl. 270)?[93] Billinge's west front is uncannily similar to a passage in Antonio da Sangallo the Younger's model for St Peter, Rome (1534–46), which was engraved in 1546 and again in 1715 (pl. 301), though I am unable to offer firm evidence that Sephton can have been aware of either.[94]

He probably had access to Continental architectural pattern books and prints. His equally odd west front at Hoole, Lancashire (pl. 302), seems to have been inspired by Serlio (pl. 303). In this connection it is worth noting Henry Dormer's use of a similar motif in his earlier proposal for a new tower at Burton Overy, Leicestershire (pl. 304).[95] Moreover, Billinge's most surprising internal feature, the treatment of the apsidal chancel (pl. 300), which according to the contract of 1716 was to be approached by an 'Ascent of Two Steps Strengthened by Three Corinthian Pilasters . . . Two at the Entrance One in the Middle . . . betwixt the two Windows', thereby positioning the middle pilaster on axis with the west door, rather than an example of provincial ineptitude, may be the result of an idiosyncratic reading of Robert Trevitt's well-known engraving of St Paul's Cathedral (pl. 305). Here the north arcade of the choir has been 'removed' to expose a panorama of participants at the General Thanksgiving service in 1706 and in the process setting askew the angle of the apse in such a way that might lead a viewer unfamiliar with the actual space to read the fluted Corinthian pilaster that lies between the middle and southernmost of the three windows (pl. 361) as separating only two windows

299 Henry Sephton. South-west view, St Aidan, Billinge, Lancashire, 1716–18, prior to eastern extension, 1908. Wigan Archives Service, 577/9.

300 Henry Sephton. Contract drawing for 'The South Prospect of Billing Chapel' as well as west and east elevations with plans, now St Aidan, Billinge, Lancashire, 1716. Pen and ink and wash. Wigan Archives Service, D/DZ A13/8.

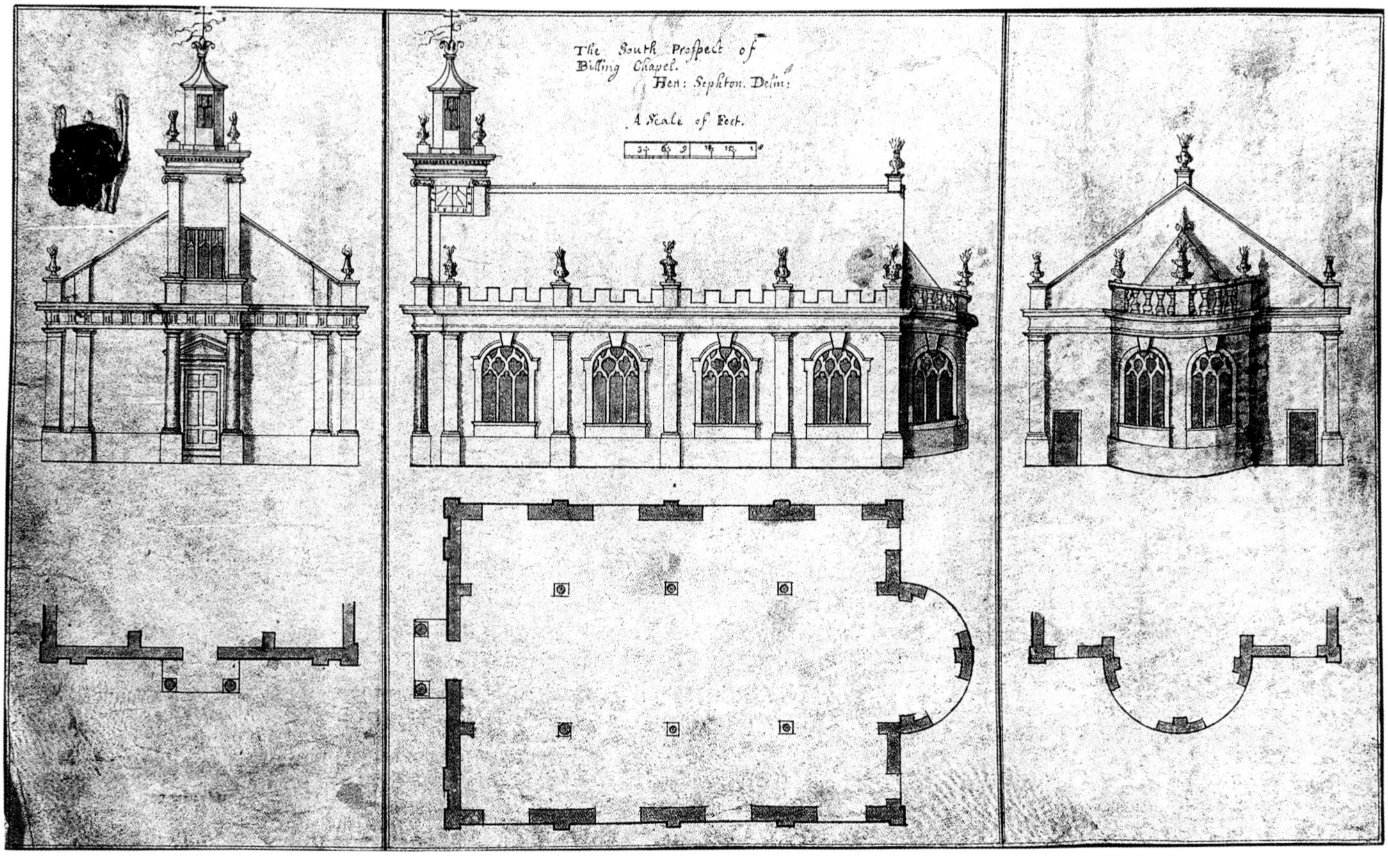

and, therefore, aligning the pilaster to the central gates of the railing and facing along the principal east–west axis of the interior.[96] As executed (pl. 306), the middle section of wall was widened to receive paired pilasters in order better to accommodate the communion table. Despite these intriguing parallels and possible models, nothing in British church design up to that time prepares one for the extraordinarily novel approach of this architect.

Sephton's next ecclesiastical commission, an unrealised scheme of 1738 for a new chapel of ease attached to the estate of Samuel Cheetham at Rochdale, Lancashire,[97] is a beautiful refinement of the Billinge formula, for which two alternative designs were offered, both conventionally planned, five-bay rectangles with projecting west towers and chancels but treated with a now-ubiquitous Sephtonian quirkiness. In one of striking originality (pl. 307), the robust façade of brick with dressed stone, with a great expanse of flat, unrelieved, largely un-fenestrated surfaces, is a dramatic and courageous substitute for the classical order as a means of achieving monumentality. The middle door is given prominence by block rustics; the frontispiece is crowned by an octagonal, ogee-domed bell turret, while a Serliana lights the chancel.[98] Along the side elevations, the double tier of windows divided by pairs of vertical mullions is separated by full-height clasping buttresses, a sole concession to medievalism.[99] The gothic alternative (pl. 308), with crocketed pinnacles rising from clasping buttresses and modified three-light tracery, while perhaps inspired by the Woodwards' Alcester, Warwickshire (pl. 312), has Wilsonian round-headed windows (pl. 271), as well as Doric nave columns and a Serliana-lit chancel. These perhaps coincidental similarities suggest that Sephton may have been an energetic explorer of church activity in the north-east. Apparently, both schemes were too maverick, since the erected church of 1739–44 (demolished 1911) was a conservative, rather clumsy building with a puny belfry and slim Doric gallery columns rising from grotesquely squat, elephantine ones. Sephton is unlikely to have been its architect.

Enfield's *An Essay Towards the History of Leverpool* (2nd edition, 1774) praised St Thomas's 'simple, elegant, and beautiful appearance [with its] well proportioned [tower ornamented] in the Grecian stile' (pl. 309). Nevertheless, in the now post-Bentham era it was understandably condemned for the 'four couplets of Corinthian columns [with] Gothic pinnacles, which seem to have no affinity with the rest of the structure, unless they be meant as a transition from the Grecian architecture below [with the paired pilasters repeated as free-

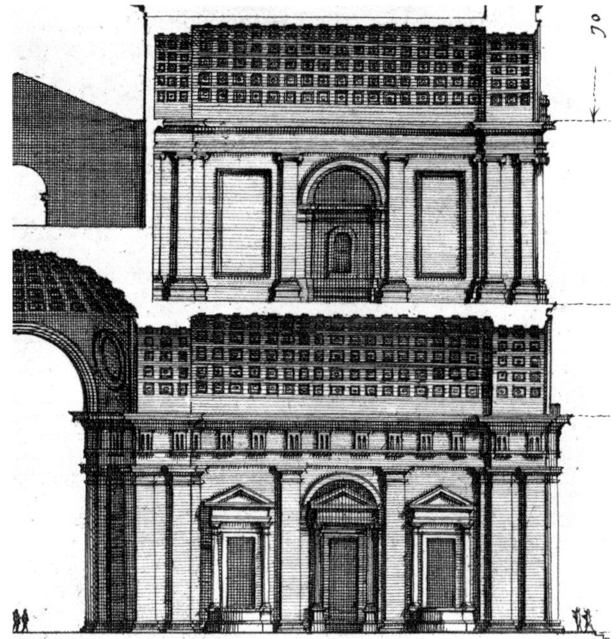

301 Alessandro Specchi. Detail of ground and first floors of north-west tower, 'Latus Basilicae Partes Eivsdem Interiores et Exteriores Osendens' of Antonio da Sangallo the younger's wooden model for St Peter, Rome, 1534–46, in Bonanni 1696, Tabula 16, P.56.3. Engraving. RIBA Library Photographs Collection (EW 499.E.e.74).

standing columns on the tower], to the Gothic spire above'.[100] Sephton was not alone among his northern contemporaries to favour this juxtaposition (pl. 311).[101] His last major work, rebuilding the dilapidated west tower of medieval St Mary, Lancaster (1753–4; pl. 310), entailed erecting 'a distinct building of itself and not . . . built upon any part of the Church Wall'.[102] Here he combined circular windows and cherubs' heads with a variety of largely convincing gothic features, for we have arrived at the era of Francis Price's influential publication *A Series of particular and useful Observations, Made with great Diligence and Care, upon that Admirable Structure, The Cathedral-Church of Salisbury* (1753).

Alcester, Warwickshire (pl. 312), built by the brothers Edward and Thomas Woodward of Chipping Campden, Gloucestershire, in collaboration with Francis Smith (who, with his older brother, William, were executant masons at St Mary, Warwick), is a straightforward separation of contrasting styles, with an entirely gothic exterior – the contract of 1730 specifying 'Buttresses Battlements and . . . Cross Iron barrs to Each pinnacle'[103] – and an interior dominated by rows of Doric columns dividing nave and aisles (pl. 313). This is an

302 (*above*) Henry Sephton. West front and tower, St Michael, Hoole, Lancashire, 1722.

303 (*right*) Design for a 'loggia' or 'portico' in Peake 1611,'The fourth Booke', Chapter 6, fol. 27, of Serlio 1537, detail. Engraving.

304 (*far right*) Henry Dormer. Design for 'The West Front of Burton-Overy Steeple' (St Andrew), Leicestershire, 1706–7. Pen and ink and coloured wash. Governing Body of Christ Church, Oxford, Wake Letters, 3, f. 253.

305 Robert Trevitt. 'A Prospect of the Choir of the Cathedral Church of St. Paul on the General Thanksgiving the 31st of Decemr. 1706. Her Majesty and both Houses of Parliament present', London, published 1710. Coloured engraving. London Metropolitan Archives (Guildhall Library).

306 Henry Sephton. Interior towards the chancel, St Aidan, Billinge, Lancashire, 1716–18, with later galleries, prior to chancel remodelling. Wigan Archives Service, 67779/2.

307 Henry Sephton. Design for the west front and interior towards the chancel of classical alternative, St Mary, Rochdale, Lancashire, 1738. Pen and ink and wash. Lancashire Record Office, DD1423/5.

308 Henry Sephton. Design for the north elevation of gothic alternative, St Mary, Rochdale, Lancashire, 1738. Pen and ink and wash. Lancashire Record Office, DD1423.

309 (*left, top*) Edward Rooker after P. P. Burdett. South elevation, St Thomas, Liverpool, Lancashire, in Enfield 1774, following p. 44. Engraving. Henry Sephton architect, 1747–50, demolished 1907.

311 (*above*) Henry Sephton. West tower, St Mary, Lancaster, Lancashire, 1753–6.

310 (*left, bottom*) Richard Axon. South-west view, 'St. Mary's Church Manchester', Lancashire, 'May [?]7th'. Pen and ink and wash. Chetham School Library, Manchester. Timothy Lightoler architect, 1753–62, demolished 1890.

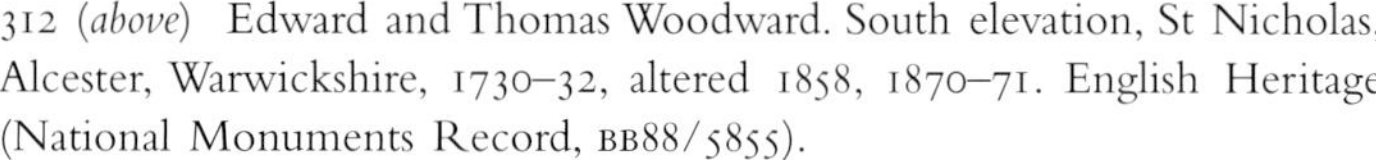

312 (*above*) Edward and Thomas Woodward. South elevation, St Nicholas, Alcester, Warwickshire, 1730–32, altered 1858, 1870–71. English Heritage (National Monuments Record, BB88/5855).

313 (*above right*) Edward and Thomas Woodward. Interior towards chancel, St Nicholas, Alcester, Warwickshire, 1730–32, altered 1858, 1870–71. English Heritage (National Monuments Record, BB88/5856).

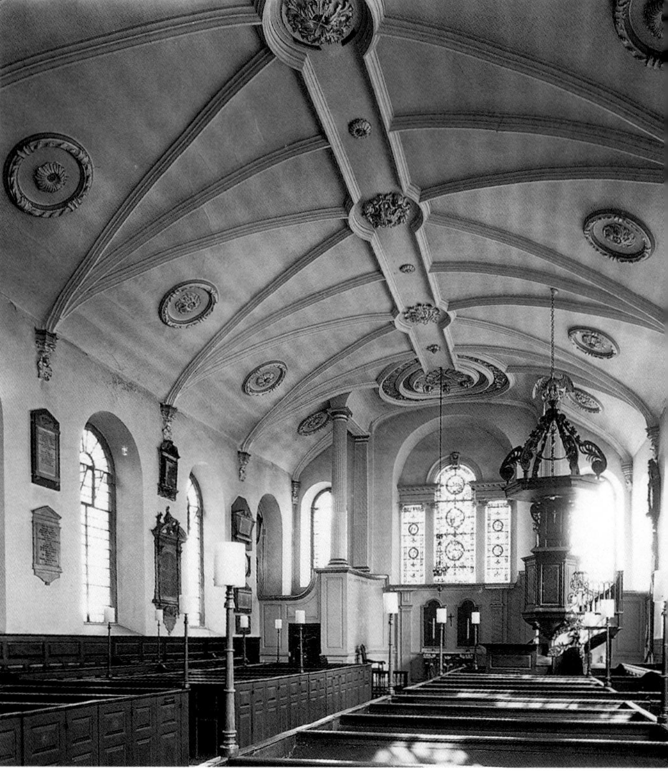

314 (*right*) Edward and Thomas Woodward. Interior towards chancel, St Swithin, Worcester, Worcestershire, 1733–6. English Heritage (National Monuments Record, BB84/894).

315 Frederic Nash. Interior towards chancel with choir screen, Canterbury Cathedral, Kent, 1805. Watercolour, detail. The Royal Museum and Art Gallery, Canterbury. Sir James Burrough, 1732–3, dismantled 1820.

316 Charles Woodfield. Choir screen, Winchester Cathedral, Hampshire, 1714. Engraving. Inigo Jones architect, 1637–8, dismantled 1820.

early British manifestation of a solution perhaps of French origin.[104] At St Swithin, Worcester, the melding is more eccentric. The external Palladian body, with fluted Doric pilasters and round-headed windows, is attached to the medieval west tower, while the single-cell interior (pl. 314) combines a Venetian-windowed chancel defined by fluted Doric columns and pilasters raised on tall screen walls separating the sacred space from flanking lobbies, with the body covered by a shallow segmental sexpartite vault springing from corbels to prominent circular central panels, the equivalent of ridge-rib bosses, with additional bosses used as isolated paterae, all executed in plaster.[105]

By the 1730s the obsessive baroque of Hawksmoor's high altar at York Minster (pl. 286) had shifted to Palladian solutions in the work of the next generation. Sir James Burrough, Master of Gonville and Caius College, Cambridge, and amateur architect, modelled his choirscreen at Canterbury (pl. 315) on Inigo Jones's iconic stone structure at Winchester (pl. 316). Embellished with Hubert Le Sueur's bronze statues of *James I* and *Charles I* (both cathedral benefactors), it served as a triumphal introduction to the gothic high altar.[106] The central arch at Canterbury, however, was glazed and blocked at the bottom by a communion table, leading one visitor to complain that it 'has no Opening through it, so that the large part of the Church, east of the Altar, is entirely excluded from View'. The flanking bays featured folding doors surmounted by moulded panels embellished with a rich panoply of ornament: cherubs' heads, festoons, flowers, rosettes, shields, olive and palm branches, bounded by the Corinthian order, which reinforced the triumphal form and had a 'Noble Effect'.[107]

In the 1730s the tide also began to turn in favour of stylistic homogeneity, the earliest expression of which

317 (*above*) John Harris. 'The Inside of the Cathedral Church of St Peter's York' towards the chancel, in Drake 1736, p. 525. Engraving. Repaving by Richard Boyle, 3rd Earl of Burlington and William Kent architects, 1731–33.

318 (*left*) J. Basire. 'Roman Pavement at Aldburgh', Yorkshire, in Drake 1736, pl. 24, detail. Engraving. Leeds Library and Information Service.

was the refurbishment of York Minster. The inaugural improvements of the newly installed dean, Richard Osbaldeston, centred on replacing the old paving, where 'an innumerable quantity of gravestones . . . enriched with . . . images . . . in brass . . . shone like embroidery'. The work was executed by William Kent, an 'eminent painter and architect', under the direction of Richard Boyle, 3rd Earl of Burlington, Lord Lieutenant of the East and West Ridings of Yorkshire, leader of the English Palladian movement, though with no track record as a church designer.[108] The new geometrical pattern (pl. 317), in which corridors and angles of intricately criss-crossing blue and white stone slabs are carefully aligned to both the central axis and the edges of the aisle piers, was characterised as 'a kind of *Mosaick*, thought properest for a *Gothick* building'.[109]

The source of inspiration was one of a group of Roman tessellated floors recently unearthed at nearby Aldburgh, a property owned by the Minster, reported and illustrated by the York historian Francis Drake (pl. 318), who associated this new work with the city's celebrated Roman origins. He alluded to the Minster in his book, *Eboracum* (1736), dedicated to the Architect Earl, as 'a structure, in a truer and noble taste of architecture, than, in all probability, the *Roman* EBORACUM could ever boast of. Your Lordship's great knowledge in this Art, soars up to the Augustan age and style'.[110]

In complete contrast is Kent's unreserved commitment to gothic in his independent design for the archbishop's throne, stall fronts and pulpit (pls 163, 319) erected in the choir, rich with a repertory of authentic medieval motifs compiled in a form that, through engravings, became the standard pattern during the eighteenth century (pls 174, 213).

Kent went on to replace the west face of the medieval pulpitum at Gloucester Cathedral with a new organ screen (pl. 320) for Bishop Benson, a cousin of the antiquary Browne Willis. His starting point seems to have been the thirteenth-century north transept screen,[111] now enriched with candelabrum, fluted pilasters, pinnacles, pineapples and polygonal panels, with a range of crocketed ogee arches of a type readily accessible from medieval tombs (pl. 166) refashioned into what was termed a 'Gothic colonade'.[112] This cacophony was tempered by the classical discipline of Palladio's Basilica at Vicenza (pl. 322), itself a casing of a gothic structure, familiar from *I quattro libri* and known to Kent first-hand from his visit to the city in 1714.[113] Was this a volte-face? Walpole condemned Kent for demonstrating 'no more there than he did anywhere else how to enter into the true Gothic taste', but in this instance this may have been a misunderstanding of the architect's attentions. The new screen's transparency helped relieve what Walpole described as the romanesque nave's 'outrageously plump' early twelfth-century piers and arches, which are brutally juxtaposed with mid-thirteenth-century Early English gothic vaulting and the celebrated cloisters' glorious late fourteenth-century Perpendicular, regarded by Stukeley as 'beautiful beyond any thing I ever saw'.[114] For Kent this might have justified a Palladian response (Palladio and romanesque being both the progeny of ancient Rome), which refigured the cathedral's interior in a Hawksmoorian stylistic sequence, the equivalent of that already achieved at Westminster (p. 311).[115] Kent's screen enjoyed an interesting progeny in work by Fuller White, a carpenter from Weybridge, Surrey (employed at nearby Oatlands, where Kent undertook work for

319 John Vardy after William Kent. 'A Pulpit in the Cathedral at York', Yorkshire, in Vardy 1744, pl. 51. Engraving. W. Kent architect, 1737–42, destroyed in 1829 fire.

320 John Vardy after William Kent. 'A Screen Erected before the Choir in the Cathedral Church of Gloucester', Gloucestershire, in Vardy 1744, pl. 49. Engraving. W. Kent architect, 1740–41, dismantled 1820.

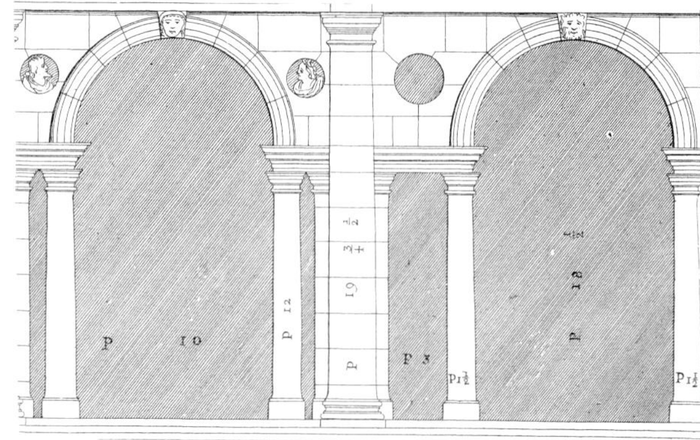

322 'Of the Basilica's of our times', Vicenza, Italy, in Ware 1738, Third Book, pl. xx, detail. Engraving. A. Palladio architect, 1545–80.

321 (*left*) Fuller White. Churchyard gateway, St Nicholas, Newbury, Berkshire, 1770. English Heritage (National Monuments Record, BB88/6581).

323 Samuel Hieronymus Grimm. View towards the altar, Cowdray House chapel, Sussex, July 1786. Pen and ink and wash. © The British Library Board, Kaye Collection, Add. MS 5675, f. 90. Architect unknown, perhaps James Gibbs, 1729–?52, destroyed in 1793 fire.

the Earl of Lincoln in 1745). Baumber church, Lincolnshire (1760), where the earl held the living, features a pared-down version of the screen, composed of three bays of single, elongated octagonal piers supporting anorexic crocketed ogee arches.[116] Ten years later White rang the changes in a pair of churchyard gates at Newbury, Berkshire (pl. 321), inspired by the celebrated romanesque arches removed from Shobdon church, Herefordshire, and re-erected with pointed and ogee forms as an eye-catcher in the park (1746–56, perhaps under Kent's direction).[117]

On the fringe of these experiments is the elusive Catholic chapel created within the medieval core of Cowdray House, Sussex (destroyed by fire in 1793). Its designer is unrecorded, no building accounts survive and its date remains imprecise, though sometime between 1729 and 1752 seems most likely and certainly no later than 1769, the first known reference to it as 'one of the finest of its kind, adorned in a very magnificent manner'.[118] This is confirmed in the sole visual record (pl. 323), drawn in July 1786, the year in which the disillusioned owners, the 7th Viscount Montagu, defected to Anglicanism and his wife turned Methodist.[119] The original client, Anthony Browne, 6th Viscount (died 1767), inherited in 1717 and immediately commissioned paintings for the Great Staircase from G.-A. Pellegrini, who returned to Venice at the end of 1719, and for the hall from Roberto Clerici and Louis Goupy, around 1722.[120] The chapel altarpiece, *Christ's Resurrection* by Giacomo Amigoni, was presumably executed during his sojourn in England (1729–39), but could have been supplied later from Italy.[121] It may be significant that the chapel was not mentioned during visits either by William Stukeley in 1722 or by Jeremiah Milles, who admired Pellegrini's work in 1743, though as a senior Anglican cleric he may not have enjoyed admittance to this inner sanctum.[122] Its double-storeyed, 24 by 50 foot space, leading directly from the main staircase, had its lower walls wainscoted in plain, gilt-trimmed mahogany, above which were flamboyantly ornamented panels painted white and gilt.[123] Ionic pilasters with fluting between volutes and astragals dividing the wall panels at the west end relate to an engraving published in D. de' Rossi's *Studio d'architettura civile . . . di Roma* (1702),[124] while the quirky crown of the altarpiece is a hallmark of Roman late baroque church façades, notably Alessandro Galilei's San Giovanni in Laterano (1732–6).[125] This repertory suggests the possible involvement of the Roman-trained Catholic James Gibbs, who was working with his team of Swiss *stuccatori* before 1733 for the recusant 8th Duke of Norfolk at Arundel Castle, a dozen miles to the south-east. Indeed, the altarpiece is comparable to the Norfolk ormolu tabernacle,[126] while the chapel ceiling is close to examples published as plate LVI in Gibbs's *The Rules For Drawing the Several Parts of Architecture* (1732). Yet what made the ensemble unmistakeably English was the mahogany altar rail of interlaced ogees and the 'light and elegant' baldachin with cusped and flattened quatrefoils supported on extravagantly slender iron columns surrounding the altar table.[127] This was an attempt to harmonise with the sixteenth-century gothic windows and owes much to Richard Bentley's Great Parlour chimneypiece at Strawberry Hill (1754), and his proposals for the ante-chapel at The Vyne, Hampshire of 1756.[128] Of course, one cannot rule out the possibility that the chapel evolved over the decades in stages under the direction of more than a single architect.

Allerton Mauleverer, Yorkshire (pl. 325), is one of the oddest-looking, most intriguing creations of Georgian hybridisation, the subject of much fanciful and con-

324 Heinrich Hulsbergh after Henry Flitcroft. 'The Elevation of the . . . Portico . . . with the West Front', St Paul's Cathedral, London, in Kent 1727, vol. II, pl. 56. Engraving. Inigo Jones architect, 1633–42, demolished 1678.

tentious speculation, yet an accurate stylistic identification and how it was interpreted are at the very heart of the nature of eighteenth-century medievalism. The history of the previous church on the site is unclear. Apparently of twelfth-century origins, by 1620 it fea-

325 John Vardy. West front, St Martin, Allerton Mauleverer, Yorkshire, *c.*1745–52.

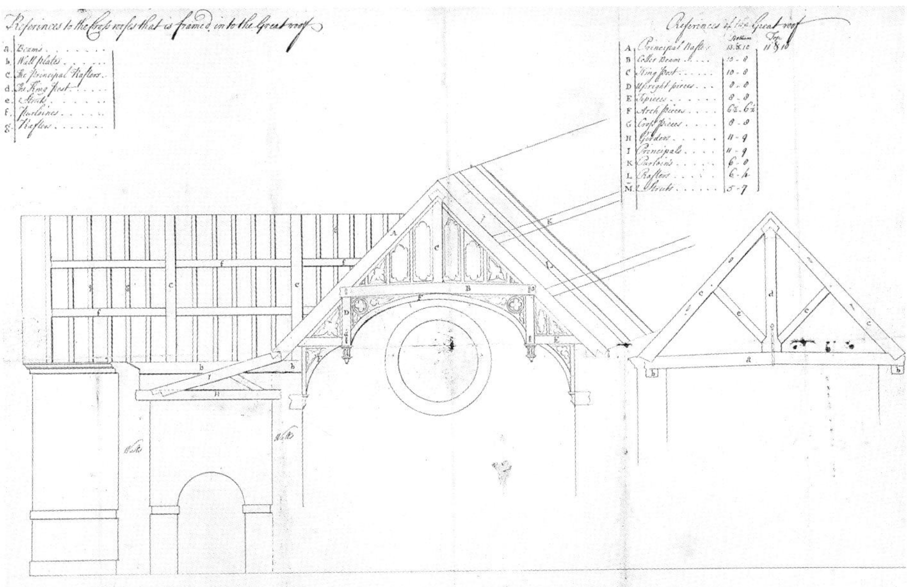

326 John Vardy. Design for the 'Cross roofes that is framed into the Great roof', St Martin, Allerton Mauleverer, Yorkshire, *c.*1745. Pen and ink. West Yorkshire Archives Service (Leeds), Acc 1493.

tured a 'high quyer' and a 'north quyer' (transept), but in 1633 was 'out of repair and wanteth many utensils'.[129] Yet, nothing was done until the 1740s, when most of the medieval fabric was razed in preparation for a new build by the lord of the manor, Richard Arundell, Surveyor-General of the Office of Works, half-brother of the architect 9th Earl of Pembroke and MP for Knaresborough, which he secured through the auspices of Lord Burlington. A confirmed classicist, he commissioned John Vardy in 1746 for a design (unrealised) for a splendid Kentian Palladian mansion en suite with the church.[130] Its crossing tower and west front sporting a gabled upper storey dominated by large circular and round-headed windows flanked by lower, slightly advanced outer bays with broad, flat framing piers, have led to a modern consensus that the church represented

327 George Dance Sr. Interior towards the crossing and chancel, St Mary, Faversham, Kent, 1754–8. English Heritage (National Monuments Record, AA50/8869).

a rare instance of romanesque revival.[131] These features, however, appear more or less in the same arrangement in the upper storey of Inigo Jones's west front of pre-Fire St Paul's Cathedral as engraved in Kent's *The Designs of Inigo Jones*, to which Arundell subscribed (pl. 324).[132] Vardy, who moved in this Palladian circle and had just published *Some Designs of Mr Inigo Jones and Mr Wm Kent* (1744), was aware that Jones had famously encased the medieval building in classical veneer, which is reflected at Allerton, where not only is the body detailed in gothic, including a reset chancel window of medieval date, but also the nave is covered by an elaborate hammerbeam roof, recorded in working drawings (pl. 326) intended for construction rather than historical record, as the carpenters' and joiners' proposals make clear.[133]

In 1754, as a spin-off of restoration activity at Canterbury three years earlier (pl. 178), George Dance Sr stabilised the frail gothic carcass of nearby Faversham church by insinuating a wholly classical endoskeleton along the central spine and transepts (pl. 327), causing him much professional anguish, as we have noted in chapter 10. To 'prevent bad consequences' he resisted preserving the old, jerry-built crossing piers as an 'injudicious' solution to reinforcing the central tower. He also dismissed the option of dismantling fewer than all four crossing piers without removing the nave arcade as 'whimsical . . . very absurd if not impractible . . . unworkmanlike, and contrary to all Rules of Art'.[134] Dance's transformation, which the Vestry believed added 'Great Beauty', is a quiet, masculine sweep of Doric columns raised on pedestals originally level with the tops of the pews, with deep entablatures of widely spaced triglyphs between long panels of stucco-festooned garlands. Dance bound the entablatures to the crossing wall by inserting a slender return atop a vertical extension of the outer half-pilasters attached to piers supporting the main arch – a quirky solution of subtle sophistication. He removed the 'Mullions and Crocket Work' of the pointed-arch aisle windows (re-gothicised in 1874). Clerestories with lunette windows 'enriched with Egg and ffllowers', a motif derived from Palladio via Henry Flitcroft's St Olave, Southwark (pls 565–6), combined with 'Ionick Modilion Cornish all Round the . . . Middle Aisle' and the walls and ceiling painted white, completed the decoration.[135] The four crossing arches were rebuilt as slimmer but sturdier triumphal arch-like structures, with oculi inserted on the transept sides, recalling the Paduan-inspired interior of the architect's St Leonard, Shoreditch (pls 575–6). Such blatant disregard for stylistic homogeneity suggests that both client and architect (a no-nonsense City of London practitioner trained in the building trades, who rarely consorted with medieval vocabulary) comfortably preferred the practical stability inherent in classical forms over the visually fragile though aesthetically appropriate gothic.

Debates about stylistic propriety reached a climax during the 1760s with issues surrounding the altarpiece of King's College chapel, Cambridge. Conflicts were already evident as early as the 1720s, when James Gibbs, though ranking the chapel as a 'beautiful building of the Gothic taste the finest I ever saw', nonetheless promoted a classical structure, while the spectacular choirscreen and stalls of 1533–5, one of the iconic masterpieces of the inaugural phase of the English renaissance, was condemned as 'the most impertinent music gallery which cuts [the interior] in two and destroys the unity of the design'.[136]

John Adam, visiting King's in 1759, thought it 'excels everything here . . . perhaps everything of the kind . . . we know of', and eight years later, when James Essex's involvement in the altarpiece still hung in the balance, the College agent in London put forward the candidature of his brother James Adam, who promised to undertake the project 'with Taste and in a manner . . . suitable to the Grandeur of the Chapple'.[137] Following Continental practice he offered stylistically alternative schemes.[138]

328 James Adam. 'Design for a Skreen for Kings College [chapel] Cambridge', Cambridgeshire, detail, 1768–9. Pen and ink and wash. Sir John Soane's Museum, London, AD 31/22.

The classical version (pl. 328), which was seen as a mirror of the 'style of the Screen & other inside wood Work', mixed antique motifs – an apsidal distyle temple portico with grotesque panels and the major order a hybrid featuring capitals based on the Temple of Aesculapius in Robert Adam's *Ruins of the Palace of the Emperor Diocletian at Spalatro* (1764), and eclectic shafts combining fluting and scales – with wholly domesticated flanks comprising ornamental, recess-panelled pilasters and 'drawing-room' doors.[139] The alternative scheme (pl. 329) is more puzzling even within the often busy, bizarre world of Adamesque gothic. The centrepiece is an obsessively pseudo-medieval filigree brimming with saintly statues, arcades, roses, bratticing, crockets and cusps recalling Milan Cathedral (pl. 330), a medieval marvel already mentioned as a specimen of both ornamental excessiveness and stylistic hybridism (pp. 187, 296), as well as Robert Adam's Alnwick Castle chapel.[140]

The College authorities expressed concern that there was 'no Stopping the Imagination of these *Virtuosi*, especially when fixed with so noble a Subject', particularly regarding the issue of the altarpiece's loftiness, which 'so very much obscurred [the] Lower part of the

2 Design of a Skreen for King's College Cambridge

329 (*above*) James Adam. '2d Design of a Skreen for King's College [chapel] Cambridge', Cambridgeshire, 1768–9. Pen and ink and wash. Sir John Soane's Museum, London, AD 31/23.

330 (*left*) Exterior of the choir, Santa Maria Maggiore (Duomo), Milan, Italy, begun 1386. Courtauld Institute of Art, 855/39/(3A).

331 Thomas Malton after Sir Robert Taylor. 'A South East View of a Design for a Church, intended for Long Ditton, Surry' (St Mary), gothic version, 1778. Engraving. Courtauld Institute of Art.

332 Thomas Malton after Sir Robert Taylor. 'A South West View of a Church built at Long Ditton Surry' (St Mary), classical version as built, 1778. Courtauld Institute of Art. Demolished by 1878.

Eastern Window' filled with splendid sixteenth-century stained glass depicting the *Passion of Christ*. Despite hints of official dissatisfaction, Adam 'adhered to his original Thought', defending his proposal by pointing out that the 'Pinnacles and Battlements [form a] Sort of Fret-Work' in which the 'Appearance of the painted Glass thro' the Intersties is no bad Effect'. He further recommended constructing the screen with 'best season'd Riga Timber [painted in a] fine Stone Colour', or alternatively of 'Composition made to resemble Stone . . . worked up upon the Spot by Men sent by Him' (presumably the artificial material cast from moulds that Mrs Eleanor Coade began manufacturing in 1769), which had the virtues of 'Durability [in] Work designed to last for Ages [and] lightening the Expence'. The provost was unconvinced; Adam received £79 2s. 0d. for drawings and was dismissed, paving the way for James Essex's official appointment as architect in 1770.[141]

Sir Robert Taylor, architect to the Bank of England, followed suit in 1778 by proposing both gothic and classical schemes for replacing the ruinous medieval church at Long Ditton, Surrey,[142] which were engraved and set in idyllic countryside with elegantly dressed strollers as if already actually built (pls 331–2). Both employed identical Greek-cross plans. One features thirteenth-century-style tracery windows, quatrefoil and embattled gables and a striking octagonal bell turret merging effortlessly into a needle spire with cinquefoil and sunk quatrefoil openings, an entirely Taylorian

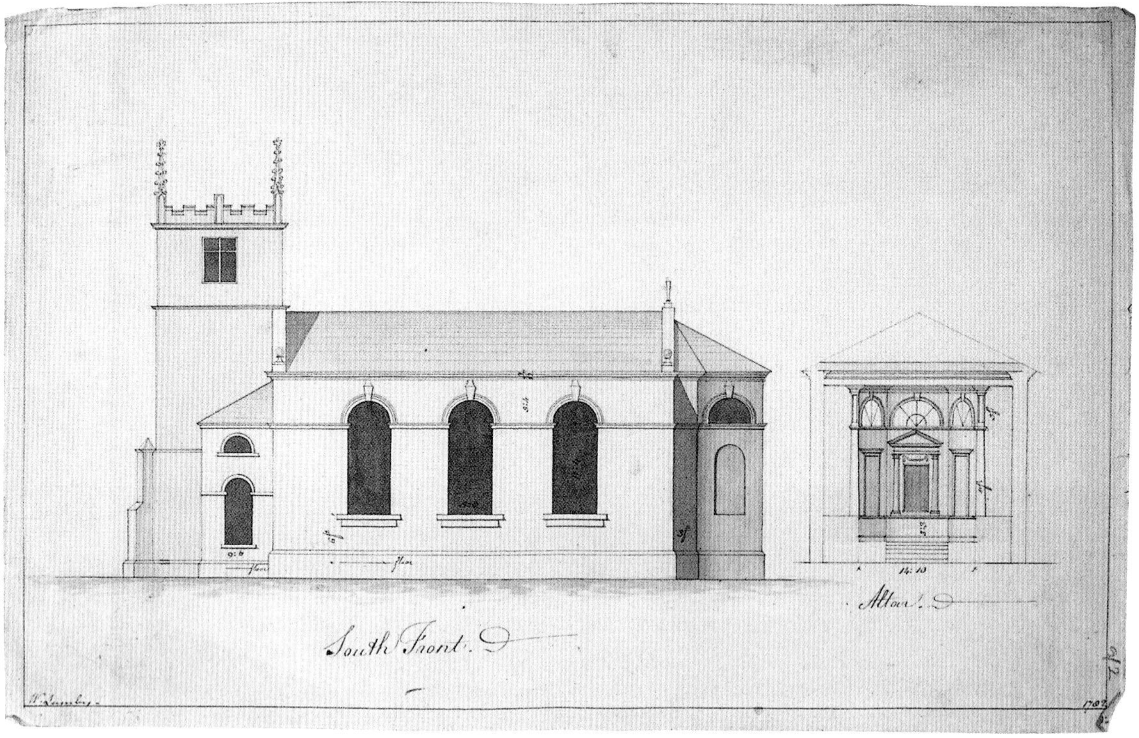

333 William Lumby. Design for the 'South Front' and 'Altar', St Vincent, Burton By Lincoln, Lincolnshire, classical version, 1781–2. Pen and ink and coloured wash. Lincolnshire Archives, Par 9/2/2a.

334 William Lumby. Design for the 'South Elevation', St Vincent, Burton By Lincoln, Lincolnshire, gothic version, 1782. Pen and ink and coloured wash. Lincolnshire Archives, Par 9/2/5.

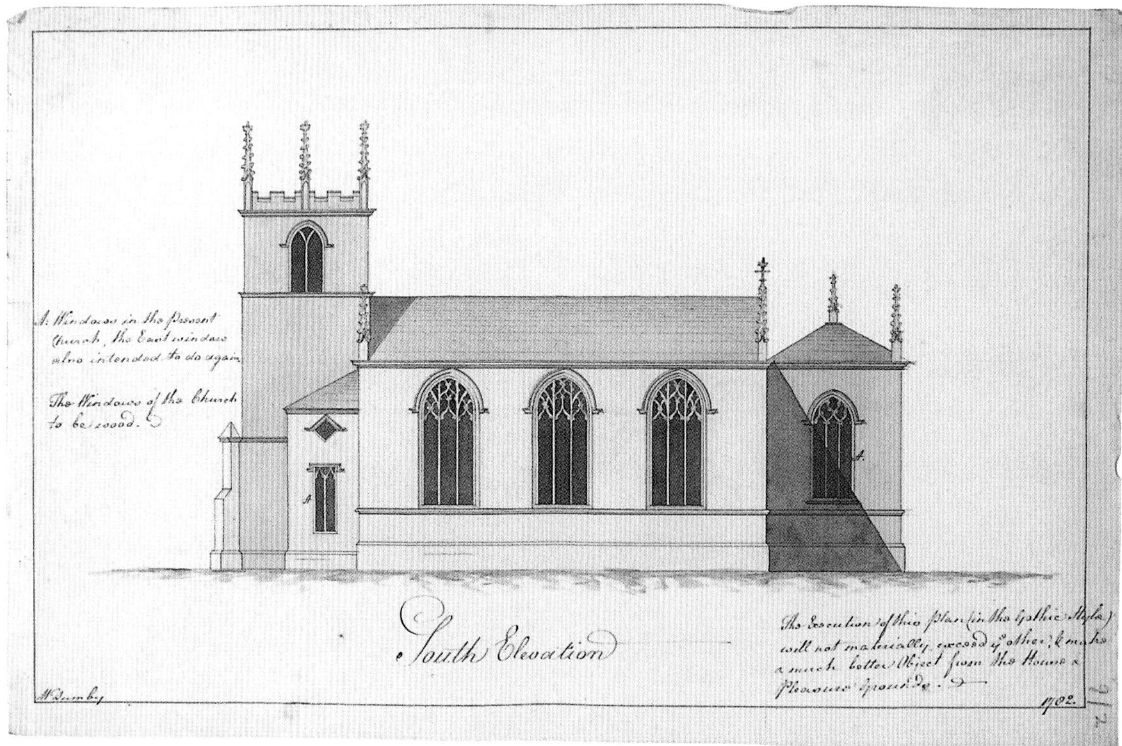

invention.[143] The alternative has a column-screened apsidal chancel on the pattern of Taylor's villas and an entrance with a Diocletian window set in a recessed arch derived from Roman baths (he owned a copy of Burlington's *Fabbriche Antiche disegnate da Andrea Palladio*, dated 1730 but issued several years later), enriched by bold jambs and voussoirs, and crowned by a powerful tempietto in the manner of the Choragic Monument of Lysicrates (as reconstructed in Stuart's and Revett's *The Antiquities of Athens*, published from 1762, also found in his library).[144]

William Lumby, Essex's talented clerk of the works and draughtsman at Lincoln Cathedral, also presented alternative replacements for the medieval body and chancel at Burton-By-Lincoln, whose late seventeenth-century gothic tower was in both cases to be preserved. The classical option (pl. 333) includes a polygonal chancel lit by lunettes. The other (pl. 334) features windows (marked A on the precisely rendered presentation drawing) that were intended 'to do again', with instructions that the 'Execution of this Plan (in the Gothic Style) will not materially exceed the other, & make a much better Object from the House & Pleasure Grounds'.[145]

Hybridism was hardly the prerogative of the architectural elite. At Buckingham, following Browne Willis's abortive attempt in 1737 to 'Exalt again' the 163-foot-high medieval spire blown down in 1699, and 'like Absolom's Pillar perpetuate the raisers' name to all generations beyond all other achievements, buildings, and monuments', only the collapse of the crossing tower in 1776 finally coerced the Vestry into rebuilding the entire church (pl. 335). The design is attributed to Francis Hiorne, who made improvements at St Mary, Warwick, between 1769 and 1779.[146] His building at Buckingham lacked subtlety. The exterior was an artless classical preaching box with a crenellated parapet, the interior a version of Wren's St James, Westminster, its chancel window an unhappy marriage between the interior Serliana externally transmogrified into a tripartite gothic frame surmounted by a pediment. A case of Jekyll and Hyde.[147]

George Steuart, a Highlander practising in London and Shropshire from the 1770s, exploited the idioms of his neoclassical contemporaries, notably James Wyatt's use of tenuous pilasters and fenestration framed in shallow blind arches, which at Wellington led to a highly original and daring treatment. On the exterior (pl. 336) he inserted between each of the aisle and gallery windows a recessed panel embellished with carved rosettes and floriated diagonals sandwiched between panelled lintels and fluted sills. The anticipatory function of this unique treatment is revealed in the original interior (pl. 337), prior to radical Victorian remodelling, where its position and pattern were mirrored in the filigreed, cast-iron fronts of the galleries, attached to slender, cast-iron, quatrefoil columns: technological innovations coming to the aid of historicism.[148]

335 R. Jones. 'The North Prospect of Buckingham Church', SS Peter and Paul, Buckinghamshire, undated. Engraving. © The British Library Board, K.Top. VIII. 6. Francis Hiorne architect, attributed, 1777–80. Altered 1860s.

St Paul, Bristol (pl. 338), its exterior 'built in the Gothic taste, the inside partly Gothic and partly modern', started out as James Allen's 'elegant design of the Grecian Order' but abandoned as too expensive in favour of Daniel Hague's rival 'Gothic Order'.[149] Hague was then completing the Hope Chapel (pl. 339), an upper-class Nonconformist enterprise (all seats for sale) founded by Lady Hope and the Countess of Glenorchy, a 'regular modern gothic' preaching box. Its identical panelled corner pilasters also distinguish St Paul's 169-foot-high west tower, recalling the diminishing stages

336 (*above*) George Steuart. Design for 'North Elevation', All Saints, Wellington, Shropshire, 1787. Pen and ink and wash. Staffordshire and Stoke-on-Trent Archive Service, B/C/5/1781.

337 (*right*) George Steuart. Interior towards the chancel, All Saints, Wellington, Shropshire, 1787–90, prior to 1898–9 remodelling. Shropshire Records and Research Unit, B4960.

of the then more than 100-year-old Royal Exchange, London.[150] The interior mixes gothic arches and an organ case 'suitable to the stile of the church' with 'fancied capitals' loosely based on the Tuscan order and a fashionable Adamesque ceiling.[151]

At Ettington, Warwickshire, despite the inhabitants objecting in Parliament to the replacement of their ancient parish church, which was 'in the most material Parts . . . very substantial . . . and capable of being repaired',[152] Evelyn Shirley, lord of the manor, entertained alternative designs for a new church submitted by two architects. Henry Couchman (pl. 340) largely repeated his twenty-year-old St Bartholomew, Binley (pl. 523), while Thomas Johnson, architect of St Nicholas, Warwick (pls 223–4), virtually mimicked his rival, changing only the form of the west tower and the shape of the openings (pl. 341); this was the version that was erected in 1806. George Richardson's pretty little Palladian church at Saxby, Leicestershire (see illustration on the back of the jacket), built for Revd Robert Sherard, 4th Earl of Harborough (for whom he also designed Teigh and Stapleford, pls 228, 229), sports an awkward tower combining urn-capped buttresses and a needle spire with lucarnes.[153]

The progress of hybridism through the century is encapsulated in the changing attitudes towards Hawksmoor's improvements at Beverley Minster (*circa* 1716–20). At first much admired,[154] by 1771 Arthur Young was unconvinced by '*modern* decorators' who had 'ideas of

338 James Allen and Daniel Hague. South-west view, St Paul, Portland Square, Bristol, Somerset, 1787–94.

339 Samuel Hieronymus Grimm. 'Chapel at the Hotwells. July 1788', Hope Chapel, Bristol, Somerset. Pen and ink and wash. © The British Library Board, Kaye Collection, IV, Add. MS 15540, f. 185. Daniel Hague architect, 1786–8, remodelled 1838.

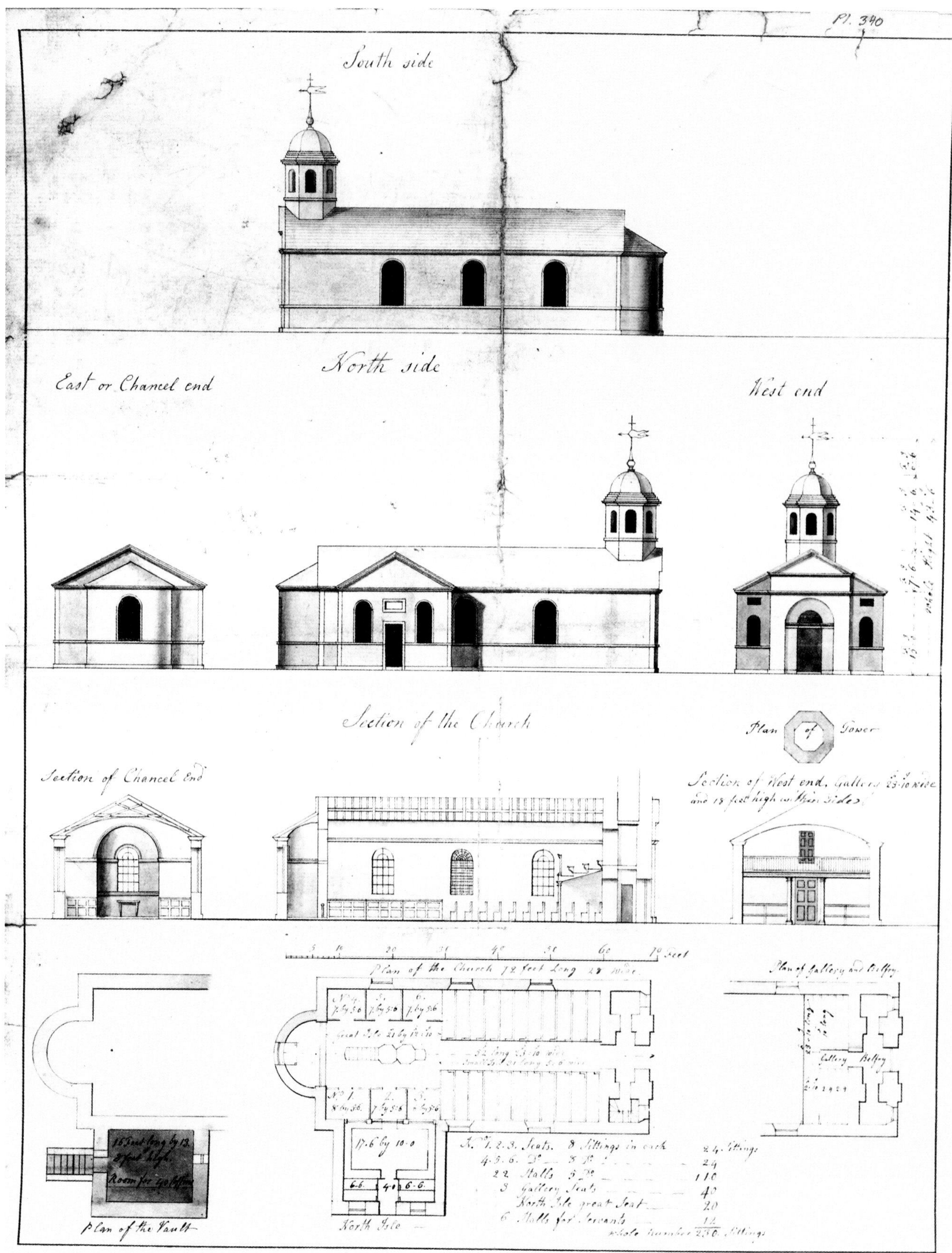
Pl. 340
South side
North side
East or Chancel end
West end
Section of the Church
Plan of Tower
Section of Chancel End
Section of West end. Gallery 23-10 wide
and 18 feet high within side
5 10 20 30 40 50 60 70 Feet
Plan of the Church 72 feet long 28 wide
Plan of Gallery and Belfry
Gallery Belfry
Great Isle 21 by 12-10
52 long 23-10 wide
No. 1.2.3. Seats. 8 Sittings in each 24 Sittings
4.5.6. Do 8 Do 24
22 Stalls 5 Do 110
8 Gallery Seats 40
North Isle great Seat 20
6 Stalls for Servants 12
whole number 230 Sittings
17-6 by 10-0
North Isle
15 Feet long by 13
8 feet high
Room for 40 Coffins
Plan of the Vault

neither beauty nor propriety', evinced by the west door reminiscent of a 'cake-house' (pl. 288) and carrying '*Grecian* ideas into the very choir of the *Gothic* cathedral' with its altarpiece in a 'stile I know not what' (pl. 287). This was confirmed by Carter, who reckoned the 'superb structure [of] antient splendour [had] not escaped the invidious marks of contempt [in the] truly-ridiculous jumble of the great tower . . . terminated with an ogee octangular dome' (pl. 276).[155] Torrington, never a fan of classicism, warned that if you 'attempt something Grecian and novel . . . you ruin church building'.[156] There was, however, a third route, neither classical nor gothic yet one rarely considered by architectural historians.

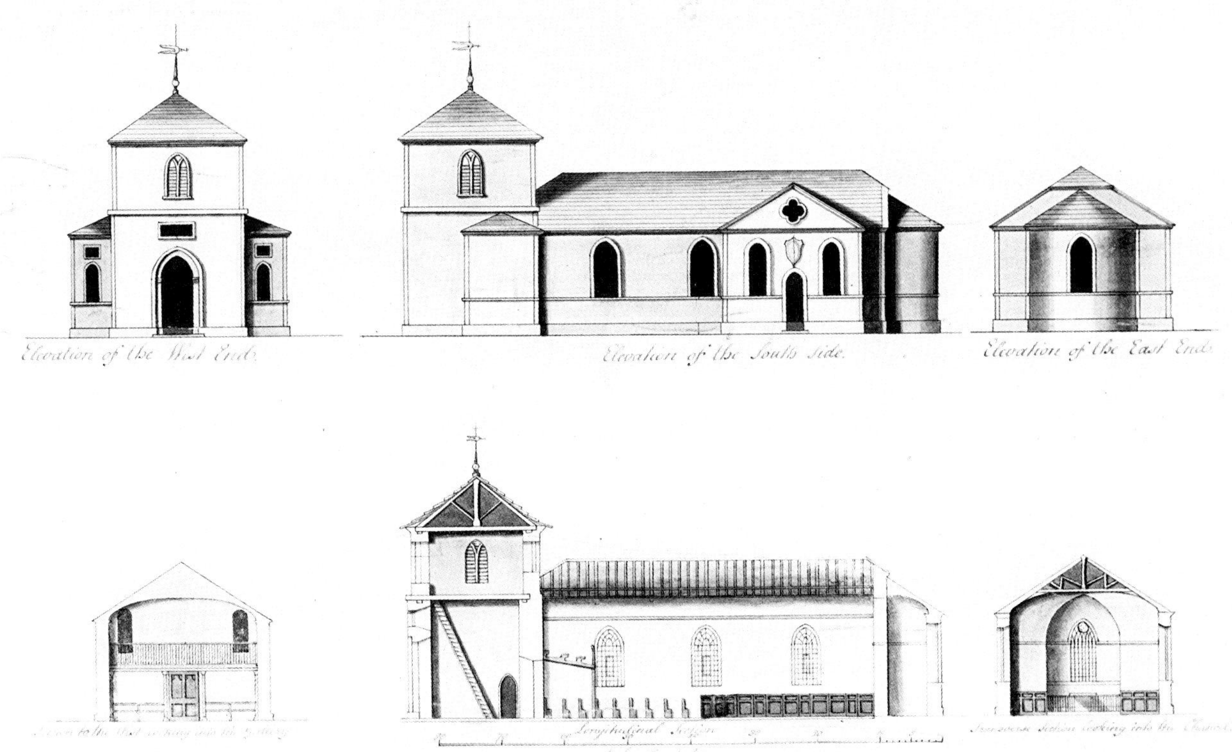

341 Thomas Johnson. Executed design, Holy Trinity, Ettington, Warwickshire, detail, 1795. Pen and ink and wash. Warwickshire Record Office, DR106v.

340 (*facing page*) Henry Couchman. Proposed plans, elevations and sections design, Holy Trinity, Ettington, Warwickshire, 1794. Pen and ink and wash. Warwickshire Record Office, DR106.

Eighteen

ROMANESQUE INTERLUDE

curious specimens of what has been called Saxon and Anglo-Norman architecture
. . . well-authenticated accounts . . . of their building, and alterations . . .
of great use to the History of Architecture in England[1]

Romanesque – or, to use pre-Rickmanian parlance Saxon (a common moniker for Norman) – the architectural style dominant in Britain between the seventh and twelfth centuries, was described by the poet Thomas Gray as possessing 'great solidity, heaviness, and rude simplicity [where the] height [of] massy piers . . . is . . . far too short for their diameter [and] round headed arches unusually wide beyond just proportion . . . and extraordinary narrow intercolumns'.[2] The young John Carter defined romanesque, which he called gothic, as 'brought by the Goths into Germany in the fifth century . . . exceeding massive, heavy, and coarse'.[3] The more discerning James Bentham in his history of Ely Cathedral (1771), however, observed that 'Some Writers call all our ancient Architecture without distinction of round and pointed Arches, *Gothic*: though I find of late the fashion is to apply the term solely to the latter', thus clarifying distinctions within an indiscriminate historical umbrella between early Saxon and French post-Conquest Norman.[4] By the 1790s John Milner, in his history of Winchester, observed that 'buildings of former times are distinguished by the Saxon, the Norman, the plain Gothic, the ornamental Gothic, the florid Gothic [Rickman's renamed Early English, Decorated and Perpendicular], and the Fantastic' (or mannerist),[5] while Thomas Hardwick Jr's meticulously rendered set of drawings of St Bartholomew-the-Great, Smithfield, London (1790–91), identified the 'Parts shaded dark [as] original . . . Saxon Work . . . a degree lighter . . . the first kind of . . . Gothic Architecture . . . still lighter . . . Gothic Work of Henry the Eights time', with the 'Modern Buildings . . . distinguished by . . . Red Tints'.[6] The truth is that in the eighteenth century the extent of Norman rebuilding was not widely understood; many antiquarian accounts of major churches identified the earliest remaining work, associated with the round rather than the pointed arch, with the time of the founder, that is, very often before the Norman Conquest, as we shall see later in this chapter dealing with attitudes towards pre-gothic cathedrals. It took several generations to put together an agreed corpus of this architectural style. Nor was romanesque universally admired. Bishop Lyttelton expressed ambivalence about 'round balls and other such vile ornaments' on Norwich Cathedral's twelfth-century west front.[7] Yet it attracted considerable interest.[8]

Between 1719 and 1721 Peter Tillemans and Thomas Eayre produced a remarkable series of views of Peterborough Cathedral (1118–1500).[9] By 1800 the antiquary Sir Richard Colt Hoare had found it 'one of the most interesting buildings I have seen, as it contains so many specimens of architecture from the early Saxon to the late ornamented Gothic', and he could not have been alone in feeling that he had never experienced a 'building of such grand and perfect Saxon architecture' as Durham.[10] Dart's large folio, 260-page, magnificently illustrated *History and Antiquities of The Cathedral Church of Canterbury* (1726), among the earliest publications of its kind in the history of architecture, evocatively described, as if a popular guidebook, the visitor entering the cathedral 'suddenly struck after an awful and solemn manner, at the Grandeur and Spaciousness of the . . . wide, lofty and high Nave' and the 'majestically Noble . . . Choir'.[11]

How were these deliberations and enthusiasms, which occupied British attention throughout the century, translated by eighteenth-century architects into

342 (*facing page*) Robert Grumbold and perhaps Sir Christopher Wren.
Restored north-west section of the north transept, Ely Cathedral, Cambridgeshire, 1699–1701.

343 Daniel King, 'The West Prospect of the Cathedral Church of Rochester', Kent, in King 1672, pl. 9. Engraving.

building activity?[12] No clear trend or consistent pattern emerges; rather, sporadic examples demonstrating a variety of approaches and solutions culminating in S. P. Cockerell's wonderful one-off 1790s transformation of ruinous twelfth-century Tickencote, Rutland, into a functioning place of worship. But the beginning of this story was if nothing else dramatic.

On 28 March 1699 the north-west section of Ely Cathedral's north transept succumbed, the result it was thought of damage sustained during an earlier earthquake. The dean, determined not to begin repairs 'till we know how to finish [and thus] justifie [the chapter] agt all [the world's] envy, malice, and capriciousness', travelled to London in August to 'consult the ablest builders, and have their opinion' on proposals (untraced) submitted jointly by Robert Grumbold, a leading Cambridge master mason, and a 'boston [Lincolnshire] Mason', later identified as a Mr Colthrop. He was repeating a process we have seen followed at St Mary, Warwick (p. 201). The Archbishop of Canterbury advised showing the scheme to Wren, whose uncle had been Bishop of Ely, but not finding the architect in residence, Dean Lambe proceeded to St Paul's Cathedral, then reaching the climax of its building programme, to confer with the 'Cheif Mason and director of . . . work', who knew Grumbold. According to Lambe's account, Samuel Fulkes 'commends his ingenuity' but reckoned his 'estimate for roofing, plumbing etc is extravagant'. On the other hand the mason recommended embracing 'without hesitation [Colthrop's] very fair, full, simple and plain' proposal in which 'nothing is omitted', especially since the 'repair is no peice of curious workmanship but plain walling wch every Mason that has served his time with an able workman knows how to performe and because the great peer, if need be, may be done by a journey man, wch he can send from London'. Fulkes also advised re-erecting the 'greatest part . . . of new stone [and] put on the same cap . . . that was upon it before, for that is not an ornament only, but a mighty strength, even as good as a Buttress, by reason of its weight'. He recommended if possible building 'upon the old foundation [and] perpendicular and not thrust the new wall into the old, but bring . . . old to . . . new'. Lambe subsequently showed Grumbold's scheme to Wren, who counselled making 'all Window frames of new stone; but good old stone is as good as new, for all other uses', and promised to question him in person on these matters. Grumbold was contracted in 1700 and work finished in the following year at a cost of £1,668.[13]

The metropolitan hold on the project is confirmed by the restoration itself (pl. 342). This entailed inserting a rusticated round-headed door (based on Wren's tower entrance of St Mary-le-Bow, pl. 484). At first glance this might seem a stylistically sympathetic choice on historical grounds in response to the adjacent romanesque openings, but only if one disregards the model of the mullion and transom window above in Wren's Trinity College library, Cambridge (1676–84).[14] Considering Wren's scepticism regarding the inherent structural defect of medieval crossing piers – expressed in his 'Report on Salisbury Cathedral' of 1668: 'For this reason this forme for Churches hath been rejected, by Moderne Architects abroad, who use the better & Roma[n] Forme of Architecture'[15] – it is hardly to be expected at this early date that he would sanction reviving authentic forms at Ely.

The situation at twelfth-century Rochester Cathedral, Kent, was somewhat different (pl. 343), the fabric having suffered storm damage in 1703 and condemned for being in 'very mean [and] slovenly condition' and making 'a miserable appearance on the outside; The Tower . . . bad . . . the Spire worse, gouty and low; the Inside . . . little better, the Pillars . . . large; the height little, the side Isles narrow . . . the Windows smal and poor'. This was the major, sustained romanesque renovation programme of the century.[16] In 1716 William Dickinson (then Westminster Abbey's under-surveyor) recommended a raft of repairs, followed by John James, who in 1730–31 designed a new crossing vault composed of pendants, flowers and oak leaves – reflecting Hawksmoor's bell hole at Westminster Abbey (pl. 284), but in a 'peculiarly disgusting . . . Grecian stile' (ancient Greece and Rome being interchangeable terms signifying a classical commonality). However, this may have been a case of James subscribing to Hawksmoor's notion of romanesque having evolved out of the Roman tradition (see pp. 348–9).[17] Then, between 1735 and 1751 Charles Sloane, among much else, erected two massive, ungainly buttresses against the south-east transept (anticipating John Nash's ungainly solution at St David's Cathedral in the 1790s, pl. 241).[18]

The principal architectural activity at Rochester occurred during the years 1760–66 under the direction of Henry Keene, while serving as the surveyor of Westminster Abbey. His enlightened survey of the fabric, the most comprehensive devoted to any romanesque cathedral in the eighteenth century, stressed 'reinstating' the two towers atop the eastern gable with 'new Stone as they were originally [repairing the] Octagonal Pinnacles and new facing [the] decay'd . . . Angle Coinstones'. Moreover, the 'handsomest way of repairing' the north-west transept was to 'reinstate the Columns, and dressings to the Windows, as they were Originally', but with a proviso that 'if the Expence . . . shou'd be Sufficient objection, it may be done in a plainer manner by omitting the Columns' and substituting the capitals with 'a projecting Corbel; according to the Stile of the Building'. Securing the 'considerable bulg'd' walls of the main body entailed a method 'which shou'd have been done at the Original building, & indeed I much wonder it was not, as most of the buildings of this kind are done so', as well as replacing damaged buttresses in the 'Same Stile', and so on. Keene believed that if executed along these lines 'in a proper, & workmanlike manner' the fabric 'will appear as it had been so done at the first building, And Consequently be no unsightly Appearance'. Finally, the 'much crackt & torn' west end required rebuilding to make it 'as handsome . . . & much more Uniform than . . . at present; & . . . so preserve the Stile of the building, that it cannot be discovered but that it is in its original State'.[19] This was a remarkably confident claim for this date and by one of the premier gothicists of his age, though due to subsequent remodelling campaigns it is unclear what was actually executed. The priorities given to stylistic homogeneity and material conservation should be contrasted to Daniel Asher Alexander's palliative of 1799, which followed a traditional formulaic solution.

Yet, however laudable was such uniformity it was not always achieved. Following partial destruction by fire in 1700 of the splendid romanesque church at Leominster, Herefordshire, the parish petitioned that there would be 'Great disfatisfaction [if the fabric] should be any waye Lessened either in length or Breadth Considering it being an Ancient and noble Structure' and pressed that the 'Ancient Walls may be kept standing'.[20] Furthermore, while it was reported in 1756 that most of the 'old church, of Saxon architecture' still stood, the new addition was 'very fine . . . Gothic [with] light . . . windows' including a large western one, 'the members of which are so fine that . . . on . . . finding they began to give way outwards, [the builders] practiced two very light buttresses up against the pillars . . . to strengthen it, which is a singular thing'.[21]

During the 1740s and 1750s two church projects evoked extraordinary romanesque responses. In John Vardy's preliminary proposal for Allerton Mauleverer, Yorkshire (pl. 344), prior to arriving at his executed

344 John Vardy. Preliminary plan, elevations and section design, St Martin, Allerton Mauleverer, Yorkshire, *c.*1745. Pen and ink and wash. West Yorkshire Archives Service (Leeds), Acc 1493.

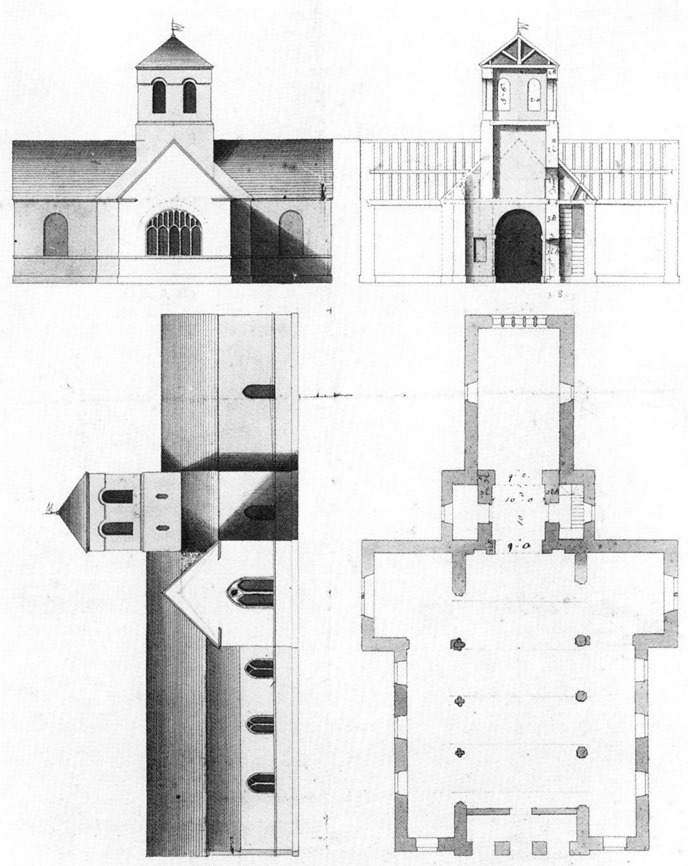

345 Henry Keene. West front, St Mary, Hartwell, Buckinghamshire, 1752–53. English Heritage (National Monuments Record, CC44/439).

Keene's new church at Hartwell of 1752–3 (pl. 345) is described in the builders' accounts as being 'in the Saxon Manner'. While the term, as we have seen, then carried various stylistic connotations ranging from Saxon through Norman to Early English,[24] further entries suggest a vocabulary distinctly separate from the ubiquitous 'Gothick Arches' that pervades the accounts, as in the case of the (now destroyed) altar 'in the Saxon manner the Moldings Composed of small unusual Members . . . Circulr Circular heads of Niches . . . the Communion Table with 6 Small Columns' and so on.[25] Singularly Saxon, too, are the polylobe, radial-traceried, blind wheel windows prominently placed on three ele-

346 Charles Lyttelton. 'The East Front of Barfreston Church in Kent', 1749, in MS 'Drawings of Saxon Churches'. Pen and ink and wash. Society of Antiquaries of London.

Jonesian solution (pls 324–5), the five-bay front (for which there is no elevation drawing) features an unusual tripartite arcaded *in antis* entrance that brings to mind the romanesque Benedictine church at Marmoutier, Alsace,[22] prompting speculation that it is perhaps a conscious reflection of Allerton's pre-1745 fabric (of unknown appearance), which had been erected by the Benedictine monks attached to twelfth-century Marmoutier Abbey in Normandy.[23]

vations, based on ancient examples such as Barfreston, Kent (pl. 346). It can hardly be coincidental that in the same year, 1749, that Keene assisted Sanderson Miller in preparing designs for Hagley Hall, Worcestershire, for its owner Baron Lyttelton,[26] the latter's younger brother, Charles Lyttelton, Dean of Exeter, was compiling a 'Book [of] several original Drawings, for the most part taken from the Door Ways &c of English Country Churches . . . such as are Executed in the

Style of Architecture which prevail'd here in the Saxon & first Norman Ages, before the introduction of the Gothick', with an important aside: 'This is the only Collection of Saxon Buildings that Ever was Made', which includes this hitherto neglected building. As its president in 1782, Charles Lyttelton bequeathed the book to the Society of Antiquaries of London.[27]

Lyttelton's precocity aside, it was not until the final decade of the century that the value of romanesque as a separate historical style to be exploited on behalf of contemporary church design was fully appreciated, most spectacularly in Samuel Pepys Cockerell's triumphant resurrection of Tickencote, Rutland (pl. 347), an uncommonly well-preserved twelfth-century chancel venerated by the Georgians for its antiquity and the 'surprizing manner' of its external architectural detailing. The petition for improvements of 1791 stressed its status as 'perhaps the most Ancient Saxon Building in Britain' and a determination to 'repair or rebuild . . . upon the Old foundations . . . to preserve the uniformity of Ancient Architecture'. In the following year Torrington thrilled to a situation where previously the fabric was 'almost pull'd down' to one where it was 'now rebuilding . . . from the old model exactly'. He hailed it as a 'model of Saxon Architecture . . . ages after all others of the stile were gone' and recommended it as a paragon 'if a nobleman wants to rebuild a church'. The shift away from gothic is particularly striking. Cockerell, who otherwise showed no interest in romanesque, was commended for achieving 'more purity . . . than . . . usually found in attempts of the sort'.[28] He apparently followed the advice of John Carter, who had surveyed the church in 1780 on behalf of the Society of Antiquaries, preparing carefully rendered drawings and noting that though the 'great part' of the chancel had previously been 'havocked' it remained 'fully sufficient to enable a "religious" restoration'.[29]

Significantly, there was no intention of preserving the ruined gothic body to create a picturesque ensemble in the manner of, say, the much lauded Croyland Abbey, Lincolnshire, with its Norman south aisle and gorgeous gothic west front,[30] or as Nash was doing concurrently at St David's (pl. 241). Because Tickencote's reformed fabric is stylistically unadulterated, Cockerell's precise

347 (*above right*) Samuel Pepys Cockerell. South chancel elevation, SS Peter and Paul, Tickencote, Rutland, 1791–92.

348 (*right*) John Carter. 'Geometrical elevation of part of the north side of the Nave of St. Peters church Northampton', 1782, in Bray 1783, p. 367, pl. VIII. Engraving.

349 James Gibbs. Inner vestibule door, Lincoln Cathedral, Lincolnshire, 1725, with colonnettes added by James Essex, 1775. English Heritage (National Monuments Record, BB49/2542).

contribution remains unclear. The antiquary Colt Hoare was 'much puzzled to give a description [since] so much in the old Saxon style and so many of the old ornaments made use of and others, as I imagine, scraped so as to appear new, that it requires a very nice eye to distinguish the modern from the antique'.[31] The external, five-tiered east front may be no more than a tidying up of the original, mirrored by a tall, central recess with narrow mouldings and clustered angle columns on the previously blank west front. The strange, shallow relief arches of the middle chancel bay recklessly splattered with diamond-shaped lozenges and the frieze below the eaves with an incised pattern of repetitive ragged-edged egg-and-dart-like ornament hardly seems credible as anything other than Cockerell's invention. On the other hand, the serrated-edged windows either imitate original work or perhaps are authentic masonry reused, since a similar motif appears at St Peter, Northampton, as recorded in Carter's drawings published in 1783 (pl. 348). This approach may well have been inspired by Bentham's ground-breaking book of 1771, *The History and Antiquities . . . of Ely*, which celebrates Saxon culture as 'the first Settlement of Christianity in Britain', and the Norman 'Door at the West End of the Cloister' (pl. VII) features a similar decorative treatment as the frieze.[32] Finally, there is the compelling treatment of Tickencote's rectangular body with what might be interpreted as a wayward giant Doric order engaged column rising from podium to frieze and dividing each bay, creating a subliminal pseudoperipteral temple form reminiscent of some transformed antique survival.

This feature, together with characteristic ranks of round arches on piers, would have prompted many Georgian observers to appreciate fundamental romanesque vocabulary as an authentic bridge from ancient Roman to post-medieval classicism. Occasionally the distinction was blurred, as when the *Gentleman's Magazine* in 1736 advocated that San Marco, Venice, was 'not much unlike' St Paul's Cathedral.[33]

Yet the discerning James Essex approvingly reported to his fellow Antiquarians that Lord Burlington had given him 'leave to say that Lincoln is by far the noblest Gothic [that is, partly romanesque] structure in England [and] whoever had the conducting of it was well acquainted with the noblest buildings of old Rome and had united some of their greatest beauties in that one work' (pl. 157).[34] It might well have been this belief that had prompted James Gibbs in repairing the cathedral's west towers in 1725 to introduce round-arched doors in the new internal supporting walls erected across the west end (pl. 349), echoing the lofty twelfth-century arches of the west front.[35] An early exercise in neo-Norman. Hawksmoor's intention in issuing a large engraved plan and panorama of Norman St Alban's abbey church, Hertfordshire, in 1721 (pl. 350) was to raise funds towards restoring the Reformation-ravaged fabric (which Celia Fiennes described as 'so worn away that it mourns for some charitable person to help

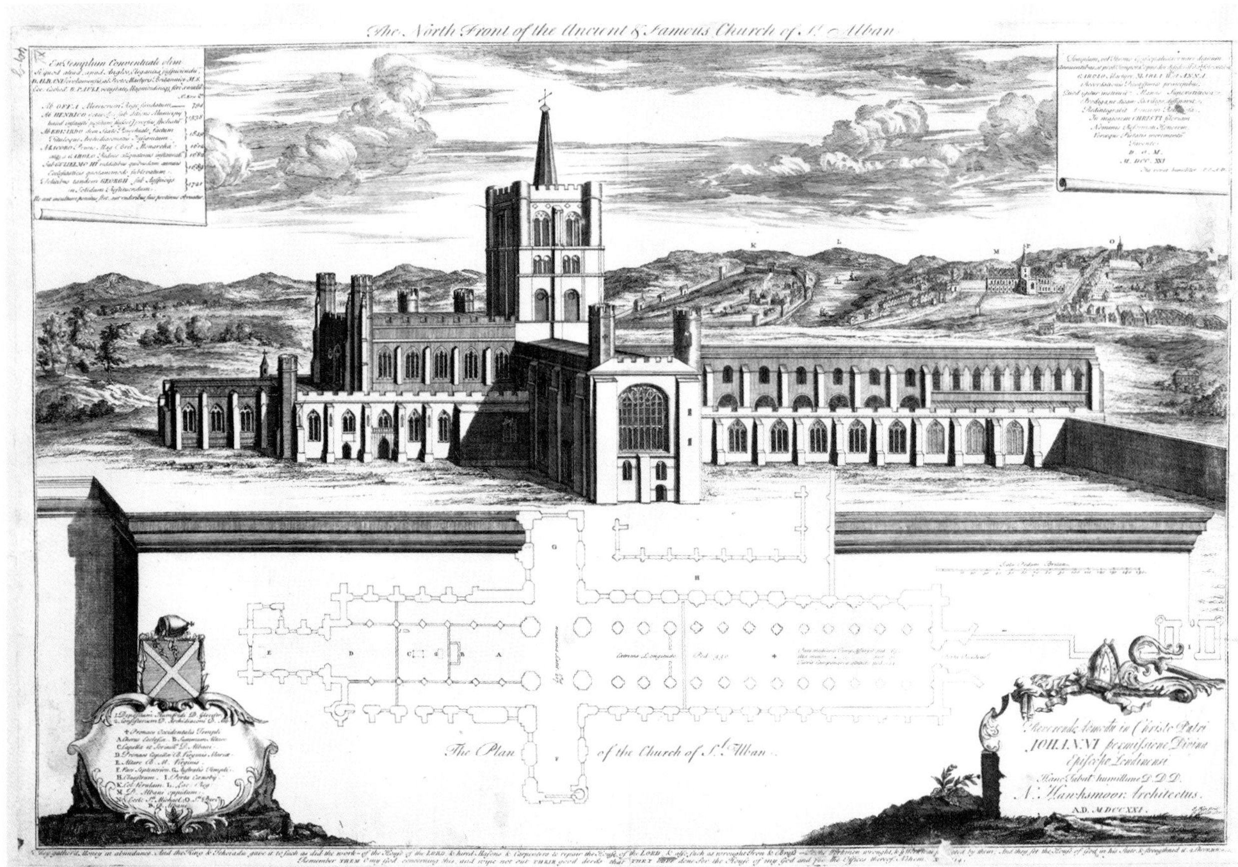

350 Jan Kip and G. Pulette after Nicholas Hawksmoor. 'The North Front [and] Plan of the Ancient & Famous Church of St. Alban', Hertfordshire. Engraving. © The British Library Board, K. Top. xv. 49.g

repaire it').[36] This is amplified in his letter to the Bishop of London in which the image, unlike the building itself, has been not only protected 'If Hen. 8 comes again' but also immortalised. Included in the landscape is 'the famed Site of the Ancient [Roman] Verulam [and the] New Towne which has arose, from the fall, of the Protomartyr St Alban'.[37]

The remodelling of romanesque St Chad, Stafford (in the nineteenth century returned to a medieval appearance), by the west Midland master builder and architect Richard Trubshaw had two distinctive features, both representing a different aspect of Georgian reinterpretation of the style. The west front, shown as a vignette in his presentation drawing (pl. 351), is without fenestration and unusually austere (Trubshaw agreed to

351 (*right*) Richard Trubshaw. Design for remodelling the west front, St Chad, Stafford, Staffordshire, detail, 1743–5. Pen and ink and wash. William Salt Library, Stafford, Hickin Papers 319/2/40.

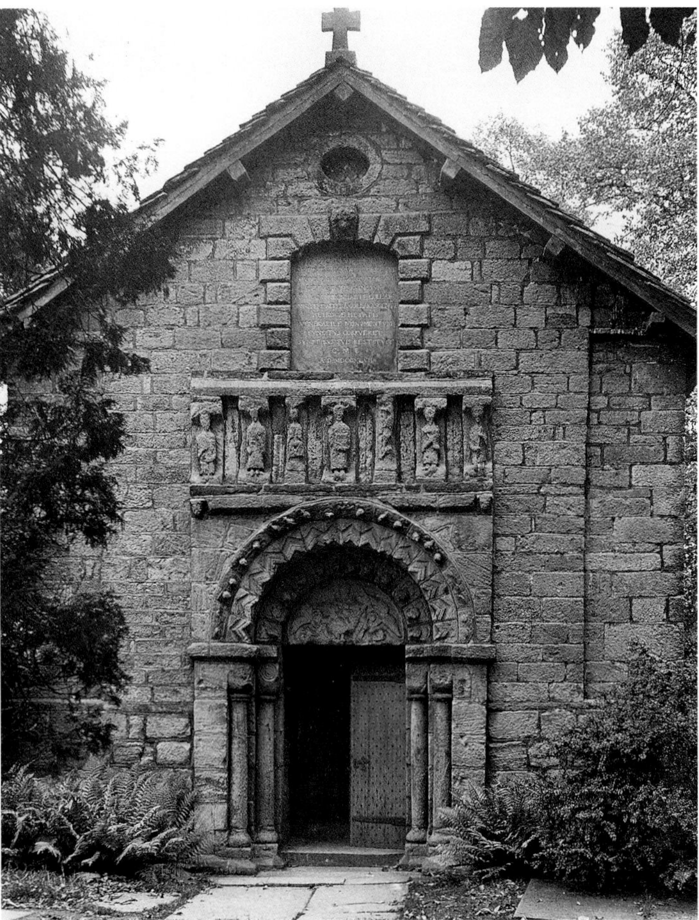

352 Architect unknown. West front, Prestbury Chapel, Cheshire, 1747, with reinstated Norman portal. English Heritage (National Monuments Record, AA63/00146).

undertake the remodelling in the 'best & most frugal manner'), with a pedimented gable, stepped buttresses and keystoned doorway of almost Vanbrughian boldness.[38] The accompanying plan reveals that the entrance consisted of a typically romanesque grouping of recessed colonnettes.[39] Internally, Trubshaw directed that the crossing pillars should be 'cut down . . . Straight' to accommodate a rusticated plaster chancel arch as part of a classical overhaul of the nave, which in its simplicity preserved the outline of its romanesque forebears.[40] A contrasting approach is represented by the 'great curiosity' of Prestbury, Cheshire, 'restored' at the expense of Sir William Meredith in 1747 'lest a venerable monument of primitive piety should utterly perish', so proudly inscribed in a rusticated elliptical arch over the reinstated Norman doorway (pl. 352).[41] The arch is derived from a 'modern Profile, executed in 1724' published in Robert Morris's *An Essay In Defence of Ancient Architecture* (1728), as a demonstration of 'a Composition of Deformity, the Result of even the most ignorant Pretender to Knowledge of Building . . . in a direct Opposition to the Rules of ancient Architecture . . . a Science visibly decaying, and overrun and trampled on by insulting Barbarity and Ignorance'.[42] It is unclear whether an intentionally ironic juxtaposition was intended.

William Stukeley proposed to the Society of Antiquaries of London in 1755 that Hereford Cathedral's surveyors 'kept more closely to the most antient British-Roman manner, which they had both from the Romans, before they left our island, and from the later Romans from Rome; when our Saxon ancestors, upon their first coming here, had well nigh ruined all antient Roman fabrics among us'.[43] In 1758 Charles Lyttelton recognised a link between the 'Alcove or Semi-circle' of Norwich's and Peterborough's choir ends and the 'pattern of the famous Basilica of Constantine at Rome'.[44] His 'Ichnography of the Vault under the Choir and side Isles of Worcester Cathedral [in] Drawings of Saxon Churches' is identified as 'the form of the Antient Basilica's at Rome – particularly Constantine's wch was the Model on which the Earliest Christian Churches were built'.[45] James Bentham described Saxon architecture as in the '*Roman* manner, and . . . the same that was then used at Rome . . . and in other parts of the Empire'.[46] *An Accurate Description and History of the Cathedral and Metropolitical Church of St Peter, York* (1790) suggested that 'In the *Anglo-Norman* Age all their Arches made Use of in Churches were nearer to the *Roman* Taste than the acute Ox-Eye Arch, which came afterwards into Fashion.'[47] William Wilkins, in 'A Description of the [twelfth-century] Church of Melbourne in Derbyshire', suggested that the earliest Christian churches converted from Roman basilicas were models for 'our oldest Saxon Churches'[48] – just as for the Grand Tourist Edward Knight, early twelfth-century Angoulême Cathedral in France was 'very much in the Grecian [Roman] manner'.[49]

In practice, these historical associations produced the uniquely extraordinary scheme for rebuilding the ruinous parish church at Kelso, Scotland (pl. 353), which had been first erected in 1649 within the ruins of the great twelfth-century abbey, commemorated by the dated pediment crowning the north transept front.[50] James Nisbet, a local architect-builder, offered to attach a rectangular, astylar body to the transept's inner face, its richly patterned romanesque porch serving as the main entrance, with internal stairs giving access to the galleries, the circular turrets and gable renewed in an almost Hawksmoorian gesture, its weathered stonework perhaps plastered and whitewashed, and the round-

353 James Nesbitt. Design for the 'Elevation to the North [of a new church] with the old Steeple', Kelso Abbey, Borders, Scotland, 1770–71. Pen and ink and wash. National Archives of Scotland, RHP 8466/4.

headed and circular features reiterated on the new building, with its Tudor hood-moulds and raised classical tablets.[51] Conversely, Stukeley saw Durham Cathedral's 'semicircular windows and arches, and great round pillars and very thick [walls], without buttresses [as] somewhat Roman degenerate';[52] Thomas Warton, in *Observations on the Fairie Queene of Spenser* (1754), saw the style as 'an adumbration or a rude imitation of the genuine Grecian or Roman manner',[53] leading Sir William Chambers to believe that 'All that is called Saxon & Norman is absolutely nothing more or less than roman Architecture the same Semicircular Arches the Same Columns with attempts at the same capitals & ornaments by men without power of execution without Judgement or taste.'[54] Such erratic perceptions nevertheless helped anchor allegiances resolutely to the antique classical tradition, which is the subject of Part Four.

Part Four

THE CLASSICAL TRADITIONS

facing page Nicholas Hawksmoor. North elevation of tower, west elevation of bridge, south elevation of body design for a new Chapel, Greenwich Hospital, London, detail of pl. 356

354 Anonymous. South elevation, St George, Bloomsbury, London, early nineteenth century. Pen and ink and wash. Author's collection. Nicholas Hawksmoor architect, 1716–31, restored 2002–6.

Nineteen

'BEHOLD! AUGUSTA'S GLITT'RING . . . TEMPLES RISE'[1]

One might expect a sanctity of style,
August and manly, in a holy pile,
And think an architect extremely odd
To build a playhouse for the church of God:
Yet half our churches, such the mode that reigns,
Are Roman theatres or Grecian fanes[2]

Modern perceptions of British eighteenth-century Anglican architecture are inevitably jaundiced. On the one hand medieval ventures had been sidelined – clearly inaccurately, as we have seen – partly owing to a latent Victorian prejudice against inauthentic gothic but also because all the leading architects of the eighteenth century, apart from a core of diehard gothicists (Essex, Keene, Miller, Walpole and Wyatt), designed primarily in a variety of classical styles on which their national reputations relied. On the other hand, there remained residual Victorian mistrust of the inherent paganism of classical vocabulary, as well as unhealthy Popish associations.

The period 1700 to 1730 witnessed a prodigious campaign to create the most magnificent group of classical churches ever seen in Britain, with the first decade climaxing with the completion, after thirty-five years construction, of St Paul's Cathedral, the outstanding ecclesiastical building achievement since the end of the middle ages. The following twenty-five years realised eleven of the proposed fifty New Churches, the so-called Queen Anne Churches, in London, Westminster and the suburbs (pl. 354). Despite their limited success in terms of actual numbers built, they are perhaps the single greatest British architectural enterprise of the century. However, rather than belonging to one stylistic hegemony, as traditionally portrayed in architectural histories, they range from full-blown Continental baroque essays to English modifications of this practice with an underlying classicism, especially in the work of Thomas Archer, James Gibbs and Nicholas Hawksmoor, to reinterpretations of so-called 'Primitive Christian' ideas through reawakened interest in late antique, post-pagan theological discourses and early church building, to a resurrection of antique temple forms for Christian worship, culminating in its first phase in St Martin-in-the-Fields. Between the 1730s and 1760s Palladian patterns were embraced, from Palladio's reconstructions of Roman architecture published in *I quattro libri d'architettura* (1570), which appeared in several English editions from 1715, to his highly influential Venetian churches, as well as those of Inigo Jones's London icons, as reinterpreted by Henry Flitcroft, George Dance Sr, James Paine, Roger Morris and others. Concomitant with these progressive developments was a sustained interest in old-fashioned Wrenian and Gibbsian vocabulary. During the remainder of the century avant-garde church forms were inspired by the precepts of international neoclassicism anchored in an archaeological revival of the antique past. Yet, as we shall discover, these ideas did not spring fully formed around mid-century, as textbook interpretations have claimed, but were the climax of an historically longer continuity stretching back as early as the 1710s, during the full flowering of English baroque. So, let us begin this architectural odyssey.

355 James Smith. Ground plan design for an unspecified cathedral-like church, undated. Pen and ink and wash. RIBA Library Drawings Collection, Q2 45.

> Where must [the architect go to seek] considerable instruction and improvement . . . for a more superb structure than . . . the grand and stately immensity of Saint Paul's cathedral?[3]

Of his masterpiece (pl. 2), 500 feet long, 340 feet to the top of the crossing dome, 2,292 feet in circumference, costing £736,752, the 85-year-old Sir Christopher Wren informed the authorities that

> throughout all my schemes of this colossal structure, I have religiously endeavoured to follow . . . the principles [of] the best ancient Greek and Roman architecture . . . and, if I glory, it is in the singular mercy of God, who has enabled me to begin and finish my great work so conformable to the ancient model.[4]

Even during construction it was proclaimed 'one of the most Spacious and Magnificent Cathedrals that ever yet was built in the World'.[5] John Evelyn reckoned 'that if the whole *Art* of *Building* were lost, it might be *recovered* and *found* again in St *Paul's* [among] those . . . Monuments of [Wren's] Happy Talent and extraordinary Genius', while J. Pote's *The Foreigner's Guide* (1729) lauded the building's combination of technological and artistic mastery: its 'Amplitude, Splendour, Solidity, Figure . . . fine Iron Work . . . Pavement of . . . Marble' and so forth.[6] A glance at Document 223 reveals that it was the most talked about and illustrated English ecclesiastical building in the eighteenth century.[7] Almost immediately on completion in 1710 it elicited spectacular responses. James Smith, an Edinburgh-based Catholic who had spent the years 1671–5 at the Scots College in Rome training for the priesthood, but instead turned to a career in architecture, produced a group of unrealised designs for an unspecified colossal church (though perhaps no more than virtuosi exercises).[8] One, known only in plan (pl. 355), has St Paul's-like semicircular side porches flanking a central dome, a narrow, projecting apsidal chancel, domed aisles and a diminutive screen-portico at the west end, as well as oddities such as the quartets of slim, pilastered nave piers and domed rooms immured in the pair of massive choir piers, presumably serving as vestries. Similarities between other related Smith designs and a proposal of 1712 by Colen Campbell, a fellow Scots, for an unrealised church for Lincoln's Inn Fields, London, published in *Vitruvius Britannicus* (1715; pl. 515), suggest that the whole group may date from these seminal years of the initial phase of the Fifty New Churches programme.

St Paul's encyclopaedic architectural vocabulary, implied by Evelyn, appealed particularly to Hawksmoor, who had served as Wren's personal clerk and draughtsman at the cathedral from 1691 to 1712. This found expression in his extravagantly untenable ventures for the Royal Hospital at Greenwich, built to accommodate wounded and disabled seamen as well as for the relief and maintenance of widows and the education of orphans of men slain in the defence of the Nation, a microcosm of one class of society given heroic architectural presence, in which the chapel played a central role. Despite an early decision (*circa* 1697) to situate it within the projected south-east (Queen Mary) block of Wren's palatial complex (its ultimate location), between 1711 and 1728 serious attention first focused on the idea of erecting an imposing detached structure at the end of the broad, grassy spine stretching southward from the Thames on gradually rising ground as a solution to creating a more spectacular climax than that offered by Inigo Jones's blocky, low-lying Queen's House (1616–25). This could have been achievable only by removing this Palladian icon either altogether or building deeper into Greenwich Park. Among several alternative studies two are particularly memorable.

One (pl. 356), presented as composite elevations without a corresponding plan, separated the soaring, nearly free-standing campanile on the hospital side of the 'New Road' connecting Greenwich to Woolwich, its giant pilasters reiterating the centrepiece of the King William Block (by Wren and Hawksmoor, 1698–1707), from the sanctuary block on the park side, linked by a covered bridge with its cloistered pedestrian walkway. Progress along the central axis would have been regal. The campanile, accessed by a broad flight of steps into a lobby through a triumphal arch emblazoned with evangelist groups, trophies and trumpeting *putti*, thence across the bridge, its proscenium-like opening giving a view westward to the aligned portico of Hawksmoor's St Alfege nestled in the nearby village (pl. 401), and finally arriving within the domed, presumably Greek-cross-plan sanctuary, with the communion table placed in one of the arms beneath a semi-dome. The powerfully rusticated basement and centrepiece of the elevation shown in the drawing are anchored by antique altars like those at St Alfege. The consoled tabernacle window surrounds recall St George, Hanover Square (pl. 430), suggesting that John James, who had been employed at the Hospital from 1705 as store-keeper and jointly with Hawksmoor as clerk of the works, may have contributed to this scheme. The composition as a whole, of course, is worryingly undisciplined.

The other Hawksmoor essay (pl. 357) features a vast, 260 by 360 foot, Berninesque transverse oval courtyard hardly lacking in timidity. Its quadrants sweep dramatically towards the gently elliptical hexastyle temple portico framed by richly articulated, towered bays *à la* St Paul's west front.[9] All this, however, forms no more than a separate screen funnelling towards an enclosed bridge (a development of pl. 356) leading into the north transept of the 185 by 300 foot Greek-cross-plan chapel. A more complexly columned temple portico on the west side advances through an elaborate sequence of colonnaded, apsidal-ended lobbies in the manner of St Paul's Morning Chapels, on axis with the communion table set within a spacious chancel illuminated by deep-set embrasured windows. The crossing is surmounted by a panelled dome on richly pilastered piers alternating with large windows that would have flooded the central space with light, looking forward to the treatment of the King William and Queen Mary blocks. Hawksmoor's imagination knew no bounds and reminds one that these schemes are contemporary with the ostentatious conglomerate European churches of George Bahr's Frauenkirke in Dresden, J.-B. Fischer von Erlach's Karlskirche in Vienna and Filippo Juvarra's Superga near Turin.[10]

Thomas Archer, who in the 1690s enjoyed the advantages of travel to Italy, by way of The Netherlands and France, in 1705, during the final decade of St Paul's construction, entered court circles as the financially lucrative Groom Porter controlling gaming tables in the royal palaces.[11] In 1709 he was invited by the building committee of St Philip, Birmingham, which included his brother, Andrew Archer of nearby Umberslade Hall, to prepare designs for a new town-centre parish church. Though Thomas is not mentioned in the surviving parish records, which consist only of summary building accounts for 1709 to 1717 and are useful mainly for identifying the participating craftsmen, he is referred to in *Vitruvius Britannicus* (1715), published in the year of consecration, as the 'ingenious [architect who] Invented [what] is justly esteemed a very beautiful Structure' (pl. 12).[12] Given the paucity of grandiose baroque models before the launch of the New Churches programme in 1712, it is unsurprising that he turned for inspiration to St Paul's. Archer's heroic tower base with its full segmental pediment (pl. 358) relies on Wren's early study for the upper north transept end,[13] the side elevations on his regularly spaced pilasters set against rusticated walls, and the western and eastern overdoors (pl. 439) on the cartouches decorating the frieze dividing the

356 Nicholas Hawksmoor. North elevation of tower, west elevation of bridge, south elevation of body design for a new Chapel, Greenwich Hospital, London, undated. Pen and ink and wash. The Bodleian Library, University of Oxford, MS Top. Oxon.a.37*, f. 11.

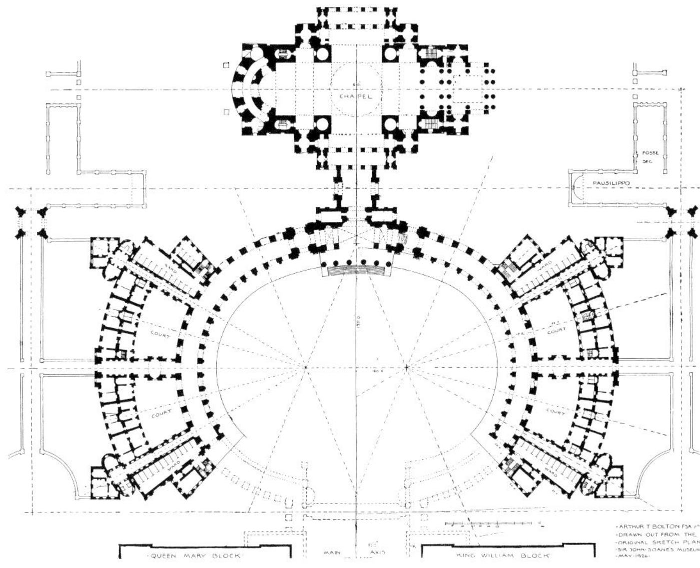

357 (*right*) Nicholas Hawksmoor. Design for a new Chapel with forecourt, Greenwich Hospital, London, plan redrawn from original Sir John Soane's Museum, London, sketch, in WS, VI, 1929, p. 87.

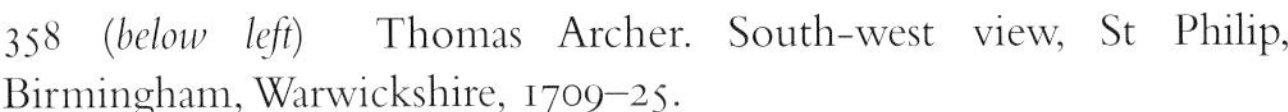

358 (*below left*) Thomas Archer. South-west view, St Philip, Birmingham, Warwickshire, 1709–25.

359 (*below right*) John Talman. Design for an imaginary church ('Turris Fortissima'), 1704. Pen and ink and black chalk. Westminster Abbey Muniments.

cathedral's two main storeys (pl. 2), while the door-cases themselves strike a powerful foreign note in their explicit echo of Borromoniesque motifs derived from D. di Rossi's *Studio d'architettura civile . . . di Roma* (1702).[14] John Talman, who spent long periods in Italy between 1699 and 1723, pursued similar architectural interests (pl. 359).[15] Both Archer's and Wren's interiors (pls 360–61) have fluted piers, rosette-enriched arches and semicircular chancels articulated by fluted Corinthian pilasters (St Philip's was radically remodelled in 1883–4).

The initial optimism expressed by Alexander Pope for the ambitious programme launched two years earlier to erect fifty new churches in London, Westminster and suburbs –

360 (*left*) Henry Harris. Interior towards the chancel, St Philip, Birmingham, Warwickshire, *c.*1825, prior to 1883–4 remodelling. Lithograph. © Birmingham Museums and Art Gallery, 1708. Thomas Archer architect, 1709–25.

361 (*below left*) J. V. Schley. Interior towards the chancel, 'La Communion des Anglicans a Saint Paul [Cathedral, London]' , detail, 1736. Engraving. Author's collection. Sir Christopher Wren architect, 1675–1710.

Behold! Augusta's glitt'ting spires increase,
And Temples rise, the beauteous works of Peace[16]

– at the end of operations in 1734, with only eleven fully consummated – St Mary-le-Strand by James Gibbs; St John, Westminster, and St Paul, Deptford, by Thomas Archer; St Alfege, Greenwich, St Anne, Limehouse, St George, Wapping, Christ Church, Spitalfields, St Mary Woolnoth and St George, Bloomsbury, all by Hawksmoor, as well as St John, Horselydown, and St Luke, Old Street, in partnership with John James (representing the five outstanding metropolitan church designers of the time) – had deflated to 'shall half the new-built churches round thee fall?', confirming Joseph Addison's more realistic suspicion that 'church-work is slow, church-work is slow!'[17] The programme's full panoply of activities, from the Commissioners' and building committee's weekly meetings concerning design issues, appropriating sites, appointing surveyors and contracting craftsmen to chronicling the progress of work, paying bills and so forth, which survive in sixty-one exceptionally detailed volumes deposited in Lambeth Palace Library, unrivalled in British architectural history (unearthed *circa* 1950 and still awaiting comprehensive systematic investigation), may be summarised as follows.

1710

28 November: the roof of medieval St Alfege, Greenwich, collapsed, leading to an Act of Parliament (Stat. 9, Annae, c.22) establishing the building commission and granting funds financed by an extension of the post-1666 tax on coal imported into London, with each church to cost £10,000.

1711

21 September: fifty-two Commissioners appointed, including Thomas Archer, John Vanbrugh and Sir Christopher Wren;

28 September: commission commenced;

3 October: call to parishes 'desirous to proceed in so pious and usefull aworke';

10 October: Nicholas Hawksmoor and William Dickinson appointed co-surveyors; Wren, Vanbrugh and George Hickes presented designing and building guidelines.

1712

11–16 July: Commissioners adopted proposals;

22 December: call for church models to be delivered by 14 January 1713.

1713

13 August: Dickinson resigned;

18 November: James Gibbs appointed co-surveyor with Hawksmoor.

1714

1 August: Queen Anne died, succeeded by George I.

1715

February–March: Whig majority in general election;

2 December: new Commissioners appointed, excluding Archer, Vanbrugh and Wren.

1716

5 January: Gibbs dismissed; John James appointed co-surveyor with Hawksmoor;

25 December: £86,575 1s. 5d. spent on erecting nine churches.

1727

24 November: new Commissioners appointed, no architects included.

1732

17 February: £8,734 2s. 1½d. available for completing the programme,

1733–4

Programme finished.

1757

Commission closed.[18]

Historians have tended to investigate this body of churches en bloc under the general remit of English baroque. Indeed, there is ample evidence of both shared participation and treatments within this genre. Archer, Dickinson, Gibbs, Hawksmoor and Vanbrugh each submitted designs for the prominently island-sited St Mary-le-Strand. One working drawing shows two superimposed plans by Dickinson of nearly identically sized but entirely different rectangular forms: an under-plan featuring a rectangular west porch linked to the body by boldly concave walls inspired by Wren's Greek-cross design of 1668 for St Paul's Cathedral, and an over-plan distinguished by a six-column half-rotunda porch encompassing a cylindrical tower closely resembling Archer's St Paul, Deptford, as built. The latter and a Hawksmoor design for an unidentified church, as well as Gibbs's successful Strand church, all probably looked to the cathedral's transept porches.[19] Moreover, a note on one of Hawksmoor's drawings for St Alfege, Greenwich, concerning the pedimented roof standing proud of the west tower, instructs: 'If what [James Grove, carpenter] has provided for [St George] Wapping . . . Cannot Serve at [St Anne] Limehouse – then we must be content to put it upon Wapping.'[20] Nevertheless, it seems more valuable to recognise within this extraordinary body of buildings the diversity of architectural ideas and sources. Little, too, has been said regarding their influence beyond London or their place in the wider European scene. For these reasons I have chosen to distribute the New Churches schemes among a series of chapters, some strictly outside the usual baroque catchments, such as the revivals of antique temple and early Christian forms and proto-Palladian experiments. But first we must consider the Commissions' complex workings.

Greenwich parish was unable to raise the estimated rebuilding expense totalling £6,260 4s. 2d., since

> Most of the great Houses upon the East Side of the Park, and down the Hill, to the Town . . . now stand Empty . . . Nine Parts in Ten of the Inhabitants are Seafaring-men, and Watermen, who subsist only on their Labour and Pay, and have no Manufacture [and] by the late and present War [with France], and Storms at sea, the Widows and Orphans . . . about 3,000, have become a Charge to the rest of the Parish for their Subsistence.[21]

Parliament therefore passed its financial Act of 1710, a matter of some import. Swift reckoned on some 300,000 inhabitants in London lacking churches who 'either stay at home, or retire to the Conventicles',[22] and the anonymous pamphleteer of *A Proposal for the Building of Tabernacles* railed against the 'Many Score Thousands of People, who scarcely in their whole lives so much as Peep into a Church'.[23] An unrealistic projected expenditure of £10,000 per building, more appropriate for Wren's smaller City Churches (pl. 510), with the final bills ranging from £16,940 0s. 4d. for Woolnoth, £18,260 5s. 9d. for Greenwich, £20,106 8s. 7d. for the Strand, £22,087 14s. 0d. for Deptford, £25,885 0s. 4d. for Wapping and £31,251 4s. 8d. for Limehouse, to whopping sums of £40,602 0s. 6d. and £40,875 14s. 0d. for Spitalfields and Westminster (see Appendix B), produced a deficit of £66,685 5s. 7½d. as early as 1721. This prompted petitions for topping up, leading inevitably to a drastic reduction in success rates.[24] Bloomsbury, the last of the grand churches, which cost £23,791 14s. 3d., suffered increasing financial difficulties and design restrictions. As a measure towards tighter control the surveyors were ordered at the beginning of construction in 1713 to 'report in Writing Monthly, of the State and progress of Every Work that is Carrying on'.[25] One remedy was to convert existing chapels into parochial churches, but here there were problems. Aylesbury Chapel, Clerkenwell, was recommended as capable of 'conveniently' holding 1,000 persons and possessing 'very good' approaches, yet nothing was done, while Poplar would require 'considerable Reparations in the Roof, Covering, Stone, Windows, paving, pewing, and Galleries, besides . . . it has no Tower at the West End which perhaps will be thought necessary if it be made parochial'.[26] Hawksmoor succeeded in regenerating St George's Chapel, Queen's Square, Holborn (1706), between 1711 and 1723, but the cost of £2,033 8s. 6d. was considered 'very Expensive' and the Commissioners 'made a Standing Order that the Surveyors shall at no time hereafter, presume to execute any Design without first presenting a Plan and Estimate'.[27] In 1721 the co-surveyors' annual salaries were cut from £200 to £150 and restored only in 1726.[28] In the same year a Bill was put before the Commons to enable the Commissioners to build in brick as well as in stone,[29] and two years later they considered a proposal for 'furnishing Bath-Stone for Building at a Cheaper Rate than can be done with Portland-Stone'.[30] In response to a report in 1717 that Parliament was to be petitioned suggesting 'ten Old Churches in the City now ruinous, may be rebuilt & esteemd a part of the fifty new Churches', the Commissioners were 'unanimously of Opinion' that it was 'against the design & Intention' of the 1710 Act.[31] The effect of insufficient funds on the aesthetic character of some of the churches was occasionally noted. In 1718 the surveyors recommended that 'A Stop should be put to the extravag[an]t. Carvings' inside St Mary-le-Strand (pl. 379).[32] Archer's design for the Deptford altarpiece, pulpit and reading desk delivered in 1721 was considered 'very expensive', and John James, a parson's son and the surveyor appointed to replace Gibbs, was ordered to 'reduce it into as plain and cheap a form as the work already done upon it, will allow'.[33] In 1725 Hawksmoor was hauled in over the 'affair of the Decorations' of Bloomsbury steeple – the lions, unicorns, festoons, crowns and royal statue (pl. 354) – which he installed without the Commissioners' 'directions or Privity', and while they agreed that 'Some Sort of Decorations were necessary in these Places', the surveyor was admonished 'to be more carefull for the future how he Engages this Board in any Such Expenses without their Directions and consent on pain of bearing the Charges . . . himself'.[34]

Even so, parishes were occasionally incautious. The rector of St Luke, Old Street, confessed in 1745 that 'the money was not laid out with Frugality & Discretion. The [churchyard] Walls being carried up much higher then was needful . . . wth Iron Gates & Palisadoes. (wth Stone Piers & a small Watch-house of stone in the Center) instead of a Brick Wall; which was a great addition to the Expence.'[35] The financial crisis was summed up in the following admission:

> the Expence of building with stone, purchasing Scites for Churches, Church yards and ministers Houses, is so very great, and does so far exceed the Calculations formerly made; that the [building] Comittee conceive it will be utterly impracticable to build one Half of the Churches at first proposed, tho they be at liberty to Employ the whole Sum as it now stands.[36]

A number of parishes petitioned government for financial aid. St Mary Woolnoth, next to the Royal Exchange, had lost its medieval church in the Great Fire, and having been partly rebuilt was by 1711 'so ruinous, and weak, that the Inhabitants dare not go to Church, for fear it should fall upon them'. The cost of rebuilding was estimated at £6,500, which it was unable to raise because of the 'many poor Families, in Alleys, who receive Relief'.[37] The 2,154 parishioners of St Mary-le-Strand, having long been without a church (demolished in Edward VI's reign) and obliged to worship in the small, medieval Savoy Chapel, procured 'a Draught' for a new church holding a congregation of 1,500 (untraced), estimated to cost £7,500 in 1711.[38] Inevitably, gross overspending combined with overburdened bureaucracy, serendipitous policies and profligate preparations of designs led to a degree of realisation in inverse proportion to the programme's ambitions.

On 21 September 1711 some fifty Commissioners were appointed to regulate this operation, including the archbishops of Canterbury and York, numerous bishops and other leading churchmen, government ministers, City officials and a nucleus of professional men, notably Wren (in his capacity as Surveyor of the Queen's Works) and his son, Christopher Jr (Chief Clerk of the Works), as well as John Vanbrugh (Comptroller of the Works) and Thomas Archer. Later, Archer wrote of having been 'no useless Commissioner, and . . . the models and designs I have made . . . have not betrayed my ignorance'.[39] The designing and supervision of construction were the responsibilities of co-surveyors: the first, appointed on 10 October 1711, were Hawksmoor and Dickinson, both intimately connected to Wren's activities at St Paul's Cathedral and the City Churches, their annual salaries set at £200 excluding charges for 'making Wooden Modells, opening of Ground, and Travelling . . . beyond the Parishes where any of the New intended Churches are to be built'.[40] Inaugural activities revolved around locating 'proper Scites for Churches – Church Yards and Ministers houses' – the territory ranged from Islington in the north to

Lambeth and Woolwich in the south, from Stepney, Limehouse and Poplar in the east to Westminster in the west – and furnishing site plans for the Commissioners' consideration.[41] Many deemed inappropriate on grounds of faulty geology, difficult access or excessive purchase prices proceeded no further. Some included proposed church plans, largely Dickinson's contributions, and while some are conservative, rectangular, towered basilicas on the pattern of Wren's St James, Piccadilly (pl. 478), others are full of invention (pl. 8). In 1726 the surveyors secured their original salaries by demonstrating that their responsibilities

> far exceeded that of former Years, and has taken up much more attendance than was required at the first Foundations of the Churches, when the work was chiefly confin'd to the Mason Bricklayer & Carpenter; but being now branch'd out and spread among all the artificers, carries with it much more additional trouble, in measuring the Works drawing Plans for the new Parishes, making up and Examining the Books and paying the numerous Artificers.[42]

What precise control did the surveyors have over the design of their churches? At Greenwich during the few, critical weeks between mid-July and early August 1712 schemes were submitted not only by Hawksmoor but also by James (not yet appointed its carpenter), and while his was disallowed, the Commissioners were not against receiving unsolicited suggestions and told him he was at 'Liberty to propose any other Plan'. Hawksmoor's was verbally corrected by the Commissioners, then improved by Archer and even after finally receiving approval underwent further modifications.[43] Similar vacillations concerning St Mary-le-Strand are evident over a longer period, beginning with a plan drawn by Dickinson in July 1713, followed by a wooden model by Gibbs billed in February 1714 but rejected, then the approval of Archer's design in April, which rose to ground level during the summer, when the Commissioners again had a change of heart, which was resolved only in November when Gibbs and Vanbrugh submitted new schemes and the former's was finally chosen (pl. 378).[44] Moreover, a lot in Hawksmoor's sale catalogue of 1740 containing twenty-four Strand designs, of which most have so far not been located, confirm that he also contributed (pls 407–8).[45] Comparison between the two demonstrates the widely disparate approaches of competing architects.

During 1712 the Commissioners attempted to bring order to these confusing operations by establishing liturgical and architectural guidelines. Counsel was received from the 80-year-old Wren 'after long Experience' as a church designer, which he offered as 'a transient View [of the New Churches] Affair; not doubting but that the Debates of the worthy Commissioners may . . . give me occasion to change, or add to the Speculations', and from Vanbrugh, who, though not having yet designed a church, incorporated palatial chapels into the fabrics of both Castle Howard, Yorkshire (1705–6), and Blenheim Palace, Oxfordshire (1705–31).[46] Together they represent the polarities of early eighteenth-century viewpoints.

The conservative, pragmatic Wren calculated that each church

> must be large; but still, in our reformed Religion, it should seem vain to make [them] larger, than that all who are present can both hear and see. The Romanists . . . may build larger Churches, it is enough if they hear the Murmur of the Mass, and see the Elevation of the Host, but ours are to be fitted for Auditories. I can hardly think it practicable to make a single Room so capacious, with Pews and Galleries, as to hold above 2000 Persons, and all to hear the Service, and both to hear distinctly, and see the Preacher. I endeavoured to effect this, in . . . *St James's, Westminster*, which . . . is the most capacious . . . that hath yet been built . . . though very broad, and the middle Nave arch'd up . . . the whole Roof rests upon the Pillars, as do also the Galleries; I think it may be found beautiful and convenient, and as such, the cheapest of any Form I could invent [pl. 478].[47]

Emphasis was placed on the choice of materials: good, well-burnt bricks; Portland or Roche Abbey stone, though 'not without their Faults', for doors and windows; 'Cockle-shell-lime well beaten with Sand; the more Labour . . . the better and stronger the Mortar'; marble 'will prove too costly for our Purposes, unless for Altar-pieces'; 'good oak . . . Roofs . . . the best; because it will bear some Negligence [or] good Yellow Deal . . . a Timber of Length, and light, and makes excellent Work'; 'Our Tiles are ill made . . . Slade not good; Lead is certainly the best and lightest Covering [and] most preferable'. In these respects the New Churches are essentially de luxe versions of the practical, post-Fire City Churches and represent little break from that tradition.

By contrast, Vanbrugh pursued more emotive, heroic visions.

> Since . . . the fifty new Churches the Queen has gloriously promoted . . . shoud not only serve for the

> Accommodation of the Inhabitants, in the performance of their Publick Religious Duty: but at the same time remain Monuments to Posterity of Her Piety & Grandeur And by consequence become Ornaments to the Towne, and a Credit to the Nation . . . That amongst the several kinds of Buildings by which Great Citys are Adorn'd; Churches, have in all Ages, and with all Religions been placed in the first Rank. No Expenses has ever been thought too much for them; Their Magnificence has even been esteem'd a pious expression of the Peoples great and Profound Veneration towards their Deitys, and the contemplation of that Magnificence has . . . augmented the Veneration.

Moreover,

> That they may be form'd for the utmost duration both in respect of the material, the Solidity of their Walls, and the Manner of their Construction: The extraordinary Expence of which is so small. That in a Church of Ten thousand pounds cost, it turns upon five hundred, whether it shall be crippled in a hundred years, or stand like a Rock a Thousand.

Both architects were in agreement as to the 'Situation of the Churches'. Wren proposed that

> they be brought as forward as possible into the larger and more open Streets, not in obscure Lanes [with] Such Fronts as shall happen to lie most open in View . . . adorned with Porticos, both for Beauty and Convenience . . . which, together with handsome Spires, or Lanterns, rising in good Proportion above the neighbouring Houses (of which I have given several Examples . . . of different Forms [untraced]) may be of sufficient Ornament to the Town, without a great Expence for enriching the outward Walls of the Churches, in which Plainness and Duration ought principally, if not wholly, to be studied.

Vanbrugh emphasised that they

> be ever Insulate. This do's not only give them that Respectfull Distinction & Dignity which Churches Always ought to have; but it makes the Access . . . easy, and is a great Security from Fire [and] That they may be so plac'd, to be fairly View'd at such proper distances . . . to shew their Exterior Form, to the best Advantage, as at the ends of Large and Strait Streets, or on the Side of Squares and Open Places [and] all Accommodated and Adorn'd with Portico's; no part in Publick Edifices being of greater use, nor no production in Architecture so solemnly Magnificent.

Unsurprisingly, the two differed in the churches' exterior impact. Vanbrugh believed that the

> necessary dispositions in the usefull part of the Fabrick, shoud be made consistent with the utmost Grace that Architecture can produce, for the Beauty of it: which . . . shou'd generally be express'd in a plain, but Just and Noble Stile, without running into those many Divisions and Breaks which other buildings for Variety of uses may require; or such Gayety of Ornaments as may be proper to a Luxurious Palace.

This was perhaps a criticism directed towards St Paul's Cathedral and the more ambitious City Churches. While Wren pressed for moderation, 'because great Towers, and lofty Steeples, are sometimes more than half the Charge of the Church', Vanbrugh emphasised that

> for the Ornament of the Towne, and to shew at a distance what regard there is in it to Religious Worship; every Church . . . may have a Tower . . . High and Bold Structures, and so form'd as not to be subject to Ruin by fire, but of such Solidity and Strength, that nothing but Time, and scarce that, shou'd destroy them.

As we shall see, it was this latter direction that the surveyors robustly pursued, resulting in a group of churches of a scale and luxury hardly seen in Protestant London apart from the recently completed cathedral. Above all, Vanbrugh argued that

> for the Lights, there may be no more than what are necessary for meer use, many Windows making a Church cold in Winter, hot in Summer, and being very disagreeable and hurtful to the sight. They likewise take off very much, both from the Appearance & reality of strength in the Fabrick; giving it more the Air of a Gay Lanthorn to be set on the Top of a Temple, than the Reverend look of a Temple itself; which shou'd ever have the most Solemn and Awfull Appearances both without and within, that is possible.

This embryonic notion of a Christian church in the form of an antique temple became one of the most compelling avant-garde innovations of the programme, as we shall discover in chapter 21.

The Revd George Hickes, a lecturer at Lincoln College, Oxford, biblical scholar and member of a clerical circle interested in early Christian architecture, was critical of Vanbrugh's omission of consideration of the chancel, which Hickes advised raising two or three steps above the nave floor and to be 'free from all fixed seats, but have such as may easily be brought in at the time of . . . communion', or baptismal fonts, which 'may be placed towards the west end . . . near the tower', or in vestry rooms. He also had much to say about liturgical orientation, perhaps in response to Wren's maxim that 'Nor are we . . . too nicely to observe East or West in the Position, unless it falls out properly'. (Vanbrugh did not allude to this crucial issue.) Hickes believed that

> The situation of . . . churches East, and West according to the ancient manner of building . . . ought to be observed . . . If money is not to be spared to make these buildings strong, gracefull and magnificent . . . neither is it to be spared to buy a little ground to make room for the situation of them.[48]

This had been one of the Commissioners' initial concerns.

On 20 November 1711, having debated 'whether in determining Scites . . . any . . . Shou'd be approved, when the Church cannot be built East and West', they resolved that no such site be 'pitched up . . . without Speciall reasons . . . to be peticularly approved of'.[49] Recently, geophysicists Jason Ali and Peter Cunich of Hong Kong University, employing a digital compass function of a KVH DataScope, demonstrated that at Limehouse and Spitalfields (as well as Gibbs's later St Martin-in-the-Fields) true alignment was so accurate that it could feasibly have been achieved only using a declination-corrected compass (with the other New Churches all facing east to varying degrees), an exercise probably assisted by Edmond Halley, of comet fame, who was one of the Commissioners.[50] This emphasis was to produce striking architectural novelties at Greenwich, Bloomsbury and Westminster. On 16 July 1712 the Commissioners agreed to adopt 'Insular' sites, as well as eastern rooms to hold vestments and vessels, a western vestry for parish business, fonts, 'Single . . . pewes . . . of equal height, so low that every person . . . may be seen either kneeling or Sitting, and so contrived that all . . . may stand or kneel towards the Communion Table' (located in the eastern chancel), 'Moveable Forms . . . so contrived in the middle Isles, as to run under the . . . pewes, and draw out into the . . . Isle' and chancels 'raised three steps'. Of particular architectural interest they pressed for 'handsome Porticoes to each Church [and] one general design or Forme . . . for all the fifty New intended Churches, where the Scites will admit . . . The Steeples or Towers excepted'.[51] There had never been in Britain such a comprehensively singular architectural vision for church design.

The ensuing design preparation, meticulously charted in the Commissioners' papers, is well represented by both working and presentation drawings, as well as by sixteen wooden scale models, all produced for the Commissioners' approval.[52] Models were first called for on 18 June 1712, probably after the Wren-Vanbrugh-Hickes proposals but before the final resolutions of 16 July, described above. They began to be delivered early in 1713 to the new headquarters in Lincoln's Inn Fields, where they were available for viewing by the Commissioners 'or such persons as they . . . bring wth them, & by no other person'.[53] Makers included the joiner John Tufnell, who received £7 10s. 0d. for 'a Modell . . . in Wainscott' and £19 for 'another . . . in Clear deal and Pair Tree Mouldings, [both] according to the Designe of Mr: Dickinson', perhaps associated with 'Mill Bank Church' (St John, Westminster), and John Smallwell, for 'Modells . . . p Mr Archers Orders', £100 15s. 0d., and, 'according to . . . Vanbrughs Designs', £50 5s. 0d., as well as £14 6s. 9d. for '2 Steeples', which were painted by a Mr Hargrove for £4 16s. 0d.[54] By 1715 it was decided that no church would be 'begun untill a plan, or Modell, and an Estimate' was approved, and would 'not be altered, without the directions of the Board'.[55] However, these objects are fraught with interpretive difficulties. With the Commissions' closure in 1759 they were transferred to Westminster Abbey, where in 1826 C. R. Cockerell drew a plan and elevation of early proposals for Limehouse and the Strand (pls 369, 410).[56] Schematic plans of thirteen models were prepared for Professor T. L. Donaldson's Royal Academy lectures, which were published with descriptions and dimensions in 1843, of which only three corresponded to executed churches.[57] By 1826 some were displayed in the Museum of Construction, South Kensington, but subsequently vanished (with the exception of two, both for St Mary-le-Strand, pl. 112).[58] What of the churches themselves?

Functioning as both a Commissioner and an architect, Archer was one of the first to benefit from the New Churches guidelines. St Paul, Deptford (recently restored to its original state), and St John, Westminster (gutted by fire in 1742 and by enemy bombs in 1940, then in 1968 remodelled internally as a performing venue), were designed and built simultaneously between 1712 and 1730. They are recognisably the work of the same hand – the surveyors were instructed to follow his directions 'in all matters relating to the building' (with James, in his capacity as carpenter, making 'a drawing Board for drawings to be carry'd before Mr Archer').[59] Both churches also underwent intercessions during their respective design stages by other architects,

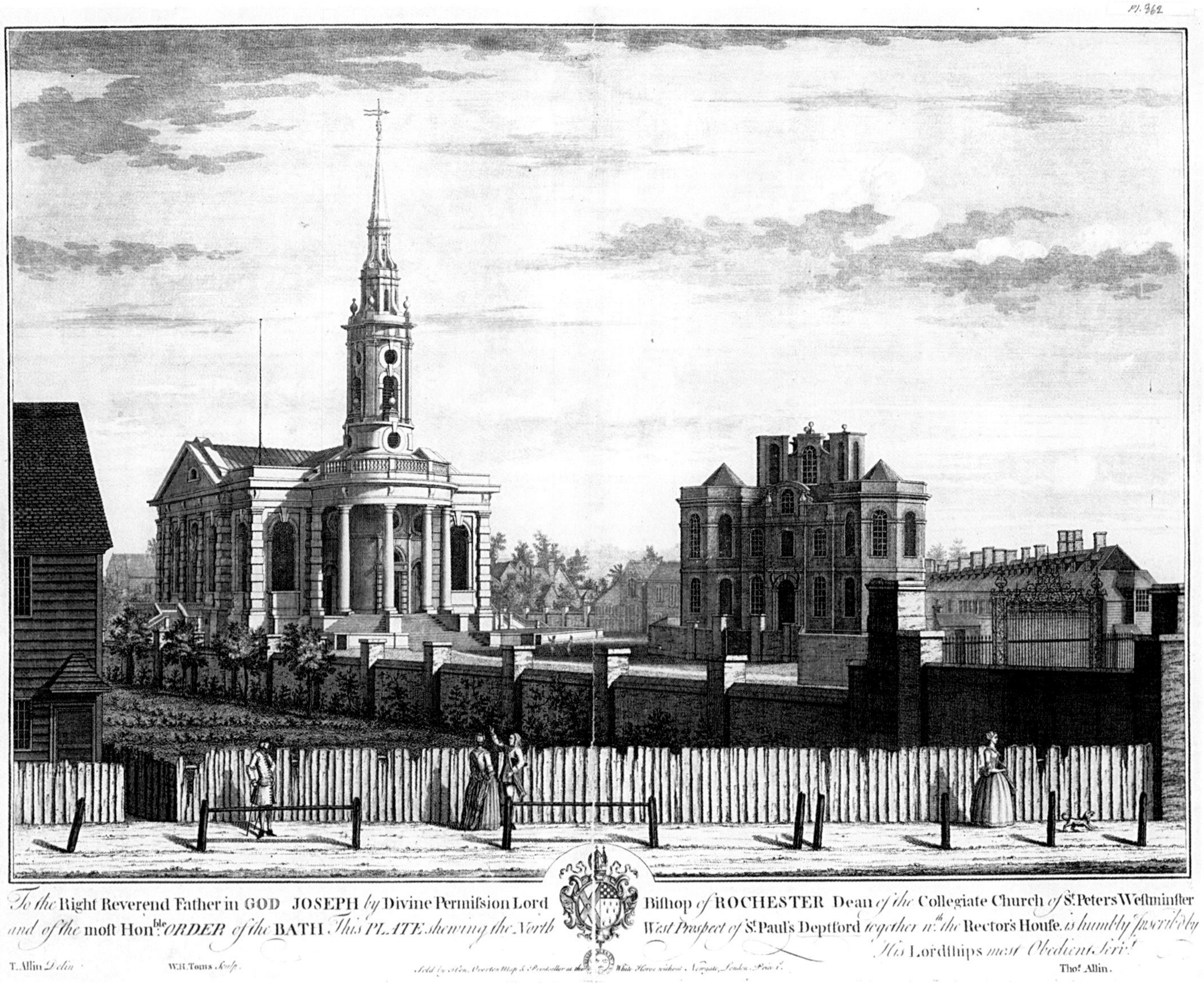

362 William Henry Toms after Thomas Allin. 'North West Prospect of St Paul's Deptford together wth: the Rector's House', London, undated. Engraving. © The British Library Board, K.Top. XVIII.18.k. Thomas Archer architect, 1713–30, parsonage demolished 1883.

Hawksmoor at Deptford, Dickinson at Westminster, though the specifics remain unknown. Yet, the churches as built hardly resemble one another.

Both suffer from the loss of their preparatory wooden models and most of their drawings; nor are their early construction histories straightforward. The Commissioners' minutes reveal that at Deptford (pl. 362) the semicircular staircase platform and 'Breaks' on the side elevations erected by the masons during 1712–13 were pulled down and reset 'in another disposition' to accommodate basement windows, and that when the platform was 'ready to receive' the pilaster bases several estimates for finishing the front were submitted. One at £952 2s. 0d. consisted of '2 Stone Lanterns omitting the great Tower', another for a 'Portico of 5 entre-Columns' at £200 15s. 6d. each, or £952 2s. 0d. for '2 Stone Lanterns [omitting] both the great Tower and Portico'. The Committee chose 'one Large Tower and a Lantern' costing £2,350 12s. 3d.[60] Archer's surviving plans of 1712 show him experimenting with alternative treatments of the tower base. Rejecting the ubiquitous rectangle in favour of an uncommon semi-detached cylinder, by 15 April 1714 his design for a Tuscan four-columned half tempietto was under construction.[61] The square, compact body of the church powerfully bound by block rusticated pilasters, treated on the side elevations as nascent engaged temple porticoes raised on perrons, on the west front bursts open to expose the naked tower base shooting through the porch into a soaring monolith. This gorgeous, dramatic gesture is quite unlike Wren's transept porches at St Paul's Cathedral (pl. 2), which provided the incentive, and perhaps owes more to baroque Rome, which Archer may have visited *circa* 1691.[62] Roman sources may also account for the robust treatment of the interior (pl. 364), where the narrow semicircular chancel echoes the porch to create an emphatically central plan. The use of Corinthian giant order engaged columns to emphasise the dynamic canted walls in the corners of the main space, producing an overall ovoid contour, and the bands of densely foliated plasterwork on the ceiling recall Borromini's San Carlo alle Quattro Fontana (pl. 363).[63]

St John, Westminster, was no less complex (pl. 365). Where the extrovert motif of twin towers first proposed for Deptford was reduced to a single, central structure, at Westminster they were doubled atop both identical north and south porticoes to form what was popularly known as Queen Anne's Footstool, later given the *coup de grâce* by Dickens's description of the building, 'resembling some petrified monster, frightful and gigantic, on its back with its legs in the air'.[64] This novelty was apparently the outcome of a logistical reckoning. Located near the Thames, the church experienced geological problems at the outset. Despite boring into a 'Bed of Lome and Clay . . . at present full of water Occasion'd . . . by Springs which boyle up from . . . Gritt or quicksand', the surveyors concluded that the foundation 'lyes very firm and hard at bottom [and is] capable to bear the Fabrick'. This proved untrue. In 1714 it had to be reinforced with hard flints, chalk and mortar 'beat together with heavy Mallets or Bootles' and in 1716 the carpenter furnished a roof model with 'diagonal Trusts [and] Flatts in the Towrs for the Masons to Strike out

363 'Spaccato Interiore della Meta Chiesa di San Carlo alle Quattro Fontane', Rome, in Rossi and Rossi 1711, pl. 18. Engraving. Francesco Borromini architect, 1638–41.

364 Thomas Archer. Interior towards the chancel, St Paul, Deptford, London, 1713–30. English Heritage (National Monuments Record, CC75/00617).

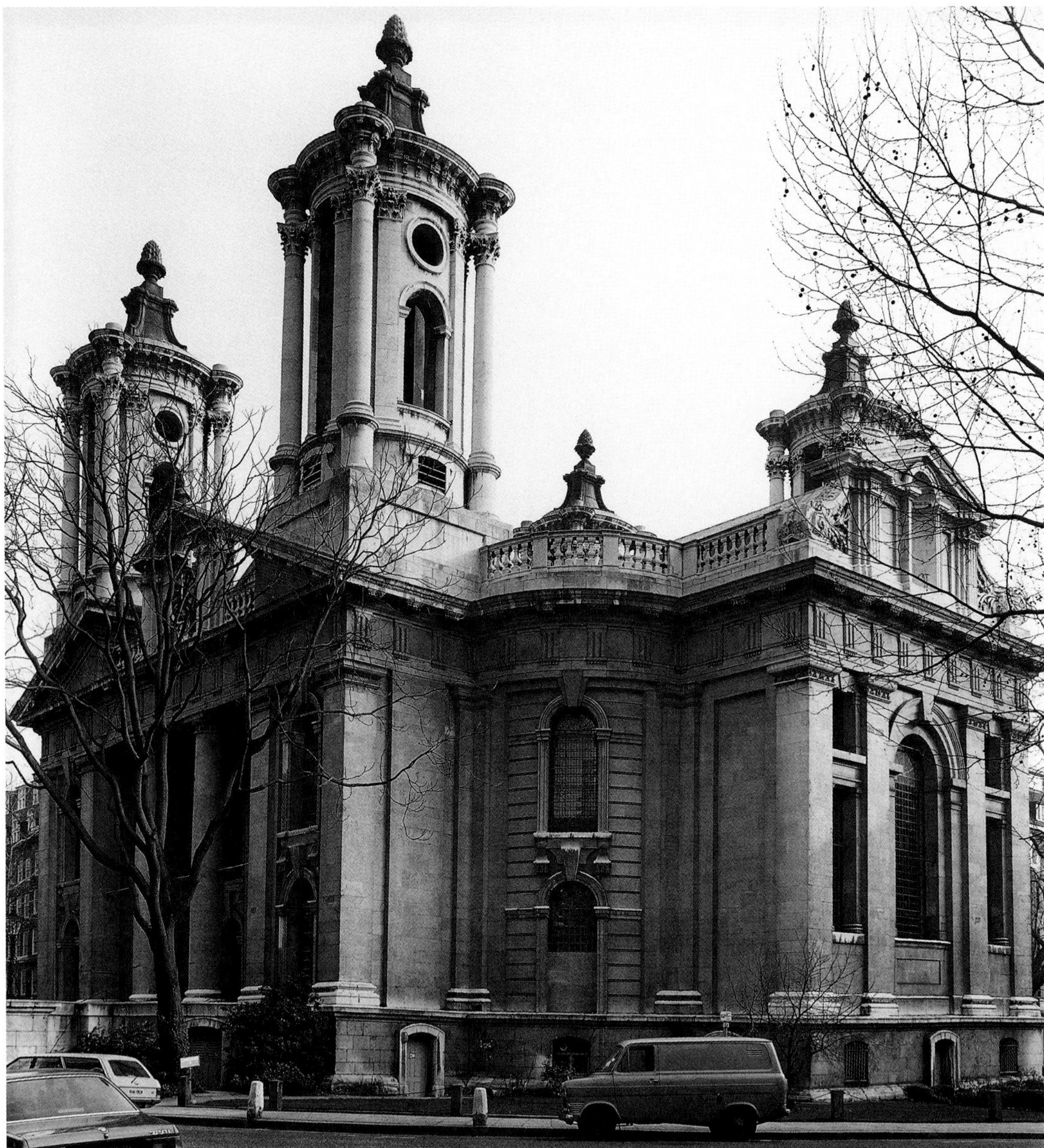

365 Thomas Archer. South-west view, St John, Westminster, London, 1712–28. English Heritage (National Monuments Record, DD88/163).

their Circles, For Keeping the Towers upright'. In May Archer was 'inclined to believe the Foundations will bear the Tower', yet in 1719–20 the bricklayers were 'Stopping . . . holes & Cracks within the Church occasion'd by . . . Settling . . . Walls' and not until the following year did the building show 'no farther Signs of Settling'.[65] This was achieved by lowering the towers and replacing balustrades and pinnacles of an earlier scheme with concaved lead domes,[66] and transferring the masonry walls of the bell openings punctured by arched and circular openings (a composition derived from the crossing colonnades of St Paul's Cathedral) from the north and south faces to the east and west so that the bulk of their weight bore down on the flanks of the portico buttressed by solid, boldly concave intermediary bays. Yet, these physical measures failed visually to rescue the towers from a sense of structural fragility: they perch precariously astride the sloping edges of the portico pediments, like the infamous 'asses ears' added in baroque times to the ancient Roman Pantheon (which had been converted in 609 to Santa Maria ad Martyres).[67] Furthermore, the already gaping *in antis* porticoes' insubstantiality are exacerbated by tabernacles breaking into and deconstructing the pediments, leaving only vestigial corners and interrupted sections of balustrade. It might be imagined that at least one of the enclosures was intended to house Queen Anne's statue, as Hawksmoor had planned at St Anne, Limehouse, but for the fact that the scheme (described on pp. 376, 379) had been abandoned several years earlier, in Summer 1714, immediately following the monarch's death.[68] What saves this apparent vulnerability is the binding presence of the boldly masculine Doric order.

This was Hawksmoor's domain. He was the innovative genius of the New Churches programme, the only surveyor to serve a full, twenty-two-year term, producing not only most of the drawings and models but eight of the eleven built churches.[69] Orders to attend the Commissioners and building sub-committee 'every time they meet' is a measure of his unassailable position.[70] Yet, two of the leading architectural commentators of the period found his admittedly sometimes bizarre modes difficult to grasp. Langley confusedly characterised the Stepney churches – Spitalfields, Limehouse and Wapping – as 'a mean between the Greek [that is, classical] and Gothique', while Ralph, too, lumped them together as 'mere Gothique heaps of stone, without form or order [which] meet with contempt from the best and worst tastes alike [and] not to be looked at without displeasure', for which Spitalfields 'deserves the severest condemnation, in that 'tis built at a monstrous expence, and yet is . . . one of the most absurd piles in Europe'.[71]

The Stepney churches, though very different in appearance, were designed and built in tandem, their models delivered on 4 February 1713, their final rectangular forms evolved during the succeeding year, their foundations laid and perimeter walls raised during 1715–16, at the same time resolving the forms of fronts and towers, their most striking features, which underwent a sequence of radical adjustments.[72] This is especially true of Spitalfields. By 1714 the west elevation (pl. 367) had evolved into a plain but powerful frontispiece in which three entrance bays are recessed into a shallow astylar slab articulated by slender sections of wall that read as monumental pilasters without capitals. This rare instance of early Georgian minimalism has a parallel in Roman baroque.[73] Hawksmoor contemplated surmounting this with either a short, slender, tame tower crowned by an octagonal lantern, or a taller, broader bulk anticipating the erected monolith. When the carcass of the body reached its main cornice in 1719, he rethought the superstructure (pl. 368) as a monumental Serliana repeated on both front and back linked by deeply concave sides, surmounted by a broach spire, a typically ambiguous Hawksmoorian fusion of pyramid and obelisk, the 'Gothique' element of the building inspired by authentic medieval examples (pl. 294). When construction reached the sills of its second tier of niches a further model was produced, with estimates for finishing the steeple with a 'plane Spire' at £1,000, and attaching to the frontispiece a prostyle portico of 'four Tuscan pillars [in the] plainest manner [and] least Expence that can be' (£700), an echoing Serliana crucially buttressing the vast masonry pile above.[74] The interior (pl. 366) is as close Hawksmoor ever came to recreating the heroic, opulent buildings of late antiquity such as the Temple of Bacchus at Baalbek, which he would have known through his friend the Revd Henry Maundrell, who had visited in 1679 and for whom 'it strikes the Mind with an air of Greatness beyond anything that I ever saw before . . . eminent proof of the Magnificence of the ancient Architecture'. Hawksmoor had supplied an imagined reconstruction for his *Journey from Aleppo to Jerusalem* (1714).[75]

In one of the models of 1713 for St Anne, Limehouse (pl. 369), the Tuscan hexastyle *in antis* temple portico with solid outer bays recalls both St Alfege, Greenwich (pl. 404), and St John, Westminster (pl. 365), while additional, distyle porches located in the middle bays of the north and south elevations result in a combined longitudinal and central plan. The crown of the west tower (pl. 370) is a cubic version of St Paul's Cathedral (pl. 2), counterpoised by diagonal piers on the bell stage and echoing the pier-buttresses enwrapping the partly submerged rotunda porch below. Stylistic bias aside, Langley offered an insightful contemporary evocation of the church as 'a most surprising beautiful structure [displaying] a solemn solidity' from afar, while closer to 'one of the most airy, light, elegant, and magnificent buildings in this kingdom, [the tower] the most solemn reverend aspect' from the front, while at an angle 'the most gay and airy', confirming that Hawksmoor was entrenched in Vanbrugh's rather than Wren's camp.[76]

The experiments at Spitalfields and Limehouse reached fruition at St George, Wapping (the interior was gutted in the Blitz of 1941). The west frontispiece and tower (pl. 371) form a single, subtly graduated slab climaxing in an octagonal lantern. Langley lauded this 'magnificent pile . . . wherein simplicity and grandeur are so well connected together, as I have yet seen in any composition of the ancients, [the] groupe of square columns affix'd to a cylinder, each supporting an ornament in a manner of an altar, on which the ancients made their offerings'.[77] These offer a vital clue to Hawksmoor's intentions of exploiting funereal symbolism. An early study explored the possibility of surmounting the body's roof with a stepped pyramid, which at St George, Bloomsbury (pl. 354), is associated with the Tomb of Mausolus at Halicarnassus in Asia Minor, one of the Seven Wonders of the Ancient World.[78] Though ultimately rejected at Wapping, the mighty, double-storey, rotunda-shaped chancel (pl. 372) evokes Theodoric's Mausoleum at Ravenna, of *circa* AD 526 (pl. 395).[79]

The potential of transferring Wapping's frontage to a cramped City site is strikingly proclaimed at St Mary Woolnoth, where private properties packed closely round the church led Hawksmoor to create a small, compact building, only 60 by 65 feet, of astonishing virility and originality (pl. 373). The pre-modern site exposed only the north elevation along Lombard Street and the west front facing St Swithin's Lane, which blocked the now-familiar open vista from Cheapside and the Mansion House.[80] Hawksmoor's combined

367 Nicholas Hawksmoor. Design for west front and steeple, Christ Church, Spitalfields, London, 22 April 1714. Pen and ink and wash. © The British Library Board, K.Top. 124 Supplement. 50.

366 (*left*) Nicholas Hawksmoor. Interior towards chancel, Christ Church, Spitalfields, London, 1714–29.

368 (*facing page*) B. Cole. 'The North West Prospect of Christ Church, Spittelfields', London. Engraving. Author's collection. Nicholas Hawksmoor, architect, 1714–29.

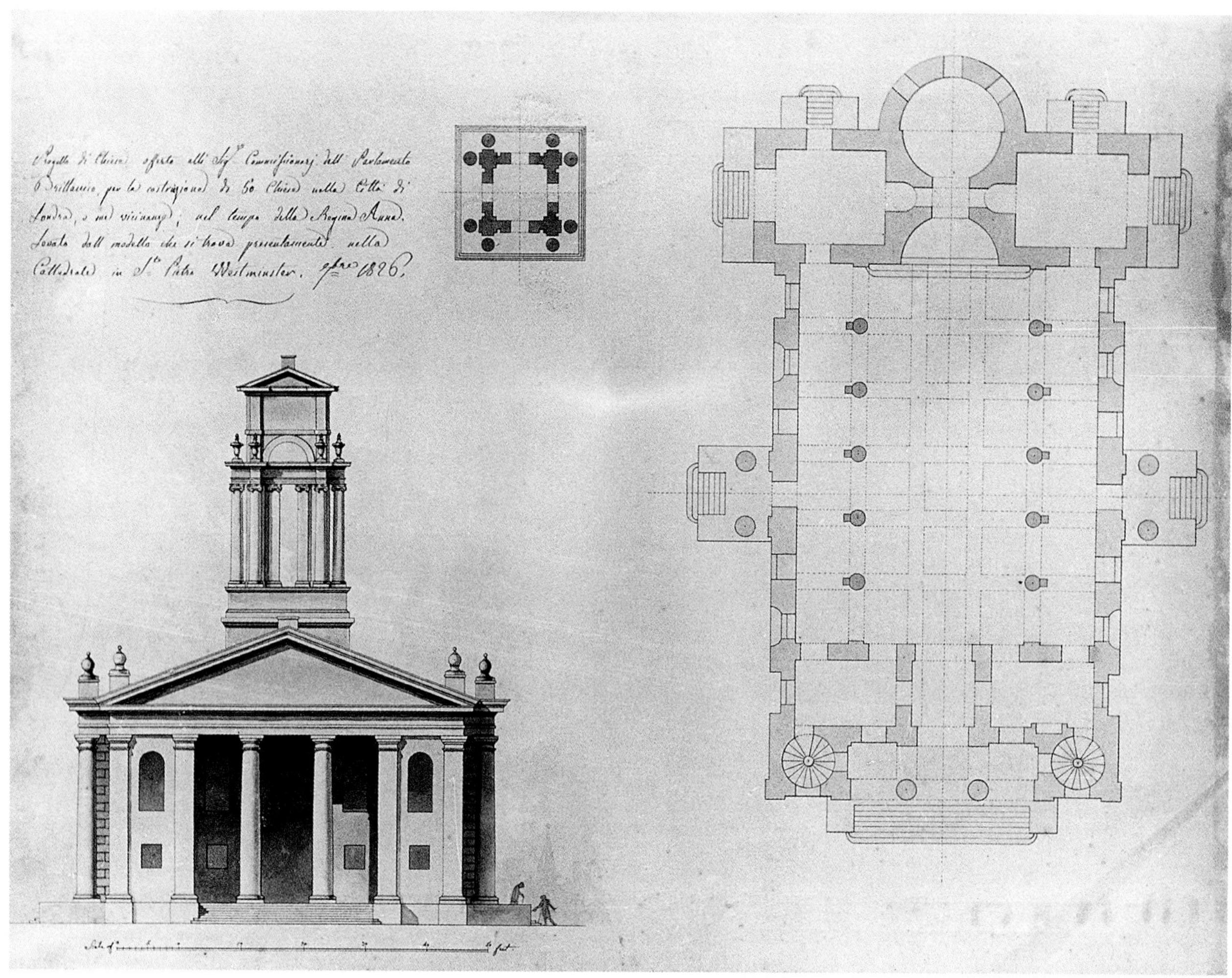

vestibule and tower base, originally fully visible only from acute angles, rises 95 feet but protrudes just 12 feet forward of the west wall of the body and is attached to it by a shallow spur containing slim side doors so that it hardly intrudes on to the pavement or deprives the interior of valuable congregational space. Indicative of this was the Commissioners' order that 'the projecture of Cornice . . . upon the West End of the steeple . . . be made as small as possible'.[81] Along the windowless Lombard Street elevation, effectively minimising traffic noise on one of the City's busiest mercantile thoroughfares, three huge, blind, illusionist, Borrominiesque tabernacles lie within the thickness of the wall. This is among the most electrifying passages in all Hawksmoor churches (pl. 374).[82]

The last of Hawksmoor's early executed churches, St George, Bloomsbury, is also located on an urban site, then, as now, set among existing buildings.[83] The rectangular ground with a pronounced north–south axis was accessible only northward towards Little Russell

369 (*above*) Charles Robert Cockerell. Plans and west front of the wooden model, St Anne, Limehouse, London, 1826. Pen and ink and wash. Victoria and Albert Museum, E. 3026-1909. Nicholas Hawksmoor architect, 1713.

370 (*facing page top left*) Nicholas Hawksmoor. West front and tower, St Anne, Limehouse, London, 1714–29.

371 (*facing page top right*) Nicholas Hawksmoor. West front and tower, St George-in-the-East, Wapping, London, 1714–29.

372 (*facing page bottom*) Nicholas Hawksmoor. East elevation, St George-in-the-East, Wapping, London, 1714–29.

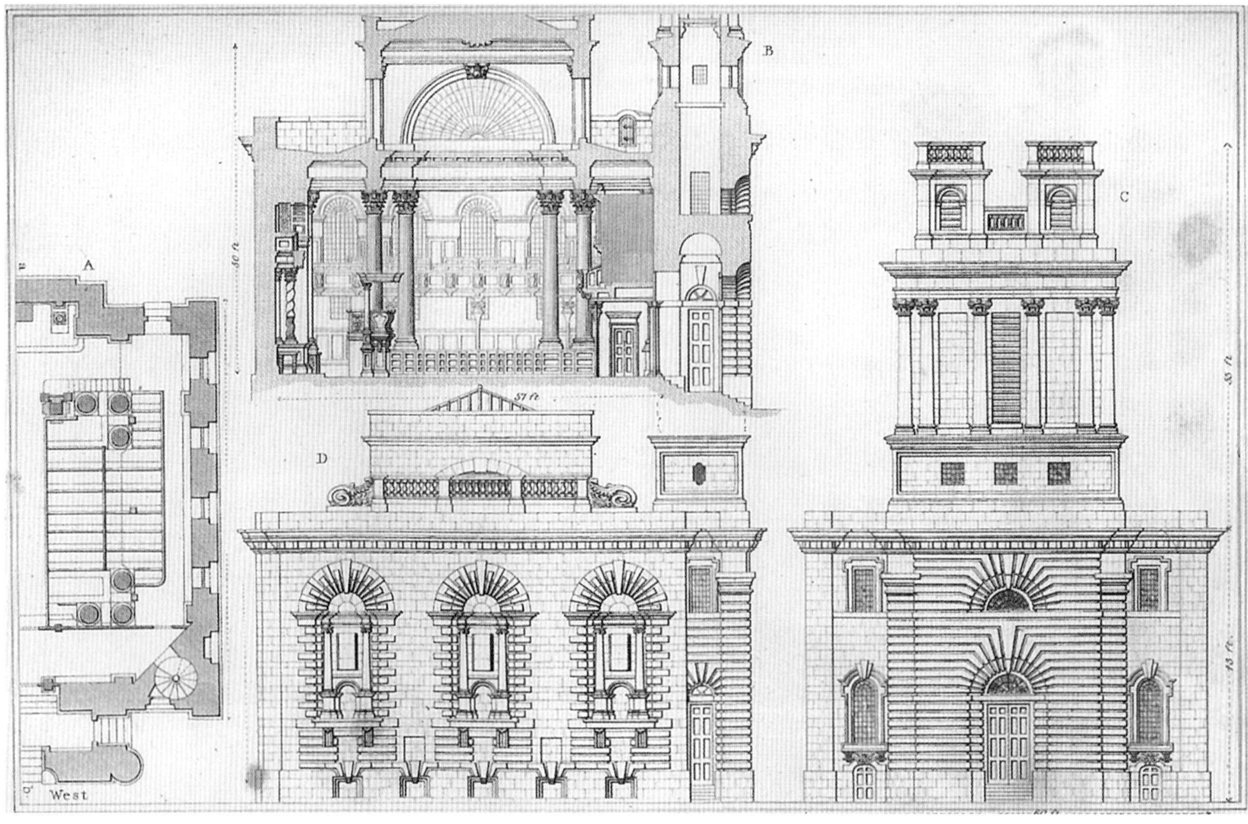

373 (*above*) John Le Keux after J. B. and T. Bradberry. Plan, section, north and west elevations, 'Church of St. Mary Woolnoth', London, 1 November 1823, in Britton and Pugin 1825, vol 1, following p. 9. Engraving. Nicholas Hawksmoor architect, 1716–31.

374 (*left*) Nicholas Hawksmoor. North elevation niche, St Mary Woolnoth, London, 1716–31.

Street and southward towards the wider Hart Street (present-day Bloomsbury Way), which marked the obvious entry points. In one preliminary scheme (pl. 375) the building, resting on a substantial platform containing burial vaults, consists of a rectangular body orientated on the west–east axis, with the liturgically eastern chancel raised on three steps (designated by a Latin cross). This central space is approached from both north and south through identical elliptical lobbies externally in the form of half *tempietti* (their columns together forming an interrupted ovoid), each crowned by a domed lantern and accessed by staircases. In this they resemble St Paul, Deptford (pl. 362). Beyond are twin, semicircular 'aisles' flanked by circular staircases leading to galleries. The west elevation features an additional entrance in the form of a colossal Serliana.[84]

375 Nicholas Hawksmoor. Plan and elevation of preliminary design, St George, Bloomsbury, London, ?1716. Pen and ink and wash. © The British Library Board, K.Top. XXIII.16.2.1.

This extrovert solution evolved into the more practical but equally unorthodox configuration of the executed building (pl. 354). Here a majestic, south-facing hexastyle temple portico leads under the galleried aisle into the longitudinal west–east orientated nave with its narrow eastern apsidal niche nurturing a splendid high altar (pl. 376) on axis with a secondary entrance within the tower base attached to the middle of the west elevation. The nave is sandwiched between galleries, with the space beyond the northern one designated for the ritual of baptism. The almost exclusive use of the Corinthian order carried associations with rulership stretching back to antiquity.[85] This notion is reinforced by the 11-foot-high statue of *George I* dressed in Roman armour, carved for £90 in 1724–5 by the master mason Edward Strong Jr. It crowns a stepped steeple that Hawksmoor would certainly have seen as the belated fulfilment of Wren's beloved but rejected Great Model for St Paul's Cathedral of 1673, with its Halicarnassus lantern and apostolic statue atop the vestibule dome (pl. 476). Bloomsbury is replete with antique references, from the Baalbek-inspired portico,[86] to the Pantheonic corbel cornice and the briefly considered covering of the body 'in the form of a Cupola instead of a Flat Roof',[87] to the external double-storeyed north end reminiscent of the Roman Colosseum.[88] Nor is it likely to have escaped the architect's notice that the church was erected on a former Roman site.[89]

If Hawksmoor offered fabulous reconstructions of ancient Rome in modern London, Gibbs, during a comparatively brief period as co-surveyor between his election in November 1714 by a Tory-dominated Commission and his dismissal in January 1716 under a new Whig regime following the Jacobite failure, created a Protestant version of Roman Catholic splendour. Born in Aberdeen into a mercantile Catholic family and destined for the priesthood, he instead trained in Rome at the Accademia di San Luca under the papal architect Carlo Fontana between 1704 and 1709. Fontana had already realised his most important ecclesiastical work: the twin churches in the Piazza del Popolo, in collaboration with Bernini (1673–4), and Carlo Rainaldi's San Marcello al Corso (1682–4), a summation of the Jesuit double-storey façade, and the publication of the magnificently illustrated account of St Peter's, *Il Tempio Vaticano e sua origine* (1694) by Carlo Fontana, subsequently concentrating on providing elaborate temporary structures for royal funerals.[90] This opening decade was particularly active in reaffirming the golden age of baroque church design.[91]

Gibbs left a fascinating manuscript account, 'A few Short Cursory Remarks on some of the finest Antient and modern Buildings In Rome, and other parts of Italy', dealing with the wide range of religious architecture that interested him, including the Pantheon and Diocletian's Baths (converted into Christian churches); St Peter's, which 'clames the first place'; Orazio Grassi's Sant'Ignazio, 'very beautifull . . . the Ceiling . . . elegantly painted in perspective by [Andrea] Pozzo . . . the Altar and Chaple of St Lois Gonzaga an exterordinary fine One . . . very rich and Magnificent'; Bernini's Sant'Andrea al Quirinale, 'a most beautifull fabrick . . . Oval form, very plain on the outside . . . the Inside . . . finished in a Most expensive Manner . . . altho . . . not very large . . . reckoned one of the best finished Churches in Rome'; Vignola's and Della Porta's Il Gesù, 'an exterordinary fine building . . . in The Ceiling . . . finely done in Stucco . . . All the Chapels and altars . . . fine varigated Marble of a good taste, and well executed'. This is followed by a lengthy description of Pozzo's altar to St Ignatius, Borromini's and Rainaldi's Sant'Agnese in Piazza Navona, 'a Greek Cross . . . Crouned with a Cupola and the front . . . adorned with tuo fine Campaniles . . . altogether a very noble fabrick', and so on.[92] Gibbs's impressive private library included three crucial architectural pattern books: *Il Tempio Vaticano*, D. and G. G. de' Rossi's *Studio d'architettura civile . . . di Roma* (1702– 21) and *Disegni di vari altari e cappelle nelle chiese di Roma* (1713).[93]

It was in this unique context – Gibbs was the first recorded British architect to have received a professional training abroad – that the most Italianate of all the New Churches was created, St Mary-le-Strand, which he described proudly as 'the first publick Building I was employed in after my arrival from *Italy*; which being situated in a very publick place, the Commissioners . . . spar'd no cost to beautify'.[94] But this was achieved only after a complicated procedure in which three surveyors and two Commissioners prepared at least six different designs in the space of seventeen months between 15 July 1713 and November 1714. This included one by Archer with a six-column, semicircular version of his Deptford portico, in response to the Commissioners' request for a one-off 'Steeple in [the] form of a Pillar . . . at the West end of the Church . . . with the Queens Statue on the top . . . instead of . . . Statues . . . upon . . . 50 Churches' as previously agreed.[95]

Meanwhile, negotiations were opened with John Talman, then in Italy, for commissioning an over-life-

376 (*facing page*) Nicholas Hawksmoor. Interior of the chancel with high altar, St George, Bloomsbury, London, 1716–31, restored 2003–6. World Monuments Fund, Britain.

size bronze statue from the leading Medici sculptor in Florence, G. B. Foggini, which three months later it was decided to reposition as the crown of a 250-foot-high, 15-foot diameter column sited to the west of the church opposite old Somerset House in the Strand, the main thoroughfare linking Westminster to the City, for which Gibbs prepared a design (pl. 377).[96] This incorporated a large relief depicting the Commissioners presenting the scheme to the enthroned monarch, with the church under construction in the background (pl. 377a). Unidentifiable relief bands (perhaps depicting episodes from Stuart history) cover the shaft, a modern version of the Roman column of Trajan, described by Gibbs as 'one of the finest peeces of Architecture . . . now extant in the world . . . erected . . . in honour to that great Emperour, when he was carrying on his . . . warr against the Dacians and had overcome . . . their King', just as Anne had done to the French and Louis XIV with the Treaty of Utrecht in 1713. This and other ancient monumental columns also carried Christian connotations that made them acceptable landmarks in the modern papal city.[97] London as the New Rome! The location again changed after the queen's untimely death on 1 August 1714, the ascendancy of George I and his Whig government and the inevitable abandonment of the Strand column. In November Gibbs's scheme for St Mary was approved as 'the most ornamental, and propperest for that situation' (pl. 378). The 50-foot-wide 'island' site sandwiched between the Strand and Holywell Street meant it was (and remains) the smallest and slimmest of the New Churches, measuring 48 by 123 feet. Within the limited 38-feet-wide interior, neither galleries nor their side entrances could practically be provided.[98]

Nor was there scope for the sort of monumentalising that makes Hawksmoor's and Archer's churches so memorable, though St Mary's fully exposed exterior was ripe for elaborate, small-scale Roman baroque treatment that could be closely scrutinised by the public passing along the busy thoroughfare. In contrast to Hawksmoor's astylar solidity, Gibbs set pedimented windows framed by engaged columns in the upper register, with the lower 'solid to keep out Noises from the Street . . . adorned with Niches'.[99] These were to be filled with statues, transforming the church into a colossal antique sarcophagus, with the queen's figure mounted on the summit of the semicircular portico, as if having stepped triumphantly through the vaulted Serliana to appear before her subjects.[100] Following Anne's death Talman suggested to the Commissioners that the church 'shou'd be so managed as to serve as a sort of Honorary Monument or Mausoleum'.[101] The restricted Strand site further forced Gibbs to treat the single-cell interior with an all-encompassing homogeneity (pl. 379), the side walls reiterating the external architectural divisions and the west front echoed in the sumptuous Italian baroque-inspired chancel arch.[102]

Many of these features reappeared in the Duke of Chandos's contemporary chapel at Cannons House, Middlesex. Visitors' descriptions, inventories, the sale catalogues issued prior to its demolition in 1747, surviving but re-sited furnishings and Gibbs's presentation drawings (pl. 380) hint at an interior of unrivalled splendour, recalling the Roman baroque churches Gibbs knew first-hand from his student days.[103] The family pew, raised on a screen of marble Doric columns and accessed directly from the palatial mansion's private apartments, was covered by a canopy with '*crimson velvet hangings* laced with gold'. The monumental paired Corinthian fluted pilasters articulating the walls, an innovation in Gibbs's religious work, can be traced to Borromini's remodelled nave of San Giovanni in Laterano (1646–50).[104]

The amateur Jacobite architect Lord Mar, writing from exile in France in 1716, congratulated his protégé on his 'fair daughter in the Strand', not doubting 'her proving the most complete little damsel in town'. Its Italianate attractions were manifest in William Kent's letter of 1718 from Rome to his English patron requesting views of it for himself and the architect Giacomo Mariari.[105] As a student at the Accademia di San Luca, Mariari (perhaps a friend of Gibbs) had won a second premium in the Corso Clementino in 1704 for a design for a Gesù-like church. In 1713 he was alerted by Kent's patron that 'if he were in England . . . he would find encouragement for . . . the humour of building encrease's wonderfully . . . there are fifty new churches to be built . . . and I do not hear yt any models are as yet fixed upon though aboundance are brought to the Commissioners'.[106] Mariari seems to have shown no interest but news of St Mary's construction from 1714 onward percolating into Italy may have borne other fruit. An intriguing suggestion has recently been put forward that the so-called Large Talman album (now in the Ashmolean Museum, Oxford), containing mainly

377a and 377b (*facing page far left and bottom right*) James Gibbs. Elevation design for the Strand Column, London, with detail of relief, 1714. Pen and ink and wash. The British Museum, Department of Prints and Drawings, 1913-12-16-9.

378 (*facing page top right*) John Harris after James Gibbs. South-west 'Prospectus Templi Stae. Mariae Londini in vico the Strand', St Mary-le-Strand, in Gibbs 1728, pl. 21.

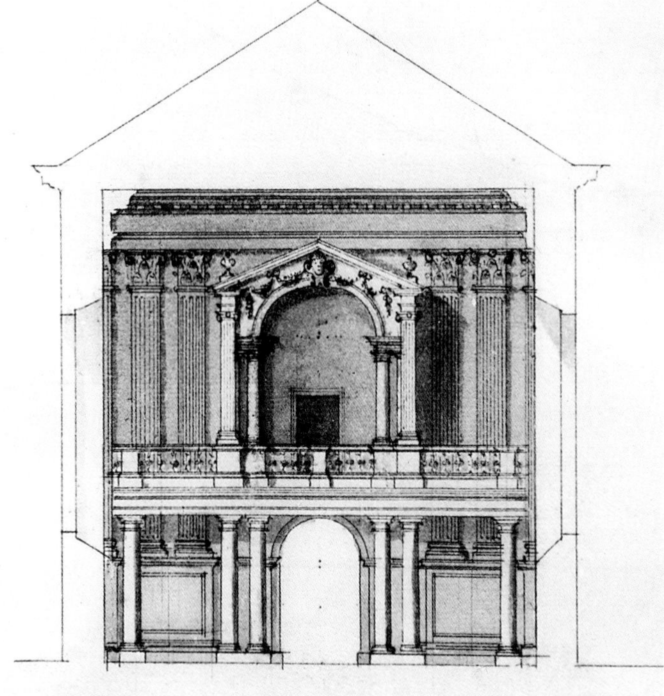

379 James Gibbs. Interior towards the chancel, St Mary-le-Strand, London, 1714–24. English Heritage (National Monuments Record, AA81/1434).

380 (*left*) James Gibbs. Design for internal east and west ends, Cannons House chapel, Middlesex, 1716. Pen and ink and wash. London Metropolitan Archives, Stowe Collection 262/50/60-61.

plans and elevations of Roman churches, might have been compiled by the connoisseur to allure certain members of the Tory-dominated New Churches Commissioners to the attractions of Italian design.[107]

Gibbs's initial success in securing the co-surveyorship may have enticed the 23-year-old Florentine architect Alessandro Galilei, at the start of his career and in search of lucrative employment beyond Italy, to London in the summer of 1714, soon after the queen's death, arriving at the very moment of a radical shift in English architectural ideas from the 'Fancy' of Tory baroque to the 'correct taste' of classicism, as we shall see in chapter

21. Unsolicited, he prepared, though apparently never presented, a group of exceptionally flamboyant circular, centrally planned church designs, among his earliest recorded work, of which plate 381 typically relies on a broad, eclectic spectrum of influences from renaissance and seventeenth-century Roman and Florentine models. These are distinguished by domes with lanterns, which as Elizabeth Kieven, the leading Galilei scholar, demonstrates, do not feature in English ecclesiastical designs, with their preference for porticos topped with towers.[108] It is, of course, inconceivable that such alien, overtly papistical proposals, devoid of even basic Anglican architectural and liturgical requirements, would have been tolerated, particularly after December 1715, when the Commission re-formed under an anti-baroque Whig regime in which Archer, Vanbrugh and Wren no longer served and Gibbs was ousted from his surveyorship (though not from further, unofficial participation in the completion of his only church, which was finally consecrated in 1724). Failing to attract work, Galilei returned to Florence via Ireland in 1718.

Meanwhile, some of the New Churches designs developed in two significantly different directions, both inspired by the classicism of late antiquity.

381 (*left*) Alessandro Galilei. West front design for an unidentified London church, 1714–15. Pen and ink and wash. Archivio di Stato, Florence, Galilei N.14/N/2, Box 109/48, f. 318.

382 William Halfpenny. South elevation and section design for the Protestant Cathedral, Waterford City, Waterford, Ireland, 1739. Pen and ink and wash. RIBA Library Drawings Collection, Shelf B3, f. 6.

Twenty

EARLY CHRISTIANITY REVIVED

upon the conversion of Constantine, many . . . basilicae . . . were given to the Church, and turned into . . . Christian assemblies[1]

The fashioning of new churches in early Christian forms reached its imaginative apogee in the unrealised proposal for a Protestant Cathedral for Waterford city, Ireland, in 1739 (pl. 382), though fascination with the idea had much earlier origins. In 1735 Hawksmoor reminded the dean and chapter of Westminster that in fourth-century Rome 'most . . . Temples . . . were either demolish'd or the Christians then esteem'd 'em prophane [and] They did make use of some of the Basilica's for Churches'.[2] At the launch of the New Churches venture on 31 November 1711, seven months before the Commissioners either formally adopted the final version of the Wren-Vanbrugh-Hickes proposals (pp. 364–5) or designated potential sites, Hawksmoor took the initiative with his 'Basilica after the Primitive Christians', which, though only a sketch plan, was worked up in considerable detail and is exceptional in the history of Western ecclesiastical architecture (pl. 383). The site selected was the 'fields' at the intersection of Hare Street and Brick Lane, Bethnal Green, in north-east London, with the church orientated 'East and West' (item A) and the 60-foot-wide Bacon Street renamed Church Street (R). Insistent that there be 'No burying in the Church – or near it on the outside – but seperately', he designated the 'way into the Cemetery, Sleeping place or place of Sepulchres' (N), the 'Burying place' in the churchyard (O), a hemicycle 'Cloyster for inscriptions' (P) and at right angles the 'Dormitory, or Cemetery' with its own entrance (Q), all located in an area east of the church, one of the benefits of building on the outer fringe of urban London.[3] The congregational nucleus is a carefully ordered complex within an 'Enclosure . . . to keep off filth Nastyness & Brutes' (F) surrounded by a 30-foot-wide 'open place' (L) approached on three sides (M). At each corner are, respectively, a 'Ministers house' (G), 'Parish Vestry' (H) and sexton's and reader's residences (I, K). 'The place for the font for the Converts . . . in the Porch' (B) is semi-detached at the west end of the church's rectangular body, leading under the 'womens Gallery [and] Stairs' (E) in a laterally projecting block, echoed at the east end by 'Vestrys for the Sacred Robes – and holy vessells' (D), with the semicircular chancel beyond (C). For Hawksmoor this ensemble represented the fullest expression of an Eusebian 'Manner of Building the Church as it was in the fourth Century in the purest times of Christianity'.[4]

Early Christian forms were revived as a palliative for 'the sumptuousness and magnificence' of Caroline design, which some churchmen regarded as 'not at all sutable to the times of the Gospels, nor according to the simplicity of the primitive Christian worship'.[5] According to Joseph Bingham's *Origines Ecclesiasticae; or, The Antiquities of the Christian Church* (1711), an English translation with commentaries of the *Ecclesiastical History* by the fourth-century Arian bishop of Caesarea, Eusebius, Constantine's creations, such as the Church of the Holy Apostles in Constantinople, 'vastly high . . . all its walls covered with marble, its roof overlaid with gold, and the outside . . . with gilded brass', are compared to earlier fabrics of the apostolic age, which were 'very simple and plain' and erected at a time when, according to Isidore of Pelusium, 'there were no such beautiful temples, but yet the Church was crowded with divine and heavenly graces, than in these days, when temples are adorned with all kinds of marble, but the Church is deprived of all those spiritual gifts'.[6]

The significance of Eusebius in British eighteenth-century religious life is attested by the inclusion of the bulky tome of the *Ecclesiastical History*, priced £1 1s. 6d., in the wainscot press of books compiled by the Society for the Promotion of Christian Knowledge dis-

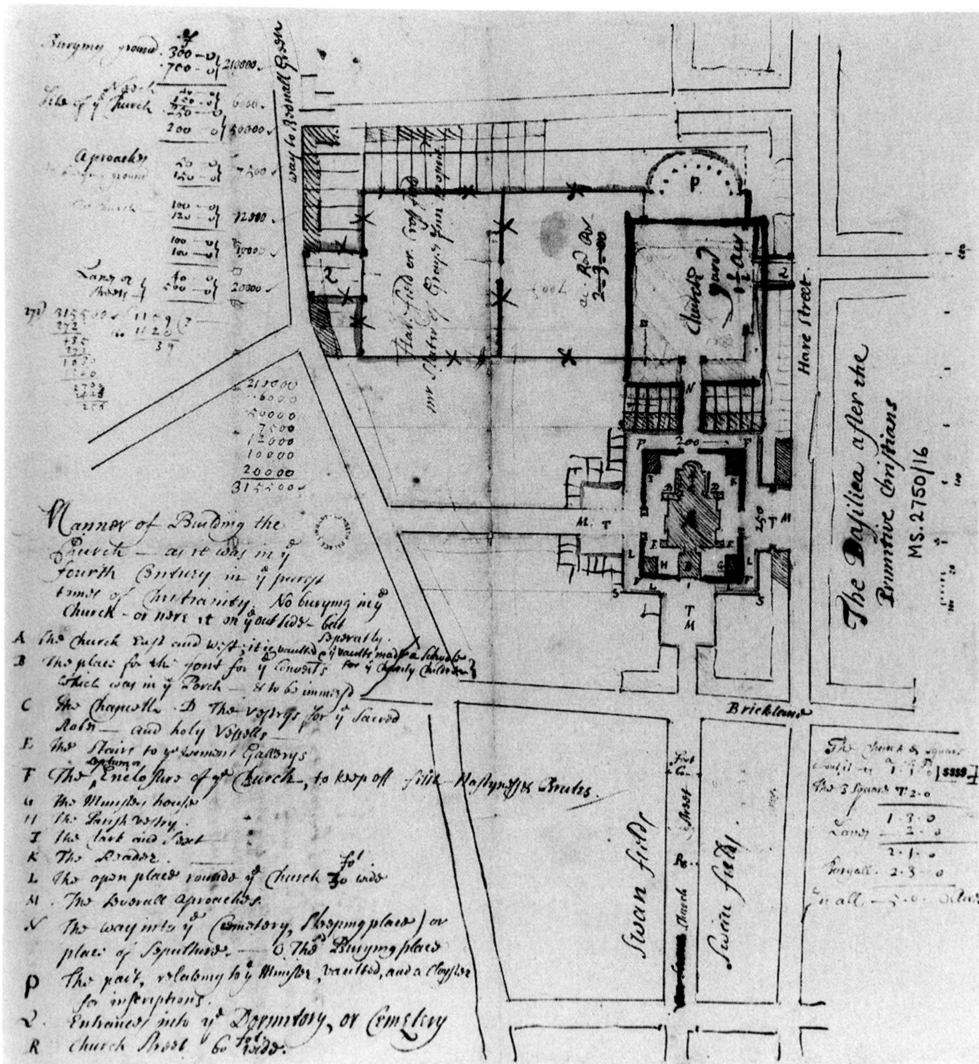

383 Nicholas Hawksmoor. Design for 'The Basilica after the Primitive Christians', Bethnal Green parish, London, 1711. Pen and ink. Lambeth Palace Library, MS 2750/16.

tributed to parochial libraries across England from 1709.[7] If Hawksmoor, by jumping the gun, so to speak, failed to realise his 'Primitive Basilica' at Bethnal Green, his famed historical precocity (see p. 304) in giving architectural expression to Bingham's writings nevertheless proved important in spreading these ideas beyond the metropolis.

John Wood Sr successfully exploited Eusebian ideals in his restoration of remote Llandaff Cathedral, Glamorgan (1734–52). He was idiosyncratic for his time in associating aspects of medieval churches with Old Testament buildings – Noah's Ark, Moses's Tabernacle and Solomon's Temple, for example, in the case of Bath Abbey. Moreover, he claimed that the cathedral's internal intercolumniation answered what Vitruvius called 'Areostylos [with] the whole Edifice . . . really and truly an *Egyptian Hall* of the *Dorick* Order sustaining the *Corinthian*, turned into the Figure of a Cross, under *Gothick* Dress'.[8] At the heart of his Llandaff scheme was a conviction that the original, pre-gothic fabric had been 'beyond doubt the most ancient *Church* in *Britain*', dating from the second century AD, a time when the inhabitants built 'Temples . . . in the Roman Taste, [subsequently] converted into *Churches*, when Christianity began to prevail'.[9] The underlying architectural inspiration arose from Wood's admittedly dubious claim that the 'East Part' of the ancient cathedral was 'built to imitate *Solomon's Temple*', both having identical dimen-

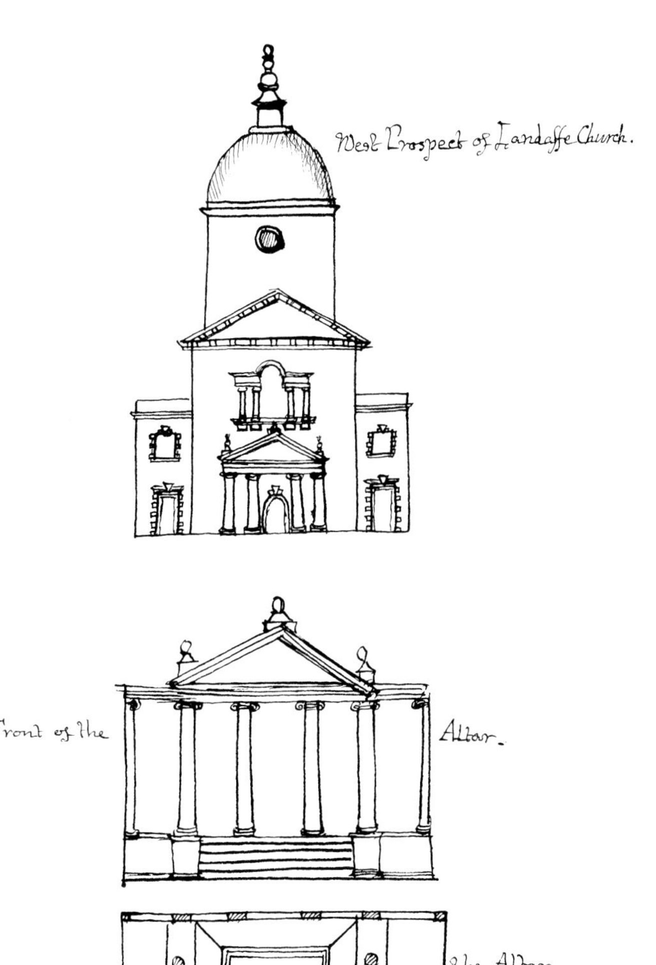

384 (*left*) William Cole after John Wood Sr. Design for the 'Cathedral of Landaffe . . . West Prospect', 'Front of the Altar' and 'Top of the Altar', Llandaff, South Glamorgan, Wales, 1736, as copied 1757, detail. Pen and ink. © The British Library Board, Add. MS 5829, f. 48v.

386 (*above*) Calvert Jones. Interior of choir and chancel, Llandaff Cathedral, South Glamorgan, Wales, in Ollivant 1860. Engraving. John Wood Sr. architect, 1736–52.

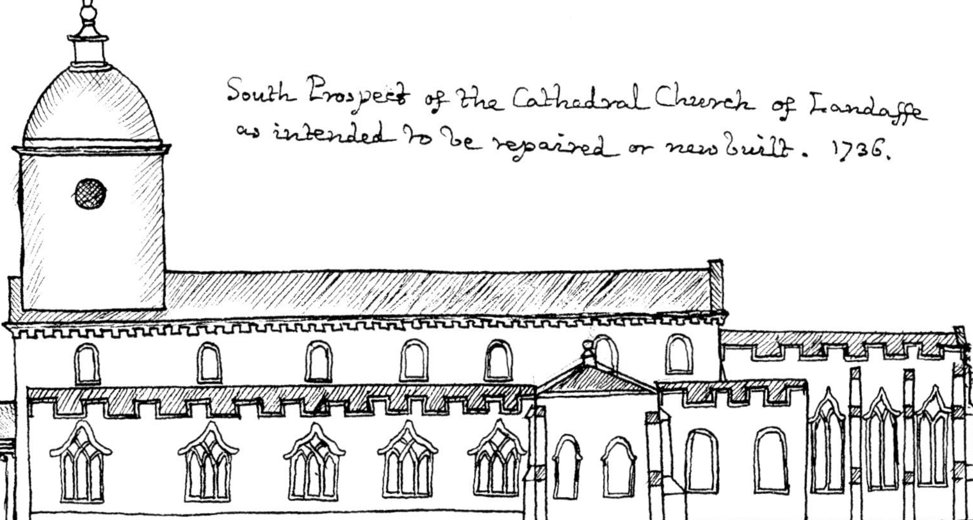

385 (*left*) William Cole after John Wood Sr. Design for the 'South Prospect of the Cathedral Church of Landaffe as intended to be repaired or new built. 1736', Llandaff, South Glamorgan, Wales, as copied 1757. Pen and ink. © The British Library Board, Add MS 5829, f. 49v.

sions (150 by 75 feet), and he suggested that if English medieval churches were 'stripped of their licentious Ornament [their] Gothick Dress . . . the Beauty of the Proportions observed by the Antients wou'd appear, in the strongest Manner, in them'.[10] From a description and record drawings of Wood's lost rebuilding scheme supplied by the Cambridge antiquary William Cole to his friend Browne Willis (pls 384–5), we learn that two-

387 Thomas Atkinson. Bar Convent chapel (Catholic), York, Yorkshire, interior towards sanctuary, 1765–91.

388 Giovanni Battista Piranesi. 'Tempio di Bacco' (Baptistery of St Costanza, St Agnese fuori le Mura), Rome, in Piranesi 1756, pl. XXI, detail. Engraving. Erected *c.*320.

thirds of the old structure, which was missing its roof by 1723, was re-covered to produce 'a more regular & exact Proportion'.[11] This left the ruined unregenerate nave and aisles to form the equivalent of an early Christian atrium (defined by Eusebius as 'a court open to the air . . . surrounded by cloisters').[12] The medieval transepts were demolished; five surviving 'old gothic Windows' on the side aisles were preserved (as Hawksmoor had recommended in his scheme for St Giles-in-the-Fields of 1730, pl. 296), while others, including the clerestory, were re-fenestrated as round-headed arches in wood, which were 'vastly cheaper, & look as well as the Gothick'. Perhaps because the fabled early date of the historical buildings selected as models (see above) preceded the invention of the bell (assigned to the fifth century AD), Wood's initial idea of a prominent, domed west tower was abandoned.[13] This left an austere, astylar, pedimented block with a diminutive tetrastyle temple portico and a Serliana, components reminiscent of Gibbs's Marylebone Chapel (pl. 506). Wood had resided in nearby Oxford Street between 1725 and 1727. The nave was lit from clerestory windows. Moreover, the front recalled the Roman Curia in the Imperial Forum (AD 287–305), which had been Christianised in the seventh century and dedicated to St Adrian, while the combination of pedimented front and columnar portico had a precedent in the early Christian Santa Maria in Trastevere as rebuilt in the twelfth century, of which the original portico was refashioned in 1701–2 by Carlo Fontana, Gibbs's master during the second half of the same decade.[14]

Internally, Llandaff's refurbished body (pl. 386) was an 'exceeding Fine . . . very stately & beautiful Room' with twin, distyle aedicule pulpit and bishop's throne (perhaps based on the Apostle's *tropaion* beneath St Peter, Rome) facing one another across the entrance to the chancel, with its 'large Arch . . . enriched with fine Fret work . . . in Stucko'.[15] Lit by high-level fenestration including Serliana at both east and west ends, and covered by a groin vault, with diffused light lower down drawn from arches opening on to the gothic side aisles, this space rose gently in a series of stepped tiers: two from nave to choir, three to chancel, five to the altarpiece. This was enclosed by a miniature Corinthian tetrastyle temple-like tabernacle, with its rear wall closing off the gothic Lady Chapel and articulated by Ionic pilasters.[16]

While Wood's transformed cathedral must have seemed a daringly radical experience to contemporary worshippers in rural Wales, critical responses were unfavourable: 'a medley of absurdities . . . a strange building . . . more like an Assembly Room or Town Hall than a sacred place', 'ridiculously absurd! a Christian altar . . . rais'd under the Portico of a Heathen Temple', 'like a ball room, with venetian windows', 'a pigeon-house . . . burlesque on what ought to be looked upon with veneration'.[17] John Carter, visiting in 1804, described the choir as 'lost in modern Ionic columns, entablatures, pediments, circular-headed windows, truss corbels, and Pantheon groins, [the high altar] composed after the manner of a Garden Pavilion, with double rows of columns, coved roof, and a balustrade'.[18] Failing to understand Wood's historical context, the fabric was demolished and rebuilt wholly in gothic in the mid-nineteenth century.

The Roman Catholic chapel secreted in the upper floor of the convent of the Most Adorable Trinity (Bar Convent) in York (pl. 387), designed by a local Catholic architect, Thomas Atkinson, miraculously survives as a beautiful and unusual cruciform space culminating in a 25-foot-diameter sanctuary covered by a low, ribbed dome decorated with gilt plaster palm branches and a frieze of eucharistic devices, lit from a central oculus of yellow tinted glass painted with the emblem of the Holy Spirit, the whole supported on eight fluted free-standing Ionic columns. It is said to have been designed 'after a model procured from Rome' by a friend of the mother superior, Ann Aspinal.[19] This was most likely Santa Costanza (pl. 388), the domed rotunda-baptistery erected by the first Christian emperor, Constantine, for his daughters Costanza and Elena (consecrated in 1254 as a church), attached to the fourth-century basilica church of Sant'Agnese fuori le Mura, an apt choice for the York nunnery, which, too, is located just outside the town walls, beyond Micklegate Bar.[20]

A crucial early Christian architectural element identified by Bingham to resurface in the eighteenth century was the 'baptisterium' located in the western narthex or 'Exhedra', which Hickes promoted as being 'after the ancient manner . . . that the . . . practice of immersion may be revived in the Church of England'.[21] Hawksmoor exploited it forcefully at Limehouse, where in one of the preliminary models its rotund form was placed behind the apsidal chancel, but in a volte-face (pl. 389) the ensemble was transferred to the west end and executed in that position (pl. 370). Dr Thomas Mangey, chaplain to the Bishop of London (one of the New Churches Commissioners), in his consecration sermon for Holy Trinity, Sunderland, entitled *The Holiness of Christian Churches*, delivered on 4 September 1719 and subsequently published, alluded to Eusebius' description of Paulinus' fourth-century basilica church at Tyre, comparing the diligence and bounty of the rector, Daniel Newcombe, in erecting the new building (1719–21) to 'the Christians in the first Ages . . . in adorning their Churches'.[22] During the years 1735–8 a semi-detached domed rotunda was added to the east end (pl. 461) into which Newcombe proposed re-siting the high altar 'under a canopy of inlaid work, supported in front by two fluted . . . Corinthian . . . pillars'.[23]

The most fully developed expression of this idea, again unrealised, was the remarkable set of designs for a new Protestant cathedral at Waterford City, Ireland (pl. 382), commissioned in 1739 by Bishop Thomas Milles from the English architect William Halfpenny. Milles had previously been Regis Professor of Greek at Oxford and published an edition of the works of the early saint Cyril of Jerusalem, though the extraordinary notion of attaching an octagonal baptistery to the west

389 Nicholas Hawksmoor. Design for the plan and interior south elevation, St Anne, Limehouse, London, 1714. Pen and ink and wash. Victoria and Albert Museum, E.3011-1909.

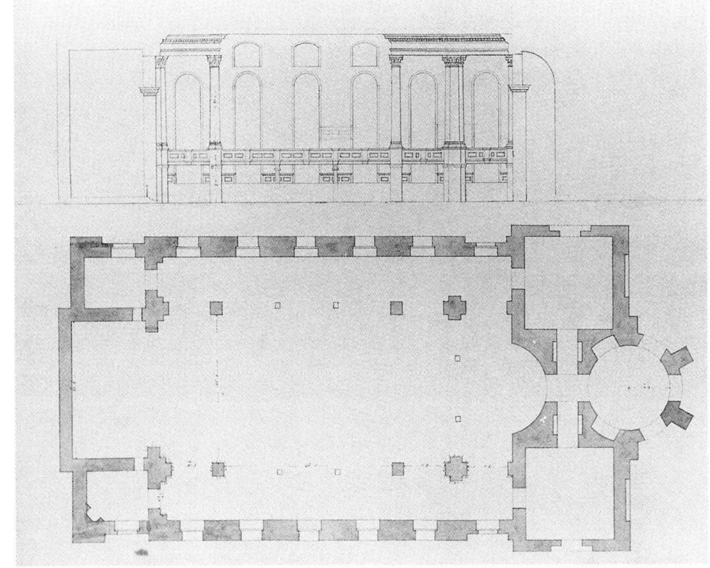

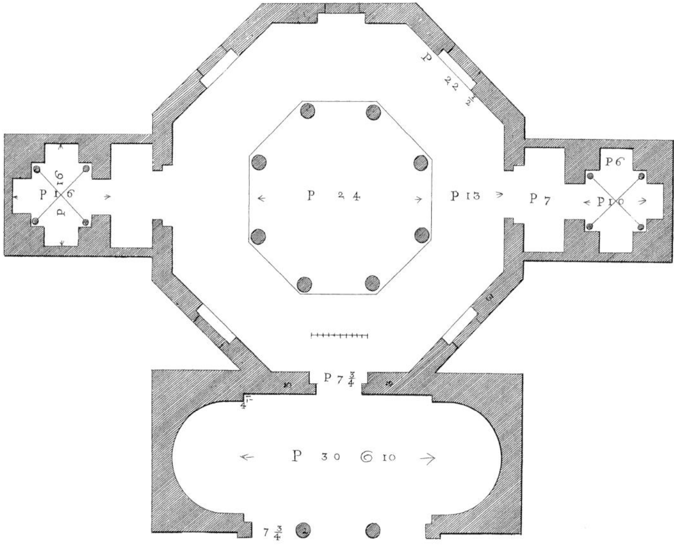

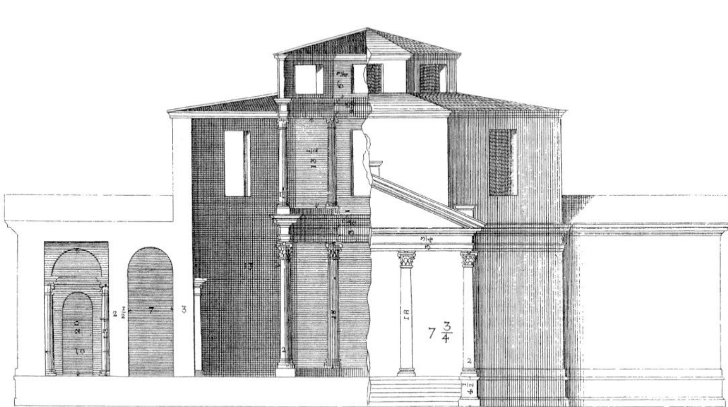

end of the body was probably chiefly determined by his two Grand Touring nephews, Jeremiah Milles, precentor of Waterford (1737–44), and Richard Pococke, vice-general of the Waterford and Lismore diocese (1734–44). In Italy in 1734 they had paused at Ravenna to see the fifth- and sixth-century basilicas of Sant'Apollinare Nuova and Sant'Apollinare at Classe, the tomb of Galla Placidia and San Vitale, which Milles described to his uncle as 'much the most beautiful [church] in the city. It is an Octagon . . . the roof is very valted'.[24] Journeying on alone, in 1737 he visited the mid-sixth-century basilica-planned cathedral at Parenzo (modern Porec) on the Istrian coast, described in his manuscript diary as 'a very ancient building' preceded at its west end by an attached but self-contained octagonal baptistery 'now uncovered, and not made use of'. News of this extremely rare survival of an early Christian arrangement reached the Milles at Waterford and formed the basis of Halfpenny's proposals.[25] Here the baptistery is covered by a steeply pitched roof surmounted by a cupola probably inspired by the twelfth-century Baptistery at Florence, which Milles and Pococke saw in the winter of 1733–4, while the exterior has a curiously old-fashioned but characteristically Halfpenny mixture of baroque and Palladian motifs, with overall an appropriately 'primitive' austerity that was uncommon even by normal Irish Protestant standards of the time. Bishop Milles's death on 12 May 1740 prevented his extraordinary project coming to fruition.[26]

A group of centrally planned churches based on iconic early Christian buildings, which, according to Eusebius, appeared during Christianity's 'first age' and featured an exedra containing the font, were 'very capacious because . . . there were usually great multitudes to

390 (*above left*) Reconstruction of 'the Baptisterium of Constantine', San Giovanni in Laterano, Rome, Italy, in Ware 1738, Fourth Book, Chapter XVI, pl. XLII. Engraving. Erected *c.*432–40.

391 (*left*) James Booth. Exterior east elevation, St Martin, Stoney Middleton, Derbyshire, 1758–9.

393 (*facing page bottom left*) John Adam. Design for 'Elevation and ground Plan of a circular Church at Inveraray', Scotland, 1758. Pen and ink and wash. From the Saltoun papers deposited in National Library of Scotland, MS 17879(3), f. 101.

394 (*facing page bottom right*) John Adam. Design for 'Section and Plan of the Gallery of a circular Church at Inveraray', Scotland, 1758. Pen and ink and wash. From the Saltoun papers deposited in National Library of Scotland, MS 17879(2), f. 100.

392 (*left*) Giovanni Battista Piranesi. 'Vedute dell' interno del Tempio di S. Stefano Rotundo', Rome, Italy, in Piranesi 1756. Engraving. Erected fifth century AD.

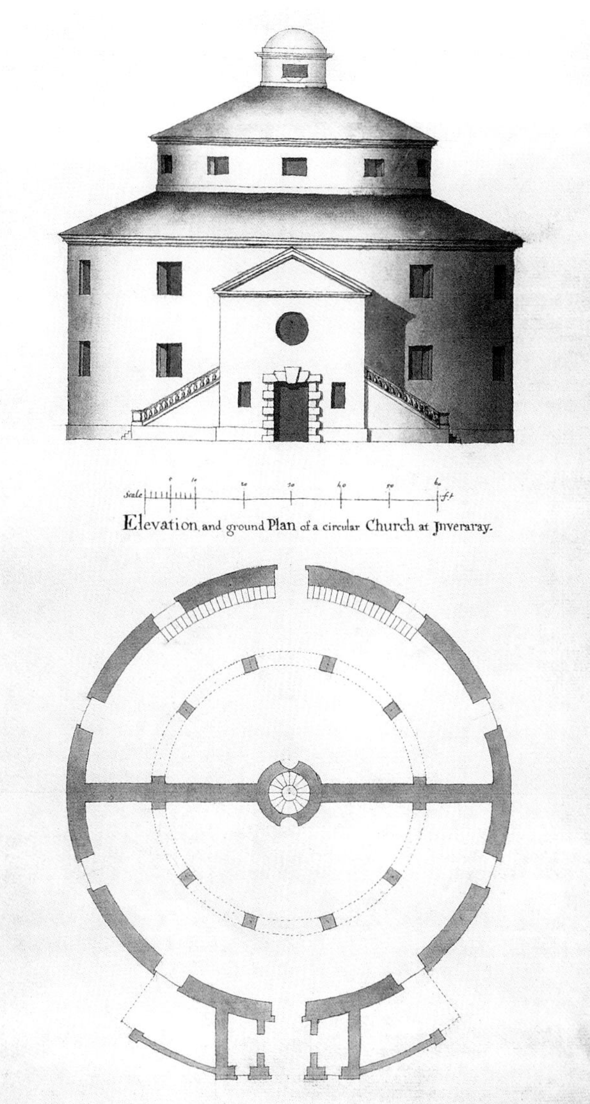

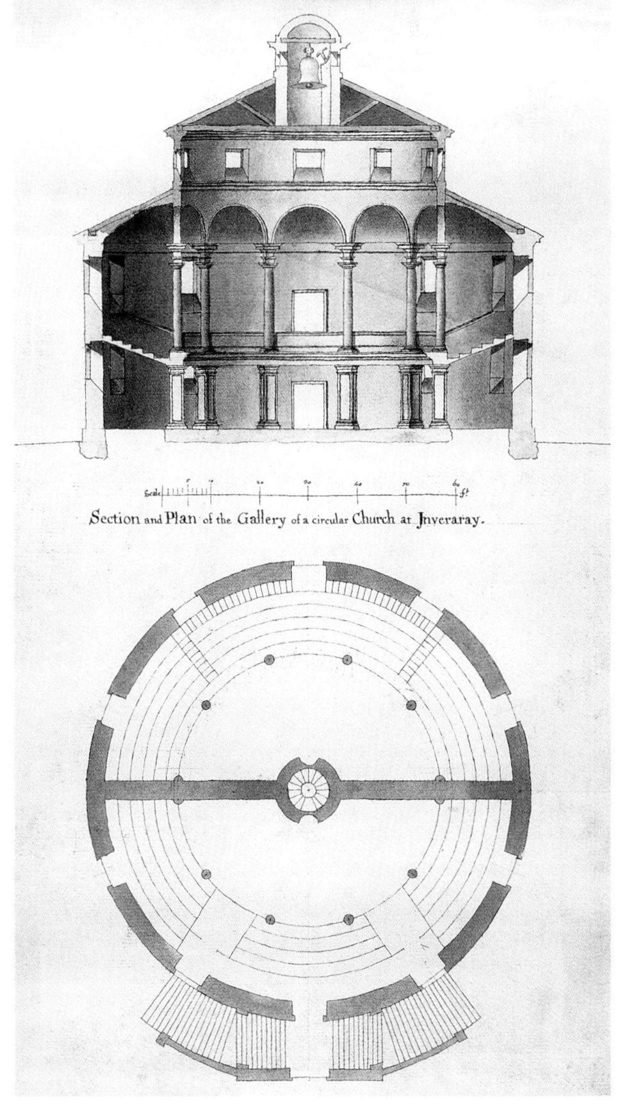

be baptized at the same time' and distinctive in lying separate from the church. He cited Constantine's baptistery adjacent to San Giovanni in Laterano (pl. 390).[27] Palladio had recommended it for being 'beautifully designed'; Gibbs found it 'intire and very handsom . . . having two Rows of columns over each other . . . with an Attic a top, to help to give light to it . . . it's a most elegant peece of building, and much admired by all who see it'.[28] The octagonal body of Stoney Middleton, Derbyshire (pl. 391), attached to the surviving medieval west tower, may have been dictated by its location near a famous warm springs believed to possess curative powers and by inference associated with the Lateran model.[29] Piranesi's *veduta* of the interior of Santo Stefano Rotondo, a well-preserved fifth-century church that largely escaped later alterations, published in *Le antichità romane* in 1756 (pl. 392), with its tribute to Robert Adam, a copy of which accompanied the architect on his return to Scotland in early 1758, may well have been the starting point for a church planned for Archibald Campbell, 3rd Duke of Argyll's New Town at Inveraray (pls 393–4), designed later in the same year by John Adam.[30] The unique arrangement of the prototype, wherein a lofty circular central space surrounded by an Ionic colonnade bisected by a straight wall supported on Corinthian dosseret arches, suited Inveraray's requirements of subdividing the space crosswise to accommodate both Gaelic/ Presbyterian and English/ Anglican congregations in separate quarters under one roof.[31] The austerely astylar, 90-foot-diameter cylinder is punctuated by small, frameless windows; the projecting, pedimented porch of the 'Inglish Church', recalling one of the surviving transepts at Santo Stefano, features outside staircases leading to 'His Gracese Galery', the traditional Scottish laird's loft. The solid 'Middle wall Deviding the Church' into independent hemicycles has pulpits for each half inserted into a common circular stairwell, giving access to a domed bell turret hidden above the flat ceiling. The duke's death in 1761 put a hold on the project until the 1790s, when a wholly different solution was erected.[32]

395 (*left, top*) Mausoleum of Theodoric, Ravenna, Italy, *c.*520.

396 (*left, centre*) Unknown artist. Colebrooke Mausoleum, Chilham, Kent, detail, 1759. Watercolour. © The British Library Board, K.Top. XVIII, f.11-3. Sir Robert Taylor architect, 1752–5, demolished 1862.

397 (*left, bottom*) 'Templum Sanctor. Silvani et Bonifaccii Via Salaria', Rome, in Aringhi 1659, Book IV, Chapter XXXVII, p. 110, detail. Engraving.

Predictably, close links existed between early Christian and Georgian mausoleum forms. That for Theodoric at Ravenna, a former capital of the Christian Roman empire in the West, where the 'stupendous large . . . stone . . . wch covers the whole top [comprises] Pedestals on wch stood the statues [of] 12 Apostles . . . now transported to Venice', secured an unequivocal Christian identity for the eighteenth century (pl. 395).[33] Hawksmoor described his similar early study (1726) for the Mausoleum at Castle Howard, Yorkshire, as 'a Small Chapel with Six Small Rooms, under it, for the Accomodation of 6 old women (or 6 old men) . . . to Live in . . . by way of an almshouse [serving as] Curators . . . to clean, sweep and Lock [the building and shew it] to Strangers', but as the scheme evolved 'a Sacellum or Chapel' was added within the main structure, with 'windows . . . to enlighten the Chapell, but not . . . seen within doors'.[34] Sir Robert Taylor's Colebrooke family mausoleum attached to the east end of Chilham church, Kent (1752–5; pl. 396), erected at a cost of £2,000, instilled a sense of fear and awe. A huge astylar rotunda, measuring 42 feet diameter, rose from a splayed base with oculi, with a deep internal entablature bearing emblems of mortality and crowned by an oddly shaped, top-lit dome glazed with panes of coloured glass, its 12-feet-thick walls lined with forty-two 'Cavaties for the Reception of the Coffins' and a plastered wood floor over an echo chamber. Its source lay in the tomb chamber of SS Silvani and Boniface engraved in Paolo Aringhi's *Roma subterranea novissima* (1659), a copy of which was in the family library (pl. 397).[35]

Robert Adam's Shelburne Mausoleum at Bowood, Wiltshire (1761–4; pl. 398), with its Romano-Christian sarcophagus cocooned within one of the arms, and John Carter's similar, self-contained building published in *The Builder's Magazine* (1774; pl. 399), are both based on the Mausoleum of Galla Placidia, Ravenna (*circa* 425). Encapsulating a circular, Santo Stefano-like rotunda with late Roman–early Christian inspired polylobed adjuncts, Carter penetrated to the heart of the prototype: 'A Mausoleum, though seldom used among the moderns, among the antients was a place solely appropriated for the depositing of their dead', their ashes 'gathered in a urn, and placed in small niches in the catacombs'. The landing, marked E, was 'where the corpse is rested during the ceremony', the pair of flanking polylobes (I) 'Porches . . . for the reception of those who wait to see the ceremony'.[36]

398 Robert Adam. 'Design of a Mausoleum & Chapple for Bowood Park', Wiltshire, detail, 1761–4. Pen and ink. Sir John Soane's Museum, AD 39/75.

399 John Carter. 'Plan and Elevation of a Design for a Mausoleum', in 'A Society of Architects', *The Builder's Magazine*, 1774, pl. XIX. Engraving.

400 Anonymous. 'A Representation of the Comet that Appear'd on January: ye 26. &. &. 1743/4 in the Evening. Taken near St Martins-Church in the Strand', published 4 February 1744. Engraving. Private collection. James Gibbs architect, 1722–7.

Twenty-One

THE RISE OF TEMPLE-FORM CHURCHES

> the old way of building churches is capable of most if not all the state, and grace of Architecture, And as that way . . . was the most ancient: so it is most fit to be imitated, And the same modelle will serve for building little, as well as great churches.[1]

The seeming contradiction of a Christian place of worship taking the form of a pagan classical temple blazed across the London sky like some prophetic comet (pls 400, 416), though as in the case of the buildings in the previous chapter the idea had an ancient pedigree. In a translation and commentary on Eusebius, *Origines Ecclesiasticae; or, The Antiquities of the Christian Church* (1711), the Revd Joseph Bingham recounted how the fifth-century Roman emperor, Honorius, issued laws forbidding further destruction of urban pagan temples and gifted survivors to the Church, so that they would 'become another thing from what they were in former ages, that is, more noble and stately edifices, more rich and beautiful'. As an example he cited Honorius' father, Emperor Theodosius, who 'turned the famous temple of Heliopolis [the now-ruined colossal first-century AD Temple of Jupiter at Baalbek] into a Christian church'.[2] Alexander Pope remarked that the popes 'spared some of the Temples [in Rome], by converting them to churches'.[3] Gibbs in Rome in 1707 mentioned the temples of Bacchus (Sant'Agnese fuori del Mura); Fortuna Virilis (Santa Maria Egiziaca), 'almost intire and altho . . . small very beautifull . . . the finest Antient Ionick building in Rome'; Antoninus and Faustina (San Lorenzo in Miranda), 'of Late I hear they have put a new Roofe upon it and made it a Christian Church . . . a very handsome front to the body of the Temple within the Antient portico, which looks very pictureske by seeing the new front . . . through the old Ruind portico of the Temple'; and the Pantheon (Santa Maria ad Martyres), 'the most intire of all the Antient Roman Buildings . . . the fine portico was added . . . by Marcus Agrippa . . . the Temple and Portico . . . built att different times, as may be seen by the two Pediments . . . likewise by the joining of the portico to the old building looking on its flank ways'. These all provided evidence of the mutability of even the most revered antique monuments, which Gibbs was to apply to the designing process of his masterpiece, St Martin-in-the-Fields, as we shall discover later in this chapter.[4] By the early eighteenth century descriptions and illustrations of important Greek and Roman temples were widely known in Britain. For example, in 1721 the amateur architect Henry Herbert, 9th Earl of Pembroke, provided the Revd William Stukeley with the dimensions of 'some Greek Temples in Sicily'.[5]

Christian repossession and conversion of pagan temples also enjoyed the sanction of the two most influential architectural writers of the renaissance. Alberti, in *De Re Aedificatoria* (1485), described how from the pagan notion that 'the Temple of various Gods ought to be built in various Forms . . . our Countrymen by Degree got into a Way of making use of Basiliques . . . for their Places of Worship [where] the Altar had a very great Air of Dignity when set in the Place of the Tribune', a raised apsidal space, which evolved into the chancel. He then observed that

> In the whole Compass of the Art of Building there is nothing in which we ought to employ more Thought, Care and Diligence than in the Layout and adorning a Temple [meaning a church] because not to mention that a Temple well built and Handsomely adorned is the greatest and noblest Ornament a City can have . . . Men are moved by the Purity of beautiful Materials, and raised by them to Reverence and Devotion for the Deity to which they are sacred. It is certain that Temples may be of great Use for stir-

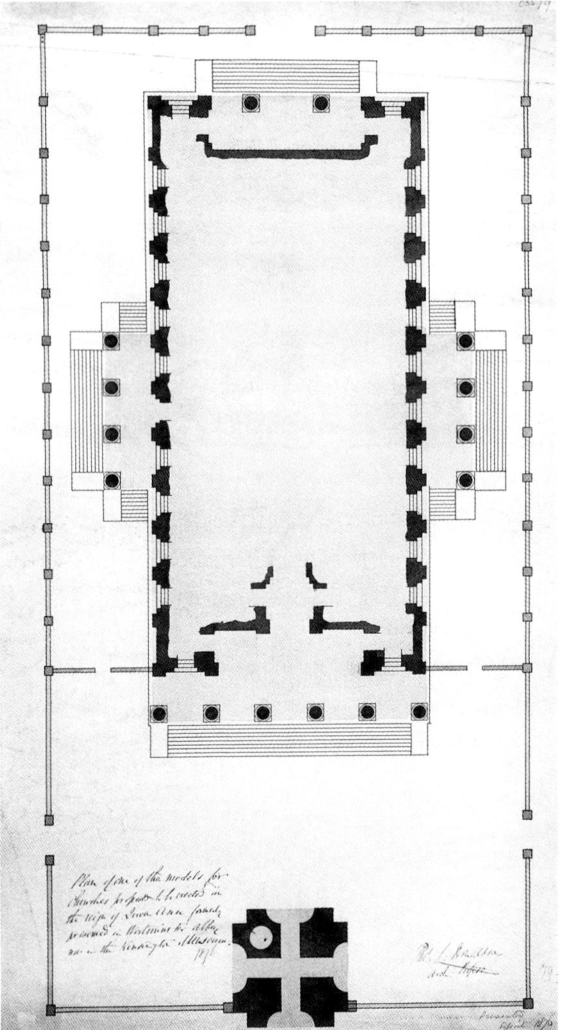

401 (*above*) Nicholas Hawksmoor. South-east view, St Alfege, Greenwich, London, 1712–26.

402 (*left*) Thomas Leverton Donaldson. Plan of wooden model No. 4, St Alfege, Greenwich, London, 1843 (west is right). Pen and ink and wash. RIBA Library Drawings Collection, OS5/9(4). Nicholas Hawksmoor architect, 1712.

> ring up Men to Piety, by filling their Minds with Delight, and Entertaining them with Admiration of their Beauty.
>
> For this Reason I would have the Temple made so beautiful, that the Imagination should not be able to form an Idea of any Place more so; and I would have every Part so contrived and adorned, as to fill the Beholders with Awe and Amazement, at the Consideration of so many noble and excellent Things, and almost force them to cry out with Astonishment: This Place is certainly worthy of God![6]

Palladio, in the preface to the Fourth Book of *I quattro libri d'architettura* (1570), devoted largely to reconstructions of Roman temples, wrote:

> If any building should have effort and labor expended on it . . . this should be done for temples in which the Creator and Giver of all things, God . . . must be adorned and praised . . . to the utmost of our abilities . . . men . . . must above all consider the dignity and grandeur of God . . . since He is the ultimate good and perfection; it is supremely appro-

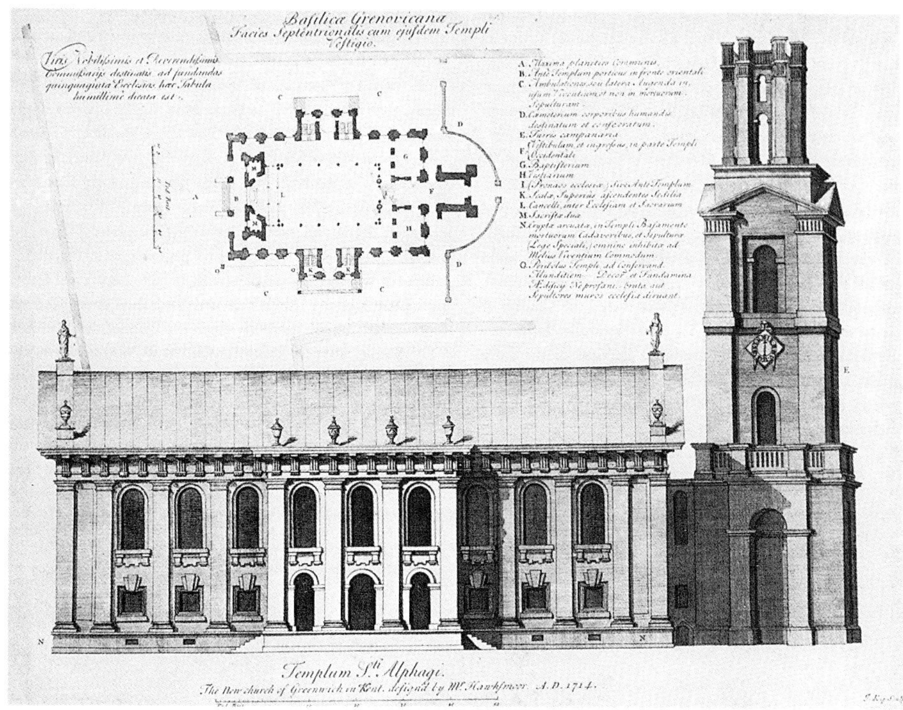

403 (*above*) Jan Kip. Plan and north elevation, 'The New Church of Greenwich in Kent', 1714. Engraving. The Bodleian Library, University of Oxford, Gough Maps 13. Nicholas Hawksmoor architect, 1712–26.

priate that everything dedicated to Him should be made to the highest level of perfection of which we are capable.

Palladio's aim was to demonstrate 'the form and ornament of many antient temples . . . so that anyone can understand the form and ornament with which churches must be built'. In Chapter II, 'On the Shapes of Temples', he recommended they have 'wide porticoes and taller columns than those needed in other buildings . . . ample and beautiful proportions; because all grandeur and magnificence is required for divine worship . . . so perfectly that . . . those who enter . . . will be astonished and stand there with their spirits raised when contemplating their grace and beauty'; or, as an English translation put it, 'remain in a kind of extasy', and he advocated the Pantheon as 'perfectly adapted to demonstrate the unity, the infinite existence, the consistency, and the justice of God'.[7]

The most common antique Roman temple form – a rectangular body defined by either peripteral (freestanding) or pseudoperipteral (attached) giant order columns or pilasters supporting a pitched roof pedimented at both ends – first appeared in English churches in 1712 at Hawksmoor's St Alfege, Greenwich (pls 401, 403–4).[8] The Leeds antiquary Ralph Thoresby, visiting in 1714, at which stage the carcass was erected and roofed and the interior ready for plastering, with

404 Jan Kip. 'Templum St. Alphagi, apud Grenovicenses orientem Spect', 1714. Engraving. The Bodleian Library, University of Oxford, Gough Maps 13. Nicholas Hawksmoor architect, 1712–26.

the medieval west tower still intact, bestowed on this 'most noble' church the crowning accolade that its temple portico was 'like that of [Inigo Jones's St Paul] Covent Garden, but much more stately' (pl. 512). Such majesty was reinforced by the Commissioners' early decision to build in ashlar, instilling on St Alfege and Hawksmoor's other New Churches a Roman grandeur absent in all but a few of Wren's brick and stone-trimmed London churches.[9]

To arrive at this highly original concept, Hawksmoor's ideas underwent a radical transformation from the trial-run Bethnal Green (pl. 383) through two preliminary wooden models (responding to the Commissioners' general call on 18 July 1712), of which the only surviving visual evidence are Donaldson's lecture plans of 1843, which lack the detailed treatments of the lost originals. Each features a combination of hexastyle prostyle and distyle *in antis* porticoes. The significance of the sudden, prophetic appearance of this impressive motif cannot be overestimated. Rejection of Wren's Great Model for St Paul's Cathedral (1673–4), with its heroic temple portico and his avoidance of the feature in all fifty-two London parish churches, meant that previous to the 1710s such a structure had rarely been seen in the metropolis.

The most innovative of the models (pl. 402) was for a double-storey, twelve-bay pseudoperipteral body, 160 feet long (if built), each bay defined by giant order Roman Doric pilasters, as at Birmingham (pl. 12), with additional tetrastyle prostyle porticoes on perrons in the middle of the long elevations, and a 28-foot-square, 76-foot-high tower completely detached from the body, which has the effect of preserving the temple form's integrity. This was an offshoot of Bethnal Green (and like it the church was contained in an 'Enclosure') and a novelty Hawksmoor was also exploring at King's College chapel, Cambridge,[10] which may have had origins in Wren's St Mary-le-Bow, of which Hawksmoor made an engraving (pl. 484).[11] On 6 August 1712 the executed revision was approved (pl. 403). The body was brought closer to a re-cased medieval tower attached by narrow spurs rising to the level of the capitals, with total pseudoperipterality preserved by lifting the entire body on a low podium (the 'Peribolius Templi' designated in Kip's engraving) and covered by a continuous pitched roof unobstructed by parapets. The choice of Doric subscribed to Fréart's perception of this order, representing '*Solidity* [which] ought not to [be employed] but in great massy Buildings . . . as . . . the Outside of *Churches* . . . where the Delicateness of the Ornament is neither convenient nor profitable'. The giant order continues round the advanced north and south porches (described in Eusebian language as 'Scalae Superius ascendentes Sedilia').[12] Hawksmoor reduced the solidity of the 'cella' wall by filling the intercolumniation with large windows linked by oversized, deeply shadowed keystones and aprons. Due to the existing unorthodoxy of the site, the west tower with its principal entrance was located in the churchyard, while the chancel faced towards the main thoroughfare and demanded its own architectural emphasis in the form of a full temple front *in antis* incorporating secondary doors leading into the aisles. As an afterthought Hawksmoor broke through the entablature of the pediment with an arch forming a monumental Serliana to reveal Queen Anne's statue (proposed on 25 June 1713) ensconced in a niche (pl. 404).[13] This would have aligned with Hawksmoor's proposed 'Via Regia' leading to his huge new chapel for Greenwich Hospital (pl. 357). Likely sources include Wren's preliminary study for the west front of St Paul's Cathedral dating from the 1690s, during Hawksmoor's tenure as draughtsman, and the fourth-century AD peristyle of Diocletian's Palace at Spalato (Split), which was incorporated in the Christian cathedral and illustrated in Wheler's *A Journey into Greece* (1682).[14] This Christian–pagan blend is reinforced by the four stone 'Altars Carv'd to stand upon the Pedestals before the East Portico each having Cherubs Heads and Festoons of Drapery' (pl. 401).[15]

St Alfege was the first British church to respond fully to Vanbrugh's call to create 'the Reverend look of a Temple'.[16] While in his capacity as a Commissioner, Vanbrugh participated only nominally as a designer (unlike Archer), and none of his New Churches drawings or models has been traced. However, independently his Newcastle pew (1723–5) attached to the south side of St George, Esher, Surrey, is a semi-transparent double tetrastyle Corinthian temple portico-like screen based on reconstructions of the Portico of Octavia in Desgodetz's *Les Edifices antiques de Rome* (1682).[17]

It was left to Gibbs, who had previously enthused on Rome's ancient temples for being 'so extremely fine and Noble . . . that nothing can come up to them in Cost nor beauty', to consummate this ideal in the New Churches.[18] On 14 May 1713, several months before being appointed co-surveyor, he offered unsolicited an astonishingly overt design, delivered as a model on 9 June (pl. 405): an Ionic peripteral temple of six by twelve columns with full pediments at both ends, raised on a single, all-encompassing stepped podium. Measuring (if built) 88 by 188 feet, Donaldson proclaimed it 'a splendour of architecture which has never been realized for churches in this country, and which . . . would

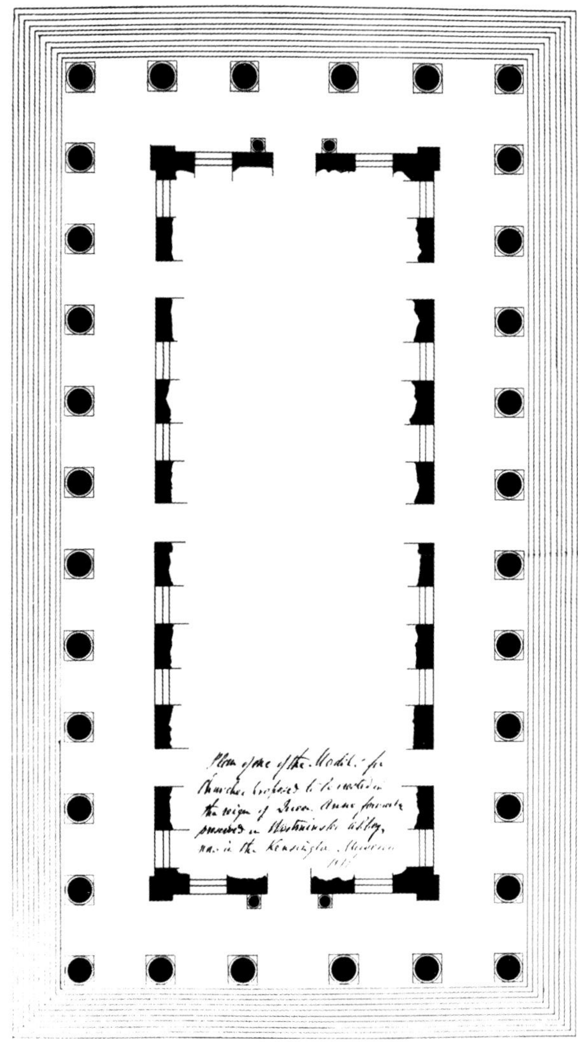

405 Thomas Leverton Donaldson. Plan of wooden model no. 9 for an unspecified 'Church with a Colonade round it of Ionick Order Steeple and inside finishing Complete', London, 1843. Pen and ink and wash. RIBA Library Drawings Collection, OS5/9(9). James Gibbs architect, 9 June 1713.

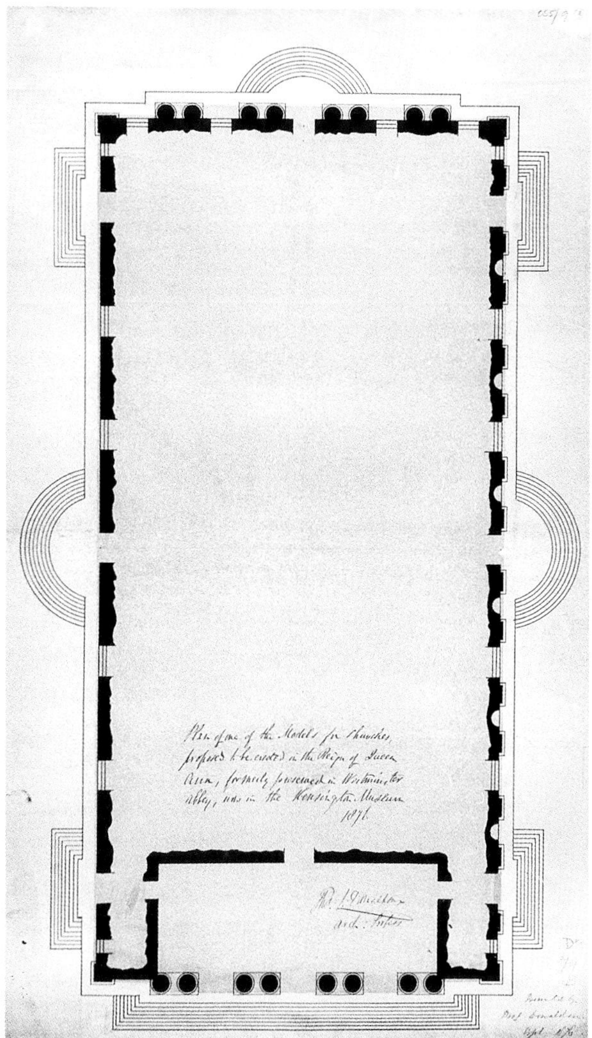

406 Thomas Leverton Donaldson. Plan of wooden model no. 12 for an unspecified 'Church Ornamtd. with pillasters of the Corinthian Ordr . . . Inside finished wth. Corinthian pillars Supporting the Roof all complete', London, 1843. Pen and ink and wash. RIBA Library Drawings Collection, OS5/9(12). James Gibbs architect, 24 July 1713.

in point of date have given us priority over the Madeleine at Paris' (begun 1806).[19] The inspiration may have been the long-vanished Temple of Diana at Ephesus as reconstructed from Pliny's account by Wren, who described it as 'a most surprizing Example of the *Grecian* Magnificence . . . two hundred and twenty Years in building . . . the first Instance of the Use of the *Ionick* Order'.[20] Wren, who had been 'for some time acquainted with Mr Gibbs, and have had opportunity's to observe his knowledge in Architecture', was his chief supporter in securing the coveted surveyorship in November 1714.[21] Apparently, only provision for the ubiquitous tower rising from the west end of its pitched roof disturbed the temple's antique purity. The source of this now-familiar but eccentric union of temple and tower, which had never before occurred in European ecclesiastical architecture, is obscure, but may have origins in the Ottoman transformation of the Athenian Parthenon from its original peripteral form (having already been converted to a Christian basilica in the sixth century) into a mosque by the addition of a soaring, independent minaret, which in engraved views appears to rise from the roof end.[22]

Gibbs's other design of 14 May 1713, delivered as a model on 24 July and also now known only in plan (pl. 406), would have been the largest of the New

407 Nicholas Hawksmoor. West elevation design, St Mary-le-Strand, London, 1713. Pen and ink and wash. City of Westminster Archives Centre, G131(6).

Churches at 92 by 192 by 70 feet and treated as a pseudoperipteral temple. At the west end an *in antis* portico of coupled Corinthian columns flanked by twin towers represented a return to Wren's cathedral (pl. 2), with the ensemble repeated, though now engaged, at the east end, and here too emphasised by a duo of towers, producing an Archerian silhouette (pl. 365). The paired order is repeated as giant pilasters along the flanks.[23]

408 Nicholas Hawksmoor. South elevation design, St Mary-le-Strand, London, 1713. Pen and ink and wash. City of Westminster Archives Centre, G131(7).

During the volatile period between the Act of Parliament for building a new church in the Strand (15 July 1713) and Gibbs's final approved design (4 November 1714), various proposals were also submitted by Archer, Dickinson, Vanbrugh and Hawksmoor (pls 407–8).[24] At cursory glance Hawksmoor's design of cubic body and prominent attic looks like a forerunner of St Mary Woolnoth, designed in 1716 (pl. 373), though without the mandatory tower. (Might this have been another of the architect's favoured detached structures?) The tiered niches filling the north and south elevations, however, which closely resemble his reconstruction of the Temple of Bacchus at Baalbek published in Maundrell's *Journey from Aleppo to Jerusalem* (1714 edition), as well as the stately Corinthian hexastyle portico, add a distinctive temple air.[25] This becomes unequivocal when the building is viewed along the full length of the side elevations (which the Strand island site would have permitted) to reveal the west portico seemingly bisecting the wider body then re-emerging at the east end to form the chancel in the pseudo-peripteral manner of the temples of Fortuna Virilis and of Antoninus and Faustina in Rome and the Maison Carrée in Nîmes (pl. 412).[26]

Hawksmoor's temple forms grew increasingly complex and deliberately more ambiguous within his preferred dual-axial planning, reaching a climax at St George, Bloomsbury (1716–31). This was largely due to the peculiarity of the site, surrounded by already existing three-storey domestic buildings to the west and east, each separated by narrow passages, and to the north defined by Little Russell Street, leaving only the thoroughfare of Hart Street (present-day Bloomsbury Way) to the south as the natural position of the principal entrance, marked by a prominent Corinthian hexastyle temple portico, the first to appear in a London church.[27] This led into an heroic interior, a square within a square, dominated on all sides by giant Serliana screens, that along the east centring on the chancel, with its magnificent mahogany reredos (pl. 376, reinstated to its original position in the recent World Monuments Fund restoration refiguration) and aligned to a monumental tower attached to the middle of the west elevation, incorporating within its base a secondary entrance. In this way the liturgical imperative of an eastern apse and the geographical one of a southern approach are reconciled. By contrast with the open-

409 Nicholas Hawksmoor. Part plan and west elevation design, 'S. George Bloomsbury', London, 1716. Pen and ink and wash. London Metropolitan Archives (Guildhall Library, H4/GEO).

ness of the interior, the outside is dominated by clear masses of plain surfaces, with each of the four elevations treated entirely differently. A close examination reveals Hawksmoor's hierarchical treatment of the principal components. The deep, Pantheonic south portico, with its delicate dentil and rosette entablature, has a second unembellished pediment rising directly behind over the higher, central clerestory. The portico, attached by engaged columns to the main block, is dressed with plainer but bolder scroll brackets in the entablature continuing along the east elevation. The shorter northern projection (enclosing the vestry and parish room beyond a second Serliana) is articulated by double tiers of Corinthian pilasters and engaged columns (reminiscent of the Roman Colosseum), with the smaller, enriched entablature reasserted: an organisation hinted at in Hawksmoor's nascent Strand offering (pl. 408). Finally, there is the wholly astylar demeanour of the tower base, articulated only by plain bands and stringcourses.[28] Hawksmoor allowed few concessions to homogeneity, as if these separate components had collided, especially poignant where the south portico and

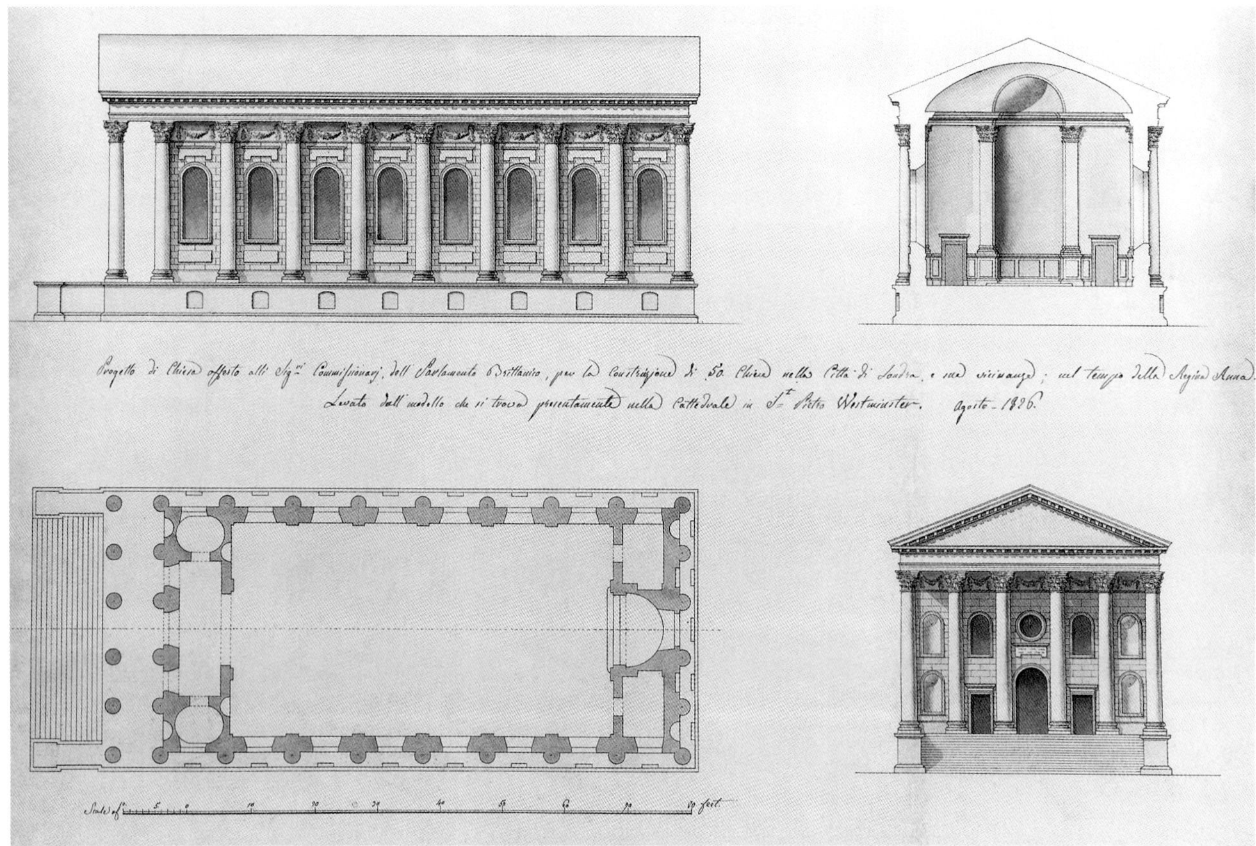

410 Charles Robert Cockerell. Plan, section and elevation of 'Modell of a Church 3 Quarts Columns of the Corinthian Order', 1826, St Mary-le-Strand, London. Pen and ink and wash. Victoria and Albert Museum, E.3024-1909. James Gibbs architect, 4 February 1714.

north projection meet the body, which itself carried an antique authority: the Roman Pantheon (pl. 671), as young Gibbs had accurately observed, where the 'Temple and Portico wer built att different times, as may be seen by the two Pediments, that built by Agrippa standing befor the Old one, as likewise by the joining of the portico to the old building looking on it flank ways'.[29] Nonetheless, St George's temple form endures, as revealed in a hitherto unpublished study for the west elevation (pl. 409), which probably dates to mid-1716, exposing an aspect of the church normally unseen in its full breadth due to the confined position. This antique resonance is reinforced by the dramatic exploitation, via Wren (pl. 476), of the long-vanished Mausoleum of Halicarnassus in Asia Minor, one of the Seven Wonders of the Ancient World, as the crown of the tower. An independent group of related Hawksmoor studies is particularly germane in that the substructures are monumental peripteral and pseudoperipteral temple forms.[30]

By contrast, Gibbs handled temple forms more straightforwardly, more radically in his first Strand exercise, represented by a model submitted on 4 February 1714 (pl. 410), the earliest detailed evidence of his architectural treatment of churches.[31] The uninterrupted pseudoperipteral Corinthian structure is anchored in the three celebrated antique temples in Rome and Nîmes mentioned above, but modified to accommodate Christian worship, most notably by reducing the portico's depth to a token screen to maximise internal space in what would have been the smallest of the New Churches (44 by 106 by 44 feet high), and by introducing tall, arched windows in the 'cella' walls to provide sufficient daylight. In turn, these expose failures in achieving unity of design. The portico's intercolumniation is one-third less than that of the body, weakening the profile; the western openings and niches are double-storeyed, with the unhappy result that their sills are unaligned with those along the side elevations. Gibbs attempted to remedy such inconsistencies by adding raised panels below the side windows, a motif retained in the executed building (pl. 378). The temple form was further jeopardised by raising an unspecified tower from the west end of the roof, as in the earlier

Ionic peripteral model (pl. 405), a solution that later re-emerged to pay striking dividends.[32]

In an unsolicited scheme by Gibbs's unfriendly rival Colen Campbell, who failed to secure an official place on the Commission, these crucial problems were wholly disregarded.[33] His 'New Design of my Invention for a Church in the Vitruvian Stile' published in *Vitruvius Britannicus* (1717; pl. 411), dedicated to one of the New Churches Commissioners, William Wake, who succeeded as Archbishop of Canterbury in the same year, was intended both as a manifesto of the avant-garde direction he envisaged ecclesiastical architecture moving in and a thinly disguised attack on St Mary-le-Strand, both Gibbs's model and the church as then under construction (pls 410, 378). An academically authentic adaptation of an antique temple, the accompanying text gives chapter-and-verse of its '*Prostile, Hexastile, Eustile* . . . Aspect which by Vitruvius, Palladio, and the general Concent of the most judicious Architects, both Ancient and Modern, is esteem'd the most beautiful and useful Disposition, being a Medium between the *Picnostile* and *Areostile*, the first being too close and the last too open'.[34] It relies closely on the triple-deep portico of the Maison Carrée (pl. 412), with only the order changed, as well as on its three-quarter-columned, unfenestrated rusticated walls, which would have made daytime services inconvenient. It was antithetical to Gibbs's executed church (pl. 378) in that it

> abstained from any Ornaments between the Columns, which would only serve to enflame the Expence and clog the Building. In those admirable Pieces of Antiquity, we find none of the trifling, licentious, and insignificant Ornaments, so much affected by some of our Moderns. The Ancients placed their chief Beauties in the justness of the Intercolumniations, the precise Proportions of the Orders and the greatness of Parts; nor have we one Precedent either from the *Greeks* or *Romans*, that they practiced two Orders, one over another in the same Temple in the Outside . . . much less to divide it into little Parts; and whereas the Ancients were contended with one continued [western] Pediment . . . we have no less than three in one Side where the Ancients never admitted any. This Practice must be imputed either to an entire Ignorance of Antiquity, or a Vanity to expose their absurd

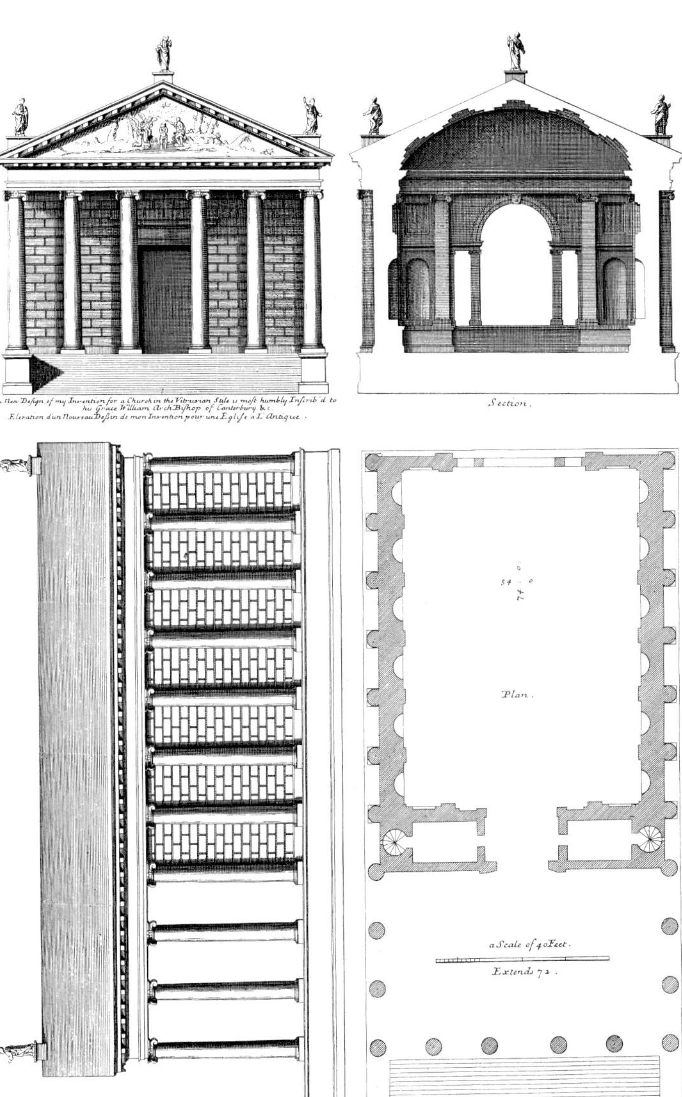

411 (*above*) Heinrich Hulsbergh after Colen Campbell. 'New Design of my Invention for a Church in the Vitruvian Stile' in C. Campbell, *Vitruvius Britannicus*, 1717, pl. 27. Engraving.

412 (*right*) François Girard. 'La Maison Quarree a Present L'Eglise des Grands Augustins', Nimes, France, detail, 1689. Engraving. The Bodleian Library, University of Oxford, Gough Maps 44, f. 213, picture 344. Erected *c.*1–10 AD.

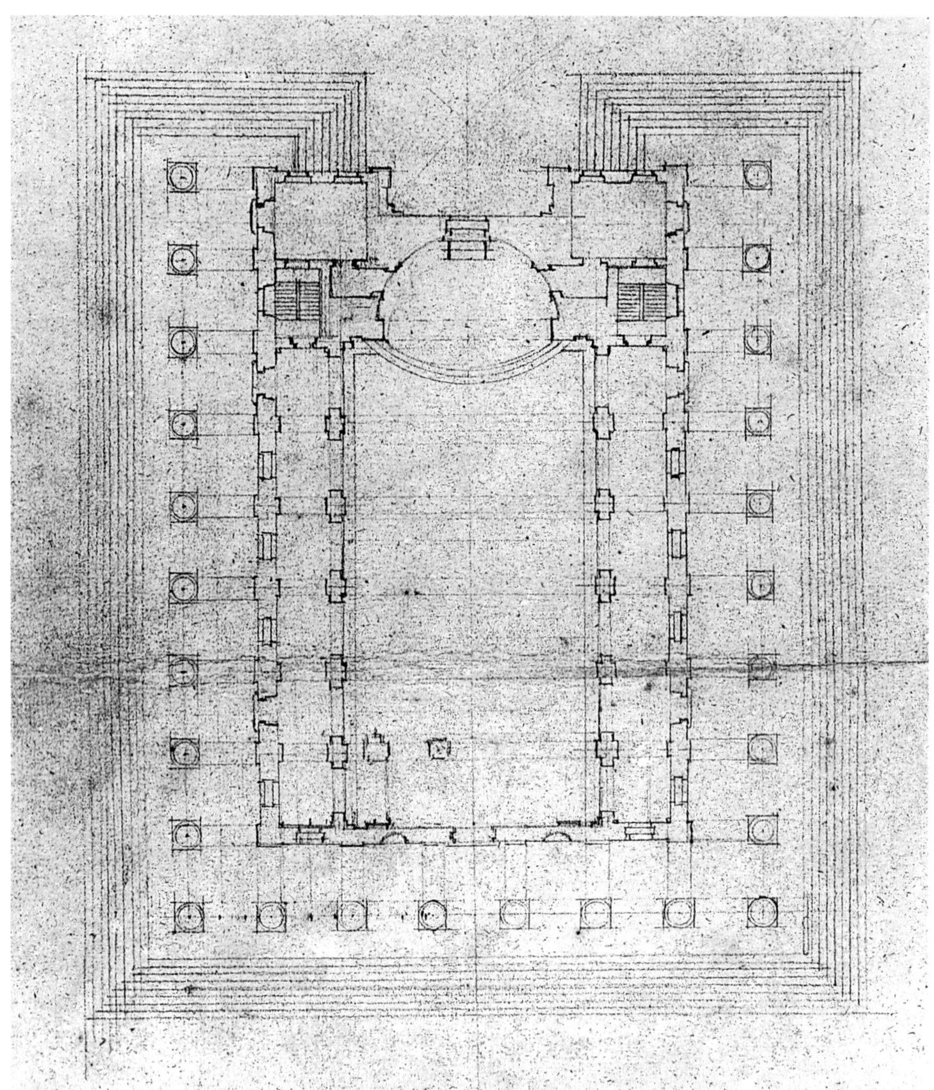

413 Alessandro Galilei. Plan design for an unidentified London peripteral doric church, detail, 1714–15. Pencil. Archivio di Stato, Florence, Galilei N.14/N/2, Box 109/48, f. 328.

> Novelties, so contrary to those excellent Precepts in *Vitruvius*, and so repugnant to those admirable Remains the Ancients have left us.[35]

There is no steeple and only the *Baptism of Christ* relief in the west pediment hints at the building's religious function. The interior has a continuous coffered barrel vault based on the Roman temple of Venus and Rome, which Palladio commended for its 'very carefully constructed and beautifully designed stucco compartments', while the windowless walls are articulated by repetitive pilasters and niches in the manner of Palladio's 'Corinthian Halls . . . with [engaged] columns on pedestals' and the Temple of Venus (or Diana) at Nîmes.[36] This austerity is poignant in the light of Hawksmoor's later remark to the Dean of Westminster that 'The primitive Christians, wanted Churches, they wou'd not, or cou'd not make use of the Temples of the Gentiles, how cou'd they? For the Cells of their Temples, were small and dark.'[37] To reconcile Christian requirements Campbell felt compelled to introduce a large, alien '*Venetian* Window' at the east end in order to 'sufficiently illuminate the whole Church'. In any case, the scheme would certainly have been too radical for the Commissioners' taste.[38]

Experiments in such extreme antique classicism were almost entirely conducted within the English Protestant sphere – no Continental equivalent then existed to my

414 Alessandro Galilei. West front design for an unidentified London peripteral doric church, 1714–15. Pencil. Archivio di Stato, Florence, Galilei N.14/N/2, Box 109/48, f. 316.

415 Alessandro Galilei. Interior west to east section design for an unidentified London peripteral doric church, 1714–15. Pencil. Archivio di Stato, Florence, Galilei N.14/N/2, Box 109/48, f. 317.

knowledge.[39] George Berkeley, the celebrated philosopher and divine, produced a peripteral temple-form church as the centrepiece of his visionary 'City of Bermuda' in the West Indies in the 1720s (pl. 729), the outcome of a visit to the Greek Doric temples of Sicily in 1718, which prompted him to expound, remarkably for this early date, 'that the old Romans were inferior to the Greeks, that the moderns fall infinitely short of both grandeur and simplicity of taste'.[40] This goes some way to account for the unlikely appearance of Alessandro Galilei's astonishingly avant-garde New Churches essay of 1714–15 for an externally fully formed Doric octastyle peripteral temple (pls 413–14). Perhaps it was motivated by the failure to attract interest in his unsuitably overt Italian baroque offerings (pl. 381) and access to Gibbs's Ionic peripteral model of 1713, then displayed in the Commissioners' Lincoln's Inn Fields headquarters (pl. 405).[41] In Galilei's scheme the abruptly discontinued colonnade at the east end leaves the chancel wall externally exposed, rare in antiquity but implicit in Palladio's reconstruction of the ruined Temple of Mars the Avenger in Rome, where rear columns were unnecessary since the building abutted the forum's perimeter wall.[42] Inside (pl. 415), the full-height, undemonstrative apsidal chancel with its coffered semi-dome framed by giant order pilasters, the heroic climax of the basilica, recalls the Temple of Venus and Rome, the subject also of Palladio's reconstruction.[43]

No European architect of the early eighteenth century so fully embraced the archaeological potentials of the rectangular temple-form church, marking the pinnacle of this brief, remarkable episode, a unique phenomenon in European classicism of the time. While only Greenwich was realised of the pseudoperipteral forms (pls 403–4), it would be true to say that each of the various experiments described in this chapter led inevitably to the creation of the most daringly original and influential of all temple-churches, St Martin-in-the-Fields, standing on the cusp between the baroque and the neoclassical (pl. 416).

> O *Gibbs*, whose Art the solemn Fane can raise,
> Where *God* delights to dwell, and *Man* to praise[44]

The year 1726 marked a momentous juncture in the development of Georgian classical church design. On 20 October, at the consecration of St Martin's, the vicar, Dr Zachariah Pearce, preached a sermon in which he denied that the display of 'Idolatrous or Supersitious' features 'can mislead true Piety' and exonerated Gibbs of the charge of sinking into Popishness levelled against him during the building of St Mary-le-Strand.[45] Alexander Gordon, the Scottish antiquary, in the preface to *Itinerarium Septentrionale; or, A Journey Thro' most of the Counties of Scotland, And Those in the North of England*, published around the same time, expressed his belief that if the

> fine Humour for Architecture [inspired by] the august Remains of so many Monuments of Grecian and Roman Buildings [including] elegant Temples; yet standing in the Forum Romanum . . . subsist in the Nation, and such Buildings as the great Artist Mr Gibbs has adorn'd London with, continues to be carried on, very few Cities in Europe (Rome excepted) will contend with it for Magnificence.[46]

Gordon was not alone in praising this consummate modern Christian reinvention of an antique pseudoperipteral temple form. The Palladian theorist Robert Morris, detecting that in classical porticoes 'something Majestick strikes the Imagination', compared St Martin's with

> some of the ancient Temples of *Greece*, in the works of Vitruvius, or the *Pantheon* at *Rome* [where] you will discover true elegance of Design, and a happy refinement of Taste. To see Buildings of more than 2000 years distance in Date be thought worthy of Imitation, shows not only the excellency of Architecture in those Times, but the Genius of this present Age, who can divest themselves of modern Error, to trace the Paths of Antiquity.[47]

The Frenchman André Rouquet, in *The Present State of the Arts in England* (1755), went so far as to describe Gibbs's portico as 'borrowed from a Greek temple without any alteration. By this choice, the architect has shewn the elegancy of his taste, and the solidity of his judgment.'[48] The process during 1720 to 1722 of reaching a final design for this, the principal Hanoverian church, is supported by an abundance of parish documents, drawings, a magnificent wooden model and the largely unaltered building itself, which together reveal Gibbs's inventive genius in integrating the essential components of portico, body and steeple, his most original and beautiful architectural idea.[49] A vital clue to this complex business comes from Pearce's 'An Essay on the Origin and Progress of Temples', published alongside his consecration sermon, in which he puts forward the notion that in ancient times temples 'became covered entirely with Roofs, and closed at Top; and . . . then the Porticos . . . were built on the Outside', but that these features were not 'contrived at once, and

416 John Harris after James Gibbs. Plan and south-west 'Perspective View of St. Martins Church', St Martin-in-the-Fields, London, in Gibbs 1728, pl. 1. Engraving.

brought to their Perfection as soon as they were thought of . . . more likely . . . they advanced by Steps and Degrees'.[50]

The monumental hexastyle temple portico began in early 1721 as a full-width Ionic columnar screen placed close to the west wall, as had those on the Ionic and Strand models (pls 405, 410) and in schemes by Hawksmoor and Galilei (pls 402, 413). The first bay of the side elevations is aligned directly beneath the steeple, which rises from the peak of the pitched roof (an idea already tried in Gibbs's model of 1713, pl. 405). This bay is differentiated only by a diminutive distyle pedimented porch, a motif repeated in the last bay at the east end. Giant order Ionic pilasters separate the intervening, double-storey windowed bays. In subsequent variations the order becomes Corinthian, with its potent ancient religious resonance – 'Roman Architecture, and the Corinthian Order owe their Perfection to the excellent *Structure*' of Solomon's Temple.[51] The building eventually evolved into the 'Approved Design' of 23 May 1721, from which an elaborate wooden model was made (pl. 113). Then followed an inspired sequence of subtle modifications. The overall width of the hexastyle portico was reduced by 20 feet, exposing narrow sections of solid wall between it and the corners of the body. At the conjunction of the portico's roof and the wider one of the body the crowning open balustrades turn inward towards the front of the steeple base. The corresponding western bays were widened by 5 feet and recessed from the main line of pilasters to accommodate a pair of free-standing, giant order columns *in antis*, creating a visually powerful substructure for the steeple in which diminutive versions of the articulation are repeated, here slightly projecting from the block.[52] On 31 October 1721 the Commissioners ordered the steeple base raised 'higher then is Expressed in the Modell but left to the Judgment of Mr Gibbs how much higher'. On 3 November 1722, after construction on the body began, they considered alterations to the portico 'Expressed . . . in a plan . . . prepared for that purpose' and on 4 January 1723 'unanimously approved . . . the proposed alteration of the breadth of the portico . . . more than . . . in the Originall Modell', finally arriving at the executed composition (pl. 416). This involved increasing the portico's depth by 12 feet in order to insert an additional column in both outer rows, resulting in creating a bolder Pantheonic-Bloomsbury form (pl. 409), reminiscent also of Hawksmoor's Strand design (pl. 408). Now the total height of the steeple from pavement to tip of spire equals the full length of the building, with the portico's revised two-column profile, set back from the body, reiterated in the pair of columns *in antis* at each end, as revealed in the accompanying plan (pl. 416). It says much about Gibbs's talent as a designer that, despite the steeple's soaring prominence, the building still retains a powerful temple presence.

The interior underwent correspondingly dramatic changes (pl. 417). The doubled portico columns and paired *in antis* ones seem to penetrate the rectangle and continue as shorter though still monumental columns separating nave and aisles (echoing the external pilasters), blurring the transition to the narrower, shallow chancel by concave penultimate bays. These are given special prominence by piercing the walls with large, theatre-like boxes occupied by the royal family, accessed by private column *in antis* entrances.[53] To affirm this columnar continuity the Wrenian system of columns on piers (for example, at St James, Westminster) was rejected in favour of giant orders with gallery fronts attached midway up the shafts, an ensemble of perhaps authentic antique origin.[54] Relying on a system termed the dosseret entablature block derived from Santa Costanza in Rome (pl. 388) via Wren's St Bride, Fleet Street (1671–8), Gibbs isolated the capitals with their entablature sections and sprung arches that merge into the barrel-vaulted ceiling, opening up expansive vistas from the galleries and allowing daylight to flood into the body. An anti-classical solecism and previously rarely appearing in post-antique Western architecture, the dosseret came to signify a specifically Hanoverian imagery, with a probable source in Holy Trinity, Wolfenbüttel, Lower Saxony (1705–19).[55]

Later times have come to regard St Martin's as the Georgian church par excellence, but initially it was severely criticised. James Ralph in *A Critical Review of the Publick Buildings, Statues and Ornaments In, and about London and Westminster* (1734), while admiring the 'elegant and august' portico, the steeple 'as one of the most tolerable in town', the 'very fine effect [of the] round columns, at each angle . . . in the profile of the building [and the] remarkably elegant' east end, faulted how 'the architect . . . in compliance to the galleries . . . revers'd the order of the windows, it being always usual to have the large ones nearest the eye, and the small . . . on the top'. Batty Langley in the *Grub-street Journal* of the same year thought the elevations might have been 'the finest ranges of pillasters and columns yet erected, either by ancients or moderns, had not their magnificence been . . . interrupted by those ridiculous block rustics in the architraves of the windows, which are of small dimension, and have no affinity with the

417 George Bickham after Thomas Malton. View towards the chancel of 'The Inside of St. Martin in the Fields in the Liberty of Westminster', London, undated. Engraving. Author's collection.

whole', hence known popularly as a 'Gibbs surround',[56] adding: 'Besides, rustics are properly the ornament of the Tuscan order . . . and this is a sufficient proof, that to introduce rustics with the Corinthian order, is a great absurdity'. In *Ancient Masonry* (1736), Langley identified the mannerist source of the rusticated block and ridiculed Gibbs's 'very pretty Invention [which] would better become a Frontispiece to a Pastrycook's shop, than they do the Windows and Doors to . . . St *Martin in the Fields*, as being analogous to the rusticated Edges of Pasties and pies'. Its origin lay in the Italian renaissance.[57] Moreover, the internal dosseret made the columns 'seem to be crowded with capital super capital', while his condemnation of the use of internal giant order columns highlights one of the central issues of adapting antique temple forms to modern churches.

> As the ancients deemed it an absurdity to introduce two heights of rooms, within the height of one order . . . so I think 'tis as absurd to place the galleries in a church to cut against the shafts of columns . . . this destroys the beauty of the columns, by hindering them from being seen clear throughout their entire height.[58]

Such anomalies, however, did not prevent St Martin's becoming the most influential church pattern in the English-speaking world.

Though Gibbs intended *A Book of Architecture* (1728), which devoted the first fifteen plates to St Martin's, to be 'of use to such Gentlemen as might be concerned in Building, especially in the remote parts of the Country, where little or no assistance for Designs can be procured',[59] in late 1721 the building committee forbade anyone to record the model, so that it was not until mid-1726, when the church neared completion and its scaffolding was finally removed, that the public caught its first sight of 'indisputably the most magnificent Parochial Church in *London*'.[60] Nonetheless, its appearance was already well known among those involved with other church building activities, most notably Sir William Dawes, a New Churches

COLL. REG. OXON. CONSPECTVS CAPELLÆ ET REFECTORII, AD AVSTRVM

418 Joseph Smith. South elevation design, 'Coll. Reg. Oxon. Conspectus et Refectorii, Ad Austrum', Queen's College chapel, Oxford, Oxfordshire, undated. Engraving. Author's collection. George Clarke and William Townesend architects, 1708–19, except tower.

Commissioner (from 1712 in his capacity as Bishop of Chester, then from 1715 until his death in 1727 as Archbishop of York).[61] On 1 November 1719 he consecrated Queen's College chapel, Oxford (begun 1708), designed by William Townesend and George Clarke (also appointed a Commissioner in 1712).[62] The main elevation (pl. 418), combining chapel and hall within a unified Roman Doric pseudoperipteral ensemble owing much to St Alfege, Greenwich (pl. 403), is additionally interesting in respect to an early, unrealised suggestion for crowning the prostyle portico with a steeple duplicating Carlo Rainaldi's abortive but engraved bell-towers for St Peter, Rome, a nod to the Italianate taste celebrated by Gibbs.[63]

Furthermore, a month earlier, on 2 October 1719, Dawes issued a faculty for erecting an entirely new church in Sheffield, Yorkshire, directing its thirty-seven-man building committee to 'procure a model . . . to be made or Drawn' for his approval, a practice de rigueur in London but still rare in the provinces.[64] Between 1720 and 1725 the carcass of the body and the tower base were constructed, perhaps to the design of Ralph Tunnicliffe of Rotherham, but with the interior left unfinished until 1772 due to prolonged bickering among various parish factions (recounted in Doc. 161, pp. 467–8). Demolished in 1938, it was a substantial building of rare sophistication for its time and place (pl. 421). Pseudoperipteral Roman Doric, constructed entirely of stone and measuring 70 by 125 feet, with a tower rising 117 feet, it was almost identical in size to St Alfege, which was clearly its main inspiration (pl. 403), though bereft of pedimental ends and a solid parapet, which would have made it a true temple form.[65] The full-height order was echoed internally (pl. 422) by free-standing Corinthian columns supporting galleries in the manner of St Martin-in-the-Fields, while the arcuation and fluted pilasters of the chancel still subscribed to a composition popularised at St Paul's Cathedral (pl. 361). The first congregation must have been electrified by this new breed of classical church, long used to worshipping in the medieval parish church, previously the only House of God in the industrial town, while 'Notwithstanding all possible Care . . . to make it Capable of Containing one of the largest Congrega-tions in this Kingdome [has become] irregular . . . crowded and darkened with old Lofts and Pews like a Scotch kirk.'[66]

Dawes's faculty of 1722, authorising the building of a new church in nearby Leeds, also directed the building committee, which included his son-in-law, to

419 (*above*) Benjamin Cole. South elevation of wooden model for Holy Trinity, Leeds, Yorkshire, 1 April 1723 (now lost), in Thoresby 1724, following p. 42. William Etty architect, 1723–7.

420 (*right*) William Halfpenny. South-west view, 'Church [Holy Trinity] . . . of my Invention for Leeds in Yorkshire', 1723, in Halfpenny 1725. Engraving.

'procure a plan or Modell . . . made or drawn, and Approved of, by Us'.[67] When the project was launched in 1714, Ralph Thoresby, the distinguished local antiquary involved in the operation, travelled to London in search of inspiration. He, too, was captivated by St Alfege, Greenwich – 'a most noble . . . new church . . . with pillars in the front, like that of [St Paul] Covent Garden, but much more stately'[68] – and through connections with the Society for Promoting Christian Knowledge, which shared premises in Lincoln's Inn Fields with the New Churches Commissioners, saw the display of the 'curious and noble models of many churches proposed to be built', with their preponderance for temple forms.[69] Nothing further happened at Leeds until 1723, when William Halfpenny submitted a design, which he subsequently published without explanation (pl. 420).[70] This is an amalgamation of St Martin-in-the-Fields (whose periphery walls were rising at the time) (pl. 416), Colen Campbell-like open pedimented windows (pl. 515)[71] and an open colon-

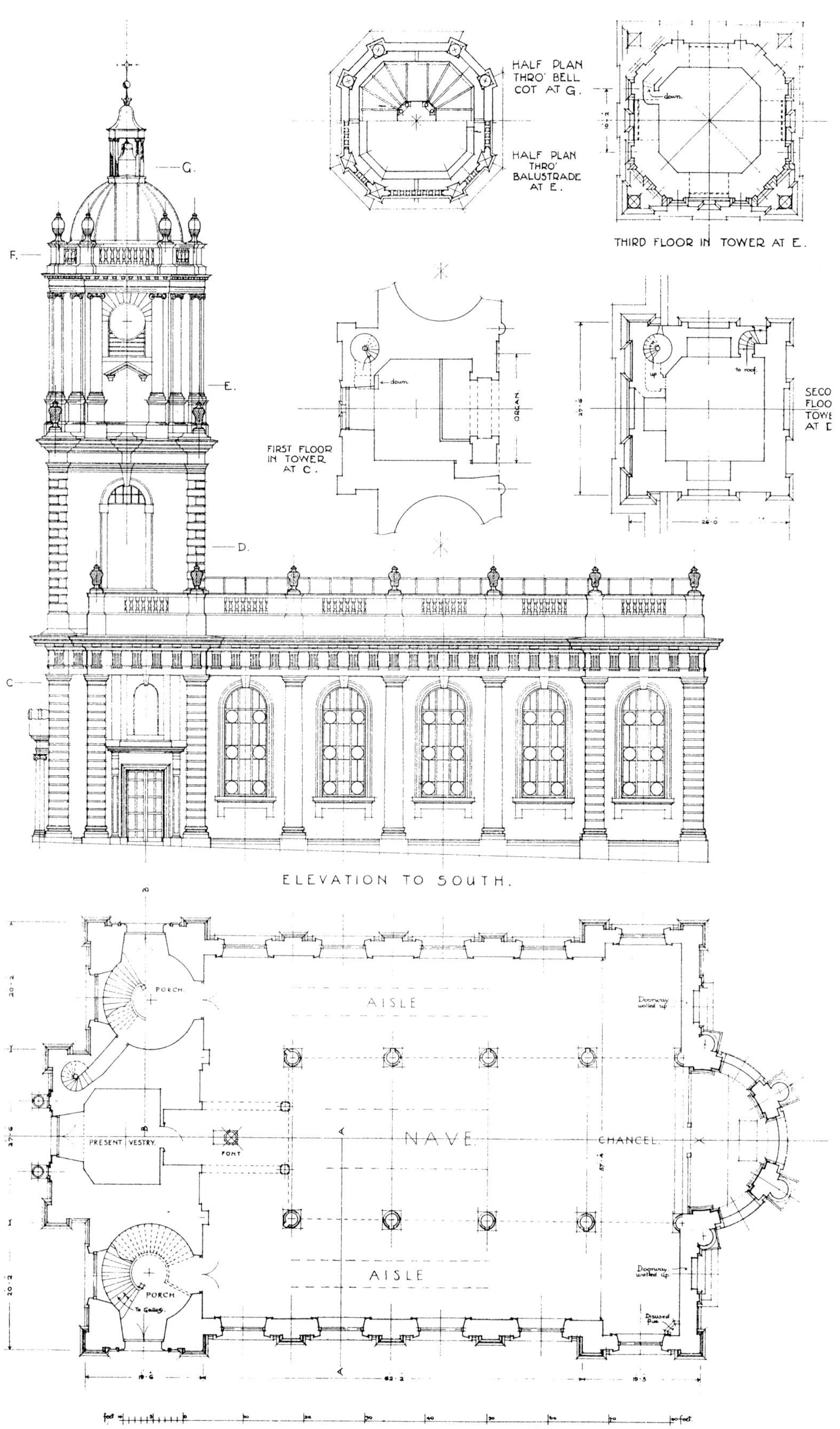

421 J. Lombardini Northam. Plans and south elevation, St Paul, Sheffield, Yorkshire, in *Building News*, vol. 100, 23 June 1911, pp. 876–7, fig. 61. Ralph Tunnicliffe, attributed, and John Platt II architects, 1720–72, demolished 1938.

422 Ralph Tunnicliffe, attributed and John Platt II. Interior towards chancel, St Paul, Sheffield, Yorkshire, 1720–72, demolished 1938. English Heritage (National Monuments Record, BB48/1358).

naded bell stage surmounted by a pyramidal roof suggesting familiarity with ancient Greek tomb architecture in Asia Minor.[72] The preferred design was by the leading York architect William Etty, who had been working under Vanbrugh at Castle Howard since 1701, made occasional journeys to London and exhibited a penchant for the Roman Doric.[73] He received £19 19s. 0d. on 1 April 1723 for supplying a wooden model (untraced), subsequently engraved (pl. 419), which was described to Thoresby as intended 'for our Workmen to go by . . . I believe you'll be surprised when I tell you we have got the north side 4 yards high . . . and our Work-men hopes . . . to Rear in Good time the next Summer [which] I believe is better news to you then that of Rosting bishops'.[74] While the alternating pedimented aisle windows look back to St Mary-le-Strand (pl. 378), the 'Gibbs-surround' door cases, as well as the internal echo of the giant order pilasters as free-standing columns supporting gallery fronts and the chancel's Serliana, a leitmotif of the new classicism, though clearly an afterthought, suggest knowledge of St Martin-in-the-Fields.

The first appearance of a temple-form church (again devoid of end pediments) in north-west England was St George, Derby Square, Liverpool, 1725–34 (pl. 38), the masterpiece of the architect-alderman Thomas Steers, a Londoner who settled in the town in 1709 but continued to own property at Rotherhithe, just up the Thames from Greenwich, where he might well have observed St Alfege under construction.[75] Nor is it insignificant that he supplied the Sheffield committee with vital building information for their proposed new church sometime in the 1720s.[76] At St George he enriched these prototypes by adding three-quarter columns over pairs of half-pilasters along the side elevations, strengthened at the corners by paired orders and throughout by projecting pedestals, entablature sections, panelled parapets and vases. One incidental yet compelling detail binds St George to the London New Churches. An early description noted the 'remains of eight paintings of saints . . . long since defaced' in the upper stage of the tower, shown in the above view as blank surfaces, which may have derived from the 'Black Marble Slabs on the apertures of the East Turrets' of St Anne, Limehouse, on the north bank of the Thames immediately opposite Rotherhithe.[77]

During the 1720s Gibbs asserted his presence as an innovative church designer in the provinces with All Saints, Derby (pl. 423). Here the preservation of the magnificent 178-foot-high Perpendicular west tower excluded the possibility of repeating the successful London formula but allowed him to explore an alter-

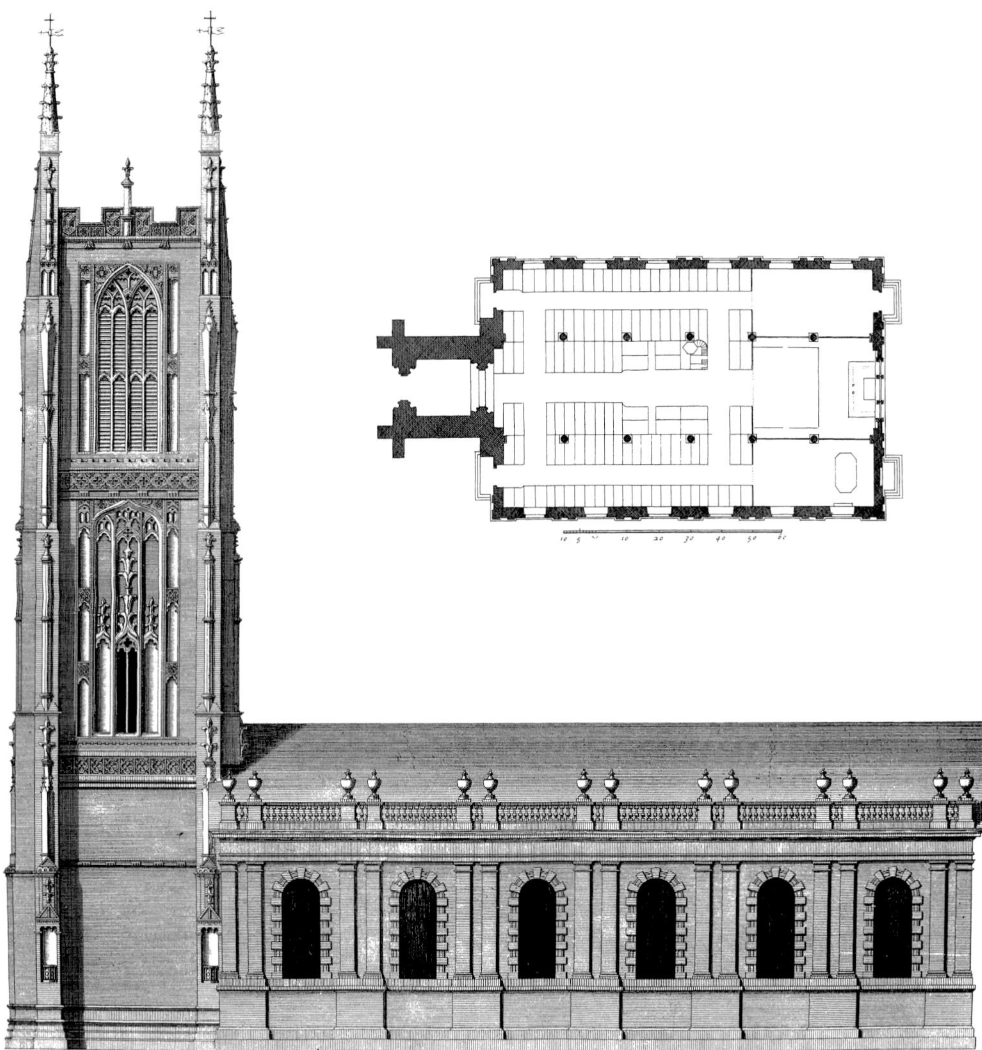

423 Heinrich Hulsbergh after James Gibbs. Plan and south elevation, 'The Church of Allhallows in Derby', Derbyshire, in Gibbs 1728, pl. 26. Engraving. James Gibbs architect, 1723–8, altered 1967–72; tower, early sixteenth century.

native pseudoperipteral temple form of paired Tuscan pilasters and St Martin-like block-rustic windows sandwiched between a deep podium and an unbroken entablature reinforced by a full-width pediment at the east end (pl. 424), a St Martin's variation (pl. 425). The pilasters, however, which an early visitor perhaps justifiably condemned for looking 'mean [and] too small for the building & of no significance',[78] neither perform the decisive structural role nor so precisely echo the internal columnar arrangement as they do in London. Here the important innovation is the omission of side galleries, which Gibbs insisted was 'more beautiful', since both galleries and pews 'clog up and spoil the Inside of Churches, and take away from the right Proportion, which they otherwise would have, and are only justifiable as they are necessary'.[79] Preference was given for incorporating the chancel within the two eastern bays of the body, enclosed by wrought-iron screens, resulting in a single space covered by an unbroken, all embracing roof.

Gibbs's intention that *A Book of Architecture* (1728), where Derby is represented by two engravings, would have an impact far beyond the metropolis, as expressed in the pattern book's introduction quoted earlier, was fulfilled at All Saints, Gainsborough, Lincolnshire (pl. 426), designed and constructed by Derby's 'Master builder' Francis Smith of Warwick. Here, too, the medieval west tower was preserved, while the body was rebuilt to a larger size and 'in an different Manner', enveloped by identical bays of block-rustic windows

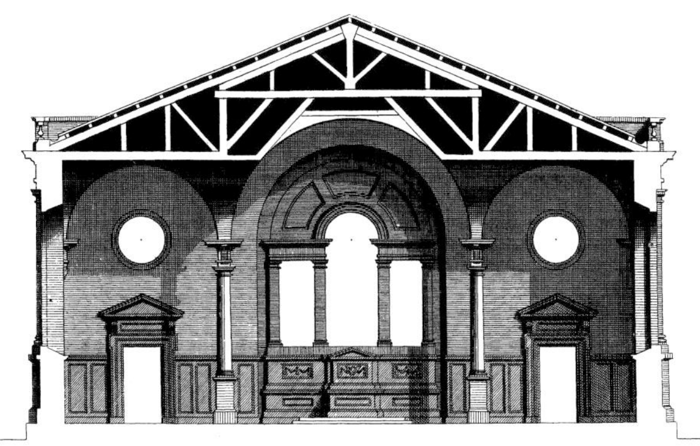

The East end of the New Church att Derby.

424 (*above left*) Heinrich Hulsberg after James Gibbs. 'Section' and 'East end', All Hallows or All Saints (now Cathedral), Derby, Derbyshire, in Gibbs 1728, pl. 27. Engraving. J. Gibbs architect, 1723–8, altered 1967–72.

425 (*top right*) James Gibbs. East elevation, St Martin-in-the-Fields, London, 1721–7.

426 (*above right*) Francis Smith. South-east view, All Saints, Gainsborough, Lincolnshire, 1734–44.

(taller above shorter) separated by giant Tuscan pilasters but without the now-superfluous *in antis* bays. The triple choir – 'Ancient Gothick Buildings . . . much too low for answering any new Design' – was replaced by 'a Cove only'.[80] The Revd Pococke found the effect 'rather heavy' but liked the interior 'handsomely fitted with galleries', which are attached to giant order Corinthian columns, though they support straight entablatures appropriate for an uncommonly ambitious but not extravagant country church.[81]

In Glasgow, which Defoe lauded as 'a city of business . . . the cleanest . . . beautifullest, and best built . . . in Britain, London excepted',[82] St Andrew (pl. 427), the first new church erected there since the Reformation and conceived on an unprecedented scale (70 by 130 feet), received the full Gibbsian panoply of prostyle hexastyle portico, lofty tower, Corinthian pseudoperipteral body and glamorously decorated interior complete with dosseret columns (pl. 429). Its launch conveniently coincided with the reissue of *A Book of Architecture* in 1739. The contract for gallery fronts specifies that they 'conform to Saint Martines . . . in the Fields',[83] a consanguinity widely recognised at the time. One commentator even claimed the 'inside excels St Martin's [with the] Stucco ornaments . . . in a finer taste'; Thomas Pennant counted it 'one of the very

427 Allan Dreghorn. South-west view, St Andrew, Glasgow, Strathclyde, Scotland, 1739–57. Andersonian Library.

428 Allan Dreghorn. South-east view, St Andrew, Glasgow, Strathclyde, Scotland, 1739–57.

few exceptions to the slovenly and indecent manner in which the house of God, in Scotland, are kept'.[84] Aspirations to rival the English capital are self-evident in the choice of fine materials, particularly mahogany for the internal panelling and furnishings, the richness of rococo plaster decoration and pride in recording the achievements of the principal craftsmen, including the stone carver David Caution, responsible for the opulent Corinthian and Composite capitals, entablatures, scrolled modillions and so forth; Thomas Clayton, a 'stucco worker' based at nearby Hamilton; and David Easton, proprietor of a local silk manufactory, who supplied crimson and blue velvet for the upholstery. However, the building was hardly free of faults. The yellow sandstone from East Cowcaddens was 'extremely bad . . . in many Places entirely green [which] takes off greatly from the beauty', as well as disturbing the classical unity, and by 1796 the decayed sections were replaced by 'more durable' specimens, causing a patchiness still blemishing the fabric (pl. 428). The 'very handsome . . . large elegant porch [is] much disfigured by the slender square tower with petter-pox [*sic*] top . . . too little tapered towards the top', rising 170 feet from the pavement but wholly unintegrated with the body. This was, it was claimed, 'owing to the Obstinacy

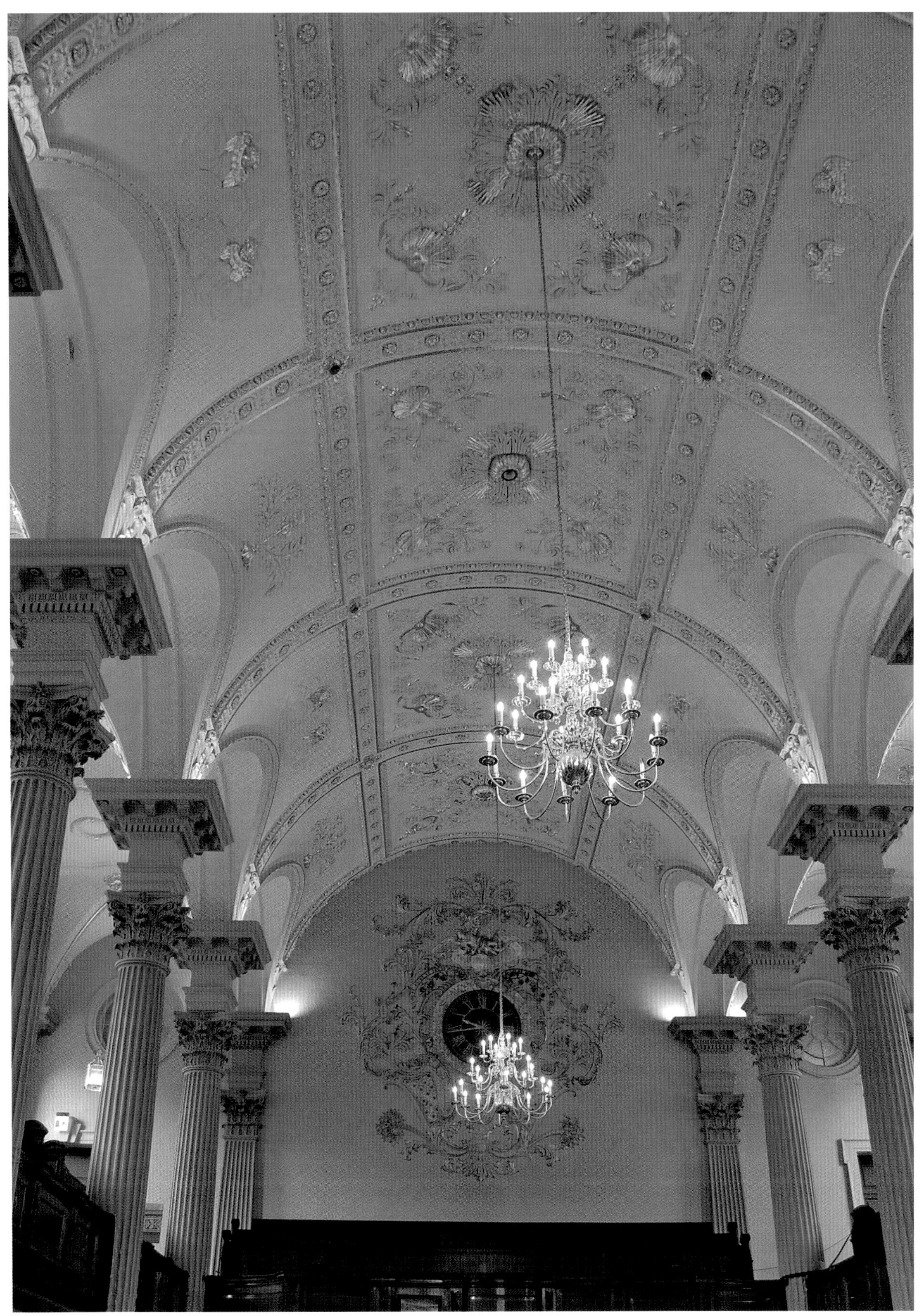

429 Allan Dreghorn. Interior towards west, St Andrew, Glasgow, Strathclyde, Scotland, 1739–57, following restoration in 2009. Courtesy Glasgow City Council, 0283.jpg.

430 (*above*) John James. Design for north elevation, St George, Hanover Square, London, *c.*1720. Pen and ink and wash. RIBA Library Drawings Collection, J9/2.

431 (*left*) John James. Detail of north-west elevations, St George, Hanover Square, London, 1720–28.

& Ignorance of the People [who controlled construction], not to any Blunder of the Architect'.[85] Can this be true? And, if so, was it a misdemeanour that also explains a similar waywardness at St Anne, Manchester (pl. 444)?

As early as the 1720s there was an inclination towards dissipating fully fledged temple forms, as seen in instances of proscribed pediments. Symptomatic of this breakdown is St George, Hanover Square, John James's only major independent London church (pl. 11), which reveals his penchant for disengaging rather than integrating crucial elements and his awkward methods of resolving formal issues in late New Churches design. In his precisely rendered presentation drawing (pl. 430), a rarity among his surviving preparatory material, the north (Great Maddox Street) elevation is articulated by isolated, Woolnoth-like tabernacles (pl. 374) set against plain astylar walls but lacking Borrominiesque excitement. Though several writers commented on similarities with St Martin-in-the-Fields (pl. 416),[86] the hexastyle temple portico is more Hawksmoorian than Gibbsian in its lack of unity, more closely resembling Bloomsbury (pl. 354), hardly surprising since the church was designed and built during the time that James and Hawksmoor shared the surveyorship.[87] Nor is there anything of Gibbs's fluid integration of portico, body and steeple; rather, James treated each as independent, disconnected components (pl. 431), so much so that it is questionable if the temple-form solution was even in his mind. At Limehouse, Hawksmoor inserted the lateral, pedimented-ended attic blocks between body and steeple to signify bays containing the principal entrance lobbies flanking the circular baptistery[88] – the equivalent to St Martin's powerful *in antis* doors leading to gallery staircases – while also lending visual stability to the soaring steeple. By contrast, James's attic surmounts a slightly projecting bay whose internal function is unclear. His steeple is unprepossessing in a church catering for an affluent West End parish.[89] Unlike St Martin's (pl. 417), nothing of this treatment anticipates the interior (pl. 432), which depends entirely on existing Wrenian formulas, with the nave, aisle, gallery and chancel ceilings differently patterned and entirely segregated from one another. For James, this marked the fulfilment of his earlier aspiration to gain the surveyorship,

432 Frederick Nash. Interior towards west of St George, Hanover Square, London, *c.*1810. Watercolour. London Metropolitan Archives (Guildhall Library), 19641. John James architect, 1720–28.

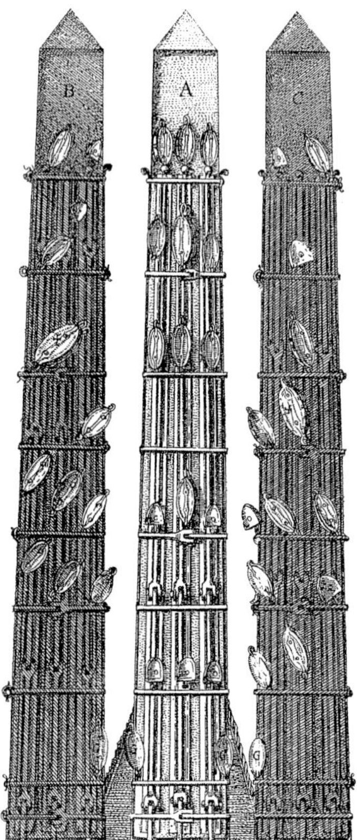

not as an Assistant for when my Designs & Estimates will be continually Subject to their [the co-surveyors'] Inspection and Reports; but to be upon the Same foot as They are . . . that I may once in my life have an Opportunity of Shewing that the Beautys of Architecture may consist with the greatest plainness of the Structure, and that Estimates of Cost may be made with as much exactness as was required by the Grecians.[90]

James's and Hawksmoor's collaborative experiments at St Luke, Old Street, and St John Horselydown (both 1727–33) concentrated on the fundamental temple components of all-embracing pedimented roofs covering rectangular bodies purged wholly of the classical order, the result of financial constraints imposed on the last of the New Churches, in which the Commissioners ordered that they be built 'as cheap as possible'.[91] The redeeming feature of the first (pl. 433) is its monolithic, obelisk-shaped west tower, lofty and imposing without incurring the excessive costs associated with the fancy structures of some of Wren's and Gibbs's creations, yet deserving 'some applause [for] being the only one of its kind in this kingdom'.[92] It has antique connotations without any precise precedent for its fluted shaft, which was carved *in situ*,[93] though it might be fruitful to see a direct source in the colossal Egyptian obelisk in Piazza San Pietro, which in Domenico Fontana's account of 1590, a copy of which Hawksmoor owned, is shown temporarily secured to wooden capstans by parallel lifting ropes (pl. 434).[94] Horselydown's equally unique tower (pl. 435) may have grown out of the Commissioners' unfulfilled resolution to erect St Mary-le-Strand's steeple 'in the Form of a pillar' crowned by Queen Anne's statue.[95] The Hawksmoor-James version was described as 'an insulate column . . . in the manner of . . . TRAJAN' in Rome, though 'had it been larger and higher (as the beauty and magnificence of such columns consist in their largeness) would have had a

433 (*above left*) Nicholas Hawksmoor and John James. North-east view, St Luke, Old Street, London, 1727–33, bombed 1940, restored as concert hall 1998.

434 (*left*) 'Finito che fv il Castello, La Gvglia vi si Tiro sotto Tanzo, Inanzi', the Vatican obelisk, Rome, in Fontana 1590, pl. 28, detail. Engraving.

435 (*facing page*) J. W. Edy after John Buckler. North-west view, St John and Vestry, Southwark, London, 1 June 1799, detail. Engraving. © The British Library Board, K.Top. XXVII-52-1. Nicholas Hawksmoor and John James architects, 1727–33, bombed in Blitz 1940, church demolished 1948.

most glorious effect'.[96] In the body the sundering of standard classical forms is stronger: main walls abruptly projecting and recessing, Serliana serving as side entrances rather than illuminating chancels, roof pediments broken by grand consoles and interrupted by tower bases.

Looking again beyond London, John Price Sr and Jr's St George's Chapel, Great Yarmouth, Norfolk (pl. 13), with its giant order pilasters, Doric and Corinthian on the west and east, both surmounted by broken-bottom pediments, while on the north and south taller, isolated, aggressively full Doric with dosseret entablatures supporting a feeble parapet, the four elevations separated by polylobed bays, is a quirky disintegration of the temple form.[97]

The awkward site of John Harvey's St Michael Extra Muros, Bath, at the intersection of two thoroughfares (pl. 436), with the ensuing breakdown of symmetry and ill-advised introduction of a prostyle tetrastyle portico, was publicly trashed by John Wood Sr (whose rival design had been rejected) as a 'whimsical Fabrick . . . in a Taste so peculiar to himself, that the very Journey-

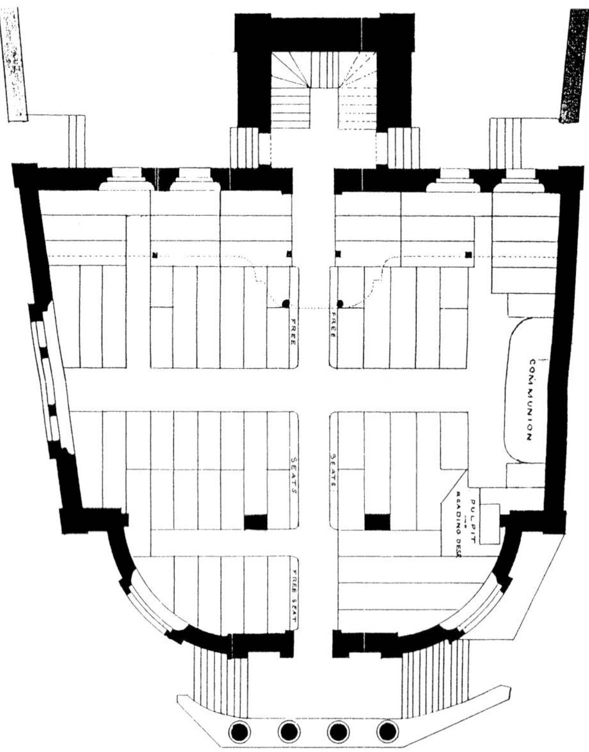

436 (*left*) G. P. Manners. Plan, St Michael Extra Muros, Bath, Somerset, 1834. Pen and ink and wash. Lambeth Palace Library, Incorporated Church Building Society, 1643. John Harvey architect, 1739–55, demolished 1835.

437 (*below*) William Halfpenny. North-west view, Redland Chapel, Bristol, Somerset, 1742, detail. Pen and ink and wash. © The British Library Board, K.Top. CXXIV, supp. cat. f. 37. John Strahan, W. Halfpenny and Thomas Paty architects, 1740–43.

438 David and William Hiorne. West front, Holy Cross, Daventry, Northamptonshire, 1752–9.

men Workmen, to mortify him, declared that a Horse, accustomed to the Sight of good Buildings, was so frightened at the odd Appearance . . . that he would not go by it till he was hoodwinked'.[98] At Redland Chapel, Bristol (pl. 437), the engaged tetrastyle Ionic portico with an unusually wide central intercolumniation features corner quoins that separate it from a wholly different, astylar system on the side elevations, and is crowned by a bulky, domed bell turret of indeterminate origin.[99] It is, nonetheless, a perfect proprietary jewel. At Daventry, Northamptonshire (pl. 438), David and William Hiorne of Warwick, who collaborated with the Smiths (Gibbs's executor at Derby), designed a façade combining St Martin and Gibbs's Fellows' Building, King's College, Cambridge, in which the giant Tuscan pilasters are so widely spaced and the entablature discontinued on the flanks that it no longer reads as a temple form. This led the Cheshire architect William Baker, visiting in 1759, to observe somewhat bewilderedly that it was 'built with a Bad yellow couler stone & windo to small – a body . . . to Low & Steeple crouded with work yet Clumsy – no connector betw the Cornice of Chancell & of pillars & Gallery'.[100]

HOLY COMMUNION
EVENSONG
THE PROVOST
SERVICES DAILY

Twenty-Two

BAROQUE BEYOND LONDON

Here *Towns*, and *Spires*, and *Hills* o'er *Hills* extend;
There *Shady Groves*, and *Lawns*, the Prospect end.
Through lavish *Ornaments*, the Fabrick shines
With wild Festoons of Fruits, and clustering Vines:
Luxuriant Decorations fill each Space,
And vast incumbrance; void of *Rules* or *Grace*;
Without Coherence crowded in each Place.[1]

Gibbs's brilliant transformation of the antique temple was not the only church form that attracted an enthusiastic audience outside the capital. The avowed aim of the New Churches Commissioners' press calls for building proposals was 'as an Encouragement to Workmen in the Country as well as Towne', thereby spreading metropolitan baroque throughout the Nation.[2] One of its striking products is what the architectural commentator Robert Morris condemned as Hawksmoor's '*wild Heap* of inconsistent Things'.[3] Others, however, found much to admire. According to *The Foreigner's Guide* (1729), Limehouse (pl. 370) was 'built in a handsome Manner',[4] and the often cantankerous Batty Langley, writing in the *Grub-street Journal* (1734), thought it 'a most surprising beautiful structure [of] such simple beauty, that I don't know where to produce its parallel'. Wapping (pl. 371) was a 'magnificent pile . . . wherein simplicity and grandeur are as well connected together, as I have yet seen in any composition of the ancients'.[5] *Parentalia* (1750) proclaimed Woolnoth (pl. 373) 'very substantially performed by the ingenious and skilful Architect Mr *Nicholas Hawksmoor*',[6] and Dodsley's and Dodsley's *London and Its Environs Described* (1761) believed Spitalfields (pl. 367) 'though . . . not without faults, yet . . . worthy of great praise; it being singular, and built for ages', while Walter Harrison's *A New Universal History, Description and Survey of the Cities of London and Westminster* (1775) described the one as 'bold and majestic' and the other as 'very handsome . . . solid and well-proportioned'.[7] Precisely how these achievements, reaching a climax in Thomas Archer's St Philip, Birmingham (pl. 439), were disseminated is demonstrated in three widely scattered provincial churches, in Oxford, Manchester and Whitchurch, Shropshire.

An engraved scheme by Michael Burghers for replacing the medieval fabric of All Saints, Oxford, destroyed by the collapse of the tower in 1700, to the design of Henry Aldrich, Dean of Christ Church, amateur architect and one of the rebuilding trustees, datable not earlier than 1704 (pl. 440), is remarkable as a pioneer and unusually confident transformation of the standard Anglican astylar preaching box coming into fashion outside the metropolis (pl. 485).[8] The whole exterior is enwrapped by a repetitious treatment of paired pilasters and tall windows (echoed in the interior), with stately prostyle temple porticoes in the westernmost bays of both the High Street and Turl Street elevations.[9] The steeple combines elements from St Mary-le-Bow (pl. 484) and St Antholin, Watling Street, London,[10] but its bold, horizontal rustication had not appeared previously in English churches and, indeed, the reduction of the lavish articulation of Wren's St Paul's Cathedral (pl. 2) to parish size was also unprecedented.[11] The church rose between 1706 and 1711. Visiting in 1710, Zacharias Conrad von Uffenbach was struck particularly by the 'uniform style [of this] beautiful edifice'.[12] Aldrich died in 1710, just as the building fund dried up and before his tower could be finished; nothing further happened until 1717, when the Bishop of Durham (former Rector of Lincoln College, the institution attached to the parish) gave £200

439 (*facing page*) Thomas Archer. South-east entrance, St Philip, Birmingham, Warwickshire, 1709–25.

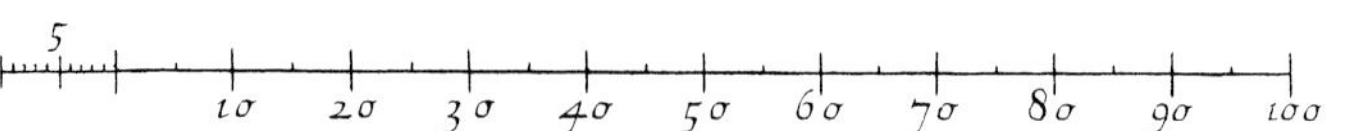

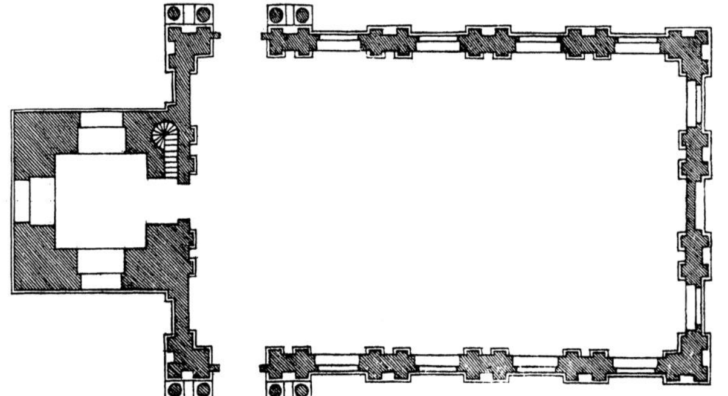

440 Michael Burghers. Plan and south elevation, 'All Saints in Oxford', Oxfordshire, 1700–4. Engraving. The Bodleian Library, University of Oxford, Gough Maps 44, p. 56, f. 107. Henry Aldrich architect.

441 Nicholas Hawksmoor. Design for west tower, All Saints, Oxford, Oxfordshire, *c.*1717. Pen and ink and wash. London Metropolitan Archives (Guildhall Library, GR.2.1.2, f. 17).

towards its completion. The University called in Hawksmoor (already involved in schemes for All Souls and Queen's Colleges and the Clarendon Building), whose reputation as an ecclesiastical innovator would have been confirmed by George Clarke, Aldrich's successor at Christ Church and the University's MP from 1717, who had served as a New Churches Commissioner between 1712 and 1715.[13] Among several surviving Hawksmoor schemes, the most dramatic (pl. 441) was for a 177-foot-high structure with a lofty first stage framed by monumental fluted Doric piers (as he also contemplated introducing at Greenwich Hospital chapel, pl. 356), incorporating an *in antis* porch in the manner of Carlo Maderno's west front of St Peter, Rome, and an upper stage in the form of a colossal

442 Nicholas Hawksmoor. Design for west tower, All Saints, Oxford, Oxfordshire, *c.*1717. Pen and ink and wash. The Bodleian Library, University of Oxford, MS Top. Oxon. a.48, f. 74.

443 John Sturt. 'A Circular Design in Perspective', St Ignatius, Rome, 1680, in James 1707, fig. LXVI. Engraving.

antique Roman altar (like those carved by Edward Strong Jr at St Alfege, Greenwich, pl. 401).[14] In the event, the rusticated lower stages of Aldrich's scheme were built (1718–20) but with Hawksmoor's spire-crowned tempietto. A preliminary study in which the superstructure is surrounded by free-standing statues (pl. 442) suggests that he may have turned to Andrea Pozzo's temporary Quarantore tabernacle set up in Sant'Ignazio in Rome for Holy Week in 1680 (pl. 443).[15] Hawksmoor's probable authorship of the altar-piece has already been noted (pl. 80).

Burgher's subscription engraving (pl. 440), issued to raise £4,800 needed for rebuilding, must have reached Manchester in the north of England during preparations to erect St Anne, the first new church in the town since the middle ages (pl. 444), which Stukeley reckoned incorrectly was 'after the London models' – the point being that there was no existing local pattern on which the client might anchor expectations.[16] The architect was probably John Barker of Rowsley, Derbyshire.[17]

On 23 January 1712, six months before St Anne was consecrated, William Smith, a leading Staffordshire builder and architect, was contracted to rebuild the recently destroyed medieval parish church of St Alkmund, Whitchurch, Shropshire, 'according to a designe drawn by John Barker' (pl. 445).[18] His building estimate specified internal dimensions of 88 by 62 by 38 feet high and a treatment 'after the Doricke Order', both features closely linking it to St Anne. Moreover, it was to have 'two hight's of windows [if the client] shall be so minded', though Smith amended this to 'one hight . . . Runde the Church ech windoe . . . 23 foot high and 8 foot wide with a plane pillostar Runde ech'. St Philip, Birmingham, comes to mind, as do the apron-like panels hanging from the main cornice (pl. 12), where Smith acted as contractor. The interior (before suffering badly in the nineteenth century from losing its north and south galleries and being stone-lined (pl. 446)), with its giant order Doric columns and fluted Corinthian pilasters in the chancel (the latter ultimately inspired by St Paul's Cathedral (pl. 361)), is more assertive than the similar Manchester interior and perhaps represents Smith's individual contribution. It is pertinent that among the subscribers to the rebuilding was Sir Orlando Bridgeman, donating £2 3s. 0d., who

444 Joseph Smith. 'The North Prospect of St. Ann's Church in Manchester', Lancashire, 1732. Engraving. © The British Library Board, K.Top. XVIII-18-d. John Barker architect, 1708–12.

445 John Barker. South elevation and west tower, St Alkmund, Whitchurch, Shropshire, 1712–13.

446 John Barker. Interior towards the chancel, St Alkmund, Whitchurch, Shropshire, 1712–13, before removal of galleries in 1972. English Heritage (National Monuments Record, AA52/10006).

had contributed £20 to the building fund for Birmingham and was kinsman to Sir John Bridgeman, a member of its building committee, where William Smith (with his brother Francis) were acting as contractors. He had also negotiated for the purchase of roof and scaffolding timber in 1712 from another Whitchurch subscriber, the Earl of Cholmondeley.[19]

Whitchurch was a prestigious commission which attracted national interest, since the town lay strategically on the main route from London and Birmingham to Liverpool and across the Irish Channel to Dublin. Among the other subscribers were Viscount Middleton, Lord Chancellor of Ireland, the Archbishop of Armagh, Lord Primate of Ireland, the bishops of Clogher, Londonderry and Waterford, and Jonathan Swift, Dean of St Patrick's, Dublin (who contributed £5 7s. 6d.).

Alessandro Galilei's failure to find favour with the New Churches Commissioners prompted him to try his luck in Ireland. Robert, 1st Viscount Molesworth, an Irish MP at Westminster, who had brought the young architect to England in 1714, within two years attempted to secure his participation in rebuilding St Werburgh, Dublin. The most recent new church undertaking in the city, St Mary (1701–4), designed by Sir William Robinson, Surveyor-General of the Royal Works in Ireland, is rectangular with concave bays preceding the chancel in the manner of St Clement Danes (1680–82), the corresponding internal columniation handled far less confidently than Wren's dynamic, interlocking sweep, and the large, impressive chancel window features a lugged, scroll-ended frame based on St Mary Aldermanbury in London (1670–76).[20] Provincial imitators of metropolitan Protestant baroque icons were not uncommon and often acknowledged at the time. For example, St Peter, Liverpool (1700–04), was 'after [the] model [of] St Andrew Holborn' (pls 485–6); the same source was cited for St Anne, Manchester, though in fact, as we have seen, it derived from All Saints, Oxford (pls 440, 444); the contract for the internal ceiling of St George, Great Yarmouth, Norfolk (1714), specified that it be 'Coved in the manner of St Clement Danes Church in the Strand',

and the chancel of St Andrew, Penrith (1719–23), 'after the manner of S. Pauls [Cathedral], London'.[21] Provincial imitators of Roman Catholic models were inevitably scarce – the unique English example of the Rainaldi-parroted steeple proposed for Queen's College chapel, Oxford (1708–19), not unexpectedly failed to materialise (pl. 418). Their blatant appearance in Dublin must surely be linked in some way with Galilei's brief appearance there in 1718, when he designed nearby Castletown House in the form of an Italian *palazzo*.[22]

The conservative archbishop, William King, objected to employing a foreign papist for St Werburgh and awarded the job to the Surveyor-General, Thomas Burgh, who apparently though ironically designed its west front (pl. 447) as a close copy of Francesco da Volterra's Santa Chiara in Rome (1627–8).[23] While unrecorded in prints, it was perhaps known in Ireland through Molesworth's brother, John, who was British envoy extraordinary to the Tuscan court between 1711 and 1714, during which he had visited Rome.[24] Furthermore, the façade of St Ann, Dublin (pl. 448), replicated Volterra's and Carlo Maderno's San Giacomo degli Incurabili (1590–1601), with a spire based on Borromini's Sant'Agnese in Piazza Navona (1653–66).[25] Galilei's involvement, if any, with either church, both of which represent a dramatic shift away from Wrenian solutions, remains unclear. Molesworth reported despondently that the Irish were 'uncapable of comprehending what an artist Galilei is', and he returned permanently to Italy in August 1719.[26]

The unsettling spectacle of Catholic-inspired churches was unique neither to Dublin nor to London. James Gibbs's first patron, John Erskine, 6th Earl of Mar, who as Secretary of State for Scotland had been instrumental in securing his post as New Churches surveyor in 1713, was himself an exceptionally talented 'amateur' architect, spending the last seventeen years of his life exiled in Italy, France and the Southern Netherlands for his pivotal military role in the Jacobite Rising. During these years he made several designs for enlarging and recasting the old, undistinguished parish church at Alloa, Clackmannanshire, adjacent to his ancestral estate.[27] Though Mar travelled widely in Italy during 1717–19 and Pope Clement XI presented him with a volume of plans of St Peter's Basilica,[28] the Alloa schemes show influences from French and Netherlandish architecture seen during his final residence in Northern Europe. In Antwerp in 1730 he produced a strikingly Gallic design (pls 449–50) with a vermiculated frontispiece on the south elevation facing the churchyard, and on the north, towards a 'New street to be made', a robust porch of one-quarter and three-quarter engaged Tuscan giant order columns with rusticated shaft bands.[29] Inside, the deep chancel is filled by the family loft screening a magnificent obelisk monument surrounded by a regal double staircase leading to Mar's dining room, private tribune, 'closet for devotion & study', minister's apartment and so on. The earl wrote to his son from Chillon in 1726 bestowing 'liberty to alter [the design] of yr own fancie wt the advice [of] yr acquaintance Mr Gibbs', but its overt Catholicism would have found little sympathy in post-Jacobite Presbyterian Scotland, and his death at Aix-la-Chapelle in 1732 frustrated its progress beyond the drawing board.[30]

Among the successful New Churches architects, John James made a significant impact beyond the metropolis. In securing the coveted post of master carpenter at St Paul's Cathedral in 1711, he had claimed to possess the 'Advantage of a better Education in the Latin Italian and ffrench Tongues, a competent Share of Mathematicks and Ten Years Instruction in all the practical parts of Building'.[31] This is confirmed in the publication of *Rules and Examples of Perspective Proper for Painters and Architects* (1707), an English translation of Andrea Pozzo's *Perspectiva Pictorum et Architectorum* (1693), and *A Treatise of the Five Orders of Columns in Architecture* (1708) after Claude Perrault's *Ordonnance* of 1693.[32] He also played a notable role as a New Churches surveyor from 1716, though his single, independent London work, St George, Hanover Square (pls 430–32), as we have seen, exposed difficulties encountered in competing on a grand scale with Hawksmoor and Gibbs. Clearly, he was more comfortable dealing with modest suburban churches (pls 433, 435, 487–8), where his preference for plain walls, isolated pilasters and large, arched fenestration proved particularly suitable for congregations holding fashionable aspirations but limited funds.

Following the collapse of the medieval parish church at Twickenham in 1713, the vicar, Samuel Pratt (Dean of Rochester, whose bishop, Thomas Sprat, was a New Churches Commissioner, which accounts for his involvement in restoring the cathedral),[33] invited James to rebuild the body on the old foundations abutting the surviving west tower (as at Greenwich, James's parish). Twickenham, on the Thames in Middlesex, was then a sophisticated 'Earthy *Elesium*': Henrietta Pye wrote of

> its Air Balmy, clear, and beautiful; The whole Place is one continued Garden. Plenty and Pleasure are the Ideas convey'd by its large Fields of Corn and its verdant Meadows . . . The Genius of the inhabitants inclines not towards Commerce, Architecture seems

447 Bowles. 'The Front of St. Warburghs Church', detail, in Charles Brooking, *A Map of the City and Suburbs of Dublin*, Ireland, 1728. Engraving. Architect unknown.

448 Bowles. 'The Front of St. Anns Church', detail, in Charles Brooking, *A Map of the City and Suburbs of Dublin*, Ireland, 1728. Engraving. Architect unknown.

their chief Delight; in which if any doubts their excelling, let him sail up the River and view their lovely Villas beautifying its Banks, Lovers of true Society, they despise Ceremony, & no Place can boast more Examples of domestic Happiness.[34]

Contemporaries thought St Mary's a 'fine *Dorick* Building . . . may vye with any Country Church in England' (pl. 451),[35] and the temple form, with its Greenwich-inspired (pl. 401) 'two Additionall Breaks on the North and South Sides', is handled with noble sim-

449 John Erskine, 6th Earl of Mar. 'Designe for enlarging the Church of Alloa. Antwerpe Aprile 1730. The South ffront', St Mungo, Alloa, Clackmannanshire, Scotland. Pen and ink and wash. National Archives of Scotland, Mar and Kellie Papers, 13258/33.

450 John Erskine, 6th Earl of Mar. Ground plan 'Designe for Enlarging the Church of Alloa. Drawen at Antwerp Aprile 1730', St Mungo, Alloa, Clackmannanshire, Scotland. Pen and ink and wash. National Archives of Scotland, Mar and Kellie Papers, 13258/35.

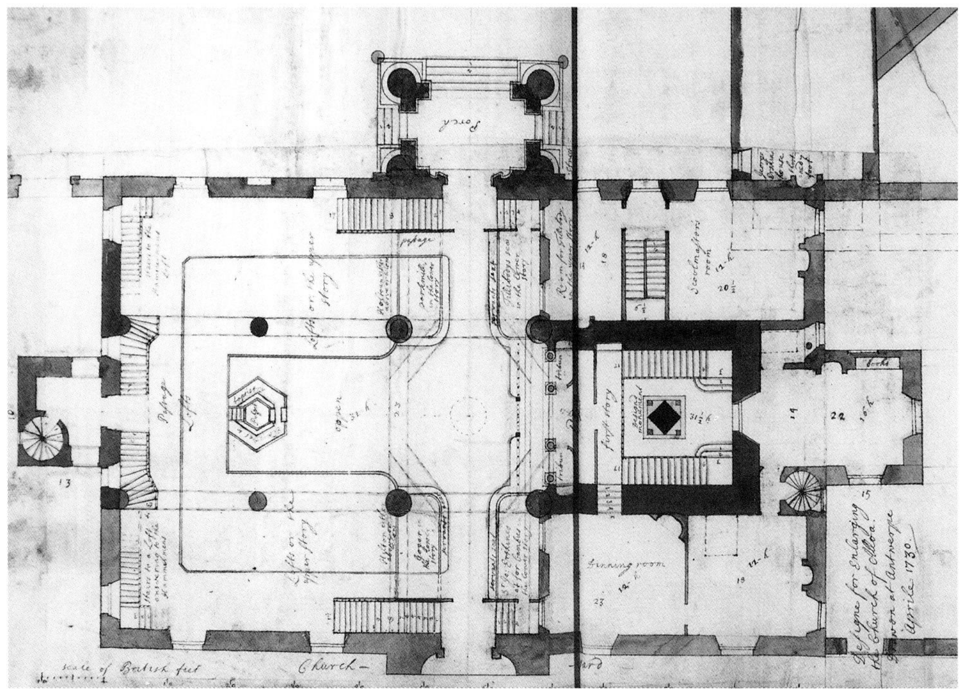

plicity.[36] The pediments on the west end and subsidiary flanks, however, collide with the old tower, and the classical integrity is further diminished by the cheaper alternative choice of brick with minimum stone dressings (pl. 134).[37] On the evidence of similarities between Twickenham and the undated, long-lost, poorly documented May Fair Chapel, Curzon Street (pl. 1), with its pseudoperipteral temple form of Ionic giant order pilasters eccentrically combined with a metope-embellished Doric entablature, and its geographical closeness to James's St George, Hanover Square, one might speculate that here too he was the architect.

Perhaps because of difficulties in modernising the Elizabethan mansion at Cannons, Middlesex, and having just dismissed William Talman, his original, cantankerous architect, James Brydges, lord of the manor, turning his attention in late 1713 to the nearby medieval parish church at Whitchurch, favoured replacement by an entirely new building (pl. 452), designed by James, who was now advising on the house.[38] Again, the middle bays of the long elevations project, though not so boldly as either Twickenham or Greenwich. They are only hesitantly emphasised by full-height pilaster strips, their wide syncopation under-

451 (*above*) John James. South elevation, St. Mary, Twickenham, Middlesex, 1714–17.

452 (*below*) John James. Plan, section and elevations design, St Laurence, Whitchurch, Middlesex, 1713. Pencil, pen and ink and wash. Henry E. Huntington Library and Art Gallery, San Marino, California, Stowe Maps and Plans Box 15.

453 John James. South-west view, St George's Chapel, Tiverton, Devon, 1714–33. English Heritage (National Monuments Record, AA55/1234).

454 John James. South elevation, St Laurence, Whitchurch, Middlesex, 1714–15.

mining any inherent peripteral temple form, further exacerbated by the suggestion, lightly pencilled, of an alternative treatment (or perhaps an early idea for the addition of the family mausoleum) beyond the east end, of rusticated pilasters and apron panels over single-storey windows, as at Birmingham (pl. 12). James successfully repeated the composition at the astylar, yellow Purbeck stone St George's Chapel, Tiverton (pl. 453).[39] But finally Brydges decided to retain the old west tower (pl. 454), providing a more emphatic public entrance on the south elevation, marked by astragal-moulded pilasters and projecting sections of cornice, which is repeated at the windowed east end, with the intervening bays slightly set back and aprons hung below the sills. The result is a church echoing James's scheme for refacing the mansion, which could be seen at the opposite end of a formal avenue.[40] The internal treatment increased proportionately to the client's rising social status (from Earl of Caernarvon to the 'Princely Chandos', paymaster to the troops), with Brydges informing his architect that he was 'considering the manner of placing the pews in the body . . . & would have them . . . as they are in the cathedral, three rows on each side . . . as . . . in Paul's'.[41] The exquisitely carved chancel screen (pl. 455) is a version of Wren's striding the Morning Prayer chapels (pl. 456).[42]

Similarities between Whitchurch and St Mary, Abbots Ann, Hampshire (1715–21), built for Thomas 'Diamond' Pitt, East India merchant and New Churches Commissioner,[43] makes it very likely that James was the architect, and through this connection his influence spread to distant Blandford St Mary, Dorset, where Pitt's father was rector. According to John Bastard (who with his brother, William, were leading architects at nearby Blandford Forum), he and 'everybodey in this cuntry . . . was shown [a measuring method] by . . . John James of Greenwich, [who] was Oaften at ower house'.[44] The Bastards made their mark as distinguished church designers with the rebuilding of SS Peter and Paul, Blandford Forum, the medieval fabric having perished with the rest of the town in a devastating fire on 4 June 1731 (p. 136).

The new church (pl. 457), built entirely of stone, was 'done in a very genteel taste; so yt there are few in England exceed it'.[45] Its debt to James is evident in the slightly projecting, pedimented frontispiece with prominently quoined corners (pl. 453), and the more monumental, pedimented Doric distyle south porch, which creates a dual axiality, one of the hallmarks of the New Churches, and particularly recalls Greenwich (pl. 401) and Twickenham (pl. 451).[46] Among other works belonging to the Jamesian style is St Rumbald, Stoke

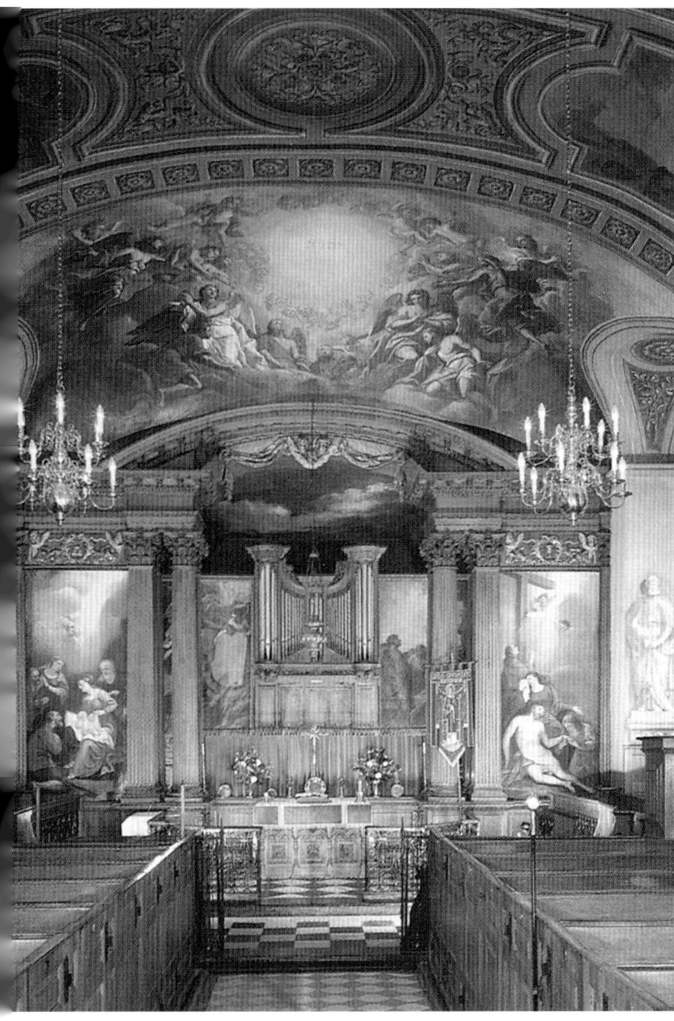

455 (*left*) John James and James Gibbs. Interior towards the chancel, St Laurence, Whitchurch, Middlesex, 1714–20.

456 (*below left*) Robert Trevitt. 'A View to the Morning Chapel in the Cathedral Church of St Paul', London, 1702–3, detail. Engraving. The Pepys Library, Magdalene College, Cambridge, PL 2972/163.

Doyle, Northamptonshire (1721–7), associated with a local surveyor named Thomas Eayre, whose preliminary study (pl. 458) retains Wrenian motifs (the south door and concave walls between body and chancel), abandoned in the more austerely executed building.[47]

457 (*above*) John and William Bastard. North-west view, SS Peter and Paul, Blandford Forum, Dorset, 1733–9.

A significant rapport was forged in the north of England between Vanbrugh and William Etty, whose architect father, John, had enjoyed close links with Wren and the Office of Works in London since the 1680s (see p. 149). From 1701 until the end of building operations in the 1730s William served as Vanbrugh's clerk of the works at Castle Howard – Hawksmoor observing that he was then 'but young, tho' he soon improved, and so would any man of common capacity

458 Thomas Eayre. Design for 'The South Upright Front &c.', St Rumbald, Stoke Doyle, Northamptonshire, ?1722. Pen and ink and wash. Shropshire Record and Research Centre, Hunt of Boreatton Papers, 6000/17808.

in so Noble a Building'.[48] It must have been the contribution of its owner, Charles Howard, 1st Earl of Carlisle, to the public subscription in 1716 towards rebuilding the 'very Crazy & Ruinous' body of the medieval parish church at Penrith, Cumberland, where he was a landowner, that accounts for Etty's involvement there.[49] Though he is mentioned in the parish records only once – on 19 August 1719 'Mr Etty, Lord Carlisle's architect' received £3 15s. 3d. 'for coming over to Survey the church [and] his Expences at the George & at a Meeting of the parishioners' – at the very least he was consulted about the design and, as other evidence suggests, was more than likely the designer.[50] One of the unusual features of this preparatory activity was the parish's obligation to provide 'a proper & Convenient Modell . . . of the church as it is intended to be New built' for the Bishop of Carlisle's 'perusal & approbation' (untraced).[51] While this term might equally apply to a drawing, 5s. paid to 'Richardson for Painting the Church Model' confirms that in this case it was a three-dimensional object. Still a rarity in the hinterlands (this may be the earliest documented example), such wooden models had recently become common practice among the New Churches in London, as we have seen (p. 149). Significantly, its Commissioners included both the Bishop of Carlisle (formerly rector of St Mary-le-Bow, London) and William Dawes, Archbishop of York, who subscribed to the Penrith rebuilding in 1716 and also promoted the building of Holy Trinity, Leeds, for which Etty made a wooden model in 1723 (pl. 419).[52]

St Andrew, Penrith, dazzling in its local red sandstone, is among the most original country churches of the period (pl. 459). The eight-bay north and south elevations of double-storeyed, round-headed windows with plain surrounds and exaggerated, triple-block keystones hung from sections of coursing, derived from the internal west courtyard windows at Castle Howard, which Etty supervised building.[53] Now they are set tightly in narrow bays between slightly advancing, abnormally broad Tuscan pilasters, which are visually the equivalent of Vanbrugh's flat sections of wall. These rest on a continuously chamfered rusticated basement. The corners of the body are strengthened by wider rusticated piers (increased from 5 ft 2¼ in. to 5 ft 9 in.), with their returns marked by conventional quoins. A dominating, triple-arched window at the east end (pl. 460) – an uncommon pattern but present at Wren's St Mary, Ingestre, Staffordshire (1673–9) – with short entablatures over the sidelights to create a sort of Serliana, and the whole enclosed in an arch framed by full-height, confidently moulded Tuscan piers, is a stately, monumentalising gesture also learnt at Castle Howard. The novelties of the exterior continued inside, where the aim was to create 'a Regular & Capacious Fabrick . . . more . . . Ellegant & Convenient than the former'.[54] Here the committee favoured a 'regular & uniform Chancell' of two bays deep, narrower than the

459 William Etty. South-west view, St Andrew, Penrith, Cumberland, 1721–3.

461 William Etty. South-east view, Holy Trinity, Sunderland, County Durham, 1720–27.

460 William Etty. East elevation, St Andrew, Penrith, Cumberland, 1721–3.

462 William Etty. West front, Holy Trinity, Sunderland, County Durham, detail, 1720–27.

body and with a slightly recessed concave centrepiece, described as 'One Semicircle or Alcove, after the manner of S. Pauls London', a building Etty knew well, since his father had been the agent for supplying its roof timbers.[55]

In 1719 Etty became Vanbrugh's clerk of the works at Seaton Delaval, Northumberland.[56] He combined activities there with designing and building a church for the newly created parish at Sunderland (pl. 461) further along the coastline, which had emerged as 'a

463 Sir William Wilson. South-west view, Job Marston's Chapel, Hall Green, Birmingham, Warwickshire, 1704.

Large and populous Town' of 6,000 souls situated at the 'Mouth of A Navigable River . . . a place of great Trade & Commerce'.[57] Unlike Penrith, his responsibilities here are recorded unequivocally in numerous payments for work, totalling £3,220 4s. 7¾d., some carried out in partnership with Isaac Mansfield, a well-established plasterer who divided his practice between York and London, where he was employed at several of the New Churches.[58] Also dependent on Castle Howard in the choice of powerful Tuscan pilasters with projecting sections of entablature and a boldly rusticated, concave door-case (pl. 462), Sunderland is architecturally less resolved and confident than Penrith. In particular, the keystones of the round-headed windows hang uncomfortably from a narrow cornice and inept vertical stone strips in the parapet, while both ends are so awkward as to suggest an unfinished exterior.[59] The interior, by contrast, is a pioneering expression of emerging Palladianism (the subject of chapter 24).

464 Francis Smith. South-east view of the chancel, St Lawrence, Chicheley, Buckinghamshire, 1708–9.

The appearance soon after 1700 of the brothers William and Francis Smith as church architects is demonstrated in two notable works. Job Marston's chapel, near Birmingham (pl. 463), where they served as 'undertakers' of a design by Sir William Wilson, collaborators on the influential St Mary, Warwick (pl. 270), combines the use of red brick with stone dressing characteristic of modest Wren-period London churches and archaicisms such as diamond-shaped recesses in the bell-tower. Corner quoins and slender pilasters between tall, round-headed windows along the side elevations mark their early appearance in the provinces.[60] Working independently, as at Chicheley, Buckinghamshire (pl. 464), Francis Smith's chancel-mausoleum for Sir John Chester, 4th Baronet, whose wife died in 1704, is an impressive essay employing late baroque motifs such as monumental Corinthian corner piers, tall segmental pedimented windows (the gothic tracery is a later interloper) and Warwick-inspired scallop-headed niches set on gadrooned aprons.[61]

Between the second and fourth decades of the eighteenth century, inspired particularly by Whitchurch (pl. 445), Francis Smith perfected his signature composition exemplified by Burton upon Trent, Staffordshire (pl. 465), and St Peter at Arches, Lincoln (pl. 466), its essence captured by a visitor to the latter in 1742:

> The New Church . . . has one row of arch'd Windows, Cornice & Ballustrade, the East End is Circuling, the breadth of the Church is not great, but yet it has 3 Isles made of Dorick Pillars, from the Capitalls of which springs Arches from Pillar to Pillar, the Cieling above the Arches is covered [coved] & then Flat, that of the side Isles wholly flat.[62]

This became synonymous with mid-Georgian churches in the Midlands, though by the time the Revd Jeremiah Milles visited Francis's late church at Monmouth (1736–7), in 1742 he found the formulaic interior 'not a good taste. tho there appears to be the Affection of it'.[63]

Following Francis Smith's death in 1738, the pattern was passed on to Richard Trubshaw, a master builder from Haywood, Staffordshire, the next village to Ingestre, where in the 1670s Wren had designed a new church in a sophisticated, up-to-date, metropolitan classical style, which in turn reinforced Trubshaw's own predilections.[64] As a young man in the 1710s, Trubshaw had lived in Oxford, amidst a flurry of ecclesiastical building activity, where he acquired a copy of the first volume of Colen Campbell's *Vitruvius Britannicus* (1715) illustrated with a variety of churches (pls 513–15).[65] In the early 1740s he came into contact with both James Gibbs and William Smith Jr.[66] Trubshaw's own churches maintain the Smiths' dour rectangularity, single range of arched windows, panelled aprons and spare use of Tuscan pilasters, accented by *oeil-de-boeufs* (pl. 467).[67]

465 William and Francis Smith. North elevation, St Modwen, Burton-on-Trent, Staffordshire, 1719–26.

466 Samuel Hieronymus Grimm. South-west view, 'St Peter in the Arches. Lincoln Augt. 1784' , Lincolnshire. Pen and ink and wash. © The British Library Board, Kaye Collection, v, Add. MS 15541, f. 155. William and Francis Smith architects, 1720–24. Re-erected differently on another city site, 1936.

In the towns and villages around Birmingham, galvanised by its close network of architects and builders, St Philip, Birmingham (pl. 12), admired throughout the century, proved hugely influential on a group of sparsely documented though evocative Midland churches erected between its completion in 1725 and

467 (*right*) Richard Trubshaw. South elevation, Holy Trinity, Baswick, Stafford, Staffordshire, 1738–42.

468 Architect unknown. South elevation, St Peter, Gayhurst, Buckinghamshire, 1724–8.

469 Architect unknown. North-east view, St Peter, Gayhurst, Buckinghamshire, 1724–8. English Heritage (National Monuments Record, AA58/2816).

the 1750s. But, such an examination brings with it a cautious note to treat these attributions of authorship solely on similarities of motif with circumspection, when probably the most that one can infer is that they share a common vocabulary rather than necessarily the same designer. To appreciate this pivotal phenomena we must first look at an example on the edge of the region, St Peter, Gayhurst, Buckinghamshire, among the most completely preserved country house churches of the period (pl. 468).[68] Its engaged columns and pilasters, relieved at the corners by horizontal channelled piers, all rising from individual pedestals supported on a rusticated platform, its south door with a lugged frame surmounted by a raised, segmental pediment, and its north frontispiece (pl. 469) facing the Elizabethan mansion composed of horizontal channelling articulated by triangular and segmental pediments, derive from Pierre Le Muet's *Manière de Bien Bastir* (1647), a celebrated seventeenth-century French pattern book (pls 470–71). The uncommon form of the south door frame reappeared at Dudley near Birmingham (pl. 472), a little-studied church resplendent with decorative quirks.[69]

Neither Gayhurst nor Dudley have identifiable architects, but Castle Bromwich (pl. 474), also near Birmingham, may hold vital clues. Here the medieval structure was completely encased in a classical skin of brick and stone at the expense of Sir John Bridgeman, whose father, together with Lady Bridgeman and Orlando Bridgeman, subscribed a total of £70 towards erecting St Philip, while the parish contributed a further £4 0s. 6d.[70] The building contract of 1724 identifies Thomas White of Worcester as the 'Carver' and he very likely also served as designer. A particularly telling idiosyncrasy is the gadrooned segmental-shaped window apron, a motif that particularly appears on Worcester buildings where he acted as carver, and is also a feature of his church monuments.[71] The elliptical-bottomed window aprons of the Castle Bromwich tower and the roll-moulded windows used throughout are identical to those on the Worcester Guildhall (1721–5, architect unknown), where White was paid as principal stone carver.[72] Perhaps the most pertinent link between Gayhurst, Dudley and Castle Bromwich is that Bridgeman's relative, Lady Wilbraham of Weston Park, a somewhat mysterious amateur architect with an obscure *œuvre*, possessed a copy of Godfrey Richards's *The First Book Of Architecture. By Andrea Palladio* (1663), which departed from the original in incorporating an 'Appendix Touching Doors and Windows, by Pr Le Muet', that is, *Augmentations De Nouveaux Bastimens Faits En France*.[73]

470 Pierre Le Muet. 'Elevation de la face du Corps de Logis' of a town house, in P. Le Muet, Manier De Bastir, 1623, pl. 95. Engraving.

471 Pierre Le Muet. 'Face sur le Rue de L'Hostel Davaux a Paris', detail, in P. Le Muet, *Augmentations De Nouveaux Bastimens Faits En France*, 1647, pl. 28. Engraving.

one of James Gibbs's alternative St Mary-le-Strand designs published in *A Book of Architecture* (1728).[75]

Though unnamed in contemporary building accounts, White seems the most likely candidate as architect, and he was perhaps the guiding spirit behind

472 William Smith Sr., attributed. South-west view, St Edmund, Dudley, Staffordshire, 1724–39.

473 Thomas White, attributed. South-west view, St Nicholas, Worcester, Worcestershire, 1728–35. English Heritage (National Monuments Record, BB70/1339).

Finally, the 'large . . . very populous and busy' city of Worcester had subscribed £30 15s. 0d. towards building St Philip,[74] and unsurprisingly a version of its west elevation (pl. 358) was adopted by the Vestry of St Nicholas in 1728 for its imposing Archerian frontispiece (pl. 473). Buck's panorama of 1732 suggests that the massive tower originally intended bore a close resemblance to Birmingham, but due to financial constraints its construction did not begin until 1734–5, then 'According to a modell [to which] some Addition and Alteration' was made, resulting in an inflated version of

474 Artist unknown. South-west view, St Mary, Castle Bromwich, Warwickshire, detail, undated. Birmingham City Archives, Aylesford Collection, 1, f. 67. Thomas White architect, attributed, 1724–7.

nearly the entire group of Midland churches described here, all of which deserve further exploration.[76]

Simultaneously, the 1730s and 1740s witnessed a gradual decline of interest in baroque patterns. The immoderation of the New Churches designs had already come under fierce critical attack. Having already publicly condemned the 'affected and licentious' work of Bernini and the 'wild extravagant . . . Borromini . . . who has endeavoured to debauch mankind with his odd and chimerical Beauties',[77] Colen Campbell made indirect but unambiguous derision of St Mary-le-Strand (pl. 378) in 1717 for its aggregation of 'two Orders, one over another . . . in the Outside', which divided the building into 'little Parts [and] no less than three [pediments] in one Side [which] must be imputed either to an entire Ignorance of Antiquity, or a Vanity to expose their absurd Novelties, so contrary to those excellent Precepts in *Vitruvius*, and so repugnant to those admirable Remains the Ancients have left us'.[78] Then, in 1734 Batty Langley thought it 'strange that the out-side . . . should be divided into two orders . . . since no galleries are erected within' (pl. 379); furthermore, that the bands of coffering are 'something curved, but not enough; much too near the eye, and much too full of ornament', while the pediment whose function was to carry off water was employed absurdly over the chancel arch 'where no Rain can fall'.[79] James Ralph disapproved of St John, Westminster (pl. 365), for being 'in a very particular taste [with] a great mixture of beauty and caprice . . . 'tis to be sure a fatal mistake, to endeavour at an excellence, and then err so wide of the mark as to stumble on deformity; all false ornaments become faults instantly, and only serve to make an absurdity more conspicuous'.[80]

475 Thomas Gilbert. South-west view, St George Reforne, Portland, Dorset, 1753–66.

476 Jakob Schynvoet. 'View of the Cathedral Church of St Paul Lond: according to the First Design of the Architect Sr Christopher Wren Knt', the Great Model, 1673, detail, 1726. Engraving.

477 Edward Rooker after P. P. Burdett. North-west view, St Paul, Liverpool, Lancashire, in Enfield 1774, following p. 44. Engraving. Timothy Lightoler architect, 1765–9, demolished 1923.

St Paul's Cathedral (pl. 2) alone was immune to proscription. Despite Campbell's initial attack and the vicissitudes of taste, it remained a universal icon, filling 'the imagination with a pleasing astonishment'; 'surveying this stupendous Monument of our Country's Genius, the Imagination is filled with a lofty kind of Admiration'; 'Lost in thought for some time wth. Regard to the Sublime taste & Grandeur yt. are to be observed in yt. Glorious structure'; 'the finest Protestant church in the world'; and so on.[81]

St George Reforne, Island of Portland, Dorset (pl. 475), designed by Thomas Gilbert, a Liveryman of the London Masons Company, whose ancestors had supplied Wren with stone quarried on the site, probably out of pride turned for inspiration to the cathedral's nave, with its apsidal-ended Morning Chapels, west towers, central domical crossing springing from canted corner piers and apsidal chancel. Perhaps heeding Hogarth's reservations that it was 'full of . . . swarms of . . . little inconsistent objects',[82] what is most striking about Portland is that, while retaining St Paul's silhouettes, Gilbert stripped both outside and in of decoration, leaving the massive astylar walls almost primitively austere, as if the church were some solitary structure crowning the arid, sublime, sea-surrounded summit like a beached Noah's Ark.

Parentalia recounts how Wren, observing the public obsession with 'Grandeur . . . endeavour'd to gratify the Taste of the *Connoiseurs* and Criticks, with something coloss and beautiful' in the shape of the Great Model (pl. 476). According to his son Christopher Jr, in 'private Conversation [he] always seem'd to set a higher Value on [this design] than any he had made before or since' and would have built it with 'Chearfulness, and Satisfaction' but for its rejection by conservative cathedral clergymen. Stephen Wren, his grandson and *Parentalia*'s publisher, hoped that it would be carefully preserved 'as an eminent and costly Performance, and a Monument . . . of the skill of the greatest Geometrician and Architect of his Time'.[83] It was accordingly placed on public display in the cathedral library, accessible for a modest admission charge.[84] The west portico and domed vestibule divorced from the main centrally planned body, as shown in this cropped image of the 1726 engraving, was resurrected as an independent building in St Paul, Liverpool (pl. 477), a stately stone structure in the middle of the newly created St Paul's Square, a kinship not lost at the time.[85] Though following current neoclassical fashions in favouring the taller, slimmer columns and wider central intercolumniation recommended in William Chambers's *A Treatise On Civil Architecture* (1759) and the division of the main walls into contrasting stratas of vigorously horizontal channelling and smooth ashlar advocated by progressive French architects of the time,[86] and proclaimed 'one of the finest [churches] in England', it failed to 'stand the test of critical examination'. The cupola was 'by no means striking; it does not rise in a bold stile; its being ribbed into an octagon, is disadvantageous; nor is there simplicity enough in the lantern' (though Wren's baroque *oeil-de-boeuf* surrounds in the dome were reduced to the simplest geometry in the engraving and omitted altogether in execution). Furthermore, there was 'a great heaviness in the breadth of the space between the capitals of the pillars and the cornice'.[87]

Spiritually, mainstream baroque had already ceased by 1744, when St John, Westminster, was restored internally following a devastating fire two years earlier, as recorded in a contemporary painting, which 'burnt with that Fierceness that in about two Hours it entirely consumed all the inside of the . . . Church and the Roof, and left nothing standing but the Stone Walls'.[88] Archer, the original architect, still alive though in country retirement, was passed over in favour of James Horne, an experienced but hardly inspired Palladian church designer, who supervised the restoration. The building accounts reveal that he reinstated some original features, such as the 'new Circular Roof on the South West Tower . . . with a Pine Apple . . . fully to answer those already upon the other Towers', 'cut out and make good with Portland Stone all the Door Cases that are any way damaged' and so on.[89] Elsewhere, there are conspicuous changes, introducing austerities undoubtedly made in the name of economy for which the classical idiom was better suited. The Vestry decided to remove permanently the twelve full-height columns standing proud of the perimeter walls because they were 'so much damaged as not to be capable of being repaired', so destroying Archer's complex, dramatic, column-filled space (restored in the years 1965–8 following the gutting of the church in an air raid in 1941). Though the proposal for framing the roof specified 'Circular Angles, to answer the Plan', Horne did not recreate Archer's coved structure, which John Grove, the carpenter responsible for erecting it in 1716–18, described as 'in many respects very Different from what hath been done in any other Church'. Instead, a flattish ceiling was installed with 'streight & circular Beams . . . Four pieces of Ornament in the Spandrells with a proper Imbossment [and] a Flower in the Center . . . Twelve Feet Diameter and Two Feet Imboss', where the original flower had measured less than half that size.[90] A later commentator thought the 'nearly flat ceiling most clumsily and inelegantly divided into heavy squares, and an immense circle with a huge flower in the centre. The Sacrarium is extremely plain, and the altar not worth describing . . . the pulpit is extremely ugly.'[91]

By the close of the century New Churches baroque found only grudging championship. J. P. Malcolm's *Londinium Redivivum; or, An Ancient History and Modern Description of London* (1803–7) is characteristic. St George, Wapping, was 'an *outré* ecclesiastical building'; St Anne, Limehouse, attempted 'more than Grecian architecture will permit', though this 'strange jumble of architecture certainly has a majestic outline'; Christ Church, Spitalfields, 'proceeded according to a set [of rules] exclusively [Hawksmoor's] own', the tower 'ponderous beyond example', the windows 'diminutive and ungraceful'; the proportions of St George, Bloomsbury, 'are not quite correct', while 'the Attick baffles all description: it is the external wall of a prison . . . under one of the clumsiest . . . ceiling in Europe'. St Mary-le-Strand's interior was 'far inferior to the exterior in grandeur and proportion' and its west front suffered 'bad taste'.[92] John Soane's Royal Academy student lectures, delivered from 1809, had much to say about the Strand's misdemeanours. 'For want of fixed principles' Gibbs 'mistook confusion for variety [and] crowded together so many small parts without sense that the mind is fatigued and embarrassed by their smallness, whilst the number of them prevents the eye from resting upon any of them.' He showed a 'fondness and blind attachment [to the] licentious introduction of pediments' and the Borrominiesque 'false taste, or rather want of taste [for] overcharged' composition.[93] Perhaps Adam Fitz-Adam had good reason to conclude in 1754 that were 'queen Anne . . . to reign again, and fifty new churches to be really built, I doubt, if in this dissolute age, this . . . might not be called her Majesty's FOLLY'.[94] This marked the end of mainstream baroque in Britain.

478 Heinrich Hulsberg after Anthony Griffin. 'North Front of . . . St James Westmr: with Lower & upper Plans', London, undated. Engraving. © The British Library Board, K.Top. XXIII-20-a. Sir Christopher Wren (body) and Edward Wilcox (steeple) architects, 1676–99.

Twenty-three

THE PERSISTENCE OF WRENIAN AND GIBBSIAN PATTERNS

Wren . . . is the most intelligent and learned man in England . . . he hath been most concerned in contriving the most beautiful churches in London[1]

[Gibbs's] Draughts of useful and convenient Buildings and proper Ornaments; which may be executed by any Workman who understands Lines[2]

Sir Christopher Wren's national reputation as an ecclesiastical designer rested, according to the Leeds antiquary Ralph Thoresby, on his work as 'the unparalleled architect of . . . more churches . . . than, perhaps, any one person in the world ever did',[3] totalling fifty-two in addition to St Paul's Cathedral, an achievement 'not parallel'd in any City of the World'.[4] Above all, there was the pattern offered by his most favoured church, St James, Westminster (1676–99; pl. 478), which enjoyed important ramifications beyond its heyday and persisted in the conservative repertory throughout the eighteenth century. Though there was unnecessarily ruthless destruction at the hands of Victorian iconoclasts and the vagaries of modern warfare, significantly the sole eighteenth-century victim was the interesting classical–gothic hybrid of St Christopher-le-Stocks, Threadneedle Street (pl. 479).[5] It was sacrificed in the name of security (an over-reaction to the Gordon Riots in June 1780), but also to provide much needed space for the expanding Bank of England next door. During 1780–82 a convoluted dispute raged between the Vestry, advised by George Dance Jr, surveyor of the City of London, and the Bank, represented by its architect, Sir Robert Taylor. The Vestry, on recommendation from its valuers, Richard Norris and Samuel Wyatt, asked 6,000 guineas for the property, countered by Taylor's 4,000 guineas, which Wyatt rejected. Taylor objected to both Dance and Robert Mylne, surveyor of Blackfriars Bridge, serving as arbitrators, so the choice fell on Kenton Couse, architect of Holy Trinity, Clapham. The Bishop of London, siding with Parliament against his own

479 Sir Christopher Wren and William Dickinson. South elevation and tower design, St Christopher-le-Stock, London, 1669–1714. Pen and ink and wash. © The British Library Board, K.Top. 124 Supplement 52.

parish, resulted in its total demolition in 1784, the first ecclesiastical scapegoat of Mammon and corporate takeover.[6]

Critics expressed misgivings about some of Wren's most celebrated churches. James Ralph in *A Critical Review of the Publick Buildings, Statues and Ornaments In, and about London and Westminster* (1734) reckoned that St Bride's steeple (pl. 266) 'wants variety . . . the first and last orders are almost the same'.[7] Langley's repost in the *Grub-street Journal* of the same year[8] considered the columns of Bow steeple (pl. 484) to be 'of strange composition, their bases being Tuscan, their shafts Ionic, with astragals of monstrous size and surprizing projection; an error which I could not have thought Sir CHRISTOPHER . . . would have permitted to pass', their capitals 'of very bad workmanship, and . . . very disagreeable effect', while the internal 'double columns, whose solid shafts intersect and cut into each other' – conjoined like Siamese twins – was 'a most barbarous and ignorant practice [and should have been] entirely clear of each other, which would have been both stronger, and more elegant architecture'. Holborn's tower (pl. 486) made a 'very disagreeable . . . figure [and is] disproportioned to the body . . . being too small a diameter, much too high, and withal too heavy in its upper part'; had its base been encased in stone 'of such reasonable thickness and strength, as would have made its diameter . . . proportionable to the present height, and thereon placed a noble and lofty spire; then this edifice would have been a great ornament to that part of the city'.[9] Nevertheless, Bow steeple was a 'masterpiece in a peculiar kind of building, which has no fix'd rules to direct it, nor is it to be reduced to any settled laws of beauty'; it was 'as perfect as human imagination can contribute or execute, and till we see it outdone, we shall hardly think it to be equall'd'.[10] Interestingly, the tradition of Wren's towers and spires continued into the post-1818 era as an alternative to the Greek revival types.[11]

Wren's churches, remarkably diverse in appearance, were widely known early on: Edward Hatton's *A New View of London; or, An Ample Account of that City* (1708) devoted 495 pages to them, mainly describing altarpieces,[12] followed by James Paterson's *Pietas Londinensis; or, The Present Ecclesiastical State of London* (1714),[13] *A New Guide to London; or, Directions to Strangers; Shewing the Chief Things of Curiosity and Note in the City and Suburbs* (1726) and *The Foreigner's Guide; or, A necessary and instructive Companion Both for the Foreigner and Native, in their Tour through the Cities of London and Westminster* (1729), with parallel English and French texts, which hint at the buildings' general artistic character: St Bride's steeple 'one of the best in London', St Clement Danes's interior a 'well contrived . . . Disposition', with many others 'fine, convenient, and decently Magnificent'.[14] In addition, there were city histories and architectural tracts, the most notable being Ralph's *Critical Review* and Langley's replies, as mentioned above, Stephen Wren's *Parentalia; or, Memoirs of the Family of the Wrens* (1750), with William Maitland's *The History and Survey of London from its foundation to the present time* (1756), comprising 122 engraved views, Thomas Osborne's *English Architecture* (1758) and R. Dodsley's and J. Dodsley's *London and Its Environs Described* (1761), among the earliest representations.[15] These reaffirmed Wrenian values for later generations. For example, Osborne described All Hallows, Thames Street (pl. 480), with its

> simple noble [tower which] always pleases the eye . . . There runs through the whole the idea of strength and solidity . . . The walls are plain and massy; the ornaments are few and simple; the apertures . . . are not numerous . . . the windows are plain, with strong simple cases . . . The genius of a great architect discloses itself in the least as well as the greatest things. Sir Christopher is to be respected as much for this tower as many larger works; and the succeeding architect may take it as a model.[16]

As did, among others, Richard Colley in his quiet yet confident remodelling of medieval Quatt, Shropshire (pl. 481).[17]

Stockton-on-Tees, County Durham, erected 'a very Beautiful New Church [at a] very great Expence' (pl. 482), which for its location and date is unusually sophisticated in both the choice of vocabulary and the regularity of design. An undated, perhaps spurious document in the parish records claims that 'Mr Wrenne . . . advised' the vicar on the design, which was executed by a 'guilde of masons' under a master builder named Richard Wrangham, a member of the Vestry. The consecration sermon preached in 1712 alluded to 'the commendable zeal for building Churches which distinguished the reign of Queen Anne', a reference to the New Churches programme on which both Wren and Nathaniel Crewe, Bishop of Durham (who consecrated the church), served as Commissioners between 1711 and 1715.[18] Wren's possible link is reinforced by the richly moulded, concave jambed west door and pedimented tripartite window of the brick and stone-quoined west tower, echoing his St Clement Eastcheap – nothing remotely like this had previously appeared in the north – and the distinctive tripartite windows with glazed arches on the west front and regimented along the

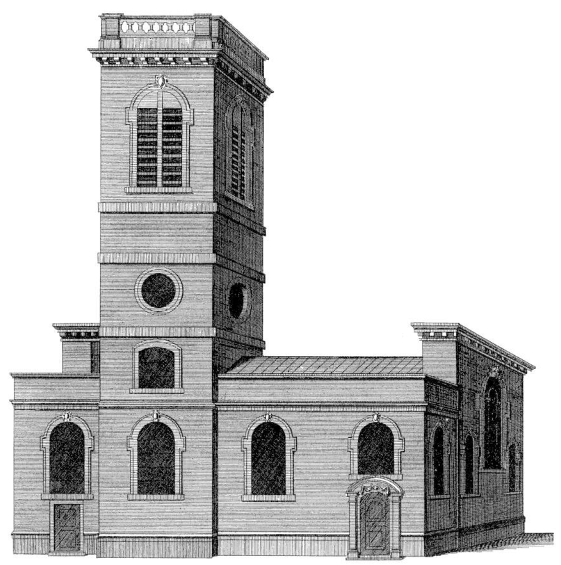

480 Benjamin Cole. 'The Parish Church of All Hallows the Great in Thames Street', London, in Maitland 1756, vol. II, p. 1054. Engraving. Author's collection. Sir Christopher Wren architect, 1676–83, demolished 1894.

481 Richard Colley. South-west view, St Andrew, Quatt, Shropshire, 1766–71.

north and south elevations, which derive from St Bride, Fleet Street (pl. 266), and which enjoyed popularity in the north-east of England at this time, as we have seen (p. 299).[19] There are, however, good reasons to believe that William Etty, who had close connections with London and moved up and down the coast undertaking commissions during these years (see pp. 299–300), may also have been directly involved. Honiley, Warwickshire (1723; pl. 102), traditionally given to Wren (who died on 25 February of that year), may be the work of his son, Christopher Jr, who had been resident at nearby Wroxall Abbey since 1713 and served as chief clerk in HM Office of Works and as a New Churches Commissioner.[20] Another intriguing provincial link with Wren and his London circle is offered by Wilsthorpe, Lincolnshire, of 1715 (pl. 483), the doorcase, circular window and balustrade of its idiosyncratic west and north fronts clearly cognisant of the view of St Mary-le-Bow showing the arcade fronting Cheapside proposed in 1671, subsequently abandoned but engraved after a drawing by Hawksmoor in 1721 (pl. 484). The tower's blocked, fluted pilasters recall columns 'extraordinaries et symboliques' in C. A. D'Aviler's *Cours d'Architecture* (1691), a copy of which Wren owned.[21]

Beyond these individual excursions, certainly among many that could be cited, three Wren churches command particular authority as unimpeachable models:

482 Sir Christopher Wren and William Etty, attributed. West front and tower, Stockton-on-Tees parish church, County Durham, 1710–12. English Heritage (National Monuments Record, A44/14108).

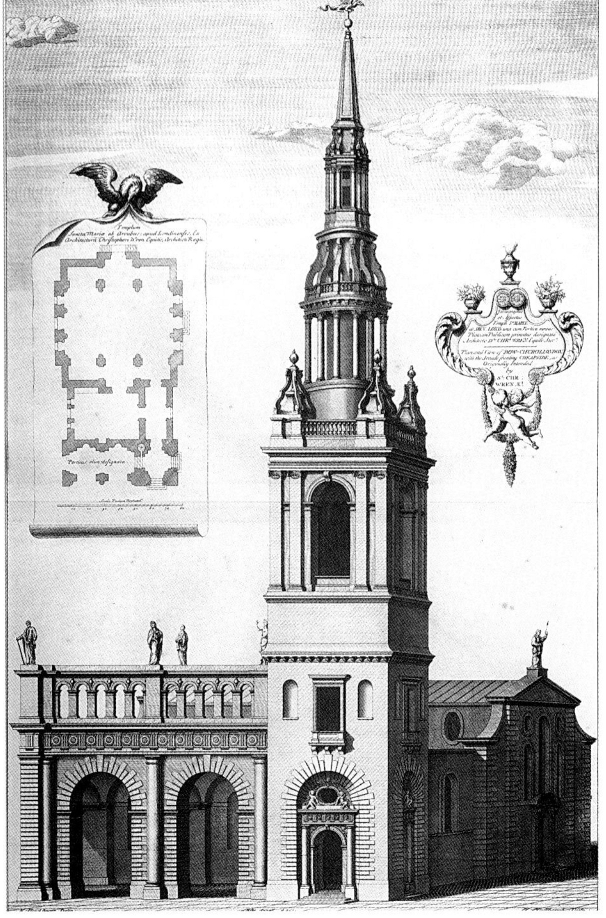

St Andrew, Holborn, St James, Westminster, and St Stephen Walbrook.

St Peter, Liverpool (1698–1704; pl. 485), the first post-Reformation church erected in this fast-growing mercantile town, which even then was described as a 'London in miniature',[22] was built probably to the design of a local mason named John Moffat 'after the patirn of St: Andrews' Holburn' (pl. 486).[23] Both churches feature pairs of domed vestry pavilions at the east end, side galleries on a pier and column system, barrel-vaulted naves and shallow chancels with a broad arched altarpiece (Richard Prescott's elaborate naturalistic carving at St Peter's a near replica of Grinling Gibbons's at St James, Westminster) lit by double-tiered, three-light windows, the upper one a Serliana, probably its first appearance in Liverpool. Notwithstanding, Holborn was built of Portland stone, Liverpool of local red sandstone, reflecting their costs of £9,000 compared to £3,500 respectively. Since Wren encased the existing medieval tower only in 1703–4, this left the Liverpuddlians free to devise their own, octagonal solution (originally also crowned by flaming torches) with the peculiarly inverted squinch-like corner transitions derived from Wren's St Swithin, Cannon Street (1677–85), their potential awkwardness avoided by overlaying delicately scrolled brackets.[24] Holborn became so firmly fixed as an ideal in the public mind that the Mancunian John Byrom commended it as 'the model, I believe, of the new church at Manchester', that is, St Anne (pl. 444), when, as we have seen (p. 425), its source was in fact All Saints, Oxford (pl. 440).[25]

Wren's promotion in 1712 of his Westminster church for its capaciousness, convenience, cheapness and beauty (p. 363), supported by a comprehensive engraving (pl. 478), secured its lasting influence, with at least one notable version built in each decade of the century.[26] The basic rural formula was established by John Price Sr of Richmond across the River Thames at All Saints, Isleworth (1705–7, gutted 1943, rebuilt 1963–70), its consecration sermon stressing 'Its Native Beauty, without any Embellishment of Art . . . sufficient to recommend . . . to the Applause of all Men, and to their Imitation . . . so far as a good Example can Influence and Invite' and praising the vestry as 'Visible in the Elegancy of this Noble Structure . . . beyond our

483 (*above*) Architect unknown. West elevation, St Faith, Wilsthorpe, Lincolnshire, 1715. English Heritage (National Monuments Record, BB50/00580).

484 (*left*) Heinrich Hulsbergh after Nicholas Hawksmoor. 'Plan, and View of Bow-Church, London with the Arcade fronting Cheapside, as Originally Intended by Sr: Chr: Wren, Kt', 1721. Engraving. Proposed 1671.

485 (*above*) John Moffat. South-east view, St Peter, Liverpool, Lancashire, 1698–1704. Liverpool Record Office, Z6H/26, photographed 1890, demolished 1922.

486 (*left*) Benjamin Cole. 'The North Prospect of St. Andrew's Church in Holborn', London, 1754, in Maitland 1756, vol. II, p. 1059. Engraving. Author's collection. Sir Christopher Wren architect, 1684–6.

Expectation, and without Example . . . made more Commodious, and more Beautiful by your pious Care and Conduct'.[27] The modesty of John James's St Mary, Rotherhithe (pl. 487), one of the failed candidates among the New Churches, sprung from the poverty of the Thames-side parish, which had suffered severe losses among the family heads either at sea or imprisonment abroad during the Anglo-French wars, making it impossible to raise locally the sum of £4,597 5s. 8d. needed for building.[28] The internal order, therefore, is the plainer Ionic (pl. 488); the galleries are attached to the back of full-height columns supporting a straight entab-

lature; the vault is subdivided by simple mouldings. In 1746, a month after James's death, the Vestry agreed to erect a new west tower, a 'very elegantly . . . well-constructed' Piccadilly-like structure crowned by a spired tempietto designed by Lancelot Dowbiggin, the son of a St Andrew Holborn 'gentleman'.[29]

The public sale in 1749 of more than two hundred Wren drawings for churches,[30] followed by 'A Catalogue, short Description, and general Dimensions, of Fifty-one parochial Churches of the City of London, erected according to the Designs, and under the Care and Conduct of Sir Christopher Wren' published in *Parentalia* (1750), alongside his recommendations of 1712, prompted a reawakening of critical interest, reaffirming again the crucial importance of the Holborn-

487 (*left*) Benjamin Cole. North-west view, 'The Parish Church of St. Mary at Rotherhithe', London, in Maitland 1756, vol. II, p. 1383. Engraving. Author's collection. John James, Benjamin Glanville and Lancelot Dowbiggin architects, 1714–48.

488 (*below*) Gideon Yates. View of interior towards the chancel of St. Mary, Rotherthithe, London, 1826. Watercolour. Southwark Local Studies Library, Gardner Collection PB304. John James architect, 1714–15.

Westminster pattern as a bulwark of conservative design now almost entirely oblivious of emerging neoclassical tastes. St Andrew (pl. 486) is praised as 'beautiful, and spacious', its 'plainness . . . regularity and symmetry of parts . . . produce a simple beauty . . . its length, breadth, and height, are in good proportion; its windows regular, of reasonable dimensions, and at tolerable good distance; and crowned with a handsome balustrade . . . The in-side is very light, airy and beautiful'.[31] The 'Beauty' of St James (pl. 478) lay in the vault's division into 'Pannels of Crocket and Fret-work', the cornice supported on twelve columns, the galleries, door-cases, especially that fronting Jermyn Street, and the double tier of eastern tripartite windows, the upper a Serliana.[32] These qualities are further asserted in Osborne's *English Architecture* (1758): St James is 'plain but well ordered, and well fashioned', while St Andrew is

> plain but not inelegant . . . no parade of columns, nor other of the nobler articles; but . . . an uniformity . . . which cannot fail to give the judicious eye satisfaction . . . The openings . . . regularly placed . . . very well proportioned to the piers . . . though without ostentation . . . and . . . have consequently a very good effect . . . there is an air of knowledge and truth in the whole building . . . It is plain that the architect has done all he intended to do.

By this time and particularly in London the models had grown so familiar that architectural invention largely concentrated on steeples. A spectacular example is St Mary, Islington (pl. 489). Rising from a conventional square base is a short octagonal stage supporting a domed tempietto of eight free-standing Corinthian columns with block rusticated shafts, crowned by an obelisk spire. The *Gentleman's Magazine* praised this work by the 'ingenious Mr *Doubikin*' (Lancelot Dowbiggin) for its 'air of elegance and novelty, which makes it universally admired'.[33]

Other solutions for enhancing the fundamental pattern included introducing a temple portico on the High Street elevation of St Mary, Lewisham (pl. 490).[34] Just as the Holborn-Westminster pattern was fading into an ultra-conservative formula, it received a new

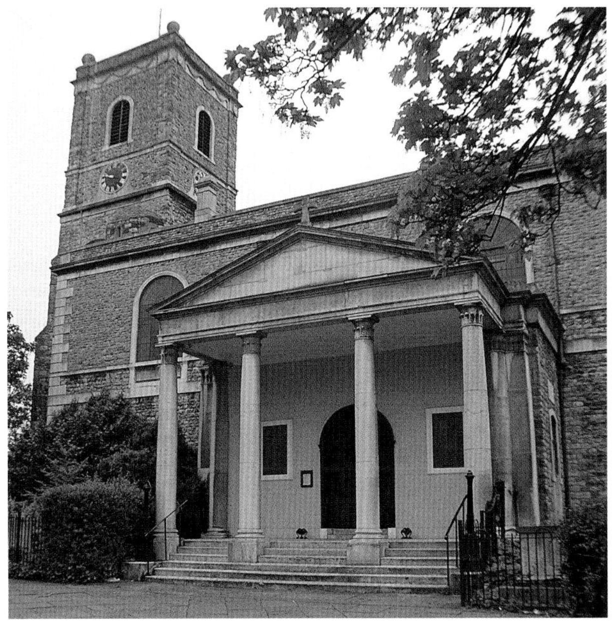

489 (*above*) Benjamin Cole. 'North East Prospect of the Parish Church of St. Mary at Islington', London, in Maitland 1756, vol. II, p. 1370. Engraving. Author's collection. Lancelot Dowbiggin architect, 1750–54, destroyed in Blitz, 1940, except tower.

490 (*right*) George Gibson Jr. South elevation, St Mary, Lewisham, London, 1773–7.

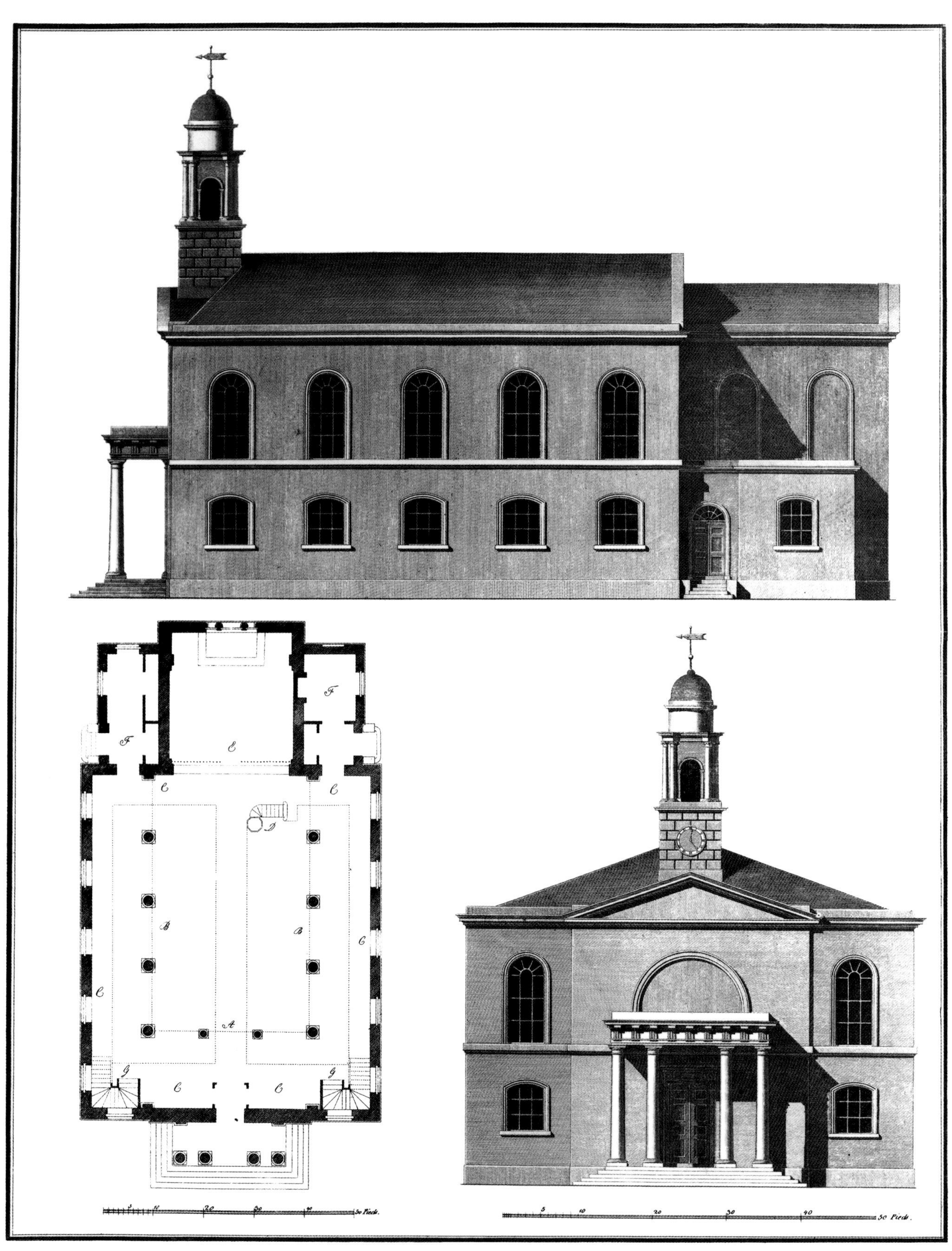

491 Cougel after Schwender. Plan, west and south elevations, St Mary, Wanstead, Essex, in Stieglitz 1800, pls 53–4. Engraving. Author's collection. Thomas Hardwick Jr. architect, 1787–90.

lease of life in the early churches of Thomas Hardwick Jr, a pupil of Sir William Chambers and the Royal Academy Schools, who, despite visiting Italy during the late 1770s, remained anchored in an earlier classical tradition, sustained by his worthy restorations of Inigo Jones's St Paul, Covent Garden, in 1788–9 and 1796–8, and St James, Westminster, in 1788–9 and 1803–4. The latter's Vestry minutes are a rare document of the sympathetic care taken in replenishing an iconic Wren church. Particularly instructive is Hardwick's provision for 'proper Boarding' to prevent Grinling Gibbons's meticulously carved reredos from 'receiving Injury', and covering the fabric-lined pews under the north gallery reserved for divine service during repairs, as well as the organ, its loft and clock, with matting and paper 'to prevent any Injury being done to them'. The brazier was ordered to 'take down and Relacquer all the Chandelier Branches and Sockets which have been Lacquered before', a 'proper Person [was employed] to wash with Soap and Water the Marble Monuments', and Robert Johnson received £20 3s. 0d. for 'cleaning Velvet Fringe &c'.[35]

Hardwick's earliest church, St Mary, Wanstead, Essex (pl. 491), surviving unaltered, is notable for the high quality of its workmanship, the

> very best Portland stone free from vents or sanholes . . . Purbeck Steps of the best quality . . . Black & white marble paving . . . well rubbed grounded and part polished . . . All . . . done . . . to the Satisfactn. of . . . the Architect [with] no bad Materials of any Sort be made Use of . . .

which the *Gentleman's Magazine* reckoned was the result of 'much study and attention to propriety in every part . . . and may be considered as a pattern church to any parish in the kingdom'.[36]

Although praised as 'so constructed as to command the praise of the judicious . . . promise a very lasting duration . . . and . . . serve the succeeding race of architects as a model in what manner they are to conduct themselves', Wren's oddly shaped churches – the elongated decagon of St Benet Fink (1670–75, demolished 1846), the coffin of St Olave Jewry (1671–9, demolished 1887) and the domed octagonal St Antholin, Budge Row (1687–9, demolished 1874) – found no imitators.[37] The exception was St Stephen Walbrook (pl. 492), a rectangle enclosing a dome floating above eight slender columns surrounded by a forest of eight further supports defining perimeter aisles to form a combined longitudinal and centralised complex. Here 'the genius of the great . . . Wren triumphs, superior to all praise!', a 'masterpiece' where 'Perhaps *Italy* itself can produce no modern building that can vie with this in taste or proportion: there is not a beauty which the plan would admit of, that is not to be found here in its greatest perfection'. *The London and Westminster Guide* (1768) encouraged visitors 'to feast [their] Eyes on the Triumph of Art'. Robert Adam viewed it 'with doubly the pleasure that I had before'. James Bridges of Bristol believed it was 'esteem'd by all Architects that have seen it, as a matchless Pile of Art'.[38] It was explored most ingeniously by two little-known architects, Robert Dingley and Thomas Wiggens Jr.

In the euphoria of launching one of the outstanding socio-architectural schemes of the eighteenth century (complementing the contemporary London Hospital for Foundlings), Dingley, a Foundling Hospital governor, promoted his own design for a 'New Magdalen House', presented as a pair of large sanguine engravings (pls 493–4). It had its beginnings in a *Proposal for the Relief and Employment of Friendless Girls and Repenting Prostitutes* (1758) by Jonas Hanway (Dingley's business partner in a St Petersburg sugar refinery and fellow member of the Society of Arts in London) as a place 'where they may pass their time in comfort and safety [and] treat them with such regard, as shall convince them that nothing more is meant than their own happiness'.[39] The 50-foot-square chapel was to form the free-standing centrepiece within an impressive quadrangular complex of dormitory and service blocks linked to them on either side of a broad avenue by cloister-like arcades. As at the Foundling Hospital, separation of inmates and visitors was to be carefully organised, in this case by a clever division of the arcaded approaches by spine walls, with public access along the inner passages leading to a ground-storey vestibule, and inmates along outer circuits connecting the main blocks to circular staircases culminating in an overhead gallery. The chapel exterior was inspired by Burlington's villa at Chiswick (a choice undoubtedly dictated by the fact that the Architect Earl, together with Roger Morris, had designed Kirkby Hall in Yorkshire, 1747–55, for Stephen Thompson, Dingley's brother-in-law).[40] The interior, requiring a religious rather than domestic configuration, is based on Walbrook (pl. 492), in which eight Corinthian columns support a polylobed, compartmented dome, with Dingley transferring Wren's semicircular vestibule to form the apsidal chancel. In the event, Joel Johnson's less seductive, conventional octagonal chapel was erected in the years 1769–72.[41]

In 1761 Wiggens won the Society of Polite Arts' premium for a design for improving the exterior of

Sr. Christopher Wren Archt.
George Marshall Delin. et Sculp.
A Perspective View of the inside of St. Stephens Church in Walbrook London.

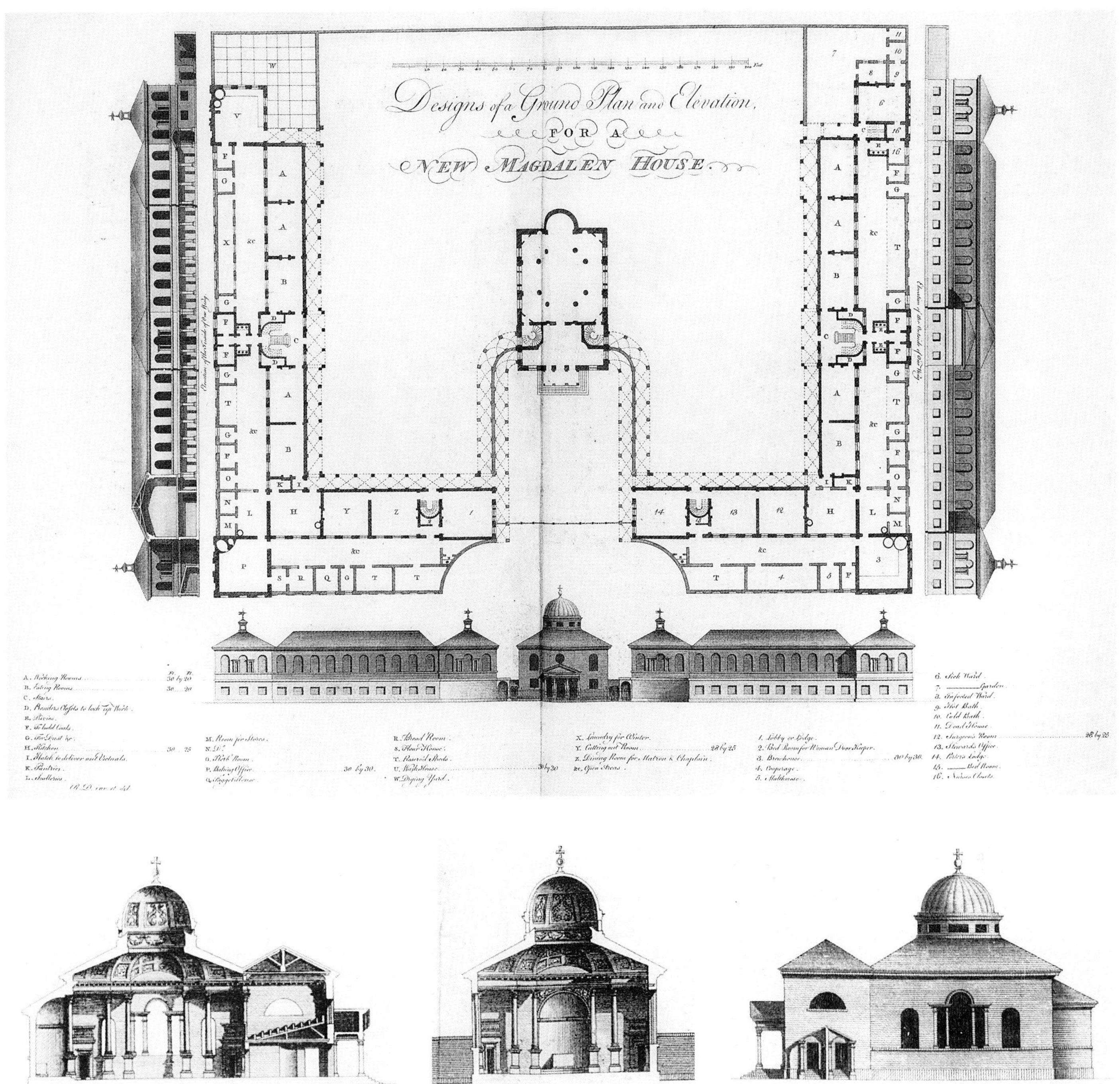

493 (*top*) Robert Dingley. 'Designs of a Ground Plan and Elevation, for a New Magdalen House', Southwark, London, 1758, unrealized. Engraving. The Bodleian Library, University of Oxford, Gough Maps 20, f. 60B.

494a, b and c (*above*) Robert Dingley. 'Section', 'Section cross' and 'Side Elevation' of the Chapel for Magdalen House, Southwark, London, 1758, unrealized. Engraving. The Bodleian Library, University of Oxford, Gough Maps 20, f. 61.

492 (*facing page*) George Marshall. 'Perspective View of the inside of St. Stephens Church in Walbrook London', detail, *c.*1740. Engraving. London Metropolitan Archives (Guildhall Library, Pr 552/STE). Sir Christopher Wren architect, 1672–1714.

495 Thomas Wiggens Jr. West front 'Design of the Outside of St. Stephen Walbrook . . . presented to the Society of Polite Arts Feby. 1761 . . . Adjudged the best For Which a Premium of Twenty Guineas was given', unrealised. Pen and ink and wash. Sir John Soane's Museum, 47/9/1.

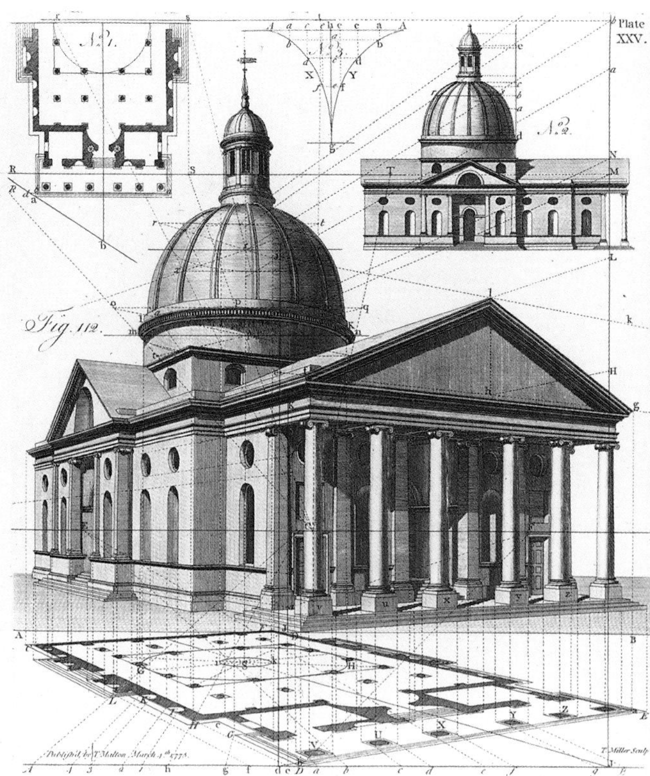

496 T. Miller. Design for 'exterior Building, adapted to St. Stephen's Walbrook, but of a different Order', London, 4 March 1775, in Malton 1779, pl. XXV, fig. 112. Engraving.

St Stephen (pl. 495). Contributions were also offered by Jacob Le Roux, a London architect and speculative builder, in the same year, and by Edward Belk of Titchfield Street in 1762, both exhibited at the Free Society of Artists but now untraced. These all responded to criticism of Wren's original building: while conceding that it was 'certainly the most elegant edifice of its magnitude [he had] ever designed', Langley nevertheless believed that 'a very material [beauty] is wanting, namely, the entrance should have been with a grand portico, on that [north] side next Stocks-market'. The Dodsleys worried that the 'large dome . . . cannot be seen to advantage . . . hid by the Mansion-house' (erected 1739–42 on that site).[42] Wiggens virtually transformed the exterior, replacing the existing jumble of tower, vestry and internal staircase that provided an awkward passage from pavement to body by attaching to the west end a monumental prostyle temple portico raised on a perron. The inspiration was Wren's Great Model for St Paul's (pl. 476), exemplifying 'an eminent and costly performance, and a Monument . . . of the Skill of the greatest Geometrician and Architect of his Time'. The windowless, rusticated west wall derived from Inigo Jones's pre-Fire cathedral (pl. 324), which in 1738 still 'stirred up a laudable Zeal'. The twin towers recall those embellishing the present cathedral (pl. 2). The dome is ribbed and crowned by a lamentably oversized lantern to supply additional height. Wiggens's scheme, while demonstrating the confusion resulting from over-reliance on engraved sources, represented what, if erected, would have marked the unique appearance of a prostyle temple portico on the City Churches.[43]

Thomas Malton Sr, who had exhibited drawings of Wren's church at the Society of Artists in 1764 and 1766, took this idea even further in 1775 (pl. 496). He heeded Langley's advice by introducing prominent side entrances, reforming the dome and lantern into a more prominent spherical shape, regularising the asymmetrical west end by flanking the apsidal entrance with a pair of vestry rooms articulated by doors, niches, circular windows and Ionic pilasters, and screening the entire elevation with a low-lying hexastyle Ionic temple portico. This helped to lessen the steep ascent from the street into the body, where an additional row of columns has been inserted between the dome and the east wall to balance the existing arrangement at the west end. Wren's baroque masterpiece has been mutated into a building that belongs unequivocally to the conservative branch of Palladianism.

This trend is epitomised in a contemporary view of the interior of an unidentified church dating from the late eighteenth or early nineteenth century (p. vi). Here the division into ground floor and gallery lit by segmental and round-headed windows reflects an arrangement popularised at St Andrew, Holborn (pl. 486), and St James, Westminster (pl. 478) – the undecorated simplicity of walls and ceiling, with their bland scheme of white and stone colours, the austerity of the great architect's Protestant approach. More up-to-date features include Tuscan columns, with marbleised shafts, rising on tall bases from the tops of the box pews to support streamlined, elegantly moulded transverse beams on which the gallery floors rest, the double recessed rectangular panels of the gallery fronts, and the tripartite Ionic reredos lit by a Diocletian window filled with richly coloured, geometric patterned painted glass.

It is worth remembering that provincial architects and builders looked to metropolitan models outside Wren's *œuvre*. Sir James Lowther wrote from London in 1714 regarding Holy Trinity, Whitehaven, Cumberland (1714–15, demolished), that he 'had a great deal of discourse' and secured the goodwill of the Archbishop of York and his soon-to-be-consecrated successor, the Bishop of Chester, Sir William Dawes, both of whom were New Churches Commissioners and 'very wel pleas'd & extream ready to promote this good design of a new Church'. Lowther described his own preferred seating arrangement after 'the Modell of a chappel in Devonshire Street', that is, St George the Martyr, Queen's Square (1705–6), a chapel of ease to St Andrew, Holborn. He ended his letter encouragingly: 'I shall in a very few days see several more Churches & draughts.'[44] St Andrew-by-the-Green, Glasgow (pl. 497), the first Episcopalian place of worship erected in Scotland, was described as 'a very handsome oblong Square . . . on the Model of the Churches of London'.[45] There were several close ties with the capital. Of the nine 'Directors or Managers' – four merchants, a bookseller, dyer, vintner, tobacconist and sugar baker 'of the Episcopal persuasion residing in or near the City of Glasgow' – appointed in 1750 to purchase the site and 'employ masons wrights and others for building and finishing [the work in] such a manner as they shall judge best', Alexander Oswald's London merchant relative, Richard Oswald, recommended employing a

497 Andrew Hunter, attributed. South-east view, St Andrew-by-the-Green, Glasgow, Strathclyde, Scotland, 1750–51.

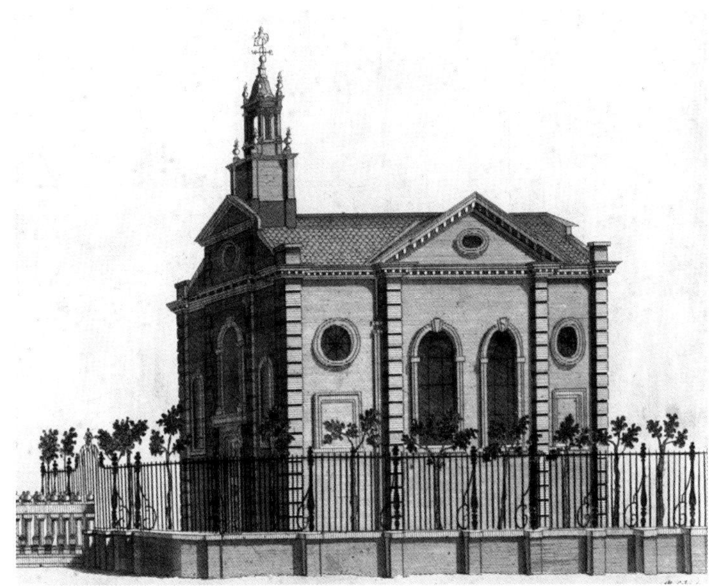

498 Benjamin Cole. 'The South West Prospect of the Sweeds Church in Princes Square Ratcliff-highway', London, in Maitland 1756, vol. II, p. 1026. Engraving. Author's collection. Architect unknown, 1729, demolished *c.* 1920.

solicitor to obtain 'a Brief in favour of the chappel' from the Bishop of London, who in turn provided 'a proper Clergy-man . . . of his Lordships nomination'. Moreover, Andrew Stalker, the treasurer, who contracted with the builders, was a bookseller and, thus, in a favourable position to receive intelligence about London architectural trends.[46] The 'Model' chosen was very likely the Swedes' Church (pl. 498). Both feature

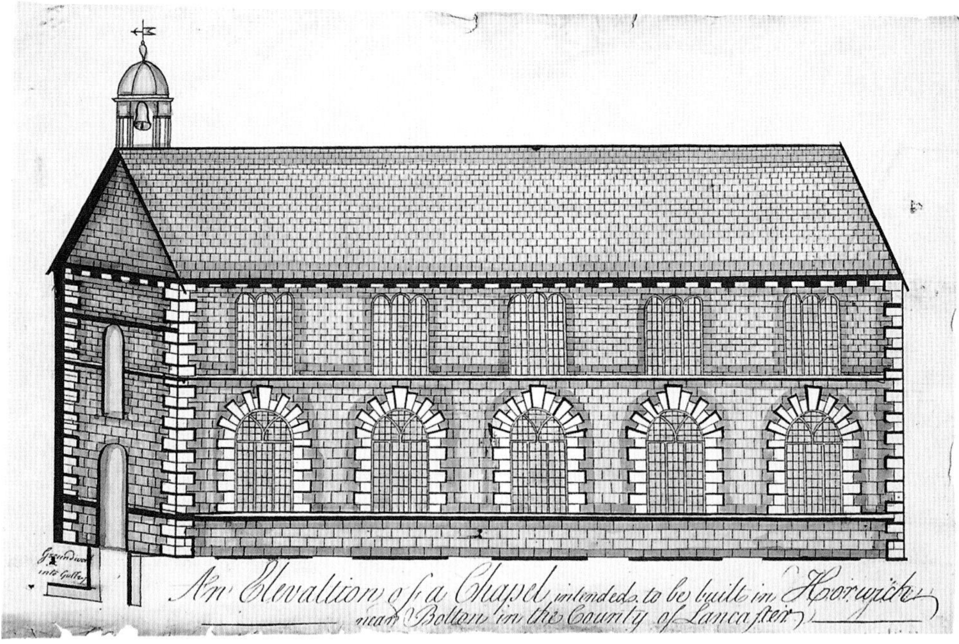

499 Architect unknown. 'An Elevation of a Chapel intended to be built in Horwich near Bolton in the County of Lancashire', *c.*1776. Pen and ink and wash. Lancashire Record Office, QSP 2046/18.

pediments with round windows on all four elevations, accentuated by 'bold . . . rustic' pilasters without capitals.[47]

As the century progressed Wren's churches came to epitomise a conservative bulwark against the *avant gardism* of the younger generation, nowhere more explicitly voiced than in Langley's counterblast to Ralph in 1734 regarding St Clement Danes. The former preferred Wren's columns on piers to Gibbs's giant order interrupted by galleries, the architrave resting on the capitals to Gibbs's St Martin-in-the-Fields's dosserets, while he abhorred Gibbs's completion of St Clement's tower with a 'small cupola [and] small black [block] rustics [in a] low mince-pye taste'.[48] Wrenian patterns, thus, remained favourites among conservative clients, their architects and builders, and though as the decades progressed they became anachronisms, strays in historical limbo, by their very number they are worthy of remembrance.

The same is true of James Gibbs's churches and their progeny. Behind these lay Wren's exemplars, for it is indicative that as Gibbs struggled under stiff competition to secure the surveyorship of St Martin's in 1720 he escorted the building committee on a study tour of St James, Westminster, St Andrew, Holborn, St Clement Danes, St Stephen Walbrook, St Martin Ludgate and St Magnus Martyr.[49] Gibbs gave pride of place to his three seminal churches – St Martin-in-the-Fields, Marylebone Chapel (subsequently St Peter, Vere Street, now offices) and All Saints, Derby – in *A Book of Architecture* (1728, second edition issued in 1739). St Martin's immediately identifiable feature, its lofty, multi-tiered steeple (pl. 416), for which nine alternative published patterns were offered and whose influence travelled far beyond Britain (see chapter 30), were widely imitated by architects and builders, ringing the changes in a sort of equivalent to eighteenth-century musical practices of improvising cadenzas.[50] Two other hallmarks also remained in vogue: the 'Gibbs surround' and the dosseret column, infusing a Gibbsian flavour in buildings, too numerous to deal with in the present book, that otherwise bear little resemblance to the models. Much of their appeal dwells in enhancing plain, provincial churches across the social spectrum.

In a trio of like-minded schemes for Walmersley (1767), Bradshaw (1774) and Horwich (*circa* 1776; pl. 499), all located within a five-mile radius of Bolton, Lancashire, clearly by the same unknown hand, where the parishes were unable to raise funds because they were 'greatly Burdened with poor . . . Cottagers . . . Labourers and common work people in the Cotton Manufactory [who were] chiefly Tenants at Rack Rents', the block rustic came into its own.[51] But also at St Paul, Birmingham (1776–9, pl. 500), erected as the centrepiece of an affluent new private estate development,[52] and at Donibristle House chapel (1729–35; pl.

500 Hancock after Pickering. South-west view, 'St Paul's Chapel', Birmingham, Warwickshire, in Hutton 1783, p. 116. Engraving. Roger Eykyn architect, 1776–9.

501), built for Charles Steward, 6th Earl of Moray, by Alexander McGill of Edinburgh, who subscribed to *A Book of Architecture*. Its octagonal, open-crown cupola was perhaps a homage to the famous seventeenth-century steeple of St Giles Cathedral, Edinburgh, an emblem of Scottish nationalism during the uncertain times between the first (1715) and second (1745) Jacobite uprisings.[53]

Gibbs's dosseret system, his personal leitmotif introduced at St Martin and at the Marylebone Chapel (pls 417, 502), where the columns support polylobed panels of plasterwork derived from the Baths of Augustus, Rome,[54] was still thriving as late as the 1740s in the exquisite Kirkleatham Hospital chapel, Yorkshire, created for Chomley Turner (pl. 503). This miniature St Martin's is embellished with black, white and variegated marble paving and a magnificent twelve-arm gilt-wood chandelier purchased in 1747 at the sale of Gibbs's defunct chapel at Cannons. The ironwork of the communion rails, the west gallery fronts and the rococo pew locks are exceptionally stunning. The Serliana of the apsidal chancel is hung with painted glass by William Price, including a copy of the *Adoration of the*

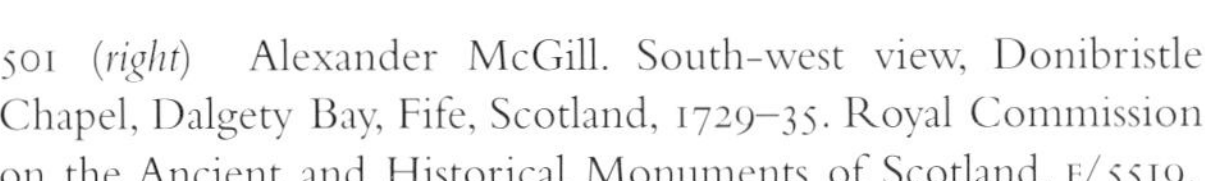

501 (*right*) Alexander McGill. South-west view, Donibristle Chapel, Dalgety Bay, Fife, Scotland, 1729–35. Royal Commission on the Ancient and Historical Monuments of Scotland, F/5519.

502 James Gibbs. Interior towards west, Marylebone or Oxford Chapel (St Peter), St Marylebone, London, 1721–26. English Heritage (National Monuments Record, A44/281, photographed 1941, before alterations).

503 James Gibbs. Interior towards chancel, Sir William Turner's Hospital Chapel, Kirkleatham, Yorkshire, 1741–60.

Magi from Cannons, flanked by standing figures of Turner ancestors.[55] John Robert's Protestant Cathedral, Waterford (1774–92; pl. 504), sports fully fledged neo-classical capitals, with the potential clash of engaged columns at the chancel arch avoided by suspending the entablature section on consoles.[56] Great Badminton, Gloucestershire (pl. 505), is a particularly gorgeous example, its spacious, open, well-lit arrangement intended to direct the eye uninhibited both axially and diagonally to Michael Rysbrack's grand figurative tombs to the dukes of Beaufort at the eastern ends of the aisles.[57]

Gibbs's chapel at ease on Edward Harley's St Marylebone Estate (1721–4; pl. 506), too, spawned a significant progeny. A 'Jewel of its Kind',[58] the astylar temple form, a type developed during the same decade on a larger scale at Old Street (pl. 433), is here distinguished by a diminutive Doric porch and a bell turret rising over the west end of the roof. This quickly became an *idée fixe*.[59] Grosvenor (or Audley Street) Chapel (1730–32) on the adjacent Mayfair Estate (pl. 1) was designed by Benjamin Timbrell, Gibbs's favourite

504 (*facing page top*) John Roberts after Thomas Malton Sr. 'Inside of the Cathedral of St. Peter's Waterford', County Waterford, Ireland, undated. Engraving. © The British Library Board, K.Top. 55-17-d. J. Roberts architect, 1774–92.

505 (*facing page bottom*) Charles Evans and Thomas Wright. Interior towards chancel, St Michael, Great Badminton, Gloucestershire, 1783–7. English Heritage (National Monuments Record, BB98/01599). Chancel rebuilt 1875.

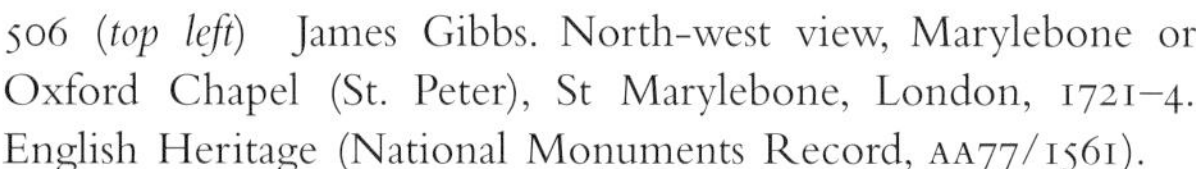

506 (*top left*) James Gibbs. North-west view, Marylebone or Oxford Chapel (St. Peter), St Marylebone, London, 1721–4. English Heritage (National Monuments Record, AA77/1561).

507 (*above left*) James Horne. Design for 'East End of Christ Church', Southwark, London, 1738. Pen and ink and wash. © The British Library Board, K.Top. XXVII-50-e. Erected 1738–41, destroyed in Blitz, 1941.

508 (*top right*) John Carr, attributed. West elevation, Westgate Chapel, Wakefield, Yorkshire, 1751–2.

509 (*above right*) Robert Morris. Design for Colegate Octagon Chapel (Presbyterian), Norwich, Norfolk, 1753. Pen and ink and wash. Norfolk Record Office, FC13/80, no. 9.

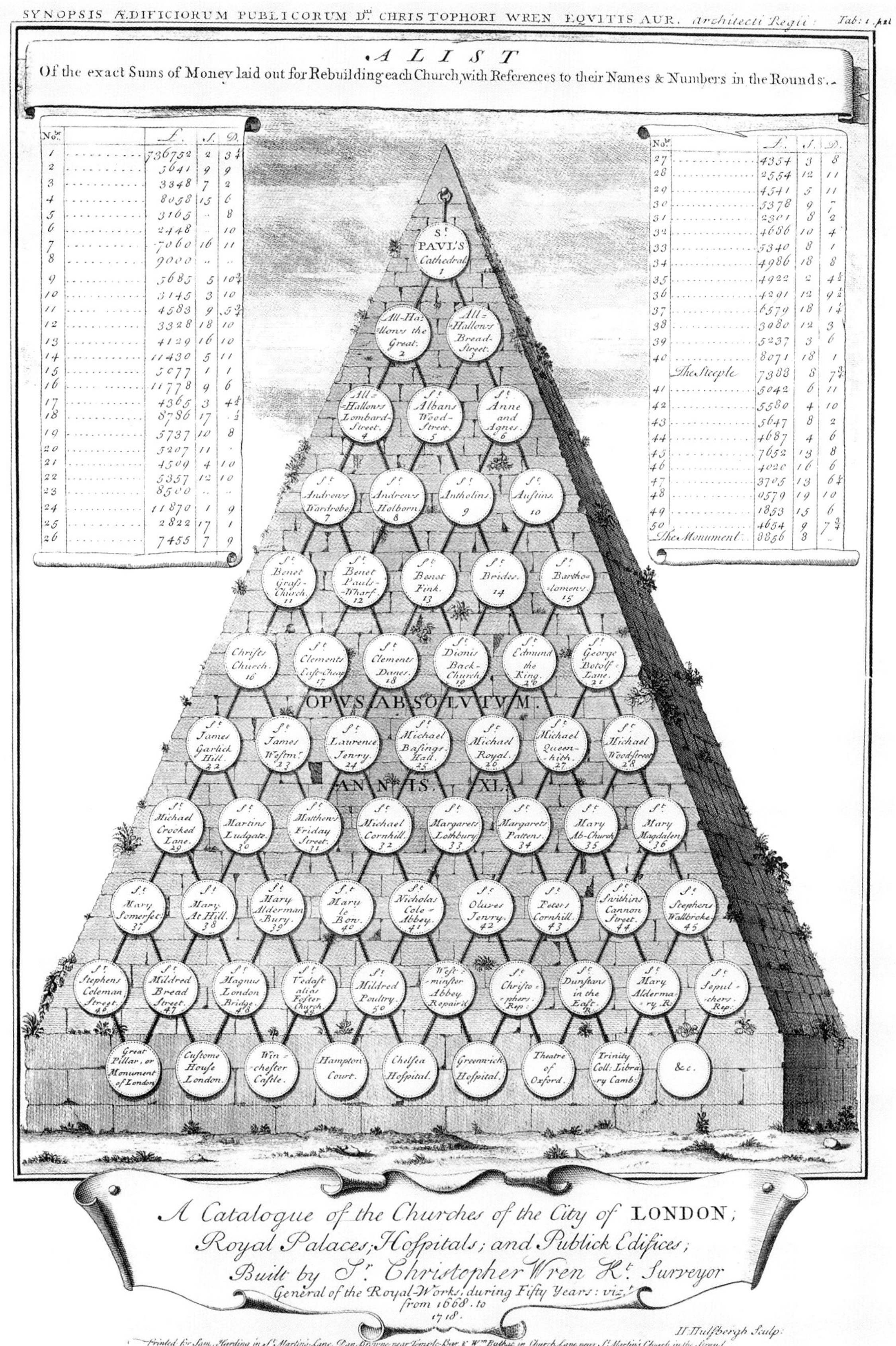

510 Heinrich Hulsbergh. 'A Catalogue of the Churches of the City of London . . . Built by Sr. Christopher Wren Kt . . . from 1668. to 1718' with 'A List Of the exact Sums of Money laid out for Rebuilding', 1729. Engraving.

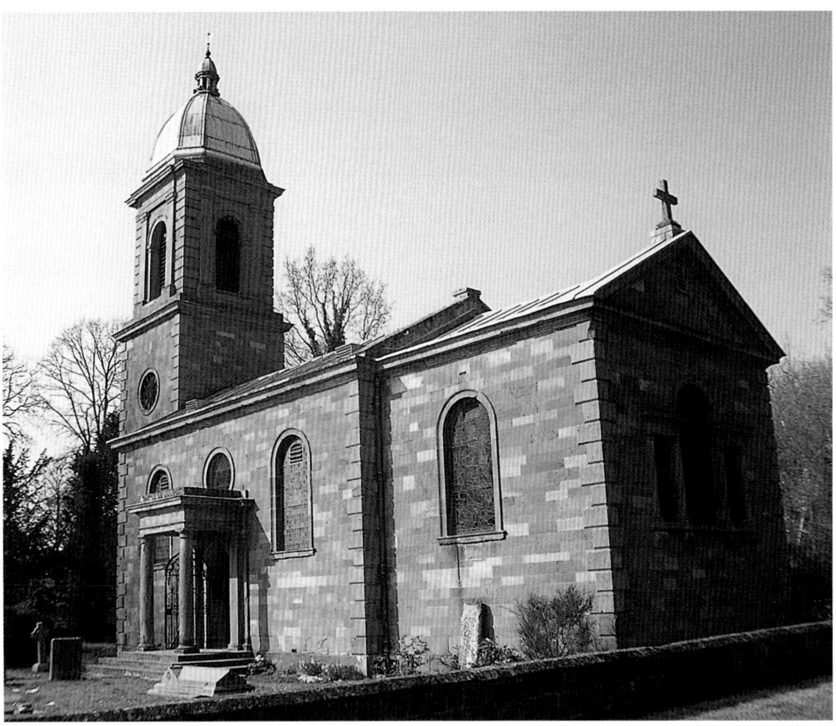

511 James Gibbs. St Mary, Patshull, Staffordshire, 1742–3, tower remodelled 19th century.

carpenter employed at both Marylebone and St Martin's and a subscriber to *A Book of Architecture*.[60] Nearby Berkeley Chapel (*circa* 1750, demolished; pl. 1), by a second-generation Palladian, William Jones, was a closer copy of the prototype.[61] Marylebone also features a prominent Serliana to mark the eastern chancel, which Gibbs recommended as 'proper to be placed at the end of Churches'.[62] James Horne, who worked under Gibbs at St Bartholomew's Hospital and King's College, Cambridge (and whose draughtsmanship is similar enough to speculate that he may have been a pupil or assistant), repeated this formula at Christ Church, Southwark (pl. 507).[63]

Westgate Chapel, Wakefield, Yorkshire (1752–3; pl. 508), erected by wealthy, influential Presbyterians, replaced an old fabric that had become 'ruinous' and due to its 'very Low . . . Situation . . . so Subject to Inundations that it was . . . Unwholesome and Dangerous to assemble there for the . . . Exercise of . . . Worship'.[64] The balance between plain structure and fashionable architectural accents accorded with the denomination's aspirations, which were perfectly expressed in the opening sermon, delivered in 1752 by the minister of Mill Hill Chapel, Leeds:

> Our saviour came into the world to settle religion upon its primitive foundations . . . He that thinks God is like himself, will naturally honour him in a way that he apprehends would be pleasing to himself . . . If he imagines that he delights in pomp and magnificence, he will honour him with such costly obligations and superb structures . . . as he presumes will be pleasing to a being of that turn of mind . . . it is not the grandeur of an edifice . . . not the fancied holiness of its materials and utensils, or all the rich and showy ornaments which art and fancy may contrive or opulence procure, that determines his residence to any place . . . though commodiousness ought first to be consulted, yet in an age in which a taste for elegance in almost all things else prevails, I see not why a discreet and moderate degree of the *same taste* may not be allowed *in this*; especially *among us*, whose worship has sometimes been ignorantly held in contempt for the *meanness* of our places . . . *This house*, not inelegantly furnished, is an evidence and will be a monument of a pious munificence.[65]

The architect may have been the young John Carr, the most talented member of an established stone masons' dynasty based at nearby Horbury, employing a Gibbsian repertory plagiarised from *A Book of Architecture* in Langley's *Treasury of Designs*, which fortuitously was published in 1740.[66] The repertory also appeared in the work of Robert Morris, a relative of the architect

Roger Morris, who was baptised at St Martin-in-the-Fields and a St Marylebone resident between 1724 and 1730, the year of Gibbs's greatest activities there. Robert, who reckoned Gibbs 'may be said, most Times in Dress to please / And few can decorate with greater Ease',[67] in 1753 sent an offering for the Colegate Nonconformist Chapel, Norwich (pl. 509), a luxurious (for that sect) rectangle combining St Martin and Marylebone Chapel motifs. It was rejected, however, in favour of one by Thomas Ivory (pl. 581).[68]

The financial crisis springing from the burst of the South Sea Bubble in 1720, the exorbitant total cost of realising less than a dozen of the intended fifty New Churches (see Appendix B), exacerbated by war with Spain over Gibraltar in 1728, led to the premature abandonment of this over-ambitious programme in 1734. St Martin-in-the-Fields, too, represented a formidable expense at £33,661 16s. 7¾d.[69] By comparison, Wren's SS Anne and Agnes, among the cheapest, costing £2,348 0s. 10d., and St James, Westminster, at £7,000, both with modest towers and largely of brick construction, demonstrated the economic benefits to the parish of adopting more sobre Wrenian solutions. While the pyramidal table of building costs issued in 1749 (pl. 510) is inaccurate and represents only a selection of the City Churches, it is poignant that the list with costs alone was reissued at the outbreak of the Seven Years War in 1756 and again in 1784 following the American War of Independence, when building trades were hampered by a scarcity of materials.[70] This retrenchment is embodied in Gibbs's last and plainest English church at Patshull, Staffordshire (1742–3; pl. 511), stone-built yet devoid of the classical order but for its diminutive Tuscan porch, as well as of ornament (the top stages of the tower are nineteenth-century additions), and most closely resembling Wren's All Hallows, Lombard Street.[71] Patshull was erected during the destabilising years between the conflict with Spain in 1739 (the War of Jenkins's Ear) and impending hostilities with France in the years 1744–8 and the Jacobite Rising of 1745–6, which inflated construction costs.[72] These events were important in paving way for a transition in church design to Palladianism, which came hard on the summit of baroque around 1730, a stylistic sea change unparalleled in eighteenth-century Europe.

The East prospect of St. Paul Church Covent Garden to the Great Square.

Elevation Oriental de L'Eglise du St. Paul Couvent Garden du coté de la grande Place.

512 Heinrich Hulsbergh after Colen Campbell. ‘The East prospect of St. Paul Church . . . The West prospect of Covent Garden . . . Great Square’, London, in Campbell 1717, pls 21–2, detail. Engraving. Inigo Jones architect, 1631–3.

Twenty-four

PALLADIAN PROTOTYPES

here . . . the reigning taste is Palladio's style . . . and a man is an Heretick
that would talk of Michel Angelo . . . You must dilligently copy
all the noted fabricks of Palladio for those very draughts would introduce
you here and without them you may despair of success[1]

That useful barometer of popular architectural fashion, James Ralph's *Critical Review* of 1734, condemned the most extrovert baroque creation of the New Churches programme, Archer's St John, Westminster (pl. 365), for its 'fatal mistake, to endeavour at an excellence, and then err so wide of the mark as to stumble on deformity', where the architect had only to have 'once thought of [the] rule [that] all false ornaments become faults instantly, and only serve to make an absurdity more conspicuous'.[2] For emerging Palladian classicism, simplicity was fundamental:

> Here buildings boast a robe, tho' rich yet chaste
> The robe of judgment, and of ripen'd taste
> Convenience here is mix'd with manly grace
> Yet ornament but holds the second place[3]

– embodied in Inigo Jones's iconic St Paul, Covent Garden (pl. 512), and in the Venetian churches of his great predecessor Andrea Palladio (pl. 518).

Ralph was not the earliest architectural commentator to rebel against baroque. Colen Campbell in the introduction to the first volume of *Vitruvius Britannicus* (1715), in an attempt to redirect taste radically, pantheonised 'the *great* Palladio, who has exceeded all that were gone before him, and surpass'd his Contemporaries, whose ingenious Labours will eclipse many, and rival most of the Ancients', together with his English follower, 'the *Famous* Inigo Jones'. This celebrated manifesto opens with an attack on two baroque icons: 'Majestic' St Peter's Basilica in Rome (Bramante, 1506, Michelangelo, 1547, Carlo Maderno, 1609–16) and 'Noble' St Paul's Cathedral in London (Wren, 1675–1710), 'beyond Exception . . . the second Church in the World'. British interest in the former was particularly strong at this time. For example, in 1710 John Talman, who had prepared a design for elaborate marble paving under St Paul's dome, wrote from Rome concerning making 'sevral drawings' of St Peter's and in the following year purchased 'a set of most rare prints of St Peters which shew curiositys . . . you see in no other prints', and he also made 'some wonderful drawings of St Peters all in colours which the Pope has a design to see'. He described a painting by Giuseppe Chiari depicting a group of British gentlemen just 'come from Rome' presenting Queen Anne with 'models of the chief buildings both sacred & secular as St Peters Vatican & the Capitol'.[4] Rivalry between these two great buildings began with St Paul's rebuilding in the 1660s, when it was 'contended, that for the Honour of the Nation, and City of *London*, it ought not to be exceeded in Magnificence, by any Church in Europe'.

> Earths Cabinet of Rarities, famed *Rome*,
> No longer now, remains without compare;
> Since *British* Architecture dares presume
> To vie with the most celebrated there.

By 1699 it was 'in the judgment of Travellers . . . like to emulate . . . even *Saint Peter's*'.[5]

What makes Campbell's contribution significant is his censure of *both* buildings. St Peter's (pl. 513) was condemned for the 'excessive Height of the *Attick*', the tetrastyle Corinthian temple portico, which was 'mean for so great a Front' and demanded 'at least . . . an Hexastyle', the 'trifling . . . Breaks [and] Parts without any Proportion', while Maderno's extended nave was 'contrary to *Michael Angelo*'s Design [of] a Square [which] extreamly injured the August Appearance of the *Cupola*'. Though kinder to St Paul's (pl. 514), he seems to have taken the Earl of Shaftesbury's remark in the *Letter concerning the art or science of design* (1712), that 'Hardly . . . shou'd we bear to see . . . a new Cathedral . . . treated . . . like St PAUL's' to issue brazenly a 'new Design of my Invention for a Church in Lincolns inn Fields' (pl. 515), dated 1712, perhaps one of his unsolicited attempts to attract New Churches patronage. Had Campbell been successful, a coup de grâce of the baroque. His plan is 'reduced [to] the most perfect Figure' of a circle inscribed by a square – repudiating ovoids as represented by the most overtly baroque proposals of Alessandro Galilei (pl. 381) and avoiding both Maderno's 'error' of isolating the crossing dome far from the front façade and Wren's of lifting it upon an ungainly substructure in order to be seen near to by pedestrians. Campbell's body 'is dress'd very plain, as

513 (*left*) Colen Campbell. 'The Elevation of St. Peters Church at Rome', Italy, in Campbell 1715, pl. 6, detail. Engraving. Donato Bramante, Antonio da Sangallo, Michelangelo, Carlo Maderno and Gian Lorenzo Bernini architects, 1513–1640.

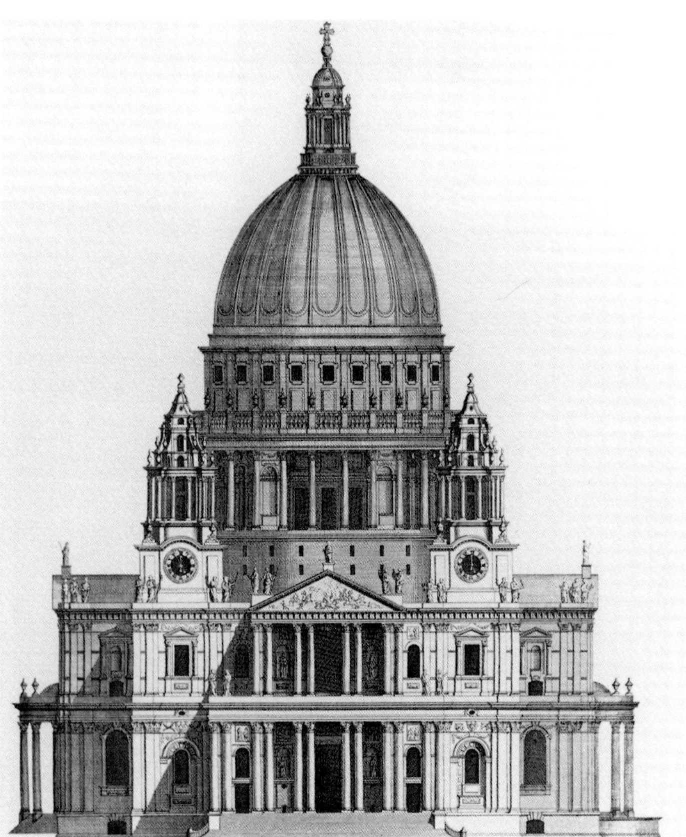

514 (*below left*) Colen Campbell. 'The West Prospect of St. Paul's Church' (Cathedral), London, in Campbell 1715, pl. 4, detail. Engraving. Sir Christopher Wren architect, 1675–1710.

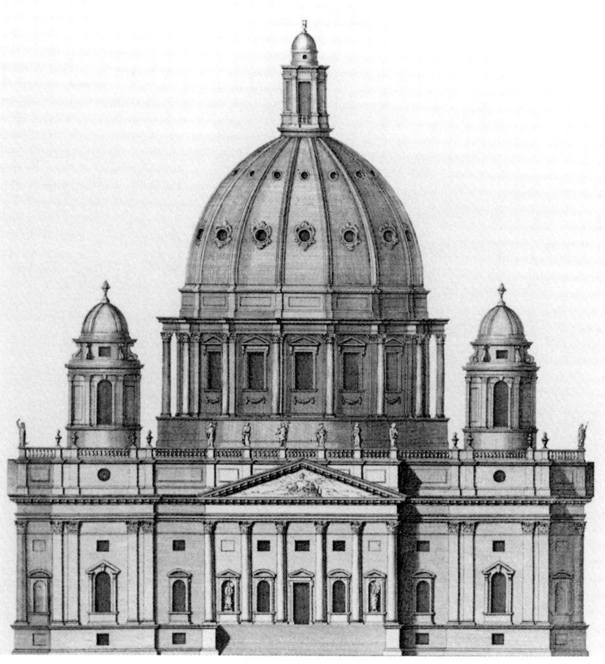

515 (*below right*) Colen Campbell. West elevation, 'A new Design of my Invention for a Church in Lincolns in Fields', London, in Campbell 1715, pl. 9, detail. Engraving. C. Campbell architect, 1712.

516 (*far left*) William Etty. Interior towards the west, St Andrew, Penrith, Cumberland, 1719–23. English Heritage (National Monuments Record, A43/5640).

517 (*left*) Andrea Palladio. Plan and section reconstruction of the Temple of Jupiter, Rome, Italy, in Leoni 1721, Book 4, Chapter XII, p. XXX. Engraving. Leeds Library and Information Service.

most proper for the sulphurous Air of the City, and, indeed, most conformable to the Simplicity of the Ancients'. This is expressed above all in plain windows set against expanses of undecorated wall and a 'regular Hexastyle [portico of a] single *Corinthian* Order, supported by a full Basement, and finished with an Attick and Ballustrade'. (Particularly disliking double-storeyed St Mary-le-Strand (see p. 401), Campbell adopted St Peter's monumental order.) The ensemble is repeated, without staircases, on the other three elevations, a sort of ecclesiastical version of Palladio's Villa Rotunda. The drum of the central dome is 'adorned with a single Colonade of detached Columns', but most significantly different is the relationship between the dome and the twin west towers. At both St Peter's and St Paul's the triumvirate overlap, whereas Campbell 'removed the Angular Towers, at such a distance, that the great *Cupola* is without any Ambarass', a decisively anti-baroque separateness.[6] One of the schemes to benefit clearly from this visual isolation, as well as the tabernacle windows flanking the portico, was Wiggens's Walbrook proposal of 1761 (pl. 495).

The manifesto also made a significant impact beyond London. At Penrith, Cumberland (1719–23; pl. 516), William Etty eschewed the ubiquitous Wren–Gibbs patterns of internal galleries attached to either columns on piers or a giant order in favour of a daringly new system of repetitive double tiers of Tuscan columns, the bases of the lower range set directly on the pavement and supporting the gallery undersides, the upper range rising from their top rails to full entablatures supporting the flat ceiling. This is the earliest recorded appearance in British church architecture of Palladio's reconstruction of a Roman temple arrangement as illustrated in Giacomo Leoni's pioneer English translation, fortuitously published in 1719–20 (pl. 517). In 1722 a local painter, Matthias Read, decorated the 'Cornish Round the top . . . with foliage in the frize and bulks between the Medallions' as a means of enhancing its antique character.[7] Here the precedent is Palladio's reference to the Temple of Jupiter's exterior 'cornice . . . beautifully designed [with] the frieze . . . carved with foliage'.[8] Etty was no stranger to fashionable pattern books: his father had subscribed to John James's 1707 translation of Andrea Pozzo's *Rules and Examples of Perspective Proper for Painters and Architects*, he himself to William Kent's *The Designs of Inigo Jones* (1727) and Gibbs's *A Book of Architecture* (1728), while Etty's York colleague William Thornton, as well as several contributors to the Penrith building programme, subscribed to Leoni's Fourth Book, dealing with temples. It is worth recording that the scion of Palladianism, Lord Burlington, who promoted Kent's book (illustrated by drawings in the earl's collection) and who owned property in Penrith parish, was both a financial contributor to and a member of its building committee.[9] Finally, at Holy Trinity, Leeds (pl. 419), where Burlington, in his capacity as Lord Lieutenant of the East and West Ridings, was a leading subscriber to the building fund,[10] in contradiction to the window hierarchy popularised at St Martin's (pl. 416), Etty heeded the Burlingtonian criticism of its 'revers'd . . . order . . . in complaisance to the galleries [while it was] always usual to have the large ones nearest the eye, and the small by way of *Attick Story*', as exemplified by Campbell's pioneer Palladian villa at Newby (now Baldersby) Park, near York (1718–21), where Etty served as clerk of the works.[11] Lewis Stephens, Archdeacon of Barnstable, in his consecration sermon of 1727, associated the new church with the

> very plain and simple [qualities of the] first Religious Places [of Christianity, which were] without the Ornaments of costly Stones, and without the Art of Workers in Wood, and Workers in Brass [and even] a decent Neatness . . . and . . . Majestic Plainness, which is in itself least Expensive, and most becoming, and somewhat resembles the plain and simple Majesty of God in all the Works of the Creation.

In effect, a loosely disguised anti-baroque agenda.[12]

Palladio's Il Redentore, Venice (1576–80), according to Dr Samuel Sharp's *Letters from Italy . . . In the Years 1765, and 1766* (1766), was

> a curious instance of the power of art; for though it is not to be ranked amongst the rich and expensive churches, abounding neither in gold nor marble, yet the simplicity and elegance of its structure had a wonderful influence on us the moment we enter within the door, and convinced us how deservedly *Palladio* is admired, and how possible it is to taste the beauty of proportion and design, without having studied the rudiments of the art.[13]

On his momentous Grand Tour of Italy in 1719 Burlington counted San Giorgio Maggiore (pl. 518) as 'one of the most beautiful buildings in the world', and perhaps with the baroque clustering at the much-disliked St Paul's Cathedral in mind, observed that on the west front Palladio had 'placed at the corners, a single pilaster, which stands angular, and fronts each side. I never saw it anywhere practiced before, but it has a very good effect, and hinders that confusion which coupled pilasters frequently occasion in angles'.[14] By 1720–21 the earl had acquired many original Palladio drawings.[15] Their early influence is evident in the work of the Scottish Catholic architect James Smith, perhaps prepared as a bid to attract the New Churches Commis-sioners (pl. 519), where on each of four fronts groups of paired engaged columns and pilasters frame a central pedimented and arched opening. The corner obelisks may derive from one of Palladio's unexecuted schemes for the façade of San Petronio, Bologna.[16]

The appeal of Palladio's churches to avant-garde Anglican sensibilities lay in his statements in *I quattro libri d'architettura* concerning their kinship with 'ancient buildings' of classical Rome, as in the example of Il Redentore, where a hybrid Ionic-Corinthian order 'placed as ornaments at the door' was derived from Constantine's baptistery at San Giovanni in Laterano, and also their expression of Christian belief, as with San Giorgio, whose Latin-cross plan represented 'in the eye of onlookers, that wood from which our Saviour was hung'.[17] But the book excluded Palladio's own ecclesiastical *œuvre* and the first published measured drawing of San Giorgio in the history of art did not appear until William Kent's *The Designs of Inigo Jones* (1727), the sole foreign building to be included, where it is described as 'the famous Church . . . so deservedly admired by all good Architects'.[18] This coincided with mounting British deprecation of Venetian baroque churches. In *Some Observations made in Travelling Through France, Italy, &c. In the Years 1720, 1721, and 1722* (1730), Edward Wright pressed readers to discriminate between Santa Maria della Salute (1630–37, by Longhena) and San Moisè (1668, by Tremignon), which were 'overcharg'd [and] encumber'd with extravagant Ornament', and Palladio's churches, 'built in regular Orders of Architecture, and in a good Taste'.[19] In William Halfpenny's design for an unidentified Irish church (pl. 521),

518 Heinrich Hulsbergh after Henry Flitcroft. 'The Front of . . . Santo Giorgio at Venice', Italy, in Kent 1727, vol. II, 1727, pl. 59. Engraving. Andrea Palladio architect, 1564–80.

519 James Smith. Design for the front of an unknown church, undated. Pen and ink and wash. RIBA Library Drawings Collection, J14(5) 63.

inspired by San Giorgio's trilobed plan (pl. 522), the self-contained, apsidal-ended vestry rooms are expressed only externally. That he specifically consulted Kent's book is demonstrated in the vignette studies for the west tower, one of which features a scroll-bracketed octagonal spire copied from Inigo Jones's St Paul's Cathedral (pl. 324), while another with a ball-fortified parapet recalls the flanking screen walls at San Giorgio.

Gibbs, who had visited Venice sometime between 1703 and 1709 and delighted in the 'most beautifull' San Giorgio by Palladio, 'the great Restorer of Architectur',[20] and who subscribed to Kent's book, was especially attracted to the separation of the west façade from the campanile positioned to the rear of the eastern choir. This was a solution he applied to his last church, St Nicholas, Aberdeen (pl. 520), where he replaced the dilapidated romanesque nave, which after the Reformation, with the high altar no longer the focus,

520 James Gibbs. Design for 'The West Front of ye Church of St Nicholas', Aberdeen, Aberdeenshire, Scotland, 1741. Pen and ink. Ashmolean Museum, Oxford, Gibbs Collection, III.131. Erected 1741–55.

521 William Halfpenny. Plan and elevations design for an unidentified church, perhaps for Waterford City, Co. Waterford, Ireland, *c.*1730s. Pen and ink and wash. RIBA Library Drawings Collection, Shelf B3, f. 4.

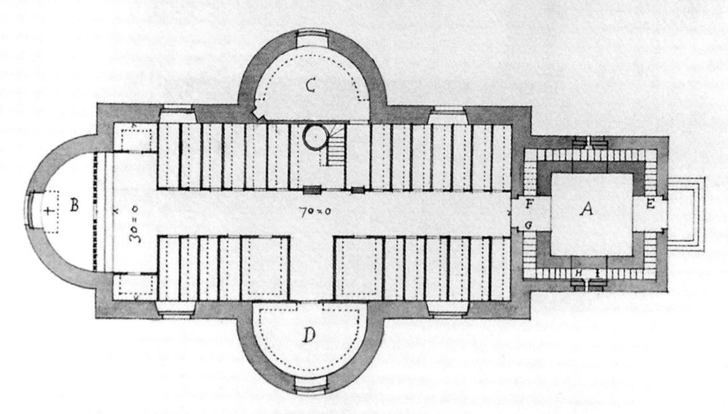

522 (*below*) Heinrich Hulsbergh after Henry Flitcroft. 'The Plan of . . . Santo Giorgio at Venice', Italy, in Kent 1727, vol. II, 1727, pl. 57. Engraving. Andrea Palladio architect, 1564–80.

523 (*facing page*) Henry Couchman and Lancelot 'Capability' Brown, attributed. South-west view, St Bartholomew, Binley, Warwickshire, 1771–3.

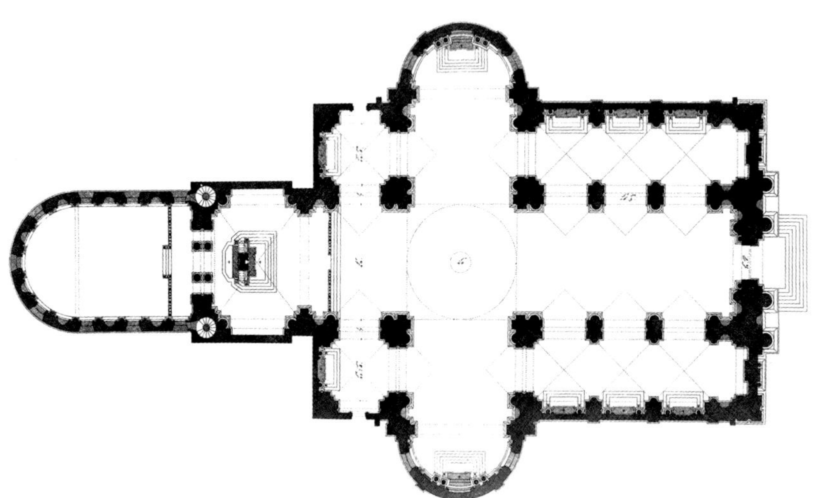

524 William Blackburn. Interior towards the east. Lewin's Mead (Unitarian) Chapel, Bristol, Somerset, 1788–91, converted to offices 1987.

was walled off from the choir, transepts and lofty crossing tower to form a separate sanctuary. This allowed for an unencumbered façade of interlocking pediments divested of engaged columns and pilasters, though not of their latent presence, since the contract specified an 'upper cornice under the high roof . . . according to the Doric order'.[21] In this context it should be noted that Wren occasionally swayed towards Palladian rhetoric, for example, citing St Mary-le-Bow's interior (1670–75) as modelled 'after the Templum Pacis', that is, the Basilica of Maxentius and Constantine in Rome, as published in *I quattro libri*.[22] More to the point, the external east end of St George, Botolph Lane (1671–6, demolished 1904), is based, as Gibbs did at Aberdeen, on Palladio's interlocking pedimented blocks (pl. 518).[23]

A singularly self-confident interpretation of this system at Binley, Warwickshire (pl. 523), an exquisite gem built for the 6th Earl of Craven, was apparently a collaborative effort between Lancelot 'Capability' Brown and Henry Couchman, the latter a former assistant to a leading Palladian architect from Norwich, Matthew Brettingham. Described in the local press as a 'noble fabric, for neatness, elegance, and beauty . . . not surpassed, nor scarce equalled, by any . . . in the Kingdom', here the familiar composition is softened by an arched and columned *in antis* porch derived from reconstructions of Roman baths published in Burlington's *Fabbriche Antiche disegnate da Andrea Palladio* (1730).[24] Couchman repeated the composition two decades later (pl. 340). The *in antis* motif was employed to stunning effect at Lewin's Mead Unitarian Chapel, Bristol (1788–91; pl. 524), where it is repeated in the centre of the west front, both side elevations and triplicated along the entire rear wall, flooding the interior with light.[25]

The buildings of Palladio's English 'protégé' also enjoyed a significant progeny.

Where *Covent-garden*'s famous Temple stands,
That boasts the Work of Jones' immortal Hands;
Columns, with plain Magnificence, appear,
And graceful Porches lead around the Square[26]

On 20 October 1711 the prescient John James wrote to his mentor, John Sheffield, 1st Duke of Buckingham, of his desire for 'an Opportunity of Shewing that the Beautys of Architecture may consist with the greatest plainness of the Structure [which] has scarce ever been hit on by the Tremontani [Italianates] unless by our famous Mr. Inigo Jones'.[27] Written in thanks for supporting his application for the coveted post of New Churches surveyor (which he secured only in 1716) and on the eve of the spectacular culmination of English late baroque church architecture (see chapter 19), James was elsewhere experimenting with adapting Jones's ecclesiastical masterpiece, St Paul, Covent Garden (1631–3; pl. 512), to his earliest known church, St George, Deal, Kent (1706–16; pls 525–6).

Though not mentioned in the parish records until 1712, he was most likely the designer, for among the inaugural subscribers to the building fund in 1706 was his client at nearby Waldershare, Sir Henry Furnese, while another, the ill-fated Rear-Admiral Sir Cloudesley Shovell (shipwrecked and drowned in 1707), would have known James in his capacity as store-keeper and assistant clerk of works since 1705 at the Royal Hospital for Seamen at Greenwich.[28] There is an unmistakable Jonesian debt in this plain yet uncommonly sophisticated building: the domed belfry rising over the chancel pediment (at St Paul it is placed at the west end), the ensemble of door and windows, both circular and round-headed, along the flanks (a treatment James also used in his contemporary church at Chalfont St Peter, Buckinghamshire) and the prominent dentil cornice (the Deal building contract of 1712 specifying a 'Parpett Wall round three Foot above the Cornish [but] found by the judgement of Skilfull Workmen to be of great prejudice' was replaced by 'plain moudillion Eves [which] will be of much more service').[29]

This initial Jonesian revival coincided with renewed professional interest in St Paul's. In 1707 Dr David Gregory, Savilian Professor of Astronomy at Oxford, wrote to Andrew Fletcher in London apologising for

525 John James and Samuel Simmons, attributed. East elevation, St George's Chapel, Deal, Kent, 1706–16.

526 John James and Samuel Simmons, attributed. South elevation, St George's Chapel, Deal, Kent, 1706–16.

not answering his letter because 'I was putt off from month to month by Mr Hawksmore, who is the only person that I can hear of has the draught of Covent Garden Church . . . I now send it you [and] hope it will satisfye all that you have to doe with it.' Fletcher was contemplating building some sort of structure about which his friend sought advice from Wren, who thought there was 'no doubt . . . but what you propose may be done . . . this is, "Upon a building 26 feet broad Walls comprehended a Roof may be laid protecting ten feet over the . . . walls to each hand . . ." '.[30] Hawksmoor's drawing (untraced) was perhaps related to the engraving published in Henry Maundrell's *Journey from Aleppo to Jerusalem* (1714), where it is described as 'the Temple at Covent Garden' and 'Compared upon the same scale wth. the Temple of Balbeck'.[31] Particularly admired was the Tuscan portico attached to the east end of the body facing towards the Piazza, called 'magnificent' in 1714 and three years later 'the only Piece the Moderns have yet produced, that can admit of a just Comparison with the Works of Antiquity, where a Majestick Simplicity commands the Approbation of the Judicious'.[32]

Accolades reached fever pitch in the 1720s, spurred by Burlington's gift in 1727 of £300–£400 towards restoring the portico 'to its primitive form . . . out of regard to the memory of the celebrated Inigo Jones, and to prevent our countrymen being exposed for their ignorance', which resulted in a structure 'now one of the finest in the world'.[33] The precise nature of this work is unclear, and although marking the earl's rare excursion into the ecclesiastical arena (the other concerned repaving York Minster, pl. 317), it stamped the church with renewed Palladian authority, reinforced by the writings of Ralph and Langley in 1734, which launched the first critical debates on the building. The former, encapsulating the Jonesian ideal, regarded it as

> without a rival, one of the most perfect pieces of architecture that the art of man can produce: nothing can possibly be imagin'd more simple, and yet magnificence itself can hardly give greater pleasure: this is a strong proof of the force of harmony and proportion; and at the same time a demonstration that 'tis taste and not expence which is the parent of beauty.

He did express reservations, however, about the 'defect . . . in the form and manner of the windows, which are not only in a bad gusto, but out of proportion', that is, too big.[34] Langley, while refuting this on grounds that

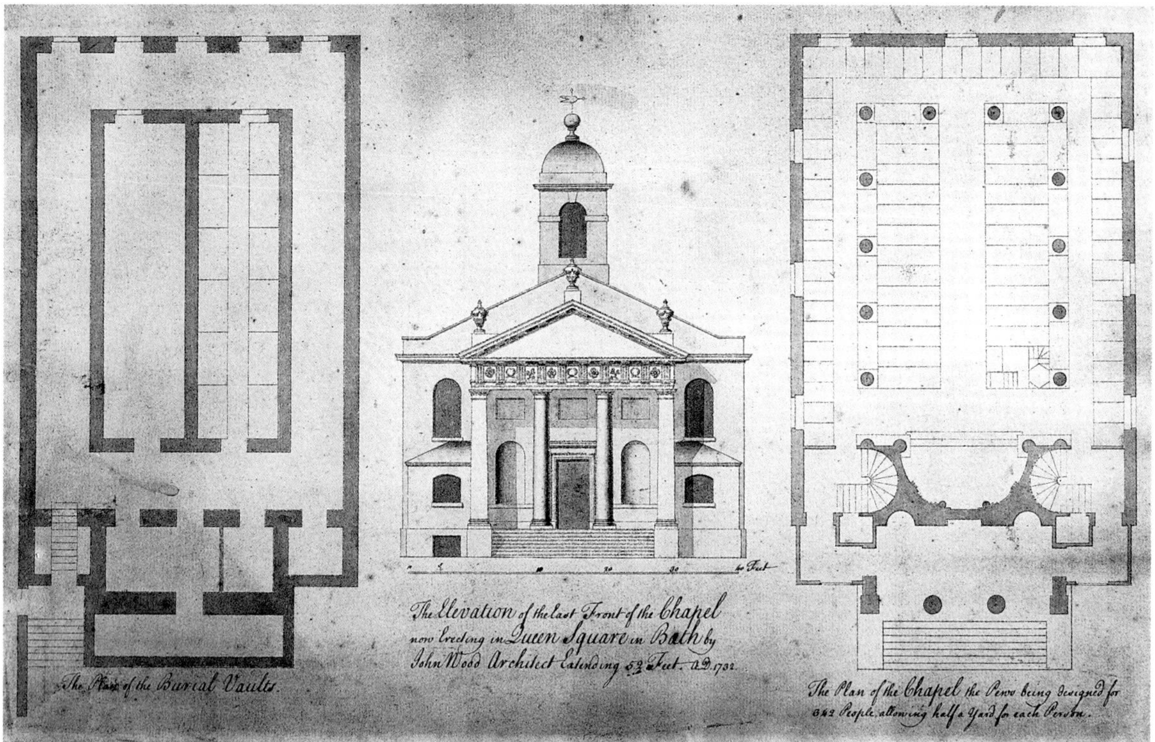

527 John Wood Sr., 'The Elevation of the East Front of the Chapel now Erecting in Queens Square in Bath by John Wood Architect', 'The Plan of the Burial Vaults', 'The Plan of the Chapel', St Mary's Chapel, Bath, Somerset, undated. Pen and ink and wash. Victoria Art Gallery, Bath, BATVG: PD:1926.32. Erected 1731–4, demolished 1875.

they 'are made to illuminate so large a space', agreed that the portico 'has really a solemn aspect, which in its simple beauty is not to be paralleled by any that I know in or about London'. Yet he expressed other misgivings: the unnecessary corner 'angular modillions [are] a mistake, as having a very ill effect'; the 'grand doors' at the east and west ends 'would have been much more simple and grand, had they been made with . . . architraves only' but no consoles; the 'rustics at the quoins . . . are entirely false; being made by square blocks . . . whose dimensions on both sides are equal, instead of being headers and stretchers alternately, which makes the best bondage'; the 'extraordinary projecture of the cornice . . . is . . . sometimes too great; the modillions . . . seeming to be overloaded, and to stand in need of some help by way of truss &c. to assist them in sustaining so great a weight'.[35] This last censure failed to grasp one of St Paul's essential features, the deeply overhanging roof cornice supported on long, slender modillions, which was described in 1733, in their reincarnation at St John Horselydown (pl. 435), as a 'span . . . beyond the walls; such as *Covent-Garden* . . . which gives a kind of shelter',[36] and in the same year was associated with a '*Barn*' – later mythologised by Horace Walpole in the story of the client, the Earl of Bedford, insisting on a chapel but 'wou'd not go to any considerable expence [and] not have it much better than a barn', to which Jones famously replied: 'you shall have the handsomest barn in England'.[37] For Georgians the feature codified the crucial association with English Palladianism's renewal of so-called primitive forms, which now began to attract imitators up and down the land.

Perhaps the earliest exponent was John Wood Sr, who lived in London between 1725 and 1727, an industrious period of ecclesiastical building that witnessed not only Burlington's restoration but also the late and more classicising phase of the New Churches programme (St George, Hanover Square, St Luke, Old Street, and St John Horselydown), as well as the completion of St Martin-in-the-Fields and the Marylebone Chapel, near to Wood's residence. In 1727 he returned to his home town of Bath, where his first ecclesiastical venture was St Mary's proprietary chapel in Queen Square (pl. 527), an innovative private urban development of palatial Palladian terrace residences, which 'raised such . . . Spirit in People to build near the Chapel' and which the press proclaimed 'will exceed any in England'.[38] The unorthodox orientation of the chapel due to its location in the south-west corner, with its temple portico facing eastward as the termination of Wood Street – a choice unlikely to have been encumbered by existing restrictions since the land was formerly pasture – was quickly recognised as aping Covent Garden.[39] Rather than adopting its well-publicised rustic Tuscan portico, however, Wood gave it the majestic sophistication of that 'incomparable *Dorick* Master-piece' at Albano near Rome, a fragment of Roman temple incorporated in the church of Santa Maria as recorded in John Evelyn's *A Parallel Of The Antient Architecture With The Modern*.[40]

With its sham central door, access to the interior was by entrances pierced in the portico's side walls, leading somewhat awkwardly through low passages on either side of the chancel, with its 'semi-elliptical dome [embellished by] four three-quarter columns',[41] into galleried side aisles, as at the much larger, more spacious St Alfege, Greenwich (pl. 403). No view of the interior is known but Wood's plan, measuring 67 by 48 by 36 feet high, shows a pew arrangement accommodating 342 tenants on the main floor and galleries; and later visitors described the galleries and roof supported by 'Ionic Pillars, the Pedestals as high as the Pews'. The 'Windows are sashed; a double Row of them . . . but a narrow Gallery going all round . . . separate them and makes the Place much handsomer and more Church-like'; the 'richly carved . . . Canopy of the Pulpit is supported by two small Pillars [the] very decent . . . Altar-Piece painted white and the carvings and proper Members of the cornices and Mouldings gilded'.[42]

At Well, Lincolnshire, of 1733 (pl. 528), an estate chapel set in a contemporary Elysian landscape on axis with the front of Well Vale House (*circa* 1725), the seat of James Bateman, a Lord Mayor of London and subscriber to the crucial second volume of *Vitruvius Britannicus* (1717), the prototype's corner piers are discarded in favour of a conventional temple portico. No building accounts survive and the identity of the architect remains a mystery.[43]

Two years later the Drapers' Company of London commissioned a scheme for Bancroft's Almshouses, Mile End Road, financed by a bequest from Francis Bancroft as a placatory gesture for a dissolute career as a notorious mercenary employed by the City Council, who would summon people before the Lord Mayor on the most trivial misdemeanours, pillage rich and poor alike and

> so effectually incurred the hatred & ill will of the Citizens of all denominations, that the Persons who attended his Funeral Obsequies [in 1726], with great difficulty, saved his Corpse from being jostled off the Beareres shoulders . . . by the inraged Populace, who . . . rang . . . the Bells . . . for joy at his unlamented death, a deportment heretofore unheard of among the London Rabble.[44]

528 Architect unknown. North-east view, St Margaret, Well, Lincolnshire, 1733.

The 'Articles for Building' of 23 May 1735 refer to a surveyor named William Barrett 'having drawn' a design for 'Intended Buildings' (untraced), which was rejected as 'larger than needful', and Edward Porter, a carpenter, who 'Delivered . . . Proposals' to the Company but who was not necessarily their author.[45] On the evidence of draughtsmanship the drawings attached to the contract (pl. 529, compared with pl. 577), as well as stylistic features, the most likely candidate for architect is George Dance Sr, who had already designed and erected Bancroft's flamboyant tomb house (1726, demolished) in St Helen, Bishopsgate (pl. 530), the earliest of his documented works.[46] The almshouses' centrepiece comprised the chapel flanked by a schoolroom and masters' houses, with the detached, right-angled outer blocks containing residences. This represented the earliest metropolitan adaptation of St Paul, Covent Garden (pl. 512). Here, however, a slimmer, more feminine Ionic order was preferred for the portico, with a second pair of outer pilasters that share a common pedestal, repeating the central *oeil-de-boeuf* over the arches set into the side walls linking it to the body

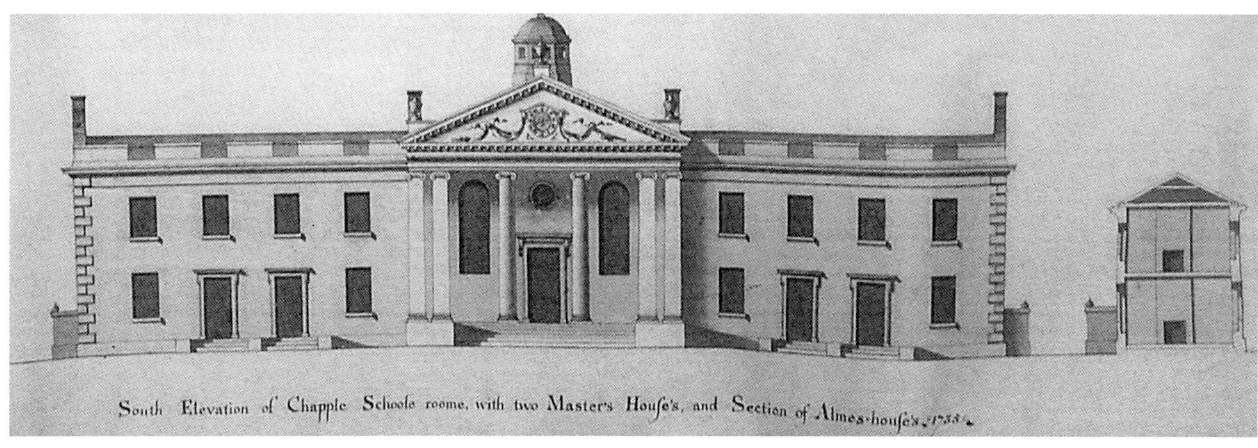

529 George Dance Sr, attributed. 'South Elevation of Chapple Schoole roome, with two Master's Houses and Section of Almes-house's', Bancroft's Almshouses, Mile End Road, London, detail. Pen and ink and wash. Drapers' Company, London, 1735, E.IV.58. Erected 1735–7, demolished 1880s.

(conspicuous in other pre-demolition views) and rejecting the exaggerated modillion in favour of a conventional block cornice, a more conservative treatment perhaps responding to Langley's recent condemnation of Jones's church 'having an ill effect'.[47]

These changes are interesting in the light of Stephen Riou's later, rather dubious and irrelevant claim that the prototype

> would not have incurred the disgrace it has in the opinion of many people, if the portico had been adorned with Ionic columns; the cornice of the entablature then would have been still plainer, and without that appearance of a barn's eves, from the monstrous projecture of the joists; the expenses would not have run higher, excepting in the workmanship of four Ionic capitals.[48]

Dance also selected a shorter, domed, octagonal bell turret based on one in Kent's *The Designs of Inigo Jones*.[49] The 31 by 28 by 20 foot high interior incorporates a pair of rear doors with *oeil-de-boeufs* over.[50]

530 N. Smith. 'Bancroft's Monument in the Church of St. Helen, Bishopsgate Street', London, 20 May 1794, in J. T. Smith, *Antiquities of London*, 1791–1800, pl. 87, detail. Engraving. Drapers' Company, London. George Dance Sr. architect, 1726, demolished.

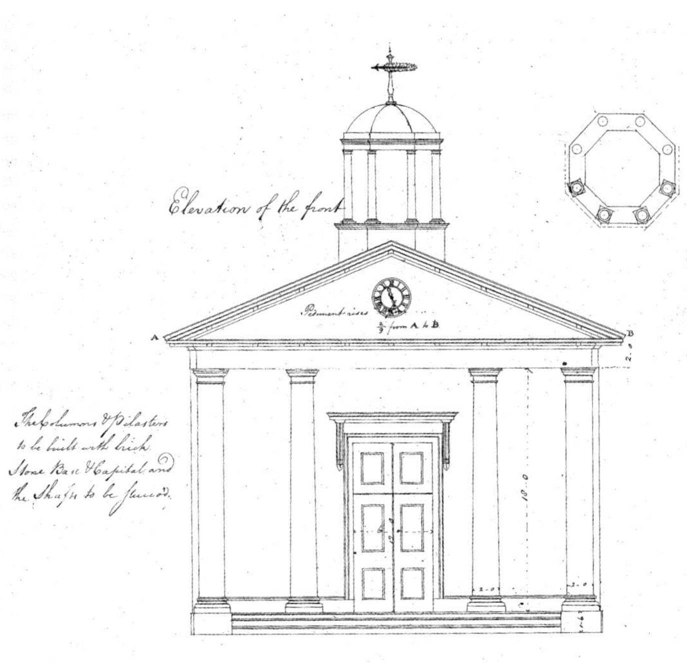

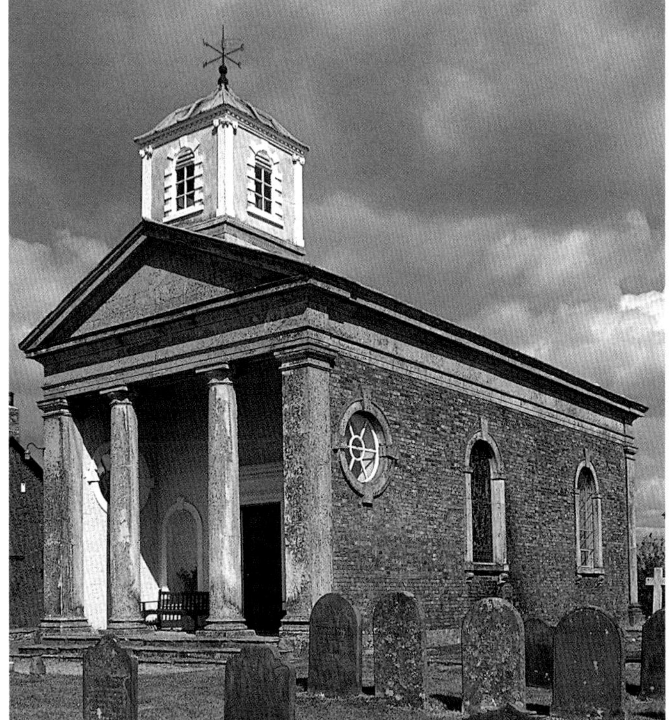

531 (*above left*) Architect unknown. Entrance elevation design for 'One of the Duke of Portland's Chapels in Marybone q. Quebeck', perhaps Quebeck Chapel, St Marylebone, London, undated. Pen and ink and wash. City of Westminster Archives Centre, Ashbridge Collection 545.

532 (*left*) Architect unknown. South-west view, St Helen, Saxby, Lincolnshire, 1773.

533 (*above right*) John Hagger. Design for 'Elevation of the front' and cupola plan, St John, Epping, Essex, 1780. Pen and ink. Essex Record Office, D/019/29. Erected 1780–87, demolished 1832.

The Jonesian façade formula was repeated in an unsigned, undated design perhaps associated with the Duke of Portland's St Marylebone Estate (pl. 531)[51] and with a variation at Saxby, Lincolnshire (pl. 532), also by an unknown architect, who favoured the side oculi made fashionable at Bancroft's while reasserting Jones's Tuscan order.[52] At Epping, Essex (1780–87; pl. 533), John Hagger articulated the solid return walls of the 'Loggia' with shallow external recesses, repeated in the eastern bays to mark the position of the vestry and staircase

534 (*above*) John Watson Jr. South-west view, Horsforth Chapel, Leeds, Yorkshire, 1750–58. West Yorkshire Archives Service (Leeds), Parish Records 85. Demolished 1884.

535 (*top*) Sir Thomas Robinson and John Carr. South-west view, St Mary, Rokeby, Yorkshire, 1761–78, vestry nineteenth century.

536 (*above*) Sir Thomas Robinson. North-east view, St Mary, Glynde, Sussex, 1763–6.

rooms flanking the chancel. Galleries raised on Tuscan columns screen both the west and east ends of the body. Despite provisions for money-saving features specified in the 1780 drawings – a stuccoed brick carcass with the loggia columns, pilasters and wall of 'patent Water Cement', 'Patent Slating', wooden internal columns, cornices and gallery fronts, '2d. Cost Crown Glass' and so forth, the estimated expense of £1,498 19s. 6d. proved too steep, and it is unclear what, if any, part of the scheme was carried out.[53]

Other aspects of Covent Garden, to do with its external astylar chastity, were also explored. John Watson's Horsforth Chapel, Leeds (1750–58; pl. 534), executed in uniform, crisply cut ashlar blocks, had doubly recessed windows, a late Palladian motif whose appearance was then still a rarity and which is used here with almost Hawksmoorian bravado. In place of a portico was a shallow recessed centrepiece inspired by Burlington's York Assembly Rooms façade (1731–2, rebuilt 1828), in turn based on reconstructions of Roman baths in the earl's *Fabbriche Antiche disegnate da Andrea Palladio* (1730).[54] This had already appeared on James Paine's chapel pavilion at Cusworth Hall, Yorkshire (1749–50; pl. 585), where Watson was employed as mason, but at Horsforth the insertion of a blind balustrade above the attached Ionic screen anticipates a corresponding internal gallery externalised, a symbolic porch. The interior was a single cell with an unsupported ceiling, as at Covent Garden, but with the west gallery on brackets and a half-domed apsidal chancel.[55]

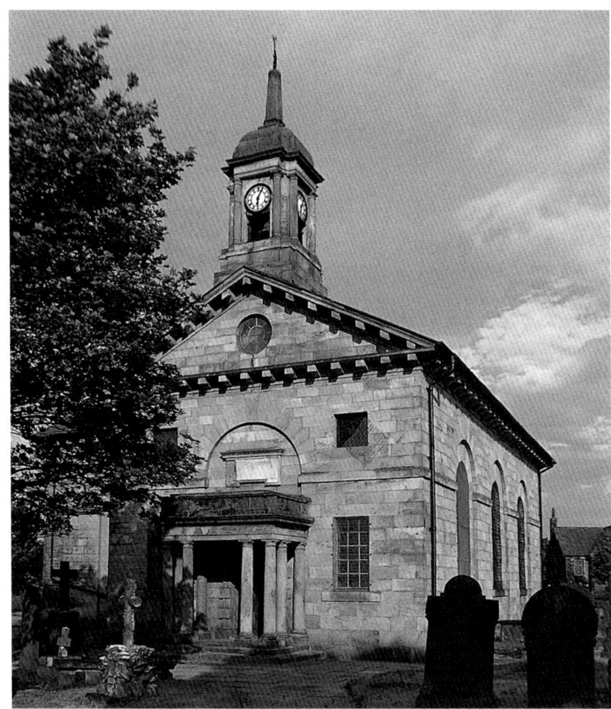

537 John Carr. South-west view, St John Evangelist, North Bierley, Yorkshire, 1766, porch added 1878.

538 John Joshua Kirby. Design for 'Plan & Elevation of Kew Chapel with the proposed Alterations', Surrey, February 1768. Pen and ink and wash. © The British Library Board, K.Top. XL-46-h.

St Paul's was exploited by the amateur Burlingtonian architect Sir Thomas Robinson, whose London residence was adjacent to Jones's Whitehall Banqueting House, at two almost identical churches. Little is known about Rokeby (1761–78; pl. 535), on his Yorkshire estate, because Robinson's personal papers were destroyed after his death.[56] Glynde, Sussex (1763–6; pl. 536), built for Sir Richard Trevor, Bishop of Durham, on the other hand, is well served by accounts and drawings. Here the contrast between precisely cut Portland stone dressings and 'Gaigd flint Worke', recessed 9 inches from the external wall plane, together with the 'Enrich't Cornice with Husks & flowers' and a plasterwork ceiling of 'Gallops & Flowers', has an appropriately geometric Jonesian sophisticated rusticity conforming to the popular perception of Covent Garden's 'primitive form'.[57] A specification for the 'inverted Position of the Altar Piece, being placed nearly in the West End of the Church', resulting from the building's unorthodox orientation, also recalls Covent Garden.[58] Trevor's achievement is praised in an anonymous verse 'On the Church which is now buildings at Glynd':

Thou Great and Good, who rear'st this beauteous fane,
The praise confer'd shalt o'er thyself regain;
Tho' rolling years eraze each mouldering stone,
Thy worth shall be beyond that period known;
Few have with thy superior fate been born,
To honour God and human kind adorn.[59]

Mid-Georgian paring down of Jones's model to the bare bones of a pedimented but unporticoed front while retaining an emphatic entrance feature and prominently dentilated projecting cornice, which has 'a bold and striking appearance, owing to the great effect of Shade it occasions',[60] also characterises John Carr's St John Evangelist, North Bierley, Yorkshire (pl. 537),[61] and J. J. Kirby's unrealised scheme of 1768 for extending the west front of Kew, Surrey (pl. 538).[62]

539 Thomas Hardwick Jr. Design for the 'Elevation of the West, or Principal Front of the Chapel and Houses', St James, Hampstead, London, 1790. Pen and ink and coloured wash. City of Westminster Archives Centre, D715, f. 517. Erected 1789–93, demolished 1965.

With Jones's Georgian reputation firmly secured by the 1740s, Covent Garden remained in ascendancy. Robert Morris wrote of

> . . . JONES more justly knew the Eye to charm,
> To please the Judgment, and the Fancy warm

and

> Of Jones you'll learn Magnificence, and Grace[63]

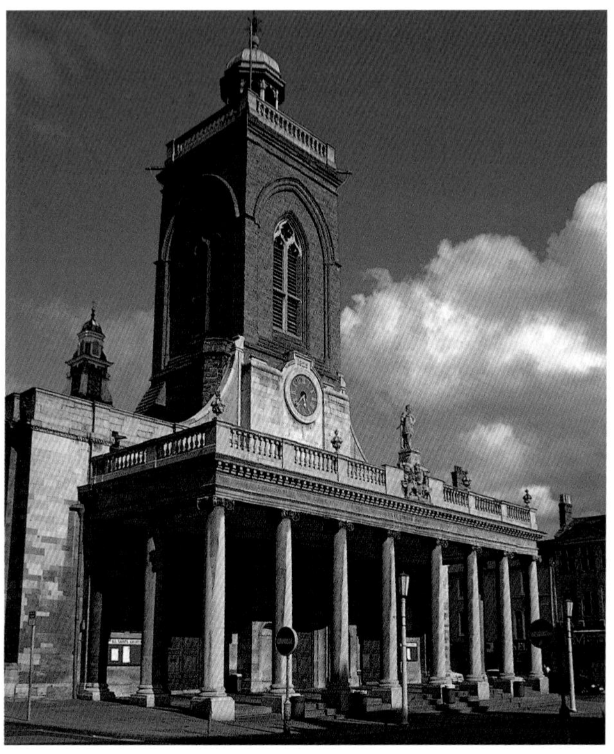

540 (*left*) Henry Bell attributed. West portico, All Saints, Northampton, Northamptonshire, 1677–1701. Medieval tower.

William Shenstone wrote to Lady Luxborough in 1775: 'How many are there, besides myself, whose eyes oblige them . . . to be more delighted . . . with the front of Covent-Garden Church than with St Paul's Cathedral. Such is the force of truth, exemplified by that of proportion.' The former was further praised in 1795 as 'Built by that Celebrated Architect Inigo Jones . . . remarkable for its Majestic Simplicity, which never fail'd to Attract the Eye of the Curious.'[64] Moreover, by then it had come to the vanguard of popular appreciation. Between 1787 and 1791 the old fabric was given a major overhaul by Thomas Hardwick Jr, the leading late Georgian conservative classicist architect. This included re-ceiling the portico, casing the external brick walls with Portland stone 'to prevent the great inconvenience and frequent expence of repairing the Stucco', replacing the original tile roof with Westmorland slate, removing the externally projecting staircase blocks, re-stuccoing the internal walls, installing a new plaster ceiling, extending the side galleries to the east wall and making new screens at the west end.[65] At the close of operations the press observed that the immense cost of the repairs could have been reduced if the structure had been rebuilt from its foundations, but 'no men were to be found . . . so deficient in understanding as to propose rebuilding a church, which for a century and a half, has been the admiration of scientific men, from all quarters of the globe', and that it was 'one of the most perfect pieces of art ever produced in this country'.[66] During these years Hardwick looked to its secular Piazza elevations (pl. 512) as the model for St James, Hampstead (pl. 539), a burial chapel to the Westminster mother church.[67] Tragically, on 17 September 1795 Covent Garden church was gutted by an accidental fire, 'which raged with so much uncontrolled fury that not a fragment of wood . . . escaped destruction' (pl. 101).[68] It was hoped that 'This relique of one of our first architects may . . . be restored without any deviation from their original plan', which was done successfully again under Hardwick's direction.[69]

There were other Jonesian adventures. We have already seen how John Vardy at Allerton Mauleverer reconfigured the upper part of St Paul's Cathedral (pls 324–5) and William Halfpenny selected its details (pl. 521). As the final gesture in rebuilding fire-ravaged All Saints, Northampton, destroyed in a town fire in 1675, an impressive un-pedimented octastyle Ionic portico *à la* St Paul's Cathedral was added across the west front *circa* 1683–1701 (pl. 540). The choice by the merchant-orientated town was no doubt anchored in Jones's belief that the 'ancients yoused Porticoes for Commoditie of the people and to walke without the Cell . . . and to give magistie to temple'.[70] The change of order at Northampton may reflect English thinking that Corinthian was 'laciviously deck'd like a Courtezan', while Vitruvius 'would not have set . . . *Tuscan* before

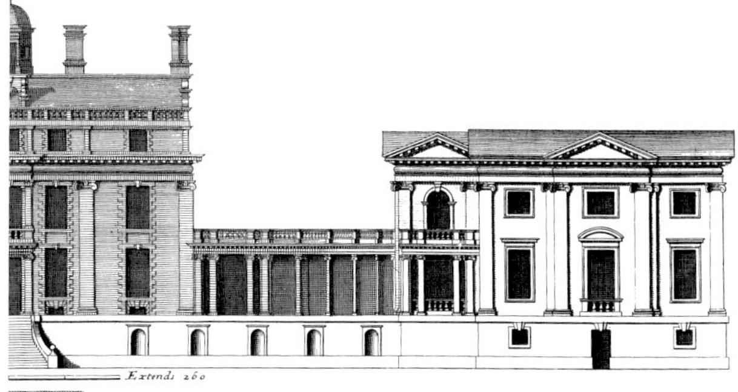

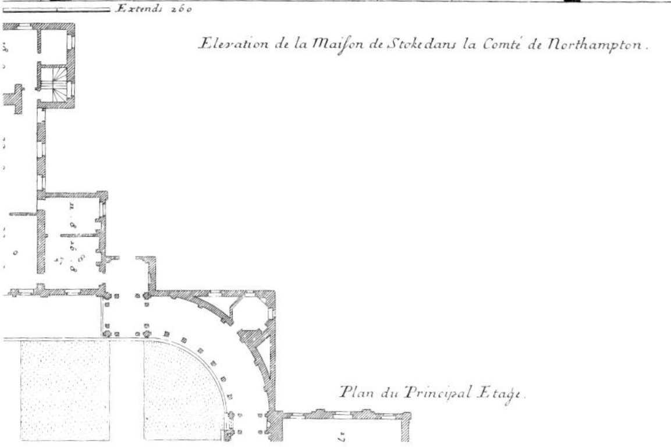

541 (*above*) Heinrich Hulsbergh after Inigo Jones. 'The Elevation of Stoke Park in Northamptonshire', chapel pavilion, in Campbell 1725, pl. 9, detail. Engraving. I. Jones architect, *c.*1630.

542 (*below*) Edward Wing. South-east view, St Michael, Aynho, Northamptonshire, 1723–5. English Heritage (National Monuments Record, AA50/3345).

543 J. Lodge after James Meader. 'A North-West View of Greenwich Church', St Alfege, Greenwich, London, 20 September 1771. Engraving. © The British Library Board, K.Top. XVII-1-3-W-1. Nicholas Hawksmoor (body) and John James (tower), architects, 1712–30.

the *Portico* of a *Church*' (as Jones had done at Covent Garden), whereas Ionic was 'composed after the *Module* of a feminine Beauty' and epitomised '*Decorum*'.[71]

Thomas Cartwright, who between 1707 and 1714 had commissioned Thomas Archer to remodel Aynho Park, Northamptonshire, with its accents of Borrominiesque embellishments,[72] following Colen Campbell's malediction against Italianate baroque in the preface to the first volume of *Vitruvius Britannicus* (Cartwright subscribed to Leoni's *The Architecture of A. Palladio*, 1715–21), changed direction and probably sanctioned the selection of Jones's Stoke Park chapel (pl. 541), located only 18 miles distant, as the model for rebuilding his medieval church (pl. 542).[73] His architect, Edward Wing, a local carpenter and builder who proudly proclaimed that the scheme presented in 1723 was 'all of his own drawing',[74] substituted Jones's Ionic for the bolder Tuscan order.

A defining moment in re-routing taste from Hawksmoorian baroque to Jonesian classicism occurred in 1729–30 when, after years of vacillation, the New Churches Commissioners banished the upper stages of Hawksmoor's powerful monolithic tower intended as the climactic beacon of Greenwich church (pl. 403) in favour of John James's stylistically mismatched, out-of-scale, multi-tiered solution (pl. 543), amalgamating the middle stages of St Martin-in-the-Fields (pl. 416) and the domed Corinthian tempietto of Jones's Whitehall Palace scheme published a few years earlier (pl. 544).

544 James Cole after Henry Flitcroft. Design for 'The Cupola in large with the Plan', Whitehall Palace, London, in Kent 1727, vol. 1, pl. 27. Engraving. Inigo Jones, architect, proposed *c.*1638.

The Banqueting House at Whitehall, 'the first Room in the World . . . designed by the immortal *Jones* [who] has introduced Strength with Politeness, Ornament with Simplicity, Beauty with Majesty',[75] which alone survived the fire of 1698, when it was converted into the Chapel Royal (pl. 545), was the model for the first interior of Greenwich Hospital chapel, designed by its surveyor, Thomas Ripley, a member of HM Office of Works, a post previously held by Jones. In 1727 the Hospital governors, rejecting Hawksmoor's grandiose suggestions for a detached chapel on the central axis (pl. 357), resolved to incorporate it within the colonnaded north wing of Queen Mary Building, echoing the Painted Hall in Wren's King William Building opposite, with both great rooms dramatically signalled by twin domes rising over their respective vestibules. This, in turn, reflected the proposal to duplicate the Banqueting House across the central courtyard of the unrealised scheme for Whitehall Palace, which Kent had published in *The Designs of Inigo Jones* (1727), to which Ripley was a subscriber.[76] The Greenwich interior, recorded in a unique engraved view (pl. 546), consisted of a two-storey double cube of 100 by 50 by 50 feet (just short of the Banqueting House's 110 by 55 by 55 feet), lit on both long walls by ranges of rectangular windows separated by narrow galleries cantilevered on elongated scroll consoles, reserved for use by the officers. Yet, this was not a straightforward copy of Jones. Ripley favoured a more complicated ceiling pattern.[77] He also avoided introducing engaged columns and pilasters between the windows, perhaps heeding criticism of the 'very ill Effect [of the] diminished Pilasters [with] Entablatures . . . broken over' on the Banqueting House façades, which (in neo-Palladian terms) are 'very great Absurdities, notwithstanding it was designed by so great a Master, and is, by many esteemed a perfect Piece of Architecture'.[78] Ripley concentrated monumentality

545 A. Pugin and T. Rowlandson. Interior view, Banqueting House, Whitehall, London, early nineteenth century. Coloured engraving. RIBA Library Drawings Collection. Inigo Jones architect, 1619–21, converted to Chapel Royal, 1698.

on the twin pair of fluted engaged Composite columns raised on tall pedestals flanking the chancel arch (perhaps repeated on the west wall), recalling plate 58 in *The Designs of Inigo Jones* for Temple Bar, London (1636–8), 'in the Manner of a Triumphal-Arch [where] the Height of the middle Opening is twice the Breadth', as also it was here.[79] Its internal five-sided wall featuring pedimented tabernacles, ornamental panels and a coffered half-dome might have been lifted from plate 72 in the same publication, a section of the Saloon at Burlington's Chiswick villa. The Hospital governors instructed Ripley to finish the chapel 'in an Elegant manner suitable to the other Parts [of this] magnificent National Building'.[80] Eyewitnesses reported 'a most elegant showy room, all the Pillars & mouldings both on the sides & Cieling . . . profusely gilt & carved', white walls and 'the proportions exceedingly beautiful . . . the ceiling of the altar . . . representing cherubims [painted in an] elegant [manner] perhaps worthy of the pencil of Albano himself', as well as the four gallery overdoors with 'Sacred history' pieces, all by Robert Brown.[81] Billeted in the very heart of the enemy camp, the chapel was among the most fully realised, if not most original, Palladian church interiors, 'one of the finest rooms in England', only to vanish in the great fire of 1779.[82]

Jones's aborted design for a chapel in Whitehall Palace (pl. 547), with its varied wall and column treatments, pedimented doors, balustraded gallery and coffered half-dome recess, was the starting point for Ralph Allen's chapel at Prior Park, Bath (pls 548–9), which, despite several disastrous fires, remains redolent of clas-

546 George Bickham Jr after Thomas Malton. 'The Inside of the New Chapel in the Royal Hospital at Greenwich', London, undated. Engraving. © The British Library Board, K.Top. XVII-1-3-q. Thomas Ripley architect, 1735–51, interior gutted by fire, 1779.

sical antiquity. Its architect, John Wood Sr (whom we have already met as the creator of the Covent Garden-inspired Queen Square Chapel, Bath, pl. 527), described the double-storey room, approached along a narrow lateral corridor from the central hall and taking up the full length of the west side of the Palladian mansion, as 'all built with Free Stone [including] fixed Ornamental Parts' and composed of 'the *Ionick* Order, sustaining the *Corinthian*', which in the upper 'Tribunal Seat' increased 'in its Magnificence; and by representing Cherubims and Palm Trees, placed alternately, give them an Idea of the manner in which King *Solomon* finished the Inside of his Temple at *Jerusalem*'.[83] This is a poignant analogy because the Temple as reconstructed in renaissance treatises, particularly J. B. Villalpando's and J. Prado's *In Ezechielem Explanationes* (1596–1605), a copy of which belonged to Wood or his architect son, had been a major inspiration on Jones's concept for Whitehall Palace.[84]

At Holkham Hall, Norfolk, the chapel (pl. 550), designed by William Kent and completed after his death by Matthew Brettingham Sr, incorporates a family pew derived from Jones's Somerset House chapel, London (pl. 551). The coffered ceiling was adopted from Palladio's reconstruction of the Temple of the Sun and Moon in Rome, praised in Ware's *The Four Books of Andrea Palladio's Architecture* (1738), to which Brettingham subscribed, as 'compartments of stucco most exquisitely wrought, and of a beautiful invention'.[85]

Finally, the Queen's Chapel, St James's Palace, originally built for Charles I's Catholic queen Henrietta Maria and after 1700 occupied by a succession of foreign Protestant congregations, was confirmed as Jones's work following Burlington's acquisition in 1720 of his collection of drawings, legitimising it within the architect's canon.[86] The most memorable feature is the Serliana at the east end (pl. 552), its earliest appearance in British ecclesiastical architecture.[87] Afterwards, at Great Stanmore, Middlesex (1632), Berwick-upon-Tweed, Northumberland (pl. 265), and St Mary Matfelon, London (1672–3), and in five Wren City Churches.[88] Revived by Campbell in *Vitruvius Britannicus* (1717; pl. 411), Hawksmoor employed it in studies for Worcester College chapel, Oxford (1720), one of which is annotated 'The Rusticks [corner quoins] according to Mr Jones, at St James Chapell' (not to mention a range of other historical sources including the Arch of Constantine, the Roman Pantheon and the 'Tower of Andromachus' or Tower of the Winds, Athens,[89] and subsequently at St Luke, Old Street, and

547 (*above*) Paul Fourdrinier after Henry Flitcroft. Design for the 'Section of the Chapel', Whitehall Palace, London, in Kent 1727, vol. I, pl. 50. Engraving. Inigo Jones, architect, proposed *c.*1638.

548 (*below left*) John Wood Sr. Interior towards the gallery, Prior Park chapel, Bath, Somerset, 1734–41. English Heritage (National Monuments Record, AA46/06083).

549 (*below right*) John Wood Sr. Interior towards the chancel, Prior Park chapel, Bath, Somerset, 1734–41. English Heritage (National Monuments Record, AA46/06082).

550 (*above*) J. Miller, 'Section of the Chapel', in M. Brettingham, *The Plans and Elevations of the late Earl of Leicester's House at Holkham* (Norfolk), 1761. Engraving. Author's collection. William Kent architect, 1734–64.

551 (*left*) Paul Fourdrinier after Isaac Ware. 'Screen at Somerset house Chapel Inigo Jones', London, in Ware 1731, pl. 30. Engraving. I. Jones architect, 1630–34, demolished 1776–90.

552 (*below left*) Inigo Jones. North-east view, Queen's Chapel, St James's Palace, London, 1623–5.

553 (*below right*) Edward and Thomas Woodward. East elevation, St John, Gloucester, Gloucestershire, 1732–4.

7.

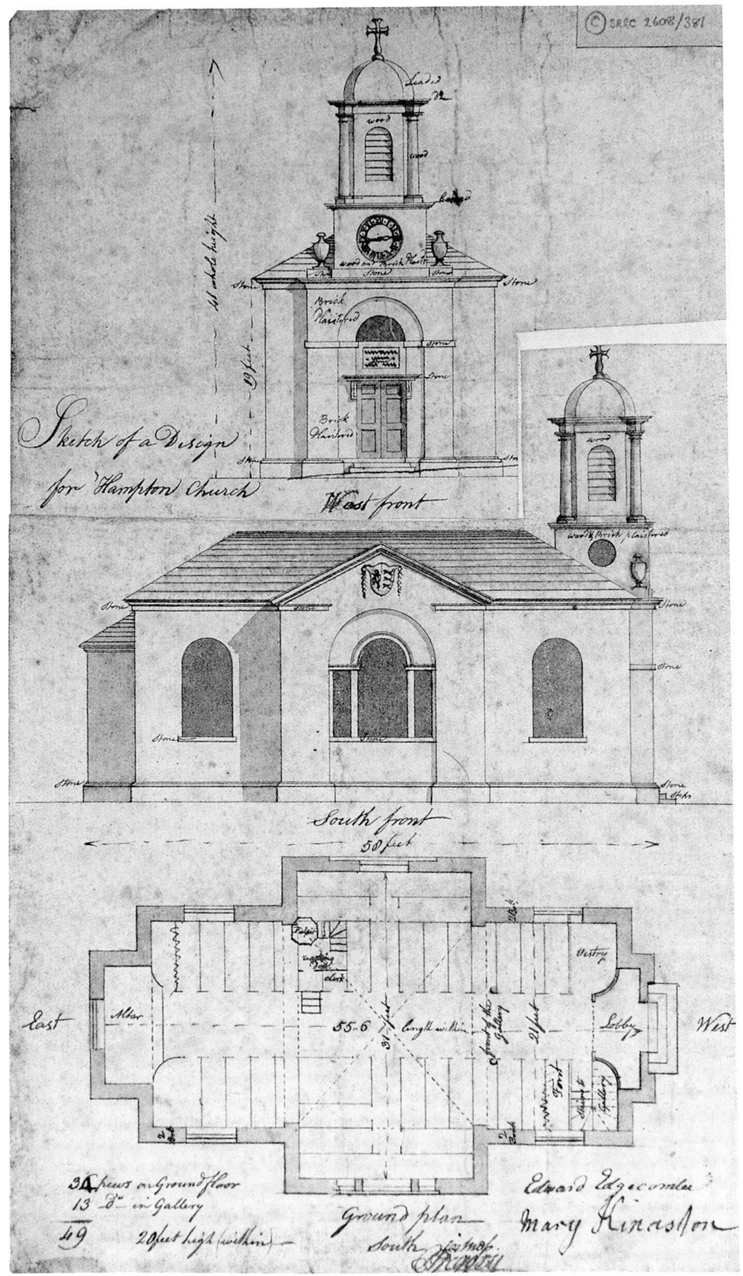

555 Edward Edgecombe. 'Sketch of a Design for Hampton Church', Welshampton, Shropshire, 28 April 1788. Pen and ink and wash. Shropshire Records and Research Unit, 2608/381, f. 8. Demolished 1863.

554 (*facing page*) George Dance Sr. Plans and longitudinal section design, St Botolph, Aldgate, London, 1741. Pen and ink and coloured wash. Sir John Soane's Museum, 14/7.

St John Horselydown; pls 433, 435), perhaps encouraged by its popularisation by Gibbs (pls 417, 424) and his advocacy as being 'proper to be placed at the end of Churches'.[90] At Holy Trinity, Leeds, it replaced the single arched window of the 1722 model.[91]

With the Serliana's appearance on the exterior east end of St Giles-in-the-Fields (1730–34), the first fully Palladian church erected in England, though with a caveat that the side lights were internally blind (pl. 563), the motif became an enduring hallmark of the style. So much so that it was employed prominently at Well (pl. 528) and Bancroft's chapels (see p. 477), both based on St Paul, Covent Garden. It was particularly worthwhile when the chancel faced towards main thoroughfares and the west end was dominated by medieval towers, as at Edward and Thomas Woodward's nearly twin churches at Worcester and Gloucester (pls 314, 553).[92] Perhaps with Isaac de Caus's unrealised 1630s Jonesian-inspired scheme for Wilton House chapel, Wiltshire, in mind, where a Serliana strides the long elevation,[93] it reappeared at Horselydown (pl. 435), St Botolph, Aldgate (pl. 554) and at Welshampton, Shropshire, by the Shrewsbury architect Edward Edgecombe, where it illuminated the centrally placed

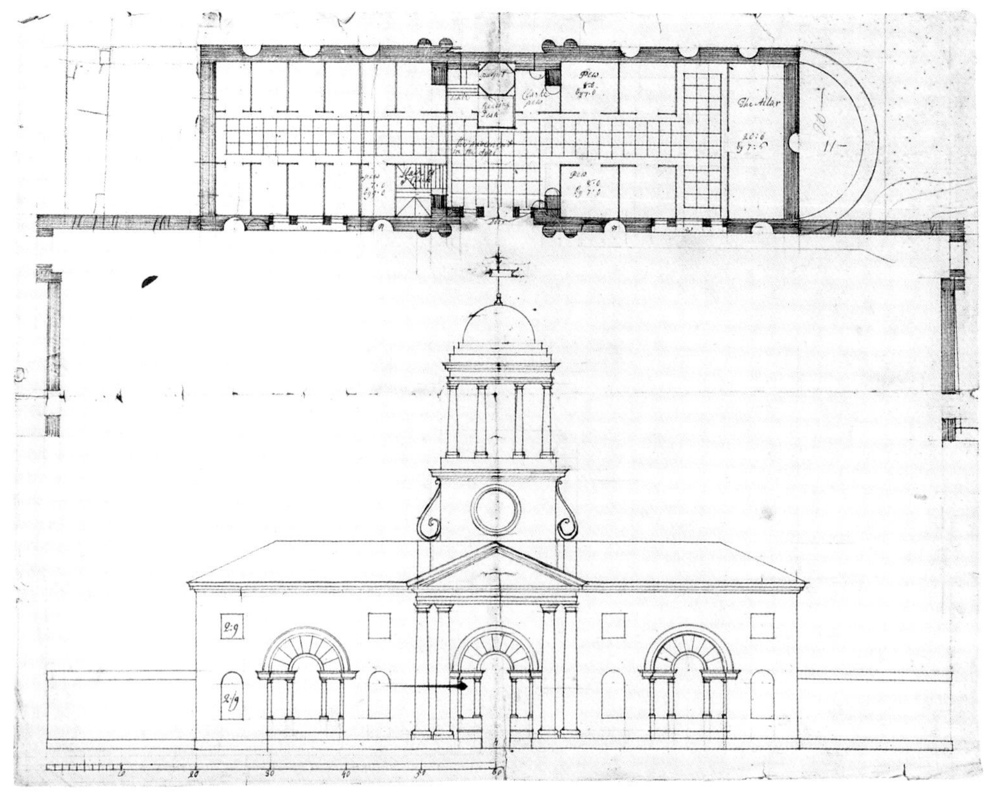

556 (*above*) Daniel Garrett. Plan and courtyard elevation design for a Chapel 'The building between the Stables at Wallington, 1751', Wallington Hall, Northumberland. Pen and ink. The National Trust, Wallington 28. Retained as stables.

557 (*left*) John Sanderson. Interior towards the chancel, All Saints, Pusey, Berkshire, 1745–6. English Heritage (National Monuments Record, AA59/1565).

preaching space (pl. 555).[94] At Wallington Hall, Northumberland, in 1751 Daniel Garrett considered using the present coach house (completed 1754) as the estate chapel (pl. 556), with three Serliana, each framed within an inclusive recessed arch in the Whitehall Palace manner, ranging across the entrance and providing the sole source of natural light.[95] At Pusey, Berkshire (pl. 557), a modest yet elegant Palladian church probably designed by John Sanderson, who was then repairing Covent Garden, they appear in their plainest form lighting the chancel and cross-axis transepts, with the latter screened from the body by more elaborate fluted Ionic versions raised on dados, derived from plate 54 in Kent's *The Designs of Inigo Jones*, to which Sanderson subscribed. No previous British church had employed the feature with such voracity.[96] But it was

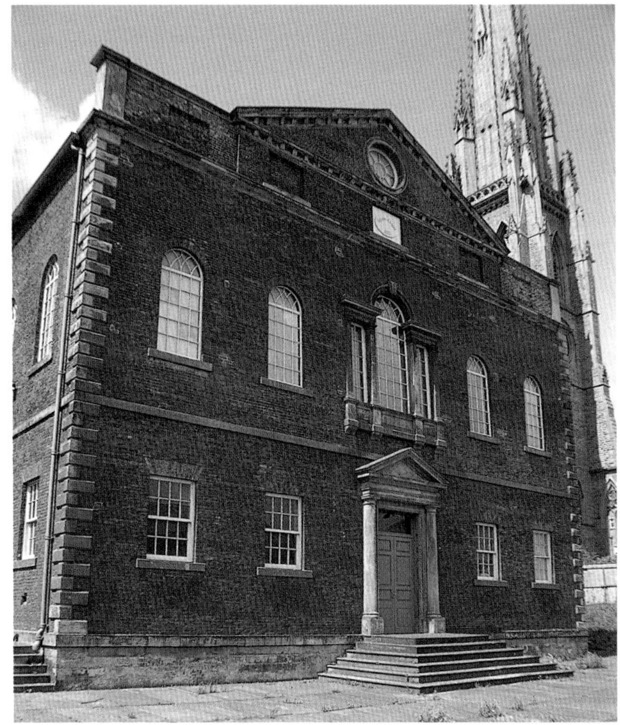

558 (*above*) Thomas Bradley, attributed. Front elevation, Square Chapel (Independent), Halifax, Yorkshire, 1771–2.

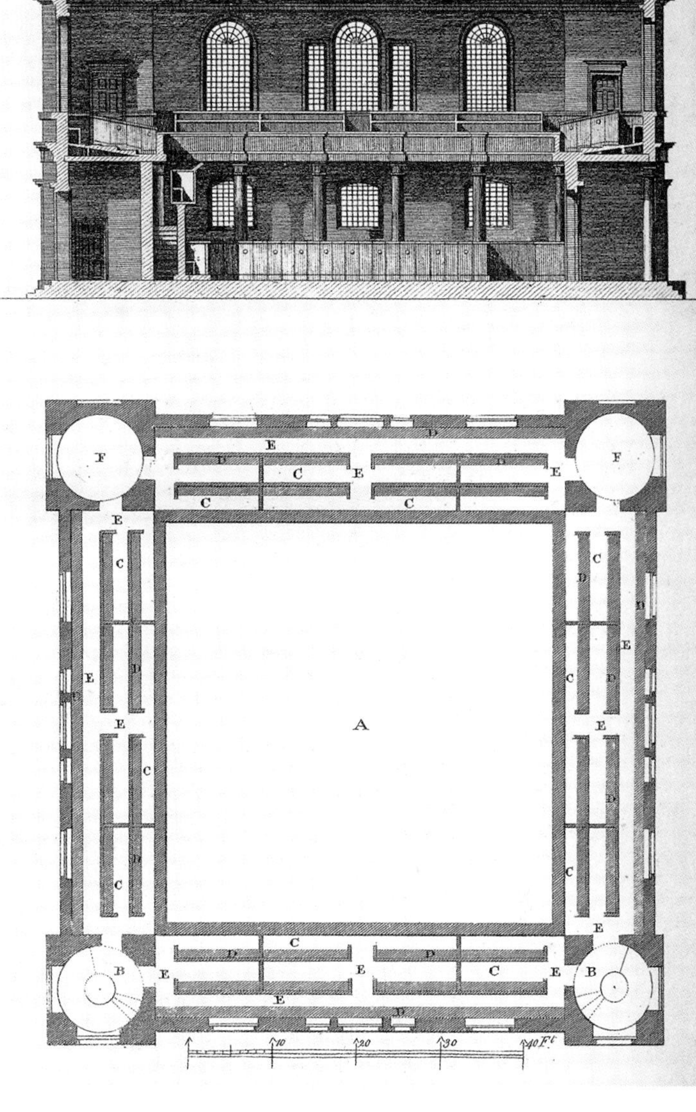

559 (*right*) G. Burder after John Carter. 'The longitudinal Section with the Plan of the Gallery Floor for a Protestant Dissenters Meeting-House', 1 October 1776, in 'A Society of Architects', *The Builder's Magazine*, 1774, pl. XCIX. Engraving.

Nonconformity, with its propensity for achieving maximum daylight, that made the best use of multiple Serliana, as in the centres of all four elevations of the Square Chapel (Independent), Halifax, Yorkshire (pl. 558), where the Revd Titus Knight, previously a dynamic preacher at one of George Whitefield's London Tabernacles, was 'actively labouring to rescue sin-slaved souls from the kingdom of darkness'.[97] The practical novelty reached a wider audience through John Carter's published design (pl. 559).

Twenty-five

THE PALLADIAN CHURCH COMES OF AGE

The Inhabitants of this Part of the moon seem
to have as Elegant Taste for Architecture as if they
had been the Earthy Disciples of
Palladio or Vitruvius[1]

– none more so than the now under-appreciated mid-Georgian City of London clerk of the works George Dance Sr, who evolved a distinctive, idiomatic mixture of familiar Palladian motifs (pl. 560).

The decision by the New Churches Commissioners to extrapolate the dilapidated medieval fabric of St Giles-in-the-Fields from its programme on the grounds that rebuilding went beyond the Parliamentary remit, and instead to place it under independent financial control, enabled the Vestry in 1730 to abandon Hawksmoor's official involvement (pls 295–6) and turn to a young and hitherto untried architect, Henry Flitcroft. Though not one of the co-surveyors, he served as clerk of the works at Westminster, Whitehall and St James's, as well as Lord Burlington's draughtsman in preparing the 136 engravings in Kent's *The Designs of Inigo Jones* (1727), which, in turn, became his architectural bible. This had the salutary effect of removing St Giles from the predominately baroque context of official church design in London up to that time.[2] Flitcroft's radically Palladian stance may have been sparked by a redolent association surviving from the old church of Inigo Jones's marble monument to the celebrated poet and translator of Homer, George Chapman (died 1634), in the then rare form of a simple antique Roman altar, which Flitcroft preserved in his new church.[3]

His rebuilding (pl. 562) marked a watershed in the history of British church architecture in featuring an exterior innovation that had not previously appeared in the building type: an unambiguous separation of the astylar body into two nearly equal-height but sharply contrasted rusticated and plain storeys completely free of the classical order. Flitcroft here appropriated Palladian domestic solutions from Jones's Queen's House, Greenwich (1616–35), and John Webb's Amesbury House, Wiltshire (*circa* 1660–61), which Georgians believed to be designed by Jones; significantly, Flitcroft made alterations to the latter around 1730.[4] In an early proposal (pl. 561), he contemplated introducing Gibbs-surround gallery windows and a lower, dome-crowned

561 Henry Flitcroft. Design for 'The North side (5)', St Giles-in-the-Fields, Holborn, London, 1731. Pen and ink and wash. RIBA Library Drawings Collection, J9/3/5.

560 (*facing page*) William Henry Toms after George Dance Sr. 'The South West Prospect of the Church of St. Leonard – Shoreditch', London, detail, 10 August 1742. Engraving. © The British Library Board, K.Top. XXIII-23-1-e. G. Dance Sr architect, 1735–40.

562 Thomas Malton Jr. North-west view, St Giles-in-the-Fields, London, *c.*1780. Watercolour. London Metropolitan Archives (Guildhall Library, 1230). Henry Flitcroft architect, 1730–34.

563 Anthony Walker after John Donowell. 'Sectional View of the Parish Church of St. Giles in the Fields', Holborn, London, *c.*1764. Engraving. Author's collection. Henry Flitcroft architect, 1730–34.

steeple, but in execution mimicked nearby St Martin-in-the-Fields (pl. 416) – Flitcroft subscribed to *A Book of Architecture* (1728) – modified only by a rusticated base and belted spire, an inexplicably awkward juxtaposition with the avant-garde body. Inside (pl. 563), he adopted the Wrenian column on pier system and Gibbsian dosseret, while at the same time introduced a series of 'Palladian' motifs, including raised panels of Doric guttae along the gallery fronts, ceiling patterns of rectangular-framed circles in the nave of a type illustrated in Isaac Ware's *Designs of Inigo Jones and Others* (1731) and in the chancel ceiling a reconstruction of the Temple of the Sun and Moon at Rome, with an open-scrolled altarpiece pediment, ornamental panels and statue-filled niches in the blind sections of a modified Serliana based on the screen and reredos of Jones's Somerset House chapel (pl. 551).[5] In this inaugural stage in the evolution of Anglo-Palladian church design these are all indicative of ambivalence on the part of the architect or the Vestry or both in precisely the stylistic direction they wished to travel. In this case the results were greatly esteemed. Shortly before St Giles's consecration on 14 April 1734, Ralph memorialised it in *A Critical Review* as 'one of the most simple and elegant of the modern structures: it is rais'd at very little expence [£10,026 15s. 9d.], has very few ornaments, and little beside the propriety of its parts, and the harmony of the whole, to excite attention, and challenge applause: yet still it pleases, and justly too'. *The London and Westminster Guide* (1768) considered: 'So chaste has the Architect been in his Execution of this Master-piece, that he has been thriftily sparing of Ornament: For this Church hath little beside the symmetric Propriety of its Parts, and the Harmony that results from the Whole, to command our Approbation.'[6]

564 G. Hawkins. South-east view, St Olave, Southwark, 1843. Pen and ink and wash. Southwark Local Studies Library, Gardner Collection, P.15497. Henry Flitcroft architect, 1737–40, demolished 1928.

Flitcroft's radicalism is self-evident if compared not only to Hawksmoor's St Giles's offering but to contemporary Continental achievements: Galilei's Madernoesque San Giovanni in Laterano (1733–6), Servandoni's Wrenian façade of Saint Sulpice, Paris (1736), Bähr's Frauenkirche, Dresden (1725–43), all still deeply embedded in the baroque, and the Asams's ravishingly rococo St Johannes Nepomuk, Munich (1733–46).[7]

Flitcroft's next church, St Olave, Southwark (1737–40; pl. 564), further explored Palladian patterns.[8] The

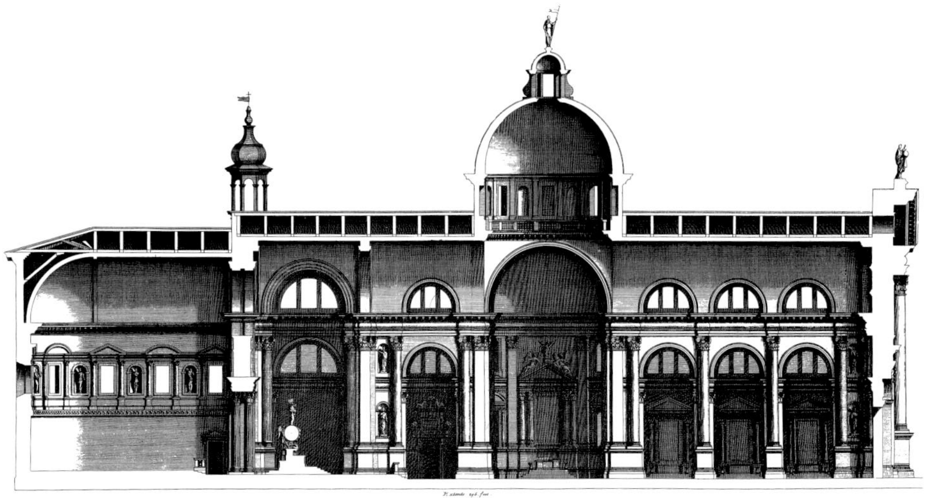

565 Heinrich Hulsbergh after Henry Flitcroft. 'A Section . . . through the Middle, length-ways', San Giorgio Maggiore, Venice, Italy, in Kent 1727, vol. II, pls 60–61. Andrea Palladio, 1564–80.

566 Henry Flitcroft. Approved design for plans and 'Section from East to West of ye Church & Steeple', St Olave, Southwark, London, 14 September 1737. Pen and ink and wash. © The British Library Board, K.Top. XXIII-32-c.

clerestory Diocletian windows derived from San Giorgio Maggiore, Venice (pls 565–6), which, uniquely among foreign buildings, was selected by Kent 'to shew that as great a Rival as that Restorer of Architecture was to the Antients, his Disciple was in no respect inferior to him', with Jones's 'own Work . . . his Monument and best Panagyrick; which remain equal Proofs of the Superiority of those two Great Masters to all others'. From the latter's recast nave aisles of pre-Fire St Paul's Cathedral come Southwark's circular windows lighting the aisle galleries, as also the quirky scrolled brackets at the east end to ease the transition from aisle to clerestory.

Flitcroft detached and isolated the aisle block to form the long, narrow, single-cell body of Stoke Edith, Herefordshire (1740–42; pl. 567), built for Thomas Foley, lord of the manor and subscriber to Leoni's *The Architecture of A. Palladio* (1715–20). Only its medieval

567 Henry Flitcroft. South elevation, St Mary, Stoke Edith, Herefordshire, 1740–42.

west tower was preserved; the Southwark oculi were re-employed above modest Jonesian doors, with single, round-headed windows salvaged from an earlier, rejected scheme.[9] The stonework exterior was originally stucco rendered 'of such Sort and Colour as [Foley] shall approve of, with Joynts drawd answerable to the Rustick Coyns'.[10] The internal western- and eastern-most bays (pl. 568) are screened by pairs of Doric columns reminiscent of Palladio's reconstructions of Roman baths, which Burlington had acquired in Italy in 1719 and subsequently published in *Fabbriche Antiche disegnate da Andrea Palladio* (sometime between 1730 and 1740).[11] The continuous entablature with metopes and triglyphs gives this simple space an austere stateliness, with the entire east wall of the chancel treated as an attached, predominately architectural altar-

568 Henry Flitcroft. Interior towards chancel, St Mary, Stoke Edith, Herefordshire, 1740–42. English Heritage (National Monuments Record, AA01568).

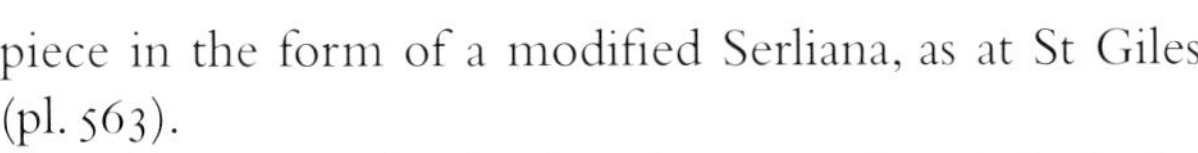

569 Henry Flitcroft. West front, St Andrew, Wimpole, Cambridgeshire, 1748–49, partly remodelled 1887.

570 Inigo Jones. North-west view, Queen's Chapel, St James's Palace, London, 1623–5.

piece in the form of a modified Serliana, as at St Giles (pl. 563).

Wimpole, Cambridgeshire (1748–9; pl. 569), built for Philip Yorke, 1st Earl of Hardwicke, the Lord Chancellor, also a remodelled medieval fabric, relished the undifferentiated, astylar treatment with quoin corners of the Queen's Chapel (pl. 570), for which Flitcroft had drawn an accurate longitudinal section in the early 1720s for Burlington.[12] Wimpole's west door is based on plate 38 in Kent's 1727 book, the altarpiece a variant of St Giles set against the solid east wall marked externally by a minimal, blind Serliana. The aim was to create a 'much more regular . . . beautiful and every way more commodious' church, though a later visitor found a 'neat but by no means elegant' building.[13] Within one generation but a change of architects and stylistic preference, the estate's places of worship moved dramatically from baroque (pl. 89) to Palladian classicism.

George Dance Sr, in his capacity as clerk of the works of the City of London from 1735 until his death in 1768, virtually an entire working career, was the most productive church architect of his generation practising in and around London. We have already seen him in action at Bancroft's Almshouses (pl. 529), St Botolph, Aldgate (pl. 554), Canterbury Cathedral (pl. 178) and Faversham, Kent (pl. 327).[14]

We first hear of him in 1724, aged around 30, as copartner with his mason father Giles, about whom little is known, and his father-in-law James Gould, a minor City builder, in connection with replacing medieval St Botolph, Bishopsgate (pl. 572), which had survived the Great Fire of 1666 but by 1714 was in so ruinous a condition as to cause fears of imminent collapse. The contentious issue of identifying the respective responsibilities of the three men is partly resolved by a careful reading of the commissioners' detailed minutes, as we have seen earlier (p. 143).[15] On 2 June 1724 Gould was appointed 'Surveyor and Clerk of All The Works [and] Measurer'; on 17 June his church plan was deemed 'most Elligible' and the committee debated the 'most

571 Giles and George Dance Sr. East door detail, St Botolph, Bishopsgate, London, 1724–8.

Convenient' location for the steeple, choosing the east end directly over the chancel, which (since the ground lay on the west side of the thoroughfare) faced Bishopsgate with access to the interior by modest flanking doors (and a further one on the south elevation within the churchyard). This was by no means a unique orientation, as we have seen at Greenwich (pl. 403), Bath (pl. 527) and Gloucester (pl. 553). On 26 October the Dances were confirmed in 'Performeing all the Masons Worke, as Specified . . . by . . . Gold', who, we may surmise from his only other documented public work (the long-vanished South Sea House in nearby Threadneedle Street, 1724–5), was responsible for the monotonous, austerely detailed, stone-dressed brick structure with unframed windows along the side and rear elevations. Subsequently, the masons proposed aesthetic improvements under the heading of 'Addition of the Work', including window architraves and corner quoins on all but the east front and fourteen carved cherub heads, etc., estimated at £480 3s. 10d. The crucial passage, dated 28 September 1726, referring to 'Extra Works done by Masons [which] over balanced their Defficiencies', including an ashlar frieze 'Enricht wth Trigliphs although Expresst plain in Designes so that it has Exceeded aggreement', carried an explanation that they 'Omitted . . . bond Stones to make the work more Beautifull' and by adding the 'Soffitta' the 'Small Window is now In A Handsome Proportion'. The 'Dorick Pillasters were Consider'd wth The Utmost Care the Benefitt, and Advantage of the Building for Which Reason, Wee could not Omitt this opportunity of Performing, what we thought so Materiall and Necessary, Towards The Increas: both of Strength, and Beauty to the Worke'. The bond stones of the doors were increased from a depth of 1½ to 3 feet to make them 'more than Equivalent'. They concluded that these and other 'Necessary improvements' were 'Justly done as will appear when the Roof is On . . . Wee abhord anything as a Intention to Save any Charge by Diminishing or Curtailing the Work: But on the Contrary have Always Added where wee Saw it Materiall or Necessary'. Gould concurred.[16] Some of these impositions, which surely should be credited to George Dance, forcefully transformed the original feeble effort in the light of the spectacular achievements of the New Churches (by 1726 all but Horselydown and Old Street were either completed or in advanced stages of construction). Botolph's mighty engaged Doric temple portico, which had featured in only one of Wren's City Churches (St Magnus Martyr, 1671–6), came into its own at Westminster (pl. 365) and Greenwich (pl. 401). Its massive, 80-foot-high tower rising directly behind the central pediment is full of idiosyncrasies: panelled pilasters in the first stage (which, as we will see, became one of the architect's leitmotifs), scrolled bracket buttresses in the second, a third closely dependent on Gibbs (pl. 416), the cupola a restrained Wrenian homage (pl. 2). It is pertinent that several of the craftsmen employed in those churches and at St Martin-in-the-Fields were also involved at St Botolph.[17]

Perhaps due to its transitional character the church did not fare well critically. Responding to Ralph's remark that the east front was 'more in taste than most about town; the parts 'tis composed of are simple, beautiful, and harmonious, and the whole deserves to be admired, for pleasing so much, at so little expence', Langley probably justifiably counter-blasted by observing that the

> cornices of the two doors to this front [pl. 571] . . . are broken by a kind of unmeaning tables, which are not, nor can be applied to any use, and in their forms are very disagreeable. The architraves . . . are intoler-

572 Benjamin Cole. 'The North East Prospect of the Parish Church of St. Botolph, without 'Bishopsgate', London, in Maitland 1756, vol. II, p. 1084. Engraving. Author's collection. James Gold or Gould, Giles and George Dance Sr, architects, 1724–8.

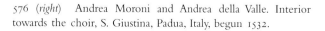

573 (*top left*) Detail of tower shown in pl. 560.

574 (*above*) Sir Christopher Wren. Arches and oculi in colonnade of drum of dome, St Paul's Cathedral, London, Erected 1700–08.

575 (*top right*) George Dance Sr. Interior bays at junction of aisle and chancel, St Leonard, Shoreditch, London, 1735–40.

576 (*right*) Andrea Moroni and Andrea della Valle. Interior towards the choir, S. Giustina, Padua, Italy, begun 1532.

> ably bad, being broken and returned, just under the cornice, where they should have been strait and entire.[18]

While unruly they are not unattractive.

> That part of the tower . . . above the pediment is much too low: if its height had been equal to its breadth, it would have given an elegance to the whole, which is much wanted; and the clumsy pilasters, at its quoins, would have had altitude proportionable to its breadths, which now are little more (if any) than five diameters in height, and therefore two degrees below Tuscan . . . those horizontal channels, so cut out, are a weakening, instead of an ornament to the building. The uppermost square . . . is a well considered part, and demands a more lofty and elegant finishing . . . which should have consisted at least of three orders of columns, pyramidically placed, sustaining a spire, &c. of easy and gradual diminution.

Langley continued: 'For 'tis the loftiness and elegancy of buildings, that make the views of cities magnificent . . . if its upper part . . . under the vase . . . was somewhat less massive, it would make it less inelegant.'[19] These misdemeanours were dealt with in Dance's next church, his most important building.

St Leonard, Shoreditch (pl. 560), designed in 1736, the year after becoming the City's clerk of works, is his most costly ecclesiastical work (at £7,485). A masculine, Portland stone, Doric temple portico, with a back wall articulated like Covent Garden (pl. 512), has its entablature extending across the whole front to form a powerful façade screen, with the giant order just turning the corner. The 192-foot-high tower is an elaborate tour de force, combining St Martin-in-the-Field's 'easy and gradual diminution', to quote Langley, and the flamboyantly scrolled, domed tempietto and spire of St Mary-le-Bow (pl. 484). Ralph described the latter as having 'no fix'd rules . . . nor . . . settled laws of beauty [and] esteem'd . . . a delightful absurdity [but] beyond question as perfect as human imagination can contrive or execute, and till we see it outdone, we shall hardly think it to be equall'd'.[20] This eminently suited Dance's idiosyncratic nature. One detail in particular, the arch and oculi-pierced walls linking the tempietto columns to the cylindrical core (pl. 573), which derived from St Paul's Cathedral dome colonnade (pl. 574), reappears in the four corners of the nave (pl. 575) as transitions from the solid end walls to the dosseret columns dividing it from the aisles (which originally supported galleries and owed much to nearby Christ Church, Spitalfields). On this hugely magnified scale the ensemble brings to mind Santa Giustina, Padua (pl. 576), which pertinently two popular English guidebooks of the period mistakenly attributed to Palladio.[21] Dance's design for an unknown church (pl. 577), though smaller in size (closer to his two other London churches, at Aldgate and Bethnal Green), lies somewhere within this group. Its most interesting novelty is the range of three oculi in the upper level of the engaged Ionic temple portico, a motif that appears in several designs in Robert Morris's *Rural Architecture* (1750), to which Dance subscribed.[22]

577 George Dance Sr. West front design for an unidentified church, undated. Pen and ink and wash. Collection Canadien Centre d'Architecture, Montreal, DR1983,0449R.

Morris made his reputation as a leading publisher of Palladian architectural treatises and pattern books, with

a small but distinguished output as a practising architect, most notably as a designer of octagonal buildings, which belong to an attractive but neglected church sub-group.[23] These should be explored before turning to the remaining leading Palladian church advocates (James Paine and Roger Morris).

The form is particularly associated with the Wesleyans, most famously Heptonstall Chapel, Yorkshire (1764; pl. 578).[24] It has an architectural pedigree in Italian renaissance pattern books such as Sebastiano Serlio's *Tutte l'opere d'architettura et prospetiva* (1547) and in Palladio's recommendation for centralised temples of round, quadrangular, hexagonal, octagonal or more plans, 'which, when . . . done with beauty and suitable proportions, and distinguished by elegant and ornamental architecture . . . deserve to be praised [and where] one ought carefully to observe, that all the angles be equal'.[25] Equally potent were a wide range of Dutch seventeenth-century churches.[26]

578 (*top*) Architect unknown. Wesleyan Chapel, Heptonstall, Yorkshire, 1764.

579 (*above*) William Sands. Entrance elevations, St James, Moulton Chapel, Lincolnshire, 1722.

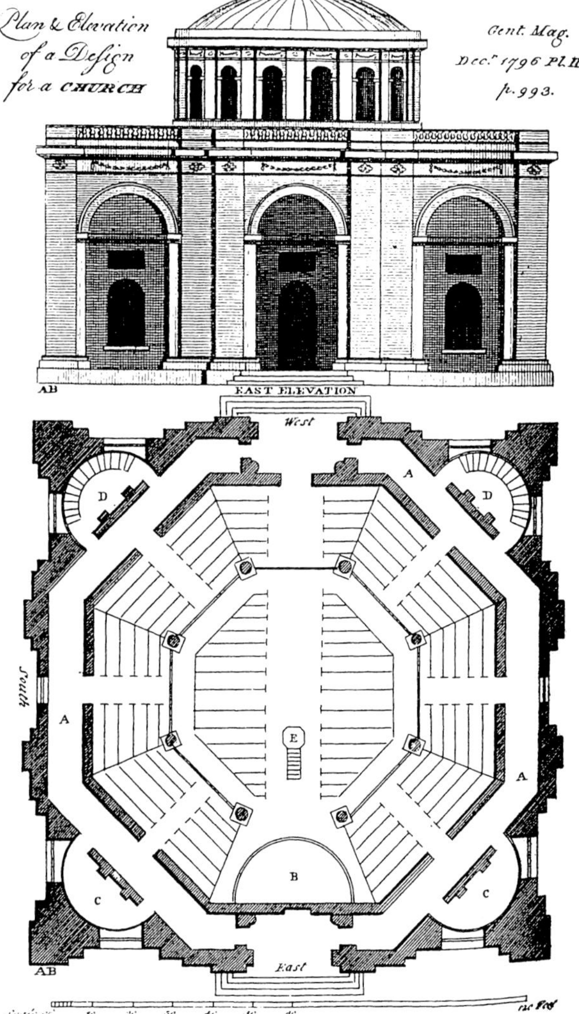

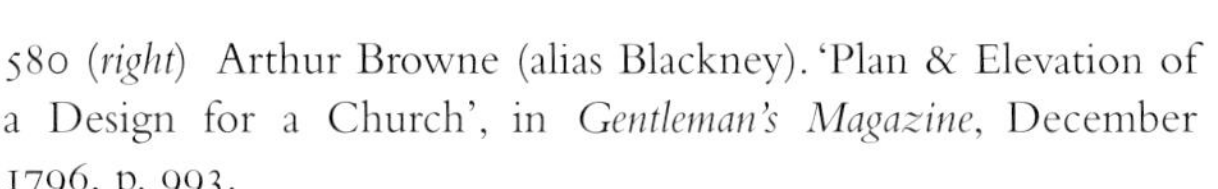

580 (*right*) Arthur Browne (alias Blackney). 'Plan & Elevation of a Design for a Church', in *Gentleman's Magazine*, December 1796, p. 993.

581 James Sillett. View of the entrance fronts, Colegate Octagon Chapel (Presbyterian), Norwich, Norfolk, 1828. Coloured stipple engraving. Author's collection. Thomas Ivory architect, 1753–6.

The form gained an Anglican foothold as early as 1722 at St James, Moulton Chapel, in the Lincolnshire fenland (pl. 579), where Dutch workmen had been involved in drainage systems since the sixteenth century. Designed for the impropriator, Maurice Johnson, a member of the Gentleman's Society of Spalding and the Society of Antiquaries of London, the architect was a local man, William Sands.[27] Its practical advantages are demonstrated in a scheme for an unspecified church by Arthur Browne of Norwich (pl. 580), described as a

> Convenient & elegant Design [with a] passage quite round it, which communicates with every part, and gives every person an opportunity of entering at that part . . . nearest to their pew without disturbing the congregation [while the] double wall will prevent the congregation being disturbed by carriages, which is often disagreeable in large towns.

The pulpit is so positioned that 'if the manner in which sound expands is considered [it brings] many within the compass of the preacher's voice, and . . . as well suited for hearing as any that can be adopted'.[28] This reflects the radically new thinking on Nonconformist design emerging in the 1750s, epitomised in the Octagon Chapel (Presbyterian), Norwich, the *magnum opus* of the genre, where it may have had a particularly powerful resonance. The congregation was founded in 1580 by Robert Browne, who with his followers, the Brownists, took refuge from persecution at Middelburg in the Netherlands, where the Protestant Oostkerk (1647–67) is a magnificent brick and stone octagon crowned by a huge dome with cupola. Dutch ties were retained when the congregation resettled in Norwich in the eighteenth century.[29]

Initially, the building committee favoured rectangularity (pl. 509), but by late 1753 interest had shifted to octagonal forms, with a design supplied by Morris (pl. 582), who advocated Presbyterian sentiments of 'Purity and Simplicity [with preferences for] Plainness and Utility to Gaiety and Ornament', and a belief that 'if you will be lavish in Ornament, your structure will look rather like a Fop, with a Superfluity of gaudy Tinsel, than a real Decoration'.[30] In turn, this was

582 Robert Morris. Plan and elevation design, Colegate Octagon Chapel (Presbyterian), Norwich, Norfolk, 1753. Pen and ink and wash. Norfolk Record Office, FC13/80 no. 1.

583 F. Schenck. Interior towards the east, Colegate Octagon Chapel (Presbyterian), Norwich, Norfolk, in J. and E. Taylor, *History of the Octagon Chapel, Norwich*, 1848. Lithograph. Norfolk Record Office, FC13/81. Thomas Ivory architect, 1753–6.

superseded in 1754 by Thomas Ivory's design (pl. 581), which was erected and opened on 12 May 1756.[31] Its Ionic portico, projecting over the entire perron to form a sort of *porte-cochère*, while providing additional cover, is visually unsatisfactory, and the building triumphs only in the unexpectedly surprising dynamic of the interior (pl. 583), with its eight richly carved and fluted, giant order Corinthian dosseret columns supporting a panelled saucer dome, inspired by Gibbs's Round Design for St Martin-in-the-Fields published as plates 11–12 in *A Book of Architecture* (1728). Its success clearly depended on this particular treatment. Morris had responded to criticism of a chapel design he published in *Rural Architecture* (1750), 'that the inner Part should have been a Circle . . . and the Roof spherical, that the Sound striking in the Angles, will render it confused, and reverberate from a Roof Octagular in the Plan, very unintelligible to the Audience' as an 'Objection of little Weight [since] the Angles are small, and nearly approaching to a Circle'.[32] Another competitor, Thomas Rawlins, believed of his own contribution, published in *Familiar Architecture* (1768), that there 'may indeed be some Reason to object [because] the Arches are to be supported with large angular Jambs forming an Isle . . . round them, which may cause a confused Reverberation of the Voice interrupted by the Piers', yet added: 'But this will not be the case where Columns are introduced.'[33]

The impact of Ivory's interior was described by John Wesley in 1757:

> I was shown [the] new meeting-house, perhaps the most elegant one in Europe. It is eight-square, built of the finest brick . . . The inside is finished in the highest taste, and is as clear as any nobleman's saloon. The communion-table is fine mahogany; the very

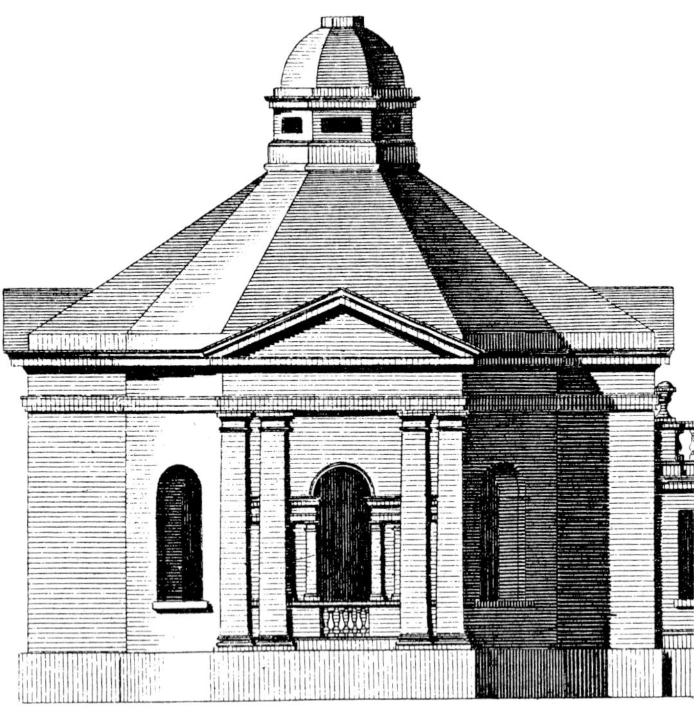

584 T. White after John Woolfe. 'Principal Front of...Buckland [chapel] in Berkshire', in Woolfe and Gandon 1767, pl. 93. Engraving. John Wood Sr and Jr architects, 1755–7.

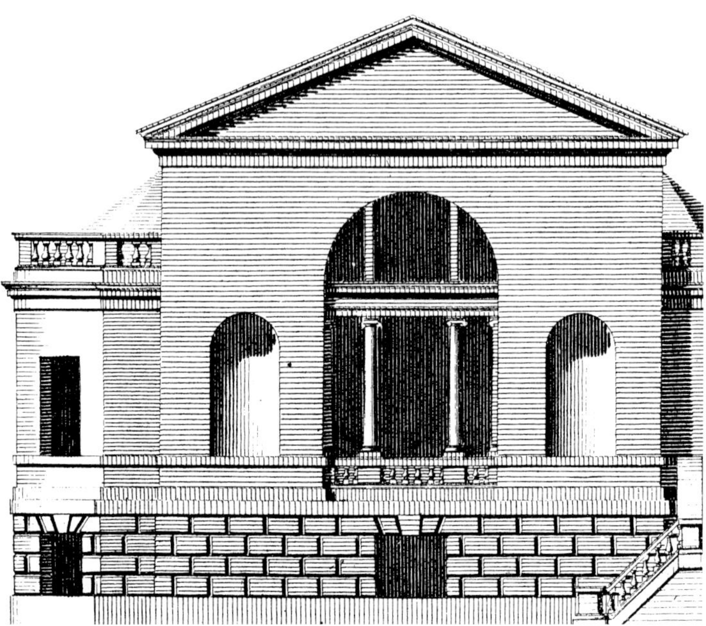

585 J. White after John Woolfe. 'South Front of Cusworth [chapel] . . . near Doncaster in Yorkshire', in Woolfe and Gandon 1767, pl. 89. Engraving. James Paine architect, 1750–54.

> latches of the pew-doors are polished brass. How can it be thought that the old, coarse gospel should find admission here?[34]

On at least one occasion octangularity was adopted as innocuous camouflage for a country house Catholic chapel, at Buckland House, Berkshire (1755–7), designed by the Woods of Bath for Sir Robert Throckmorton, 4th Baron (pl. 584), an externally sedate Palladian pile hardly hinting at its internal richness of door frames, Serliana, aedicule niches, pilasters and exquisitely carved floral friezes.[35]

Yet another beautiful experiment from this middle decade is James Paine's first outstanding ecclesiastical work, the chapel at Cusworth Hall, Yorkshire (1750–54; pl. 585). Measuring only 24 by 30 feet, it is, like Buckland, contained in one of the twin wings added to the central block (1742–4, by George Platt II) situated 'on an eminence in the midst of a pleasant park, and commanding extensive views . . . over the adjacent country'.[36] Paine wrote in 1750 to the owner, William Wrightson, High Sheriff of the West Riding of Yorkshire promising to

> finish the Chaple in a very Gentiel taste viz Columns inserted in the wall, supporting a Entablature Adorn'd with Gentill enrichments: & Above the entablature a handsom cove with a few Gentiel Ornaments in it. I propose the Alter table to stand within the Bow which being supported with Columns Also will Produce a fine effect . . . I hope the Design will Please you & if the expense rises higher than you Propose I can lessen it by finishing it Plainer.

A few months later: 'as I have your Building very much at heart, I cou'd not think of leaving any thing unstudyed, and therefore revised every Part and have made Quite a new disposition of the intended parts, which as Well as the reducing the expence, will produce a more Harmonious Effect then the former'.[37] The garden front is a disengaged bay of Burlington's Roman baths-inspired façade of York Assembly Rooms (1731–2), to which Paine substituted the broken pediment for a continuous one and added a lower poly-lobed chancel to the outer flank.[38] One of the masters of the early phase of English rococo, the internal walls (pl. 586) are delicately modulated advancing and receding surfaces framed by syncopated Ionic pilasters, half, three-quarter and free-standing Ionic columns, with a billowing, compartmented plasterwork ceiling surrounding an irregular octagonal painting of the *Ascension* by Francis Hayman, whose art was admired for its 'utmost Grace and Delicacy . . . beautiful Colouring [and] the most lively Expression of Character'.[39] The chancel,

586 James Paine. Interior towards the chancel, Cusworth Hall chapel, Doncaster, Yorkshire, 1750–54. English Heritage (National Monuments Record, AA56/01680).

screened by the now almost ubiquitous Serliana, here crowned by a floridly festooned and scrolled pediment, has a playful plasterwork apse modelled by the celebrated Joseph Rose Sr, who also fashioned the frame of Hayman's *Good Samaritan* altarpiece, recalling nothing so much as the vocabulary of contemporary engraved trade cards.[40]

In 1753 Paine began working at Gibside, County Durham, the magnificent landscape garden created by George Bowes, who may have been the author of a mausoleum-church scheme dated 1736–7 intended to commemorate his first wife of only two months, who had died in 1724, age 14. This survives only in plan and is a remarkable 30-foot-diameter, 54-foot-high domed rotunda approached by identical tetrastyle temple porticoes on perrons placed on the three cardinal points, with the chancel lit by a Serliana, perhaps inspired by the Pantheon-like San Simeon Piccolo, Venice.[41] This

distinctive and noble form was fashionable at the time, as Canaletto demonstrated (pl. 587).[42] The unrealised proposal was one of the seeds of Paine's ecclesiastical masterpiece (pl. 588), situated on what he described as the 'end of a most beautiful terras which commands extensive views of the adjacent country, and of the valley through which the *Derwent* runs'.[43] It is a daringly original reworking of Palladio's Tempietto at Maser (1580), the Barbaro family church adjacent to

587 (*left*) Antonio Canaletto. *A Domed Church Seen through a Ruined Arch*, detail, *c.*1753–5. Oil on canvas. Private collection, England.

588 (*below*) James Paine. Entrance elevation, Gibside Chapel, County Durham, 1760–76.

589 (*facing page top*) J. Morris after C. Ebdon. 'Section of the Chapel & Mausoleum', Gibside, County Durham, in Paine 1767, vol. I, pl. LXIX. Engraving.

590 (*facing page bottom left*) J. Morris. Plan, Gibside Chapel, County Durham, in Paine 1767, vol. I, pl. LXVII. Engraving.

591 (*facing page bottom right*) Architect unknown. Interior towards the choir, Santa Maria Mater Domini, Venice, Italy, *c.*1502–15.

Chris.r Ebdon delin
5
10
20
30
40 Feet

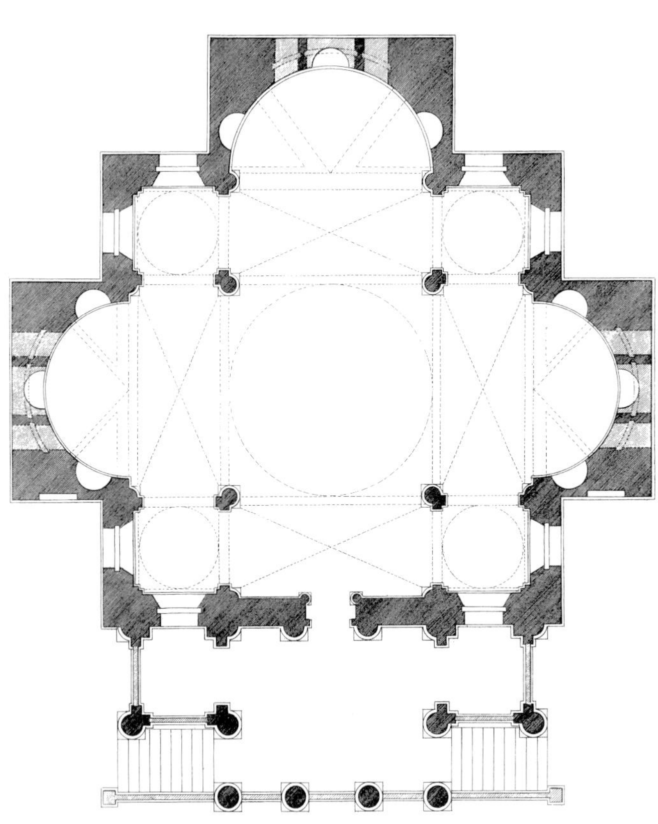

their villa, which, though not yet engraved, was probably known to Paine, if not first hand from his Italian travels in 1755–6, then through Flitcroft's measured drawings made for Burlington.[44] He simplified the prototype by flattening the external north, south and east arms, concentrating illumination in high-level Diocletian windows, removing the lantern from the crossing dome on drum and reducing the Corinthian hexastyle temple portico to Ionic tetrastyle. On the other hand, the entrance front is more complex, with a semi-enclosed porch inserted between portico and body, its outer bays pierced by balustraded arches on adjacent elevations suggested by the return walls at Maser, and at Gibside serving as viewing loggias. Festoons embellishing the drum were redeployed from Maser's intercolumniation. The internal Greek-cross plan (pls 589, 590) with apsidal-ended arms, domes on pendentives covering both the central crossing and the corner chapels, and quarter-engaged Corinthian columns attached to the chapels' inner angles framing elegant, round-headed arches springing from shorter pilasters so closely resemble the distinctive treatment of Santa Maria Mater Domini in Venice (pl. 591) that it seems inconceivable that Paine did not know of it.[45]

His unrealised and hitherto unnoticed design for Warden, Northumberland (pl. 592),[46] exposes the confusions in adopting Palladianism to Georgian church architecture: the domestic stratification of storeys interrupted by Gibbs-surround gallery windows (which, with the dome-capped tower, is a late reflection of Flitcroft's preliminary scheme for St Giles-in-the-Fields, pl. 561);[47] intimations of astylar temple forms contaminated by a monumental, shallow arched recess breaking into the roof pediment, one of Paine's signature motifs;[48] and a diminutive, pediment-less portico. Nor was Paine alone in struggling with this problem as more Palladian patterns became common currency.

St Lawrence, Mereworth, Kent (1743–6; pl. 593), handicapped by a puzzling history due to insufficient documentation, reveals a failure to achieve stylistic homogeneity when over-relying on fashionable archetypes. The client was John Fane, 7th Earl of Westmorland, of nearby Mereworth House (Colen Campbell's 1720–25 adaptation of Palladio's Villa Rotunda). The architect was probably Roger Morris, a relative of Robert Morris, who had first-hand knowledge of the architecture of Vicenza and Venice, which he visited in 1731–2 and probably again in 1744, and whose London residence in Leicester Fields lay conveniently midway between St Martin-in-the-Fields, St Giles-in-the-Fields and Covent Garden, from where much of his ecclesiastical repertory originated. St Lawrence has been aptly described as 'a goulach of famous London churches'.[49] The rustic rag and sandstone body with its deep modillion eaves is a more faithful rendering of Covent Garden than we have seen in other Georgian imitations, which led one commentator not only to acknowledge the model but also to claim Mereworth 'more splendid'.[50] Yet, it is also curiously different, with ranges of identical, unframed, heavily key-block, rectangular windows, which at the east end (pl. 594) flank a central, round-headed opening (a sort of Jonesian deconstructed Serliana featured frequently in *The Designs of Inigo Jones*, 1727, to which Morris subscribed) and a big Diocletian window (favoured by Palladio but never placed by him within the pediment, though with other Italian precedents[51]). Horace Walpole associated the 'vast Doric pillars' of the west porch with the smaller, delicate Ionic south porch (later removed) of Wren's St Clement Danes, but its carefully integrated modillion eaves suggests it might be read better as an open, semicircular version of Covent Garden (pl. 512).[52] The Tuscan west door with its deep entablature and lunette of radiating tapered glazing bars recalls Palladio's San Francesco della Vigna, Venice. The first stage of the wayward steeple rising unabashedly out of the body's wider, westernmost side bays (paying no attention to Gibbs's use of integrated columns *in antis*), with its corner quoins and distinctive windows in which the imposts are unsupported by jambs, is of a piece with the body and presumably belongs to the original concept. In 1734, however, Langley could not agree with Ralph's assessment of Covent Garden as 'one of the most perfect pieces of architecture that the art of man can produce' on the (perhaps dubious) grounds 'that if a steeple of proper dimensions was raised above the pediment, 'twould be a very great improvement to the whole',[53] though Jones left no indication of such a consideration, thus facilitating the possibilities of assorted solutions. Mereworth's position on low ground made a compelling need for a soaring structure within the landscape.[54] It is usually suggested that the erected upper stages, dating from a separate, slightly later building campaign, were copied from St Martin-in-the-Fields (where Morris was baptised), though, in fact, apart from the isolated triangular pediments on consoles in Mereworth's clock stage (from pls 29–30 in *A Book of Architecture*, 1728, to which Morris was a subscriber), it precisely follows Flitcroft's unexecuted steeple proposed for St Giles in 1733, where, too, the steeple and body are similarly at odds.[55] Perhaps rightly, the irritated Walpole condemned St Lawrence's structure as 'designed for the latitude of Cheapside, and is so tall, that the poor church curtseys under it, like Mary

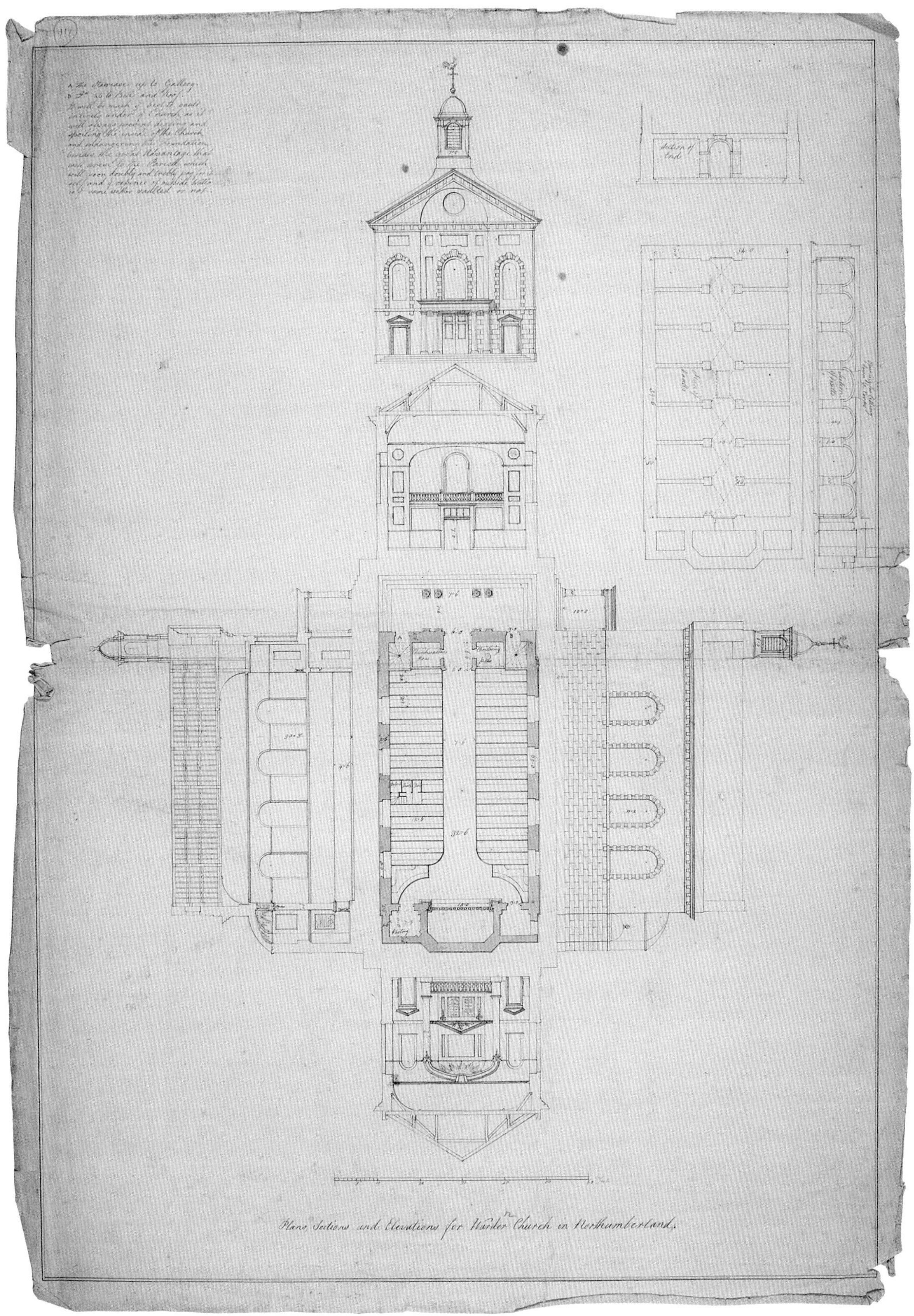

592 James Paine. Design for 'Plans, Sections and Elevations for Warden Church in Northumberland' (St Michael), before 1765. Pen and ink. The National Trust, Wallington Hall, no. 111.

594 Roger Morris. South-east view, St Lawrence, Mereworth, Kent, 1743–6.

Rich in a vast high-crown hat'. He also attacked the interior as 'the most abominable piece of tawdriness that ever was seen, stuffed with pillars painted in imitation of verd antique, as all the sides are of Siena marble: but the greatest absurdity is a Doric frieze, between the triglyphs of which is the Jehovah, the I.H.S. and the dove'.[56] Yet, this interior was revolutionary for its day. Originally free of box pews,[57] its large eastern Diocletian window and wide, barrel-vaulted nave painted with imitation coffering, supported on close-set, baseless Doric columns with a deep, full entablature, continuing as half-columns on the west and east walls and also on the outer walls of the narrow side aisles, with their flat, rosette-painted ceilings, altogether create the appearance of an antique Roman temple.[58] Nonetheless, an anomaly arises in the mitigation of this austere avant-gardism by the rococo flamboyance of William Price's heraldic painted glass filling the windows (pl. 595), further confirmation that the building belongs to the pre-archaeological phase of British classicism.

Nothing at this date in church architecture could be further removed from, say, Fuga's façade of Santa Maria Maggiore, Rome (1743), or the German Neumann's Vierzehnheiligen interior, near Bamberg (1743–72); indeed, across the Continent architects continued to be enamoured with the ideas of Berniniesque baroque.[59] But in the 1750s Europe, and particularly France, reinvented the antique in a succession of radical experiments, which became the universal measure of Western avant-gardism.[60] The following chapters explore their impact in Britain.

595 William Price. Enamel painted glass window, St Lawrence, Mereworth, Kent, 1752.

593 *(facing page)* Roger Morris. South-west view, St Lawrence, Mereworth, Kent, 1743–6.

596 Bellicard after Jacques-Gabrielle Soufflot. West elevation 'Vue de la Nouvelle Eglise de Ste. Genevieve' (later the Pantheon), Paris, 1757, detail. Engraving. Author's collection.

Twenty-six

THE FIRST NEOCLASSICAL CHURCHES

[A] pagan temple dedicated to *Cybele*, and all the gods,
and afterwards consecrated to the *Virgin Mary*, and all the saints
. . . tho' . . . the most ancient, is not withstanding the most intire
of all the remains of antiquity[1]

British neoclassicism burgeoned from the experiments of mid-eighteenth-century French architecture, most memorably at Sainte Geneviève (the Panthéon), Paris (pl. 596), with its exclusive use both externally and internally of free-standing columns rather than piers and arches, and its own, independent discoveries of the Roman and Greek past.

After the hiatus of St Martin-in-the-Fields in the 1720s there followed a persistent succession of peripteral and pseudoperipteral temple-form church adventures. The most prophetic were voiced in the *Grub-street Journal* in 1734 by Batty Langley, writing under the pseudonym Hiram, architect of Solomon's Temple at Jerusalem. He advocated the notion that 'Porticos of large columns have', in Vanbrughian parlance, 'a majestic aspect, and fill the eye with solemn grandeur [and] nothing contributes so much to the grandeur of a front'; furthermore, that 'all public buildings, where columns . . . are introduced, they should be of large dimensions, and few parts; for it is thereby that majesty is expressed'.[2] He made a poignant distinction between antique and Palladian classicism, between the 'truly grand and magnificent' entablature of Gibbs's St Martin's, which continues 'intire throughout [the church's] whole length, according to the ancient manner' (pl. 416), and the 'false' treatment of Inigo Jones's Whitehall Banqueting House (then serving as the Chapel Royal), where it is 'broken into many parts [and] infinitly short of that grandeur'.[3] He then courageously demonstrated, though unfortunately failed to illustrate, how that consummate example of English baroque, St Paul's Cathedral (pl. 2) – about which he was apparently of two minds, criticising many of its features in the *Journal* of 1734 while redeploying its west front and crossing dome for an 'extremely jejune' design for the London Mansion House in 1735[4] – might be metamorphosed into an antique temple.

Placing himself in Wren's shoes ('had I been the architect'), he recommended two solutions for preventing the interior falling 'very short of that grandeur in the height of its ceilings' that the master had allowed. One introduced a double tier of columns with windows between in the upper range 'after the Egyptian manner', from which rose a 'semicircular groin'd ceiling . . . curiously divided into compartments, enriched with carved ornaments', expressing 'a grandeur which words are not able to describe'.[5] Here Galilei had already offered a way forward (pl. 415), yet one never pursued. The other solution supplanted Wren's column-enhanced piers in the nave, which Langley considered 'rather too massy, and fill up the space with too much solidity', with groupings of two pairs of Corinthian columns sharing a single square plinth shadowed by 'small pillasters, with their composite imposts and architraved arches . . . excluded' and the intercolumniation reduced so as to accommodate more columns but the apertures enlarged to increase the 'lights and shadows', producing 'an open, light, and elegant aspect [and] adding very greatly to the perspective view from the west entrance'. In the raised choir the column bases would stand directly on the floor so that 'the rays of sight, at the west entrance, would have had one continued series of parts in the columns, throughout the whole length, that would have produced a most surprising and beautiful appearance', although the continuity of the full classical order would be broken.[6]

Langley's recommendation for transforming the cathedral's (for him) clumsy baroque exterior into a

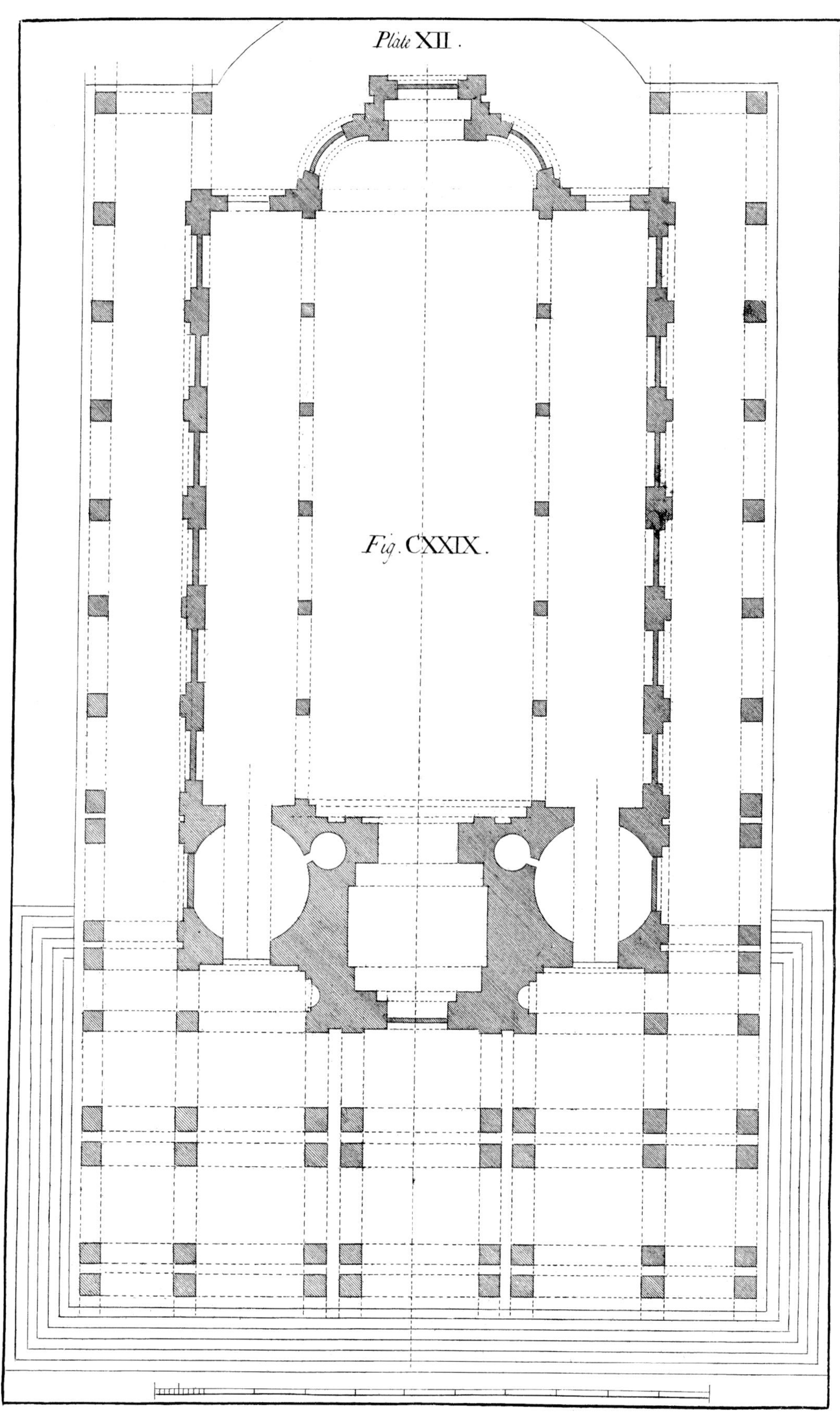

597 Batty Langley. Plan proposal for ensconcing Thomas Archer's St Philip, Birmingham, Warwickshire, from Campbell 1715, pl.10, within an antique peripteral temple, in Langley 1736, pl. XII, fig. CXXIX. Engraving.

'truly magnificent pile' is even more extraordinary. He would encapsulate its entirety in a colossal, 180 by 500 foot, peripteral temple, restructuring Wren's main walls straight from front to rear by reducing the depth of the transepts to form a rectangular body, 71 foot high, with 7-foot-diameter Corinthian columns ranged ten across the west front, projecting 41 feet forward and crowned by a colossal pediment (he does not indicate if the west towers would be preserved), and seventy-one along the north and south sides, with corresponding pilasters attached to the walls. This 'spacious colonade of prodigious length', supporting a 28-foot-high entablature crowned by a statue over each column, was linked by balustraded parapets. Only Wren's semicircular chancel and his great dome rising above its peristyle drum over the central crossing would remain untouched, in order to bring daylight directly into the interior. The total effect 'would have filled the eye with solemn awe and surprising grandeur . . . not . . . parallelled by any building now subsisting in the world' and outshine in size if not in columniation the long-vanished colossal Temple of Diana at Ephesus, the Fifth Wonder of the Ancient World.[7] Nor would it have escaped Langley's notice that St Paul's was believed to stand on the site of a Roman temple dedicated to Diana.[8] Later, the double columns of Wren's west front were criticised as offensive and 'contrary to the usual Mode of the Ancients', while the neoclassical architect James Wyatt expressed preference for 'only *one range* of pillars instead of Pillars over Pillars'.[9] On a slightly more practical though no less fantastic level, in 1736 Langley republished plate 10 from *Vitruvius Britannicus* (1715), the plan of Archer's St Philip, Birmingham (pl. 597), confuting its baroque carcass by encircling the west, north and south elevations with a deep, forest-like peristyle of single, coupled and quadrupled columns on pedestals, precisely aligned with the existing articulation, again exposing only the chancel, with the whole building raised on a podium. Unfortunately, neither a corresponding elevation nor an explanation accompanies this demonstration.[10] Related to this was the notion of the classical column as an independent architectural element. Already in 1734, for example, Langley condemned Wren's use in St Bride's of 'double columns whose solid shafts intersect and cut into each other [in effect a polylobed pier as] a most barbarous and ignorant practice', preferring 'columns in pairs . . . which would have been both stronger, and more elegant architecture'.[11]

It was also during the 1730s that the British began systematic visits to Roman sites beyond Italy. The Revd Richard Pococke, Vice-General of the Waterford and Lismore diocese (later Bishop of Ossory and Meath), travelled to Egypt, Palestine, Syria, Mesopotamia, Turkey and Greece between 1737 and 1741, publishing his judgmental observations in the two-volume *A Description of the East, and Some other Countries* (1743–5), richly illustrated with both peopled, picturesque views and analytical plans and elevations of Roman and Greek buildings, a presentation which was to become de rigueur after 1750. The Temple of Bacchus at Baalbek, for example, was 'deservedly admired as one of the most beautiful pieces of antiquity that remains' (pl. 598).[12] By the end of the decade images of antique temples had become commonplace. In 1749 a 'Grand, Curious and Splendid Representation of the [Doric] Temple of Apollo, at Delphos [Delphi] in Greece . . . adorn'd with every Thing that can render it pleasing to the Spectator, having curious Pillars of Lapis Lazuli, and embellish'd with Painting in an elegant Manner' (untraced), toured by a Mr Yates of London, was 'displayed at the Black Boy in Edgbaston Street, Birmingham'.[13]

It is worth noting here that the impact of pioneer neoclassical treatises based on first-hand, archaeological investigations of antique classical buildings is well demonstrated by the rapid use made of Robert Wood's highly acclaimed *The Ruins of Palmyra* (1753), the result of an English expedition to the Levant undertaken in 1750–51 with the aim 'to produce things as they found them'. The plate devoted to the temple ceiling, with its combination of central palmette-leafed rosette encircled by repeated, diminutive octagonal coffers, was painted *trompe l'œil* across the entire nave ceiling of West Wycombe church in 1761 under the guidance of the lord of the manor, Sir Francis Dashwood, 2nd Baronet, a leading spirit of the Society of Dilettanti, which had sponsored both the expedition and the publication.[14]

By mid-decade revolutionary ideas advocated by French theoreticians had reached English readers. Marc-Antoine Laugier's chapter entitled 'On the Style in Which to Build Churches' in his influential *Essai sur l'Architecture* (1753), an English edition of which appeared in 1755, wrote: 'Since our churches are meant to receive into their midst a multitude bringing with them the religious image of the God they are going to worship, these churches give the architect scope for working on a large scale and do not in any way restrict the nobility of his concepts', yet in France 'so few of our churches deserve our enlightened interest', which convinced Laugier that 'until now we have not developed the right style for this class of building'. He was particularly critical of G. N. Servandoni's façade of Saint Sulpice, Paris, begun in 1732 (pl. 720), modelled on St Paul's Cathedral (pl. 2), and offered an ideal church that would be

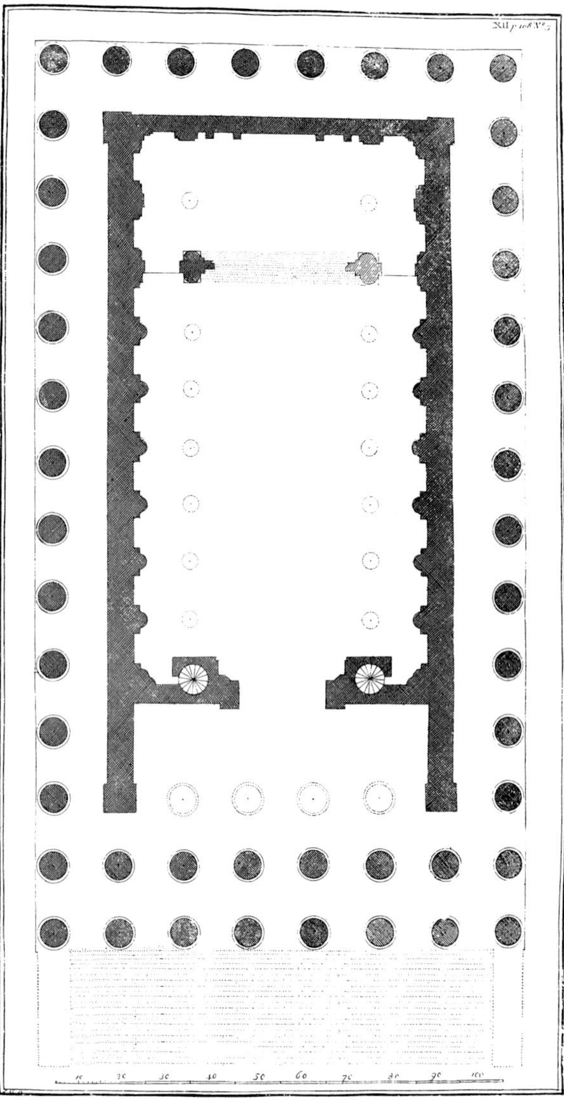

598 'A View' and 'A Plan of the Temple of Baalbeck' (Temple of Bacchus), Lebanon, second century AD, in Pococke 1745, vol. II, pls XII–XIII. Engraving. Leeds University Library, Special Collections.

> entirely natural and true; everything . . . reduced to simple rules and executed according to great principles: no arcades, no pilasters, no pedestals, nothing awkward or constrained . . . [the] barrel vault loses all heaviness . . . since it has no transverse ribs which would appear to weight down heavily . . . The whole building is extremely elegant and delicate . . . nothing is superfluous, nothing is bulky, nothing is offensive . . . The best way of decorating the main front . . . is to build a portico across the whole width of the nave and aisles.

Furthermore, the 'column must be free-standing so that its origin and purpose are expressed in a natural way [and] must rest directly on the floor . . . Pilasters are only a poor representation of columns [and] are never necessary.'[15]

Stephen Riou, the first English architectural writer to take up these avant-garde temple ideas (though not the prophetic baseless columns), was a London architect of French Huguenot extraction who had spent several years in Italy, Greece and Asia Minor.[16] In *The Grecian Orders of Architecture. Delineated and Explained from the Antiquities of Athens* (1768) – a reference to Stuart's and Revett's pioneer publication of 1762 – he included two schemes for 'magnificent [churches in] great and opulent cities' dated in the previous year.

any edifice, in all likelihood, be undertaken with a view to exceed by its immensity, or in rich materials, [yet] it may not be impossible to imagine one of superior disposition, with chaser decorations' in a 'Grecian' mode. Here the twin west towers rise 'without interruption to the pediment' of the hexastyle portico, allowing the

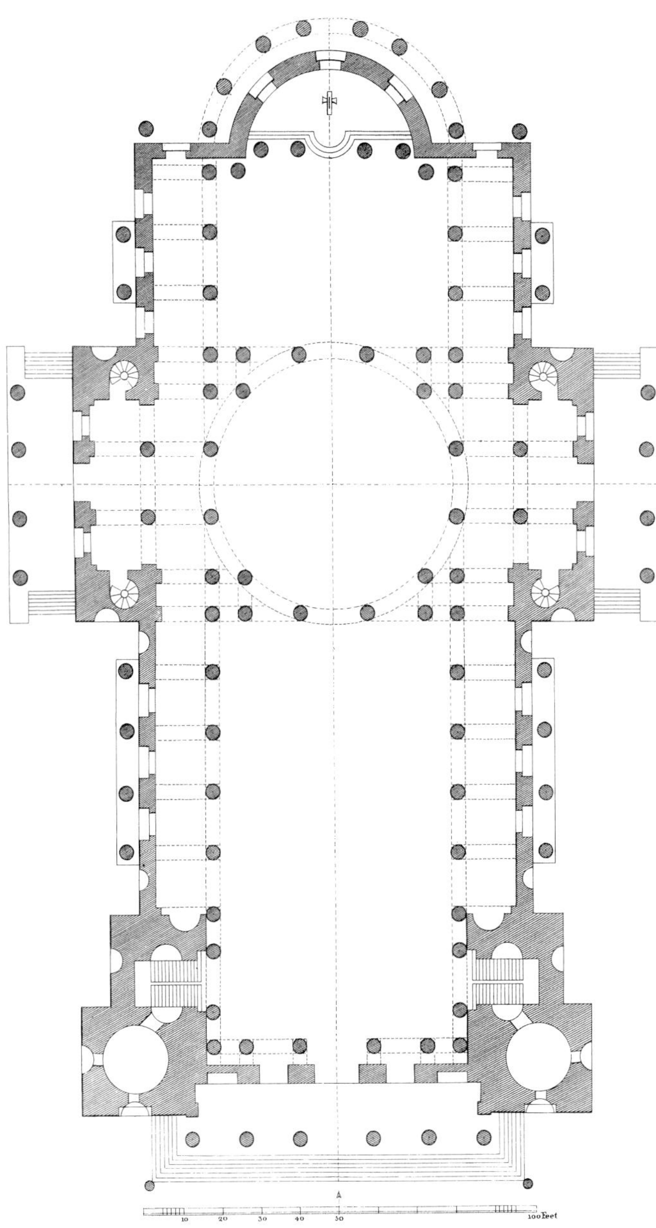

599 Stephen Riou. Design for the plan of a 'magnificent church', 1767, in Riou 1768, vol. II, pl. II. Engraving. RIBA Library Photographs Collection.

600 Stephen Riou. Design for 'The Fore-Front' of a 'magnificent church', 1767, in Riou 1768, vol. II, pl. III. Engraving. RIBA Library Photographs Collection.

central crossing dome to appear 'in its full breadth'. Additional porticoes attached to the transepts 'advance beyond the towers'. Insisting that 'nothing contributes more to the majesty of a building [than an] insulated' column, he also introduced single and ranges of two, four and eight free-standing Corinthian columns placed close to the perimeter walls serving as buttresses, which answered 'all the purposes of those rude Gothic masses'.[18] Perhaps taking a clue from Campbell's contrast between St Paul's Cathedral and his 'new Design of my Invention' for Lincoln's Inn Fields (pls 514–15), Riou's constituent parts might fruitfully be compared to Hawksmoor's similar, rejected design for St George, Bloomsbury (pl. 602), a half-century apart, where dome and tower still slightly overlap and masonry walls still dominate. Interestingly, while the two most celebrated Parisian churches 'now building' – Soufflot's Sainte Geneviève (begun 1757; pl. 596), and Contant d'Ivry's

Internally (pl. 599), the entire length and width of the nave is defined by ranges of single, free-standing columns with an aggregated quartet, in place of piers, at four cardinal points round the central crossing, with each of their inner ones forming part of a circular, full-height colonnade from which rises a solid, 60-foot-diameter domed rotunda. Riou thought this 'invention of suspending the cupola in the air gives an additional variety for sacred edifices'.[17] Externally (pl. 600), the building was a response to St Peter, Rome: 'never will

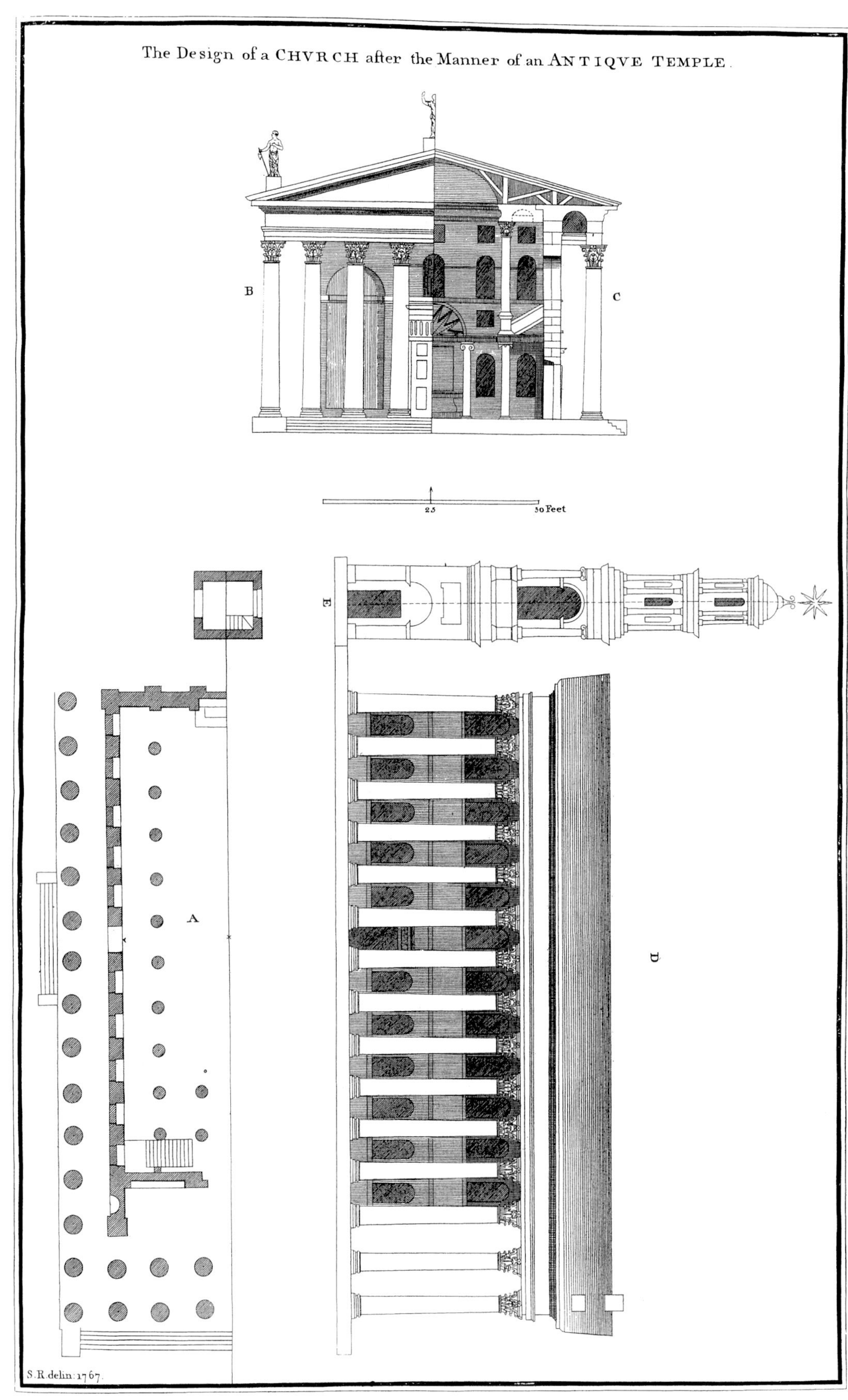

601 Stephen Riou. 'The Design of a CHURCH after the Manner of an ANTIQUE TEMPLE', 1767, in Riou 1768, vol. II, pl. I. Engraving. RIBA Library Photographs Collection.

Madeleine (begun 1763) – 'deserve the attention and applause of the publick', Riou observed that 'though intended to revive the antique disposition of insulated columns, if examined from the designs published, do not seem to promise that purity which might have been introduced'.[19]

His other and if anything more remarkable design is for a peripteral 'CHURCH after the Manner of an ANTIQUE TEMPLE' (pl. 601), 27 by 150 feet, with Corinthian columns encircling the pronaos, double-rowed in front but column-less at the east end in order, unlike either Galilei's or Langley's similar designs (pls 414–15, 597), to accommodate a steeple 'placed at a small distance, and detached from the back front', but on axis 'for the sake of symmetry', perhaps no more than coincidentally resembling Hawksmoor's early Greenwich model, then displayed in Westminster Abbey (pl. 402). The ever-popular solution of St Martin-in-the-Fields, which Riou condemned because the steeple appears 'to stand upon the roof, and to have no other support', was discarded in order to preserve the integrity of the temple form: 'no incumbrance should be admitted that could destroy the beauty of the portico and the anti-temple: therefore the pediment or roof should not be loaded with that Gothic part of our churches, a tower and its spire'.[20] The most distinctive feature of the interior is the reduction of the standard elements of the classical order by 'omitting the frieze and cornice' of the lower range of columns and springing the barrel-vaulted ceiling from 'a plinth above the cornice' of the upper range.[21] Riou may have read Laugier's description of an ideal church, where there was placed

> all around the nave, transept and choir the first Order of isolated columns standing on low socles [and with] a straight architrave terminated by an ogee of moderate projection and erected over this a second Order [with a] complete straight entablature and, directly over it without any sort of attic . . . a plain barrel vault without transverse ribs. Then, around the nave, crossing, and choir . . . columned aisles which form a true peristyle . . . covered by flat ceilings.

602 Nicholas Hawksmoor. Design for the entrance front, St George Bloomsbury, London, 1715. Pen and ink and wash. © The British Library Board, K.Top. XXIII-16-2-b.

Elsewhere, he advocated doors and windows of simple square shape without mouldings, thereby excluding 'irregular spaces [and] bizarre ornaments'.[22] How these avant-garde ideas were translated into actual buildings is demonstrated in two crucial pioneer ecclesiastical endeavours of the early 1760s, Nuneham and All Hallows, London Wall, both of which were unprecedented as English church forms and, moreover, survive largely in their original states.

603 George Dance Jr. Interior towards the chancel, All Hallows, London Wall, London, *c.*1800. Watercolour. London Metropolitan Archives (Guildhall Library), 1765–7.

Twenty-seven

'RULES & STANDARTS OF THE MODERNS': CHURCHES OF THE 1760s AND 1770s

these Stupendous & lasting Works of the Ancients have something of a particular Charm & Majesty no where to be met with in Modern performances, which give them such an excellent éclat that they justly become the Rules & Standarts of the Moderns by which they ought to coppy after, & attract both the Attention & Admiration of every assiduous & inquisitive Artist, and the fittest Objects for the advancing of his improvement.[1]

Early visitors to All Hallows, London Wall (1765–7), must have been startled by the unfamiliar appearance of its novel and exquisite Grecian interior (pl. 603). It was, however, not the first expression of this radically new departure, which the British helped to pioneer. The church at Nuneham, Oxfordshire (1762–4; pl. 604), was most likely designed by Simon, 1st Earl of Harcourt, the owner of Nuneham Park and a founder-member of the Society of Dilettanti, which had sponsored the momentous Greek excursion between 1751 and 1754 undertaken by his co-architect, James 'Athenian' Stuart, and the latter's collaborator, Nicholas Revett, which resulted in the publication of *The Antiquities of Athens* (1762–), the first accurate survey of Greek classical monuments.[2] This parish church-cum-garden pavilion is a spartan, monochromatic rectangle partly screened on its main elevation by a hexastyle unfluted Ionic version of the tetrastyle temple on the Ilissus (450 BC), which had been converted into a Christian church but abandoned in the seventeenth century and finally demolished *circa* 1780, though not before being surveyed and recorded by Stuart and Revett as 'among those works of antiquity which best deserve our attention' (pl. 642).[3] Nuneham's 'portico', however, is deceptive: lacking corresponding openings on the back wall (the existing door and window frames are blind), it serves only as a narrow veranda for viewing the panorama of lush parkland. The actual entrance is on the short end marked by a diminutive Ionic half-rotunda (a common Georgian garden feature), echoed by a projecting semicircular chancel opposite, with the central space crowned by a dome on a tall drum lit by Diocletian windows. A surprised Horace Walpole aptly described the building as 'the part of a temple acted by a church'.[4]

604 James Stuart and Simon, 1st Earl of Harcourt. North-west view, All Saints, Nuneham Courtenay, Oxfordshire, 1762–4.

605 George Dance Jr. South elevation, sections of nave and aisle, vaulting design for All Hallows, London Wall, London, 1765. Pen and ink and wash. RIBA Library Drawings Collection, J3/17-1.

In 1765, at the start of a long, fruitful career and within months of returning from five intensive years' study in Rome, George Dance Jr produced an unusually confident preliminary scheme for All Hallows, London Wall (pl. 605).[5] In it he brilliantly assimilated the heroic monumentality of ancient Roman groin-vaulted assembly buildings, such as the Basilica of Maxentius and Constantine and the so-called Temple of Peace, which, interestingly, had been the subject of the Corso Clementino of the Accademia di San Luca in 1762.[6] This choice is curious considering the severely restricted site for the proposed church, sandwiched between a remnant of ancient masonry and the thoroughfare of London Wall. Indeed, his 60-foot-wide structure, far exceeding the available ground, suggests that this early idea may even have been prepared while Dance was still in Italy, without benefit of an accurate survey, rumours of an intended rebuilding perhaps reaching him from his father, who then still served as the City's clerk of the works.[7] The executed building (pl. 606), curtailed to a compact 33 foot width, abandoned the domed corner blocks (reminiscent of St Andrew, Holborn, pl. 486) and the central door letting directly on to the road, while reducing the tall window space to lunettes set high up in the arches of extremely shallow blind recesses, no more than a delicately linear shadow of the previous scheme. The sole entrance, an unpretentious distyle Doric door, is placed at the slim west end, surmounted by a domed tempietto based on the Temple of Vesta at Tivoli, of which Dance had made numerous measured and reconstruction studies.[8]

Though previously there had been few comparably chaste church exteriors erected in the City,[9] it is inside that Dance's radical neoclassicism is fully manifest (pl. 603). Soane, who worked in his office between 1768 and 1771 and was profoundly influenced by the building, later described it as an 'example of refined taste' compared to the poverty of 'some of our modern churches'.[10] The single cell of almost early Christian simplicity, with its high-level windows attracting daylight from above the surrounding roofs, while muting traffic noises, has delicate, fluted Ionic engaged columns attached to the bare walls carrying a continuous, flat band that is intentionally ambiguous. Its position directly over the capital suggests the isolated architrave of a missing entablature, but its greater height and anthemion ornament hint at a frieze embellished by a decorated astragal (not part of the traditional classical frieze). Soane specifically associated this reductionism of the entablature with J.-L. de Cordemoy's idea that the frieze and cornice should be suppressed because they blocked light.[11] Laugier advocated that 'the frieze and cornice can only be used jointly and with the architrave', whereas 'only the architrave could . . . be used singly'.[12] Springing from projecting blocks above the columns, the thin, weightless surface of the barrel vault billows tent-like, its panels decorated with highly original, Greek-like low-relief plasterwork, its ribs reduced to flat bands framed by bead and reel. The coffering of the unannounced chancel derives from the apses of the Temple of Venus and Rome, which Palladio praised as having 'very carefully constructed and beautifully designed stucco compartments'.[13] Above a modest

606 George Dance Jr. South-west view, All Hallows, London Wall, London, 1765–7.

607 Interior view of 'Clare Hall Chapel', Cambridge, Cambridgeshire, in Rudolph Ackermann, *History of the University of Cambridge*, vol. 1, 1814, pl. 35. Coloured engraving. James Burrough and James Essex, 1763–9.

communion table hangs Nathaniel Dance's painting of *Ananias Restoring Sight to St Paul*, after Pietro da Cortona, presented by the artist (George's brother) and framed with 'such Ornaments in Plaister Work as he shall think fit'. The body is paved with Portland stone and black marble squares, 'all of an equal Size set in the Diamond Fashion'.[14] To provide the maximum unobstructed seating, the pulpit (without sounding board, since its auditory function is performed by the ceiling itself) is mounted in the middle of the north wall, with access through a door leading into the vestry (demolished 1890), a semicircular room projecting from the exterior wall over the foundation of an existing Roman bastion. The extent to which young Dance had turned his back on Palladianism is apparent when his interior is compared to contemporary Clare College chapel, Cambridge (pl. 607), the last work of the 72-year-old Sir James Burrough, externally still dependent on Gibbs's nearby Senate House (1721–30), internally covered by a barrel vault with small, repetitive, rosetted coffering.[15]

608 Giovanni Paolo Pannini, *Interior of the Pantheon, Rome*, *c.*1734. Oil on canvas. National Gallery of Art, Samuel H. Kress Collection, Washington D.C.

Returning from Italy to launch his career in London precisely one year before the younger Dance set out for that Mecca, Robert Adam also committed himself from the beginning wholeheartedly to neoclassicism.[16] Their transforming goals were largely the same. Robert described St Peter, Rome (pl. 513), as

> a very noble building and not admired without justice . . . the proportions are so well affixed to particular parts and to the whole that though a monstrous building it has a very opposite air, neither being heavy nor huge to appearance . . . like the face of a man or woman which has something pleasing, well-proportioned and sweet in it, in spite of some bad features, pock-pits and other little failings. It has some gross faults, many small ones. Fine on the whole though without the grandeur or nobility of the antique.[17]

His architect brother, James, in Italy between 1760 and 1763, reported on modern Italian architects

> struggling to produce effect by means of excess of breaks, for this reason they crowd pilasters on the top of pilasters and break their entablatures into trifling parts . . . so that the eye is quite fatigued with a long examination of minute parts that seem to be pieces put together by chance. This defect is . . . most palpable in the admired parts of St Peter's [front, which] tho' in reality of colossal grandeur, appears little and trifling to the instructed eye.[18]

The brothers' draughtsman, George Richardson, who was James's travelling companion, wrote from Rome in 1762 of the 'Splendor and glory of the Buildings of the Ancient Romans . . . which . . . convey the greatest Idea of their Grandeur', offering the advice that opened this chapter. In particular, the Pantheon (pl. 608)

> excited my greatest Curiosity . . . its grandeur and magnificence far surpass'd my Ideas & infinitely excell'd every other piece of Architecture that ever I had beheld. There is grandeur true proportion and harmony thro' the whole & there I gaz'd with wonder & admiration first at its lofty & Noble Elevation & then at the excellent Beauty & Magnificence of the inside . . . That Structure is most certainly one of the finest in the World & challenges the greatest Attention. Its ancient form still remains with little other Alterations than Rob'd of its numerous Monuments, amongst all the Ancient Temples, it is the best preserv'd & was one of the most considerable ones. Its superior Magnitude and great Solidity has certainly resisted the Injuries of time & defy'd the Violence of Barbarians . . . The Pantheon's stately Columns & Lofty Dome are still the Admiration of every one & have unparallel Majesty.[19]

Robert, too, observed that 'the greatness and simplicity of [its] parts fills the mind with extensive thoughts, stamps upon you the solemn, the grave and the majestic and seems to prevent all those ideas of gaiety or frolic which our modern buildings admit of and aspire'.[20] Its conversion for Christian liturgy (in the seventh century) made it additionally attractive as a church model.[21]

Sometime in the early 1760s Adam adapted Santa Maria Rotonda for the chapel of the proposed new Lock Hospital in Grosvenor Place, Westminster, which specialised in the female treatment of

> Syphilitic Maladies . . . supported by the voluntary contributions of gentlemen, who have had the humanity to consider, that pain and misery, however produced, entitle frail mortals to relief . . . in imitation of the munificence of the Almighty, who causes his sun to shine on the evil and the good, afford relief equally to the innocent and the guilty.[22]

The centrepiece of a stately complex of wings and pavilions (pl. 609) is reminiscent of Piranesi's imaginary reconstruction in *Il Campo Marzio dell'antica Roma* (1762; pl. 611), published to commemorate the Italian's election as Fellow of the Society of Antiquaries of London and dedicated to 'Roberto Adam Britann Architecto Celeberrim'.[23] His portico is an *in antis* version of the pre-Christian Pantheon (without the pair of clumsy bell-towers added in the seventeenth century) flanked by aedicule windows based on its internal tabernacles, just as the blind medallions in the portico echo internal marble veneers (pl. 608). Langley recommended it in *Ancient Masonry* (1736) as 'one of the most simple and grand Composition I ever saw', which he offered 'as an Example for Help to Invention'.[24] The ox-head and garland frieze encircling the rotunda comes from the Temple of Fortuna Virilis (Santa Maria Egiziaca) in Rome.[25] An 88-foot-diameter outer dome covers an inner one of 62 feet (pl. 610), entirely undecorated and rising directly from a powerful, uninterrupted entablature supported on a ring of giant Corinthian columns encircled by a galleried aisle. Adam omitted the Pantheon's plastered and panelled attic presumably in response to doubts expressed about its antiquity, which were part of a current controversy surrounding the restoration of the interior, at the same time taking on board Carlo Fontana's hypothesis that

609 Robert Adam. Design for the 'Elevation of Lock Hospital Chapel', London, detail, early 1760s. Pen and ink and wash. Sir John Soane's Museum, AD 38/16.

610 Robert Adam. Design for the 'Section of Lock Hospital Chapel', London, early 1760s. Pen and ink and wash. Sir John Soane's Museum, AD 38/16.

611 Giovanni Battista Piranesi. 'Elevazione del Pantheon, e degli altri edifizi che gli eran vicini', in *Il Campo Marzio dell' Antica Rome*, 1762. Engraving.

originally the 'place of these pilasters was supplied by . . . Caryatids . . . which the antiquarians have sought for in vain [so] it is impossible to conceive where these [figures] could be placed'.[26] Adam placed a figural pair against the upper section of the columns flanking the entrance into the rotunda. The only source of daylight is provided from the glazed oculus of the dome, a practice sanctioned by no less an authority than Sebastiano Serlio, who recommended that 'any one who wants more light [in churches] could make an opening in the apex of the vault, covered by sheets of glass in a pyramid shape so that snow and ice would not gather there'.[27] An alternative scheme for the Lock Hospital, however, has neither oculus nor side windows, relying entirely on artificial lighting, the resulting gloom perhaps intended to disguise the terrible ravages wrought by venereal disease on the unfortunate inmates.

In Adam's first built church, for Sir William Harbord of Gunton Hall, Norfolk (pl. 612), which survives largely intact, the Tuscan order of the tetrastyle portico was adapted from the Corinthian apteral temple of Augustus and Rome at Pola, Istria (AD 2–14), which the architect visited in 1757 on his journey to Spalato (Split). Adam encircled his otherwise astylar block with an entablature to reinforce the temple form.[28] To this he intended adding, as suggested in a preparatory drawing, the distinctive fluted frieze found on the ruin known as the Incantada at Thessaloniki, recorded by Stuart and Revett in 1754 (pl. 614), which Adam embellished with a rosette above each column.[29]

Adam took this composition a further, more accomplished and beautiful stage in an unrealised design for Wonersh, Surrey (pl. 613), perhaps dating as early as 1767, when he was involved at nearby Wonersh House for Sir Fletcher Norton Bt.[30] Here the Incantada frieze of the tetrastyle portico is repeated intermittently along the remaining elevations, perhaps broken by undecorated sections; on the portico and slightly projecting pedimented centrepieces of the sides and rear are raised panels with Doric guttae, a reminder of the absent Doric order on astylar walls, along which float niches and oculi, and both tabernacle and tripartite Diocletian windows linked by narrow guilloche bands. Here, a bold, new Adamitic church architecture has arisen.

Of about the same time must date an unidentified design, represented solely by a front elevation of a church (pl. 615), composed of a prostyle, unpedimented Doric porch raised on a perron, surmounted by a multi-tiered steeple, the second stage of which repeats the Incantada motif in a diminutive tetrastyle Ionic temple, and crowned by a domed tempietto.[31] The origin of this unusual structure seems to be a watch-tower engraved in Leoni's English edition of Alberti's *De Re Aedificatoria* (1485), published in 1726 and again in 1739 and 1755 (pl. 616).[32]

William Chambers was also active as a church designer in the 1760s, having encountered Continental classicism by a more circuitous route via Paris (1749–50) and Italy (1750–55), Robert Adam reporting from Rome that his future rival had already gained a reputation as 'a prodigy for Genius, for Sense & good taste'.[33]

The austere exterior of his German Lutheran Church in The Savoy, Westminster (1766–8), erected by permission of George III (pl. 617) to Chambers's design, gave no hint of the inside, where a St Martin-in-the-Fields system of dosseret columns was enriched by an elegant decorative vocabulary learnt as J. F. Blondel's pupil at the Ecole des Beaux-Arts in Paris. This is explicit particularly in the carver's bills: 'Ionic Capitals . . . after the Antique', 'Alter piece . . . with . . . Laurel Swags . . . Tyed with Knotts of Ribband', 'Laurel Branches with Leaves and berries', and those of the plasterers: 'Ornaments in Center of Chapel . . . branches of Olive Leaves . . . round Medalln Palm Branches Scroles . . . drapery round Head under alter Window . . . Scrowl'd Ornaments in Soffits wh Branches of Hyacinct . . . Laurel Leaves & Berries to Swelling Eliptical Soffit'.[34] This up-to-date Gallic vocabulary immediately filtered down to provincial architects like Timothy Lightoler of Warwick, who, in the Octagon Chapel, Bath (1766–7; pl. 618), with its slender, unfluted

612 Robert Adam. Design for the 'Side View of Gunton Chapel', (St Andrew), Gunton, Norfolk, 1766. Pen and ink. Sir John Soane's Museum, AD 43/12.

613 Robert Adam. South elevation 'Design for Wonersh Church', St John Baptist, Surrey, *c.*1767. Pen and ink and wash. Sir John Soane's Museum, AD 30/109.

Ionic columns and leaf-festooned oval windows, catered to an upper-class congregation. A Salopian lady attending in 1794 sat in one of the railed semicircles 'round a nice parlour looking fire . . . carpeted all over . . . too unlike a church to be comfortable'.[35]

By 1770, therefore, the principal neoclassical treatments that were to redefine British church architecture were firmly in place: peripteral, pseudoperipteral and apteral temple forms, domed rotunda and other central planning, monumental prostyle and *in antis* porticoes,

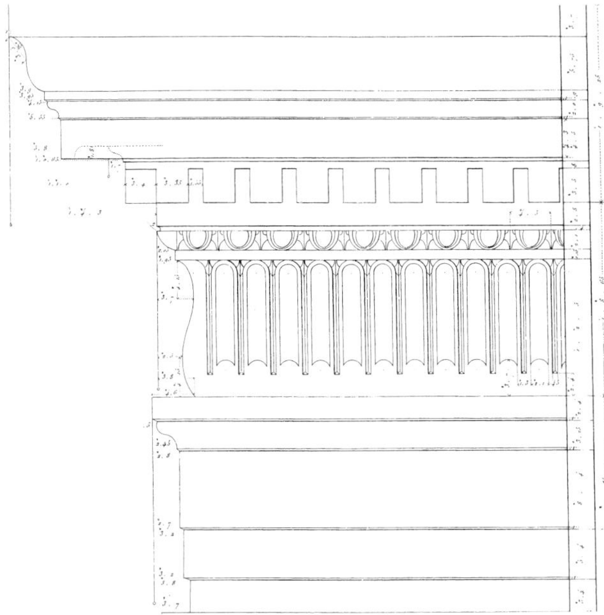

614 (*above*) The Incantada, Thessalonica (Salonica), third century AD, in Stuart and Revett 1795 (1825 edition), vol. III, chapter XI, pls XLVI–XLVII, detail. Engraving.

616 Bernard Picart. Design for a watchtower, in Leoni 1755, vol. VIII, Chapter V, pl. 48. Engraving. L. B. Alberti, architect, 1485.

avant-garde internal architectural and decorative patterns, sedate ornament and, above all, the sense of an Enlightenment society at peace in a built environment recreating ancient Rome. How were these treatments developed over the next three decades?

In 1774 Chambers advised his former pupil Edward Stevens, then in Rome (where he died the following year):

615 (*left*) Robert Adam. West front design for an unidentified church, undated. Pen and ink and wash. Sir John Soane's Museum, AD 21/47.

617 Sir William Chambers. Design for a 'Section from East to West', German Lutheran Church, London, 1766. Pen and ink and wash. City of Westminster Archives Centre, 90/7. Erected 1766–8, demolished 1875.

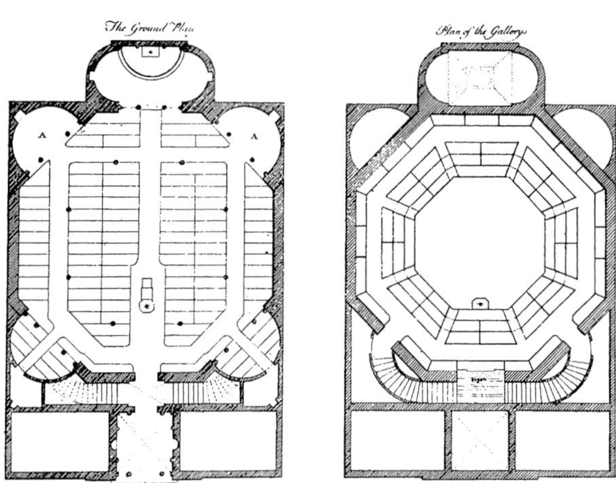

618 William Lindley after Timothy Lightoler. 'The Plans and Section of the New Octagon Chappel at Bath', Somerset, 1786. Engraving. T. Lightoler architect, 1766–7, demolished.

> Do not . . . begin to study where you ought to leave off, and instead of formg a taste upon those noble remains, whence the great Masters of the fifteenth & Sixteenth Centurys collected their knowledge; trifle away time, in Collecting poor Ornaments, & extravagant forms, from the vestiges of Barbarous Ages. our taste here has already been sufficiently Vitiated by this unlucky mistake.[36]

This accorded with intellectual perceptions of Continental architectural trends, epitomised in the travel notebook of John Mitford MP, who toured France and Italy during 1776–7. He found contemporary French buildings 'less charged with ornament than that of many of their predecessors. Profusion still accompanies their embellishments but it is a more modest profusion, & less ostentatious', exemplified by Sainte Geneviève, Paris (pl. 596), which he regarded as 'very magnificent, solid . . . highly ornamented, but ornamented with judgment' compared to Saint Sulpice (pl. 720), 'disfigured by the quantity of unecessary stone' and an 'elegant portico [which] entirely loses its dignity from the weight of two unmeaning towers. The hand of taste is preparing to overthrow these disgusting heaps of stone'. Piedmontese buildings, Chambers's 'vestiges of Barbarous Ages', that is, Bernini's and Borromini's art, 'suffered sometimes to run wild in the decorations . . . with the strangest turned columns that the extravagance of fancy ever exposed', referring to Juvarra's Superga, Turin. St Peter, Rome (pl. 513), always a contentious building, suffered from having the plan of a 'small church, & that the architects have only made a Brobdignag of a Lilliputian without giving additional dignity by the increase of size . . . In general the design is too simple, & the ornaments too complicated', while the 'poverty of the entrance appears a glaring defect. The naked unmeaning space between affords no pleasure', the 'ridiculous columns' of Bernini's Baldacchino 'have the appearance of four fat dropsically women'.[37]

The 1770s opened auspiciously with Chambers's proposal for replacing the plain, brown brick parish church

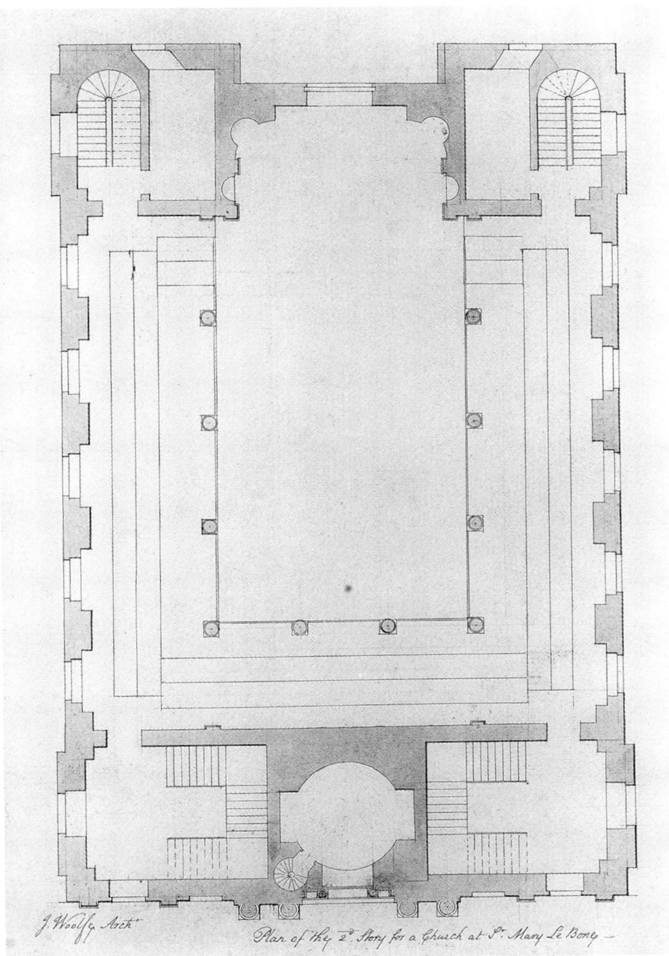

619 John Woolfe. Design for a 'Plan of the 2d. Story for a Church at St. Mary Le Bone', London, 1770, unrealised. Pen and ink and wash. London Metropolitan Archives (Guildhall Library, M/MAR/10a).

of St Marylebone (1741–2) with an ambitious circular, domed building of decisively fashionable French taste, though not without some struggle. A call for designs in 1770 produced schemes from, among others, John Woolfe, best remembered as joint author with his architectural partner, James Gandon, of the fourth and fifth volumes of *Vitruvius Britannicus* (1767, 1771), who designed little, and what looks from the surviving plans (pl. 619) to be a conventional, galleried rectangle with a two-storey west front, the lower astylar with recesses and niches, the upper with pilasters and an engaged tetrastyle temple centrepiece framing a Serliana with solid side lights.[38] It is far removed from Chambers's grand offering.

Appointed surveyor on 2 July 1770 and taking full advantage of a site in the centre of the newly laid-out Manchester Square, during the following years he prepared 'a Bushell of Sketches [and] no less than 6 different Designs all . . . large & complicated consequently very Difficult to contrive & tedious to execute'.[39] The most accomplished is a centrally planned domed rotunda (pl. 620), which, despite his initial misgivings – 'the Solidity of the Work requires so many Precautions which effect the Conveniency of the Building' – after modifications 'managed it so as to have very little Solid to occupy Space within . . . so that it will be equally convenient'. It received approval in 1771.[40] The press claimed that it was 'a rotunda . . . from a curious design in Italy'.[41] This may be misleading. Chambers had, it is true, advised his young, ill-fated pupil Edward Stevens, in Rome in 1774, to 'endeavour to unite the grand manner' of Michelangelo and Vignola, with the 'elegance, Simplicity, and purity' of Peruzzi and Palladio; Bernini's 'Compositions are not in the Severe Sublime Style of Antiquity, but they are always Ingenious, graceful, & full of Effect'; Palladio and Scamozzi 'require your particular attention: Study them carefully, and correct that bold, luxuriant, and perhaps licentious style, which you will have Acquired at Rome, Florence, Genoa, and Bologna, by their Simple, chase, but rather tame manner'; avoid Naples, Vanvitelli, Fuga and

620 Sir William Chambers. Design for the entrance front, St Mary, St Marylebone, London, 1770–74. Pen and ink and coloured wash. Victoria and Albert Museum, 2206.

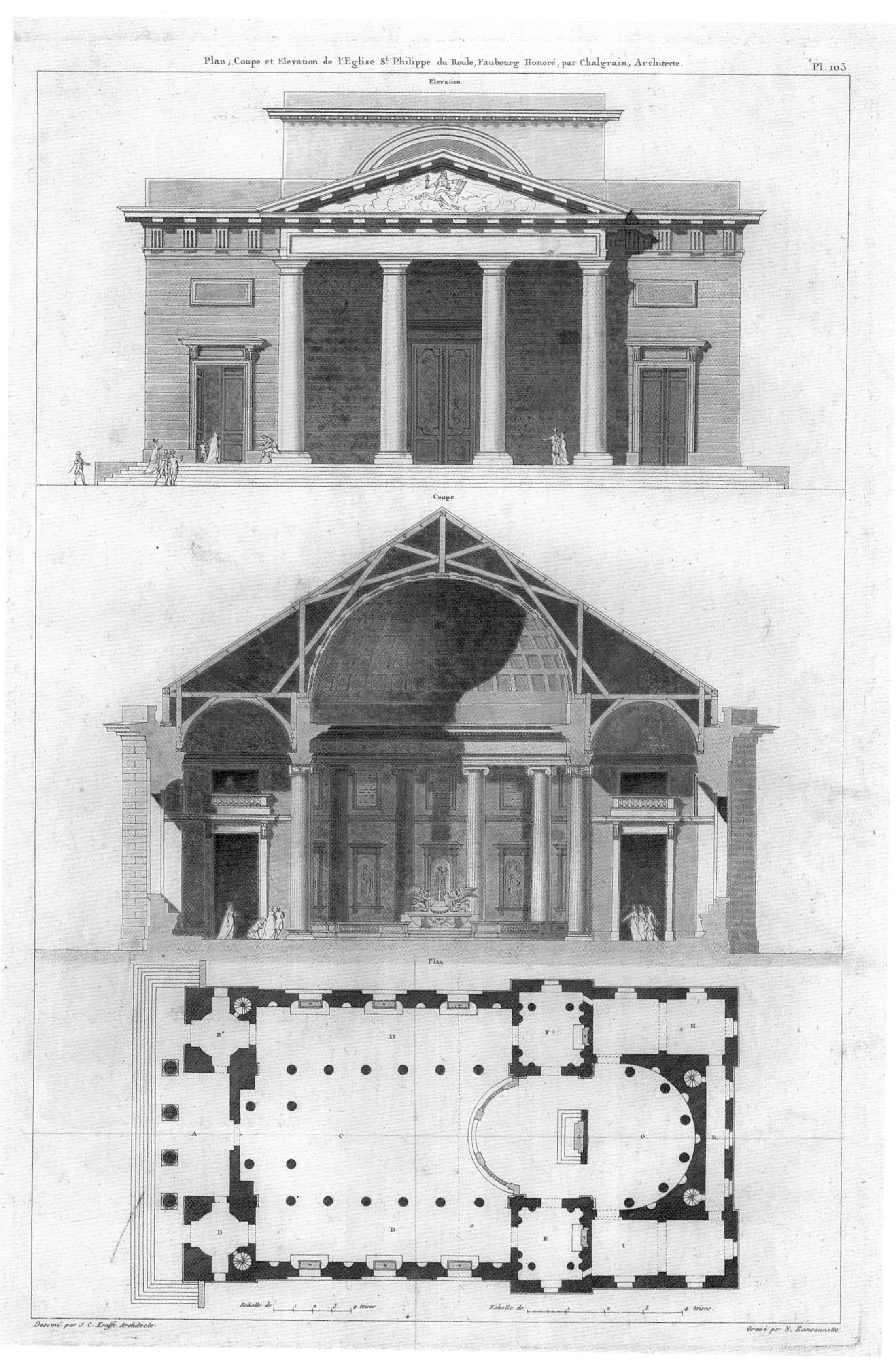

621 N. Ransonnette after J. C. Krafft. 'Plan, Coupe et Elevation de l'Eglise St. Philippe du Roule', Paris, France. Hand-coloured engraving. Author's collection. Jean-François-Thérèse Chalgrin architect, 1764–84.

622 Thomas Ivory. 'Section of the South Side of the Chapel of the New Blue Coat Hospital', Dublin, Ireland, 1776. Pen and ink and coloured wash. © The British Library Board, 71365. Erected 1772–83.

> other Blockheads of less fame . . . as you must Boromini, with all the later Architects; excepting Salvi, who without any general principles, sometimes fortunately stumbled upon the right, as appears by part of his Domenican Church at Viterbo . . . forget not Piranesi . . . he is full of Matter; extravagant 'tis true, often absurd, but from his overflowings you may gather information.[42]

The surviving designs, however, are firmly anchored in current Ecole des Beaux-Arts practices. The powerful Doric *in antis* portico, with the entablature wrapping round the flanking staircase blocks, owes much to J.-F.-T. Chalgrin's Saint Philippe-du-Roule (pl. 621).[43] It reveals how far Chambers had moved away from the stance expressed in *English Architecture* (1758), condemning the use of Tuscan (a simplified Doric) as the 'coarsest' of the orders.[44] His dome resting on an uninterrupted colonnaded drum, employing Laugier's favourite paired columns, may represent a response to the dispute that had erupted in 1769 concerning the stability of the proposed crossing dome of Sainte Geneviève, prompting Soufflot's rethink of his original more baroque solution of 1757 (pl. 596) in favour of the erected neoclassical structure.[45] It was hoped that Chambers's 'desireable work . . . and noble object . . . will . . . appear . . . with a magnificence proper for the religious worship of an opulent people' – the scheme, which was to seat 1,500 and cost £15,000, was promoted by the local nobility – but his disappointment in its abandonment in 1774 found expression when he could not 'wth: Decency accept [the] trifling' design fee of £120.[46]

Chambers's other major ecclesiastical endeavour of the decade, the chapel at Trinity College, Dublin (1775–93), echoes Nicola Salvi's use of internal paired pilasters.[47] This, in turn, is reflected in Thomas Ivory's nearby Blue Coat School chapel (1776; pl. 622), where earlier one of the governors had been 'intriguing busily to have an application made to my favorite . . . Sr Wm. Chambers' for a design.[48]

The modernity of Chambers's idiom is blatantly obvious compared, for example, to the contemporary but provincially awkward St Mary, Birmingham (1771–4; pl. 623), which the biased local press nevertheless inflated as

> admirably well adapted for Hearing [and] executed in a masterly Manner, Witness that surprizing Roof which is the Wonder of the Age, and covers an

623 Henry Burn. View of St Mary, Birmingham, Warwickshire, detail, *c.*1842. Engraving. English Heritage (National Monuments Record, BB86/7409). Joseph Pickford architect, 1771–4, demolished 1925.

> Octagonal Building of upwards of eighty Feet Diameter, without one Pillar to support it, and every other Part so expeditiously and well performed, as rebounds greatly to the Honour of that celebrated and ingenious Architect, Mr Joseph Pickford, whose Merit is inexpressible.[49]

Nor was Thomas Atkinson's Shrewsbury Hospital chapel, Sheffield (1775; pl. 624), built for the 9th Duke of Norfolk, with its deep-set arched recesses robustly articulated by over-sized voussoirs and apron-like panels, in the forefront of mainstream fashion. Though constructed of 'rather beautiful stone', John Wesley, something of an octagon pundit, thought that 'one may safely say there is none like it in [Yorkshire]; nor, I suppose, in the world'.[50]

In 1771 Robert Adam proposed a grandiose, multi-pavilion scheme for redeveloping the site to the east of Lincoln's Inn Fields for the Society of Lincoln's Inn (pl. 625), which entailed replacing a haphazard group of medieval and Stuart buildings, preserving only the mixed-style chapel with its undercroft, presumably on grounds that it was widely believed to be Inigo Jones's work (pl. 264). This he camouflaged in a Maison Carrée-inspired envelope (pl. 412) raised on a rusticated basement, screened on the west, towards the Fields, by a prostyle temple portico leading into a circular lobby and staircase, and on the east end, towards Chancery Lane, by a large, fan-crowned Serliana set in a dummy wall standing just proud of the old gothic aperture.[51]

The celebrated Roman temple had attracted renewed interest during the 1760s and 1770s. Tobias Smollett published an evocative description a few years after visiting Nîmes in 1763: it 'enchants you with the most exquisite beauties of architecture and sculpture . . . The proportions . . . are so happily united, as to give it an air of majesty and grandeur, which the most indifferent spectator cannot behold without emotion . . . Without all doubt it is ravishingly beautiful. The world cannot parallel it.'[52] Charles-Louis Clérisseau, a French architect with whom Adam had visited Dalmatia in 1757 and collaborated in the production of *Ruins of the Palace of the Emperor Diocletian at Spalatro* (1764), made plans, elevations, sections and views in 1768–9 (later published in *Antiquities de la France: premier partie, monumens des Nismes*, 1778). Pertinently, in 1771, the year of the Lincoln's Inn commission, Clérisseau appeared in London, and a sculptor named Dubourg exhibited a 'model of the temple of Fortuna Virilis; a ruin' (its Roman cousin) at the Society of Artists.[53]

Five years later the rectangular temple form reappeared in another unrealised metropolitan church inte-

624 Edward Blore. View of Shrewsbury Hospital Chapel, Sheffield, Yorkshire, in Hunter 1819, p. 179. Thomas Atkinson architect, 1775, demolished 1825.

625 Robert Adam. 'Perspective View of the Front towards Chancery Lane', Society of Lincoln's Inn Chapel, London, 1771. Pen and ink and wash. Sir John Soane's Museum, AD 28/14.

grated in the residential terrace of Durham Yard within the Adam brothers' ill-fated Adelphi development on ground lying between the Strand and the Thames.[54] The entrance front (pls 626–7), an *in antis* variation of the Lock Hospital chapel (pl. 609), is almost overwhelmed by elaborate, diminutive, antique-style decorations of the sort found in abundance in the 247 plates of Piranesi's *Le Antichità Romane* (1756), praised by Adam as 'the greatest fund for inspiring and instilling invention in any lover of architecture that can be imagined'.[55] From that source and from *Il Campo Marzio dell'antica Roma* (1762), dedicated to Adam, comes the Portico of Octavia motif of a panel-overlaid architrave and frieze, used by Adam for a dedication inscription to the 'DIVINO ARCHITECTO', which also appears at Lincoln's Inn (pl. 625). The Aesculapius-inspired fluted and foliated Corinthian capital derives from Adam's own *Spalatro*.[56] In the light of Chambers's cautious remarks about Piranesi, quoted above, it is Adam's decorative proliferation that is one of the salient differences between the two rivals.

Durham Yard is further distinctive for its partially glazed barrel-vaulted ceiling, since fenestration along the side walls was prohibited by adjacent buildings. This exploitation of an essentially domestic device of top lighting, a selection of which appears in *The Works in Architecture of Robert and James Adam* (1773), was explicitly expressed in his next ecclesiastical work, located on the Essex estate of Richard Rigby at Mistley. A French aristocratic visitor recognised intimate associations between the 'new church built from the designs of Mr [Robert] Adam, an excellent architect', the mansion (also by Adam, since demolished), the nearby village and their shared pastoral setting, describing the ensemble as 'a very small place, fifty houses at most, which are so well built and so spruce that you see at a glance that . . . the whole town and a superb house and fine park . . . all belong to the same owner'; the windows on the mansion's main front 'frame a delightful view: the estuary formed by the [Stour] river-mouth . . . bordered on both banks by well-cultivated fields and embellished with houses, farms', while he 'never saw anything more elegant' than the church, which 'serves as an eye-catcher from the house'.[57]

In a preliminary design (pl. 628), internal ranges of Ionic pilasters rising from dado rails, and side apses screened by pairs of columns, recall the famous library room at Kenwood House, London (1767), while the centre of the body is covered by a richly decorated and top-lit saucer dome, and daylight also filters down from oculi in the subsidiary spaces of the lobby and chancel.[58] These theatrical features, as well as the decorative plasterwork, were omitted in execution, creating an interior that 'is all one conception, with

626 Robert Adam. Entrance front 'Design of a Church for Durham Yard', The Adelphi, London, 1776. Pen and ink and wash. Sir John Soane's Museum, AD 44/95.

no ornament' and an exterior designed 'with simplicity and delicacy'.[59]

Adam was, as we have seen at Lincoln's Inn (pl. 625), a master of disguise. With great ingenuity he transformed an existing body at Mistley (1729–35; architect unknown), described as 'an absolute antique temple, with a portico' (pls 629–30).[60] He removed the middle bays of the long elevations and inserted projecting, internally columnar screened apsidal transepts, added shallow temple porticoes raised on low platforms, perroned on the south towards the mansion and false towards the estuary (serving the same purpose as the Nuneham veranda). Viewed in profile, the refreshed fabric looked like an amphiprostyle temple bisecting the centre of the body. Furthermore, at both ends he added twin, tempietto-topped accents (the sole features to survive the demolition of 1852).[61] These were buttressed by pairs of free-standing columns supporting sections of projecting entablature, which have two obvious antique Roman sources: the Forum of Nerva and the tepidarium of the Baths of Diocletian, which had been converted by Michelangelo into Santa Maria degli Angeli in 1561, then further remodelled in 1749 to become one of Adam's essential architectural quarries.[62] In 1755 he reported 'making an exact plan' of the church, which had been 'fitted up by [Luigi] Vanvitelli . . . I think it may be greatly helped and will make a noble design so that sooner or later I will make a new design for it with all the alterations in the antique style'.[63] The idea of employing seried, free-standing columns placed close to perimeter walls as structural buttresses also recalls Riou's exercise of 1767 (pls 599 and 600).

Never before had the temple form been manipulated in such a complex, interlocking and dramatic fashion, firmly setting Adam apart from other leading innovators of the decade. This is only too obvious when compared to John Tasker's contemporary Catholic chapel at Lulworth Castle, Dorset (pl. 631), for Thomas Weld, the richest recusant in England. A remodelling of a domes-

627 Robert Adam. Design for 'Section of a Church for Durham yard', The Adelphi, London, 1776. Pen and ink and wash. Sir John Soane's Museum, AD 44/76.

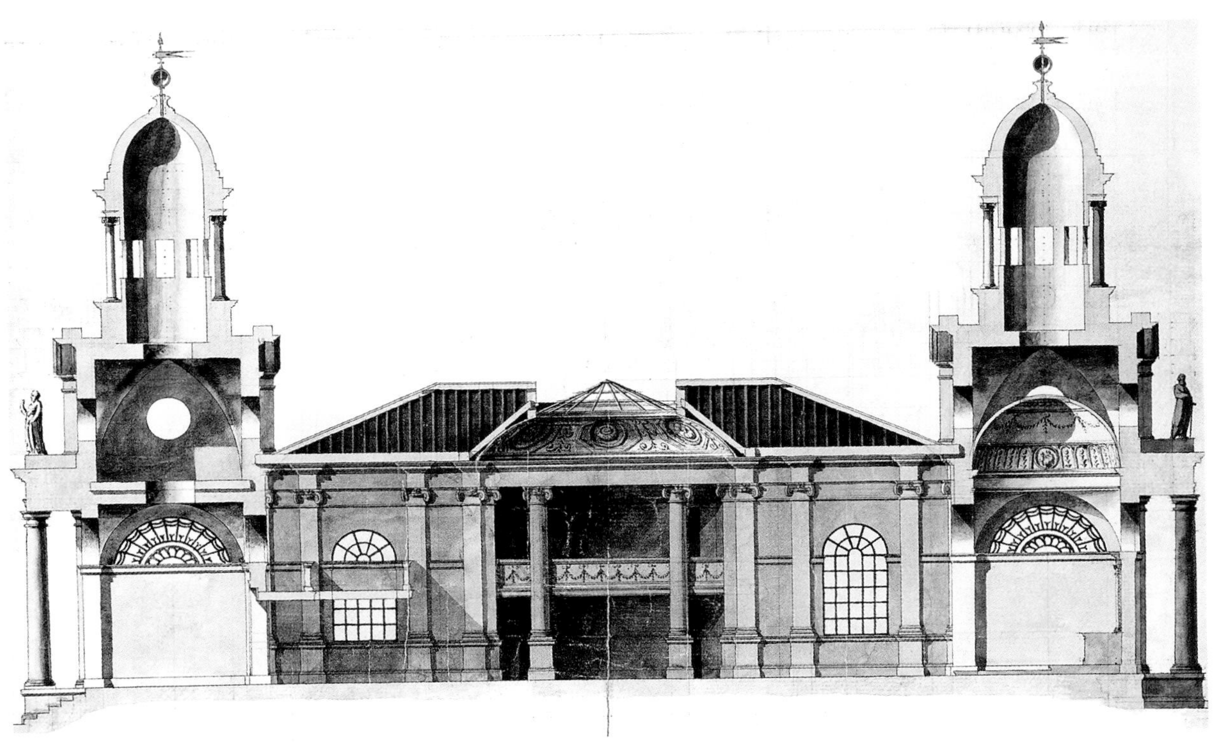

628 Robert Adam. Design for 'Section through Mistley Church', St Mary, Mistley, Essex, 1776. Pen and ink and wash. Sir John Soane's Museum, AD 41/68.

629 Thomas Vivares after Robert Adam. 'South-West View of the Parish Church of Mistley in Essex', 1776, in Adam 1779, vol. II, pl. 75. Engraving. R. Adam architect, 1776–7, demolished 1852 except towers.

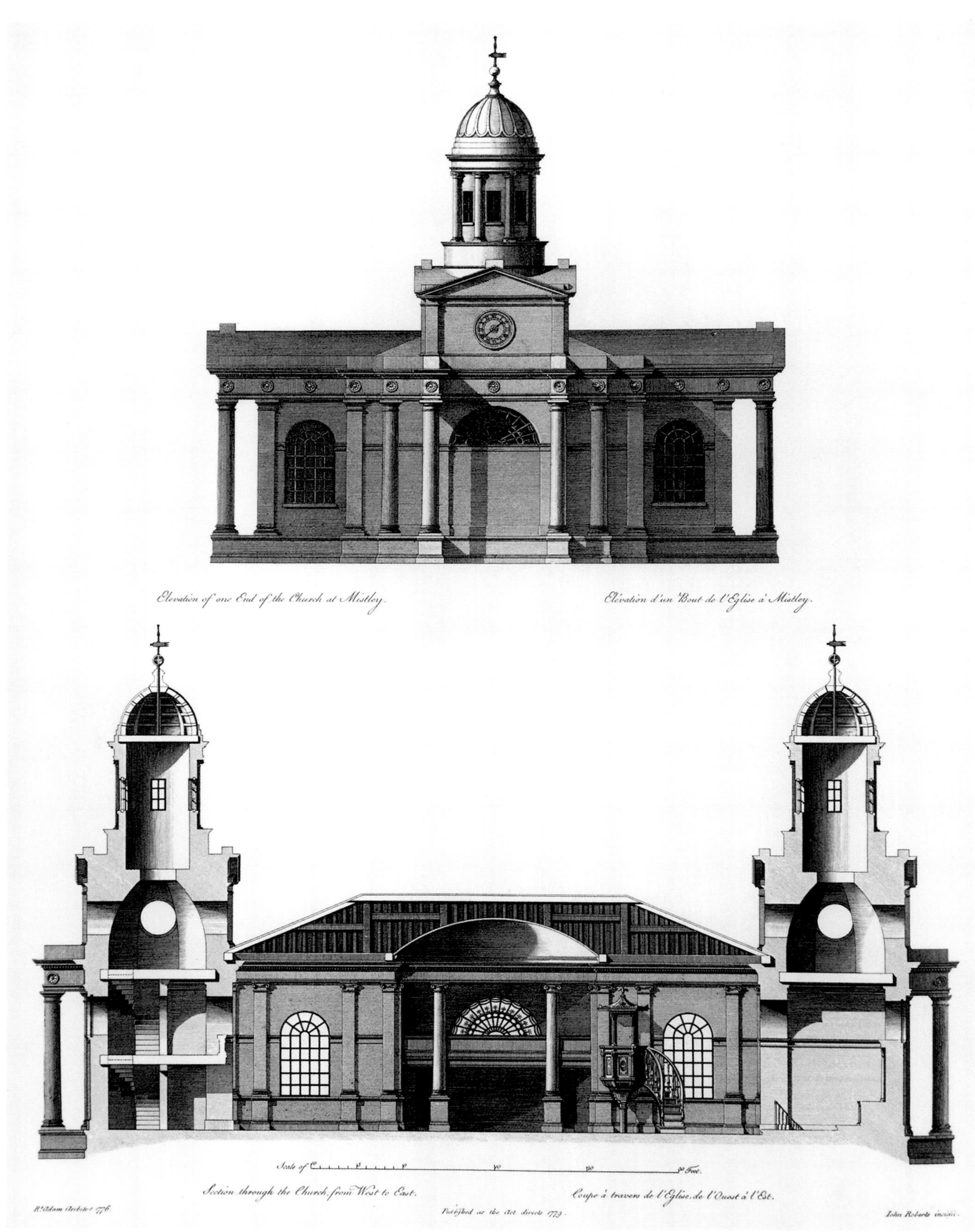

630 John Roberts after Robert Adam. 'Elevation of one End of the Church at Mistley' and 'Section through the Church from West to East', 1776, in Adam 1779, vol. II, pl. 74. Engraving. R. Adam architect, 1776–7, demolished 1852 except towers.

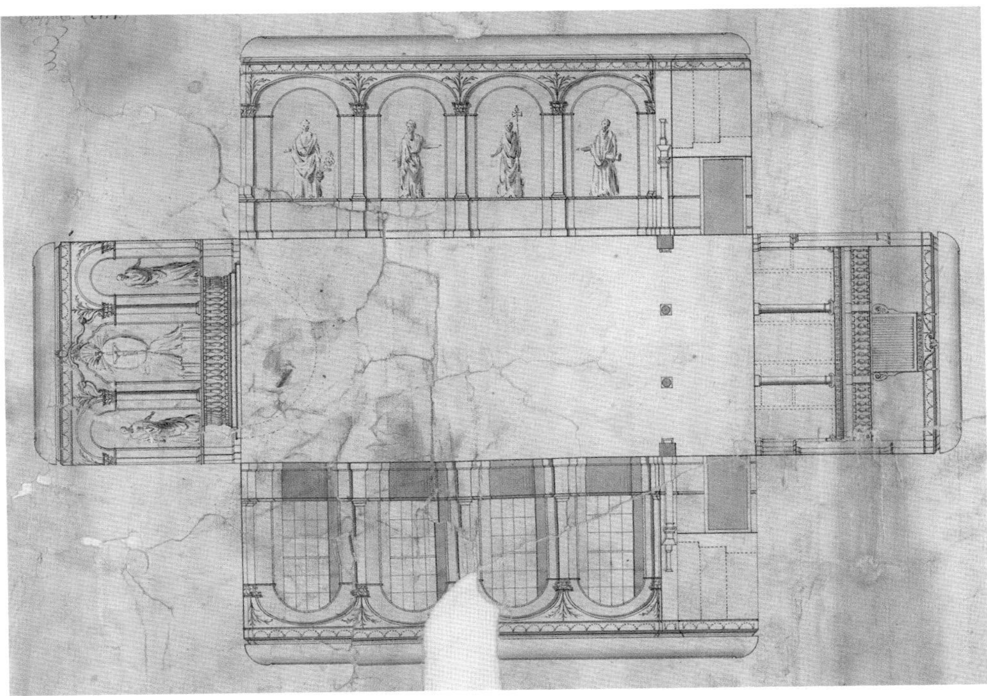

631 John Tasker. Plan and internal elevations design, Lulworth Castle chapel (Catholic), Dorset, 1776. Pen and ink and coloured wash. Dorset Record Office, Lulworth D/WCL/P54. Erected 1776–82, remodelled as dining room 1785.

tic room of 1743–6 by the Bastards of Blandford, it preserved the arrangement but divided the walls into Corinthian blind arcades embellished with palm branches, and the high altar with a 'Rich frame with gothick head'. The walls were painted 'Dead white', the rails blue, and the space was well lit by four large double brass chandeliers and numerous sconces. The overwhelming effect was of gilding, sometimes using 'Burnished Gold', of nearly every decorative element: the frieze with swags of flowers tied by knotted ribbons and paterae, the dentil cornice, fluted imposts, elliptical fluted mouldings, palms, capitals, ceiling flowers, pulpit, 'Two Carved frames & open brass Work cutt in Leaves', 'I.H.S. & Glory', 'Four Fancy scrole Iron pannels . . . to . . . Altar Rails', 'Four Iron Diamond pannells between' and a 'Figure of King David', the traditional paraphernalia of English Catholic places of worship.[64]

The Piranesian opulence hinted at but abandoned at Mistley was fulfilled at Wardour Castle chapel for Henry Bellings, 8th Earl of Arundell, with assistance from the English Jesuit father John Thorpe, whom we met in chapter 2. The two had toured Italy together between 1758 and 1760, and their voluminous correspondence constitutes a remarkable document of cosmopolitan Anglo-Catholic Italianate taste, of which Wardour, housing some of the most magnificent furnishings to have reached England and still surviving *in situ*, is unequivocally the masterpiece.[65] Thorpe forewarned his protégé that if he aimed to 'satisfy every one, the chapel will be no better than a pretty house for a Harlequin', and wisely recommended avoiding 'gaudiness and trumpery' if he wished 'to have the most elegant Chapel in England'.[66]

Arundell had commissioned James Paine, to whose first volume of *Plans, Elevations and Sections, of Noblemen and Gentlemen's Houses* (1767) he had subscribed, to design a grand neoclassical mansion at Wardour, in which the chapel terminating the western pavilion started out as a rectangle with apsidal ends, that at the east containing the family tribune raised on Ionic columns (pl. 632). In 1774, with the chapel's final form still fluid, Thorpe turned for advice to a Venetian-born architect, 'full of genius & fire [who] made his studies under Palladio, & the best models of antiquity . . . His name is [Giacomo] Quarenghi, but is better known [as] *Palladio's* Shade, upon account of his passion for that great man.'[67] He had been a prizewinner in the Corso Clementino of 1771 of the Accademia di San Luca in Rome for his scheme for a 'Chiesa cattedrale per una grande città' in the form of a Greek cross with apsidal

632 (*top*) James Paine. Interior towards the west gallery, Wardour Castle chapel (Catholic), Wiltshire, 1767–89. © *Country Life*, 688534.

633 (*above*) James Paine and John Soane. Interior towards the chancel, Wardour Castle chapel (Catholic), Wiltshire, 1767–90. © *Country Life*, 688378.

ends.[68] This was not pursued, but Quarenghi received the commission for the high altar, which was completed in 1776, as described earlier (p. 35). Thorpe advised:

> When the ornaments are executed, pleased to have all the proper parts strongly determined, that they may preserve a fine Chiaro Obscuro. You have several excellent workmen in Stucco; & no small part of the beauty of the Chapel will depend upon the . . . perfection of what they . . . do in it. If the Pillars &c of the Tribune be finished in wood & stucco, the same ornaments are to be carefully executed.[69]

He explained that 'Roman Altars . . . are isolated, having a passage quite round them, & in no wise joined to the building'.[70] The articulation of the apsidal wall is similar to Quarenghi's drawing of almost Piranesian opulence (pl. 634).[71]

634 Giacomo Quarenghi. 'A transverse Section of the Sanctuary' design, Wardour Castle chapel (Catholic), Wiltshire, detail, 1775. Pen and ink and wash. Wiltshire and Swindon Archives (Courtauld Institute of Art, 706/31(5)).

With Paine's retirement in 1788, aged 71, and his death in the following year, the completion of the east end was entrusted to John Soane, who had spent the years 1778–80 in Italy and now took full advantage of

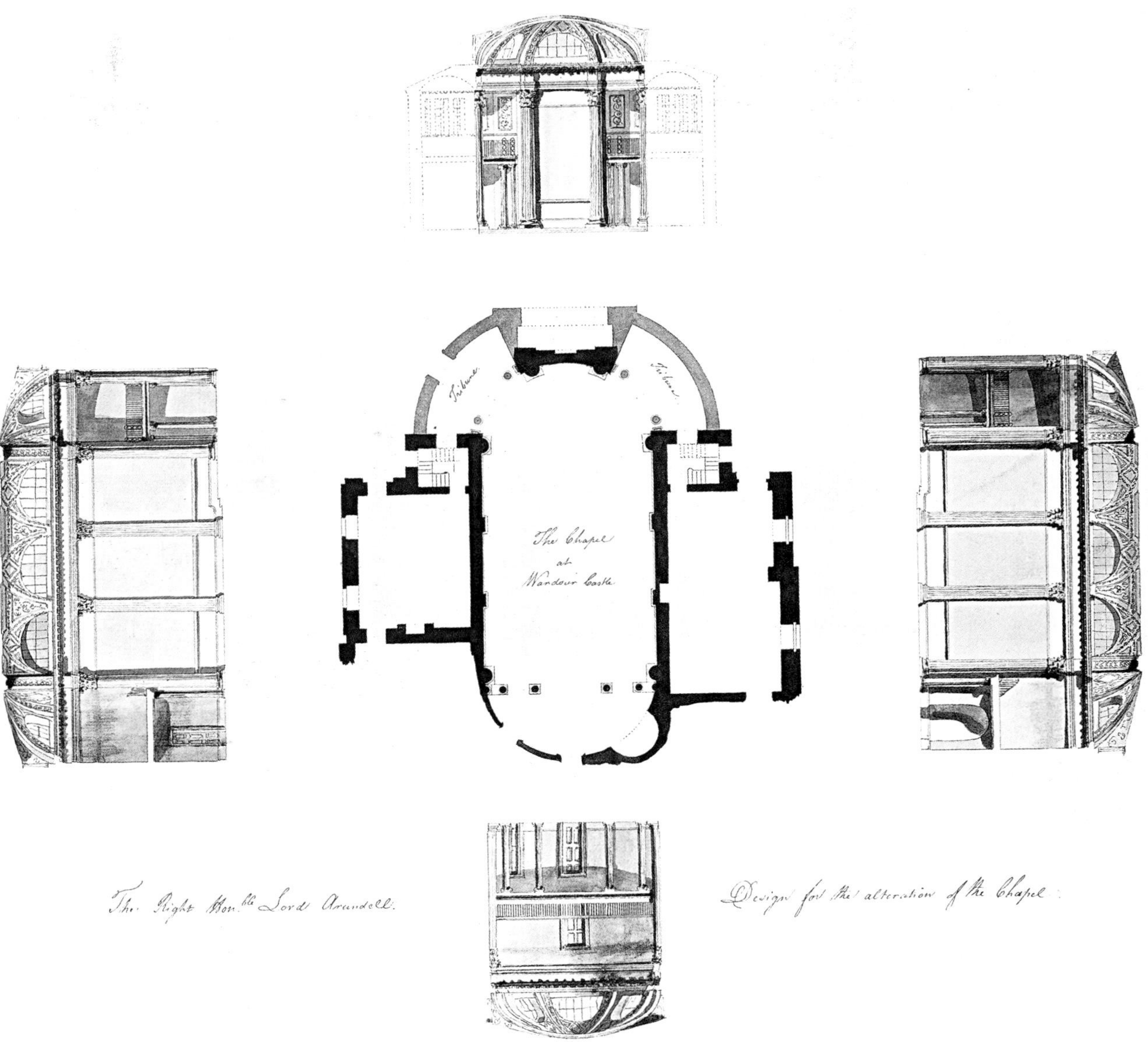

635 John Soane. 'Design for the Alteration of the Chapel', Wardour Castle, Wiltshire, 26 April 1788. Pen and ink and wash. Sir John Soane's Museum, 47/2/53.

Thorpe's recommendations by preserving the lines of Paine's chancel but regrouping the engaged columns and opening out the flanks to create segmental-ended tribunes raised on paired columns facing each other across the altar space, now transformed by a saucer dome and lit by arched windows in the attic, the one over the altar painting illuminated by Francis Eginton's painted glass of the *Holy Trinity* with glory and cherubs (1802). In a preliminary design (pl. 635), he experimented with flanking tribunes placed diagonally to the island altar, perhaps inspired by the 'very ruined temple outside Rome' where the side chapels 'converge towards the centre', as illustrated in Serlio's *Tutte l'opere d'architettura et prospetiva* (1540),[72] an arrangement already used with striking effect by Nicholas Revett (pls 645–6). It is to him and his confrère, William Newton, that we now should turn.

Trained under two conservative Anglo-Palladians, William Jones and Matthew Brettingham, by 1765 young Newton was experimenting with St Paul's Cathedral-like structures updated by French neoclassical planning.[73] The following year he was in Rome, though little is known about this sojourn, and in 1771 he published the first English translation of Vitruvius.[74]

636 William Newton. 'Elevation of the West Front of the Design for Battersea Church' (St Mary), London, 1774. Pen and ink and wash. RIBA Library Drawings Collection, K9/10(7).

None of this, however, fully explains his choice of a remarkably avant-garde classicism for new churches at Battersea and London Wall, both dated to 1774–5.

The construction of a bridge across the Thames at Battersea in 1771–2, opening up south-west London to rapid development, encouraged St Mary's Vestry to rebuild their medieval parish church. Newton's offering was described as 'approv'd by the most eminent Surveyor in England, & is different from any yet executed'.[75] The novelties displayed in his presentation drawing (pl. 636) set in a riverside arcadia are intoxicating. The west front is a distyle *in antis* portico raised on a perron flanked by solid walls with tripod-enhanced niches. The uncanonical order – Ionic with an acanthus band and short section of fluting above the astragal – derives from James Gandon's Nottingham County Hall (1769–72), published in *Vitruvius Britannicus* (1771).[76] Viewed from the front, only the relief with Christ in a mandorla and the Latin dedication signify the building's Christian function. From

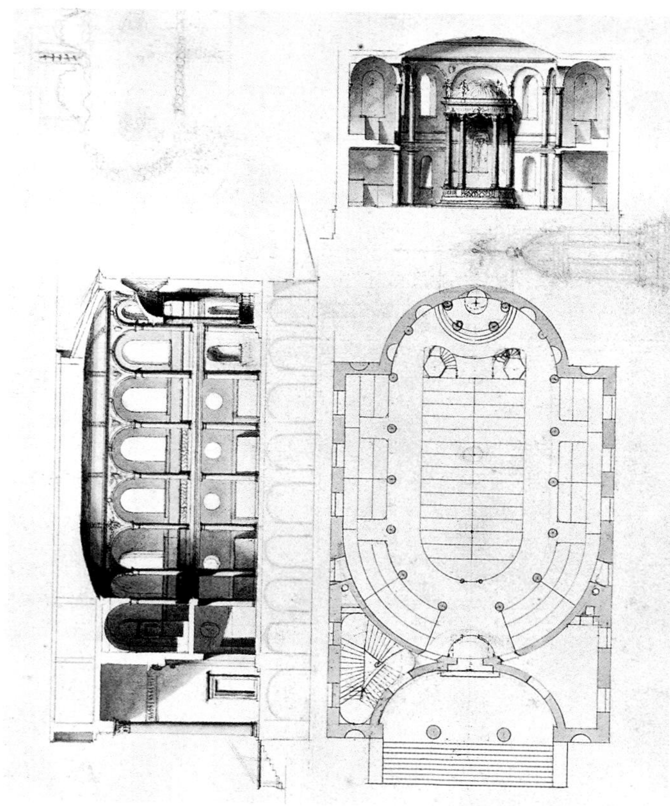

637 (*right*) William Newton. Plan and sections design, St Mary, Battersea, London, detail, 1774. Pen and ink and wash. RIBA Library Drawings Collection, K9/10(1).

638 William Newton. 'Elevation of the South Side' design, St Mary, Battersea, London, 1774. Pen and ink and wash. RIBA Library Drawings Collection, K9/10(8).

each end of its central panel, framed by a plain cyma, the order's architrave *alone* extends across the upper wall then turns the corner (pl. 638), no more than the brief width of an absent pilaster whose shaft is suggested elusively by the abrupt halt of the string-course dividing the two storeys of the side elevations. Perhaps this eccentricity was suggested by the first-century BC monument of M. Vergilius Eurysaces in Rome, which also features ranks of circular openings.[77] The double-storey, semicircular chancel with tiered round-headed arches is reminiscent of several early Christian churches in Rome, notably Santa Sabina.[78] Attached to the chancel end is a tall, slender steeple, Newton's response, like Hawksmoor's and Riou's before him (pls 403, 601), to the problem of divorcing the temple body from its ubiquitous bell-tower. Newton crowned his structure with a fussily decorated tempietto recalling the Roman monument of the Julii at Saint-Rémy-de-Provence in France, but here freakishly shot through with a conical spire.[79] The portico screens an apsidal *in antis* porch, a popular domestic feature since the 1730s but never before used on the exterior of a British church.[80] This led into an elongated oval body (pl. 637) with double-tiered columns defining the aisles and galleries, their fronts in the form of serpentine-fluted antique sarcophagi, continuing round the apsidal chancel as engaged orders, with the middle section breaking forward as a domed half-tempietto altar canopy. This unusual idea of a semi-independent columnar structure inserted into the chancel may have its origin in

639 William Newton. West front design, St Alphage, London Wall, London, 1775. Pen and ink and wash. RIBA Library Drawings Collection, K9/11(2).

640 (*below*) William Newton. Plan and 'Section of the Church of St. Alphage. London Wall', London, 1774. Pen and ink and wash. RIBA Library Drawings Collection, K9/11(3).

Piranesi's abortive schemes for remodelling the presbytery of San Giovanni in Laterano (1763–7), featuring a semicircular screen.[81] Compared to Adam's Durham Yard church of two years later (pls 626–7), Newton's plainer walls, more discrete decoration and slimmer pedimental proportions reveal the extent he was moving towards imitating the elegant austerity of Greek architecture. It may be pertinent that St Mary's minister at the time, the Revd William Fraigneau, had previously been Cambridge University Professor of Greek?[82] Two weeks after receiving this exceptional offering, the building committee 'unanimously' approved the extremely mundane Palladian design of its own surveyor, Joseph Dixon.[83]

Undeterred, Newton presented an equally radical scheme for rebuilding St Alphage, London Wall (pl. 639), a section of ruined masonry in his presentation drawing symbolising its ancient urban context. A low, full-width, Battersea-like west pediment crowns a distyle *in antis* portico with corner piers, as in the Athenian Treasury at Delphi (485 BC), while adapting an unfluted version of the Ionic column of the temple on the Ilissus (*circa* 450 BC), as reconstructed in *The Antiquities of Athens* (1762).[84] St Alphage is among the earliest documented expressions in Western church architecture of Greek taste, but even more remarkable

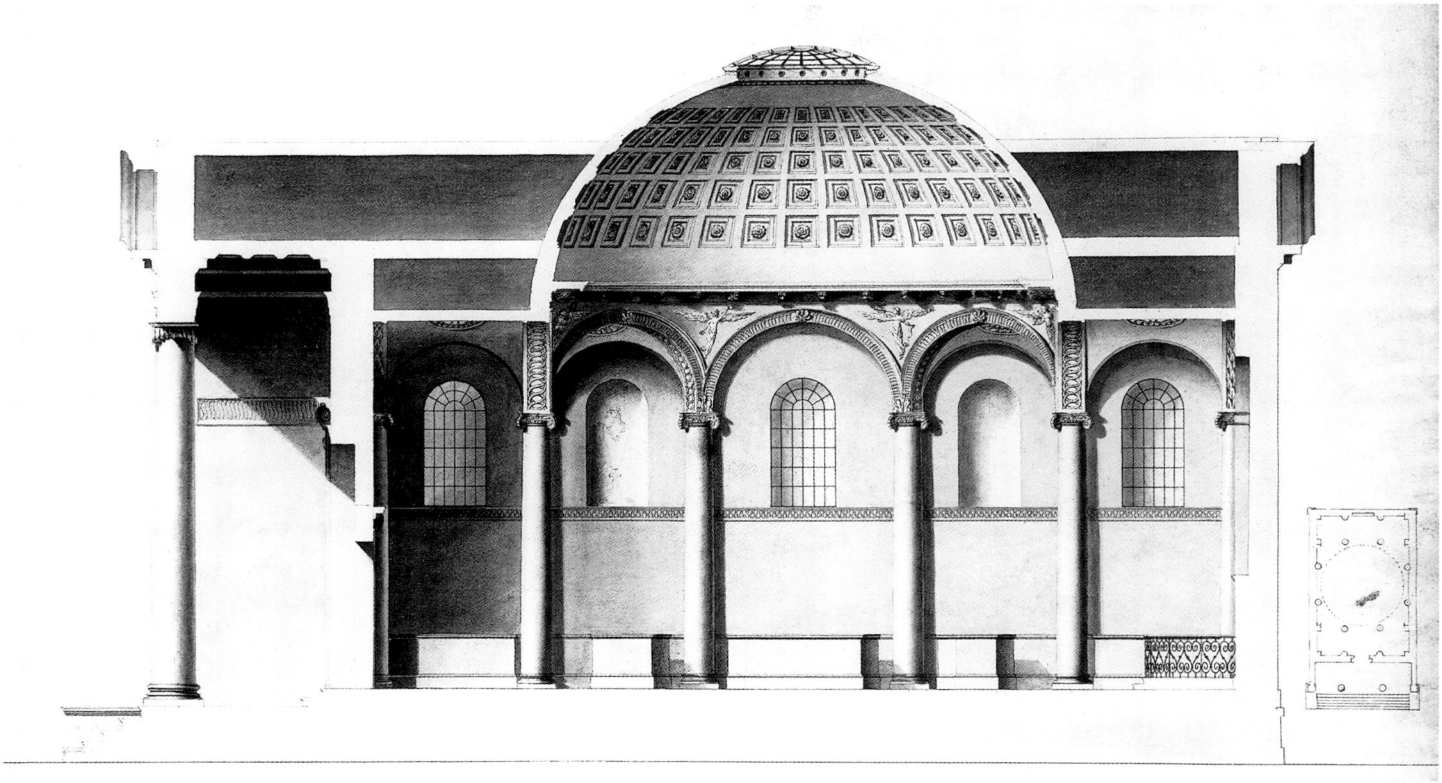

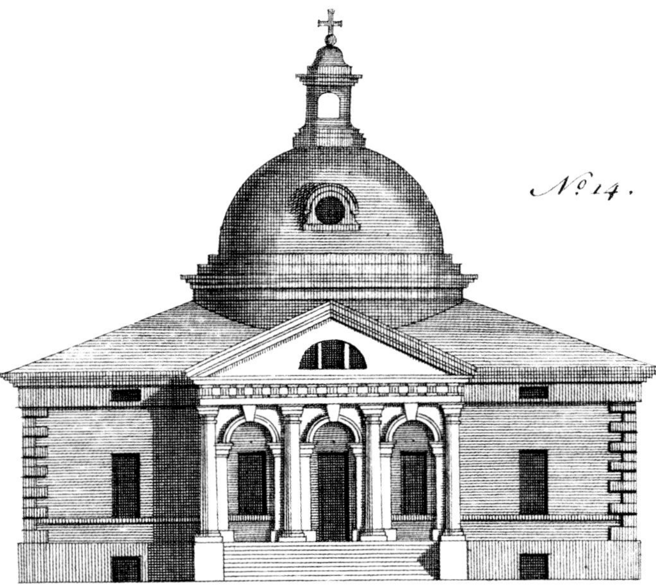

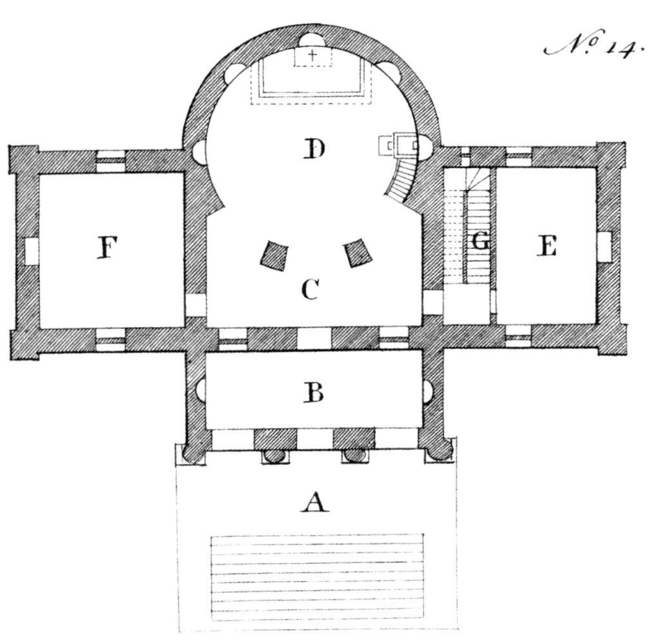

641 Parr after William Halfpenny. Plan and elevation of an unidentified chapel, in W. Halfpenny, *A New and Compleat System of Architecture*, 1749, pl. 20, no. 14, detail. Engraving. RIBA Library Photographs Collection.

is its internal interpolation of an eight-bay, Pantheon-like domed rotunda into the apteral rectangular cella (pl. 640), a homage to Wren's St Stephen Walbrook (pl. 492), though now with Ionic columns standing directly on the floor.[85] Though experiments in merging rotunda and rectangle were anticipated in published patterns (pl. 641), in a neoclassical context this seeming anachronism has its origin in J.-D. Leroy's *Les Ruines des Plus Beaux Monuments de la Grèce* (1770), and in *The Antiquities of Athens*, for which Stuart published both a

642 James Stuart. 'View of the Temple on the Ilissus', Athens, Greece, 1750–60s, detail. Gouache. RIBA Library Drawings Collection, SD145/2. Engraved in Stuart and Revett, 1762, vol. I, pl. I.

carefully measured reconstruction of the Ilissus temple and a topographical view of its condition, prior to destruction in 1778, for which his gouache also survives (pl. 642). The accompanying text refers to the fabric having incurred 'some barbarous additions [which] transformed it into a church' (dedicated to St Mary on the Rock); that is, the porch was infilled with masonry, windows were cut into the solid external side walls and a dome was inserted into the east end of the cella.[86]

Newton's pioneering marriage of Greek and Roman forms has a slightly later parallel in the combination of post-and-lintel and domical systems that characterise Ayot St Lawrence, Hertfordshire (1778–9; pl. 643), the only erected church by Revett, who had studied Greek buildings first hand in the 1750s. The *Gentleman's Magazine* proclaimed it 'One of the most singular exertions of [his] genius . . . in a style of Architecture not

643 Nicholas Revett. West front, St Lawrence, Ayot St Lawrence, Hertfordshire, 1778–9.

644 Nicholas Revett. North and east elevations, St Lawrence, Ayot St Lawrence, Hertfordshire, 1778–9.

645 Nicholas Revett. East elevation, St Lawrence, Ayot St Lawrence, Hertfordshire, 1778–9.

confined to any one Grecian model'.[87] Like Mistley, Ayot formed a picturesque feature in the pastoral landscape of the lord of the manor's estate. Reporting its consecration, the *Magazine* described the 'new church, on the Grecian model . . . built . . . at the sole expence of Sir Lionel Lyde, bart', which was attended by the neighbouring nobility, gentry and 'many hundred persons of all denominations from different parts of the county . . . preceded by a band of music . . . when they arrived at the church, the doors were thrown open (each of the populace eager to enter first)', after which 'the company . . . returned to the mansion-house,

646 Nicholas Revett. Interior towards the chancel, St Lawrence, Ayot St Lawrence, Hertfordshire, 1778–9. English Heritage (National Monuments Record, B90/775).

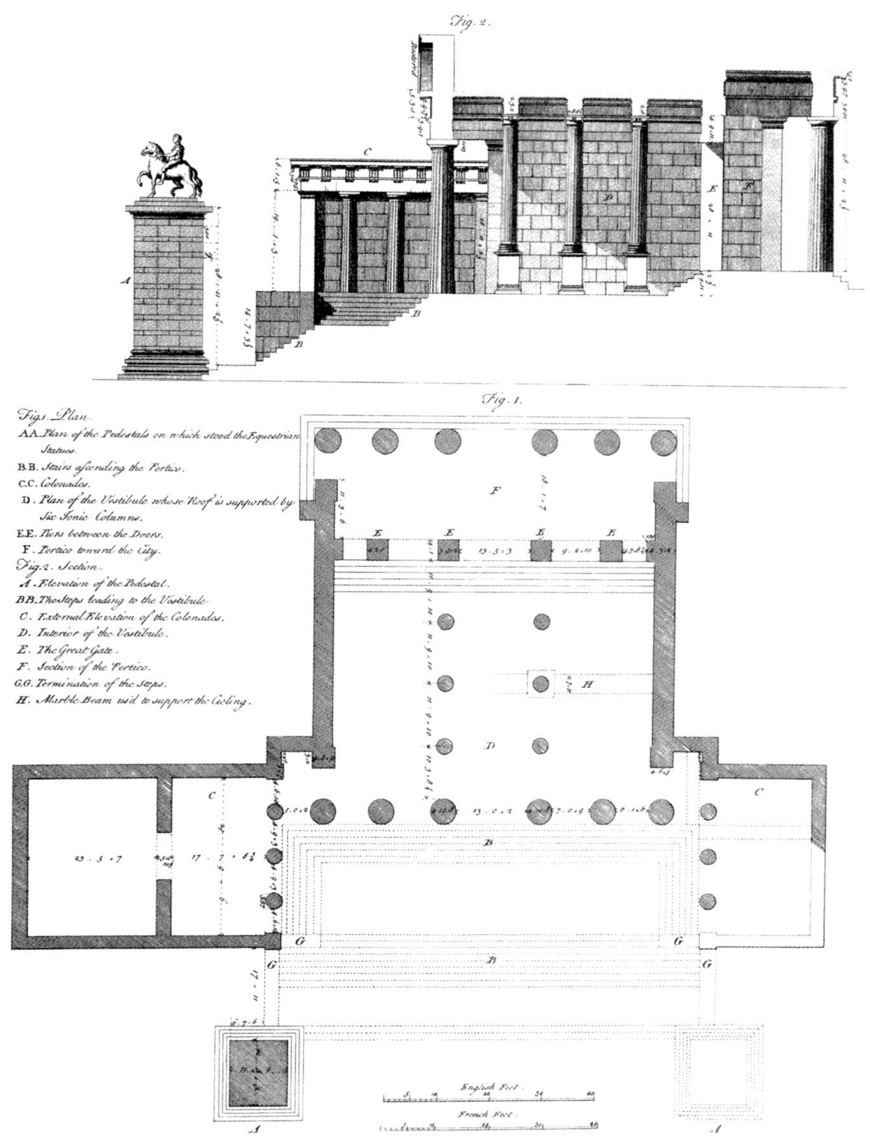

647 Plan, elevation and section reconstruction, Propylaen, Acropolis, Athens, Greece, in Robert Sayer, *Ruins Of Athens*, 1759, pl. 26. Engraving.

where an elegant dinner was provided [then] dispersed in the adjoining fields, where they diverted themselves in innocent rural games, to the close of day, and at last parted highly delighted with the pleasure they had received'.[88]

The portico and pronaos is the earliest built instance of a British church using the Greek Doric temple form, its order with plain shaft and narrow bands of fluting at top and bottom deriving from the celebrated amphiprostyle Temple of Apollo at Delphi (426 BC), which Stuart and Revett recorded in 1753.[89] The use made of this model, however, is unorthodox, because though the entablature wraps round the whole central structure, its metopes and triglyphs cease abruptly along the sides just behind the flanking colonnade screens, where the rendering suddenly gives way to bare brickwork (pl. 644). Yet since the pedimented transepts and semicircular chancel interrupt the temple continuity in a way that excludes an ornamental frieze and the whole complex is immaculately constructed, this must be read as a self-consciously finished product of Revett's adherence to the Society of Dilettanti's undoctrinaire approach to combining Greek and Roman architectural ideas.[90] The unconventionally beautiful polygonal shapes, exposed spanning arches, flat arched windows and isolated passages of stonework of the rear elevations (pl. 645), uncamouflaged expressions of a complex internal planning, conjure up the ancient brick buildings that proliferate in Rome and are minutely depicted in Piranesi's engravings. The interior (pl. 646) elaborates on these two merged antique systems: the centrality created by shallow transepts are reinforced in the flat ceiling by an illusionist coffered crossing dome (compared to the real structure in Newton's London Wall scheme, pl. 640).[91] The deep, double-tiered entablature is based on the Propylaea of the Athenian Acropolis (pl. 647). In adapting the church's funereal function, rather than providing a conventional burial vault (as shown in plate 638, for example), Revett extended the portico along its flanks by ranges of shorter Delos columns, an ingenious arrangement probably also inspired by the Propylaea, where the secondary screens are at right angles to the central portico.[92] Both lateral spines terminate in open, square pavilions containing the Lydes' memorial urns,[93] and were originally each crowned by a tempietto (removed 1832), perhaps Revett's response to Mistley (pl. 629).[94]

Twenty-eight

GREENWICH HOSPITAL CHAPEL

difficult to imagine a room more grandly and beautifully proportioned[1]

On 2 January 1779 Thomas Ripley's twenty-five-year old chapel interior was devastated by fire. Over the next decade it was remodelled into 'a masterpiece of taste . . . an example of enriched Grecian architecture, which almost defies competition in any part of Europe'.[2] It marked the first occasion in Britain when the exquisite beauties of ancient Greek architectural ornament, inspired by accurately measured drawings and archaeological reconstructions, were applied on such a lavish scale, creating one of the most significant and beautiful avant-garde rooms in Europe, which miraculously still remains in a pristine state (pls 648–9).[3] Its unique stature was recognised at the time: 'the greater part of the . . . works are of a kind & in a Style not in common use so that every thing was to be Studied & Invented, not only the Designs of the several parts & Members, but even in many Cases the Methods of executing them'. When the Hospital governors complained that construction was taking too long, the clerk of the works and the presiding genius, William Newton, replied that it was being 'executed in [an] excellent & Masterly manner' and warned that, although the Hospital was

> suffering a loss, in the gifts of Visitors . . . its attraction . . . will depend on its merit. if in order to have it expeditiously finished, it should be so hurried in designing & execution that the several parts be ill considered. Void of Taste, & poorly worked, instead of the Loss of a year or two, the Loss to the Hospital might be perpetual, by the Object being thought unworthy of attention.[4]

Notwithstanding the fulsome documentation and the survival of some 136 working and presentation drawings, a contentious issue remains in identifying the respective contributions made by the architects involved. The conceptual framework was undoubtedly the responsibility of the 69-year-old James Stuart, whose comprehensive reassessment in 2006 confirms his reputation as a dazzling interior designer and decorative painter rather than as an architect (with the exception of his activities in the realm of garden buildings) and as co-author, with Nicholas Revett, of the seminal first two volumes of *The Antiquities of Athens* (1762–87).[5] Stuart's first clerk of the works at the Hospital, Robert Mylne, claimed that 'through Infirmity or some other Cause', apparently a crippled hand, he had been entrusted with preparing the drawings, but a misunderstanding between them led to this crucial activity passing quickly to William Newton, with Mylne lamenting that he regarded it 'absolutely repugnant to the design . . . I had conceived and meant to execute'. The latter 'continued to produce all the Designs [except for a handful or so given to Stuart on grounds of draftsmanship] as well as . . . superintend the Execution'. This accounts for the motive that 'induced [Newton] to accept the Situation which appears beneath his rank as an Artist, and . . . give up his other appointments and professional engagements'. Newton had anticipated succeeding to the Hospital surveyorship on Stuart's death in 1788, but he was passed over in favour of first Sir Robert Taylor, who died in post the same year, and then John Yenn, leaving Newton in 'Sole direction' of completing the chapel 'according to the original intention [with] Taylor taking no part whatever'. In the following year, he was paid his full fee of £1,100, and due to ill health retired to Devon to 'take the benefit of Sea-Bathing'.[6] He wrote to the Hospital governors that 'it cannot hurt . . . Stuart now in his Official Capacity as it might have done when living therefore there is no reason for concealing the truth if his friends should desire his fame to be increased by

648 (*facing page*) James Stuart and William Newton.
View towards the entrance, Greenwich Hospital chapel, London, 1781–91. © *Country Life*, 688331.

649 Page. View towards the chancel, 'The New Chapel, Greenwich Hospital, Engraved . . . from an original drawing', undated. © The British Library Board, K.Top. XVII-1-3-r. James Stuart and William Newton architects, 1781–91.

what is not due to it & belongs to another'. Newton argued that they

> surely dont mean to desire me to be guilty of or accessory to a Fraud . . . & a very disgracefull act to all Concerned, & would Injure my reputation I can no more justly attribute my works & errors to others, than assume those of others as my own . . . Should [they] wish to Insist upon letting all the designs . . . pass as being . . . Stuarts . . . the public & posterity would know better, indeed the public know it already . . . all the workmen & Officers . . . & even the King knows – it cannot be concealed whose designs they are . . . The Drawings themselves will bear Evidence that Stuart could not do them. & the numerous first thoughts & sketches will also [confirm] whose they were.[7]

In his book *The Architecture of M. Vitruvius Pollio* (1791), Newton went so far as to suggest that the 'only part' in which Stuart 'had any share were the ornaments of the ceiling, the frame of the altar picture and the balustrades used in the two side galleries; these with the carving of some stone mouldings, taken from Greek examples in his *Antiquities of Athens*, were all that he determined; the remainder were my designing, or my selection'.[8]

Even under these circumstances, however, the pairs of giant order engaged Corinthian columns flanking the altarpiece (and presumably their echo at the west end, for which no pre-1779 record is known) were no more than a matter of veneering the fire-stained shafts of Ripley's structure, with a renewal of their damaged capitals, while the narrow side balconies accommodating naval officers merely reinstated their predecessors, though with the ornament of the balustrades and the thirty-two cantilevered iron and timber consoles updated (pl. 650). The aridity of the Palladian architecture required only overlaying with gorgeous ornament, egg and dart, bead and reel, anthemions and palmettes on the galleries, rosettes on the west door frame and leaf and tongue on the pulpit's medallion surrounds, which derive straight from the Erechtheum, as Newton

rightly acknowledged.[9] An un-acrimonious parallel seems to have existed at Westminster Abbey during the 1710s and 1720s, where William Dickinson became amanuensis and draughtsman to the shaky-handed octogenarian Wren, while independently contributing his own ideas (see p. 203). A closer look at Greenwich suggests something of the same relationship between Newton and Stuart.

650 (*left*) James Stuart and William Newton. Gallery detail, Greenwich Hospital chapel, London, 1781–91. English Heritage (National Monuments Record, WI 58, © The Warburg Institute, London).

651 (*below left*) James Stuart and Benjamin West. Pulpit, Greenwich Hospital chapel, London, 1781–91.

652 (*below right*) Elevation and section reconstruction, Choragic Monument of Lycratise, Athens, Greece, in Stuart and Revett 1762, vol. I, Chapter iv, pl. xxiv, detail. Engraving.

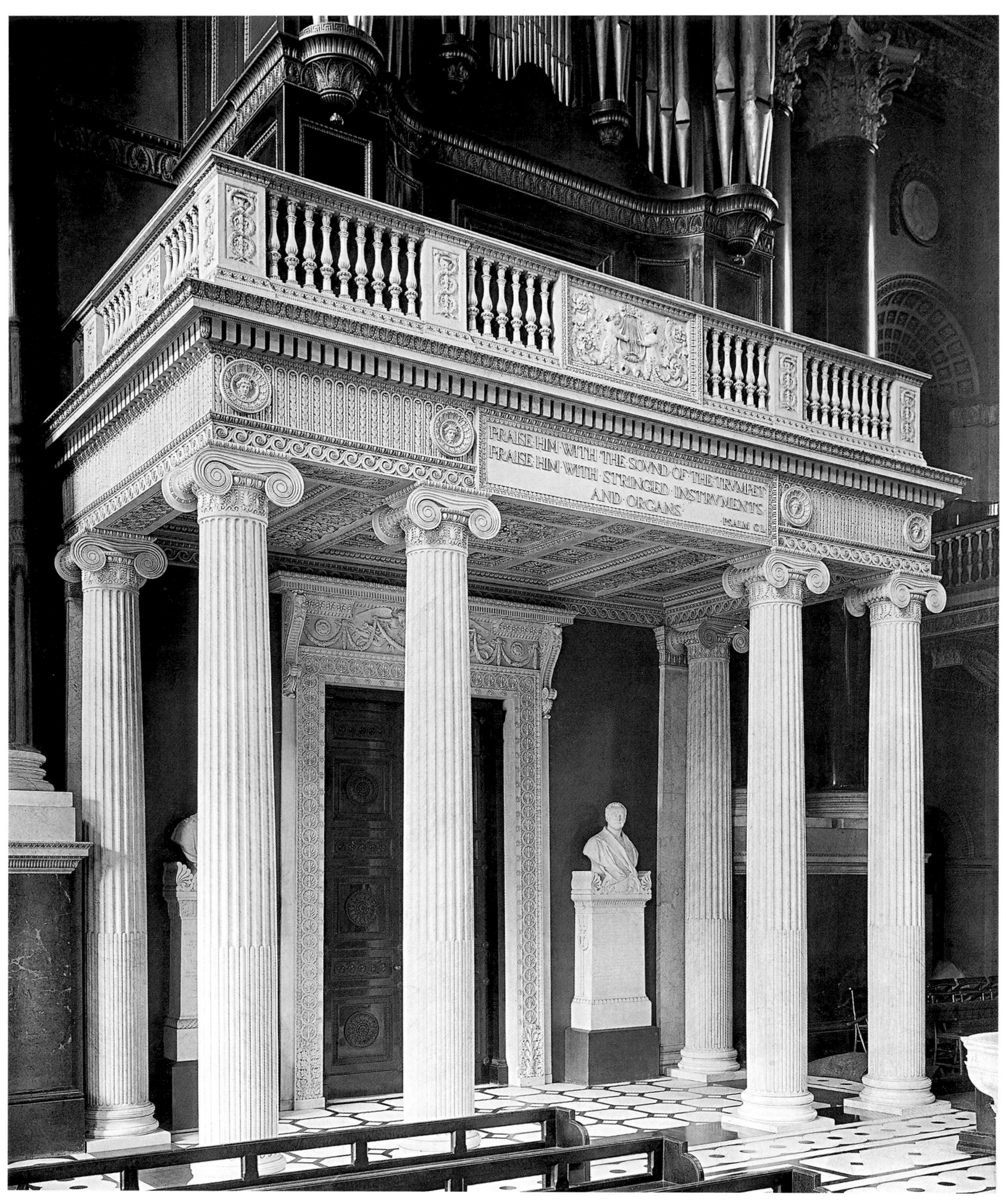

653 James Stuart and William Newton. West gallery, Greenwich Hospital chapel, London, 1781–91. English Heritage (National Monuments Record, CC40/00060).

The exquisite cylindrical pulpit (pls 648, 651), an entirely original concept that broke radically with the traditional tub mounted on a central stem, was cleverly adapted from the Choragic Monument to Lysicrates, Athens (pl. 652), less its foliated domical crown. Removing the masonry enclosure below the capitals freed the column shafts and bases; the upper intercolumniation of tripods was replaced by a deeper band decorated with six Coade-stone relief medallions designed by Benjamin West (the American-born painter trained in Rome and future president of the Royal Academy). The figurative frieze of the entablature was refashioned as repetitive palmettes and scrolls taken from 'Antiq: Chapr: 2. plate 6 fig:' in Richard Chandler's, Nicholas Revett's and William Pars's *Ionian Antiquities* (1769–).[10] It is significant that Revett finally relinquished the relevant drawings to the Society of Dilettanti in 1782, which were then lent to Stuart for a year as source material.[11] He is also most likely to have had access to unpublished views of the first-century BC (so-called) Tomb of Hiero, or Theron, at Agrigentum in Sicily, the model for the companion reader's desk (now in storage), a novel square box with fluted engaged corner columns supporting a continuous entablature.[12] Some of Stuart's chapel designs underwent modifications in execution. The fluted shafts and lotus-leaf capitals of the west gallery (pl. 653), based on the so-called Tower of the Winds at Athens, were revised to the Ionic order of the Erechtheum's north porch, now supporting the Incantada frieze so admired by both Newton and Adam. The lion's heads and dolphins specified in the contract of 1786 for the pair of carved and bronzed wood candelabra, a form with origins in Piranesi's *Vasi, candelabri, cippi, sarcofagi, tripodi, lucerne, ed ornamenti antichi* (1778) rather than Greek furniture, were changed to *putti* heads and seahorses (pl. 648).[13]

The Hospital 'Board' (building committee) was responsible for the iconographic programme, executed by its teams of painters, the most distinguished being West, and sculptors, notably John Bacon Sr, which consisted of two appropriately reciprocal themes. One was based on the Old and New Testament accounts of the life of Christ, with figures of the *Prophets*, *Evangelists* and *Apostles*, including six medallion reliefs embellishing the pulpit depicting episodes from St Paul's life, to whom the chapel is dedicated. The other, centred on West's colossal altar painting of *St Paul Shaking the Viper from His Hand after the Shipwreck* (1789), containing fifty over-life-size figures, and other marine motifs, such as the candelabra seahorses symbolic of sailors and Christianity, and the plaster dolphins under the galleries, together with anchors, compasses, oars, rudders and tridents in the marble pavement, are reminders of the naval function of the Hospital, which, according to a contemporary guidebook (for the room was opened to visitors), 'cannot fail to having the proper effect on the minds of seafaring men and impressing them with the due sense of their past preservation . . . present comfortable situation and support in this glorious asylum for naval misfortune and naval worth'.[14]

Reinforcing the chapel's stunning interior was the Stuart circle's belief in superlative building construction evinced by 'the great judgment' shown in surviving Greek architecture.[15] It was also observed at the time that Newton throughout his long clerkship continued 'to preserve consistancy & Uniformity of Design'.[16] It is these qualities that make the room still so potent.

654 Richard Morrison. Design for completing the west tower, Cashel Cathedral, Co. Tipperary, Ireland, 1791. Pen and ink and coloured wash. Hampshire Record Office, Normanton Papers, 21 M57/B14/8. Body by John Morrison, attributed, 1763–83.

Twenty-nine

THE FINAL DECADES, 1780–1800

In ancient times it was great and meritorious to raise the temple, the portico, and other public edifice. How great the advantage and glory that accrued to the Roman name and empire from their buildings.[1]

During the last twenty years of the eighteenth century architects of unusually inventive skills produced an almost endless variety of classical church patterns – rectangular temple and basilical forms, centrally planned Greek crosses, rotundas, octagons and polygons – bringing to fruition a century and more of experiments and creating some of the most vigorous, imaginative and elegant ecclesiastical architecture in Europe (pl. 654).

The uninterrupted popularity of temple-form churches in Britain throughout the eighteenth century is embodied in successive transformations of St Swithin, Walcot, Bath.[2] The first improvements necessitated by severe storm damage to the medieval fabric in 1739 were undertaken by one of the churchwardens, Robert Smith, the successful rival to John Wood Sr, a parishioner (who won the commission by a vote of fifteen to nil). Wood had proposed an esoteric structure 37½ by 23 feet, the same dimensions as Moses' Tabernacle incorporating the Ark of the Covenant, making it 'a perfect Example of that glorious Edifice' on the grounds of his (historically dubious) claim that the old church was on the site 'of a Pagan High Place that answered the exact Size and Form' as its biblical ancestor.[3] Between 1775 and 1783 a proposal to re-case the body in contrasting smooth and rusticated storeys in the Palladian manner of St Giles-in-the-Fields was rejected in favour of giant order Ionic pilasters rising from a deep podium to a straight entablature enwrapping the whole building (pl. 116). Then between 1789 and 1792 the building was enlarged and the tower completed with a bold columnar emphasis, and the pedimental presence of the temple body implied in the tower's second stage. All these phases are carefully represented in John Palmer's 1789 presentation drawing (pl. 655).

The 1780s was marked by a resurgence of conservative Palladian plainness partly prompted by economic factors. During the years between 1779 and 1784 net public expenditure nearly doubled net income, exacerbated by war with France, Spain and the Dutch Republic, Britain's increasing losses in the American colonies, climaxing with a reluctant granting of independence in 1783, and the outbreak of the French Revolution in 1789.[4]

James Wyatt's first independent ecclesiastical work, the Kentish Town Chapel, London (1779; pl. 656), was praised as 'a successful instance of the superior effect of simplicity in architecture. The stile . . . is elegantly plain; the portico partakes somewhat of the grand.'[5] This manner had been learnt between 1762 and 1768 from his Venetian teacher, Antonio Visentini, whose studio specialised in producing large numbers of accurately measured, finely rendered plans and elevations of Venetian churches by Palladio and his followers, principally for British consumption.[6] Kentish Town's short pedimented transepts, while obviously inspired by Ayot St Lawrence (pl. 644), eschewed Revett's Greek avant-gardism for Jonesian Palladianism (pl. 512). Perhaps this was motivated by the chapel's location on the west side of Kentish Town Road, which preconditioned the portico's placement on the east end. The treatment is quieter, more chaste; Jones's oculi, flanking doors and windows are replaced by austere recessed panels and vacant niches, his outer piers with return walls by free-standing, more elegantly proportioned columns (eight rather than seven times the height of the shaft diameter), with evenly spaced intercolumniation, and the signature modillion eaves abandoned altogether.[7]

Wyatt explored these ideas further in St Peter, Manchester (1788–94, demolished 1907; pls 657–8), as a

655 John Palmer. Design for addition of vestries, lobby and west tower, St Swithin, Walcot, Bath, Somerset, 1789. Pen and ink and wash. Somerset Record Office, D/P/wal SW 8/4/1.

656 James Wyatt. North-east perspective design, Kentish Town Chapel, London, 1779. Pen and ink and coloured wash. Camden Local Studies and Archives Centre, Heal Collection, A.VI.37. Erected 1780–84, rebuilt 1845.

rare amphiprostyle temple, having both front and rear porticoes, which responded to its central position in a newly created square on the edge of town with the north portico terminating the prospect of fashionable Moseley Street, a Kentish Town variant with the portico raised on a rusticated podium, the body encircled by more richly articulated pilasters and the south portico facing open fields (the site of the Peterloo massacre of 1818), but with its middle bay enclosed to form a lobby and tower base flanked by open, porch-like bays. Wyatt preferred this solution to St Martin-in-the-Fields's camouflaged structure, which he condemned as 'bad'.[8] The anomaly of the needle spire (also a peculiarity of the design ilustrated in plate 655) in this case was apparently imposed by the client, the architect preferring a dome. No view of the interior is known, but a guidebook of 1816 described it as 'a Model of elegance and taste' with the communion table and pulpit placed opposite one another in shallow east and west transepts equidistant between the two porticoes, beyond which were galleries, creating a decisively centralised orientation.[9]

Benjamin Henry Latrobe, the leading English-born architect practising in the United States from 1796, highlighted in a letter to his colleague Thomas Jefferson the stylistic and compositional difficulties of adopting the antique temple form:

> In Grecian architecture I am a bigoted Greek . . . Whenever therefore the Grecian style can be copied without impropriety I love to be a *mere*, I would say a *slavish* copyist, but the *forms*, and the *distribution* of the Roman and Greek buildings which remain, are in general inapplicable to the objects and uses of our public buildings. Our religion requires churches wholly different from their temples . . . altho' the want of a *belfry* . . . rendered them a *necessary* appendage to the church, yet I cannot admit that because the Greeks and Romans did not place elevated cupolas upon their temples, they may not, where necessary, be rendered also beautiful . . . The question would be as to its real or apparent utility in the place in which it appeared: for nothing in the eye of good taste (which ought never to be at warfare with good sense) can be beautiful which appears useless or unmeaning.[10]

These poignant issues were largely resolved through a process of adjustment and refinement by Willey Reveley towards the end of his brief career (cut short by his death at the age of 39 in 1799), at All Saints,

657 John Palmer. South-east view of St Peter, Manchester, Lancashire, detail, *c.*1820. Pen and ink and wash. Manchester Central Library Archives, M16/2/2. James Wyatt architect, 1788–94, demolished 1907.

658 John Palmer. Plan, St Peter, Manchester, Lancashire, *c.*1820. Pen and ink and wash. Manchester Central Library Archives, M16/2/3. James Wyatt architect, 1788–94, demolished 1907.

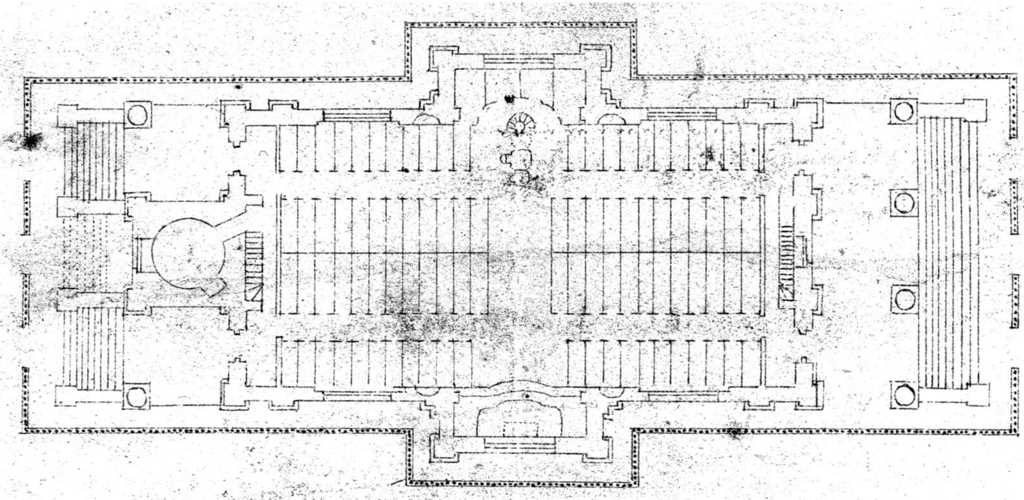

grandeur of the Parthenon, or the still more masculine character of the great temple of Pesto.'[13] During editorial preparations of the third volume of *The Antiquities of Athens* (1794), a publication he praised as among the 'precious additions to the stock of genuine Grecian architecture' and to which he appended a personal attack on Chambers's dismissal of Greek architectural principles out of both prejudice and antipathy, and reaffirmed his own wholehearted championship of the 'gusto Greco', 'The Athenian Reveley', as he was nicknamed, struggled at Southampton to preserve the temple form against a parochial and woefully inexperienced building committee.[14] He resisted its indecisiveness whether or not to have a prominent portico

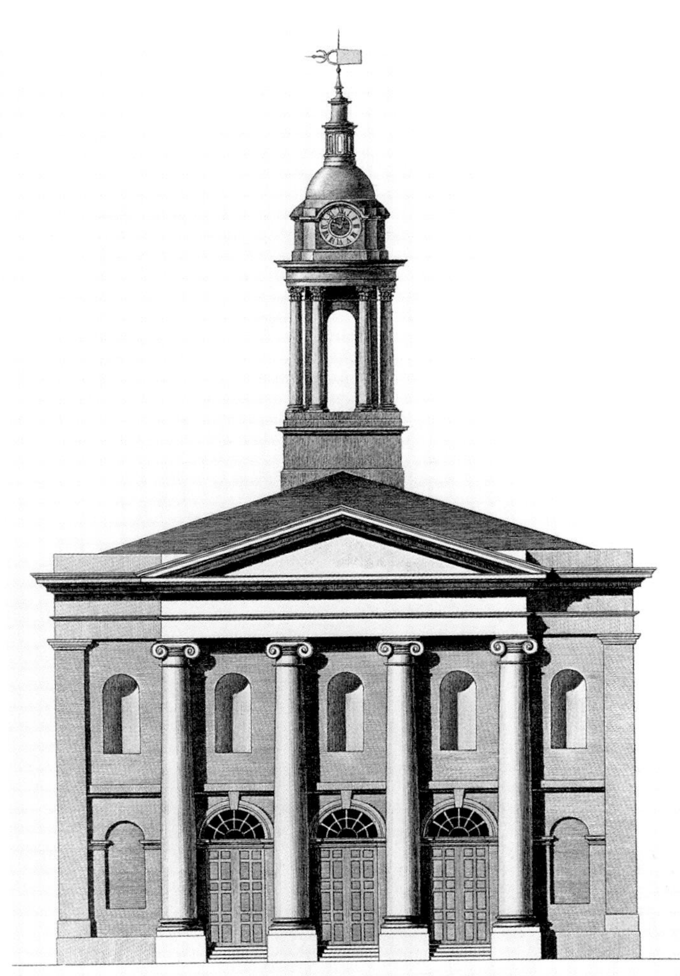

659 Ranzonette after Schwender. West front, All Saints, Southampton, Hampshire, in Stieglitz 1800, pl. 23. Engraving. RIBA Library Photographs Collection. Willey Reveley architect, 1790–95, destroyed in Blitz, 1940.

660 West elevation reconstruction, Erechtheum, Acropolis, Athens, Greece, in Stuart and Revett 1787, vol. III, ch. II, pl. XXVII, detail. Engraving. Erected 421–405 BC.

Southampton, Hampshire (1790–95; pl. 659). Having served as Chambers's assistant clerk of works at Somerset House, London (1776–7), the most important British public building of its age, he travelled in Italy, Greece and Egypt during the years 1784–8, making drawings of buildings that became 'universally known to all the lovers of art, and admirers of classic Antiquity'.[11] Though approving of Roman temples such as the Maison Carrée, Nîmes as 'really . . . a very beautiful piece of architecture' (pl. 412),[12] subsequent excursions to Paestum and following in the footsteps of Stuart and Revett convinced Reveley of the superiority of the Greek over the Roman Doric order: 'Let those who prefer the later Doric indiscriminately, and entirely reject the Grecian, try whether they can, with their slender order, produce the chaste and solid

on grounds of obstructing the pavement by citing St George, Hanover Square (pl. 11), and James Wyatt's Oxford Street Pantheon as exemplary because a portico 'shews the building to more advantage, & is not found any objection'.[15] He contemplated introducing a hexastyle portico stretching across the entire west front, perhaps having in mind the Temple of Athena Polias at Priene as reconstructed in the first volume of the Society of Dilettanti's *Ionian Antiquities* (1769), before returning to his inaugural hexastyle solution.[16] Here the Greek Ionic order was preferred, since the capitals 'shine with a decided superiority over all the Roman Ionics . . . the few specimens . . . now remaining at Rome are of so little merit', and only Stuart's and Revett's 'discovery of the antiquities of Greece . . . brought into notice the admirable specimens of Ionic architecture, which have ever since met with so much attention from the best informed architects as well as connoisseurs'.[17] The result is a graceful engaged portico set against a windowless west front framed by Doric corner pilasters resembling the west elevation of the Erechtheum illustrated in *The Antiquities of Athens* (pl. 660).

Chambers's insinuation, according to Reveley, that the Parthenon 'would gain considerably with respect to beauty by the addition of a steeple' in the tradition of St Martin-in-the-Fields (pl. 416), was utterly rejected by the younger architect since a 'judicious observer of the fine arts would scarcely be more surprised were he to propose to effect this improvement by adding to it a Chinese pagoda', an aspersion on Chambers's structure at Kew Gardens.[18] Furthermore, though 'one of the best in London', Gibbs's church 'is no more than a very inferior imitation of the Greek prostyle temple, and will not enter into the slightest degree of comparison with the chaste grandeur, the dignified simplicity, and sublime effect of the Parthenon'.[19] Reveley reacted to this curious debate by positioning All Saints' turret over the projecting eastern chancel block, separating it from the main roof as a way of preserving the integrity of the temple body.[20]

In Italy, Reveley had rejected both Palladian and baroque architecture, for example, condemning the west front of St Peter, Rome (pl. 513), as 'too full of breaks & littlenesses & void of unity & grandeur . . . nobody can . . . be struck with an effect of grandeur by such trivial & ill contrived attempts at novelty & variety'.[21] Nor was he prepared to sanction Soufflot's handling of Sainte Geneviève (pl. 596), then nearing completion:

> The portico so far as it approaches to the antique is grand, but many french ornaments &c destroy a good deal the effect of it particularly two columns stuck on at each end as if on purpose to disfigure it . . . The flanks are almost Gothick or so far from the Greek & Roman as to seem composed by their excessive ugliness on purpose to serve as a foil to the Portico.[22]

By contrast, All Saints' exterior possesses an uncommon austerity, as *The Southampton Guide* (1805) makes clear:

> Around the church runs an entablature, supported on each flank by the same kind of pilasters as finish the angles. These stand on a plain basement, without any projection, and greatly strengthen the walls . . . exactly where the bearings of the roof rest. The south flank [facing a side street] . . . is lighted by sixteen windows, in two ranges [with] plain neat sashes [each separated by giant Doric pilasters]. The north flank, being hidden by the houses to which it adjoins, has no windows, and the church is very sufficiently lighted without them.[23]

In effect, a modified pseudoperipteral temple.

Antique solutions were also sought for the interior (pl. 661). The open, cella-like space was covered by a single-span ceiling, with the gallery supports minimised, and the triumphal altarpiece that occupied the entire back wall of the shallow chancel dramatically top-lit from windows scooped into its coffered vault based on the Roman arch of Trajan at Beneventum, near Naples, which Reveley had visited in 1785.[24] The whole interior was to be 'whited . . . so as to leave [it] perfectly compleat'.[25] Here is the antithesis of everything found contemptible at St Peter's:

> I never was in my life struck at the first entrance of any building . . . The prodigious quantity of gilding with the variety of marbles of different colours, raise in the mind all those ideas which are produced by richness & grand confusion . . . The forms are . . . lost by the variety of colours, which also disguise the beauties of the architecture which are but few in this building . . . It is difficult to conceive how a pile so full of faults the most striking can astonish & delight mankind as this does.

It was 'quite different from the effect of simple grandeur, produced by great unity & real fine architecture'.[26] All Saints' impact on visitors is well described in *The Southampton Guide*:

> Grecian pilasters, similar to those on the outside, but with more ornamented capitals, are also made use of within the walls. Their mouldings are continued quite round the building; and from this, as an impost, with a gentle rise of only eight feet, springs the arched ceiling, which is a segment of a circle, ornamented with square sunk pannels. No heavy columns, no protruding beams, intercepting the sight and sound, are employed in the support of this ample [61-foot-wide] roof. It is indeed a noble performance, seldom perhaps excelled in boldness of design.

It concluded that this 'elegant modern structure . . . on a plan of chaste and noble simplicity . . . does honour to the genius of its architect'.[27] This was all part of Reveley's campaign 'to build A Church without faults',[28] though its destruction by enemy bombs in 1940 and the lack of the architect's original designs, as well as an inadequate photographic record, now make

661 Willey Reveley. Interior towards the chancel, All Saints, Southampton, Hampshire, 1790–95, photographed before Blitz, 1940. Southampton Archives.

such an assessment almost impossible. A contributor to the *Gentleman's Magazine* in 1801 was of the opinion that 'the application of Grecian temples to the purpose of Christian churches' represented by All Saints, as well as Revett's Ayot St Lawrence, 'have greatly failed'.[29] This, however, could not be said with regard to the 35-year-old Thomas Telford's first and finest church at Bridgnorth, Somerset, an astonishing debut.

St Mary Magdalene (1788–96; pl. 662) was to a significant extent a reaction to what Telford condemned as the 'very expensive contrivance' of St Chad, Shrewsbury, which 'by no means answers [the] best judges . . . expectation as to grandeur' (pl. 679).[30] This was expressed not without bias since his presage of the medieval fabric's imminent collapse in 1788 had gone unheeded by the authorities and the lucrative job of rebuilding went to his rival, George Steuart.[31] Despite Telford's inexperience – when his Bridgnorth design was submitted to Parliament for approval he enquired if it had undergone 'any criticism in London' and 'observations that . . . could tend to improvement' – from the start he was adamant as to the certainty that 'a new Church is most advisable [since] if any part [of the old one] should be preserved, that part would still remain suspicious and be very improper for connecting with the new Work'.[32] He also selected, after surveying nine different town sites (see p. 18), the old churchyard standing high and 'very romantic on the Banks of the Severn', acropolis-like, in order to exploit the building fully in the round. While built on part of the medieval foundations, the new fabric had its axis reorientated to face north, filling the end of East Castle Street, with the tower 'seen in all directions', which he regarded as 'more ornamental to the town'.[33]

Here he developed a subtle, telescopic composition never before seen in Britain, and the most original transition from portico to body since St Martin-in-the-Fields. On the entrance front a Tuscan tetrastyle engaged temple portico, though occupying a space only 4 feet deep, has a prostyle presence resulting from the way its supports change from three-quarter columns to nearly full piers, perhaps a reference to Covent Garden church (pl. 512), then undergoing restoration and much in the news.[34] The piers then turn the corners to meet narrow sections of masonry with flat, intermediary piers that frame side walls containing doors leading into lobbies and staircase units. These, in turn, connect with short walls and further flat piers marking the corners of the body, before finally embarking on the quieter, more spacious rhythms of paired pilasters and single windows along the east and west elevations. The vestry and chancel walls were simplified, pedimented but door-less versions of the front. Tying all these components together is a continuous entablature and podium,

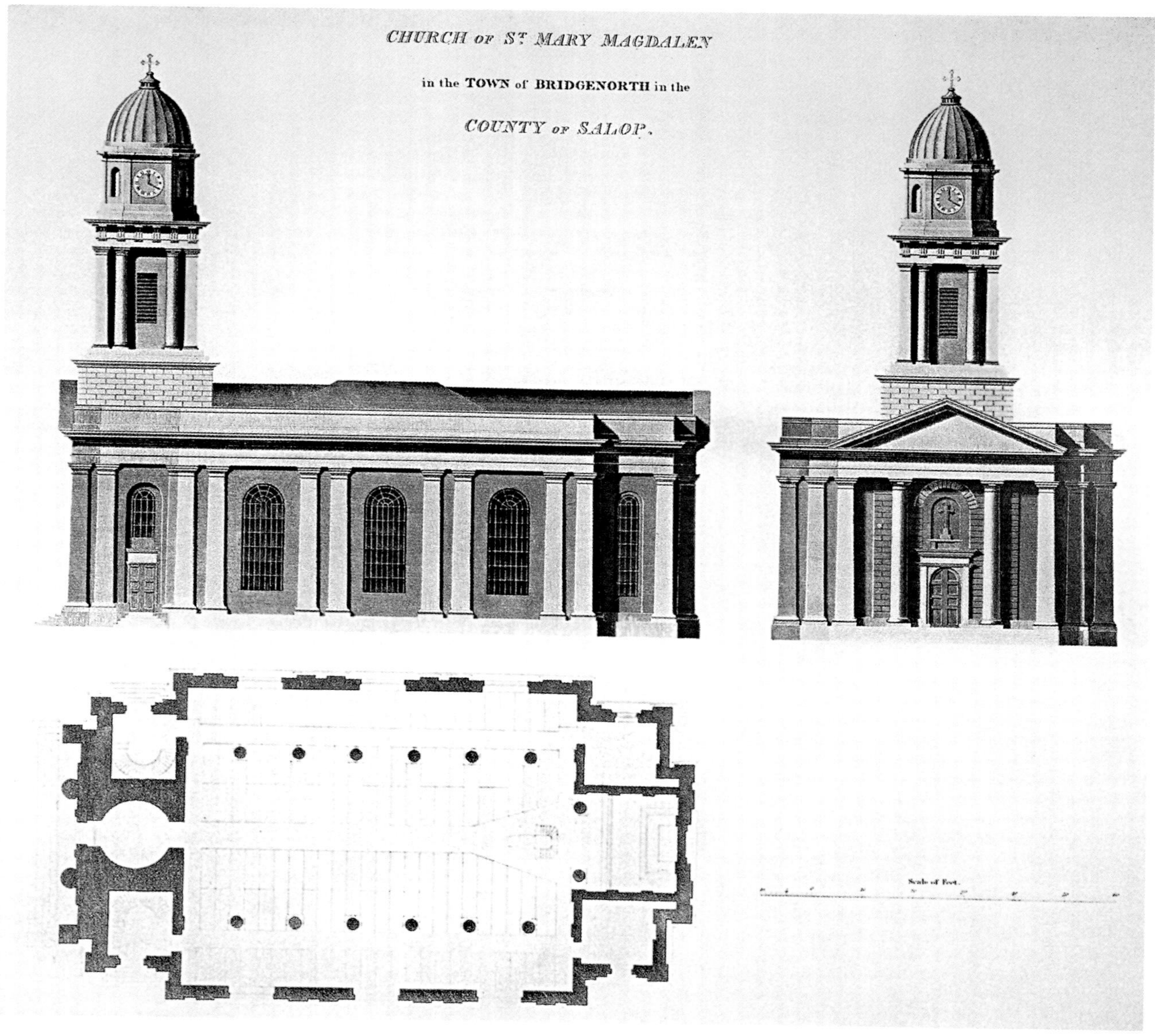

662 Thomas Telford. Plan, entrance and north elevations, 'Church of St. Mary Magdalen in . . . Bridgenorth . . . Salop', Shropshire, in Rickman 1838, pl. IX. Engraving. Ironbridge Gorge Museum Trust. Erected 1788–96.

which, as specified in the builders' contract, 'run in a straight line along the Portico [and] break round each Pilaster but . . . receive two Pilasters along each side and round the Chancel end'.[35] Telford disliked clerestories because 'two rows of windows convey the notion of their being two heights of apartments [which, with] the other small divisions become an offensive number of thriving parts', whereas here 'the body of the Church is brought forward distinctly, the plain Order reaches the whole height of the side Walls, and instead of ten small Windows there are three very large ones on each side. By this means it is hoped that the attention will be drawn to the body . . . as one great and undivided apartment.'[36] Behind the portico a central section of wall, slightly wider than the middle bay and divested of the recessed, cross-embellished overdoor shown in plate 662, forms a shallow, entirely sunk-jointed rusticated screen set against the plain, main wall (pl. 663). Early in 1792 Telford reported:

> In making a Copy of the Elevation [drawing] . . . I have discovered that by ten minutes work I can much improve the Base of the Tower . . . all the alteration I have made has been the rusticating the Base

> . . . and the wall below, it is done on purpose to add the appearance of Neatness to the Base . . . and to shew it connects with the Wall . . . altho' it is a very trifle . . . the Plan is likely to be more & more approved by judges.[37]

The bell stage is a Doric version of the portico, identical on all four faces, recalling the well-preserved mausoleum of the second century AD at Mylasa (Milas) in Turkey, which Richard Chandler, who visited it during the 1760s, observed was 'now open' but originally 'closed with marble pannels'.[38]

During the designing process Telford avidly consulted architectural pattern books. On 31 March 1792, while the House of Commons deliberated on the building petition, he borrowed from Shrewsbury School library the second volume of the English 1721 edition of Bernard de Montfaucon's *L'Antiquité Expliquée* (1719), devoted to temples including Jupiter Capitolinus, the 'most celebrated Temple in Rome', with its Doric portico standing before an entirely rusticated, windowless wall, and the Maison Carrée, 'a Model of the best Architecture' (pl. 412), with columns 'all round the Temple, that project or jut-out', which are echoed in Telford's specification for pilasters 'all round to project . . . before the face of the finished wall'.[39] Underpinning this beautiful conception and assuring an essential neoclassical homogeneity and crispness, Telford turned to the first volume of *The Antiquities of Athens*, also borrowed from the same source, which demonstrates in the reconstructed Stoa the sparsity of ornament and 'depth of the channels in the rustic', reinforcing his experience as a mason working on Chambers's Somerset House.[40] Looking forward to a great engineering career, he scrutinised choices of building stone, rejecting a local red sandstone in favour of an appropriately whiter variety, and demanded a high standard of technical proficiency. The foundation was to be of

> Stones laid Flat and Close to . . . breaking Joints not only on the Outside but quite thro' the Wall . . . with proper projections to take the plinths and Pilasters . . . The outside of the whole . . . worked with squared Ashler properly tool'd or stroked . . . all the offsetts . . . worked with a weathering to let the water run off . . . the walls . . . built with good scabbled stones and in regular courses well bedded . . . The Parapet . . . of cleansed Stone . . . laid so as the water shall fall towards the Roof . . . all bad and insufficient Materials . . . rejected by the . . . Surveyor and all bad work . . . taken down and replaced with good at the Expence of the . . . Contractors.[41]

663 (*top*) Thomas Telford. Entrance front, St Mary Magdalen, Bridgenorth, Shropshire, detail, 1788–96.

664 (*above*) Thomas Telford. Interior towards the west, St Mary Magdalen, Bridgenorth, Shropshire, 1788–96, west gallery added 1889.

Bridgnorth has an uncommonly wide and spacious nave (pl. 664), with side aisles of the same height, separated by ranges of single Ionic columns supporting a continuous entablature and uninterrupted by galleries (that at the entrance end is a Victorian intrusion). According to the builders' contract, the tall windows were glazed with 'best Bristol Crown Glass' set in thin

cast-iron bars painted in 'Oil of an Iron colour', with the walls 'finished with rough Stucco', the ceilings 'plastered three Coats . . . and sett white' and the woodwork painted 'in Oil of an Oak colour'. For 'the better preservation of uniformity', pews were not permitted to be painted, lined or raised in height, and no monuments were 'at any time [to] be erected . . . in the . . . new church . . . or on the outside walls'.[42] The original, square chancel (remodelled 1872–6) framed by a pair of columns standing proud of the side walls

665 (*left*) Unknown artist. View of 'St Botolph without Aldersgate Street', London, detail, *c.*1815. Pencil, London Metropolitan Archives (Guildhall Library, 1467). Nathaniel Wright architect, 1787–92.

666 (*below*) Nathaniel Wright. Interior towards the west, St Botolph, Aldersgate, London, 1787–92. English Heritage (National Monuments Record, AA61/2776).

667 Joseph Bonomi. Perspective design of interior towards the chancel, Spanish Ambassador's Chapel (Catholic), Manchester Square, St Marylebone, London, 1792, demolished 1802. RIBA Library Drawings Collection.

was unfenestrated in order to accommodate paintings or statuary both over the altar and to each side. A skylight recessed in a white plastered dome glazed with 'best Bristol Crown Glass in Cast Iron Barrs [with] plain painted or stained Glass' alone illuminated this space.[43] Telford's debt to Saint Philippe-du-Roule, a potent Parisian neoclassical landmark, is self-evident (pl. 621).

Elsewhere, other aspects of astylar temple-form rectangularity were investigated, in particular the antique basilica, a church with the central vessel higher and wider than the aisles and with a clerestory, derived from the Roman assembly hall adapted for Christian worship. In the case of St Botolph, Aldersgate, London (1787–92), this had been preceded by a 1750s Palladian remodelling of a 'very much damnified' medieval fabric, which was now heightened and re-roofed as an indifferent brick structure compared to 'a brew house' (pl. 665).[44] This, however, utterly belies the brilliantly redecorated interior by Nathaniel Wright, a successful City carpenter in his only documented church (pl. 666). Lying on the west side of the street with access from either side of the apsidal chancel lit by a prominent Serliana, echoed at the eastern entrance by a segmental-shaped organ loft (the instrument supplied by Samuel Green in 1788), the four-bay body with nave and galleried aisles defined by a traditional column on pier arrangement, and lunette windows cutting into the vault in the manner of Wren's nearby Christ Church, Newgate (1677–87), is unequivocally up-to-date in its detailing. The piers support only a low-relief scrolled frieze and Corinthian columns rising from a narrow ledge directly above, with separate, slightly recessed gallery fronts. Such omissions from the orthodox components of the classical order look back to Dance Jr's nearby All Hallows, London Wall (pl. 603).[45]

Joseph Bonomi's Spanish Ambassador's chapel in Manchester Square, London (1792; pl. 667), was deeply rooted in those early Christian basilicas in Rome refashioned in the eighteenth century, such as Santa Cecilia in Trastevere (founded in the fifth century and given an engaged temple portico front by Ferdinando Fuga in 1741–2) and San Paolo fuori le Mura (begun in 384, the subject of a 'Restauro in forme moderne' for the Corso Clementino of 1758 at the Accademia di San Luca, of which Bonomi's teacher, Antonio Asprucci, was a member).[46] Bonomi's interest in these ancient adaptations was rekindled during a brief return

668 John Le Keux after Thomas Taylor. North-west view, St Paul, Leeds, Yorkshire, in Whitaker 1816, p. 69. Engraving. Thomas Johnson architect, 1791–4, demolished 1906.

669 (*below left*) Thomas Johnson. South-east view, Holy Trinity, Halifax, Yorkshire, 1795–8, now offices.

670 (*below right*) James Whittle. South-west view, St Wilfrid Chapel (Catholic), Preston, Lancashire, 1791–3. Lancashire Library, Preston, 1287-7. Demolished 1880.

visit to Rome in 1783 (when he was made an Accademia associate), with the Corso entry for an 'Altro ordine per S. M. sopra Minerva'. This was an eighth-century foundation rebuilt in the gothic period where Filippo Volpi had inserted a barrel-vaulted ceiling enriched with Pantheon-like coffering and prominent lunette windows at the east end, motifs that reappear in Bonomi's chapel.[47] Furthermore, the altarpiece was framed by geometric marble panels, a common sight in Roman churches but at this time probably unique in England.[48]

Finally, a miscellany of British churches retaining hints of temple origins. Cashel Cathedral in Ireland (pl. 654) has an Ionic articulation along the body and in the pedimented entrance centrepiece but with corner quoins disconnecting the two columnar sections. Its tower was finished in 1791.[49] The Ionic engaged temple front of St Paul, Park Square, Leeds (1791–4; pl. 668), erected on the western edge of the town within sight of open fields, perhaps prescribed to Batty Langley's delightful dictum that

> as *public buildings* are erected for different purposes, the order after which they are to be built should be considered . . . therefore . . . if a church in the country, the Ionic will be most proper, having its freeze enriched with leaves, and the volutes of its capitals with festoons of fruits and flowers, alluding to its rural situation.[50]

The architect Thomas Johnson, a pupil of James Wyatt, advertised in the local press in 1787 that while residing in Rome (1785–6) he had 'seen all the principal Cities

of Italy', together with a 'Tour through France', and now intended settling in Leeds with a 'View to Improvement in his Profession' by giving 'Proof . . . in uniting Taste with Oeconomy' and joining 'Elegance to Convenience'. He was probably the first professional architect to practise in the town.[51] Johnson's other major church, at Halifax, Yorkshire (1795–8; pl. 669), also employing slender Ionic pilasters in the upper storey, has a prominent, pedimented centrepiece comprising a Wyattesque tripartite lunette window framed by recessed, nearly free-standing columns raised over a rusticated basement with a deep-set lunette illuminating the internal altarpiece. The steeple lies semi-detached on the south side.[52] Similar recessed fenestration articulated the long street elevation of St Wilfrid, Preston, Lancashire (1791–3; pl. 670), designed by the Mancunian James Whittle, one of the earliest free-standing Catholic churches built in the provinces, the outcome of a new ecumenical spirit in government. The sedate though imposing 60 by 90 foot red brick, stone-trimmed block with full pedimental ends was free of the Anglican imposition of a bell-tower, which was still prohibited to the faith, and therefore took on the largely unblemished appearance of an astylar temple.[53]

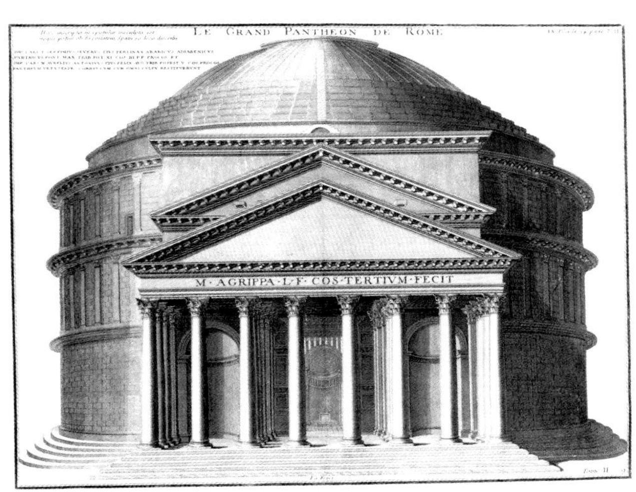

671 'Le Grand Pantheon de Rome' restored, in Montfaucon 1719, vol. II, pl. 9. Engraving. Author's collection. Erected *c.*118–*c.*128.

672 William Sibbald. West front design, St Andrew, Edinburgh, Midlothian, Scotland, detail, undated. Pen and ink and wash. Royal Commission on the Ancient and Historical Monuments of Scotland, Calendar House, EDD/195/6. Andrew Fraser (body), W. Sibbald (tower) architects, 1785–7.

In a memorandum of 1785 from Rome, Willey Reveley warned of the hazards of adapting the pagan rotunda to modern Christian usage, dismissing the famous baroque ovoid-planned Sant'Andrea al Quirinale, San Carlo alle Quattro Fontane and Santa Maria di Montesanto for having 'a very bad effect', and observing of Santa Maria dell'Assunzione at Ariccia that 'the greatest merit of this fine work of Bernini is, that it is something like the Pantheon . . . in the general form, but infinitely worse in all its parts. it is a very bad copy of one of the finest buildings in the world' (pl. 671).[54] The initiative to reinvigorate the form for Anglican worship, which had failed in London, first with Gibbs's 'Round Design' for St Martin-in-the-Fields (pl. 675) and latterly with Chambers's St Marylebone (pl. 620), passed into the hands of more determined, adventurous provincial authorities in the 1780s and 1790s.

The first of these was St Andrew, Edinburgh New Town (1785–7; pl. 672), with a design history confused

673 T. Dick. East view, All Saints, Newcastle-upon-Tyne, Northumberland, *c.*1820. Engraving. © The British Library Board, K.Top. XXXII-57-a. David Stephenson architect, 1786–96.

by incomplete documentation and uncertain involvement of several architects, of whom Andrew Frazer seems to have been the guiding hand, with William Sibbald responsible for the steeple's final form, apparently an afterthought.[55] The latter was a particularly troublesome issue in Presbyterian Scotland: one of the heritors of nearby St Cuthbert (1789–90), which sported a similar superstructure, remarked: 'I never will consent to the expenditure . . . of one single shilling for the purpose of building a Steeple or any such superfluous whimsical additional building.'[56]

No such difficulties were suffered at All Saints, Newcastle upon Tyne (1786–96), hailed as a 'truly grand church . . . with . . . exceedingly beautiful and rich . . . ornamental architecture . . . one of the most striking resemblances of the Grecian and Roman architecture . . . and . . . for ages, a proof of the good taste and munificence of the parishioners', notable particularly for its 'lofty steeple, the height [202 feet] and numerous enrichments of which justly excite admiration' (pl. 673).[57] This was the outcome of an architecturally enlightened Vestry that welcomed competitors whose professional experiences were anything but parochial. One of them, Thomas Harrison, had studied in Rome between 1769 and 1776, making numerous drawings of antique buildings, as well as schemes for altering St Peter's sacristy and the Piazza del Popolo.[58] His Newcastle proposal (untraced) was of a uniquely semicircular form with a tetrastyle Doric temple portico flanked by steeples at the extremities of the straight elevation, which reminded a contemporary of the 'ground part . . . of a noble structure . . . at Rome', presumably the Theatre of Marcellus.[59] This can be associated with an undated, more expansive design still among the architect's papers (pl. 674).[60] It is a Serlian demonstration that in the Marcellian theatre are 'found forms as beautiful as any I have ever seen in ancient ruins [with a cornice] very far from Vitruvian doctrine', leading to a conclusion 'that it is not enough to say "I can do it because the ancients did it" [since] even if the ancient architect was licentious, we must not be so', and, in turn, to warn readers that while Vitruvius is 'an infallible guide and rule . . . anyone who . . . had seen the wonderful works built by the Greeks . . . would judge [them] better by far than those of the Romans'.[61]

But Newcastle was not ready for Harrison's Continental avant-gardism and preferred a more familiar native solution by David Stephenson, a local man trained at the Royal Academy Schools in London during 1782–3. His now-lost inaugural design was described as 'an elipse, with a colonade of coupled columns, of the Ionic order, the length of the whole south front, over the colonade an attic, from which rises a dome', which was approved in 1786 but 'considerably altered' in execution.[62] The striking result (pl. 673), sited spectacularly above the steep north bank of the River Tyne, is an original and dramatic rethinking of Gibbs's published St Martin-in-the-Fields 'Round Design' (pl. 675). Stephenson's tetrastyle fluted Doric portico, derived from the early Roman Republican temple of Hercules at Cori (Lazio), the shaft of its hybrid order rising directly from a base devoid of torus, fillet and apophyge in the Greek manner,[63] though stately in itself, is nevertheless diminished by the bulk and loftiness of the steeple (202 feet high, a proportion of 1 to 5), nearly twice that of St Martin's (1 to 3). The dramatic voids created by diagonally placed Tuscan columns standing proud of the upper cores may inten-

674 Thomas Harrison. Entrance front design, All Saints, Newcastle-upon-Tyne, Northumberland, ?1786. Pen and ink and wash. Grosvenor Museum, Chester 1959.79.8.

675 James Gibbs. South elevation design for a 'Round church', St Martin-in-the-Fields, London, 1720, in Gibbs 1728, pl. 15. Engraving.

676 David Stephenson. West entrance, All Saints, Newcastle-upon-Tyne, Northumberland, 1786–96.

tionally have been a foil to the flying buttressed, medieval tower of nearby St Nicholas (now the cathedral), then the two most prominent structures of the Newcastle skyline.[64] Flanking the portico the single-storey Morning Chapel and vestry form a delicate screen of paired Ionic pilasters laid against rusticated walls with tripartite fan-lit windows executed in elegantly detailed golden sandstone, which continue along the sides and merge with the bulging units of the oval body articulated by single, dosseret pilasters and tall windows surmounted by panelled and blind balustraded attics, forming an eastern chancel and a western entrance (pl. 676). Behind and above rises the double-storeyed rotunda, pilastered below, astylar above, sweeping amphitheatre-like round the north side, 'the curvature of which is remarkably elegant'.[65] The distinctly different and sometimes disconnected shapes and articulations, particularly the use of Doric and Ionic orders of varying sizes agitating across the exterior, give the building an undisciplined (or perhaps a more apposite term would be a picturesque) yet exciting, uniquely Stephensonian character. Thomas Sopwith, who served as churchwarden during construction and published the first definitive study of the building in 1826, has left a compelling description of its impact, which is worth quoting fully (pls 677–8). The portico leads into 'a lofty vestibule of circular form, having a noble vaulted roof, supported by eight coupled Ionic pilasters . . . enriched with . . . chaste and elegant decorations [and] carved foliage work', lit by Diocletian windows in the vault; the order is painted white as 'a chaste contrast to the stone colour of the walls'.

> On entering the [body] the spectator is pleased and surprised by the union of elegance and convenience. The beautiful curvature of the pews, the fine perspective of the columns . . . the cast iron, cased with mahogany [and reiterating those of the portico] . . . which support the gallery, the chaste and elegant ornaments of the chancel, and the numerous windows . . . combined in producing an effect rarely equalled in ecclesiastical structures of modern date. On advancing further into the church . . . an aisle of considerable width, flagged with large stones, descends by four steps to the level of the . . . central part of the church, and continues along three sides of the fourteen pews which form the auditory . . . separated from an aisle, the floor of which is . . . raised a few inches [and] small gates . . . At the north end of a floored aisle ascends by four steps to a passage extending nearly round the church. . . . Less picturesque, but no less curious or beautiful, is the

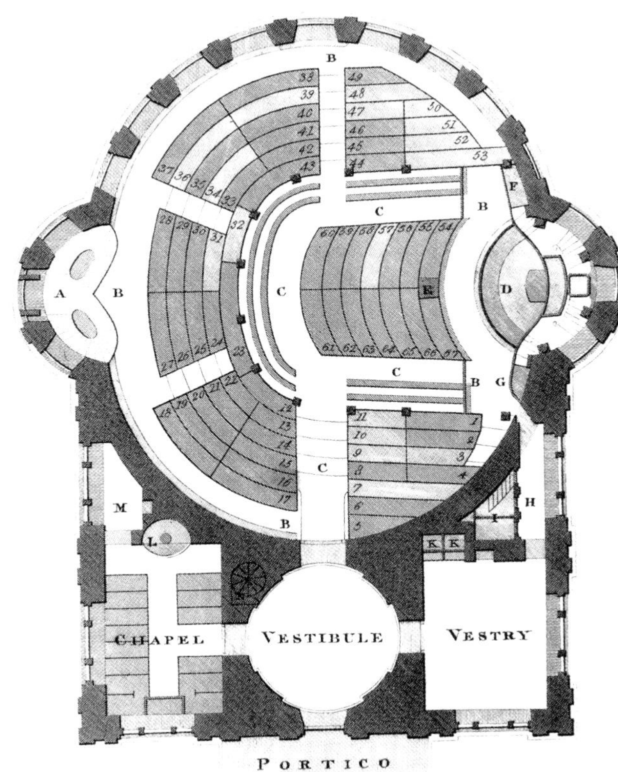

appearance of the church when viewed from the chancel, as it is here that the whole of the auditory is presented to the view . . . The regularity and compactness of every part . . . are peculiarly striking. . . . The gallery is uncommonly spacious . . . lighted by . . . fifteen windows: the bars are of cast iron [of] light and elegant . . . appearance. . . . Immediately above . . . an Ionic cornice, exceedingly beautiful and rich, with massive and highly ornamented modillions, extends round the church. From this extends a coved ceiling possessed of singular beauty . . . thrown into twelve compartments, divided into ribs, which diverge from an ellipse in the centre . . . from the middle of which the chandelier is suspended.[66]

Despite the seemingly ideal form of the Pantheonic body for a city 'daily increasing in its population and opulence',[67] the church came under criticism as early as 1794 on grounds of 'the disadvantage to which all circular buildings are subject, – that of drowning the voice of the preacher, and rendering it impossible for

677 (*left*) David Stephenson. Ground plan, All Saints, Newcastle-upon-Tyne, Northumberland, in Sopwith 1826, following p. 95.

678 (*below*) David Stephenson. Interior towards the west, All Saints, Newcastle-upon-Tyne, Northumberland, 1786–96. English Heritage (National Monuments Record, 130/4).

679 (*top*) George Steuart. South-west view, St Chad, Shrewsbury, Shropshire, 1789–92.

680 (*above*) George Steuart. North elevation, St Chad, Shrewsbury, Shropshire, 1789–92.

those who are seated at any distance from him to hear his discourse'. Nevertheless, it was regarded as a 'most beautiful modern building' perhaps supplemented by a local belief that the ancient dedication to All Saints originated in the Roman name for this part of Newcastle – Pampedon, after the Pantheon in Rome, dedicated to all the gods, hence All Saints.[68]

The adoption of St Martin's 'Round Design' at St Chad, Shrewsbury (1789–92; pl. 679), caused heated discussions between the building committee and its architect, George Steuart, and led the bishop who consecrated the church on 20 August 1792 to comment that while admiring 'the beauty & the neatness of the Building . . . it wants the solemnity necessary in a place of worship. I almost conceive I am entering a Theatre' – a contrary aspect of All Saints that Sopwith made abundantly clear in his description quoted above.[69] Torrington thought St Chad 'ugly . . . improper, and would better suit a Pantheon – a Ranelagh or a drawing room'; Robert Southey compared its 'preposterous' 100-foot-diameter body and small circular lobbies to 'an overgrown spider'.[70]

The creation of this splendid church began spectacularly on 9 July 1788, when the medieval crossing tower suddenly collapsed and destroyed most of the fabric (see p. 139), energising the parishioners into erecting an expensive new building, costing £17,752. Relocated just outside the town wall, on high ground overlooking an oxbow of the River Severn, it is confined to a narrow strip of virgin ground running south to north, with the chancel facing north rather than east. The approach from the town centre is dominated by the weighty ensemble of Tuscan temple portico, tempietto tower and flanking vestry blocks. The rotundas of the staircase lobby and body are revealed gradually as they unfold along the western elevation, catching the full flood of afternoon sun, intensified by the use of 'best Grinshill Free Stone', a local pale-coloured, fine-grained, siliceous sandstone resistant to weathering and capable of being worked to a smooth surface with sharp detailing.[71]

The basic St Martin components are treated as independent forms of contrasting astylar and plain, richly rusticated and plastered surfaces in carefully stratified storeys, while Steuart abandoned altogether Gibbs's gradually diminishing, multi-tiered steeple for a bolder, two-staged structure, necessitated by having to accommodate a ring of twelve bells, modelled on the Roman building known as the Tour Magne at Nîmes, but with 'Antique Ionic Capitals' probably inspired by Stuart's and Revett's reconstruction of the temple on the Illisus (pl. 642).[72] In place of St Martin's giant order, St Chad's

681 George Steuart. Interior towards the chancel with original pulpit and desk *in situ*, St Chad, Shrewsbury, Shropshire, Shropshire Records and Research Centre, B3769.

body is surrounded by evenly spaced, paired pilasters raised on a tall, rusticated basement forming a grand sweep interrupted only by a large Serliana lighting the rectangular chancel contained within the rotunda circumference (pl. 680). 'The Church is a most beautiful piece of Architecture', reported a visitor in 1794,

> The Body . . . is a perfect Circle . . . No spouts are to be seen on the outside to convey the water down from the top. But at the East end I observed the mouth of two spouts upon the surface of the ground which were conveyed within the walls & it happening to rain at the time I was there I could hear the water falling down, & see it discharged at the . . . mouths.[73]

Inside, the south to north axis processes through three increasingly large and grander round spaces towards the triumphal-arched chancel (pl. 681). The concentrically arranged box pews and exceptionally thin, wood-encased cast-iron columns allowed uninterrupted views to the pulpit, desk and font, originally grouped together in the central arena.

Where Steuart and Stephenson had taken Gibbs's 'Round Church' designs to their most complex conclusions, Jesse Gibson, a minor City of London architect, reduced the portico-vestibule-tower-body ensemble to a few, compact, simple geometric elements, at St Peter-Le-Poer (1788–92; pl. 682), the only domed rotunda church built in the metropolis in the eighteenth century. The small site in Broad Street had no churchyard and was engulfed by terrace houses, which left only the church's entrance front exposed. An Ionic engaged tetrastyle temple portico, with its flanking pilasters, formed a shallow, single-storey screen across

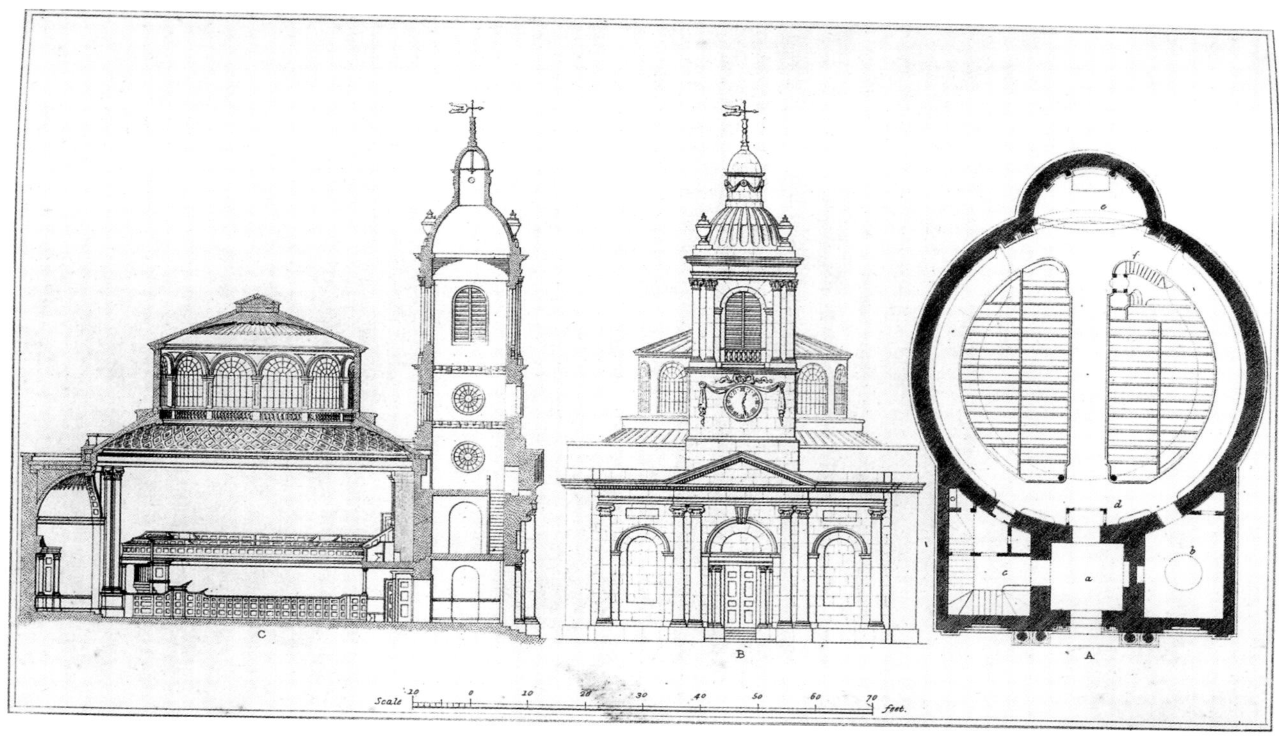

682 John Le Keux after T. Bradberry. Plan, west elevation, longitudinal section, St Peter-Le-Poer, London, 1 September 1825, in Britton and Pugin 1828, vol. II, pl. 2, following p.76. Engraving. Jesse Gibson architect, 1788–92, demolished 1908.

683 Exterior reconstruction of S. Costanza (called the Temple of Bacchus), Rome, in Ware 1738, Fourth Book, pl. LXII. Engraving. Erected second quarter fourth century.

this entire elevation, while the rest of the upper body was camouflaged by a ponderous, square tower forced to the front edge immediately behind the pediment so that it was only after passing through the tiny lobby that the grand gesture of the rotunda was revealed. This 55-foot-diameter by 30-foot-high room of 'light and beautiful appearance' was obsessively naked, with only a narrow gallery attached along three-quarters of the perimeter wall, which was entirely void of windows (prohibited by the site).[74] Early commentators commended this treatment since such fenestration was 'certainly any thing but ornamental or appropriate in modern churches [since they] interfer sadly with classical chasteness of design'.[75] Gibson avoided the criticism sometimes levelled against the Roman Pantheon of introducing pedimented tabernacles in the interior. Soane, who had climbed to the latter's oculus to make detailed studies in 1778–9, later wrote that as 'an hypaethral temple . . . open in the centre' (pl. 608) the altars of the Pantheon 'require roofs to protect them from the weather', and yet 'no example, however respectable, can justify the adoption of that which is repugnant to common sense, and to those first principals which every man should comprehend'.[76] St Peter-Le-Poer's apsidal chancel framed by monumental, fluted pilasters rose only to the height of the main entablature, thereby also avoiding a controversy mentioned in Palladio, who was 'absolutely positive' that in the Pantheon the central chapel opposite the entrance, despite its arch breaking into the pilasters of the attic, was integral with the ancient fabric and not, as some believed, 'enlarged in line with the requirement in

684 J. Wells. Approved perspective design, St Mary, Banbury, Oxfordshire, 6 September 1790. Engraving. The Bodleian Library, University of Oxford, G.A.Oxon.a.76, ff. 11/12. Samuel Pepys Cockerell architect, 1790–97.

Christian times that there should be a main altar larger than the rest'.[77] Gibson omitted the attic altogether, instead raising his tautly coved ceiling, with its diamond coffers inspired by the Temple of the Sun and Moon in Rome, directly from the entablature and in turn surmounting it with a 32-foot-diameter, saucer-domed clerestory ringed by twelve windows, the sole source of natural light. This was based on the early Christian mausoleum-church of Santa Costanza in Rome as reconstructed by Palladio (pl. 683).[78]

In the 1790s Samuel Pepys Cockerell, who was then remodelling St Margaret, Westminster, in its final Georgian gothic guise (pls 246–7), produced two highly unusual hybrid rotunda churches. The exterior of Banbury, Oxfordshire (1790–97; pl. 684), conflated the portico of St Paul, Deptford (pl. 362), and the tower of Long Ditton (by Robert Taylor, his master, pl. 332), encircling its base with pairs of prominent Italian renaissance-inspired scrolled buttresses.[79] The Roman Doric order is set against rusticated walls constructed of local Hornton stone with the plinth 'axed perpendicularly on the face worked out of the old stone . . . the Ashler rustic work twelve Inches thick . . . the plain Ashler work eight inches thick [and] the Ionick Capitals in the Columns of the Tower projecting ¾ of the diameter in a bold strong manner', according to the masons' contract.[80] This robust treatment led to a comparison of the church being 'more like a gaol than a Christian temple', a building suitable only for 'the exhibition of gladiators or of wild beasts in ancient Rome

685 Samuel Pepys Cockerell. North-east view, St Martin Outwich, London, 1795–8. Photographed prior to demolition, 1874. English Heritage (National Monuments Record, AA75/01930).

but . . . totally unfit for a Christian church'.[81] Indeed, it was physically heavy as well. The *Gentleman's Magazine* reported in 1794 how, as workmen were 'drawing up a large cornice stone, the tackle suddenly gave way . . . when, owing to the great projection of the stones in the lower row of cornice, and the small hold they have on the wall, the weight of the falling stone forced several of them out of their place'. This had tragic human consequences, as we have seen (pp. 137–8).[82]

686 W. G. Smith. Ground plan, St Martin Outwich, London, in William Thornbury, *Old and New London*, vol. 1, 1883, p. 534. Samuel Pepys Cockerell architect, 1795–8, demolished 1874.

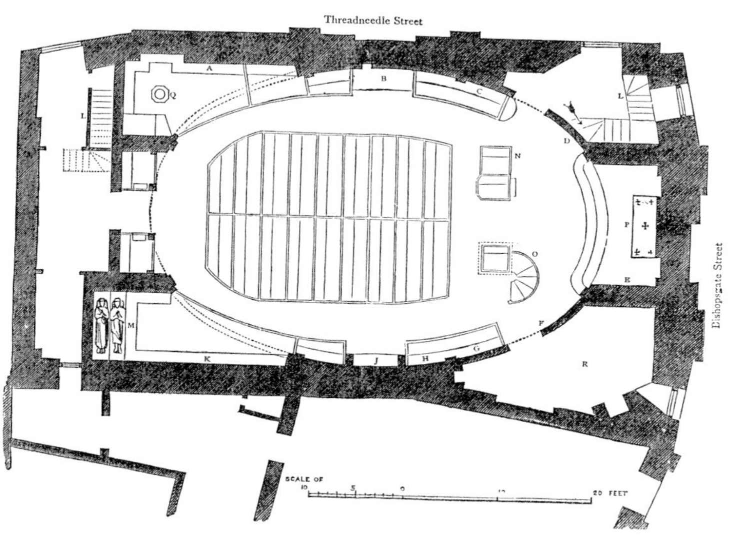

Cockerell's St Martin Outwich, London (1795–8; pl. 685), was one of the most eccentric churches of the period, described as 'a complete representation of a goal, accompanied by marks of extreme strength, very ill suited to its diminutive outline'.[83] He had inherited a small, irregular medieval site (48 by 74 feet) at the busy intersection of Bishopsgate and Threadneedle Streets, with only those two elevations capable of architectural treatment, the west and south being obscured by buildings. The simple domed tempietto belfry, therefore, was placed at the east end of the church. To abate traffic noises the lower walls, except for small windows lighting the lobby and vestibule to either side of the chancel, are solid, horizontal channelled masonry articulated by pilaster-like piers and blind recesses. Daylight came from Diocletian windows in the oval clerestory and its short, projecting north and east arms. J. P. Malcolm, in *Londinium Redivivum* (in the fourth volume of 1807), described the interior (pl. 686) as

> a complete oval, which, though not a common form for a church, has an excellent effect; [its] West end . . . has a deep recess, the whole intercolumnation in width; [the] Sacrarium resembles the Western recess in outline . . . but the sides are plain. Three steps lead to the altar . . . Each angle of the [main] walls, which make nearly a square, compose a gallery, fronted by neat railings, and ornamented with brackets [with a] very pleasing effect produced by . . . suspending the branches before each gallery.

Four fluted pilasters on the north and south have 'Cherubims between volutes for capitals . . . connected by a strange substitute for an entablature, formed by carved fluting, with roses in the centre of the arch; [the ceiling] is a semi-oval, with very bad pannel of the same figure, enclosing a large flower'. The chancel was paved with 'highly-polished veined marble, the ground a bright yellow, and the veins white and purple', its steps covered by a rich Wilton carpet; 'two very correct copies of antique stools, ornamented with purple drapery, stand on the platform'; the arched communion table 'in imitation of red marble, spotted with white, with a very high polish [and] caryatide winged boys, whose arms are crossed on their breasts . . . painted white, though of stone [with two] dark velvet cushions'.[84] Few churches of this decade anticipated the stunningly florid character of fully blown Regency classicism so vividly.[85]

Octangularity, which had first appeared in recent British churches early in the century (pl. 579) and gained a foothold in the 1750s (pls 578, 581–4), reached an apogee during these last two decades. In 1782–3 that itinerant evangelising wonder and leading light of the Countess of Huntingdon's Connexion, the Revd Roland Hill, son of a Shropshire baronet, erected the Surrey Chapel in Southwark as his London headquarters, the first effort of a minor architect named William Thomas (pls 689–90).[86] Measuring 85 feet in diameter and capable of accommodating 5,000, it was a version of the Norwich Octagon, originally doubled to sixteen sides, achieving almost full rotundity but subsequently reduced to eight, with a top-lit dome supported on an equal number of slender cast-iron columns forming a nearly circular gallery. To maximise the seating, vestibule, vestry and gallery staircases were contained in circular pavilions attached at cardinal points to the outer perimeter. Even so, Thomas inadequately anticipated the huge crowds attracted to Hill's sermonising and in execution these appendages were refashioned into bigger, inelegant boxes, while the dome, at first internally ribbed and coffered, was stripped of ornament and rose from segmental arches rather than a straight entablature.[87] The steeply pitched roof echoes Robert Adam's reconstructed Temple of Jupiter at Spalato (pl. 687), long in use as a Christian cathedral, about which he observed that the 'Form . . . in Temples . . . is uncommon in the ancient Buildings of the Romans . . . But having found the Roman Stamp upon the Tyles . . . there was no Room left to doubt its Antiquity.'[88]

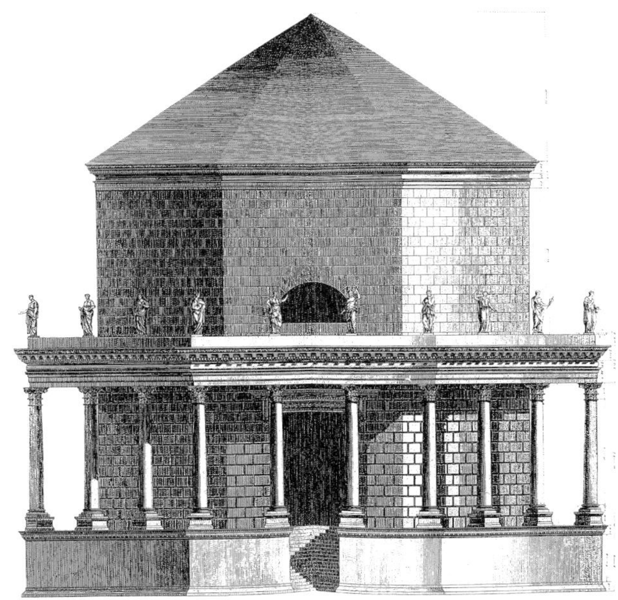

687 'Geometrical Elevation of the Temple of Jupiter', Diocletian's Palace, Spalatro, Dalmatia, in Adam 1764, pl. XXIX. Engraving.

At Steuartown in northern Edinburgh, on land in the New Town acquired between 1785 and 1791 by David Steuart, a merchant and former Lord Provost, Adam proposed building an octagonal-bodied church (pl. 688) with identical tetrastyle temple porticoes on the west and east sides (the eastern one with a blind door backing against the communion table) and enclosed tetrastyle porches on the north and south

688 Robert Adam. 'Design for a Church for the North part of Edinburgh', St George Chapel (Episcopal), Steuartown, Lothian, Scotland, detail, 1785–91. Pen and ink and wash. Sir John Soane's Museum, AD 44/99.

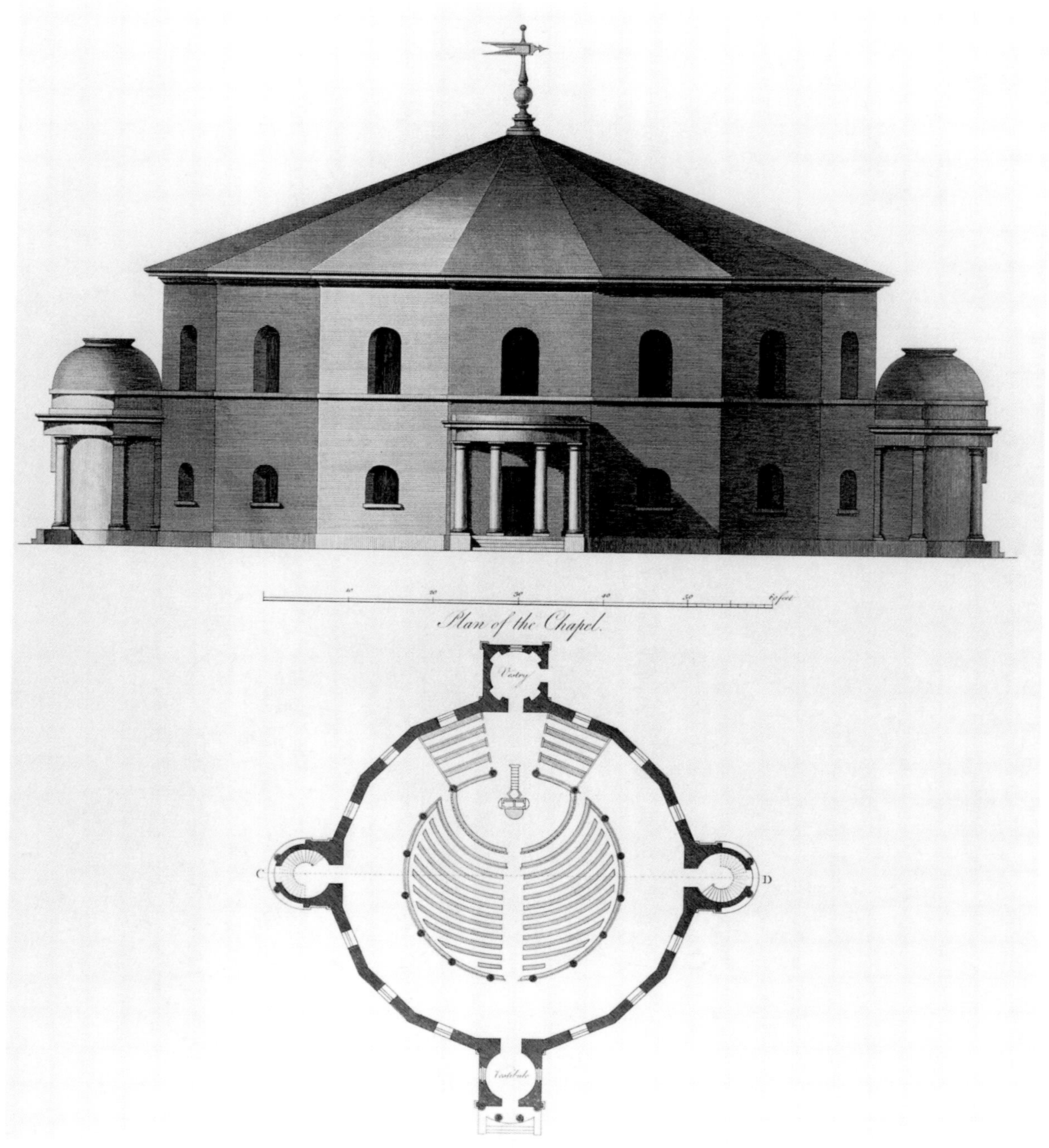

689 J. Miller. 'The Plan and Elevation of the West Front of Surrey Chapel in St Georges road Southwark', London, 1 February 1783, in Thomas 1783, pl. xx. Engraving. W. Thomas architect, 1783, destroyed in Blitz, 1940.

forming a double axis recalling Palladio's Villa Rotunda. A delicately ornamented band below the entablature runs round the body, dividing the ground and attic storeys, with a diminutive, Mistley-like domed turret crowning the octagonal roof, which reinforces both centrality and symmetry (pl. 629).[89] In an unrealised scheme for the Gaelic-speaking congregation at Cromarty (*circa* 1783; pl. 691), Adam chose a hybrid Doric pilaster to emphasise the pair of tetrastyle engaged temple porticoes. Along the projecting side walls the order is discontinued, but a notion of pseudoperipterality is preserved in single triglyphs in

690 A. Pugin and W. J. White after Rudolph Ackermann, 'Interior of Surry Chapel', Southwark, London, 10 May 1812. Aquatint engraving. London Metropolitan Archives (Guildhall Library, 19469). William Thomas architect, 1783, destroyed in Blitz, 1940.

691 Robert Adam. Design for the 'Elevation of one Side of a Church for George Ross Esqr. Near Cromarty', Highlands, Scotland, detail, *c.*1783. Pen and ink and wash. Sir John Soane's Museum, AD 45/45.

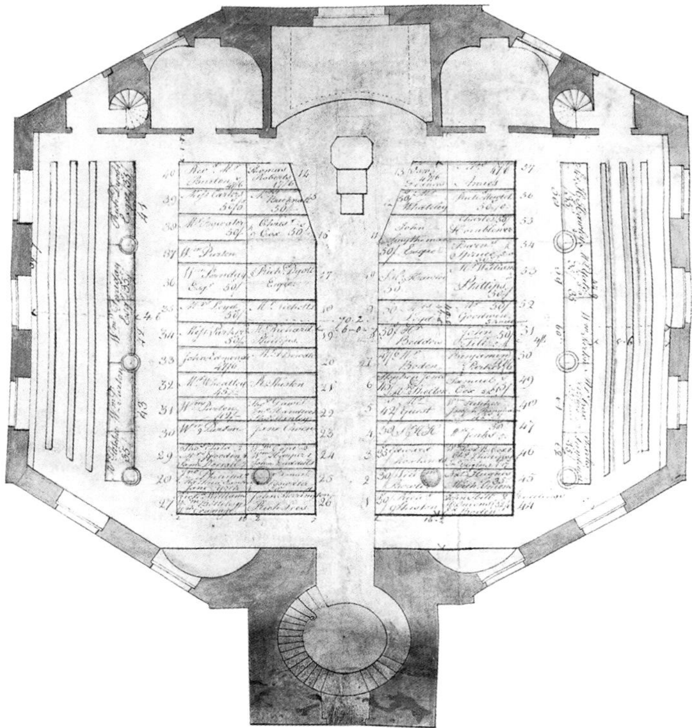

692 (*above*) Thomas Telford. Plan design, St Michael, Madeley, Shropshire, 20 January 1794. Pen and ink and wash. Shropshire Records and Research Centre, 2280/6/57. Erected 1793–7.

693 (*left*) Thomas Telford. Entrance front, St Michael Madeley, Shropshire, 1793–7. Shropshire Records and Research Centre, B238A.

the entablature placed directly over the positions where pilasters would otherwise be expected, a conceit of Italian renaissance origin.[90] No other British architect seems to have employed this particular deconstruction device, though it has kinship with Newton's absent pilaster at Battersea (pl. 638).

Octangularity proved particularly apt at Madeley, Shropshire, with a congregation denominated Methodist that frequented the Anglican parish church, where in 1764 John Wesley had preached in a medieval building so small that a window near the pulpit was removed to allow worshippers to congregate in the churchyard.[91] A visitor in 1792 reported that the interior was 'ill contrived . . . the Walls supporting the . . . tower taking up much room obscuring the Minister from part of the Congregation & other parts . . . are inconvenienced by heavy & low galleries'.[92] Telford described his new church of 1793–7 as of 'very peculiar construction' (pl. 692),[93] where 'Galleries being . . . considered absolutely necessary, the design was made with the view of forming and lighting the body . . . independent of them. For this purpose it was made 70 foot by 50 foot, from which a space at each end of the four angles is cut off, to admit of large windows.'[94] The resulting twenty windows on two storeys, in addition to one in the chancel, all with thin iron frames, are positioned nearest to the central space occupied by a triple-decker pulpit; there were no awkward, dark corners. Curve-ended vestry rooms tucked into the two eastern angles flanking the chancel mirror elliptical recesses on either side of the west door. A majestic tower rises over the square portico (pl. 693). The inherent sobriety of Nonconformity – the celebrated Evangelical vicar John Fletcher and his successor, who had devoted decades to the spiritual welfare of a rural community struggling to find its way in the new mechanised world of the nearby Ironbridge iron manufactories – with its emphasis on rational geometry and rejection of ornamental embellishment, is perfectly expressed in this building. The subtly engaged pedimented porch, chunky tower and cast-iron gallery columns produce an economical dignity entirely suitable to the no-nonsense nature of a church serving this early industrial heartland.[95]

Horbury parish church, Yorkshire (1789–94; pl. 694), designed by John Carr towards the end of his enormously successful career, was financed and built by him for a reported £10,000 as a homage to the otherwise modest village of his birth, a rare expression of Georgian private philanthropy, proudly proclaimed in both the pedimental inscription – 'JOHANNES CARR, ARCHITECTUS GLORIA DEO IN EXCELSIS' – and the fine engraved view by Malton published in 1791. The local press considered it 'the handsomest building of it size in the country', reflecting 'the highest honor' on the architect; at the consecration on 18 May 1794 'a thousand of the inhabitants . . . conducted him into the Church'.[96] The circumstances of the enterprise offered scope for an unorthodox plan (pl. 695): an elongated octagon with internally semicircular east and west apses (a variation on Adam's Cromarty, pl. 691), rectangular lobbies projecting from the middle of the north and south elevations, with each of these cardinal adjuncts screened by pairs of Corinthian columns from the central, barrel-vaulted congregational space.[97] The southern spur serves as the principal entrance emphasised by a monumental, engaged Ionic tetrastyle temple portico facing the main street, while the tower rises from a square base attached to the west end. This results in an externally irregular Greek cross with an internal

694 (*above*) Thomas Malton after John Carr. 'Elevation of the Church at Horbury near Wakefield', St Peter, Horbury, Yorkshire, 1 November 1791. Engraving. Author's collection. J. Carr architect, 1789–94.

695 (*below*) John Carr. Plan, St Peter, Horbury, Yorkshire. J. Carr architect, 1789–94.

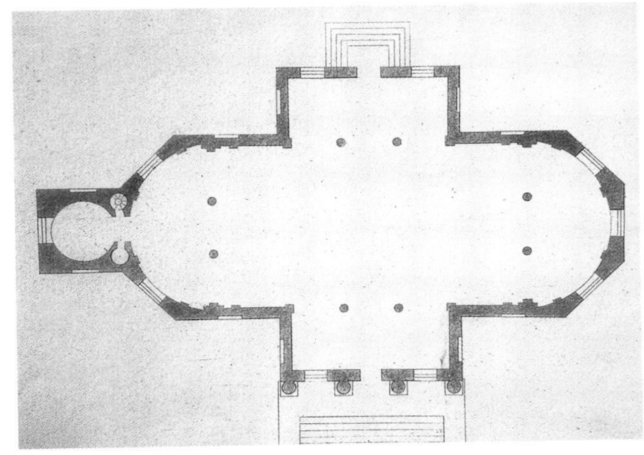

696 Reville and van Mael after Schwender. South elevation, St Mary, Paddington, London, in Stieglitz 1800, pl. 45. Engraving. RIBA Library Photographs Collection. John Plaw architect, 1788–91.

697 Reveille and van Mael after Schwender. Plan, St Mary, Paddington, London, in Stieglitz 1800, pl. 46. Engraving. RIBA Library Drawings Collection. John Plaw architect, 1788–91.

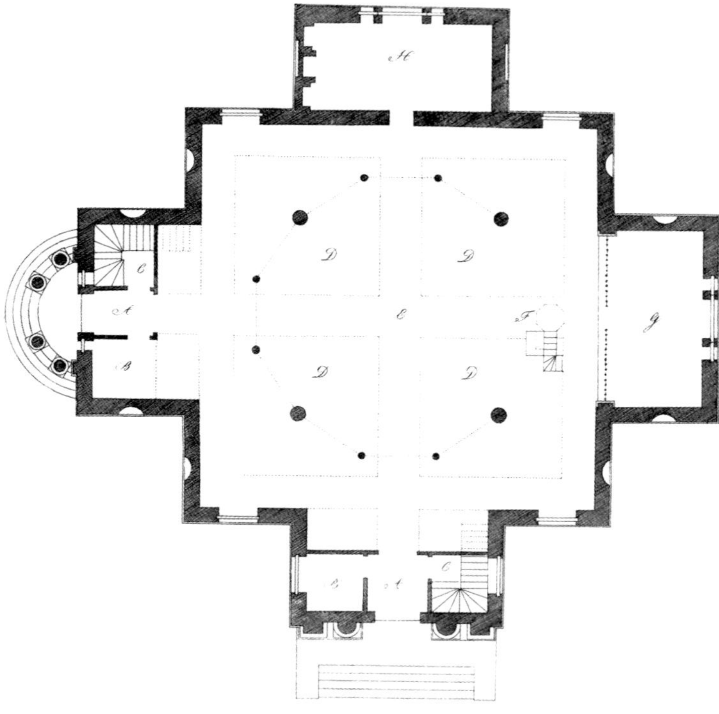

double axis that disorientated an early visitor: supposing (correctly) that the portico marked the building's front, which therefore ought to have been located at the west end, 'what can be more incongruous' than the steeple at one end and 'at the other a kind of anomalous termination utterly unknown to the good taste of antiquity'.[98]

The Greek-cross plan, with its four equal-length arms, possessed special poignancy in the eighteenth century for its particular association with early Christianity and such buildings as the so-called Mausoleum of Galla Placidia at Ravenna (*circa* 425).[99] The former imperial capital, which by the eighteenth century had shrunk to a backwater, still attracted occasional British visitors, including John Talman during 1714–16 and Robert Adam in 1755–6.[100] Equally pertinent, the pattern provided models for grand renaissance churches, most famously Santa Maria delle Carceri in Prato, the Madonna di San Biagio at Montepulciano and Sant'Eligio degli Orefici in Rome.[101] In England, the quintessential early example is the Unitarian Chapel in York (1692).[102]

698 John Plaw. Interior towards west, St Mary, Paddington, London, 1788–91.

699 John Plaw. Interior section towards the west design, St Mary, Paddington, London, 1788. Pen and ink. Victoria and Albert Museum, DD7E.3007-1909.

At St Mary, Paddington Green, London (1788–91; pls 696–7), John Plaw, best remembered for Belle Isle, his Pantheon-like villa on Lake Windermere, cleverly inserted a domed, central-planned, light-filled space within an austerely geometric, sharp-edged Greek cross. *The Ambulator; or, A pocket companion in a tour round London* (1800) commended it as 'a beautiful structure [which] does the highest credit to the taste of the architect'. Its pastoral position in the middle of the green, 'on an eminence, finely embosomed among venerable elms', may have encouraged different treatment for each of the four arms, as if they are isolated pavilions set in a landscape garden:[103] on the south an engaged Tuscan portico of Portland stone in the manner of St Paul, Covent Garden (pl. 512, undergoing restoration in 1788–93); on the west a smaller, Tuscan half-rotunda porch with a Diocletian window breaking into the upper pediment; on the north a projecting, rectangular vestry with tripartite and Diocletian windows; and on the east an identical projection but with a large Serliana illuminating the chancel. Plaw's daring internal acrobatic structure (pl. 698), demonstrable in a recently identified section working drawing (pl. 699), immediately ran into aesthetic difficulties. An unnamed but

700 Joseph Bonomi and perhaps Heneage Finch, 4th Earl of Aylesford. South-west view, St James, Great Packington, Warwickshire, 1789–92.

'very eminent Architect' to whom the design was submitted for comment in 1788 considered 'the Elevation has not sufficiently in its present Form the Air & appearance of a parish Church [and was] referred back to Mr Plaw to remedy this Fault by making the Cupola more in the Manner of those to be found in Cathedrals, only avoiding what is Gothic', and also suggested that the bells and clock 'might be more commodiously placed over the Entrance without the necessity of building a Tower or Spire. This would . . . tend to give the Building a more characteristic appearance.' Plaw apparently disregarded these recommendations.[104] Worse was to follow. The masons' and carpenters' contracts for internal work specified an elaborate experimental structure of 'Great [and] lesser [columns] bored through the Heart', plinths and piers intended to secure the delicate system of supports rising tier-upon-tier to the flat and taut, paper-thin, Soanian saucer domes on pendentives and segmental arches to create an airy, skeletal interior seating 4–5,000 people 'commodiously'.[105] Instead, it precipitated a structural crisis involving 'Several Sinkings of the Arches', which Plaw assured were 'not dangerous', though subsequently the central vault together with the upper arches and cornice fell in, crushing the supporting piers. Plaw proposed rebuilding the north arch and part of its piers. Two independent surveyors claimed the problem was 'a Defect in the Design', the arches 'not being supported with sufficient Buttments' and suggested alterations that 'will not prevent the Building being finished according to the Section originally designed'. The building committee also 'censured' Plaw for 'Defects in the Plan', to which he 'apologized . . . for all past Misconduct . . . and said he was willing to do any Thing in future to oblige'.[106]

At the opposite extreme is Great Packington, Warwickshire (1789–92), a collaboration between Heneage Finch, 4th Earl of Aylesford, of nearby Packington Hall, and his architect, Joseph Bonomi, whom we have already met in connection with the Spanish chapel (p. 573). A previous proposal, perhaps dating as early as 1766 and intended for the 3rd Earl, attributable to Henry Couchman, the architect of Binley (pl. 523), is a clumsy variation on St Martin-in-the-Fields, but the son, who had toured Italy, was made of sterner stuff and the erected building is one of the most architecturally advanced and original churches of its day in eighteenth-century Europe (pl. 700).[107] Built largely of rich red brick, without the use of timber in the spirit of ancient Roman construction, and though only 63 feet square yet looking immensely monumental (pl. 701), it rejects not only a steeple but also a prominent entrance (the *in antis* loggia with flanking octagonal lobbies shown in his presentation drawing was ultimately abandoned). Instead, it relies for impact on huge, unframed Diocletian windows flanked in the outer bays by diminutive versions stacked like a Roman columbarium, stressing the church's extra-mortuary function. The exterior resembles certain Venetian renaissance churches, probably not coincidentally, since the Bonomi family originated in Venice and the architect had visited the city on his journey to England in 1784.[108] There is, however, no obvious prototype for the sandstone, domed-capped sarcophagi-like blocks rising over the corner bays – functionless except on a symbolic level yet strikingly picturesque in the Packington landscape. In the Greek-cross interior the sole concessions to ancient Rome are the Pantheonic pedimented altarpiece and the groin vaults springing from four freestanding columns placed close to the walls, which relate to a perspective of the tepidarium of Diocletian's Baths as imagined before conversion by Michelangelo into Santa Maria degli Angeli, drawn by the 4th Earl after Desgodetz's *Les Edifices antiques de Rome* (1682) and perhaps his contribution to the design.[109] But it is to Bonomi that the interior owes the solemnity of un-pilastered walls, the reduced cornice, the powerfully coffered barrel vaults of the short arms, plastered brick

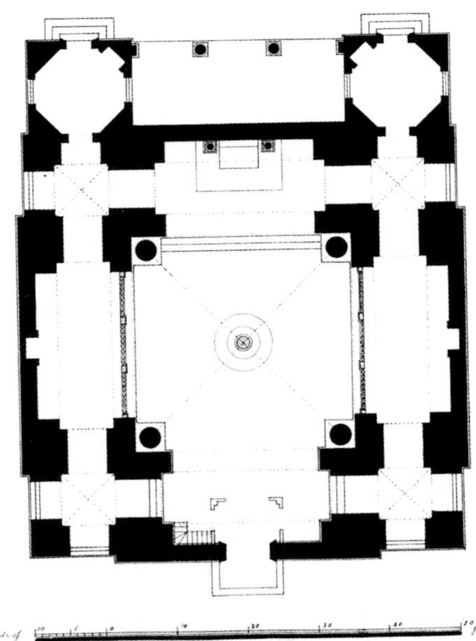

701 Joseph Bonomi and perhaps Heneage Finch 4th Earl of Aylesford. Plan, west front, section towards the east 'Design for a Parish Church built at Great Packington, Warwickshire…begun…1789 & finished…1792', St James. Pen and ink and wash. RIBA Library Drawings Collection, E6/8/1–2.

702 Orazio Porta. Half-section and elevation design for a church, *c.*1600, in The Vasari Album owned by Robert Adam. Pen and ink and wash. Sir John Soane's Museum, Picture Room, case 87, no. 681.

painted in imitation of ashlar throughout and the subtly raised perimeter corridors. Above all, the stocky, fluted, primitive Greek Doric columns derived from the fifth-century BC Temple of Neptune at Paestum, which Bonomi studied first-hand in 1784, marking their first appearance in an executed British church.[110] Willey Reveley perfectly evokes the order's impact:

> the causes of the sublime may easily be perceived. The simplicity of the basement, the sweeping lines of the fluting . . . and grand straight lines of the entablature crossing in their directions the graceful ones of the fluting . . . all contribute to this striking effect . . . There is a certain appearance of external duration . . . that gives a solemn and majestic feeling . . . masculine boldness . . . awful dignity and grandeur.[111]

Robert Adam's exploration of the form has its origins in two renaissance architecture albums that he possessed, one previously owned by Vasari, the other by G. B. Montano, both rich with examples (pl. 702).[112] Moreover, his father, William, had designed a beautiful Greek-cross-planned church with a central domed rotunda at Hamilton, Lanarkshire, in the years 1731–4

703 William Adam. North-east view, Hamilton parish church, Lanarkshire, Scotland, 1731–4, steeple, 1748, interior altered 1926.

(pl. 703), which must have found sanctuary in the heart of his brilliant progeny.[113] In Robert's scheme at Lasswade, Midlothian (1791; pls 704–5), concave-fronted lofts occupy all four arms, each firmly supported on paired Tuscan columns, with the inner angles of the piers trimmed to form an uninterrupted, fully integrated space. It is not known why the heritor rejected this elegant design in favour of a quite ordinary Greek-cross building clearly not designed by Adam.[114]

In Adam's last and most prestigious ecclesiastical commission, for the new, cathedral-like St George, Charlotte Square, Edinburgh (1791; pl. 706), which was to form the climax of the east–west axis through the New Town, the origin of the complex amalgamation of temple-form body with interconnecting square, rectangular and apsidal internal spaces lay in his early caprices drawn in Italy in the 1750s and in lateral twin-towered Mistley (pl. 629).[115] As finally developed, an elaborate octastyle temple portico of coupled Corinthian columns and a lofty dome on drum complement his New Building of Edinburgh University (begun 1786), the centrepiece of the Old Town.[116] The room sequence (pl. 707) recalls the scenographic distribution of the Vasari Album designs and the numerous schemes for St Peter, Rome, to which Adam returned at the end of his life.[117] He died suddenly on 3 March 1792, before work began in Charlotte Square, though a similar church, designed by Robert Reid, was erected there in the years 1811–14.[118]

Adam's younger contemporary, John Soane, introduced Picturesque notions to these complex patterns, reaching their *ne plus ultra* in his unrealised 'Sepulchral Church' at Tyringham, Buckinghamshire (1796–1800; pl. 708). Its triangular form derived from Laugier's rec-

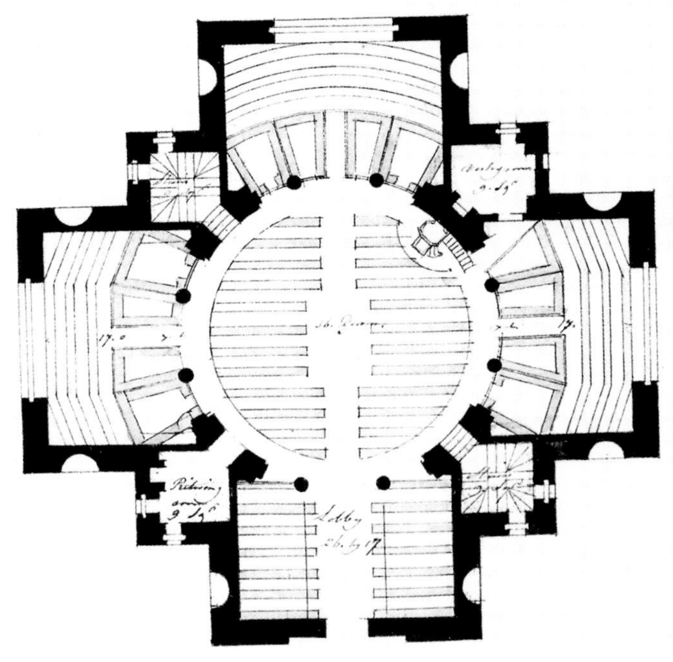

704 (*above left*) Robert Adam. 'Lateral Elevation of a New design for the Church of Laswade', Midlothian, Scotland, detail, 1791. Pen and ink and wash. Sir John Soane's Museum, AD 33/79-80.

705a and b (*above right and right*) Robert Adam. 'Section through [and] Ground Plan of the Church of Laswade', Midlothian, Scotland, 1791. Pen and ink and wash. Sir John Soane's Museum, AD 33/81-82.

706 Robert Adam. Entrance front and part plan 'Design of the West side of Charlotte Square extending 522 feet with the great Church in the Center, & 5 or 6 Houses on each side of it', St George, Edinburgh, Lothian, Scotland, 1791. Pen and ink and wash. Sir John Soane's Museum, AD 32/4.

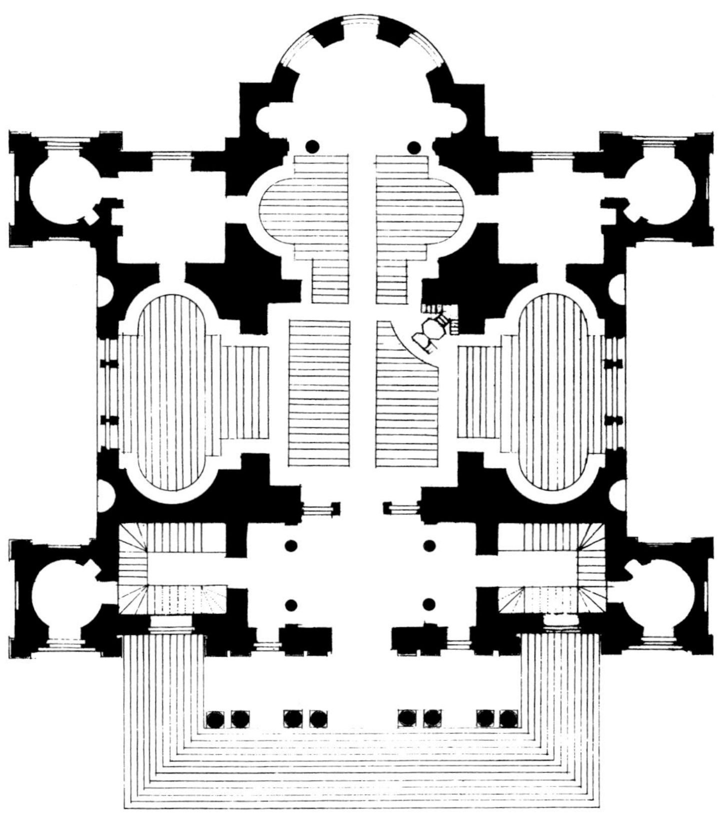

707 Robert Adam. 'Plan for the Church in Charlotte Square Edinburgh' (St. George), Lothian, Scotland, 1791. Pen and ink and wash. Sir John Soane's Museum, AD 32/5.

ommendation in *Essai sur l'Architecture* (1753): 'one can give churches all forms imaginable . . . All geometrical figures, from the triangle to the circle, can serve to vary continuously the composition.' He condemned those critics for whom

> inventions are troublesome and incapable of bringing forth anything new. No doubt at all, it is easy to erect over the plan of an equilateral triangle a church which will look most attractive. This is how I would set about it. I inscribe in the triangle a circle that gives me the outline of a dome . . . At the three angles I construct three rotundas which gives me three sanctuaries where I place three altars. In the center of each of the three facades I make an opening for a door which produces three entrances each having an altar facing them.[119]

Gandy's perspective with 'Moonlight effect' reveals how the sculpture of *Charity with Children* would be backlit against geometrical painted glass, and the illuminated lantern serve as a religious beacon. The interior (pl. 709) is an arresting image of a Georgian church in operation, the preaching focused on the central, triangular, light-filled space covered by a canopied dome with its integrated pendentives resting on segmental arches.[120]

Nowhere is the range of architectural solutions more dramatically demonstrated than in the series of proposals for replacing the dilapidated medieval church at Hackney between 1779 and 1814 by Soane's close friend, James Spiller, a pupil of James Wyatt. This north-east London suburb was then a prosperous parish of 9,500 souls with a substantial community of wealthy

708 (*above*) Joseph Michael Gandy. View of the 'Sepulchral Church', Tyringham, Buckinghamshire, undated. Watercolour. Sir John Soane's Museum, P269. Sir John Soane architect, 1796–1800.

709 (*right*) Joseph Michael Gandy and A. van Assen. Interior view of the 'Sepulchral Church', Tyringham, Buckinghamshire, undated. Watercolour. Sir John Soane's Museum, 13/5/7. Sir John Soane architect, 1796–1800.

City merchants, where the 'necessity of erecting a more spacious' church was compelling because the local Dissenting chapels had been 'very considerably enlarged before the new church was thought of; and as Nonconformists are seldom deficient in zeal, it is no unusual thing with them to wait upon strangers, and offer them the best accommodation, &c. upon the first coming among us'.[121]

One scheme (pl. 710), capable of holding 2,500, featured paired, free-standing columns tied to the octagonal body by entablature sections, an externalising of the Temple of Jupiter at Spalato (which Adam himself had adapted at Mistley, pl. 629),[122] the column-

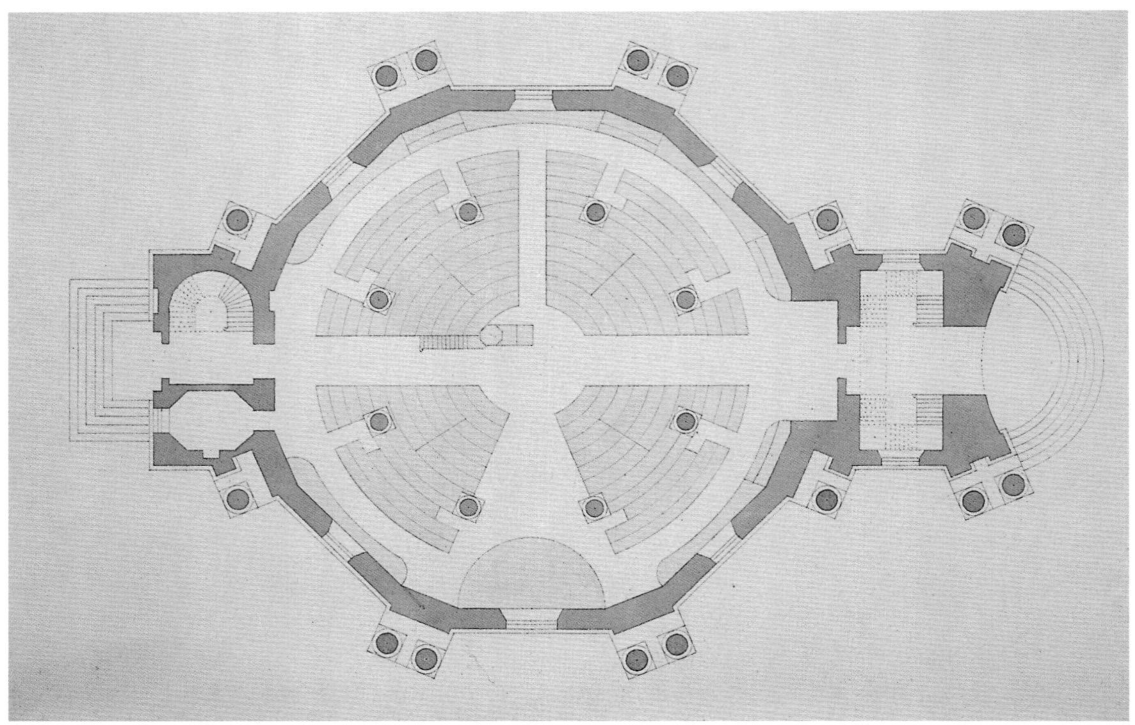

710 (*above*) James Spiller. Design 'upon the Principal of an Octagon', west is to the left, St John, Hackney, London, 1791. Pen and ink and wash. Sir John Soane's Museum, 47/10/22

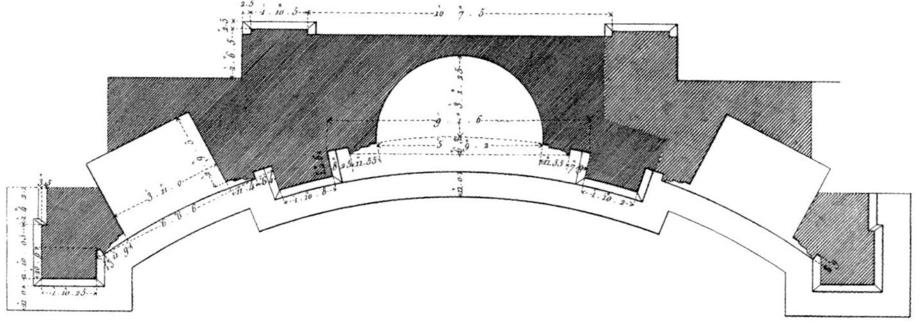

711 (*right*) View of 'The Monument of Philopappus' with plan reconstruction, in Stuart and Revett 1794, vol. III, ch. V, pl. XXIX. Engraving. Erected AD 114–16.

encircled exterior anticipating the columnar rotunda inside. The strikingly unusual concave front was probably inspired by the Monument of Philopappus, Athens (pl. 711).[123] The executed building (pl. 712) is a Greek cross 'in the plainest manner', 'simplex mundities', seating 2,125 and costing £10,000, begun in 1792 and opened within five years, though the tower was not completed until 1814.[124] Constructed of yellow stock brick with minimum stone dressings and deeply dentilled, Covent Garden-inspired pediments crowning all four arms (two have since been removed), the walls are wrapped by broad, slightly projecting Tuscan piers linked by arches rising through two storeys, a Soanian homage as well as a stern, unrelenting treatment widespread in late Roman and early Christian brick architecture.[125] A large central space covered by a single-span cross vault with galleried aisles accommodated 2,125 (pl. 713).

This treatment accords with a general trend in late neoclassicism memorialised in James Lewis's *Original*

712 James Spiller. South-east view, St John, Hackney, London, 1792–1814, before removal of side pediments, 1955. English Heritage (National Monuments Record, B45/00054).

713 James Spiller. Interior towards the chancel design, St John, Hackney, London, 20 June 1791. Pen and ink and wash. Sir John Soane's Museum, 47/10/31. Erected 1792–1814.

714 (*top*) John Tasker. East view, St Mary's Chapel (Catholic), Lulworth, Dorset, 1786–90.

715 (*above*) John Tasker. South-west view, St Mary's (Catholic) Chapel, Lulworth, Dorset, 1786–90.

716 (*above right*) John Tasker. Ground plan, St Mary's Chapel (Catholic), Lulworth, Dorset, in Hutchins 1796, 2nd edition. Engraving. Erected 1786–90.

Designs in Architecture (1780), to which Spiller subscribed. In the introductory commentary on the history of Greek architecture it advocated as part of a programme of national church building the application of 'strength, convenience and beauty [as] the principal objects to be attended to', cautioning the first not to 'degenerate into heaviness', the next becoming 'futile when over nice, and decoration when too profuse . . . to terminate in confusion'.[126]

A particularly striking experiment in polyform planning survives intact in the Welds' Catholic chapel in the grounds of Lulworth, Dorset (1786–90; pls 714–15), erected after George III sanctioned the venture (pro-

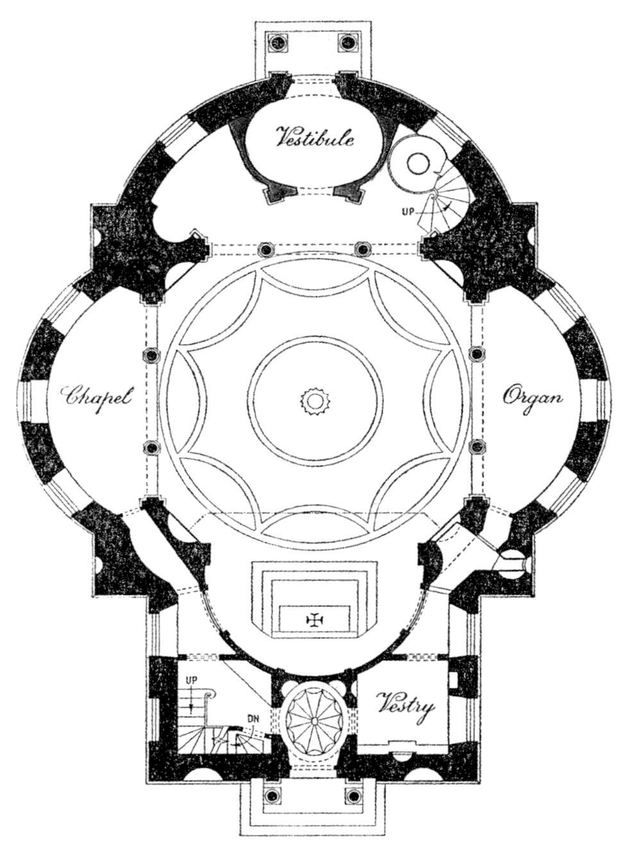

vided it was disguised as the family mausoleum). This charming, deceptively secular-looking building reminded Fanny Burney of 'a Pantheon in miniature' (that is, James Wyatt's Oxford Street place of social entertainment, 1769–72, which in turn derived from Hagia Sophia in Constantinople).[127] The chapel at Lulworth (pls 716–17) is characterised by a complex layering of varied shapes, comprising a square marked by the four external, vase-crowned piers, a circle defined by the central saucer dome, a Trinity-imbued cloverleaf formed by three galleried side apses and a chancel – with its marble and gilt-metal high altar supplied from Rome in 1787 – embedded in a rectangular arm with its domestic façade facing towards the castle, as if some innocuous garden pavilion.[128]

717 John Tasker. Interior towards the west, St Mary's Chapel (Catholic), Lulworth, Dorset, 1786–90. (From Little 1966, pl. 36).

On 15 August 1790 the chapel was consecrated by John Carroll, Bishop of Baltimore. Fourteen years later he launched the building, along Lulworth lines, of the diocesan cathedral to the design of the Yorkshire-born, Washington-based architect, Benjamin Henry Latrobe, marking the climax of a century of fruitful architectural co-operation between Britain and America. This is in part the subject of the final chapter of this book.

718 Dr John Kearsley and Robert Smith. North-east view, Christ Church, Philadelphia, Pennsylvania, 1727–59.

Thirty

BEYOND BRITAIN

I preached a sermon at Great St Helen's [City of London], for erecting a church for the Saltzburghers of Georgia, and collected £33. The people gave most readily, many wishing they had more to give.[1]

Ord'd that Augustine Smith . . . send for As Good An Organ As the . . . Money shall purchase in Great Britain and to have the Same Ensured [against] the Danger of the Seas[2]

By the time Tee Yee Neen Ha Ga Row and his fellow Iroquois chieftains (according to Joseph Addison's satirical account) undertook their celebrated visit to St Paul's Cathedral in 1710, intercontinental ecclesiastical links were in full swing, and within a generation sophisticated architectural patterns flowered in the American colonies (pl. 718). By the very nature of British expansion abroad and the spread of ideas through pattern books and other printed material during the eighteenth century, Anglican church design made its way around the globe. Three extraordinary visions of Wren's masterpiece – a building running through this book as a recurring expression of British architectural prestige – hint at this wider international esteem: William Marlow's *Capricco: St Paul's and a Venetian Canal* (pl. 719) proclaimed its Italian ancestry;[3] Addison's account established an early colonial consciousness of homeland church building of the highest standard;[4] and Lord Lyttelton's *Poem by a young Nobleman of distinguished Abilities, lately deceas'd* (1780), regarding 'the State of England, and the once flourishing City of London. In a Letter from an American Traveller, dated from the ruinous Portico of St Paul's, in the year 2199, to a friend settled in Boston, the Metropolis of the Western Empire', inferred some future relocation of Enlightenment classicism in the New World.[5] The cathedral was the first post-medieval ecclesiastical structure significantly to influence architectural thought beyond its shores, and especially in France. J. Pote's *The Foreigner's Guide; or, A necessary and instructive Companion Both for the Foreigner and Native, in their Tour through the Cities of London and Westminster* (1729), with parallel English and French texts, hailed it as 'equal if not superior to any [church] in Europe'. Its impact is forcefully declared on the façade of Saint Sulpice, Paris (begun 1733; pl. 720), designed by the Florentine-born Giovanni Niccolò Servandoni, who had spent the years 1722–4 in London.[6] Pierre Patte's attack on Sainte Geneviève, Paris, published in 1770, the outcome of a special excursion to London two years earlier to measure the cathedral, prompted the former's architect, J.-G. Soufflot, to alter his original baroque dome (pl. 596) in favour of a classically Wrenian solution.[7] He also exhibited a drawing of Wren's St Mary-le-Bow steeple at the French Academy in 1770.[8] The Danish architect Laurids de Thurah proposed for the Fridenchs Kirkes, Christianshavn (pl. 721), a steeple combining elements from St Mary-le-Strand and St Martin-in-the-Fields derived from Gibbs's *A Book of Architecture* (1728, second edition, 1739), a copy of which was owned by his colleague Vincents Lerche.[9] Occasionally, Italians showed interest in English churches, as when William Kent wrote from Rome in 1718 requesting a 'design' of St Mary-le-Strand for himself and an architect colleague, Giacomo Mariari.[10]

English churches increasingly attracted Continental visitors. The Swiss César de Saussure wrote enthusiastically to his family in 1725 of Henry VII's 'magnificent chapel' in Westminster Abbey.[11] The German architect Friedrich Wilhelm von Erdmannsdorf reported to Prince Leopold III Friedrich Franz of Anhalt-Dessau, creator of famed Wörlitz, that Canterbury Cathedral, which he visited in 1764, 'gave us an idea of the simplicity of English churches . . . a very vast building in the Gothic style, without the slightest ornament or paintings' (compared to 'the splendour and treasures of the Catholic church'), while Ripley's Greenwich Hospital chapel (pl. 546) was 'a beautiful work of architecture' and King's College chapel, Cambridge (pl. 190), was 'very beautiful and despite its size has no columns, the vaulting is entirely self-supporting'.[12] On approaching London in 1782 another German tourist, Karl Philipp Moritz, was dazzled as he 'drew nearer and nearer [and] the surrounding objects grew more distinct . . . St Paul's rearing above the multitude of smaller buildings like a huge mountain. . . . Westminster Abbey . . . a steeple of one church after another came into view'. 'Nothing inspired me', he went on, 'with more reverence than St George's Chapel [Windsor], it raised within me by its very appearance memories of the centuries that had flowed past while it had stood' and both inside and out 'has an aspect of the deepest melancholy'.[13] The Frenchman Françoise de la Rochefoucauld visited Westminster Abbey in 1784 (pls 6, 261), observing that Henry VII 'almost brought it to its present form, for since his day no-one has worked there until . . . Wren . . . the nave very grand and architecture wonderfully light, the west entrance [by Hawksmoor] notable'. Further afield he admired Robert Adam's Mistley, Essex (pl. 629), and Norwich Cathedral, 'a big and very heavy Gothic building . . . built by the Saxons'.[14] In the following year La Rochefoucauld and his brother travelled to Northampton, where All Saints (pl. 540) 'is built of a beautiful stone . . . its frontispiece adorned with a fine colonnade . . . and a very beautiful dome over the church'; St Paul, Liverpool (pl. 477), proved 'rather fine architecturally, but enormously heavy'; Nuneham, Oxfordshire (pl. 604), was 'a very elegant building, like a Roman temple'; Exeter Cathedral was 'beautiful' and Canterbury Cathedral (pl. 209) 'one of the most magic Romanesque buildings in Europe'.[15]

719 William Marlow. *Capricco: St Paul's Cathedral and a Venetian Canal*, *c.*1795. Oil on canvas. Tate Gallery, London, N06213.

Influences also moved in the opposite direction. An exceptionally interesting case was the amateur Scottish architect, John Erskine, 6th Earl of Mar, exiled to the Continent in 1715 following the Jacobite defeat in which he played a leading role, wandering through Italy, France and the Southern Netherlands until his death at Aix-la-Chapelle in 1732, who by his own admission was 'inflicted with the disease of building and gardening'.[16] His proposal for remodelling medieval Alloa parish church (pls 449–50), prepared at Paris in 1722 and at Antwerp in 1730, gives credence to the probability that he was employing features from the Hôpital de la Salpetrière (1660) and monastic buildings attached to Sainte Geneviève (*circa* 1720).[17] As we have also seen, the amateur Scottish architect James, 7th Earl of Findlater and Seafield, while resident in Dresden, was commissioned to supply graphic material on British buildings selected to illustrate C. L. Stieglitz's *Plans et dessins tirés de la belle architecture*, published in Leipzig, Moscow and Paris between 1798 and 1801, a survey of recent European achievements, which included All Saints, Southampton, St Mary, Paddington, St Mary, Wanstead, and Kentish Town Chapel (pls 491, 656, 696–7). A garbled story recorded in 1775, however, claiming that Lord Burlington, having acquired drawings of a much-admired but unnamed Italian church on returning from his Grand Tour (either the first in 1715 or subsequently in 1719), only to discover that it imitated St Stephen Walbrook (pl. 492), while at the same time believing that Wren had 'stole' the 'original' design since 'It revolts against the *costume* that an Italian Architect

720 Le Canu. 'Elevation du Grand Portail de St. Sulpice', Paris, France. Engraving. Author's collection. Niccolo Servandoni architect, begun 1733.

721 Laurids de Thurah, West front design, Fridenchs Kirkes, Christianhavn, Denmark, prepared for the unpublished third volume of *Den Dansk Vitruvius*, before 1755. Pen and ink and wash.

would borrow models from London', seems not only Anglophobic but highly implausible.[18]

The beginning of British architectural influence abroad was signalled by several noteworthy endeavours. The Presidency church of St Anne within Fort William, Calcutta, measuring 80 by 20 feet, erected under the jurisdiction of the Bishop of London by an unknown architect employed by the East India Company (consecrated on 5 June 1709, with the tower completed in 1716), though destroyed together with the parish papers by the Nawab of Bengal in 1756, was fortunately recorded in a view of *circa* 1730 (pl. 722). Its soaring polygonal spire crowning a square tower, and combination of circular and round-headed windows, reflected Wren's St Margaret Pattens, Rood Lane (1684–1702; pl. 723), located a short distance from the Company's City of London headquarters in Leadenhall. The introduction of a second range of circular windows in the clerestory recalls St Bride, Fleet Street (1671–1703; pl. 266), the boldly projecting apsidal chancel St Paul's Cathedral, with some form of classical porch attached to the west front. The design probably originated in the Office of Works or among the City Churches builders.[19] To this was added distinctly oriental flourishes: the whitewashed exterior deflected the sun's intense heat; the convex nave and aisle roofs helped

722 Anonymous English artist. South-east view, Fort William, Calcutta, India, with St Ann, detail, *c.*1730. Oil on canvas. Private collection.

723 Benjamin Cole. South-west view, 'The Parish Church of St. Margaret Pattens in little Tower Street', London, in Maitland 1756, vol. II, p. 1128. Engraving. Author's collection. Sir Christopher Wren architect, 1684–1703.

combat monsoons; the huge S-shaped buttresses, perhaps constructed of wrought iron, installed on the roof as part of repairs made after the tower was struck by lightning in 1724 (it was blown down in a cyclone in 1737 and never rebuilt). As 'the strongest Edifice' in the settlement, it was proposed to fortify the building against attack 'by opening portholes under the windows, which may be closed with Slight work to beat out occasionally'; the painting shows the fenestration secured by fancy ironwork.

In the American colonies during this period there was also a growing awareness of church building in the mother country. William Byrd II of Westover, Virginia (creator of one of the earliest grand Wrenian mansions in the South),[20] made an extensive tour with his English friend Sir John Perceval in 1701 that took in ecclesiastical buildings between London and the Scottish border, of which they were both admiring and critical. Ely was a 'very bewtyfull & Spacious Structure'; Durham, despite its newly refreshed and 'very neat' choir, 'extremely mean', while noting the baroque chapel at Chatsworth (1687–1704), the 'noblest' they had ever seen (pl. 84), as well as the recently built classical-style parish churches of St Nicholas, Whitehaven, Cumberland (1693; pl. 3), St Peter, Liverpool (1699–

724 (*facing page top*) Architect unknown. Design for the 'East end . . . West end or Entrance' and 'Entrance to the Chancell', St Paul, Chowan, North Carolina, 1708. Pen and ink. Lambeth Palace Library, Tenison Papers, S.P.G. f. 124.

725 (*facing page bottom left*) Architect unknown. Design for 'The Broad side [and] floor . . . of St. Pauls church in Chowan', North Carolina, 1708. Pen and ink. Lambeth Palace Library, Tenison Papers, S.P.G. f. 123.

726 (*facing page bottom right*) Architect unknown. Exploded plan for a 'Chapel or Oratory', St Michael, Croston, Lancashire, 2 July 1704. Pen and ink. Cheshire Record Office, EDA 2/4, f. 29.

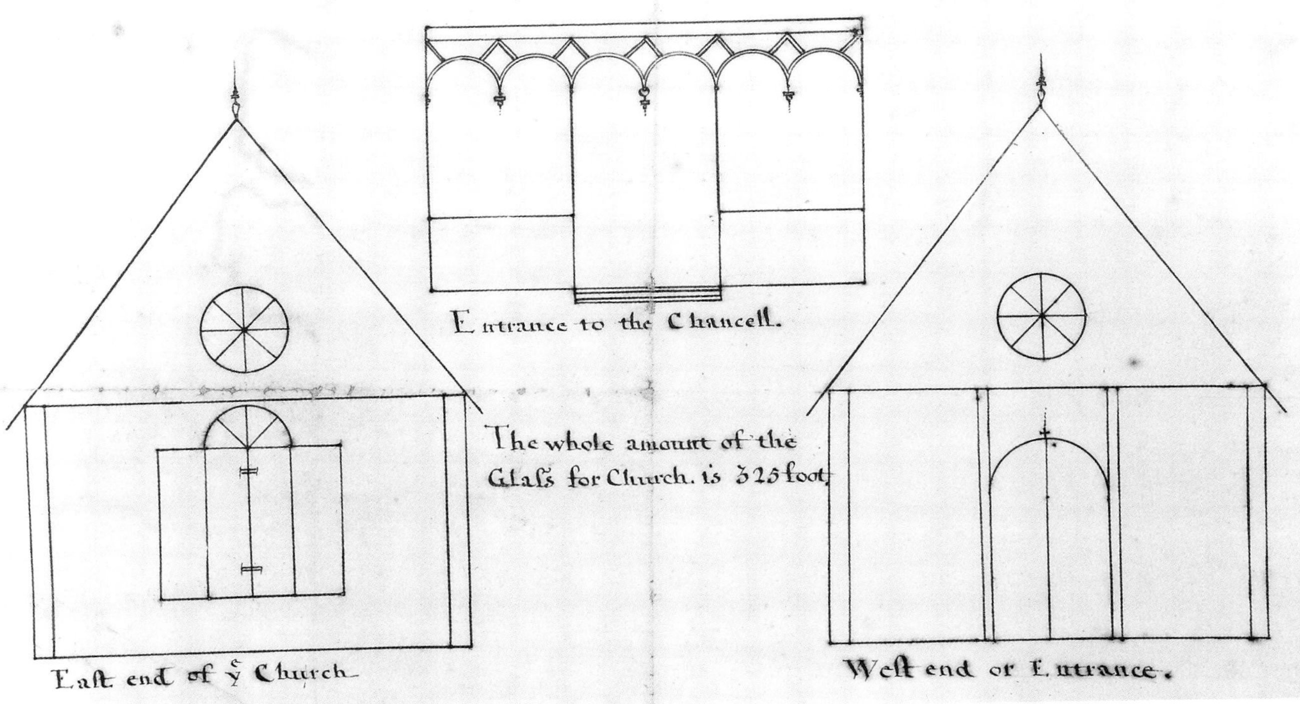
Entrance to the Chancell.
The whole amount of the
Glass for Church. is 325 foot
East end of ye Church
West end or Entrance.

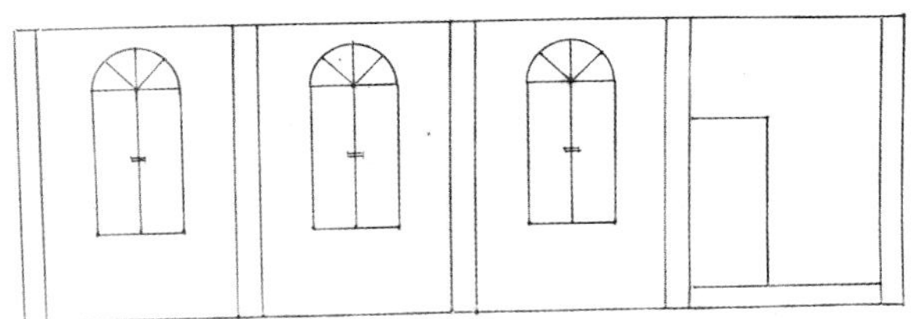
The Broad side of St Pauls church in Chowan: being 40 foot long.

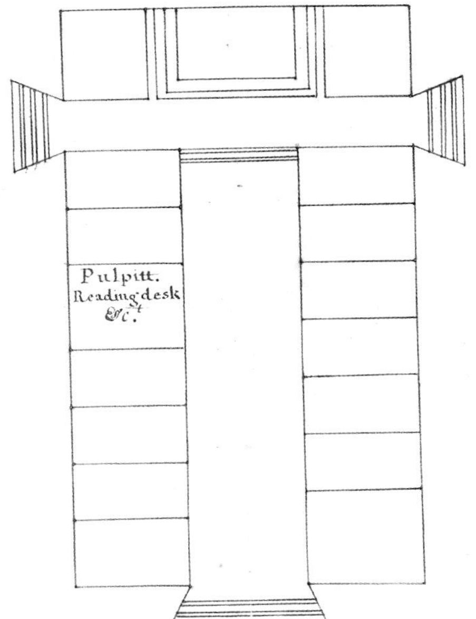
Pulpitt.
Reading desk
&c.
Church floor being 40. foot long & 24. foot wide.

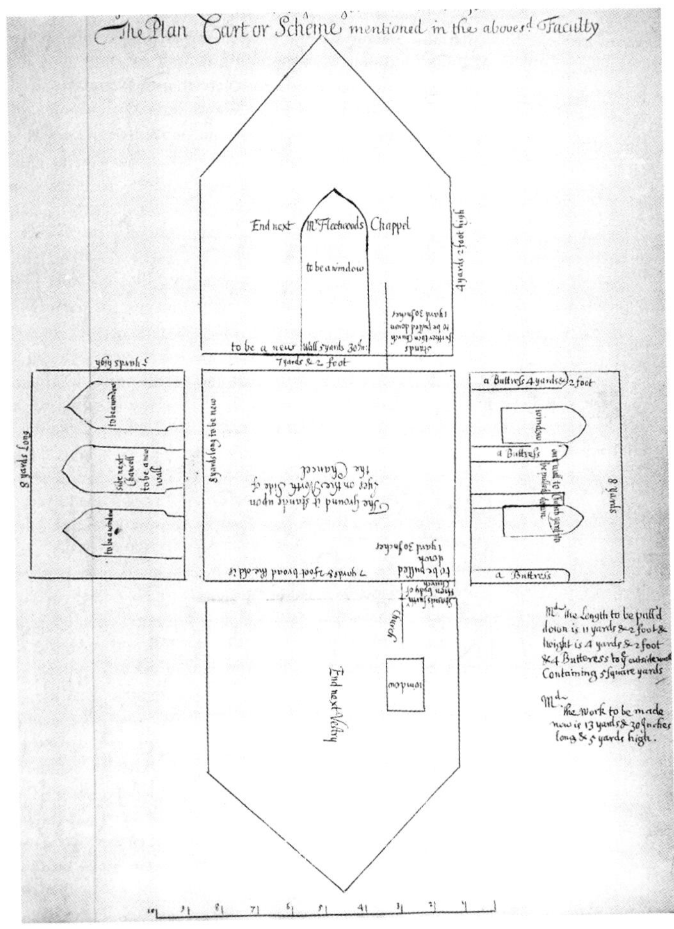
The Plan Cart or Scheme mentioned in the abovesd Faculty
End next Mr Fleetwoods Chappel
to be a window
7 yards & 2 foot
a Buttress 4 yards & 2 foot
8 yards
8 yards long
a Buttress
Md the Length to be pull'd
down is 11 yards & 2 foot &
height is 4 yards & 2 foot
& 4 Butteress to ye outside wall
Containing 5 square yards
Md
the Work to be made
new is 13 yards & 30 Inches
long & 5 yards high.

1704; pl. 485), 'very fine . . . after the patirn of [Wren's] St: Andrews [Holborn] at London [pl. 486] wch: will cost 5 or 6000 li', and the 'Very bewtyfull and magnificent' All Saints, Northampton (1697–1701; pl. 540).[21]

The parish of Chowan near Edenton, North Carolina, erected the first Anglican church in the region in 1701–2. The Vestry quickly grew disenchanted with its internal sheathing boards, even after an arbiter recommended white-washing, and the building remained unfinished, the door left open and 'all the Hogg & Cattle flee thither for shade in the summer and warmth in the Winter . . . make a loathsome place with their dung and nastiness'. In 1708 the authority, resolving to build a larger fabric, produced two sheets of drawings (pls 724–5) comprising a precisely ruled plan, section and elevation for the approval of the Bishop of London (still among his papers at Lambeth Palace). They display a typically simple rectangle, measuring 40 by 24 feet, with steeply pitched roof, shuttered windows and plain drop-arched chancel screen.[22] This failed to materialise, however, for lack of funds. The draughtsmanship and carefully ruled linear presentation with no attempt to indicate wall thickness or render volume through shading or perspective differ little from provincial English work of the time (pl. 726), in turn derived from popular pattern books such as Pierre Le Muet's *Maniere de Bien Bastir* (1647).[23] What makes the Chowan example very special is that it predates any other known colonial architectural drawings by several decades, and perhaps even represents the earliest surviving specimen.[24]

727 Architect unknown. West front design, 'St. Philip's Church in Charles Town, South Carolina', in *Gentleman's Magazine*, June 1753, p. 260. Engraving. Dating to the 'Act for Erecting a New Brick Church in Charles Town' of 1710–11.

One of the earliest major expressions of the new classicising trend resulted from an Act of 1710–11 'for Erecting a New Brick Church in Charles Town', South Carolina, which specified 'Such Height . . . Dimensions . . . Materials and in such Modoll and form as [the building committee] think fitting'. By 1713 a 'large brick Church', 100 by 45 feet, was building at a cost of £8,000, and ten years later it was described as 'a large, regular and Beautiful Building, exceeding any that are in his Majesty's Dominions in America [though] not yet entirely finished'.[25] The design, celebrated unusually in an engraving published in the *Gentleman's Magazine* (pl. 727), was wholly unexpected in the colonies for its avant-garde sophistication. Its innovative composition, a three-by-five-bay block, each separated by Tuscan Doric pilasters carrying an uninterrupted entablature, uniquely featured three tetrastyle temple porticoes projecting from the west and the western ends of the north and south elevations. Then unprecedented in America for the explicitness of its temple form, the ensemble closely reflects architectural ideas currently being promoted in the Fifty New Churches programme in London, particularly multiple entrances (pl. 402), which St Philip's chief promoter, the Revd Gideon Johnston, could have noted during his visit in the summer of 1714 to solicit financial support from Carolina merchants and the Bishop of London, one of the Churches Commissioners. Like Ralph Thoresby of Leeds during the same months, he might well have had access to the wooden models in the Commissioners' Lincoln's Inn Fields headquarters (see p. 409). Furthermore, in 1722 General Francis Nicholson, South Carolina's governor, who actively supported the church venture, gifted a consignment of cedar to the prominently porticoed St Martin-in-the-Fields (pl. 416).[26] G. Watt's *Sermon Preached before the Trustees for Establishing the Colony of Georgia in America; at their Anniversary Meeting* on 8 March 1735 held in Wren's St Bride, Fleet Street, offered further intercontinental ties.[27]

Unsurprisingly, considering London's hold on colonial architectural activity, the Wrenian tradition virtually dominated American mainstream church design. This was particularly true respecting New England.

Christ Church (Old North), Boston (cornerstone laid on 15 April 1723, two months after the great architect's death), designed apparently by William Price, an English-born, locally based printseller and member of the congregation, was modelled on St James, Westminster (pl. 478).[28] The same pattern reappeared in Richard Munday's Trinity Church, Newport, Rhode Island (1725–41).[29]

From the mid-1720s the colonial capitals began to adopt more progressive London trends. The most avant-garde is represented by the modest, red brick Holden Chapel, Cambridge, Massachusetts (1742; pl. 728), the first appearance of a classical pseudoperipteral temple-form church in the colonies, funded by the widow of Samuel Holden, a wealthy London merchant and director of the Bank of England, and probably designed by James Gibbs's acquaintance John Smibert.[30] The major achievement is Christ Church, Philadelphia (1727–59; pl. 718), then the second city after Boston, with a population increasing from 20,000 to 200,000 during the first half of the century.[31] In 1725 the Vestry petitioned the Bishop of London that the existing church of 1710–11 was ruinous and required rebuilding; fourteen years later it was reported that the 'goode design . . . for erecting a new, more large & comodious Building . . . wth much care and industry is carried out . . . the foundation of a Steeple laid, & the Body . . . on the outside almost finished', but due to insufficient funds the interior 'remains unfinished . . . A Gallery, and other conveniences should yet be added'. By 1743 work on the shell, which had been 'at a Stand . . . for many Years [was] now Proceeding . . . with great alacrity', and in the following year the building was 'happily finished', the creation of the amateur architect Dr John Kearsley. Robert Smith, a leading member of the Carpenters' Company, who had immigrated from Dalkeith in Scotland in 1749, erected the immense steeple by 1759. The total cost was £6,229 19s. 8d.[32] The monumental and sophisticated ensemble is remarkable even by London standards and, indeed, would hardly have been out of place in the Georgian metropolis. Measuring 61 by 188 feet with a 200-foot-high tower, it was then one of the largest churches in the colonies. The eight-bay body is double-storeyed, each articulated by its own order, the upper supporting a Doric entablature (repeated inside) and crowned by a series of carved wood urns imported from England in 1736. Open-bed pedimented windows and blind niches recall St Mary-le-Strand (pl. 378). Gibbs's explanation in *A Book of Architecture* (1728), that because the church 'is situated in a very publick place, the Commissioners . . . spar'd no cost to beautify it. It consists of two Orders, in the upper of which the Lights are placed; the Walls of the lower, being solid to keep out Noises from the Street, is adorned with Niches', would not have been lost on its American readers.[33] The configuration of the Christ Church site, which orientated the east end towards the main thoroughfare, produced an uncommonly showy treatment (particularly for Quaker-dominated Philadelphia), where the chancel with its St Martin-in-the-Fields-inspired giant pilasters and Serliana (its earliest known appearance in the colonies) and the separate pedimented attic bracketed by robust volutes (recalling St Andrew, Holborn) are compositionally divorced from the body and project forward as a sort of enormous altarpiece. Smith's steeple combines elements from two alternative St Martin designs in Gibbs's publication.[34]

728 John Smibert, attributed. Holden Chapel, Cambridge, Massachusetts, 1742.

In the late 1720s George Berkeley, later Bishop of Cloyne in Ireland, planned a utopian 'City of Bermuda Metropolis of the Summer Islands' (pl. 729), featuring a tetrastyle temple-form church flanked on both sides by 'Open Porticoes' and a free-standing steeple located in the centre of the square, which reflected not only ideas currently promoted by the New Churches Commissioners but also his own pioneering enthusiasm for ancient Greek architecture. He wrote as early as 1718 that

> This gusto of mine is formed on the remains of antiquity that I have met with in my travels, particularly in Sicily, which convince me that the old Romans were inferior to the Greeks, and that the

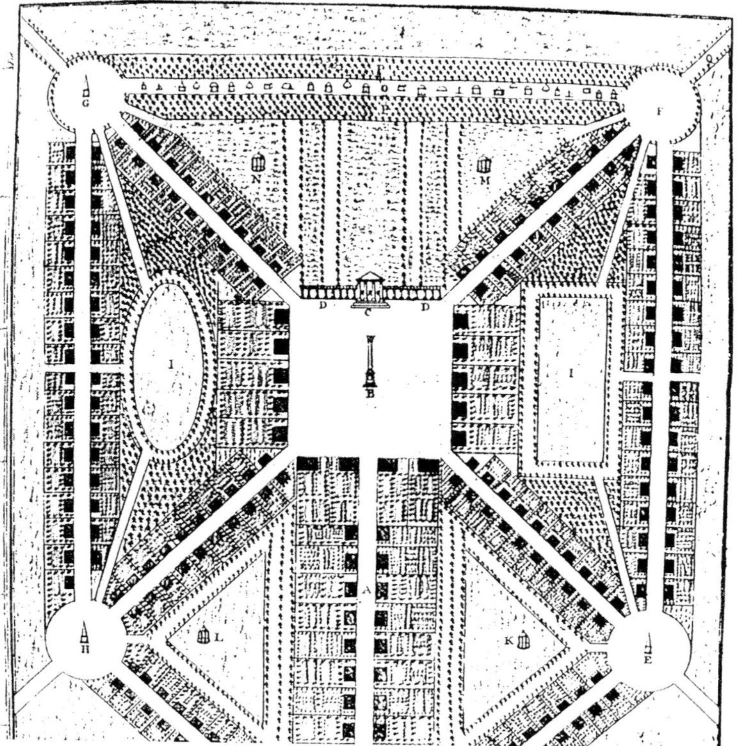

729 George Berkeley. 'The City of Bermuda Metropolis of the Summer Islands' with a church, steeple and 'Open Porticoes' (marked B, C, D), late 1720s, in Berkeley 1956, p. 111, detail (1784 edn.). Engraving.

> moderns fall infinitely short of both in the grandeur and simplicity of taste . . . there is not any one modern building in Rome that pleases me, except the wings of the capitol built by Michael Angelo, and the colonade of Berninies before St Peter's. The Church itself I find a thousand faults with, as indeed with every other modern Church here.[35]

Had the Bermuda adventure been built it would have represented an extremely early example of a composition actually realised only in 1779 at Ayot St Lawrence (pl. 643). Otherwise, Anglican churches in the Caribbean appear to have been modest affairs mired in the archaistic doldrums.[36]

During the Colonial and Federal periods, St Martin-in-the-Fields was an almost ubiquitous pattern for churches. Distinguished among its progeny is St Michael, Charleston, South Carolina (1752–61), at 60 by 130 feet by 184 feet high, only slightly smaller than its prototype (and the largest house of worship erected in the colonies), and costing an astronomical £62,000. On 22 February 1752, five days after the cornerstone was laid, the *South Carolina Gazette* announced that the church 'will be built on the Plan of one of Mr Gibson's [*sic*] Designs' (pl. 416) and ''tis tho't will exhibit a fine Piece of Architecture when compleated'. To ring the changes, the tower was based on Wren's St Bride, Fleet Street (pl. 266). The designer was Samuel Cardy, perhaps with involvement of the English-born Rhode Island-based architect Peter Harrison during one of his excursions south.[37]

The absence of contemporary accounts and drawings has made the designing history of St Paul, New York City, fraught with problems (pl. 730). It was built in two campaigns, the first in 1764–6 under the elusive Thomas McBean, who was responsible for the body with its Serliana lighting the chancel and probably the monumental tetrastyle Ionic temple portico projecting eastward towards Broadway (a variation on the orientation of St Alfege, Greenwich, pls 403–4), and the second in 1794 under J. C. Laurence and T. Colbourne (the former having previously practised in London), who added the Gibbsian steeple at the west end facing into the churchyard. The interior subscribes to St Martin's giant order dosseret system (pl. 417).[38]

The First Baptist Meeting House, Providence, Rhode Island, was designed by Joseph Brown, who owned a copy of *A Book of Architecture*. The *Providence Gazette* for 10 June 1775 reported that the steeple specifically derived from 'the middle Figure in the 30th Plate of Gibbs designs', which a subsequent owner, Thomas Dawes, a leading contemporary Boston architect, had inscribed 'Providence' over that example.[39] In this context it is particularly worth noting that Gibbs's celebrated book, first published by the author in 1728 (with a proposed parallel French text abandoned), priced 4 guineas by subscription, became increasingly available as a reissue in 1739 by a consortium of London booksellers who sold off the remaining stock at 3 guineas and charged £2 10s. 0d. for the new edition.[40] Both were advertised by Boston, Charleston, New York and Philadelphia booksellers on eight occasions between 1760 and 1789, the belated availability contributing to a conservative solution, firmly anchored in the Palladian tradition of a half-century earlier, not merely persistent but endemic in colonial church design.[41] Thus, around 1770 we see Thomas Jefferson using a plan for an octagonal chapel in Robert Morris's *Select Architecture* (1755) as the model for a similar, unexecuted building.[42] Moreover, the first church design published in an American pattern book, Asher Benjamin's *The Country Builder's Assistant* (1797), closely resembles the earliest ecclesiastical work of Charles Bulfinch, at Pittsfield and Taunton, Massachusetts (1790–93), whose vocabulary can be traced back to early Georgian England.[43]

730 C. Milbourne, *North-east view, St Paul's Chapel, New-York City, New-York*, detail, 1798. Watercolour. Collection of The New-York Historical Society, acc. no. 1953.63. Thomas McBean (body, 1764–6), James Crommelin Laurence and T. Colbourne (steeple, 1794–6), architects.

Of particular importance to colonial churches was ringing the changes of the eighteen alternative steeple designs associated with St Martin, St Mary-le-Strand, St Clement Danes and Marylebone Chapel offered in the A *Book of Architecture*.[44] The last building (pl. 506), much imitated in Britain (chapter 23), also found favour abroad, not only through the published designs but also via the celebrated example of St Paul, Halifax, Nova Scotia (1749–50), then a newly founded settlement under the supervision of the Board of Trade and Plantations in London, most likely designed by Gibbs himself in his capacity as Architect of the Ordinance (1727–54) as the first Anglican parish church erected in what is now Canada, which still stands though in an altered state. Its original appearance is captured in an engraving of 1764 (pl. 731).[45] The promoter, Governor Edward Cornwallis, and the Church of England missionary the Revd William Tutty both acknowledged the identically sized London chapel as their model.[46] Correspondence reveals that the church was framed in Boston, transported by ship to Halifax and erected on a pre-prepared stone foundation, perhaps employing carpenters from the naval garrison at Annapolis, Maryland.[47] The technology, favouring timber cladding rather than brick with stone dressings, marks one of the major material differences between Georgian church construction in England and New England.[48]

732 Peter Harrison. West front, King's Chapel, Boston, Massachusettes, 1749–54.

731 John Fougeron and Richard Short after Dominic Serres. View of 'the Church of Saint Paul. . . at Halifax in Nova Scotia', Canada, detail, 1 March 1764. Engraving. James Gibbs architect, attributed, 1749–50, altered nineteenth century.

Peter Harrison, following training in his native Yorkshire, probably among Lord Burlington's northern coterie, arrived at Newport, Rhode Island, in 1739–40, reinforcing ties during brief return excursions to England between 1742 and 1744. By the end of his career in 1775 he possessed a personal library of some 700 volumes, including twenty-nine architectural titles, among them William Halfpenny's *The Art of Sound Building* (1725), William Kent's *The Designs of Inigo Jones* (1727) and Gibbs's *A Book of Architecture* (1728), which together formed the foundation of his heroic ecclesiastical work.[49] His monumental concept for the new Anglican King's Chapel, Boston (1749–54; pl. 732), is revealed in a letter of 15 September 1749 to the rector, which enclosed a set of six drawings (untraced):

> The Body . . . (as you directed) is as Plain as the Order of it will possibly admitt of; but the Steeple is fully Decorated, and I believe will have a beautifull effect. The Inside is likewise design'd Plain, and as regular as can be contrived from the Dimensions you limited me to [65 by 100 feet]. From these hints, you

733 Architect unknown. West elevation, Chowbent Chapel (Independent), Atherton, Lancashire, 1721–2.

> may perhaps be able to answer the Objections of such the Committee and others, who may not be conversant with Drawings, or have not a Taste in Things of this Nature.

He pleaded 'that no material Alteration is made in the Execution, as it is very possible by that means the Symmetry of the Whole may be destroy'd'.[50] The body's double tier of round-headed windows recalls the Marylebone Chapel; a near-contemporary description suggests that the proposed steeple was an unpractical, flamboyant variant of St Martin-in-the-Fields.[51] The exterior colonnade of six by three Ionic columns enclosing the tower base, echoed by paired pilasters on the body, an unprecedented and daring solution in colonial church design, reveals Harrison's awareness of English trends in temple-form structures (described in chapter 21) and perhaps also the Jonesian-inspired All Saints, Northampton (pl. 540).[52] Though the Boston Vestry contacted Ralph Allen, proprietor of the Bath stone quarries in Somerset, in November 1750, his estimate of £1,200 for supplying Ionic and Corinthian columns, pilasters and mouldings, and an offer to send craftsmen (lately employed in building Bristol Exchange) to Boston if paid travel expenses and home wages, proved too expensive.[53] Instead, local Quincy hewn granite was used, contributing to an unusually spartan sense of permanence rare in colonial churches at the time (where timber or brick construction was largely favoured), imposing an Old World character on the building.

The Southern States preferred brick with stone dressings, a simple rectangle articulated by plain round-headed windows in the English Nonconformist tradition epitomised by Chowbent Chapel, Atherton, Lancashire (1721), the Dissenting heartland (pl. 733).[54] The classic American example, James Wren's Pohick church, Truro Parish, Fairfax County, Virginia (1769–73; pl. 734), is the most beautiful and best documented of a distinctive regional group.[55] The surviving Vestry minutes provide an excellent notion of the designing and construction of such a colonial fabric. While Wren received 40s. for designs and Daniel French £877 as 'undertaker', the building cost was paid in huge quantities of tobacco, such as 34,900 lb specified in 1769, and certain building materials were indigenous, such as 'Cypress Shingles' for roofing. Though the interior was whitewashed, the 'Wooden-work . . . neatly Painted of the proper [unnamed] Colours' and the external 'rub'd Bricks at the returns of . . . the Windows . . . so near as possible the same colour with the Arches', it would be misleading to imagine that this was a sort of Puritan achromatic, as some modern restorations have attempted to suggest, since the Vestry also ordered craftsmen to 'gild the Ornaments within the Tabernacle Frames the Palm Branch and Drapery on the Front of the Pulpit also the Eggs on the Cornice of the small Frames', as well as furnish the pulpit, desks and com-

734 James Wren. West front, Pohick Church, Truro Parish, Fairfax County, Virginia, 1769–73.

munion table with 'Crimson Velvett with Gold Fring' and prayer books bound in 'blue Turkey Leather'. The raised stone font was carved by William Copein for £6, 'according to a Draught in the 150th plate of Langleys Designs being the uppermost on the left hand', that is, *The City and Country Builder's and Workman's Treasury of Designs* (1740), a copy of which perhaps belonged to the Revd Lee Massey, who was appointed minister on returning from England in 1766.[56] More comprehensive evidence of colonial colouring is provided by the bill for repainting St Paul, Halifax, Nova Scotia, in the years 1786–8, entailing 2,585 feet of mahogany colour, 2,455 feet of white and stone colour, 46 feet of marbling, 93 feet of chocolate, 355 feet of brown and 243 feet of green for the 'Venetian Blinds of the Spire'.[57] There is also the advertisement in the *New-York Gazette* of 26 September 1748 placed by the painter and glazier John Humble:

> Just imported from London . . . White lead, red lead, Spanish brown, spanish white, venetian red, English oker, spruce yellow, blue smalt, vermillion, prussian blue, india red, verdigrease, umber, white vitriol, gold and silver leaf, brushes, tools, pencils, oyl, and sundry other things relating to the business: As also all sorts of Crown window glass . . .

while John Baldwin, house painter, alerted readers of the *New-York Mercury* on 10 March 1766 that 'he will perform . . . painting, gilding, glazing &c. after the most accurate Method now followed in London, Viz. Dead White, and all Sorts of shining Colours, in the most beautiful and exquisite Manner'.[58]

The Society of Friends ('Quakers') transferred a largely standardised, inexpensive form unchanged from the mother country. A description of 1816 of the Philadelphia congregations' 'refined architectural simplicity, solidity, and extreme cleanliness [as] admirable features of their temples', with pews painted 'ash-grey', might easily stand for the type.[59]

Transatlantic intercourse among architects and builders was undoubtedly more commonplace than surviving documents suggest. Probably not untypical was the case of George Harrison, a London-trained marble worker, who advertised in the Philadelphia press in 1746 that he 'had the Honour to be employ'd by several Gentlemen in England as a Surveyor, in the Designing, Making Draughts of, and Superintending their Building'.[60] He may be the person of the same name who subscribed to Gibbs's *A Book of Architecture* (1728) and was perhaps a relative of John Harrison, who was one of the founders of Christ Church, Philadelphia, in the 1690s and perhaps its first architect. His son Daniel worked on the new building during the years 1726–40; Henry Harrison was a Vestryman and churchwarden.[61] There is no evidence that this dynasty was related to Robert Harrison, who supplied a design for St Andrew, Penrith, Cumberland, in 1720, and no more than a fascinating coincidence that the successful architect of the church was William Etty of York, who enjoyed professional links with Wren, Vanbrugh, Burlington and Colen Campbell,[62] and who may have been Peter Harrison's master. He, in turn, seems to have introduced into the colonies the technique of treating woodwork with sand-textured paint to imitate stone, as employed in King's Chapel, Boston, and the Redwood Library, Newport. It is a technique that he was very likely familiar with in Gibbs's Kirkleatham Hospital chapel, Yorkshire (1741–60; pl. 503).[63]

Henry Flitcroft ('Burlington Harry') supplied a design for an Anglican church for Savannah, Georgia, in 1738 (the year he designed St Olave, Southwark, pl. 564)[64] in response to a resolution that 'Covent Garden Church [pl. 512] happening to be well known' to the promoters was 'recommended . . . as a Model . . . to work by, as well for its being deemed a Curious piece of Inico Jones, as because the Work will come much Cheaper for being so very plain . . . the less we vary from it the better'. The association in Palladian design between simplicity and affordability particularly suited the colonial spirit. In this case, however, its appearance is unrecorded, nor was it realised.[65]

In the opposite direction it says much that James Ralph, author of the influential, pioneering *Critical Review of the Publick Buildings, Statues and Ornaments In, and about London and Westminster* (1734), which offered provocative commentaries on churches (as well as other building types), was an American who settled in England in 1725.[66] In 1760 James Bridges submitted a design for St Nicholas, Bristol, based on a 'Plan I saw executed, when on my travels through . . . Pensilvania, in America' during 1755–6, though the drawing is untraced and the identity of the model remains a mystery.[67] In 1763 he departed for the West Indies and obscurity. In 1786 the *Gentleman's Magazine* described the recently completed Bethesda Chapel, Dorset Street, Dublin, for the Swadlers, or Methodists, as 'built upon the plan of an edifice of that appellation in America, erected by the labours of . . . Mr Wesley', that is, Bethesda Orphan House (1740–42, destroyed 1773), near Savannah, Georgia, which incorporated a chapel on the ground floor of a typically American timber-frame, hipped-roof, colonnaded, farm-like building crowned by a bell-tower, but, in fact, hardly resembling its purported Dublin progeny.[68] More substantial are the

Anglo-American churches of two leading colonial architects, Charles Bulfinch and Benjamin Henry Latrobe.

Bulfinch, the great Boston architect, whose 'genius [and] liberal education . . . improved by a tour through Europe' between 1785 and 1787, immediately thereafter designed the Hollis Street Church in Boston (pl. 735). One may speculate that its novel combination of *in antis* temple portico and twin west towers, an unprecedented innovation in America, derived from some of the wooden models made for the London New Churches in the early decades of the century, which he may have seen displayed in Westminster Abbey (since lost), including Gibbs's Corinthian pseudoperipteral temple, itself a rare form in Britain (pl. 406).[69] The publication of the Boston building in 1793 led to a brief flowering of the formula, which included the First Presbyterian Church, Baltimore, Maryland, by James Dalrymple and John Mosher (1789–95, demolished 1859); the First Congregational Church, Providence, Rhode Island, by Caleb Ormsbee (1795–1814, demolished); and the North Dutch Reform Church, Albany, New York, by Philip Hooker and Elisha Putnam (1796–9, since altered), the last of which was commended in the local press as 'a superb and elegant building . . . in the most modern style'.[70]

Nowhere is this interaction better demonstrated than in Latrobe's ecclesiastical career. Born at the Moravian settlement at Fulneck, Yorkshire, and employed as draughtsman to Samuel Pepys Cockerell before emigrating in 1796 to the fledgling United States, he quickly emerged as the leading architect of the Federal period. In 1790 he had married the daughter of the Revd William Sellon, builder and proprietor of the Portman Chapel, St Marylebone (1779, demolished 1970), a simple brick box distinguished by a prominent Serliana set above a ground storey of round-headed doors recessed in shallow arches, a treatment later much favoured by Latrobe.[71] During his early professional career in London, launched in 1784, two churches that he would have known first-hand proved particularly influential. John Plaw's Greek-cross-planned St Mary, Paddington (pl. 696), located a short distance from Latrobe's Fitzrovia residence, led to St John, Washington, DC (pl. 736), which he described as 'a smart thing enough, at which the natives stare exceedingly, because it does not in the least resemble a barn' – a reference to the deeply dentilled eaves derived from Inigo Jones's St Paul, Covent Garden (pl. 512), which had also been likened to a barn and which Thomas Hardwick Jr had restored in 1788–9, during Latrobe's London years. Of St John's he further observed that it 'has the form of a Cross and is covered with a dome . . . a pretty thing [which] has a celebrity beyond all bounds [and] has made people religious who were never before at Church, [the style] extremely simple, but out of the

735 South-west view, Hollis Street Church, Boston, Massachusetts, in *The Massachusetts Magazine*, 1793. Engraving (from E. V. Gillon Jr., *Early Illustrations and Views of American Architecture*, 1971, pl. 69). Charles Bulfinch architect, 1787–8, altered 1810, demolished 1897.

736 Benjamin Henry Latrobe. View of St John, Washington D.C., 1815. Pencil, pen and ink and watercolour. Maryland Historical Society, Baltimore, 269/B2. Erected 1815–16, altered 1820–22.

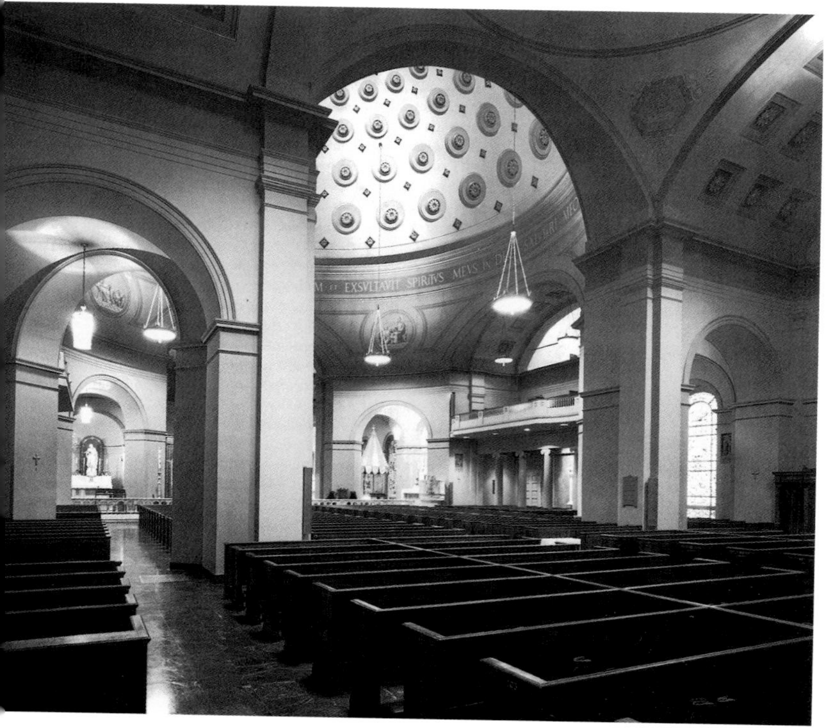

737 Benjamin Henry Latrobe. Interior, Baltimore Cathedral (Roman Catholic), Maryland, 1804–21.

738 (*below left*) Benjamin Henry Latrobe. 'Section, showing the Choir & Transept', Baltimore Cathedral (Roman Catholic), gothic alternative, detail, 1805. Pencil, pen and ink and watercolour. Archives of the Archdiocese of Baltimore, 283/B3.

739 (*below right*) James Wyatt. South-east view, St Swithin, East Grinstead, Sussex, 1788–92. Photographed *c.*1908. West Sussex Record Office, PH1613.

usual track of form [which] gains daily more approbation'.[72]

This was the late neoclassical vocabulary adopted for Latrobe's masterpiece, the externally temple-porticoed, twin-towered Baltimore Catholic Cathedral (1804–21; pl. 737), internally based on the Lulworth chapel (pl. 717), which, as we have seen, was consecrated by Bishop Carroll of Baltimore in 1790 (p. 601). The architect explained to Carroll and the building committee that

> The Veneration which the Gothic cathedrals generally excite, by their peculiar style, by the associations belonging peculiarly to that style, and by the real grandeur, and beauty which it possesses, has induced me to propose the Gothic style of building [though] impracticable to the uses of common life, while the Greek and Roman . . . has descended from the most magnificent temples to the decoration of our meanest furniture. On this account, I conceive that the former has a peculiar claim to preference . . . my *habit* rather inclining me to the latter . . . Roman taste . . . while my reasonings prefer the first.[73]

Latrobe's gothic alternative (pl. 738)[74] brings me to the second church with which he would have been familiar, St Swithun, East Grinstead, Sussex (pl. 739), rebuilt by James Wyatt after the collapse of the old west tower in 1785 destroyed the entire fabric. In 1792, while building nearby Greek revival Hammerwood Lodge and working nearby at Wyatt's gothic Sheffield Place, Latrobe negotiated the purchase of redundant scaffolding from the church.[75] About this he later wrote from Philadelphia to his brother in Yorkshire:

> I forget the Year in which I went to Bath, Bristol, Wells and Salisbury . . . I am obliged . . . to design from memory. I cannot here procure a single *technical* account or representation of a Gothic Building of any superior merit [so little did the medieval tradition then interest Americans[76]]: but the style, and even the detail is so impressed on my imagination that I hope to succeed, in escaping the censure you so justly bestow upon Wyatt.[77]

This presumably refers to the attacks against Wyatt's restoration of Salisbury and Durham cathedrals and attempts to blackball him from membership of the powerful Society of Antiquaries of London on grounds that 'he is but half-learned (which is worse than being totally ignorant) with respect to the style of the middle ages [and] by admitting him . . . we shall appear in the face of our contemporaries and of all posterity, to sanction a system which tends to deprive us of the very subject of our study', as reported in the *Gentleman's Magazine*.[78] He was admitted in 1797, however, by a full meeting, which included Latrobe's old master, S. P. Cockerell, who thought Wyatt

> possessed infinite taste and ingenuity – but . . . had not the feeling or conceptions so original and bold as those of Vanbrugh and that Dance [Jr] excelled all the present Architects in *appropriate invention*. His designs explained the purpose for which the building was intended. The finishing & decorations of Wyatt are generally beautiful, but his outside designs are blocks of stone.[79]

Thus, in this lengthy and complex historical voyage through British eighteenth-century church architecture we have, so to speak, come full circle.[80]

Appendix A

'SOME OBSERVATIONS MADE IN A JOURNEY, BEGUN JUNE THE 7TH AND FINISH'D THE 9TH. 1742'

Anon., 'Some Observations made in A Journey, begun June the 7th and finish'd July the 9th. 1742', British Library, Add. MS 22926, ff. 2–80v. A small folio with numerous church plans.

The excursion began and ended at Norwich, Norfolk, passing through Suffolk, Kent, London, Middlesex, Berkshire, Oxfordshire, Northamptonshire, Derbyshire and Lincolnshire, visiting: Woodbridge (f. 6), Gravesend (f. 9v), Rochester (f. 10), Canterbury (f. 13–v), Woolwich (f. 17v), St Anne, Limehouse (f. 19), St Paul, Deptford (ff. 19v–20), Greenwich Hospital (f. 19v), St Mary, Rotherhithe (ff. 20v–21), Southwark: St George, St Olave, Christ Church (ff. 21–2), Marylebone parish church (ff. 23v–24), St Stephen Walbrook (ff. 24v–25), St Mary Woolnoth (f. 25v), St Mary Abchurch (f. 26–v), St Magnus Martyr (f. 26v), Christ Church, Newgate (f. 28–v), St Botolph, Bishopsgate (f. 29–v), St Leonard, Shoreditch (f. 29v), St George, Radcliffe, Wapping (ff. 30v–31), St Anne, Limehouse (f. 31v), Christ Church, Spitalfields (f. 32–v), St Luke, Old Street (ff. 32v–33), St Bride, Fleet Street (ff. 33v–34), St Clement Danes (ff. 34v–35r), St Mary-le-Strand (ff. 35v–36), St Martin-in-the-Fields (f. 36–v), St Paul, Covent Garden (ff. 36v–37), St James, Westminster (f. 38–v), St George, Hanover Square (f. 40–v), St Giles-in-the-Fields (ff. 40v–41), St George, Bloomsbury (f. 41–v), Chelsea Hospital (f. 42v), Hampton Court Palace (f. 51), Windsor Castle (f. 53), Eton College (f. 53), Oxford: Pembroke College (f. 56v), All Souls College (f. 56v), University College (f. 57), Queen's College (f. 59–v), Trinity College (f. 59v), All Saints (f. 63), Northampton (ff. 71v–72), Derby (f. 73–v), Lincoln: Cathedral (f. 80–v), St Peter (f. 80v). Individual entries quoted in the corresponding documents on the CD-rom attached to the back board.

Appendix B

TOTAL CONSTRUCTION COSTS OF SELECTED NEW-BUILT CHURCHES

Arranged in chronological order, with dates of completion. Numbers within parentheses refer to the documents recorded on the CD-rom attached to the back board

1704 St Peter, Liverpool, Lancashire, £3,500 (Doc. 120)
1713 St Alkmund, Whitchurch, Shropshire, £4,287 4s. 2d. (Doc. 195)
1716 St Mary, Deal, Kent, £2,554 12s. 4d. (Doc. 62)
1724 St Peter at Arches, Lincoln, £3,373 14s. 4d. (Doc. 116)
1724 St Andrew, Penrith, Cumberland, £3,094 5s. 0d. (Doc. 147)
1727 St George, Wapping, London, £25,885 0s. 4d. (Doc. 260)
1727 St Martin-in-the-Fields, London, £33,661 16s. 7¾d. (Doc. 269)
1728 St Botolph, Bishopsgate, London, £10,444 1s. 8½d. (Doc. 215)
1728 St George, Hanover Square, London, £19,078 16s. 3d. (Doc. 245)
1729 Christ Church, Spitalfields, London, £40,602 0s. 6d. (Doc. 259)
1730 Holy Trinity, Leeds, Yorkshire, £4,963 12s. 5d. (Doc. 112)
1731 St Mary Woolnoth, London, £16,940 0s. 4d. (Doc. 221)
1731 St John, Westminster, London, £40,875 14s. 0d. (Doc. 267), additional post-fire remodelling in 1745: £3,920 8s. 8d.
1733 St Giles-in-the-Fields, London, £8,436 19s. 6d. (Doc. 229)
1740 St Olave, Southwark, London, £5,210 7s. 1d. (Doc. 250)
1744 St Botolph, Aldgate, London, £5,536 2s. 5d. (Doc. 214)
1744 All Saints, Gainsborough, Lincolnshire, £5,230 12s. 8¼d. (Doc. 82)
1749 Quaker Meeting House, Bristol, Somerset, £2,091 (Doc. 36)
1752 Christ Church, Bristol, Somerset, £1,500 (Doc. 34)
1754 St Mary, Islington, London, £7,340 (Doc. 240)
1757 Octagon Chapel, Norwich, Norfolk, £5,254 (Doc. 137)
1758 Holy Cross, Daventry, Northamptonshire, £3,486 2s. 5½d. (Doc. 61)
1760 St Andrew, St Andrew-by-the-Green, Glasgow, Scotland, £1,110 (Doc. 85)
1767 All Hallows, London Wall, London, £2,941 (Doc. 208)
1772 Square Unitarian Chapel, Halifax, Yorkshire, £2,000 (Doc. 94)
1780 SS Peter and Paul, Buckingham, Buckinghamshire, £7,000 (Doc. 44)
1790 St Mary, Wanstead, Essex, £9,150 (Doc. 187)
1792 St Chad, Shrewsbury, Shropshire, £17,752 (Doc. 166)
1792 St Peter-Le-Poer, London, £4,000 (Doc. 224)
1793 St Paul, Leeds, Yorkshire, £10,000 (Doc. 113)
1795 St Andrew, Edinburgh, Scotland, £5,183 6s. 11d. (Doc. 74)
1795 All Saints, Southampton, Hampshire, £9,744 19s. 6d. (Doc. 167)
1796 St Mary Magdalene, Bridgnorth, Shropshire, £6,827 11s. 9d. (Doc. 31)
1796 All Saints, Newcastle upon Tyne, Northumberland, £27,000 (Doc. 135)
1797 St Mary, Banbury, Oxfordshire, £22,000 (Doc. 10)
1799 St John, Hackney, London, £28,479 5s. 2d. (Doc. 237)
1800 St Martin Outwich, London, £5,256 17s. 1d. (Doc. 218)

Abbreviations used in the Notes to the Text

Buildings of England	volumes by counties, N. Pevsner et al.
Buildings of Ireland	volumes by counties
Buildings of Scotland	volumes by counties
Buildings of Wales	volumes by counties
Doc., Docs:	Refers to DOCUMENTS on the CD-ROM attached to the inside back board; see also 'List of Documents on the CD-ROM' on pages 785–7 below
Gibbs Collection	Eight volumes of drawings in the Ashmolean Museum, Oxford (see Friedman 1984, p. 289)
Grub-street Journal	British Library, Burney Newspapers 306.b [on microfilm]
Journals of the House of Commons	various volumes
RCHM	Royal Commission on Historical Monuments
RCHME	Royal Commission on Historical Monuments of England
RIBA Catalogue	*Catalogue of the Drawings Collection of the Royal Institute of British Architects*, various volumes
SMIF	St Martin-in-the-Fields: Minutes of Commissioners for Rebuilding the Church, 1720–24 (419/309). Accounts, 1720–27 (419/310), Accounts, 1721–7 (419/311), in City of Westminster Archives Centre
VCH	*The Victoria History of the Counties of England*, various volumes
Wren Society	20 vols, 1924–43

Notes to the Text

PREFACE

1 Summerson 1970, p. 353; Gwynn 1776, p. 45 (see chapter 21, note 58), paraphrased in Riou 1768, p. 69; Friedman 1984, pp. 55–70.
2 N. Pevsner's *A History of Building Types* (1976), for example, excludes ecclesiastical architecture altogether as a category. It is indicative that M. Whiffen's pioneering *Stuart and Georgian Churches: The Architecture of the Church of England outside London, 1603–1837* (1948) remained the only publication devoted to an overview of the subject until the appearance of the present writer's *The Georgian Parish Church: 'Monuments to Posterity'* (2004), a concise survey of the major developments of Anglican architecture during the eighteenth century, supported by in-depth studies of six churches representing the chief styles of the period: baroque St John, Westminster; classical St Paul, Sheffield, Yorkshire; gothic St Margaret, Westminster; Palladian St Bartholomew, Binley, Warwickshire; Greek revival Ayot St Lawrence, Hertfordshire; and Roman revival All Saints, Newcastle upon Tyne. A sort of preamble to the present book.
3 Ward 1993, pp. 242–3.
4 Pennant 1772, p. 131.
5 Ireland's impressive church building operations are diligently if summarily chronicled in Lewis 1837, which records the enormous benefits of the First Fruits (*Journals of the House of Commons*, xv, pp. 323, 337, 352–3, 617).
6 *Gentleman's Magazine* (February 1785), p. 92.
7 *The Royal Commission on Historical Manuscripts Repositories in Great Britain*, current edition.
8 See Bill 1979.
9 A good example of this approach, subscribed to in the present book and the author's other related writings, is Berry 2004.
10 A recent claim in Pears 1988, p. 139, that the period 'saw the amount of construction of new buildings by the church fall to an extremely low level', is unsustainable.
11 See Huelin 1996.
12 See Stell 1986, 1991, 1994, 2002; Butler 1999.
13 *The Ecclesiologist*, II (1843), p. 173; Brandwood 1987, pp. 60–61, pl. 63. Simon Bradley (private communication to the author) observes that the condemnation of pews was part of a 'churchwarden culture', wide and deep in cleri cal and antiquarian circles before the nineteenth century.
14 Britton and Pugin 1825–8, vol. I, p. 92. *London Guide* [1876], quoted in Hibbert 1988, p.125.
15 *Our Mutual Friend* (1847), book II, chapter I.
16 Salmon et al. 2005.
17 Doc. 223: 1709, 1733.
18 Doc. 223: 1714, 1716, 1741.
19 Morris 1728, pp. 2–3.

ONE CHURCHSCAPES

1 Georges Simenon, *The Man Who Watched the Trains Go By* [1938], Penguin Classics, 2004, p. 66.
2 On All Saints, Newcastle upon Tyne, Northumberland (1786–96), see Baille 1801, p. 271.
3 Doc. 223: 1739.
4 G. Crabbe, *The Borough* [1810], in Betjeman 1959, p. 23.
5 Pope 1732, p. 18. For further discussion, see Friedman 1991.
6 Pope 1966, p. 48, line 377, and Anon., '*A Description of* LONDON', *Gentleman's Magazine* (September 1739), p. 491.
7 Hogarth 1997, p. 47.
8 Anon., 'Fairy Fort; or, The Pleasures of an Aire', in Barton 1739, p. 22.
9 *The Spectator*, VII, no. 620 (15 November 1714).
10 Doc. 223: 25 June 1740.
11 Anon. 1726, p. 35 (Doc. 223).
12 Anon. 1750, pp. 13, 33. Also 'How beautiful does our land now look, from the spires and steeples' (Torrington 1934–8, vol. II, p. 342, 27 June 1791).
13 Fougeroux MS, p. 24.
14 See also, for example, 'A New and Extra Prospect of the North Side of the City of London, taken from . . . Islington August 5th. 1730' (British Museum, Crace 32–62).
15 From 'The Country Seat', an unpublished poem of 1727 (National Archives of Scotland, Edinburgh [formerly The Scottish Record Office], GD184404, in Piggott 1970, p. 115). A 'Tower, remarkable only for its Altitude, as a MARK to direct People to the Places of their Abode, and where to assemble for religious Purposes' (Wood 1741, p. 33). A site plan of Hatton Gardens, Holborn, of 1712 endorsed by William Dickinson is annotated 'the platforme of the Royall Oake is on a hill and that the Church and Steeple will be a prospect from Holborne, Saffron hill, Hockly Hole, Clerken well green, And all the fields Northwards, from Islington, St. Pancrass, from ye Lower end of Grays Inn Lane, Liquorpond Street Leather Lane and Severall

other places not Mentiond' (Lambeth Palace Library, London, MS 2750/7–8; Rocque 1746–7, 4Ab–c).

16 Doc. 269: Ralph 1734. Soane thought they produced 'a contrast with the pilasters, and a breadth of light and shadow that satisfies the classical eye' (Watkin 1996, p. 610). Reeves 1764, p. 79, suggested that 'had the front . . . a full opening to the [Royal] Mews, it would have a most noble effect' (Doc. 269: 1764). In Scotland, Gibbs's soaring steeple served duty as civic markers, most conspicuously on William Adam's Dundee town house, 1732–4 (RCAHMS 1996, pp. 202–3, citing other examples); also Berwick-upon-Tweed Town Hall, Northumberland, 1750–55, by the Londoners S. and J. Worrall (*Buildings of England: Northumberland*, 1957, p. 90, pl. 56b). Gwynn (1766, p. 85) reckoned St Martin 'wants nothing but the advantage of being seen in the manner proposed' in plate II (p. 45), where the Royal Mews was cleared to create 'King's Square' (the future Trafalgar Square), with an octagonal centrepiece embellished by a statue of George III, surrounded by 'elegant houses . . . a street of seventy feet in width . . . opened opposite to St Martin's-Church (which is the width of the Portico) giving a noble view of the front'. Moreover, 'The lower part of St. Martin's-Lane is widened, especially that fronting the Church, in order to give room for coaches to turn, and the buildings which are about the church are detached, forming a regular paved square, from which carriages are excluded; some of the houses are also thrown back in a line with the body of the church, by which means the portico will project and have a fine effect . . . at the present the expence bestowed on the exterior part of that church answers very little purpose, there being no point from whence it can possibly be seen to advantage, which is greatly to be lamented, as this is undoubtedly one of the most magnificent in London' (pp. 92–3), as well as 'A spacious street . . . carried down to Hungerford-Stairs from the south-east angle of St. Martin's-Church, in which case the church will be seen from the Thames' (p. 94).

17 Among the 'Reasons' put forward in 1715 for rebuilding St Giles (Doc. 229). In Hogarth's engravings of *The First Stage of Cruelty* and *Gin Lane*, both 1751, the steeple is seen rising over the roofscapes. Plate II in Gwynn 1766 shows St Giles 'disencumbered and . . . seen from five different stations' (p. 81); furthermore 'if the lines of Tottenham-Court-Road were continued as in the plan, it would give a fine view of St. Giles's-Church, the strong dotted lines continued from Oxford-Road to High-Holborn shew what a prodigious improvement might be made by joining those two streets in that manner, instead of the aukward curve made at Broad St. Giles's, which answers no end but that of obliging passengers of all kinds to go out of their way; and this would make one of the noblest street in Europe if well built' (p. 93).

18 Downes 1977, p. 257.

19 *Gentleman's Magazine* (April 1761), p. 182. The steeple of St Michael, Stamford, Lincolnshire, was erected by Thomas Eayre according to a faculty of 16 April 1761; it was demolished in 1832 (Lincolnshire Archives, Lincoln, F.B.I, ff. 249–51).

20 Brice 1759.

21 Attributed to Jonathan Swift (Prior 1860, p. 381).

22 Doc. 270: 12 September 1717.

23 Price 1753, pp. 61–2. Around Christmas 1734 the 'ceremony of throwing bread and cheese among the people . . . was performed on Paddington church steeple' (Doc. 246: 22 December 1734).

24 Epitaph on his monument at St Mary (Friedman 1994).

25 Doc. 269: June 1727; Doc. 64: October 1732; *Gentleman's Magazine* (December 1735), p. 735, respectively.

26 British Library, Add. MS 15,776, ff. 1–279; Add. MSS 14256–9; Pococke 1750, 1760, 1887, 1995.

27 Torrington 1934–8, vol. IV, p. 115, 3 June 1789.

28 Doc. 272: 1731 (*The Metamorphoses of the Town*).

29 *The Spectator*, dedication, p. iv, preface, pp. iii–iv, xi–iii, xv.

30 Doc. 272: 1764, p. 26, adding: 'The whole is shewn for three-pence each person' (p. 68).

31 Doc. 272: 1782.

32 Doc. 272: 1785.

33 Doc. 272: 4 March 1794. In 1728, however, a French visitor 'would not dare speak of the majority of the monuments . . . the use [marble] has been put to here is perhaps worse than anywhere else in the world' (Fougeroux MS).

34 Doc. 223: 26 May 1712, 16 December 1725, 1726, 28 August 1761, 9 March 1794, respectively.

35 Doc. 223: 1782; Farington 1978–84, vol. III, p. 790, 8 March 1797, adding: 'The doors & Windows of St Peters at Rome are opened every day'.

36 Leicestershire Record Office, DE 2415/1, 'Proceedings of the Society at Church Langton Founded by . . . Revd William Hanbury', f. 17, 1 March 1773 (nineteenth-century transcript).

37 Doc. 223: 27 April 1711. Addison indirectly alluded to this Vitruvian origin of the classical order (Rykwert 1972).

38 Doc. 223: 6 March 1716.

39 Doc. 223: 1728, 1726, 24 March 1762, 1711–12, 1734, 22 August 1734. Defoe (1991, p. 143) suggested that Wren 'would have added a circular piazza . . . after the model of that at Rome [Bernini's Piazza San Pietro], but much more magnificent, and an obelisk of marble in the centre . . . exceeding any thing that the world can now shew of its kind . . . of modern work'. Gywnn (1766, p. 38) remarked that 'the want of a proper space for viewing the building compelled the architect to execute it in the manner he has done; this may be a fact, but it is pity that such a trifling consideration had any weight at all with him. Had he pursued his own better judgment as to the propriety of the building, it might have one time proved the means of obtaining a proper point of view for this vast design, and necessity might have obliged the publick to do that which nothing but necessity can ever force them to do, for as yet very little attention has been paid to publick magnificence', and 'too little attention has hitherto been given to the obtaining of space and giving freedom to the air; a more striking instance of the bad effects of this neglect cannot be given, than in that of St Paul's Church, the members and ornaments of which in many places are entirely choaked up with soot, which misfortune is owing to its being pent up with buildings' (pp. 122–3).

40 Lines 11–14, 17–19: Darwin 1985, p. 761.

41 Soo 1998, pp. 112–18; Downes 1977, pp. 257–8.

42 Tavernor and Schofield 1997, p. 215.

43 Doc. 233: 23 October 1711. For Archer's particular fondness for paths emanating outwards from buildings to form multiple allées, exemplified by several seventeenth-century Netherlandish gardens that he visited in the 1690s, see Lawrence 2010, pp. 40–43.

44 Tavernor and Schofield 1997, pp. 264–7.

45 *De Re Aedificatoria* [1486], trans. Rykwert, Leach and Tavernor 1991, pp. 195–6, 199.

46 Smith 2003, pp. 132–3, Book IV, Chapter V.

47 Lambeth Palace Library, MS 2690, p. 42, July 1712.

48 Wren 1750, p. 267. Ralph 1734, p. 4, observed that Wren proposed placing churches 'in such a manner as to be seen at the end of every vista of houses, and dispersed in such distances from each other, as to appear neither too thick, nor thin in prospect; but give a proper heightening to the whole bulk of the city, as it filled the landscape'.

49 At the Commissioners' first meeting, on 3 October 1711, 'proper places' for sites were considered; on 31 October they ordered 'one of the best, and Largest mapps' of London; on 7 November Wren, Vanbrugh and others were 'desired to view the Scites agreed upon by the Surveyors, and report their opinion'; on 21 November they agreed to 'Reserving a liberty to alter such Scites as occasion shall require' (Lambeth Palace Library, MS 2690, ff. 1, 9, 11, 15).

50 Downes 1977, p. 257. 'The Insular situation of churches wth large, and spatious Areas about them (as this ingenious Architect observes) is most convenient' (Revd George Hickes, 'Observation on Mr Vanbruggs Proposals About Buildinge the New Churches', in Du Prey 2000, p. 139). Gwynn (1766; p. 81) recommended St George, Bloomsbury be 'detached and disencumbered from the buildings; and streets opened north and south', St George, Hanover Square 'disencumbered from buildings . . . that it may be properly seen' (p. 82), St John, Westminster 'opened to the Thames' (p. 92), and 'the narrow parts of Drury-Lane . . . widened, especially that next the New-Church', St Mary-le-Strand (p. 98).

51 Doc. 253. The site chosen was to become Manchester Square.

52 For a full account, see Friedman 1976. Column designs were also prepared by Archer (Lambeth Palace Library, MS 2724, ff. 4, 6, 8, 24) and Hawksmoor (Downes 1959, p. 277 no. 143, pl. 79b).

53 Soane MS, vol. 26, ff. 24–5, 41. The three radiating streets are the vie Babuino, Corso and Ripetta. This appraisal was shared by Wright 1730, vol. I, pp. 195–6, and Smollett 1981, p. 239.

54 Lambeth Palace Library, MS 2690, f. 1r–v; MS 2727, f. 4. A list was drawn up on 2 November (MS 2690, back, f. 5), ratified on 7 November (MS 2690, f. 11).

55 Doc. 216: 16 March 1716.

56 Lambeth Palace Library, MS 2690 back, ff. 6, 8–9, 26; MS 2724, f. 27.

57 *Wren Society*, XVII (1940), p. 45, with a postscript: 'The prejudice that Devonshire House would receive by such a building is the greatest objection'.

58 These plans form part of Lambeth Palace Library, MS 2750.

59 The Commissioners never purchased the property.

60 *Wren Society*, VI (1929), pl. XV top. A traveller in 1742 remarked that Hawksmoor's St Anne, Limehouse, was 'built with a view to come within the Visto' of Greenwich Hospital (Doc. 258).

61 Dickinson reported on the feasibility of the site on 7 March 1712 (Lambeth Palace Library, MS 2724, f. 30) and presented 'Plans, and Draughts' on 2 March 1713 (MS 2693, f. 65; MS 2690, f. 75). Rocque 1746–7, 13CC.

62 Doc. 260: 29 July 1714; also Lambeth Palace Library, MS 2714, ff. 111–13; MS 2750/26, a site plan of 1711 endorsed by Dickinson, annotated: 'any one of these houses [along Ratcliffe Highway] may be purchased at a Reasonable Rate'. Two other alternative plans (MSS 2750/80–81) indicate an 'open place' on the south, 64 and 164 feet respectively, bound by properties annotated 'This may remain in the Mercers Company'. Rocque 1746–7, 15AA–b; Downes 1959, p. 175. As built, the church was approached only from a narrow lane linked to Cannon Street and today lies open to Ratcliffe Highway because of the clearance of Second World War damage.

63 Doc. 221: 1761.

64 Doc. 267: 12 January 1713.

65 Doc. 245: 11 March 1720.

66 Doc. 245: Stewart (1771) thought the portico 'seen in profile, enriches and beautifies the whole', but it mortified Malcolm 1803–7, vol. IV, p. 232, since the body, flanked by 'brick buildings almost in contact with it[, was] without a possibility of being seen' and its 'magnificent and finely proportioned portico . . . which would do honour to Rome or Florence' was relegated to 'one corner of a pitiful street', adding that the church 'is most unadvisedly and most absurdly placed. If the front had been on either side of the square, the portico and steeple would have had an excellent effect . . . The Commissioners . . . were ignorant of every principle of taste, and governed by a contemptible spirit of parsimony . . . by accepting of a site utterly unfit for a grand church'.

67 Tavernor and Schofield 1997, p. 215.

68 Downes 1959, pp. 121–5, figs 16–18, 282–3, 285; White 1997, pp. 84–93; Hart 2002, pp. 187, 191, pls 276–7.

69 Downes 1959, pp. 117–21, 281–2, pl. 38; Hart 2002, pp. 187, 191–2, 196, pls 278, 288; Giedion 1952. When in 1721 Gibbs planned the Public Building, a grouping of Senate House, Consistory and Royal Library to the north of King's, he justified non-alignment in order 'to bring the middle opening of the intended Library the South Building must come wtin 18ft: or ther abouts of Kings College Chapell, which I believe that College will not suffer for many reasons which are obvious' (Cambridge University Library, CUR, f. 16, letter of 2 May 1728; Friedman 1984, pp. 225–30, 294–5, pls 250–52).

70 Doc. 24: 1778, 1783.

71 Doc. 23: 4 April 1777.

72 Based on a plan by 'Le Quoy, Architect to Louis XV' advertised in *Aris's Birmingham Gazette*, 9 November 1772, as an 'admirable Piece of immense Labour, the only Thing of the Kind in the World', displayed at Mrs Sawyers, 11 The Square. The identity of Le Quoy remains obscure.

73 Burkett and Sloss 1995, pp. 1–2, 61–8, pls 11–15, 24–6.

74 Graves 1905, vol. III, p. 30, 1771, no. 125, 'view of part of the Polygon, now building at Southampton'; 1772, no. 138,

'design for a publick chapel and shop, forming a forum intended to be built, in the Polygon' (untraced). 'Plan of Southampton and . . . Polygon' with 'Plan of . . . Intended Polygon' vignette (*Southampton Maps from Elizabethan Times*, item 8, in Southampton Archives). *The Southampton Guide*, 4th edn, 1789, pp. 79–80, noting that this 'assemblage of elegant buildings was devised, about the year 1768 by Mr *Leroux*, an architect of Great Russell Street', London.

75 Russell and Price 1769, vol. I, p. 320. Defoe (1991, p. 28, pl. 19) claimed that it has 'the finest key in England, if not in Europe, not inferior even to that of Marseilles itself' (Doc. 92). The Town Hall committee resolved to build on 10 May 1715; Price Sr and Jr were contracted to construct it 'according to a draft and plans' (untraced); on 7 August 1716 a sum of £80 was transferred from the chapel fund for purchasing lead; the total cost was £880. Both committees included Captain Artis, Majors England and Ferrier, Captain Wakeman and the Chamberlains (Preston 1819, pp. 22, 30, 190–92); the Town Hall contained a lobby, parlour and domestic quarters (Preston 1819, pp. 192–8; Colvin 2008, p. 830). The church was enclosed in a palisade with provision for 'Streets, enlightened in the dark Nights' (*Journals of the House of Commons*, vol. XIX, p. 419).

76 Doc. 112. On 9 July 1710 Henry Robinson, William Cookson and William Milner, future prominent members of the Holy Trinity building committee, agreed with 'Mr: William Etty of York Architect for the repair of the Moot hall . . . He performing the same Exactly according to the Draught by him and given in' for £140 (untraced; West Yorkshire Archives Service [Leeds District Archives], Leeds Pious Uses Committee, 1664–1788, Part I, f. 151). For Pontefract, see Linstrum 1978, pp. 189, 313, pl. 248; Colvin 2008, pp. 493, 919.

77 Young 1770–71, vol. II, p. 167. Enfield marked the church as the focal point of 'The Diagram or Series of Great Triangles by which the most eminent places in the Map of the Environments of Leverpool were projected' (Doc. 119: 1774).

78 *The Fleece*, Book III [1757], in Johnson 1779, 53, p. 92.

79 Williamson 1894, p. 67.

80 Doc. 113: 3 November 1792. Burial was confined to a vault beneath the church, where by 1842 'the moisture . . . exuded from the [corpses attracted] millions of black flies' (Beresford 1988, p. 272).

81 According to the *Grub-street Journal*, no. 244 (29 August 1734), p. 1. This Elysium, 'one of the most pleasant and healthy situations' (Wright 1797, p. 25), by 1834 had sunk to 'one of the meanest . . . most unpleasant in . . . Leeds' due to smoke from the nearby Oil Gas Works Co. (Baines and Newsome, *General Commercial Directory . . . of Leeds*, 1834, vol. I, p. 171).

82 Soo 1998, p. 91. See Hawksmoor's estimated cost of purchasing and demolishing these properties (Doc. 272: 30 November 1724), with their removal recorded in site plan Westminster Abbey Muniments, no. 2.

83 Doc. 268: Ralph 1734, pp. 55–6, 61–3. Gwynn (1766; p. 90) claimed, 'King-Street in its present form is entirely destroyed, and a new street opened to the north door of the Abbey, one side of which is in a line with the square proposed to front the Abbey; the proposed improvement of a square opposite to the Cathedral will not only have a fine effect in point of view, but will also be the means of removing that intolerable nuisance of a green-market, which according to the unaccountable tastelessness of modern undertakers, is almost thrust under the very wall of the church, when it was impossible to turn around without observing a number of situations much better adapted for the purpose. It is hardly possible to imagine that so fine a building as the Abbey was originally intended to be crouded up with little paultry hovels. Dr. Wilcox . . . swept away all those houses which stood close to the church.'

84 *Grub-street Journal*, no. 241 (8 August 1734), p. 1.

85 *Grub-street Journal*, no. 238 (18 July 1734), p. 1. This has a Palladian origin: the temporary structures for the triumphal entry of Henri III of France to Venice in 1574 (Puppi 1975, pp. 406–8, pls 570–84).

86 Compare Wren 1750, p. 313, and Jeffery 1996, fig. 121. This clever alteration had its downside and the Committee was obliged to 'consult Mr Wyatt . . . relative to removing the Nusance in the Recesses under and round the . . . Steeple' (Guildhall Library, London, MS 2791/1, f. 258, 20 March 1770). See Gwynn 1766, p. 106.

87 Rocque 1746–7, 11ca; Malcolm 1803–7, vol. III, p. 397; Ralph 1734, p. 37; Doc. 265: 17 December 1793, 1799. See Gwynn 1766, p. 98.

88 Leicestershire Record Office, DE 2415/1, ff. 8–11, 13–14, 27, 130–33. Prophet 1982.

89 Doc. 31: 5 November, 15–16, 20, 28–9 December 1791, 19 January, 11 March 1792.

90 Defoe 1962, vol. I, pp. 200–06.

TWO THE ARCHITECTURE OF RELIGION

1 Moritz 1987, pp. 114–15, in 1782.

2 Macky 1722, vol. I, p. 95.

3 Wolcot 1795, lines 9–14, 18–20, referring to 'The place of Mr Rowland Hill's Chapel', Surrey Chapel, Southwark, London (Doc. 251). Pls 689–90 in the present publication.

4 Friar 1996, pp. 81, 85, 116–17, 125–7, 135, 366, 373–4, 465.

5 Friar 1996, pp. 33–4, 138–9, 359–60, 424–5, 444; Rupp 1986, pp. 108–51. See also Currie, Gilbert and Horsley 1977; Mather 1985; Shorney 1996.

6 No equivalent to the present survey yet exists for the pre-1700 period, but see Whiffen 1948; Summerson 1970; Hay 1957; Downes 1966; Airs 1982; Morrice 1982; Mowl and Earnshaw 1988; Jeffery 1996; Friedman 1997b; Bradley and Pevsner 1997; Finney 1999; Guillery 2005; Ricketts 2007; Worsley 2007; Colvin 2008.

7 Ward 1993, vol. IX, p. 164; vol. XVI, p. 296. The ugly old woman 'seen walking . . . to *Covent-Garden* Church, with a starved Foot-boy behind carrying her Prayer-book' was associated by Tom Jones (the eponymous hero of Henry Fielding's 1749 novel) with Hogarth's print of *Morning* from *The Four Times of Day* set (Shesgreen 1983, pp. 109–16). See also the related Gravelot-Hulett engraving *Owen Farrel the Irish Dwarf*, published on 27 May 1742, and L. P. Boitard, *The Covt: Garden Morning Frolick* and *He and*

His Drunken Companion Raise a Riot in Covent Garden, all with views of the church (British Museum, Crace, 18, nos 92, 94–5).

8 Torrington 1934–8, vols II, p. 347 (1791), III, p. 204 (1793), p. 171 (1792).

9 Green 1796, p. 140.

10 *Gentleman's Magazine* (March 1778), p. 137; (July 1768), p. 346, respectively.

11 Moritz 1987, pp. 126–9, at Nettlebed, Oxfordshire.

12 Archbishop Herring, 1743 (Ollard and Walker 1928–31, vol. I, pp. 2–3); Whitkirk, Leeds, 9 July 1762 (Thoresby Society, Leeds); Dewsbury, 1798 (West Yorkshire Archives Service, Wakefield, D9/307).

13 Jukes 1957, p. 143 (Standlake), p. 46 (Clanfield), p. 39 (Charlton on Otmoor).

14 Lambeth Palace Library, London, MS 2721, f. 70. Doc. 25.

15 *Weekly Journal or the British Gazette*, no. 114 (15 July 1727), p. 4.

16 Doc. 112: 27 August 1722, as reported by Ralph Thoresby.

17 Rochefoucauld 1784, pp. 7–8. Oliver Goldsmith facetiously reported (through the mouth of Lien Chi Altangi to Fum Hoam at Peking [Beijing]) that 'Religious Sects in England are far more numerous than in China. Every man who has interest enough to hire a conventicle . . . may set up for himself and sell off a new religion . . . Their shops are much frequented, and their customers every day encreasing, for people are naturally fond of going to Paradise at as small Expence as possible' (Goldsmith 1760–61, Letter CXI, 1760–71).

18 Anon. 1734; *Gentleman's Magazine* (July 1804), pp. 615–16.

19 British Library, 698.g.15(9), referring to St George's Chapel, with *The Case of the Patron and Rector of St Andrew's, Holbourn. In Answer to a Pamphlet*, 1722 (689.g.15[10]) and *A Reply*, 1723 (698.g.15[11]).

20 Langford 1870, vol. I, p. 113; *Gentleman's Magazine* (July 1764), p. 328; Hutton 1783, pp. 113–14; Dugdale 1819, vol. IV, p. 408; Clarke 1963, p. 83; *VCH: Warwick*, vol. VII, 1964, pp. 361–2.

21 H. Walpole, *The Castle of Otranto*, 1990, pp. 27, 104.

22 Torrington 1934–8, vol. II, p. 70, 21 June 1789.

23 Torrington 1934–8, vol. III, pp. 74–5, 14 June 1792.

24 Le Camus de Mezières 1992, pp. 159–60.

25 Doc. 67: 1 August, 11 September 1800.

26 Other interesting chapels appear in Campbell 1715–25. Among a fascinating group of exercises by the Jacobite 6th Earl of Mar made during his Continental exile following the final defeat at Sheriffmuir in 1715 is his un-realised 'Reforme of Longleat', Wiltshire, where a clutter of Elizabethan rooms in the core were to be swept away to create a 60-foot-high domed octagonal saloon linked to the west range by a central corridor culminating in a semi-circular 'Great Tribune' overlooking the chapel, with its 'Little Tribune' and 'musick room' equipped with an organ. Both he and the owner, Thomas Thynne, subscribed to *Vitruvius Britannicus*, which records the mansion (Campbell 1715–25, vol. II, pl. 69). See also 'Tinley Draught' for Ditchley (1720; Oxfordshire Archives, DIL/I/p/1a), Friedman 1984, pp. 117, 318–19, pl. 117; Robert and James Adam at Lowther Hall, 1767 (Campbell 1715–25, vol. II; Colvin, Crook and Friedman 1980, cat. nos 85–6, pl. 23b; King 2001, vol. II, pl. 149).

27 Rykwert, Leach and Tavernor 1991, pp. 141, 146.

28 Leoni 1755, Book V, Chapter XVII, p. 105.

29 'This fine chapel is most elegantly pewed and wainscoted with cedar . . . an eagle of burnished gold supports the desk . . . The two front feet of the communion-table are carved out of the original Royal Oak . . . adorned by an Egyptian white marble chimney-piece, with an entablature, a dove pecking the olives' (Nichols 1795–1811, vol. IV, pt 2, p. 858, pl. CXXXIX, view of 1795 towards chancel showing ceiling), a clear allusion to peace. British Architectural Library, Drawings and Archives Collection, Victoria and Albert Museum, London, K10/11(1, 21–2), K10/12/11 (Richard Hayward's chimneypiece design, *circa* 1764, with entablature relief after an engraving of Castiglione's *Raising of Lazarus*, in *RIBA Catalogue: G–K*, 1973, p. 131). *Gentleman's Magazine* (April 1791), p. 305. The furnishings were transferred to Holy Trinity, Penn Street, Buckinghamshire, prior to demolition in 1951 (*Buildings of England: Buckinghamshire*, 1994, p. 597).

30 Friar 1996, p. 371; Shropshire Records and Research Unit, Shrewsbury, 4258/Ch/1/1. The furnishings included a Wedgwood black basalt font, now in the Lady Lever Art Gallery, Port Sunlight, Cheshire. Biddlesdon chapel, inscribed over the door 'Deo Patriaeque Sayer D.D.A.D. 1735', is attached to the end of the stable wing of the house, built for Henry Sayer in 1731, attributed to Francis Smith (Gomme 2000, pp. 80–81, 133–4, 515). The interior (restored 1904) features a west gallery supported on fluted Doric columns, elaborate altar rail and a pair of Gibbs-style Decalogues (*Buildings of England: Buckinghamshire*, 1994, p. 179). William Sayer, perhaps a relative, subscribed to J. Gibbs, *A Book of Architecture*, 1728, p. xxviii. See illustrations in English Heritage (National Monuments Record Centre, Swindon), AA66/2976, AA46/4121–2.

31 Anon., 'A BALLAD on *Lord* D – le's *altering his* CHAPEL *at* Grove *to a* KITCHEN', *Gentleman's Magazine* (May 1746), p. 266.

32 Defoe 1962, vol. I, p. 358. James Gibbs's designs for a royal palace featuring a large, St Martin-in-the-Fields-like chapel, is perhaps a reflection of Defoe's scheme (Friedman 1984, p. 326).

33 Oxfordshire Archives, MS Oxf. dioc. papers d.562, ff. 171–4. For an overview, see Rupp 1986.

34 *Gentleman's Magazine* (December 1799), p. 1070. This accorded with Oliver Goldsmith's perception of the Methodists in *The Citizen of the World*, who 'weep for their amusement . . . Laughter is their aversion . . . Dancing . . . is with them . . . running in a direct line to the devil . . . as for gaming . . . they would sooner play with a rattle snake's tail' (Goldsmith 1760–61, Letter CXI).

35 The pulpit was moved to the west wall during internal renovations in 1866 (Hague 1986, pp. 38–9). Built for Thomas Marriott of Ughill, the indentures dated 19 February 1743, the fabric opened on 2 June 1743 (Anon. 1987, p. 5).

36 Dorset Record Office, 3693/M1, f. 68; 3693D/M2. Brockett 1962, p. 134; Meller 1989, pp. 40–42, pl. 35; Stell 1991, pp.

79–81. The building cost £2,143 11s. 0d. It was converted to secular use in 1987.

37 Boswell 1950, p. 317, 30 July 1763.

38 Doc. 11; Rupp 1986, pp. 462–4; Lane 1971. See also Spa Fields Chapel, Islington (1768–70, remodelled 1777, demolished 1846), Guildhall Library, 8618; Welch 1975, p. 50; Welch 1972. Also the Connexion's Worcester Chapel (Chambers 1820, p. 266; *Country Life*, 28 March 1974, p. 717; 30 May 1985, p. 1492) and the coffin-shaped Grape Lane Chapel, York (1781, demolished 1963; Royle 1993, pp. 4, 23–7, 131, 145–6).

39 Friedman 1997b, pp. 157–63, figs 55–7.

40 Whitefield 1985, pp. 260–65, 277, 312, 316. 'Rev. . . . *Whitefield* not being admitted to one Pulpit in City or Suburbs, continued his Preachments at *Moorfields*, and *Kennington Common* to vast Numbers of People' (*Gentleman's Magazine*, May 1739, p. 271).

41 Whitefield 1772, p. 344.

42 Coope 1972, pp. 5–6, 183–7, 212–13, pls 214–16; Murdoch 1985, cat. nos 8, 25; *Le Temple* 1982, pp. 141–3. For Tottenham Court Road Tabernacle, see City of London, London Metropolitan Archives, Acc. 1801; *Survey of London*, vol. XXI, 1949, pp. 67, 69, 71; Phillips 1964, p. 223, fig. 304; British Museum, Crace 31/14; British Library, King's Topographical Collection, XXVII–13-a–c; *Gentleman's Magazine* (18 November 1770), p. 541; Palmer 1870, pp. 109–18; Bailey 1981, pp. 9, 29, 55, 59. For Fano, see Perrault 1684, pp. 152–5.

43 Friar 1996, pp. 291–2.

44 Podmore 1998, p. 150. Ledstone was the seat of the Countess of Huntingdon's brother and his wife, Lady Elizabeth Hastings. Wesley, visiting Fulneck in 1747, found the south front 'exceeding grand, though plain' and observed that though the 'Germans suppose it will cost . . . about £3000', he reckoned 'it will be well if it were not nearer ten' (Wesley 1909–16, vol. III, p. 292).

45 Smith 1990. An engraved plan and elevation of the mansion inscribed 'Richd. Wilkinson delin. 1743' might have served as model. The complex issue of identifying Grace Hall's architect requires further investigation.

46 Doc. 81.

47 Staffordshire Record Office, D4383/1/4, f. 86. *Journals of the House of Commons*, vol. XVIII, p. 227, 16 July 1715, reporting that on 14 July Francis Gibbins and Thomas Royston were shot dead at West Bromwich 'by those Persons who defended the Presbyterian Meeting House from being pulled down', but which was nevertheless 'burn'd to Ashes'.

48 Cennick 1745, pp. 3–4, 6, 9, 14.

49 Langford 1870, pp. 472–8. See also *Gentleman's Magazine* (July 1791), pp. 596–600, 674–6; (August 1791), pp. 694–5; Witton 1791. For the history of rioting during this period, see Gilmour 1992; Rude 1981; Walsh 1972.

50 *Leeds Intelligencer* (8 November 1791), p. 3; Linstrum 1978, pp. 192–3, pls 66, 148; Goodchild 1968.

51 Harvey 1794, p. 3. *Gentleman's Magazine* (March 1798), p. 215, reported that during repairs to Highgate Chapel, London, 'members of the Establishment attended at the nearby Dissenting meeting'.

52 Lambeth Palace Library, MS 2712, ff. 182v–183, 191v–192.

53 Particularly useful are Rupp 1986, chapter 13; Little 1966; Evinson 1998; Martin 2006; *Catholic Record Society* volumes.

54 *A Letter to the Patriot* . . . , pp. 10–11, price 3d. (Leeds Reference Library, YY.82[282]).

55 Ollard and Walker 1928–31, vol. I, p. 142; Ward 1995, pp. 209, 285.

56 Doc. 180: 24 July 1786. For the sculpture context of Lord Petre, see Craske 2007, pp. 54–5.

57 Gandy 1998.

58 Harris and Savage 1990, pp. 168–71 n.13. The commission went to George Dance Sr, the City's Protestant clerk of works.

59 *Gentleman's Magazine* (3 February, April 1779), pp. 98, 209; *London Chronicle* (1–3 June 1780), p. 536; Walpole 1937–83, vol. XXXIII, pp. 177–8, 196; *Felix Farley's Bristol Journal* (10 June 1780), p. 21; (17 June 1780), p. 3; Anon. 1781, pp. 9–10, 22–4, 27.

60 Walpole 1937–83, vol. XXIX, pp. 51–3 (4 June 1780); vol. II, p. 225 (2 July 1780), respectively. He was not adverse to Popishness, describing The Vyne's chapel as needing only a 'few pictures to give it a true Catholic air' and encouraging its owner to have a 'thousand masses said in your divine chapel' (Doc. 186: 16 July 1755, 8 June 1756).

61 Saunders 2005, p. 305.

62 Loveday 1984, p. 163.

63 Boynton 1992, pp. 364–5, 367, 371, 373–5, pls 1–3, 5. See also the splendid gilt-bronze tabernacle with an emblematic figure of the *Lamb of God* and a *Crucifixion*, crafted by the great German goldsmith Charles Frederick Kandler for the 8th Duke of Norfolk's chapel at Arundel Castle, Sussex, designed by James Gibbs, basing the *Lamb* on the baptismal font (1692–3) in St Peter's, Rome, by his master Carlo Fontana (Friedman 1984, pp. 73, 324, pl. 56; Rossi and Rossi 1702–21, vol. III, pl. 51).

64 Paine 1767–83, vol. II, pl. 73 (Leach 1988, pp. 104–5).

65 Doc. 180: *circa* 1750.

66 Doc. 180: 1739, ff. 3–9v, 12r–v, 14, 19v. For silver gilt plate, see Schroder 2008, pp. 82–4, figs 89, 94.

67 The Bar Convent Archives, York, 3B/4, 'Anecdotes of the Bar from the Year 1735', unpaginated; January, August 1742, March, June 1745, August 1750, April, July 1751, February 1752, April–June 1753, April, October 1756, April, November 1757, July 1758, September 1759, September 1760, September 1763. In May 1750 'The Chapel wainscoted at ye backs of ye Altar, & roand ye bottom, ye Pillars rails & Altar Table or drawers; steps up to ye Altar all new. New whitened & painted'. The Catholic tradition of gilt flowers for ecclesiastical ornament is discussed in Montagu 1996, pp. 17–18, figs 26–8. The Leeds antiquary and devout Dissenter Ralph Thoresby's Museum included similar relics, described as 'Romish Superstition' (Thoresby 1715, pp. 488–91).

68 Bar Convent Archives, 7B2(2), 8 December 1790.

69 Coleridge 1887, p. 190.

70 Doc. 189: 13, 17 July 1776. 'Since the superb Chapel . . . made here for the King of Poland no work of the kind has been so much so universally admired. the concourse of the Dilettante did not lessen until the tabernacle was down' (24 July 1776). Thorpe reported that the altar had

been assembled in the maker Vinelli's 'work yard . . . with all it's gilt brass ornaments [which] has a magnificent appearance' and attracted 'illustrious' members of the clergy and aristocracy, as well as 'other persons of rank, who hearing it so much praised, can not refrain from coming to look at it'; 'Artists also come with pleasure to examine a performance that is singular in it's kind & has nothing like it at Rome: they congradulate with the Architect for the novelty & elegance of the design; the choice of the materials & diligence in the execution are also commended'. The 'concourse . . . that daily go to admire [it] is so great, that I do not yet know when I shall be able, without giving offence, to have it taken down . . . The Romans universally allow that so elegant a piece of work has not for many years been seen . . . the celebrated Gawin Hamilton [Scottish painter and archaeologist resident in Rome] told me, that he did not think that anything could be better calculated to please in England'. Nonetheless, 'Capt. Mead . . . a Catholick . . . has taken charge of the Crucifix . . . His written Bill of Lading intimates . . . box not to be registered in his Cargo, & . . . more easily . . . conveyed to its adress' (Clifford of Chudleigh MSS, 28 January 1775). For Thorpe's activities at Wardour as a dealer in antiquities, see Bignamini and Hornsby 2010, vol. I, pp. 324–5.

71 Clifford of Chudleigh MSS, 22 October 1774. Bignamini and Hornsby 2010, vol. I, pp. 246–8, 325

72 Doc. 189: 6 June 1770. Ingamells 1997, pp. 169–72.

73 Doc. 189: 17 July 1767. In the manner of *Oeuvres de G.-M. Oppenord*, late 1740s (Minguet 1988, p. 154). Thorpe's fascination with old-fashioned sculpture is reflected in Pozzo's *St Ignatius* altarpiece in the Gesù (1695), a print of which he refers to on 15 December 1770, sending to Arundell (Enggass 1976, pl. I), and his acquisition for Arundell of P. E. Monnot's *Holy Family* relief of 1703 (19 March 1774, 9 June 1789).

74 Doc. 189: 20 April, 18, 30 May, 26 October 1771.

75 Doc. 189: 24 September 1774, 21 May 1777. Ingamells 1997, p. 941.

76 Doc. 189: 27 October 1787. For preliminary discussions about subject matter, see 6 June 1770, 24 December 1774, 25, 28 January, 4 February, February–March 1775, 19 October 1776.

77 Corporation Council Minutes, 5 May 1792. Girouard 1992, pp. 160–61, pl. 138; De Breffny and Mott 1979, p. 141.

78 In 1773 the local Catholic population reached 1,000 (Warren and Keegan 1993, p. 23).

79 The chapel is located in the south-east wing, shown in a house plan (North Yorkshire County Record Office, ZRL13/1/2). A floorboard inscribed 'Isaiah & Reubon Robinson worked on this Chapel in Year of Our Lord 1734' was discovered during post-1979 restoration work (Hatcher 1990, pp. 33–4).

80 Worsley 1987b, figs 5, 11; Cornforth 1967, fig. 6. For Ware's rococo, see White 1986. Compare the handwriting on the Brough drawing (pl. 28) with Ware's signed accounts of 1736 for Office of Works undertakings (Nottinghamshire Record Office, 12, 872/1–2, 5–6) and in Griffin 1992, pp. 60–70.

81 Paine was particularly partial to foliated roundels, as at Whitley Beaumont (*circa* 1752–4), the seat of his brother-in-law, Richard Beaumont (Leach 1988, p. 156, pl. 174). Carr of York also favoured this vocabulary in the 1750s (Wragg 2000, pls 7, 163).

82 De Saussure 1995, p. 203, 29 April 1729; Fougeroux MS, p. 136. The Toleration Act of 1689 'allows of no *image-worship* within ten miles of London, except it be in a foreign amb_r's chapel' (*Read's Weekly Journal*, 18 December 1725).

83 *Gentleman's Magazine* (September 1751), p. 425; (October 1789), p. 950; (23 October 1799), p. 898. The mausoleum's appearance is unrecorded but presumably reflected a temporary catafalque for Pius in Rome in 1802 (Fagiolo 1997, pp. 264–6).

84 A reversed preparatory drawing for the engraving shows *in situ* the *Christ Crucified* and two figures standing before the chancel rail, annotated: 'When I showed this drawing to Mr John Tussaud he said he had been in the Chapel many times, and that he remembered it quite distinctly.' The *St James* altarpiece is now in Budapest (Levy 1986, pp. 167–9).

85 Jeffery 1996, pp. 233–5, fig. 105; Harris and Savage 1990, pp. 182–5, fig. 51. 'If nature's taste by judgements' rule refin'd. / And apt invention, grace an artist's mind. / If such an artist's loss, demands your moans, / *Britons* lament, you've lost a second *Jones*' ('*On the Death of Mr* Wm Jones, *Architect, who died* Nov. 19, 1757', *Gentleman's Magazine*, December 1757, p. 563). Colvin 2008, p. 596.

86 Doc. 234: 1726, 1780, 1808–9. The architect's name is spelt variously 'Jaques' in 1793 (Rigaud 1984, p. 89), 'Jaque' in 1808 (Ackermann 1808–9, vol. I, p. 115) and 'Jacque' (Croft-Murray 1962–70, vol. II, p. 182).

87 The Roman Catholic Conventicle 'Our Lord in the Attic' (1663) and Oude Lutherse Kerk (1633; Kuyper 1980, pl. 81; Van Swingchem, Brouwer and van Os 1984, pp. 50–51, also pp. 14–15, 48, 118). See also St Patrick's Catholic Church, Waterford, *circa* 1740 (McParland 2001, p. 37, figs 32–3).

88 Described by the Catholic architect James Gibbs as a 'fine Church . . . prodigious large . . . ye Cupola . . . an Octagon . . . atop of which is a lanthorn . . . built by the famous Architect Philippo Brunelleschi' (Soane MS, vol. 26, f. 52); 'in a better Taste of Architecture [than gothic], by Brunellescho, the greatest Man of his Time' (Wright 1730, vol. II, p. 394). It was well illustrated in Nelli 1733 (Fanelli and Fanelli 2004, pp. 82–93).

89 For example, San Lorenzo, Turin (Meek 1988, fig. 36).

90 Friedman 1970, fig. 4. For background, see Lock 2007. Gothic was rarely favoured for English Catholic chapels, though see Stephen Wright's chapel (1764–73), Milton House, Berkshire (White 1991, p. 52; Sykes 2009).

91 Doc. 198, 1792, Milner 1798–1801/1809, vol. II, pp. 247–8.

92 For the most distinguished surviving examples, see Krinsky 1985, pp. 238–42, 389–95; Belinfante et al. 1991; Curiel and Cooperman 1990, pp. 42–55; Downing and Scully 1967, pp. 84–7. Also De Breffny 1978; Jamilly 1999; Jarrasse 2001; Kadish 1996; Kadish 2006; Lindsay 1993; Meek 1995; Tigerman 1988; Wigoder 1986.

93 'Worship towards the East is an old Christian custom, so much that the former Jews, in order to differ from them, would pray to any side except the East', citing Talmudic

authority (A.V.O., *Gentleman's Magazine*, November 1778, p. 511).

94 De Saussure 1995, p. 204, 29 April 1729; 'Touts les synagogues se ressemblent: les hommes y sont séparés des femmes, qui se placent toujours dans de tribunes élevées' (Cambry 1788, p. 73). *A New Guide to London* (1726), p. 65, advised: 'you may on a *Saturday* [the Jewish day of rest] go and see their Synagogue, which is very fine', probably referring to Bevis Marks (Doc. 212).

95 Morris 1750, pp. 7–8, pl. 47, further recommended as a 'private Dissecting-Room', an 'Auction-Room' and a library. A building for Everyman.

96 British Library, Add. MS 5810, ff. 191, 193; Add. MS 5833, f. 165r–v, William Cole in 1762, repeated by James Essex (Add. MS 6772, ff. 144, 159v), who reconstructed the Cambridge church in *Archaeologia*, VI (1781). 'St Pulken's Church att Northampton which has formerly been a Jewesh Synagogue; it is made round' (Lancaster 1912, p. 101, from Hannah Beale, 5 June 1710).

97 Quoted in Felsenstein 1995, pp. 305–6 n. 23, the subject of several contemporary satirical prints featuring the cathedral (pp. 143, 198–9, 209–10, 213–14 illus.); Miller 1986, pls 93–4; Hyamson 1951, opposite p. 129.

98 *Wren Society*, XIX (1942), pp. 12–14; Hatton 1708, vol. I, pp. 172–3. Wren's altarpiece was replaced in 1822–3.

99 Doc. 212: 12 February 1700. Its modest brick and stone-trimmed exterior recalls St Mary Abchurch (Jeffery 1996, pp. 268–70, fig. 130).

100 Jones 1988, pp. 404–5; Horne 1972, pp. 199–203; Rosenau 1979, pp. 91, 135, pls 82–3, 90, 97, 101, 111, 125–6, 128–9.

101 '*Roman Architecture*, and the *Corinthian Order* owes their Perfection to the excellent *Structure* of this *Temple*' (Lediard 1730, Book I, p. 1). Langley 1736, pl. CLXXVIII: 'Corinthian *Profiles, taken from the Temple of* Jerusalem'.

102 Doc. 217. Esnoga was the 'most splendid edifice of the kind in the known world' (*Gentleman's Magazine*, May 1778, p. 200).

103 Doc. 94: 1772: Knight 1772, pp. 3, 8.

104 Doc. 187: 8 December 1788, 24 June 1789. Bingham 1711, p. 189, citing Paulinus's great church at Tyre. W. Beveridge's ideal early Christian church of 1672 features a 'cancelli' at the head of the altar apse (Du Prey 2000, fig. 13). This resonates in Robert Bakewell's delicate iron screen separating the nave and chancel spaces in Gibbs's All Saints, Derby (1723–5; Doc. 64). In this context it is worth suggesting that the oddity of the concave cone-shaped spire on St James, Manchester (1788, demolished 1928), may have its origin in the so-called Tomb of Absalom, Jerusalem, of the first century AD (Manchester Central Library Archives, M403/3/6/1; Aston 1816, pp. 82–3; S. Slack, 'St James's Church Manchester' from the south-west, Manchester Central Library Local Studies, acc. no. 9844, architect unknown). MacDonald 1986, p. 153, pl. 139.

105 From a broadside for building a 'NEW GENERAL HOSPITAL . . . at BATH for the Reception of one hundred and fifty poor Strangers . . . 1737' (Rolls 1988, p. 16). For a general discussion, see Thompson and Goldin 1975; Richardson 1998; Stevenson 2000.

106 From an advertisement inviting building subscriptions (Nichols and Wray 1935, p. 201).

107 Doc. 227: December 1772, January 1777. Most public hospital chapels, all vanished, were simple rooms. The exceptions are Richard Castle's Lying-In, or Rotunda, Dublin (1750–57), the first of its kind in Britain, with exceptionally vivacious rococo plasterwork by the brilliant Fleming Bartholomew Cramillion (Curran 1945; Curran 1967, chapter VII; Clarke 1976, pl. 16; McDonnell 1991, pp. 9, 24, 27, 124–7; Craig 1992, pp. 140–41), and Thomas Atkinson's powerful free-standing hexagon (1775) at the Shrewsbury Hospital, Sheffield (Doc. 163).

108 Doc. 248: 17 May 1758. For a further discussion of this unrealised competition, see pp. 143, 453.

109 'This is a handsome hospital, accommodated with a very neat chapel. There is a good carved figure of the donor of this charity, fixed in the front . . . in his robes, well executed' (Green 1764, p. 241). *Buildings of England: Worcestershire*, 2007, p. 749.

110 Butler 1740. Prison literature is extensive; for its architecture, see particularly Bender 1987; Evans 1982; Pevsner 1976, chapter 10; Brodie, Croom and Davies 2002, pp. 21–53.

111 Brodie, Croom and Davies 2002, p. 29. James Neild, writing of Exeter High Gaol, Devon, asked: 'Can there be reformation of morals, where there is no Chaplain, nor any religious duties performed or encouraged? (*Gentleman's Magazine*, June 1808, p. 502). Extracts from his survey of prisons appeared in April 1807, pp. 315–16; June 1807, p. 507; August 1807, p. 727; October 1807, p. 917; May 1808, pp. 412–13; October 1808, p. 898; December 1808, p. 1059.

112 Drake 1736, p. 287; Downes 1966, pl. 498. 'Architectural discrimination, or character, in the edifice . . . has been totally neglected; and a stranger, in scanning over the three sumptuous piles . . . is at a loss to ascertain which is the roof where Justice dwells, the cells for durance vile, or the chapel' (*Gentleman's Magazine*, January 1807, p. 35).

113 Howard 1777, pp. 7, 9, 12, 15, 46, 48, 54, 76. Exemplified in G. Dance Jr's Newgate Prison, London (1770–80, demolished; Evans 1982, p. 114, fig. 49).

114 'Explanation of the Plan', in Fielding 1753, pp. 18, 33, 60–61 (Evans 1982, fig. 22); Colvin 2008, p. 427.

115 Penitentiary Act, 1779, 19. Georgii III, c.74 (*Statutes at Large*, 13, 1780, pp. 486–7, 494–7). Evans 1982, pp. 120–25, figs 50–52; Du Prey 1982, chapter 10.

116 'Postscript, Part I. Containing Further Particulars and Alterations Relative to the Plan of Construction Originally Proposed; Principally Adapted to the Purpose of a Panopticon Penetentiary-House' [1791], in Bozovic 1995, pp. 35, 41, 97–9.

117 *Builder's Magazine*, 1778, pp. 95–9.

118 Doc. 222: 28 April 1720. West and Toms 1736–9 records such commercial excrescence at St Dunstan-in-the-West and St Ethelburga, Bishopsgate (Cobb 1977, pls 6, 139).

119 Colvin 2008, pp. 980–81.

120 Doc. 118: 1774.

121 *I quattro libri d'architettura*, 1570, Book III, Chapter XX (Tavernor and Schofield 1997, p. 203).

122 Doc. 206: 1778. The present writer attributes the undated, unsigned design (Borthwick Institute of Historical Research, York University, PRY/ASP.F.17/9) to Atkinson on close stylistic similarities with his improvements of 1763–9

at Bishopthorpe Palace and church, outside York, for Archbishop Robert Hay Drummond (pl. 214). The cross of 1671 was replaced in the nineteenth century (Buttery, no date, p. 22).

123 Adding: 'It is of more consequence to consult the health of the inhabitants . . . than to employ so much attention in beautifying their town with new streets, squares, and churches' (Smollett 1985, p. 283).

124 Adam's schemes, replacing an ancient church destroyed by fire on 8 February 1793 (Denholm 1804, pp. 96–7, 165–6), are represented in Sir John Soane's Museum, London, AD 48/16–20, annotated: 'The Church may be built imeadiately but the parts tinted Grey and Red being two different designs for Shops in front give the alternative of either removing the Building and Steple towards the Street or of retaining them as they now Stand' (King 2001, vol. I, pp. 71–3, pl. 89). The scheme with 'Dwelling House in front' (Sir John Soane's Museum, AD 48/21–22; King 2001, vol. II, p. 66; Gomme and Walker 1968, pp. 62, 264, 269) is reminiscent of N. Salvi's Trevi Fountain, the centrepiece of a palace façade (begun 1732, unveiled 1762; Pinto 1986, p. 188, fig. 85). James Adam visited Rome in the years 1761–3 (Ingamells 1997, pp. 4–5). Three views by an unknown artist, of 1755–7, are in Sir John Soane's Museum, AD, Miscellaneous Sketches, Drawer 70, nos 55–7 (Pinto 1986, p. 214, figs 157–9). For Trades Hall, see King 2001, vol. I, pls 68–70. For the Scottish background, see Steven 2002.

125 Lindsay and Cosh 1973, pp. 283–6, pl. 89. Ward-Perkins 1981, pl. 59. Further evidence of business participation in church building is provided by the Bristol Society of Merchants' contribution of £150 on 4 February 1775 towards repairing St Nicholas (Doc. 40).

THREE ACCOMMODATING THE CONGREGATION

1 *The New Bath Guide*, 1761.

2 *The Spectator*, I, no. 50 (27 April 1754), p. 186; Bindman 1997, pp. 66–7.

3 Macky 1722, vol. I, pp. 305–6.

4 'Satyr upon the Neglect and Abuse of divine Worship', *Grub-street Journal* (13 April 1732), pp. 13–14.

5 Lincolnshire Archives, Lincoln, FAC10/73.

6 Camden Local Studies and Archives Centre, London, P/GB/M/1–3, f. 18, 20 October 1731.

7 West Yorkshire Archives Service (Leeds District Archives), Vestry Minute Book 36, f. 33, 31 November 1731. See also 'The Misbehaviour of . . . Young Men . . . arisen from Two Misapprehensions' at Stoke Edith (Herefordshire Record Office, E12/IV/174/9 [551]).

8 Lincolnshire Archives, DC/ciii/40/1, 19 April 1765.

9 *Gentleman's Magazine* (23 April 1789), p. 336.

10 At the Countess of Huntingdon's Connexion Chapel, Bath, 'prayers were read in a vulgar tone of voice & . . . we ventured to leave the church before the sermon began . . . The whole chapel was extremely crowded' (Plymley 1992, p. 97, 12 October 1794).

11 Rochefoucauld 1784, pp. 60–61, 66.

12 Macky 1722, vol. I, p. 93.

13 As explicity stated at Stockton-on-Tees (Doc. 172: 20 October 1719).

14 *Leeds Intelligencer* (3 March 1794), p. 3, again on 17 August 1795. See also 24 October 1769, p. 1, for Holy Trinity (Friedman 1997b, p. 99 n. 147), and the French Church, London (Murdoch 1985, no. 57).

15 Soo 1998, p. 116.

16 Oxfordshire Record Office, MS DD PAR Banbury c.6, ff. 67v–68v; a.1 CR, 2 June 1797.

17 Doc. 22: 29 August 1774; on 22 June 1779, 136 'kneelings' raised 2s. 6d. to 2s. 7d. each, bringing in an annual rent of £199 14s. 6d. Richard Kains allocated 'Sitting in . . . North Gallery Markt No 1 for . . . two Shillings' at Blandford Forum (Dorset Record Office, PE/BF/VE1/1, 2 November 1740). The 'new Table of Fees . . . wrote fair according to . . . Estimate of . . . Robert Ross Painter at Four Guineas & an half' at St Magnus Martyr, London (Guildhall Library, MS 2791/1, f. 259v, 19 April 1770).

18 Birmingham Library Services Archives Division, *Local Notes and Queries*, 1890–94, f. 201, 5 October 1715. See also Clarke 1963, p. 22. Wright 1730, vol. I, p. 203, noted a comparable hierarchy in Italy, where pews did not exist: 'The People kneel upon the bare Marble; only Ladies of the first Quality, and Ambassadors Ladies, have Cushions', while at Lent 'they fill the middle . . . with Benches, and stretch a Canopy of Canvas quite over Preacher and People, a little higher than the Pulpit, partly for warmth, and partly to assist the Voice of the Preacher, more than what the Canopy of the Pulpit alone could do'.

19 Worcestershire Record Office, 3696/2, f. 367, 8 April 1735.

20 Manchester Central Library Archives, M403/3/6/1, 15 September 1788.

21 Birmingham Library Services Archives Division, DRO 35/40, 8 May 1781.

22 In 1776, quoted in Smith 1976, p. 14. The practice of curtaining pews is illustrated on p. vi of the present book. The priest at Claughton Chapel, Lancashire, ruled against 'Nails on any consideration allowed for Hats in the Wall' (Lancashire Record Office, RCC 12/15, in 1792). For this practice, see the gallery front in Friedman 2004, fig. 77.

23 Cumbria Record Office, D/Lons/W2/1/47. The church was erected 1713–15. Devonshire Street Chapel is probably St George, Queen's Square (Rocque 1746–7, 3Bb), altered 1717–20 (Colvin 2008, p. 500).

24 Penrose 1983, pp. 44, 72–3, 20, 30 April 1766, adding: 'at present the rich and great assemble here, because Service begins later, and (there being no Sermon) is much shorter; and . . . having but one Door . . . is much warmer'. Nonetheless, 'it is not half big enough to contain the People who would be glad to attend'.

25 Nottinghamshire Archives, PR4295, 17 December 1732. These were to be 'Built Uniform and commodious'.

26 Cumbria Record Office, PR/79/88, 1 October 1779, with seating plan of 1777 (PR/79/87).

27 West Yorkshire Archives Service, Bradford, SPST11/4/2/8, 10 November 1758. Doc. 100.

28 Richard Wilson's opinion, 24 August 1769 (Leeds Reference Library, SR 283, 4275, C765, pp. 25–7). Friedman 1997b, pp. 105–6.

29 Staffordshire Record Office, D917/3/5/11, 31 May 1791; D917/3/5/13, 23 May 1791. On 15 February it was claimed that the church 'is large enough to hold and conveniently contain the whole of the Congregation . . . the present Old Seats . . . are quite sufficient to contain the whole of the Inhabitants', which the vicar and churchwardens 'know and believe in their conscience to be true' (D917/3/5/11).

30 Letter from W. Jackson, 24 May 1791 (Staffordshire Record Office, D917/3/5/13). On 24 September he allowed the faculty to pass, though only 'provided the reading Desk and Pulpit remain in the place they now are on or nearly on the same Spot [since they] are now situated in a commodious part of the Church and . . . if . . . removed and set . . . at either the West or East end . . . they would be in an incommodious situation in so much that many of the parishioners . . . would be deprived of the Benefit of hearing the Minister so well as they now do', adding that if removed they 'ought to be set in the Centre of the . . . Church against the North Wall . . . which would make it more commodious . . . to hear divine Service performed'. Only now was rebuilding sanctioned (D917/3/5/1 and D917/3/5/11). 'Plan and Elivation of Milwich Church' (D917/3/1), Clarke 1963, p. 101.

31 Nicolson 1877, pp. 147, 152, 20 March 1704.

32 Clarke 1963, pp. 214–15, in 1718.

33 Camden Local Studies and Archives Centre, P/GB/M/1–3, f. 19, 9 December 1731. A seating plan of 1780 for Rowner, Hampshire, designates pews for various farm workers (Portsmouth City Record Office, CHU 46/4/1).

34 Hackney Archives Department, P/J/1, f. 306, 15 April 1799. Pew-openers are discussed in *Gentleman's Magazine* (June 1806), p. 519; (August 1806), pp. 727–8.

35 Young and Young 1986, p. 15.

36 *RCHME: Northamptonshire*, vol. VI, 1984, p. 2, fig. 13.

37 Oxfordshire Archives, Oxfordshire Diocesan Papers, c.654, ff. 29–31, 1761 (Yates 1991, p. 203, plan 13). See also 'Plan of the Church at Wonersh', 1781, with impropriator's pew adjacent to the pulpit, minister's seat across the aisle, servants in separate boxes between them and parishioners seated beyond (Surrey Record Office, PSH/WON/12/18).

38 At St George, Bloomsbury, in connection with a 'Complaint of want of room for Pews; (the reason given . . . for Setting up a new Gallery without acquainting the Comm[issione]rs.)', 300 were 'easily Seated' on the floor, 90 in galleries, with 'Spacious Isles in the body . . . for the poorer Sort of People' (Lambeth Palace Library, London, MS 2713, f. 134, 5 May 1732).

39 Petition of 1738 (*A Short History of St Mary's Church*, undated, p. 8).

40 Warwickshire Record Office, DR87/88, f. 46, 15 August 1780.

41 Cheshire Record Office, EDP 89/4, in 1741.

42 Sheffield Archives, B/5(3), November 1800.

43 Northamptonshire Record Office, Faculty Register I, f. 184, in 1723.

44 Bristol Record Office, SF/A12/1, f. 19v, 29 September 1748. See also St Mary, Warwick (Doc. 190: 1703), and Horsforth Chapel, Leeds (Doc. 100: *circa* 1759). At Church Langton, Leicestershire, 'Boys [were given] portable forms arranged parallel to the steps leading to the altar' (Leicestershire Record Office, DE 2415/1, f. 16, 1 March 1773). A specimen of this now-rare furniture type may still survive in the now-redundant St Michael, Bristol.

45 Guildhall Library, MS 4526/2, 14 June 1720.

46 Farington 1978–84, vol. II, p. 547, 12 May 1796. Until its ruination in the 1950s Hartwell preserved its original, 200-year-old benches (pl. 169, this publication).

47 Lancashire Record Office, RCC l 2/15, in 1792.

48 Jukes 1957, pp. 141–2, in 1738.

49 Lancashire Record Office, QSP 1817/1, 12 October 1760. The parishioners of Bradshaw, Lancashire, were unable to raise £1,107 3s. 0d. for rebuilding their church among 'Chiefly Tenants at Rack Rents . . . greatly Burdened with poor' (Doc. 30: 21 April 1774).

50 Printed sheet, quoted in Vincent 1890, p. 149; *Journals of the House of Commons*, vol. XXXIII, p. 281, 13 March 1739.

51 Thoresby 1724, postscript and conclusion, pp. 246–7.

52 Matthews 1794, p. 75. *The New Bristol Guide* (1799), p. 121, adding: 'their dialect was the roughest and rudest in the nation'.

53 Bristol Record Office, 04225/1, 1750, 22 November 1752, 14 May 1754. Gomme, Jenner and Little 1979, p. 149 ill.

54 Borthwick Institute of Historical Research, York University, FAC, 1769/5, with pew plan.

55 Plymley 1992, pp. 105, 109 (5 October 1796, 1799), 113–14 (25 January 1807). For a wider discussion, see Ripley 1985.

56 Swift 1747, pp. 26–7. See the numerous petitions and faculties, 1660–1800, relating to Cheshire, Cumbria, Lancashire and Yorkshire churches in Cheshire Record Office, Bishop's Registers, EDA 2/3–10, as well as Horsforth Chapel, Leeds, *circa* 1756 (Friedman 1997b, fig.38).

57 Doc. 112: 22–30 April 1751. Grafton Wilks, linen draper, 'says that if he could not have Room to sitt . . . he would go to the presbyterian Meeting House' (Borthwick, CP I, 1323).

58 Doc. 112: 4, 6 July (with plan), 21 November, 5 December 1751, 20 February, 12, 15 March, 15 June 1752, 28 October, 11 November 1755. For Scott, see Whitaker 1816, p. 45. A detailed account of this debate is chronicled in Friedman 1997b, pp. 96–100, fig. 30. The galleries were subsequently removed.

59 National Archives of Scotland, Edinburgh (formerly The Scottish Record Office), HR 479/4/1, RHP 176/3–5, 9.

60 Atkyns 1712, pp. 10–11.

61 Nottinghamshire Archives, PR 4295, 17 December 1732.

62 Oxfordshire Archives, MS Oxford Diocesan Papers, c.456, f. 92, 22 April 1738.

63 Borthwick Institute of Historical Research, Fac.Bk.1, ff. 257–8, 12 November 1757; ff. 365–6, 7 November 1763. See also 1700 and 1744. Addleshaw and Etchells 1948, p. 81; *Buildings of England: North Riding*, 1966, pp. 392–5, pl. 54a; Chatfield 1979, pp. 151–4; *Country Life* (12 May 1988), p. 141, pls 7–8; Yates 1991, p. 101. The inappropriately boxy warts of a similar provision are recorded in a view of St Peter, Leeds, before its demolition in the 1830s (Friedman 1997a, fig. 1).

64 Borthwick Institute of Historical Research, D/C FAC 1789/2b, 8 June 1789.

65 Cambridgeshire Record Office, P39/6/21, after 1724.
66 Torrington 1934–8, vol. III, p. 28, 2 June 1792.
67 Howel 1718, vol. I, pp. 1–2.
68 Neve 1726, p. 69.
69 Perriam 1973, no. 35; Stell 1994, pp. 44–5.
70 Camden Local Studies and Archives Centre, P/GB/M/1–3, f. 21, 8 May 1734.
71 Sir John Soane's Museum, London, AD 44/100, and this publication pl. 688. National Library of Scotland, Edinburgh, MS 14835, ff. 76–77v, 18 March 1793.
72 Including 'Cutting & making up with Thread & Labour', 5 June 1779 (Buckinghamshire Records and Local Studies Service, D/DR/12/61).
73 Doc. 268: 22 January 1799.
74 Doc. 269, Doc. 51: 1747, Doc. 109, respectively.
75 Hutchinson 1776, vol. I, pp. 320–24.
76 Dodsley and Dodsley 1761, vol. III, p. 41. Doc. 229.
77 Doc. 268: 3 November 1757, 1758, 8 February 1759, 1761.
78 On 6 February 1779 (Taylor 1925, p. 337). A companion watercolour to the view of an unidentified church interior (author's collection) illustrated on p. vi records not only pulpit and reading desk candlesticks but also brass sconces fixed to pew railings with bell-shaped glass cloches suspended above.
79 Guildhall Library, MS 4073/1, 29 May 1789.
80 West Yorkshire Archives Service, Bradford, SpSt11/4/2/16, undated.
81 Torrington 1934–8, vol. II, pp. 48–9, in 1789.
82 City of Westminster Archives Centre, H806, f. 122, 26 March 1794. See Doc. 271: 12 December 1790.
83 Shropshire Records and Research Unit, Shrewsbury, 1048/63, ff. 132–3, 21 February 1793.
84 Burne 1958, p. 206, 28 November 1749.
85 J. N., 'Of warming Churches', *Gentleman's Magazine* (February 1755), pp. 68–9; See also *Gentleman's Magazine* (January 1756), pp. 32–3. Penrose 1983, p. 116, 16 May 1766: 'I cannot help wondering, that we should hear everyday, that People are afraid to go to Church, because the Churches are cold; when in that we have now been at, and in the Square Chapel all Things are contrived, as it were on purpose, for the sake of Warmth.'
86 'Description of the Pensylvania Fire-Places', *Gentleman's Magazine* (October 1781), pp. 453–4. See also Harris and Savage 1990, p. 467. In 1749 Peter Kalm reported from America on 'the New Invented Pennsylvania Fire-places . . . a . . . Stove, which not only provides plenty of heat, saves fuel and brings fresh air into the room, but is so constructed that the flame may be seen . . . cast of iron . . . The size varies and so does the price' (Benson 1937, pp. 652–3, 8 December 1749. An English edition was published at Warrington, Lancashire, in 1770).
87 Doc. 224: 11 January, 4 April 1792, 20 February 1793.
88 At Bath (1773), the 'roof having no supporters, making it very light, spacious and elegant . . . has . . . two . . . Buzaglo's stoves' (*New Bath Guide*, undated, p. 35). At Lewisham 'Mr: Buzaglo' received £22 3s. 0d. 'for a Buzaglo to air the Church continually', 27 March 1778 (Doc. 243). However, it was too expensive for St Mary-at-Hill (Banham 1997, vol. II, p. 1240). The vast space of Leeds parish church chancel was heated in this manner (Friedman 1997b, fig. 3).
89 Doc. 268: 22 January 1799.
90 Birmingham Library Services Archives Division, MS 11R81, f. 18, 14 April 1777. Colvin 2008, pp. 1193–4. A system put in action by his younger brother, James, at Dodington, Gloucestershire, is recorded in his rare working drawing (Doc. 67: 1805).
91 Malcolm 1803–7, vol. II, p. 550, in 1803.
92 Anon. 1825, p. 18, while observing that 'much of the beauty of contrasts is lost when the building is not Gothic . . . and of a venerable appearance; it being there that the splendid taste of some of the modern churchwardens most distinguish itself'. Also plates 2, no. 12: '*How to carry the Pipe of a Stove on the outside of a Chancel with the best effect*. Pierce the upper part of the east window, and carry an elbow of the pipe through it, joining the chimney on with a gentle angle to . . . the chancel roof [showing] much *effect, beauty* and *boldness* in the plan', a 'sublime idea' (p. 30). For an actual example, see Croydon parish church (British Library, vol. XL–12A, print of 1806). A hand-coloured copy of this publication (author's collection) inscribed on the title label in an old hand 'by the Mr Hares Augustus & Julius', clergymen brothers, the latter Archdeacon of Lewes (Bradley 2000, pp. 33–5), though there is no proof of authorship.
93 Doc. 238. See 'Time Piece . . . for the Inside of Churches' (Langley 1740, pl. CXXXIX) and the now-lost rococo dial attached to St Magnus Martyr's tower, 1765 (Simon 2003, p. 52, fig. 4).
94 Some samples may be identified in the Furniture, Textiles and Fashion Department, Victoria and Albert Museum, London.
95 Humphrey 1728, p. 6; Fougeroux MS, p. 85.
96 Doc. 51: 12 June 1747, lots 4–10. Doc. 109. Subsequently sold.
97 Thoresby 1715, pp. 40, 248–9.
98 Fiennes 1982, p. 224.
99 Doc. 223.
100 Hodnet: Shropshire Records and Research Unit, 2275/79, 6 October 1732. Portsmouth City Record Office, CHU 4/2/1, 1755. King's: Doc. 50: 25 January, 2, 27 March 1755. Westminster: Secker 1988, p. 19, Malcolm 1803–7, vol. IV, p. 22, in 1738.
101 Warwick: Doc. 191: 15 August 1780. Cornhill: Doc. 222: 30 September 1789. Gainsborough: Doc. 82, Addleshaw and Etchells 1948, p. 167, in 1746.
102 Ward 1995, p. 216.
103 Windsor: Doc. 201: 1775; Anon. 1774, pp. 213–14. Hastings: *Gentleman's Magazine* (August 1786), p. 650. Banqueting House: Doc. 262: 20 September 1734.
104 Doc. 85: 22 August 1755. See also Doddington, Lincolnshire (Doc. 66: 19 January 1775).
105 Guildhall Library, London, MS 601/1, 18 November 1773.
106 Gloucester: Walpole 1937–83, vol. XXXV, pp. 153–4, September 1753. Westminster: City of Westminster Archives Centre, E.2421, ff. 36, 38, 26 July, 11 October 1757. Guildford: Surrey History Centre, Woking, PSH/GU.HT/16/1, 17 October 1763. All Hallows: Malcolm 1803–7, vol. III, p. 67, in 1765. St Peter-Le-Poer: Doc. 224: 2 May 1792.

107 Penrose 1983, p. 32, 13 April 1766. Following childbirth they underwent 'Churching', a form of thanksgiving that released them 'back into the world' of church life (Friar 1996, pp. 33, 111).

108 *Buildings of England: North Somerset and Bristol*, 1958, p. 81. Randall 1980, p. 123, pl. 153.

109 Shropshire Records and Research Unit, Deeds 9973, 1 February 1744.

110 Shropshire Records and Research Unit, Deeds 9973, 1 February 1744; contract dated October 1744 (Deeds 13408). The sculptor is Henry Cheere (Craske 2007, pp. 277–8, fig. 132).

111 A 'handsome altarpiece containing the creed, Lord's prayer, and ten commandments in gold letters, on a black ground in stucco between two Corinthian pillars' (Hutchins 1774, vol. I, p. 539); craftsmen's payments are recorded in Dorset County Record Office, PE/ABB/CW/1, 1748–51. *RCHME: Dorset*, vol. I, 1952, pls 57, 66.

112 Doc. 87: 13 March 1734.

113 Bray 1783, pp. 239–40.

114 Nichols 1795–1811, vol. IV, pt 2, p. 901, *circa* 1797; the plate was stolen in 1765.

115 'Vidua's Wish; or, One Thing wanting', in Barton 1739, p. 41.

116 Bennet, no date; Rupp 1986, pp. 462–86.

117 Thoresby 1724, p. 248, epitaph on monument in Ledsham church by Peter Scheemakers; Friedman 1997b, pp. 7–9, 43, 60–65, 80–81, 157–8. Scott 1983. Doc. 112.

118 Clarke 1963, p. 62.

119 *Aris's Birmingham Gazette* (19 September 1772), p. 3. Doc. 22.

120 Doc. 182: 1792.

121 Surrey History Centre, PSH/GU.HT/16/1, 14 October.

122 On 13 June 1751 (*Walthamstow Antiquarian Society*, 14, 1926, p. 33).

123 Guildhall Library, MS 601/1, 8 November 1751.

124 Portsmouth City Record Office, CHU 4/2/1, in 1755.

125 'Account of . . . Earl of Litchfield Churchwarden . . . 1757', f. 4r (Alex Cobbe archive).

126 Staffordshire Record Office, D3785/2/1, in 1760–61.

127 Doc. 165: 25 September 1795.

128 Hampden 1940, pp. 164–5.

129 *The Spectator*, II, no. 98 (22 June 1711), p. 69.

130 *Gentleman's Magazine* (Sunday, 8 September 1775), p. 451.

FOUR THE VICAR'S LIFE

1 *Gentleman's Magazine* (October 1786), p. 983. Such aspirations were expressed in 'A Letter from a Clergyman in *Derbyshire*, to his Friend at *Cambridge*': 'You know, my good Friend, that I . . . crav'd A bare hundred a year, with a neat little house, And a garden adjoining' (*Gentleman's Magazine*, December 1735, p. 730), or 'Between the smooth descent of yonder hills, Deep in the vale with tufted trees beset . . . There stands a Country Parson's calm retreat' ('The Country Parson', *Gentleman's Magazine*, January 1737, p. 52).

2 Walpole 1937–83, vol. XXVIII, pp. 165, 107; Wragg and Wragg 1956; Wragg 2000, p. 108, pls 89–90.

3 Nichols 1795–1811, vol. II, pt 2, pp. 664, 666, pl. CXII. *Buildings of England: Leicestershire*, 1984, pp. 236–64, pl. 47b.

4 Anon. 1810, pp. 5–9, citing 53-year-old James Marshall, curate of Ireby, Cumberland, with ten children and an annual income of £25 (p. 11).

5 Taylor 1985.

6 Anon., *The Curate's Inventory* [1739], in Barton 1739, pp. 81–3, 85.

7 Friar 1996, pp. 476–7. Ollard and Walker 1928–31, vol. II, p. 121, 136; vol. III, pp. 110, 177; vol. IV, p. 53; vol. I, p. 79, respectively. Irthington, Cumberland, 'lyes in most Scandalous Ruins. It fell in the time of the present Vicar, Mr *Goslin*; who is the wretched and beggardly father of ten poor Children' (Nicolson 1877, p. 52, in 1703). Torrington 1934–8, vol. IV, p. 28, reported on 21 May 1794 that James Webster, rector at Meppershall, Bedfordshire, built a new rectory in 1762, 'convenient and sufficiently good – but placed in a dismal country upon a wretch'd soil, in a starving village, with roads nearly impassable: (Nothing but force could set me down in such a place)'.

8 Act of Parliament, Stat. 1 Georgii I, c.10; *Journals of the House of Commons*, vol. XV, pp. 323, 337, 352–3, 617; Friar 1996, p. 181; De Breffny and Mott 1979, pp. 136–7; Best 1964.

9 *Journals of the House of Commons*, vol. XXXV, pp. 670, 785, 800–01; vol. XXXVI, pp. 405, 539; vol. XXXVIII, p. 565; *Gentleman's Magazine* (June 1776), pp. 252–4. Act of Parliament, Stat. 17, Georgii III, c.53 (103). Friar 1996, p. 181. An unusually well-documented example of the Act in operation is offered by improvements made to Bromsberrow rectory, Gloucestershire, 1800–02, including designs (Birmingham Library Services Archives Division, Barnard 930, 931, 932, 933/1).

10 For an overview, see Bax 1964; Savidge 1964; Brittain-Catlin 2008.

11 Bax 1964, pp. 113, 115 ill. A large group of topographical views of the type is in Hertfordshire Archives and Local Studies, Hertford, VI, f. 347.

12 See also Aheron 1754, and W. Halfpenny and J. Halfpenny [1752], in Harris and Savage 1990, nos 9, 12–13; Bax 1964, pp. 114–15.

13 Lambeth Palace Library, London, MS 2690, ff. 5, 37, 2 November, 18 December. On 12 July 1712 the Commissioners resolved to site them as close to the church as possible (ff. 42–3).

14 Lambeth Palace Library, MS 2697, f. 665, in 1717.

15 Lambeth Palace Library, MS 2692, f. 155, 15 April 1738, under John James's direction.

16 Lambeth Palace Library, MS 2714, f. 124; MS 2701, ff. 356, 488, in 1729–32. The others were St Mary-le-Strand and St Michael, Cornhill.

17 Lambeth Palace Library, MS 2691, ff. 17–18, where Archer referred to it on 23 April 1718 as 'very convenient, according to the foundations already laid [and] Unless another piece of ground is bought . . . I am of opinion that there can't be a better forme, nor a prettier building' (MS 2717, f. 100). Jeffery 1993. The polygonal bays were probably the inspiration for the garden elevation of Hawksmoor's Fournier Street vicarage (1725–9), next to Christ Church, Spitalfields (Lambeth Palace Library, MS 2690, f. 169; MS

2713, f. 43; MS 2721, ff. 90–105; MS 2701, ff. 26, 28, 261–2, 343–7; MS 2691, f. 387), Downes 1959, p. 276, no. 74; Girouard et al. 1989, pp. 49–66; *Survey of London*, vol. XXVII, 1957, pp. 199–204.

18 Lambeth Palace Library, MS 2692, ff. 110–13; MS 2749, item 8, nos I–IX, inscribed 'All the fronts are carry'd up with Grey Stock bricks, sound e Good neatly and strongly performed'.

19 Lambeth Palace Library, MS 2749, item 8.

20 Centre for Kentish Studies, Maidstone, DRb/AC1.

21 For example, Bell Hall, Naburn, Yorkshire (1680), and Eagle House, Mitcham, Surrey (1705; Worsley 1995, figs 37, 40). Other schemes for which architects' drawings survive include 'An intended Steward's or Parsonage House' (1769; National Trust, Wallington, Northumberland, 96); Buckden, Huntingdonshire, 16 December 1783, by Jacob Leroux (Lincolnshire Archives, Lincoln, MG A4); Beckenham, Kent (Rowan 1985, pp. 66–7; King 2001, pp. 122, 253, pl. 261); Thomas Robinson's Bigby, Lincolnshire (1779–80; *Gentleman's Magazine*, April 1800, pp. 321–2 illus.).

22 *Gentleman's Magazine* (February 1746), p. 100. '*Romano*' refers to the renaissance architect Giulio Romano.

23 British Library, Add. MS 5834, f. 179, 14 February 1763, with a lengthy description and numerous sketches of the parsonage and outbuildings (ff. 179–91). The vocabulary is that of B. Langley and T. Langley, *Gothic Architecture, Improved*, 1747. 'A. Z.', 'Remonstrance in Favour of the Inferior Clergy', *Gentleman's Magazine* (September 1795), p. 718: 'My friend supposes, as the *Dig.* and his wife are *remarkably elegant* persons, of *true taste*, that he wishes the handsome sashed bow-windows taken out, and the miserable wretched old casements *replaced*, to give the vicarage of T******** the appearance of *Gothic structure*'. The rectory was rebuilt in 1834 (Colvin 2008, p. 486).

24 Dickins and Stanton 1910, pp. 20–21, 20 March 1735. For an overview, see Addison 1947.

25 De Saussure 1995, pp. 132–3, 29 May 1727.

26 Moritz 1987, pp. 7, 37– 8.

27 Torrington 1934–8, vol. IV, p. 54, 13 June 1794; see also p. 194.

28 Anon., 'On a Country Vicar carrying his Wife behind him, to visit his Parishioners', *Gentleman's Magazine* (October 1757), p. 469, and 'Y.', 'Epigram On a Dissolute Clergyman', *Gentleman's Magazine* (April 1785), p. 309. Anon. 1810, p. ix, touches on the right of tithes, which 'has ever been the unexpiated crime of our Clergy. It has made them *avaricious* and *worldly-minded* . . . this system of decimation is the high road to national ruin'.

29 *The Spectator*, V, no. 353 (15 April 1712), pp. 138–9.

30 *Gentleman's Magazine* (11 February 1769), p. 107. See also *Gentleman's Magazine* (December 1777), p. 566; (July 1784), pp. 532–3.

31 Simon 2003, pp. 13, 54, fig. 7.

32 Foster 1981, p. 231. Bagot 1784, pp. 10–11 (Jacob 1979; Guy 1979). See also *Gentleman's Magazine* (December 1764), p. 592; (January 1767), p. 27; (August 1784), p. 576; Keene, Burns and Saint 2004, fig. 38.

33 Alethea 1776.

34 Friar 1996, pp. 476–7.

35 Campbell 1990, p. 27.

36 City of London, London Metropolitan Archives, P71/TMS/213, f. 123, 5 April 1708.

37 Ward 1993, vol. XV, p. 264 [1709].

38 *Gentleman's Magazine* (1 January 1764), p. 42.

39 Cumbria Record Office, D/Lons/W2/3/49, 21 May 1751. St James, an architecturally exemplary church, was erected 1751–3 (Collier 1991, p. 21; Crossland 1971, pl. 34; *Country Life*, 9 October 1975, p. 917, fig. 4).

40 Doc. 64: *Doctor H _ Vindicated*, 1728; *Review Of the Proceedings*, 1728, p. 10.

41 Doc. 240: 11 February 1748–5 February 1751.

FIVE FUND-RAISING AND OTHER PUBLIC AFFAIRS

1 Concerning building St George, Deal, Kent, in Anon. 1713 (*Deal, Walmer, Dover and Kentish Telegram*, 21 September 1867, quoting S. Pritchard, *History of Deal*, undated).

2 *Journals of the House of Commons*, vol. XIII, pp. 711, 772, 871, 888–9, 29 January–11 May 1702; XIV, pp. 11, 17, 34, 68–9, 172, 31 October 1702–2 February 1703. For an overview, see Chalkin 1984.

3 Doc. 253: 24 February 1741.

4 Ollard and Walker 1928–31, p. 2.

5 Oxfordshire Archives, c.654, ff. 27–8, 29 December 1760. The suggestion was not pursued.

6 Friar 1996, p. 67

7 Doc. 167: 27 September, 19 October 1791, 7 March 1792.

8 Doc. 237: 21 December, 28 August 1795.

9 Doc. 112; Friedman 1997b, pp. 58–62.

10 Doc. 161; Friedman 2004, pp. 75–6.

11 Doc. 24: 1712–14, 1725.

12 City of Westminster Archives Centre, Acc. 90/7, 25 June 1766.

13 Malcomson 2003, pp. 36–51; Rankin 1972.

14 Lincolnshire Archives, Lincoln, 10/1, ff. 1–2.

15 Doc. 64: 16 April 1722; Cox and Hope 1881, pp. 35–8; *Weekly Journal*, no. 234 (20 April 1723), p. 1377.

16 *Leeds Mercury* (17 December 1782), p. 3.

17 Nicolson 1877, pp. 142–3. Cumbria Record Office, WPR/15/3, ff. 14–15. The new church was built in 1726–7 (*Buildings of England: Westmorland*, 1967, p. 223, pl. 98).

18 City of Westminster Archives Centre, SMIF 419/311, f. 109, 6 April 1724.

19 Gwent Record Office, churchwardens' accounts, 1673–1745, 4 April 1743. The church, costing £987 (Chalkin 1984, p. 292), was built 1736–7, demolished *circa* 1880 (Gomme 1985–8; Gomme 2000, pp. 56–7, 84, 421, 423–4, 539; Kissack 1975, pp. 110–13, 123, pls 12a–b).

20 Leicestershire Record Office, DE 2493/6/3, 16 January–25 June 1752; DE 2493/6/1, 25 May 1753, 2493/6/2.

21 Birmingham Library Services Archives Division, IIR81, ff. 7, 12, 24, 26–8. See Doc. 23.

22 Pope 1731, lines 142–3, n. 'The false Taste in *Music*, improper to the subjects [of chapel worship], as of light airs in churches, often practised by the organist, *&c*.'. 'As some to church repair, / Not for the doctrine, but the music there' (Pope 1711, vol. I, 342).

23 Nichols and Wray 1935, pp. 202–4; *Gentleman's Magazine* (April 1751), p. 185; (May 1751), p. 233; (April 1752), p. 189.

24 Wakefield: *Leeds Intelligencer*, 1 September 1767. Birmingham: Langford 1870, p. 159, 12 September 1768. Beverley: *Judas Macchabaeus: A Sacred Drama. As it will be perform'd at the opening of the Organ in the Minster At Beverley, On Thursday the 21st of September, 1769. The Music Compos'd by G. F. Handel, Esq.*, including a twenty-two-page libretto (Burton Constable Hall copy). Oxford: *Gentleman's Magazine* (5 July 1774), p. 328.

25 Birmingham: Langford 1870, vol. I, p. 165, 7 September 1778. Birmingham Library Services Archives Division, 202200A, *A Grand Selection of Sacred Music, To Be Performed On Wednesday April 27, 1791, For Defraying the Expences of A Window in Stained Glass, For An Altar Piece in the Said Chapel*, 1791, with librettos and names of singers. Furthermore, *Grand Miscellaneous Concert at The Theatre . . . For defraying the Expences of a Window in Stained Glass for an Altar Piece in St Paul's Chapel*, 28 April 1791 (202200B).

26 Simon 1985, pp. 99–109; Jenkins 1999, pp. 2, 168, etc.

27 Defoe 1991, p. 170, repeated in Pote 1729, p. 150, and Anon. 1774, p. 52. Macky 1722, vol. II, p. 5, commented that it 'hath a Choir of Vocal and Instrumental Musick, as the Royal Chapel'; *Weekly Journal; or, British Gazette* (3 September 1720) 'had divine Worship perform'd in it with an Anthem on Monday last, it being the first time of its being opened'.

28 *Gentleman's Magazine* (February 1733), pp. 94, 97.

29 Baldwin 1990, pp. 239–41; De Saussure 1995, pp. 26–7, 17 September 1725.

30 Doc. 272: 26 May 1784.

31 Doc. 272: *Gentleman's Magazine* (June 1787), p. 545.

32 *Gentleman's Magazine* (May 1771), p. 235.

33 Friar 1996, pp. 111–12, 309–10. See Farmer 1735, pp. 9–10, under 1735, and at Whitkirk, Leeds, on 10 January 1747 (West Yorkshire Archives Service [Leeds District Archives], PAR 53, f. 11). MacDermott 1948; Nettel 1977; Temperley 1979; Turner 1997. Information kindly supplied by Peter Howell. A characteristic publication is Brady and Tate 1725, which carries a preface of 1698 referring to royal permission to 'Use [this] New Version of the Psalms . . . *in all* Churches, Chapels and Congregations . . . *done with so much* Judgment *and* Ingenuity . . . *it may take off that unhappy Objection, which has hitherto lain against the* Singing Psalms; *and dispose that Part of Divine Service to much more* Devotion' (author's collection). The phenomenon, which survived into the nineteenth century, is famously described in Thomas Hardy's *Under the Greenwood Tree*, 1872. For modern performances, see *Vital Spark of Heav'nly Flame Music of Death and Resurrection from English Parish Churches and Chapels, 1760–1840* (Hyperion, CDA67020) and *Vital Spark Present Vital Spark* (Dog Rose, CECD001).

34 Smollett 1985, p. 269.

35 Leeds Library, *MS Leeds Charities*, f. 39, 17 March 1708.

36 Giving as example Cannock, Staffordshire (*Gentleman's Magazine*, April 1797, p. 336; June 1797, pp. 469–70).

37 Doc. 172: 20 October 1719, December 1750.

38 See particularly Wilson 1979, pp. 75–80; Clutton and Niland 1963; Plumley 1966.

39 Downes 1988, pp. 166–70; Keene, Burns and Saint 2004, pp. 224–6, figs 147–9, 154–5, 329.

40 *New Bath Guide*, undated, p. 33, replaced 1838 (Vallance 1947, p. 27).

41 Doc. 16: 1 October 1750.

42 John Goodchild Collection, Wakefield, M/51. See also Robert and William Gray's organ of 1791 at St Chad, Shrewsbury, and James Palmer's case design for St Swithin, Bath (Doc. 17: 1783).

43 Doc. 52: 8 July 1784.

44 West Yorkshire Archives Service (Leeds District Archives), PAR 53, f. 20, 27 April 1782.

45 Pope 1731, line 29. Flanders 2007, pp. 274–5.

46 Ward 1993, vol. XIV, p. 250.

47 York Minster Library, H7, f. 109v, 28 April 1735. See also the situation at Glasgow (*Gentleman's Magazine*, May 1764, f. 248) and Bath (Anstey 1766, p. 24).

48 *The Spectator*, III, no. 205 (25 October 1711), pp. 138–9; V, no. 338 (28 March 1712), pp. 75–6. See, however, *The Spectator*, VII, no. 503 (7 October 1712), pp. 110–11. Also 'Rusticus', 'On the Abuse of Psalmody in Church', *Gentleman's Magazine* (February 1741), pp. 82–3; 'Observations on Church Musick', *Gentleman's Magazine* (May 1757), p. 220.

49 Vertue 1930–55, vol. III, p. 8, 1722.

50 Torrington 1934–8, vol. II, p. 206, 22 June 1790. *The Spectator*, I, no. 29 (3 April 1711), p. 108 [Addison 1754].

51 *Grub-street Journal*, no. 57 (4 February 1731), reprinted in *Gentleman's Magazine* (February 1731), p. 51.

52 Torrington 1934–8, vol. IV, pp. 139–40, 8 June 1789.

SIX FROM THE CRADLE TO THE GRAVE

1 *Gentleman's Magazine* (April 1749), p. 181.

2 Boswell 1950, pp. 112, 55, 62, 74–5, 109–10, 147, 233, 237, 248, 253, 289.

3 Thoresby 1715, pp. 39, 41.

4 Hutton 1785, pp. 35–6.

5 Paterson 1714, pp. 285, 291, adding 'a Coffee-House, Tavern, or Exchange, will be thronged; while a few and small Number go up to the Temple at the House of Prayer; and the Minister thinks it not worth his while to attend on so few. And thus the Life of Religion is like to vanish in this carnal and profane Age' (pp. 292–3).

6 Curtis 1979, p. 414.

7 *The Spectator*, V, no. 372 (7 May 1712), p. 218. Also *The Spectator*, I, no. 14 (16 March 1711), pp. 56–7, where the under-sexton requested that '*Punchinello* . . . chuse hours less canonical. As things are now, Mr *Powell* [the puppeteer] has a full congregation, while we have a very thin house.'

8 Paterson 1714, Introduction.

9 *The Spectator*, II, no. 112 (9 July 1711), p. 112. Secular matters were announced in church: 'An order of council concerning cattle was issued . . . which are to be read in every church, chapel, &c' (*Gentleman's Magazine*, March 1748, p. 137).

10 Defoe 1728, p. 41. 'General Fast day, was observ'd here

with all the Regularity and Decency imaginable. All the Churches were crowded with such numerous Congregations as are seldom seen, who by their silent Attention, shew'd how sensible they were of the Occasion which brought 'em together. The Shops were shut up throughout the whole Town, except those of one particular Sect; and the Streets and Alehouses remarkably free from loose, disorderly People, during the whole Day' (*Leeds Intelligencer*, 10 February 1756).

11 *Weekly Miscellany*, 28 December 1734; reprinted in *London Magazine* (December 1734), p. 658.

12 Garretson 1701, pp. 26–7.

13 *The Spectator*, V, no. 380 (16 May 1712), pp. 246–7; VI, no. 458 (15 August 1712), pp. 237–8; VI, no. 460 (18 August 1712), p. 246.

14 *The Spectator*, II, no. 129 (28 July 1711), p. 175; III, no. 175 (20 September 1711), p. 29. See also *The Spectator*, IV, no. 259 (27 December 1711), p. 35, and IV, no. 272 (11 January 1712), p. 83.

15 Reprinted in *Gentleman's Magazine* (May 1734), p. 266; also 'The *Preachers* . . . have an abrupt Way of ending their Discourse . . . while . . . People, *stare, wonder*, and know *nothing of the Matter*'.

16 *The Spectator*, IV, no. 282 (23 January 1712), p. 118. See also IV, no. 284 (25 January 1712), pp. 126–7; IV, no. 296 (8 February 1712), p. 169; VII, no. 515 (21 October 1712), p. 161.

17 Reported in *The London Spy*, 1725 (Ward 1993); quoted in McMaster 1916, p. 85. Ward 1993, vol. I, p. 16, also wrote about the dark side of churchgoing: 'a Water Lane Protestant who when at church seems most devout, yet is picking the pocket of some over-penitent Christian who is so zealous at his prayers that he neglects to watch, and whilst he has God in his heart has the devil tumbling about his breeches'.

18 Friar 1996, p. 279.

19 The wedding venue is unrecorded, though the architecture is reminiscent of St Martin (Paulson 1971, vol. I, pp. 224–5, pl. 84). For an autograph copy in the Philadelphia Museum of Art, see Friedman 1984, pl. IV.

20 Vertue 1930–55, vol. III, p. 68.

21 Croker 1884, vol. I, pp. 312–16. The decor created in the same venue for George III's marriage to Queen Charlotte of Mecklenburg-Strelitz on 8 September 1761 was even more sumptuous, described as 'very handsomely decorated . . . hung with Crimson Velvet laced & fringed with Gold. On the sides were very fine pieces of Tapestry of the Cartoons put up in the manner of Pictures with Frames of broad Gold Lace. Round the altar piece was a broad border of Gold flower'd Tissue and the steps &c of the Altar was covered with Silver Tissue. On one side of the Altar was a Throne for the King & Queen of Crimson Velvet adorn'd with Gold Lace & fringe of Carving and Gilding . . . lined with Silver Tissue' (Northumberland 1926, pp. 31–2).

22 Fagiolo 1997, p. 34.

23 D. Vickers, notes and libretto accompanying Hyperion recording CDA 67701/2 of 2008.

24 Sheffield Local Studies Library, file, press report.

25 Doc. 19: 9 September 1726, carved by William Thornton of York. Friar 1996, pp. 33, 202–4.

26 Doc. 245: 25 March 1724–25 March 1725.

27 See his fixture of 1729 at Dulwich College chapel, London (Friedman 1984, p. 305). By 1740 they were plagiarised by Batty Langley, who recommended that 'to be grand, [they] should be erected on a spacious Ascent of three Steps, that . . . during the Performance . . . the Priest may be elevated above the Congregation' (Langley 1740, p. 22, pl. CL). See also Langley 1738.

28 *Gentleman's Magazine* (3 July 1763), p. 359 (Purchas 1994). This curious triadic object, on the border between rococo and the antique, perhaps derives from a Roman bronze lucerna in an English collection illustrated in G. B. Piranesi, *Vasi, candelabri, cippi, sarcophagi, tripodi, lucerne, ed ornamenti antichi*, 1778 (Ficacci 2000, pl. 803).

29 Nichols 1795–1811, vol. II, pt 1, p. 340; Addleshaw and Etchells 1948, p. 66.

30 Whitehead 1757.

31 Pope 1733, lines 375, 380–84.

32 As recorded on engraved funeral tickets, which were commercially printed leaving blank spaces for hand-written personalised invitations. Litton 1991, pls 3, 9, 79; Llewellyn 1991.

33 Fagiolo 1997 and Fagiolo dell'Arco 1997. See particularly the obsequies surrounding the exiled James II of England held in 1702 at San Lorenzo in Lucina, Rome, where the façade was draped in black (Fagiolo 1997, pp. 9–10, figs 6–7).

34 *Gentleman's Magazine* (January 1789), p. 81.

35 *Gentleman's Magazine* (December 1737), pp. 763–4; Westminster Abbey Muniments, 6274. At St Mary, Nottingham, the pulpit and desk were 'put into Mourning with black Bayes or flannel in a Devout manner' (Nottinghamshire Archives, CA7708, f. 98, 4 December 1737).

36 *Gentleman's Magazine* (April 1751), pp. 184–5. He died of pneumonia, aged 44. The pulpit and mayor's pew in St Nicholas, Newcastle upon Tyne, were draped in black to mark the passing (Sykes 1833, p. 199, 20 March 1751).

37 *Gentleman's Magazine* (November 1760), pp. 539–40. Similar arrangements were made for the royal children (Westminster Abbey Muniments, 48262, 48058, 48496, 48502, 49393; *Gentleman's Magazine*, November 1765, pp. 535–6). The communion table, pulpit, desks and three cushions in St Botolph, Aldersgate, London, were 'putt into Mourning' to mark the king's passing (Guildhall Library, City of London Corporation, MS 3863/1, f. 34).

38 Anon., 'LINES *suggested by Mr* PITT's *Funeral in* Westminster Abbey', *Gentleman's Magazine* (April 1806), p. 358.

39 Hearne 1906, pp. 222, 225–6, 252–4; Roscoe 1999, figs 32–3.

40 *Gentleman's Magazine* (July 1778), pp. 333–4; Walpole 1937–83, vol. XXXIII, p. 19, 9 June 1778.

41 Hampden 1940, p. 341. Robert Adam's triumphal white marble tomb commissioned by the widower to 'the best of wives' was erected two years later (King 2001, p. 369, pl. 532).

42 *Gentleman's Magazine* (October 1780), pp. 472–3.

43 Goldsmith 1760–61, Letters XII–XIII. See also Rouquet 1755, pp. 64–5.

44 Rochefoucauld 1785, p. 182 n. 12. See Craske 2007.

45 On 19 June and July 1755, p. 324, respectively, adding: 'the Chinese taste . . . already introduced into our gardens . . . building, and . . . furniture, will also soon find its way into our churches'. The issue of classical-style tombs in gothic churches is discussed in Milner 1798–1801/1809, vol. II, pp. 14–15.

46 Anon. 1731, p. 16 (British Library, T.0156[14]). 'In Westminster abbey, frigid or dormant, indeed, must be the faculties of that man, who does not contemplate with secret satisfaction the monuments of those great and illustrious personages who have adorned the annals of our country' (*Gentleman's Magazine*, Supplement 1799, p. 1100). They were by no means universally admired: Abbé Fougeroux, visiting in 1728, 'would not dare speak of the majority of the monuments . . . the use [marble] has been put to here is perhaps worse than anywhere else in the world' (Fougeroux MS, p. 22).

47 Dart 1723, vol. I, pp. ii–iii, xxii.

48 Roscoe 1999, p. 179, fig. 33. Anon. 1726, pp. 15–16. Entrance fees doubled between 1697 and 1723 (Carpenter 1972, p. 252). 'The Dean and Chapter are no farther concerned, as to the erecting Monuments, than to give Leave for it; they apply all the Fees paid for the Ground and Monument, to the Fabrick [and] all the Profit arising from shewing the Tombs, to the Choir and Officers of the Church' (*Gentleman's Magazine*, May 1734, p. 246).

49 De Saussure 1995, pp. 31, 33, 17 September 1725.

50 *Gentleman's Magazine* (May 1737), p. 313.

51 *Gentleman's Magazine* (June 1759), p. 257; Vertue 1930–55, vol. III, p. 116; Roscoe 1999, pp. 202–4, figs 51–2.

52 Gwynn 1749, pp. v–vi. Whinney 1988, pp. 172–3, pls 115–16. Gwynn (1766; pp. 27–31), who offered an historical survey of English sculpture, regarded Westminster Abbey as 'deformed by monuments . . . The beauty of the whole is destroyed by these intrusions, and however sub-lime and beautiful some of these works may be in themselves, hardly one of them has been introduced with pro- priety, or its form and situation considered with regard to the whole structure. Some are less faulty in this particular than others, but numbers of them ought to be entirely taken away, as tending to nothing more than loading and deforming the church in the most wretched manner' (p. 124); moreover, 'The custom of erecting monuments in churches at all is an absurdity, but the practice of deforming churches merely because people can afford to pay a large tax upon vanity, is intolerable, and if the real worth of some, who figure it in holy places, was strictly enquired into, many a heap of beautiful marble, and exquisite art, would be unanimously thrust out of them as publick nuisances' (p. 113).

53 Leicestershire Record Office, DE 2415/1, ff. 8–10, 18–19, 45. Costs were hierarchical, from the first ten trustees at £1,500 each, trustees with more than twenty years service £1,000; when sites were full, 'no more Monuments shall be erected in the Church, but a Grand Mausoleum shall be built in some convenient place for the Sepulture of the Trustees and the professors for ever' (f. 10). 'The Marble Merchants at Mill Bank Westminster sell . . . White Italian . . . Statue Marble . . . in the Block 22/ per Cubic foot' (f. 22).

54 The chapel foundations were dug in 1705 (Green 1951, p. 73); in 1711 Vanbrugh estimated on finishing the chapel (Historical Manuscript Commission, *Portland*, vol. X, 1931, pp. 136–7); a proposed scheme was published in Campbell 1715–25, vol. I, pl. 62; Marlborough directed burial in the interior in his will of 1722 (Green 1951, p. 269); William Townsend contracted for 'Bragetting and finishing . . . the Plaisterer' in 1724 (p. 238); it was 'not yet completed' in 1728 (Fougeroux MS, p. 67). In May 1730 J. M. Rysbrack, who prepared various designs (Harris 1971, p. 190, pls 137–44), agreed to 'make a tomb . . . according to the model [now in Sir John Soane's Museum, London] done by [William] Kent . . . the figure of the Duke . . . seven feet high . . . The Battle upon the Basso Relievo . . . what her Grace shall direct' for £2,200 (Green 1951, p. 274). Vertue 1930–55, vol. III, p. 66, commented in 1733 that Rysbrack gave the duke 'life & likeness in . . . Marble' (Green 1971–2). The chapel was consecrated on 4 September 1731; according to the duchess, on 24 May 1732 it was 'finish'd and more than half the Tomb . . . ready to set up all in Marble Decorations of Figures, Trophies, Medals . . . in short everything that could do the Duke . . . Honour and Justice. This is all upon the Wall of one side the Chappel. The rest of it is finish'd decently substantially and very plain. And considering how many Wonderful Figures and Whirligigs I have seen Architects finish a Chappel withal, there are of no Manner of Use but to laugh at, I must confess I cannot help thinking that what I have designed for this Chappel may as reasonably be call'd finishing of it, as the Pews and Pulpit' (Green 1951, p. 160). It is 'a noble piece of architecture' (Godber 1968, p. 147). Dugdale 1819, vol. IV, p. 120; Downes 1966, fig. 37. The control of multiple monuments in an architectural setting was dramatically achieved at Warkton, Northamptonshire (Torrington 1934–8, vol. III, p. 209, 15 July 1793; Murdock 1980; Bindman and Baker 1995, pp. 299–301, 361).

55 Smollett 1985, p. 215. The *London Magazine* (February 1756), pp. 81–3, featured 'Burying in Churches pernicious'. The *Gentleman's Magazine* ran an unrelenting campaign with titles like 'Burying in Churches infectious, by reason of the Steam from putrid Carcases' (October 1736, p. 604), 'Animal Putrefaction highly pernicious' (July 1749, pp. 301–4), 'properly reprobated' (May1805, pp. 421–2).

56 Guildhall Library, MS 594/4, f. 13, 26 November. See the case of the still-intact Pennant monument, St Michael Paternoster, London, *circa* 1750, by J. M. Rysbrack (Bradley and Pevsner 1997, p. 118).

57 Lambeth Palace Library, London, MS 2724, ff. 41–2, 23 April 1714, in connection with St Alfege, Greenwich, adding the 'difference of . . . Expence in filling it up with earth, and vaulting it is not more than___ £200'.

58 *Buildings of England: London 6*, 2003, pp. 143–84; *Westminster Abbey Official Guide*, 1973. See Doc. 272: 1769.

59 Camden Local Studies and Archives Centre, London, P/PN/M/1, ff. 94, 96r–v, 22 April, 18 June 1794. The vaults are shown in a contemporary model (Doc. 255).

60 City of Westminster Archives Centre, 5/1, ff. 104–5. Nevertheless, 'Eight Vertical Air Grates, & Eight Horizontal . . . to admit air into . . . Vaults' were specified for St James's Chapel, Hampstead Road, London, 1789–93 (British Architectural Library, Drawings and Archives Collection, Victoria and Albert Museum, London, AC/HAR/Add/2).

61 *Journals of the House of Commons*, vol. XXIX, p. 495, 24 February 1763.

62 Leeds Reference Library, Parish Records Book 17, ff. 46–7, 25 May 1761.

63 Soo 1998, p. 112.

64 Downes 1977, p. 257.

65 Soo 1998, p. 113; Downes 1977, p. 258. See also George Hickes's contemporary 'Observations' (Du Prey 2000, p. 141). In 1711 the Commissioners resolved when possible to separate churches 'some distance' from cemeteries (Lambeth Palace Library, MS 2690, f. 9, back, 13 November, f. 13, 14 November).

66 Downes 1977, p. 258, pl. 55, citing the 'English manner of Interment . . . at Surrat' (Williams 2000, fig. 82).

67 Roger Gale to William Stukeley, 28 September 1743 (Stukeley 1882–7, vol. I, p. 361; Webb 1931, p. 117, 3 September 1726; pp. 119–20, 11 July 1728). Downes 1959, pp. 222–31, 283, pls 92–6. For an overview, see Colvin 1991, pp. 316–17, figs 293–4, frontispiece.

68 Doc. 108. Gibbs turned to his copy of J. B. Fischer von Erlach's *Entwurff Einer Historischen Architectur*, 1721, pl. VI (Friedman 1984, pl. 271). For an equally striking neoclassical version, see James Wyatt's Darnley Mausoleum, Cobham, Kent (1783–4), described by Soane as 'enriched with the modern Doric order . . . finished with a pyramid, not from the taste of the architect but pursuant to the will' of the 4th Earl of Darnley (Watkin 1996, p. 548). Restored 1997–2009 (Bowdler 2009).

69 *Gentleman's Magazine* (November 1761), p. 527.

SEVEN THROUGH THE WEST DOOR

1 Legrand and Landon 1806–9, vol. I, p. 38.

2 Doc. 37: *circa* 1750.

3 Smollett 1981, p. 218, Letter XXVII. A. Pozzo's *Perspectiva Pictorum Et Architectorum*, first published in 1693, appeared in several editions in various countries (Pollock 2000, pp. 329–35). Wren and Hawksmoor owned copies (Watkin 1972, p. 36 lot 542, p. 103 lot 93), as did the Leeds antiquary Ralph Thoresby (Friedman 1997b, p. 66). Interestingly, John James's English edition of 1707, *Rules and Examples of Perspective*, excluded the majority of Pozzo's studies for church interiors.

4 Soo 1998, pp. 112–18. For similar interior sections as pl. 74 and also perspectives, see Malton 1779, pl. XXX, fig. 2; Summerson, Watkin and Mellinghoff 1983, p. 112; Worsley 1991a, p. 123.

5 Doc. 40: 1798.

6 Hunter 1828–31, vol. II, p. 19, 9 January 1709.

7 Campbell 1947, p. 50, 12 March. Doc. 227.

8 Loveday 1984, p. 339. Doc. 8.

9 Doc. 270: 1728 (Gibbs 1728).

10 Malcolm 1803–7, vol. I, p. 321, in 1769; Huelin 1996, p. 82.

11 Borthwick Institute of Historical Research, York University, Reg. 35, ff. 108–9, 19 June 1731; the faculty was granted on 14 July.

12 Farmer 1735, p. 8.

13 Doc. 119: 1774.

14 Doc. 119: 1794. In 1818 Thomas Harrison inserted a low, timber and plaster saucer dome springing from the imposts of the columns, which solved the problem but marred the proportions: its 'surface enriched with panelling similar to that of the temple of Vesta at Tivoli, which has added greatly to the richness and beauty of the interior, and also had the desired effect' (*Gentleman's Magazine*, December 1829, p. 511).

15 Doc. 166: 3, 8 September 1789.

16 Shropshire Records and Research Unit, Shrewsbury, 1048/63, ff. 12–15, adding: 'there is not a doubt but [an oblong St Chad] may be Executed for some less Money . . . Yet the design has Neither the Elegance or Novelty' of the rotunda.

17 Quoted in Odom 1922, p. 97, quoting from Wesley's *Journal*, August 1788.

18 Malcolm 1803–7, vol. I, p. 21. For another viewpoint, see 'Singular Effect of removing the Cushion from a Pulpit' (*Gentleman's Magazine*, November 1780, p. 527).

19 The 11th edition, of 1747, p. 24, shows the minister preaching from a wooden barrel raised on a platform above the indolent congregation, with a view through a window to a public hanging.

20 Soo 1998, p. 115, in 1711.

21 Clarke and Colvin 1952–3, pt II, p. 94, in 1719.

22 Doc. 235: 1719–20. Friedman 1997a.

23 Doc. 52. See also the fantastical pulpit at Beverley Minster, *circa* 1724–5 (destroyed); Hawksmoor was then acting as surveyor (Doc. 19), Cobb 1980, pl. 95.

24 A recommendation of 12 April 1694 to 'make the Pulpit' for All Hallows, Lombard Street, 'both for good workmanship, carving and other ornaments, according to . . . the Pulpit now standing in *St Mary Abchurch*' (*Wren Society*, XIX, 1942, p. 3) suggests that the practice of borrowing patterns among the City churches may not have been uncommon. Langley published numerous designs, 'which the ingenious Workman may perform with Pleasure' (Langley 1740, p. 21, pls CXII–CXVII). Similar examples appear in William Pain's pattern books (Harris and Savage 1990, pp. 338–46).

25 Melville 2007, p. 196. The type is well represented by H. F. Verbruggen's pulpit of 1699 in Brussels cathedral (Gerson and Ter Kuile 1960, fig. 22B).

26 Friar 1996, p. 368. Unusually, at Great St Mary, Cambridge, Dr Rutherford, a member of the University Syndics providing a new pulpit, seemed to believe the latter useless ('Cantabrigensis', 'On the Sounding-Boards in Pulpits, &c', *Gentleman's Magazine*, August 1780, p. 364).

27 Doc. 240: 17 October 1754. As confirmed in a pre-1940 photograph (Islington Archives, 24719). See similar situations at St Peter, Nottingham (Nottinghamshire Archives, PR 4295, 19 February 1732; PR 10,893, 15 June 1784), and St Mary, Battersea (Doc. 261: 8, 15 March, 12 April 1777).

28 Doc. 39: 17 February 1780.

29 Doc. 270: 25 March 1722.
30 Doc. 163: 15 August 1781.
31 Doc. 19: 12 December 1724, 28 October 1726. Doc. 119: 1774.
32 Swift 1747, p. 27.
33 'Corinra', 'On a short Clergyman', *Gentleman's Magazine* (January 1735), p. 45.
34 Campbell 1947, p. 57. On another occasion his 'composition inclined to vehemence' (p. 81).
35 Campbell 1947, pp. 46–7, 78, 80. See also 'On hearing the Rev. Mr Dodd Preach' (*Gentleman's Magazine*, March 1768, p. 135). He was executed in 1777 for forgery.
36 *The Spectator*, VI, no. 407 (17 June 1712), p. 47.
37 Williams 1765, lines 107–11, published in 1765.
38 *Gentleman's Magazine* (September 1746), p. 490; (December 1759), pp. 575–6; (January 1760), pp. 7–8; (January 1778), pp. 18–21; (May 1779), p. 261; (February 1791), pp. 112–14.

EIGHT THE BATTLE BETWEEN DECORATION AND ADORATION

1 'The Choir', in Wright 1697, p. 9.
2 Rouquet 1755, p. 22. The absence, at least early in the eighteenth century, of spectacular altar paintings was largely due to the destructive nature of post-Reformation iconoclasm (Aston 1988; Dowsing 2001).
3 Hatton 1708, pp. 172–3.
4 Doc. 140: August 1717, 1718. Colvin 2008, p. 496; Downes 1988, pp. 157–72; Keene, Burns and Saint 2004, figs 152–3.
5 Doc. 221: 1 January 1727–25 March 1728.
6 Centre for Kentish Studies, Maidstone, U23 Q3/2.
7 'A Society of Architects', *Builder's Magazine* (1774–8), p. 229, pl. CLXIII, dated 1 March 1778.
8 Collinson 1791, vol. III, p. 9; King 2001, vol. I, p. 369, pl. 523.
9 Blum 1997, p. 79, no. 143. The prestige attached to communion vessels is manifest in the Revd Samuel Parr's instructions to his parishioners at Hatton, Warwickshire: 'the new Plate to be kept in a convenient Box, lined with green cloth, and furnished with soft paper . . . have [it] cleaned and touched very gently, so as not to hurt the fine Workmanship [and] never . . . twisted or defaced', particularly the Rundell & Co. ewer, which 'exceeds probably any other to be found in any Parish Church throughout the Kingdom [and] quite equal [the] beautiful service . . . King George . . . graciously presented to the Church of Quebec' (Warwickshire Record Office, DR 476/10, 5 December 1809).
10 Anon. 1767b, p. 13, which refers to 'drawing away the People of GOD to the Worship of Idols' (York Minster Library). D. D., 'The Commandments': '1. One GOD there is – him only shall thou fear, 2. Nor make to sculptur'd idols fruitless pray'r' (*Gentleman's Magazine*, January 1748, p. 39). For an overview, see Haynes 2006.
11 Trapp 1723 (original in British Library, 694.k.10 [20]). Trapp was vicar of Christ Church, Newgate, London. No record of Shipbourne's interior survives apart from Gibbs's and J. M. Rysbrack's splendid monument to the Barnards, to which Trapp refers ('*by a Christian Contempt of Death You have* built your own Tomb . . . *May the yet vacant Marble, in the Midst of the August Statues, and other Decorations with which it is surrounded, for many Years continue vacant*') and which remains in the rebuilt church of 1879 (Friedman 1984, pp. 72, 92, 302–3, pls 55, 83; Hussey 1958b, p. 112).
12 Lacy 1715, pp. 5, 9, 16.
13 Pearce 1727, pp. 12–13 (original in City of Westminster Archives Centre, F131/27–32).
14 Ken Spelman, Antiquarian Booksellers, York, *Engraved Trade Cards & Printed Ephemera of the XVIIIth and XIXth Centuries*, 1992, lot 129.
15 *Wren Society*, XVI (1939), p. 107. Stainton and White 1987, p. 236. The contenders were the Venetian Sebastiano Ricci and the Bolognese Marcantonio Franseschini, 'who by sinister means is now painting a Cupola for St Peter's' (Talman 1997, p. 160, 18 November 1711). Other participants were Pierre Berchett, G. B. Cattenaro, Louis Chéron and G. A. Pellegrini (Doc. 223).
16 Gwynn 1766, p. xv.
17 Wren 1750, p. 292, based on Wren's unpublished notes, states only that the 'Painting and Gilding of the Architecture over the Communion Table was intended only to serve . . . till such Time as Materials could have been procured for a magnificent Design of an Altar'. Gwynn (1766; pp. 26–7) made a strong case that 'in order to raise the art to the utmost degree of perfection in England, it is sincerely to be wished, that the narrow notion of banishing works of this nature from places of publick worship was entirely exploded; no solid reason can be given, why subjects, properly chosen, should not be painted in Protestant churches, nor can it be argued, that because those who profess the Romish religion, pay adoration to wooden saints and pictures, that those of the church of England would become guilty of a sin in looking upon a picture, merely because they found one in a place of worship, which it was never intended that should pay adoration to; nor can it be conceived, that while any one is seriously and attentively listening to the sacred history of our Saviour and his apostles, that a noble and sensible representation of the very action itself, would inspire them with any other thoughts than such as would tend to illustrate and make permanent their ideas of the relation. Possibly the contemplation of such objects might prevent the thoughts of many from wandering to others far less worthy of contemplation. The fabulous superstitious legends of pretended saints, ought, without doubt, to be for ever banished; but the life and miracles of Christ and his apostles, are surely subjects which are suitable to the church, and can never with the least shadow of reason be objected to. These would certainly be much properer decorations than painted or carved imitations of cherubims, &c. which are scattered about with the greatest profusion in almost every church in London, and particularly in St. Paul's, in which cathedral, as the dome has been suffered to be painted already, and has been so justly admired, there seems to be no reason why the decorations should not be finished according to . . . Wren's original intention, who never dreamed of the ridiculous objections that would be made

to its being executed, as appears by the many compartments, in that structure, which manifestly point out that great architect's intentions. If this miserable mean-spirited prejudice was once overcome, England might in time, in its churches and painters, vie even with Rome itself; but, till that happens, historical painting certainly never will arrive to that pitch, to which such a glorious opportunity would undoubtedly advance it.'

18 Macky 1722, vol. I, p. 300, in 1722. See related comments in Ralph 1734 (Doc. 223). Gwynn and Wale hinted at such a treatment in a publishing venture of 1751, *Six Perspective Designs for the Concave Mirrour* (the Claude Glass), one of which shows a Piranesian cathedral-like interior with a *Crucifixion* hung in the apse, which in turn reflected their manifesto of 1749 promoting a London equivalent to the Académie Royale in Paris, with its audacious suggestion that 'What is annually given to preserve and continue the *Gothic* Taste in the old Repository of Tombs at *Westminster*, would . . . be sufficient to raise among us the Taste of *Rome* and *Athens*' (Gwynn 1749, p. 74; Paul Mellon Centre, London, photograph 82/1725). The image was inspired by Piranesi's 'Vestibolo d'antico Tempio' in *Prima parte di Architecture*, 1743 (Ficacci 2000, fig.12).

19 Keene, Burns and Saint 2004, pp. 241–2, 323, 329, figs 137, 275, deal with the circumstances of the episode but offer no iconographic interpretation.

20 Stephenson 2005, pp. 101, 183–4.

21 On 1 February 1711 the renowned glass painter Joshua Price unsuccessfully petitioned the dean and chapter 'concerning . . . painting the Glass Windows' (*Wren Society*, XVI, 1939, p. 111).

22 Gwynn's *An Essay on Design* (1749, p. 74) refers to the conflict with France as 'an expensive War'. The tombs particularly reflect the international rococo repertory of L.-F. Roubiliac and J.-B. Pigalle (Bindman and Baker 1995, pp. 286–98, 311–14, pls II–III, VII, 8, 49, 172; London 1984, pp. 284–5, 297 (S21), fig. 8; Hammelmann 1975, pp. 89, 91. For Wale's painterly talents, see his *Lamentation* (1768) set in Gwynn's rococo gilt-wood frame in the altarpiece at Bledlow, Buckinghamshire, 1777 (Paul Mellon Centre, photograph). The St Paul's architectural ensemble relates to F. Blondel's *Recueil des plans, élévations, coupes et profils des églises* and *Oeuvres de Juste-Aurèle Meissonnier*, both 1727 (Minguet 1988, pp. 82, 96; Fuhring 1999, vol. II, p. 365, no. 104), and temporary festival decoration devised for Roman churches, for example, by F. Fuga in San Giovanni dei Fiorentini, 1740, and L. Vanvitelli, etc., in St Peter's, 1746, both engraved (Fagiolo 1997, pp. 110–11, 132–3).

23 Doc. 223. See also Hogarth's criticism in 1753. Green 1782, p. 38, lamented that 'by a fatality which has too uniformly attended the Public movements of the British Arts, not only St Paul's . . . has been deprived of a noble benefaction of Painting [from the Royal Academy] for the embellishment of the wide waste of its solitary inside . . . but also the Arts of the most desirable Sanctuary, in which to deposit a memorial of their Genius'. Moritz 1987, p. 74, confessed that 'on first entering . . . its emptiness damped rather than stimulated the feeling of majesty I desired. All around . . . were huge empty walls and pillars . . . There was no altar visible, nor indeed any sign to indicate that men assembled there to praise the Almighty.'

24 Fiennes 1982, p. 106. Both chapels are discussed in A. Ricketts's pioneer study of 2007, pp. 161–3, 189, 190–95, 238–9, fig. 6.10, pls XXXI–XXXII, XXXV.

25 Vertue 1930–55, vol. II, p. 36; vol. VI, p. 73. The plan of this 'extremely Magnificent' room is recorded in Campbell 1715–25, vol. I, p. 6, pls 72–3. Percival 1989, pp. 154–5, in 1701, thought it 'the noblest I ever was in . . . the sides where there is not painting wainscoted with cedar inlay'd. Tis impossible to describe the bewtyfull appearance it makes, the Ornamts: of the pulpit & Alter are of velvet imbroaderd wth: gold and Silver'. Vertue 1930–55, vol. II, pp. 36–7; vol. VI, pp. 73, 163, 'a most compleat work. of statuary painting Carvings joiners work' as 'splendid as any in a protestant Country', the collaboration of Verrio, Louis Laguerre, Caius Gabriel Cibber and Samuel Watson. *Wren Society*, XVII (1940), pp. 29–31, 35–7, pls XXXIV–XXXVI; Thompson 1949, pp. 43, 70–71, 132–8, pls 8–9, 59–60, 62; Croft-Murray 1962–70, vol. I, p. 251; Downes 1966, pl. 8; Lees-Milne 1968, p. 893, figs 8–9; Colvin 1976, p. 332, fig. 27; Jackson-Stops 1994, p. 57, figs 10–11; Ricketts 1996; Devonshire 2002, pp. 104–9.

26 Doc. 45: 1733.

27 Vertue 1930–55, vol. II, p. 30.

28 'Magnificent o'er all the Fabrick shin'd / The rich Profusion of a Royal Mind. / . . . When *Chandos* has the matchless Work design'd, / And form'd the Plan of Wonders in his Mind / O'er all the Waste, a blooming Change prevails / A Desart rising to a grand *Versailles* / . . . Rais'd by the Practice of so pure a Mind, / Religion gains the Homage of Mankind' (Humphrey 1728, pp. 6, 9–10, 17; reprinted in Gilmore 1972, pp. 42–63).

29 Doc. 51.

30 Doc. 194.

31 Gibbs owned a copy of D. de' Rossi, *Studio d'architettura civile . . . di Roma* (Friedman 1984, p. 329).

32 Doc. 196: *circa* 1721. Thornhill proposed the same subject for All Soul's College chapel, Oxford, *circa* 1714 (Doc. 141: 1715–16).

33 Fougeroux MS, p. 63.

34 Doc. 51: 15 May, 12 June 1747.

35 Doc. 51: 22 June 1747, undated. St Mary, Fawley, was remodelled, perhaps under the direction of its lord of the manor, John Freeman, an amateur architect. On 22 June 1747 George Shakespear, master carpenter, purchased furnishings from Cannons chapel (Doc. 51: 1747, lots 53–7, 60–61) and measured the plan: 'Wall Wainscot 6 by 6 = 54 feet . . . Front pews 39.11 with . . . circular end . . . Weight of 2 lat wagons with . . . pews & rails' (Gloucestershire Record Office, Strickland of Apperley papers D1245/FF 38A5); Baker and Baker 1949, p. 145. On 7 July 1748, with medieval Fawley church 'very Incommodious for the parishioners[, Freeman] intends adding a Step up to the Doors of the North c South sides . . . take the porch away . . . make the Entrance on the west . . . put the pulpit on the South side . . . Change the pews from East to West . . . make the Gallery in the Belfry with a Convenient Stair case . . . for him . . . and . . . family . . . ceil the Church

make four proper Windows instead of the wholes . . . take the Old font out of the passage . . . being a very bad one . . . put one made of Marble in a more Convenient place . . . make some other little Alterations for . . . beautifying the Church' (Buckinghamshire Record Office, D/A/X/9, ff. 154–8). Bodleian Library, University of Oxford, MS Top. Bucks a.1, f. 34, exterior south-west view. The fabric was altered in 1882–3 (*Buildings of England: Buckinghamshire*, 1994, p. 325). Dugdale 1819, vol. I, p. 152; Clarke 1963, p. 54; Tyack 1986, p. 5, pl. IX.

36 Verrio had died in 1707, Laguerre in 1721, Bellucci in 1726, Thornhill in 1734, Pellegrini in 1741; Ricci returned home in 1716, Grisoni in 1724, Chéron in 1725, Amigoni in 1739. Sleter, who settled in England in 1719, died here in 1775 (Croft-Murray 1962–70, vol. I, pp. 236, 250, 265; vol. II, pp. 163, 170, 214–15, 253–5, 264, 277).

37 For example, G. Sardi's San Pasquale Baylon, 1744–7 (Mallory 1977, p. 61, pls 95–6, 99). See also his Santa Maria del Rosario, Marino (Varriano 1986, p. 160, pl. 96). Gibbs is known to have kept abreast of current Roman architecture throughout his career (Friedman 1984, p. 2).

38 Doc. 91: 13 February 1751, 6 June 1752, September 1756, 10 November 1762.

39 Cambridge: Doc. 50: 17 December 1780, 25 March 1781 (King's); for other colleges, see Willis and Clarke 1886, vol. I, p. 195, vol. II, p. 146; *RCHME: City of Cambridge*, vol. II, 1959, p. 154, pl. 223; Vertue 1930–55, vol. VI, p. 18; Dugdale 1819, vol. I, p. 219; *Buildings of England: Suffolk*, 1961, p. 206. Oxford: Dugdale 1819, vol. IV, pp. 96, 100. Paterson 1714 provides a comprehensive list for London City Churches.

40 Thompson 1760, pp. 62, 65.

41 Vertue 1930–55, vol. I, p. 39; Cruickshank 2003, p. 43.

42 *RCHME: City of Cambridge*, vol. I, 1959, pls 112, 117; Croft-Murray 1962–70, vol. II, p. 164. His painted staircase at Powis House, London (destroyed), was 'calculated only to please at a Glance, by an artful Mixture of gay Colourings, but have no Solidity, and will not bear Examination' (*Gentleman's Magazine*, June 1734, p. 316).

43 Quoted in Houfe 1977, p. 729.

44 Vertue 1930–55, vol. III, p. 157. Doc. 227: 30 December 1747, 30 November 1748. It was replaced in 1801 by Benjamin West's *Christ Presenting a Little Child*.

45 Doc. 141: 1771, 1782.

46 Swift 1747, pp. 47, 140.

47 [W. Fleetwood], *A Letter to an Inhabitant of the Parish of St Andrew's Holbourn, about New Ceremonies in the Church*, 1717, British Library, 689.g.15(7). Fleetwood is identified as author of this anonymous pamphlet in *Gentleman's Magazine* (November 1735), p. 652.

48 *Gentleman's Magazine* (May 1781), pp. 207–8.

49 Quoted in Black 1992, pp. 269–70, 241. See an early eighteenth-century view of the Earl of Leicester admiring the interior of the Gesù, Rome (Haynes 2006, pl. 3).

50 Defoe 1962, vol. I, pp. 141–2.

51 Rocque 1746–7, p. 22.

52 Welton 1714a; Welton 1714b; Welton 1714c; Dr Thomas Barlow, 'THE CASE Concerning setting up IMAGES or Painting of them IN CHURCHES, 1714, Images an Abomination to the Lord. Or, Dr KENET'S REASONS For Pulling Down the Altar-piece at White-Chapel, The Whole Tryal and Examination of Dr Welton, Rector of White-Chapel, and the Church-Wardens', *The Flying-Post; or, The Post-Master*, 20–22 and 24–7 April 1714 (British Library, 1418.r.34[7]). The controversy is discussed in Walpole 1937–83, vol. XIII, p. 86, 15 October 1735; P. Q., '*On* Dr. Welton's *famous Altar-piece in* White-Chapel *Church*', *Gentleman's Magazine* (September 1784), p. 644; (October 1784), p. 729; Malcolm 1803–7, vol. IV, pp. 447–8, noting the 'obnoxious picture is now the altar-piece of St Alban's Abbey Church', since removed. Haynes 2006, pp. 126–7, 134, suggests political agendas behind the controversy.

53 Doc. 114.

54 Doc. 265: 4–7 September 1725, pp. 3–6, 10, 15–16, adding: 'never before was any popish Saint put over the Communion Table in a Protestant Church . . . A great many . . . have only the Pictures of *Moses* and *Aaron* on each side the Commandments' (p. 21, October 1725).

55 Doc. 241: 6 August 1735.

56 Loveday 1984, p. 240, in 1736; 'one of the best pieces of . . . Thornhill' (Pococke 1750, vol. I, p. 92, in 1750); 'a large . . . noble altar piece' (Hutchins 1774, vol. I, p. 415). *RCHME: Dorset*, vol. II, pt 2, 1970, p. 334, pl. 178; Haynes 2006, pl. 29. A version hangs in St Peter, Dunstable, Bedfordshire, given in 1722 (*VCH: Bedfordshire*, vol. III, 1912, p. 366).

57 Doc. 38. Wright 1730, vol. I, p. 251, recorded the Raphael 'so well known by the Prints . . . that I need say nothing of it. As to the Execution . . . 'tis highly finish'd and the drawing Part throughout most admirable. The Colouring . . . very mellow. The Expression in the Figures . . . very strong . . . that of . . . *Christ* . . . most delicate: the whole affords an inexpressible Pleasure'. King 1982, pl. 24.

58 Doc. 38: 20 May 1766, August 1772.

59 Doc. 201: May 1788, referring to executed work at nearby St George's chapel, also 'striking proof of the abilities of the artists of this country . . . Wonderful specimen of Modern taste' (17 October 1790).

60 Doc. 200. Ingamells 1997, pp. 194–5, 990–92. For example, the attic figures recall both La Monnaie, Paris, and the Trevi Fountain, Rome, which reappear on Somerset House, London (Harris 1970, pls 153, 156; Harris and Snodin 1996, pl. 25).

61 Pressley 1983, p. 15.

62 Doc. 201.

63 Doc. 236: 23 December 1782, 18 August 1786, 27 February 1788, 1 January 1795.

64 Doc. 201: 16 March 1794.

65 Doc. 143: November 1777, 1778, 23 June 1781. Haskell and Penny 1981, p. 243.

66 Doc. 143: 1782. A 'finer combination was never produced by Reynolds . . . Among the shepherds . . . are . . . portraits of . . . Reynolds, and Jervais. The colouring . . . is temperate, though rich, and the whole approximates more nearly to nature than any effort of glass-painting before' (Dugdale 1819, vol. IV, p. 94).

67 Doc. 143: October 1785, 11 May 1783, 12 July 1779, 6 October 1785.

68 Doc. 145: 8 July 1781.

69 Cotton 1859, pp. 58–9; Armitage 1959, p. 55.

70 Torrington 1934–8, vol. III, p. 28, 2 June 1792. Doc. 202: 2 July 1781. The press condemned the 'evil-minded . . . wicked Persons' who stole painted glass from Gloucester cathedral in 1798 (Doc. 86).

71 The 'glaring colours, rendered still more glaring by transparency is said to throw the mind into that serious temper, which is peculiarly adapted to the indulgence of devotion . . . Such an effect it may perhaps produce, in a great degree, on minds subject to superstition and fanaticism . . . yet why light, one of the most glorious works of creation, should refrigerate the ardour of religion in the rational and dispassionate possessor of it, no good reason can be assigned' (Knox 1778).

72 *Birmingham Gazette*, 28 July 1800 (Langford 1870, vol. II, pp. 121–2). For his working method, see Doc. 142: 1793–5.

73 Doc. 23: 9 March 1785, 1786, 8 December 1789, 10 January 1791, 2 May 1791. Warner 1802, vol. II, p. 224, in 1802 considered 'the execution transcends all praise'.

74 *York Courant*, 15 October 1795; *Leeds Intelligencer*, 19 October 1795. Brighton 1967–8; Brighton 2004; Brighton 1991. For his working method, see Doc. 7: 1722–4.

75 Shearman 1965, vol. I, pp. 217–19 no. 32; vol. II, pl. 35a; Friedman 2004, p. 113, pl. 32. Doc. 21.

76 Docs 130, 272: 1721, 25 March 1722–4.

77 For example, see Wayment 1980. For William Price's method of installation, see Doc. 61: 23 October 1755.

78 Doc. 268: 10 June 1758–21 January 1761. Similar arguments were expressed in Hole's *Sermon Preached in the Parish-Church of Werrington, Devon*, 1743, pp. 7, 12 (British Library, 1026, f. 8, no. 9).

79 Warwickshire Record Office, DR 476/10, 5 December 1809, several months after Napoleon had defeated Austria at Wagram. For further reading, see Armitage 1959, chapter 7; Lee, Seddon and Stephens 1976, pp. 142–5; Archer 1979; Archer 1985; Cowen 1985; Lloyd 1992; Osborne 1993.

NINE THE 'FATE OF SUBLUNARY THINGS'

1 *Gentleman's Magazine* (March 1784), p. 201.

2 Swift 1709, pp. 56–7.

3 *Weekly Journal; or, The British Gazette* (15 June 1727), p. 4.

4 Doc. 229: 14 February 1718, petition regarding St Giles-in-the-Fields, London, rebuilt 1731–4.

5 Doc. 62: end 1709.

6 Doc. 244: 6 April, 16 October 1711. See Herman and Guillery 2004, figs 7.2–3.

7 Preface to Thoresby 1724.

8 Jukes 1957, pp. 80–81, in 1738, referred to as Heyford At Bridge.

9 Gloucestershire Record Office, D678 57D/282, 26 March 1737.

10 *Journals of the House of Commons*, vol. XXV, p. 293, 17 February 1747.

11 Lancashire Record Office, DR Ch 37/51/ 1 and 2. Cumbria Record Office, DX/748/182, 4 August 1745.

12 *Gentleman's Magazine* (March 1751), p. 139.

13 Lambeth Palace Library, London, MS 2691, f. 378, 25 March 1726.

14 Doc. 104: 18 August 1710.

15 *Journals of the House of Commons*, vol. XXVII, pp. 505–8, 9 March 1756. Dodsley and Dodsley 1761, vol. III, p. 240. The church was destroyed by enemy bombing in 1940–41, except the tower. Harrison 1775, p. 548 illus.

16 Ollard and Walker 1928–31, vol. I, pp. 2–3.

17 Nicolson 1877, pp. 21–2, 91.

18 Shropshire Records and Research Unit, Shrewsbury, MS 6862, f. 32r–v, 25 July 1793; ff 33–34v, 23 March 1794. View (6009/26). *Buildings of England: Shropshire*, 1958, pp. 76–7.

19 Doc. 80: 1729.

20 *Leeds Intelligencer* (2 September 1760), p. 3.

21 Bishopthorpe MSS, Bundle 28, no. 151, 29 October 1767, typescript (West Yorkshire Archives Service [Leeds District Archives], Clark MSS, vol. 23). The 'local family' may have been Lady Elizabeth Hastings, Huntington's sister-in-law.

22 Wesley 1909–16, vol. VI, p. 206, 2 August 1778.

23 Cheshire Record Office, EDA 2/4, ff. 269–82, 12 February 1714.

24 Doc. 238: 21 December 1795.

25 Doc. 258: 25 June 1712; Lambeth Palace Library, MS 2712, ff. 80, 182v–183, in 1724.

26 Lambeth Palace Library, MS 2717, f. 31, 8 October 1725.

27 Ward 1993, vol. XII, p. 220, in 1709.

28 Doc. 66: 20 September 1770.

29 *VCH*: *Warwickshire*, vol. III, 1945, p. 122; *Buildings of England: Warwickshire*, 1966, pp. 312, 484; Downes 1966, p. 109, pl. 483; Thompson and Thompson 1988. There are no known building accounts. For a further discussion, see chapter 22.

30 The Vestry petitioned on 29 December 1790 that the medieval church half a mile from Kinoulton was 'Ancient . . . in so ruinous a Condition that no Duty has been performed therein . . . for upwards of Twenty years'; the town's chapel 'likewise in a State of Decay . . . very unsafe . . . Dangerous . . . And . . . too small'; that the earl 'at his own sole Charge' will rebuild on the latter site 'one New Church agreeable to the plan . . . annexed' (Borthwick Institute of Historical Research, York University, Fac.1792/1a). The faculty was granted on 3 February–8 March 1791 (Fac. 1792/1c; Reg. 38, ff. 227r–229r; Nottinghamshire Archives, PR 24,190/1). William Maclellan, carpenter, William Mew, mason, both of Mansfield, contracted on 17 March 1792 to 'build an entire new church' for £1,432 10s. 0d. (Leicestershire Record Office, DE 3214/256/13). The site was conveyed on 3 April (Fac. 1792/1d; Reg. 38, ff. 261r–264r). Legg's designs (1792/1e–g). *Buildings of England: Nottinghamshire*, 1951, p. 89.

31 Bedford Estate Office, London, R3/1772 June, no. 21, 16 June 1772. It is unclear whether the scheme (untraced) was carried out (Pickford 1994, p. 97).

32 W. Woolston referring to medieval St Mary, Adderbury, Oxfordshire, with its 160-foot-high spire (*Gentleman's Magazine*, March 1800, pp. 209–10 ill.). For a fuller discussion, see Friedman 2006.

33 Referring to the destruction of the town of Blandford

Forum, Dorset, including its medieval church, 4 June 1731 (Hutchins 1774, vol. I, pp. 78–9).

34 Defoe 1991, p. 21, pl. 16.

35 *Gentleman's Magazine* (August 1768), p. 393, 24 July. Of storm-wrecked Cranbrook, Kent: 'When lightning vivid thro' the aether spreads, / And aweful thunder rolls above our heads, / In the bright flash we view the brighter God, / Who sends this token of his power abroad; / And in the stroke which rends the passive air / We hear his voice that fills the world with fear; / Then, 'midst the dangers which our lives surround, / Our shield of safety on his arms is found' (*Gentleman's Magazine*, September 1787, p. 824).

36 *Gentleman's Magazine* (November 1791), p. 1055.

37 Quoted in Curtis 1979, pp. 286–8, 290–92, 294.

38 Dugdale 1819, vol. IV, p. 308.

39 Renwick 1911, pp. 20–21, 13–14 January 1740.

40 *Gentleman's Magazine* (18 March 1770), p. 138.

41 Doc. 26: 4 June 1731. A temple-like memorial commemorating the disaster was erected soon after in the churchyard.

42 See also Nichols 1795–1811, vol. II, pt 2, 1798, pp. 467–8. An engraving of Speldhurst, Kent, shows the church aflame on 20 October 1791 (Friedman 1996a, pp. 68–9, fig. 2).

43 Doc. 271: 22 September 1795, 22 March 1796. Malcolm 1803–7, vol. IV, pp. 220–21.

44 Doc. 158: 5–6 June 1741.

45 Shropshire Records and Research Unit, MS 6863, f. 26, 28 January 1793 Visitation; British Library, Add. MS 21,018, f. 286, ill. See also Westbury (Shropshire Records and Research Unit, MS 6001/372, II, f. 5).

46 Doc. 207: 1753, 24 May, 1 December 1754. Balston 1945. For Woodstock, 31 August 1777, it was ordered to 'lay six or more fire Plugs in . . . proper Places of the Tower to keep them in repair . . . in Case of a Calamity of fire they may all be ready to use' (Oxfordshire Archives, MSS.D.D.Par. Woodstock, c.12, f. 324).

47 Durham County Record Office, EP/SU HT5/2, f. 188, 9 April 1765.

48 'A most violent . . . tornado . . . beat open the door . . . though a very strong one' at St Paul, Hammersmith, London, 'and the chandelier becoming a conductor to the lightning . . . past . . . through the church, and beat out a very large Gothic window' (*Gentleman's Magazine*, November 1780, p. 537). 'An account of the effects of lightning in the *Danish* church, in *Well-Close square* . . . Dec.3, 1753; with explanations by Mr Benjamin Franklin' (*Gentleman's Magazine*, January 1757, pp. 22–3). Some were sceptical: 'The natural philosophers . . . believe . . . Franklin has invented a machine of the size of a toothpick-case, and materials, that would reduce St Paul's [Cathedral] to a handful of ashes' (Walpole 1937–83, vol. XXVIII, p. 287, to William Mason, canon of York).

49 *Gentleman's Magazine* (January 1769), p. 50.

50 Stukeley 1882–7, vol. II, pp. 369–70, 8 February 1750. He was the author of *The Philosophy of Earthquakes, Natural & Religious*, 1750. The greatest quake in recorded history followed by a tsunami, which destroyed Lisbon, the Portuguese capital, on 1 November 1755, including numerous churches, profoundly impacted on England, which enjoyed long-standing trade relations (Paice 2008).

51 Printed tract quoted in Vincent 1890, p. 149. The church was rebuilt in the years 1727–39. See also St Leonard, Shoreditch, London (Doc. 238: 1716).

52 *Gentleman's Magazine* (11 July 1777), p. 293.

53 Doc. 10.

54 Doc. 98: 17, 20 April 1786, 10 August, July 1787; Britton 1831, p. 46.

55 Doc. 166: 12 July 1788.

56 Doc. 127: 17 September 1794.

57 Le Neve 1717–19, vol. IV, pp. 210–11.

58 Nottinghamshire Archives, PR 5697, 11 September 1736; Borthwick Institute of Historical Research, Reg. 35, ff. 169v–170. Throsby 1790, p. 324, reported one man killed and others wounded.

59 Dugdale 1819, vol. IV, p. 316.

60 Nichols 1795–1811, vol. IV, pt 2, p. 606, pl. XCIX.

61 *Gentleman's Magazine* (January 1800), p. 79; (May 1800), p. 432; Plumptre 1992, p. 189; Briggs 1991, pp. 51, 100, 121, 126–7; British Library, King's Topographical Collection, XIII, 11–b, c; Williams 1931, pls III–IV; Friedman 1996a, pp. 72–3; Friedman 2006, p. 75, fig. 3.

TEN ARCHITECTS AND BUILDERS

1 Introduction to Chapter IV, 'On the Style in Which to Build Churches', *An Essay On Architecture*, 1753 (Laugier 1977, p. 100).

2 Neve 1726, pp. iii–iv, 12–13. See also the link between building and 'our Blessed SAVIOUR' (p. 57). Harris and Savage 1990, pp. 331–7. Neve established the pattern for later published interpretations: E. Chambers, *Cyclopaedia*, vol. I, 1728; Anon., *The Builder's Dictionary*, 1734, accredited by Nicholas Hawksmoor, John James and James Gibbs, the three leading church architects of the age; Samuel Johnson, *A Dictionary of the English Language*, 1755. Colvin 2008, pp. 15, 17, 19.

3 Gibbs 1728, pls 1–31, 110, 145–6. Introduction, p. i. A significant number of builders and craftsmen appear in the list of subscribers (pp. xxvi–xxviii). Colvin 2008, pp. 20–21, 24.

4 Colvin 2008, p. 37.

5 Doc. 82: February 1735, 1734. For York, see Doc. 207: 21 June 1713.

6 Doc. 79: 5 July, 15 April, 15 May, 31 May 1754. The rival plan is probably Sir John Soane's Museum, London, Drawings vol. 19, no. 26.

7 Doc. 268: 6 February 1735.

8 Doc. 136: undated entry following 1739–40.

9 Hackney Archives Department, D/F/TYS/13, ff. 10–11, 29, 75–6.

10 Doc. 248: 17 May, 7 June 1758.

11 Doc. 215: 18 July 1734, 1758.

12 Doc. 215: 16 September 1724, 28 September 1726.

13 Doc. 223: 14 February, 25, 29 August 1707.

14 Quoted in Lang 1956, p. 239.

15 Defoe 1991, p. 143.

16 Doc. 272: 1 February 1724, 29 January 1725, 1 February 1727. See also 18 March 1735.

17 Doc. 228: 26 November 1725. For the bust at All Soul's College, Oxford, see Hart 2002, fig. 3.

18 Nottingham University Library, NeL 1,098. Doc. 18.

19 Doc. 165: 16 December 1794.

20 Wandsworth Local History Library, MS 568, f. 160, 21 April 1772. Doc. 261.

21 Doc. 214: 11, 15 May 1741. However, a proposal for the architect 'to attend the Work every Hour the Building shall be carrying on or send a sufficient Deputy [was] passed in the Negative'.

22 Doc. 167: 19 January 1792, 20 June 1796.

23 Doc. 167: 8 June 1791, following 22 June 1791. Paine circulated his political manifesto from 13 March 1791.

24 Doc. 167: following 17 January 1792, 18, 20 March 1793, 20 June 1796, 1 June, 12 December 1797, 17 December 1798.

25 Doc. 127: 22 October 1793.

26 Doc. 167: 23 November 1793.

27 Doc. 165: 1 March 1794.

28 Doc. 237: 20 February 1797. It was finally erected in 1812–13. See also St Paul, Deptford (Doc. 244: 16 October 1711, during the Anglo-French war, 1702–13), Westminster Abbey (Doc. 272: 11 June 1739, during the War of Jenkins's Ear) and Peterborough cathedral (Doc. 148: 1772, during the American War of Independence).

29 Doc. 23: 14–16 April 1776.

30 Doc. 179: 20 August 1741, 11 January 1742, following 29 December 1740, 1742–3.

31 Doc. 214: 15 May 1741. At Durham cathedral George Nicholson was ordered to draw the exterior to 'serve as Canvas to . . . mark out . . . necessary Alterations' (Doc. 70: 29 November 1777, 1780).

32 Doc. 214: 24 December 1744.

33 Doc. 31: 29 March 1792, 2 November 1797. All these drawings have vanished.

34 James Gibbs was particularly fond of this method (Friedman 1984, pls 35, 37–8).

35 One might speculate that Sephton learnt his skills through contacts at Preston or Wigan (the latter close to his residence at Billinge), which were centres of polite society during the first half of the century, rather than at Liverpool or Manchester, which emerged as prominent artistic scenes only after 1760 (Walton 1987, pp. 80–81). I am grateful to Edward Morris for directing my attention to these possible links.

36 Campbell 1715–25, vol. I, pls 44, 59–60, both similarly signed 'Ca Campbell Delin:'. Sephton's drawing is in University of Hull, Brynmor Jones Library, Everingham Papers DDEV/73/13j. Hussey 1958a, figs 1–2.

37 This was apparently Sephton's normal practice: for example, in 1716 he received 10s. 9d. 'for plotting out Burial-places in ye Church & Church-yard' of St Mary, Eccleston, Lancashire, 2s. 6d. for 'transcribing ym. again upon Parchment' (Lancashire Record Office, PR 2695/17). He had a local reputation as a draughtsman, for example, charging 10 guineas for 'haveing drawn some draughts' of another architect's scheme for St George, Liverpool, untraced (Doc. 118: 2 November 1726).

38 Colvin 2008, pp. 1058–9.

39 Gibbs 1728, pls 1–31, 110–37, 146, pp. i–ii.

40 Doc. 80: 25 February 1726, 18 February 1729; Bodleian Library, University of Oxford, MS Willis 52b, f. 158.

41 Doc. 8: November 1723.

42 B. Taylor, *Linear Perspective* . . . (first published 1715); the second edition (Taylor 1719) 'endeavour'd to make everything so plain, that a very little Skill in Geometry may be sufficient to enable one to read this Book by himself' (British Architectural Library, Drawings and Archives Collection, Victoria and Albert Museum, London, e.g., 818 and 819, Preface p. viii).

43 Doc. 196: 24 July 1719, 17 May 1721; Doc. 137: 14 January 1754; Doc. 50: March 1768, 26 March 1769, also 27 October 1769.

44 Doc. 48: 26 October–13 November 1706.

45 Anon. 1734, vol. II, under 'MODEL', repeated in Aheron 1754, Book III. See also Langley 1736; Gwynn 1752, Second Letter, p. 19; Leoni 1755, Book II, Chapter I, p. 22.

46 Keene, Burns and Saint 2004, pl. III. 'But since a Work like this must slowly rise, / And few may live to see it built out-right, / To satisfy this Generation's Eyes, / Behold in little a Prophetick Sight / What miracle of Art will grow from hence, / And Challenge through the World a Parallel, / When the bare Model only, for Expence, / And real value, does so far excell?' (Anon. 1677, pp. 7–8).

47 Lambeth Palace Library, London, MS 2690, f. 34; f. 217, 19 May 1715.

48 Doc. 270: 4 February 1716.

49 Doc. 259: 1716–17, 1725–6.

50 Doc. 258: 1724–5.

51 Doc. 267: 25 June 1729–25 March 1731.

52 Lambeth Palace Library, MS 2690, ff. 54–6, 67, 286, 291; MS 2693, ff. 17, 20, 72.

53 A particularly early example is the now-lost model for St Nicholas, Whitehaven, in remote Cumberland, made in 1686 in London, notable because the erected church (1687–93, demolished) resembled a standard Wrenian form (see chapter 23).

54 Doc. 147: 12 October 1720. For a further discussion, see chapter 22.

55 Doc. 112: 13 April 1723.

56 Doc. 229: 1731. Doc. 231: 8 December 1744. Doc. 191: Easter 1777.

57 For references to 'models', see Index; for further discussions, see Wilton-Ely 1965; Wilton-Ely 1968; Wilton-Ely 1967; Wilton-Ely 1969. For their European background, see Reuther and Berckenhagen 1994; Millon 1994; Millon 1999.

58 Doc. 166: 15–29 November 1789, 31 January, 17 February 1791, 3 July 1794. Fees for designing only were generally modest. Gibbs received £25 for All Saints, Derby, in 1726 (Hutton 1791, pp. 152–3). Robert Taylor was paid £31 10s. 0d. for Wallingford (Berkshire Record Office, D/P 139/6/3), Telford £147 10s. 8d for Bridgnorth on a total expenditure of £8,659 12s. 8½d. (Doc. 31: 1798). Chambers, who produced many designs for St Marylebone, hampered by interference and never executed, requested 5 per cent on total building costs (Doc. 253: 9 June 1772, 16 February 1774).

59 Doc. 34: July 1786. Doc. 167: 20 January 1792. At Penrith, Cumberland, the 'Able . . . Experienced Workmen' included William Dobson, Robert Harrison and Robert Monkhouse, who also prepared drawings, now lost (Doc. 147: 3 October 1716, 12 October 1720). The architect was probably William Etty.
60 Doc. 269: 27 February, 24 March 1722.
61 Doc. 272: 1735.
62 Doc. 28: 25 October 1725.
63 Hewlings 2000. A possible exception was Lady Elizabeth Wilbraham of Weston Park, Staffordshire, who may have designed her local parish church, 1700–01, though she has not found entry in Colvin 2008. Harris and Hradsky 2007, pp. 7–8.
64 Doc. 272: 29 January–29 September 1707, 22 June 1710, 25 March 1716.
65 Doc. 220: 20 August 1705.
66 Doc. 267: 2, 9 November 1744.
67 Doc. 83: September 1768.
68 Doc. 136: October 1783.
69 City of Westminster Archives Centre, E.2419, f. 338.
70 *RCHME: Northamptonshire*, vol. VI, 1984, p. 16, pl. 57. The Ten Commandments at Barnwell, according to an inscription, were 'painted by her own hand . . . 1714 in the 70th. year of her age / She was the daughter of Sir Gilbert Pickering / Baronet and / Elizabeth Mountague his wife' (Bridges 1791, vol. II, p. 393, also pp. 267, 385).
71 Doc. 166.
72 Doc. 261: 13 December 1777.
73 Doc. 98: 14 January 1792.
74 Doc. 270: 12 September 1717.
75 He was not alone. John Tuffnell and his son, Edward, both master masons at Westminster Abbey, share an impressive monument incorporating a portrait bust, located in the cloister; the sculptor was probably the latter's son, Samuel (Roscoe 2009, pp. 1284–5).
76 Doc. 238: 1740.
77 Doc. 231: 4 May 1745. On 7 March 1748 Lee was ordered to 'make good all . . . pointing at . . . own Expence'.
78 Doc. 231: 15, 22 September 1755.
79 Doc. 105: 3 November 1756, 17 February 1757.
80 Gloucestershire Record Office, D2700, QP4/6/1, 21 September 1782.
81 Simon 2003, p. 53.
82 St Alfege, Greenwich, 1715 (Lambeth Palace Library, MS 2697, f. 259); St Mary-le-Strand, 1717 (f. 461); Christ Church, Spitalfields, 1724–5 (MS 2700, f. 108).
83 Doc. 269: 5 September 1724, 25 October 1725. Doc. 221: 25 March 1724–25 March 1725.
84 Doc. 270: 1 January–31 December 1717, 25 March 1722–25 March 1723.
85 Doc. 272: 1 April 1769. Doc. 246: 5 December 1789 (City of Westminster Archives Centre, Church Book of Entries of Contracts, f. 7).
86 Copied into Grove's work book (British Library, Add. MS 30092, f. 155). Friedman 2004, fig. 41.
87 Lambeth Palace Library, MS 2726, f. 23v, 11 July 1727.
88 Doc. 231: 4 May 1745.
89 Lincolnshire Archives, Lincoln, Fac 3/17, in 1767.
90 In 1791 (Rowntree 1951, pp. 38–9).
91 Doc. 245: 13 September 1723, 12 October 1724, 16, 18 January 1725. In 1719 Henry Turner, carpenter and former mayor of Rochester, Kent, was dismissed 'from every working for the [cathedral] on account of his very unfair dealing by it' (Doc. 155).
92 Doc. 223: April, 5 May, 24 October 1711, 25 January 1712.
93 Doc. 221: 19 March 1719.
94 Doc. 66: 10, 17 July 1774.
95 Doc. 239: 27 October–10 November 1727.
96 Doc. 167: 30 March, June 1790. His identity is unlikely ever to be known.
97 Doc. 187: 10 October 1796. A sum of £321 5s. 11d. was outstanding from a total of £661 3s. 4d.
98 Doc. 95. Thomas left debts of £2,183 10s. 8d. against savings of £4 15s. 0d. in 'pocket & house' (East Riding Archives and Local Studies, Beverley, DDCC/43/127). The family residence, 20 Andrewgate, which Thomas may have designed, is a large, imposing, elegantly detailed pile (Nuttgen 1970, p. 47, no. 64).
99 *Wren Society*, XV (1938), pp. 79, 105, 107; XVI (1939), pp. 100–01, 119, 129.
100 Doc. 269: 24 March, 31 July 1722, 2, 6 May 1723.
101 Doc. 215: 15 November 1726.
102 Colvin 2008, p. 331.
103 *Gentleman's Magazine* (April 1754), p. 230; repeated in Russell and Price 1769, vol. II, p. 238.
104 Nichols 1795–1811, vol. II, pt 2, 1798, p. 495, 8 January 1735.
105 Doc. 98: 3 February 1790.
106 Doc. 10: 29 August 1794. For other human catastrophies, see Docs, p. 383, 2 September 1786 (All Saints, Newcastle upon Tyne); p. 632, 1797 (York Minster); p. 973, 1 February 1724 (Westminster Abbey).

ELEVEN ON BUILDING AND MAINTENANCE

1 Doc. 79: 8 April 1754 (Faversham, Kent). Leeds Reference Library, Parish Records Book 17, ff. 12–13, 23 February 1759 (St Peter, Sowerby, Yorkshire). Doc. 240: 14 April, 13 June 1787.
2 Docs 221, 228, 235, 239, 244, 245, 249, 256, 258–60, 267, 270. The history of St Mary, Banbury, Oxfordshire, during the 1790s, too, is replete with evidence of intimate details relating to both materials and construction (Doc. 10).
3 Doc. 37: 22 May 1742.
4 Doc. 31: 17 October 1792.
5 Doc. 42: 24 June 1790.
6 Doc. 19: 3 September 1733.
7 Doc. 239: 1729–31.
8 Doc. 136: 22 November 1756. Doc. 70: February 1779.
9 Doc. 223: 13 October 1719, 31 December 1719–24 June 1720, 3 December 1720–24 June 1721, *circa* 1776.
10 West Yorkshire Archives Service (Leeds District Archives), DB 209/28, 7 December 1765. They also lent '9 Scaffold deals at 2d', totalling 1s. 6d., charging 4d. for carriage.
11 Doc. 272: 30 September 1769.
12 Doc. 235: 1719.

13 Shropshire Records and Research Unit, Shrewsbury, QS/6/1, File 1, no. 72, 27 September 1736.

14 Doc. 117: 15–18 March 1725, 20 September 1726.

15 Lambeth Palace Library, London, MS 2690, f. 179, 21 July 1714.

16 Doc. 239: 1 January 1727–25 March 1728. City of Westminster Archives Centre, Proceedings of Vestry 1741–52, 1 June 1741 (St John, St Marylebone, London).

17 Cheshire Record Office, P12/12/1, f. 94.

18 Doc. 19: 3 June 1721, 10 August 1717.

19 Leicestershire Record Office, 2D 31/309, 19 February 1736.

20 Doc. 24: 1 July 1709–19 September 1711.

21 Seed 1907, pp. 41–2.

22 Doc. 231: 4 May 1745. For a comprehensive account, see Brunskill 1990.

23 Lambeth Palace Library, MS 2717, ff. 83–4, Hawksmoor and James, report of 10 December 1713.

24 Lambeth Palace Library, MS 2723, ff. 15, 33.

25 Doc. 267: 9 November, 16 December 1713, 15 April 1714.

26 Doc. 246: 17 December 1780. Similar technical perfection was sought in the masonry work, which specified the 'whole . . . of neat grained portland stone free from Vents or course Shells neatly and accurately worked . . . well set . . . cramped Joggled . . . plugged and run with lead' (5 December 1789).

27 Thomas Hardwick Jr, then restoring fire-damaged St Paul, Covent Garden, also considered the claim 'without foundation' (Doc. 246: 11, 25 May 1789).

28 Doc. 246: 8 February, 15 December 1790, 25 February 1791, 22 April, 11, 15 May, 19 October, 16, 30 November, 7, 28 December 1789.

29 Doc. 167: undated (1793) specification, 27 July 1793. He, too, called for the use of 'best portland Stone free from flaws and . . . Defects of all Sorts'.

30 Doc. 221: 25 March 1724–25 March 1725.

31 Doc. 228: 25 March 1724–25 March 1725. Later removed, they were re-carved and installed in 2005.

32 Doc. 270: 1 January 1714–31 December 1715.

33 Doc. 235: 25 March 1731–24 June 1732. Among the ornamental carvers employed here was Joseph Wade, King's Carver in His Yards at Deptford and Woolwich, whose elaborately decorated marble monument in Rotherhithe parish church testifies to his high status (*Buildings of England: London 2*, 1983, p. 53).

34 Doc. 112: 21 December 1723.

35 Clarke and Colvin 1952–3, pt 1, p. 82.

36 Guildhall Library, City of London Corporation, MS 3204/2, 28 January 1778. For John Liardet's patent oil cement of 1773 manufactured by the Adam brothers, see Harris and Savage 1990, pp. 295–6, and 'patent Water Cement' used at Epping, Essex (Doc. 76: 1780).

37 Doc. 187: 8 December 1788–22 October 1789. Kelly 1990; Guilding 2008.

38 'Vases and Pine Apple on . . . Cupola . . . to be of . . . Codes Composition . . . painted as the Cupola' at Paddington (Doc. 246: 5 December 1789).

39 See particularly Price 1735, pp. 15–22, pls G–N*, though unspecified. Harris and Savage 1990, pp. 39–40, 374–7.

40 See especially Langley 1740, pls 12–14 (citing St Alfege, Greenwich, and St Paul, Covent Garden), and Langley 1741, pls 88–94, respectively. Harris and Savage 1990, pp. 262–80. *The Builder's Dictionary* (Anon. 1734, vol. II) devoted twenty-four pages to kinds of timber, seasons for felling, methods of seasoning, preserving and measuring. Yeomans 1992.

41 Doc. 4: *circa* 1745. It was hardly coincidental that Vardy was responsible for preparing the celebrated perspective view (1749) of the interior of the Great Hall at Hampton Court Palace, with its elaborate Tudor timber hammerbeam roof (Thurley 2003, pl. 267).

42 Doc. 246: 5 December 1789.

43 Doc. 166: 6 May 1790.

44 Doc. 158: 30 January, 25 June, 29 August 1737.

45 Doc. 237: 19 September 1791. The Hackney design was approved on 7 March 1791. Russia's acquisition of 28 March was wrongly assumed to possess strategic importance in the Black Sea, prompting Pitt to request increased naval spending.

46 Doc. 215: 7, 15, 22 July 1726.

47 Doc. 15: 1742.

48 Soo 1998, pp. 114–15. St Mary-at-the-Wall, Colchester, was covered with '55 sqr. of . . . Dutch Glaz'd pantiles' (Doc. 56: 14 May 1713).

49 Bristol Record Office, 04225/1, 1 August 1752. The church, designed by Samuel Glascodine, was built in the years 1751–4 (Gomme, Jenner and Little 1979, pl. 117).

50 Doc. 167: 22 October, 12, 26 November 1791, 1793. Benjamin Wyatt recommended a 'New Method of Slating almost as flat as lead which is the best . . . 4 C.Wt . . . go as far as half a Ton', for St Paul, Birmingham (Doc. 23: 14 April 1777).

51 Doc. 250: 12 October 1738; Doc. 97: 1759; Doc. 10: 1 December 1790.

52 Doc. 79: 8 April 1754.

53 Soo 1998, p. 114.

54 Doc. 97: June 1753–September 1754.

55 Bingham 1711, p. 589.

56 Doc. 260: 6 March 1718; Doc. 259: 1 February 1732.

57 Doc. 259: 9 November 1721. For rare pictorial evidence of the process of roof covering, see Temple 1992, pp. 72–3.

58 Odom 1919, p. 87.

59 Doc. 117: August 1764.

60 Saint 2007, pl. 49; Bradley and Pevsner 1997, p. 99.

61 Doc. 235: 1 January–31 December 1716, 1 January–31 December 1717.

62 Doc. 270: 1718–19.

63 Doc. 245: 25 March 1724.

64 It closely resembles that at St Paul's Cathedral (Saunders 2001, p. 145).

65 Harris 1960, pls 6–25.

66 Doc. 64: 2 January 1731.

67 Doc. 38: 1710.

68 Churchyard gates at Wrexham, 1720–24; Ruthin, Clwyd, 1722; Oswestry, Shropshire, 1738 (Edwards 1977, pp. 25, 44–51 ill.).

69 West Yorkshire Archives Service (Bradford District Archives), DB 204/28, 1764–6; Doc. 100: 1758–9.

70 Ionides 1999, pp. 261–6; Trinder 1977.

71 Shropshire Records and Research Unit, 2275/76, 92, 97.
72 Doc. 192: 16 July 1790. The interior was drastically altered in 1899.
73 The remaining openings were 'glazed with New Castle seconds Glass' (Doc. 165: 1793, 17 April, 14 December 1795).
74 Clarke 1963, p. 226, pl. 8.
75 Doc. 166: 21 August 1790. 12 May 1791 (the press notice further specifying glazing with 'Sound London, or Newcastle Crown Glass'), 11 June, 12 August 1791. In addition, a waggoner named Powell charged £6 per ton for carriage 'on a Timber . . . platform made for that purpose'. Based in London, Steuart preferred employing metropolitan craftsmen for some of his commissions, which were largely located in Shropshire.
76 Doc. 158: May 1759, September 1762. Occasional designs survive, such as ones by R. Barber for Thaxted, 14 May 1757 (Essex Record Office, D/P16/62), and G. Dance Jr (Findlay 1985, back cover).
77 Essex Record Office, D/D QS 140, f. 11, September 1786.
78 Lambeth Palace Library, MS 2697: 1 July 1717–25 March 1719, f. 22, priced 2s. 6d.
79 City of London, London Metropolitan Archives, P71/TMS/213, f. 101, 11 March 1703. Guildhall Library, MS 601/1, 28 March 1769.
80 Doc. 235: 1 January–31 December 1717.
81 Doc. 267: 16 November 1744.
82 Doc. 174: 7 May 1754.
83 Doc. 236: 5 September 1781.
84 Doc. 117: 1799.
85 Doc. 52: 1751. For an account of the profession, see Saunders 2005.
86 Doc. 223: 1710.
87 *Gentleman's Magazine* (March 1735), p. 134, citing the *Gazette*. Palmer and Palmer 1992, p. 207.
88 Doc. 10: 1 December 1790.
89 Soo 1998, p. 114, in 1712.
90 Doc. 244: 23 May 1716. Blackheath, near Deptford and Greenwich.
91 'Deduct from Stone Molding what may be made of Stocco about 500 Feet wch. will cost 4d. p foot less than Stone', £8 6s. 8d., at Horsforth Chapel, Leeds (West Yorkshire Archives Service [Bradford Archives], SP ST 11/4/2/7, *circa* 1756).
92 Doc. 228: 25 March 1725–31 December 1726. For Stoneleigh, see Shakespeare Birthplace Trust, DR 18/3/47/55 (29 September 1744); Gomme 2000, pp. 311, 564–6, figs 182–3.
93 Doc. 97: 2 December 1755.
94 Doc. 89: following 19 January 1786.
95 Buckinghamshire Record Office, D/DR/12/61, 30 April–12 August 1785. The fabric was altered in the years 1870–88 (*Buildings of England: Buckinghamshire*, 1994, pp. 129–31). A variety of equipment was provided, including 'Molds, Pluggs, and Trussels', 'Frames for the Plaisterers to form the Corinthian Capitals', 'Bees Wax for the . . . Molds', 'a Chimney to the Out-yard for the Plasterers use' at St Luke, Old Street (1732–3; (Lambeth Palace Library, MS 2701, f. 521), St George, Hanover Square (1723–5; MS 2700, f. 3); Audley End (1769; Essex Record Office, D/Dby A27/1), St John, Wakefield, Yorkshire (John Goodchild Collection, 'Account', 20 September 1794), St George's Chapel, Queens Square, London (1717–19; Lambeth Palace Library, MS 2697, f. 16). For an overview, see Beard 1975.
96 Addison 1761, p. 47.
97 Gibbs 1728, p. v, pl. 6 (Friedman 1984, pl. 45). Banham 1997, vol. 1, pp. 55–8.
98 Friedman 2004, p. 90, fig. 79, pl. 30.
99 Doc. 267: 26 October–9 November 1744.
100 Doc. 235: 4 June 1719.
101 Lambeth Palace Library, MS 2716, f. 54, in connection with St Mary-le-Strand. Since Webster is not mentioned further, his bid was presumably unsuccessful.
102 Uffenbach 1928, pp. 24–5; Colvin 1983, pls 26–7.
103 Doc. 269: 10 July 1722.
104 Doc. 231: 24 September 1753, 15 September 1755.
105 Northampstonshire Record Office, Capron Deposit, 25 July 1723. Edward Ward rebuilt the medieval church in the years 1722–7 (Faculty Register 1, ff. 161v–166; 304 P/23; Shropshire Records and Research Unit, D 17791); Eayre's set of designs (Shropshire Records and Research Unit, 6000/17808–13). Whiffen 1948, p. 39, pl. 29, 118; Clarke 1963, pp. 133–4; Downes 1966, pp. 109, pl. 485; *Buildings of England: Northamptonshire*, 1961, pp. 414–15.
106 See also Trinity College chapel, Oxford (1691; Colvin 1983, pls 26–7). Wren's and Talman's proposed flooring of St Paul's Cathedral (1707–10) are exceptional in their lavishness for the period (Downes 1988, pp. 178–80; Talman 1997, pp. 57, 106, 153, pl. 5; *Wren Society*, XIII, 1936, p. xi, pl. XXX). *Grub-street Journal*, no. 244 (29 August 1734), p. 1, ridiculed the idea of 'granite and porphyry, intermixt with lapis lazuli, and all the several kinds of costly stones in Mosaic manner'.
107 St David, Pembrokeshire, was 'sadly disfigured by the custom generally adopted through many parts of Wales of digging graves within . . . by which the level is raised and rendered very uneven' (Hoare 1983, p. 45, 13 June 1793). Worcester was exceptional for its 'fine white-stone floor, which adds greatly to the beauty . . . since . . . no graves are suffered . . . there' (Green 1764, p. 56).
108 Doc. 52: following 29 May 1768.
109 Doc. 207: 26 August 1734, 25 July 1735.
110 Doc. 117: September 1778, November 1779.
111 Doc. 77: 28 April 1794.
112 Swete MS, vol. 1, f. 92, 1783–4.
113 Doc. 7: 14 September, 28 November 1772.
114 Pococke 1750, 8 June 1751.
115 Doc. 272: 26 August 1769. Doc. 10: 1 December 1790.
116 Doc. 235: 24 June 1714, 1715.
117 Doc. 167: 27 July 1793.
118 Doc. 41: 4 December 1787.
119 Aston 1816, pp. 82–3, in 1788.
120 Doc. 31: 17 October 1792.
121 Doc. 167: 1793.
122 'Remarks on St George's Church, Hanover Square', *Gentleman's Magazine* (September 1807), p. 832.
123 Nicolson 1877, p. 82.
124 Bristow 1996 and Bristow 1977 hint at the extraordinary discoveries to be made in the ecclesiastical sphere.
125 'A few handfuls of sea salt, mixed with about one cwt. of

lime . . . used in white wash, will make it adhere to the wall and destroy insects' (*New York Mercantile Advertiser*, 16 April 1803, quoted in Gottesman 1965, p. 276).

126 Quoted in Leoni 1755, p. 149, also observing that 'Marble, with which we are told *Nero* built a Temple to *Fortune* . . . was so white, so clean and transparent, that even when all the Doors were shut the Light seemed to be enclosed within' (pp. 118–19). Ancient classical temples were a main source of inspiration for Anglican design (see the present publication, chapter 21).

127 Leoni 1715–20, Book Four, Part First, Chapter II, p. 7, paraphrased in Ware 1738, p. 82.

128 Defoe 1991, vol. I, 1748, p. 326.

129 York 1768, pp. 48–9, 51.

130 Doc. 52: 27 September 1794. Carter complained that it altered and mutilated ancient churches (December 1798).

131 Hoare 1983, p. 108, 1 June 1799.

132 Richards 1973, p. 108. The south elevation of St Botolph, Knottingley, Yorkshire (remodelled 1750–55), retains its whitened exterior (Borthwick Institute of Historical Research, York University, Reg. 36, ff. 162v–164. Ryder 1993, p. 164).

133 *Gentleman's Magazine* (March 1753), p. 140.

134 He specified 'the Modell of the Great Wreaths over the mid Isle of the Choire Stone Colour' at St Paul's (*Wren Society*, XIV, 1937, p. 142); 'all flatt worke, painted in stone colour' at St Andrew, Holborn, 5 October 1686 (*Wren Society*, X, 1933, pp. 105–6).

135 Doc. 214: 1708.

136 Doc. 259: 1723–4.

137 Doc. 229: 9 June 1731.

138 Doc. 109: 29 October 1748. The 'wash for [Lady Luxborough's] Summer House of a Stone-Colour. You may try the Colour first on an hot Brick on which it will dry immediately. You have a good Sand near you. It should be done twice at least' (Shenstone 1939, pp. 286–7, 8 August 1750). For a discussion of the technique as used in America, see chapter 30.

139 Lounsbury 1994, p. 354.

140 Doc. 10: 11 April 1797. East Riding Archives and Local Studies, Beverley, PE 60/1, 16 August 1730. Doc. 222: 18 January 1790.

141 Doc. 272: 29 January–29 September 1707.

142 Doc. 269: 13 September 1721.

143 Doc. 222: 21, 28 June, 19 July 1775.

144 Clarke 1963, p. 80, in 1783.

145 Doc. 10: 11 April, 3 May 1797. See also the trade card of Upton, Shrewsbury, painter and undertaker (Doc. 165: 20 October 1795). The colour was composed of umber and white lead (Lounsbury 1994, p. 395).

146 Buckinghamshire Record Office, D/DR/12/61, 30 April–12 August 1785. This was part of Samuel Wyatt's refurbishment of 1778–85, altered 1890 (Bray 1783, pp. 3–4; *Buildings of England: Buckinghamshire*, 1994, pp. 129–31).

147 Doc. 230: 25 June 1790. Bristow 1996, p. 175, fig. 185, and following p. 276, samples 19–20. Bignamini and Hornsby 2010, pp. 151–4. British awareness of Continental schemes is evident in Edward Dewes's observation of 1776 that Dijon cathedral was 'wash'd with a kind of collour betwixt . . . cream & . . . light pink which seemd a fashionable collour' (Bodleian Library, University of Oxford, MS Eng.misc. d. 213, f. 153).

148 Westminster Abbey Muniments, 34515, f. 52r–v, in 1727. Doc. 125: 4 July 1780.

149 Doc. 244: 25 March 1724–25 March 1725. Southampton Archive, D/PM/9/4/5/8, f.1 7v, in 1795.

150 Doc. 155: 14 December 1731.

151 Doc. 50: 6 March 1759.

152 Richard Wooddeson of Reading, 'On Goody Biddice, who cleans the Church and the Assembly-Room', quoted in Loveday 1984, p. 46.

153 Bingham 1711, p. 170. See also Willmott 1885, pp. 222, 245–6.

154 *Gentleman's Magazine* (May 1766), p. 210. It was still in poor condition in 1800 (Hodgkinson 1992, p. 145).

155 Torrington 1934–8, vol. II, p. 357, 2 July 1791.

156 *Gentleman's Magazine* (April 1798), p. 274.

157 Leicestershire Record Office, 1D41/18/21, f. 10, 6 September 1775; Shropshire Records and Research Unit, MS 6861, f. 115v, 15 June 1797.

158 Lambeth Palace Library, MS 2691, f. 397, 19 January 1727; Owen 1994, p. 221, in 1787; Leicestershire Record Office, 1D41/18/21, f. 109, in 1789.

159 Leicestershire Record Office, 1D41/18/21, f. 115, 17 August 1776 (similarly at Desford in 1779, f. 55v); Essex Record Office, D/P 245/5/2, 29 September 1798.

160 Nash 1781–2, vol. I, pp. 4–5.

161 Burne 1958, p. 206, 28 November 1749. See Friedman 2004, pl. 24.

162 Doc. 19: 6 July 1726.

163 Hampstead Parish Church Trustees Minutes, 1744–96, f. 142, 12 October 1747. Doc. 231.

164 Nicolson 1877, p. 91.

165 Polwhele 1793–1806, vol. II, p. 236, in 1793.

166 Doc. 136: 30 March 1772.

167 Westminster Abbey Muniments, 34515, f. 35v, in 1724–5. Six ladders priced at 18s. 6d. were supplied by Francis Price, the carpenter in charge of improvements at Salisbury cathedral in 1740 (Wiltshire Record Office, D1/27/3/2/4).

168 Doc. 266: 2, 11 June 1789.

169 York Minster Library, E2/PV, 22 February 1779.

170 Doc. 272: 1713.

171 Colvin 2008, p. 1164.

172 Doc. 240: 9 July 1786, 14 April, 13 June 1787.

173 Doc. 57: 3 March 1789, 25 June, 17 July 1793, 15 March 1794.

174 Fougeroux MS, pp. 18–21; Campbell 1947, p. 43, 3 March 1775. 'Every blackening church appalls', lamented William Blake in *Songs of Experience*, 1794.

175 Campbell 1715–25, vol. I, p. 3, pl. 9.

176 Doc. 70: 1786.

177 Doc. 52: following 29 May 1768. Surface scraping was recommended as a preservative at St Margaret, Westminster (Doc. 268: 6 February 1735).

178 Doc. 98: 1704; Derbyshire Record Office, D643, A/PW/1/1, 3 December 1770; Doc. 271: 25 August 1797.

179 Doc. 124: 2 April 1793.

180 Doc. 167: 21 December 1798.

181 Essex Record Office, D/P 245/5/2, 31 January 1795.
182 Leicestershire Record Office, ID41/18/2, f. 109, in 1789.
183 Durham University Library, DCD, Chapter Acts 1725–41, f. 163, 14 March 1741 (Bedlington); Lincolnshire Archives, Lincoln, Billinghay PAR 9/3, 8 May 1742; East Riding Archives and Local Studies, BC/II/7/8, f. 319v, 16 November 1795 (Beverley).
184 Doc. 105: 3 November 1756.
185 Leeds University Library, Department of Manuscripts and Special Collections, MS Dep 1980/1/88, 1, 4 September 1724, charging 4d.; Guildhall Library, MS 25539/12, f. 105, 4 December 1714 (All Hallows); City of Westminster Archives Centre, H 805, f. 480, 17 March 1787.
186 Doc. 259: 25 June 1729–25 March 1731.
187 *Wren Society*, XV (1938), pp. 59–60, 1 April–30 June 1700; p. 113, September 1704.
188 Doc. 19: 27 February, 20 June 1717, 2 August 1718, 13 July, 24 August 1719.
189 *Gentleman's Magazine* (February 1799), p. 94. In 1736 Hawksmoor's obituarist (and son-in-law) claimed that the machine was the architect's 'own Invention', which prompted widow Thornton to set the record straight by issuing plates 137–8 as a reaffirmation of her husband as the true 'man of great genius' (Doc. 19: 25 March 1736, 1 July 1740).

TWELVE 'RABIES GOTHORUM'

1 Or 'Gothic rage', from Corbet Owen, *Carmen Pindaricum*, 1669, reprinted in *Musarum Anglicanarum analecta*, 1721 and again in 1747 (*Oxford Dictionary of National Biography*, vol. XLII, pp. 187–8).
2 Reeves 1764, p. 26.
3 Doc. 272.
4 In a letter of September 1753 to Richard Bentley concerning Worcester cathedral (Walpole 1937–83, vol. XXXV, p. 150).
5 The bibliography relating to ecclesiastical gothic is extensive; see particularly Clark 1928; Beer 1948; Colvin 1948; Summerson 1970, chapter 24; Lang 1966; Davis 1974; Frew 1980; Georgian Group 1983; McCarthy 1987; Worsley 1995, chapter IX; Brooks 1999, chapters 1–2, 4; Charlesworth 2002; Sweet 2004, particularly chapters 1, 3, 7.
6 Peck 1727, pp. 52–4. He 'would only suggest a thought to better judges' based on the disposition of steeples. A valiant attempt to chronicle the development of medieval styles was offered in Dallaway 1806, Sections I–II.
7 Soo 1998, p. 40.
8 Referring to Perpendicular. Published in Rawlinson 1719; Wren 1750, pp. 304–6; Price 1753, pp. 16–18 (Soo 1998, pp. 61–3).
9 Soo 1998, pp. 79–80, 82–3, 85. In the account published in *Parentalia* (Wren 1750), Christopher Wren Jr added: 'what we now vulgarly call the *Gothick*, ought properly and truly to be named the *Saracenick Architecture refined by the Christians*' (p. 306). In *The Expedition of Humphrey Clinker*, 1771 (Smollet 1985, p. 214), Matthew Bramble remarks to Dr Lewis on 'ancient churches in different parts of the kingdom, which used to be called monuments of Gothic architecture; but it is now agreed, that this stile is Saracen . . . and, I suppose, it was first imported into Europe from Spain, great part of which was under the dominion of the Moors'.
10 F. Blondel in *Cours d'architecture*, Book 1, 1675, p. 4, wrote of the 'superb buildings' of ancient Rome 'brought down' and replaced by an 'excessive and intolerable way of building, which our Fathers employed for a long time by the name of Gothick Architecture' (quoted in Bizzarro 1992, pp. 30–31). Describing Notre Dame during a visit to Paris in 1718, an Englishman commented that the gothic 'manner . . . gradually declin'd' from the mid-thirteenth century 'into a barbarous & shocking taste: About the reign of our King Hen 8th: it sunk' (British Library, Add. MS 45,059, f. 107).
11 Soo 1998, pp. 82–3.
12 Evelyn 1696, pp. 9, 26, added to his English translation of R. Fréart, *Parallele de l'architecture antique et de la moderne* [1650], first published in 1664, quoting pp. 9, 26 from the editions of 1723 or 1733 (Harris and Savage 1990, pp. 196–201). Evelyn had republished in *Parallele* Henry Wotton, *The Elements of Architecture*, 1624, which attacked the pointed arch 'both from the natural Imbecility of the sharp Angle itself, and likewise for [its] very Uncomeliness' and thought it 'ought to be exiled from judicious Eyes, and left to [its] first Inventors, the *Goths* . . . amongst other Reliques of that barbarous Age' (Theorem V, p. xiv).
13 Colvin and Newman 1981, p. 14, also expressing the same sentiments (p. xxiii).
14 Addison 1761, pp. 224–5, 1701–3.
15 Peck 1727, pp. 52–4.
16 Quoted in Piggott 1985, p. 56. This prejudice persisted in some quarters until the end of the century – 'At what time, previous to the literary production of Sir C. Wren [published in Wren 1750], do we read of the term *Gothic*, as being applied to stigmatise our ancient and national architecture . . . which at present is degraded by the low and barbarous name of GOTHIC Architecture!' (*Gentleman's Magazine*, January 1801, p. 33) – and well beyond.
17 Evelyn 1696, p. 10 (see note 12). 'Gothick Architecture [which failed to show] good taste in its chimerical ornaments, has nevertheless much solidity and wonder because of the artifice of its workmanship, as one can see in the cathedral churches of Paris, Reims, Chartres' (D'Aviler 1691, pp. 384–5, quoted in Bizzarro 1992, p. 36).
18 Colvin and Newman 1981, pp. 15, 22 (see note ••).
19 Soo 1998, p. 85.
20 Laugier 1977, pp. 76–7. Author's preface. Thomas Lediard's 1730 English edition of J. B. Fischer von Erlach's *Entwurff Einer Historischen Architectur* (1721) stated in respect to 'Gothick Building [that] there are certain general Principles in Architecture, which can by no Means be laid aside, without offending the Eye [including] that the Weaker must be supported by the Stronger'. James Essex, a leading English gothicist, observed that 'the Gothick Architects endeavoured in all their works to surprise by an apparent weakness' (British Library, Add. MS 6772, f. 272, in 1764).

21 Gloucestershire Record Office, D2002/2/4/1, John Mitford's MS travel diary, ff. 119–20.

22 Pope 1715, lines 119–20.

23 Under 'Gothic'. The edition of 1703 omits an entry on gothic. According to Harris 1704 (unpaginated), 'Gothick, in Architecture, is an Order so far different from the Ancient Proportions and Ornaments, that its Columns are too massy in a form of vast Pillars, or as slender as Poles, having Capitals without any certain Dimensions, carved with the Leaves of Brank-Usine, Thistles, Coleworths, etc.'.

24 Stukeley 1882–7, vol. III, pp. 379–80.

25 Doc. 272: 23 January 1738. Hawksmoor had died in 1736.

26 Doc. 78: 1723.

27 Doc. 117: 1769.

28 Price 1794, pp. 50–51.

29 The literature is extensive; see particularly Denslagen 1994; Jokilehto 1999.

30 Anonymous, 'Upon Viewing the Charges of Rebuilding St: Magdalens at Wolveston, 1716' (Durham County Record Office, EP/WO21).

31 Thoresby Society, Leeds, for St Mary, Whitkirk.

32 Nicolson 1877, pp. 22, 124–6. See also Bridekirk (pp. 81–2) and Caldbeck (pp. 94–5).

33 Shropshire Records and Research Unit, Shrewsbury, MS 6862, ff. 32–3, 25 July 1793. Thomas Telford's report of 23 March 1794 stated that the proprietor, Lord Clive, 'would lend . . . his Assistance [and] give whatever was proper'. See also Cleobury Mortimer (MS 6860, f. 48, 9 April 1794). The work was carried out by Telford in 1793 (Childe 1878, p. 54; views in British Library, Add. MS 21,018, ff. 19–20).

34 From a letter to the patron of the living, Lord Howard of Audley End, appealing to the church 'as a most valuable part of his Lordship's own Property and Inheritance and well becoming the Sender of his Station and Situation' in an attempt to convince him to 'bear One half' of the total cost of £6,000; he offered £1,000 and wished the parish success in 'keeping this noble Structure firm on its legs' (quoted in Rowntree 1951, pp. 37–8). The architect for repairs was R. W. F. Brettingham.

35 *Gentleman's Magazine* (October 1802), pp. 901–3. Adding insult to injury, 'as in many antient churches, by some strange perverseness, the service is not performed in the choir but in the nave'. Placido Columbani, a Milanese architect practising in England and a prolific publisher of decorative pattern books, repaired the church in 1799–1800 (Colvin 2008, pp. 271–2). Even the more stylistically correct medievalism of Kineton, Warwickshire (1756), by Sanderson Miller was considered by the Victorians as being 'almost irretrievably damaged by work of the lowest form of debased Gothic' as an excuse for remodelling it (1873–80) in a more 'authentic' manner (*The Architect*, 18 March 1882). Titchmarsh 1983.

36 British Library, Add. MS 5957, f. 23v, September 1735; Pococke 1750, vol. I, p. 151, 23 October 1750; Penrose 1983, p. 155, 2 June 1766. It was 'the most beautiful' of cathedrals (Defoe 1991, p. 117); 'grand . . . and beautiful . . . a superb Gothic work' (Rochefoucauld 1785, p. 159); 'one of the most superb pieces of Gothick architecture in this kingdom' (Collinson 1791, vol. III, p. 398); 'one of the finest Cathedrals in England . . . outside has a most venerable appearance . . . western front is very magnificent . . . much admired for ancient Gothic imagery' (*New Bristol Guide*, 1799, p. 173). However, *The New Bath Guide*, undated, p. 58, remarked that the front 'has ever been admired for its antient imagery . . . but the taste being rudely Gothic, it does not strike a common observer with either elegance or simplicity; the outside carries a venerable and awful look'. Bristol 'by the Generosity and Zeal' of the dean and chapter 'is so well Adorn'd, that it wants for no Cost or Art to render it beautiful, and is daily improving, and may be said to be kept in as good Repair as any Church whatsoever', though it was regarded, certainly unfairly, as 'truly no elegant Structure, being reputed one of the meanest Cathedrals in the Kingdom' (Willis 1717–30, p. 762).

37 A visitor in 1725 thought it 'makes not a much better figure than the [ruinous] church at Hexham. So much of the west end as is left standing is converted into a parish church . . . and is in a poor and wretched order (or rather disorder) as I ever saw any' (Doc. 53: 1725, 1727, 1764–5; see also 1783–6). Chester fared little better: 'very clumsy' and of 'mean appearance' due to the 'red, sandy, ill looking stone which takes much of the beauty of it, and . . . yielding to the weather, seems to crumble . . . which much defaces the building'. It underwent few improvements (Loveday 1984, p. 254, in 1737; *Gentleman's Magazine*, September 1764, p. 410; Defoe 1991, p. 202). A visitor of 6 October 1735 likened the stone to 'Petrified Mudd' (British Library, Add. MS 5957).

38 Evelyn 1707, p. 13; Harris and Savage 1990, pp. 196–201.

39 Doc. 31: 15 December 1791.

40 Lincolnshire Archives, Lincoln, F.B.1, f. 13, 14 April 1740.

41 Borthwick Institute of Historical Research, York University, FAC 1764/1a, 10 April 1764; the rector was otherwise 'willing to defray the whole Expence of . . . rebuilding'. The faculty was passed on 25 May (FAC 1764/1c). The chancel measured 44 by 18 feet.

42 Lincolnshire Archives, FAC 9/74, 20 May 1765, with before and after sketches.

43 Brand 1789, p. 247. The galleries, pews and pulpit were removed, the chancel dismantled and the altar screen pushed eastward (Baille 1801, p. 230), adding 'In short, every old erection was levelled, except the organ gallery'. Simon Bradley (letter to author, 18 September 2008) suggests this may be 'an instance of the taste for through-vistas, as implemented by Wyatt at Salisbury [Doc. 158: 1787–92] to antiquarian dismay'.

44 *Gentleman's Magazine* (July 1806), pp. 617–18.

45 Loveday 1890, p. 148; Stukeley 1882–7, vol. III, pp. 416–17; *Gentleman's Magazine*, Supplement 1745, pp. 681–2. National Library of Scotland, Edinburgh, MS 5371, ff. 196–209r. Pennant 1769, p. 55. The duke died on 20 February 1754.

46 Society of Antiquaries of London, 'A General List of The Members of the Society of Antiquaries, London, from MDCCXVII inclusive to Michaelmas MDCCXLVII'. Piggott 1985; London 2007.

47 *Oxford Dictionary of National Biography*, vol. LIX, pp. 372–5.

48 Wiltshire Record Office, D1/27/3/1, 2 September 1736, 16 May 1737.

49 Wiltshire Record Office, D1/27/3/1, 8 July 1742; *Oxford*

Dictionary of National Biography, 2004, vol. 59, pp. 372–5. This had to wait until 1776–7, when Francis Hiorne created an elegant, accurate gothic ensemble (Bodleian Library, University of Oxford, MS D.D.Radcl.c.51; Swete MS, vol. V, f. 22; Dugdale 1819, vol. I, p. 183; Clarke 1963, p. 207; *Buildings of England: Buckinghamshire*, 1994, p. 552).

50 Doc. 44: 3 October 1737.

51 Clarke 1963, pp. 129–30.

52 In the new building he hung an engraved portrait of Thomas Willis inscribed 'In honour of thy memory, blessed shade, / Was the foundation of this chapel laid' (Dugdale 1819, vol. I, p. 182).

53 Doc. 207: 1769.

54 Doc. 158: 1722.

55 Swift 1726, pp. 78, 112–13.

56 Fiennes 1982, p. 84. 'Grantham's soaring spire salutes the skies' (Anon. 1782, p. 17). Worsley 1987a.

57 An early nineteenth-century reference quoted in Taylor 1875, p. 156.

58 Peck 1727, p. 53.

59 Stukeley 1776, vol. I, p. 59, December 1713; Loveday 1984, p. 254, 1737; British Library, Add. MS 30,172, f. 12, 1794; Defoe 1991, p. 205, pl. 154, Stukeley's sketch of 1712. In 1798 John Carr of York considered Wrexham 'one of the most beautiful Gothick structures I ever beheld' (Myerscough 2000, p. 69).

60 *Newcastle Courant* (21–8 July 1750), p. 2, 17 July 1750; Durham County Record Office, EP/DA. SC 36, f. 390, 16 June 1752. Hutchinson 1823, vol. III, p. 224, observed that in rebuilding the 'old ornaments, the rolls at the angles [were] omitted . . . which deprived it of much beauty'. Whittaker and Clark 1971, p. 18.

61 Quoted in Cox 1875, p. 95. He estimated the cost at £1,050 10s. od.; the improvement was not carried out.

62 Fiennes 1982, p. 36.

63 Soo 1998, pp. 62, 67–9, 72–4.

64 Price 1753, pp. 32–3, 36, 38–9, 41.

65 'Lucius', 'SARUM. A Poem', *Gentleman's Magazine* (May 1740), p. 255 (Doc. 158).

66 Price 1735, pp. 33–4, pl. PQ, 'founded on a serious perusal of some of the most celebrated ones about *London*', probably including Wren's St Antholin, St Margaret Pattens and St Swithin (Cobb 1977, pp. 39–40 nos 34–6; Harris and Savage 1990, pp. 374–7), as well as Salisbury. About the right-hand design on p. 34 he observed that 'Lanthorns, or large openings, render a spire weak, unless care be taken in the performance', that is, in F and H 'the ogee roof, by its spreading helps to embrace and strengthen the whole the better', while in G and L the diagonal braces 'bolted or screw'd together, prevent the weight of the materials or the force of the wind, from separating them'. Both sheets were reproduced in reverse in Langley 1736, pl. CCCLXXXIX, as 'By Mr F. Price'.

67 Greene 1965, pp. 94–5, 99–100. West subscribed £10. *Gentleman's Magazine* (December 1792), p. 1077.

68 Clarke 1963, p. 15. The church reopened in 1758.

69 Colvin 2008, pp. 249–50, 1126.

70 Worcestershire Record Office, BA 348/5Q.

71 Doc. 203.

72 Doc. 57: 3 May 1789.

73 Guildhall Library, City of London Corporation, MS 3204/1–2, 1778. Wren 1750, p. 317 ill.; Godwin 1839, vol. I, pp. 4–8, 11 ill.

74 See Payne 1987, and publications listed in Documents.

75 West Yorkshire Archives Service (Bradford District Archives), 74D 83/1/20/a, f. 5 (*Bradford Archives* 1996, p. 57, ill.).

76 Stukeley 1776, vol. I, pp. 31–2, adding: 'the lantern at top is very beautiful, and the thinness of the stone-work is admirable', with north-west view dated 29 August 1722 (pl. 19). A 'noble and lofty [tower] . . . not only beautiful by land, but . . . very useful at sea to guide pilots into that port' (Defoe 1991, p. 216), 'the highest and best proportion'd that ever I saw' (British Library, Add. MS 38,448A, ff. 36–7, 1741 tour), 'a magnificent specimen of a fine gothic taste' (Pennant 1769, p. 14), 'admiring with all my eyes, and a strained neck, the beauty, grandeur, and loftiness of the tower of Boston Church, a building of most wonderful workmanship' (Torrington 1934–8, vol. II, p. 244, 3 July 1790), 'tower . . . said to have been built after the model of . . . the great church of Antwerp' (Dugdale 1819, vol. III, p. 603), that is, St Maria (1352–1521).

77 *Journals of the House of Commons*, vol. XVI, p. 55. See the case of Hulsberg's engraving of 1725 of All Saints, Derby (pl. 423), subsequently published in Gibbs 1728 (Doc. 64: 18 February–14 December 1725, 1728).

THIRTEEN THE BEGINNINGS OF EIGHTEENTH-CENTURY GOTHIC

1 'Mr Hawkesmoor's defence of the style of his work at Westminster Abbey', 1735 (Westminster Abbey Muniments, 24878, f. 1).

2 Doc. 190. Wren's work at Westminster Abbey and a small number of London City Churches (Jeffery 1996) puts the lie to the careless belief that he was 'no admirer of Gothic' (Denslagen 1994, p. 219).

3 Tyack 1998, p. 23; *Buildings of England: Lincolnshire*, 1989, pl. 46; Jeffery 1996, fig. 110.

4 Geraghty 2000, pp. 12, 113 no. 162.

5 Paterson 1714, pp. 236–7.

6 'O', 'On Westminster-Abbey', *Gentleman's Magazine* (September 1737), p. 565.

7 Doc. 272: 18 March 1735.

8 Neve 1726, under 'Gothic'.

9 Doc. 272: 1713.

10 Obituary, *Whitehall Evening Post*, 28 February 1725. See also Dickinson's 'Substantial repair' to the romanesque cathedral of Rochester, Kent, 1716–18, costing £1,161 17s. od. (Doc. 155: 5 May, 26 June 1716).

11 Doc. 272: 1709.

12 Doc. 272: 1734 (Ralph).

13 Cocke 1995, pp. 16–27.

14 Beauvais, which lies between Calais and the capital, is not mentioned on the itinerary (Whinney 1958), though for links between its cathedral and St Paul's, see Keene, Burns and Saint 2004, pp. 22–3, and Murray 1989, chapter VII, p.

105 n. 51, cover, pls 38–9; Wilson 1990, p. 252, pls 191–2. A closely related example is Martellange's south transept front of Orléans cathedral, *circa* 1620 (Brooks 1999, p. 23, pl. 11).

15 Soo 1998, p. 85.

16 Doc. 272: 25 December 1719, 4–5, 29 January and 29 September 1720, 22 May and 7 October 1721, 23 February and July–November 1723.

17 Doc. 272: Westminster Abbey Muniments (P) 902. A variation crowned by a spire carried on flying arches (Westminster Abbey Muniments [P] 912A–B, *circa* 1722) recalls St Dunstan-in-the-East, the erection of which Dickinson had supervised (Jeffery 1996, pp. 238–9). See John Talman's related sketch (Victoria and Albert Museum, London, 92.D.60B).

18 King 1672, pls 75–6. Doc. 115.

19 Soo 1998, pp. 61–78, citing 'eminent Structures' such as those of Vienna and Strasbourg (Nussbaum 2000, pls 44, 145).

20 *Wren Society*, XI (1934), p. 116, in 1724.

21 Westminster Abbey Muniments, 35495, 21 March 1723.

22 Doc. 272: 4 May 1725.

23 Frankl 2000, pls 29, 261; Nussbaum 2000, pls 86, 145.

24 Downes 1959, p. 278, pl. 45.

25 Doc. 272: 18 March 1735.

26 Doc. 272: 6 March 1735.

27 Doc. 272: 6 March 1735.

28 An alternative design for the west front (Westminster Abbey Muniments, no. 8) features the gable screened by a stylistically unauthentic baroque bauble.

29 Middleton 1962–3, pp. 297–8, 318–19, pls 39e, g, 42c–d; Henderson 1967, pl. 115; Fossier 1997, pp. 495–7; see also Saint Louis, Poissy, 1700–11 (pp. 502–5).

30 Doc. 153.

31 Doc. 115: 1722, 1724.

32 Doc. 70: 1735.

33 Doc. 117: 29–30 April, 20 September, 22 October 1726. On 25 April 1732 James specified in rebuilding the medieval spire of St Michael, Southampton, that since it 'is taking down somebody should be employed to take the Exact Size of everything that the same may be built agn:' (Doc. 168).

34 Doc. 155: 26 June 1716.

35 Doc. 52. Perhaps including William Emmett, who lived at Bromley, Kent, and who from 1702 published a series of engravings of St Paul's Cathedral (Colvin 2008, pp. 358–9).

36 Doc. 52: 24 March 1705, 1726. The spire is recorded in King 1672 and in an incised diagram dated 1702 on the south choir aisle wall.

37 Doc. 272: 1759, repeated 1761.

38 Doc. 268: 31 October 1734, 11 February 1799, 1761.

39 Doc. 268: 6 February 1735; 16, 21 May, 4 September 1735; 1737. There is no record of its internal appearance.

40 Talman 'apply'd himself to Ecclesiastical rarities, and [made] Draughts of whatever he found most remarkable in all the Churches where he travell'd' (Talman 1997, p. 22, pls 3–4, 16, 28–30, 33–8, 40–45, 51). These are summarised in Colvin 2008, pp. 1007–8, and on www.talman.arte.unipi.it, which included a now-lost volume of 'about 300 drawings of Churches etc. in Italy'. Collareta 2008. Ingamells 1997, pp. 924–6.

41 Doc. 141. White 1993, pls 278, 319, 372. Talman's pursuit of historical continuity is continued in his design for the axially aligned hall, which features a large history painting of Henry VI in Parliament confirming the foundation of the college to Chichley (Colvin 1964, p. 8 no. 42, pl. 54).

42 Stukeley 1776, vol. I, p. 44, in May 1712.

43 Doc. 141: 17 February 1715.

44 Atkyns 1712, pp. 82, 126; Colvin 1999, p. 226, figs 182–3. See also Sherston, Wiltshire, 1730–33, and Berkeley, Gloucestershire, 1749–53 (Colvin 1999, figs 184–5).

45 Doc. 28. Verey 1976, pl. 33.

FOURTEEN GOTHIC IN TRANSITION

1 Whitehead 1753.

2 Hart 2002, pp. 3–4. Craske 2004, chapter 3.

3 Doc. 272: 8 March 1735.

4 Doc. 272: 6 March 1735, 11 July 1734.

5 Anon. 1734, vol. I, under 'Gothic Architecture'. For further reading, see Harris and Savage 1990, pp. 265–8; Lang 1966, p. 256; Rowan 1975.

6 Langley 1742, pp. 6–7.

7 Sir John Soane's Museum, London, AL 39D (Harris and Savage 1990, p. 271, pl. 1), signed 'Jno Carr 1770'.

8 The medieval fabric was transferred to the Corporation in 1722; in 1772 the 'whole chapel was repaired and beautified' (Barrett 1789, pp. 343–4 ill.); in December 1777 the dean and chapter granted leave 'to erect a portico at the front door', completed in 1778 for £92 10s. 6d. (Latimer 1887–1908, vol. II, p. 431). Dr Timothy Mowl has pointed out (letter to author, 7 March 2005) a close resemblance to the existing gothic arcade added by James Paty (died 1779) to Stoke Park, Bristol, *circa* 1760–61 (Mowl 1991a).

9 Doc. 207: 22 December 1737, February, 14 October, 6 December 1740, 3, 26 February, 4 July, 14 November 1741. For contemporary gothic work at York by Kent and perhaps his circle, see Friedman 1995. Kent, born at Bridlington, Yorkshire, is likely to have known Bishop Cosin's gothic woodwork in Auckland Castle chapel, County Durham, 1661 (Worsley 1995, p. 180, fig. 209).

10 See particularly the chapter house canopies and choir-stalls (Brown 2003, figs 2.38, 5.79; *Buildings of England: York*, 1957, pl. 12b).

11 Hildyard 1755, p. 143.

12 Doc. 164: September 1756. Richard Bentley and J. H. Müntz, who were employed at Strawberry Hill, together designed Richard Bateman's gothic residence at Old Windsor, Berkshire (1759–62; McCarthy 1987, pp. 104–11, pls 140, 142–7).

13 Doc. 164: 8 May 1746, 28 February 1748, 18 February 1750, 28 March 1752, 1753.

14 Doc. 179: 1749, 1752 (Tetbury), Doc. 197 (Wimpole), Doc. 173: 27 May 1740 (Stoke Edith). Flitcroft designed the Gothic-style Alfred's Tower (1772) at Stourhead, Wiltshire (Colvin 2008, p. 382), and perhaps 'The Towers', Redlynch, Somerset (1751–5; Colvin 2009, pp. 2–3, fig. 1). He visited Westminster Abbey on 2 June 1722 (Doc. 272).

15 For Esher, see Harris 1998b, nos 20–23, pl. 9; Mowl 2006, ill. following p. 170. For Langley, see pls VIII, XXIV, XLIII.

Versions of the *tabula ansata* panels (R. Hewlings in Barnard and Clark 1995, pp. 116, 118, fig. 47a) appear on the Thompson Mausoleum, Little Ouseburn (1743), attributed to Roger Morris, a member of the Burlington–Kent circle (*Buildings of England: Yorkshire: The West Riding*, 2009, pp. 575–6, pl. 77) and at St Margaret, Westminster, in 1758 by Kenton Couse, Flitcroft's protégé (Friedman 2004, fig. 78). Walpole 1937–83, vol. XXXV, p. 487, 6 May 1778, advised a client building in 'the *esprit du Gothique* [to] copy the pattern exactly, of which there are many in Dart's *Westminster* or *Canterbury*' (Dart 1726). The 'Care . . . Taken [with] as Much Decency as Possible and as Little Molestation as Possible' in Sanderson Miller's remodelled Adlestrop (1758–65) is exemplary (Colvin 2008, p. 694). Of the considerable modern literature on Shobdon (Doc. 164), the late Sir Howard Colvin most recently offered the best considered assessment: 'an anthology of Kentian designs, some perhaps by Kent himself . . . some perhaps assembled by . . . Bateman with the help of an informed committee' (Colvin 2009, p. 8). Kent's gothic work is examined in Colvin 2008, pp. 613–16; Barkley 1984, pp. 3–5, illustrations to Spenser's *The Faerie Queene*, published in 1751; McCarthy 1987.

16 The Court of King's Bench, Westminster Hall, 1739, removed *circa* 1825 (Vardy 1744, pl. 48; Vardy 1742, pl. XXXII). A variation is Keene's Shelburne Pew, All Saints, High Wycombe, Buckinghamshire, 1754, now in Wycombe Abbey School (Addleshaw and Etchells 1948, pl. V; Harris 2007, pl. 68).

17 According to Leland (Tatton-Brown and Mortimer 2003, p. 1).

18 Warwickshire County Record Office, CR 136B/1785 (McCarthy 1987, fig. 174). The triple-canopied bishop's pew in the south-west corner recalls John of Eltham's monument, removed in the late eighteenth century (Binski 1995, pp. 177–8, fig. 233). The arcades of triangular crowned stalls are also a familiar abbey motif (Dart 1723, vol. II, pp. 12–13, 30; Binski 1995, figs 149–50, 155, 157, 168–9). Doc. 96.

19 Doc. 202: 18 May 1750, September 1753.

20 Davis 1974, pp. 91, 138; Whiffen 1948, p. 70; Humphrey 1991, p. 113. For a full account, including documents and designs, see Friedman 2002.

21 Doc. 97.

22 Tyack 1998, pp. 113, 141–2.

23 Harris 1998a.

24 Cocke 1995, pl. 10. Keene probably designed the equally elaborate Harte-Dyke monument at Lullingstone, Kent (Craske 2004, pp. 64–5, fig. 36). The daughter of Sir Thomas Dyke of Lullingstone Castle was married to William Lee, cousin of Sir William Lee of Hartwell (Smyth 1851, p. 96).

25 Doc. 86: September 1753, having provoked similar accolades in 1722, 1736 and 1783–4.

26 G. Vertue after Ride, *The Market-Cross at Chichester* (Friedman 2002, p. 149). Keene may have known Ride, who resided during part of his career in Westminster (Colvin 2008, pp. 868–9) and was the author of a poem, 'Westminster Abbey', in praise of tombs (*Gentleman's Magazine*, August 1755, p. 373).

27 *Buildings of Scotland: Lothian*, 1978, pp. 213–14, pl. 30; King 2001, vol. I, pp. 356–7, pl. 512; vol. II, p. 11, pl. 13; Royal Commission of Ancient and Historic Monuments of Scotland, A 7546 (Edinburgh University, Department of Architecture measured drawing).

28 Stukeley 1882–7, vol. III, p. 416, 18 August 1739. Maggi 2002; Fleming 1962, p. 22.

29 The bald church accounts record in 1759: 'Repairing . . . Leads & Windows', £1 11s. od.; 'Edwd. Bilton for Iron Work about Church', £2 10s od. (West Yorkshire Archives Service [Leeds District Archives], P31, Parish Records 21). Sir John Soane's Museum, AD 50/86–87 (Fleming 1962, p. 266, pl. 87), Adam was employed at Harewood House in the years 1758–71 (Colvin 2008, p. 50).

30 Doc. 58.

31 These recall Carbrooke, Norfolk (Lever and Harris 1993, pl. 68).

32 Significantly, Brown's Croome Court (1751–2) involved the participation of Sanderson Miller, one of the principal architects of Georgian gothic (Colvin 2008, p. 694).

33 Doc. 52: 1746–7, 1751.

34 Brown 1999, pl. 146.

35 Colvin 2008, pp. 884–5; Toynbee 1927, pp. 2, 5, 10, 14.

36 Doc. 174: 29 June 1792.

37 Doc. 159.

38 Parish records for both churches have vanished, resulting in confused building histories. Regarding Manchester: Act of Parliament granted in 1753 to defray the cost of building on ground adjacent to Deansgate (*Journals of the House of Commons*, vol. XXVI, p. 556, 7 February, and pp. 594–5, 16 February); foundation stone laid on 28 April 1768 (Manchester Central Library, Q283, 43733 Ma 9); Edward Byrom petitioned Parliament on 24 January 1769 that 'Trade, Commerce . . . Manufactures, within . . . Town . . . for several Years past greatly increased', also population at 'Upper End . . . *Deansgate* . . . which lies at . . . great Distance from . . . Churches and Chapels within . . . Town . . . of great Benefit and Utility . . . if another . . . built . . . already begun to erect . . . now at . . . own Expence carrying on . . . proposes to finish in . . . proper, decent . . . commodious Manner', requested Bill to enclose land for churchyard, granted (*Journals of the House of Commons*, vol. XXXII, pp. 133–4), passed Stat. 9, Georgii III, c.60; consecrated 7 July 1769 (Q283 42733 Ma 9). Described in Aston 1816, pp. 79–82; various views (Manchester Central Library, 67044, 67069, 6866, 23833 interior towards chancel. For Liverpool: Act of Parliament granted in 1762 to build two new churches, Lightoler's St Paul (Doc. 119) and St John; latter foundation stone laid on 24 June 1775 (*Gore's General Advertiser*, in Peet 1901, pl. V); consecrated in 1783 (Picton 1873, vol. II, pp. 210–11, attributed incorrectly to Thomas Lightoler). Described in Picton 1886, pp. 276–7; Moss 1794, pp. 84, 90; Wallace 1794, pp. 146–7; Troughton 1810, pp. 379–80; *Country Life* (19 March 1987), p. 109.

39 Preface to Halfpenny and Halfpenny 1752; also pl. 16, 'a Lodge or Keepers House fit for a Park, Forrest, &c', in Lightoler 1762.

40 Doc. 11: 10 October 1766, letter to John Chute of The Vyne, Hampshire.

41 Doc. 11: 22 April, 16 March 1766.

42 To Richard Bentley, August 1756 (Walpole 1937–83, vol. xxxv, p. 266).

43 Elizabeth Parkin of Ravenfield Hall (altered by Carr *circa* 1760–70, demolished) petitioned for a faculty 'to pull down & Rebuild the . . . Chapel . . . at her own Expense agreeable to a plan . . . annexed' (York Minster Library, Chapter Acts, 1747–56, H9/1, f. 116, 19 April 1755); Hunter 1819, p. 184; Wragg 2000, p. 195, fig. 206. She also financed the building of a similar church at Woolley near Bath (1761), an estate inherited from her uncle William, attributed to John Wood Jr (Bath and North East Somerset Record Office, D/P/wooly 2/1/1, 16 November 1757; Clarke 1963, p. 77; *Buildings of England: North Somerset and Bristol*, 1958, p. 345, pl. 31b).

44 Doc. 65: April 1797. See also St Andrew, Boynton, Yorkshire (1767–3; Doc. 29).

45 Doc. 43: 11 September 1758, 1799.

46 Doc. 40: 1760, 26 January 1769.

47 The sustained repetition of windows derives from St John-on-the-Wall, the tracery from St Peter, both in Bristol (Gomme 2000, pls 37–8, 42).

48 Doc. 50. Brown 2003, fig. 2.16.

49 For example, Lowick, Northamptonshire, and Gressford, Denbighshire (Allen 1932, pls 37, 45).

50 Essex Record Office, D/P 16/6/1, February 1757. Morant 1768, vol. II, p. 445. Wing's design (1757) is in Northampton Public Library, Local Collection.

51 Doc. 106: 1790.

FIFTEEN A NEW SPIRIT OF 'TRUEST GOTHIC TASTE'

1 Dallaway 1806, p. 81.

2 Langley 1742.

3 Willis 1717–30, vol. II, p. 3.

4 Fiennes 1982, p. 79, in 1697 (with, pp. 80–81, views from D. Loggan, *Cantabrigia Illustrata*, 1690).

5 Doc. 50: 1722, 2 October 1735, 1733, 1765 (Cole).

6 Doc. 50: 10 January 1771, 1784.

7 Doc. 50: 1788, 1796–1800. See also Watkin 1996, p. 555.

8 Society of Antiquaries of London, *Minute Book from 1 Janry. 1718 to 26 Octr. 1732*, vol. I.

9 Evans 1956, p. 206; Crook 1995; London 2007, pp. 123–41, 159–61.

10 A large collection of Lyus's drawings of Suffolk churches (1782–6) is in Ipswich Borough Council Museums and Galleries (*Country Life*, 20 August 1992, p. 59). For Grimm, see British Library, Kaye Collection; Payne 1987, pl. 27.

11 King 1672; this publication, pl. 150.

12 Preface to Willis 1717–30, vol. I, pp. vi–vii.

13 Adams 1983, pp. 78–80.

14 Dart 1726, pp. 26, 29–30.

15 Peck 1727, pp. 53–4.

16 *Gentleman's Magazine* (June 1789), p. 500, pl. III, fig. 7. For background, see Usher 2007.

17 Saint Nicaise, Reims (*Gentleman's Magazine*, April 1773, p. 164), Evreux cathedral (April 1783, p. 308), Lisieux cathedral (October 1783, pp. 813, 818) and multiple views of Sées cathedral, Normandy (May 1786, p. 359), the last published in connection with Ducarel and Warburton 1778.

18 Middleton 1962–3; Laugier 1977.

19 Talman 1997, pp. 107, 157. 'John Talman: An Early Eighteenth Century Collector of Drawings', curated by C. M. Sicca, University of Pisa, Paul Mellon Centre for the Study of British Art, London, 2005; Centre photographic file; WWW.TALMAN.ARTE.UNITPI.IT; Sicca 2008, pp. 1–75. For Santa Croce (founded 1294–5), see White 1993, pp. 30–34.

20 Society of Antiquaries of London, Minute Book, vol. V, p. 216, 2 March 1748/9. For the unfinished building at the end of the middle ages, see Germann 1972, pl. 51.

21 Walpole 1937–83, vol. XIII, p. 163, 21 April 1739, to Richard West; Walpole 1937–83, vol. I, p. 103, 18 January 1766, to William Cole, responding to the latter's observation: 'I never was more pleased in my life with a Gothic building than with the Cathedral of Amiens: everything so light and elegant, and the doors so richly ornamented with figures' (vol. I, p. 101). Frankl 2000, pp. 61–4, 67–8, 119–23, 130–33, pls 27–9, 34, 88–90, 101–4.

22 Bodleian Library, University of Oxford, MS Eng.misc.d.213, ff. 13–14, 39, 65, 73–4, 133–5, 174. Ingamells 1997, p. 297. For the above buildings, see Frankl 2000, pls 27–9, 43–4, 94–6, 107–8, 116, 123, 152–4, 169–70, 178–9, 200, 230, 235–6. 267; Wittkower 1974a, chapters I–III; Bekaert 1987, pp. 80–95.

23 Soo 1998, pp. 34–92.

24 Vertue 1930–55, vol. VI, p. 196, in 1742.

25 Harris and Savage 1990, pp. 374–6; Colvin 2008, p. 829. Republished in 1774.

26 Hogarth 1997, chapter VIII, p. 48.

27 Defoe 1991, vol. II, p. 130.

28 Walpole 1784, preface, p. I.

29 For example, J. H. Müntz, architect of the Gothic cathedral, Kew, adapted a 'Gothick Door at St Alban's Abbey, Hertfordshire to one in the Villa's Gallery' (McCarthy 1987, p. 84, pl. V). Crook 1973; Snodin, Wainwright and Calloway 1980; Calcraft and Viscardi 2007.

30 Doc. 107. The Hardinge family had owned the manor of Canbury and the rectory and advowson of All Saints, Kingston, since 1671 (information from Surrey History Centre, Woking). Compare Bentley's design to McCarthy 1987, pls 32–3. Nicholas Hardinge was a member of the Society of Antiquaries of London.

31 Walpole's brief history of The Vyne (Hampshire Record Office, 31M 57/652, f. 14, 18 March 1793).

32 Doc. 186: 1, 16 July 1755.

33 Walpole 1937–83, vol. IX, p. 216.

34 I am grateful to Dr Adam White for insights on this sculpture (letter to author, 9 March 2006). The tomb chamber was 'built . . . to receive the fine tomb . . . of his ancestor' (Walpole 1937–83, vol. XXXV, p. 642, 18 March 1793). Chute's internal staircase at The Vyne (1770) derives from Ashburnham House, Westminster School (*circa* 1662), attributed to John Webb (Bold 1989, pp. 151–2, pl. 99); he also remodelled The Vyne (1654–7; Bold 1989, pp. 170–74).

35 Doc. 186: May 1789.

36 Brown 1999, p. 123, pl. 98.

37 Doc. 177: 23 October 1771, 22 December 1772, 20 January

1773, 28 May, 8, 19 June 1774, 17 April 1779, 1784. For the Abbey shrine, see Foster 1991, pl. 68; Binski 1995, pp. 98–104, fig. 134.

38 Ware 1738, Fourth Book, Chapter VI, p. 86 (Tavernor and Schofield 1997, p. 221); Ward-Perkins 1981, pp. 66–7, pl. 30. Doc. 177: 29–31 October 1774.

39 Doc. 177: 28 May, 29–31 October 1774, 4 June 1779, 30 May 1780, 1784 *Description*. This is confirmed in John Carter's watercolour recording the centrally sited shrine dominating the interior with its trefoil- and quatrefoil-panelled pilasters supporting a fan-vaulted ceiling inspired by that in Henry VII's chapel in Westminster Abbey (Snodin 2009, p. 137, fig. 163). For other views of the Chapel in the Wood, see Snodin 2009, figs 28–9, 286.

40 Doc. 88. Perhaps not coincidentally, Bentley had prepared a design *circa* 1755 for a Strawberry Hill-inspired gothic gateway into Trevor's episcopal residence at Bishop Auckland, County Durham, which was superseded in 1760 by one by Robinson (McCarthy 1987, pls 29, 35). Bishop Trevor was the dedicatee of pl. XLV, dated 1767, in Bentham 1771.

41 Colvin 2008, pp. 1052–3. Kuyper 1980, pp. 24–6, figs 7A–B, pls 60, 62. The Nieuwe Kerk had been well known to the English since the Commonwealth; a sketch by the Royalist architect Robert Hooke is in British Library, Add. MS 5238.

42 Doc. 272: 1734. Cocke 1995, pl. II. See also Bentley's Isleworth Teahouse (McCarthy 1987, pl. 38).

43 Dugdale 1819, vol. II, p. 353. A later owner condemned it for being in the '*Strawberry Hill Gothic* . . . fashion . . . a mode of decoration sufficiently objectionable under any circumstances, but perhaps never adopted with less judgment or a worse effect' than here (Braybrooke 1836, p. 127).

44 Morant 1768, facing p. 140. *Buildings of England: Essex*, 1954, p. 123, pl. 48a; Essex Record Office, D/D BY A30/11, 9 October 1770.

45 British Library, Add. MS 5834, f. 57v.

46 Bentham 1771, pp. ii–iii, 282.

47 Walpole 1937–83, vol. I, pp. 190–91. This was published as the 'Account of the Old Conventual Church at Ely'.

48 Colvin 2008, p. 362, listing his various publications. See also Cocke 1975; Cambridge 1984; Brown 1985, pp. 98–113.

49 British Library, Add. MS 6762, f. 16v.

50 Doc. 117. Essex's Lincoln survey report of 1764 (British Library, Add. MS 5842, f. 169). Doc. 117: August 1764.

51 Doc. 117: 14 September 1774, 29 March 1775. In a letter of March 1778 concerning a new link across Eton's schoolyard connecting the hall to the medieval chapel (unrealised), Essex explained: 'I have made the Elevation . . . as near as they [the authorities] would permit of the same stile as the College & propose the whole be of Brick and stone mixt, as they are in the old buildings' (Connor 1993, pp. 9–10), an attitude in diametric contrast to, say, Wren's imposition of the wholly classical Honywood Library (1674–5) into Lincoln cathedral's gothic cloisters (Colvin 2008, p. 1159).

52 Walpole 1937–83, vol. I, pp. 208–9, 3 January 1771.

53 Walpole 1937–83, vol. XXVIII, p. 306, 2 May 1777, to Revd William Mason, precentor of York Minster; Walpole 1937–83, vol. I, p. 46, 22 May 1777, to Cole.

54 Doc. 50: 1701, 1709, 1718, 1735, 1742.

55 Miller was architect of the gothicised Lacock Abbey, Wiltshire (1754–6), the restored medieval Kilkenny cathedral, Ireland (1756–7; Doc. 105), and Pomfret House, London (1758–60), which Walpole later likened to King's College chapel (Doc. 50: 1757, 6 March 1759, 1779). Colvin 2008, pp. 692–5.

56 Doc. 50: 6 March 1759.

57 Walpole 1937–83, vol. XXXV, p. 487, 6 May 1778.

58 Doc. 53.

59 Doc. 50: 1 November 1765, 1766.

60 Doc. 50: 2–3 January 1771. For builders' estimates, see 1773–5.

61 Doc. 50: 14–27 March 1775.

62 'Plans and Heads of an Intended History of Gothic Architecture', 1770 (British Library, Add. MS 6771, f. 200r). See Walpole 1937–83, vol. I, p. 211, 10 January 1771; Walpole 1937–83, vol. II, p. 304, 31 January 1781, 17 February 1782.

63 Doc. 117: 6 March 1759.

64 Doc. 117: 1734. See also 1701, 1703, 1720–21, 1722, 1730, 1740, 1741–3, 1758, 16 May 1762, 1769, 1772.

65 Doc. 117: 1755, 1765–6. See also the related *Last Judgement* porch (1258–80) at the south-east corner of Lincoln, which gave direct access to the choir space immediately behind the altar (Willis 1717–30, vol. III, preceding p. 1). John Carter's undesignated, undated Lincoln-inspired high altar design is in the Victoria and Albert Museum, London, W.102a, D.18–1886.

66 Doc. 117: 22 November 1779, 9 August 1783.

67 Doc. 117: 14 September 1774, 8 March 1775.

68 Doc. 117: 8, 29 March 1775, 7 April 1776.

69 Bennett 1997, p. 30.

70 Doc. 117: 9 August 1783. Cocke 1975, p. 90. The object is untraced.

71 Doc. 75.

72 Doc. 75: July 1757.

73 Doc. 75: 14 June 1759. Bentham 1771, p. 285, observed that the presbytery occupied one-third of the interior and 'in respect of Elegance, Proportion, and Decoration, may justly be accounted one of the choicest and most perfect remains of Gothic Architecture . . . fell into disuse after the Reformation [yet] found on trial to be better adopted in all respects to the purpose of Reading and Hearing, as well as the Organ and Voice, for performing the several parts of Divine Service'.

74 Doc. 75. Willis 1717–30, vol. III, p. 334.

75 Doc. 75: 14 June 1759. Bentham 1771, p. 285, reiterated that 'when the Whole is finished, there is no doubt this Church will be . . . rendered one of the most elegant and magnificent in the Kingdom'.

76 Doc. 75: 1 November 1770.

77 Bishop Wren was elevated in 1636, when Christopher was four years old (Bentham 1771, pp. 200–01).

78 *Grub-street Journal*, no. 233 (29 August 1734), pp. 1–2.

79 Doc. 75: 25 November 1768. Bentham 1771, p. 214.

80 Doc. 50: 6 March 1759.

81 Doc. 75: 14 June, 7–9, 12 July, 3, 11 August 1769, 24 March, 20, 28 November, 15 December 1770, 3 January 1771.

82 Bentham 1771, pp. 282, 285. Most was swept away by the Victorians.

83 Doc. 199.
84 Doc. 63.
85 British Library, Add. MS 5842, f. 164, in 1784. An unusually sensitive, fully gothic chancel was added to Laughton, Sussex (1764–5), by John Morris, a Lewes stonemason and surveyor, to his own design, represented by an accomplished drawing corresponding closely to the surviving fabric (Berry 2004, figs 6–7).
86 Doc. 52: 1768, February 1770.
87 Doc. 207.
88 Doc. 162: 1735, 7 November 1722, 29 September 1772.
89 Doc. 207: 24 February, 26 April 1794.
90 Doc. 207: 1703, 26 June 1740, 1769.
91 Despite references in Nichols 1795–1811, vol. II, pt 2, 1798, pp. 665–6, 685–92, and detailed accounts in Hill 1867, pp. 118–47, and Prophet 1982.
92 Prophet 1982, p. 99. Adding, 'Not like St. Paul's beneath whose ample dome / No thought arises of the life to come: / For, though superb, not solemn is the place, / The mind but wanders o'er the distant space, / Where 'stead of thinking on the God, most men / Forget his presence to rememeber *Wren*.'
93 Colvin 2008, p. 829, including the years 1768–9. In 1773 Hanbury proposed an annual benefaction of £16,000 towards 'Building and Founding [a] College at Oxford for . . . training . . . Youth for Holy Orders . . . on Heddington Hill . . . It shall consist of 2 or 3 large Quadrangles . . . a very superb Collegiate Gothic Church . . . having ornamental Steeples &c. – in . . . Cathedral Stile . . . laid out in the best taste . . . a perfect model of Grandeur, Elegance, and Beauty' (Leicestershire Record Office, DE 2415/1, ff. 28–9), a scheme still unrealised at the time of his death in 1778.
94 Leicestershire Record Office, DE 2415/1, ff. 5–8, 30.
95 Harrison 1775, pp. 130–31.
96 Accompanied by his architect son, Theodosius, Keene visited at Brussels Notre Dame de la Chapelle (1190–1483), the cathedral of SS Michael and Gudula (thirteenth–fifteenth centuries), with 'very fine windows painted with Historical Subjects the best I ever saw' by van Orley, and Mechelen cathedral (1342–*circa* 1520), with 'a large Gothic Steple . . . part . . . destroy'd by lightning' (British Library, Add. MS 60,356, ff. 12, 14). Blyth 1990, pp. 176–8, 219–20, 234–5, pl. 25.
97 Doc. 272: 21 October 1769, 1773, 21 July 1774, 10, 31 July 1775. The design is reproduced in Doc: p. 997.
98 Keene's improvements were anticipated by Gwynn 1766, pp. 125–6: 'the church would be vastly improved if those mean stalls in the choir were taken down . . . and enrich the choir by suitable Gothick stalls decorated in character with the rest of the church . . . the choir might also be widened by throwing the stalls back upon a line with the middle of the columns; this would give it a proportionable width to the length which would be gained by the removal of the [Whitehall] altar . . . whenever any repairs are made in the building every particular whatever should be restored as near as possible to its original form, and it is great pity that the whole cathedral is not put into a more respectable condition . . . if . . . an elegant Gothick dome [were] raised from the nave . . . and the whole inside . . . painted of an uniform clean stone colour . . . it would then become a most beautiful pile, and be deservedly esteemed one of the finest things of the kind perhaps in Europe'. Poignant evidence of Keene's influence is offered at Farnell on Farnwell, Angus, Scotland (1788–9), the London-based Scottish architect James Playfair's only foray into church gothic. His private 'Journal of Architecture' reveals that, worried over the commission, he modified the design in consultation with the heritor, Sir David Carnegie, and in the final stage visited Westminster Abbey to seek out an appropriate 'Exemplar' (National Library of Scotland, Edin-burgh, Adv. 33.5.25, f. 22v, 11 January 1789). The quatrefoil panels of the west gallery suggest that he looked at Keene's choir furnishings of 1775 (Macaulay 1975, pp. 256–8, pl. 135; Cocke 1995, p. 137).
99 The pre-ruined west front is recorded on the cover of the *Parish Magazine Bishopthorpe*, March 1863. A plan of 1878 (Borthwick Institute of Historical Research, York University, BIS 14) corresponds to the still-intact foundations. *Country Life* (14 September 1961), p. 568, fig. 3.
100 Doc. 206. The scheme was rejected in favour of Belwood's design of 1781.
101 Lincolnshire Archives, Lincoln, DAC/A/4/13, Essex to bishop, 8 March 1775.
102 Doc. 6: Skrine in 1795.
103 Snodin, Wainwright and Calloway 1980, p. 40.
104 Doc. 6: 1775.
105 Percy 1775, advertisement and pp. 16–17: 'Then, scoop'd within the solid rock,/Three sacred Vaults he shows;/The chief a Chapel, neatly arch'd,/On branching Columns rose./Each proper ornament was there,/That should a chapel grace;/The Latice for confession fram'd,/And Holy-water Vase./Up to the Altar's ample breadth/Two easy steps ascend;/And near a glimmering solemn light/Two well-wrought Windows lend./Besides the altar rose a Tomb/All in the living stone;/On which a young and beauteous Maid/In goodly sculpture shone./A kneeling Angel fairly Carv'd/Lean'd hovering o'er her breast;/A weeping warrior at her feet;/And near to these her Crest'. Engraved title page by I. Taylor after S. Wale illustrates this scene.
106 Doc. 6: 1799.
107 Doc. 6: 1775. Of the original furnishings only the gothic armchair and lectern (*circa* 1780), both versions of ones designed by Adam for Croome church in 1761, survive at Alnwick (5 December 1780).
108 Harris and Savage 1990, pp. 130–33; Crook 1995; Colvin 2008, pp. 231–3.
109 *Builder's Magazine* (1774), pp. 229, 63–4.
110 *Builder's Magazine* (1774), pls CX, CXIII, CXVI, CXIX, CXXIV, CXXVI, CXXX, pp. 59, 61, 63–5, 67, 69, 71. For a detailed analysis, see Friedman, in preparation.
111 For example, St Peter, Leeds (1837–41; Webster 1991, pl. 29a). I am grateful to Dr Webster for discussions on this subject.
112 Described as 'highly ornamented, and executed by . . . Van Gelder . . . under the direction of Mess. Carters, who are reckoned among the first statuaries of this Kingdom [and]

esteemed by connoisseurs one of the completes pieces of sculpture in this Kingdom' (Hutchins 1774, vol. I, pp. 148–9 illus., vol. II, p. 146). Vangelder was attached to the Carter family workshop in Piccadilly, where John Carter also trained (Roscoe 2009, pp. 1308–9, 215–16). The church's door frame is inscribed 'J. F. 1776' for James Frampton, the client and date of completion (Dorset Record Office, FRA/E68; *RCHME: Dorset*, vol. II, pt 1, 1970, p. 174, pls 112–13). In 1790 unspecified masonry work costing 13s. 7d.; April 1792, William Shepherd 'making . . . New Mouldings over . . . West Window' etc., £5 14s. 1d. (Dorset Record Office, PE/MTN/CW/1/1). North aisle added 1841, west porch 1848, damaged Second World War (*RCHME: Dorset*, vol. II, pt 1, 1970, p. 174). *A Short History of St Nicholas Moreton*, 1984 [guidebook]; *Buildings of England: Dorset*, 1972, pp. 300–01, pl. 79.

113 The similar hall arrangement of the choir of the Temple Church, City of London (*circa* 1220–40; Bradley and Pevsner 1997, pp. 132–6, pl. 4), was recorded in a perspective perhaps drawn by James Gibbs (Christ Church, Oxford, inv. 1140).

114 Doc. 191. Colvin 2008, p. 581.

115 Doc. 179. Dugdale 1819, vol. II, p. 451, noted that the columns 'support nothing, as the principal on which the roof of [Wren's Sheldonian] Theatre at Oxford was constructed, has been applied to this building'.

116 Port 2006, pls 82, 100, 102, 143, 172, 215.

117 Doc. 179: 1791. Hiorne repeated this composition at Stony Stratford, Buckinghamshire (1776–7, subsequently altered), described by Swete MS, vol. V, f. 22, as possessing a 'remarkably handsome' east window, 'pillars . . . light, and beautiful beyond description . . . of the most elegant Gothic Architecture I ever saw'. Bodleian Library, MS D.D. Radcl.c.51, 1 May 1777; Dugdale 1819, vol. I, p. 183; Clarke 1963, p. 207; *Buildings of England: Buckinghamshire*, 1994, p. 552; National Monuments Record Centre, English Heritage, Swindon, AA66/2578, nineteenth-century interior photograph.

SIXTEEN 'ANCIENT GOTHIC IN ALL ITS RICHEST ORNAMENTS'

1 Richard Colt Hoare on Durham cathedral, 15 July 1800 (Hoare 1983, pp. 143–4).

2 Torrington 1934–8, vol. I, pp. 170–71, 15 July 1784.

3 Colvin 2008, p. 1062. 'The choir lately beautifd. in the Gothic style' (British Library, Add. MS 30,172, ff. 10v–11, in 1794); largely remodelled in the nineteenth century (*Buildings of Wales: Clwyd*, 1986, pp. 435–40).

4 *Gentleman's Magazine* (February 1783), pp. 138–9, responding to *Gentleman's Magazine* (October 1782), pp. 480–82; (January 1783), p. 37.

5 Doc. 171.

6 'The superior lightness and sharpness of the ornamental parts are immediately apparent, as no stone can be wrought to so exquisite a finish' (Dugdale 1819, vol. I, pp. 117–18).

7 Doc. 63: 1786–93; Doc. 187: 8 December 1788, 7 April, 25 May, 22 October 1789.

8 Doc. 201: January 1787 under 29 December 1786.

9 Walpole 1937–83, vol. II, p. 363, 9 October 1791.

10 Doc. 201: 16 December 1796, 4 August 1790.

11 Ionides 1999, pp. 260–66. At St Alkmund 'All the Iron Work was cast by the Coalbrook-Dale Company' (*Shrewsbury Chronicle*, 30 October 1795, p. 3).

12 Doc. 165: 5 August, 23 December 1793, 15 May, 24 June 1794, 22 November 1793.

13 Friedman 1996a, p. 122, pl. 35.

14 For example at Much Wenlock in 1737, Welshampton in 1786, St Chad, Shrewsbury, in 1791 and Bridgnorth in 1792 (Friedman 1996a).

15 Hoare 1983, p. 169, 15 May 1801, though the pulpit, originally sited in the central aisle, was 'so injudiciously placed as to obstruct the view of the window on entering the church'. Eginton based his composition on a 1792 engraving of Guido Reni's *Assumption of the Virgin*, then in the Electoral picture gallery, Düsseldorf (*Gentleman's Magazine*, March 1743, p. 154), now in Alte Pinakotek, Munich (Pepper 1984, p. 284, pl. 213).

16 Doc. 165: 23 December 1793, 4 January, 7 November 1794. I am grateful to Revd Richard Hayes for alerting me to recent restoration discoveries (correspondence of 17 November 2008).

17 British Library, Add. MS 5845, f. 114v, with a long description, attributing the work to an English architect (ff. 121v–122v). Frew and Wallace 1986; McCarthy 1987, p. 17; Charlesworth 2002, vol. II, pp. 14–32; Smith 1968, pp. 52–6, pls 12–15, 27; Dias et. al. 2002, pp. 92–7.

18 Murphy 1795, preface, p. i. Colvin 1991, pp. 180–84, figs 167, 169. For Conyngham's 'Sketches of Batalha' (Society of Antiquaries, London), see Ostergard 2001, p. 119, fig. 7–2.

19 Linstrum 1973, p. 41 no. 19, but not a record of Batalha, as stated. Linstrum notes links between Wyatt and Conyngham.

20 Doc. 211. Malcolm 1803–7, vol. I, p. 303, claimed that the church was 'by very far the best attempt of modern days to imitate the *Saracenic*, Gothic style, I have seen'. Kalman 1971, p. 150, cites York Minster chapter house, though only a single space, with the tracery pattern based on Durham cathedral kitchen. The suggestion by Lever 2003, p. 417, of a possible source in the renaissance church of Santa Maria della Pace, which Dance drew in Rome in 1759–61, is unconvincing.

21 Murphy 1795, preface, pp. i, 16. The cusped arch of the altar recess (unrealised) featured in Dance's design, which Lever 2003, p. 87, pl. 23.6, associates with his London Guildhall façade (pl. 45); it also features at Batalha (Smith 1968, pl. 13).

22 'Memoirs of Thomas Jones', *Walpole Society*, 32 (1951), pp. 40, 59, 62, 65, 68. Graves 1905, vol. II, p. 280, 1786 no. 41, 1788 no. 261. Hardwick's father, Thomas Sr, also an architect, was involved with work at Hereford cathedral in 1786 (Doc. 98), while Thomas Jr was associated with John Carter at Canterbury cathedral in 1791 (Doc. 52) and exhibited in 1781 no. 541, 'Elevation of a church'; in 1794 no. 641, 'Design for . . . west front of a church'; in 1795 no. 670, 'Design for a church in South Wales' (Graves 1905, p.

385). Johnes's father, of Croft Castle, Herefordshire, subscribed to Bentham's *Ely* (1771). Old Hafod church was demolished 1799 and built anew by James Wyatt in 1803 (Colvin 2008, p. 1181; Yerburgh 2000, pp. 32–3). Hardwick's (?)Hafod church studies – plan, west front and section – formerly in A. P. Lyons's collection (present whereabouts unknown; recorded in Courtauld Institute of Art photographs 783/12/33, 35–6; Colvin 2008, p. 480 n. 1). Johnes's penchant for gothic octagons at Hafod is revealed in Yerburgh 2000, pp. 14–15; Inglis-Jones 1960, foll. p. 156. See the related eastern chapel-mausoleum at St Mary, Debden, Essex (1791–3), by John Carter (Doc. 63: 1791–3, 1797).

23 National Library of Scotland, Edinburgh, MS 14835, ff. 76–77v, 18 March, and ff. 78–9, 17 April 1793. A chandelier is also discussed. King 2001, vol. I, p. 71, pls 86–8, draws a parallel between the vault pattern and Southwell Minster chapter house.

24 Rowan 1985, pls 62, 64.

25 Denholm 1804, pp. 170–71. Sir John Soane's Museum, London, AD 1/145; 54/IV/252–54. Gomme and Walker 1968, p. 264, pl. 38; Tait 1993, pp. 167–8, fig. 143; King 2001, vol. I, pp. 73–5, pl. 90.

26 Doc. 157. See also Nash's St Non, Llanerchaeron, Cardiganshire, 1798 (Mansbridge 1991, p. 52).

27 Hoare 1983, p. 224, 2 July 1802.

28 Collinson 1791, vol. I, p. 74, for Charles Spackman, whose residence was attached to the chapel's south side.

29 Dugdale 1819, vol. IV, p. 198; *The Historic & Local New Bath Guide*, 1801, p. 50. It was illuminated by Thomas Barker's painted glass of the *Last Supper* over the altar and apostles' heads in each of the twelve upper windows (McCallum 2003, pp. 25, 53, 55, 74, 80–81). Palmer's Christ Church, Walcot, Bath (*circa* 1796–8), is a conventional, evenly bayed rectangle satiated with pinnacled buttresses, providing a link between Lightoler's earlier Liverpool church and some of the 1818 Commissioners' efforts, such as John Pinch Jr's St Saviour, Bath (Ison 1948, pp. 79–80; Plymley 1992, p. 115, pl. 6; Port 2006, pp. 204–5, pls 184, 187).

30 Doc. 207: 1770, 1786; see also Skrine 1795.

31 The complete set of drawings in British Architectural Library, Drawings and Archives Collection, Victoria and Albert Museum, London, H3/1, ff. 1–32 (*RIBA Catalogue*, vol. VIII, 1972, pp. 93–4).

32 Charlesworth 2002, vol. II, pp. 33–43, frontispiece. Rykwert 1972, pp. 82–7. Buchanan 1999, pp. 170–71, fig. 10.1. Charles Beazley turned to this much-admired specimen for finishing off Faversham parish church (1794–9; *Gentleman's Magazine*, July 1799, pp. 553–4). The *Gentleman's Magazine* wished for 'a design more consonant to the original style of the whole building. It stands an additional proof how difficult it is to imitate the true style of Gothic architecture' (Doc. 79: August 1799).

33 Bartell 1800, pp. 43–6.

34 Doc. 268: 12 December 1798, 22, 31 January 1799.

35 Friedman 2004, fig. 84.

36 Doc. 268: 17 February, 24 July 1801, 27 August, 5, 12 November 1802. Robinson 1979, pp. 157–60.

37 Doc. 268: September 1802.

38 Doc. 268: *Gentleman's Magazine*, Supplement 1799, September 1802.

39 Doc. 52: December 1798, Doc. 148: 5 June 1789, April 1799.

40 However, see Parlington, Yorkshire (pl. 30), and Milton Manor House, now Oxfordshire, by Stephen Wright, 1764–72 (Oswald 1948, p. 1330, fig. 2; White 1991, p. 52 ill; Boynton 1992, p. 370).

41 Doc. 198: Milner in 1792. For a fuller account, see T. Friedman, 'John Carter and the Georgian Struggle for Gothic Authenticity', forthcoming.

42 'The general idea was to give a modern imitation of the English, or pointed style, with its corresponding decorations in the middle ages' (Dugdale 1819, vol. II, p. 556).

43 Soane 1788, p. 9.

44 Carter's design for a combined market cross and martyrs' monument for Smithfield, London, *Builder's Magazine* (1774), pl. CVIII, pp. 57–8 (Crook 1995, fig. 3), suggests that he had known the Winchester structure by that date, perhaps via a print of 1741 (*VCH: Hampshire*, vol. V, 1912, p. 6). Friedman 2010.

45 Shaw 1798–1801, vol. I, p. 13.

46 Doc. 272: 26 May 1784, June 1785.

47 Doc. 268.

48 *Gentleman's Magazine* (November 1801), p. 1001; Supplement 1798, pp. 1104–5.

49 Doc. 115: November 1795.

50 Hoare 1983, p. 196, 30 July 1801.

51 *Gentleman's Magazine* (April 1801), pp. 311–13; (April 1807), pp. 321–4.

52 Doc. 98: 2 June 1788, 8 July, 31 August 1786, 19 March 1787. No drawings for Hereford survive.

53 Doc. 98: 17 September 1788, 3 February, 5 March 1790, February 1793.

54 Doc. 98: July 1793, July 1795. The spatial organisation anticipated Wyatt's Fonthill Abbey, Wiltshire, 1797–1812 (demolished 1825), which included a 'monastic' chapel, its ceiling 'entirely gilt . . . with delicate fan-work . . . resting upon a slender pillar', with four 25-foot-high windows filled with Eginton's painted glass depicting saintly figures, the room preceded by a 'Revelation Chamber' dominated by William Beckford's tomb 'viewed through wire gratings' (Farington 1978–84, vol. III, pp. 1091, 1117; Dugdale 1819, vol. IV, p. 465). The front of Hereford was rebuilt in the years 1902–8 in an inappropriate, vociferous Decorated gothic.

55 Doc. 158: 6 October 1789.

56 Doc. 158: 25 November 1758, 3 August 1790.

57 Doc. 158: 21 October 1789, 1738 (Loveday).

58 Doc. 158: 10 December 1789.

59 Doc. 158: 20 February 1791.

60 Doc. 143: July 1789.

61 For Wyatt's links with Westmacott, including the monument to John Oglander in New College chapel, see Busco 1994, p. 7.

62 Doc. 143: 1773, letter to the painter William Peckitt.

63 Doc. 143: February 1793.

64 *Gentleman's Magazine* (August 1801), p. 707.

65 Doc. 142: 22 November 1793, 15 July, 6 December 1794.

Eginton's design for a new window (White 2001, pl. 3) possesses a gorgeously filigreed richness recalling illustrations in Murphy 1792, to which Wyatt was a subscriber.

66 Doc. 70.

67 Pococke 1993, p. 37, in 1660; Doc. 70: 1725.

68 Coldstream and Draper 1980, pls XII, XIIID–E.

69 Doc. 272: 10, 31 July 1775.

70 Doc. 232: 1797.

71 *Gentleman's Magazine* (January 1802), p. 31. Crook 1995, pp. 80–90; *Oxford Dictionary of National Biography*, vol. x, pp. 356–8.

72 Doc. 148: 5 June 1789, 1790.

73 *Gentleman's Magazine* (January 1802), p. 32; Shipley 1990, pp. 87–8, 101.

74 Crook 1995, pp. 88–90, figs 6–8, 11–17, 19–22; Colvin 2008, pp. 231–3.

75 Farington 1978–84, vol. II, p. 414. He later blamed Barrington, 'who has seated himself as prime *imitator* and *preserver* of our ancient architectural glories', yet ordered that 'All this work must come down' (*Gentleman's Magazine*, January 1802, p. 31).

76 *Gentleman's Magazine* (December 1801), p. 1093; (April 1802), p. 327; (March 1802), pp. 228–9; (May 1802), p. 400.

77 *Gentleman's Magazine* (March 1802), p. 229.

78 *Gentleman's Magazine* (December 1803), p. 1122; (November 1803), pp. 1021–2.

79 *Gentleman's Magazine* (May 1802), p. 402.

80 *Gentleman's Magazine* (June 1802), p. 496.

81 *Gentleman's Magazine* (July 1801), p. 613.

82 *Gentleman's Magazine* (July 1801), pp. 613–14; (August 1800), pp. 736–7; also (January–May 1803), pp. 31–3, 118–19, 204, 317–18, 423–6. See also Evans 1956, pp. 206–14.

83 The 'Dissertation' was returned unread to Milner in 1798 (*Gentleman's Magazine*, Supplement 1798, p. 1108).

84 Durham University Library, Archives and Special Collections, *DCD*, Chapter Acts, 1800–1818, f. 59, 21 July 1806, though on 21 November 1808 'Plaistering . . . the East side of the . . . Tower [was] discontinued' (f. 86).

85 *Gentleman's Magazine* (August 1803), pp. 735–6. See also October 1798, p. 825.

86 *Gentleman's Magazine* (October 1799), pp. 830–31; (November 1799), p. 945. For a later Georgian perspective, see John Soane's Royal Academy Lecture VIII (Watkin 1996, p. 600).

87 *Gentleman's Magazine* (September 1790), p. 788.

88 Doc. 272: 1790.

89 Doc. 201: 1782–5.

90 As dramatised in Copley's celebrated painting of 1779–81 (Prown 1966, chapter XII, fig. 392).

91 Binski 1995, p. 177, pl. 233. The setting of Carter's proposal is confirmed by the abbey's distinctive wall treatment.

92 Burnage 2007, chapter 3. An article in *The Connoisseur*, no. 7 (1755), propounded that ancient philosophers revived and visiting Westminster Abbey 'would be induced to fancy [themselves] in a *Pantheon* of the heathen gods [and that this] modern taste (not content with introducing *Roman* temples into our churches)' should be stopped, otherwise 'we may soon expect to see our churches, instead of being dedicated to the service of religion, set apart for the reception of the heathen Gods' in preference to 'the present absurd mixture of the several objects of Pagan and Christian belief [which] must be shocking to every serious beholder'. In turn, this led to a proposal to erect 'a separate place distinct from our churches, for the reception of . . . monuments' (*Gentleman's Magazine*, July 1755, pp. 303–4).

SEVENTEEN THE 'BASTARD BREED'

1 Laugier 1977, pp. 8, 100–01, in 1753.

2 Defoe, vol. II, 1761 edition, p. 137, on the style of Westminster Abbey's west towers.

3 Reid 1802, p. 222.

4 Pyne 1823, vol. II, chapter XVIII, pp. 241–6. Doc. 231.

5 Doc. 272: 6 April 1710. It was dismantled in 1820 and destroyed, apart from the figurative sculpture.

6 *Wren Society*, VII (1930), pp. 81–6. The dean and chapter considered it as 'a lasting Monument to [Anne's] Royal Munificence' (*Wren Society*, XVIII, 1941, p. 165). Gwynn (1766, p. 124) remarked on the 'unpardonable . . . absurdity . . . more tasteless . . . and a greater piece of deformity than . . . all the [Classical] monuments . . . no other than that disjointed, unconnected attempt at magnificence . . . the marble altar; there never was any thing more absurd than the thought of decorating a Gothick building with Greek or Roman architecture, manners so essentially different that it is utterly impossible there should ever be the least harmony subsisting between them. The truth is, the present altar ought by all means be taken down and the whole thrown open to the east end of the abbey.'

7 'That this splendid work was worthy of the queen, and a magnificent gift, cannot be disputed; but that it has spoiled the *keeping* of the building is equally beyond dispute. White polished marble is as foreign to the decayed stone surrounding it, as the Grecian architecture is to that of the Abbey' (Malcolm 1803–7, vol. I, pp. 87–8).

8 *Wren Society*, VII (1930), p. 84. *Dickinson's Memorandum Book*, 'Apr: 7th 1718 Altar peice for Gt: Waltham neere Langley in Essex' (*Westminster Abbey Muniments*, 51554, f. 4r–v).

9 *Wren Society*, VII (1930), pp. 83–5. His son, Samuel Tufnell, a City magnate, had recently acquired Langleys, a property near Great Waltham (see note 8, above).

10 Doc. 16: 25 September 1725, 3, 9, 20 May 1726. Roger Davis and John Smallwell, joiner to HM Office of Works, employed on St Paul's Cathedral choir and west towers (*Wren Society*, XV, 1938, pp. xix–xxi, 10–11, 18–19, 49, 62, 74–5, pls 71–3), erected in Canterbury cathedral choir pews 'in as good workmanship manner as . . . in the Choire of . . . St Paul London', priced at the same rates (Doc. 52: 7 December 1704). Numerous other classical intrusions are illustrated in Randall 1980.

11 'If Inigo [Jones] ever deserved censure, it was certainly for that monstrous absurdity of mixing the Roman and Gothick architecture which he did in erecting a portico of the Corinthian order to the west-end of the Gothick

church of St. Paul' (p. 36); Wren was 'guilty of the same impropriety . . . in mixing Gothick with Roman architecture' (p. 42); in discussing James Gibbs's work at King's College, Cambridge, the 'custom of mixing Gothick and Modern architecture in the same pile . . . has . . . been practiced in the university of Oxford, with great success, and serves to shew that very little attention is paid to taste and elegance in places where one would expect to find hardly any thing else . . . Gibbs has also given another instance of this erroneous practice at [All Saints] Derby, where he has to a fine rich Gothick steeple, added a church of the Tuscan order' (p. 46).

12 'Gothicism and the restoration of that architecture, and not of the bastard breed, spreads extremely in this part of the world' (to Richard Bentley, on Worcester cathedral, September 1753, Walpole 1937–83, vol. XXXV, p. 150). 'The rage of repairing, beautifying, white-washing, painting, and above all, the mixture of Greek (or Roman) ornaments in Gothic edifices. This well-meant fury has been, and will be little less fatal to our ancient magnificent edifices, than the Reformation and the Civil War' (to James Bentham, 1765, quoted in Carritt 1948, p. 312).

13 British Library, Add. MS 6761, f. 69r.

14 Neve 1726, pp. 154–5, 197, paraphrased in Aheron 1754, book III, under 'Modern'.

15 Vertue 1930–55, vol. I, p. 148, in 1713. For the Continental context, see Wittkower 1974a; Middleton 1962–3. Hart 2002, pp. 60, 63–4.

16 Wright 1730, vol. II, pp. 461–2. See also Addison 1761, pp. 27–8. The neoclassical architect Willey Reveley, visiting in 1785–6, thought the 'edifice . . . entirely void of that mathematical knowledge so aparent in Kings Colledge Chapel Cambridge & many other Gothic structures. It is also much inferiour in its general taste & what is worse than all is half gothic, & half bad Roman [mannerist] architecture . . . The whole will be an abominable mixture' (British Architectural Library, Drawings and Archives Collection, Victoria and Albert Museum, London, REW/1, f. 101). Perhaps the earliest instance in ecclesiastical theory is C. Cesariano's *Di Lucio Vitruvio Pollione de Architectura* (1521), where Vitruvius's rules are superimposed on the late fourteenth-century riotous gothic Milan cathedral (Wittkower 1974a, figs 24–7). For other Continental hybrids, see Santa Maria Novella and the cathedral, Florence (Heydenreich and Lotz 1974, pls I, 21), Saint Etienne-du-Mont and Saint Gervais (Brunel et al. 1995, pp. 224–8, 249–51). Wittman 2006, citing also Saint Merri, Saint Nicolas-des-Champs, Saint Germain-l'Auxerrois, which had their internal gothic piers clad or re-cut as classical columns (figs 1–2).

17 Fleming 1962, p. xvi, fig. 12; Tait 1993, p. 165; Tait 2008, no. 57, see also no. 79.

18 Doc. 223. Keene, Burns and Saint 2004, pp. 175–85. See also his proposed termination of the crossing tower by an ogee dome rising from Serliana arcades (Anderson 2007, pl. 13; Worsley 2007, pl. 13).

19 Doc. 232. According to Vertue 1930–55, vol. VI, pp. 61–2, Jones conceived the chapel 'to be after the Greek rule or Roman' but the client 'woud . . . have it done after the old manner of Building' so Jones 'has artfully varyd by modifying the Gothick manner to the Rules of the Tuscan order . . . wherein he has showd great skill and Judgement . . . from a small hint to me by an old Surveyor of his dayes I have recovered this particular but have represented it to the Curious of the present Age both Noblemen Gentlemen & Archytects. by words & a drawings . . . which may one day be published and added to other . . . Jones printed examples. Of his skill & merrit'; see also Vertue 1930–55, vol. I, pp. 14, 137, and vol. V, p. 73. Colvin 2008, p. 252. A reflection of this is William Stukeley's unrealised 'design I made at Duke of Montagu's command . . . for his intended interment in a chapel at Weekley church [Northamptonshire]', dated July 1744, with Tuscan corner-engaged columns supporting fan vaulting (Bodleian Library, University of Oxford, MS Top. Gen. d.14, f. 50r).

20 Farington 1978–84, vol. III, p. 1106, 8 December 1798. See note, below.

21 *Gentleman's Magazine* (November 1758), p. 517.

22 Walpole 1826–8, vol. I, pp. 194–200. Predictably, John Carter also thought 'no true considerate admirer of Grecian architecture can with confidence maintain that such *medley work* shews real taste, it can only shew a love of novelty, which will always reflect a disgrace on the intruder of Grecian architecture on Gothic remains' (*Builder's Magazine*, 1774, p. 100).

23 Harris and Savage 1990, pp. 196–201. Addison asked his readers to 'reflect on the disposition of mind he finds in himself, at his first entrance in the *Pantheon* at *Rome*, and how the imagination is filled with something great and amazing; and, at the same time, consider, how little, in proportion, he is affected with the inside of a *Gothic* cathedral, though it be five times larger than the other; which can arise from nothing else but the greatness of the manner in the one, and the meanness in the other' (*The Spectator*, VI, no. 415, 26 June 1712, p. 77).

24 Soo 1998, pp. 48, 50, 53, figs 13–15. Downes 1988, pls I–III, VII–XI (the Warrant Design). Wren's pre-Fire design (before September 1666) already featured a monumental domed crossing rising above the medieval body.

25 *Gentleman's Magazine* (May 1781), p. 217.

26 Hart and Hicks 1996, pp. 306–7, 310–15, further popularised in A. Palladio, *I quattro libri d'architettura*, 1570 (Tavernor and Schofield 1997, pp. 203–5). See, for example, St John, Great Stanmore, Middlesex (1632; Mowl and Earnshaw 1995, pp. 8–9, pl. 2), St Mary Matfelon, Whitechapel (1672–3; Guillery 2005, p. 88, figs 14–16) and various Wren City Churches (Jeffery 1996, figs 17, 36, 75, 119, 141, 181).

27 Colvin 2008, pp. 365, 1205. *Wren Society*, XVIII (1941), p. 68. Fuller 1799, following p. 182, recording the original form of the west and north aisle windows, remarked that some 'approach nearer that of the Venetian than to any other kind'. Others are similar to St Katherine Cree, London (1628–31; Bradley and Pevsner 1997, p. 94, pl. 20). For an alternative dating, see Mowl and Earnshaw 1995, pp. 14–15, pl. 4.

28 *Wren Society*, XIII (1936), p. 33; XV (1938), pp. 3, 25, 28, 46, 52.

29 Hatton 1708, vol. I, p. 172.

30 Saumarez Smith 1990, pp. 60, 86. Perhaps Etty consulted an early study by Palladio for the Basilica in Vicenza featuring a range of such *piano nobile* fenestration, which had been acquired by Jones in Italy and by the 1680s had passed into the hands of John Oliver, assistant surveyor at St Paul's (Lewis 1981, pp. 106–7, cat. no. 61; Harris and Higgott 1989, p. 22).

31 Doc. 160. Cobb 1980, pls 97, 104, 107–9; *Wren Society*, XIX (1942), p. 57, pls XV–XXIV. See related work at nearby Abbots Bromley, 1698, attributed to John Barker (Gomme 2000, p. 405); James Hill's Bishop's Cleeve, 1699–1700 (Gloucestershire Record Office, P 46 VE 1/1; National Monuments Record Centre, English Heritage, Swindon, BB54/1246); Thomas Wilkinson Sr's Ripple, 1713 (Worcestershire Record Office, 850 Ripple BA 348/5Q; *VCH: Worcestershire*, vol. III, 1913, p. 486).

32 For example, at St Michael, Spurriergate (*RCHME: York: Historic Buildings of the Central Area*, 1981, pl. 37). A brief granted on 5 February 1719 to collect £1,732 upwards for repairs to St Hilda (recorded *circa* 1678, Tyler 1971, p. 50 no. 17) involved the choir 'almost entirely unroofed . . . steeple, pillars . . . walls . . . so much decayed by length of time . . . whole fabrick will inevitably fall to . . . ground, unless speedily prevented' (Mackenzie and Ross 1834, vol. I, p. 473). The decision was taken on 22 September 1721 to retain the length and breadth of the present building, flatten the roof pitch by 4–6 inches, take down and rebuild the north wall 'but in fear of . . . cash arising from . . . brief may not answer . . . expectation . . . wall . . . referred until . . . last . . . church . . . new flagged, pued . . . whitened . . . in respect to . . . glory of . . . antiquity of . . . church, what repairs . . . windows may want . . . be wrought after . . . same model as . . . now are . . . chancel . . . referred until . . . Earle of Scarborough's consent . . . got in writing . . . steeple both in . . . outside . . . repaired (Mackenzie and Ross 1834, vol. I, pp. 473–4). Six commissioners viewed the church on 5 May 1724: 'Opinion . . . Roof . . . taken down . . . New Cover'd with . . . flat roof of wood . . . Lead . . . present Chancell consisting of Twenty three yards . . . one Half Length within . . . Walls taken down . . . Rebuilt five yards Long . . . Roof of . . . Chancel . . . flatt . . . Cover'd wth Lead . . . vestry . . . pull'd Down . . . Rebuilt on . . . south side of . . . Chancel . . . Pews . . . pull'd Down . . . Rebuilt', also stated in Vestry petition to the Bishop of Durham (Durham University Library Archives, Durham Diocesan Records, Faculty Papers 60). The bishop granted the petition on 22 May 1724 to reduce the 23½ yards long chancel to 5 yards within the walls of the body (Mackenzie and Ross 1834, vol. I, p. 474, ill.; Sykes 1833, p. 140). Pococke 1760, p. 249, noted 'buttresses to . . . west . . . formed porch . . . isles . . . refitted with . . . sort of Venetian window in imitation of . . . Gothic'. H. Grimm, undated drawings (British Library, Add. MS 15,539, ff. 146–8).

33 Book IV, f. 184r–v (Hart and Hicks 1996, p. 366). Though placed high up at Warwick, these curious capitals originally stood out by a provision for 'whiteing' on 26 August 1701; see also 13 February 1706 (Doc. 190). That Wilson probably had access to this publication is reinforced by echoes on the west tower of arched carriage openings on three sides and shell-headed niches, derived from the Arch of Janus Quadriform in Rome, of the fourth century AD (Book III, ff. 97v–98r; Hart and Hicks 1996, pp. 192–3).

34 Thomson 1984, p. 187; Blunt 1957, pp. 28–9, pl. 21A; Stankovitch 1995; Perouse de Montclos 1994, pp. 433–9.

35 There is no record of Wilson having travelled abroad, nor apparently was the Paris church illustrated before 1704, though he may have had access to some intermediary source. In 1701–2 the Scottish architect Alexander Edward visited Paris to 'observe and take draughts of the most curious and remarkable . . . Edifices'; he attended a funeral at Saint Eustace (Colvin 2008, pp. 343–4). See also the apsidal windows of Saint Pierre, Caen, 1528–45 (Blunt 1957, pl. 4A). An interesting parallel to St Mary's stylistic mixture on a comparably ambitious scale is the contemporary University Church, Würzburg, Germany (1696–1703), where monumental giant order pilasters enwrapping the body and lower part of the prominently projecting west towers are tempered by delicate late gothic-style window mullions, perhaps a conscious homage to the first builder-patron (1582–91), Bishop Mespelbrunn, renowned for his preference for the middle ages as an expression of his desire to restore the old, pre-Reformation faith (Hempel 1965, p. 43, pl. 90; Longo 1985, pp. 48–52, illus).

36 Doc. 190: July 1785.

37 Downes 1959, p. 8.

38 Du Prey 2000, p. 93; Hart 2002, pp. 62–4. For Hawksmoor's brand of hybridism, in which gothic is tempered by the classical disciplines of symmetry, harmony and regularity, where at the abbey he employed classical architectural terms such as 'pediment' to describe the west gable and 'Calceoli' (acanthus leaves of the Corinthian capital) the crockets, see Hart 2002, pp. xii, 62.

39 Doc. 52: 1742. Bishop Trelawney's throne (1706) in Winchester cathedral was later criticised for the 'defect . . . that the Corinthian order is ill assorted with the Gothic stile of the choir' (Doc. 199: 1706).

40 Engraved in F. Bonanni, *Numismata Summorum Pontificum Templi Vaticani Fabricam*, 1696, pl. 49 (Mander 1998, pp. 26–42, pl. 26).

41 Frontispiece. Hawksmoor subscribed to J. James's English edition, *Rules and Examples of Perspective Proper for Painters and Architects*, 1707. By 1704 he may also have owned the 1693 edition, as well as C. Fontana's *Templum Vaticanum*, 1694, and D. de' Rossi's *Studio d'architettura civile . . . di Roma*, vol. I, 1702 (Watkin 1972, p. 103 lot 93, p. 104 lots 118, 125). For the motif of giant scrolls rising from the column groups, see S. Cipriani's temporary catafalque for King James II erected in San Lorenzo in Lucina in 1702 (Fagiolo 1997, pp. 10–11).

42 Doc. 235: 1704; *Wren Society*, XV (1938), pp. xxii–iii. Compare drawings (Downes 1988, pp. 168–9, 171–2) with Canterbury. The joiner John Smallwell, who was then executing the choir-stalls and had been paid £142 towards making the bishop's seat and throne in St Paul's (*Wren Society*, XV, 1938, pp. xxii–iii, 18–19), may also have been involved at Canterbury (see under 7 December 1704). See

also Hawksmoor's high altar design for York Minster (this publication, pl. 286).

43 Doc. 19: 1733.

44 Doc. 19: undated following 1739.

45 Doc. 117: 15–18 March 1725, described as 'octangular lanterns' (29–30 April 1726). Gibbs added stone cupolas to Houghton Hall's corner pavilions in the years 1725–8 (Friedman 1984, pp. 105–7, pl. 100).

46 Doc. 117: 29–30 April, 20 September 1726.

47 Doc. 158: 3 September 1790.

48 Doc. 158: 24 August 1736, illus. p. 997. At Upton-upon-Severn, Worcestershire, the spire of the old church was removed in 1755 and replaced with Anthony Keck's domed octagon based on Gibbs 1728, pl. 31 (Worcestershire Record Office, 850, 6218/9, ff. 1, 29v; *Buildings of England: Worcestershire*, 2007, p. 641, pl. 81).

49 Doc. 158: 1746. *Gentleman's Magazine* (May 1786), p. 359, ill., commented on the 'dome over the choir [of Sées cathedral, Normandy] taken down two years ago, at which time the small spire . . . was erected in its place. This injudicious alteration is a plain proof of a want of taste in Gothick architecture. A dome gives the idea of lightness, magnificence, and space; but one is at a loss to conceive how a spire . . . can be supported when placed on the ridge of a building.'

50 Doc. 272: 1713.

51 Doc. 272: 17 January, 6 December 1724.

52 Dart 1723, vol. I, pp. xxii–iii, xxviii.

53 Finelli and Finelli 2004, pp. 63–98. The cathedral was already the subject of considerable historical scrutiny as well as of English veneration. James Gibbs, visiting sometime between 1703 and 1709, noted the 'Cupola was . . . looked upon to be the boldest peece of Archtectur in Italy' (Soane MS, vol. 26, f. 52). English interest in Italian domes is reflected in J. Addison's remark of the one on Siena cathedral (1284–1377) as 'nothing in this City so extraordinary . . . which a Man may view with Pleasure after he has seen St *Peter's* [in Rome], though it is quite of another Make, and can only be looked upon as one of the Master-pieces of *Gothic* Architecture' (Addison 1761, p. 224). Wilson 1990, pl. 197.

54 Downes 1959, pp. 8–9; Watkin 1972, pp. 45–105.

55 Denslagen 1994, pp. 133–7, pl. 49. The type is also represented by Saint Germain, Argentan (Olivier-Michel and Gisler 1966, p. 34, pl. 5) and the abbey church at Kladruby, now Czech Republic, 1712–18 (Galmiche 1989, pp. 29–35, 84–5).

56 *Buildings of England: Surrey*, 1990, p. 330; Blatch 1997, pl. 175. Ockham Park is among the least well documented of Hawksmoor's works. The north chapel, 1734–5, sometimes attributed to him (Downes 1959, pp. 210–14, 278), may be the work of Thomas Hinton, his under-surveyor at Westminster, 1725–46. For the King monument, see Craske 2007, pp. 409–13, fig. 194. For the painting, see De Grazio and Garberson 1996, pp. 35–9; Baetjer and Links 1989, pp. 256–9, pls 75–6; Liversidge and Farrington 1993, pp. 98–9; Beddington 2006, p. 196, no. 70.

57 Notably Shepton Beauchamp, Somerset (Dunning 1996, p. 174; Leedy 1980, pp. 17, 200, pl. 65, as well as p. 187, pl. 64). An alternative design (City of Westminster Archives Centre, Box 53; Downes 1959, pl. 86a) mounted the dome on an expanded platform with imposing corner pinnacles to anchor the crossing piers, which also features a radical reworking of the north transept front, only recently completed to a Wren-Dickinson design but not an unqualified success: it 'has the appearance of a tad pole with five tails' (*Grub-street Journal*, no. 271, 6 March 1735, p. 1).

58 Doc. 272: 6 December 1724. See Rocque 1746–7, pp. 11–12. Rivalry between these two metropolitan landmarks grew during the eighteenth century. In 1709 Ward (1993, vol. VIII, p. 148) compared 'the greatness of that huge, huge, huge Cathedral, which is big enough to hold more souls than Westminster Abbey, though it is not half so venerable'. In 1782 Moritz (1987, p. 26) wrote: 'In contrast with the round, modern, majestic cathedral . . . there rises . . . the long medieval pile of Westminster Abbey with its enormous pointed roof' (also p. 30). For a graphic comparison, see Harrison 1775, ill. following p. 324.

59 Doc. 207: 1726. Hawksmoor owned a copy of D. de' Rossi, *Studio d'architettura civile . . . di Roma* (Watkin 1972, p. 104, no. 125).

60 Doc. 207: 1726.

61 Doc. 19: 1732. Hawksmoor's colleague, William Thornton, sketched the tomb (24 August 1719). *Buildings of England: York*, 1995, pp. 290–91, pl. 24. William Collins's life-size statues of *King Aethelstan* and *St John of Beverley* were added in 1781, now re-sited elsewhere in the Minster.

62 Other contemporary baroque furnishings included Thornton's pulpit, 1722–5 (vanished), and font cover, 1726 (surviving). Links between Beverley and York were strong: among subscribers in 1718 to the latter's repairs were the Archbishop of York, Dean Henry Finch, Thomas Jubb, the chapter registrar, and Thomas Lamplugh, canon evidentiary. Thornton operated from a York workshop; stone was quarried from the ruins of St Mary's Abbey there; and William Etty valued Beverley's carpentry work in 1724 (Doc. 207).

63 Doc. 19.

64 Doc. 19: 27 November 1725. Gent 1733 associated the galleries with the fictitious church of St Alban, Rome, apparently confused with a similar order illustrated in Evelyn 1664, chapters IV–V, the 'incomparable *Doric* Master-piece . . . discover'd at Albano' near Rome, but having fluted shafts as in the preceding plate, recording 'one of the most excellent Pieces . . . in the *Baths* of *Dioclesian* at Rome'.

65 Doc. 272: 1 March, 1 June 1728, 14 May 1729. This had replaced a blank wall with Tuscan gates crowned by elaborate obelisks set up in the years 1680–1700 (Cocke 1995, pp. 128–9, pls 91–3).

66 Doc. 50: 28 March 1713, 1735.

67 Hart 2002, pls 30, 81, 269.

68 Doc. 222. Jeffery 1996, figs 72, 74. Wren's Cornhill body of 1669–72 had been attached to the surviving medieval tower until structural faults forced the Vestry to rebuild in 1715–17 under William Dickinson's direction.

69 Doc. 222: 1734.

70 Doc. 222: 1758.

71 Doc. 102. 'A Catalogue of Books In . . . Petre's Library at Thornton . . . 1742' (Essex Record Office, D/DP Z4).

See his designs for garden pavilions at Worksop, Nottinghamshire (*Country Life*, 15 March 1973, pp. 680–82, figs 9–12). Giacomo Leoni served as architect for remodelling Thorndon Hall, 1733–42, demolished 1763. Relevant documents for Ingrave are untraced, perhaps lost during James Paine's rebuilding of the mansion, 1764–70, or in the fire of 1878. The Petre parish church was at Ingatestone, with the family chapel incorporated in the mansion.

72 The tower form relates to a distinctively medieval Essex type: Castle Hedingham, Tolleshunt Major, West Ham and Gestingthorpe (Fitch 1996, pls 32, 34, 36, p. 94). The frieze is a hallmark of several Vanbrugh buildings: his Greenwich residence (1718–19), Eastbury, Dorset (1718), Kensington Palace Water Tower (1722–4), as well as the Great Store, Chatham Dockyards (begun 1717), by an unknown Board of Ordnance architect, perhaps under Vanbrugh's direction (Downes 1977, pls 102–5, 133, 135, 148). The last is located directly across the Thames from Ingrave.

73 Throsby 1790, p. 136; Whiffen 1948, p. 67, pl. 88; *Buildings of England: Leicestershire*, 1984, p. 159; Brandwood 1987, pp. 30–31, pl. 13. An unprecedented eastern inspiration cannot be ruled out: numerous pagodas illustrate Nieuhof 1669, which includes a section devoted to Christian presence in the country (Appendix, pp. 69–72).

74 Doc. 259: 1734; see also 1742, 1775.

75 Doc. 258, 259, 260: 11 July 1734. For Langley's examples of spires atop classical towers, pilfered from Francis Price's *The British Carpenter* (1733), see Langley 1736, pl. CCCLXXXIX, observing that the former 'would have been better, had this Master omitted [the latter], they being a manifest Proof of a Barrenness of Invention'.

76 Doc. 153: 18 March 1735.

77 'John Aislaby Esqr Mayor of Ripon hath acquainted . . . this Chapter that the Corporation of Ripon . . . intends to build an Obeliske in the Markett place there and to doe other things for the Ornament of the . . . Towne and desirdus to contribute towards the Charge thereof. It is therefore Ordered That the Deane and Chapter of this Church shall pay according to their Respective Proportions to be deducted out of their Respective Salaryes Twenty Pounds to be thus divided vizt. The Deane £4-4s-2½d The Sub Deane 3-3-2 Mr. Lamplugh 2-2-1¼' and five others of the same latter amount (Leeds University Library, Department of Manuscripts and Special Collections 1980/1/42, Chapter Acts, f. 61, dated 1702). Hewlings 1981, pls 26–8. The spire was 'fir'd by Lightning' on 5 December 1593, and 'blown down by a violent Wind, much undamaging the arched Roof of the Choir, and other Places' on 8 December 1660, then left unrestored due to financial mismanagement (Gent 1733, p. 118), noting Aislabie 'generously repair'd the Fabrick, particularly St *Wilfrid*'s Steeple', though the only evidence of this among the surviving papers is a 7s. 6d. bill of 4 September 1724 from Francis Cundall for supplying '6 Ropes for tyein up the Skaffel in the Great Steple' (Leeds University Library, Department of Manuscripts and Special Collections, 1980/1/88.1). However, Buck's view of 1745 shows an entirely steepleless building (Hyde 1994, p. 52, pl. 64).

78 'For true it is, nothing can be more absurd than mixing one taste with the other, as is too commonly the case, for instance, the towers of Westminster abbey, what a medley of Grecian and Gothic architecture there is!' (J. Carter, in 'A Society of Architects', *Builder's Magazine*, 1774, p. 100).

79 Doc. 229: 7 December 1711, 1715, 1730.

80 Du Cerceau 1988, pp. 128–39.

81 Weinreb and Hibbert 1983, p. 710.

82 Quoting a letter of 1711 (Colvin 2008, p. 565). For James's Jonesian churches, see chapter 24.

83 Doc. 272: 1738.

84 Doc. 268: *Gentleman's Magazine*, 1799.

85 Doc. 259. Hart 2002, pp. 170–71, fig. 245, citing the similar mannerist conceit on the Uffizi, Florence (1560; Satkowski 1993, pls 51, 63).

86 He was responding to Ralph's recommendation to remove the church together with 'little hovels' encumbering the abbey's north side to allow Henry VII's Chapel to 'come into play' (Doc. 268: 6 February, 6 March 1735, 1734).

87 Doc. 168: 25 April 1732. He explained the circumstances for rebuilding St Margaret's in the *Daily Journal* (28 February 1735). Nevertheless, at Stratford-le-Bow, London, the Vestry was aware that the stone fabric was 'upwards of four hundred Years', yet permitted James to replace the upper stage, 1727–9, in brick with stone dressings in a combination of medieval battlements and Gibbs-surround windows (Lambeth Palace Library, London, MS 2691, ff. 443, 445, 447–8; MS 2716, ff. 1 53, 155; Jeffery 1986, pp. 276, 315; Hibbert 1988, p. 180 ill.).

88 Doc. 64: 1728.

89 The motives of committed medievalists in promoting classicism are sometimes more difficult to reconcile, as in the case of Browne Willis at Fenny Stratford, pls 141–2 (Doc. 80).

90 Doc. 150. Information courtesy Revd T. Steel. Daniel Sephton (1714–1759) was among the best tomb sculptors then practising from Manchester (Roscoe 2009, [p. 1116]).

91 Wigan Archives Service, D/DZ A13/8, 11 December 1716, mentions stone 'Gotten Out of a Certain Delff in Billinge'. Another Henry Sephton of Billinge 'Delfman' is listed on 13 February 1797 (D/P/6/24/12). In 1724 our Henry resided at Rainford, 3 miles from Billinge, also certainly designing as well as building nearby Wigan Grammar School, 1720–23 (demolished 1882), where a Corinthian giant order was combined with thirteenth-century-style windows (AB/Wig, ff. 8, 21; MS 'History of . . . Town & Borough of Wigan . . . with Anecdotes collected and Recollected by Thomas Whitehouse', 1828, f. 69; photograph 67230/2).

92 Doc. 20: 11 December 1716.

93 Sephton favoured urn-capped corners at St Mary, Eccleston, begun 1716, and perhaps St Mary, Tarleton, 1719, both in Lancashire. The latter's previous building history is recounted in Cheshire Record Office, EDA 2/4, ff. 337–8. The fabric of 1719 was connected with an Act of Parliament of 1720 making the River Douglas navigable and is presumably the Douglas Chapel mentioned frequently in the Eccleston churchwardens' accounts (Lancashire Record Office, PR 2695/17); indeed, Ferrand Hodgson, curate of Eccleston, signed a Tarleton document in 1716 (EDA 2/4, f. 346).

94 One of Sephton's chief patrons, James Stanley, 19th Earl of

Derby of Knowsley Hall, Lancashire, toured Italy in 1723–4, describing a visit to the Vatican and acquiring a drawing or engraving of the 'Cupilo of St Peter's Church' (Russell 1987, pp. 150, 152–3). Sephton repeated this formula at nearby St James, Darwen, Lancashire, in 1722, reversing the emphasis by placing paired Doric pilasters at the ends of the side elevations. Lancashire Record Office, PR 2878/2/14; H. P. Horner, 'Report on the State of the Chapel of Ease at Over Darwen', 5 December 1851; A. Proctor, *The History of Darwen Chapel, or St James' Church, Darwen*, undated, ill. (published copies in Lancashire Record Office, box, Darwen P/23); *Buildings of England: North Lancashire*, 1969, p. 113; Buchanan 1978, pl. 11.

95 Doc. 48.

96 The Bolds of Bold Hall, Prescot, Lancashire, long-standing members of Parliament (Namier and Brooke 1964, p. 99), were presumably recipients of Trevitt's commemorative engraving, making it potentially available to Sephton.

97 Doc. 154.

98 The first feature was perhaps derived from a 'Rustick Door from Palladio, *much used by the Modern Architects*' in W. Halfpenny's *Practical Architecture*, 1724, p. 26 (with editions published in 1730 and 1736; Harris and Savage 1990, pp. 226–7). The turret is repeated in Sephton's companion design for a service block at Cheetham's nearby Castleton Hall (Lancashire Record Office, DDX/1423/11–14), in what was envisaged as an ambitious ensemble of a sort already noted at Great Yarmouth (Doc. 92: 1715) and Leeds (Doc. 112: 1723). The Hall was remodelled in 1719 (*VCH: Lancashire*, vol. V, 1911, pp. 202–3).

99 For a similar front, see Aston-By-Sutton, Cheshire, 1736–40, perhaps Sephton's design (Cheshire Record Office, P128/6/11; Richards 1973, pp. 796–805, pl. 802), National Monuments Record Centre, J. L. Birchall measured drawings.

100 Doc. 121: 1774.

101 St Mary, Deansgate, Manchester, demolished 1890–92, is problematic. Petitioned for building on 17 February 1753 (Manchester Central Library Archives, M 39/2/16/1), with an Act of Parliament passed, Stat. 26, Georgii II, c.45 (*Gentleman's Magazine*, April 1753, p. 198), and a press call on 24 April for tenders 'according to the plan and dimensions of Knots ford [Knutsford, Cheshire, see below] . . . except . . . cased with stone' (Clarke 1963, p. 45); foundation stone laid on 16 July, consecrated 29 September 1756 (M 403/2/1–5); panels inscribed 'THIS SPIRE, was built by the voluntary Subscription of y. Inhabitants of MANCHESTER, in ye Year 1762 the first Stone laid by EDWARD BYROM Esqr. then BORROUGHREAVE the Revd. Mr. DOWNES Rectr. T: Lightoler Archt . . . John Jackson Mason' (Manchester Central Library Archives, *St Mary's Church, Manchester Scrap Book*, MS F 283 4273 M 390, p. 259; *Manchester City News*, 6 December 1902). The tower apparently had several alternative spires before dismantling in 1854 (Manchester Central Library Local Studies 120, 3717, 9799, 20960). The church was demolished in 1890–92. St John, Knutsford, Cheshire, 1741–4, was designed by John Gatlive (Cheshire Record Office, P7/8/1, ff. 1–3; Pococke 1750, vol. II, p. 9; Dugdale 1819, vol. I, p. 332; Aikin 1795, p. 423; Richards 1973, pp. 195–6; Crossley 1942, pp. 40–41; Hall 1963, p. 56; *Buildings of England: Lancashire*, 1971, pp. 250–51; Morant 1989, pp. 143–4).

102 Doc. 110: 27 June 1753.

103 Doc. 3: 10 March 1730. John Morgan, rector of Alcester, subscribed to Price's *Salisbury*, 1753.

104 For example, Guillaume Henault's remarkable, unrealised project of 1718 for the Benedictine church, Orléans, about which he wrote: 'Le gothique et l'entique . . . sont reunis en un mesme corps d'ouvrage'; that is, a Sainte Chapelle-like exterior and a Versailles-like interior (Middleton 1962–3, vol. I, pp. 318–19, pls 42c–d).

105 Doc. 205.

106 Harris and Higgott 1989, pp. 248–50, fig. 80; Gotch 1928; Vallance 1947, pp. 51–2; Colvin 1973–6, vol. V, p. 311. It was 'very handsomely performed by . . . Jones' (British Library, Add. MS 5957, f. 16, in 1735), 'a very handsome Screen of Portland stone designed by Inigo Jones, & everyway worthy of him . . . the ascent to it by steps . . . makes it appear to advantage' (Add. MS 16,776, f. 260, in 1743). Vardy 1744, pl. 3.

107 Doc. 52: 1732, 1737, 1742. Interestingly, from mid-century the Winchester screen's prestige as an appropriate model began to wane: 'tho' exceeding beautiful, yet to join *Roman* with *Gothic* Architecture, is a solecism. One would imagine, that *Inigo's* Pride would not deign to let him give into *Gothic* Building; for in repairing Part of old *Paul's*, he, as far as was practicable, *Romaniz'd* that Building' (Defoe 1962, p. 263); 'very plain, and neat, but not all in the Church or Gothic style' (Torrington 1934–8, vol. I, pp. 79–80, 25 August 1782); the 'view towards the choir . . . intercepted by mean or incongruous objects; a Grecian screen . . . of a different hue from the rest of the stonework, and shut up with a modern panelled door and fanlight, fitter for a tavern than a cathedral. In these, and such like faults, which are the effect, not of necessity, but of choice, we discover the bad taste of modern ages. Formerly the appearance of the sanctuary . . . was rendered more striking, by being seen through the glade of Gothic pillars and arches, supporting the ancient pulpitum' (Milner 1798–1801/1809, vol. II, p. 24).

108 Doc. 207: Drake 1736.

109 Doc. 207: Drake 1736. In 1792 Torrington thought it 'might be invented by a school boy for his kite'.

110 Doc. 207: 1736. Burlington's revolutionary Assembly Rooms, York, 1731–2, based on Palladio's reconstruction of an Egyptian Hall, was seen as a modern successor to the ancient Praetorian Palace, the foundations of which still survive beneath the Minster.

111 Welander 1991, pp. 112, 378.

112 Doc. 20: 1757.

113 Harris and Savage 1990, pp. 352–65; Ingamells 1997, pp. 569–71.

114 Doc. 86: 17 September 1721, September 1753.

115 According to Dallaway 1806, p. 78 note u, Kent contemplated (what the former regarded as a 'bizarrerie') fluting the nave's shafts but abandoned the scheme when he discovered the cores filled with rubble. However, no contemporary reference to this is known (Doc. 86: 1741–4).

116 Doc. 18: 1773. White presumably was responsible for the entire church.

117 Zarnecki 1993; Headley and Meulenkamp 1999, p. 269.

118 Russell and Price 1769, vol. I, p. 119; Ricketts 2007, pp. 32–3, figs 3.3–5.

119 Bence-Jones 1992, pp. 61–2. British Library, Add. MS 5675, f. 17 (Grimm's exterior views of the house of 1781). Goodall 2009.

120 Croft-Murray 1962–70, vol. II, pp. 191, 213, 254. Stukeley 1776, vol. I, p. 202, noted the work of all three artists at Cowdray *circa* 1722.

121 Croft-Murray 1962–70, vol. II, pp. 163–5. *Vetusta Monumenta* 1747–90, vol. III, p. 1, refers to an 'opportunity to save the altar-piece by Amigoni' in 1793. Dugdale 1819, vol. IV, p. 378.

122 Stukeley 1776, vol. I, p. 202, though he noted 'walls painted with architecture by Roberti . . . statues by Goupe . . . staircase by Pelegrini [and] a long gallery with the twelve apostles as big as the life'. British Library, Add. MS 15,776, f. 226, in 1743.

123 *Vetusta Monumenta* 1747–90, vol. III, p. 13. Calcined plaster fragments survive attached to the walls (*Country Life*, 9 January 1992, p. 66).

124 Rossi and Rossi 1702–21, pl. 139, G.-A. de' Rossi's Palazzo Celsi.

125 Kieven 1991b, pp. 100, 104, 126–7, pls 23, 28, 50–51.

126 Friedman 1984, pl. 56. Compare also to the Lutheran's church, Augsburg (Picart 1733, following p. 362).

127 *Vetusta Monumenta* 1747–90, vol. III, pp. 9, 13.

128 McCarthy 1987, p. 173, pls 216–17.

129 Butler 1978, pp. 180, 182, fig. 1, Doc. 4.

130 Doc. 54. The house plan and elevation are inscribed 'J:V: 1746, for Mr. Arundell' (Brown 1985, pl. 151).

131 Doc. 4: bibliography under Speight 1894; Clarke 1963; Carter 1976; Butler 1978; *Buildings of England: Yorkshire: The West Riding*, 1986, p. 78; Aslet 1989.

132 Harris and Higgott 1989, pp. 238–42, figs 76, 78. The crossing tower echoes Vanbrugh's Nunnery, Greenwich (1719–20, destroyed; Hart 2008, pl. 328).

133 Doc. 4: following 1746. In 1749 Vardy engraved the interior of the hammer-beamed Great Hall at Hampton Court Palace after Kent's drawing. 'A coloured view of the gothick hall at Hampton Court, from drawing made on the spot, and engraved by Mr Vardy, when clerk of the works in that palace' (1745–6) was exhibited at the Society of Artists in 1762 (Graves 1905, p. 266 no. 211). Harris 1998b, p. 35 no. 44.

134 Doc. 79: 8 April, 15 May 1754.

135 Doc. 79: 18 April, 15 May 1754. Dance disdained others giving 'directions to colour the ground of the Freese [as] quite out of Character' (9 September 1756).

136 Doc. 50: 1724, 1728, 2 October 1735.

137 Doc. 50: 1759. The third brother, Robert, was then involved in furnishing Croome church (this publication, pl. 174).

138 Rival designs for completing the west front of San Petronio, Bologna (begun 1390), by Palladio favouring classicism and Giulio Romano favouring gothic (neither of which were adopted), the drawings for which still remain in the church, were traced by young Soane in 1779 (Du Prey 1982, p. 164, figs 6.7–18; Wittkower 1974a, chapter IV).

139 Navarra 2001, p. 224, pl. XLIX. The repertory is found in other Adam work (King 2001, vol. I, pls 23, 440, 467, 476).

140 Wittkower 1974a, chapters I–II. Neither James nor Robert Adam are recorded as stopping at Milan during their Italian journeys, though James travelled from Turin to Venice in 1760 (Ingamells 1997, pp. 4–6). The cathedral was dismissed by many British visitors: Addison 'had heard so much [about it], but was never more deceived in my Expectations' (Addison 1761, p. 27). The architect Willey Reveley found it 'entirely void of that mathematical knowledge so apparent in Kings College Chapel . . . & many other Gothic structure [as well as] much inferiour in its general taste' (British Architectural Library, Drawings and Archives Collection, Victoria and Albert Museum, London, REW/1, f. 101, in 1785–6). John Carr, visiting Alnwick in 1795, was informed by his host that the chapel walls were painted 'after' Milan cathedral (Doc. 6).

141 Doc. 50: 25–6 March, 18 April, 18–27 October 1769.

142 Doc. 123.

143 He added an identical spire turret at St Peter, Wallingford, Oxfordshire (1776–7), to a plain classical body (1760–69) by an unknown architect, the interior of which Taylor completed with his signature ceiling of shallow recessed octagonal and diamond panels. The stylistic shift may have resulted from intercessions by the subscribers for rebuilding, who included the bishops of Salisbury and Winchester, the Hawksmoorian gothic All Souls College, Oxford, and its Recorder, William Blackstone, the eminent jurist (Clarke and Colvin 1952–3, pt II, pp. 100–01; Berkshire Record Office, D/P 139/6/3; Binney 1984, p. 79; *Buildings of England: Berkshire*, 1966, p. 248, pl. 9a; *Country Life*, 17 September 1970, p. 696).

144 Soros 2006, fig. 7–23. Gibson 1973, nos 34, 67–8. The Library's sole publication devoted to medieval architecture is item 11, J. Dart, *Westmonasterium*, vol. II, 1723. Malton's view of the classical design was the source for John Fidel's Kingston Bagpuize, Berkshire, now Oxfordshire (1798–1800; working drawings in Wiltshire Record Office, D1/61/4/38; Bodleian Library, University of Oxford, MS Top. Berk. c.50, f. 71r–v; *Murray's Architectural Guide: Berkshire*, 1949, p. 78, pl. 110; Clarke and Colvin 1952–3, pt I, pp. 94–5; Clarke 1963, p. 116; *Georgian Group Annual Report*, 1994, p. 19).

145 Doc. 46: 1781–2.

146 Doc. 44: 3 October 1737. Doc. 190 (Warwick). In 1762 Francis's father William Hiorne ineptly remodelled the west front of medieval St Mary, Nottingham, crenellating the lower side aisles but replacing large expanses of tracery with big, round-headed windows surrounded by a central classical pediment and inserting Doric and Gibbs-surround doorcases; the fabric was re-gothicised in 1843 (Colvin 2008, p. 522; Harwood 2008, p. 36, pl. 27).

147 Two notable treatments of the Serliana, above all other Palladian motifs symbolising the Georgian approach to modernising medieval fabrics, are Quarley, Hampshire (1723), by William Benson (Bold 1988, p. 22, pl. 21) and Nether Hampton, about which Torrington 1934–8, vol. II, p. 110, remarked in 1789: 'To one remaining Gothic isle . . . has been added a Venetian brother; proving which

looks best; the venerable Goth, or the tasteless Italian' (*RCHME: Churches of South-East Wiltshire*, 1987, pp. 161–2, pls 371–2).

148 Doc. 192.

149 Doc. 41: 17 December 1787, Shiercliffe 1793.

150 Summerson 1970, pl. 154.

151 Doc. 41: 1799. Matthews 1794, pp. 51, 80; Gomme, Jenner and Little 1979, p. 176; Mowl 1991a, p. 100. St Paul was thought to resemble 'a Grecian building at a distance . . . when examined, an attempt to imitate the Pointed style is observable, which it as little resembles as the [thirteenth-century] tower of St Mary Redcliffe [Bristol] does the dome of St Pauls', London' (Malcolm 1807). At King's Norton, Leicestershire (1757–61), unreservedly committed to a comprehensive, precociously authentic gothic, neither client nor architect hesitated in furnishing the interior entirely in a classical mode (Doc. 106).

152 Doc. 77: 27 February 1795.

153 At Stapleford 'is a model of Saxby church [untraced], which his Lordship [4th Earl of Harborough] is now rebuilding (Throsby 1789, p. 150); 'when finished, it will doubtless grace his lordship's domain' (Throsby 1790, p. 152); 'a pretty little church . . . a handsome spire . . . of free-stone', the tower dated 1788 (Nichols 1795–1811, vol. II, pt 1, pp. 311–12, pl. LIII). The interior was 'ravaged' in 1874 (*Buildings of England: Leicestershire and Rutland*, 1984, p. 367, p. 52; Colvin 2008, pp. 861–3).

154 Doc. 19: 4 October 1731, 1732, 1733, 1734, 1 July 1740, 1758, 1769.

155 Doc. 19: 1771, 1790.

156 Torrington 1934–8, vol. III, p. 219, 27 July 1793, referring to St Leonard, Over Whitacre, Warwickshire (1766), by William Hiorne, which originally had a west tower apparently crowned by a bullet-shaped dominal feature (Birmingham Library Services Archives Division, Aylesford, I, f. 254), remodelled into a spire in 1850 (*Buildings of England: Warwickshire*, 1966, pp. 368–9, pl. 42a).

EIGHTEEN ROMANESQUE INTERLUDE

1 *Gentleman's Magazine* (15 February 1791), p. 132, William Porden, architect, on St Mary de Haura, New Shoreham, *circa* 1130, or St Nicholas, Old Shoreham, *circa* 1140; St Andrew, Steyning, *circa* 1170, all in Sussex (*Buildings of England: Sussex*, 1965, pp. 276–81, 285–7, 337–40, pls 16a–b, 17b, 18).

2 Gray 1814 (Bizzarro 1992, pp. 76–7).

3 In 'A Society of Architects', *Builder's Magazine* (1774–8), p. 229.

4 Bentham 1771, p. 37. Extracts appeared in Bentham 1772 and Nash 1781–2, vol. I, pp. 597–8.

5 Milner 1798–1801/1809, vol. I, p. 448.

6 Society of Antiquaries of London, Red Portfolio London A–B, f. 12. John Carter applauded this exercise in preserving the building as the triumph of 'an able Architect and Antiquary . . . done in the teeth of the would-be-Innovators' set on demolition (*Gentleman's Magazine*, March 1809, p. 227). Guildhall Library, City of London Corporation, MS 3990/4, ff. 8, 10–11, 212, 225, 1790–1808; Godwin 1839, vol. I, pp. 10–14 ill.; Clarke 1966, p. 5.

7 Doc. 136: 1750; in 1758 he noted the buildings 'entirely . . . one style of Architecture . . . generally termed . . . Saxon'.

8 For example, Talman 1997, pls 40–43, devoted much effort to recording Italian specimens, particularly San Marco, Venice.

9 Bailey 1996, pp. 144–60; *Buildings of England: Northamptonshire*, 1968, pp. 305–20, pl. 12.

10 Hoare 1983, pp. 143, 117–18. Others lamented the ignominious destruction of lesser Saxon churches such as the long ruinous Flatworth, Nottinghamshire (demolished 1773), with its 'materials . . . taken to mend the roads, build bridges, erect pig-sties &c' (Dugdale 1819, vol. IV, p. 139).

11 Doc. 52: 1726, pp. 29–30. See also John Bakker's oil painting of *The Canterbury Quire* (*circa* 1696–1712) in Royal Museum and Art Gallery, Canterbury.

12 For recent studies, see Cocke 1973; Cocke and Dodwell 1984; Bizzarro 1992.

13 Doc. 75: 20, 23 August 1699, undated, 14 July 1700, 1702.

14 The Bow entrance also appears on the tower of 1684 of St Leonard, Deal, Kent, architect unknown (*Buildings of England: North East and East Kent*, 1969, p. 269; *Country Life*, 26 April 2001, p. 126).

15 Soo 1998, p. 68.

16 Doc. 155: 1730 (Loveday), 1742 (British Library).

17 Doc. 155: 26 June 1716, 1730, 26 July 1731, November 1799.

18 Doc. 155: 1735–51.

19 Doc. 155: 10 October 1760.

20 Herefordshire Record Office, AM 40/1, 14 January 1702.

21 Pococke 1750, vol. II, pp. 223–4, September 1756. See also Dugdale 1819, vol. II, p. 595.

22 Haug 1962, pls 42, 221b.

23 Butler 1980. This historical link may account for the distinctive hood moulds of the crossing tower.

24 Doc. 97. Langley referred to the 'Saxon Manner' in *Ancient Architecture*, 1747 (Harris and Savage 1990, p. 271 no. 410). Thirteenth-century Salisbury was considered by Thomas Warton as being in the 'Saxon Stile [or] a sort of Gothic Saxon' (Warton 1754, p. 186).

25 Doc. 97: 1752–5.

26 Brown 1985, p. 214.

27 Cocke and Dodwell 1984, p. 47 no. 511. The drawings, dated 1749–66, also include Iffley, Oxfordshire (no. 514), the subject of a view in *Gentleman's Magazine* (June 1791), p. 499.

28 Doc. 182: 1727, 29 August 1791, 29–30 May 1792, 1796.

29 Doc. 182: 1780, 1806.

30 Described as a 'magnificent [cathedral] of the first style; semicircular arches, great pillars' (Stukeley 1882–7, vol. II, p. 211, 24 July 1749), Croyland was recorded by the above 1730–49 (Stukeley 1882–7, vol. I, pp. 42, 232, 266, 370; vol. II, pp. 306, 309–10), and James Essex's 'Drawings for the Hist: of Architecture' (British Library, Add. MS 6776, ff. 44–6). See 'Observations on Croyland Abbey and Bridge', in Nichols, *Bibliotheca Topographica Britannica* (*Gentleman's Magazine*, July 1784, pp. 525–6); Pennant 1769, p. 14;

Russell and Price 1769, vol. I, p. 375; R. G.'s (?Richard Gough) poetic 'History of Croyland' (*Gentleman's Magazine*, March 1784, p. 201); and Torrington 1934–8, vol. II, pp. 219–21. *Buildings of England: Lincolnshire*, 1989, pp. 238–41, pl. 25.

31 Doc. 182: 1800.

32 Introduction, pp. 1–31, including 'Historical Remarks on the *Saxon* Churches', and p. 35. Bray 1783, pp. 366–7, remarked that St Peter was 'very deserving of notice . . . a perfect remain of the Saxon building'. The *Gentleman's Magazine* devoted illustrations to Saxon churches at Orford, Suffolk (August 1788, p. 702), Threekingham, Lincolnshire (October 1791, p. 906), Lullington, Somerset (October, November 1794, pp. 893, 993), reflecting an upsurge of public curiosity.

33 Doc. 223: September 1736.

34 Quoted in Carritt 1948, p. 222.

35 Doc. 117: 15–18 March 1725. See also 29 April 1726.

36 Fiennes 1982, p. 118.

37 Doc. 156: 14 June 1721. In 1734–5 Hawksmoor succinctly summed up the abbey's romanesque character.

38 Doc. 170: 19 May 1743. Trubshaw had spent his formative years in Oxford, where he married in 1714 and may have been employed in building Blenheim Palace. In Oxford he purchased a copy of *Vitruvius Britannicus*, the first volume (1715) of which featured Vanbrugh's King's Weston, Castle Howard and Blenheim (Colvin 2008, p. 1058).

39 As at Lincoln cathedral and St Mary, Tutbury, Staffordshire (Shaw 1798–1801, vol. I, p. 59, pl. V).

40 Doc. 170: 19 December 1743, 1744. John Douglas's powerful octagonal belfry, 1744, attached to the 1185 body of Leuchars, Fife, followed a similar format (*Buildings of Scotland: Fife*, 1988, p. 308, pl. 11; Colvin 2008, p. 330).

41 The 'very ancient chapel . . . having become ruinous through ages, part of its having already fallen, and the rest upon the point of falling . . . The capitals on each side of the door are a sort of Gothick composit, there are several figures on it in bas-relief' (Pococke 1750, vol. I, p. 212, 12 June 1751). Dugdale 1819, vol. I, p. 345; Richards 1973, pp. 282–3; Bilsborough 1991, pp. 146–8; Salter 1995, p. 64.

42 Morris 1728, pp. 87–9. Kaufmann 1955, p. 26, fig. 16.

43 Doc. 98: 30 October 1755.

44 Dickins and Stanton 1910, p. 396. Ward-Perkins 1981, pls 289–90.

45 Doc. 202: 1750.

46 Bentham 1771, p. 25. See also *Gentleman's Magazine* (February 1794), pp. 113–14.

47 Drake 1790, p. 53.

48 *Archaeologia*, XIII (1798), pp. 300–01.

49 Worcestershire Record Office, 000293. Conant 1966, pp. 221–2.

50 Doc. 103. Cavers 1993, p. 66, pl. 50.

51 Cruden 1986, pp. 45–52, pls 12–15, and *RCHMS: Roxburghshire*, vol. I, 1956, pp. 240–45. An octagonal church was erected on an adjacent virgin site (Doc. 103).

52 Stukeley 1776, vol. II, p. 71, in 1725.

53 Warton 1754, p. 245.

54 British Architectural Library, Drawings and Archives Collection, Victoria and Albert Museum, London, CHA. 1/12. vi.

NINETEEN 'BEHOLD! AUGUSTA'S GLITT'RING . . . TEMPLES RISE'

1 Pope 1713, lines 377–8.

2 Cawthorn 1771.

3 *Gentleman's Magazine*, Supplement 1799, p. 1099.

4 Doc. 223: 28 October 1717.

5 Harris 1699, p. 2.

6 Doc. 223: 1706 (this edition dedicated to Wren), 1729.

7 Doc. 223. For a fulsome account of the cathedral's eighteenth-century reputation, see Keene, Burns and Saint 2004, chapters 28, 42.

8 British Architectural Library, Drawings and Archives Collection, Victoria and Albert Museum, London, J14(5) 54–65. Colvin 2008, pp. 949–53; Sicca 1980, p. 47, no. 24; Roberts 1991. Design J14(5)61 is linked with St Peter's Basilica; interestingly, the *concorsi* held for architectural students at the Accademia di San Luca – 'Chiesa a pianta centrale' (1677), 'Chiesa con edifici annessi' (1678), 'Chiesa con due companili' (1679) – show the continuing domination of the Michelangelo-Maderno building (Marconi, Cipriani and Valeriani 1974, vol. I, under dates; Smith 1984; Smith 1993, chapter II). If erected, pl. 355 would have measured overall 1,000 by 610 feet, that is, approximately twice the length and breadth of the present cathedral.

9 Reminiscent of an unrealised Greenwich Hospital scheme of the 1690s (Pevsner 1961, p. 29, pls 1–3) and the model of 1715 for the New Sacristy of St Peter's (Hager 1998). See also Wren's projected quadrant arcade for St Paul's *piazza* (*Wren Society*, III, 1926, pls XXXI–XXXII; VI, 1929, p. 83, pl. XXI; VIII, 1931, pls XVIII, XIX).

10 Magirius 2005; Aurenhammer 1973, pp. 132–4, pls 85–96; Millon 1999, pp. 571–4.

11 Colvin 2008, pp. 71–3. For Archer's Continental itinerary, see Lawrence 2010.

12 Doc. 24: 1715.

13 Downes 1988, p. 59 no. 10.

14 Hawksmoor owned a copy of this book (Watkin 1972, p. 104 lot 125).

15 In 1727 Samuel Gale praised Talman's record drawings of 'Sacred Temples' as having 'touched the heavenly Beauties [and] Lights . . . Thrown in upon . . . the Antique Roofs . . . rich embellished . . . Altars . . . all gloriously transmitted to Posterity, whilst Brittan admires & emulates Greece & Rome' (Sicca 2008, p. 47). Ingamells 1997, pp. 924–6. Davidson 2008, p. 93, figs 17–18. Talman converted to Catholicism in 1708–9.

16 Pope 1713, lines 377–8, perhaps referring to the New Churches as the happy outcome of the Treaty of Utrecht signed on 31 March 1713, ending the Anglo-French War.

17 Pope 1734, line 119. *The Spectator*, V, no. 383 (20 May 1712), p. 257. Furthermore, 'were her late majesty queen Anne . . . to reign again, and fifty new churches to be really built, I doubt if in this dissolute age, this also might not be called her Majesty's FOLLY' (*The World By Adam Fitz-Adam*, vol. II, 1757, 14 February 1754, pp. 213–14, reprinted in *London Magazine*, 1754, p. 80).

18 Bill 1979, with an introduction by H. Colvin, revised from Bill 1950. Port 1986. The Papers (Lambeth Palace Library, London) are available on fourteen reels, World Microfilms

Publications. See also Summerson 2003, chapter 6; Downes 1959, chapters X–XII; Downes 1966, pp. 98–105.

19 Geraghty 2007, p. 49 no. 52, p. 68 no. 81, p. 118 nos 171, 172.

20 Downes 1959, p. 175.

21 *Journals of the House of Commons*, vol. XVI, p. 580, 6 April 1711.

22 *The Examiner*, 42, 24 May 1711 (Davis 1941, p. 160).

23 Manuscripts bound in volume of printed pamphlets (British Library, Bills 357B.4.91).

24 Lambeth Palace Library, MS 2691, ff. 136–7, 19 January 1721. For expenditures, see MS 2693, f. 86; MS 2711, f. 77.

25 Lambeth Palace Library, MS 2690, f. 131.

26 Lambeth Palace Library, MS 2690, f. 284; MS 2691, f. 207 in 1716, 1723; MS 2690, f. 391 in 1718. Poplar (1654) was not rebuilt until 1776.

27 Lambeth Palace Library, MS 2691, f. 88, 21 January 1720.

28 Lambeth Palace Library, MS 2691, ff. 145, 387–8.

29 Lambeth Palace Library, MS 2691, f. 366, 4 February 1726.

30 Lambeth Palace Library, MS 2691, f. 366; MS 2692, ff. 1–2.

31 Lambeth Palace Library, MS 2690, f. 327, 11 April 1717.

32 Doc. 270: 20 November 1718.

33 Doc. 244: 26 January 1721. James described himself as 'a Parson's Son' in a letter of 20 October 1721 (Bodleian Library, University of Oxford, MS Rawl. B376, ff. 8–9).

34 Doc. 228: 12, 26 November 1725. In fairness to Hawksmoor, he was no more than developing an aborted proposal of 1713 to provide individual statues of Queen Anne for all fifty New Churches (see pp. 376, 379).

35 Doc. 239: 20 March 1745.

36 Lambeth Palace Library, MS 2691, f. 378, 25 March 1726.

37 Doc. 221: 6 April 1711.

38 Doc. 270: 6 April 1711. Lambeth Palace Library, MS 2716, f. 13, described the Savoy Chapel as 'but one isle [with] no more allotment than eight or nine pews, and a Small part of a Gallery for servants', with a steeple or bells, the approach 'dangerous for coaches, and noisomly Scandalous every way'.

39 Historical Manuscript Commission, *Portland*, vol. X, 1931, pp. 145–7, 16 March 1713. Bill 1979, p. xxiii, for a full list of Commissioners.

40 Lambeth Palace Library, MS 2690, ff. 2, 63; MS 2693, ff. 38, 41.

41 Lambeth Palace Library, MS 2690, back f. 5. Forty-seven sites were drawn (plans in MS 2750). For a typical exploratory plan in a crowded urban site, see Geraghty 2007, p. 117 no. 170.

42 Lambeth Palace Library, MS 2691, ff. 387–9.

43 Doc. 235: 4, 9 July 1712. James was appointed carpenter on 11 March 1713 (Lambeth Palace Library, MS 2690, f. 75).

44 Doc. 270: 15 July 1713, 4 February, 29 April, 1 July, 2, 4 November 1714.

45 Watkin 1972, p. 82 no. 36. A substantial number of unspecified 'Designs for different Churches' by Hawksmoor, now untraced, highlights the difficulty of a too-detailed interpretation of his contributions as the longest serving surveyor. Jeffery 1994, p. 12, suggests that All Soul's, Oxford, Wren Collection I. 58, perhaps represents James's Strand submission of pre-29 April 1714.

46 *Wren Society*, IX (1932), pp. 15–18; Downes 1977, pp. 257–8; Du Prey 2000, pp. 133–7; Soo 1998, pp. 112–18. Only Wren's 'Letter to a Friend' was published in the eighteenth century (Wren 1750, pp. 318–21). For Vanbrugh's rare excursions as a church designer beyond his New Churches involvements, see an unidentified, attributed scheme (*circa* 1712–14) and the Newcastle pew, Esher, Surrey (1723–5; Hart 2008, pp. 95, 111, figs 138, 167).

47 It cost £8,500 (Doc. 266: 1750).

48 Du Prey 2000, pp. 140, 142. For Hickes, see pp. 37–8, 56–8, 62–5.

49 Lambeth Palace Library, MS 2690, back f. 13; MS 2690, f. 15.

50 Ali and Cunich 2005a; Ali and Cunich 2005b; Ali 2005.

51 Lambeth Palace Library, MS 2690, ff. 42–3; also MS 2693, ff. 5–6 (Du Prey 2000, pp. 143–4).

52 '16 [models] of Churches', with vellum labels, of which two models and all labels survive (Lambeth Palace Library, MS 2724, 8, 20–25, in 1733).

53 Lambeth Palace Library, MS 2690, ff. 34, 65–7; MS 2693, ff. 17, 72. On 13 July 1716, 50s. were spent for 'Shelves with . . . Iron work upon which the models stand' (MS 2690, f. 286).

54 Lambeth Palace Library, MS 2724, ff. 1, 4, 22 October 1712; MS 2708, f. 9, 6 June 1717.

55 Lambeth Palace Library, MS 2690, f. 217, 19 May 1715.

56 'I sincerely hope . . . that a time will come when Westminster Abbey . . . will be open to the free inspection of the public, who may . . . see the works of ancient and modern art, without being invited to pay for the exhibition of wax-work and models of churches', which should be presented to the Society of Artists (Smith 1949, p. 184).

57 Donaldson 1843, giving dimensions based on a scale of ¼ inch to a foot, with their 'architectural features made out with considerable care, and the whole of the internal fittings . . . accurately and minutely modelled . . . easily seen, as the roofs are fitted with hinges'; they were 'not very materially injured [but had] no inscriptions upon them to indicate the name of the architect, the date, or destination of the churches'. His lecture plans are in British Architectural Library, Drawings and Archives Collection, Victoria and Albert Museum, London, X16/11,1–7 (Bill 1979, p. xviii).

58 Jeffery 1986, pp. 63–4; Jeffery 1995, pp. 81–96, 135–6, provides a history of the models and documentary evidence for their interpretation.

59 Doc. 244: 16 July 1713; Lambeth Palace Library, MS 2697, f. 162, 1714–15.

60 Doc. 244: 1 January 1712ff., 10 December 1713.

61 Doc. 244. A transitional plan shows the porch attached to the body by half-columns (British Library, King's Topographical Collection, XVIII,18–I) rather than block rusticated piers, further evidence of the subtle progress towards the final design.

62 For example, the unexecuted scheme of 1669 for a colonnaded apse at Santa Maria Maggiore (Marder 1998, pp. 311–14, pls 286, 288). Colvin 2008, p. 71.

63 Archer's preliminary plan (British Library, King's Topographical Collection, XVIII,18–a) introduced a large circular ceiling moulding rather than the executed square panel. Complaints that the pulpit and desks were 'very

Difficult and Troublesome to execute' (Lambeth Palace Library, MS 2698, ff. 35–8) indicate the over-elaborateness of the interior (Friedman 1997a, pp. 88–9).

64 Doc. 267: 1731. C. Dickens, *Our Mutual Friend*, 1865, Book the Second, chapter 1.

65 Doc. 267: 3, 9 January 1713, 23 June 1714, 1 January–31 December 1716, 25 March 1719–25 March 1720, 1721. Chamberlain commented in 1769–70 that the towers were erected that the 'whole might sink equally'.

66 Friedman 2004, fig. 42.

67 Marder 1998, p. 225, pl. 209; removed in 1883.

68 Doc. 258. Friedman 2004, fig. 48. Archer here is adapting a distinctive composition derived from the Villa Aldobrandini (1598–1603), engraved in 1699 (Frank 1966, pl. 135), which he had already introduced at Roehampton House, Surrey, 1710–12 (Campbell 1715–25, vol. I, pl. 81). Dr Elizabeth Kieven, the foremost Alessandro Galilei scholar, does not accept the attribution to him of the east front of Kimbolton, with its similar pedimental treatment, traditionally given to Archer, suggested in Thurley 2006, p. 70, pl. 5).

69 Dallaway 1806, p. 147, claimed 'his genius runs riot amongst steeples', referring to St Anne, Limehouse, and St George, Bloomsbury. Watkin 1972, pp. 81–98, itemises some 185 'Designs of different Churches', including a number for Westminster Abbey, not all traced. Ralph 1734, p. 6. See Downes 1959; Worsley 1995; Du Prey 2000; Hart 2002, among the more considered and dispassionate of a rich and growing literature on the architect.

70 Lambeth Palace Library, MS 2693, f. 69; MS 2690, f. 79, 23 March 1713.

71 *Grub-street Journal*, no. 237 (11 July 1734), p. 1.

72 Docs 258–60.

73 F. Borromini's Propaganda Fide (Rossi and Rossi 1702–21, vol. II, pl. 9). See also J. C. Schlaun's similar use of the treatment at Münster (1724–9; Hempel 1965, pl. 136).

74 Doc. 259: 25 March 1719, 25 March, 12 July 1725.

75 Hart 2002, pp. 39–47, fig. 52. Ward-Perkins 1981, pp. 314–21, pls 202–5. Hawksmoor repeated some features in his abortive scheme of 1730 for St Giles-in-the-Fields (Doc. 229).

76 Doc. 258: 11 July 1734.

77 Doc. 260: 11 July 1734. Based on C. G. Cibber's 'Incence Potts', 1700, at the south transept entrance to St Paul's Cathedral (*Wren Society*, XV, 1938, p. 62, pl. 26), also used by Hawksmoor at Greenwich (Hart 2002, p. 154, pl. 210).

78 Hart 2002, p. 155, pls 73–6, 177, 192, 214.

79 Krautheimer 1986, pp. 269, 272–3, pl. 234. For John Talman's interest in the Mausoleum *circa* 1712–16, including G. A. Grisoni's view, see Sicca 2008, pp. 211–12, figs 72. 109. Worsley 1995, pp. 61–3, pls 75–7, demonstrates that even Hawksmoor's 'most outlandish un-Classical' churches like Wapping were inspired by imaginative reconstructions of ancient classical temples exhibiting a penchant for semi-circular apses, giant porticoes and towers of a sort published in the early seventeenth century by J. A. du Cerceau and G. B. Montano, the latter present in Hawksmoor's private library (Watkin 1972, p. 103 lot 96).

80 Hart 2002, pls 182, 242. Rocque 1746–7, 13ba. The effects of the restricted site are recorded in compensation claims for damage to Robert Burgess's adjacent residence in 1717 (Lambeth Palace Library, MS 2690, f. 351). Doc. 221: 5 March 1719, 11 August 1720, 13 March 1724.

81 Doc. 221: 6 May 1719. One is reminded of Jacob van Campen's Nieuwe Kerk, Haarlem (Kuyper 1980, pp. 16–18, figs 4–5, pls 37–40).

82 One of his studies show statues filling the niches (Hart 2002, pl. 258) in the manner of San Giovanni in Laterano (Rossi and Rossi 1702–21, vol. I, pl. 63); see also the Falconieri tomb, San Giovannni dei Fiorentini (Rossi 1713, pl. 16).

83 Rocque 1746–7, 3AC.

84 Compare to Hawksmoor's unsuccessful Proposal VI for Queen's College chapel, Oxford, 1708–9 (Doc. 144; Downes 1959, fig. 12E, pls 30a–b).

85 Discussed in Du Prey 2000, p. 110.

86 Stukeley 1882–7, vol. III, p. 9, claimed that 'Hawksmoor made the portico . . . in imitation, and of the size, of that at Balkeck', the Temple of Jupiter (Ward-Perkins 1981, pp. 316–17, pls 202–3).

87 Doc. 228: 25 March 1722, 13 June 1723.

88 This building was the subject of renewed interest in Hawksmoor's time, with the scheme for a circular, domed church set in its bowels, published in *L'Anfiteatro Flavio*, 1725 (Hager 1973).

89 Society of Antiquaries of London, Minute Book 1718–32, I, p. 55, recorded the gift of a Roman aqueduct pipe taken '3 years ago in digging the Foundation of the *new Church Bloomsbury*'.

90 Curcio 2003. The funeral of Emperor Leopold I in Santa Maria dell'Anima, 1705, and for King Pedro II in Sant'Antonio de' Portoghesi, 1707 (Braham and Hager 1977, pp. 35–6, pls 68–9, 150–89, 199–223, 563–4; Fagiolo dell'Arco 1997, pp. 19–20, 23–5. Placzek 1982, vol. II, pp. 92–9; Varriano 1986, pp. 151–5, pls 91–2.

91 The Accademia's early Corso Clementino competitions for students centred on such themes as a 'Rilievo una nicchia' and a 'Facciata' for San Giovanni in Laterano (1702–4). Marconi, Cipriani and Valeriani 1974, vol. I, nos 63–71, 78–81, 123–34, 145–52; Kieven 1991b. Among Continental architectural drawings owned by Gibbs is an anonymous copy of Fontana's Lateran proposal, notable for the reassertion of the free-standing column, which had progressively vanished from the Italian repertory (Friedman 1984, p. 37, pl. 13). The young but already brilliant architect Filippo Juvarra was among Gibbs's contemporaries in Fontana's circle and he was to visit London in 1720 (Placzek 1982, vol. II, p. 527).

92 Soane MS, vol. 26, ff. 13–17, 22, 31–7. See Blunt 1982.

93 Friedman 1984, pp. 328–9.

94 Doc. 270: 18 November 1713. Gibbs 1728, p. vi. It 'will shew . . . posterity, that the period when it was built afforded architects who might have done honour to Italy' (1761).

95 Doc. 270: 29 April 1714. Archer's Deptford portico was approved on 15 April 1714 (Doc. 244).

96 Doc. 270: 9 April, 1, 6 July 1714. For additional material not cited in above Document, see Blackett-Ord 2001, pp. 89–90, and Longstaffe-Gowan 2009, pp. 57–8, fig. 5.

97 Trajan's was topped by a 13-foot-high gilt bronze statue of

St Peter, the column of Antoninus Pius with one of St Paul, another excavated in the Campus Martius and proposed to be erected at the Trevi Fountain with St Clement's statue (unrealised) and a 59-foot-high column from the destroyed Temple of Peace re-erected in front of Santa Maria Maggiore with a figure of the *Virgin* (Soane MS, vol. 26, ff. 24–6). Archer and Hawksmoor also prepared column designs, the former now untraced, the latter inspired by Wren's Fire Monument, 1671–6.

98 Nevertheless, James proposed erecting galleries (Doc. 270: 26 July 1723), though none was installed until *circa* 1818, then removed in 1828 (City of Westminster Archives Centre, MS G1004).

99 Gibbs 1728, p. VI. In this respect, however, Gibbs failed (see Doc. 270: Anon. 1726 [*New Guide to London*, p. 29] and 7 November 1734).

100 Gibbs's fondness for semicircular entrées is evident from his observation of Bernini's Sant'Andrea Quirinale as 'a most beautifull fabrick . . . the portico . . . is a Masterpeece of Art' (Soane MS, vol. 26, f. 34). The 'Westwerk'-like form may have derived from Bernini's Contessa Matilda tomb, and the similar Carlo Fontana scheme (unexecuted) for Queen Christina, both in St Peter (Marder 1998, pl. 164; Braham and Hager 1977, pp. 56–60, pls 33–4).

101 Doc. 270: 8 September 1714 (Friedman 1976, p. 53). Sicca 2008, pp. 46, 48, 137–8, 143–8.

102 Compare to the Corsini chapel, Santa Maria del Carmine (1675–83), Florence (Colvin 1991, fig. 190). Gibbs visited 'the fine Churches' of the city sometime between 1703 and 1709 (Soane MS, vol. 26, ff. 52–3). Gwynn (1766; p. 46) thought St Mary-le-Strand 'an expensive rich design without the least appearance of grandeur, which is occasioned by its being divided into too many parts, a building may be made in parts very elegant and very rich, and yet very inelegant in the whole, which is the case of this church, the division of the building into two orders has destroyed its grandeur, the steeple is a confused jumble of rich parts piled one upon another, without any regard to the shape of the whole, and has this additional fault . . . it appears to stand upon the roof of the church.'

103 Doc. 51. For example, Santa Maria in Via Lata, San Lorenzo in Lucina and San Crisogono in Trastevere (Blunt 1982, pp. 68–9, 120–22, pls 46–7; Fagiolo 1997, pp. 6, 9–10; Rossi and Rossi 1702–21, vol. III, pl. 42).

104 Rossi and Rossi 1702–21, vol. I, pl. 62. Braham and Hager 1977, pp. 86–7. The niches in the main piers received apostolic statues carved under Carlo Fontana's direction beginning in 1703, the year he began training Gibbs. One can only speculate on the chapel's plain, red brick and stone-dressed exterior, measuring 25 by 70 feet, for which there is no pictorial evidence. Its appearance may be reflected in Gibbs's Wimpole Hall chapel (Doc. 196) and his unrealised design for Kiveton House chapel, Yorkshire, 1741 (Friedman 1984, p. 321), as well as William Smith's Capesthorne House chapel, Cheshire, 1720–23 (Cheshire Record Office, EDA 2/4, f. 408, 4 September 1722; Richards 1973, pp. 87–9 ill.; Gomme and Gomme 1969; Gomme 2000, pp. 31, 36, 333–4, 414, 518). Echoes may survive at St Mary, Avington, Hampshire (1768–71), built for the Marquess and Marchioness of Caernarvon, Chandos relatives, which still possesses a crimson velvet and gold lace braided covered copy of Baskett's Bible and Prayer Book inscribed 'Canons' (*St Mary the Virgin Avington*, 1977, guidebook; Hunt 1961; Clarke 1963, p. 62; Chatfield 1979, pp. 44–6; Hampshire Record Office, 21M65/17F/1, 22M69A/PR1 back).

105 Doc. 270: 1716, 8 June 1718. See also 1761. In 1717 Kent painted the ceiling of San Giuliano del Fiamminghi (Mowl 2006, pp. 57–8, colour pl.).

106 Marconi, Cipriani and Valeriani 1974, vol. I, 1704, nos 126–8. Blackett-Ord 2001, pp. 103–4, 14 May 1713.

107 Cinza Maria Sicca, a leading Kent scholar and member of the John Talman Project research team based at Pisa University, verbally to the present writer (15 October 2008). Talman 1997, pp.183, 186.

108 Kieven 2008, pp. 5–7,11–14, figs 6–8, 12–13. His sources included Nigetti's façade of 1637 for the Ognissanti, Silvani's of 1648 for Santi Michele e Gaetano (Goy 2002, p. 242), Caccini's single-storey arcaded porch of 1601–4 for Santissima Annunziata (Cresti 1992, pp. 134–5, also p. 142; Dee 1968, pls 13, 17). The related ground plan and section (Archivio di Stato, Florence, Galilei N.14, N/2, Box 109/48, ff. 319, 328), inscribed 'People 736 in all the Galleries and all the Body of the Church 2450 wch makes in all 736/3780 People'. One of Galilei's English patrons suggested in 1719 that 'it would be for your service to present Lord Chancelor with the draft of your Churches' (Toesca 1952, p. 216), but the finished drawings have vanished and only sketches survive in Florence (as above, ff. 316–19, 323, 325–9, 334); Kieven 1973; Placzek 1982, vol. II, pp. 145–9; Kieven 2008; Sicca 2008. See chapter 22, note 22.

TWENTY EARLY CHRISTIANITY REVIVED

1 Bingham 1711, p. 8. Santa Maria sopra Minerva (*circa* 800, 1280s), for example, was built on the 'site of what was once the Temple of Minerva Calcidica' (Hart and Hicks 2006, p. 128; Blunt 1982, p. 94).

2 Westminster Abbey Muniments, 24878 (Downes 1959, p. 255). R. Neve's definition of a basilica as 'a large Hall, with Portico's, Isles and Tribunal, where the Kings administered Justice . . . but . . . applied now-a-days . . . to Churches' (Neve 1726) was repeated in *The Builder's Dictionary* (Anon. 1734), under Basilic, where it was endorsed by Hawksmoor.

3 Doc. 256.

4 These links are expounded brilliantly by Du Prey 1989 and more fully in Du Prey 2000. See also Doll 1997. Peter King, one of the New Churches Commissioners, published *An Enquiry into the Constitution, Discipline, Unity and Worship of the Primitive Church*, 1691, while the Revd George Wheler, author of *An Account of the Churches . . .* (Wheler 1689), for whom Hawksmoor had illustrated *A Journey into Greece*, 1682, was the proprietor of a chapel in nearby Spitalfields, which was to be an unsuccessful contender for one of the New Churches sites. Knight 2000.

5 *Tracts Relating to London*, untitled, 1678 (British Library, 816.m.9.92). Such sources were not exclusively an English

preserve; for instance, see Galilei's reconstruction of a later antique martyrium, published in Florence in 1731 (Kieven 2008, p. 11, figs 10–11).

6 Bingham 1711, pp. 39–40, 43. These are themes present in Binckes 1710, preached at St Philip, Birmingham; Lacy 1715; Stephens 1727; all subsequently published.

7 Cowie 1956, pp. 53–4. Valued in total at above 20 guineas; owing to insufficient subscriptions, the libraries had reached only sixty parishes by 1723.

8 Wood 1765, pp. 308–9.

9 Wood 1741, the text composed at least from 1737 (Harris and Savage 1990, pp. 480–89). For a parallel example, see Lord Burlington's repairing of York Minster, 1730–34, based on Roman mosaics, an eminently un-gothic solution given credence as a reflection of the city's ancient classical past (Doc. 207).

10 Wood 1741, pp. 221–2. Wood owned J. B. Villalpanda's *In Ezechielem Explanantiones et Apparatus Urbis ac Templi Hierosoplomytani*, 3 vols, 1604 (Brownell 1976, Appendix III). Wood's intentions are well summarised in Mowl and Earnshaw 1988, chapter six.

11 Doc. 122: 6 February 1723, 23 November 1736.

12 Bingham 1711, p. 55.

13 Duncan 1999, p. 148. This dome may have been based on a reconstruction of the Turris Campanaria on early Christian St Peter (Bonanni 1715, p. 14).

14 Sant'Adriano marked an important station on the pilgrimage route from San Giovanni in Laterano to Santa Maria Maggiore (Kessler and Zacharias 2000, pp. 101–3, figs 94–5). For Trastevere, see Blunt 1982, p. 112; Braham and Hager 1977, pp. 77–9, figs 109–13, with fig. 111, an engraved view of 1708.

15 By AD 200 this had become the focal point of the shrine (Krautheimer 1986, p. 32, fig. 3).

16 Stevenson 1983, p. 308, suggested that the structure may have been a reflection of the altar at Hagia Sophia, Constantinople (532–7), described in Bingham 1711, p. 100, as an 'ornamental canopy . . . raised in the form of a little turret, upon four pillars at each corner'. For a similar arrangement, in which the eastern end of the roofless body of Battlefield, Shropshire (1409), was fitted out around 1749 by four Tuscan columns supporting a coved ceiling, see Shropshire Records and Research Unit, Shrewsbury, QS/1/3, f. 21v; 6001/225 (Ionides 1999, pp. 219, 284; Carr 1994, pls 122–3; Fletcher 1889, pp. 22–3).

17 Doc. 122: 1774, 1783–4, 1787, 1794.

18 *Gentleman's Magazine* (February 1804), p. 126; (March 1804), p. 216.

19 Bar Convent Archives, 4J3; Coleridge 1887, p. 178. On 26 January 1769 Aspinall reported the chapel 'not yet finished . . . Thanks to God . . . almost at . . . end of this great affair' (p. 187); on 27 April 'we enter'd . . . New Chapel' (Archives: 3B/4), cost including the convent buildings, also designed by Atkinson, £3,216 7s. 6d. (Archives: *Annals of The Bar Convent Museum*, 8, undated, chapter 24); Midsummer 1791: 'Certificate . . . recorded . . . roman Catholic Chapel' (3B/15). Interior shown in nineteenth-century print by H. Brown (Bar Convent Archives), partly remodelled in 1815 (7B3/12); sacristy enlarged in 1837, redecorated in 1969 (*RCHME: York*, vol. III, 1972, pp. 40–41, fig. 42, pl. 139). Kirkus 2000; Bar Convent Archives: *The History of the Bar Convent*, undated.

20 Krautheimer 1986, p. 67, fig. 28. Gibbs described it as 'a very fine Antient Building a little way out of Rome . . . of Circular forme . . . very elegant . . . commonly called the Temple of Bacchus . . . now . . . a Christian Church . . . it is intire . . . has a Cupolo supported by twenty four granite Columns in cuplets . . . all the members enriched . . . Capitells . . . of the Composite Order, finely wrought, in good taste . . . well worth . . . seeing and studying . . . Degodez has given an exact plan upright and section' (Soane MS, vol. 26, f. 19). See also Tavernor and Schofield 1997, pp. 297–9. It was also the model for St Peter-Le-Poer, London (1788–92; Doc. 224, pls 682–3).

21 Du Prey 2000, p. 140, figs 13–14, 30.

22 Mangey 1719, pp. 17–18.

23 Doc. 178. He died before work was completed; the room is now bare. See Kenton Couse's failed attempt to introduce a pair of domed octagons of undesignated function attached to the east end of the aisles of Holy Trinity, Clapham, London (Doc. 242).

24 Gloucestershire Record Office, D 2663/28, 15–26 May 1734.

25 British Library, Add. MS 22,994, f. 47. Krautheimer 1986, pp. 278–80, fig. 242, discussed in Friedman 1998a, pp. 27–8, pl. 14. Pococke's preceding diary (Add. MS 19,940) bears the annotation 'part of my sons travels Copyed for Mr. Jer. Milles'.

26 San Lorenzo, Milan (*circa* 378), rebuilt following its collapse in 1573 but retaining the original foundations (Krautheimer 1986, pp. 78–81, pls 35–7), described by Gibbs, who visited it between 1703 and 1709, as 'a very fine structure of an octagonal forme . . . well finished . . . inside, with . . . many ornaments' (Soane MS, vol. 26, f. 59), may have been a source for an undated design for a colossal church (Harris 1998b, pp. 26–7 no. 18).

27 Bingham 1711, pp. 54, 63, 116–19; Krautheimer 1986, pp. 90, 92, pl. 47.

28 Tavernor and Schofield 1997, Book V, pp. 61–3. Soane MS, vol. 26, f. 20.

29 Doc. 176. The circular gallery windows linked by straight coursings derive from the internal dome of Gibbs's round St Martin-in-the-Fields (Gibbs 1728, pl. 12); a Gibbs-surround door on the south side, now blocked up, is recorded in a view in *Gentleman's Magazine* (July 1803), p. 621. The source of the Diocletian windows of the octagonal clerestory is Burlington's Chiswick villa (Kent 1727, vol. I, pls 70–73). Stony Middleton's designer, James Booth, served as James Paine's master mason at Chatsworth, the seat of Burlington's son-in-law, the 4th Duke of Devonshire, who contributed to the church rebuilding fund (Leach 1988, p. 179).

30 Ficacci 2000, p. 195, pl. 183; an exterior view appeared in *Varie vedute di Roma antica e moderna*, 1748, p. 81, pl. 38. Wilton-Ely 1993, p. 27, with Robert's portrait on the frontispiece to volume II.

31 Krautheimer 1986, p. 92, pls 48–9. A reference in 1758 to Argyll's nearby seat, Inveraray Castle, 1745–60, as 'in some

[unspecified] particulars is said to bear a strong resemblance to Solomon's Temple' (Burrell 1997, p. 83), strengthens the case for ancient models lying behind the church.

32 Adam's 'Estimate for Building . . . Circlear Church', 13 November 1758 (National Library of Scotland, Edinburgh, MS 17688, ff. 41r–42v). The present rectangular, temple-form church was built to Robert Mylne's design, 1792–1802 (Lindsay and Cosh 1973, pp. 151, 165, 267, 282–6, 319, pls 53b, 58, 89).

33 Revd Richard Pococke, 15–26 May 1734 (Gloucestershire Record Office, D 2663/28). Colvin 1991, fig. 112; Campbell 2004, vol. II, no. 203. Krautheimer 1986, pl. 234.

34 Webb 1931, pp. 117–19, 3 September 1726, 11 July 1728, ill.

35 Canterbury Cathedral Archives and Library, Canterbury, Kent, DCb/EF/1, 24 October 1754 faculty. *Gentleman's Magazine* (September 1809), pp. 825–7 ill.; Dugdale 1819, vol. III, p. 159. 'There could hardly have been a more emphatic gesture of the pretensions of the [London banking] family to become the ancients of the future than the building of a tomb fit for the earliest Christians' (Craske 2007, p. 373), poignantly describing it as 'a work of Piranesi-like terror'. See also Aringhi 1659, Book III, Chapter XXII, p. 313.

36 King 2001, vol. I, pp. 325, 366, figs 456–7, 520. Krautheimer 1986, pp. 181–2, figs 144–6. The building was noted early in the century by Talman 1997, pp. 24–5; Addison 1761, pp. 75–9. Jeremiah Milles observed that 'At . . . upper end . . . is a marble sarcophagus, very large in wch they say her body lyes' (Gloucestershire Record Office, D 2663/28, 15–26 May 1734). The *Builder's Magazine* (1774), pp. 9–10, pls XIX, XXI, added: 'reviving this custom [of] the antients . . . will not be amiss [because it] will have an elegant appearance, in whatever situation it is placed; and more decent and reverential than the present method of depositing the body . . . in an irreverent manner in a poisonous vault under a church, the resort of rats and other vermin, which fills the mind with very disagreeable sentiments . . . We have not introduced windows, thinking it more suitable . . . to have lamps placed in different parts . . . which will cast a religious gloom over the whole place, and inspire . . . proper ideas for the awful scene'; see also pp. 81, 84, pls CL, CLVI.

TWENTY-ONE THE RISE OF TEMPLE-FORM CHURCHES

1 G. Hickes, 'Observations on Mr Vanbruggs Proposals About Building the New Churches' (Du Prey 2000, p. 139).

2 Bingham 1711, pp. 46–50; Ward-Perkins 1981, pp. 314–17, pl. 203.

3 Pope 1743, pp. 531–2.

4 Soane MS, vol. 26, ff. 3, 19–20, 29. His lengthy description of the Pantheon, ff. 3–17, includes a plan, elevation and section copied from *Il Tempio Vaticano* (Curcio 2003, pp. 307–9). Of Fortuna Virilis he added: 'now in the possession of the Armenians . . . Desgodetz has given plans and uprights' (f. 20; Desgodetz 1682). For the above, see Tavernor and Schofield 1997, pp. 241–7, 260–63, 285–99.

5 Stukeley 1882–7, vol. I, p. 64, 29 May 1721. William Catlyn of Kingston-upon-Hull, Yorkshire, is recorded as having left 'A Book of Architecture of Ancient Rome' to the library of Holy Trinity parish church in 1709 (Colvin 2008, p. 238).

6 Book VII, Chapter III, as quoted in Leoni 1755, pp. 136–7.

7 Tavernor and Schofield 1997, pp. 213, 216–17, 285–6. Ware 1738, p. 82.

8 A few years earlier his scheme for Queen's College chapel, Oxford (1708–9), took the form of a laterally orientated rectangle with a monumental hexastyle Corinthian temple portico stretching across the south elevation (Doc. 144: Proposition A). From an earlier age is Webb's unexecuted design for a large temple-form church, in the possession in the early eighteenth century of the amateur architect George Clarke, joint Secretary to the Admiralty and secretary to Prince George of Denmark (Harris and Tait 1979, pp. 1–2, 69–70 nos 160v–164, pl. 112; Whinney 1943, p. 38a).

9 Doc. 235: 14 July 1714, 9 July, 6, 13 August 1712. This was strengthened by whitewashing the whole interior (1 January–31 December 1715, ditto 1719).

10 Doc. 50.

11 Some notion of the impact of this separation is evident, ironically, in the present state of St George, Wapping, where the west tower stands isolated from the Blitzed but partly rebuilt body at its eastern end (forming a new sanctuary, complete with its entrance façade), with an intervening open courtyard.

12 Evelyn 1664, p. 14.

13 The physical, not to say visual power of the resulting Serliana is attested by the carpenter's memorandum for supplying temporary 'Centering to the great Architraves . . . requiring very strong Stuff to bear the weight' (Doc. 235: 1 January–31 December 1714).

14 Downes 1988, pl. 33; Colvin 2008, p. 496; Ward-Perkins 1981, pl. 309.

15 Doc. 235: 1 January–31 December 1717. Hart 2002, fig. 210.

16 For a related, unexecuted Hawksmoor design, see Geraghty 2007, pp. 118–19 nos 172–3.

17 Desgodetz 1682, p. 165, pl. 1 (Friedman 1984, pl. 103). Whistler 1954, p. 155; Clarke 1963, p. 81; Downes 1977, p. 118, p. 152; Beard 1986, pp. 59, 136, pl. 86; Blatch 1997, figs 83, 142; Hart 2008, p. 239, figs 351–2; Langham-Carter, no date, p. 3.

18 Soane MS, vol. 26, f. 70.

19 During 1713–14, however, Hawksmoor proposed recasting medieval Oxford as a Roman town, including a 180 by 125 foot peripteral temple of eight by fourteen columns raised on a podium, and an alternative 150 foot square of twelve by fourteen columns with an independent campanile, called the 'Capella Universitatis' (Hart 2002, p. 194, figs 276–7, 282–3, 285). Gibbs submitted unsolicited 'Several Draughts for Churches', 14 May 1713 (Lambeth Palace Library, London, MS 2690, f. 87): pear tree wood 'Modell of a Church with a Colonade round it of Ionick

Order Steeple and inside finishing Complete' £25, 9 June 1713 ('James Gibbs's bill for Modells', MS 2708, f. 7; MS 2724, f. 2); listed 6 August 1733, 'No. 2 A Model with a Peristilum by . . . Gibbs' (MS 2724, ff. 4, 6, 8, 11), described by Donaldson 1843, no. 9, as 'imitation of . . . hexastyle peripteral Ionic temple . . . lofty steeple, rising over . . . pediment of . . . front portico at . . . short distance from . . . front . . . steps form . . . total height of 1½ in . . . order 11½ in. high; to top of pediment 16 inches. Total width, 22 inches, total length 47 inches', scale ¼ in. to 1 ft. Bill 1979, p. xviii, no. 9; Friedman 1984, pp. 303–4, pl. 30. For Madeleine, see Braham 1980, p. 256, pl. 345.

20 The temple measured 425 by 220 feet, with 127 columns, each 60 feet high (Soo 1998, pp. 169–73, figs 35–6), Hart 2002, figs 71a–b.

21 Friedman 1984, pp. 9–10.

22 During the Turkish regime the Acropolis was virtually inaccessible to non-Muslims, though see Spon 1678 (Tournikiotis 1994, pl. 14; also pl. 15: Fanelli 1707). Wren owned a copy of Spon (Watkin 1972, p. 24, lot. 318).

23 Pear-tree wood 'Model' £28 listed on 24 July 1713 ('James Gibbs's bill for Models', Lambeth Palace Library, MS 2708, f. 7), 6 August 1733, 'No 5 A Large model by . . . Gibbs' (MS 2724, ff. 2, 4, 6, 14), described by Donaldson 1843, no. 12, as 'very large model, of . . . Corinthian order . . . front represents a tetrastyle . . . disposition, with coupled columns . . . pediment over . . . tower at each of . . . four angles . . . One side of . . . flanks . . . plain, but . . . other . . . en-riched', 23 by 48 in., scale ¼ in. to 1 ft. Bill 1979, p. xviii, no. 12; Friedman 1984, p. 304. Surely not coincidentally, on 30 April 1713 Archer had delivered his St John, Westminster, 'Modell . . . wth: four Towers' (Doc. 267). Batty Langley stressed that 'as *public buildings* are erected for different purposes, the order . . . should be considered . . . if a church . . . in a city, the Corinthian . . . contains the properest emblem of the elegancy and riches' (*Grub-street Journal*, no. 244, 29 August 1734, p. 1).

24 Doc. 270: 15 July 1713 (Dickinson), 10 June 1714 (Archer), 2 November 1714 (Vanbrugh, untraced). Pls 407–8 in Hawksmoor's hand, though inscribed on verso 'For St Mary in ye Strand by J. King', presumably John King, a member of the building committee, 7 September 1712–2 December 1715 (Lambeth Palace Library, MS 2690, f. 58, MS 2711, f. 3; Bill 1979, p. xxiii), who may only have sponsored or delivered the design. Friedman 1984, p. 61, pl. 34.

25 Hart 2002, figs 52, 133. Compare the grouping of columns, piers and pilasters to Palladio's reconstruction of the early Christian, though thoroughly pagan-looking temple of Clitumnus near Spoleto (Tavernor and Schofield 1997, pp. 241–7, 310–14).

26 Cruickshank 1996, pp. 231, 237. It is topical that in 1718 Gibbs's former chief private patron, John Erskine, 6th Earl of Mar, designed a house with an elevation based on the Maison Carrée (Colvin 2008, p. 361).

27 Defoe 1991, vol. II, 1761 ed., p. 135, claimed this as 'the first Building wherein was introduced a Portico after the Manner of the ancient Temples'.

28 The features described above are illustrated in Downes, Amery and Stamp 2008, pp. 7, 12, 30 (parish map of 1720), 31, 38, 40–43, 48–9, 60, 666–7, 69, 71; Rocque 1746–7, 3AC.

29 Soane MS, vol. 26, f. 3. MacDonald 1976; Hart 2002, figs 61–2, 72, 183, 244, 259–60, 262–3.

30 Geraghty 2007, pp. 120–21, nos 175–8. Thornton 1784, p. 463, observing the lack of affinity of the building's parts, found the 'injudiciously . . . very large' lions and unicorns over the smaller columned stage 'preposterous' (Doc. 228: 1784).

31 Doc. 270. Recorded in 1826, subsequently vanished.

32 Dickinson experienced no such difficulties in his Ionic tetrastyle pseudoperipteral scheme (*circa* 1711–13; Geraghty 2007, p. 119, no. 174), perhaps associated with the Strand commission.

33 On 25 June 1712 'Mr. Campell deliver'd the Comittee Several Designes for New Churches for their consideracon' (Lambeth Palace Library, MS 2693, f. 11), presumably the inept British Architectural Library, Drawings and Archives Collection, Victoria and Albert Museum, London, nos 80.1–6, all but 5–6 inscribed 'Mr Cambell' (Harris 1973, p. 19, figs 172–7), and 'A new Design for a Church in Lincolns-Inn Fields' (1712), dedicated to Dr Lancaster, vicar of St Martin-in-the-Fields (Campbell 1715–25, vol. I, p. 3, pls 8–9).

34 See Glossary, under intercolumniation. Palladio described the eustyle of the Ionic temple of Diana, Ephesus, as 'the most beautiful and suitable kind of intercolumniation' (Tavernor and Schofield 1997, p. 32), as well as 'beautiful and elegant' (p. 219).

35 Campbell 1715–25, vol. II, pp. 1–2. In fairness to Gibbs, he intended designing a baroque rather than an 'antique'-style church.

36 Tavernor and Schofield 1997, pp. 248–50, 114, 116, 330–33, respectively, Palladio preferring a dedication to one of the Roman 'underworld deities' because 'the door . . . was at the front in such a way that [the cella] could not receive light from any direction'.

37 Westminster Abbey Muniments, 24878, dated 1723–35, quoted in Downes 1959, p. 255.

38 In Campbell 1715–25, vol. II, pls 82–3. Campbell published without comment a huge, free-standing domed chapel for Greenwich Hospital, though he did not pursue the scheme further during his tenure as Hospital surveyor (1726–9; Doc. 236).

39 A. Tirali's portico to San Nicolò da Tolentino (1706–14) and G. Scalfarotto's San Simeon Piccolo (1718–38), both Pantheon-inspired, are possible exceptions (Howard 1987, pp. 197–9, figs 105–6).

40 Ingamells 1997, pp. 81–2. Chaney 1998, p. 324.

41 Galilei's modern biographer, Dr Elizabeth Kieven, draws attention to a strong, long-standing predilection for 'the beautiful and simple architecture of the ancients' (Galilei's own words in 1723) enjoyed by the Florentine intellectual avant-garde in which he, together with his English friends and patrons resident there, moved (Kieven 2008, pp. 1–5). See also Kieven's reconstruction of a church project of 1716 featuring multiple, prostyle tetrastyle temple porticoes surrounding a domed octagonal body (p. 11, fig. 9).

42 Tavernor and Schofield 1997, pp. 225–32. Galilei's English

supporter, Thomas Hewett, wrote to him at Florence on 21 February 1720: 'I wish you could visit Rome once more & there very exactly take the Dimensions of the antique buildings especially those of the Grecian & best Taste, but don't meddle with the Gothique or mixt [styles] which are indeed "alla Italian" ' (Toesca 1952, pp. 217–18). This led to his radically classical façade of San Giovanni in Laterano (1733–6; Wittkower 1999, vol. III, pp. 13–15, pl. 13), a work that later interested both Gibbs (Soane MS, vol. 26, f. 40) and the Society of Antiquaries of London (Minute Book, II, f. 121, 4 December 1735).

43 Tavernor and Schofield 1997, pp. 248–50, called the Temple of the Sun and Moon (136, 307BC–12AD). Ward-Perkins 1981, p. 421, pl. 284.

44 From *The Wanderer*, 1729, lines 157–8 (Savage 1962, p. 134).

45 Doc. 269. See also 1729. Doc. 270: 13 January 1716.

46 Friedman 1984, p. 39, for a fuller reference.

47 Morris 1734, p. 132.

48 Rouquet 1755, pp. 95–6. Soane instructed his Royal Academy students that St Martin's 'Majestic . . . portico . . . with a noble flight of steps reminds us of an ancient temple of the best times', comparing it to the temple on the Ilissus and the gate to the Roman Agora, as well as to Saint Geneviève (the Panthéon), Paris (Watkin 1996, p. 610, pls I, 67). St Martin was synonymous with the definition of a portico: '*Portico* . . . the Front of a Church, &c. where *Columns* are detached from the Building, as the *west* End of St. *Martin's*' (Aheron 1754, Book III). As a member of the Society of Antiquaries of London, Gibbs would have known that he was building on a Roman site. William Stukeley reported to the Society on 2 May 1722 that 'the Roman building in St Martins Church was an Arch Built of Ro. Brick'; on 20 December 1722 he visited 'to see St Martins new Ch. [Lord Winchelsea] brought a couple of Roman brick found there'; on 28 July 1725 he showed a drawing of an ancient glass vase found in a coffin while 'digging the foundation of the Portico' on 17 March (Society of Antiquaries of London, Minute Book, I, pp. 61–2, 68, 151, 170).

49 Doc. 269. Friedman 1984, pp. 61–6, pls 35, 37–42.

50 Doc. 269: 20 October 1726, pp. 33, 15, respectively.

51 Lediard 1730, Book I, p. 1.

52 The origin of this composition was very likely the tower of Antonio da Sangallo's church at Montepulciano (1518–19), from where Gibbs also adapted the pyramid spire (Friedman 1984, pl. 41; Hermans 1987). The deployment of St Martin's paired giant order pilasters as bracketing agents at the ends of a façade dominated by a temple portico is also demonstrated in Gibbs's contemporary Cambridge Senate House, 1721–30 (Friedman 1984, pl. 253).

53 This interlocking system is graphically demonstrated in Britton and Pugin 1825–8, vol. I, pp. 42–5, ill.

54 See C. Perrault's reconstruction of the long-vanished Basilica at Fano based on Vitruvius's description (Perrault 1684, Livre V, pp. 152–5), Friedman 1984, p. 68, pl. 47.

55 Hempel 1965, p. 222, pl. 134B. This issue is discussed in Bury 1992, its significance in the eighteenth century in Arciszewska 2002, pp. 332–3.

56 Doc. 269: 3 October 1734. Gibbs's alternative reading on the model's north elevation of unadorned window frames set against rusticated walls was rejected by the building committee.

57 Doc. 269: 1736, p. 227, pl. XLVI, fig. III; fig. I is 'a Design of *Vignola's* . . . not to be commended, he having destroyed the natural Course of the Architrave and Freeze, for the Sake of making the key-stones monstrously high and narrow'. Wittkower 1974b. However, that Langley did not object in principle to the motif is apparent in his many published plagiarisms for secular use, including '*Rusticated Windows in all their Varities* . . . wherein the young Student will find much Pleasure and Delight' (Langley 1736, p. 340, pl. CCCLXI).

58 Doc. 269: 5 September 1734. Langley's solution was to adopt the 'much more natural . . . method' of Wren's St Andrew Holborn and St Clement Danes, 'where the galleries are supported by square pillasters' so the columns are presented 'in their utmost beauty' (3 October 1734). Gwynn (1766; p. 45) thought Gibbs at St Martin-in-the-Fields 'acquitted himself upon the whole tolerably well. The church . . . is esteemed one of the best in this city, though far from being so fine as it is usually represented to be, the absurd rustication of the windows, and the heavy sills and trusses under them are unpardonable blemishes, and very improperly introduced into this composition of the Corinthian order, as it takes away the delicacy which should be preserved in this kind of building. The steeple itself is good, but it is so contrived that it seems to stand upon the roof of the church, there being no appearance of its continuation from the foundation, and consequently it seems to want support . . . being formed by internal sweeps makes the angles too acute, which always produces an ill effect . . . Upon the whole [the] church is composed in a grand stile of one order, the portico is truly noble.'

59 Introduction, Gibbs 1728.

60 Doc. 269: 21 November 1721, May 1726, 1729.

61 Bill 1979, pp. xxiii–xxiv.

62 Doc. 144.

63 Illustrated in F. Bonanni, *Numismata Summorum Pontificum Templi Vaticani Fabricam*, 1696, a copy of which was in the library of Clarke's Oxford friend, the architect Dean Aldrich (Hiscock 1960, p. 25, pl. 28). McPhee 2002, fig. 145. An alternative, wholly English structure was erected above an engaged temple portico.

64 Doc. 161. Apparently, no model was produced. For the full building history, see Friedman 2004, chapter III.

65 In this context Simon Bradley has suggested that the use of the giant order 'seems more like a spill over from house architecture, where it had been the most exciting new fashion of the 1700s' and also cites Continental architects 'from Juvarra to Christopher Dientzenhofer . . . deploying [the motif] on their churches, without obvious echoes of the temple model' (Bradley 2005, p. 75). Of course, neither observations, while correct, take into account the fundamental notion of the temple-form church pervading English ecclesiastical architecture at this time.

66 Doc. 162: 2 October 1719, 1735.

67 Doc. 112: 25 August 1722.

68 Doc. 235: 14 July 1714.

69 Thoresby 1830, vol. II, p. 244, 29 July 1714. Society for Promoting Christian Knowledge, Archives, London, Minute Book IV, ff. 4–5, 193–4.
70 Doc. 112: 8 May 1723.
71 Campbell 1715–25, vol. I, pl. 9, a motif described in Halfpenny 1724, pp. 43–4, as 'taken from the works of the Moderns'. The tower door is based on Campbell's Burlington House gateway (1718–19; Campbell 1715–25, vol. III, pl. 25).
72 The Temple of Jupiter at Melasso and Hawksmoor's sketch of Wren's reconstructed Mausoleum at Halicarnassus, which he described as 'firm, yet airy' (Montfaucon 1721–2, vol. II, pl. V item 5, and 'Of the Sepulchre of Mausolus King of Caria' in Wren 1750; Soo 1998, p. 187, fig. 44; Friedman 1997b, fig. 17). Thoresby owned copies of Montfaucon and *Vitruvius Britannicus* (Piggott 1974, pp. 5, 36–8).
73 Saumarez Smith 1990, pp. 86, 137. A letter of 23 April 1725 refers to Etty visiting London 'in Hopes to see something that might be newer fashioned' (University of Kingston-upon-Hull Archives, DDHA 14/25–26).
74 Doc. 112: 15 May 1723.
75 Peet 1932, pp. 189, 228.
76 Doc. 120: under 25 June 1704 (Friedman 2004, pp. 67–8).
77 Doc. 118: 1774 (Enfield). Doc. 258: 25 June 1729–31. Hart 2002, figs 202, 247. Belfry windows filled with black marble also appear at St Luke, Old Street (Doc. 239: 25 March 1731).
78 Doc. 64: 1742.
79 Doc. 64: 1728 (Gibbs 1728).
80 Doc. 82: 22 July 1724.
81 Doc. 82: 22 October 1760
82 Defoe 1991, pp. 330–31.
83 Doc. 84: 9 March 1753.
84 Doc. 84: 1772, 1775. See also May 1766.
85 Doc. 84: 1758, 25 May 1760, 1772, 1797.
86 Doc. 245: 1728, 1729.
87 Doc. 228: 3 May 1716.
88 Hart 2002, pls 2, 239, 248.
89 Hanover Square was 'the most frequented Part of the Town by Quality' in 1722 (Macky 1722, vol. II, p. 4). The Vestry included the Duke of Devonshire, Earl of Coventry, Sir William Lowther, Sir Robert Walpole (Lambeth Palace Library, MS 2691, ff. 336–8, 31 May 1725).
90 Bodleian Library, University of Oxford, MS Rawl. B376, ff. 8–9, 20 October 1711.
91 Docs 239, 249: 9 June 1727.
92 Doc. 239: 8 August 1734. For Wren tower costs, see Jeffery 1996.
93 Doc. 239: 25 June 1729–25 March 1731.
94 Watkin 1972, p. 104 lot 104. On 20 February 1723 'Dr Knight brought a fine pair of Cavalier ffontana's [engravings] raising the great Obelisk before St Peters Chh. At Rome' (Society of Antiquaries of London, Minute Book, I, p. 84). For other iconographic readings of this and Horselydown's Ionic tower, see Hart 2002, pp. 100–01, pls 184–6, 219–20.
95 Doc. 270: 29 April 1714. However, the *Grub-street Journal*, no. 241 (8 August 1734), p. 1, remarked of Wren's St Antholin (1687–8, razed 1874) as having 'a lofty spire, crowned with an Ionic capital; a manner of finishing not to be produced in any other building about this city, and which is both elegant and magnificent'. Jeffery 1996, pp. 206–8, frontispiece.
96 Doc. 249: 11 July 1734. The medieval-style spire of St Andrew, Worcester, crowned by a Corinthian capital (1751; Doc. 203), is a reflection.
97 The dynamic polylobed plan has a parallel, perhaps coincidentally, in William Dickinson's plan of 1711–13 for an unidentified church for St Margaret, Westminster, parish (Lambeth Palace Library, MS 2750/57; Friedman 2004, fig. 52). Yarmouth's interior is strikingly similar to Wren's St Clement Danes, London (Doc. 92).
98 Doc. 15: 1742.
99 Doc. 37. The portico recalls Cesare Cesariano's reconstruction of a prostyle temple in *Di Lucio Vitruvio Pollione de Architectura*, vol. III, 1521, pl. 2 (Thoenes 2003, p. 71 item 4), which also features a prominent semicircular apse, corresponding to Redland's chancel, with its coffered barrel vault derived from the Temple of Peace (Basilica of Maxentius), Rome, illustrated in Ware 1738, Fourth Book, pp. 86–7, pl. II.
100 Doc. 61: 8 April 1759.

TWENTY-TWO BAROQUE BEYOND LONDON

1 Morris 1742, p. 6. Colvin 2008, pp. 704–5.
2 Lambeth Palace Library, London, MS 2690, f. 85, 7 May 1713.
3 Morris 1742, p. 15.
4 Doc. 258.
5 Doc. 260: 11 July 1734.
6 Doc. 221.
7 Docs 221, 259.
8 Dating All Saints is based on the fact that the Revd Dr Timothy Halton, listed as a trustee on an earlier scheme engraved by Sturt (identical to the above except in the positioning of the main north and south entrances in the middle bays), vacated his post as Provost of Queen's College in 1704 (*VCH*: *The University of Oxford*, vol. III, 1954, p. 137).
9 The latter may have origins in F. Mansart's Val-de-Grâce, Paris, as engraved in the *Grand Marot*, a copy of which Aldrich owned (Hiscock 1960, pl. 18).
10 Jeffery 1996, frontispiece, fig. 140.
11 However, see Aldrich's Trinity College chapel, Oxford, 1691–4, aligned by the Turl Street entrance to All Saints (Colvin 1983, pp. 29–32, figs 26–7). One of the builders, Bartholomew Peisley III, was grandson of a local mason who supplied stone for the cathedral, while Edward Strong, who served there as master mason, donated £30 15s. 0d. worth of stone from his Oxfordshire quarries for All Saints' porticoes (Doc. 140: 2 April 1700, 1711, October 1718). Fortuitously, St Paul's was the subject of engravings by William Emmett issued in 1702 (*Wren Society*, XIV, 1937, pls XIII–XV).
12 Doc. 140: 5 October 1710.

13 Colvin 2008, pp. 253–4.

14 The order is based on Diocletian's Baths, Rome, recommended in Evelyn's 1707 English edition of Fréart 1650, pp. 22–3, as 'one of the most excellent Pieces of *Architecture* . . . of so noble a Composition, and so Regular, that it's nothing inferior to that which went before'. See also Hawksmoor's unrealised High Street front for Queen's College, 1708–9 (Downes 1959, p. 279 no. 241, pl. 28).

15 Hawksmoor, as well as several members of Oxford colleges, were subscribers to James's English editions of 1707 (Watkin 1972, p. 103 lot 93). Fagiolo dell'Arco 1997, p. 510.

16 Doc. 129: December 1713. William Dawes, a New Churches Commissioner (Bill 1979, pp. xvii–xix) and Visitor of Queen's College, Oxford, was then Bishop of Chester, the diocese responsible for Manchester (Friedman 1997b, p. 83; Friedman 2004, p. 62).

17 The original west tower, recorded in 1732 (Doc. 129), so closely resembles Abbots Bromley, Staffordshire, 1702–7, that this interesting church may also be Barker's work (Staffordshire Record Office, D1209/1/2, f. 275; Gomme 2000, p. 405).

18 Doc. 195; untraced.

19 Recorded on a benefaction board in the church (K. Barnard and D. Barnard, 'Monumental Inscriptions of St Alkmund's Church Whitchurch Shropshire', typescript, 1987, church archives CH7). Doc. 195: 28 January 1712.

20 McParland 2001, p. 44, pls 45–7. Robinson visited London in 1674, 1677 and 1679 (Loeber 1981, pp. 88–9, 95). Loeber 1979, p. 58, pl. 11a.

21 Doc. 120: 1703; Doc. 129: 1713, 1752; Doc. 92: 24 March 1714; Doc. 147: 1719.

22 McParland 2001, pp. 9, 182–3, fig. 1. Galilei has also been associated with the enigmatic garden temple at Drumcondra near Dublin, based on Roman baroque church façade elements (Howley 1993, p. 140, pls 226–7). In January 1714, before setting out for England, Galilei examined Carlo Fontana's collection of architectural designs, including many for churches, then deposited in the Vatican; in 1762 it was acquired by Robert Adam's brother James, then in Rome, on behalf of the royal collection, now deposited in Windsor Castle (Sicca 2008, p. 200).

23 Loeber 1981, p. 36; McParland 2001, p. 45, figs 49–50; Blunt 1982, pp. 29–30.

24 Ingamells 1997, p. 666. The ungainly domed superstructure, owing much to Wren's St Magnus Martyr (Jeffery 1996, fig. 43), was not erected; a version of St Mary, Islington, was put up (1766–8; Severens 1992–3; Loeber 1979, p. 54; McParland 2001, pp. 45, 216 n. 162, fig. 49; *Gentleman's Magazine*, November 1754, p. 529; Craig 1992, pp. 178–9, pl. XXVII.

25 Blunt 1982, p. 48; Wittkower 1999, vol. II, pl. 66. San Giacomo was engraved in Falda 1665–9, vol. III, pl. 26, and Rossi 1684, pls 56–8. St Ann's Italian origin was common knowledge. Lewis 1837, vol. I, p. 553, described it as 'designed from a church in Rome'. Only the lower storey and mezzanine were realised, rebuilt in 1868. A third Dublin façade initiated by King, St Nicholas Within (begun 1707, rebuilt *circa* 1837), also had Roman origins (*Gentleman's Magazine*, May 1786, p. 390, fig. 9).

26 Toesca 1952, p. 211. Italianate motifs lingered in the door case of St Mark, Pearse Street, Dublin (1729–52), copied from G. B. Vignola, *Regola delli cinque ordini d'architettura*, 1562 (Harris and Savage 1990, pp. 458–62; McParland 2001, fig. 5). For Molesworth's continuing interest in Galilei's Italian churches, see Toesca 1952, pp. 219–20. A fuller account of Galilei's Irish sojourn must await the publication of Elizabeth Kieven's biography.

27 Doc. 5. Colvin 2008, pp. 359–62. Gibbs very likely designed the pair of marble wall monuments for St Mungo, Alloa (now re-sited in the nearby mausoleum), commemorating recently deceased members of the Erskine family (Royal Commission on Historical Monuments, Scotland, photographs A80209–10; *Buildings of Scotland: Stirling and Central Scotland*, 2002, pp. 134–5); oval cartouches embellished with flamboyant cherubs' heads, scrolls, leaves and coats of arms of a Roman baroque type (Millon 1984), which Gibbs, who must have known Juvara in Rome, particularly relished (Gibbs Collection, vol. 1, ff. 54–5, 65, 70, and Gibbs 1728, p. xxiv, pls 128–35). I am grateful to Margaret Stewart for alerting me to the Alloa monuments, making them possibly Gibbs's earliest executed works. For Gibbs–Mar relations, see Friedman 1984.

28 Ingamells 1997, pp. 638–9; Colvin 2008, p. 360, untraced.

29 The latter appear at Saint Jean-en-Etienne aux Minimes (1700–15), Notre-Dame du Finistère (1708–30), Brussels, and the Jesuit church of St Loup, Namur (begun 1621; Hubert 1998, p. 36; Vlieghe 1998, pl. 378). Mar's scheme 'Drawen at Paris Octob: 1722' (The National Archives of Scotland, Edinburgh [formerly The Scottish Record Office], PHR 13258/31) was perhaps inspired by L. Le Vau's and P. Le Muet's Hôpital de la Salpetrière, Paris (1660; Minguet 1988, pp. 173–4).

30 Doc. 5: March 1726.

31 Doc. 223: 24 October 1711.

32 Harris and Savage 1990, pp. 242–3.

33 Bill 1979, p. xxiii.

34 Pye 1760, pp. 46, 52.

35 Doc. 184: 1722.

36 Doc. 184: 30 April 1714, echoing Hawksmoor's estimated cost at Greenwich of 'Carrying . . . two Arcades or Breaks on the North and South Side' (Doc. 235: 23 February 1713).

37 At Greenwich brick was rejected in favour of ashlar (Doc. 235: 9 July 1712).

38 Doc. 51: November 1713.

39 Doc. 183.

40 City of London, London Metropolitan Archives, ACC 262/50/59 (Friedman 1996c, p. 115, fig. 1; Jenkins 2007, fig. 9).

41 Doc. 194: 7 September 1714.

42 St Paul's screens (Downes 1988, figs 196–7; *Wren Society*, XIV, 1937, pl. XXV) were also models for similar structures at Cruwys Morchard, north Devon (*Buildings of England: North Devon*, 1952, p. 80, pl. 24b), and St Paul's Walden, Hertfordshire (1727), erected by Edward Gilbert, a member of the Grocers' Company, London (*Buildings of England: Hertfordshire*, 1953, p. 229, pl. 20b; Whitelaw 1990, p. 119).

43 Bill 1979, p. xxiv, appointed 2 December 1715. Doc. 1.

44 Letter dated 6 July 1752 (Beamish, Hillier and Johnstone 1976, pp. 57, 62, cited in Jeffery 1986, p. 190).

45 Doc. 26: 1735–42 (Milles).

46 St Mary, Charlton Marshall, Dorset, 1713–15, a medieval fabric remodelled by the brothers' father, Thomas Bastard, features Doric arcades separating the nave and north aisle that might have been lifted from James 1707, figs XLV–XLVI.

47 Represented by a set of unsigned drawings (Shropshire Records and Research Unit, Shrewsbury, 6000/17808–17813). The client, Edward Ward, was the son of the Chief Baron of the Exchequer and one of the original 1696 subscribers towards building Greenwich Hospital, James's territory (*Dictionary of National Biography*, vol. XX, pp. 768–9; Colvin 2008, pp. 564–8). For Stoke's building history, see Shropshire Records and Research Unit, D17791, H/1419 Hunt of Boreatton Papers 17789; Northamptonshire Record Office, Faculty Register 1, ff. 161V–166, 304P/23, ff. 1–8, 24, 28, Capron Southwick Deposit). Whiffen 1948, p. 39, pls 29, 118; *Buildings of England: Northamptonshire*, 1961, p. 415, pl. 37; Downes 1966, p. 109, pl. 485.

48 Saumarez Smith 1990, p. 60. William was in London in 1703 consulting with Vanbrugh and Hawksmoor (p. 86).

49 Doc. 147: 3 October 1716.

50 Doc. 147. However, this evidence is not so conclusive as it may seem (Colvin 2008, p. 366). William Dobson, Robert Monkhouse and Robert Harrison were paid for drawings, unspecified and untraced, on 12 October 1720 (Doc. 147). Under comparable circumstances at Holy Trinity, Leeds, unquestionably designed by Etty, Benjamin Maxwell was paid on 12 November 1723 for 'drawing draughts & offering to undertake to make the roof' (Doc. 112).

51 Doc. 147: undated letter following 19 December 1719.

52 Doc. 147: 3 October 1716. See also St Paul, Sheffield (Doc. 161).

53 Downes 1977, pl. 32. Fiennes 1982, p. 198, in 1698 remarked that the stone 'look'd so red . . . at my entrance into the town [that she] thought its buildings were all of brick . . . but after found it to be the collour of the stone which I saw in the Quarrys look very red', and which to Hoare 1983, p. 138, 7 July 1800, 'gives it a very heavy appearance'.

54 Doc. 147: 1717–18, 10 November 1722.

55 Doc. 147: undated letter following 19 December 1719. *Wren Society*, XIII (1936), p. 33; XV (1938), pp. 3, 25, 28, 46, 52.

56 Downes 1977, p. 103. James Mewburn of Seaton was negotiating for timber to be transported from York by boat in October 1719 (house archives).

57 Doc. 178: Act of Parliament of 1719. George Causfield, who was paid £133 2s. 11d. for 'ffree stone worke' at Sunderland, which was measured by Etty (undated payments, 1720), was a mason based at Seaton Sluice, the Delaval estate wharfage (Colvin 2008, p. 238).

58 Doc. 178: undated payment, 1720. Beard 1981, p. 270.

59 Downes 1977, pls 6, 8. A similar combination of elements marks the chapel frontispiece of Fountaine Almshouses, Linton-in-Craven, Yorkshire, 1720 or 1721. The founder, Richard Fountaine, a timber merchant who supplied building materials for Castle Howard, strengthens an attribution to Etty as architect. Downes 1966, p. 111, fig. 499, and Downes 1977, p. 122, pls 6, 8, attributes the design to William Wakefield of York. No building accounts or other relevant papers for the almshouses are known. The small central chapel is lit by a Serliana. The closely similar rusticated Tuscan porch, 1726, at St Andrew, Newcastle upon Tyne, Northumberland, may also be Etty's work (Baille 1801, p. 258; Honeyman 1941, p. 141, pl. X, 3; McCombie 2009, p. 170, pl. 117).

60 Whitehead 1992; Gomme 2000, pp. 405, 559. Compare to St Thomas, Southwark, 1699–1703 (Jeffery 1996, pp. 353–5, fig. 187).

61 Downes 1977, p. 95, pl. 233; Tanner 1961; *Buildings of England: Buckinghamshire*, 1994, p. 245; Gomme 2000, pp. 350–51, 520, pl. 269.

62 Docs 116, 47.

63 British Library, Add. MS 15,776, f. 134, adding that the Shire Hall (1724, by Fisher of Bristol) was 'built I believe by a worse Architect'. *Buildings of Wales: Gwent/Monmouthshire*, 2000, p. 401, pl. 72. For the Smiths' other churches, see Colvin 2008, pp. 941–2; Gomme 2000.

64 Plot 1686, pp. 297–8, described Ingestre as 'uniform and elegant . . . with a well proportiond *Tower* . . . ceiled with the finest plaister, garnisht . . . with deep and noble Fretwork', accompanied by an engraved view (*Wren Society*, XIX, 1942, p. 57, pl. XV). The client, Walter Chetwynd, was Wren's fellow-member of the Royal Society.

65 Campbell 1715–25, pls 3–11, including St Philip, Birmingham.

66 Trubshaw, Gibbs and Smith each worked at Catton Hall, Derbyshire (Friedman 1984, pp. 146–7, 298).

67 Doc. 169. For Trubshaw's other churches, see Friedman 2001; Colvin 2008, pp. 1058–9.

68 Wrighte, lord of the manor, applied to the Bishop of Lincoln for a licence to replace the 'very old, uncomely . . . ruinous' church at his own expense (Anon., *History of Gayhurst*, undated). A faculty was issued on 23 March 1725 to rebuild in 'a more Beautiful . . . Handsome Manner [fitted up] very Decently' (Clarke 1963, p. 53). Inscribed on the west tower: 'Gloriae Dei Omnipotentis, Georgius Wrighte Armiger (Nathan Wrighte Equistis Aurati, hand ita pridern Magni Sigili Angliae Cultodis Filius natu maximus) hujus Manerij nec non adjacentis Villae de Stoke-Goldington, primus ex Genere suo Dominus Ecclesiam hanc, quam vivus instaurare in animo habuit, moriens begavit. Anno Donmn. 1728'. Partly restored in 1883. R. Tunstall measured drawings, 1949 (National Monuments Record Centre, English Heritage, Swindon, photographs); restored 1960–73 (Whiffen 1948, pp. 39–40, pl. 38; Downes 1977, pp. 108, 110, pls 264–5, 482; Chatfield 1979, pp. 13–15 ill.; *Buildings of England: Buckinghamshire*, 1994, pp. 84, 335–6, pl. 67). For the Wrighte monument in the church, see Craske 2007, pp. 129–30, fig. 72.

69 Le Muet appeared in an English edition by Robert Pricke, *The Art of Fair Building* (Harris and Savage 1990, pp. 288–9). *VCH: Staffordshire*, vol. III, 1913, p. 102; Chandler and Hannah 1949, pp. 136–7; Roper 1968, p. 9; Gomme

2000, pp. 410, 413, 526, pl. 256. The four-bay body dominated by tall, round-headed windows follows a familiar William Smith Sr arrangement (Whitchurch, Shropshire, pl. 445; St Peter at Arches, Lincolnshire, pl. 466), while the scrolled consoles linking the lower and upper stages of the tower recall Abbots Bromley (1702–7, architect unknown). Staffordshire Record Office, D 1209/1/2, f. 275, D 3924/1/11; Shipman 1979, p. 5; Gomme 2000, p. 405.

70 Doc. 54: 1707–10. Bridgeman's outstanding involvement was noted on 13 February 1711.

71 For example, Britannia House, *circa* 1725 (*Buildings of England: Worcestershire*, 2007, pl. 75) and the tomb to Henrietta Wrottesley (died 1719), signed 'White' (Thomas 1737, p. 84 ill.). The open-bedded, segmental pediment with advancing corners raised on panelled strips framing a raised panel at Castle Bromwich is echoed in White's Brydges tomb (*circa* 1742), Bosbury, Herefordshire (Whiffen 1945, p. 1005 ill.).

72 *Wren Society*, XVIII (1941), p. 189, pl. XIII.

73 Harris and Savage 1990, pp. 352–5.

74 Stukeley 1882–7, vol. III, p. 279, 4 September 1721. Doc. 24: 27 September 1714, 3 October 1715.

75 Gibbs 1728, pl. 31. Doc. 204.

76 A local reflection of the St Philip–St Nicholas frontispieces is All Saints (1737–42), probably designed by Richard Squire, with White's bust of Bishop Hough set in the east pediment (*Journals of the House of Commons*, vol. XXIII, pp. 33, 48; *Gentleman's Magazine*, May 1738, p. 274; Worcestershire Record Office, 899:13, BA 3762; Green 1764, p. 220; *Wren Society*, XVIII, 1941, pl. XIV; Roscoe 2009, p. 1375; Whiffen 1945, p. 36, pl. 140; Downes 1977, p. 108, pl. 467; *Buildings of England: Worcestershire*, 2007, p. 317, pls 77, 82). St Thomas, Stourbridge (1727–9), located between Worcester and Birmingham, was probably designed by the Birmingham builder William Westley Jr, who was employed at St Philip (Doc. 24: 7 October 1709, 16 May, 21 October 1711; Colvin 2008, p. 1106; Worcestershire Record Office, 850/8520/5[1]; Chambers 1979, pp. 5–9, 13–14, 19, 28–9, 31–2 item 8 (Dudley Archives and Local History Service); Whiffen 1948, p. 37, pl. 40; Downes 1977, p. 109, pls 472–3; *Buildings of England: Worcestershire*, 2007, p. 268, pl. 76). Stourbridge and Swinford parishes subscribed £16 0s. 9d. towards the above, on 27 September 1714. Joseph Westley, presumably a relative, was employed at Castle Bromwich, 1724–6 (Doc. 54).

77 Campbell 1715–25, vol. I, Introduction.

78 Campbell 1715–25, vol. II, p. 2, entry for pl. 27, Campbell's Vitruvian Church.

79 Doc. 270: 7 November 1734, 1741.

80 Doc. 267: 1734.

81 Doc. 223: 1758, 1759, 28 August 1761, 1775.

82 Doc. 223: 1753.

83 Wren 1750, p. 282. By 1759 the model had 'suffered to run to Decay' (Doc. 223: *Historical Account*).

84 Doc. 223: 3d. in 1726 (*New Guide to London*).

85 Doc. 119: 1794 (Moss, Wallace), 1795 (Aikin).

86 Chitham 1985, p. 35. Neufforge 1757–68, vol. V, 56e Cayée, and *Supplement*, XLIIe Cahier and XLIIIe Cahier.

87 Doc. 119: 1769, repeated 1771 (Young 1770–71).

88 Friedman 2004, pl. 53.

89 Doc. 267: 29 September 1742, 16, 23 November 1744.

90 Doc. 267: 1716 memorial, 29 September 1742, 4, 25 June, 26 October, 16, 23 November 1744, 18 May 1745. Friedman 2004, fig. 56.

91 Malcolm 1803–7, vol. IV, p. 168, in 1807.

92 Malcolm 1803–7, vol. III, p. 479; vol. II, p. 82; vol. III, p. 387; vol. II, p. 418; vol. IV, p. 283, respectively.

93 Watkin 1996, pp. 610, 541, 646.

94 *The World By Adam Fitz-Adam*, vol. II, 1757, dated 14 February 1754.

TWENTY-THREE THE PERSISTENCE OF WRENIAN AND GIBBSIAN PATTERNS

1 Sir George Wheler on proposals to build Spital Square Chapel in 1693 (*Survey of London*, vol. XXVII, 1957, pp. 101–2). The chapel was erected in 1714.

2 Introduction to Gibbs 1728 (Harris and Savage 1990, p. 212).

3 Thoresby 1830, vol. I, p. 341; vol. II, p. 20, in 1701 and 1709.

4 Paterson 1714, introduction. Listed in Colvin 2008, pp. 1161–5; Jeffery 1996.

5 Destructions listed in Huelin 1996. Paterson 1714, p. 66, praised St Christopher as 'very neat, decent and beautiful' following improvements to the steeple, which included 'pulling down . . . from . . . top of . . . Battlements to . . . 2d. Floor', adding '3 New Storys inside . . . outside, wth . . . Gothick Battlements . . . 4 pine[apple]s . . . 4 pinnacles 28 ft. high each . . . whole worke beginning top of . . . first old floor . . . carry'd up in new worke 99 f: . . . to . . . top of . . . pinnacles', for which Edward Strong Jr received £2,050 2s. 1½d., witnessed by William Dickinson (Guildhall Library, City of London Corporation, MS 25539/12, ff. 36–8, 9 October 1712); Jeffery 1996, p. 228.

6 Guildhall Library, MS 4425/2, 26 October, 15 November 1780, 20 February, 10 April, 3, 11, 13 December 1781; Bank of England Archives, M5/748, ff. 87–97 (March 1781, 1784), G4/23, ff. 245, 251, 257 (31 January–28 March 1782). Bradley and Pevsner 1997, p. 101; Huelin 1996, p. 46; Abramson 2005, pp. 85–7, figs 66, 73.

7 Ralph 1734, p. 23.

8 Harris and Savage 1990, pp. 265, 381–5.

9 *Grub-street Journal*, no. 245 (5 September 1734), p. 1.

10 Ralph 1734, pp. 13, 23. Wren's judicious handling of Holborn's internal arches is also commended in Langley 1736, p. 363, pl. CCLXXX.

11 Port 2006, pls 141, 157.

12 Hatton 1708, pp. 95–580.

13 Largely repeated in *The Pocket Remembrancer; or, A Concise History of the City of London*, *circa* 1750.

14 Pote 1729, pp. 54, 58. A third edition, *The Foreigner's Guide*, 'Revised, Corrected, Improved, and brought down to the present Time', appeared in 1752.

15 Listed in Adams 1983. Several churches were represented by single-sheet engravings, for example, St Bride (*Wren Society*, XVIII, 1941, pl. VII).

16 Osborne 1758, p. 30.

17 On 1 July 1766 Colley of Bridgnorth delivered a 'true Estimate . . . with plans [untraced] for a new Church & Steeple at Quatt' specifying '3 Stone door cases . . . 5 Cemicurculer window ends . . . 2 Curculer Windows with Cornish', glass, plaster, lead, tiles, pewing, etc., a total of £1,126 1s. 6d. (Shropshire Records and Research Unit, Shrewsbury, 4237/Ch/ 29b–c); early views (Shropshire Records and Research Unit, 6001/372, II, f. 31, 11 August 1790; 6009/163); Glynne 1997, p. 81; Ionides 1999, p. 283, pl. 12-A1; *Country Life* (8 March 1979), pp. 634–7, fig. 2. See also John Olley's Emmanuel Almshouses chapel, Westminster (1699–1701), Guildhall Library, Rep. 106, f. 119, John Deane mason (Colvin 2008, pp. 759–60). Olley's 'Prospect', 'Ground Plot', plan, elevation of 'Emmanuel Hospital Founded by . . . Lady Dacres', City of London (London Metropolitan Archives, Court of Aldermen, vol. 109, f. 612). Extensively repaired in 1846, demolished in 1893 (Paul 1984, pls i–ii; Hobhouse 1971, p. 146 ill.). *The Case of the Inhabitants of the Parish of St Mary Woolnoth, London*, undated (British Library, 816.m.9.[108]), fabric report by 'able Surveyors', including Olley (*Wren Society*, XIX, 1942, p. 35).

18 Doc. 172: following 6 June 1710, 1711 Act of Parliament, 21, 23 August 1712. Brewster 1796, pp. 121–2; Bill 1979, p. xxiii. Wren's family originated at Binchester, 15 miles from Stockton (*Wren Society*, XVIII, 1941, p. 181).

19 For another early appearance of this motif, see Henry Bell's North Runcton, Norfolk, 1703–4 (Anon., 'Bell of Lynn: A Contemporary of Sir C. Wren', RIBA Essay Medal, 1928; *BAC*, X(079)E, pp. 15–16, measured drawings; Colvin and Wodehouse 1961, pp. 55, 57; Whiffen 1948, p. 21; *Buildings of England: Norfolk 2*, 1999, p. 573, pl. 96.

20 Colvin 2008, p. 1155; Bill 1979, p. xxiii.

21 Kruft 1994, p. 138, pl. 85; Watkin 1972, p. 27, lot 376. Hulsbergh's Bow engraving is dated 1721, in Du Prey 2000, pp. 106, 160 n. 66. Little is known of Wilsthorpe's building history: Edward Curtis, lord of the manor, 'lately at his own charge rebuilt' it (Lincolnshire Archives, Lincoln, Fac 9/20; Clarke 1963, p. 209). The front is dated 1715. The fabric was altered in 1862–3, including window mullions and the addition of a spire (*Buildings of England: Lincolnshire*, 1989, pp. 801–2). The arcaded parapet with flanking urns also appears in a church design associated with Vanbrugh (Hart 2008, fig. 167).

22 'A large fine town [with] 24 streets . . . faire and long [with] houses of brick and stone built high and even [and] abundance of persons . . . very well dress'd and of good fashion . . . its London in miniature as much as ever I saw any thing [though with only] one Church' (St Nicholas), observed Celia Fiennes in 1698 (Fiennes 1982, pp. 183–4). The population had reached 5,714 by 1700 (Enfield 1774, p. 28).

23 Doc. 120: 1701.

24 Jeffery 1996, fig. 183.

25 Doc. 129: 1752.

26 Sir James Lowther recommended St James, Westminster, as the template for St Nicholas, Whitehaven (1687–93, demolished), based on a model prepared in London in 1686 (untraced, architect unknown), which the congregation opposed, the patron retorting: 'let the Towne please themselves, I only tell you wt is most approved in London' (Cumbria Record Office, D/Lons/W2/1/21, 27 April, 21 September 1686). Collier 1991, pp. 30, 34, pl. 14.

27 Gery 1707, Dedication, pp. 14, 22. Sir Orlando Gee bequeathed £500 'towards . . . *Rebuilding or Repairing* . . . at . . . discretion of Trustees', 25 May 1705; on 15 October the nobility and gentry 'subscrib'd so liberally as gave Encouragement to proceed . . . Orders . . . for workmen to prepare . . . Schemes and Proposals', delivered on 9 December; on 27 January 1706 'Trustees . . . consider'd . . . several Persons, approv'd . . . *John Price* of *Richmond* and concluded with Him'; on 18 February the 'old Church [was] taken down' (Bodleian Library, University of Oxford, MS Rawl. B389c, f. 22). Exterior views published in Harrison 1775, p. 567, pl. 88; Thornton 1784, following p. 488; *Gentleman's Magazine* (December 1799), pp. 1025, 1027. *Buildings of England: London 3*, 1991, p. 429.

28 Doc. 252: 7 December 1711.

29 Doc. 252: 19 June 1746, 1748, 1775.

30 Watkin 1972, p. 42, lot 31: 'A Hundred and fourteen large and finished Drawings of *St Paul's, Bow*, and other Churches in *London*'; lot 34: 'An hundred Drawings and Sketches of *London* Churches'. Geraghty 2007, p. 3.

31 Doc. 226: 1750; Doc. 266: 1750. Ralph (1734) considered St Andrew's interior 'neat . . . well-finish'd, as the manner and taste it is form'd in will allow'.

32 Doc. 266: 1750.

33 Doc. 240: February 1754.

34 The church was 'distinguished for its beautifull neatness and simplicity' (Doc. 243: June 1788). Such porticoes were also favoured at Clapham Common (pl. 74) and St Mary, Newington, London (1792–3, demolished 1876), by Francis Hurlbatt (Lambeth Palace Library, London, VH79/111/1–4; Manning and Bray 1804–14, vol. III, p. 451; *Buildings of England: London 2*, 1983, p. 576; Clarke 1966, pp. 168–9).

35 Doc. 266: 2, 11 June, 1 August 1789, 11 February 1790.

36 Doc. 187: 5 July 1787, 7 April 1789, July 1790.

37 Osborne 1758, p. 17. For an insightful analysis, see Bradley and Pevsner 1997, pp. 126–9, pl. 30. Jeffery 1996, pp. 206–8, 214–16, 324–5, figs 83–4, 89, 170–71.

38 Doc. 225: 1768 (referring to Wren as 'our English Vitruvius'), 1734, 1754, 1760.

39 Doc. 248: 18 February, 6 September 1758.

40 Doc. 248: 13 April 1758, p. 139. Colvin 2008, p. 151.

41 For a similar design, see 'a small Church or Chapel 50 *ft.* Diameter within, and 32–6 to the Center of the Dome, which is supported by eight Columns', in Rawlins 1768, p. 30.

42 Doc. 225: 8 August 1734, 1761. Wren's early, unexecuted study for the church incorporated just such a feature (Furst 1956, pp. 22–4, pls 29–30).

43 It had parallels on the Continent: the subject of the Grand Prix of the 1760 French Concours was an 'église paroissiale [with a] portail sur une place' (Perouse de Montclos 1984, p. 71), while the Concorso Clementino in Rome of 1762 was a porticoed 'Facciata per la chiesa di S. Adriano al Campo Vaccino' (Marconi, Cipriani and Valeriani 1974, vol. I, nos 612–25).

44 Cumbria Record Office, D/Lons/W2/1/47, 23 March 1714. Rocque 1746–7, Bb. The Whitehaven building subscription was launched on 1 February 1713 (Whitehaven Library, Church Book, Accounts of Building); on 12 February 1714 Lowther expressed willingness to donate a site (Chester Record Office, EDA 2/4, ff. 269–82); the church was erected by October 1715 (Cumbria Record Office, D/Lons/W2/1/59–60) for £1,900 (Chalkin 1984, p. 295); it was destroyed in a fire in 1871 (Burkett and Sloss 1995, pp. 11–12). Collier 1991, p. 15. St George was founded as a chapel of ease in 1706 (Paterson 1714, pp. 86–7; Clarke 1966, p. 84); on 16–17 October 1711 it was a 'Large Spacious building' capable of holding 2,000 and made a parochial church (Lambeth Palace Library, MS 2690, f. 4 and back f. 1), though Hawksmoor reported on 23 October that the thin walls 'make whole Edifice Ruinous' (MS 2724, f. 119v); he subsequently made it 'convenient . . . for Divine Worship', 1717–23 (MS 2697, ff. 9–25; MS 2690, ff. 347, 350; MS 2724, ff. 61v, 65, 132v); Downes 1959, p. 277 nos 95–7. It was remodelled in the years 1817–68 (Clarke 1963, pp. 208–9).

45 Doc. 85: 25 May 1760.

46 Doc. 85: 15 March, 3 May 1750, 26 September 1751.

47 Rocque 1746–7, 14a–b. The 'front . . . carried up flat with niches and ornaments . . . on summit . . . a pediment . . . body . . . divided into . . . central part projecting forwarder than . . . rest, and two sides . . . central part has two tall windows terminated by . . . pediment . . . in . . . midst . . . an oval window . . . sides . . . only . . . compartment below with . . . circular window above . . . corners . . . wrought in . . . bold, plain rustic . . . tower rises square from . . . roof . . . at . . . corners . . . urns with flames . . . turret in . . . lanthorn form with flaming urns . . . covered with . . . dome . . . ball . . . fane, in . . . form of . . . rampant lion' (Dodsley and Dodsley 1761, vol. V, pp. 228–9). The furnishings are now in the Swedish Church, Harcourt Street, St Marylebone (*Buildings of England: London 3*, 1991, p. 605).

48 Doc. 265: 31 October 1734.

49 Doc. 269.

50 Gibbs 1728, pls 1, 3, 7, 9–10, 12, 14–15, 29–30.

51 An 'Elevation of the South Front' and plan for Walmersley attached to a petition of April 1767 (Lancashire Record Office, QSP 1906/50) is linked to a Manchester Justice of the Peace report of 7 May on the 'very antient [chapel] so ruinous . . . so great danger of falling [which] must be wholly taken down and rebuilt' for £1,063 18s. 7d. (1906/48). It was rebuilt in 1883 (*Buildings of England: Lancashire I*, 1969, p. 100). Doc. 30 (Bradshaw), Doc. 101 (Horwich). It is unclear if these three schemes were carried out since the buildings all vanished in the nineteenth century without visual record. The duplication of almost identical designs may reflect a regional economic policy, as in the case of Henry Sephton's twin chapels at Billinge and Darwen, Lancashire (Docs 20, 60). The 'Gibbs surround' entered the Irish pattern book repertory in J. Aheron's *A General Treatise of Architecture*, 1754 (Whiffen 1948, p. 34), which he was compiling by 1745 (Harris and Savage 1990, pp. 104–7). A handsome example is Ballymore, Co. Donegal, 1752 (McParland 2001, p. 44, fig. 44).

52 Doc. 23.

53 Doc. 68. Fawcett 1994, pp. 162–3, 189, fig. 6.2.

54 Doc. 254. Illustrated in Montfaucon 1719 (Friedman 1993, pl. 118).

55 Doc. 109: 12, 22 June 1747. See also Gibbs's unsuccessful design of 1730 for St Giles-in-the-Fields (Doc. 229).

56 William Halfpenny's designs of 1739 to build the cathedral anew came to nought (Friedman 1998a), nor did Thomas Ivory's for rebuilding the medieval steeple in 1773 (Corporation Council Minutes). Robert's scheme was selected in 1774 and implemented by 1792 (Girouard 1992, pp. 159–60, pls 133, 136) at a cost of £5,397 (Lewis 1837, vol. II, p. 690); there were various nineteenth-century alterations (p. 691): Galloway 1992, pp. 216–17. Roberts repeated the dosseret motif as a giant order in the nearby Catholic cathedral (1792–3; Galloway 1992, p. 221; Girouard 1992, pp. 160–62, pl. 138).

57 Doc. 89. See also St John, Hampstead, London (1744–7; Doc. 231); Christ Church, Bristol (1786–91; Doc. 34); Wanstead, Essex (1787–90), with its rich, crisply detailed artificial Coade stone capitals (Doc. 187); St Martin, Worcester (1768–72; Worcester Record Office, b850, 5234/5; *Journals of the House of Commons*, vol. XXX, p. 7; Anon. 1808, p. 71; Kingsley 1988, p. 140); cost £2,215 (Chalkin 1984, p. 287), altered 1855–6 (Clarke 1963, p. 209). Whiffen 1948, p. 55, pl. 59; *Buildings of England: Worcestershire*, 2007, pp. 713–14.

58 Doc. 254: 1729.

59 See Gibbs's St Giles, Shipbourne, Kent (1722–3, demolished 1880; Soane MS, vol. 26, f. 96; British Library, 694.k.10[20]; Whiffen 1948, pl. 52; *Country Life*, 16 November 1958, p. 112; Friedman 1984, pp. 72–3, 258, 302–3, pl. 55). William and David Hiorne's St Bartholomew, Birmingham, 1747–50 (*Ariss's Birmingham Gazette*, XII, no. 611; *Gentleman's Magazine*, July 1764, p. 328; Hutton 1783, p. 113; Dugdale 1819, vol. IV, p. 408; Langford 1870, vol. I, pp. 16, 25, 113, 207), restored 1893, demolished 1937–43 (*VCH: Warwickshire*, vol. VII, 1964, pp. 361–2).

60 Rocque 1746–7, 9B–CB; City of Westminster Archives Centre, C766a, ff. 157, 160, 163, 167–8, 183 (Clarke 1963, pp. 195–6), *Survey of London*, vol. XXXIX, 1977, pp. 10, 19, 23, 29, 104, 118–19, 132, 157, fig. 7, pls 1, 12b; vol. XL, 1980, pp. 290, 298–302, figs 68–70, 76a–d; Colvin 2008, pp. 1042–3.

61 Colvin 2008, p. 596.

62 Gibbs 1732, p. 34, pl. XLVIII.

63 Doc. 247. Horne's other London churches, St Katherine Coleman (1739–42, demolished 1927) and St Mary, Ealing (1739, demolished 1866), relied heavily on the use of Gibbs surrounds, less so Holy Trinity, Guildford, Surrey (1741–63; Colvin 2008, pp. 54–5). See also S. Leadbetter's Portland or Foley Chapel (later St Paul), Great Portland St, St Marylebone (1758–66, restored 1883, demolished 1908) for the 3rd Duke of Portland (City of Westminster Archives Centre, Ashbridge 243/525–6; Guildhall Library, 55374; *The Builder*, 25 April 1908, p. 482 ill.). Park Street Chapel,

Mayfair (1762), built by the carpenter John Spencer and William Timbrell on land acquired by the latter's father, Benjamin Timbrell, in 1739 (*Survey of London*, vol. XXXIX, 1977, pl. 49a–b). St Anne's Chapel, Newcastle upon Tyne (1764–8), by W. Newton (*Newcastle Courant*, 2 October 1762, p. 2; 3 September 1768, p. 2; Harvey 1794, pp. 23–4; Dugdale 1819, vol. III, p. 721; Sykes 1833, pp. 244, 251–2; Allsopp 1967, pp. 36–7 ill.; *Twelve Newcastle Churches*, 1982; *Buildings of England: Northumberland*, 1992, p. 413). St Mary, Battersea, London (1767–77), by J. Dixon and R. Dixon, with a temple *porte-cochère* (Doc. 261: 15 August 1774).

64 December 1750 (J. Goodchild, 'The Building of Westgate Chapel, Wakefield', 1975, MS, Goodchild Collection, Wakefield).

65 Yorkshire Archaeological Society, Leeds, 129 G4, pp. 2, 18–19, 27, 31–2.

66 Harris and Savage 1990, p. 276. See particularly pls XXI, XXXIV, XL, LII. John was then collaborating with his 'Architect' father, Robert Carr, and in 1748 launched an independent practice at Huthwaite Hall, where the Gibbsian door frame derived from Langley 1740, pl. XXVII (Wragg 2000, pp. 163–4, fig. 2; Colvin 2008, pp. 221–3). Linstrum 1978, p. 199, pl. 155.

67 Colvin 2008, pp. 704–6. Morris 1742, p. 14.

68 Doc. 137: 29 December 1753, 7 January, 20 February 1754.

69 Doc. 269: 1726.

70 *Gentleman's Magazine*, Supplement 1756, p. 602; July 1784, pp. 449–50. Harris and Savage 1990, p. 508.

71 Jeffery 1996, pp. 184–6, 356. It cost £8,058 15s. 6d. (pl. 510).

72 Doc. 146. Its cost is unrecorded. John Lane's St Marylebone parish church (1741–2, demolished 1952), a decimated version of the Marylebone Chapel, costing £1,051 19s. 0d., was sanctioned by Edward Harley, lord of the manor, on grounds that he would 'Concurr . . . in any reasonable proposal [only if] done without over burthening the Inhabitants with any unnecessary Charge; especially at this time when provisions of all kinds bear so high aprice' (City of Westminster Archives Centre, Proceedings of Vestry, 1741–52, f. 12, 17 March 1741, 1752–68, f. 339). Rocque 1746–7, 1cb; S. H. Grimm, exterior view (British Library, Add. MS 15,542, f. 135).

TWENTY-FOUR PALLADIAN PROTOTYPES

1 John Molesworth in England to Alessandro Galilei in Italy, 31 January 1726 (Toesca 1952, p. 220).

2 Doc. 267: 1734, referring to the lack of chastity in handling the quadruple towers.

3 Henry Jones, *Clifton*, 1766; 'PALLADIO's stile in PATTY's plans appear', quoted in Ison 1952, p. 42, referring to a Bristol suburb and the architect Thomas Paty.

4 Talman 1997, p. 8, fig. 5, p. 117 (letter 104), p. 135 (letter 156), p. 139 (letter 169), p. 154 (letter 200); see also pp. 24, 26–7, 146; Friedman 1975.

5 Doc. 223: 1751; J. Wright, 'The Rebuilding' [1677], in Wright 1697, p. 8; Harris 1699, p. 2. Comparative dimensions were published throughout the eighteenth century.

6 T. P. Connor, 'A Study of Colen Campbell's *Vitruvius Britannicus*', 1977 (Bodleian Library, University of Oxford, MS D. Phil c2645), pp. 100–01, associates this with G. Alessi's Santa Maria di Carignano, 1549–72, illustrated in Rubens 1658, pls 62–3. The radical makeover of Campbell's scheme is demonstrated when compared to an undated design by James Smith, more richly worked and closer to St Peter's, which once belonged to Campbell (British Architectural Library, Drawings and Archives Collection, Victoria and Albert Museum, London, x8/12). Gwynn (1766; p. 38) remarked 'With regard to [St Paul's] turrets . . . it must be confessed, they are light and elegant, but with respect to grandeur, their upper parts consist of rather too many divisions, which produces something like confusion, and, if they had been more spread, or set further apart, it would given a grace to the west-front of the church, and it would have prevented their falling in the view upon the peristylum of the dome.' Joining the debate comparing the two great fabrics he considered St Paul's 'in some respects, superior to that of St. Peter's at Rome; the west-front is designed more in character, that is, it has more the appearance of a building designed for publick worship. St. Peter's rather gives the idea of a front of a palace, and the pediment is mean and trifling; the dome of St. Paul's is more elegantly shaped, nor is there any comparison between the lanterns on the top; that of St. Peter's is heavy and clumsy, and produces an ill effect, but the body of the church, being composed of one order, is very grand and noble, though it suffers by an introduction of parts which are rather too minute. The interior parts of St. Peter's are many of them extremely noble, and the monuments and decorations are grand, and introduced with a decorum and propriety, which no way effects or deforms the building, a consideration hardly ever attended to in this country. The high altar . . . designed and executed by the celebrated Bernini, is perhaps the noblest work of its kind that ever was performed: This truly magnificent decoration is most judiciously placed under the centre of the dome, and produces the finest effect imaginable; in short, nothing trifling or unbecoming the dignity of the church is suffered to be place in it; but notwithstanding the profusion of elegance and grandeur which are displayed in this celebrated building, there are many defects, and some capital errors to be found in the design . . . the grand isle . . . is one continued arched vault, without variety, the whole being composed of pannels and roses, and the windows are broken into it, in so aukward a manner, that they appear rather to be after-thoughts, and are entirely unconnected with the decorations of the ceiling . . . Wren's judgment pointed out this tasteless deformity, and the superiority of the grand isle of St. Paul's, in this respect, is very apparent, in which the windows are regularly introduced into the ceiling, and the architecture forms the most noble frames, which he designed for the reception of paintings' (pp. 39–40). Furthermore, 'the dome of St. Peter's . . . is composed of the same materials with the rest of the building, and consequently has a much grander effect than that of St. Paul, which is covered with lead; for which reason the dome of St. Paul's . . . ought to be painted of a stone-colour, which would bring the turret and the body . . . into harmony, and

produce an effect in the whole that would greatly contribute to the grandeur of its appearance in every point of view' (p. 83).

7 Doc. 147: 30 June 1722, now vanished. The term 'bulks' presumably refers to buranium (garlanded ox skulls) in a Doric frieze.

8 Tavernor and Schofield 1997, p. 253, referring to pl. 43.

9 Doc. 147: 3 October 1716. Harris and Savage 1990, pp. 348–52. Etty's contemporary church at Sunderland, with its equal-height nave and aisles separated by lofty Corinthian columns rising from pedestals to straight entablatures, might be the first high colonnaded hall church in English post-medieval architecture (Doc. 178).

10 Doc. 112: 7 January 1722.

11 Doc. 269: 1734. Campbell 1715–25, vol. III, p. 9, pl. 46. Boynton 1970, p. 137. Etty also adopted its lugged frames.

12 Doc. 112: pp. 5, 21. Note Gent's observation that the church was 'not yet Adorn'd with any Tombs or Monuments'.

13 Letter III, dated Venice, September 1765 (Sharp 1766, p. 13). Ingamells 1997, pp. 850–51. Boucher 1994, pp. 196–200.

14 Annotated in one of Burlington's copies of *I quattro libri*, 1570 (Harris 1994, pp. 62–4 no. 82). San Giorgio continued to interest architects: W. Collins exhibited 'The Church of Sancto Georgio, at Venice by Paladio' (Graves 1907, p. 62, 1773 no. 81); Soane praised it and Il Redentore as 'most beautiful specimens of refined taste' (Watkin 1996, p. 560).

15 Colvin 2008, p. 149. Lewis 1981, pp. 190–98.

16 Puppi 1975, p. 404, pl. 574. Smith travelled in Italy in the 1670s (Colvin 2008, p. 949). Colvin 1974 deals with Smith's role in the emergence of Palladian domestic architecture.

17 Tavernor and Schofield 1997, pp. 273–5, 216.

18 Kent 1727, vol. I, advertisement; vol. II, pls 57–61. However, topographical views of all Palladio's churches appear in D. Lovisa, *Il gran theatro delle pitture, e prospettiva di Venezia*, 1717, 1720 (Bonannini et al. 1993).

19 Wright 1730, vol. I, pp. 48, 61. Howard 2002, pls 117–22, 126–8, 136.

20 Soane MS, vol. 26, f. 54.

21 Doc. 2: 25 February 1752. Gibbs's alternative design (Gibbs Collection, Ashmolean Museum, Oxford, IV. 4) is in the manner of Palladio's San Francesco della Vigna, Venice, also devoid of an integrated campanile. See also John Smyth's Redentore-inspired St Thomas, Dublin, 1758–62 (Pool and Cash 1780, pp. 90–92; O'Dwyer 1981, p. 68).

22 Doc. 220: 1750, Soo 1998, pp. 173–8, figs 37–8. Beard 1982, pl. 140. See also his observation on Palladio as authority for the layout of the Temple of Mars Ultor, Rome (Soo 1998, pp. 180–83, also pp. 3–4, 6, 15).

23 Jeffery 1996, fig. 115.

24 Doc. 21: 19 July 1773. The pedigree is discussed in Friedman 2004, chapter V. See also the east end of Francis Hiorne's St Bartholomew, Tardebigge, Worcestershire (1775–7), before Victorian remodelling (Birmingham Library Services Archives Division, Aylesford Collection, II, f. 218). Brown was Craven's architect at Benham Place, Berkshire (Colvin 2008, p. 168).

25 Doc. 35.

26 Gay 1716, p. 33, lines 25–8.

27 Bodleian Library, University of Oxford, MS Rawl. B376, ff. 8–9.

28 Doc. 62: 14 June 1706, 22 October 1707, 26 June 1712. Colvin 2008, pp. 564–5. James designed Waldershare House, 1705–12 (Brushe 1994, p. 8). The attribution of St George to Samuel Simmons, a Deal builder involved in its construction from 1707 (Colvin 2008, p. 924), seems less likely.

29 Doc. 62: 11 August 1712. Jeffery 2001, figs 1–5. Covent Garden's original brick carcass was 'rendered over' by 1708, and the belfry erected 1708–10 (Doc. 271).

30 National Library of Scotland, Edinburgh, MS 16502, ff. 208–9, 21 April 1707, including a detailed specification and diagram (f. 208v).

31 Hart 2002, pl. 59.

32 Doc. 271: 1714 (Paterson 1714), 1717 (Campbell 1715–25). See also Gay 1716. The portico was based on Palladio's reconstruction in D. Barbaro, *I dieci libri . . . di M. Vitruvio*, 1556 (Summerson 1990, p. 46, pl. 27). Even the arch-baroque Thomas Archer succumbed to the form in the south transept addition (1717) at St Mary, Hale, Hampshire, his parish church, in sympathy and homage to the Covent Garden-inspired front (1631–2), attributed to Jones (Whiffen 1973, pp. 31–2; Colvin 2008, pp. 73, 590).

33 Doc. 271: 22 April 1727, 1729, 1736. A plan and east-front variant appears in an allegorical homage to the architect on the frontispiece of Kent 1727 (Anderson 2007, fig. 101).

34 Doc. 271: 1734.

35 Doc. 271: 3 October 1734. He published a measured elevation and roof section in 1736.

36 Doc. 249: 1733 (Price).

37 Doc. 271: 1733, 1765. The earliest reference associating St Paul's with a barn dates to 1728.

38 Doc. 14: 3 February 1731, 25 March 1732.

39 Doc. 14: 1739, 1779. Ison 1948, pls 1–2, fig. 32.

40 Evelyn 1664, Chapter V, pp. 24–5 (Harris and Savage 1990, pp. 196–201), discussed in Wood's MS 'The Origin of Building' (Bath Reference Library, f. 73v), noted in Brownell 1976, pp. 31–2, who suggests that Wood's figural metopes perhaps derive from Jones's Whitehall Palace scheme (Kent 1727, vol. I, pl. 11). Dugdale 1819, vol. IV, p. 198, claimed: 'Wood . . . formed its plan from that of an ancient temple at Athens'.

41 Wright 1864, p. 259.

42 Doc. 14: 1739, 28 April 1766.

43 The house is attributed to Henry Flitcroft, Burlington's chief draughtsman (Jackson-Stops 1972: 14 December, figs 1, 5; 21 December, figs 9–11). William Beckford similarly built 'opposite to the grand front' of Fonthill Redivus, Wiltshire (then thought to have been Jones's work, destroyed in a fire in 1755), and forming 'a good termination of the prospect . . . a Church [Holy Trinity, Fonthill Gifford] on the plan of Covent Garden' in 1747–8, demolished 1866 (Pococke 1750, vol. II, p. 47, 2 July 1754), closely resembling Well (Clarke 1963, pp. 85, 141; Rutter 1823, pp. 97, 103; Ostergard 2001, pp. 140, 301, 349–50, figs 3–4, 3–8; J. Buckler view [Wiltshire Architectural Society Collection]; 'New Church at Fonthill Gifford', *London Illustrated News*, 29 September 1866, pp. 303–5).

44 Doc. 210: 15 December 1726, according to the text accompanying pl. 530.

45 Doc. 210. For William Barrett, see Tetbury, Gloucestershire (Doc. 179: 28 July 1742).

46 Doc. 210: 15 December 1726.

47 Doc. 271: 3 October 1734. Dance's cornice is based on Jones's Queen's Chapel, St James's (1623–5; Worsley 2007, fig. 127).

48 Riou 1768, pt II, p. 69, adding: 'We don't presume to attack the reputation of the great architect, but the meanness of those who tied up his hands.'

49 Kent 1727, vol. II, pl. 21, 'A principal Front of . . . a Square Building'. It was erected to a more traditional form.

50 The timber construction of the roof is a slight variation on Covent Garden and a plate in Price 1735, p. 15, pl. G, B (Yeomans 1992, fig. 25), also used by Henry Flitcroft at St Giles-in-the-Fields, 1730 (fig. 24). Bancroft owned property in Chiswick (Wing 1987, p. 16), so may have known Burlington. For the building type, see Godfrey 1950; Berridge 1985; Howson 1993.

51 Stiff Leadbetter was associated with the estate, 1740–60s (Worsley 1991b). The Quebec Chapel referred to in the pencil inscription on pl. 531 was built to a different design (Clarke 1963, p. 190, pl. 15).

52 The faculty stated: 'Chancell . . . become ruinous . . . decayed . . . cannot effectually be repaired but must be entirely taken down and rebuilt . . . proposed to erect . . . entire new Chancell . . . cover with flat Tiles, as . . . at present . . . finish inside in . . . decent . . . handsome manner', granted 2 September 1773 (Lincolnshire Archives, Lincoln, Fac.3/37), restored in 1869 (*Buildings of England: Lincolnshire*, 1989, p. 622, pl. 95). Yates 1991, p. 46; Thorold 1989, p. 161.

53 Doc. 76.

54 Woolfe and Gandon 1767–71, vol. IV, p. 9, pl. 79, 'a lasting monument of his lordship's taste in architecture'. Wittkower 1948.

55 In the manner of Campbell's Banqueting House, Studley Royal, Yorkshire, *circa* 1729. Horsforth's vicar, John Morfitt, who was active in promoting the rebuilding, was a cousin of John Aislabie, creator of the Palladian paradise at Studley and Burlington's Deputy Lord Lieutenant of the East and West Riding (Laurence 1986, p. 18; Greeves 1988 p. 51 ill.). Doc. 100.

56 Vestry 'Presentmt . . . We have . . . decent place to perform divine service in . . . Sir Thomas proposes to build . . . new Church this year' (West Yorkshire Archives Service [Leeds District Archives], RD/CB8/10/1761/1); 'Church . . . rebuilding, at . . . Expence of . . . Proprietor . . . will be finished without Expence to . . . Purchaser' (*London Evening-Post*, 27–9 June 1765); 'will soon be finished, 8 May 1768 (RD/CB/10/1768); church 'in Ruins for several years . . . divine service could not be performed [Robinson] erected at . . . own expense . . . new Church now . . . property [of J. S. Morritt who] proposed to give two acres . . . opposite . . . to build . . . at . . . own Expence . . . new Rectory . . . agreeable to . . . plan . . . annexed' (untraced), 12 June 1775 (North Yorkshire County Record Office, North Allerton, PR/ROK4); designed by Isaac Ware (Bax 1964, p. 115); font designed by Robinson, 1775 (*Country Life*, 19 March 1987, p. 79, fig. 19). Church completed for Morritt by John Carr, consecrated 30 May 1776 (Clarke 1963, p. 86; Wragg 2000, p. 198); Robinson died on 3 March 1777 (Colvin 2008, p. 882). Exterior view, 1845 (Leeds University Library, Department of Manuscripts and Special Collections, Churches of Diocese of Ripon, III, f. 31); chancel remodelled 1877 (*Buildings of England: West Riding*, 1967, p. 310). Worsley 1999.

57 Doc. 271: 27 April 1727.

58 Doc. 88: 1763, February 1764, 1765.

59 Doc. 88: undated (East Sussex Record Office, GLY 951a).

60 Malton 1779, dated 1775, p. 211.

61 Linstrum 1978, p. 189, pl. 144; *Buildings of England: West Yorkshire*, 1967, p. 136; Wragg 2000, pp. 114–15, pl. 100. Porch added in 1828.

62 Doc. 104. See also Otterden, Kent (1753–4; Doc. 139), perhaps designed by the lord of the manor, the Revd Granville Wheler, a subscriber to Kent 1727.

63 Morris 1742, pp. 14, 25.

64 Doc. 271: 1775, 5 November 1795.

65 Doc. 271: 17 March, 16 April 1787. Britton and Pugin 1825–8, vol. I, p. 113, suggests that the whole building was put into a state of complete repair and 'the original simplicity of the outline was strictly preserved'. However, there is a lack of detailed visual evidence of the internal appearance apart from the generalised representation in Campbell 1715–25, vol. II, and a fleeting reference to repairing ceiling 'flowers'.

66 Doc. 271: 3 November 1789, 1792.

67 Doc. 230.

68 Malcolm 1803–7, quoted in Bumpus, no date, vol. II, p. 83.

69 Doc. 271: 17 September 1795. Hardwick replicated his Covent Garden portico, introducing a more prominent steeple, at St John, Workington, Cumberland, 1823 (*Buildings of England: Cumberland*, 1967, pl. 61; *Country Life*, 26 December 1991, p. 48).

70 Allsopp 1970, p. 39, Book Four, p. 8; bequeathed in 1736 by George Clarke (p. ix). At St Paul's Cathedral it functioned as 'an Ambulatory for People, who, by walking in the Body . . . were wont to disturb the Service' (Newberry 1759, p. 16).

71 Wotton 1624, p. x; Evelyn 1696, p. 14; Evelyn 1664 (Harris and Savage 1990, pp. 19–201). All Saints' body was rebuilt in an imposing Wrenian idiom (1677–80) by Henry Bell (*Wren Society*, XIX, 1942, pp. 58–9, pls XXVII–XXVIII). Hawksmoor's sketch of 1680–83 shows a Corinthian por-tico before one was added (*RIBA Catalogue: G–K*, 1973, p. 100 [9]). Lever and Richardson 1984 suggests a dubious attribution to Hawksmoor (discussed in Hart 2002, p. 21, fig. 19; Colvin 2008, p. 116). Fiennes 1982, pp. 116, 228, described 'two rows of stone pillars at the entrance . . . not quite finished' in 1697, but so by *circa* 1701. The portico, crowned by John Hunt's statue, is inscribed 'This Statue Was Erected in Memory of King Charles II. Who Gave a Thousand Tun of Timber Towards the Rebuilding of This Church and To This Town Seven Years Chimney Money Collected In It. John Agutter Mayor Humf Northton fecit'. Whiffen 1945, pp. 17–20;

Buildings of England: Northamptonshire, 1961, pp. 308–9, pls 10a, 20a.

72 Downes 1966, pl. 197.

73 Oswald 1953; Summerson 2000, pp. 116–18, pls 55–6. Illustrated in Campbell 1715–25, vol. III, p. 7, pl. 9: 'This Building was begun by *Inigo Jones*; the Wings, and Collonades, and all the Foundations, were made by him; but the Front of the House was designed by another Architect'. An earlier, more crucial link for Cartwright may have been provided by Tillemans, who drew views of Aynho Park and church on 12 July 1721 and of Stoke Park on 10 August 1721 (British Library, Add. MS 32,467, ff. 8, 10, 237; Bailey 1996, pp. 9, 11, 195). Worsley 2007, pp. 111–13, pl. 129.

74 Doc. 8: 8 August 1723. In a preliminary study (Northamptonshire Record Office, Peterborough Diocesan Records, Faculty Reg. I, f. 184), Wing contemplated upper-level circular windows and a door surround based on the Covent Garden church.

75 Doc. 262: 1715.

76 Kent 1727, vol. I, pls 3–4, 51, the Banqueting House marked B, the chapel marked C, measuring 110 by 55 feet, with north and south galleries raised on columns and an altarpiece against the east wall.

77 One he had already used in the dining room at Wolterton Hall, Norfolk, begun in 1727, for Horatio, 1st Lord Walpole, brother of Ripley's powerful chief patron, Sir Robert Walpole, who had recommended him for the Greenwich Hospital post (A. Klausmeier to author, 1 May 1999, also noting similar window frames in the Marble Hall and Saloon and almost identical consoles in the main staircase at Robert Walpole's Houghton Hall). A similar ceiling is illustrated in Ware 1731, pl. 20.

78 Langley 1736, pp. 312–13, pl. CCLXXXIX.

79 Kent 1727, vol. I, pl. 58; Harris and Higgott 1989, pp. 251–3. Ripley may also have known Jones's preliminary designs for the Banqueting House, with its 'Great Niche' reserved for the royal throne, and for the Star Chamber, Palace of Westminster (pp. 98–100, 110–11).

80 Doc. 236: 26 May 1747. Externally, the astylar courtyard elevation of the chapel (Bold 2000, pls 157, 169, 212) does not resemble Wren's brick and stone block, but adopted the division into rusticated basement and smooth upper storey pioneered in Henry Flitcroft's recently completed St Giles-in-the-Fields (this publication, pl. 562).

81 Doc. 236: 1775, 19 August 1754, 1769. Brown (died 1753), a student of Laguerre and Thornhill's chief assistant in painting St Paul's Cathedral dome, who also painted the chancel of St Andrew Undershaft, 1726, to 'general Applause' (Croft-Murray 1962–70, vol. I, p. 263; vol. II, pp. 32, 36, 322).

82 Doc. 236: 1769.

83 Doc. 13: 1765. Compare Jones's plan for Whitehall chapel (Kent 1727, vol. I, pl. 4) and Prior Park.

84 Rosenau 1979, pp. 94–5, pls 97, 99–100; Tigerman 1988, Book III, pl. 16. *A Catalogue of a Valuable and Select Collection of Books of Antiquities, Architecture, etc . . . the Property of Mr Wood, Architect, Late of Bath, Deceased*, Christie's, London, 8 June 1795, lot 107: 'Villalpandus in Ezekiel, 3 vols' (Pollock 2000, pp. 469–74).

85 Ware 1738, Book Four, Chapter X, p. 91, pl. XXIII. At Holkham the band of modillions and rosettes normally found on the soffit of the Corinthian order is unconventionally relocated as an isolated element at the top of the walls.

86 Doc. 264. The drawings were purchased from John Talman on 4 May 1720; soon afterwards Burlington's draughtsman, Henry Flitcroft, made a measured sectional drawing (Harris and Higgott 1989, pp. 23, 182–4 no. 51, fig. 50; Harris 1981, p. 115, pls 136–7).

87 Worsley 2007, chapter 9. Palladio never employed it in his executed churches, though it features in unexecuted designs for the façade of San Petronio, Bologna, of 1572–9 (Puppi 1975, pp. 403–6, pls 574–6), in the eighteenth century deposited in the church, where they were traced by Soane in 1779 (Du Prey 1982, p. 164). Serliana also appear in work by Serlio (Hart and Hicks 1996, p. 410), Giulio Romano's San Benedetto, Polirone, *circa* 1540 (Gombrich et al. 1989, pp. 538–43), and Vasari's Badia delle Sante Flora e Lucilla, Arezzo, 1565 (Satkowski 1993, pp. 88–91, fig. 27, pls 182–3, 187–90).

88 Mowl and Earnshaw 1995, figs 2, 14. Guillery 2005, p. 88, fig. 15. Wren's St Andrew, Holborn, St James, Piccadilly, St Mary-at-Hill, St Mildred Poultry, St Olave Jewry (*Wren Society*, IX, 1932).

89 Doc. 145.

90 Gibbs 1732, p. 34, pl. XLVIII; repeated in Langley 1740, p. 18, pl. LI; Langley 1736, pp. 279–80, pl. CLXXI; and Ware 1756, Book IV, Chapter 23, p. 467.

91 Doc. 112.

92 Docs 87, 205. At Thomas Woodward's St Anne, Bewdley, Worcestershire (1745–8), the eastern Serliana faces towards the broad main street (*Buildings of England: Worcestershire*, 1968, p. 84, pls 3, 81).

93 Harris and Tait 1979, p. 48 no. 111, pl. 92, previously (*circa* 1705–34) in the architect George Clarke's collection at Oxford (pp. 1–2) and so perhaps regarded as Jones's work.

94 Docs 193, 214, 249. Similar examples include Samuel Bell's St Andrew, Dundee (1772–4; Hay 1957, fig. 26; Walker and Ritchie 1987, p. 113, pl. 91); John Wood Jr's St Nicholas, Hardenhuish, Wiltshire (1777–9; *Gentleman's Magazine*, 4 November 1779, p. 563; Wiltshire Architectural Society, J. C. Buckler view; *Country Life*, 3 February 1950, pp. 319–20; Clarke 1963, pp. 117, 184; Parker and Chandler 1993, pp. 89, 154); William Marshall's Longdon (Doc. 124) and Bourton-on-the-Water (1784–94, body rebuilt 1872–91; Gloucestershire Record Office, P55 VE2/1; Bigland 1989–95, vol. I, 1791, p. 232 ill.; Clarke 1963, p. 61; Verey 1976, p. 179; *Buildings of England: Gloucestershire I*, 1999, pp. 188–9, pl. 81; Picktorn, no date); Pain 1791, pls 133–5.

95 The scheme was abandoned with the decision in 1753 to erect a chapel at nearby Cambo, Garrett's drawing (also at Wallington) showing a starkly plain Palladian church with minimalist Serliana (Cornforth 1970, p. 858, fig. 10; Leach 1974, fig. 5). Similar treatments appear in Aheron 1754, pl. 14, and Morris 1750, pl. 49, a 'Plain . . . Church for a pretty populous Town', perhaps originating in Serlio's 'temples which suit Christian customs' (Hart and Hicks 1996, pp. 424–5). Multiple Serliana are employed dramatically in the Magdalen House Chapel, London (1769; Doc. 248), and

Kensington Chapel, Bath (Somerset Record Office, D/P/wal sw 8/4/1; Ison 1948, pp. 78–9, fig. 13)

96 Doc. 152: 18 June 1746. Sanderson, who designed Pusey House (*circa* 1750) for J. A. Pusey, and owned a copy of G. Leoni, *The Architecture of A. Palladio* (1715–20), lived in Covent Garden (Colvin 2008, p. 899).

97 Doc. 94. Crabtree 1836, p. 271; C. E. Seager, 'Square Chapel and Church, Halifax', undated, unpublished typescript.

TWENTY-FIVE THE PALLADIAN CHURCH COMES OF AGE

1 An Irish cleric visiting Bath, 7 August 1772 (British Library, Add. MS 27,951, f. 77).

2 Ironically, Flitcroft was to serve as surveyor of St Paul's Cathedral during the years 1746–56 (Doc. 223).

3 Doc. 229. A drawing of the old church is inscribed: 'This monument . . . to George Chapman Poet. By his Affectionate Friend Inigo Jones Architect it stands in St. Giles . . . church yard against the South Side of the church as it did to the old church till. 1730. so its placed again and adjoyning to the new builded Church' (Bodleian Library, University of Oxford, Gough Maps 44, f. 158). The monument is recorded in f. 158v and N. Smith's engraving of 15 June 1795 (National Monuments Record Centre, English Heritage, Swindon); it is now preserved within doors.

4 The Queen's House has 'a noble rustick Basement' (Campbell 1715–25, vol. I, p. 4, pl. 15). Amesbury, 'designed by *Inigo Jones* . . . Here is a bold rustick Basement' (Campbell 1715–25, vol. III, p. 7, pl. 17), inscribed 'I: Jones Architectus' in Kent 1727, vol. II, pl. 8. Stukeley 1776, vol. I, p. 137, noted that Amesbury was 'built by Inigo Jones, and deservedly to be admired: some new works are added to it under the direction of my lord Burlington, possessor of his spirit, and a noble collection of his designs'. Bold 1989, pp. 94–100, pls 63–4. The domestic nature of Flitcroft's vocabulary elicited a single rebuke from Ralph 1734, p. 101, that of 'the smallness of the doors' at the west end of the church 'and the poverty of appearance that must necessarily follow'.

5 Ware 1731 (dedicated to Burlington), pls 15–18, 28–30; Leoni 1715–20, Book IV, p. 22, pl. XXVI item A.

6 Doc. 229: 1734, 1768. Ralph, *A Critical Review of the Publick Buildings*, was issued on 11 April 1734 (Harris and Savage 1990, p. 382).

7 Wittkower 1999, vol. III, pp. 14–15, figs 12–13. Kalnein and Levey 1972, pp. 288–9, figs 252–53, also pl. 254. Hempel 1965, pp. 184–6, 196–8, figs 113, 115, 121.

8 Doc. 250.

9 Kent 1727, vol. I, pl. 53. Doc. 250: British Library, King's Topographical Collection, XXIII–32–e.

10 Doc. 173: 7 November 1740.

11 Hewlings 1995, figs 27c, 38–40.

12 Harris and Higgott 1989, pp. 182–4 no. 51.

13 Doc. 197: 23 April 1748. From the same stable are St James's Chapel, Walton Hall, Warwickshire, 1750 (Birmingham Library Services Archives Division, Aylesford Collection, III, p. 224; *VCH: Warwickshire*, vol. IV, 1947, pp. 196–7 ill.), and L. Brown's Compton Verney, 1770–80 (Shakespeare Birthplace Trust Record Office, Stratford-upon-Avon, Warwickshire [now Shakespeare Birthplace Library and Archives], DR 98/1802, ff. 79, 114–15; Bolton 1913, p. 535 ill.; Tyack 1975, p. 9), bellcote added 1855 (*Buildings of England: Warwickshire*, 1966, p. 240).

14 In addition, Dance was involved with St Matthew, Bethnal Green, 1742–6 (Doc. 257), the Great Synagogue, Aldgate, 1765–6 (Doc. 217), and incidental work at St Luke, Old Street, 1733 (Doc. 239), St Edmund the King, 1733 (Harrison 1986, pp. 6–7), Guildhall Chapel, 1736 (Stroud 1971, p. 238), St Katherine Coleman, 8 August 1739 (Guildhall Library, City of London Corporation, MS 1133, f. 3v), St Bride, Fleet Street, 29 June 1750 (Guildhall Library, MS 6554/5, f. 156v), St Dunstan-in-the-West, 20 November 1751 (Guildhall Library, MS 2973, 27 November 1751–7 June 1753, MS 3016/4, f. 30; Lever 2003, pp. 408–9), St John, Wapping, 9 March 1756, where he delivered a gruesome prognosis of extreme decrepitude (*Journals of the House of Commons*, vol. XXVII, pp. 505–8).

15 Doc. 215. One set of minutes (Guildhall Library, MS 4526/2, unlisted in Colvin 2008, pp. 294, 438) has hitherto not received due attention. No drawings for St Botolph are known.

16 Doc. 215: 23 June 1725, 28 September, 12 October 1726.

17 Doc. 215: 16 September 1724, 19 August, 28 September 1725. There were reports of some craftsmen 'Guilty of . . . Great Neglect' and poor craftsmanship.

18 Doc. 215: 18 July 1734. The motif of a panelled overdoor framed by scrolled brackets derives from St Paul's Cathedral (Downes 1988, pl. 128).

19 Doc. 215: 18 July 1734; see also 1758, 1761.

20 Doc. 220: 1734; see also 1728 (St Mary-le-Bow).

21 Addison 1761, p. 55, and Wright 1730, vol. I, p. 39. The Revd Jeremiah Milles, visiting in 1734, thought it 'by much the most beautiful [church] in Padua' and noted the 'arms & names of several Englishmen, who had taken their degrees here' (Gloucestershire Record Office, D 2663/28). Dance's handsomely composed Doric doors flanking the chancel may have been modelled on Morris 1728, opposite p. 60, which acknowledged 'that great Architect *Andrea Palladio*, whose Works testifying his Genius, it seems needless to praise' (p. xiii). Lotz 1995, p. 162, pls 258–9. A remarkable design by Willey Reveley features a colossal Bow-like steeple (sold Christie's, December 1982, in Colvin 2008, p. 857, untraced).

22 Morris 1750, pls 18, 23, 28, 36, 39.

23 Colvin 2008, pp. 704–5. Harris and Savage 1990, pp. 317–24.

24 Chapman and Turner [1974]; Linstrum 1978, pp. 197, 199, pl. 154; Stell 1985, p. 22, 24A. When John Wesley preached in the octagonal chapel at Rotherham, Yorkshire (1761, demolished), he remarked that it was a 'Pity our houses, where the ground will admit . . . should be built in any other form' (Wesley 1909–16, vol. IV, pp. 474, 478, 29 August; Stell 1985, p. 22), and at the Methodist Conference of 1770 recommended it as 'best for the voice, and on many accounts more commodious than any other' (White

1964, p. 114). By the late 1770s it had become a standard for the sect. Outside Wesleyan circles notable examples include the Temple Court Octagon Chapel, Liverpool, 1763, demolished 1820 (Enfield 1774, p. 47; Wallace 1794, p. 148), First Presbyterian Church, Belfast, 1781–3 (Brett 1976, p. 4), Paradise Street Unitarian Chapel, Liverpool, 1791, demolished (Wallace 1794, pp. 152–4), Zion Chapel, Leeds, 1796, demolished 1952 (Friedman 1997b, pp. 157–63, figs 55–7).

25 Hart and Hicks 1996, pp. 408–13; Ware 1738, p. 81.

26 For example, Oostkerk, Middelburg, 1647–67, by B. F. Drijfhout and P. Post (Ozinga 1929, figs 20–25, pls 1, 3, 32–8, 62–3); Van Swingchem, Brouwer and van Os 1984, pp. 58–9; Kuyper 1980, pls 45–53.

27 Inscribed over the west door: 'Christ, the beginning and the ending for all eternity; to the Father, the Son, and the Holy Ghost. Of his own free gift, Johnson, the donor, rebuilt and restored, in the year of the salvation of men, 1722'. John Talman's studies for Italianate improvements to the chapel survive in the Spalding Gentlemen's Society, Spalding, Lincolnshire (Harris 2008, p. 121). A chancel was added in 1886. Dr John Lord suggests (12 September 2008, letter to author), given Johnson's antiquarian interests, a possible precedent for St James in the octagonal, brick Red Mount Chapel (1485), King's Lynn, Norfolk (*Buildings of England: Norfolk 2*, 1999, pp. 472–4, pl. 33). Other early, unidentified examples include an undated plan, section and elevation (Cumbria Record Office, Lowther archives, III.16, fig. 86); 'Project of a Church 1726' (Downes 1967, p. 29 no. 104); Killin, Perthshire, 1743–4, by John Douglas (The National Archives of Scotland, Edinburgh [formerly The Scottish Record Office], Survey 657, bundle 2; Colvin 2008, p. 330); Ayot St Peter, Hertfordshire, 1751 (Hertfordshire Archives and Local Studies, Hertford, D/P/11/29/1 and Oldfield drawings, vol. II, f. 239; Brushe 1977, figs 3–4); Hartwell, Buckinghamshire, 1753–6 (Doc. 97, this publication pl. 168). Thomas Prowse's St Mary, Berkley, Somerset, 1749–53, features an octagonal dome supported on four Ionic columns contained within a square block (Collinson 1791, vol. II, pp. 203–4; *Country Life*, 19 May 1988, pp. 168–71, figs 2, 7).

28 *Gentleman's Magazine* (December 1796), p. 993, being recommended to the parishioners of traffic-ridden St Clement Danes, London. Browne also published a design for Lord Nelson's octagonal mansion (*Gentleman's Magazine*, February 1799, p. 97, pl. 1). Colvin 2008, p. 172.

29 Friedman 2003, p. 58, fig. 5. See the reference to wainscot staining 'procured . . . from an Artist in Holland' (Doc. 137: 9 August 1754).

30 Morris 1750, title page and Preface. Thomas Rawlins's contribution of 1753 to the Octagon Chapel competition (Rawlins 1768, pp. 29–30, pl. XLIV) stressed its 'very plain Outside . . . a very advantageous Structure for Hearing' (Friedman 2003, fig. 17); see also pls XLVII–XLVIII, an octagonal variation of Wren's St Stephen Walbrook.

31 Doc. 137.

32 Morris 1750, p. 5, pls 31–2.

33 Rawlins 1768, p. 30.

34 Wesley 1909–16, vol. IV, p. 244, 23 November 1757. A direct reflection is the Independent Chapel, Colchester, Essex, 1763–7, demolished 1862, for which Robert Godfry received £1 1s. 0d. for a 'Plan & Estimate' on 1 August 1765 and for which a card model was supplied (Essex Record Office, D/NC 52/5/2; National Monuments Record Centre, BB 75/3768–71; Blaxhill 1938, pp. 19–23 ill.). Thomas Ivory designed Colchester Theatre in 1764 (Colvin 2008, p. 559).

35 Hussey 1955, pp. 204–7, figs 366–7; Mowl and Earnshaw 1988, pp. 176–8. The laterally placed twin pavilions reflect Vanbrugh's Eastbury, Dorset, 1725, demolished 1775 (Hart 2008, fig. 285).

36 Woolfe and Gandon 1767–71, vol. IV, p. 10, pls 88–9, to which Paine subscribed (p. 12).

37 Doc. 59: 18 January, 3 June 1750.

38 Burlington's front (Woolfe and Gandon 1767–71, vol. IV, pl. 79) was destroyed in 1828.

39 C. Ranger, *The Gray's Inn Journal*, 9 February 1754, pp. 116–17.

40 Snodin 1986. Compare the picture frame with Paine's design for a pier glass for Nostell Priory, Yorkshire, where Rose was employed in these same years (London 1984, M9).

41 Doc. 83. San Simeon, 1718–38, by G. Scalfarotto, is the subject of Vicentini's engraving after Canaletto (*Prospectus Magni Canalis Venetiarum*, 1735, pl. XI; Links 1971; Bomford and Finaldi 1998, pp. 20–27, pl. 17).

42 Beddington 2006, cat. no. 64. William Bowes of Streatham Castle, County Durham, a relative, visited Venice in 1717 (Ingamells 1997, p. 113).

43 Paine 1767–83, vol. I, p. 19.

44 Ingamells 1997, p. 731. Based on now-untraced Palladio originals (Sicca 1980, pp. 36–7 no. 5; Proyoyeur and Proyoyeur 1982, pp. 175–6 nos 191–3). Measured drawings of the Tempietto were not published until 1783, in O. Bertotti Scamozzi, *Le fabbriche e i disegni di Andrea Palladio*, vol. IV, pls IX–XI (Leach 1988, pls 139–40). An undated, unidentified Paine church design (*RIBA Catalogue: O–R*, 1976, p. 15 no. 9, fig. 7) adventurously blends elements from Palladio's San Giorgio Maggiore, Il Redentore and Le Zitelle, Venice.

45 Antonio Viscentini's studio, which specialised in producing great numbers of orthographic drawings of Venetian buildings for the English market between 1740 and 1760, recorded Santa Maria in more than one set of plans, elevations and sections (McAndrew 1974, pp. 7–11, 33 no. 121, fig. 77). The church's formula was influenced by Mauro Codussi, Palladio's great Venetian predecessor (Franzoi and Di Stefano 1976, pp. 60–61; Goy 1997, pp. 184, 187). Paine visited Venice during 1755–6 (Ingamells 1997, p. 731).

46 Doc. 188. Sir Walter Blackett, lord of the manor, was Paine's patron at Wallington Hall in 1755 (Leach 1988, pp. 212–13). Between 1752 and 1766 he also worked at Blagdon, Gosforth and Belford, all in Northumberland, and at Gibside, County Durham (pp. 174–5, 185–7). Compare the handwriting on the Warden drawing with Leach 1988, pl. 153.

47 As a resident of St Martin's Lane, London, from 1754, Paine is certain to have known St Giles, while as clerk in HM

Office of Works responsible for Jones's Queen's House, Greenwich, would have come into contact with Flitcroft (Colvin 2008, pp. 766–7).

48 See Kirkstall Grange, Leeds, 1752, and 5 Market Place, Pontefract, *circa* 1750–55, both in Yorkshire (Leach 1988, pls 28, 104).

49 *Buildings of England: West Kent and the Weald*, 1969, p. 406. Rocque 1746–7, 10cb, 11Ab. Ingamells 1997, pp. 683–4. The façade of Morris's Council House, Chichester (1731), derived from Palladio's San Giorgio Maggiore and Il Redentore; Wilton Lodge (*circa* 1731–2) from San Francesco della Vigna (Parissien 1990, pp. 51–2, figs 2–3; Colvin 2008, pp. 705–9). Parissien 1990, pl. 23.

50 Dugdale 1819, vol. III, p. 216.

51 For example, S. Maria di Carignano, Genoa (Lotz 1995, fig. 207).

52 Walpole 1937–83, vol. XXXV, pp. 143–4. Newman (*Buildings of England: West Kent and the Weald*, 1969, p. 406) compares it with Archer's St Paul, Deptford.

53 Doc. 271: 1734, 3 October 1734.

54 The 'situation is very bad: the country about it very uneven & much enclosed & the house is situated in the very lowest ground . . . unluckily enough' (British Library, Add. MS 15,776, ff. 197–8, in 1743).

55 Friedman 1997c, fig. 18.

56 Doc. 132: 5 August 1752, while the house 'is so perfect in a Palladian taste, that I must own it has recovered me a little from Gothic'.

57 'Here are no pews, but seats, as on the continent' (Dugdale 1819, vol. III, p. 216). Yates 1991, p. 36.

58 It relates particularly to J. B. Fischer von Erlach's reconstruction of the long-vanished Temple of Jupiter at Olympia, Third Wonder of the Ancient World, published in Fischer von Erlach 1721, Book I, pl. V, 1721; the English translation of 1730 (Lediard 1730, pp. 6–7) noted that Pausanias's account did not identify the order: Fischer chose Corinthian as 'one of the most magnificent', but admitted that 'we learn from other Historians that [they were] Dorick', thereby giving authority for its use at Mereworth.

59 Norberg-Schulz 1974, pls 95, 423.

60 Braham 1980, chapters 1, 5; Bergdoll 2000, pp. 23–32.

TWENTY-SIX THE FIRST NEOCLASSICAL CHURCHES

1 *Gentleman's Magazine* (August 1751), p. 344, referring to the Roman Pantheon, with interior view.

2 *Grub-street Journal*, no. 238 (18 July 1734), p. 1; no. 258 (5 December 1734), p. 1; no. 237 (11 July 1734), p. 1. In *Lectures on Architecture*, 1734, pp. 114–15, Robert Morris wrote of the temple portico's power of vesting 'Grace and Nobleness to a Design'. Riddell 1990, p. 82.

3 *Grub-street Journal*, no. 249 (3 October 1734), p. 2; no. 256 (21 November 1734), p. 1. Summerson 2000, pl. 18.

4 Doc. 223: 26 August 1735; Colvin 2008, p. 630.

5 *Grub-street Journal*, no. 244 (29 August 1734), p. 1. The reference is to 'On Egyptian Halls' in Palladio's *I quattro libri d'architettura*, 1570 (Tavernor and Schofield 1997, pp. 117–18), which Burlington adopted at York Assembly Rooms, 1731–2.

6 *Grub-street Journal*, no. 249 (20 August 1734), p. 1. Langley favoured the Corinthian order because it was 'naturally more lofty, and richer in composition [and] contains the properest emblem of elegance and riches', therefore most appropriate for a 'cathedral in a city'.

7 *Grub-street Journal*, no. 243 (22 August 1734), p. 1. The temple as reconstructed in Von Erlach 1721 measured 425 by 200 feet, 'adorn'd on the Out-& Inside with 127 *Columns* of the most exquisite Marble, 60 Foot in Height' (Lediard 1730, First Book, p. 8, pl. VII).

8 'Antiquaries suppose that the Temple of *Diana* stood formerly . . . where St *Paul's* Cathedral is now erected' (*Gentleman's Magazine*, October 1738, p. 523). See also Doc. 238: 5 September 1796. This is unlikely (Keene, Burns and Saint 2004, p. 4).

9 Doc. 223: 1759, 7 November 1797. Gwynn (1766; pp. 37–8) criticized the 'division of the building into two orders [as] undoubtedly a great fault, it would have had a much nobler effect, had one only been used; as it is, the lower part of the church seems to be the work of one master, and the dome of another, the peristylum of which is very fine, and perfectly adapted to finish one single order, but, as it is, appears too heavy; the lower part of the church is extremely elegant, but does not harmonize with the upper part, the columns of the peristylum being much larger, in proportion to their distance, than the columns of the portico. Indeed one of the most capital errors in the construction of this church is, the neglecting to shew the proper dependency of one part upon the other, and a regular harmonious gradation from the foundation to the summit of the super-structure; perhaps if the disproportion between the length and breadth of the whole building had not been so great, it might have produced a more noble effect, a more elegant shape, and an opportunity of forming the due connection between the dome and the lower part of the building, which now seems to stand in need of such an union, by the former appearing to rest upon the roof.' Like Langley, Gwynn seems to have been theoretically preparing St Paul's for a neoclassical transformation. Interestingly, he condemned Gibbs's St Mary-le-Strand because 'the whole being divided into two orders, the parts of each are small, and the subordination (without which there can be no greatness of manner) is destroyed. Had such a portico as that of St. Martin's Church been placed there, and the church been like that composed only of one order, it is very easy to conceive what a different effect it would have had upon the spectator' (p. 44).

10 See also William Stukeley's reconstruction of Solomon's Temple at Jerusalem (1731–4), in which the Holy of Holies amalgamated Christ Church, Spitalfields, and St Martin-in-the-Fields (Du Prey 2000, pp. 105, 130, figs 57–8).

11 *Grub-street Journal*, no. 245 (5 September 1734), p. 1. Beard 1982, pl. 158.

12 Conversely, the Temple of Augustus and Rome at Mylasa (Melasso), which combines a Corinthian portico with foliage-based columns and an Ionic colonnade round the

cella, 'may be looked on as bad taste' (Pococke 1743–5, vol. II, pp. 108, 110, pls X–XX, and p. 61, pl. LV). McCarthy 1996.

13 Langford 1870, p. 48, quoting from the local press. In December 1750 Birmingham was hailed as 'A Town which Virgil's self might nobly own' and linked to 'Athens, in Days of Yore, for Arts was fam'd, / And Rome's immortal Glory stands proclaim'd . . . Thus blest with every Grace the Powers can give, / May Birmingham long flourish, and e'er live' ('A Prologue (spoke at the Theatre in Birmingham, in praise of the town by Mr. Brodin)', Langford 1870, pp. 42–3).

14 Harris and Savage 1990, pp. 491–5; Wiebenson 1969, pp. 25–33, 92–7, pl. 3; Purchas 1994. The painter Giuseppe Borgnis repeated the ceiling pattern in the entrance hall of the nearby mansion (Knox 2001, pp. 11–12, 48–56; Kelly 2009, p. 132, figs 72–3).

15 Laugier 1977, pp. 15–16, 100–02, 104, 115. In Chapter I, 'General Principles of Architecture', p. 13, the Maison Carrée's beauty resides in its being 'a rectangle where thirty columns support an entablature and a roof – closed at both ends by a pediment – that is all; the combination is of a simplicity and a nobility which strikes everybody'.

16 Ingamells 1997, pp. 813–14. He met James Stuart and Nicholas Revett in Smyrna in 1753 (Colvin 2008, p. 869; Harris and Savage 1990, pp. 390–93).

17 Riou 1768, pt II, p. 70, adding that 'if executed with due regard to the simple principles of the antique, makes an agreeable contrast in a prospect, with the other buildings of a town; how happily have they been introduced in the finest pictures of Claude and Poussin'. Riou's externally colonnaded chancel and internal column screens may show an awareness of church designs in Neufforge 1757–68, vol. VI, 70e cahier, p. 417, pl. 3; vol. VII, 74e cahier, p. 492, pl. 4, and 73e cahier, p. 436, pl. 4.

18 This arrangement derived from a ruined 'Stoa or Portico . . . Commonly Supposed To Be The Remains Of The Temple of Jupiter Olympius . . . one of the most considerable remains of Athenian magnificence' recorded and reconstructed in Stuart's and Revett's *The Antiquities of Athens*, 1762–94, vol. I, chapter V, pls XXXI–XXXII. Also, compare pls 599–600 (this publication) with Robert Hampden's undated 'Idea of a cathedral' (Kenworthy-Brown 2008, fig. 3).

19 Braham 1980, pp. 33–6, 50–52, 73–82, pls 34, 58, 89. Riou compared his treatment in pls 599–600 with the 'beautiful example' of Wren's St Stephen Walbrook.

20 Riou believed that Gibbs had 'a better opportunity than most artists, to display his talents in the grand style of architecture [at] St. Martin-in-the-Fields . . . But the taste of this architect has thrown no new light upon the art' (Riou 1768, pt II, p. 57: 'Remarks Concerning Publick and Private Edifices, with Designs').

21 The arrangement of Ionic and Corinthian columns supporting narrow side galleries is based on Palladio's reconstruction of the Temple of Jupiter on the Quirinale, Rome, where also there are no columns at the rear since the temple abutted a partition wall (Tavernor and Schofield 1997, pp. 253–9).

22 Laugier 1977, pp. 103, 32–3 (Chapter I, Article V: 'Windows and Doors').

TWENTY-SEVEN CHURCHES OF THE 1760S AND 1770S

1 George Richardson on ancient Roman buildings, 11 July 1762 (National Library of Scotland, Edinburgh, MS 3812, f. v).

2 Harris and Savage 1990, pp. 439–50.

3 Stuart and Revett 1762–94, vol. I, chapter II, p. 29. Lawrence 1983, pp. 172–3, pls 139–40.

4 Doc. 138: 9 August 1773.

5 Doc. 208. In Rome he was 'full of business . . . measuring the Antiquities, practising Drawing with assiduity, & studying Geometry, very closely [and] thinking of drawing all the most beautiful Antique Entablatures with their . . . many fine Ornamented Freezes, Capitals & Bases pretty large & make out the Ornaments, Measures & taste of Workmanship, in the most elegant distinct & exact manner possible' (British Architectural Library, Drawings and Archives Collection, Victoria and Albert Museum, London, Da Fam/1/1, ff. 1, 21, letters to his father of 4 October 1760 and 10 April 1762). Ingamells 1997, pp. 273–4.

6 Marconi, Cipriani and Valeriani 1974, vol. I, nos 626–40.

7 The site measured 40 by 405 feet maximum (Lever 2003, p. 84). Discussions about replacing the decrepit medieval church were in hand by 6 September 1764 (Doc. 208); Dance returned to London in December of that year (Ingamells 1997, p. 273). Dance Sr apparently helped prepare the competition drawings of 8 May 1765.

8 Lever 2003, pp. 66–71.

9 Its accomplishment is evident compared to Dance's undisciplined, quirky, unrealised scheme for St Martin, Outwich (1765–8), previously attributed to Dance Sr (Lever 2003, pp. 85–8, figs 22.4–5).

10 Watkin 1996, pp. 527, 223, pl. 99; Worsley 1995, fig. 335.

11 Watkin 1996, pp. 140–41.

12 Laugier 1977, p. 42.f

13 Tavernor and Schofield 1997, pp. 248–50; Ward-Perkins 1981, pl. 284; Lever 2003, p. 83.

14 Doc. 208: 11 July 1766. 'The inside is extremely simple, without pillars, or division of any kind . . . It is the extreme richness of the great arch adorned with a beautiful arrangement of stucco, most fancifully combined with a frieze of scrolls and shells, that arrests the spectator's attention' (Malcolm 1803–7, vol. II, p. 67).

15 Doc. 49. A later reflection of London Wall is St Mary, Lewisham (1775–7), by George Gibson. Either he or his architect father had been unsuccessful contenders in the London Wall competition of 1 May 1765 (Doc. 208); conversely, Dance prepared a scheme for Lewisham (untraced) on 18 October 1773, ten months prior to the approval of Gibson's design (Doc. 243).

16 Adam returned on January 1758; Dance set out the following December (Ingamells 1997, pp. 5–6, 273).

17 Quoted in Fleming 1962, p. 145. Adam's library included

'views of St Peters . . . by Mr R. Adam, Piranesi, Clerisseau, &c.' (Watkin 1972, p. 170, lot 28).

18 Manuscript essay on architecture, 1762, quoted in Fleming 1962, p. 316.

19 National Library of Scotland, MS 3812, f. 1v, 11 July 1762 (Ingamells 1997, p. 811).

20 Quoted in Fleming 1962, p. 145. Adam drew the building in 1756 (pls 57, 61 in the latter publication).

21 James Essex remarked: 'If few R[oma]n Temples were built on a Circular plan there are some which demand our notice, as being attributed to Constantine or for having been Heathen Temples, & dedicated to Christianity . . . The Pantheon was the most remarkable' (British Library, Add. MS 6772, f. 140v).

22 Dodsley and Dodsley 1761, vol. III, pp. 322–3, the original chapel having opened on 31 January 1747 (British Library, King's Topographical Collection, XXVII–28, view). Following the closure of the Lock Hospital, Southwark (Medvei and Thornton 1974, p. 352; Weinreb and Hibbert 1983, p. 465), Adam prepared designs (Sir John Soane's Museum, London, AD 38/16–20; King 2001, vol. II, pp. 16–7, pl. 24). Erected to another scheme by an unknown architect (British Museum, Crace, 34, f. 25; Shepherd 1829, p. 122).

23 Ficacci 2000, pls 483, 534. Adam owned a plan, elevation and sections of the Pantheon drawn by G. B. Montano (Fairbairn 1998, vol. II, pp. 553, 644 nos 1133–4).

24 Langley 1736, p. 285, pl. CLXXIX.

25 Tavernor and Schofield 1997, pp. 260–63.

26 *Gentleman's Magazine* (March 1759), pp. 101–2; furthermore: 'As for the attic, there is great reason to doubt of its antiquity, and to suspect that the pilasters are of that kind of ornaments distinguished by the appellation of *modern antiques* . . . But granting the pilasters to have been of the best age of architecture, they were two years ago broken to pieces, and fallen into ruins' (Curcio 2003, p. 309). The anonymous article, responding to a lengthy historical survey in *Gentleman's Magazine* (January 1759), pp. 9–12, ending with a note on 'a monstrous project . . . for modernizing it all over' in 1757, reported that 'No alteration is proposed except in the dome, the attic, and the pavement. The balustrade of the sanctuary . . . has been new done already; but there is no reason that this should at all disgust the antiquarians'; the dome long stripped of ornament offers 'nothing to the view but rough masonry of a dark dirty complexion . . . and . . . raises the idea of an edifice falling to ruin, rather than of the magnificence of ancient architecture', ending: 'In a word, it is to be wished that this project had never taken place.'

27 Hart and Hicks 1996, p. 409. George Richardson noted on the Pantheon: 'There are no Windows for the Admission of light as the Spacious Lanthorn on the top of the famous Dome well supplies the whole Temple with Abundance of Light' (National Library of Scotland, MS 3812, f. 1v, 11 July 1761). See also *Gentleman's Magazine* (August 1766), p. 367. The oculus was glazed as part of the recent improvements, *Gentleman's Magazine* (March 1759), p. 102, admitting 'that the large aperture of the dome is extremely incommodious to the congregation. Together with snow and rain, catarrhs and rheumatisms are too apt to descend through it; but to close it up with a cupola, is not only to exclude much of the light, but likewise to surcharge the edifice with a most ridiculous addition.'

28 Ingamells 1997, p. 8. The temple is reconstructed in Palladio (Tavernor and Schofield 1997, pp. 319–22), recorded in its ruined state in Piranesi's *Alcune vedute di archi trionfali* (Ficacci 2000, pls 96–7) and in much-praised measured drawings by Stuart and Revett in 1750, for engraving (Harris and Savage 1990, p. 440; Wiebenson 1969, pp. 81–2, pl. 5).

29 Stuart's and Revett's reconstruction appears in the third volume of *The Antiquities of Athens*, 1794, chapter XI, pls XLVI–XLVII (Harris and Savage 1990, p. 441). Adam's copy of the first volume, published in 1762, was inscribed 'This superb copy was presented to Mr Adam by the Author' (Watkin 1972, p. 189, lot 139), suggesting a friendship that could have allowed Adam to have seen Stuart's preparatory drawings for the Incantada by 1766. The Bishop of Norwich granted a faculty on 19 April 1766 for the old church 'greatly out of repair . . . to pull down . . . Rebuild . . . in . . . substantial . . . handsome manner at [Harbord's] own Cost . . . making [it] fit and comodious' (Norfolk Record Office, DN/FCB 3/1), Sir John Soane's Museum, AD 43/11–15 (King 2001, vol. I, pp. 68–9, pls 79–81), opened 1769, interior rearranged 1894 (*Buildings of England: Norfolk 1*, 1997, pp. 534–5, pl. 80).

30 The church is poorly documented. Sir John Soane's Museum, AD 30/109–11 (King 2001, pp. 58, 181, 183, 204). It was rebuilt in 1793 for £600 by an unknown architect in a dismally pedestrian manner (Surrey Record Office, PSH/ WON/12/21–22), Manning and Bray 1804–14, vol. II, p. 113; Clarke 1963, p. 144; *Buildings of England: Surrey*, 1990, pp. 447–8; Blatch 1997, pp. 222–3, fig. 212.

31 Sir John Soane's Museum, AD 21/47; a closely related design, vol. 54, series IV, nos 174–5. King 2001, vol. II, p. 63, pl. 69.

32 Leoni 1755, pp. 170–71, pls 45–7, Book VIII, Chapter V, 'Of Towers and their Ornaments': 'The greatest Ornaments are lofty Towers placed in proper Situations, and built after handsome Designs . . . a Way of Building which I extremely commend . . . because each Story growing less and less all the Way up, conduces both to Strength and Beauty, and by being well knit one into another, makes the whole Structure firm . . . some Architects, about half Way of the Height . . . have adorned it with a Kind of Portico with insulate Columns', featuring 'a square Superstructure like a little Chapel [and a] circular Portico . . . covered with a Cupola'. Harris and Savage 1990, pp. 107–9.

33 Colvin 2008, p. 239.

34 Doc. 263: 15 November 1766, 23 April 1767.

35 Plymley 1992, pp. 99–100 (Doc. 12).

36 British Library, Add. MS 41,136, ff. 8v–9v. Colvin 2008, pp. 984–5.

37 Gloucestershire Record Office, D 2002/3/4/1, ff. 28–9, 111, 180, 185. Ingamells 1997, p. 664.

38 Doc. 253: 23 June 1770. The composition relies on domestic work (Gosforth, Northumberland, *circa* 1755–64, and Fetherstonhaugh's Whitehall residence, 1754–8, by Paine

1767–83, pls XVII–XVIII, XXVII–XXVIII, to which Woolfe subscribed). In the 1750s he served as Paine's office clerk (Colvin 2008, pp. 1149–50). The Duke of Portland, who donated the St Marylebone site, subscribed to *Vitruvius Britannicus* (Woolfe and Gandon 1767–71, vol. V).

39 Doc. 253: 16 February 1774.

40 Doc. 253: 3 August, 6 September 1770, 12 February, 16 July 1771.

41 Doc. 253: unidentified press clipping of 1771, adding that it 'will exceed in size that of St Martin's', that is, Gibbs's 'Round Design' for St Martin-in-the-Fields published in Gibbs 1728, pls 8–15. Can this be a reference to Juvarra's Superga near Turin, of 1716–31 (Millon 1999, pp. 112, 116–19, 348, 366–8, 671–4), a city visited by Chambers sometime between 1750 and 1755 (Ingamells 1997, pp. 194–5)?

42 British Library, Add. MS 41,136, ff. 8v–9v, 5 August 1774. For Santa Maria dei Gradi, Viterbo, renovated in 1733, see Kieven 1993, cat. 93.

43 Braham 1980, pp. 132–3, pls 169–70.

44 Chambers 1758, p. 15, in connection with the spire of St Bride, Fleet Street.

45 Petzet 1961, pls 24–7. The dispute began with Pierre Patte's attack in *Mémoires sur les objets des plus importans de l'architecture*, 1769, a copy of which Chambers owned (Watkin 1972, p. 118, lot 38), following Patte's visit to survey St Paul's Cathedral dome in 1768 (Braham 1980, p. 78).

46 Doc. 253: 1771 (Stewart), 16 February 1774. A new church was eventually built in the years 1813–17 by his pupil Thomas Hardwick Jr.

47 For example, in his study for transforming the early Christian basilica of San Paolo fuori le Mura, 1758 (Kieven 1991a, cat. 74). For Dublin, see Lewis 1837, vol. I, p. 552; Harris 1970, pp. 96, 206, pls 149, 151.

48 Doc. 69: following 7–12 January 1773, Caldwell to Charlemont.

49 Doc. 22: 24 August 1774. For a more balanced assessment, see 1783.

50 Doc. 163: 28 February 1785, 15 August 1781.

51 A. T. Bolton suggested that Adam chose the Lincoln's Inn composition out of respect for Jones, who had masked medieval St Paul's Cathedral in classical dress (Bolton 1917, p. 115). The composition is almost identical to Adam's Society of Arts façade, Adelphi (1772; Allan 1974, pp. 28–9, pl. 4b), with additional embellishments including free-standing statues, relief medallions and a reappearance of the much-prized Incantada fluted frieze in the entablature.

52 Smollett 1981, pp. 83–4, adding: 'I am astonished to see it standing entire, like the effect of inchantment, after such a succession of ages, every one more barbarous than another', partly quoted in *Gentleman's Magazine* (June 1766), p. 261.

53 Graves 1907, p. 82, no. 213. The model is untraced. Clérisseau remained in England probably until 1775 (McCormick 1990, pp. 135–6, 147–63).

54 Rocque 1746–7, IIA–Bb. Stewart 1771, p. 34, reported in 1771: 'the embellishments and improvements . . . carrying on admid the ancient ruins of Durham yard, is a sample of what may be done in that way'. 'Design of . . . Church . . . intended to be built in Durham yard' inscribed 'DIVINO ARCHITECTO DEO OPTIMO OMNIPOTENTI' (Sir John Soane's Museum, AD 10/64, 44/95–98, alternative 35/27–31), erected to another scheme of unknown appearance (King 2001, vol. I, pp. 77–82, pl. 91; vol. II, pp. 60, 66, pls 67–8; Stillman 1988, vol. II, pp. 439, 454–5). In June 1772 a run on banks patronised by Adam, which threw the Adelphi project into confusion (King 2001, vol. II, p. 33), may explain the frustration of the chapel project.

55 Ingamells 1997, pp. 5–8.

56 Navarra 2001, pl. XLIX. For a further discussion of this design, see Rowan 2007, pp. 58–9, nos 35–7, who also considers the 1776 Adam office proposal (unrealised) for a more conservative, Palladian chapel for the Revd Toplady, a Calvinist, at the Adelphi (pp. 58, 60, no. 38).

57 Doc. 133: 1784 (Rochefoucauld 1784, pp. 115, 119–20, pls 21–5). For house (demolished 1835), landscape and village, see Rochefoucauld 1784, pp. 115–22; King 2001, vol. I, pp. 249, 344–6, pls 356–7, 492–3; Muilman 1769–72, vol. VI, p. 31 ill. Rigby was MP for Essex and Paymaster to the Forces.

58 The decorative scheme was also used in Mistley Hall (King 2001, vol. I, pls 356–7), further linking the two buildings. Among Adam's drawings collections is F. J. Belanger's study for Lansdown House gallery, London (1779; Sir John Soane's Museum, AD 68/5/5), with an almost identical top-light.

59 Rochefoucauld 1784, p. 119. King 2001, vol. I, pls 83–4.

60 Doc. 133: 1745. Its outer walls with their external and internal Tuscan pilasters are indicated in Adam's published plan (King 2001, vol. I, pl. 83) and preserved in his remodelling.

61 Twin-towered churches were unusual but not unique: see Alloa church (Doc. 5), which Robert may have known since his father included Mar's Royal Palace design in *Vitruvius Scoticus*, pl. 110 (Friedman 1986, fig. 19).

62 Ficacci 2000, pls 79, 193, 920, 966.

63 Clerk MS, 7 June 1755, quoted in Fleming 1962, p. 352, illustrating 'Another view of the Carthusian Church at Rome' (pl. 63).

64 Doc. 125. The *David* is now in the present chapel in the grounds (Doc. 126).

65 Ingamells 1997, pp. 29–30, 939–42. Bignamini and Hornsby 2010, vol. I, pp. 324–5.

66 Doc. 189: 11 February 1775, 15 January 1774, 28 January 1775.

67 Doc. 189: 22 October, 9 March 1774. Thorpe referred to 'his merit of invention', 17 August 1774.

68 Marconi, Cipriani and Valeriani 1974, vol. I, nos 704–6. His free-standing, basilical 'grande cappella . . . Per Arundel . . . un Palazzo di campagne' culminating in a Santa Costanza-like rotunda (Angelini et al. 1984, p. 23, fig. 9, without citing documentation), was probably based on Constantine's church of the Holy Sepulchre, Jerusalem (Krautheimer 1986, pp. 60–63, pl. 27B). Interestingly, on 20 April 1771 Thorpe offered Arundell 'a neat model of the Church of the H. Sepulchre' from the late Thomas Wagstaffe's collection (Ingamells 1997, p. 970). Quarenghi's beautiful interior of Santa Scolastica, Subiaco (1771–4), fea-

tures, like Paine's chapel, plain walls articulated by the classical order supporting a deep entablature with lunette windows over (Angelini et al. 1984, figs 5–7).

69 Doc. 189: 24 December 1774

70 Doc. 189: 10 October 1769.

71 Thorpe thought Piranesi 'has done more for the honour of the Antiquities of Rome, & for the fine Arts in general than any other Artist whatever' (Ingamells 1997, p. 941). He acquired for Arundell Piranesi's *Diverse maniere d'adornare i cammini*, 1769 (Doc. 189: 20 April, 18 May 1771). On 15 February 1775 he alerted Arundell to 'Two candelabri with Piranesi that would suit your chapel very well, tho . . . of marble, & antique'. Quarenghi departed for Russia in 1779 (23 October).

72 Book III, pls XXX–XXXI (Hart and Hicks 1996, vol. I, pp. 121–2).

73 Stillman 1988, vol. II, pl. 320.

74 Ingamells 1997, pp. 706–7. *The Architecture of M. Vitruvius Pollio* (Harris and Savage 1990, pp. 464–6).

75 Doc. 261: 11 July 1774. The 'most eminent Surveyor' may have been Sir William Chambers, then Controller of the King's Works (Colvin 2008, p. 1218).

76 Woolfe and Gandon 1767–71, vol. V, pls 76–7 (McParland 1985, pl. 10). Its origin is the Temple of Jupiter order illustrated in Robert Adam's 1764 book on Spalatro, pl. XXXVI.

77 Colvin 1991, p. 96, pl. 91.

78 Krautheimer 1986, pp. 171–4, figs 135–6.

79 Colvin 1991, pl. 48.

80 For example, William Kent's Temple of Venus, Stowe, *circa* 1731 (Ware 1731, pl. 47) and C.-N. Ledoux's Hôtel Guimard, Paris, (1770–71), and Château Louveciennes pavilion (1771; Braham 1980, pls 226–7, 230–31).

81 Placzek et al. 1972, pp. 34–5. The provenance of the set after 1767 until the twentieth century is unrecorded.

82 Taylor 1925, p. 406.

83 Doc. 261.

84 Stuart and Revett 1825–30, vol. I, chapter 2, pt I (Lawrence 1983, pls 139–40, 142). Newton's intermixed Ionic and Tuscan orders call to mind the west front of the Erechtheum, which was illustrated in J. D. Le Roy's *The Ruins of Athens*, vol. II, 1759, pl. XVI, fig. 1, reprinted in Piranesi, *Delle magnificenza ed architettura de' romani*, 1761 (Ficacci 2000, pl. 471). It was also illustrated in Stuart and Revett 1762–94, vol. II, edited by William Newton.

85 Leroy credited the introduction of domes to Greek architecture (Middleton 2003, p. 32). Newton sketched Walbrook church (British Architectural Library, Drawings and Archives Collection, Victoria and Albert Museum, London, L9/52, *RIBA Catalogue: L–N*, 1973, p. 143 item 95), perhaps in connection with this commission.

86 Lawrence 1983, pp. 171–3, figs 139–41 (Soros 2006, pp. 127–9, figs 3–24, 25, 26).

87 *Gentleman's Magazine* (July 1804), p. 691; (September 1804), p. 860.

88 Doc. 9: 28 July 1779.

89 The temple was published in Stuart and Revett 1762–94, vol. III, chapter XII, pls LI–LII. Revett employed the same order in the portico of Standlynch, now Trafalgar House, Wiltshire, 1766 (Wiebenson 1969, pl. 45; Kelly 2009, p. 137, figs 116–18). The 'colonnes du celebre Temple d'Apollo' is illustrated in Leroy 1759 (Wiebenson 1969, p. 70, pl. 39).

90 Worsley 1995, p. 306, rather than Stillman's unlikely suggestion that the building remains unfinished (Stillman 1988, vol. II, p. 434).

91 The diagonal spurs flanking the chancel once interested Soane (pl. 635); see this chapter, note 73.

92 Stuart's and Revett's reconstruction was published in *The Antiquities of Athens* (Stuart and Revett 1762–94, vol. II, chapter V). Of it Willey Reveley speculated in the preface to vol. III, p. 14: 'The small temples, which on each side form the wings of the Propylaea, possibly contributed to render the central part more solid, by the appearance of a lateral support . . . while in every other respect they must have increased the general dignity of the whole, and, by the smaller dimensions of their parts of the same order, have added to the consequence of the central range of columns. The magnificence of this entrance . . . must have been extreme when in its original perfection'.

93 Doc. 9: 26 November 1789.

94 For a fuller discussion of Ayot St Lawrence, see Friedman 2004, chapter VI.

TWENTY-EIGHT GREEENWICH HOSPITAL CHAPEL

1 The Frenchman Maximilien de Lazowski visiting on 9 May 1785 (Rochefoucauld 1785, pp. 229–30).

2 Ackermann 1808–9, vol. III, p. 246.

3 'For truly classical design, in which no ornament is applied but from an antique example, the chapel of Greenwich hospital, as restored by the Athenian Stuart, has no rival in England, I might also add, in Italy. So pure a taste and so characteristick a magnificence should be consulted and adopted in all ecclesiastical structures, that may be hereafter erected upon the Grecian model' (Dallaway 1806, p. 219).

4 British Architectural Library, Drawings and Archives Collection, Victoria and Albert Museum, London, NEW/1/7/2(i), 'A Short account of the progress of restoring the Chapel & Dome of Greenwich Hospital'. Doc. 236: 19 August 1754.

5 Soros 2006; Colvin 2008, pp. 998–1003.

6 Doc. 236: 9–11 February, May, 10 September 1782, 2 February, 22, 27 September 1789, February 1790.

7 British Architectural Library, Drawings and Archives Collection, Victoria and Albert Museum, London, MS NEW/1/8/4–6. Newton died on 6 July 1790. His executor enquired if the governors were 'not of Opinion notwithstanding . . . Stewart was the regular Surveyor . . . but owing to his advanced age or infirmity, incapable of performing the duties of the office, that the designs . . . were almost wholly if not intirely of the invention selection & arrangement of . . . Newton?' (NEW/1/8/2 [i]). See also Doc. 236: 24 August 1790, 30 November, 2 December 1791.

8 Doc. 236: 9–11 February, 14 March, 14 August, 10 September 1782, 22 September 1789 Advertisement. British Architectural Library, Drawings and Archives Collection,

Victoria and Albert Museum, London, NEW/1/8/9. Of numerous preparatory drawings, only Stuart's for the east and west walls and the ceiling survive (Doc. 236: 14 March 1782).

9 Lawrence 1983, pp. 213–21.

10 Doc. 236: 27 February 1788.

11 Harris and Savage 1990, pp. 431–7, 445.

12 Sir John Soane's Museum, London, 47/6/10. Knight described it as 'a small pyramidal Building . . . raised upon a pedestal and has an Ionic Column, fluted, projecting from each Angle, but the Entablature is Doric' (Stumpf 1986, p. 44, pl. 17), Ward-Perkins 1981, pp. 287, 265. Stuart was an 'Associate' of the antiquary Matthew Nulty, who together with Robert Mylne undertook an expedition to Sicily in 1757, where they visited Agrigentum (Ingamells 1997, pp. 693–4, 717, 910).

13 Watkin 1982a, pls 76–7. Ficacci 2000, pp. 582–633.

14 Doc. 236: 27 February 1788, 18 August 1786, 1 January 1795.

15 In the preface to Stuart and Revett 1762–94, vol. III, p. 11, the editor, Willey Reveley, observed that the 'perfect state in which those monuments remain, which have not been destroyed by violence, is one proof of the judgment with which they were constructed', citing the Choragic Monument of Lysicrates in vol. I as 'now entire, a circumstance arising chiefly from the great judgment shewn in its construction'.

16 British Architectural Library, Drawings and Archives Collection, Victoria and Albert Museum, London, NEW/1/8/2(i), 1/8/8, f. 5. A contemporary reflection of this is James Wyatt's scheme for modernising the early Georgian chapel of Worcester College, Oxford, 1783–91 (Doc. 145).

TWENTY-NINE THE FINAL DECADES, 1780–1800

1 Soane 1788, Introduction, p. 1.

2 Doc. 17.

3 Wood 1742, pt II, p. 29. Mowl and Earnshaw 1988, p. 127. The medieval church measured 21 by 16 feet (Root 1992, pp. 6–7). For the ancient Tabernacle, see Meek 1995, p. 27.

4 In 1775 expenditure was at £10,365 compared to income at £22,112, but in 1779 it rose to £19,714 compared to £11,853 and in 1782, £29,234 to £13,765 (Gregory and Stevenson 2000, p. 269).

5 Doc. 255: 19 July 1784. The church was rebuilt in 1845.

6 McAndrew 1974.

7 Perhaps an even more direct source is a sheet of studies for a proposed church by John Webb, though inscribed 'Inigo Jones' (the eighteenth century favouring an attribution to the master rather than the pupil), then already in the collection of Worcester College, Oxford, where Wyatt redecorated the chapel, 1776–90 (Harris and Tait 1979, pp. 1–2, 66 nos 151A–E; Whinney 1943, p. 149, pl. 40a).

8 Farington 1978–84, vol. III, p. 918.

9 Doc. 131. Aston 1816, pp. 87–8.

10 Latrobe 1984–8, vol. II, pp. 428–9, 21 May 1807, citing the Lantern of Demosthenes, Athens, of 'which nothing of the kind can be more beautiful, as not less beautiful if mounted upon a magnificent Mass of architecture'.

11 'Obituary of remarkable Persons', *Gentleman's Magazine* (July 1799), p. 627.

12 British Architectural Library, Drawings and Archives Collection, Victoria and Albert Museum, London, REW/1, f. 281v, visiting 12 July 1787. Reveley owned C. L. Clérisseau, *Antiquities de la France*, 1778 (Christie's 1801, p. 5, lot 118; British Architectural Library, Drawings and Archives Collection, REW/1).

13 Stuart and Revett 1762–94, vol. III, p. 15, Reveley as editor, citing the Theatre of Marcellus and the Colosseum, Rome, as specimens of the Roman Doric 'void of character and strength'; p. 13 n. b describes the Paestum temple, which he visited on 20–25 February 1785 (Ingamells 1997, pp. 807–8). Salmon 2000, pp. 43, 237 n. 20, 238 n. 86, pl. 26.

14 Reveley remarked: 'Though I can add nothing to the high reputation of Grecian art, it seems incumbent on me . . . not to pass, wholly unnoticed, the observation . . . given to the world by . . . Chambers' (Stuart and Revett 1762–94, vol. III, preface, dated September 1794, pp. 11, 16); furthermore, he observed in Chambers's *A Treatise on the Decorative Parts of Civil Architecture*, 1791, the 'complaint of the disproportionate architraves in the Grecian architecture is ridiculous' (p. 15) and 'the very contemptuous manner in which Sir William treats all the admirers of Grecian art' (p. 16). Harris and Savage 1990, pp. 446–9. For Reveley's difficulties with the committee, see pp. 144–5.

15 Doc. 167: 25 January 1792.

16 Chandler, Revett and Pars 1769–1915, vol. I, chapter 2, pl. V (Middleton et al. 1998, p. 301).

17 Preface to Stuart and Revett 1762–94, vol. III, p. 15.

18 Harris 1970, pl. 35.

19 Preface to Stuart and Revett 1762–94, vol. III, pp. 12–13.

20 See also a similar design for an unidentified church, 1794–5 (Lukacher 2006, pl. 7).

21 From 'Observations made on the spot'. Reveley wrote of St Peter that 'The coupled columns round it are clumsy & too wide asunder . . . The windows are too large & by their enormous size give a trifling appearance to the colums . . . the breaks in the [attic] pilasters are too trifling to have any effect . . . The [dome's] ribs are too heavy, large & complicated; such preposterous masses upon a dome are not only the destruction of its general form but approach the size of columns . . . ornaments [of the dome windows] should have been . . . more simple as they are to be seen at a great distance. The Lanthorn is too complicated . . . The small cupolas . . . are very ill placed . . . They are very ugly compositions . . . The front . . . is perhaps as full of faults as any thing of the size can be', etc. (British Architectural Library, Drawings and Archives Collection, Victoria and Albert Museum, London, REW/1, ff. 65–6).

22 British Architectural Library, Drawings and Archives Collection, Victoria and Albert Museum, London, REW/1, f. 116, observed 'when I passed through Paris (1788)'.

23 *The Southampton Guide*, 1805 (eighteenth edn), pp. 34–5.

24 Ingamells 1997, p. 807. Friedman 2002, pp. 84–5, fig. 7, discusses a possible preliminary design for the interior with features reminiscent of Greenwich Hospital chapel.

25 Southampton Archives, D/PM 9/4/2/15/1, f. 16.
26 British Architectural Library, Drawings and Archives Collection, Victoria and Albert Museum, London, REW/1, ff. 73r–v, 86v.
27 *The Southampton Guide*, 1804, pp. 34–6.
28 'An Architect Whose sole View is to build A Church without faults' (Southampton Archives, D/PM/ 9/4/2/13).
29 D. H. [David Hughson?], 'Reveley's Classical Drawings', *Gentleman's Magazine* (May 1801), pp. 419–20.
30 Doc. 31: 7 February 1792.
31 Doc. 166.
32 Doc. 31: 29 March 1792, 15 December 1791.
33 Doc. 31: 13, 19 January 1792. Friedman 1996a, pl. 21.
34 Doc. 271.
35 Doc. 31: 17 October 1792.
36 Undated letter, quoted without source in Rolt 1958, p. 39.
37 Doc. 31: 31 January, 7 February 1792.
38 Colvin 1991, p. 39, fig. 33. *Travels in Asia Minor* [1775], in Chandler 1971, p. 113; drawn by his travelling companion, William Pars, pl. IX, it was engraved for the second volume of *Ionian Antiquities* (Chandler, Revett and Pars 1769–1915, vol. II [1797], p. xxxix, pl. 24). Telford consulted the first volume (1769) during a trip to London, where he 'met with the Antiquities of Athens and Ionia . . . examined most of the Editions of Vitruvius, some as early as 1511 – and . . . saw some splendid Ed. of Palladin and Inigo Jones Architecture [etc.] so that with the information I was before in possession of. I think I have a tolerable good general notion of Architecture' (The Ironbridge Gorge Museum, Letters of Thomas Telford, I, 10 March 1793; Friedman 1996a, p. 130 note 103).
39 Doc. 31: 17 October 1792. Montfaucon 1721–2, vol. II, pp. 42, 72–3, pls 5, 13. Shrewsbury School Library, MS Borrowing Book 1736–99, p. E (Friedman 1996a, p. 130 n. 103).
40 Rolt 1958, p. 25.
41 Doc. 31: 17 October 1792. Scard 1990, p. 63.
42 Doc. 31: 17 October, 30 March 1792.
43 Dugdale 1819, vol. IV, p. 157, noted 'a very handsome Grecian altar-piece', since vanished. Doc. 31: 17 October 1792. The chancel skylight is a feature Robert Adam favoured but failed to implement at Mistley (this publication pl. 629).
44 Doc. 213: 6 April 1711, 1775. Godwin 1839, vol. II, p. 5.
45 Malcolm 1803–7, vol. II, p. 548, observed in 1803: 'there is something defective in the pillars . . . which support the side galleries . . . they are neither Tuscan nor Doric . . . the frieze above them is without a cornice'.
46 Mâle 1960, pl. 102; Blunt 1982, p. 28; Placzek 1982, vol. I, p. 112; Marconi, Cipriani and Valeriani 1974, vol. I, nos 551–69, of which V. Bracci's entry, nos 557–62, features nave colonnades supporting continuous entablatures replacing the original arcading (Mâle 1960, pp. 238, 241–2, pls 37, 74, 82). For a view of the chapel's triple-storey exterior, with the centrepiece of the upper storeys in the form of an engaged tetrastyle temple portico, see Craven 1964, p. 19.
47 Marconi, Cipriani and Valeriani 1974, vol. I, nos 850–52.
48 Rice 1997, particularly figs 42, 132, 149. Hughson 1817, vol. II, p. 279, observed of Bonomi's chapel: 'its classic purity of style, is admired by all lovers of architecture'.
49 Richard Morrison's presentation drawing is inscribed 'This plan was approved of & adopted . . . 8th day of July 1791'. McParland and Rowan 1989, p. 54, pls 46–7.
50 Doc. 113: *Grub-street Journal*, no. 244 (29 August 1734), p. 1, adding: 'if a church or cathedral in a city, the Corinthian, which being naturally more lofty, and richer in composition . . . contains the properest emblem of elegancy and riches'.
51 *Leeds Intelligencer*, 5 June 1787. Ingamells 1997, p. 560. Colvin 2008, p. 582.
52 Doc. 93.
53 The altarpiece presented to the 'eye . . . an interesting spectacle . . . enclosed within a capacious niche, embellished on each side by two massy . . . composite . . . columns . . . enriched by three paintings in Chiaro Scuro relief . . . and . . . angels . . . looking down from the roof of the niche, listening with reverence and . . . devotion to the divine mysteries celebrated below' (Whittle 1821, quoted in Doc. 151: Warren and Keegan 1993, pp. 35–6). See also Whittle's closely related, towered Anglican church at nearby Blackburn (Doc. 25).
54 British Architectural Library, Drawings and Archives Collection, Victoria and Albert Museum, London, REW/1, ff. 118v, 165v. Wittkower 1999, vol. II, pls 29–36, 49–54, 128–9.
55 Doc. 74.
56 The National Archives of Scotland, Edinburgh (formerly The Scottish Record Office), HR 152/2, ff. 5–6, 9 April 1789, referring to it as an object of 'decoration and fancy'.
57 Doc. 135: 1801; Oliver 1831, p. 89.
58 Ingamells 1997, pp. 467–8; Colvin 2008, p. 488.
59 Doc. 135: 1 June 1786. Hart and Hicks 1996, pp. 136–9.
60 This drawing, in turn, is closely related to Harrison's Chester Castle, a competition won in 1786, the first and final designs submitted between 28 February and September (Ockrim 1988, pp. 59, 416 pl. 2.3), erected 1792–1801. J. Gondoin's anatomical theatre of the Ecole de Chirurgie, Paris, 1769–74, could have provided a suitable arrangement for the internal seating (Braham 1980, pp. 137–43, pls 176, 178–80). Harrison's twin tempietto towers are similar to one he added to Lancaster Town Hall, 1782–3 (Friedman 2004, fig. 117).
61 Hart and Hicks 1996, pp. 136–7.
62 Doc. 135: 2 June 1786.
63 Reconstructed in Piranesi's *Antichità di Cora*, 1764, pl. VI (Ficacci 2000, pls 590–603), Friedman 2004, p. 138, fig. 118.
64 Sopwith 1826, p. 79, observed that these features 'justly excite the admiration of the stranger, after contemplating the venerable memorial of past ages presented by St Nicholas' steeple, turns with pleasure to observe so fair a monument of the taste and munificence of modern times'.
65 Mackenzie 1827, p. 308.
66 Sopwith 1826, pp. 87–93.
67 *Gentleman's Magazine* (April 1791), p. 325.
68 Bourne 1725, pp. 88–9. For a fuller discussion, see Friedman 2004, chapter VII.
69 The two buildings were closely linked. Owen 1808, p. 181, thought St Chad's plan 'extremely novel . . . though not absolutely unique [since a] church very nearly similar was erected a few years previous . . . at Newcastle'.

70 Doc. 166: 20 August 1792, 20 July 1793, referring to Ranelagh Gardens Rotunda, Chelsea (1742). Southey in 1839, quoted in Rolt 1958, p. 22.

71 Doc. 166: 30 November 1789. Scard 1990, pp. 3, 12.

72 Doc. 166: 21 June 1798. Clérisseau 1778, pl. LVIII (Friedman 1996a, p. 96, pl. 16). Stuart and Revett 1762–94, vol. I, pp. 29–35, pls VIII–XI. Robert Adam sketched the Tour Magne in its ruined state in 1754 (Tait 2008, pl. 25).

73 Doc. 166: 25 July 1794.

74 Doc. 224: 1 December 1792.

75 J. M. Moffatt and W. H. Leeds in Britton and Pugin 1825–8, vol. II, p. 76.

76 Sir John Soane's Museum, London, 45/3/29–31 (Du Prey 1982, pp. 132–3, fig. 7.4); Victoria and Albert Museum, London, 3436.183 (Du Prey 2000, cat. no. 4). Watkin 1996, p. 540.

77 Tavernor and Schofield 1997, pp. 285, 293.

78 Tavernor and Schofield 1997, pp. 250, 298.

79 Notably Sangallo the Younger's circular project for San Giovanni dei Fiorentini, Rome, *circa* 1520, in *Libro d'Antonio Labacco*, 1552, pl. 23 (Hopkins 2000, fig. 58a). A modified portico and tower were built 1818–22 to the design of his son, C. R. Cockerell.

80 Doc. 10: 1 December 1790.

81 Doc. 10: August 1800; J. H. Parker, 1840.

82 Doc. 10: 29 August 1794. The internal columnar distribution follows Wren's St Stephen Walbrook, while employing Gibbs's St Martin dosseret entablature. Cockerell was Taylor's pupil at the time when the latter built the similarly composed Transfer Office in the Bank of England, London (1765–8; Binney 1984, fig. 11).

83 Malcolm 1803–7, vol. IV, pp. 410–12.

84 Malcolm 1803–7, vol. IV, pp. 410–12.

85 For useful overviews, see Watkin 1982b, chapter 4; Morley 1993.

86 Doc. 251. It suffered an ignominious afterlife as a boxing ring before its destruction in the Blitz in 1940.

87 In imitation of James Gibbs's Radcliffe Library, Oxford, illustrated in his *Bibliotheca Radcliviana*, 1747, pls IX, XIX (Friedman 1984, pl. 276).

88 Navarra 2001, p. 220, pls XXVII–XXIX. Its enclosing covered colonnade, sections of which survived into the eighteenth century, offered a pattern for portico treatments.

89 Sir John Soane's Museum, AD 44/99–102. King 2001, vol. II, p. 66. A similar 'chapelle ou petit temple peut être exécuté sur une place plantées d'arbres', architect unnamed, appears in Stieglitz 1800, pls X–XI.

90 For examples, Madonna dell'Umiltà, Pistoia, and Santo Stefano della Vittoria, Foiano della Chiana near Arezzo, where in both cases they are still associated with pilasters (Satkowski 1993, pp. 61–7, pls 134, 136). Adam owned O. Porta's drawing of the latter (Fairbairn 1998, vol. II, pp. 476, 511–12, no. 748). He would probably also have known the motif on the entrance screen of Santa Maria del Priorato, Rome, 1766 (Wilton-Ely 1993, fig. 87). It reappeared in Adam's undated design for a very plain octagonal church for the Welsh antiquary Thomas Johnes, presumably for his seat at Stanage, Powys (Sir John Soane's Museum, AD 34/91–94, King 2001, vol. II, pp. 63, 67). His Cromarty drawings include Sir John Soane's Museum, AD 45/44–49 (King 2001, vol. II, pp. 18, 58, 63, pls 70–71; Nightingale 1977, fig. 6). The church was built in 1783 by an unknown architect to a different design (*Buildings of Scotland: Highlands*, 1992, p. 398, pl. 4). For a structure similar to Adam's design, see Rawlins 1768 (to which James Adam subscribed), pl. XLV, 'Design for a Person of Quality, of an octangular Church . . . to be placed on an Eminence at a small Distance from the Mansion, for the use of his Family, and a Parish that has but few Inhabitants; to be finish'd with a Cove-Cieling'. Its uncommon tower suggests that Rawlins, a Norwich architect trained in London, may have been aware of current French trends such as those published in Neufforge 1757–68.

91 Trinder 1977, p. 46.

92 Doc. 127: 15 December 1792.

93 Lawson 1980, p. 9.

94 Brewster 1830, p. 644.

95 Trinder 1973, pp. 267–71, and Trinder, no date, pp. 2–4. So successful was this design that Telford duplicated it in the adjacent parish of Malinslee (1804–5; Friedman 1996a, p. 106, pl. 24).

96 Doc. 99: 18 May, 27 June 1794. Carr's monument in the church refers to him as 'rightly counted among the most famous Masters of this art . . . if you wish to know how outstanding he was in generosity and piety, in ability and knowledge, look upon this hallowed Church, erected thanks to his most praiseworthy munificence' (Wragg 2000, p. 100).

97 Carr and Adam were employed contemporaneously (1758–71) at Harewood House near Leeds (Colvin 2008, pp. 50, 225).

98 Whitaker 1816, p. 295, adding: 'the exterior . . . presents nothing to the eye but a beautiful and majestic portico misplaced'; preferably the tower should have been 'wholly detached from the building [forming] a gateway into the churchyard' (p. 296), reviving a solution offered at the start of the century by Hawksmoor for St Alfege, Greenwich (this publication, pl. 402).

99 Krautheimer 1986, pp. 181–3, pls 144–6.

100 Talman 1997, pp. 24–5, pls 16, 51; Fleming 1962, pp. 180–82, pl. 47; Ingamells 1997, pp. 6–7, 924–6. Neither, however, specifically mentions the mausoleum.

101 Furnari 1993, pp. 27–8, 30–31, 35. Serlio published two examples in *Tutte l'opere d'architettura et prospetiva* (Hart and Hicks 1996, pp. 125, 417).

102 *RCHME: York: Historic Buildings in the Central Area: A Photographic Record*, 1981, p. 8, pl. 66 no. 32. Willis, no date, p. 3; Seymour 1992, p. 65.

103 Anon. 1800, p. 131. See also its reappearance in Plaw's *Ferme ornée* (1795; this publication, pl. 17).

104 Doc. 246: 29 July 1788.

105 Doc. 246: 5 December 1789, 20 May 1788.

106 Doc. 246: 19 October, 2, 16, 30 November 1789, 8 February 1790.

107 Doc. 90: 1766–80. Ingamells 1997, p. 436, under Guernsey.

108 Meadows 1988, p. 7. Particularly Santa Lucia on the Grand Canal, destroyed in the nineteenth century, and San Lorenzo Monache, with a façade of red brick (Franzoi and

Di Stefano 1976, pp. 100–02, 466–77, pls 134, 137, 679, 690).

109 Bonomi exhibited several views of the Pantheon in 1785–6 (Graves 1905, vol. I, p. 237). Aylesford owned two copies of Desgodetz (Binney 1971, p. 112, fig. 4).

110 Bonomi explored the effect of raised aisles in an abortive design of 1776 for the New Sacristy, St Peter's, Rome (Meadows 1988, p. 7, pl. 2). In November 1789 he designed a sarcophagus monument to Earl Waldegrave for Packington (Doc. 90), a subscriber to T. Major, *Les Ruines De Paestum, Ou De Posidonie, Dans La Grande Grece*, 1768. Bonomi's radicalism is all too evident when compared to James Wyatt's Dodington Park parish church-cum-family mausoleum (1797–1805), where the central space of the Greek cross is articulated by free-standing Doric corner columns with fluted Greek shafts but Roman capitals and neck bands, from which spring a Pantheon-like coffered dome. The interior is richly decorated in coloured marbles accented with inlaid brass, gilt mouldings and crimson velvet (Doc. 67).

111 Stuart and Revett 1762–94, vol. III, preface, pp. 13–14.

112 Fairbairn 1998, vol. II, pp. 400, 554, nos 681–6, 826, 836, 1093, 1231.

113 Adam 1811, pls 12–13. Here the east and west arms form enclosed staircase units with only the north and south arms open to the central arena; the turret is a later addition (Lowrey 1990).

114 Doc. 111.

115 Fleming 1962, pls 70, 74; Tait 1996, pp. 40–42, no. 52 ill.

116 King 2001, vol. I, pl. 60.

117 Fairbairn 1998, vol. II, no. 827. Millon 1994, pp. 598–627.

118 Colvin 2008, pp. 46, 848. For St George, see Sir John Soane's Museum, AD 10/51–56, 32/4–7; *Scots Magazine*, 76 (1814), p. 166; Youngson 1966, pp. 189–91, pl. 15; Rykwert and Rykwert 1984, p. 99, pl. 208; King 2001, pp. 6, 63–6, pls 72–3; converted to West Register House, 1968–70.

119 Chapter IV: 'On the Style in Which to Build Churches' (Laugier 1977, pp. 119–20).

120 See also the central apartment at Chillington Hall, Staffordshire, initially intended as the Catholic chapel (1788), redesigned in the same year as the saloon when Thomas Clifford apostatised following marriage to a Protestant (Soane 1788, pls 12, 16); for his unrealised scheme for a free-standing chapel and chaplain's apartment at Chillington (1786), see Sir John Soane's Museum. 41/79v–80. The dome was iconised in the Four Per Cent Office (1793–7; Abramson 2005, figs 115, 123).

121 *Gentleman's Magazine* (December 1795), p. 982, noting the pew rentals 'is upwards of 33,000 l. a year'. Hackney Archives Department, M40841, mentions families that 'go to Price's and Palmers' meetings who were bred to the Church of England's worship and would go to Church if they could be accommodated there'.

122 Doc. 237: 24 January 1791. Navarra 2001, pls XXVI, XXXIII–XXXIV.

123 Though not illustrated until Stuart and Revett 1762–94, vol. III, the building was listed in the publication's *Proposal* of 1751 (Wiebenson 1969, p. 83). A picturesque view appeared in R. Sayer, *Ruins of Athens*, 1759, p. 22, pl. 5. A not unrelated example appears in R. Wood, *The Ruins of Balbec*, 1757, pls XLII–XLVI, the third-century AD Temple of Venus, the author pertinently observing that 'the lower . . . story is at present converted into a Greek church' (p. 27).

124 Doc. 237: 4 April 1791, 9 May 1796.

125 For example, the Basilica at Trier (Ward-Perkins 1981, pl. 297), Santa Sabina, Rome, Mausoleum of Galla Placidia and San Giovanni Evangelista, Ravenna, and Sant' Apollinare in Classe (Krautheimer 1986, pls 135, 145, 147, 240).

126 Other church-designing subscribers to vol. II (1797) included Bonomi, Carr, S. P. Cockerell, James Gandon, Thomas Hardwick Jr, John Palmer, Giacomo Quarenghi, George Richardson, Soane and James Wyatt.

127 Doc. 126: 8 August 1789. Weld visited the Pantheon on 4 May 1772 (Dorset Record Office, D/WLC/AF 11); it was destroyed by fire in 1792 (Colvin 2008, p. 1173). Krautheimer 1986, chapter 9. The recently completed chapel in the castle (this publication pl. 631) was subsequently refurbished as a dining room.

128 Bignamini and Hornsby 2010, vol. I, p. 325.

THIRTY BEYOND BRITAIN

1 Whitefield 1985, p. 198, in 1739. This was the Bethesda Orphan House, Savannah, 1740–42, destroyed 1773 (Lane 1990, pp. 20–21, ill.).

2 For Petsworth parish church, Poplar Spring, Gloucester County, Virginia, 13 June 1735 (Mason 1945, p. 251).

3 Wilton and Bignamini 1996, p. 290.

4 See p. 8. They also visited St Paul, Covent Garden, and the Queen's Chapel, St James's Palace, both by Inigo Jones (Bond 1952, pp. 2, 9).

5 Reviewed in *Gentleman's Magazine* (February 1780), p. 89. This was politically forecast by Cornwallis's momentous surrender to Washington's army at Yorktown in 1781 and two years later by British recognition of American independence.

6 Middleton 1962–3, vol. I, pp. 278–80, pls 38a–c; Middleton 1968, p. 46, pls 8–9. Willey Reveley regarded Servandoni's façade as 'one of the best pieces of Modern Architecture that I have seen [but] I do not like the placing a wall in the second order over columns in the lower one as it is in appearance unsolid' (British Architectural Library, Drawings and Archives Collection, Victoria and Albert Museum, London, REW/1, f. 115r–v).

7 Patte 1770. Patte and N. H. Jardin measured St Paul's in 1769 (Doc. 223. Middleton 1968, p. 53). Jardin's Frederikskirken, Copenhagen, was similarly influenced (Middleton 1968, p. 53; Donnelly 1992, p. 161, pl. 4.42). The church was completed in 1894 (Woodward 1998, pp. 43–4). John Carr's unrealised scheme of 1769 for a large courtyard chapel in his Hospital do San Antonio, Oporto (Wragg and Wragg 1959, pp. 127–8, fig. 2; Wragg 2000, pp. 33, 39, 46–7, 187, pl. 99), was based on St Paul's Great Model via St Paul, Liverpool (Doc. 119). John's brother, Samuel Carr, was a prebendary of St Paul's Cathedral (Wragg 2000, p. 4).

8 Middleton 1968, p. 154, untraced. Fougeroux MS, p. 24, observed that London steeples 'built of good stone and in an agreeable variety of designs' were 'more worth seeing than the churches themselves . . . When you have seen one, you have seen a hundred'. French commentators and critics generally condemned St Paul's Cathedral. Foucheroux considered the dome of St Peter's in Rome 'infinitely superior', St Paul's 'insufficiently high inside', the whole building 'too heavy' while 'accrued smoke' blemished the 'whiteness and polish of the Portland stone', leading to his advice that it would be 'very wise not to follow the Model' (Doc. 223: 1728). Abbé le Blanc thought Wren 'only reduced the plan of St Peter's . . . to two thirds of it's size [with] very ill observed . . . proportions [and] throughout the whole, wherever he deviates from his model . . . has committed the greatest errors'. J. D. LeRoy regarded it 'inferior in beauty of form to . . . St Peters . . . though St Peters front has some faults, yet having but one order is composed in a much nobler taste'.

9 Friedman 1984, p. 265, pl. 294. The church as erected has a differently designed steeple. See also Lerche's Vor Frue Kirke, Copenhagen (1731–42). Donnelly 1992, pp. 158–9, fig. 4.39.

10 Doc. 270: 8 June 1718, perhaps in connection with thoughts of competing in the London New Churches programme (see p. 379).

11 Doc. 272: 17 September 1725.

12 Weiss 1997, pp. 44, 47, 62. The Gothic House, Worlitz, 1773–6, features wall paintings of English buildings including York Minster (Feist 1973, pl. 30), copied from F. Vivares's engraving of 1750 after J. Baker's view (Aylmer and Cant 1977, pl. 171B; Murray et al. 1990, p. 112), as well as views of Westminster Abbey, Fountains Abbey and Lincoln cathedral, based on similar popular prints.

13 Moritz 1987, pp. 25, 114–15, 140–41. He added: the 'disgusting boar who showed me round . . . for a shilling ruined the impression of the place itself by his claptrap'.

14 Rochefoucauld 1784, pp. 7–8, 13, 115–23, 209.

15 Rochefoucauld 1784, pp. 141, 163, 233.

16 Colvin 2008, pp. 359–62. Friedman 1986.

17 Doc. 5. The hospital's entrance portal (Minguet 1988, pp. 173–4); Sainte Geneviève's circular windows (Evans 1964, pl. 455). The National Archives of Scotland, Edinburgh (formerly The Scottish Record Office), Mar and Kellie papers, RHP 13258, confirms that Mar was in contact with an Aachen-based architect (Köven 1983). For Mar's own spectacular monument planned for Alloa church he had almost certainly studied Michael van der Voort's Precipiano tomb in Malines cathedral (Webb 1954, p. 3), as well as Arnold Quellin's Oxinden tomb, Wingham, Kent (Vigar 1995, p. 144; Friedman 2010). In 1730 Mar was in contact with 'Mr Bourchet Sculptur at Antwerpe' (RHP 13258), probably Michiel van der Borcht (Lawrence 1981, p. 352, no. 293).

18 Doc. 225: 2 April 1775, Dr Thomas Campbell, an Irish cleric. Ingamells 1997, pp. 160–61.

19 Rocque 1746–7, 13Ca. Jeffery 1996, pp. 262–4, 222–5. St Anne's site was designated in 1704 (Losty 1990, pp. 20–22, 24, 29, 32, pls 1–2, 7–9; Losty 2004, pp. 143, 147, pl. 11.3; Cotton 1980, pp. 20, 60, 270, 352, 381–2; Neill 1984, p. 371).

20 Erected 1730–40 (Pierson 1976, pp. 73–8, figs 35–9).

21 Perceval 1989, pp. 84, 119, 128, 140, 154, 161.

22 Bishir et al. 1990, pp. 41–3. The church was erected to a different design, 1736–48 (Lane 1985, pp. 26–7, 48; Bishir 1990, p. 38, figs 1.50–1.52). Window glass was obtained in England (Kornwolf 2002, vol. II, p. 827). For comparable churches of similar date, see St James, Goose Creek, Berkeley County, South Carolina (1708), and St Paul, Wye Mills, Talbot County, Maryland (1717; Kornwolf 2002, vol. II, figs 5.59a–c, 6.100a–b).

23 Wiebenson 1993, pp. 260–61. The Croston 'Plan Cart or Scheme' by an unknown draughtsman (this publication, pl. 726) is attached to the 1704 licence for erecting the 'Beconsall Chapel or Chancel' belonging to Thomas Hesketh of Rufford, 'being very ruinous, as well as incomform & incommodious to ye Chancel & Nave . . . be taken down . . . & new Walls with Windows plac'd therein' (Cheshire Record Office, EDA 2/4, ff. 28–9). Demolished 1866–7 (*VCH: Lancashire*, vol. VI, 1911, pp. 82–3).

24 O'Gorman et al. 1986, pp. 33–8 nos 1–2, cites a plan and elevation for the Pennsylvania Statehouse dated 1732 and other drawings of the 1750s.

25 Revd. Gideon Johnston, 'Representation' to the Bishop of London for financial support' (Rutledge 1959, p. 112).

26 Kornwolf 2002, vol. II, p. 861; Friedman 1994, p. 279. St Philip's interior was based on Wren's St Mary-le-Bow (*Wren Society*, IX, 1932, pl. XXXV). A reference of 1761 linking it to the 'Jesuit's Church at Antwerp' (Kornwolf 2002, vol. II, p. 862) may relate to the western turrets of Sint-Carolus-Borromeuskerk (1615–21; Vlieghe 1998, fig. 374). Lane 1984, pp. 24–5; Lounsbury 1994, pp. 27, 32, 59, 112, 134, 141, 192, 259, 287, 298, 319, 326, 334, 367, 388, 402, 410.

27 The sermon was published in 1736 (British Library, 942.e.9[4]).

28 Morrison 1952, pp. 431–3, figs 362–6; Peabody 1979; Mallary 1985, pp. 61–3; Kornwolf 2002, vol. II, pp. 970–71, figs 7.13b, 7.14(i). Robert Twelves's Old South Meeting House (1729–30) has a spire similar to that recorded in the Griffin-Hulsberg Westminster engraving (Kornwolf 2002, vol. II, fig. 7.15a).

29 In December 1725 the churchwardens determined that a 'Plaisterer should be sent for from Boston for greater certainty of having it handsomely Plaistered' (Anon. 1930, p. 5). The congregation was organised in 1698 by Francis Nicholson (see note 26), then Lieutenant Governor of New York (Friedman 1984, p. 279). Morrison 1952, pp. 442–4, fig. 370; Downing and Scully 1967, pp. 50, 54–7, pls 52–5; Pierson 1976, pp. 98–102, figs 58, 60–62; Kalman 1976, pp. 90–91; *Trinity Church, Newport*, undated guidebook; Kornwolf 2002, vol. II, pp. 1026–8, figs 7.98a–e.

30 It is a condensed version of his Fanueil Hall, Boston (1740–42), derived from Gibbs 1732, 2nd edn, 1739, pl. XXXI (Friedman 1984, pp. 272–3, pls 305–6). The chapel's vaulted interior, as described in 1763, had 'on either side of the middle aisle . . . ranges of seats with backs made wholly of oaken wood and rising one above the other to the side walls'. The windows were originally shorter and the exter-

nal door frame was added in 1850 (Bunting 1985, pp. 25–7, figs 14–15). Morrison 1952, p. 465, fig. 388. Saunders 1995, pp. 43–5, 53, 114–16, figs 122–3. Kornwolf 2002, vol. II, p. 986, fig. 7.34e. Abramson 2005, pp. 31, 49.

31 Morrison 1952, p. 510. Bushman 1993, pp. 169–80.

32 Morrison 1952, p. 537; Dorsey 1952, pp. 128–35; Shoemaker 1953, pp. 189–90; Tatum 1961, p. 30; Rose 1963, pp. 340–41; Millar 1968, pp. 118–19; B. B. Garvan in Philadelphia 1976, p. 33; Kornwolf 2002, vol. II, pp. 1190–93, figs 8.87a–f.

33 Gibbs 1728, p. vi, pls 16–21. Doc. 270.

34 The pulpit (Dorsey 1952, p. 132; Kennedy 1982, p. 115), made in 1770 by John Folwell for £70 (Shoemaker 1953, p. 194 n.), is based on Langley 1740, p. 21, pl. CXVI, 'which the ingenious Workman may perform with Pleasure', a copy of which was acquired by Smith in 1751 and others were advertised by local booksellers in 1760 and later (Garvan in Philadelphia 1976, p. 32 note; Schimmelman 1999, pp. 71–3 note).

35 Berkeley 1956, p. 111. The column-shaped steeple conjures up his admiration for the Piazza del Popolo, Rome, visited in 1717–18, that it 'is contrived to give a traveller a magnificent impression of Rome upon his first entrance . . . the two beautiful Churches . . . standing on either side of the . . . Corso . . . carrying the eye in a strait line through the middle of the city' (E. Chaney, 'George Berkeley's Grand Tours: The Immaterialist as Connoisseur of Art and Architecture' in Chaney 1998, pp. 314–16, 340–42, fig. 56). The 'Cypress Walk' or 'Walk of Death', marked O, in Bermuda, where 'monumental urns or Obelisks might be erected', described in Kippis 1778–93, vol. III [1784], may have been the basis of Thomas Hardwick Jr's proposal for a formal burial ground with bordered walks and a water system located behind St James's Chapel, Hampstead, London, 1789–93 (Doc. 230: City of Westminster Archives Centre, D1715, f. 509).

36 They suffer from a limited literature: Acworth 1949, pls 7, 17, 31, 39, 48; Robertson 2004, chapter 8, with bibliography. I am grateful to Eric Goldstein and Melanie Hall for assistance in this matter.

37 Morrison 1952, pp. 408–10. Cardy's obituary refers to the 'ingenious Architect [who] undertook and compleated the Building of St. Michael's Church' (*South Carolina Gazette*, 31 January 1774). Williams 1951; Dorsey 1952, pp. 102–5; McKee 1964; Millar 1968, pp. 103–5; Lane 1984, pp. 55–7, 162–3; Friedman 1984, p. 280, pl. 317; Ravenel 1992, pp. 5, 29–31, 33–4, 37, 67, 82–4, 120; Jacoby 1994, pp. 25–7; Kornwolf 2002, vol. II, pp. 863–5, figs 6.42a–d, noting that building materials were imported from England. An interesting aside is the Memorial to Lady Anne Murray (daughter of the Earl of Cromarty) of 1768–72 in the First Scots Presbyterian Church, Charleston, remarkable for uniquely retaining its original marbleised paintwork over a New England white-pine carcass made up of rococoised elements from a chimneypiece overmantel published in Gibbs's *Rules For Drawing the several Parts of Architecture*, 1732, which first appeared in the Charleston Library Society catalogue of 1770 (pl. LI [far right]; Heckscher and Bowman 1992, pp. 172–3, pl. 116; Schimmelman 1999, p. 32).

38 Rose 1963, pp. 142–7; Millar 1968, pp. 143–5; Friedman 1984, p. 280, pls 314, 316; Kornwolf 2002, vol. II, p. 1125, figs 8.4a–f. According to *Notes on Members St Andrew's Society of State of New York By William M. MacBean (1852–1924)*, New York Historical Society, 69, the MacBean clan were prominent in the Jacobite Risings of 1715 and 1745, two serving under John Erskine, 6th Earl of Mar (Gibbs's early patron); Donald MacBean was in America by 1757, Alexander McBean (died 1765), a New York vintner. Thomas's relation to the above is unknown. See Laurence and Colbourne's advertisement in the *New-York Advertiser*, 5 April 1796 (Gottesman 1954, p. 192). Laurence's steeple drawing is illustrated in Gilchrist 1972, p. 13 no. 10. There is no record of Laurence at work in Britain.

39 Hitchcock 1939, pp. 23–5, pls 9–12, 15; Millar 1968, pp. 177–8; Benes and Zimmerman 1979, pp. 28, 119 no. 21; Friedman 1984, p. 280, pl. 318; Kornwolf 2002, vol. II, pp. 1047–8, figs 7.125a–f. St Martin's progeny further includes J. McComb's and I. McComb's St John Chapel, New York (1803–7, demolished 1918), and A. Benjamin and I. Town's First Congregational Church, New Haven, Connecticut (1812–14; Friedman 1984, pp. 281–2, pls XVI, 319).

40 Friedman 1984, pp. 259, 261, as advertised in the *London Evening Post*, 14 February 1740 (British Library, Burney 350b [on microfilm]) and *Leeds Mercury*, 6 June 1738.

41 Schimmelman 1999, pp. 31–2, 164. Likewise, two other Palladian source books featuring church designs, W. Kent, *The Designs of Inigo Jones* (1727) and W. Halfpenny, *The Art of Sound Building* (1725), are not listed until 1793 and 1796 respectively (Schimmelman 1999, pp. 169, 172).

42 Morris 1755, pl. 31, p. 5. *Select Architecture* is listed from 1760 (Schimmelman 1999, p. 168). Adam 1976, cat. no. 24.

43 Benjamin 1992, pl. 27. For Benjamin, see Placzek 1982, vol. I, pp. 176–9. Kirker 1969, pp. 25–31.

44 Isaac Fitch of Lebanon, Connecticut, and Peter Harrison, Thomas Jefferson and John Smibert of Boston possessed copies (Friedman 1984, pp. 272–80). Abbreviated forms of St Martin-in-the-Fields appeared in India (St John, Calcutta, 1788), Canada (Holy Trinity Cathedral, Quebec, 1799–1803, by W. Hall and W. Robe, employing English craftsmen) and Australia (by the English-born Francis Greenway, transported under sentence of death for forgery in 1812). Nilsson 1968, pls 14–15, 55–8, 61b; Friedman 1984, p. 281; Kalman 1994, pp. 187–9, pl. 4.51; Kornwolf 2002, vol. III, pp. 1263–4, figs 9.2a–c; Ellis 1953; Dupain 1980. See the closely related Meetinghouse, Lebanon, Connecticut (1804–7; Jaffe 1975, pp. 294–6, figs 202, 204).

45 In June 1749, 2,576 settlers emigrated from England to Halifax; mostly cockneys, they were described by the Revd William Tutty, the Church of England missionary, as 'a set of profligate Wretches . . . so deeply sunk into all kinds of Immorality, that they scarce retain the Shadow of Religion' (Kalman 1994, p. 104). The site for the church was established by July 1749. Tutty reported on 2 November: 'the blessed sacrament has not yet been administered here, because divine service has hitherto been performed in the open air, but as soon as the Governor's [Edward Corn-

wallis] dining-room is finished, it is proposed to make use of that till a church can be erected', and on 17 March 1750: 'The want of it is a great inconvenience as the . . . room . . . is not large enough to contain one fifth of those who would be glad to assemble themselves together' (Harris 1949, p. 12). *Gentleman's Magazine* (14 July 1750), p. 459, speculated at the foundation-stone laying that it 'will be the handsomest [church] in America', similarly reported in the *Boston Weekly News Letter*, 14 July 1750. Pierson 1976, pp. 98–102; Friedman 1984, pp. 277, 279, pl. 313; Kornwolf 2002, vol. III, pp. 1341–2, figs 9.128a–b.

46 Cornwallis noted on 15 March 1750: 'the plan is the same with that of Marybone Chapel', Tutty on 17 March: 'exactly the model of Mary'bone Chapel' (McAleer 1993, p. 24). They were comparably sized: London at 55 by 90 feet, Halifax at 56 by 90 feet. Gibbs enjoyed the patronage of a former governor, Richard Phillips (1717–49), for whom he built Stanwell Place, Middlesex, by 1750 (Friedman 1984, pp. 279, 316).

47 They remarked on 27 July 1749 concerning the building of the Governor's House: 'I have constantly employed all the carpenters I could get from Annapolis' (Kalman 1994, p. 105); on 29 September that the church 'is now framing at Boston'; on 15 March 1750: 'I expect the Frame of the Church will be here next month from New England'; on 10 July: 'The Church . . . now setting up will cost £1,000, by the estimate sent . . . from Boston'; on 18 July that 'The Frame of the Church is now erecting & I am in hopes that we shall be able to assemble in it in about 2 months time, which will be a great happiness' (McAleer 1993, pp. 11, 24).

48 For all-timber construction, see Benes and Zimmerman 1979, pp. 123–4 nos 34–5. Anon. 1975. Other American offspring of the Marylebone Chapel include St Peter, Philadelphia (1758–61, steeple rebuilt 1842), with Robert Smith contracting on 5 August 1758 to 'Erect . . . in a Workman like manner . . . of good Merchantable Bricks [with] Gable Ends . . . in the Pedements . . . Rustick Work at each Corner . . . good English Glass for the . . . Sashes . . . the whole outside . . . painted . . . with three different Coats of paint of a good stone Colour' for £2,310. The minister, William McClenachan, had been ordained in London in 1755 (Dorsey 1952, pp. 136–9; Eisenhart 1953, pp. 190–91, fig. 2; Kornwolf 2002, vol. II, pp. 1193–4, figs 8.88a–b); James Wren's Christ Church, Alexandria, Virginia, 1767–73, its pedimented Serliana derived from Langley 1740, pl. LI, copies of which were available from 1754 (Schimmelman 1999, pp. 73–5 n.); St Matthew, Hillsborough, North Carolina, 1768, attributed to John Hawks (Lane 1985, p. 51; Bishir et al. 1990, p. 84; Kornwolf 2002, vol. II, pp. 614, 841, figs 4.76a–d, 6.22).

49 Bridenbaugh 1949, pp. 3, 168–70; Jordy and Monkhouse 1982, p. 4; Placzek 1982, vol. II, pp. 321–3. Harrison's private and business papers, including drawings, were destroyed at the time of his death.

50 Harrison listed a plan, west and east elevations, section 'Breadthways', plans of steeple and pews (Kornwolf 2002, vol. II, p. 973), responding to a request for providing 'a handsome church' not requiring 'any great Expense or Ornaments, but chiefly aim at Symmetry and Proportion' (Morrison 1952, p. 451); Dorsey 1952, pp. 176–9.

51 The 'elegant and lofty steeple of two square stories and an octagonal spire. The first story . . . of the Ionick order, with sixteen fluted coupled columns and pilasters . . . The second . . . of the Corinthian order, formed of eight fluted single columns . . . The spire . . . finished in the richest manner. The columns with their entablature, which project from the body of the steeple, to support highly finished and ornamental urns' (*Geographical Gazetteer of 1784*, quoted in Morrison 1952, p. 452).

52 It has been suggested that the internal ranges of paired fluted Corinthian dosseret columns, which is not part of the British tradition, were inspired by N. Nicole's Sainte Madeleine (1746–66; Graf Kalnein and Levy 1972, p. 292, pl. 255), which Harrison may have seen during his visit to Besançon in 1748 (J. F. Millar, *Peter Harrison (1716–1775)*, May 1999, p. 3, printed by the author). Friedman 1984, p. 277, pl. 311.

53 Boyce 1967, pp. 195–6, with the Vestry letter enclosing a sketch of King's College chapel (untraced) and a reference to Allen's 'noble Design . . . lately executed in building and endowing a Chapel' at his own expense, that is, St Nicholas, Bathampton, Somerset, where the 'south aile . . . was rebuilt about . . . 1754 by Ralph Allen esq.; who at the same time repaired and beautified the whole' (Collinson 1791, vol. I, p. 118). The church, designed by Richard Jones, was rebuilt in 1858 (Colvin 2008, p. 594). The Bristol Exchange and Market (1741–3) was designed by John Wood Sr (Mowl 1991a, pp. 42–5 ill.); craftsmen listed in Gomme, Jenner and Little 1979, p. 148.

54 Wright 1921, p. 17; Hague 1986, chapters 1–2; Stell 1994, pp. 75–8.

55 Upton 1986, chapter 5.

56 *Minutes of the Vestry Truro Parish, Virginia, 1732–1785*, 1955, pp. 98–9, 114–18, 121–2, 129, 134–5. Langley's pl. CL, p. 22: 'Of Christening Fonts . . . which to be grand, should be erected on a spacious Ascent of three Steps that . . . during the Performance of Baptism, the Priest may be elevated above the Congregation'.

57 'William Lawlor's Acct of Sundry Work' (McAleer 1993, p. 51 n.3).

58 Gottesman 1970, pp. 348, 350.

59 Cazort 2003, p. 98; Butler 1999.

60 Cohen 1986, p. 18. He is not the George Harrison mentioned in Colvin 2008, p. 485, though perhaps a relative.

61 Moss 1976, pp. 38, 537.

62 Doc. 147: 12 October 1720.

63 Doc. 109. The technique, which may have had metropolitan origins (see Doc. 220: 17 July 1724), was widely popular: 'You will no doubt make the wash for your Summer House of a Stone-colour. You may try the Colour first on an hot Brick on which it will dry immediately. You have a good Sand near you. It should be done twice at least' (Shenstone 1939, pp. 286–7, to Lady Luxborough, 8 August 1750).

64 Doc. 250.

65 William Stephens, quoted in Lounsbury 1994, p. 232. Colvin 2008, p. 384.

66 Harris and Savage 1990, pp. 381–5.

67 Doc. 40.

68 *Gentleman's Magazine* (March 1786), pp. 217–18 ill.; Lewis 1837, vol. I, p. 555; Lane 1990, pp. 20–21; Kornwolf 2002, vol. II, pp. 937–8, fig. 6.150. Converted to a cinema in 1913 (O'Dwyer 1981, p. 74 ill.).

69 Kirker 1969, pp. 6–7, 17–21, fig. 3, quoting the *Columbia Magazine*, II (April 1788), p. 178. Kornwolf 2002, vol. III, p. 1433, fig. 10.38. The discontinuance of the Doric entablature along the side elevations of the Boston church may owe something to St Leonard, Shoreditch (this publication pl. 560).

70 Hayward and Shivers 2004, pp. 59–61. Bucher and Wheller 1992, pp. 31–2, 54–62, cover, figs 9, 20–21, 23–7, reproducing the contract and drawings. Kornwolf 2002, vol. III, pp. 1434–5, figs 10.40 and 10.45. See the related if odd St Andrew, Leonardtown (1766), perhaps designed by the English trained joiner Richard Boulton (Dorsey 1952, p. 82; Lane 1991, pp. 42–5, 48 illus.).

71 Latrobe 1977, pp. lxxv, 201, 205. For Portman Chapel, see petition to build of 19 June 1779 (City of Westminster Archives Centre, 5/1, ff. 199–201), west view (Ashbridge 242/514), James Gandon's sketch of 'Roof to . . . Chapel near . . . Portman Square' (National Library of Ireland, Dublin, Fitzgerald Kenny Album, III, MS 22016), *Buildings of England: London 3*, 1991, p. 596.

72 Letters of 8 November 1815, 19 December 1816, 4 June 1817 (Latrobe 1984–8, vol. III, pp. 702, 842, 891). Cohen and Brownell 1994, pp. 565–6, 661–70, col. pl. 15a, figs 211–17. It is worth noting that Plaw designed a house in South Third Street, Philadelphia (1786, demolished; Colvin 2008, p. 810). Latrobe might also be seen as updating planning long-established in the Southern colonies, most notably at Christ Church, Lancaster County, Virginia (1732–5; Dorsey 1952, pp. 72–5; Upton 1986, figs 5, 90–100, 117).

73 Latrobe 1984–8, vol. II, p. 58, 27 April 1805; Kornwolf 2002, vol. III, figs 10.46a–c; Cohen and Brownell 1994, pp. 431–91. In defence of the Pantheonic form as built and its greater acoustical benefits, Latrobe cited the Octagon Chapel, Bath, and the Surrey Chapel, London, as 'the best adapted to the ease of hearer and speaker, and also as containing the most space within the least quantity of walling' (Latrobe 1984–8, vol. I, pp. 400–06, *circa* 1803). The radicalism of the executed cathedral is evident when compared to Town's and Davis's Eglise du Saint Esprit, New York (1831–4; Peck 1992, p. 19, figs 28–9, pls 17–18), which adopted the interlocking plans of Greek temple and Roman rotunda explored by William Newton at St Alphage, London Wall, in 1774 (Doc. 209). The stylistic range and planning variety of early nineteenth-century American religious buildings is well illustrated in Liscombe 1985.

74 Cohen and Brownell 1994, pp. 434–5 note. It owes something to medieval Kirkstall Abbey, Leeds, close to his birthplace (Friedman 1997b, pp. 170–72).

75 Doc. 75: 29 September 1792, 27 May 1793.

76 However, see the American Joshua Gilpin's observations on Gloucester cathedral (Doc. 86: 1796).

77 Latrobe 1984–8, vol. I, p. 19, 6 February 1805.

78 *Gentleman's Magazine* (August 1797), p. 638. See also *Gentleman's Magazine* (October 1797), pp. 811–13; (November 1797), pp. 930–31; (Supplement 1797), p. 1089; (September 1800), pp. 813–14; and Farington 1978–84, vol. III, pp. 860, 864–5, 880, 889, 909, 913, 919–20, 922, 924, 932, 935–7, 945–7, 950–55, 980, 986, 994.

79 *Gentleman's Magazine*, Supplement 1797, p. 1122. Farington 1978–84, vol. III, p. 1087, 10 November 1798.

80 For useful surveys of ecclesiastical America, see Kalman 1976; Kennedy 1982; Howe 2003.

Bibliography

PRIMARY SOURCES

For details regarding variant titles and other editions of early architectural books listed below, see Harris and Savage 1990; Schimmelman 1999; *The Mark J. Millard Architectural Collection*: Middleton et al. 1998, Pollock 2000; Wiebenson 1993

ABA: see Gibbs 1728

Ackermann 1808–9
R. Ackermann, *The Microcosm of London*, 3 vols, 1808–9

Ackermann 182
R. Ackermann, *The History of the Abbey Church of St. Peter's Westminster, its Antiquities and Monuments*, 2 vols, 1812

Adam 1764
R. Adam, *Ruins of the Palace of the Emperor Diocletian at Spalatro*, 1764

Adam 1773–9
—, *The Works in Architecture of Robert and James Adam*, 2 vols, 1773–9

Adam 1811
W. Adam, *Vitruvius Scoticus*, 1811

Adams 1983
B. Adams, *London Illustrated, 1604–1851*, 1983

Addison 1754
J. Addison, *The Spectator*, nos 1–634 [1711–12], 1754

Addison 1761
—, *Remarks on Several Parts of Italy, &c. In the Years 1701, 1702, 1703*, 1761

Aheron 1754
J. Aheron, *A General Treatise of Architecture: In Five Books*, 1754

Aikin 1795
J. Aikin, *A Description of The Country from thirty to forty Miles around Manchester*, 1795

Alethea 1776
Alethea, 'Advice to a Young Clergyman', *Gentleman's Magazine* (January 1776), pp. 37–8

Alexander 2008
D. Alexander, 'George Vertue as an Engraver', *Walpole Society*, 70 (2008), pp. 207–517

Allsopp 1970
B. Allsopp, ed., *Inigo Jones on Palladio being the notes by Inigo Jones in the copy of I Quattro Libre dell Architettura di Andrea Palladio 1601 in the Library of Worcester College Oxford*, 1970

Ambulator: see Anon. 1774

Anon., no date
Anon., *A Concise and Accurate Description of the University, Town, and County of Cambridge*, undated

Anon. 1677
—, *Ecclesia Restaurata: A Votive Poem to the Rebuilding of St Paul's Cathedral*, 1677

Anon. 1710
—, *The Screw-Plot Discover'd: or, St Paul's Preserv'd*, 1710 [British Library, 1078.4.14. (9)]

Anon. 1713
—, *Deal in an Uproar*, 1713

Anon. 1726
—, *A New Guide to London; or, Directions to Strangers; Shewing the Chief Things of Curiosity and Note in the City and Suburbs*, 2nd edn, 1726 [British Library, 577.d.3]

Anon. 1731
— [Elizabeth Thomas], *The Metamorphoses of the Town: or, A View of the Present Fashion: A Tale*, 1731 [British Library, T.1056 (14)]

Anon. 1734
—, *The Builder's Dictionary; or, Gentleman and Architect's Companion*, 2 vols, 1734

Anon. 1750
—, *St Paul's Cathedral: A Poem. In Two Parts: Part I. Relating to the Cathedral; Part II. The Prospect from the Gilded Gallery*, 1750 [British Library, 11630.b.7. (2)]

Anon. 1767a
—, *A Companion To every Place of Curiosity and Entertainment In and about London and Westminster*, 1767

Anon. 1767b
—, *Twenty-four Errors of the Romish Church dissected: Shewing A Protestant's Reasons Why he will not be a Papist. By Way of Question and Answer*, 1767

Anon. 1774, 1800

—, *The Ambulator; or, The Stranger's Companion in a Tour around London; Within the Circuit of Twenty-five Miles . . . Collected by a Gentleman for his private Amusement*, 1774; *Ambulator: or, A pocket companion in a town named London*, 9th edn, augmented, 1800

Anon. 1781

— [Member of Middle Temple], *Trial of the Right Honourable George Gordon, Commonly called Lord George Gordon, on a Bill of Indictment for High Treason*, 1781

Anon. 1782

—, *Viator, A Poem; or, A Journey from London to Scarborough By the Way of York*, 1782

Anon. 1789, 1805

—, *The Southampton Guide*, 4th edn, 1789; 18th edn, 1805

Anon. 1808

—, *A Concise History of Worcester*, 1808

Anon. 1810

—, *The Curate: A Poem*, 1810

Anon. 1825

—, *Hints to Some Churchwardens, With a Few Illustrations, Relative to the Repair and Improvements of Parish Churches. With Twelve Plates*, 1825 [attributed to A. Hare and J. Hare, in present author's possession]

Anstey 1766

C. Anstey, *New Bath Guide*, 1766

Aringhi 1659

P. Aringhi, *Roma Subterranea Novissima*, 2 vols, 1659

Aston 1816

J. Aston, *A Picture of Manchester*, 1816

Atkyns 1712

R. Atkyns, *The Ancient and Present State of Glostershire*, 1712

Badeslade and Rocque 1739

J. Badeslade and J. Rocque, *Vitruvius Britannicus*, vol. IV, 1739

Bagot 1784

L. Bagot, *A Charge delivered to the Clergy at the Primary Visitation of Lewis Lord Bishop of Norwich*, 1784

Bailey 1996

B. A. Bailey, ed., *Northamptonshire in the Early Eighteenth Century: The Drawings of Peter Tillemans and Others*, 1996

Baille 1801

J. Baille, *An Impartiall History of the Town and Country of Newcastle upon Tyne, and its Vicinity*, 1801

Baker MS

'William Baker Account book & Diary, 1748–59', unknown private collection, transcription courtesy A. Gomme. *See* Morrice 1993

Barlow 1714

Dr Thomas Barlow, '*The Case Concerning Setting up Images or Painting of them in Churches . . . Images an Abomination to the Lord. Or, Dr Kenet's Reasons for Pulling Down the Altar-pieces at White-Chapel, The Whole Tryal and Examination of Dr Wetton, Rector of White-Chapel, and the Church-Warden*', 20–22, 24–7 April 1714

Barrett 1789

W. Barrett, *The History and Antiquities of the City of Bristol*, 1789

Bartell 1800

Edmund Bartell Jr, *Observations upon the Town of Cromer, Considered as A Watering Place, and the Picturesque Scenery in its Neighbourhood*, 1800

Barton 1739

R. Barton, *Farrago: or, Miscellanies in Verse and Prose*, 1739 [British Library, 11631.d.20]

Benjamin 1992

A. Benjamin, *The Country Builder's Assistant* [1797], facsimile edition, 1992

Benson 1937

A. B. Benson, ed., *Peter Kalm's Travels in North America*, 1937

Bentham 1771

J. Bentham, *The History and Antiquities of the Conventual and Cathedral Church of Ely From the Foundation of the Monastery, A.D. 673 To the Year 1771*, 1771

Bentham 1772

—, 'Characteristics of Saxon and Norman Architecture', *Gentleman's Magazine* (April 1772), pp. 166–8

Berkeley 1956

The Works of George Berkeley, Bishop of Cloyne, ed. A. A. Luce and T. E. Jessop, vol. VIII, 1956

Betjeman 1959

J. Betjeman, ed., *Altar and Pew: Church of England Verses*, 1959

Bigland 1989–95

R. Bigland, *Historical, Monumental and Genealogical Collections, Relative to the County of Gloucester*, ed. B. Frith, Gloucestershire Record Society, 8 vols, 1989–95

Bill 1979

E. G. W. Bill, *The Queen Anne Churches: A Catalogue of the Papers in Lambeth Palace Library of the Commission for Building Fifty New Churches in London and Westminster, 1711–1759*, 1979

Binckes 1710

W. Binckes, *The Christian Synagogue; or, The Original, Use and Benefit of Parochial Churches*, 1710

Bingham 1711

J. Bingham, *Origines Ecclesiasticae; or, The Antiquities of the Christian Church* [1708–22], in *The Works of The Rev. Joseph Bingham, MA*, ed. R. Bingham, London, 1843, vol. III: 'Contents of the Eight, Nine and Tenth Books of The Antiquities of the Christian Church' [1711]

BL, Add. MS 22926: *see* Appendix A

Black and Harris 1778
Black and Harris, *The Rudiments of Architecture* [1778], ed. D. M. Walker, 1992

Blackett-Ord 2001
C. Blackett-Ord, 'Letters from William Kent to Burrell Massingberd from the Continent, 1712–1719', *Walpole Society*, 63 (2001), pp. 75–109

Bonanni 1715
P. Bonanni, *Numismata Summorum Pontificum Templi Vaticani Fabricam Indicantia*, 1715

Bonannini et al. 1993
A. Bonannini et al., *Venezia 1717, Venezia 1993: immagini a confronto*, 1993 [engraved views by D. Lovisa]

Boswell 1950
J. Boswell, *Boswell's London Journal, 1762–1763*, ed. F. A. Pottle, 1950

Bourne 1725
H. Bourne, *Antiquitates Vulgares; or, The Antiquities of the Common People*, 1725

Brady and Tate 1725
N. Brady and N. Tate, *A New Version of the Psalms of David, Fitted to the Tunes Used in Churches*, 1725

Braham and Hager 1977
A. Braham and H. Hager, *Carlo Fontana: The Drawings at Windsor Castle*, 1977

Brand 1789
J. Brand, *History and Antiquities of the Town and County of Newcastle upon Tyne*, vol. 1, 1789

Bray 1783
W. Bray, *Sketch of a Tour into Derbyshire and Yorkshire*, 2nd edn, 1783

Brewster 1796
J. Brewster, *Parochial History and Antiquities of Stockton upon Tees*, 1796

Brice 1759
A. Brice, *The Grand Gazetteer*, 1759

Bridges 1791
J. Bridges, *The History and Antiquities of Northamptonshire*, 2 vols, 1791

Brighton 1991
J. T. Brighton, 'William Peckitt's Commission Book, 1751–95', *Walpole Society*, 54 (1991), pp. 334–453

Britton 1831
J. Britton, *The History and Antiquities of the Cathedral of Hereford*, 1831

Britton and Pugin 1825–8
— and A. Pugin, *Illustrations of the Public Buildings of London*, 2 vols, 1825–8

Burrell 1997
Sir William Burrell's Northern Tour, 1758, ed. J. G. Dunbar, 1997

Butler 1740
Bishop Joseph Butler, *A Sermon Preached Before the Right Hon. The Lord Mayor, the Court of Aldermen, the Sheriffs, and the Governors of the Several Hospitals of the City of London*, Easter Week, 1740

Cambry 1788
J. Cambry, *De Londres et De Ses Environs*, 1788

Campbell 1715–25
C. Campbell, *Vitruvius Britannicus*, 3 vols, 1715–25

Campbell 2004
I. Campbell, *The Paper Museum of Cassiano dal Pozzo, Series A: Antiquities and Architecture. Part Nine: Ancient Roman Topography and Architecture*, 3 vols, 2004

Campbell 1947
T. Campbell, *Dr Campbell's Diary of a Visit to England in 1775*, ed. J. L. Clifford, 1947 [Thomas Campbell, Irish clergyman]

Carter 1797–1817
'An Architect' [John Carter], 'On the Pursuits of Architectural Innovation', *Gentleman's Magazine* (1797–1817) [various articles listed individually in Crook 1995, pp. 80–89]

Cavers 1993
K. Cavers, *A Vision of Scotland: The Nation Observed by John Slezer, 1671 to 1717*, 1993

Cawthorn 1771
J. Cawthorn, *Of Taste: An Essay* [1761], in *Poems*, 1771

Cennick 1745
J. Cennick, *An Account of a Late Riot at Exeter*, 1745

Chambers 1728
E. Chambers, *Cyclopaedia; or, An Universal Dictionary of Arts and Sciences*, 1728

Chambers 1820
J. Chambers, *A General History of Worcester*, 1820

Chambers 1758
W. Chambers, *English Architecture; or, The Publick Buildings of London and Westminster*, 1758

Chandler 1971
Richard Chandler: Travels in Asia Minor, 1764–1765, ed. E. Clay, 1971

Chandler, Revett and Pars 1769–1915
R. Chandler, N. Revett and W. Pars [Society of Dilettanti], *Ionian Antiquities*, 4 vols, 1769–1915

Charlesworth 2002
M. Charlesworth, ed., *The Gothic Revival, 1720–1870: Literary Sources and Documents*, 3 vols, 2002

Christie's 1801
A Catalogue of The Capital, Truly Valuable and Interesting Collection of Drawings, Prints, Book of Prints, &c. &c. Of that distinguished Artist and Civil Engineer, The Athenian Reveley, Christie's, 11–12 May 1801

Clérisseau 1778
C.-L. Clérisseau, *Antiquities de la France: premier partie, monumens des Nismes*, 1778

Collinson 1791
J. Collinson, *The History and Antiquities of the County of Somerset*, 3 vols, 1791

Colvin 1964
H. M. Colvin, *A Catalogue of Architectural Drawings of the 18th and 19th Centuries in the Library of Worcester College, Oxford*, 1964

Colvin, Crook and Friedman 1980
—, J. Mordaunt Crook and T. Friedman, *Architectural Drawings from Lowther Castle Westmorland*, 1980

Colvin and Newman 1981
— and J. Newman, eds, *Of Building: Roger North's Writing on Architecture*, 1981

Concise and Accurate Description: see Anon., no date

Cowie 1956
L. W. Cowie, *Henry Newman: An American in London, 1708–43*, 1956

Croker 1884
J. W. Croker, ed., *Memoirs of the Reign of George II*, 3 vols, 1884

Crull 1711
J. Crull, *The Antiquities of St Peter's; or, The Abbey-Church of Westminster . . . Adorned with Draughts of the Tombs, curiously Engraved*, 1711

Curcio 2003
G. Curcio, ed., *Il Tempio Vaticano, 1694: Carlo Fontana*, 2003

Dallaway 1806
Revd J. Dallaway, *Observations on English Architecture: Military, Ecclesiastical, and Civic*, 1806

Dart 1723
J. Dart, *Westmonasterium; or, The history and Antiquities of The Abbey Church of St Peters Westminster*, 2 vols, 1723

Dart 1726
—, *The History and Antiquities of The Cathedral Church of Canterbury*, 1726

Darwin 1985
E. Darwin, *Visit of Hope to Sydney Cove, near Botany-Bay* [1789], in *The New Oxford Book of Eighteenth Century Verse*, ed. R. Lonsdale, 1985

D'Aviler 1691
A. C. d'Aviler, *Cours d'architecture*, 1691

Davis 1941
H. Davis, ed., *The Prose Works of Jonathan Swift*, vol. III, 1941

Dee 1968
E. E. Dee, *Views of Florence and Tuscany by Giuseppe Zocchi, 1711–1767*, 1968

Defoe 1728
D. Defoe, *Augusta Triumphans; or, The Way to make London the most Flourishing City in the Universe*, 1728

Defoe 1962
—, *A Tour Through the Whole Island of Great Britain* [1724–6], 2 vols, 1962 [Everyman's Library, 1761 edn]

Defoe 1991
Daniel Defoe: A Tour Through the Whole Island of Great Britain [1724–6], ed. P. N. Furbank and W. R. Owens, 1991

Denholm 1804
J. Denholm, *The History of the City of Glasgow and Suburbs*, 3rd edn, 1804

De Saussure 1995
A Foreign View of England in 1725–1729: The Letters of Monsieur César De Saussure to His Family [1902], trans. and ed. Madame van Muyden, 1995

Desgodetz 1682
A. Desgodetz, *Les Edifices Antiques De Rome: Dessinés Très Exactement*, 1682

Dickins and Stanton 1910
L. Dickins and M. Stanton, *An Eighteenth-Century Correspondence*, 1910 [various authors, to Sanderson Miller]

Dodsley and Dodsley 1761
R. Dodsley and J. Dodsley, *London and Its Environs Described*, 6 vols, 1761

Downes 1967
K. Downes, 'The King's Weston Book of Drawings', *Architectural History*, 10 (1967), pp. 7–88

Downes 1988
—, *Sir Christopher Wren: The Design of St Paul's Cathedral*, 1988

Dowsing 2001
The Journal of William Dowsing: Iconoclasm in East Anglia during the Civil War, ed. T. Cooper, 2001

Drake 1736
F. Drake, *Eboracum; or, The History and Antiquities of the City of York*, 1736

Drake 1768, 1790
—, *An Accurate Description and History of the Cathedral and Metropolitical Church of St Peter, York*, 2nd edn, 1768; 3rd edn, 1790

Drake 1788
—, *Eboracum: or, The History and Antiquities of the City of York*, 2 vols, 1788

Ducarel and Warburton 1778
A. Ducarel and T. Warburton, *Some account of the Alien Priories and of such lands as they are known to have possessed in England and Wales*, 1778

Du Cerceau 1988
J. A. Du Cerceau, *Les Plus Excellents Batiments de France* [1576–9], fascimile, ed. D. Thomson, 1988

Dugdale 1819
J. Dugdale, *The New British Traveller; or, Modern Panorama of England and Wales*, 4 vols, 1819

Eboracum: *see* Drake 1788

Encyclopedia Britannica 1771
Encyclopedia Britannica; or, A Dictionary of Arts and Sciences, 1771

Enfield 1774
W. Enfield, *An Essay Towards the History of Leverpool*, 2nd edn, 'with Additions', 1774

Evelyn 1664
J. Evelyn, *A Parallel Of The Antient Architecture With The Modern*, 1664 [translation of Fréart 1650]

Evelyn 1696
—, *An Account of Architects and Architecture*, 1696

Evelyn 1707
—, Evelyn 1664, with addition of *An Account of Architects and Architecture*, 2nd edn, 1707

Fagiolo 1997
M. Fagiolo, *Corpus delle Feste a Roma*, vol. II: *Il Settecento e l'Ottocento*, 1997

Fagiolo dell'Arco 1997
M. Fagiolo dell'Arco, *Corpus delle Feste a Roma*, vol. I: *La festa barocca*, 1997

Fairbairn 1998
L. Fairbairn, *Italian Renaissance Drawings from the Collection of Sir John Soane's Museum*, 2 vols, 1998

Falda 1665–9
G. B. Falda, *Il nuovo teatro delle fabriche di Roma*, 4 vols, 1665–9

Fanelli 1707
F. Fanelli, *Atene, Attica*, 1707

Farington 1978–84
The Diary of Joseph Farington, ed. K. Garlick and A. Macintyre, vols I and II, 1978; vol. III, 1984

Farmer 1735
J. Farmer, *The History of the ancient Town, and once Famous Abbey, of Waltham, In the County of Essex*, 1735

Farr 1992
M. Farr, *The Great Fire of Warwick, 1694: The Records of the Commissioners Appointed under an Act of Parliament for Rebuilding the Town of Warwick*, 1992

Ficacci 2000
L. Ficacci, *Giovanni Battista Piranesi: The Complete Etchings*, 2000

Fielding 1753
H. Fielding, *Proposal for Making an Effectual Provision for the Poor, For Amending their Morals, and for Rendering them useful Members of the Society*, 1753

Fiennes 1982
The Illustrated Journeys of Celia Fiennes, 1682–c.1712, ed. C. Morris, 1982

Fischer von Erlach 1721
J. B. Fischer von Erlach, *Entwürff Einer Historischen Architectur*, 1721; see under Lediard 1730

Fontana 1590
D. Fontana, *Del modo tenuto nel transporters l'obelisco vaticano*, 1590

Fossier 1997
F. Fossier, *Les Dessins du fonds Robert de Cotte de la Bibliothèque national de France*, 1997

Fougeroux MS
Abbé Pierre-Jacques Fougeroux, 'Voiage D'Angleterre D'Hollande et de Flandre fait en L'année 1728', Victoria and Albert Museum, National Art Library, MS 86 NN 2 [with modern English translation]

Fréart 1650
R. Fréart, *Parallèle de l'architecture antique et de la moderne*, 1650; see under Evelyn 1664

Friedman 1976
T. Friedman, 'Foggini's Statue of Queen Anne', in *Kunst des Barock in der Toskana: Studien zur Kunst unter den letzten Medici*, ed. K. Lankheit, 1976, pp. 39–56

Friedman 1986
—, 'A "Palace worthy of the Grandeur of the King": Lord Mar's Designs for the Old Pretender, 1718–30', *Architectural History*, 29 (1986), pp. 102–33

Friedman 1996b
—, 'The Eighteenth Century Disaster Print', in *The Image of the Building*, ed. M. Howard, Papers from the Annual Symposium of the Society of Architectural Historians of Great Britain of 1995, 1996, pp. 67–82

Friedman 2002
—, 'Henry Keene and St Mary, Hartwell', in *Gothic Architecture and its Meanings, 1550–1830*, ed. M. Hall, 2002, pp. 134–56, 187–207

Fuller 1799
J. Fuller, *The History of Berwick upon Tweed*, 1799

Garretson 1701
J. G. Garretson, *The School of Manners; or, Rules for Childrens Behaviour*, 1701

Gay 1716
J. Gay, *Trivia; or, The Art of Walking the Streets of London*, 1716

Gent 1730
T. Gent, *The Antient and Modern History of the Famous City of York*, 1730

Gent 1733
— *The Antient and Modern History of the Loyal Town of Rippon*, 1733

Geraghty 2007
A. Geraghty, *The Architectural Drawings of Sir Christopher Wren at All Souls College, Oxford: A Complete Catalogue*, 2007

Gery 1707
R. Gery, *Sermon Preach'd in the Parish-Church of Isleworth . . . At the First Opening . . . after . . . Rebuilding, 2 March 1707*

Gibbs 1728
J. Gibbs, *A Book of Architecture*, 1728

Gibbs 1732
—, *Rules for Drawing the Several Parts of Architecture*, 1732

Gibbs 1739
—, *A Book of Architecture*, 2nd edn, 1739

Gibson 1973
D. J. Gibson, *Books from the Library of Sir Robert Taylor in the Library of the Taylor Institution, Oxford: A Checklist*, 1973

Gilmore 1972
T. B. Gilmore, *Early Eighteenth Century Essays on Taste*, 1972

Glynne 1994
S. Glynne, *Sir Stephen Glynne's Church Notes for Somerset*, ed. M. McGarvie, 1994

Glynne 1997
—, *Sir Stephen Glynne's Church Notes for Shropshire*, ed. D. C. Cox, 1997

Glynne 2007
—, *The Yorkshire Church Notes of Sir Stephen Glynne (1825–1874)*, ed. L. Butler, Yorkshire Archaeological Society, Record Series, CLIX, 2007

Godber 1968
J. Godber, *The Marchioness Grey of Wrest Park*, Bedfordshire Historical Record Society, XLVII, 1968 [contains Philip Yorke's travel journal, 1744–63, pp. 125–63]

Goldsmith 1760–61
O. Goldsmith, *The Citizen of the World* [1760–61], in *Collected Works of Oliver Goldsmith*, ed. A. Friedman, vol. II, 1966

Gottesman 1954
R. S. Gottesman, *The Arts and Crafts in New York, 1779–1799: Advertisements and News Items from New York City Newspapers*, 1954

Gottesman 1965
—, *The Arts and Crafts in New York, 1800–1804: Advertisements and News Items from New York City Newspapers*, 1965

Gottesman 1970
—, *The Arts and Crafts in New York, 1726–1776: Advertisements and News Items from New York City Newspapers*, 1970

Graves 1905
A. Graves, *The Royal Academy of Arts: A Complete Dictionary of Contributors*, 4 vols, 1905

Graves 1907
—, *The Society of Artists of Great Britain, 1760–1791: The Free Society of Artists, 1761–1783: A Complete Dictionary of Contributors*, 1907

Gray 1814
T. Gray, *Architectura Gothica* [1754], 1814

Green 1764
V. Green, *A Survey of the City of Worcester*, 1764

Green 1782
—, *A Review of the Polite Arts in France, At the Time of their Establishment under Louis the XIV, Compared with their Present State in England*, 1782

Green 1796
—, *The History of Worcester*, 1796

Greene 1965
L. Fox, ed., *Correspondence of Revd Joseph Greene*, Historical Manuscripts Commission, 1965

Griffin and Lincoln 1993
D. G. Griffin and S. Lincoln, *Drawings from the Irish Architectural Archive*, 1993

Gwynn 1749
J. Gwynn, *An Essay on Design*, 1749

Gwynn 1752
—, *The Qualifications and Duty of a Surveyor explained in a Letter*, 1752

Gwynn 1766
—, *London and Westminster Improved, to which is Prefixed a Discourse on Publick Magnificence*, 1766

Halfpenny 1724
W. Halfpenny, *Practical Architecture*, 1724

Halfpenny 1725
—, *The Art of Sound Building*, 1725

Halfpenny and Halfpenny 1752
— and J. Halfpenny, *Chinese and Gothic Architecture Properly Ornamented*, 1752

Hampden 1940
J. Hampden, ed., *An Eighteenth-Century Journal: Being a Record of the Years 1774–1776*, 1940

Hardwick 1977
N. Hardwick, ed., A *Diary of the Journey through the North of England Made by William and John Blathwayt of Dyrham Park in 1703*, 1977 [translation of P. de Blainville, *A relation of the journey of the gentlemen Blathwayt into the north of England*]

A. and J. Hare 1825
Augustin and Julius Hare, *Hints to Some Churchwardens, with a Few Illustrations, Relative to the Repair and Improvement of Parish Churches*, 1825

Harris and Savage 1990
E. Harris and N. Savage, *British Architectural Books and Writers, 1556–1785*, 1990

Harris 1704
J. Harris, *Lexicon Technicum*, 1704

Harris 1960
J. Harris, *English Decorative Ironwork from Contemporary Source Books, 1710–1836*, 1960

Harris 1971
—, *A Catalogue of British Drawings for Architecture, Decoration, Sculpture and Landscape, 1550–1900, in American Collections*, 1971

Harris 1973
—, *RIBA Catalogue: Colen Campbell*, 1973

Harris and Higgott 1989
— and G. Higgott, *Inigo Jones: Complete Architectural Drawings*, 1989

Harris and Tait 1979
— and A. A. Tait, *Catalogue of the Drawings by Inigo Jones, John Webb and Isaac De Caus at Worcester College, Oxford*, 1979

Harris 1699
W. Harris, *Description of the King's Royal Palace and Garden at Loo, Together With a Short Account of Holland*, 1699

Harrison 1775
W. Harrison, *A New Universal History, Description and Survey of the Cities of London and Westminster*, 1775

Hart and Hicks 1996
V. Hart and P. Hicks, *Sebastiano Serlio on Architecture: Volume One: Books I–V of 'Tutte L'Opere D'Architettura et Prospetiva' by Sebastiano Serlio*, 1996

Hart and Hicks 2006
— and —, *Palladio's Rome: A Translation of Andrea Palladio's Two Guidebooks to Rome*, 2006

Harvey 1794
J. Harvey, *Sentimental Tour through Newcastle*, 1794

Hasted 1797–1801
E. Hasted, *The History and Topographical Survey of the County of Kent*, 1797–1801

Hatton 1708
E. Hatton, *A New View of London; or, An Ample Account of that City*, 2 vols, 1708

Hearne 1906
Remarks and Collections of Thomas Hearne, Oxford Historical Society, vol. VII, 1906

Hildyard 1755
J. Hildyard, *An Accurate Description and History of the Metropolitan and Cathedral Churches of Canterbury and York*, 1755

Hoare 1983
The Journeys of Sir Richard Colt Hoare through Wales and England, 1793–1810, ed. M. W. Thompson, 1983

Hodgkinson 1992
A Lancashire Gentleman: The Letters and Journals of Richard Hodgkinson, 1763–1847, ed. F. Wood and K. Wood, 1992

Hogarth 1997
W. Hogarth, *The Analysis of Beauty* [1753], ed. R. Paulson, CT, 1997

Hole and Wilson 1761
W. Hole and T. Wilson, *The Ornaments of Churches Considered, With a Particular View to the late Decoration of the Parish Church of St Margaret Westminster*, 1761

Houfe 1977
S. Houfe, 'A Taste for the Gothick: Diaries of the Countess of Pomfret', *Country Life* (24 March 1977), pp. 728–34

Howard 1777
J. Howard, *The State of Prisons in England and Wales*, 1777

Howel 1718
L. Howel, *A Compleat History of The Holy Bible . . . Adorn'd with about 150 Cuts, engraved by J. Sturt*, 3rd edn, 1718

Hughson 1817
D. Hughson, *Walks through London, including Westminster and the Borough of Southwark, with the Surrounding Suburbs*, 2 vols, 1817

Humphrey 1728
S. Humphrey, *Cannons: A Poem. Inscrib'd to His Grace the Duke of Chandos*, 1728

Hunter 1819
J. Hunter, *Hallamshire: The History and Topography of the Parish of Sheffield in the County of York*, 1819

Hunter 1828–31
—, *South Yorkshire: The History and Topography of the Deanery of Doncaster*, 2 vols, 1828–31

Hutchins 1774
J. Hutchins, *The History and Antiquities of the County of Dorset*, 2 vols, 1774

Hutchinson 1776
W. Hutchinson, *An Excursion to the Lakes in Westmorland and Cumbria*, 1776

Hutchinson 1823
—, *The History and Antiquities of the County Palatine of Durham* [1785–94], 3 vols, 1823

Hutton 1783
W. Hutton, *An History of Birmingham*, 1783

Hutton 1785
— *A Journey from Birmingham to London*, 1785

Hutton 1791
—, *The History of Derby*, 1791

Hutton 1795
—, *An History of Birmingham*, 3rd edn, 1795

Hyde 1994
R. Hyde, *A Prospect of Britain: The Town Panoramas of Samuel and Nathaniel Buck*, 1994

Ingamells 1997
J. Ingamells, *A Dictionary of British and Irish Travellers in Italy, 1701–1800*, 1997

J. N. 1755
J. N., 'Of warming Churches', *Gentleman's Magazine* (February 1755), pp. 68–9

James 1707
J. James, trans., A. Pozzo, *Rules and Examples of Perspective Proper for Painters and Architects* [1693], 1707

Johnson 1755
S. Johnson, *A Dictionary of the English Language*, 1755

Johnson 1779
—, *The Works of the English Poets with Prefaces Biographical and Critical*, vol. 1, 1779

Jordy and Monkhouse 1982
W. H. Jordy and C. P. Monkhouse, *Buildings on Paper: Rhode Island Architectural Drawings, 1825–1945*, 1982

Jukes 1957
H. A. L. Jukes, ed., *Articles of Enquiry Addressed to the Clergy of the Diocese of Oxford at the Primary Visitation of Dr Thomas Secker, 1738*, Oxfordshire Record Society, XXXVIII, 1957

Kent 1727
W. Kent, *The Designs of Inigo Jones Consisting of Plans and Elevations of Publick and Private Buildings*, 2 vols, 1727

Kieven 1991a
E. Kieven, *Architettura del Settecento a Roma*, 1991

Kieven 1991b
—, 'Il ruolo del designo: il concorso per la facciata di S. Giovanni in Laterano', in *In urbe architectus: modelli disegni misure: la professione dell'architetto di Roma, 1680–1750*, ed. B. Contardi and G. Curcio, 1991, pp. 78–123

Kieven 1993
—, *Von Bernini bis Piranesi*, 1993

King 1672
D. King, *The Cathedralls and Conventuall Churches of England and Wales orthographically delineated*, 1672 [the Gregg Press reprint of 1969 has an introduction by H. Colvin]

King 1691
P. King, *An Enquiry into the Constitution, Discipline, Unity and Worship of the Primitive Church*, 1691

Kippis 1778–93
A. Kippis, *Biographia Britannica*, 5 vols, 1778–93

Knight 1772
T. Knight, *Hhadash Hamishcan; or, The New Chapel, at Halifax, in Yorkshire*, 1772

Knox 1778
V. Knox, *Essay*, 1778

Knyff 1984
L. Knyff, *Britannia Illustrata: Knyff & Kip*, ed. J. Harris and G. Jackson-Stops, 1984

Lacy 1715
J. Lacy, *Sermon Preach'd at the Consecration of a Church in the Parish of Castle-Ton, near Sherborne, Dorset. September 7. 1715*, 1715

Lancaster 1912
W. T. Lancaster, ed., 'Letters Addressed to Ralph Thoresby FRS', *Thoresby Society*, 21 (1912)

Langley 1736
B. Langley, *Ancient Masonry*, 1736

Langley 1738
—, *The Builders Compleat Chest-Book*, 1738

Langley 1740
—, *The City and Country Builder's, and Workman's Treasury of Designs*, 1740 (1750 edn, with 'appendix')

Langley 1741
—, *The Builder's Jewel*, 1741

Langley 1742
—, *Ancient Architecture, Restored, and Improved, by a Great Variety of Grand and useful Designs, Entirely New In the Gothic Mode . . . Exceeding every Thing thats Extant*, 1742; as *Gothic Architecture, Improved By Rules and Proportions*, 1747

Latimer 1887–1908
J. Latimer, *Annals of Bristol*, 4 vols, 1887–1908

Latrobe 1977
The Virginia Journals of Benjamin Henry Latrobe, 1795–1798, ed. E. C. Carter, vol. 1, 1977

Latrobe 1984–8
Correspondence and Miscellaneous Papers of Benjamin Henry Latrobe, ed. J. C. Van Horne, 3 vols, 1984–8 [vol. 1 ed. J. C. Van Horne and L. W. Formwalt]

Laugier 1977
M.-A. Laugier, *Essai sur l'Architecture* [1753]; as *An Essay on Architecture by Marc-Antoine Laugier*, trans. W. Herrmann and A. Herrmann, 1977

Leach and Cheetham 1826
Leach and Cheetham, *Concise Description of Manchester and Salford*, 1826

Le Camus de Mezières 1992
N. Le Camus de Mezières, *The Genius of Architecture; or, The Analogy of That Art with our Sensations* [1780], ed. R. Middleton, 1992

Lediard 1730
T. Lediard, *A Plan of Civil And Historical Architecture*, 1730 [translation of Fischer von Erlach 1721; facsimile published with the Leipzig edn of 1725, 1964]

Legrand and Landon 1806–9
J. G. Legrand and C. P. Landon, *Description de paris et de ses edifices*, 2 vols, 1806–9

Le Neve 1717–19
J. Le Neve, *Monumenta Anglicana*, 5 vols, 1717–19

Leoni 1715–20
G. Leoni, *The Architecture of A. Palladio*, 4 vols, 1715–20

Leoni 1755
—, trans., *Leon Battista Alberti: The Ten Books of Architecture*, 1755

Leroy 1759
J. D. Leroy, *Ruins of Athens, with Remains and Other Valuable Antiquities in Greece*, 1759

Le Temple 1982
Le Temple: representations de l'architecture sacrée, 1982

Lever 2003
J. Lever, *Catalogue of the Drawings of George Dance the Younger (1741–1825) and of George Dance the Elder (1695–1768) from the Collection of Sir John Soane's Museum*, 2003

Lewis 1981
D. Lewis, *The Drawings of Andrea Palladio*, 1981

Lewis 1837
S. Lewis, *Topographical Dictionary of Ireland*, 2 vols, 1837

Lightoler 1762
T. Lightoler, *The Gentleman and Farmer's Architect. A New Work Containing a great Variety of Useful and Genteel Designs . . . of Parsonage and Farm Houses, etc.*, 1762

Linstrum 1973
D. Linstrum, *RIBA Catalogue: Wyatt Family*, 1973

Loveday 1890
J. Loveday, *Diary of a Tour in 1732*, Roxbrughe Club, 1890

Loveday 1984
John Loveday of Caversham, 1711–1789: The Life and Tours of an Eighteenth-Century Onlooker, ed. S. Markham, 1984

Mackenzie 1827
A. Mackenzie, *A Description and Historical Account of the Town and Country of Newcastle Upon Tyne, including the Borough of Gateshead*, 1827

Mackenzie and Ross 1834
E. Mackenzie and M. Ross, *An Historical, Topographical, and Descriptive View of the County Palatine of Durham*, 2 vols, 1834

Macky 1722, 1732
J. Macky, *A Journey Through England: In Familiar Letters From A Gentleman Here, To His Friend Abroad*, 2 vols, 1722; 2nd edn, 1732

Maitland 1756
W. Maitland, *The History and Survey of London from its foundation to the present time*, 2 vols, 1756

Malcolm 1803–7
J. P. Malcolm, *Londinium Redivivum; or, An Ancient History and Modern Description of London*, 4 vols, 1803–7 [vols I–III, 1803; vol. IV, 1807]

Malcolm 1807
—, *First Impressions*, 1807

Malton 1779
T. Malton, *A Compleat Treatise on Perspective in Theory and Practice; on the True Principles of Dr Brook Taylor* [1775], 1779

Mangey 1719
Dr T. Mangey, *The Holiness of Christian Churches*, 1719

Manning and Bray 1804–14
O. Manning and W. Bray, *The History and Antiquities of the County of Surrey*, 3 vols, 1804–14 [vol. I, 1804; vol. II, 1809; vol. III, 1814]

Marconi, Cipriani and Valeriani 1974
P. Marconi, A. Cipriani and E. Valeriani, *I disegni di architettura dell'Archivio storico dell'Accademia di San Luca*, 2 vols, 1974

Matthews 1794
W. Matthews, *The New History, Survey and Description of the City and Suburbs of Bristol; or, Complete Guide*, 1794

McAndrew 1974
J. McAndrew, *RIBA Catalogue: Antonio Visentini*, 1974

Melville 2007
J. Melville, 'A Journal of a Trip Through Part of Flanders in 1726 by John Thornhill', *Walpole Society*, 69 (2007), pp. 185–209

Middleton et al. 1998
R. D. Middleton et al., *The Mark J. Millard Architectural Collection*, vol. II: *British Books: Seventeenth through Nineteenth Centuries*, 1998

Miller 2005
The Diaries of Sanderson Miller of Radway, ed. W. Hawkes, Dugdale Society, 2005

Millon 1984
H. A. Millon, *Filippo Juvara: Drawings from the Roman Period, 1704–1714*, vol. I, 1984

Milner 1798–1801/1809
J. Milner, *The History Civil and Ecclesiastical, & Survey of the Antiquities of Winchester*, 2 vols, 1798–1801; 2nd edn, 1809

Montfaucon 1719
B. de Montfaucon, *L'Antiquite expliquée*, 5 vols in 10, 1719

Montfaucon 1721–2
—, *Antiquity Explained*, trans. D. Humphreys, 5 vols, 1721–2

Morant 1748
P. Morant, *The History and Antiquities of the most ancient Town and Borough of Colchester*, 1748

Morant 1768
—, *The History and Antiquities of the County of Essex*, 2 vols, 1768

Morgan 1986
P. Morgan, ed., *Inspections of Churches and Parsonage Houses in the Diocese of Worcester in 1674, 1676, 1684 and 1687*, Worcestershire Historical Society, NS, 12, 1986

Moritz 1783
K. P. Moritz, *Reisen eines Deutschen in England im Jahr 1782*, 1783

Moritz 1987
—, *Journeys of a German in England: Carl Philip Moritz: A walking-tour of England in 1782*, trans. R. Nettel, 1987 [translation of Moritz 1783]

Morris 1728
R. Morris, *An Essay In Defence of Ancient Architecture; or, A Parallel of the Ancient Buildings with the Moderns*, 1728

Morris 1734
—, *Lectures on Architecture*, 1734

Morris 1742
—, *The Art of Architecture: A Poem In Imitation of Horace's Art of Poetry*, 1742

Morris 1750
—, *Rural Architecture*, 1750

Morris 1755
—, *Select Architecture*, 1755

Moss 1794
W. Moss, *The Liverpool Guide*, 1794

Mouat 1775
Mouat's Journal, begun 14 January 1775, MS, The National Library of Scotland, Edinburgh (formerly in possession of F. Bamford)

Muilman 1769–72
P. Muilman, *A New and Complete History of Essex . . . By a Gentleman*, 6 vols, 1769–72

Murphy 1795
J. Murphy, *Plans Elevations Sections and Views of the Church of Batalha*, 1795

Murray et al. 1990
H. Murray et al., *York through the Eyes of the Artist*, 1990

Myerscough 2000
C. Myerscough, ed., *Uncle John Carr: The Diaries of his Great-nieces, Harriett and Amelia Clark*, 2000

Nash 1781–2
T. R. Nash, *A History of Worcestershire*, 2 vols, 1781–2

Navarra 2001
M. Navarra, ed., *Robert Adam: Ruins of the Palace of the Emperor Diocletian at Spalatro in Dalmatia* [1764], 2001

Nelli 1733
G. B. Nelli, *Descrizione e studi dell'insigne Fabbrica di S. Maria del Fiore*, 1733

Neufforge 1757–68
J. F. de Neufforge, *Recueil élémentaire d'architecture*, 8 vols, 1757–68

Neve 1726
R. Neve, *The City and Country Purchaser, and Builder's Dictionary; or, The Compleat Builders Guide* [1703], 1726; reprinted 1969

Newberry 1759
J. Newberry, *An Historical Account of the Curiosities of London and Westminster*, 1759

Newton 1791
W. Newton, *The Architecture of M. Vitruvius Pollio*, 1791

Nichols 1795–1811
J. Nichols, *The History and Antiquities of the County of Leicester*, vols II–IV, 1795–1811 [vol. II, pt 1, 1795; vol. II, pt 2, 1798; vol. III, pt 1, 1800; vol. III, pt 2, 1804; vol. IV, pt 1, 1807; vol. IV, pt 2, 1811]

Nicoll 1768
W. Nicoll, *The London and Westminster Guide, Through the Cities and Suburbs*, 1768

Nicolson 1877
Miscellany Accounts of the Diocese of Carlisle, with their Terriers Delivered in to me at my Primary Visitation by William Nicolson, Late Bishop of Carlisle [1703–7], ed. R. S. Ferguson, Cumberland and Westmorland Antiquarian and Archaeological Society, 1877

Nieuhof 1669
J. Nieuhof, *An Embassy from the East-India Company of the United Provinces to the Grand Tartar Cham Emperor of China* [1665], 1669

Northumberland 1926
The Diaries of a Duchess: Extracts from the Diaries of the First Duchess of Northumberland (1716–1776), ed. J. Greig, 1926

O'Gorman et al. 1986
J. F. O'Gorman et al., *Drawing towards Building: Philadelphia Architectural Graphics, 1732–1986*, 1986

Oliver 1831
T. Oliver, *A New Picture of Newcastle upon Tyne*, 1831

Ollard and Walker 1928–31
S. L. Ollard and P. C. Walker, eds, *Archbishop Herring's Visitation Returns, 1743*, Yorkshire Archaeological Society, Record Series, 5 vols, 1928–31

Osborne 1758
T. Osborne, *English Architecture*, 1758

Owen 1669
C. Owen, *Carmen Pindaricum*, 1669; reprinted in *Musarum Anglicanarum analecta*, 1721 and 1747

Owen 1808
H. Owen, *Some Account of the Ancient and Present State of Shrewsbury*, 1808

Owen and Blakeway 1825
— and J. B. Blakeway, *A History of Shrewsbury*, 2 vols, 1825

Pain 1791
W. Pain, *Practical House Carpenter; or, Youth's Instructor*, 1791

Paine 1767–83
J. Paine, *Plans, Elevations and Sections of Nobleman and Gentlemen's Houses*, 2 vols, 1767–83

Paterson 1714
J. Paterson, *Pietas Londinensis; or, The Present Ecclesiastical State of London; Containing An Account of all the Churches, and Chapels of Ease, in and about the Cities of London and Westminster; of the set Times of their Publick Prayers, Sacraments, and Sermons, both ordinary and extraordinary . . . To which is added, A Postscript, recommending the Duty of publick Prayer*, 1714

Patte 1770
P. Patte, *Mémoire sur la construction de la coupole projectée pour couronner la nouvelle église de Sainte Geneviève*, 1770

Payne 1987
A. Payne, *Views of the Past: Topographical Drawings in the British Library*, 1987

Peake 1611: *see* Serlio 1537

Pearce 1727
Z. Pearce, *A* Sermon *Preached at the New Parish Church of St Martin in the Fields, Westminster, Oct. 20. 1726*, 1727

Peck 1727
Revd F. Peck, *Academia Tertia Anglicana; or, The Antiquarian Annals of Stamford*, 1727

Pennant 1769
T. Pennant, *A Tour in Scotland, 1769* [1771 edn], 2000

Pennant 1772
—, *A Tour in Scotland and Voyage to the Hebrides, 1772*, ed. A. Simmons, 1998

Penrose 1983
Letters from Bath, 1766–1767, by the Rev. John Penrose, ed. B. Mitchell and H. Penrose, 1983

Perceval 1989
The English Travels of Sir John Percival and William Byrd II: The Percival Diary of 1701, ed. M. R. Wenger, 1989

Percy 1775
T. Percy, Bishop of Dromore, *The Hermit of Warkworth: A Northumberland Ballad*, 4th edn, 1775

Perrault 1684
C. Perrault, *Les Dix Livres d'architecture de Vitruve*, 1684

Perouse de Montclos 1984
J.-M. Perouse de Montclos, *'Les Prix de Rome': Concours de l'Académie royale d'architecture au XVIIIe siècle*, 1984

Petter 1974
H. M. Petter, *The Oxford Almanacks*, 1974

Phillips 1779
T. Phillips, *The History and Antiquities of Shrewsbury*, 1779

Picart 1733
B. Picart, *Ceremonies et Coutumes Religieuses De Tous Les Peuples Du Monde*, vol. III, 1733

Picton 1873
J. A. Picton, *Memorials of Liverpool: Historical and Topographical*, 2 vols, 1873

Picton 1886
—, *City of Liverpool: Municipal Archives and Records, from AD 1700 to the Passing of the Municipal Reform Act, 1835*, vol. II, 1886

Piggott 1974
S. Piggott, ed., *Sale Catalogues of Libraries of Eminent Persons, Antiquaries*, 1974

Piranesi 1756
G. B. Piranesi, *Le Antichità Romane*, 4 vols, 1756

Placzek et al. 1972
A. K. Placzek et al., *Giovanni Battista Piranesi: Drawings and Etchings at Columbia University*, 1972

Platt MS
'John Platt's Journies and his other transactions in Business' (1761–91), Rotherham Central Library, Archives (microfilm 101/F, vol. 1): *see* Potts 1959

Plot 1686
R. Plot, *Natural History of Staffordshire*, 1686

Plumptre 1992
James Plumptre's Britain: The Journals of a Tourist in the 1790s, ed. I. Clusby, 1992

Plymley 1992
E. Wilson, 'A Shropshire Lady in Bath, 1794–1807', *Bath History*, IV (1992), pp. 94–123 [Katherine Plymley]

Pococke 1743–5
R. Pococke, *A Description of the East, and Some other Countries*, 2 vols, 1743–5

Pococke 1750
—, *The Travels through England of Dr Richard Pococke, Successively Bishop of Meath and of Ossory during 1750, 1751, and Later Years*, ed. J. J. Cartwright, Camden Society, NS, I, vol. 42, 1888; vol. 44, 1889

Pococke 1760
—, 'Northern Journeys of Bishop Richard Pococke', in *North Country Diaries*, Publication of the Surtees Society, CXXIV, 1915

Pococke 1887
—, *Tours in Scotland, 1747, 1750, 1760, by Richard Pococke*, ed. D. W. Kemp, 1887

Pococke 1995
Richard Pococke's Irish Tours, ed. J. McVeagh, 1995

Pollock 2000
M. Pollock, *The Mark J. Millard Architectural Collection*, vol. IV: *Italian and Spanish Books, Fifteenth through Nineteenth Centuries*, 2000

Polwhele 1793–1806
R. Polwhele, *The History of Devonshire*, 3 vols, 1793–1806

Pool and Cash 1780
R. Pool and J. Cash, *Views of the most Remarkable Public Buildings, Monuments and other Edifices in the City of Dublin*, 1780

Pope 1711
A. Pope, *An Essay on Criticism*, 1711

Pope 1713
—, *Windsor-Forest*, 1713

Pope 1715
—, *The Temple of Fame*, 1715

Pope 1731
—, *Epistle IV: To Richard Boyle, Earl of Burlington: Argument of the Use of Riches*, 1731

Pope 1732
—, *A Miscellany on Taste. By Mr Pope, etc.*, 1732

Pope 1733
—, *Epistle III: To Allen Lord Bathurst: Argument of the Use of Riches*, 1733

Pope 1734
—, *The Second Satire of the Second Book of Horace Imitated*, 1734

Pope 1743
—, *The Dunciad in Four Books with the Prolegomena of Scriblerus and Notes Variorum*, 1743

Pope 1966
—, *Poetical Works*, ed. H. David, 1966

Port 1986
H. M. Port, ed., *The Commissioners for Building Fifty New Churches: The Minute Books, 1711–17: A Calendar*, London Record Society, 23, 1986

Pote 1729
J. Pote, *The Foreigner's Guide; Or, a necessary and instructive Companion Both for the Foreigner and Native, in their Tour through the Cities of London and Westminster*, 1729 [English/French edn; British Library, 578.b.7]

Prado and Villalpando 1596–1605
J. Prado and J. B. Villalpando, *In Ezechielem Explanationes*, 3 vols, 1596–1605

Preston 1819
J. Preston, *The Picture of Yarmouth*, 1819

Price 1735
F. Price, *A Treatise on Carpentry* [1733], enlarged as *The British Carpenter*, 1735

Price 1753
—, *A Series of particular and useful Observations, Made with great Diligence and Care, upon that Admirable Structure, The Cathedral-Church of Salisbury*, 1753

Price 1794
U. Price, *An Essay on the Picturesque*, 1794

Pye 1760
H. Pye, *A Short Account, Of the Principal Seats and Gardens, In and about Twickenham*, 1760

Pyne 1823
W. H. Pyne [as Ephraim Hardcastle], 'A Ramble on the Heath', in *Wine and Walnuts; or, After-Dinner Chit-Chat*, 2 vols, 1823

Ralph 1734
J. Ralph, *A Critical Review of the Publick Buildings, Statues and Ornaments In, and about London and Westminster*, 1734

Rawlins 1768
T. Rawlins, *Familiar Architecture; or, Original Designs of Houses for Gentlemen and Tradesmen; Parsonages; Summer Retreats; Banqueting-Rooms; and Churches*, 1768

Rawlinson 1719
R. Rawlinson, *The History and Antiquities of the Cathedral Church of Salisbury, and the Abbey of Bath*, 1719

Reeves 1764
G. Reeves, *A New History of London, From Its Foundation to the Present Year, By Question and Answer*, 2nd edn, 1764

Reid 1802
W. H. Reid, 'Hints for improving the Energy of the Pulpit', *Gentleman's Magazine* (March 1802), pp. 221–3

Renwick 1911
R. Renwick, ed., *Extracts from the Records of the Burgh of Glasgow with Charters and other Documents*, vol. VI, 1911

Reuther and Berckenhagen 1994
H. Reuther and E. Berckenhagen, *Deutsche Architektur-Modelle-Projekthilfe zwischen 1500 und 1900*, 1994

Richardson 1802–10
G. Richardson, *New Vitruvius Britannicus*, 2 vols, 1802–10 [vol. I, 1802–8; vol. II, 1808–10]

Rickman 1838
J. Rickman, *Atlas to the Life of Thomas Telford*, 1838

Rigaud 1984
'Facts and Recollections of the XVIII Century in a Memoir of John Francis Rigaud Esq., RA', *Walpole Society*, 50 (1984), pp. 1–164

Riou 1768
S. Riou, *The Grecian Orders Of Architecture. Delineated And Explained From The Antiquities Of Athens*, 1768

Roberts 1995
J. Roberts, *Views of Windsor*, 1995

Roberts 1988
M. Roberts, *The Emergence of Clarity: Images of English Cathedrals, 1640–1840*, 1988

Rochefoucauld 1784
A Frenchman's Year in Suffolk, ed. N. Scarfe, Suffolk Records Society, XXX, 1988

Rochefoucauld 1785
Innocent Espionage: The La Rochefoucauld Brothers' Tour of England in 1785, ed. N. Scarfe, 1995 [translations of François de la Rochefoucauld, *Mélanges sur l'Angleterre*, and Alexandre de la Rochefoucauld, *Journaux de voyage*]

Rocque 1746–7
J. Rocque, 'A Plan of the Cities of London and Westminster, and Borough of Southwark' [1746–7], facsimile, with Alphabetical Index, in R. Hyde, *The A to Z of Georgian London*, 1981

Rossi and Rossi 1702–21
D. de' Rossi and G. G. de' Rossi, *Studio d'architettura civile sopra gli ornamenti de porte e finestre . . . di Roma*, 3 vols, 1702–21

Rossi 1684
G. G. de' Rossi, *Insignium Romae templorum prospectus*, 1684

Rossi 1713
—, *Disegni di vari altari e cappelle nelle chiese di Roma*, 1713

Rouquet 1755
A. Rouquet, *The Present State of the Arts in England*, 1755

Rowan 1985
A. Rowan, *Designs for Castles and Country Villas by Robert and James Adam*, 1985

Rowan 1988
—, *Robert Adam: Catalogue of Architectural Drawings in the Victoria and Albert Museum*, 1988

Rowan 2007
—, *Vaulting Ambition: The Adam Brothers: Contractors to the Metropolis in the Reign of George III*, 2007

Rubens 1658
P. P. Rubens, *Palazzi moderni di Genova*, 1658

Russell and Price 1769
P. Russell and O. Price, eds, *England Displayed*, 2 vols, 1769

Russell 1997
T. M. Russell, ed., *The Encyclopaedic Dictionary in the Eighteenth Century: Architecture, Arts and Crafts*, 5 vols, 1997

Rutter 1823
J. Rutter, *Delineations of Fonthill and Its Abbey*, 1823

Rykwert, Leach and Tavernor 1991
J. Rykwert, N. Leach and R. Tavernor, trans., *Leon Battista Alberti: On the Art of Building in Ten Books*, 1991

Salmon 1748
W. Salmon, *The London and Country Builder's Vade Mecum: Or, The Compleat and Universal Architect's Assistant*, 1748; reprinted 1999

Savage 1962
The Poetical Works of Richard Savage, ed. C. Tracey, 1962

Schimmelman 1999
J. G. Schimmelman, *Architectural Books in Early America: Architectural Treatises and Building Handbooks Available in American Libraries and Bookstores through 1800*, 1999

Secker 1988
The Autobiography of Thomas Secker, Archbishop of Canterbury, ed. J. S. Macauley and R. W. Greaves, 1988

Serlio 1537
S. Serlio, *Tutte l'Opere D'Architettura et Prospetiva*, 1537

Sharp 1766
S. Sharp, *Letters from Italy . . . in the Years 1765, and 1766*, 1766

Shaw 1798–1801
S. Shaw, *The History and Antiquities of Staffordshire*, 2 vols, 1798–1801

Shenstone 1939
The Letters of William Shenstone, ed. M. Williams, 1939

Shepherd 1829
T. H. Shepherd, *London and its Environs in the Nineteenth Century*, 1829

Shepherd 1829a
—, *Modern Athens*, 1829

Shiercliff 1789
E. Shiercliff, *Bristol and Hotwell Guide*, 1789

Skrine 1795
H. Skrine, *Three Successive Tours in the North of England and Great Part of Scotland*, 1795

Smith 1746
C. Smith, *The Antient and Present State of the County and City of Waterford*, 1746

Smith 1949
J. T. Smith, *Nollekens and his Times* [1828], 1949

Smith 1833
T. Smith, *Topographical and Historical Account of the Parish of St Mary-le-Bone*, 1833

Smith 2003
T. G. Smith, *Vitruvius on Architecture*, 2003

Smollett 1981
T. Smollett, *Travels through France and Italy* [1766], ed. F. Felsenstein, 1981

Smollett 1985
—, *The Expedition of Humphrey Clinker* [1771], ed. A. Ross, 1985

Snodin 2009
M. Snodin, ed., *Horace Walpole's Strawberry Hill*, 2009

Soane MS, vol. 26
'A Manuscri By Mr Gibbs A few Short Cursory Remarks on some of the finest Antient and modern Buildings In Rome, and other parts of Italy, by Mr Gibbs while he was Studying Architectur there, being Memorandums for his oun use. 1707 and not intended to be made Public being imperfect', 'A Short Accompt of Mr James Gibbs Architect And of Several things he built in England &c. Affter his returne from Italy', Sir John Soane's Museum, London

Soane 1788
J. Soane, *Plans Elevations and Sections of Buildings*, 1788

Soo 1998
L. M. Soo, *Wren's 'Tracts' on Architecture and Other Writings*, 1998

Sopwith 1826
T. Sopwith, *A Historical and Descriptive Account of All Saints' Church in Newcastle upon Tyne*, 1826

Spon 1678
J. Spon, *Voyage d'Italia, de Dalmatie et de Grece*, 1678

Stephens 1727
L. Stephens, *A Sermon Preached On the 10th of August, 1727, at the Consecration of Trinity-Chapel, in the Town of Leeds in Yorkshire*, 1727

Stewart 1771
John Stewart (attributed), *Critical Observations on the Buildings and Improvements of London*, 1771

Stieglitz 1800
C. L. Stieglitz, *Plans et dessins tirés de la belle architecture*, 1800

Stuart and Revett 1762–94
J. Stuart and N. Revett, *The Antiquities of Athens*, 3 vols, 1762–94 [vol. I, 1762; vol. II, 1787, ed. W. Newton; vol. III, 1794, ed. W. Reveley]

Stuart and Revett 1825–30
— and —, *The Antiquities of Athens*, ed. W. Kinnard et al., 4 vols, 1825–30

Stukeley 1776
W. Stukeley, *Itinerarium Curiosum; or, An Account of the Antiquities, and Remarkable Curiosities in Nature or Art, Observed in Travels Through Great Britain* [1724], 2nd edn, with 'Large Additions', 2 vols, 1776

Stukeley 1882–7
The Family Memoirs of the Rev. William Stukeley, MD, and the Antiquarian and other Correspondence of William Stukeley, Roger and Samuel Gale, etc., Publication of the Surtees Society, LXXIII, 3 vols, 1882–7

Stumpf 1986
C. Stumpf, ed., *Richard Payne Knight: Expedition into Sicily* [1777], 1986

Swete MS
J. Swete, *MS Tour Through England and Scotland By Way of Bristol, Monmouth, Cardiff, Hereford, Warwick, Derbyshire, Lancashire, The Lakes to Scotland*, 5 vols, 1783–6 [in Leeds University Library, Special Collections]

Swift 1709
J. Swift, *A Project for the Advancement of Religion, and the Reformation of Manners*, 1709

Swift 1726
—, *Travels Into Several Remote Nations of the World. By Lemuel Guliver*, 1726

Swift 1747
—, *A Tale of a Tub* [1704], 1747

Sykes 1833
J. Sykes, *Local Records; or, Historical Register of Remarkable Events*, vol. I, 1833

Talman 1997
G. Parry, ed., 'The John Talman Letter-Book', *Walpole Society*, 59 (1997), pp. 1–179

Tavernor and Schofield 1997
R. Tavernor and R. Schofield, trans., *Andrea Palladio: The Four Books on Architecture*, 1997

Taylor 1719
B. Taylor, *Linear Perspective: or, A New Method Of Representing justly all manner of Objects As they appear to the Eye in all Situations. A Work necessary for . . . Architects . . . to Judge of and Regulate Designs by* [1715]; 2nd edition, 1719

Taylor 1985
H. Taylor, 'The Country Curate' [1737], in *The New Oxford Book of Eighteenth Century Verse*, ed. R. Lonsdale, 1985, pp. 297–9

Thomas 1737
W. Thomas, *A Survey of the Cathedral-Church of Worcester*, 1737

Thomas 1783
—, *Original Designs in Architecture*, 1783

Thompson 1760
G. Thompson, *A Description of the Royal Palace, and Monastery of St Lawrence, Called The Escurial; and of the Chapel Royal of the Pantheon*, 1760

Thoresby 1715
R. Thoresby, *Ducatus Leodiensis; or, The Topography of the Ancient and Populous Town and Parish of Leedes, and Parts Adjacent in the West-Riding of the County of York*, 1715

Thoresby 1724
—, *Vicaria Leodiensis*, 1724

Thoresby 1830
The Diary of Ralph Thoresby FRS, ed. J. Hunter, 2 vols, 1830

Thornton 1784
W. Thornton, *The New, Complete, and Universal History, Description, and Survey of The Cities of London and Westminster, The Borough of Southwark, And the Parts Adjacent*, 1784

Torrington 1934–8
The Torrington Diaries Containing the Tour Through England and Wales of the Hon. John Byng (Later Fifth Viscount Torrington) between the Years 1781 and 1794, ed. C. B. Andrews, 4 vols, 1934–8

Throsby 1789, 1790
J. Throsby, *Select Views of Leicestershire*, vol. I, 1789; *The Supplementary Volume to the Leicestershire Views*, vol. II, 1790

Toynbee 1927
P. Toynbee, *Strawberry Hill Accounts*, 1927

Trapp 1723
J. Trapp, *A Sermon Preached At Shipbourne in Kent, Upon the Opening of the New Church There; Entirely Rebuilt at the sole Expense Of the Right Honourable The Lord and Lady Barnard*, 1723 [British Library, 694.k.10 (20)]

Troughton 1810
T. Troughton, *The History of Liverpool*, 1810

Tyler 1971
R. Tyler, *Francis Place, 1647–1728*, York City Art Gallery, 1971

Uffenbach 1928
Oxford [and] *Cambridge in 1710 from the Travels of Zacharias Conrad von Uffenbach*, ed. W. H. Quarrell and J. C. Quarrell, 1928

Vardy 1742
J. Vardy, *Ancient Architecture*, 1742

Vardy 1744
—, *Some Designs of Mr Inigo Jones and Mr Wm Kent*, 1744

Vertue 1930–55
Vertue Note Books, in *Walpole Society*, I/18 (1930); II/20 (1932); III/22 (1934); IV/24 (1936); V/26 (1938); VI/30 (1955)

Vetusta Monumenta 1747–90
Society of Antiquaries of London, *Vetusta Monumenta: quae ad rerum Britannicarum memoriam conservandan: Societas Antiquariorium Londini sumptu suo edenda curavit*, 3 vols, 1747–90 [vol. I, 1747; vol. II, 1770; vol. III, 1790]

Wallace 1794
J. Wallace, *A General and Descriptive History of Liverpool*, 1794

Walpole 1784
H. Walpole, *A Description of the Villa . . . At Strawberry Hill*, 1784

Walpole 1826–8
—, *Anecdotes of Painting in England* [1762–71], ed. J. Dallaway, 5 vols, 1826–8

Walpole 1937–83
—, *Correspondence*, ed. W. S. Lewis, 48 vols in 47, 1937–83

Ward 1993
E. Ward, *The London Spy* [1698–1731]; as *The London-Spy Compleat, In Eighteen Parts*, 4th edn, 1709; ed. P. Hyland, 1993

Ward 1995
W. R. Ward, ed., *Parson and Parish in Eighteenth-century Hampshire: Replies to Bishops' Visitations*, Hampshire Record Service, XIII, 1995

Ware 1731
I. Ware, *Designs of Inigo Jones and Others*, 1731

Ware 1738
—, *The Four Books of Andrea Palladio's Architecture*, 1738

Ware 1756
—, *A Complete Body of Architecture*, 1756

Warner 1802
R. Warner, *A Tour Through the Northern Counties of England and the Borders of Scotland*, 2 vols, 1802

Warton 1754
T. Warton, *Observations on The Fairie Queene of Spenser*, 1754

Watkin 1972
D. J. Watkin, *Sale Catalogues of Libraries of Eminent Persons*, vol. IV: *Architects*, 1972

Watkin 1996
—, *Sir John Soane: Enlightenment Thought and the Royal Academy Lectures*, 1996

Webb 1931
G. Webb, 'The Letters and Drawings Relating to the Building of the Mausoleum at Castle Howard, 1726–1742', *Wren Society*, 19 (1931), pp. 111–64

Welton 1714a
R. Welton, *Church-Ornament without Idolatry Vindicated*, 1714 [British Library, 694.e.9]

Welton 1714b
—, *A Letter to the Church-Wardens of White-Chaple, Occasioned by A New Altar-Piece Set up in their Church*, 1714

Welton 1714c
—, 'An Answer to Willoughby Willey's Letter', *The Patriot*, 3–7 May 1714

Wesley 1909–16
The Journal of the Rev. John Wesley, AM, ed. N. Curnock, 8 vols, 1909–16

West and Toms 1736–9
Perspective Views of all the Ancient Churches, and other Buildings, In the Cities of London, and Westminster, and Parts adjacent, Drawn by Robert West, Engraved by Wm Hry Toms, 2 vols, 1736–9 [vol. I, 16 March 1736; vol. II, 18 March 1739]

Wheler 1689
Revd G. Wheler, *An Account of the Churches, or Places of Assembly, of the Primitive Christians, from the Churches of Tyre, Jerusalem and Constantinople Described by Eusebius*, 1689

Whitaker 1816
T. D. Whitaker, *Loidis and Elmete*, 1816

White 2001
R. White, *The Architectural Drawings of Magdalen College, Oxford: A Catalogue*, 2001

Whitefield 1772
A Select Collection of Letters of George Whitefield, ed. J. Gillies, vol. I, 1772

Whitefield 1985
George Whitefield's Journals [1756, The Banner of Truth Trust edn], 1985

Whitehead 1753
W. Whitehead, *The World*, no. 12, 1753

Whitehead 1757
—, 'Elegy II: "On the Mausoleum of Augustus", 1756, To George Bussy, Viscount Villiers, written at Rome', *Gentleman's Magazine* (February 1757), p. 84

Whittle 1821
P. Whittle, *Account of Preston*, 1821

Wiebenson 1993
D. Wiebenson, *The Mark J. Millard Architectural Collection*, vol. I: *French Books Sixteenth through Nineteenth Centuries*, 1993

Williams 1765
C. H. Williams, *Isabella; or, The Morning* [1740], 1765

Willis 1717–30
B. Willis, *A Survey of the Cathedrals of Bangor, Llandaff, St Asaph and St David* [1717–21]; *York, Durham, Carlisle, Chester, Man, Lichfield, Hereford, Worcester, Gloucester, and Bristol* [1727]; *Lincoln, Ely, Oxford, and Peterborough* [1730], 3 vols, 1717–30; reissued 1742

Willis 1742
—, *A Survey of the Cathedrals . . .*, 3 vols, 1742 [reissue of Willis 1717–30]

Willmott 1885
R. A. Willmott, ed., *The Works of George Herbert in Prose and Verse*, 1885

Wilson 1761
T. Wilson, *The Ornaments of Churches Considered*, 1761

Wittkower 1974a
R. Wittkower, *Gothic versus Classic: Architectural Projects in Seventeenth Century Italy*, 1974

Witton 1791
P. H. Witton, *Views of the Ruins of the Principal Houses Destroyed during the Riots at Birmingham*, 1791

Wolcot 1795
J. Wolcot, *The Sorrows of Sunday: An Elegy*, 1795

Wood 1741
J. Wood Sr, *The Origin Of Building; or, The Plagiarism of the Heathens Detected*, 1741

Wood 1742
—, *An Essay Towards a Description of the City of Bath*, 2 parts, 1742

Wood 1765
—, *A Description of Bath*, 2 vols in one, 2nd edn, 'Corrected and Enlarged', 1765

Woolfe and Gandon 1767–71
J. Woolfe and J. Gandon, *Vitruvius Britannicus*, vols IV and V, 1767–71

Worsley 1991a
G. Worsley, *Architectural Drawings of the Regency Period, 1790–1837*, 1991

Wotton 1624
H. Wotton, *The Elements of Architecture*, 1624

Wren 1750
S. Wren, *Parentalia; or, Memoirs of the Family of the Wrens* [1750], Heirloom copy reprint, 1965 [see also Soo 1998]

Wright 1730
E. Wright, *Some Observations made in Travelling Through France, Italy, &c. In the Years 1720, 1721 and 1722*, 2 vols, 1730

Wright 1793
G. Wright, *History of the Town and Parish of Leeds*, 1793

Wright 1797
—, *A History of the Town and Parish of Leeds, Compiled by Various Authors . . . To which are added, A History of Kirkstall Abbey*, 1797

Wright 1697
J. Wright, *Three Poems of St Paul's Cathedral*, 1697

York 1768
An Accurate Description and History of the Cathedral and Metropolitical Church of St Peter, York, vol. I, 1768

Young 1770–71
A. Young, *A Six Months Tour Through the North of England*, 4 vols, 1770–71

SECONDARY SOURCES

Abbott et al. 1972
E. Abbott et al., *Westminster Abbey*, 1972

Abramson 2005
D. M. Abramson, *Building the Bank of England: Money Architecture Society, 1694–1942*, 2005

Acworth 1949
A. W. Acworth, *Treasure in the Caribbean: A First Study of Georgian Buildings in the British West Indies*, 1949

Adam 1976
W. H. Adam, ed., *The Eye of Thomas Jefferson*, 1976

Addison 1947
W. Addison, *The English Country Parson*, 1947

Addleshaw and Etchells 1948
G. W. O. Addleshaw and F. Etchells, *The Architectural Setting of Anglican Worship*, 1948

Airs 1982
M. Airs, *The Buildings of Britain: Tudor and Jacobean*, 1982

Airs 1996
—, ed., *Baroque and Palladian: The Early 18th Century Great House*, 1996

Ali 2005
J. Ali, 'A New Angle on Hawksmoor: The East–West Orientation Rule and a Proposed Collaboration with Edmond Halley', Paul Mellon Centre, London 'Restoring Hawksmoor' Conference, 23 September 2005

Ali and Cunich 2005a
— and P. Cunich, 'Halley and the London Queen Anne Churches', *Astronomy and Geophysics*, 46/2 (April 2005), pp. 2.22–2.25

Ali and Cunich 2005b
— and —, 'The Church East and West: Orienting the Queen Anne Churches, 1711–34', *Journal of the Society of Architectural Historians of Great Britain*, 64 (March 2005), pp. 56–73

Allan 1974
D. G. C. Allan, *The Houses of the Royal Society of Arts: A History and a Guide*, 1974

Allen 1932
F. J. Allen, *The Great Church Towers of England*, 1932

Allsopp 1967
B. Allsopp, *Historic Architecture of Newcastle upon Tyne*, 1967

Amery 1988
C. Amery, *Wren's London*, 1988

Anderson 2007
C. Anderson, *Inigo Jones and the Classical Tradition*, 2007

Angelini et al. 1984
S. Angelini et al., *Giacomo Quarenghi*, 1984

Anon. 1930
'Trinity Church in Newport and Some of Its Members', *Bulletin of The Newport Historical Society*, 77 (October 1930), pp. 2–12

Anon. 1975
The Dissenting Church of Christ at St John's, 1775–1975: A History of St David's Presbyterian Church, St John's, Newfoundland, 1975

Anon. 1987
Underbank Chapel Stannington (Unitarian): A Short Account of its Earlier History, 1987

Archer 1979
M. Archer, *Stained Glass*, 1979

Archer 1985
—, *An Introduction to English Stained Glass*, 1985

Arciszewska 2002
B. Arciszewska, *The Hanoverian Court and the Triumph of Palladio*, 2002

Arciszewska and McKellar 2004
— and E. McKellar, eds, *Articulating British Classicism*, 2004

Armitage 1959
E. L. Armitage, *Stained Glass: History, Technology and Practice*, 1959

Aslet 1989
C. Aslet, 'Early History of Allerton Park', *Country Life* (26 January 1989), pp. 92–5

Aston 1988
M. Aston, *England's Iconoclasts: Laws against Images*, 1988

Atherton et al. 1996
I. Atherton et al., eds, *Norwich Cathedral: Church, City and Diocese, 1096–1996*, 1996

Aurenhammer 1973
H. Aurenhammer, *J. B. Fischer von Erlach*, 1973

Aylmer and Cant 1977
G. E. Aylmer and R. Cant, eds, *A History of York Minster*, 1977

Aylmer and Tiller 2000
— and J. Tiller, eds, *Hereford Cathedral: A History*, 2000

Baetjer and Links 1989
K. Baetjer and J. G. Links, *Canaletto*, 1989

Bailey 1981
N. Bailey, *Fitzrovia*, 1981

Baker and Baker 1949
C. H. Collins Baker and M. I. Baker, *The Life and Circumstances of James Brydges, First Duke of Chandos, Patron of the Liberal Arts*, 1949

Baldwin 1990
D. Baldwin, *The Chapel Royal: Ancient and Modern*, 1990

Balston 1945
T. Balston, *The Life of Jonathan Martin, Incendiary of York Minster*, 1945

Banham 1997
J. Banham, ed., *Encyclopedia of Interior Design*, 2 vols, 1997

Barkley 1984
H. Barkley, *Drawings by William Kent (1685–1748) from the Print Room Collection*, Victoria and Albert Museum, London, 1984

Barnard and Clark 1995
T. Barnard and J. Clark, eds, *Lord Burlington: Architecture, Art and Life*, 1995

Bax 1964
B. A. Bax, *The English Parsonage*, 1964

Beamish, Hillier and Johnstone 1976
D. Beamish, J. Hillier and H.F.V. Johnstone, *Mansions and Merchants of Poole and Dorset*, Poole Historical Trust, 1976

Beard 1966
G. Beard, *Catholic Churches since 1623*, 1966

Beard 1975
—, *Decorative Plasterwork in Britain*, 1975

Beard 1981
—, *Craftsmen and Interior Decoration in England, 1660–1820*, 1981

Beard 1982
—, *The Work of Christopher Wren*, 1982

Beard 1986
—, *The Work of John Vanbrugh*, 1986

Beddington 2006
C. Beddington, *Canaletto in England: A Venetian Artist Abroad, 1746–1755*, 2006

Beer 1948
E. S. Beer, 'Gothic: Origin and Diffusion of the Term: The Idea of Style in Architecture', *Journal of the Warburg and Courtauld Institutes*, 11 (1948), pp. 143–62

Bekaert 1987
G. Bekaert, *Landschap van Kerken*, 1987

Belinfante et al. 1991
J.C.E. Belinfante et al., *The Esnoga: A Monument to Portuguese-Jewish Culture*, 1991

Bence-Jones 1992
M. Bence-Jones, *The Catholic Families*, 1992

Bender 1987
J. Bender, *Imagining the Penitentiary: Fiction and the Architecture of Mind in Eighteenth-Century England*, 1987

Benes and Zimmerman 1979
P. Benes and P. D. Zimmerman, *New England Meeting Houses and Churches, 1630–1850*, 1979

Bennett 1997
C. Bennett, *Lincoln Cathedral*, 1997

Bennet, no date
R. Bennet, *Selina, Countess of Huntingdon: A Brief Celebration of a Remarkable Eighteenth Century Lady*, undated

Benton 1983
T. Benton, 'Wren, Dickinson and the Westminster Abbey Repairs', in *A Gothick Symposium at the Victoria and Albert Museum*, The Georgian Group, 1983

Beresford 1988
M. Beresford, *East End, West End: The Face of Leeds during Urbanisation, 1684–1842*, 1988

Bergdoll 2000
B. Bergdoll, *European Architecture, 1750–1890*, 2000

Berridge 1985
C. Berridge, *The Almshouses of London*, 1985

Berry 2004
S. Berry, 'Laughton Church Chancel and Other Major Church Alterations in and around Lewes, East Sussex, *c.*1740–1810: The Role of Architects and Local Craftsmen', *Sussex Archaeological Collections*, 142 (2004), pp. 107–13

Best 1964
C. F. A. Best, *Temporal Pillars: Queen Anne's Bounty, the Ecclesiastical Commissioners and the Church of England*, 1964

Bignamini and Hornsby 2010
I. Bignamini and C. Hornsby, *Digging and Dealing in Eighteenth-century Rome*, 2010

Bill 1950
E. G. W. Bill, 'Fifty New Churches', *Architectural Review* (March 1950), pp. 189–96

Bilsborough 1989
N. Bilsborough, *The Treasures of Lancashire*, 1989

Bilsborough 1991
—, *The Treasures of Cheshire*, 1991

Bindman 1997
D. Bindman, *Hogarth and his Times: Serious Comedy*, 1997

Bindman and Baker 1995
— and M. Baker, *Roubiliac and the Eighteenth-Century Monument: Sculpture as Theatre*, 1995

Binney 1971
M. Binney, 'A Pioneer Work of Neo-Classicism', *Country Life* (8 July 1971), pp. 110–15

Binney 1984
—, *Sir Robert Taylor: From Rococo to Neoclassicism*, 1984

Binski 1995
P. Binski, *Westminster Abbey and the Plantagenets*, 1995

Bishir 1990
C. W. Bishir, *North Carolina Architecture*, 1990

Bishir et al. 1990
— et al., *Architects and Builders in North Carolina: A History of the Practice of Building*, 1990

Bizzarro 1992
T. W. Bizzarro, *Romanesque Architectural Criticism: A Prehistory*, 1992

Black 1992
J. Black, *The British Abroad: The Grand Tour in the Eighteenth Century*, 1992

Blatch 1997
M. Blatch, *The Churches of Surrey*, 1997

Blaxhill 1938
E. A. Blaxhill, *History of Lion Walk Congregational Church, Colchester, 1642–1937*, 1938

Blum 1997
D. E. Blum, *The Fine Art of Textile: The Collection of the Philadelphia Museum of Art*, 1997

Blunt 1957
A. Blunt, *Art and Architecture in France, 1500 to 1700*, 1957

Blunt 1982
—, *Guide to Baroque Rome*, 1982

Blyth 1990
D. Blyth, *Flemish Cities Explored*, 1990

Bold 1988
J. Bold, *Wilton House and English Palladianism*, 1988

Bold 1989
—, *John Webb: Architectural Theory and Practice in the Seventeenth Century*, 1989

Bold 2000
—, *Greenwich: An Architectural History of the Royal Hospital for Seamen and the Queen's House*, 2000

Bold and Chaney 1993
— and E. Chaney, eds, *English Architecture, Public and Private*, 1993

Bolton 1913
A. T. Bolton, 'Compton Verney, Warwickshire', *Country Life* (18 October 1913), pp. 528–35

Bolton 1917
—, 'Lincoln's Inn and the Fields', *Architectural Review*, 41 (1917), pp. 111–15

Bomford and Finaldi 1998
D. Bomford and G. Finaldi, *Venice through Canaletto's Eyes*, 1998

Bond 1952
R. P. Bond, *Queen Anne's American Kings*, 1952

Boucher 1994
B. Boucher, *Andrea Palladio: The Architect in His Time*, 1994

Bowdler 2009
R. Bowdler, 'Respice finem', *The Georgian*, no. 1 (2009), pp. 12–18

Bowersock et al. 1999
G. W. Bowersock et al., eds, *Late Antiquity: A Guide to the Postclassical World*, 1999

Boyce 1967
B. Boyce, *The Benevolent Man: A Life of Ralph Allen of Bath*, 1967

Boynton 1970
L. Boynton, 'Newby Park, the First Palladian Villa in England', in Colvin and Harris 1970, pp. 97–105

Boynton 1992
—, 'Gillows' Furnishings for Catholic Chapels, 1750–1800', in *The Church and the Arts*, ed. D. Wood, 1992, pp. 363–79

Bozovic 1995
M. Bozovic, *Jeremy Bentham: The Panopticon Writings*, 1995

Brabbs 1986
D. Brabbs, *English Country Churches*, 1986

Bradford Archives 1996
Bradford Archives, 1974–1995: An Illustrated Guide to Bradford Archives, 1996

Bradley 2000
S. Bradley, 'The Roots of Ecclesiology: Late Hanoverian Attitudes to Medieval Churches', in *'A Church As It Should Be'*, ed. C. Webster and J. Elliott, 2000, pp. 22–44

Bradley 2005
—, 'Book Reviews [Friedman 2004]', *Ecclesiology Today*, 34 (January 2005), pp. 74–5

Bradley and Pevsner 1997
— and N. Pevsner, *London*, vol. I: *The City of London*, The Buildings of England, 1997

Braham 1980
A. Braham, *The Architecture of the French Enlightenment*, 1980

Brandwood 1984
G. K. Brandwood, *The Anglican Churches of Leicester*, 1984

Brandwood 1987
—, *Ancient and Modern: Churches and Chapels around Market Harborough*, 1987

Braybrooke 1836
R. Braybrooke, *The History of Audley End and Saffron Walden*, 1836

Brett 1976
C. E. Brett, *Roger Mulholland, Architect, of Belfast, 1740–1818*, Ulster Architectural Heritage Society, 1976

Brewster 1830
D. Brewster, *The Edinburgh Encyclopedia*, vol. VI, pt 2, 1830

Bridenbaugh 1949
C. Bridenbaugh, *Peter Harrison, First American Architect*, 1949

Briggs 1991
N. Briggs, *John Johnson, 1732–1814: Georgian Architect and Country Surveyor of Essex*, 1991

Brighton 1967–8
J. T. Brighton, 'William Peckitt, the Greatest of the Georgian Glasspainters', *York Georgian Society Annual Report* (1967–8), pp. 14–24

Brighton 2004
—,'William Peckitt (1731–95) and the Quest for Colour in 18th Century Glass', *British Art Journal* (spring–summer 2004), pp. 41–5

Bristow 1977
I. C. Bristow, 'Ready-Mixed Paint in the Eighteenth Century', *Architectural Review*, 161 (April 1977), pp. 246–8

Bristow 1996
—, *Architectural Colour in British Interiors, 1615–1840*, 1996

Brittain-Catlin 2008
T. Brittain-Catlin, *The English Parsonage in the Nineteenth Century*, 2008

Brockett 1962
A. Brockett, *Nonconformity in Exeter, 1650–1875*, 1962

Brodie, Croom and Davies 2002
A. Brodie, J. Croom and J. O. Davies, *English Prisons: An Architectural History*, 2002

Brooke 1853
R. Brooke, *Liverpool as It Was During the Last Quarter of the Eighteenth Century, 1775 to 1800*, 1853

Brooks 1999
C. Brooks, *The Gothic Revival*, 1999

Brown 1981
P. Brown, *Buildings of Britain, 1550–1750: South West England*, 1981

Brown 1985
R. Brown, ed., *The Architectural Outsiders*, 1985

Brown 1999
S. Brown, *'Sumptuous and Richly Adorn'd': The Decoration of Salisbury Cathedral*, 1999

Brown 2003
—, *'Our Magnificent Fabrick': York Minster: An Architectural History*, c. *1220–1500*, 2003

Brownell 1976
C. Brownell, 'John Wood the Elder and John Wood the Younger: Architects of Bath', unpublished PhD thesis, Columbia University, 1976

Brunel et al. 1995
G. Brunel et al., *Dictionnaire des églises de Paris*, 1995

Brunskill 1990
R. W. Brunskill, *Brick Building in Britain*, 1990

Brushe 1977
J. Brushe, 'Two Wayward Georgian Churches', *Country Life* (3 November 1977), pp. 1302–3

Brushe 1994
—, 'Some Designs by John James', *Georgian Group Journal* (1994), pp. 4–10

Buchanan 1999
A. Buchanan, 'Science and Sensibility: Architectural Antiquarianism in the Early Nineteenth Century', in *Producing the Past: Aspects of Antiquarian Culture and Practice, 1700–1850*, ed. M. Myrone and L. Peltz, 1999, pp. 169–86

Buchanan 1978
V. Buchanan, *A Look at Old Darwen*, 1978

Bucher and Wheller 1992
D. G. Bucher and W. R. Wheller, *A Neat Plain Modern Style: Philip Hooker and His Contemporaries, 1796–1836*, 1992

Bumpus, no date
F. Bumpus, *London Churches: Ancient and Modern*, 2 vols, undated

Burkett and Sloss 1995
M. E. Burkett and D. Sloss, *Read's Point of View: Paintings of the Cumbrian Countryside: Mathias Read, 1669–1747*, 1995

Burnage 2007
S. Burnage, 'The Work of John Bacon RA, 1740–1799', unpublished PhD thesis, University of York, 2007

Burne 1958
R. V. H. Burne, *Chester Cathedral*, 1958

Bury 1992
J. Bury, 'The Dosseret Entablature Block: An Unexplained Solecism', in *L'Emploi des ordres dans l'architecture de la Renaissance*, ed. J. Guillaume, 1992, pp. 355–64

Busco 1994
M. Busco, *Sir Richard Westmacott, Sculptor*, 1994

Bushman 1993
R. L. Bushman, *The Refinement of America: Persons, Houses, Cities*, 1993

Butler 1999
D. M. Butler, *The Quaker Meeting Houses of Britain*, 2 vols, 1999

Butler 1978
L.A.S. Butler, 'St Martin's Church, Allerton Mauleverer', *Yorkshire Archaeological Journal*, 50 (1978), pp. 177–88

Butler 1980
—, *Guide to St Martin, Allerton Mauleverer*, 1980

Buttery, no date
D. Buttery, *The Vanished Buildings of York*, undated

Calcraft and Viscardi 2007
A. Calcraft and J. Viscardi, *Strawberry Hill: Horace Walpole's Gothic Castle*, 2007

Cambridge 1984
The Ingenious Mr Essex, Fitzwilliam Museum, Cambridge, 1984

Campbell 1990
R. Campbell, 'Scotland's Neglected Enlightenment', *History Today*, 40 (May 1990), pp. 22–8

Carpenter 1972
E. Carpenter, *A House of Kings*, 1972

Carr 1990
J. L. Carr, *Churches in Retirement: A Gazetteer*, 1990

Carr 1994
T. Carr, *Shrewsbury: A Pictorial History*, 1994

Carritt 1948
E. F. Carritt, *A Calendar of British Taste from 1600 to 1800*, 1948

Carter 1976
R. A. Carter, *A Visitor's Guide to Yorkshire Churches*, 1976

Cazort 2003
M. Cazort, *Mauro in America*, 2003

Chalkin 1984
C. W. Chalkin, 'The Financing of Church Buildings in the Provincial Towns of Eighteenth Century England', in *The Transformation of English Provincial Towns, 1600–1800*, ed. P. Clark, 1984, pp. 284–310

Chambers 1979
R. L. Chambers, *St Thomas's Church Stourbridge: The Story of its Foundation*, 1979

Champness 1989
J. Champness, *Lancashire's Architectural Heritage: An Anthology of Fine Buildings*, 1989

Chandler and Hannah 1949
G. Chandler and I. C. Hannah, *Dudley As It Was and As It Is Today*, 1949

Chaney 1998
E. Chaney, *The Evolution of the Grand Tour: Anglo-Italian Cultural Relations since the Renaissance*, 1998

Chapman and Turner [1974]
E.V. Chapman and G. A. Turner, *The Heptonstall Octagon, 1764*, [1974]

Chatfield 1979
M. Chatfield, *Churches the Victorians Forgot*, 1979

Childe 1878
E. Childe, 'Cleobury Mortimer', *Transactions of Shropshire Archaeological and Natural History Society* (1878) [reprint]

Chitham 1985
R. Chitham, *The Classical Order of Architecture*, 1985

Clark 1928
K. Clark, *The Gothic Revival*, 1928

Clarke 1963
B. F. L. Clarke, *The Building of the Eighteenth-Century Church*, 1963

Clarke 1966
—, *Parish Churches of London*, 1966

Clarke and Colvin 1952–3
— and H. Colvin, 'The Rebuilding and Repair of Berkshire Churches during the Seventeenth, Eighteenth and Early Nineteenth Centuries', *Berkshire Archaeological Journal*, 53 (1952), pp. 65–99; 54 (1953), pp. 58–118

Clarke 1976
H. Clarke, *Georgian Dublin*, 1976

Clifton-Taylor 1989
A. Clifton-Taylor, *English Parish Churches as Works of Art*, 2nd edn, 1989

Clutton and Niland 1963
C. Clutton and A. Niland, *The British Organ*, 1963

Cobb 1977
G. Cobb, *London City Churches* [1942], revised edn, 1977

Cobb 1980
—, *English Cathedrals: The Forgotten Centuries: Restoration and Change from 1530 to the Present*, 1980

Cocke 1973
T. H. Cocke, 'Pre-Nineteenth-Century Attitudes in England to Romanesque Architecture', *Journal of British Archaeological Association*, 3rd series, 36 (1973), pp. 72–97

Cocke 1975
—, 'James Essex, Cathedral Restorer', *Architectural History*, 78 (1975), pp. 12–24

Cocke 1979
—, 'The Architectural History of Ely Cathedral from 1540–1840', in *Medieval Art and Architecture at Ely Cathedral*, ed. N. Coldstream and P. Draper, British Archaeological Association Conference Transactions, 1979, pp. 71–7

Cocke 1985
—, 'James Essex, 1722–1784: Archaeological Sensibility', in Brown 1985, pp. 98–113

Cocke 1986
—, 'The Architectural History of Lincoln Cathedral from the Dissolution to the Twentieth Century', in *Medieval Art and Architecture at Lincoln Cathedral*, ed. T. Heslop and V. Sekules, British Archaeological Association Conference Transactions, 1986, pp. 148–57

Cocke 1995
—, *900 Years: The Restoration of Westminster Abbey*, 1995

Cocke and Dodwell 1984
— and C. R. Dodwell, 'Rediscovery of the Romanesque', in *1066: English Romanesque Art, 1066–1200*, 1984, pp. 360–91

Cohen 1986
J. A. Cohen, 'Early American Architectural Drawings in Philadelphia, 1730–1860', in *Drawing Towards Building: Philadelphia Architectural Graphics, 1732–1986*, 1986, pp. 15–32

Cohen and Brownell 1994
— and C. E. Brownell, *The Architectural Drawings of Benjamin Henry Latrobe*, vol. II, pt 2, 1994

C-M: *see* Croft-Murray 1962–70

Coldstream and Draper 1980
N. Coldstream and P. Draper, eds, *Medieval Art and Architecture at Durham Cathedral*, British Archaeological Association Conference Transactions, 1980

Coleridge 1887
H. J. Coleridge, ed., *St Mary's Convent Micklegate Bar, York, 1686–1887*, 1887

Collareta 2008
M. Collareta, 'John Talman and the Arts of the Italian Middle Ages', in Sicca 2008, pp. 211–23

Collier 1991
S. Collier, *Whitehaven, 1660–1800*, 1991

Collinson, Ramsay and Sparks 1995
P. Collinson, N. Ramsay and M. Sparks, eds, *A History of Canterbury Cathedral*, 1995

Colvin 1948
H. M. Colvin, 'Gothic Survival and Gothic Revival', *Architectural Review*, 103 (March 1948), pp. 91–8; reprinted in Colvin 1999, chapter VIII

Colvin 1950
—, 'Fifty New Churches', *Architectural Review*, 107 (March 1950), pp. 189–96; reprinted in Bill 1979, pp. ix–xxi

Colvin 1973–6
—, ed., *The History of the King's Works*, vol. V: *1660–1782*, 1976; vol. VI: *1782–1851*, 1973

Colvin 1974
—, 'A Scottish Origin for English Palladianism', *Architectural History*, 17 (1974), pp. 5–13

Colvin 1983
—, *Unbuilt Oxford*, 1983

Colvin 1991
—, *Architecture and the After-Life*, 1991

Colvin 1999
—, *Essays in English Architectural History*, 1999

Colvin 2008
—, *A Biographical Dictionary of British Architects, 1600–1840*, 4th edn, 2008

Colvin 2009
—, 'Henry Flitcroft, William Kent and Shobden Church, Herefordshire', in *Essays in Scots and English Architectural History: A Festschrift in Honour of John Frew*, ed. D. Jones and S. McKinstry, 2009

Colvin and Harris 1970
— and J. Harris, eds, *The Country Seat: Studies in the History of the British Country House Presented to Sir John Summerson on his Sixty-Fifth Birthday*, 1970

Colvin and Wodehouse 1961
— and L. M. Wodehouse, 'Henry Bell of King's Lynn', *Architectural History*, 4 (1961), pp. 41–62

Conant 1966
K. J. Conant, *Carolingian and Romanesque Architecture, 800–1200*, 1966

Connor 1993
T. P. Connor, *Unbuilt Eton*, 1993

Coope 1972
R. Coope, *Salomon de Brosse and the Development of the Classical Style in French Architecture from 1565 to 1630*, 1972

Cornforth 1967
J. Cornforth, 'Brough Hall, Yorksire', *Country Life* (12 October 1967), pp. 894–8

Cornforth 1970
—, 'Wallington, Northumberland', *Country Life* (16 April 1970), pp. 854–8

Cornforth 1992
—, 'Putting Up with Georgian DIY', *Country Life* (9 April 1992), p. 55

Cotton 1980
H.E.A. Cotton, *Calcutta, Old and New: A Historical and Descriptive Handbook to the City* [1909], revised 1980

Cotton 1859
W. Cotton, ed., *Reynolds's Notes and Observations on Pictures*, 1859

Cowen 1985
P. Cowen, *A Guide to Stained Glass in Britain*, 1985

Cox 1875
J. C. Cox, *Churches of Derbyshire*, vol. I, 1875

Cox and Hope 1881
— and W. H. St John Hope, *The Chronicles of the Collegiate Church or Free Chapel of All Saints, Derby*, 1881

Crabtree 1836
J. Crabtree, *Concise History of the Parish and Vicarage of Halifax*, 1836

Craig 1982
M. Craig, *The Architecture of Ireland from the Earliest Times to 1880*, 1982

Craig 1992
—, *Dublin, 1660–1860*, 1992

Cranage 1912
D.H.S. Cranage, *An Architectural Account of the Churches of Shropshire*, 1912

Craske 2004
M. Craske, 'From Burlington Gate to Billingsgate: James Ralph's Attempt to Impose Burlingtonian Classicism as a Canon of Public Taste', in Arciszewska and McKellar 2004, pp. 97–118

Craske 2007
—, *The Silent Rhetoric of the Body: A History of Monumental Sculpture and Commemorative Art in England, 1720–1770*, 2007

Craven 1964
G. Craven, *The Church of Saint James, Spanish Place*, 1964

Cresti 1992
C. Cresti, *Allemandi's Architectural Guides: Florence*, 1992

Croft-Murray 1962–70
E. Croft-Murray, *Decorative Painting in England, 1537–1837*, 2 vols, 1962–70

Crook 1972
J. Mordaunt Crook, *The Greek Revival: Neo-Classical Attitudes in British Architecture, 1760–1870*, 1972

Crook 1973
—, 'Strawberry Hill Revisited, II', *Country Life* (14 June 1973), pp. 1726–30

Crook 1995
—, *John Carter and the Mind of the Gothic Revival*, 1995

Crossland 1971
J. Brian Crossland, *Looking at Whitehaven*, 1971

Crossley 1942
F. H. Crossley, 'Post-Reformation Church Building in Cheshire during the 17th and 18th Centuries', *Journal of the Cheshire and North Wales Archaeology Society*, n.s., 35/1 (1942), pp. 5–48

Cruden 1986
S. Cruden, *Scottish Medieval Churches*, 1986

Cruft and Fraser 1995
K. Cruft and A. Fraser, eds, *James Craig, 1744–1795*, 1995

Cruickshank 1996
D. Cruickshank, ed., *Sir Banister Fletcher's* A History of Architecture, 1996

Cruickshank 2003
—, *The Royal Hospital, Chelsea: The Place and the People*, 2003

Curiel and Cooperman 1990
R. Curiel and B. D. Cooperman, *The Ghetto of Venice*, 1990

Curl 1980
J. S. Curl, *Classical Churches in Ulster*, 1980

Curran 1945
C. P. Curran, *The Rotunda Hospital: Its Architects and Craftsmen*, 1945

Curran 1967
—, *Dublin Decorative Plasterwork*, 1967

Currie, Gilbert and Horsley 1977
R. Currie, A. Gilbert and L. Horsley, *Churches and Churchgoers: Patterns of Church Growth in the British Isles since 1700*, 1977

Curtis 1979
L. A. Curtis, *The Versatile Defoe*, 1979

Dance 1972
George Dance the Elder, 1695–1768, the Younger, 1741–1825, 1972

Daniell 1907
A. E. Daniell, *London City Churches*, 2nd edn, 1907

Davidson 2008
P. Davidson, '"Donec Templa Referecis": British Catholicism, Roman Antiquity, Historical Contention', in Sicca 2008, pp. 77–95

Davis 1974
T. Davis, *The Gothick Taste*, 1974

Dean 2006
P. Dean, *Sir John Soane and London*, 2006

De Breffny 1978
B. de Breffny, *The Synagogue*, 1978

De Breffny and Mott 1979
— and G. Mott, *The Churches and Abbeys of Ireland*, 1979

De Grazio and Garberson 1996
D. de Grazio and E. Garberson, *Italian Paintings of the 17th and 18th Centuries*, National Gallery of Art, Washington, DC, 1996

Dening 1923
C.F.W. Dening, *The Eighteenth-Century Architecture of Bristol*, 1923

Denslagen 1994
W. Denslagen, *Architectural Restoration in Western Europe: Controversy and Continuity*, 1994

Devonshire 2002
Duchess of Devonshire, *Chatsworth: The House*, 2002

Dias et. al. 2002
P. Dias et. al., *The Manueline: Portuguese Art during the Great Discoveries*, 2002

Dictionary of National Biography
Dictionary of National Biography, ed. S. Leslie et al., 1885–

Doig 1979
A. Doig, *The Architectural Drawings Collection of King's College, Cambridge*, 1979

Doll 1997
P. Doll, *After the Primitive Christians: The Eighteenth-Century Anglican Eucharist in its Architectural Setting*, 1997

Donaldson 1843
T. L. Donaldson, 'Some Account of the Models of Churches Preserved in Henry V's Chantry, Westminster Abbey', *The Architect, Engineer and Surveyor*, IV/47 (1 December 1843), p. 315

Donnelly 1992
M. C. Donnelly, *Architecture in the Scandinavian Countries*, 1992

Dorsey 1952
S. P. Dorsey, *Early English Churches in America, 1607–1807*, 1952

Downes 1959
K. Downes, *Hawksmoor*, 1959

Downes 1966
—, *English Baroque Architecture*, 1966

Downes 1977
—, *Vanbrugh*, 1977

Downes 1982
—, *The Architecture of Wren*, 1982

Downes, Amery and Stamp 2008
—, C. Amery and G. Stamp, *St George's Bloomsbury, London*, World Monuments Fund, 2008

Downing and Scully 1967
A. F. Downing and V. J. Scully Jr, *The Architecture of Newport, Rhode Island, 1640–1915*, 1967

Dunbar 1966
J. G. Dunbar, *The Historic Architecture of Scotland*, 1966

Duncan 1999
D. E. Duncan, *The Calendar*, 1999

Dunning 1996
R. Dunning, *Fifty Somerset Churches*, 1996

Dupain 1980
M. Dupain, *Francis Greenway: A Celebration*, 1980

Du Prey 1982
P. de La Ruffinier du Prey, *John Soane: The Making of an Architect*, 1982

Du Prey 1989
—, 'Hawksmoor's "Basilica after the Primitive Christians": Architecture and Theology', *Journal of the Society of Architectural Historians of Great Britain*, 48 (March 1989), pp. 38–52

Du Prey 2000
—, *Hawksmoor's London Churches*, 2000

Edwards 1977
I. Edwards, *Davies Brothers, Gatesmiths*, 1977

Eisenhart 1953
L. P. Eisenhart, ed., *Historic Philadelphia*, 1953

Ellis 1953
M. H. Ellis, *Francis Greenway: His Life and Times*, 1953

Enggass 1976
R. Enggass, *Early Eighteenth-Century Sculpture in Rome*, 1976

Erffa and Staley 1986
H. von Erffa and A. Staley, *The Paintings of Benjamin West*, 1986

Evans 1956
J. Evans, *A History of the Society of Antiquaries*, 1956

Evans 1964
—, *Monastic Architecture in France*, 1964

Evans 1982
R. Evans, *The Fabrication of Virtue: English Prison Architecture, 1750–1840*, 1982

Evans and Worsley 1981
W. Evans and R. Worsley, *St David's Cathedral 1181–1981*, 1981

Evinson 1998
D. Evinson, *Catholic Churches of London*, 1998

Fanelli and Fanelli 2004
G. Fanelli and M. Fanelli, *Brunelleschi's Cupola: Past and Present of an Architectural Masterpiece*, 2004

Fawcett 1994
R. Fawcett, *Scottish Architecture from the Accession of the Stewarts to the Reformation, 1371–1560*, 1994

Feist 1973
P. H. Feist, 'Neo-Classicism and Gothic Revival at Woerlitz: The Gothic House and its Gothic Room', in *Neoclassicismo: Atti del convegno internazionale: London, 1971*, 1973, pp. 31–42

Felsenstein 1995
F. Felsenstein, *Anti-Semitism Stereotypes: A Paradigm of Otherness in English Popular Culture, 1660–1830*, 1995

Findlay 1985
D. Findlay, *All Hallows, London Wall: A History and Description*, 1985

Finelli and Finelli 2004
G. Finelli and M. Finelli, *Brunelleschi's Cupola: Past and Present of an Architectural Masterpiece*, 2004

Finney 1999
P. C. Finney, *Seeing Beyond the Word: Visual Arts and the Calvinist Tradition*, 1999

Fishwick 1900
H. Fishwick, *The History of the Parish of Preston*, 1900

Fitch 1996
J. Fitch, ed., *A Select Guide to Essex Churches and Chapels*, 1996

Flanders 2007
J. Flanders, *Consuming Passions: Leisure and Pleasure in Victorian Britain*, 2007

Fleming 1962
J. Fleming, *Robert Adam and his Circle in Edinburgh and Rome*, 1962

Fletcher 1889
W. G. D. Fletcher, *Battlefield Church, Salop: An Historical and Descriptive Sketch*, 1889

Foster 1981
R. Foster, *Discovering English Churches*, 1981

Foster 1991
—, *Patterns of Thought: The Hidden Meaning of the Great Pavement of Westminster Abbey*, 1991

Foyle 2004
A. Foyle, *Bristol*, 2004

Frank 1966
C. L. Frank, *The Villas of Frascati*, 1966

Frankl 2000
P. Frankl, *Gothic Architecture*, rev. P. Crossley, 2000

Franzoi and Di Stefano 1976
U. Franzoi and D. Di Stefano, *Le chiese di Venezia*, 1976

Frew 1980
J. Frew, 'An Aspect of the Early Gothic Revival: The Transformation of Medievalist Research, 1770–1800', *Journal of the Warburg and Courtauld Institutes*, 43 (1980), pp. 174–85

Frew and Wallace 1986
— and C. Wallace, 'Thomas Pitt, Portugal and the Gothic Cult of Batalha', *Burlington Magazine* (August 1986), pp. 582–5

Friar 1996
S. Friar, *A Companion to the English Parish Church*, 1996

Friedman, J. 1993
J. Friedman, *Spencer House: Chronicle of a Great London Mansion*, 1993

Friedman 1970
T. F. Friedman, 'Romanticism and Neo-classicism for Parlington: The Tastes of Sir Thomas Gascoigne', *Leeds Arts Calendar*, 66 (1970), pp. 16–24

Friedman 1975
—, 'The English Appreciation of Italian Decorations', *Burlington Magazine* (December 1975), pp. 841–7

Friedman 1984
—, *James Gibbs*, 1984

Friedman 1991
—, '"High and Bold Structures": A Georgian Steeple Sampler', *Georgian Group Journal* (1991), pp. 6–20

Friedman 1993
—, '"Behold the Proud Stupendous Pile": Eighteenth Century Reflections of St Paul's Cathedral', in Bold and Chaney 1993, pp. 135–46

Friedman 1994
—, 'Modern Icarus; or, The Unfortunate Accident', *Church Monuments*, 9 (1994), pp. 68–71

Friedman 1995
—, 'The Transformation of York Minster, 1726–42', *Architectural History*, 38 (1995), pp. 69–90

Friedman 1996a
—, 'The Golden Age of Church Architecture in Shropshire', *Shropshire History and Archaeology*, 71 (1996), pp. 83–134

Friedman 1996c
—, 'The Palace of the Princely Chandos' in Airs 1996, pp. 101–20

Friedman 1997a
—, 'Oratorial Machines for Furniture Historians', *Furniture History*, 33 (1997), pp. 84–103

Friedman 1997b
—, *Church Architecture in Leeds, 1700–1799*, Publications of the Thoresby Society, second series, vol. VII, 1997

Friedman 1997c
—, 'Baroque into Palladian: The Designing of St Giles-in-the-Fields', *Architectural History*, 40 (1997), pp. 115–43

Friedman 1997d
—, 'James Wyatt's Earliest Classical Churches', *Georgian Group Journal*, 7 (1997), pp. 56–70

Friedman 1998a
—, 'William Halfpenny's Designs for an "Early Christian" Cathedral at Waterford', *Irish Architectural and Decorative Studies*, 1 (1998), pp. 8–33

Friedman 1998b
—, 'Thomas Hardwick Jr's Early Churches', *Georgian Group Journal*, 8(1998), pp. 43–55

Friedman 2000
—, 'The Church of St Peter-Le-Poer Reconsidered', *Architectural History*, 43 (2000), pp. 162–71

Friedman 2001
—, 'St Chad's Church, Stafford: A Young and Beautiful Virgin and her Decayed and Doting Husband', *Architectural History*, 44 (2001), pp. 258–64

Friedman 2003
—, 'The Octagon Chapel, Norwich', *Georgian Group Journal*, 13 (2003), pp. 54–77

Friedman 2004
—, *The Georgian Parish Church: 'Monuments to Posterity'*, 2004

Friedman 2006
—, '"The Fate of Sublunary Things": Lives of Medieval Churches in Georgian Times', *Architectural History*, 15 (2006), pp. 69–87

Friedman 2010
—, 'Proposals for a Protestant Martyrs Monument at Smithfield', *The Sculpture Journal*, 19.1 (2010), pp. 107–12

Friedman, in preparation
—, 'John Carter and the Georgian Struggle for Gothic Authenticity', in preparation

Fuhring 1999
P. Fuhring, *Juste-Aurèle Meissonnier: un génie du rococo, 1695–1750*, 2 vols, 1999

Furnari 1993
M. Furnari, *Atlante del Rinascimento: il disegno dell'architettura da Brunelleschi a Palladio*, 1993

Furst 1956
V. Furst, *The Architecture of Sir Christopher Wren*, 1956

Galloway 1992
P. Galloway, *Cathedrals of Ireland*, 1992

Galmiche 1989
X. Galmiche, *Santini architecte: gothico-baroque en Bohème, 1677–1723*, 1989

Gandy 1998
M. Gandy, 'Catholicism in Westminster: The Return of Papists of 1767', *Westminster History Review*, 2 (1998), pp. 19–22

Georgian Group 1983
The Georgian Group, *Gothick Symposium at the Victoria and Albert Museum, 21 May 1983* [Proceedings]

Geraghty 2000
A. Geraghty, 'Nicholas Hawksmoor and the Wren City Church Steeples', *Georgian Group Journal*, 10 (2000), pp. 1–14

Germann 1972
G. Germann, *Gothic Revival in Europe and Britain: Sources, Influences and Ideas*, 1972

Gerson and Ter Kuile 1960
H. Gerson and E. H. Ter Kuile, *Art and Architecture in Belgium, 1600 to 1800*, 1960

Giedion 1952
S. Giedion, 'Sixtus v and the Planning of Baroque Rome', *Architectural Review*, 111 (1952), pp. 217–26

Gilchrist 1972
A. A. Gilchrist, 'John McComb, Sr and Jr, in New York, 1784–1799', *Journal of the Society of Architectural Historians* (March 1972), pp. 10–21

Gilmour 1992
I. Gilmour, *Riots, Rising and Revolution: Governance and Violence in Eighteenth Century England*, 1992

Girouard 1992
M. Girouard, *Town and Country*, 1992

Girouard et al. 1989
— et al., *The Saving of Spitalfields*, 1989

Glendinning, MacInnes and MacKechnie 1996
M. Glendinning, R. MacInnes and A. MacKechnie, *A History of Scottish Architecture from the Renaissance to the Present Day*, 1996

Godfrey 1950
W. H. Godfrey, *The English Almshouse*, 1950

Godwin 1839
G. Godwin, *The Churches of London*, 2 vols, 1839

Gold 1965
S. M. Gold, *Short Account of the Life and Work of John Rowell*, 1965

Gombrich et al. 1989
E. H. Gombrich et al., *Giulio Romano*, 1989

Gomme 1985–8
A. Gomme, 'St Mary's, Monmouth: The Building of the Eighteenth Century Church', *Monmouthshire Antiquary*, 5/3 (1985–8), pp. 88–95

Gomme 2000
A. Gomme, *Smith of Warwick: Francis Smith, Architect and Master-Builder*, 2000

Gomme and Gomme 1969
— and S. M. Gomme, 'Who Designed Capesthorpe Hall?, *Transactions of the Historic Society of Lancashire and Cheshire*, 121 (1969), pp. 24–34

Gomme, Jenner and Little 1979
—, M. Jenner and B. Little, *Bristol: An Architectural History*, 1979

Gomme and Walker 1968
— and D. Walker, *Architecture of Glasgow*, 1968

Goodall 2009
J. Goodall, 'The Rescue of a Romantic Ruin', *Country Life* (17 June 2009), pp. 82–5

Goodchild 1968
J. Goodchild, *Attorney at Large: The Concerns of John Lee of Wakefield, 1759–1836*, 1968

Gotch 1928
J. A. Gotch, 'The Choir Screen in Winchester Cathedral Designed by Inigo Jones', *RIBA Journal* (24 November 1928), pp. 46–8

Goy 1997
R. Goy, *Venice: The City and Its Architecture*, 1997

Goy 2002
—, *Florence: The City and Its Architecture*, 2002

Grady 1987
K. Grady, *The Georgian Public Buildings of Leeds and the West Riding*, Thoresby Society, LXII/133, 1987

Graf Kalnein and Levy 1972
W. Graf Kalnein and M. Levy, *Art and Architecture of the Eighteenth Century in France*, 1972

Green 1951
D. Green, *Blenheim Palace*, 1951

Green 1971–2
—, 'Rysbrack at Blenheim', *Country Life* (7 January 1971), pp. 26–8; (15 June 1972), pp. 1543–5

Greeves 1988
L. Greeves, 'Tour of the Garden', in *Fountains Abbey and Studley Royal*, 1988

Gregory and Stevenson 2000
J. Gregory and J. Stevenson, *Britain in the Eighteenth Century, 1688–1820*, 2000

Griffin 1992
D. J. Griffin, 'Leinster House and Isaac Ware', in A. Bernelle, ed., *Decantations: A Tribute to Maurice Craig*, 1992, pp. 60–70

Guilding 2008
R. Guilding, 'How the Code for Coade was Cracked', *Country Life* (10 January 2008), pp. 60–61

Guillery 2005
P. Guillery, 'Suburban Models; or. Calvinism and Continuity in London's Seventeenth-century Church Architecture', *Architectural History*, 48 (2005), pp. 69–106

Gunnis *see* Roscoe 2009

Guy 1979
J. R. Guy, 'Perpetual Curacies in Eighteenth Century South Wales', in *The Church in Town and Countryside*, ed. D. Baker, Studies in Church History, 16, 1979, pp. 327–33

Hager 1973
H. Hager, 'Carlo Fontana's Project for a Church in Honour of the "Ecclesia Triumphans"', *Journal of the Warburg and Courtauld Institutes*, 36 (1973), pp. 319–37

Hager 1998
—, 'Il "Modello grande" di Filippo Juvarra per la nuova Sacrestia di San Pietro in Vaticano', in A. B. Correa et al., *Filippo Juvarra e l'architettura europea*, 1998, pp. 105–20

Hague 1986
G. Hague, *The Unitarian Heritage: An Architectural Survey of Chapels and Churches in the Unitarian Tradition in the British Isles*, 1986

Hall 1963
I. Hall, 'The Classical Architecture of Manchester, 1700–1850', unpublished PhD thesis, Manchester University School of Architecture, 1963

Hall and Hall 1979
— and E. Hall, *A New Picture of Georgian Hull*, 1979

Hallelujah 1985
Hallelujah! Recording Chapels and Meeting Houses, 1985

Hammelmann 1975
H. Hammelmann, *Book Illustrators in Eighteenth-Century England*, 1975

Harris 2001
E. Harris, *The Genius of Robert Adam: His Interiors*, 2001

Harris 1970
J. Harris, *Sir William Chambers, Knight of the Polar Star*, 1970

Harris 1981
—, *The Palladians*, 1981

Harris 1994
—, *The Palladian Revival: Lord Burlington: His Villa and Gardens at Chiswick*, 1994

Harris 1998a
—, 'Chambers's Design for the Gothic Cathedral at Kew', *Georgian Group Journal*, 8 (1998), pp. 151–6

Harris 1998b
—, *William Kent, 1685–1748: A Poet on Paper*, 1998

Harris 2007
—, *Moving Rooms*, 2007

Harris 2008
—, 'William and John Talman: Architecture and a Partnership', in Sicca 2008, pp. 97–125

Harris and Hradsky 2007
— and R. Hradsky, *A Passion for Building: The Amateur Architect in England, 1650–1850*, 2007

Harris and Snodin 1996
— and M. Snodin, *Sir William Chambers, Architect to George III*, 1996

Harris 1949
R. V. Harris, *The Church of Saint Paul in Halifax, Nova Scotia, 1749–1949*, 1949

Harrison 1986
R. H. Harrison, *The Church of St Edmund, King & Martyr, Lombard Street, City of London: A History of the Church since 1670*, Ecclesiological Society, 1986

Hart 2002
V. Hart, *Nicholas Hawksmoor: Rebuilding Ancient Wonders*, 2002

Hart 2008
—, *Sir John Vanbrugh: Storyteller in Stone*, 2008

Harwood 2008
E. Harwood, *Pevsner Architectural Guides: Nottingham*, 2008

Haskell and Penny 1981
F. Haskell and N. Penny, *Taste and the Antique*, 1981

Hatcher 1990
J. Hatcher, *Richmondshire Architecture*, 1990

Haug 1962
H. Haug, *L'Art en Alsace*, 1962

Hay 1957
G. Hay, *The Architecture of Scottish Post-Reformation Churches, 1560–1843*, 1957

Haynes 2006
C. Haynes, *Pictures and Popery: Art and Religion in England, 1660–1760*, 2006

Hayward and Shivers 2004
M. E. Hayward and F. R. Shivers, *The Architecture of Baltimore*, 2004

Headley and Meulenkamp 1999
G. Headley and W. Meulenkamp, *Follies, Grottoes and Garden Buildings*, 1999

Heckscher and Bowman 1992
M. H. Heckscher and L. G. Bowman, eds, *American Rococo, 1750–1775: Elegance in Ornament*, 1992

Hempel 1965
E. Hempel, *Baroque Art and Architecture in Central Europe*, 1965

Henderson 1967
G. Henderson, *Gothic*, 1967

Herman and Guillery 2004
B. L. Herman and P. Guillery, 'Negotiating Classicism in Eighteenth-Century Deptford and Philadelphia', in Arciszewska and McKellar 2004, pp. 187–225

Hermans 1987
J. B. Hermans, *La Descendance de la tour de l'église de la Madonna di San Biagio à Montepulciano*, 1987

Heslop and Sekules 1986
T. A. Heslop and V. A. Sekules, eds, *Medieval Art and Architecture at Lincoln Cathedral*, British Archaeological Association Conference Transactions, 1986

Hewlings 1981
R. Hewlings, 'Ripon's Forum Populi', *Architectural History*, 24 (1981), pp. 39–52

Hewlings 1995
—, 'Chiswick House and Gardens: Appearance and Meaning', in Barnard and Clark 1995, pp. 1–149

Hewlings 2000
—, 'Women in the Building Trades, 1600–1850: A Preliminary List', *Georgian Group Journal*, 10 (2000), pp. 70–83

Heydenreich and Lotz 1974
L. H. Heydenreich and W. Lotz, *Architecture in Italy, 1400 to 1600*, 1974

Hibbert 1988
C. Hibbert, *London's Churches*, 1988

Hicks 1997
C. Hicks, ed., *Cambridgeshire Churches*, 1997

Hill 1966
F. Hill, *Georgian Lincoln*, 1966

Hill 1867
J. H. Hill, *The History of the Parish of Langton*, 1867

Hiscock 1960
W. G. Hiscock, *Henry Aldrich of Christ Church, 1648–1710*, 1960

Hitchcock 1939
H.-R. Hitchcock, *Rhode Island Architecture*, 1939

Hobhouse 1971
H. Hobhouse, *Lost London*, 1971

Hodgetts 1990
M. Hodgetts, *Midlands Catholic Buildings*, Archdiocese of Birmingham Historical Commission, Publication No. 6, 1990

Honeyman 1941
H. L. Honeyman, 'The Church of St Andrew', *Archaeologia Aeliana*, 4th series, 19 (1941), pp. 96–193

Hopkins 2000
A. Hopkins, *Santa Maria della Salute*, 2000

Horne 1972
A. Horne, *King Solomon's Temple in the Masonic Tradition*, 1972

Howard 1987
D. Howard, *The Architectural History of Venice*, 1987

Howard 2002
—, *The Architectural History of Venice*, revised edn, 2002

Howe 2003
J. Howe, *Houses of Worship*, 2003

Howley 1993
J. Howley, *The Follies and Garden Buildings of Ireland*, 1993

Howson 1993
B. Howson, *Houses of Noble Poverty*, 1993

Hubert 1998
J.-C. Hubert, *Architecture du xviiie siècle en Belgique*, 1998

Huelin 1996
G. Huelin, *Vanished Churches of the City of London*, 1996

Humphrey 1991
S. C. Humphrey, ed., *Blue Guide: Churches and Chapels of Southern England*, 1991

Humphrey 2000
—, *Churches and Cathedrals of London*, 2000

Hunt 1961
J. M. Hunt, 'Restoration of a Georgian Church', *Country Life* (6 April 1961), pp. 756–7

Hussey 1955
C. Hussey, *English Country Houses: Early Georgian, 1715–1760*, 1955

Hussey 1958a
—, 'Ince Blundell Hall, Lancashire', *Country Life* (10 April 1958), pp. 756–9

Hussey 1958b
—, 'A Gibbs-Rysbrack Monument', *Country Life* (16 November 1958), p. 112

Hutton and Smith 1952
G. Hutton and E. Smith, *English Parish Churches*, 1952

Hyamson 1951
A. M. Hyamson, *The Sephardim of England*, 1951

Inglis-Jones 1960
E. Inglis-Jones, *Peacocks in Paradise*, 1960

Ionides 1999
J. Ionides, *Thomas Farnolls Pritchard of Shrewsbury: Architect and 'Inventor of Cast Iron Bridges'*, 1999

Ison 1948
W. Ison, *The Georgian Buildings of Bath from 1700 to 1830*, 1948; facsimile, 2004

Ison 1952
—, *The Georgian Buildings of Bristol*, 1952

Jackson-Stops 1972
G. Jackson-Stops, 'Well Vale, Lincolnshire', *Country Life* (14, 21 December 1972), pp. 1650–54, 1722–5

Jackson-Stops 1994
—, 'Duke of Creation', *Country Life* (7 April 1994), pp. 52–7

Jacob 1979
W. M. Jacob, '"A Practice of a Very Hurtful Tendency"', in *The Church in Town and Countryside*, ed. D. Baker, Studies in Church History, 16, 1979, pp. 315–26

Jacoby 1994
M. M. Jacoby, *The Churches of Charleston and the Low Country*, 1994

Jaffe 1975
I. B. Jaffe, *John Trumbull: Patriot-Artist of the American Revolution*, 1975

Jamilly 1958
E. Jamilly, 'Anglo-Jewish Architects, and Architecture in the 18th and 19th Centuries', *Jewish Historical Society of England Transactions*, 18 (1958), 127–41

Jamilly 1999
—, *The Georgian Synagogue: An Architectural History*, 1999

Jarrasse 2001
D. Jarrasse, *Synagogues*, 2001

Jeffery 1992
P. Jeffery, 'Originals or Apprentice Copies? Some Recently Found Drawings for St Paul's Cathedral, All Saints, Oxford and the City Churches', *Architectural History*, 35 (1992), pp. 118–39

Jeffery 1993
—, 'Thomas Archer's Deptford Rectory: A Reconstruction', *Georgian Group Journal* (1993), pp. 32–42

Jeffery 1994
—, 'Unbuilt Gibbs: A Fresh Look at His Designs for the 1711 Act Church Commissioners', *Georgian Group Journal* (1994), pp. 11–19

Jeffery 1995
—, 'The Commissioners' Models for the Fifty New Churches: Problems of Identity and Attribution', *Georgian Group Journal* (1995), pp. 81–96

Jeffery 1996
—, *The City Churches of Sir Christopher Wren*, 1996

Jeffery 1986
S. Jeffery, 'English Baroque Architecture: The Works of John James', PhD thesis, Birkbeck College, University of London, 1986

Jeffery 2001
—, 'John James at Chalfont St Peter', *Architectural History*, 44 (2001), pp. 249–57

Jenkins 1999
Simon Jenkins, *England's Thousand Best Churches*, 1999

Jenkins 2007
Susan Jenkins, *Portrait of a Patron: The Patronage and Collecting of James Brydges, 1st Duke of Chandos (1674–1744)*, 2007

Jenkinson 1917
W. Jenkinson, *London Churches before the Great Fire*, 1917

Jokilehto 1999
J. Jokilehto, *A History of Architectural Conservation*, 1999

Jones 1988
B. E. Jones, *Freemasons' Guide and Compendium*, 1988

Kadish 1996
S. Kadish, ed., *Building Jerusalem: Jewish Architecture in Britain*, 1996

Kadish 2006
—, *Jewish Heritage in England: An Architectural Guide*, 2006

Kalman 1971
H. D. Kalman, 'The Architecture of George Dance the Younger', PhD thesis, Princeton University, 1971

Kalman 1976
H. Kalman, *Pioneer Churches*, 1976

Kalman 1994
—, *A History of Canadian Architecture*, vol. I, 1994

Kalnein and Levey 1972
W. G. Kalnein and M. Levey, *Art and Architecture of the Eighteenth Century in France*, 1972

Kaufmann 1955
E. Kaufmann, *Architecture in the Age of Reason*, 1955

Keene, Burns and Saint 2004
D. Keene, A. Burns and A. Saint, eds, *St Paul's: The Cathedral Church of London, 604–2004*, 2004

Kelly 1990
A. Kelly, *Mrs Coade's Stone*, 1990

Kelly 2009
J. M. Kelly, *The Society of Dilettanti: Archaeology and Identity in the British Enlightenment*, 2009

Kendall 1998
D. Kendall, *The City of London Churches: A Pictorial Discovery*, 1998

Kennedy 1982
R. G. Kennedy, *American Churches*, 1982

Kenworthy-Brown 2008
J. Kenworthy-Brown, 'Nollekens's Monument to Bishop Trevor', *Georgian Group Journal*, 16 (2008), pp. 141–8

Kessler and Zacharias 2000
H. L. Kessler and J. Zacharias, *Rome 1300: On the Path of the Pilgrim*, 2000

Kieven 1973
E. Kieven, 'Galilei in England', *Country Life* (25 January 1973), pp. 210–12

Kieven 2008
—, 'An Italian Architect in London: The Case of Alessandro Galilei (1691–1737)', *Architectural History*, 51 (2008), pp. 1–31

Killanin and Duignan 1989
Lord Killanin and M.V. Duignan, *The Shell Guide to Ireland*, 1989

King 1982
C. King, 'The Liturgical and Commemorative Allusions in Raphael's "Transfiguration and Failure to Heal"', *Journal of the Warburg and Courtauld Institutes*, 45 (1982), pp. 148–59

King 2001
D. King, *The Complete Works of Robert and James Adam: Unbuilt Adam*, 2 vols in one, 2001

Kingsley 1988
N. Kingsley, 'Modelling in the Provinces', *Country Life* (20 October 1988), pp. 138–41

Kirker 1969
H. Kirker, *The Architecture of Charles Bulfinch*, 1969

Kirkus 2000
Sister G. Kirkus, 'A Short History of the Bar Convent', in *Aspects of York*, ed. A. Whitworth, 2000, pp. 55–70

Kissack 1975
K. Kissack, *Monmouth: The Making of a County Town*, 1975

Knight 2000
C. Knight, 'The Travels of The Rev. Sir George Wheler (1650–1723)', *Georgian Group Journal*, 10 (2000), pp. 21–35

Knowles 1953
J. A. Knowles, 'The Price Family of Glass-Painter's', *Antiquaries Journal*, 33 (July–October 1953), pp. 184–92

Knox 1995
T. Knox, 'The Model of the Kentish Town Chapel of Ease', *Georgian Group Journal* (1995), pp. 97–102

Knox 2001
—, *West Wycombe Park, Buckinghamshire*, 2001

Kornwolf 2002
J. D. Kornwolf, *Architecture and Town Planning in Colonial North America*, 3 vols, 2002

Köven 1983
K. Köven, *Johann Joseph Couven: ein Architekt des 18. Jahrhunderts zwischen Rhein und Maas*, 1983

Krautheimer 1986
R. Krautheimer, *Early Christian and Byzantine Architecture*, revised edn, 1986

Krinsky 1985
C. H. Krinsky, *Synagogues of Europe*, 1985

Kruft 1994
H.-W. Kruft, *History of Architecture: Theory from Vitruvius to the Present*, 1994

Kuyper 1980
W. Kuyper, *Dutch Classicist Architecture*, 1980

Lane 1971
M. Lane, *'The Queen of the Methodists': Selina, Countess of Huntingdon*, 1971

Lane 1984
—, *Architecture of the Old South: South Carolina*, 1984

Lane 1985
—, *Architecture of the Old South: North Carolina*, 1985

Lane 1990
—, *Architecture of the Old South: Georgia*, 1990

Lane 1991
—, *Architecture of the Old South: Maryland*, 1991

Lang 1956
J. Lang, *Rebuilding St Paul's after the Great Fire of London*, 1956

Lang 1966
S. Lang, 'The Principles of the Gothic Revival in England', *Journal of the Society of Architectural Historians*, 25 (December 1966), pp. 240–67

Langford 1870
J. A. Langford, *A Century of Birmingham Life*, 2nd edn, 2 vols, 1870

Langham-Carter, no date
R. R. Langham-Carter, *St George's Church Esher*, undated

Laurence 1986
A. Laurence, 'Upper Bank House and the Morfitts' in *The Green*, Horsforth History Guides, v, 1986

Lawrence 1983
A. W. Lawrence, *Greek Architecture*, revised edn, 1983

Lawrence 1981
C. M. Lawrence, *Flemish Baroque Commemorative Monuments, 1566–1725*, 1981

Lawrence 2010
H. Lawrence, 'The Travels of Thomas Archer: New Discoveries', *Georgian Group Journal*, vol. XVIII, 2010, pp. 35–48

Lawson 1980
J. B. Lawson, 'Thomas Telford in Shrewsbury: The Metamorphosis of an Architect into a Civil Engineer', in A. Penfold, *Thomas Telford: Engineer*, 1980, pp. 1–22

Leach 1974
P. Leach, 'The Architecture of Daniel Garrett', *Country Life* (12 September 1974), pp. 694–6

Leach 1988
—, *James Paine*, 1988

Lee, Seddon and Stephens 1976
L. Lee, G. Seddon and F. Stephens, *Stained Glass*, 1976

Leedy 1980
W. C. Leedy Jr, *Fan Vaulting: A Study of Form, Technology and Meaning*, 1980

Lees-Milne 1968
J. Lees-Milne, 'Chatsworth, Derbyshire', *Country Life* (11 April 1968), pp. 890–93

Leonard 1991
J. Leonard, *Cheshire Parish Churches*, 1991

Leonard 1993
—, *Derbyshire Parish Churches*, 1993

Leonard 1995
—, *Staffordshire Parish Churches*, 1995

Leonard 1997
—, *London's Parish Churches*, 1997

Leonard 2004a
—, *The Churches of Herefordshire and Their Treasures*, 2004

Leonard 2004b
—, *The Churches of Shropshire and Their Treasures*, 2004

Lever and Harris 1993
J. Lever and J. Harris, *Illustrated Dictionary of Architecture, 800–1914*, 1993

Lever and Richardson 1984
— and M. Richardson, 'Have Pen Will Travel', *The World of Interiors* (December 1984), pp. 140–41

Levy 1986
M. Levy, *Gianbattista Tiepolo*, 1986

Lewis 2001
D. Lewis, *The Churches of Liverpool*, 2001

Lindsay and Cosh 1973
I. G. Lindsay and M. Cosh, *Inveraray and the Dukes of Argyll*, 1973

Lindsay 1993
P. Lindsay, *The Synagogues of London*, 1993

Links 1971
J. G. Links, *Views of Venice by Canaletto*, 1971

Linstrum 1978
D. Linstrum, *West Yorkshire: Architects and Architecture*, 1978

Liscombe 1985
R. W. Liscombe, *The Church Architecture of Robert Mills*, 1985

Little 1966
B. Little, *Catholic Churches since 1623*, 1966

Litton 1991
J. Litton, *The English Way of Death: The Common Funeral Since 1450*, 1991

Liversidge and Farrington 1993
M. Liversidge and J. Farrington, eds, *Canaletto and England*, 1993

Llewellyn 1991
N. Llewellyn, *The Art of Death*, 1991

Lloyd 1992
A. Lloyd, ed., *The Painter in Glass*, 1992

Lock 2007
A. Lock, 'Sir Thomas Gascoigne, 8th Bart. (1745–1810): Catholicism, Apostasy and Yorkshire Politics', unpublished MA dissertation, Eighteenth Century Studies, Leeds University, 2007

Loeber 1979
R. Loeber, 'Early Classicism in Ireland: Architecture before the Georgian Era', *Architectural History*, 22 (1979), pp. 49–63

Loeber 1981
—, *A Biographical Dictionary of Architects in Ireland, 1600–1720*, 1981

London 1984
Rococo: Art and Design in Hogarth's England, Victoria and Albert Museum, London, 1984

London 2007
Making History: Antiquaries in Britain, 1707–2007, Royal Academy of Arts, London, 2007

Longo 1985
L. Longo, *Antonio Petrini: ein Barockarchitekt in Franken*, 1985

Longstaffe-Gowan 2009
T. Longstaffe-Gowan, 'Brazen Proclamations: The Deployment of Statuary in Some Early London Garden Squares', *Sculpture Journal*, 18/1 (2009), pp. 52–66

Losty 1990
J. P. Losty, *Calcutta, City of Palaces: A Survey of the City in the Days of the East India Company, 1690–1858*, 1990

Losty 2004
—, 'British Settlements and Trade Centres', in *Encounters: The Meeting of Asia and Europe, 1500–1800*, ed. A. Jackson and A. Jaffer, 2004, pp. 142–55

Lotz 1995
W. Lotz, *Architecture in Italy, 1500–1600*, 1995

Lounsbury 1994
C. Lounsbury, ed., *An Illustrated Glossary of Early Southern Architecture and Landscape*, 1994

Lowrey 1990
J. Lowrey, 'William Adam Tercentenary Exhibition Summer 1989', *Architectural Heritage*, 1 (1990), pp. 116–22

Lukacher 2006
B. Lukacher, *Joseph Gandy: An Architectural Visionary in Georgian England*, 2006

McAleer 1993
J. P. McAleer, *A Pictorial History of St Paul's Anglican Church, Halifax, Nova Scotia*, 1993

Macaulay 1975
J. Macaulay, *The Gothic Revival, 1745–1845*, 1975

McCallum 2003
I. McCallum, *Thomas Barker of Bath: The Artist and his Circle*, 2003

McCarthy 1987
M. McCarthy, *The Origins of the Gothic Revival*, 1987

McCarthy 1996
—, '"The dullest man that ever travelled"? A Re-assessment of Richard Pococke and his Portrait by J.-E. Liotard', *Apollo*, 143 (May 1996), pp. 25–9

McCombie 2009
G. McCombie, *Pevsner Architectural Guides: Newcastle and Gateshead*, 2009

McCormick 1990
T. J. McCormick, *Charles-Louis Clérisseau and the Genesis of Neo-Classicism*, 1990

MacDermott 1948
K. H. MacDermott, *The Old Church Gallery Minstrels*, 1948

MacDonald 1976
W. L. MacDonald, *The Pantheon: Design, Meaning and Progeny*, 1976

MacDonald 1986
—, *The Architecture of the Roman Empire*, vol. II, 1986

McDonnell 1991
J. McDonnell, *Irish Eighteenth-Century Stuccowork and its European Sources*, 1991

McKee 1964
H. J. McKee, 'St Michael's Church, Charleston, 1752–1762: Some Notes on Materials and Construction', *Journal of the Society of Architectural Historians*, 23 (March 1964), pp. 39–43

McMaster 1916
J. McMaster, *A Short History of the Royal Parish of St Martin-in-the-Field*, 1916

McParland 1969
E. McParland, 'Francis Johnson, Architect, 1760–1829', *Quarterly Bulletin of the Irish Georgian Society* (July–December 1969), pp. 61–139

McParland 1985
—, *James Gandon: Vitruvius Hibernicus*, 1985

McParland 2001
—, *Public Architecture in Ireland, 1680–1760*, 2001

McParland and Rowan 1989
— and A. Rowan, *The Architecture of Richard Morrison (1767–1849) and William Vitruvius Morrison (1794–1838)*, 1989

McPhee 2002
S. McPhee, *Bernini and the Bell Towers: Architecture and Politics at the Vatican*, 2002

Maggi 2002
A. Maggi, 'Documents Relating to Roslin Chapel', *Architectural Heritage*, 13 (2002), pp. 73–8

Magirius 2005
H. Magirius, *Die Dresdner Frauenkirche von George Bahr*, 2005

Malcomson 2003
A. P. W. Malcomson, *Primate Robinson, 1709–94*, 2003

Mâle 1960
E. Mâle, *The Early Churches of Rome*, 1960

Mallary 1985
P. T. Mallary, *New England Churches and Meeting Houses, 1680–1830*, 1985

Mallory 1977
N. A. Mallory, *Roman Rococo: Architecture from Clement XI to Benedict XIV, 1700–1758*, 1977

Mander 1998
T. A. Mander, *Bernini and the Art of Architecture*, 1998

Mansbridge 1991
M. Mansbridge, *John Nash: A Complete Catalogue*, 1991

Marder 1998
T. A. Marder, *Bernini and the Art of Architecture*, 1998

Martin 2006
C. Martin, *A Glimpse of Heaven: Catholic Churches of England and Wales*, 2006

Mason 1945
G. C. Mason, *Colonial Churches of Tidewater, Virginia*, 1945

Mather 1985
F. C. Mather, 'Georgian Churchmanship Reconsidered: Some Variations in Anglican Public Worship, 1714–1830', *Journal of Ecclesiastical History*, 36 (April 1985), pp. 55–83

Meadows 1988
P. Meadows, *Joseph Bonomi, Architect 1739–1808*, 1988

Medvei and Thornton 1974
V. C. Medvei and J. L. Thornton, *Royal Hospital of Saint Bartholomew, 1123–1973*, 1974

Meek 1988
H. A. Meek, *Guarini and his Architecture*, 1988

Meek 1995
—, *The Synagogue*, 1995

Meller 1989
H. Meller, *Exeter Architecture*, 1989

Mercer 2003
E. Mercer, *English Architecture to 1900: The Shropshire Experience*, 2003

Middleton 1962–3
R. D. Middleton, 'The Abbé De Cordemoy and Graeco-Gothic Ideal: A Prelude to Romantic Classicism', *Journal of the Warburg and Courtauld Institutes*, 25 (1962), pp. 278–320; 26 (1963), pp. 90–123

Middleton 1968
—, 'French Eighteenth-Century Opinion on Wren', in *Concerning Architecture: Essays on Architectural Writers and Writing Presented to Nikolaus Pevsner*, ed. J. Summerson, 1968, pp. 40–57

Middleton 2003
—, *Julien-David Leroy in Search of Architecture*, The Annual Soane Lecture, 2003

Millar 1968
J. F. Millar, *The Architects of the American Colonies; or, Vitruvius Americanus*, 1968

Miller 1986
J. Miller, *Religion in the Popular Prints, 1600–1832*, 1986

Millon 1994
H. A. Millon, ed., *The Renaissance from Brunelleschi to Michelangelo: The Representation of Architecture*, 1994

Millon 1999
—, *The Triumph of the Baroque: Architecture in Europe, 1600–1750*, 1999

Minguet 1988
P. Minguet, *France Baroque*, 1988

Montagu 1996
J. Montagu, *Gold, Silver and Bronze Metal Sculpture of the Roman Baroque*, 1996

Moore 1982
P. Moore, ed., *Crown in Glory*, 1982

Morant 1989
R. W. Morant, *Cheshire Churches: A Guide to the Ancient Parish Churches of the County, 1066 to 1820*, 1989

Morley 1993
J. Morley, *Regency Design, 1790–1840*, 1993

Morrice 1982
R. Morrice, *The Buildings of Britain: Stuart and Baroque*, 1982

Morrice 1993
—, 'The Payment Book of William Baker of Audlem (1705–71)', in Bold and Chaney 1993, pp. 231–46

Morrison 1952
H. Morrison, *Early American Architecture from the First Colonial Settlements to the National Period*, 1952

Moss 1976
R. W. Moss, 'The Origins of the Carpenters' Company of Philadelphia', in *Building Early America*, ed. C. E. Peterson, 1976, pp. 35–53

Mowl 1991a
T. Mowl, *To Build the Second City: Architects and Craftsmen of Georgian Bristol*, 1991

Mowl 1991b
—, 'The Castle of Boncoeur and the Wizard of Durham', *Georgian Group Journal* (1992), pp. 36–7

Mowl 2006
—, *William Kent: Architect, Designer, Opportunist*, 2006

Mowl and Earnshaw 1988
— and B. Earnshaw, *John Wood, Architect of Obsession*, 1988

Mowl and Earnshaw 1995
— and —, *Architecture without Kings: The Rise of Puritan Classicism under Cromwell*, 1995

Murdoch 1985
T. Murdoch, *The Quiet Conquest: The Huguenots, 1685 to 1985*, 1985

Murdock 1980
T. Murdock, 'Roubiliac as an Architect? The Bill for the Warkton Monuments', *Burlington Magazine* (January 1980), pp. 40–46

Murray 1989
S. Murray, *Beauvais Cathedral: Architecture of Transcendence*, 1989

Namier and Brooke 1964
L. Namier and J. Brooke, *The History of Parliament: The House of Commons, 1754–1790*, vol. II, 1964

Neave 1991
D. Neave, *Lost Churches and Chapels of Hull*, 1991

Neill 1984
S. Neill, *A History of Christianity in India: The Beginnings to AD 1707*, 1984

Nettel 1977
R. Nettel, 'Changing Face of Church Bands', *Country Life* (1 December 1977), pp. 1625–6

Nichols and Wray 1935
R. H. Nichols and F. A. Wray, *The History of the Foundling Hospital*, 1935

Nightingale 1977
J. Nightingale, 'The Threat to Cromarty', *Country Life* (11 August 1977), pp. 338–40

Nilsson 1968
S. Nilsson, *European Architecture in India, 1750–1850*, 1968

Norberg-Schulz 1974
C. Norberg-Schulz, *Late Baroque and Rococo Architecture*, 1974

Nussbaum 2000
N. Nussbaum, *German Gothic Architecture*, 2000

Nuttgen 1970
P. Nuttgen, *York*, 1970

O'Brien and Guinness 1994
J. O'Brien with D. Guinness, *Dublin: A Grand Tour*, 1994

Ockrim 1988
M. Ockrim, 'The Life and Work of Thomas Harrison of Chester, 1744–1829', PhD thesis, University of London, 1988

Odom 1919
W. Odom, *St Paul's Church, Sheffield: Its Ministers and Associations*, 1919

Odom 1922
—, *Memorials of Sheffield: Its Cathedral and Parish Churches*, 1922

O'Dwyer 1981
F. O'Dwyer, *Lost Dublin*, 1981

Olivier-Michel and Gisler 1966
F. Olivier-Michel and C. Gisler, *A Guide to the Art Treasures of France*, 1966

Olivant 1860
A. Ollivant, *Llandaff Cathedral*, 1860

Osborne 1993
J. Osborne, *Stained Glass in England*, 1993

Ostergard 2001
D. E. Ostergard, ed., *William Beckford, 1760–1844: An Eye for the Magnificent*, 2001

Oswald 1948
A. Oswald, 'The Manor House, Milton, Berks', *Country Life* (24 December 1948), pp. 330–33

Oswald 1953
—, 'Stoke Park, Northamptonshire', *Country Life* (23 July 1953), pp. 280–83

Owen 1994
D. Owen, *History of Lincoln Minster*, 1994

Oxford Dictionary of National Biography
Oxford Dictionary of National Biography, ed. H. C. G. Matthew and B. Harrison, 60 vols, 2004

Ozinga 1929
M. D. Ozinga, *De Protestantsche Kerkenbouw in Nederland*, 1929

Paice 2008
E. Paice, *Wrath of God*, 2008

Palmer and Palmer 1992
A. Palmer and V. Palmer, *The Chronology of British History*, 1992

Palmer 1870
S. Palmer, *St Pancras*, 1870

Parissien 1989
S. Parissien, 'The Careers of Roger and Robert Morris', unpublished D.Phil. thesis, Oxford, 1989

Parissien 1990
—, 'The Ecclecticism of Roger Morris', in *New Light on English Palladianism*, ed. C. Hind, Georgian Group Annual Symposium for 1988, 1990, pp. 50–63

Parker and Chandler 1993
D. Parker and J. Chandler, *Wiltshire Churches: An Illustrated History*, 1993

Paul 1984
R. W. Paul, *Vanished London*, 1984

Paulson 1971
R. Paulson, *Hogarth: His Life, Art and Times*, 2 vols, 1971

Peabody 1979
J. B. Peabody, 'The Building of Trinity Church, Boston', in *Architecture in Colonial Massachusetts*, 1979, pp. 75–86

Pears 1988
I. Pears, *The Discovery of Painting: The Growth of Interest in the Arts in England, 1680–1768*, 1988

Peck 1992
A. Peck, ed., *Alexander Jackson Davis, American Architect, 1803–1892*, 1992

Peet 1901
H. Peet, 'Brief Historical Notes on the Churches of St George and St John, Liverpool', *Transactions of the Historic Society of Lancashire and Cheshire*, 51 (1901), p. 39

Peet 1932
—, 'Thomas Steers: The Engineer of Liverpool's First Dock: A Memoir', *Transactions of the Historic Society of Lancashire and Cheshire*, 82 (1930), pp. 163–242

Pepper 1984
D. S. Pepper, *Guido Reni: A Complete Catalogue of His Work*, 1984

Perouse de Montclos 1994
J.-M. Perouse de Montclos, *Le Guide du patrimoine Paris*, 1994

Perriam 1973
D. R. Perriam, *Eighteenth Century Carlisle*, 1973

Petzet 1961
M. Petzet, *Soufflots Sainte-Geneviève und der Franzosische Kirchenbau des 18. Jahrhunderts*, 1961

Pevsner 1961
N. Pevsner, 'John Bodt in England', *Architectural Review*, 130 (July 1961), pp. 29–35

Pevsner 1976
—, *A History of Building Types*, 1976

Philadelphia 1976
Philadelphia Museum of Art, *Philadelphia: Three Centuries of American Art*, 1976

Phillips 1964
C. H. Phillips, *Mid-Georgian London*, 1964

Pickford 1994
C. Pickford, ed., *Bedfordshire Churches in the Nineteenth Century*, Bedfordshire Historical Record Society, vol. 73, 1994

Pickford 1998
—, ed., *Bedfordshire Churches in the Nineteenth Century*, Bedfordshire Historical Record Society, vol. 77, 1998

Pickford 2000
—, ed., *Bedfordshire Churches in the Nineteenth Century*, Bedfordshire Historical Record Society, vol. 79, 2000

Picktorn, no date
C. H. Picktorn, *Parish Church of St Lawrence, Bourton-on-the-Water*, undated

Pierson 1976
W. H. Pierson, *American Builders and Their Architects: The Colonial and Neoclassical Styles*, 1976

Piggott 1970
S. Piggott, 'Sir John Clerk and "The Country Seat"', in Colvin and Harris 1970, pp. 110–16

Piggott 1985
—, *William Stukeley: An Eighteenth-Century Antiquary*, 1985

Pinto 1986
J. A. Pinto, *The Trevi Fountain*, 1986

Placzek 1982
A. K. Placzek, ed., *Macmillan Encyclopedia of Architects*, 4 vols, 1982

Plumley 1966
N. M. Plumley, *The Organs of the City of London: From the Restoration to the Present*, 1966

Pococke 1993
D. Pococke, ed., *Durham Cathedral: A Celebration*, 1993

Podmore 1998
C. Podmore, *The Moravian Church in England 1728–1760*, 1998

Port 2006
H. M. Port, *Six Hundred New Churches: The Church Building Commission, 1818–1856*, 2006

Potts 1959
J. D. Potts, *Platt of Rotherham, Mason-Architect, 1728–1810*, 1959 [see Platt MS]

Pressley 1983
N. L. Pressly, *Revealed Religion: Benjamin West's Commissions for Windsor Castle and Fonthill Abbey*, 1983

Pride 1996
G. L. Pride, *Dictionary of Scottish Building*, 1996

Prior 1860
J. Prior, *Life of Malone*, 1860

Prophet 1982
J. Prophet, *Church Langton and William Hanbury*, 1982

Prown 1966
J. D. Prown, *John Singleton Copley: In England, 1774–1815*, 1966

Proyoyeur and Proyoyeur 1982
P. Proyoyeur and C. Proyoyeur, *Le Temple: representations de l'architecture sacrée*, 1982

Puppi 1975
L. Puppi, *Andrea Palladio*, 1975

Purchas 1994
A. Purchas, 'The Church of St Lawrence, West Wycombe: Ancient or Modern?', *Georgian Group Journal* (1994), pp. 65–9

Randall 1980
G. Randall, *Church Furnishing and Decoration in England and Wales*, 1980

Rankin 1972
P. Rankin, *Irish Building Ventures of the Earl Bishop of Derry, 1730–1803*, 1972

Ravenel 1992
B. St J. Ravenel, *Architecture of Charleston*, 1992

RCAHMS 1996
Royal Commission on the Ancient and Historical Monuments of Scotland, *Tolbooths and Town-houses: Civic Architecture in Scotland to 1833*, 1996

Rice 1997
L. Rice, *The Altars and Altarpieces of New St Peter's: Outfitting the Basilica, 1621–1666*, 1997

Richards and Summerson 1942
J. M. Richards and J. Summerson, *The Bombed Buildings of Britain: A Record of Architectural Casualties, 1940–41*, 1942

Richards 1973
R. Richards, *Old Cheshire Churches*, 1973

Richardson 1955
A. E. Richardson, *Robert Mylne, Architect and Engineer, 1733–1811*, 1955

Richardson 1998
H. Richardson, ed., *English Hospitals, 1660–1948: A Survey of their Architecture and Design*, 1998

Ricketts 1996
A. Ricketts, 'All the Pride of Prayer: The Purpose of the Private Chapel at Chatsworth', in Airs 1996, pp. 85–92

Ricketts 2007
—, *The English Country House Chapel: Building a Protestant Tradition*, ed. S. Ricketts, 2007

Riddell 1990
R. Riddell, '"To Introduce the *Temple* Beauties": Approaching Palladian Porticoes', in *New Light on English Palladianism*, ed. C. Hind, Georgian Group Annual Symposium for 1988, 1990, pp. 81–94

Ripley 1985
R. Ripley, 'Poverty in Gloucester and its Alleviation, 1690–1740', *Transactions of Bristol and Gloucestershire Archaeological Society*, 103 (1985), pp. 185–99

Roberts 1991
A. Roberts, 'James Smith and James Gibbs: Seminarists and Architects', in *Scottish Architects Abroad: Architectural Heritage, Journal of the Architectural Heritage Society of Scotland*, 2 (1991), pp. 41–55

Roberts 1977
J. Roberts, 'Henry Emlyn's Restoration of St George's Chapel', *Report of the Society of Friends of St George's Chapel*, 5/8 (1976–7), pp. 331–8

Robertson 2004
J. Robertson, 'Architecture of Confidence?: Spanish Town, Jamaica, 1655–1792', in Arciszewska and McKellar 2004, pp. 227–58

Robey 1997
A. Robey, 'Floor Cloth Manufacture in Knightsbridge', *Georgian Group Journal*, 7 (1997), pp. 160–67

Robinson 1979
J. M. Robinson, *The Wyatts: An Architectural Dynasty*, 1979

Rolls 1988
R. Rolls, *The Hospital of the Nation: The Story of Spa Medicine and the Mineral Water Hospital at Bath*, 1988

Rolt 1958
L.T.C. Rolt, *Thomas Telford*, 1958

Root 1992
J. Root, *The Parish Church of St Swithin Walcot: A Brief History*, 1992

Roper 1968
J. S. Roper, *Dudley: The Town in the Eighteenth Century*, 1968

Roscoe 1999
I. Roscoe, 'Peter Scheemakers', *Walpole Society*, 61 (1999), pp. 178–89

Roscoe 2009
—, *A Biographical Dictionary of Sculpture in Britain, 1660–1851*, 2009 [new edition of R. Gunnis, *Dictionary of British Sculptors, 1660–1851*, 1968]

Rose 1963
H. W. Rose, *The Colonial Houses of Worship in America*, 1963

Rosenau 1979
H. Rosenau, *Vision of the Temple: The Image of the Temple of Jerusalem in Judaism and Christianity*, 1979

Rowan 1975
A. Rowan, 'Batty Langley's Gothic', in *Studies in Memory of David Talbot Rice*, ed. G. Robertson and G. Henderson, 1975, pp. 197–215

Rowntree 1951
C. B. Rowntree, *Saffron Walden Then and Now*, 1951

Royle 1993
E. Royle, ed., *A History of the Nonconformist Churches of York*, 1993

Rude 1981
G. Rude, *The Crowd in History: A Study of Popular Disturbances in France and England, 1730–1848*, 1981

Rupp 1986
G. Rupp, *Religion in England, 1688–1791*, 1986

Russell 1987
F. Russell, 'The Derby Collection (1721–1735)', *Walpole Society*, 53 (1987), pp. 143–80

Rutledge 1959
A. W. Rutledge, 'The Second St Philip's, Charleston, 1710–1835', *Journal of the Society of Architectural Historians*, 18 (October 1959), pp. 112–14

Ryder 1993
P. Ryder, *Medieval Churches of West Yorkshire*, 1993

Rykwert 1972
J. Rykwert, *On Adam's House in Paradise*, 1972

Rykwert and Rykwert 1984
— and A. Rykwert, *Robert and James Adam*, 1984

Saint 2007
A. Saint, *Architect and Engineer: A Study in Sibling Rivalry*, 2007

St Aubyn 1985
F. St Aubyn, *A Portrait of Georgian London*, 1985; *see* Ackermann 1808–9

Salmon 2000
F. Salmon, *Building on Ruins: The Rediscovery of Rome and English Architecture*, 2000

Salmon et al. 2005
— et al., *The Professor's Dream: An Introduction and Guide to the Display*, Royal Academy of Arts, London, 2005

Salter 1995
M. Salter, *Old Parish Churches of Cheshire*, 1995

Satkowski 1993
L. Satkowski, *Giorgio Vasari: Architect and Courtier*, 1993

Saumarez Smith 1990
C. Saumarez Smith, *The Building of Castle Howard*, 1990

Saunders 2001
A. Saunders, *St Paul's: The Story of the Cathedral*, 2001

Saunders 1993
E. Saunders, *Joseph Pickford of Derby*, 1993

Saunders 2005
—, 'Biographical Dictionary of English Wrought Iron Smiths of the Seventeenth and Eighteenth Centuries', *Walpole Society*, 67 (2005), pp. 237–384

Saunders 1995
R. H. Saunders, *John Smibert: Colonial America's First Portrait Painter*, 1995

Savidge 1964
A. Savidge, *The Parsonage in England: Its History and Architecture*, 1964

Scard 1990
M. A. Scard, *The Building Stones of Shropshire*, 1990

Schroder 2008
T. Schroder, ed., *Treasures of the English Church*, 2008

Scott 1983
B. Scott, 'Lady Elizabeth Hastings', *Yorkshire Archaeological Journal*, 55 (1983), pp. 95–118

Seed 1907
T. A. Seed, *Norfolk Street Wesleyan Chapel, Sheffield*, 1907

Severens 1992–3
K. Severens, 'New Perspective on Georgian Building Practice: The Rebuilding of St Werburgh's Church, Dublin, 1754–59', *Bulletin of the Irish Georgian Society*, 35 (1992–3), pp. 3–16

Seymour 1992
B. Seymour, *York's Other Churches and Chapels*, 1992

Shearman 1965
J. Shearman, *Andrea del Sarto*, 2 vols, 1965

Shesgreen 1983
S. Shesgreen, *Hogarth and the Times-of-Day Tradition*, 1983

Shipley 1990
D. Shipley, *Durham Cathedral*, 1990

Shipman 1979
E. R. Shipman, *Saint Nicholas Church, Abbots Bromley, Staffordshire*, 1979

Shoemaker 1953
R. W. Shoemaker, 'Christ Church, St Peter's and St Paul's', in *Historic Philadelphia*, ed. L. P. Eisenhart, Transactions of American Philosophical Society, 43, pt 1, 1953, pp. 187–98

Shorney 1996
D. Shorney, *Protestant Nonconformity and Roman Catholicism: A Guide to Sources in the Public Record Office*, 1996

Sicca 1980
C. M. Sicca, 'Il Palladianesimo in Inghilterra', in *Palladio: La sua eredità nel mondo*, 1980, pp. 30–71

Sicca 2008
—, ed., *John Talman: An Early Eighteenth-Century Connoisseur*, 2008

Simon 1985
J. Simon, *Handel: A Celebration of his Life and Times, 1685–1759*, 1985

Simon 2003
—, 'Thomas Johnson's *The Life of the Author*', *Furniture History*, 39 (2003), pp. 1–64

Skempton 2002
A. Skempton, ed., *A Biographical Dictionary of Civil Engineers in Great Britain*, vol. 1, 2002

Smiles 2003
S. Smiles, 'Data, Documentation and Display in Eighteenth-Century Investigations of Exeter Cathedral', in *Tracing Architecture: The Aesthetics of Antiquarianism*, ed. D. Arnold and S. Bending, 2003, pp. 80–99

Smith 1976
E .E. F. Smith, *Clapham*, 1976

Smith and Cook 1989
E. Smith and O. Cook, *English Cathedrals*, London, 1989

Smith 1990
F. Smith, *Cusworth Hall and the Battie-Wrightson Family*, 1990

Smith 1984
G. Smith, 'The Concorso Accademia of 1677 at the Accademia di San Luca', in *Projects and Monuments in the Period of the Roman Baroque*, ed. H. Hager and S. S. Munshower, Papers in Art History from the Pennsylvania State University, 1, 1984, pp. 26–45

Smith 1993
—, *Architectural Diplomacy: Rome and Paris in the Late Baroque*, 1993

Smith 1968
R. C. Smith, *The Art of Portugal, 1500–1800*, 1968

Smyth 1851
W. H. Smyth, *Aedes Hartwelliana*, 1851

Snodin 1986
M. Snodin, 'Trade Cards and English Rococo', in *The Rococo in England: A Symposium*, ed. C. Hind, 1986, pp. 82–103

Snodin, Wainwright and Calloway 1980
—, C. Wainwright and S. Calloway, *Horace Walpole and Strawberry Hill*, Orleans House Gallery, Twickenham, 1980

Soros 2006
S. Soros, ed., *James 'Athenian' Stuart: The Rediscovery of Antiquity*, 2006

Speight 1894
H. Speight, *Nidderdale and the Garden of the Nidd: A Yorkshire Rhimeland*, 1894

Stainton and White 1987
L. Stainton and C. White, *Drawings in England from Hilliard to Hogarth*, 1987

Stalley 1999
R. Stalley, *Early Medieval Architecture*, 1999

Stankovitch 1995
A.-M. Stankovitch, 'A Reconsideration of French Renaissance Church Architecture', in J. Guillaume, *L'Eglise dans l'architecture de la Renaissance*, 1995, pp. 161–80

Stell 1985
C. F. Stell, *Calderdale Chapels*, Halifax Antiquarian Society, 1985, pp. 16–35

Stell 1986
—, *Nonconformist Chapels and Meeting-houses in Central England*, 1986

Stell 1991
—, *Nonconformist Chapels and Meeting-houses in South-West England*, 1991

Stell 1994
—, *Nonconformist Chapels and Meeting-houses in the North of England*, 1994

Stell 1999
—, 'Puritan and Nonconformist Meetinghouses in England', in *Seeing Beyond the Word: Visual Arts and the Calvinist Tradition*, ed. P. C. Finney, 1999, pp. 49–81

Stell 2002
—, *Nonconformist Chapels and Meeting-houses in Eastern England*, 2002

Stephenson 2005
D. Stephenson, *Visions of Heaven: The Dome in European Architecture*, 2005

Steven 2002
M. Steven, *Parish Life in Eighteenth-Century Scotland*, 2002

Stevenson 1983
C. Stevenson, '"Solomon Engothicked": The Elder John Wood's Restoration of Llandaff Cathedral', *Art History*, 6 (September 1983), pp. 301–14

Stevenson 2000
—, *Medicine and Magnificence: British Hospital and Asylum Architecture, 1660–1815*, 2000

Stillman 1988
D. Stillman, *English Neoclassical Architecture*, 2 vols, 1988

Stretton 1910
W. Stretton, *The Stretton Manuscripts: Being Notes on the History of Nottinghamshire*, 1910

Stroud 1971
D. Stroud, *George Dance, Architect, 1741–1825*, 1971

Summerson 1964
J. Summerson, *The Classical Language of Architecture*, 1964

Summerson 1970
—, *Architecture in Britain, 1530 to 1830* [1953], 5th revised edn, 1970

Summerson 1990
—, 'Inigo Jones: Covent Garden and the Restoration of St Paul's Cathedral' [1964]; reprinted in *The Unromantic Castle and Other Essays*, 1990, pp. 41–62

Summerson 2000
—, *Inigo Jones*, revised edn, 2000

Summerson 2003
—, *Georgian London* [1945], ed. H. Colvin, 2003

Summerson, Watkin and Mellinghoff 1983
—, D. Watkin and G. Tilman Mellinghoff, *John Soane*, Architectural Monographs, London, 1983

Sweet 2004
R. Sweet, *Antiquaries: The Discovery of the Past in Eighteenth-Century Britain*, 2004

Sykes 2009
C. Simon Sykes, 'Command Performace', *World of Interiors* (February 2009), pp. 60–61

Tait 1993
A. A. Tait, *Robert Adam: Drawings and Imagination*, 1993

Tait 1996
—, *Robert Adam: The Creative Mind: From the Sketch to the Finished Drawing*, 1996

Tait 2008
—, *The Adam Brothers in Rome: Drawings from the Grand Tour*, 2008

Tanner 1961
J. M. Tanner, 'The Building of Chichley Hall', *Records of Buckinghamshire*, 17 (1961), 1, pp. 41–8

Tate 1983
W. E. Tate, *The Parish Chest* [1946], 3rd edn, 1983

Tatton-Brown 1989
T. Tatton-Brown, *Great Cathedrals of Britain*, 1989

Tatton-Brown and Mortimer 2003
— and R. Mortimer, eds, *Westminster Abbey: The Lady Chapel of Henry VII*, 2003

Tatum 1961
G. B. Tatum, *Penn's Great Town*, 1961

Taylor 1925
J. G. Taylor, *Our Lady of Batersey: The Story of Battersea Church and Parish Told from Original Sources*, 1925

Taylor 1875
R. V. Taylor, *The Ecclesiae Leodiensis; or, Historical and Architectural Sketches of the Churches of Leeds and Neighbourhood*, 1875

Temperley 1979
N. Temperley, *The Music of the English Parish Church*, 1979

Temple 1992
P. Temple, *Islington Chapels: An Architectural Guide to Nonconformist and Roman Catholic Places of Worship in the London Borough of Islington*, 1992

Thoenes 2003
C. Thoenes, *Architectural Theory from the Renaissance to the Present*, 2003

Thompson 1949
F. Thompson, *A History of Chatsworth*, 1949

Thompson and Goldin 1975
J. D. Thompson and G. Goldin, *The Hospital: A Social and Architectural History*, 1975

Thompson and Thompson 1988
P. Thompson and P. Thompson, *St John Baptist Church, Honiley*, 1988

Thomson 1984
D. Thomson, *Renaissance Paris*, 1984

Thorold 1989
H. Thorold, *Lincolnshire Churches Revisited*, 1989

Thurley 2003
S. Thurley, *Hampton Court: A Social and Architectural History*, 2003

Thurley 2006
—, 'Kimbolton Castle, Huntingdon, Cambridgeshire', *Country Life* (30 March 2006), pp. 66–71

Tigerman 1988
S. Tigerman, *The Architecture of Exile*, 1988

Titchmarsh 1983
P. Titchmarsh, *The Parish Church of St Peter, Kineton, Warwickshire: A Brief History and Guide*, 1983

Toesca 1952
I. Toesca, 'Alessandro Galilei in Inghilterra', *English Miscellany*, 3 (1952), pp. 189–220

Tournikiotis 1994
P. Tournikiotis, *The Parthenon and its Impact in Modern Times*, 1994

Trinder, no date
B. Trinder, *John Fletcher, Vicar of Madeley during the Industrial Revolution*, undated

Trinder 1973
—, *The Industrial Revolution in Shropshire*, 1973

Trinder 1977
—, *'The Most Extraordinary District in the World': Ironbridge and Coalbrookdale*, 1977

Trowles 2008
T. Trowles, *Treasures of Westminster Abbey*, 2008

Turner 1997
C. Turner, ed., *The Gallery Tradition: Aspects of Georgian Psalmody*, 1997

Tyack 1975
G. Tyack, 'Compton Verney', *Warwickshire History*, 3 (Summer 1975), pp. 3–14

Tyack 1986
—, *Fawley, Buckinghamshire: A Short History of the Church and Parish*, 1986

Tyack 1998
—, *Oxford: An Architectural Guide*, 1998

Upton 1986
D. Upton, *Holy Things and Profane: Anglican Churches in Colonial Virginia*, 1986

Usher 2007
R. Usher, 'Chapel Royal and Symbol of the Church Militant: The Iconography of Christ Church and St Patrick's Cathedrals, Dublin, *c.*1600–1760', *Irish Architectural and Decorative Studies*, 10 (2007), pp. 200–23

Vallance 1947
A. Vallance, *Greater English Church Screens*, 1947

Van Swingchem, Brouwer and van Os 1984
C. A. van Swingchem, T. Brouwer and W. van Os, *Een huis voor het Woord Het protestant se Kerkinterieur in Nederland tot 1900*, 1984

Varriano 1986
J. Varriano, *Italian Baroque and Rococo Architecture*, 1986

Verey 1976
D. Verey, *Cotswold Churches*, 1976

Vigar 1995
J. E. Vigar, *Kent Churches*, 1995

Vincent 1890
W. T. Vincent, *The Records of the Woolwich District*, 1890

Vlieghe 1998
H. Vlieghe, *Flemish Art and Architecture, 1585–1700*, 1998

Walker and Ritchie 1987
B. Walker and G. Ritchie, *Exploring Scotland's Heritage: Fife and Tayside*, 1987

Walker 2000
S. Walker, *Historic Ulster Churches*, 2000

Walsh 1972
J. Walsh, 'Methodism and the Mob in the Eighteenth Century', in *Popular Belief and Practice*, ed. G. J. Cuming and D. Baker, 1972, pp. 213–27

Walton 1987
J. K. Walton, *Lancashire: A Social History, 1558–1936*, 1987

Ward-Perkins 1981
J. B. Ward-Perkins, *Roman Imperial Architecture*, 1981

Warren and Keegan 1993
L. Warren and F. Keegan, *Through Twenty Preston Guilds: The Catholic Congregation of St Wilfrid's, Preston*, 1993

Watkin 1982a
D. Watkin, *Athenian Stuart: Pioneer of the Greek Revival*, 1982

Watkin 1982b
—, *The Buildings of Britain: Regency*, 1982

Wayment 1980
H. Wayment, 'The Stained Glass in the Chapel of the Vyne', *National Trust Studies*, 1980

Webb 1954
M. I. Webb, *Michael Rysbrack, Sculptor*, 1954

Webster 1991
C. Webster, *R. D. Chantrell, Architect: His Life and Work in Leeds, 1818–1847*, Publications of the Thoresby Society, Second Series, 2, 1991

Weinreb and Hibbert 1983
B. Weinreb and C. Hibbert, *The London Encyclopedia*, 1983

Weiss 1997
T. Weiss, *For the Friends of Nature and Art: The Garden Kingdom of Prince Franz von Anhalt-Dessau in Age of Enlightenment*, 1997

Welander 1991
D. Welander, *The History, Art and Architecture of Gloucester Cathedral*, 1991

Welch 1972
E. Welch, 'Lady Huntingdon and Spa Fields Chapel', *Guildhall Miscellany*, 4 (1972), pp. 175–83

Welch 1975
—, *Two Calvinist Methodist Chapels: The London Tabernacle and Spa Fields Chapel*, 1975

Wells-Cole et al. 1992
A. Wells-Cole et al., *Country House Lighting, 1660–1890*, 1992

Westlake 1914
H. F. Westlake, *St Margaret's Westminster: The Church of the House of Commons*, 1914

Whiffen 1945
M. Whiffen, 'White of Worcester', *Country Life* (7 December 1945), pp. 1002–5

Whiffen 1948
—, *Stuart and Georgian Churches: The Architecture of the Church of England outside London, 1603–1837*, 1948

Whiffen 1973
—, *Thomas Archer*, 1973

Whinney 1943
M. Whinney, 'Some Church Designs by John Webb', *Journal of the Warburg and Courtauld Institutes*, 6 (1943), pp. 142–50

Whinney 1958
—, 'Sir Christopher Wren's Visit to Paris', *Gazette des Beaux-Arts*, 51 (1958), pp. 229–42

Whinney 1988
—, *Sculpture in Britain, 1530 to 1830*, rev. J. Physick, 1988

Whistler 1954
L. Whistler, *The Imagination of Vanbrugh and His Fellow Artists*, 1954

White 1964
J. F. White, *Protestant Worship and Church Architecture*, 1964

White 1993
J. White, *Art and Architecture in Italy, 1250–1400*, 1993

White 1986
R. White, 'Isaac Ware and Chesterfield House', in *The Rococo in England: A Symposium*, ed. C. Hind, 1986, pp. 175–92

White 1991
—, 'Discreet Gothick', *House and Garden* (June 1991), p. 52

White 1997
—, *Nicholas Hawksmoor and the Replanning of Oxford*, 1997

Whitehead 1991
D. Whitehead, 'A Goth among Greeks: The Architecture of Hereford Cathedral in the 18th Century', *The Friends of Hereford Cathedral*, 57th Annual Report, 1991

Whitehead 1992a
—, 'The Georgian Churches of Worcester', *Transactions of the Worcestershire Archaeological Society*, 3rd series, 13 (1992), pp. 211–22

Whitehead 1992b
—, 'Job Marston's Chapel', *Georgian Group Journal* (1992), pp. 79–81

Whitehead 1995
—, ed., *Medieval Art, Architecture and Archaeology at Hereford*, British Archaeological Association Conference Transactions, 1995

Whitelaw 1990
J. W. Whitelaw, *Hertfordshire Churches and Other Places of Worship*, 1990

Whittaker and Clark 1971
N. Whittaker and U. Clark, *Historic Architecture of County Durham*, 1971

Wickham 1965
A. K. Wickham, *Churches of Somerset*, 1965

Wiebenson 1969
D. Wiebenson, *Sources of Greek Revival Architecture*, 1969

Wigoder 1986
G. Wigoder, *The Story of the Synagogue: A Diaspora Museum Book*, 1986

Williams 1951
G. W. Williams, *St Michael's, Charleston, 1751–1951*, 1951

Williams 1931
J. F. Williams, 'The Rebuilding of Chelmsford Parish Church, 1800 to 1803', *Essex Review* (July 1931), pp. 96–104

Williams 2000
R. Williams, 'Vanbrugh's India and his Mausolea for England', in *Sir John Vanbrugh and Landscape Architecture in Baroque England, 1690–1730*, ed. C. Ridgway and R. Williams, 2000, pp. 114–30

Williamson 1894
G. W. Williamson, *John Russell*, 1894

Willis, no date
R. Willis, *Nonconformist Chapels of York, 1693–1840*, York Georgian Society Occasional Paper no. 8, undated

Willis and Clark 1886
— and J. W. Clark, *The Architectural History of Cambridge*, 3 vols, 1886

Wilson and Mee 1998
B. Wilson and F. Mee, *The Medieval Parish Churches of York: The Pictorial Evidence*, 1998

Wilson 1990
C. Wilson, *The Gothic Cathedral: The Architecture of the Great Church, 1130–1530*, 1990

Wilson 1979
M. I. Wilson, *Organ Cases of Western Europe*, 1979

Wilton and Bignamini 1996
A. Wilton and I. Bignamini, *Grand Tour: The Lure of Italy in the Eighteenth Century*, 1996

Wilton-Ely 1965
J. Wilton-Ely, *The Architect's Vision*, Nottingham University Art Gallery, 1965

Wilton-Ely 1967
—, 'The Architectural Model', *Architectural Review*, 142 (1967), pp. 26–32

Wilton-Ely 1968
—, 'The Architectural Model, 1: English Baroque', *Apollo* (October 1968), pp. 250–59

Wilton-Ely 1969
—, 'The Role of Models in Church Design', *Country Life Annual* (1969), pp. 76–9

Wilton-Ely 1993
—, *Piranesi as Architect and Designer*, 1993

Wing 1987
K. R. Wing, *A History of Bancroft's School, 1737–1987*, 1987

Wittkower 1948
R. Wittkower, *The Earl of Burlington and William Kent*, York Georgian Society Occasional Paper no. 5, 1948

Wittkower 1974b
—, 'Pseudo-Palladian Elements in English Neoclassicism' in *Palladio and English Palladianism*, 1974, pp. 168–74

Wittkower 1999
—, *Art and Architecture in Italy, 1600–1750* [1958], rev. J. Connor and J. Montagu, 3 vols, 1999

Wittman 2006
R. Wittman, 'A Bourgeoise Family Puts Its Cathedral in Order: A Fictive Debate on Notre Dame in the *Journal de Paris* in 1780', in *Fragments: Architecture and the Unfinished*, ed. B. Bergdoll and W. Oechslin, 2006, pp. 197–208

Woodward 1998
C. Woodward, *The Buildings of Europe: Copenhagen*, 1998

Worsley 1986
G. Worsley, 'The Baseless Roman Doric Column in Mid-Eighteenth-Century English architecture: A Study in Neo-classicism', *Burlington Magazine* (May 1986), pp. 331–9

Worsley 1987a
—, 'Georgian Buildings in Grantham', *Country Life* (4 June 1987), pp. 246–52

Worsley 1987b
—, 'Rokeby Park, Yorkshire', *Country Life* (19 March 1987), pp. 74–9

Worsley 1991b
—, 'Stiff But Not Dull', *Country Life* (25 July 1991), pp. 90–93

Worsley 1995
—, *Classical Architecture in Britain: The Heroic Age*, 1995

Worsley 1999
—, 'New Light on 'Long Sir Thomas', *Georgian Group Journal*, 9 (1999), pp. 1–16

Worsley 2007
—, *Inigo Jones and the European Classicist Tradition*, 2007

Wragg 2000
B. Wragg, *The Life and Work of John Carr of York*, ed. G. Worsley, 2000

Wragg and Wragg 1956
M. Wragg and R. B. Wragg, 'Two Houses By John Carr', *Country Life* (12 April 1956), pp. 752–5

Wragg and Wragg 1959
— and —, 'Carr in Portugal', *Architectural Review*, 125 (February 1959), pp. 127–8

Wright 1864
G. N. Wright, *The Historical Guide to Bath*, 1864

Wright 1921
J. J. Wright, *Story of Chowbent Chapel, 1645–1721–1921*, 1921

Wynne 1982
M. Wynne, 'Irish Stained and Painted Glass in the Eighteenth Century' in Moore 1982, pp. 58–68

Yates 1991
N. Yates, *Buildings, Faith and Worship: The Liturgical Arrangement of Anglican Churches, 1600–1900*, 1991

Yeomans 1992
D. Yeomans, *The Architect & the Carpenter*, 1992

Yerburgh 2000
D. S. Yerburgh, *An Attempt to Depict Haford in Cardiganshire*, 2000

Young and Young 1986
E. Young and W. Young, *London's Churches*, 1986

Youngson 1966
A. J. Youngson, *The Making of Classical Edinburgh, 1750–1840*, 1966

Zarnecki 1993
G. Zarnecki, 'The Future of the Shobdon Arches', *Journal of the British Archaeological Association* (1993), pp. 87–92

Glossary

Definitions of technical terms that appear in the text and Documents (CD-ROM) – except where meanings are completely obscure – are arranged alphabetically. Erratic and eighteenth-century phonetic spellings should require no more than common-sense associations on the readers' part. Sources cited: Anon. 1734 [*The Builder's Dictionary*] (Russell 1997, vol. III); Black and Harris 1778; Chambers 1728 (Russell 1997, vol. II); Curl 1980 [illustrated]; *Encyclopedia Britannica* 1771 (Russell 1997, vol. V); Friar 1996; Harris 1704 (Russell 1997, vol. I); Johnson 1755 (Russell 1997, vol. IV), Lever and Harris 1993 [illustrated]; Lounsbury 1994 [illustrated]; Neve 1726; Pride 1996; Salmon 1748; Summerson 1964 [illustrated].

acanthus ornament based on a scalloped leaf of the acanthus plant used on Corinthian and Composite capitals (Lever and Harris 1993, p. 1)
acroteria 'sharp Pinacles and spiry Battlements, which stand in Ranges about flat Buildings, with Rails and Balasters' (Harris 1704, pp. 116–17)
aedicule door, window, niche surround consisting of columns or pilasters supporting pediment (Lever and Harris 1993, p. 1)
amphiprostyle *see* temple forms
anthemion classical motif based on honeysuckle (Lever and Harris 1993, p. 2)
apertines perhaps 'Apertions' or 'Apertures', that is, an 'opening . . . to signifie, *Doors, Windows*' (Neve 1726, pp. 7–8)
apophyge concave sweep at top or bottom of a column shaft (Lever and Harris 1993, p. 2)
apron raised or sunk panel immediately below a window sill (Lever and Harris 1993, p. 2)
apteral *see* temple forms
architrave lowest division of entablature resting on column abaci (Lounsbury 1994, pp. 11–12)
areostyle *see* intercolumniation
arris sharp edge made at junction of two surfaces (Lounsbury 1994, p. 12)
ashlering 'quartering in Garrets perpendicular to Floor: up to under side of Rafters' (Neve 1726, p. 21)
astragal 'little round Moulding, which encompases Shaft of Column' or step (Neve 1726, p. 22)
astylar classical façade without columns or pilasters (Lever and Harris 1993, p. 4)
baldacchino canopy over an altar supported on columns (Lever and Harris 1993, p. 4)
baptistery room in which the rite of baptism is performed (Lounsbury 1994, p. 19)
barge 'wood slat to protect window, door from rain or flooding' (Pride 1996, p. 13)
bartisan turret corbelled out from the angle of a wall or tower (Lever and Harris 1993, p. 5)
basilica 'great Hall which had two Ranges of Pillars, and two Isles with Galleries afterwards turned into Churches' (Harris 1704, p. 122)
battlements indented parapet of alternating openings (crenellation) and solid raised parts (merlons) (Lever and Harris 1993, p. 5)
bead and reel enrichment of the astragal of classical order (Summerson 1964, p. 49)
beetles [bootles] heavy mallets to drive down piles (Pride 1996, p. 15)
block rustic *see* Gibbs-surround
blocking crowning course above cornice (Lever and Harris 1993, p. 6)
bolection moulding projecting beyond the face of an adjoining panel (Lounsbury 1994, p. 36)
bootles *see* beetles
boss ornamented projection placed at the intersection of the ribs of a vault or ceiling beams (Lever and Harris 1993, p. 7)
brads 'Nails having no spreading Heads' (Harris 1704, p. 190)
branch chandelier
brattising [bratticing] ornamental cresting usually formed of the leaves or flowers on late gothic screens (Lever and Harris 1993, p. 7)
bresummers [breastsomer, bressemer, bresstumber] timber 'pieces in outward Parts of Building, and in middle Floors into which Girders fram'd' (Chambers 1728, p. 73)
bricks 'fictitious or artificial kind of Stone in *England* made for the most part of a yellowish colour'd fat Earth, somewhat reddish [vulgarly call'd Lome]', 'Stock bricks made upon a Mould' (Neve 1726, pp. 37–8, 43; also Anon. 1734, pp. 53–62, Salmon 1748, pp. 1–18), 'Rubbed red Stock commonly called red Bubbers' (Doc. 246: 17 December 1788; *see* sammel and Spanish, below)

Brief written consent from a bishop authorising collection for charitable causes (Friar 1996, p. 67)
broach spire tapering octagon or square producing corner half-pyramids at intersections (Lever and Harris 1993, p. 36)
broached [broched, brotched] stone face worked to show horizontal or diagonal furrows with margin-draft round edges of finer, narrower draft (Pride 1996, p. 19)
bronzing 'art of varnishing wood, plaster *etc.* to give colour of bronze' (*Encyclopedia Britannica* 1771, p. 83)
bubbers *see* bricks
buzaglo *see* stove

calceolus flower [calceoli, caulicoli] '8 lesser Branches or Stalks in *Corinthian* Capital, springing out from four greater Caules or Stalks' (Anon. 1734, p. 94), or *see* crocket
cancelli *see* latticing
candleholder *see* sconce
canopy *see* type
capstand mechanism working on principle of wheel and axle
cavetto 'hollow Member, or round concave Moulding containing Quadrant of Circle used as Ornament in Cornice' (Anon. 1734, p. 93)
cella inner sanctuary of antique temple
chainplates series of connected plates built into wall for greater stability
chalder dry capacity measure
chancel 'most sacred part of Temple, or Church' (Neve 1726, p. 103); *see* latticing
chandelier *see* sconce
chiaro obscura [clair-obscure, *chiaroscuro*] 'Art of Distributing Light and Shadow' (Harris 1704, p. 196)
choirscreen partition across the part of a church separating the nave from the chancel or choir where services are performed (Lever and Harris 1993, p. 35)
Christiana *see* timbers
ciborium [cyborium] canopy over altar (Lever and Harris 1993, p. 10)
cima [scima] *see* og
clamp metal brace to strengthen masonry (Pride 1006, p. 24)
clapboard thin, riven board tapered along one side (Lounsbury 1994, pp. 81–2)
classical order column comprising base, shaft, capital and entablature, the last combining architrave, frieze and cornice. *Greek Doric*: column without base or fluted shaft; *Roman Doric*: column with base and plain or fluted shaft; *Tuscan*: simplified Doric, the plainest, most massive of the orders; *Ionic*: capital with volutes; *Corinthian*: bell-shaped capital with acanthus leaves projecting from eight small volutes, shaft normally fluted; *Composite*: capital combining Ionic volutes and foliate bell of Corinthian (Lever and Harris 1993, pp. 26, 112–18). Proportions of diameters to height: Tuscan 7 diameters, Doric 8 diameters, Ionic 9 diameters, Corinthian and Composite 10 diameters (Neve 1726, pp. 209–12; Gibbs 1732; Gibbs 1739, p. 3; Worsley 1986)
clerestory upper storey of the nave above the aisle roof, pierced with windows that light the interior (Lever and Harris 1993, p. 10)
Coade stone artificial stone composed of clay, ceramic and other material cast from moulds, manufactured during the second half of the eighteenth century by Mrs Eleanor Coade & Co., Lambeth, London (Kelly 1990)
coffer-vaulted ceiling ornamented with sunk panels (Lever and Harris 1993, p. 11)
collar-beam 'Beam fram'd cross betwixt two principal Rafters', 'Timber, which stands by Pairs meet in Angle at Top of Roof' (Anon. 1734, pp. 99, 216)
colonnette diminutive column (Lever and Harris 1993, p. 11)
colours pigments ('Catalogue of the Simple Colours', in Harris 1704, pp. 129–31; Bristow 1996)
columbarium square or circular structure internally honeycombed with small recesses (Lever and Harris 1993, p. 11)
Composite *see* classical order
conductors *see* electrical rod
console double-scrolled bracket (Lever and Harris 1993, p. 11)
Conventicle meeting of Nonconformists (Friar 1996, p. 139)
copal resin mixed in solvent to make a hard, glossy, transparent varnish used to protect wood and metal surfaces against effects of moisture, air and light (Lounsbury 1994, p. 387)
corbel carved or moulded support projecting from a wall (Lever and Harris 1993, p. 11)
Corinthian *see* classical order
corner-stones 'two Stones which stands one in each Jamb' (Neve 1726, p. 115)
coronna 'Flat-Crown Member in *Dorick* Gate' (Harris 1704, p. 134; Anon. 1734, pp. 106–7)
cramp *see* clamp
crocket one of a series of stylised leaf-form projections decorating the sloping sides of a spire, pinnacle or gable in gothic architecture (Lever and Harris 1993, p. 12)
crooks [cruik] hook on which a door or gate is hung (Pride 1996, p. 28)
cupelettes [cupolas] small domes on a drum used as a crowning feature (Lever and Harris 1993, p. 12)
cupola *see* cupelettes
cusping point formed by the intersection of two arcs in a gothic arch or tracery (Lever and Harris 1993, p. 12)
cyborium (ciborium) canopy over altar (Lever and Harris 1993, p. 10)

Dantzig *see* timbers
deal 'thin kind of fir-planks formed by sawing trunk of tree into many longitudinal divisions' (*Encyclopedia Britannica* 1771, pp. 99–100)
Decalogue The Ten Commandments (Friar 1996, p. 443)
Delf stone quarry
dentelling 'Ornament in Corniches, bearing

Resemblance to Teeth cut on little square Members' (Chambers 1728, pp. 133–4)
desk table with sloping top located at the east end of the nave and used by a clerk or reader conducting post-Reformation services (Friar 1996, pp. 371–2)
Diocletian window semicircular window divided by two mullions, the centre part larger than the sides, derived from Baths of Diocletian, Rome, also called therm or thermal window (Lever and Harris 1993, p. 13)
dipteral *see* temple forms
distyle *see* temple forms
dog nail for 'fastning Hinges close to Doors without Heads flying off' (Neve 1726, p. 206)
dormients *see* sleepers
dosseret detached section of entablature above a column or pilaster (Lever and Harris 1993, p. 14)
drum wall on which a dome rests (Lever and Harris 1993, p. 14)

echinus [ovolo] 'Member placed on top of *Ionick Capital* resembling prickly Rind of Chestnut' (Harris 1704, p. 139)
Eldorado work *see* latticing
electrical rod [conductor, Franklin, lightning rod] piece of metal attached to steeple, etc., connected to the ground by a series of long rods preventing lightning from striking a building (Lounsbury 1994, pp. 128, 150)
ells linear measure defined as 37 inches (Pride 1996, p. 32)
engaged column column attached to a wall and projecting by half its diameter (Lever and Harris 1993, p. 16)
entablature assembly of horizontal members (architrave, frieze and cornice) in a classical order, also used on a wall without columnar support (Lever and Harris 1993, p. 16)
eustyle *see* intercolumniation

fan vault arched ceiling composed of inverted concave cones overlaid with numerous ribs radiating from one support, producing a fanlike pattern (Lever and Harris 1993, p. 42)
fillet narrow rectangular moulding (Lounsbury 1994, p. 139)
filligrance work filigree
fir *see* deal
floor cloth [oil cloth] painted patterned cloth covering for floors, an early form of linoleum (Robey 1997)
flying buttress arch used to carry the thrust of a vault or roof from the walls to the outer pier or buttress to give stability to a structure (Lever and Harris 1993, p. 7)
Franklin *see* stove and electrical rod
Frederickstadt *see* timbers
free-stone stone dug on Isle of Portland, Dorset, 'much softer and whiter than *Purbeck* . . . commonly rais'd . . . in bigger Blocks'; also found in Oxfordshire 'some call *Rigate*' (Neve 1726, p. 250)
fret-work 'plain bordering round ceiling made with divers fillets or bands affording a great variety of figures by their turnings' (Black and Harris 1778, under F)
furring 'making good the Rafters Feet in Cornice when Rafters rotten, or sunk hollow towards each End nailed upon them, to make them straight' (Anon. 1734, p. 134)

gadrooned decorative pattern formed of a series of convex ridges (Lever and Harris 1993, p. 18)
Galilee vestibule reserved as chapel for penitents at the western end of an early medieval church or cathedral (Friar 1996, p. 211)
gallets perhaps galleting or chipping joints of stone externally
gavil gable (Pride 1996, p. 37)
Gibbs-surround [block rustic] blocked architrave of door, window or architrave of alternating large and small blocks of Renaissance origin popularised by James Gibbs (Lever and Harris 1993, p. 19; Wittkower 1974b, chapter 11).
glass *crown*: blown window glass of relative clarity and strength manufactured in London, Bristol, Newcastle upon Tyne and Stourbridge, Worcestershire (Lounsbury 1994, pp. 104–5, 160–61). *Bristol*: 'made at Bristol but not the Conveniency to send by Sea very rare to have any in London tho' as cheap, and better than *Newcastle* Glass'; *Newcastle*: 'kind of an Ash-colour most in use in E*ngland* but subject to Specks, Blemishes, Streaks, very often warped and crooked'; *Radcliffe* (London): 'best and clearest' (Neve 1726, pp. 145–8)
glebe land portion of land owned by an Anglican parish for the use of its minister (Lounsbury 1994, pp. 161–2)
goloss [goloso] *see* guilloche
gothic medieval stylistic phases: *Early English* (*circa* 1180–1280) with pointed arch, rib vault, lancet window; *Decorated* (*circa* 1250–1350) comprising *Geometrical* with trefoil, quatrefoil, cusped triangle tracery, and *Curvilinear* with daggers and mouchettes (*see* below), open arches, lierne vaulting [*Geometrical* and *Curvilinear* are now archaic terms]; *Perpendicular* (*circa* 1330–early fifteenth century) with strong verticals of panel tracery, four-centred arches, fan and pendant vaults (Lever and Harris 1993, pp. 13–14, 28)
grout thin fluid mortar
Greek Doric *see* classical order
guilloche repeated pattern of interlacing curved bands ornamenting classical mouldings (Lever and Harris 1993, p. 20)
guttae small conic drops under mutules and triglyphs (*see* below) of a Doric entablature (Lever and Harris 1993, p. 20)

harle aggregate mixture of gravel used for rough casting, thrown rather than trowelled on wall (Lever and Harris 1993, p. 32)
hasp metal fastener fitting over staple secured by a pin (Lounsbury 1994, p. 175)
header brick or stone laid so that the short end is exposed to the wall surface, with the long end (stretcher) extended back into the wall thickness (Lounsbury 1994, p. 176)
heritor Scottish proprietor of heritable land or building liable in payment of public burdens
hexastyle *see* temple forms

hood mould medieval projecting moulding over opening to throw off rainwater (Lever and Harris 1993, p. 21)
husk stylised bell-shaped classical motif linked to form a garland (Lever and Harris 1993, p. 21)

impost 'Capitals of Pilasters that support Arches' (Neve 1726, p. 177)
impropriator layman in possession of a living or its revenues
in antis portico recessed into a building with columns ranged with the front wall (Lounsbury 1994, p. 5)
intercolumniation space between two columns measured at the lowest part of the shaft: *aroeostyle* at 4 diameters apart; *distyle* at 3 diameters; *eustyle* at 2¼ diameters; *pycnostyle* at 1½ diameters (Lever and Harris 1993, p. 21)
Ionic *see* classical order
ising glass whitish semitransparent substance, or mica

Japanned [Japanning] 'Art of varnishing and drawing Figures on Wood' using 'Spirit of Wine Gum-Lacca Spring-water Castile-Soap Allum Mastick white Amber', etc. (Chambers 1728, pp. 238–9)
joggle fastening two adjoining members with wooden pins (Lounsbury 1994, p. 194)

keystone *see* voussoir
king post 'Timber standing upright in Middle between two principal Rafters having Strutts going to Middle of each Rafter' (Harris 1704, p. 205)
kirk alternative name for a church in Scotland (Pride 1996, p. 46)

Lady Chapel chapel dedicated to the Virgin Mary, often placed behind the high altar at the east end of a church (Lever and Harris 1993, p. 22)
lancet tall, narrow, pointed window found in gothic architecture, *circa* 1180–1280 (Lever and Harris 1993, p. 22)
lapus lazuli [lapis lazuli] complex silicate pigment containing sulphur, bright blue colour of mineral
lath and plaster thin strips of sawn wood nailed to framing members with slight gaps between to secure the base coat of plaster used in roof structures (Loundsbury 1994, p. 207)
laths 'long thin narrow slips of Wood, us'd in Tiling [roof] or Walling' (Anon. 1734, p. 159)
latticing [lattices, Eldorado work] 'Lattices or Cancelli which anciently us'd to seperate . . . *Chancel*, most sacred part of Church' (Neve 1726, pp. 103–4)
lierne vault tertiary rib in a vault employed as a decorative link between the main and tierceron ribs (Lever and Harris 1993, p.42)
lightning rod [Franklin] electrical conductor attached to roofs to prevent lightning from striking a building by providing a direct path to the ground (Lounsbury 1994, pp. 128,150)
limner practitioner of limning or 'Painting in Water-Colours and in Fresco on Walls' (Chambers 1728, p. 252)
lucarne dormer gabled window in spire (Lever and Harris 1993, p. 23)
luffer louvre board (Pride 1996, p. 50)
lugged fixing frame or pipe to a wall by a small projection (Lever and Harris 1993, p. 23)

mandorla pointed oval shape framing the figure of Christ (Lever and Harris 1993, p. 42, under *vesica piscis*)
mattocks pickaxes (Pride 1996, p. 51)
Memel *see* timbers
mensa flat stone altar-top (Friar 1996, p. 290)
metope plain or decorated space between triglyphs in a Doric frieze (Lever and Harris 1993, p. 23)
mitchels 'Purbeck stones for paving hew'd ready for Paving' (Neve 1726, p. 197)
modillion 'little Brackets set under Cornice to support Projecture of Drip' (Harris 1704, pp. 154–5)
monions [munions] 'short upright timber or metal posts dividing several Lights in Window-frame' (Neve 1726, p. 205)
mosaick work 'curious Piece of Work Assemblage of Marble, pretious Stones Pieces of Glass, *etc.* cut square cemented on Ground of Stuck in imitation of natural Colour of surprising Beauty and Durableness', also applied to coloured glass window (Anon. 1734, pp. 173–4)
mouchette curved dagger-shaped motif in curvilinear tracery (Lever and Harris 1993, p. 24)
mullion vertical member dividing a window into lights (Lever and Harris 1993, p. 24)
muntin sash bar holding edge of glass pane in a window (Lounsbury 1994, p. 238)
mutule one of a series of projecting inclined blocks under the corona of a Doric cornice and over each triglyph, sometimes hung with guttae (Lever and Harris 1993, p. 24)

obelisk *see* pyramid
octastyle *see* temple forms
oculus small round or oval window (Lever and Harris 1993, p. 26)
œil-de-bœuf round or oval 'bull's-eye' or 'ox-eye' window with radiating glazing bars (Lever and Harris 1993, p. 7)
og (ogee, ogive, cima) 'Moulding of two Members one concave other convex some resemblance to s' (Chambers 1728, pp. 288–9; Neve 1726, p. 107)
open-bed pediment low-pitched triangular gable in classical architecture with gap in centre of base (Lever and Harris 1993, p. 28)
ovolo *see* echinus
ox-eye window *see œil-de-bœuf*

pales wooden posts for rails (Neve 1726, pp. 213–14)
pallisado wood or iron 'Fence to beautifie a Place, or Walk' often with 'Heads handsomely cut' (Neve 1726, p. 214)
palmette classical ornament in the shape of a palm shoot (Lever and Harris 1993, p. 27)

pans [pantiles] roof tiles of flattened s-shaped section (Lever and Harris 1993, p. 27), 'Clay kneeded together squeez'd flat in Mould bak'd in Kiln' (Neve 1726, pp. 265–71)
pantiles *see* pans
papier mâché [stucco-paper] paper 'boiled to mash pounded vast while put into moulds of any form when tacked up painted white, or gild' (Shenstone 1939, pp. 338–9; Cornforth 1992)
patera [rosette] circular ornament resembling a shallow disk or flat medallion worked in relief (Lever and Harris 1993, p. 27)
paviour worker in paving (Neve 1726, pp. 216–18; Salmon 1748, pp. 48–53)
pediment low-pitched triangular gable finishing the end of a sloping roof in classical architecture (Lever and Harris 1993, p. 28)
pendentive concave spandrel effecting the transition from an angular to a circular plan when a dome or drum rests on the crown of supporting arches (Lever and Harris 1993, p. 28)
Pensylvania *see* stove
peripteral *see* temple forms
peristyle *see* temple forms
perron platform at the head of a flight of steps immediately preceding an entrance (Lever and Harris 1993, p. 28)
pier large masonry or brick support, often for an arch (Lever and Harris 1993, p. 29)
pinnacle tall, thin, termination of a buttress (Lever and Harris 1993, p. 29)
piscina [pissina] shallow basin with drain used for washing sacred vessels (Lever and Harris 1993, p. 29)
plaster *see* stucco
plate tracery elementary form of ornamental work in the upper part of a gothic window, having the effect of a simple opening cut out of stone infilling (Lever and Harris 1993, p. 40)
porte-cochère portico large enough to admit a carriage from the side (Lever and Harris 1993, p. 30)
Portland stone close-grained whitest Jurassic limestone quarried on the Isle of Portland, Dorset, popular from the seventeenth century onwards
prebendary title holder of cathedral benefice (Friar 1996, p. 358)
presbytery area of a church near the sanctuary (Friar 1996, p. 360)
pronaos space within a classical temple portico preceding the body or naos
prostyle *see* temple forms
pseudoperipteral *see* temple forms
pulpitum (chancel or rood screen) stone screen between the ritual nave and choir of a monastic church (Lever and Harris 1993, p. 30)
Purbeck shelly limestone capable of taking a high polish quarried in the Purbeck peninsula of Dorset, popular as a building material during the middle ages
purlines [purloins] 'pieces of Timber that lie a cross Rafters, on in side to keep them from sinking in middle' (Neve 1726, p. 228)
putti painted, carved or modelled representation of small, naked, winged boys (Lever and Harris 1993, p. 30)
pycnostyle *see* intercolumniation
pyramid [obelisk] 'Quadrangular Pyramid, very high and slender *Obelisk* has very small Base *Pyramid* very large one' (Anon. 1734, p. 177)

quatrefoil four small arcs separated by a cusp in a gothic arch or tracery (Lever and Harris 1993, p. 17)
quirk acute v-shaped groove or shadow to ogee or ovolo (Lever and Harris 1993, p. 31)
quoin [coin] 'corners of brick or stone wall If edges cypher'd off call'd Rustick-quoins' (Neve 1726, p. 229)

rabitted [rabbeting] 'planing or cutting Channels or Grooves in Boards' (Anon. 1734, p. 216)
rack rent rent equal, or nearly so, to the full value of land
rafter *see* collar-beam
reredos painting, carving or ornamentation covering the wall behind and above the altar (Lever and Harris 1993, p. 32)
reticulated tracery circles drawn at top and bottom into ogee shapes (Lever and Harris 1993, p. 40)
Riga *see* timbers
right wainscot *see* wainscot
rod [rodd] measure of length equal to 16½ feet (Lounsbury 1994, p. 309)
Roman Doric *see* classical order
rond-point streets radiating from a central circle
rose window large circular window filled with tracery arranged in a concentric or radiating pattern (Lever and Harris 1993, p. 34)
Rumford *see* stove
rustic work 'Manner . . . in Imitation of Nature . . . Columns . . . encompassed with frequent Cinctures', also piers, quoins (Neve 1726, pp. 232–3)

sacristy secure room adjacent to presbytery or chancel in an Anglican church for storing church plate and other valuables (Friar 1996, p. 397)
saddle bar [stanchion] metal bar fixed horizontally across a window to stiffen leaded glazing (Lever and Harris 1993, p. 35)
saltpetre [saltpeter] potassium nitrate crystals causing damp walls
sammel [samel] bricks that 'lie out most in Kiln where Selt-peter not digested for want of heat . . . very soft and soon moulder to dirt' (Neve 1726, p. 43)
saucer dome shallow dome with height less than its radius (Lever and Harris 1993, p. 13)
scable [scabbled, scappled] stone roughly laced with mason's scabbler, pick, chisel or hammer (Pride 1996, p. 67)
scagliola highly polished, variegated plasterwork imitat-

ing marble or other stone used to decorate walls and columns (Lounsbury 1994, p. 318)

scantling 'Measure, Size, or Standard, whereby Dimensions determined' (Chambers 1728, p. 349)

scarfed joint where two long members are joined together in the same plane by overlapping ends (Lounsbury 1994, p. 319)

scima recta *see* og

sconce candleholder attached to a wall or hung from a ceiling, also called branch or chandelier (Wells-Cole et al. 1992, pp. 35–42, cat. no. 8, fig. 24)

Serliana [Palladian or Venetian window] triple opening with the central opening arched and wider than the flat-headed side openings, first illustrated in Sebastiano Serlio, *Architettura*, 1537 (Lever and Harris 1993, p. 36; Wittkower 1974b)

slate [sclating] 'blue fossile Stone, very soft when dug out of Quarry easily cut or saw'd into thin long Squares for Covering' (Chambers 1728, p. 360)

sleepers ['dormients'] 'Oblique Rafters in Gutter' (Neve 1726, p. 241)

soalls [sole] window sill (Pride 1996, p. 73)

soffitt 'Boards over tops of windows' or 'Wainscot formed by Cross-Beams, or flying Cornices' (Neve 1726, pp. 233–4)

Solomonic column classical column with curved, twisted shaft, associated with the ancient Temple of Solomon, Jerusalem (Curl 1980, p. 109)

spandrel triangular surface between two adjacent arches (Lever and Harris 1993, p. 36)

Spanish inferior bricks made of Sea Cole ashes (Lambeth Palace Library, MS 2717, ff. 83–4)

sparrs rafters, purlin, wooden door bolt (Pride 1996, p. 73)

spriges small, thin, flat, headless nails used to hold glass in sash until the putty dries (Pride 1996, p. 74)

squinch small arch built across the angle of a square or polygon to support a dome (Lever and Harris 1993, p. 37)

stanchion *see* saddle bar

standard timber or iron upright (Lounsbury 1994, p. 348)

staple piece of U-shaped wrought iron used to receive hook, hasp or bolt (Lounsbury 1994, p. 348)

stove structure for heating a room, sometimes called Buzaglo, Franklin, Rumford or Pensylvanian (*sic*) fireplace (*Gentleman's Magazine*, October 1781, pp. 453–4; Lounsbury 1994, pp. 357–8)

stretcher *see* header

stucco [stoca, stuccho, stuco, stocco] 'Composition of Lime and Marble Powder'd very fine revived from Ancients' used for wall covering (Harris 1704, p. 215; Beard 1975)

summor [simmer, summer] principal beam in roof supporting joists, rafters, lintel (Pride 1996, p. 70)

superficial measure ['supl.'] two-dimensional length times width measurement of area (Lounsbury 1994, p. 363)

tabernacle 'among *Jews* Place wherein Ark of Covenant lodg'd' and 'temporary Church or Chapel, contrived to serve immediate Purposes of Parishioners while proper Church Repairing, Rebuilding' (Chambers 1728, p. 372)

teagle tackle used for hoisting materials

tempietto small cylindrical building with a domed core surrounded by a colonnade (Lever and Harris 1993, p. 38)

temple forms classified according to the order and the disposition of columns: *amphiprostyle* with front and rear porticoes; *apteral* with plain walls at sides, no columns; *dipteral* cella surrounded by two ranges of columns; *distyle* two columns fronting portico; *hexastyle* six columns fronting portico; *octastyle* eight columns fronting portico; *peripteral* two porticoes and side colonnades with single range of columns; *peristyle* space between columns and cella wall; *prostyle* portico in front; *pseudoperipteral* one or two porticoes and engaged columns or pilasters on sides; *tetrastyle* four columns fronting portico (Lever and Harris 1993, pp. 38–9)

tie beam horizontal member spanning the lowest section of a timber-frames roof structure (Lever and Harris 1993, p. 34)

tester *see* type

tetrastyle *see* temple forms

thean [thane] weather vane (Pride 1996, p. 79)

therm, thermal window *see* Diocletian window

tierceron secondary rib in a vault issuing from the main supports and inserted between the transverse and diagonal ribs (Lever and Harris 1993, p. 42)

tiles *see* pans

timbers varieties of native and foreign trees cut down, sawed and seasoned, called Christiana, Dantzig, elm, fir (deal), Frederickstadt, Memel, oak, Riga (Neve 1726, pp. 257–64)

timpans [tympanum] triangular or segmental surface between the enclosing mouldings of a pediment (Lever and Harris 1993, p. 41)

torus 'large round Moulding in Base of Column not unlike Edge of Quill' (Neve 1726, p. 264)

tracery ornamental work in the upper part of a gothic window or opening (Lever and Harris 1993, p. 40)

transept transverse arm of a cruciform, or Latin-cross, plan church (Lever and Harris 1993, p. 40)

transome horizontal member dividing a window (Lever and Harris 1993, p. 40)

trefoil three small arcs separated by cusps in a gothic arch or tracery (Lever and Harris 1993, p. 17)

triglyph rectangular block with two vertical grooves in the centre and half-grooves on edges placed between metopes in a Doric frieze (Lever and Harris 1993, p. 41)

turnbuckle fastening for a window casement

type [canopy, tester] flat canopy serving as a sounding-board over a pulpit (Lever and Harris 1993, p. 39)

upholder [upholsterer] furnisher of timber furniture and textiles

verde antico green coloured marble quarried in Thessaly, Greece (Bowersock et al. 1999, p. 560)
vermiculated surface of stone given the appearance of being worm-eaten (Lever and Harris 1993, p. 35)
volutes spiral scrolls in Ionic, Corinthian and Composite capitals of classical order (Lever and Harris 1993, p. 43)
voussoir [keystone] one of a series of radiating wedge-shaped stones or bricks to form an arch, of which the key-stone is the topmost (Lever and Harris 1993, p. 43)

wainscot [right wainscot, wainscote, wainscott, wainscotting] 'Pannel'd Work round (against Walls) of Room' (Neve 1726, pp. 273–4)
wall plate horizontal member placed along the top of wall to receive the ends of rafters (Lever and Harris 1993, p. 34)
weatherboarding 'nailing up with Feather-edg'd boards against *Wall*' (Neve 1726, p. 281)
whetstone fine-grained stone to give a sharp edge to cutting tools after being ground on a grindstone (Lounsbury 1994, p. 404)

y-tracery where the mullion of a window splits to form a Y-shape, characteristic of gothic *circa* 1300 (Lever and Harris 1993, p. 40)

Index

The Index incorporates the Preface, Chapters 1–30, illustrations (plate numbers are given in *italics*), Appendices A and B and the Notes (designated as n.) in the printed text, together with the Documents (prefixed Doc. or Docs) contained in the CD-ROM attached to the inside back board. Buildings are referenced by location (town and county, country when outside England) and dedication. Persons with the same surname are grouped in single entries under that surname, whether or not they are of the same family. Dedications to Saints in English-speaking countries are abbreviated as St, otherwise various spellings are given uniformly as S. Details of architects' careers and works are found in Colvin 2008 and Placzek 1982. Special emphasis is given to members of the building trades, with occupations where identified in contemporary records shown in (parentheses); where ambiguous, specified under the generic heading of 'builder'; where unknown, left blank. Owners, impropriators, trustees, benefactors, subscribers and other laymen active in church promotion are designated as clients. Jobbing painters are differentiated from pictorial and decorative artists. Books, tracts and articles (listed in the Bibliography) are generally not indexed.

Photograph Credits

Unless otherwise credited, the photographs are the author's own.

Aberdeen Art Gallery and Museums Collections: pl. 205.
All Soul's College, Oxford: pl. 148.
Andersonian Library, University of Strathclyde: pl. 427.
Archives of the Archdiocese of Baltimore, Maryland, USA: pl. 738.
Archivio di Stato, Florence: pls 381, 413, 414, 415.
Ashmolean Museum, Oxford: pls 48, 126, 134, 520.

Birmingham Local Studies Archives (Birmingham Library Services Archives): 149, 474.
Birmingham Museums and Art Gallery: pl. 360.
The Bodleian Library, University of Oxford: pls 10, 69, 141, 146, 190, 250, 352, 356, 403, 404, 412, 440, 442, 493 494a–b, 684.
Borthwick Institute of Historical Research, York University: pls 39, 103.
The British Library Board: p. xvi, pls 24, 35, 38, 42, 44a–b, 58, 61, 64, 66, 72, 80, 83, 93, 97, 100, 101, 104, 106, 107, 116, 121, 140, 162, 172, 200, 201, 252, 264, 268, 269, 286, 295, 296, 321, 323, 335, 339, 350, 362, 367, 375, 384, 385, 396, 435, 437, 444, 466, 478, 479, 504, 507, 538, 543, 546, 560, 566, 573, 602, 622, 649, 673.
The British Museum, Department of Prints and Drawings: pls 377a–b.

Camden Local Studies and Archives Centre, London: pl. 656.
Canterbury Cathedral Archives, reproduced with permission: pls 75, 178.
Castle Photographic Services, Halifax, Nova Scotia: pl. 731.
Centre for Kentish Studies, Maidstone, Kent: pls 57, 81.
Chatsworth Settlement Trust: pl. 84.
Cheshire Record Office (records in the Office are reproduced with the permission of Cheshire Shared Services and the owner/depositor to whom copyright is reserved): pl. 726.
Chetham School Library, Manchester: pl. 310.
Christ Church, Oxford, Governing Body: pl. 304.
City of Bristol Museum and Art Gallery: pl. 62.
City of Westminster Archives Centre: pls 1, 5, 68, 133, 246, 247, 407, 408, 531, 539, 617.
The Collection, Art and Archaeology in Lincolnshire, Lincoln, pl. 157.
Collection Canadien Centre d'Architecture, Montreal: pl. 577.
Country Life Picture Library, London: pls 632, 633, 648.
Courtauld Institute of Art, Conway Library, London: pls 27, 238, 273, 330, 331, 332.
Cumbria Record Office, Carlisle: pl. 47.

Dallas Museum of Fine Art, Texas: pl. 98.
Dog Rose Trust, Ludlow, Shropshire: pls 472, 588.
Dorset Record Office, Dorchester: pl. 631.
Kerry Downes: pl. 433.
The Drapers' Company of the City of London, reproduced with kind permission: pls. 529, 530.
Durham Cathedral, with permission: pls 257, 258.
Durham County Record Office, reproduced by permission of incumbent of parish church: pl. 63.

English Heritage Photo Library (National Monuments Record), Swindon, Wiltshire, by kind permission: pls 67b, 70, 76, 129, 165, 167, 168, 169, 170, 174, 177, 194, 195, 197–a, 198, 208, 223, 225, 244, 245, 271, 274, 276, 312, 313, 314, 327, 345, 349, 352, 364, 365, 379, 422, 446, 453, 469, 473, 482, 483, 502, 505, 506, 516, 542, 548, 549, 557, 568, 586, 623, 646, 653, 666, 678, 685, 712.
Essex Record Office, reproduced by courtesy of: pls 105, 533.

Fitzwilliam Museum, Cambridge: pl. 207.
Foundling Hospital, London: pl. 92.

Glasgow City Council, Dennis McCue: pl. 429.

Hampshire Record Office, Winchester: pl. 654.

Vaughan Hart: 552
Henry E. Huntington Library and Art Gallery, San Marino, California: pl. 452.
Henry Moore Institute, Leeds, Yorkshire: pls 166, 176.
The Hepworth, Wakefield, Yorkshire: pls 135, 136, 137, 138.
Hereford and the Hereford Mappe Mundi Trust, the Dean and Chapter: pl. 253.

Ironbridge Gorge Museum Trust: pl. 662.
Islington Local History Centre, London: pl. 115.

Jewish Museum, London: pl. 33.

Lambeth Palace Library, London, the Trustees: pls 8, 9, 383, 436, 724, 725.
Lancashire Library, Preston: pl. 670.
Lancashire Record Office, Preston: pls 307, 308, 499.

Leeds Library and Information Service, Yorkshire: pls 52, 94, 131, 318, 517.
Leeds University Library, Special Collections: pl. 598.
The Lewis Walpole Library, Yale University, Connecticut, courtesy of: pls 189, 191.
Lincolnshire Archives, Lincoln: pls 203, 204 (with permission of the Dean and Chapter), pls 333, 334.
Liverpool Record Office: pl. 485.
London Borough of Lambeth, Archives Department: pl. 74.
London Metropolitan Archives (incorporating the former Guildhall Library Prints and Drawings Collection): pls 34, 56, 305, 380, 409, 432, 441, 492, 562, 603, 619, 665.
John Lord: pls 528, 579.

Magdalen College, Oxford, the President and Fellows: pl. 255.
Magdalen College, Cambridge: pl. 456.
Manchester Archives and Local Studies: pl. 181.
Manchester Central Library Archives: pls 657, 658.
Maryland Historical Society, Baltimore, USA: pl. 736.
Metropolitan Museum of Art, New York: pls 65, 85.
Moravian archive, Herrnhut, Germany: pl. 26.
Timothy Mowl: pls 182, 338, 386.
Museum of London: front jacket, pl. 1.

National Archive of Scotland, Edinburgh, Scotlandsimages.com/Crown Copyright 2009: pls 46, 353, 449, 450.
National Gallery of Art, Washington D.C.: pls 282, 608.
National Library of Scotland, Edinburgh: pls 393, 394.
National Portrait Gallery, London: pls 59a-b, 108.
The National Trust © NTPL/Andreas von Einsiedel: pls 89, 193, 556, 592.
The New-York Historical Society, New York, Collection of: pl. 730.
Norfolk Library and Information Service, Norwich: pls 13a-b.
Norfolk Record Office, Norwich: pls 509, 582, 583.
Northamptonshire Record Office, Peterborough Diocesan Records: pl. 111.
North Yorkshire County Council and Information Service: pl. 267.
North Yorkshire County Record Office, North Allerton: pls 28a-c.

Philadelphia Museum of Art, Pennsylvania, bequest of Mrs William R. Mercer: pl. 79.
Pontefract Museum, Yorkshire: pl. 14.
Portsmouth City Record Office, Hampshire: pl. 45.

Rotherham Metropolitan Borough Council Archives and Local Studies, Yorkshire, copyright holder Parker Rhodes, pl. 185.
Royal Institute of British Architects Drawings Collection, London: pls 7, 20, 21, 112, 113, 196, 212, 227, 235, 243, 355, 382, 402, 405, 406, 430, 519, 521, 545, 561, 605, 636, 637, 638, 639, 640, 642, 667, 701.
RIBA Photographs Collection: 301, 599, 600, 601, 641, 659, 696, 697.

Shropshire Records and Research Centre, Shrewsbury: pls 130, 233, 337, 458, 555, 681, 692, 693.
R. J. L. Smith: pl. 232.
Sir John Soane's Museum, London, by courtesy of the Trustees: pls 40, 41, 77, 77a, 88, 173, 175, 217, 218, 234, 236, 237, 240, 263, 329, 398, 495, 554, 609, 610, 612, 613, 615, 625, 626, 627, 628, 635, 691, 702, 704, 705, 706, 707, 708, 709, 710a-b, 713, endpapers.
The Society of Antiquaries of London: pl. 346.
Somerset Record Office, Taunton: pl. 4 (an attempt has been made to contact the depositor; image used by permission of Somerset RO), pl. 655.
Southampton Archives, Hampshire: pl. 661.
Southwark Local Studies Library (now Southwark Local History Library); pls 488, 564.
Staffordshire Record Office, Stafford: pls 226, 251, 336.
Stratford-upon-Avon Record Office, Shakespeare Birthplace Trust (now Shakespeare Birthplace Library and Archives): pl. 102.

Tate, London: pl. 719.
Tullie House, Carlisle, Cumberland, pl. 199.

Victoria and Albert Museum, London: pls 91, 369, 389, 410, 620, 699.
The Victoria Art Gallery, Bath, Somerset: pl. 527.

Warburg Institute, London (Helmut Gersheim): pl. 650.
Warwickshire Record Office, Warwick: pls 224, 340, 341.
Westminster Abbey, by courtesy of the Dean and Chapter: pls 147, 151, 153, 154, 155, 213, 261, 278, 279, 283, 284, 285, 289, 290, 359.
West Sussex Record Office, Chichester: pl. 739.
West Yorkshire Archives Service, Leeds: 31, 326, 344, 534.
Wigan Archives Service, Lancashire: pls 110, 299, 300, 306.
Wiltshire and Swindon Archives, Arundel family collection: pl. 634.
William Salt Library, Stafford, Staffordshire: pl. 351.
Windsor, the Dean and Canons: pl. 259.
Worcester College, Oxford, the Provost and Fellows: pl. 158.
Worcestershire Record Office, Churchill Family Archives, Northwick Park: pl. 159.
World Monuments Fund, Britain (Angelo Hornak): pl. 376.

Yale Center for British Art, New Haven, Connecticut, USA, Paul Mellon Collection: frontispiece, pls 2a–c, 3, 96, 96.
York Museums Trust: pls 139, 211.

Documents on the CD-*Rom*

Chronological histories of 272 British places of worship contained in the CD-ROM attached to the inside back board, listed (according to the Pevsner *Buildings of England, Scotland, Wales and Ireland* series) by document number, as follows:

GREAT BRITAIN (EXCEPT GREATER LONDON)

1 St Mary, Abbots Ann, Hampshire
2 St Nicholas West, Aberdeen, Aberdeenshire, Scotland
3 St Nicholas, Alcester, Warwickshire
4 St Martin, Allerton Mauleverer, Yorkshire
5 St Mungo and Mar Monument, Alloa, Clackmannanshire, Scotland
6 Alnwick Castle chapel, Northumberland
7 Audley End chapel, Essex
8 St Michael, Aynho, Northamptonshire
9 St Lawrence, Ayot St Lawrence, Hertfordshire
10 St Mary, Banbury, Oxfordshire
11 Countess of Huntingdon's Chapel, Bath, Somerset
12 Octagon Chapel, Bath, Somerset
13 Prior Park chapel, Bath, Somerset
14 St Mary's Chapel, Bath, Somerset
15 St Michael Extra Muros, Bath, Somerset
16 SS Peter and Paul Abbey Church, Bath, Somerset
17 St Swithin, Walcot, Bath, Somerset
18 St Swithin, Baumber, Lincolnshire
19 St John Minster, Bevereley, Yorkshire
20 St Aidan, Billinge, Lancashire
21 St Bartholomew, Binley, Warwickshire
22 St Mary, Birmingham, Warwickshire
23 St Paul, Birmingham, Warwickshire
24 St Philip (now Cathedral), Birmingham, Warwickshire
25 St John Evangelist, Blackburn, Lancashire
26 SS Peter and Paul, Blandford Forum, Dorset
27 Blenheim Palace chapel and Marlborough Monument, Oxfordshire
28 SS Peter and Paul, Blockley, Gloucestershire
29 St Andrew, Boynton, Yorkshire
30 St Maxentius, Bradshaw, Lancashire
31 St Mary Magdalene, Bridgnorth, Shropshire
32 All Saints, Bristol, Somerset
33 Cathedral, Bristol, Somerset
34 Christ Church, Bristol, Somerset
35 Lewin's Mead Unitarian Chapel, Bristol, Somerset
36 Quaker Meeting House, The Friars, Bristol, Somerset
37 Redland Chapel, Bristol, Somerset
38 St Mary Redcliffe, Bristol, Somerset
39 St Michael, Bristol, Somerset
40 St Nicholas, Bristol, Somerset
41 St Paul, Bristol, Somerset
42 St Thomas, Bristol, Somerset
43 St Werburgh, Bristol, Somerset
44 SS Peter and Paul, Buckingham, Buckinghamshire
45 Bulstrode House chapel, Buckinghamshire
46 St Vincent, Burton-By-Lincoln, Lincolnshire
47 St Modwen, Burton-on-Trent, Staffordshire
48 St Andrew, Burton Overy, Leicestershire
49 Clare College chapel, Cambridge, Cambridgeshire
50 King's College chapel, Cambridge, Cambridgeshire
51 Cannons House chapel, Edgware, Middlesex
52 Christ Church Cathedral, Canterbury, Kent
53 Holy Trinity Cathedral, Carlisle, Cumbria
54 St Mary, Castle Bromwich, Warwickshire
55 St Werburg Cathedral, Chester, Cheshire
56 St Mary-at-Wall, Colchester, Essex
57 St Michael, Coventry, Warwickshire
58 St Mary Magdalene, Croome D'Abitot, Worcestershire
59 Cusworth Hall chapel, Yorkshire
60 St James, Darwen, Lancashire
61 Holy Cross, Daventry, Northamptonshire
62 St George's Chapel, Deal, Kent
63 St Mary, Debden, Essex
64 All Saints (now Cathedral), Derby, Derbyshire
65 All Saints, Dewsbury, Yorkshire
66 St Peter, Doddington, Lincolnshire
67 St Mary, Dodington Park, Gloucestershire
68 Donibristle Chapel, Fife, Scotland
69 King's Hospital (Blue Coat School) chapel, Dublin, Ireland
70 SS Mary and Cuthbert's Cathedral, County Durham
71 St Swithin, East Grinstead, Sussex
72 St Mary, Eccleston, Lancashire
73 Holyrood Palace chapel, Edinburgh, Midlothian, Scotland
74 St Andrew, Edinburgh, Midlothian, Scotland
75 St Etheldreda Cathedral, Ely, Cambridgeshire
76 St John's Chapel, Epping, Essex
77 Holy Trinity, Ettington, Warwickshire
78 SS Mary and Peter Cathedral, Exeter, Devon
79 St Mary, Faversham, Kent

80 St Martin, Fenny Stratford, Buckinghamshire
81 Grace Hall Moravian Chapel, Fulneck, Yorkshire
82 All Saints, Gainsborough, Lincolnshire
83 Gibside Chapel and Mausoleum, County Durham
84 St Andrew, Glasgow, South Clydeside, Scotland
85 St Andrew-By-The-Green, Glasgow, South Clydeside, Scotland
86 Cathedral, Gloucester, Gloucestershire
87 St John, Gloucester, Gloucestershire
88 St Mary, Glynde, Sussex
89 St Michael, Great Badminton, Gloucestershire
90 St James, Great Packington, Warwickshire
91 Great Witley chapel, Worcestershire
92 St George's Chapel, Great Yarmouth, Norfolk
93 Holy Trinity, Halifax, Yorkshire
94 Square Unitarian Chapel, Halifax, Yorkshire
95 Constable Mausoleum, Halsham, Yorkshire
96 Hartlebury Castle chapel, Worcestershire
97 St Mary, Hartwell, Buckinghamshire
98 St Ethelbert's Cathedral, Hereford, Herefordshire
99 St Peter, Horbury, Yorkshire
100 Horsforth Chapel, Yorkshire
101 Holy Trinity, Horwich, Lancashire
102 St Nicholas, Ingrave, Essex
103 Parish Church, Kelso, Borders, Scotland
104 St Anne, Kew, Surrey
105 St Canice's Cathedral, Kilkenny, Ireland
106 St John Baptist, King's Norton, Leicestershire
107 All Saints, Kingston-on-Thames, Surrey
108 St Cuthbert and Turner Mausoleum, Kirkleatham, Yorkshire
109 Sir William Turner's Hospital chapel, Kirkleatham, Yorkshire
110 St Mary, Lancaster, Lancashire
111 Parish Church, Lasswade, Lothian, Scotland
112 Holy Trinity, Leeds, Yorkshire
113 St Paul, Leeds, Yorkshire
114 St Peter, Leeds, Yorkshire
115 St Chad's Cathedral, Lichfield, Staffordshire
116 St Peter-At-Arches, Lincoln, Lincolnshire
117 St Remegious's Cathedral, Lincoln, Lincolnshire
118 St George, Liverpool, Lancashire
119 St Paul, Liverpool, Lancashire
120 St Peter, Liverpool, Lancashire
121 St Thomas, Liverpool, Lancashire
122 Cathedral, Llandaff, South Glamorgan, Wales
123 St Mary, Long Ditton, Surrey
124 St Mary, Longdon, Worcestershire
125 Castle chapel (Roman Catholic), Lulworth, Dorset
126 St Mary's Chapel (Roman Catholic), Lulworth, Dorset
127 St Michael, Madeley, Shropshire
128 Collegiate Church (now Cathedral), Manchester, Lancashire
129 St Anne, Manchester, Lancashire
130 St. John, Manchester, Lancashire
131 St Peter, Manchester, Lancashire
132 St Lawrence, Mereworth, Kent
133 St Mary, Mistley, Essex
134 St Nicholas, Newbury, Berkshire
135 All Saints, Newcastle-upon-Tyne, Northumberland
136 Cathedral, Norwich, Norfolk
137 Octagon Unitarian Chapel, Norwich, Norfolk
138 All Saints, Nuneham, Oxfordshire
139 St Lawrence, Otterden, Kent
140 All Saints, Oxford, Oxfordshire
141 All Souls College chapel, Oxford, Oxfordshire
142 Magdalen College chapel, Oxford, Oxfordshire
143 New College chapel, Oxford, Oxfordshire
144 Queen's College chapel, Oxford, Oxfordshire
145 Worcester College chapel, Oxford, Oxfordshire
146 St Mary, Patshull, Staffordshire
147 St Andrew, Penrith, Cumbria
148 St Peter's Cathedral, Peterborough, Huntingdonshire
149 St George Reforne, Portland, Dorset
150 St Mary, Prescot, Lancashire
151 St Wilfrid's Chapel (Roman Catholic), Preston, Lancashire
152 All Saints, Pusey, Berkshire
153 St Wilfrid's Cathedral, Ripon, Yorkshire
154 St Mary, Rochdale, Lancashire
155 St Andrew's Cathedral, Rochester, Kent
156 St Alban's Abbey Church, St Alban's, Hertfordshire
157 St David's Cathedral, St David's, Dyfed, Wales
158 Cathedral, Salisbury, Wiltshire
159 St Chad, Seighford, Staffordshire
160 St Germaine's Abbey Church, Selby, Yorkshire
161 St Paul, Sheffield, Yorkshire
162 St Peter (now Cathedral), Sheffield, Yorkshire
163 Shrewsbury Hospital Chapel, Sheffield, Yorkshire
164 St John Evangelist, Shobdon, Herefordshire
165 St Alkmund, Shrewsbury, Shropshire
166 St Chad, Shrewsbury, Shropshire
167 All Saints, Southampton, Hampshire
168 St Michael, Southampton, Hampshire
169 Holy Trinity, Baswick, Stafford, Staffordshire
170 St Chad, Stafford, Staffordshire
171 St Mary Magdalen, Stapleford, Leicestershire
172 Parish Church, Stockton-on-Tees, County Durham
173 St Mary, Stoke Edith, Herefordshire
174. St Michael, Stone, Staffordshire
175 Stoneleigh Abbey chapel, Staffordshire
176 St Martin, Stony Middleton, Derbyshire
177 Strawberry Hill Oratory and Chapel-in-the-Woods, Twickenham, Middlesex
178 Holy Trinity, Sunderland, County Durham
179. St Mary, Tetbury, Gloucestershire
180 St Peter's chapel (Roman Catholic), Thorndon, Essex
181 St Margaret, Thorpe Market, Norfolk
182 SS Peter and Paul, Tickencote, Rutland
183 St George's Chapel, Tiverton, Devon
184 St Mary, Twickenham, Middlesex
185 Sepulchral chapel, Tyringham, Buckinghamshire
186 The Vyne chapel, Hampshire
187 St Mary, Wanstead, Essex
188 St Michael, Newbrough, Warden, Northumberland
189 Wardour Castle chapel (Roman Catholic), Wiltshire
190 St Mary, Warwick, Warwickshire
191 St Nicholas, Warwick, Warwickshire
192 All Saints, Wellington, Shropshire
193 St Michael, Welshampton, Shropshire
194 St Lawrence, Whitchurch, Middlesex
195 St Alkmund, Whitchurch, Shropshire

196 Wimpole Hall chapel, Wimpole, Cambridgeshire
197 St Andrew, Wimpole, Cambridgeshire
198 St Peter's Chapel (Roman Catholic), Winchester, Hampshire
199 St Swithin's Cathedral, Winchester, Hampshire
200 King's Chapel, Windsor Castle, Berkshire
201 St George's Chapel, Windsor Castle, Berkshire
202 Cathedral, Worcester, Worcestershire
203 St Andrew, Worcester, Worcestershire
204 St Nicholas, Worcester, Worcestershire
205 St Swithin, Worcester, Worcestershire
206 All Saints, York, Yorkshire
207 St Peter's Minster, York, Yorkshire

GREATER LONDON

CITY OF LONDON

208 All Hallows, London Wall
209 St Alphege, London Wall
210 Bancroft's Almshouse Chapel, Mile End Road, Bancroft's Tomb, St Helen, Bishopsgate
211 St Bartholomew-the-Less, Smithfield
212 Bevis Marks Synagogue, Aldgate
213 St Botolph, Aldersgate
214 St Botolph, Aldgate
215 St Botolph, Bishopsgate
216. St Giles, Cripplegate parish
217 Great Synagogue, Aldgate
218 St Martin Outwich
219 St Mary Aldermary
220 St Mary-le-Bow
221 St Mary Woolnoth
222 St Michael, Cornhill
223 St Paul's Cathedral
224. St Peter-Le-Poer
225 St Stephen Walbrook

CAMDEN (INCLUDING BLOOMSBURY, HAMPSTEAD AND HOLBORN)

226. St Andrew, Holborn
227 Foundling Hospital chapel, Holborn
228 St George, Bloomsbury
229 St Giles-in-the-Fields
230 St James's Chapel, Hampstead
231 St John, Hampstead
232 Lincoln's Inn Chapel, Holborn
233 Lincoln's Inn Fields Church, Holborn
234 Sardinian Embassy Chapel, Holborn

GREENWICH

235 St Alfege
236 Royal Hospital chapel

HACKNEY (INCLUDING SHOREDITCH)

237 St John, Hackney
238 St Leonard, Shoreditch

ISLINGTON (INCLUDING CLERKENWELL)

239 St Luke, Old Street
240 St Mary, Islington
241 St James, Clerkenwell

LAMBETH

242 Holy Trinity, Clapham

LEWISHAM (INCLUDING DEPTFORD)

243 St Mary, Lewisham
244 St Paul

MAYFAIR

245 St George, Hanover Square

PADDINGTON

246 St Mary

SOUTHWARK (INCLUDING ROTHERHITHE)

247 Christ Church, Southwark
248 Magdalen House chapel, Southwark
249 St John Horselydown
250 St Olave, Southwark
251 Surrey Chapel, Southwark
252 St Mary, Rotherhithe

ST MARYLEBONE

253 St Mary
254 Marylebone (or Oxford) Chapel

ST PANCRAS

255 Kentish Town Chapel

TOWER HAMLETS (INCLUDING BETHNAL GREEN, LIMEHOUSE, SPITALFIELDS AND WAPPING)

256 'Basilica Church', Bethnel Green
257 St Matthew, Bethnal Green
258 St Anne, Limehouse
259. Christ Church, Spitalfield
260 St George-in-the-East, Wapping

WANDSWORTH

261 St Mary, Battersea

WESTMINSTER

262 Banqueting House (Chapel Royal), Whitehall
263 German Lutheran Church, Savoy
264 Queen's Chapel, St James's
265 St Clement Danes
266 St James, Piccadilly
267 St John, Smith Square
268 St Margaret
269 St Martin-in-the-Fields
270 St Mary-le-Strand
271 St Paul, Covent Garden
272 St Peter's Abbey

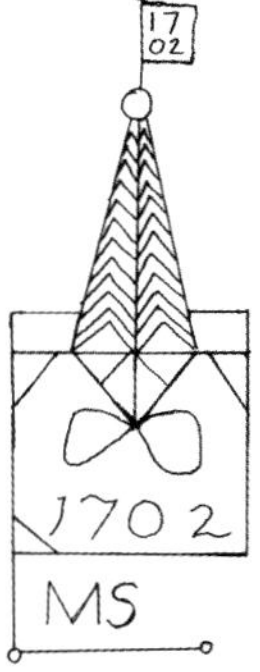

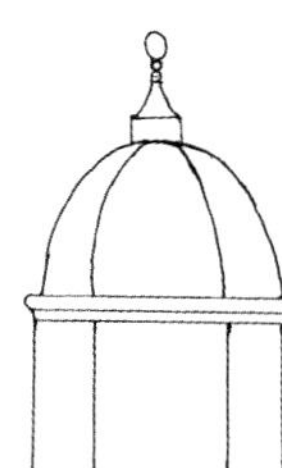

far left Canterbury Cathedral, Kent: 'representation of crossing spire incised on wall of south choir aisle, second window'. See Doc. 52, under '1702'. (Redrawn by the author)

left Salisbury Cathedral, Wiltshire: 'sketch of ... supposed covering instead of ... Pinacles'. See Doc. 158, under '24 August 1736'. (Redrawn by the author)

Abbreviations used in the Documents on the CD-Rom

For locations of parish records and other archival material, consult The Royal Commission on Historical Manuscripts, *Record Repositories in Great Britain*, published by the Public Record Office.

ABA	J. Gibbs, *A Book of Architecture*, 1728
Adshead	D. Adshead, *Wimpole: Architectural Drawings and Topographical Views*, 2007
AH	*Architectural History*, Journal of the Society of Architectural Historians of Great Britain
BAACT	*British Archaeological Association Conference Transactions*
BAL	The British Architectural Library (Royal Institute of British Architects, London)
BE	*Buildings of England*, volumes by counties, N. Pevsner et al.
BHRS	Bedfordshire Historical Record Society
BI	*Buildings of Ireland*, volumes by counties
BIGS	*Bulletin of the Irish Georgian Society*
BL	The British Library, London
BLARS	*Bedfordshire and Luton Archives and Record Series*
BLSA	Birmingham Library Services Archives
Bodleian	Bodleian Library, University of Oxford
Borthwick	Borthwick Institute of Historical Research, York University
Brotherton	Leeds University Library, Special Collections
BS	*Buildings of Scotland*, volumes by counties
Burney	London newspapers (British Library microfilm)
BW	*Buildings of Wales*, volumes by counties
CCA	Canterbury Cathedral Archives
CCALS	Cheshire and Chester Archives and Local Studies, Chester
CIA	Courtauld Institute of Art, London
CKS	Centre for Kentish Studies, Maidstone
CL	*Country Life* (periodical)
CLSAC	Camden Local Studies and Archives Centre, London
CRO	County Record Office (various)
CUL	Cambridge University Library
CWA	City of Westminster Archives
EKAC	East Kent Archives Centre, Dover
ERALS	East Riding Archives and Local Studies, Beverley
ESRO	East Sussex Record Office
GCA/Gibbs Collection	Eight volumes of drawings by James Gibbs and others in the Ashmolean Museum, Oxford (see Friedman 1984, p. 289)
GGJ	*Georgian Group Journal*
GL	Guildhall Library, London
GM	*Gentleman's Magazine*
Gomme and Maguire	Andor Gomme and Alison Maguire, *Design and Plan in the Country House: From Castle Donjons to Palladian Boxes*, 2008
GsJ	*Grub-street Journal* (British Library, Burney Newspapers 306.b, on microfilm)

HAD	Hackney Archives Department, London
HALS	Hertfordshire Archives and Local Studies
HCA	Hereford Cathedral Archives
HMC	Historical Manuscripts Commission
JAHSS	*Journal of the Architectural Heritage Society of Scotland*
JHC	*Journals of the House of Commons*, various volumes
JSAH	*Journal of the Society of Architectural Historians*
JWCI	*Journal of the Warburg and Courtauld Institutes*
K. Top.	King's Topographical Collection, British Library, London
LA	Lincolnshire Archives
LLSA	Lewisham Local Studies and Archives
LMA	London Metropolitan Archives
LPL	Lambeth Palace Library
MALS	Manchester Archives and Local Studies
MSC	Medway Studies Centre, Kent
NAS	The National Archives of Scotland (formerly Scottish Record Office), Edinburgh
NLI	The National Library of Ireland, Dublin
NLS	The National Library of Scotland, Edinburgh
NLW	The National Library of Wales, Aberystwyth
NMR	National Monuments Record Centre, English Heritage, Swindon
NYCRO	North Yorkshire County Record Office, Northallerton
PRO	The National Archives (formerly Public Record Office), Kew
QBIGS	*Quarterly Bulletin of the Irish Georgian Society*
RCHM	Royal Commission on Historical Monuments
RCHME	Royal Commission on Historical Monuments of England
RCHMS	Royal Commission on Historical Monuments of Scotland
RIBA Catalogue	*Catalogue of the Drawings Collection of the Royal Institute of British Architects*, various volumes
RO	Record Office
ROLLR	Record Office of Leicestershire, Leicester and Rutland, Leicester
SA	Sheffield Archives
SAL	The Society of Antiquaries of London
SARS	Somerset Archive and Records Service
SBTRO	Shakespeare Birthplace Trust Record Office, Stratford-upon-Avon (now Shakespeare Birthplace Library and Archives)
SHC	Surrey History Centre, Woking
SL	*Survey of London*, various volumes
SLSL	Sheffield Local Studies Library
SM	Sir John Soane's Museum, London
SMIF	St Martin-in-the-Fields: Minutes of Commissioners for Rebuilding the Church, 1720–24 (*CWA*, 419/310), Accounts, 1720–27 (419/310), Accounts, 1721–7 (419/311)
Southwark LSL	Southwark Local Studies Library (now Southwark Local History Library)
SPCK	Society for Promoting Christian Knowledge Archives, London
SRRU	Shropshire Records and Research Unit, Shrewsbury
SSTAS	Staffordshire and Stoke-on-Trent Archives Service, Stafford
TGSEY	*Transactions of the Georgian Society of East Yorkshire*
THSLC	*Transactions of the Historical Society of Lancashire and Cheshire*

UAHS	Ulster Architectural Heritage Society
VAM	Victoria and Albert Museum, London
VB	*see* Campbell 1715–25, vols I–III; Badeslade and Rocque 1739; Woolfe and Gandon 1767–71, vols IV–V; Richardson 1802–8, 1808–10 (*New Vitruvius Britannicus*); with P. Breman and D. Addis, *Guide to Vitruvius Britannicus Annotated and Analytic Index to the Plates*, 1972
VCH	*The Victoria History of the Counties of England*, various volumes
WAM	Westminster Abbey Muniments
Whitehead and Shoesmith	D. Whitehead and R. Shoesmith, *James Wathen's Herefordshire 1770–1820: A Collection of his Sketches and Paintings*, 1994
WS	*The Wren Society*, 20 vols, 1924–43, series 'Printed for the Wren Society at the University Press', Oxford
WYAS (LDA)	West Yorkshire Archives Service (Leeds District Archives)
YAS	Yorkshire Archaeological Society, Leeds
YML	York Minster Library